Copinger and Skone James on Copyright

Volume Two—Materials

COPINGER AND SKONE JAMES ON COPYRIGHT

SEVENTEENTH EDITION

By

GILLIAN DAVIES, D.L., PH.D.
of Lincoln's Inn, Barrister
Professor of International Copyright Law, Centre for Commercial
Law Studies, Queen Mary, University of London

NICHOLAS CADDICK, M.A., B.C.L.
One of Her Majestey's Counsel

GWILYM HARBOTTLE, B.A. (OXON)
of Lincoln's Inn, Barrister

SWEET & MAXWELL   THOMSON REUTERS

Published in 2016 by Thomson Reuters (Professional) UK Limited trading as
Sweet & Maxwell Friars House, 160 Blackfriars Road,
London SE1 8EZ
(Registered in England & Wales, Company No 1679046.
Registered Office and address for service:
2nd Floor, 1 Mark Square, Leonard Street, London EC2A 4EG

For further information on our products and services, visit
www.sweetandmaxwell.co.uk

Typesetting by Sweet & Maxwell electronic publishing system
and LBJ Typesetting Ltd
Printed and bound in Great Britain by CPI Group (UK) Ltd, Croydon, CR0 4YY

No natural forests were destroyed to make this product; only farmed
timber was used and re-planted

A CIP catalogue record for this book is available from the British Library

ISBN 978-0-41403-422-8

CONTENTS

PART B

RELATED LEGISLATION AND MATERIALS

PART C

Orders in Council

PART D

Tables of Parliamentary Debates

PART E

Repealed Statutes

PART F

COPYRIGHT CONVENTIONS AND AGREEMENTS

PART G

TREATY ON THE FUNCTIONING OF THE EUROPEAN UNION (TFEU)

PART H

EU DIRECTIVES

PART I

RELATED EU INSTRUMENTS

PART A

COPYRIGHT, DESIGNS AND PATENTS ACT 1988 AND RELATED MATERIALS

PART A

COPYRIGHT, DESIGNS AND PATENTS ACT 1988 AND RELATED MATERIALS

Contents

A1. Copyright, Designs and Patents Act 1988

1988 (c.48)

ARRANGEMENT OF SECTIONS
Part 1
Copyright
Chapter I
Subsistence, Ownership and Duration of Copyright

Chapter II
Rights of Copyright Owner

CHAPTER VII

COPYRIGHT LICENSING

Licensing schemes and licensing bodies

PART II
RIGHTS IN PERFORMANCES
[CHAPTER I
INTRODUCTORY]

Part III

Design Right

Chapter I

Design Right in Original Designs

Introductory

An Act to restate the law of copyright, with amendments; to make fresh provision as to the rights of performers and others in performances; to confer a design right in original designs; to amend the Registered Designs Act 1949; to make provision with respect to patent agents and trade mark agents; to confer patents and designs jurisdiction on certain county courts; to amend the law of patents, to make provision with respect to devices designed to circumvent copy-protection of works in electronic form; to make fresh provision penalising the fraudulent reception of transmissions; to make the fraudulent application or use of a trade mark an offence; to make provision for the benefit of the Hospital for Sick Children, Great Ormond Street, London; to enable financial assistance to be given to certain international bodies; and for connected purposes. [15th November 1988]

PART 1

COPYRIGHT

CHAPTER I

SUBSISTENCE, OWNERSHIP AND DURATION OF COPYRIGHT

Introductory

Copyright and copyright works

1.—(1) Copyright is a property right which subsists in accordance with this Part in the following descriptions of work—

(a) original literary, dramatic, musical or artistic works,

(b) sound recordings, films [or broadcasts], and

(c) the typographical arrangement of published editions.

(2) In this Part "copyright work" means a work of any of those descriptions in which copyright subsists.

(3) Copyright does not subsist in a work unless the requirements of this Part with respect to qualification for copyright protection are met (see section 153 and the provisions referred to there).

Note: In s.1(1)(b) the words in square brackets were substituted for the former words ", broadcasts or cable programmes" by the Copyright and Related Rights Regulations 2003 (SI 2003/2498), reg.5(2) with effect from October 31, 2003. For savings and transitional provisions, see Part 3 of those Regulations.

Rights subsisting in copyright works

2.—(1) The owner of the copyright in a work of any description has the exclusive right to do the acts specified in Chapter II as the acts restricted by the copyright in a work of that description.

(2) In relation to certain descriptions of copyright work the following rights conferred by Chapter IV (moral rights) subsist in favour of the author, director or commissioner of the work, whether or not he is the owner of the copyright—

(a) section 77 (right to be identified as author or director),

(b) section 80 (right to object to derogatory treatment of work), and

(c) section 85 (right to privacy of certain photographs and films).

Descriptions of work and related provisions

Literary, dramatic and musical works

3.—(1) In this Part—

"literary work" means any work, other than a dramatic or musical work, which is written, spoken or sung, and accordingly includes

(a) a table or compilation [other than a database],

(b) a computer program,

[(c) preparatory design material for a computer program, and

(d) a database;]

"dramatic work" includes a work of dance or mime; and

"musical work" means a work consisting of music, exclusive of any words or action intended to be sung, spoken or performed with the music.

(2) Copyright does not subsist in a literary, dramatic or musical work unless and until it is recorded, in writing or otherwise; and references in this Part to the time at which such a work is made are to the time at which it is so recorded.

(3) It is immaterial for the purposes of subsection (2) whether the work is recorded by or with the permission of the author; and where it is not recorded by the author, nothing in that subsection affects the question whether copyright subsists in the record as distinct from the work recorded.

Note: Subsection (1) is printed as amended by the Copyright (Computer Programs) Regulations 1992 (SI 1992/3233), with effect from January 1, 1993, and as further amended by the Copyright and Rights in Databases Regulations 1997 (SI 1997/3032), with effect from January 1, 1998. For savings and transitional provisions, see reg.12 of the former Regulations, and regs 26 to 30 of the latter.

Databases

[**3A.**—(1) In this Part "database" means a collection of independent works, data or other materials which—

(a) are arranged in a systematic or methodical way, and

(b) are individually accessible by electronic or other means.

(2) For the purposes of this Part a literary work consisting of a database is original if, and only if, by reason of the selection or arrangement of the contents of the database the database constitutes the author's own intellectual creation.]

Note: This section was inserted by the Copyright and Rights in Databases Regulations

1997 (SI 1997/3032), with effect from January 1, 1998. For savings and transitional provisions, see regs 26 to 30 of those Regulations.

Artistic works

4.—(1) In this Part "artistic work" means—

(a) a graphic work, photograph, sculpture or collage, irrespective of artistic quality,

(b) a work of architecture being a building or a model for a building, or

(c) a work of artistic craftsmanship.

(2) In this Part—

"building" includes any fixed structure, and a part of a building or fixed structure;

"graphic work" includes—

(a) any painting, drawing, diagram, map, chart or plan, and

(b) any engraving, etching, lithograph, woodcut or similar work;

"photograph" means a recording of light or other radiation on any medium on which an image is produced or from which an image may by any means be produced, and which is not part of a film;

"sculpture" includes a cast or model made for purposes of sculpture.

Sound recordings and films

5. [...]

Note: Section 5 was substituted for ss.5A and 5B by the Duration of Copyright and Rights in Performances Regulations 1995 (SI 1995/3297) Pt II reg.9(1) with effect from January 1, 1996. The old s.5 provided:

Sound recordings and films

"**5.**—(1) *In this Part*—

"sound recording" means—

(a) a recording of sounds from which the sounds may be reproduced, or

(b) a recording of the whole or any part of a literary, dramatic or musical work, from which sounds reproducing the work or part may be produced,

regardless of the medium on which the recording is made or the method by which the sounds are reproduced or produced; and

"film" means a recording on any medium from which a moving image may by any means be produced.

(2) Copyright does not subsist in a sound recording or film which is, or to the extent that it is, a copy taken from a previous sound recording or film."

For savings and transitional provisions, see Part III of those Regulations.

Sound recordings

[**5A.**—(1) In this Part "sound recording" means—

(a) a recording of sounds, from which the sounds may be reproduced, or

(b) a recording of the whole or any part of a literary, dramatic or musical work, from which sounds reproducing the work or part may be produced,

regardless of the medium on which the recording is made or the method by which the sounds are reproduced or produced.

(2) Copyright does not subsist in a sound recording which is, or to the extent that it is, a copy taken from a previous sound recording.]

Note: Sections 5A and 5B inserted by the Duration of Copyright and Rights in Performances Regulations 1995 (SI 1995/3297), which replaced the old s.5 with effect from January 1, 1996.

Films

[**5B.**—(1) In this Part "film" means a recording on any medium from which a moving image may by any means be produced.

(2) The sound track accompanying a film shall be treated as part of the film for the purposes of this Part.

(3) Without prejudice to the generality of subsection (2), where that subsection applies.
- (a) references in this Part to showing a film include playing the film sound track to accompany the film,
- [(b) references in this Part to playing a sound recording, or to communicating a sound recording to the public, do not include playing or communicating the film sound track to accompany the film,
- (c) references in this Part to copying a work, so far as they apply to a sound recording, do not include copying the film sound track to accompany the film, and
- (d) references in this Part to the issuing, rental or lending of copies of a work, so far as they apply to a sound recording, do not include the issuing, rental or lending of copies of the sound track to accompany the film.]

(4) Copyright does not subsist in a film which is, or to the extent that it is, a copy taken from a previous film.

(5) Nothing in this section affects any copyright subsisting in a film sound track as a sound recording.]

Notes:
(1) Subsection (3)(b) was substituted and subss.(3)(c) and (d) inserted by the Performances (Moral Rights, etc.) Regulations 2006 (SI 2006/18), Sch. para.2, with effect from February 1, 2006.
(2) Sections 5A and 5B inserted by the Duration of Copyright and Rights in Performances Regulations 1995 (SI 1995/3297), which replaced the old s.5 with effect from January 1, 1996.

For savings and transitional provisions, see Part III of those Regulations.

Broadcasts

6.—[(1) In this Part a "broadcast" means an electronic transmission of visual images, sounds or other information which—
- (a) is transmitted for simultaneous reception by members of the public and is capable of being lawfully received by them, or
- (b) is transmitted at a time determined solely by the person making the transmission for presentation to members of the public,

    and which is not excepted by subsection (1A); and references to broadcasting shall be construed accordingly.

(1A) Excepted from the definition of "broadcast" is any internet transmission unless it is—
- (a) a transmission taking place simultaneously on the internet and by other means,
- (b) a concurrent transmission of a live event, or
- (c) a transmission of recorded moving images or sounds forming part of a programme service offered by the person responsible for making the transmission, being a service in which programmes are transmitted at scheduled times determined by that person.]

(2) An encrypted transmission shall be regarded as capable of being lawfully received by members of the public only if decoding equipment has been made available to members of the public by or with the authority of the person making the transmission or the person providing the contents of the transmission.

(3) References in this Part to the person making a broadcast, [or a transmission which is a broadcast] are—

(a) to the person transmitting the programme, if he has responsibility to any extent for its contents, and

(b) to any person providing the programme who makes with the person transmitting it the arrangements necessary for its transmission;

and references in this Part to a programme, in the context of broadcasting, are to any item included in a broadcast.

(4) [For the purposes of this Part, the place from which a [wireless] broadcast is made is the place where, under the control and responsibility of the person making the broadcast, the programme-carrying signals are introduced into an uninterrupted chain of communication (including, in the case of a satellite transmission, the chain leading to the satellite and down towards the earth).]

[(4A) Subsections (3) and (4) have effect subject to section 6A (safeguards in case of certain satellite broadcasts).]

(5) References in this Part to the reception of a broadcast include reception of a broadcast relayed by means of a telecommunications system.

[(5A) The relaying of a broadcast by reception and immediate re-transmission shall be regarded for the purposes of this Part as a separate act of broadcasting from the making of the broadcast which is so re-transmitted.]

(6) Copyright does not subsist in a broadcast which infringes, or to the extent that it infringes, the copyright in another broadcast[...].

Notes:

(1) Subsection (1) was substituted and subs.(1A) and (5A) inserted, in subs.(3) the words in square brackets substituted for the former words ", broadcasting a work, or including a work in a broadcast", in subs.(4) the word "wireless" was inserted and in subs.(6) the words "or in a cable programme" repealed by the Copyright and Related Rights Regulations 2003 (SI 2003/2498), reg.4 and Sch.2 with effect from October 31, 2003. For savings and transitional provisions, see Part 3 of those Regulations. Subsection (1) previously provided:

"(1) *In this Part a "broadcast" means a transmission by wireless telegraphy of visual images, sounds or other information which—*

(a) *is capable of being lawfully received by members of the public, or*

(b) *is transmitted for presentation to members of the public;*

and references to broadcasting shall be construed accordingly."

(2) Subsection (4) is printed as amended by, and subs.(4A) was inserted by, the Copyright and Related Rights Regulations 1996 (SI 1996/2967), which replaced the old subs.(4) and inserted the new subs.(4A) with effect from December 1, 1996. For savings and transitional provisions, see Part III of those Regulations.

Safeguards in case of certain satellite broadcasts

[6A.—(1) This section applies where the place from which a broadcast by way of satellite transmission is made is located in a country other than an EEA State and the law of that country fails to provide at least the following level of protection—

(a) exclusive rights in relation to [wireless] broadcasting equivalent to those conferred by section 20 [infringement by communication to the public] on the authors of literary, dramatic, musical and artistic works, films and broadcasts;

(b) a right in relation to live [wireless] broadcasting equivalent to that conferred on a performer by section 182(1)(b) (consent required for live broadcast of performance); and

(c) a right for authors of sound recordings and performers to share in a single equitable remuneration in respect of the [wireless] broadcasting of sound recordings.

(2) Where the place from which the programme-carrying signals are transmitted to the satellite ("the uplink station") is located in an EEA State—

(a) that place shall be treated as the place from which the broadcast is made, and

(b) the person operating the uplink station shall be treated as the person making the broadcast.

(3) Where the uplink station is not located in an EEA State but a person who is established in an EEA State has commissioned the making of the broadcast—

(a) that person shall be treated as the person making the broadcast, and

(b) the place in which he has the principal establishment in the European Economic Area shall be treated as the place from which the broadcast is made.]

Notes:

(1) This section was inserted by the Copyright and Related Rights Regulations 1996 (SI 1996/2967), with effect from December 1, 1996. For savings and transitional provisions, see Part III of those Regulations.

(2) The word "wireless" was inserted into subs.(1) and the words "infringement by communication to the public" substituted for the former words "infringement by broadcasting" by the Copyright and Related Rights Regulations 2003 (SI 2003/2498), reg.5(3) with effect from October 31, 2003. For savings and transitional provisions, see Part 3 of those Regulations.

Cable programmes

7. [...]

Note: Section 7 was repealed by the Copyright and Related Rights Regulations 2003 (SI 2003/2498), reg.5(1) and Sch.2 with effect from October 31, 2003. For savings and transitional provisions, see Part 3 of those Regulations. Section 7 formerly provided:

Cable programmes

"**7.**—(1) *In this Part—*

"cable programme" means any item included in a cable programme service; and

"cable programme service" means a service which consists wholly or mainly in sending visual images, sounds or other information by means of a telecommunications system, otherwise than by wireless telegraphy, for reception—

(a) at two or more places (whether for simultaneous reception or at different times in response to requests by different users), or

(b) for presentation to members of the public,

and which is not, or so far as it is not, excepted by or under the following provisions of this section.

(2) The following are excepted from the definition of "cable programme service"—

(a) a service or part of a service of which it is an essential feature that while visual images, sounds or other information are being conveyed by the person providing the service there will or may be sent from each place of reception, by means of the same system or (as the case may be) the same part of it, information (other than signals sent for the operation or control of the service) for reception by the person providing the service or other persons receiving it;

(b) a service run for the purposes of a business where—

     (i) *no person except the person carrying on the business is concerned in the control of the apparatus comprised in the system,*

    (ii) *the visual images, sounds or other information are conveyed by the system solely for purposes internal to the running of the business and not by way of rendering a service or providing amenities for others, and*

    (iii) *the system is not connected to any other telecommunications system;*

  (c) *a service run by a single individual where—*

    (i) *all the apparatus comprised in the system is under his control,*

    (ii) *the visual images, sounds or other information conveyed by the system are conveyed solely for domestic purposes of his, and*

    (iii) *the system is not connected to any other telecommunications system;*

  (d) *services where—*

    (i) *all the apparatus comprised in the system is situated in, or connects, premises which are in single occupation, and*

    (ii) *the system is not connected to any other telecommunications system, other than services operated as part of the amenities provided for residents or inmates of premises run as a business;*

  (e) *services which are, or to the extent that they are, run for persons providing broadcasting or cable programme services or providing programmes for such services.*

(3) *The Secretary of State may by order amend subsection (2) so as to add or remove exceptions, subject to such transitional provision as appears to him to be appropriate.*

(4) *An order shall be made by statutory instrument; and no order shall be made unless a draft of it has been laid before and approved by resolution of each House of Parliament.*

(5) *References in this Part to the inclusion of a cable programme or work in a cable programme service are to its transmission as part of the service; and references to the person including it are to the person providing the service.*

(6) *Copyright does not subsist in a cable programme—*

  (a) *if it is included in a cable programme service by reception and immediate re-transmission of a broadcast, or*

  (b) *if it infringes, or to the extent that it infringes, the copyright in another cable programme or in a broadcast."*

Published editions

8.—(1) In this Part "published edition," in the context of copyright in the typographical arrangement of a published edition, means a published edition of the whole or any part of one or more literary, dramatic or musical works.

(2) Copyright does not subsist in the typographical arrangement of a published edition if, or to the extent that, it reproduces the typographical arrangement of a previous edition.

Authorship and ownership of copyright

Authorship of work

9.—(1) In this Part "author," in relation to a work, means the person who creates it.

(2) That person shall be taken to be—

[(aa) in the case of a sound recording, the producer;

 (ab) in the case of a film, the producer and the principal director;]

 (b) in the case of a broadcast, the person making the broadcast (see section

6(3)) or in the case of a broadcast which relays another broadcast by reception and immediate re-transmission, the person making that other broadcast;

(c) [...]

(d) in the case of the typographical arrangement of a published edition, the publisher.

(3) In the case of a literary, dramatic, musical or artistic work which is computer-generated, the author shall be taken to be the person by whom the arrangements necessary for the creation of the work are undertaken.

(4) For the purposes of this Part a work is of "unknown authorship" if the identity of the author is unknown or, in the case of a work of joint authorship, if the identity of none of the authors is known.

(5) For the purposes of this Part the identity of an author shall be regarded as unknown if it is not possible for a person to ascertain his identity by reasonable inquiry; but if his identity is once known it shall not subsequently be regarded as unknown.

Notes:

(1) Subsections (aa) and (ab) inserted by the Copyright and Related Rights Regulations 1996 (SI 1996/2967), which replaced the old subs.(a) with effect from December 1, 1996. The old subs.(a) provided:

"(a) *in the case of a sound recording or film, the person by whom the arrangements necessary for the making of the recording or film are undertaken;"*.

For savings and transitional provisions, see Part III of those Regulations.

(2) Subsection (2)(c) was repealed by the Copyright and Related Rights Regulations 2003 (SI 2003/2498), reg.5(4) and Sch.2 with effect from October 31, 2003. For savings and transitional provisions, see Part 3 of those Regulations. Subsection (2)(c) formerly provided:

"(c) *in the case of a cable programme, the person providing the cable programme service in which the programme is included;"*.

Works of joint authorship

10.—(1) In this Part a "work of joint authorship" means a work produced by the collaboration of two or more authors in which the contribution of each author is not distinct from that of the other author or authors.

[(1A) A film shall be treated as a work of joint authorship unless the producer and the principal director are the same person.]

(2) A broadcast shall be treated as a work of joint authorship in any case where more than one person is to be taken as making the broadcast (see section 6(3)).

(3) References in this Part to the author of a work shall, except as otherwise provided, be constructed in relation to a work of joint authorship as references to all the authors of the work.

Note: Subsection (1A) was inserted by the Copyright and Related Rights Regulations 1996 (SI 1996/2967), with effect from December 1, 1996. For savings and transitional provisions, see Part III of those Regulations.

Works of co-authorship

[**10A.**—(1) In this Part a "work of co-authorship" means a work produced by the collaboration of the author of a musical work and the author of a literary work where the two works are created in order to be used together.

(2) References in this Part to a work or the author of a work shall, except as otherwise provided, be construed in relation to a work of co-authorship as references to each of the separate musical and literary works comprised in the work of co-authorship and to each of the authors of such works.]

Note Section 10A inserted, subject to savings, transitional and review provisions, by the Copyright and Duration of Rights in Performances Regulations 2013 (SI 2013/1782), reg.4, with effect from November 1, 2013 (for savings, transitional and review provisions see regs 11–27).

First ownership of copyright

11.—(1) The author of a work is the first owner of any copyright in it, subject to the following provisions.

(2) Where a literary, dramatic, musical or artistic work[, or a film,] is made by an employee in the course of his employment, his employer is the first owner of any copyright in the work subject to any agreement to the contrary.

(3) This does not apply to Crown copyright or Parliamentary copyright (see sections 163 and 165) or to copyright which subsists by virtue of section 168 (copyright of certain international organisations).

Note: Subsection (2) is printed as amended by the Copyright and Related Regulations 1996 (SI 1996/2967), with effect from December 1, 1996. For savings and transitional provisions, see Part III of those Regulations.

Duration of copyright

Duration of copyright in literary, dramatic, musical or artistic works

12.—(1) The following provisions have effect with respect to the duration of copyright in a literary, dramatic, musical or artistic work.

(2) Copyright expires at the end of the period of 70 years from the end of the calendar year in which the author dies, subject as follows.

(3) If the work is of unknown authorship, copyright expires—

  (a) at the end of the period of 70 years from the end of the calendar year in which the work was made, or

  (b) if during that period the work is made available to the public, at the end of the period of 70 years from the end of the calendar year in which it is first so made available,

subject as follows.

(4) Subsection (2) applies if the identity of the author becomes known before the end of the period specified in paragraph (a) or (b) of subsection (3).

(5) For the purposes of subsection (3) making available to the public includes—

  (a) in the case of a literary, dramatic or musical work—

      (i) performance in public, or

      (ii) [communication to the public]

  (b) in the case of an artistic work—

      (i) exhibition in public,

      (ii) a film including the work being shown in public, or

      (iii) [communication to the public]

but in determining generally for the purposes of that subsection whether a work has been made available to the public no account shall be taken of any unauthorised act.

(6) Where the country of origin of the work is not an EEA state and the author of the work is not a national of an EEA state, the duration of copyright is that to which the work is entitled in the country of origin, provided that does not exceed the period which would apply under subsections (2) to (5).

(7) If the work is computer-generated the above provisions do not apply and

copyright expires at the end of the period of 50 years from the end of the calendar year in which the work was made.

(8) The provisions of this section are adapted as follows in relation to a work of joint authorship [or a work of co–authorship]

(a) the reference in subsection (2) to the death of the author shall be construed—

(i) if the identity of all the authors is known, as a reference to the death of the last of them to die, and

(ii) if the identity of one or more of the authors is known and the identity of one or more others is not, as a reference to the death of the last whose identity is known;

(b) the reference in subsection (4) to identity of the author becoming known shall be constructed as a reference to the identity of any of the authors becoming known;

(c) the reference in subsection (6) to the author not being a national of an EEA state shall be construed as a reference to none of the authors being a national of an EEA state.

(9) This section does not apply to Crown copyright or Parliamentary copyright (see sections 163 to [166D]) or to copyright which subsists by virtue of section 168 (copyright of certain international organisations).

Notes:

(1) This section was substituted by the Duration of Copyright and Rights in Performances Regulations 1995 (SI 1995/3297), which replaced the old s.12 with effect from January 1, 1996. The old s.12 formerly provided:

Duration of copyright in literary, dramatic, musical or artistic works

"**12.**—(1) *Copyright in a literary, dramatic, musical or artistic work expires at the end of the period of 50 years from the end of the calendar year in which the author dies, subject to the following provisions of this section.*

(2) *If the work is of unknown authorship, copyright expires at the end of the period of 50 years from the end of the calendar year in which it is first made available to the public; and subsection (1) does not apply if the identity of the author becomes known after the end of that period.*

For this purpose making available to the public includes—

(a) *in the case of a literary, dramatic or musical work—*

(i) *performance in public, or*

(ii) *being broadcast or included in a cable programme service;*

(b) *in the case of an artistic work—*

(i) *exhibition in public,*

(ii) *a film including the work being shown in public, or*

(iii) *being included in a broadcast or cable programme service;*

but in determining generally for the purposes of this subsection whether a work has been made available to the public no account shall be taken of any unauthorised act.

(3) *If the work is computer-generated neither of the above provisions applies and copyright expires at the end of the period of 50 years from the end of the calendar year in which the work was made.*

(4) *In relation to a work of joint authorship—*

(a) *the reference in subsection (1) to the death of the author shall be construed—*

(i) *if the identity of all the authors is known, as a reference to the death of the last of them to die, and*

(ii) *if the identity of one or more of the authors is known and the identity of one or more others is not, as a reference to the death of the last of the authors whose identity is known; and*

> (b) *the reference in subsection (2) to the identity of the author becoming known shall be construed as a reference to the identity of any of the authors becoming known.*
>
> (5) *This section does not apply to Crown copyright or Parliamentary copyright (see sections 163 to 166) or to copyright which subsists by virtue of section 168 (copyright of certain international organisations)."*

(2) The words in square brackets in s.12(9) were substituted by the Government of Wales Act 2006 (c.32), Sch.10 para.23, with effect from May 4, 2007.

(3) In subs.(5)(a), the words in square brackets were substituted for the former words "being broadcast or included in a cable programme service" and in subs.(5)(b), the words in square brackets were substituted for the former words "being included in a broadcast or cable programme service" by the Copyright and Related Rights Regulations 2003 (SI 2003/2498), Sch.1 para.4 with effect from October 31, 2003. For savings and transitional provisions, see Part 3 of those Regulations.

(4) In subs.(9) the words "166B" were substituted for the former words "166A" by the Northern Ireland Act 1998 (c.47), s.99 and Sch.13 para.8 with effect from December 2, 1999 (the Northern Ireland Act 1998 (Commencement No.5) Order 1999 (SI 1999/3209)), the words "166A" having been previously substituted for the original words "166" by the Scotland Act 1998 (c.46), s.125 and Sch.8, para.25 with effect from July 1, 1999 (the Scotland Act 1998 (Commencement) Order 1998 (SI 1998/3178).

(5) In subs.(8) words in square brackets inserted, subject to savings, transitional and review provisions, by the Copyright and Duration of Rights in Performances Regulations 2013 (SI 2013/1782) reg.5, with effect from November 1, 2013 (for savings, transitional and review provisions see regs 11–27).

Duration of copyright in sound recordings and films

13. [...]

Note: Section 13 was substituted for ss.13A and 13B by the Duration of Copyright and Rights in Performances Regulations 1995 (SI 1995/3297) Pt II reg.6(1) with effect from January 1, 1996. Section 13 formerly provided:

Duration of copyright in sound recordings and films

"**13.**—(1) *Copyright in a sound recording or film expires*
>   (a) *at the end of the period of 50 years from the end of the calendar year in which it is made, or*
>   (b) *if it is released before the end of that period, 50 years from the end of the calendar year in which it is released.*
>
> (2) *A sound recording or film is "released" when—*
>   (a) *it is first published, broadcast or included in a cable programme service, or*
>   (b) *in the case of a film or film sound-track, the film is first shown in public;*
>   *but in determining whether a work has been released no account shall be taken of any unauthorised act."*

Duration of copyright in sound recordings

[**13A.**—(1) The following provisions have effect with respect to the duration of copyright in a sound recording.

[(2) Subject to subsections (4) and (5) [and section 191HA(4)], copyright expires—
>   (a) at the end of the period of 50 years from the end of the calendar year in which the recording is made, or
>   (b) if during that period the recording is published, [70] years from the end of the calendar year in which it is first published, or
>   (c) if during that period the recording is not published but is made available to the public by being played in public or communicated to the public,

[70] years from the end of the calendar year in which it is first so made available,

but in determining whether a sound recording has been published, played in public or communicated to the public, no account shall be taken of any unauthorised act.]

(3) [...]

(4) Where the author of a sound recording is not a national of an EEA state, the duration of copyright is that to which the sound recording is entitled in the country of which the author is a national, provided that does not exceed the period which would apply under [subsection (2)]

(5) If or to the extent that the application of subsection (4) would be at variance with an international obligation to which the United Kingdom became subject prior to 29th October 1993, the duration of copyright shall be as specified in [subsection (2)]]

Notes:

(1) Sections 13A and 135B inserted by the Duration of Copyright and Rights in Performances Regulations 1995 (SI 1995/3297), which replaced the old s.13 with effect from January 1, 1996.

(2) Subsection (2) was substituted and subs.(3) repealed, and the words in square brackets in subs.(4) and (5) substituted for the former words "subsections (2) and (3)" by the Copyright and Related Rights Regulations 2003 (SI 2003/2498), reg.29 with effect from October 31, 2003. Subsections (2) and (3) formerly provided:

"(2) *Copyright expires—*

(a) *at the end of the period of 50 years from the end of the calendar year in which it is made, or*

(b) *if during that period it is released, 50 years from the end of the calendar year in which it is released;*

subject as follows.

(3) *For the purposes of subsection (2) a sound recording is "released" when it is first published, played in public, broadcast or included in a cable programme service; but in determining whether a sound recording has been released no account shall be taken of any unauthorised act."*

For savings and transitional provisions, see Part 3 of those Regulations.

(3) In subs.(2) first words in square brackets inserted, and in subs.(2)(b), (c), figure in square brackets substituted for figure "50", subject to savings, transitional and review provisions, by the Copyright and Duration of Rights in Performances Regulations 2013 (SI 2013/1782) regs 5, 6, with effect from November 1, 2013 (for savings, transitional and review provisions see regs 11–27).

Duration of copyright in films

[13B.—(1) The following provisions have effect with respect to the duration of copyright in a film.

(2) Copyright expires at the end of the period of 70 years from the end of the calendar year in which the death occurs of the last to die of the following persons—

(a) the principal director,

(b) the author of the screenplay,

(c) the author of the dialogue, or

(d) the composer of music specially created for and used in the film;

subject as follows.

(3) If the identity of one or more of the persons referred to in subsection (2)(a) to (d) is known and the identity of one or more others is not, the reference in that subsection to the death of the last of them to die shall be construed as a reference to the death of the last whose identity is known.

(4) If the identity of the persons referred to in subsections (2)(a) to (d) is unknown, copyright expires at—

(a) the end of the period of 70 years from the end of the calendar year in which the film was made, or

(b) if during that period the film is made available to the public, at the end of the period of 70 years from the end of the calendar year in which it is first so made available.

(5) Subsections (2) and (3) apply if the identity of any of those persons becomes known before the end of the period specified in paragraph (a) or (b) of subsection (4).

(6) For the purposes of subsection (4) making available to the public includes—

(a) showing in public, or

[(b) communicating to the public]

but in determining generally for the purposes of that subsection whether a film has been made available to the public no account shall be taken of any unauthorised act.

(7) Where the country of origin is not an EEA state and the author of the film is not a national of an EEA state, the duration of copyright is that to which the work is entitled in the country of origin, provided that does not exceed the period which would apply under subsections (2) to (6).

(8) In relation to a film of which there are joint authors, the reference in subsection (7) to the author not being a national of an EEA state shall be construed as a reference to none of the authors being a national of an EEA state.

(9) If in any case there is no person falling within paragraphs (a) to (d) of subsection (2), the above provisions do not apply and copyright expires at the end of the period of 50 years from the end of the calendar year in which the film was made.

(10) For the purposes of this section the identity of any of the persons referred to in subsection (2)(a) to (d) shall be regarded as unknown if it is not possible for a person to ascertain his identity by reasonable inquiry; but if the identity of any such person is once known it shall not subsequently be regarded as unknown.]

Notes:

(1) Sections 13A and 13B inserted by the Duration of Copyright and Rights in Performances Regulations 1995 (SI 1995/3297), which replaced the old s.13 with effect from January 1, 1996.

(2) Subsection (6)(b) was substituted by the Copyright and Related Rights Regulations 2003 (SI 2003/2498), Sch.1 para.4 with effect from October 31, 2003. For savings and transitional provisions, see Part 3 of those Regulations. Subsection (6)(b) formerly provided:

"(b) *being broadcast or included in a cable programme service;*".

Duration of copyright in broadcasts

[**14.**—(1) The following provisions have effect with respect to the duration of copyright in a broadcast [...].

(2) Copyright in a broadcast [...] expires at the end of the period of 50 years from the end of the calendar year in which the broadcast was made [...] subject as follows.

(3) Where the author of the broadcast [...] is not a national of an EEA state, the duration of copyright in the broadcast or cable programme is that to which it is entitled in the country of which the author is a national, provided that does not exceed the period which would apply under subsection (2).

(4) If or to the extent that the application of subsection (3) would be at vari-

ance with an international obligation to which the United Kingdom became subject prior to 29th October 1993, the duration of copyright shall be as specified in subsection (2).

(5) Copyright in a repeat broadcast [...] expires at the same time as the copyright in the original broadcast [...]; and accordingly no copyright arises in respect of a repeat broadcast [...] which is a broadcast [...] after the expiry of the copyright in the original broadcast [...].

(6) A repeat broadcast [...] means one which is a repeat [...] of a broadcast previously made [...].]

Notes:

(1) This section was substituted by the Duration of Copyright and Rights in Performances Regulations 1995 (SI 1995/3297), which replaced the old s.14 with effect from January 1, 1996. The old s.14 provided:

"**14.**—(1) *Copyright in a broadcast or cable programme expires at the end of the period of 50 years from the end of the calendar year in which the broadcast was made or the programme was included in a cable programme service.*

(2) *Copyright in a repeat broadcast or cable programme expires at the same time as the copyright in the original broadcast or cable programme; and accordingly no copyright arises in respect of a repeat broadcast or cable programme which is broadcast or included in a cable programme service after the expiry of the copyright in the original broadcast or cable programme.*

(3) *A repeat broadcast or cable programme means one which is a repeat either of a broadcast previously made or of a cable programme previously included in a cable programme previously included in a cable programme service.*"

(2) In subss.(1), (2), (3), (5) and (6), all references to cable programmes and programmes included in cable programme services repealed by the Copyright and Related Rights Regulations 2003 (SI 2003/2498), Sch.2 with effect from October 31, 2003. For savings and transitional provisions, see Part 3 of those Regulations.

Duration of copyright in typographical arrangement of published editions

15. Copyright in the typographical arrangement of a published edition expires at the end of the period of 25 years from the end of the calendar year in which the edition was first published.

Meaning of country of origin

[**15A.**—(1) For the purposes of the provisions of this Part relating to the duration of copyright the country of origin of a work shall be determined as follows.

(2) If the work is first published in a Berne Convention country and is not simultaneously published elsewhere, the country of origin is that country.

(3) If the work is first published simultaneously in two or more countries only one of which is a Berne Convention country, the country of origin is that country.

(4) If the work is first published simultaneously in two or more countries of which two or more are Berne Convention countries, then—

(a) if any of those countries is an EEA state, the country of origin is that country; and

(b) if none of those countries is an EEA state, the country of origin is the Berne Convention country which grants the shorter or shortest period of copyright protection.

(5) If the work is unpublished or is first published in a country which is not a Berne Convention country (and is not simultaneously published in a Berne Convention country), the country of origin is—

(a) if the work is a film and the maker of the film has his headquarters in, or is domiciled or resident in a Berne Convention country, that country;

(b) if the work is—

    (i) a work of architecture constructed in a Berne Convention country, or

    (ii) an artistic work incorporated in a building or other structure situated in a Berne Convention country,

that country;

(c) in any other case, the country of which the author of the work is a national.

(6) In this section—

(a) a "Berne Convention country" means a country which is a party to any Act of the International Convention for the Protection of Literary and Artistic Works signed at Berne on 9th September 1886; and

(b) references to simultaneous publication are to publication within 30 days of first publication.]

Note: This section was inserted by the Duration of Copyright and Rights in Performances Regulations 1995 (SI 1995/3297), with effect from January 1, 1996. For savings and transitional provisions, see Part III of those Regulations.

CHAPTER II

RIGHTS OF COPYRIGHT OWNER

The acts restricted by copyright

The acts restricted by copyright in a work

16.—(1) The owner of the copyright in a work has, in accordance with the following provisions of this Chapter, the exclusive right to do the following acts in the United Kingdom—

(a) to copy the work (see section 17);

(b) to issue copies of the work to the public (see section 18);

⌊(ba) to rent or lend the work to the public (see section 18A;]

(c) to perform, show or play the work in public (see section 19);

[(d) to communicate the work to the public (see section 20);]

(e) to make an adaptation of the work or do any of the above in relation to an adaptation (see section 21);

and those acts are referred to in this Part as the "acts restricted by the copyright."

(2) Copyright in a work is infringed by a person who without the licence of the copyright owner does, or authorises another to do, any of the acts restricted by the copyright.

(3) References in this Part to the doing of an act restricted by the copyright in a work are to the doing of it—

(a) in relation to the work as a whole or any substantial part of it, and

(b) either directly or indirectly;

and it is immaterial whether any intervening acts themselves infringe copyright.

(4) This Chapter has effect subject to—

(a) the provisions of Chapter III (acts permitted in relation to copyright works), and

(b) the provisions of Chapter VII (provisions with respect to copyright licensing).

Notes:

(1) Subsection (1)(ba) was inserted by the Copyright and Related Rights Regulations

1996 (SI 1996/2967), with effect from December 1, 1996. For savings and transitional provisions, see Part III of those Regulations.

(2) Subsection (1)(d) was substituted by the Copyright and Related Rights Regulations 2003 (SI 2003/2498), reg.6 with effect from October 31, 2003. For savings and transitional provisions, see Part 3 of those Regulations. Subsection (1)(d) formerly provided:

"(d) *to broadcast the work or include it in a cable programme service (see section 20);"*.

Infringement of copyright by copying

17.—(1) The copying of the work is an act restricted by the copyright in every description of copyright work; and references in this Part to copying and copies shall be construed as follows.

(2) Copying in relation to a literary, dramatic, musical or artistic work means reproducing the work in any material form.

This includes storing the work in any medium by electronic means.

(3) In relation to an artistic work copying includes the making of a copy in three dimensions of a two-dimensional work and the making of a copy in two dimensions of a three-dimensional work.

(4) Copying in relation to a film [or broadcast] includes making a photograph of the whole or any substantial part of any image forming part of the film [or broadcast].

(5) Copying in relation to the typographical arrangement of a published edition means making a facsimile copy of the arrangement.

(6) Copying in relation to any description of work includes the making of copies which are transient or are incidental to some other use of the work.

Note: The words in square brackets in subs.(4) substituted for the former words ", television broadcast or cable programme" and ", broadcast or cable programme" by the Copyright and Related Rights Regulations 2003 (SI 2003/2498), reg.5 with effect from October 31, 2003. For savings and transitional provisions, see Part 3 of those Regulations.

Infringement by issue of copies to the public

18.—(1) The issue to the public of copies of the work is an act restricted by the copyright in every description of copyright work.

[(2) Reference in this Part to the issue to the public of copies of a work are to—

(a) the act of putting into circulation in the EEA copies not previously put into circulation in the EEA by or with the consent of the copyright owner, or

(b) the act of putting into circulation outside the EEA copies not previously put into circulation in the EEA or elsewhere.

(3) References in this Part to the issue to the public of copies of a work do not include—

(a) any subsequent distribution, sale, hiring or loan of copies previously put into circulation (but see section 18A: infringement by rental or lending), or

(b) any subsequent importation of such copies into the United Kingdom or another EEA state,

except so far as paragraph (a) of subsection (2) applies to putting into circulation in the EEA copies previously put into circulation outside the EEA.]

[(4) References in this Part to the issue of copies of a work include the issue of the original.]

Notes:

(1) Subsections (2) and (3) are printed as amended by, and subs.(4) was inserted by,

the Copyright and Related Rights Regulations 1996 (SI 1996/2967), which replaced the old subss.(2) and (3) and inserted the new subs.(4) with effect from December 1, 1996. The old subss.(2) and (3) provided as follows:

"(2) *References in this Part to the issue to the Public of copies of a work are [except where the work is a computer program] to the act of putting into circulation copies not previously put into circulation, in the United Kingdom or elsewhere, and not to—*

(a) *any subsequent distribution, sale, hiring or loan of those copies, or*

(b) *any subsequent importation of those copies into the United Kingdom;*

except that in relation to sound recordings and films the restricted act of issuing copies to the public includes any rental of copies to the public.

(3) *References in this Part to the issue to the public of copies of a work where the work is a computer program are to the act of putting into circulation copies of that program not previously put into circulation in the United Kingdom or any other member State, by or with the consent of the copyright owner, and not to*

(a) *any subsequent distribution, sale, hiring or loan of those copies, or*

(b) *any subsequent importation of those copies into the United Kingdom;*

except that the restricted act of issuing copies to the public includes any rental of copies to the public."

For savings and transitional provisions, see Part III of those Regulations.

(2) The words in square brackets in the old subs.(2) and the old subs.(3), inserted by the Copyright (Computer Programs) Regulations 1992 (SI 1992/3233), with effect from January 1, 1993. For savings and transitional provisions, see reg.12 of those Regulations.

Infringement by rental or lending of work to the public

[**18A.**—(1) The rental or lending of copies of the work to the public is an act restricted by the copyright in—

(a) a literary, dramatic or musical work,

(b) an artistic work, other than—

(i) a work of architecture in the form of a building or a model for a building, or

(ii) a work of applied art, or

(c) a film or a sound recording.

(2) In this Part, subject to the following provision of this section—

(a) "rental" means making a copy of the work available for use, on terms that it will or may be returned, for direct or indirect economic or commercial advantage, and

(b) "lending" means making a copy of the work available for use, on terms that it will or may be returned, otherwise than for direct or indirect economic or commercial advantage, through an establishment which is accessible to the public.

(3) The expressions "rental" and "lending" do not include—

(a) making available for the purpose of public performance, playing or showing in public [or communication to the public];

(b) making available for the purpose of exhibition in public; or

(c) making available for on-the-spot reference use.

(4) The expression "lending" does not include making available between establishments which are accessible to the public.

(5) Where lending by an establishment accessible to the public gives rise to a payment the amount of which does not go beyond what is necessary to cover the operating costs of the establishment, there is no direct or indirect economic or commercial advantage for the purposes of this section.

(6) References in this Part to the rental or lending of copies of a work include the rental or lending of the original.]

Notes:

(1) This section was inserted by the Copyright and Related Rights Regulations 1996 (SI 1996/2967), with effect from December 1, 1996. For savings and transitional provisions, see Part III of those Regulations.

(2) The words in square brackets in subs.(3)(a) substituted for the former words ", broadcasting or inclusion in a cable programme service" by the Copyright and Related Rights Regulations 2003 (SI 2003/2498), Sch.1 para.6 with effect from October 31, 2003. For savings and transitional provisions, see Part 3 of those Regulations.

Infringement by performance, showing or playing of work in public

19.—(1) The performance of the work in public is an act restricted by the copyright in a literary, dramatic or musical work.

(2) In this Part "performance," in relation to a work—

(a) includes delivery in the case of lectures, addresses, speeches and sermons, and

(b) in general, includes any mode of visual or acoustic presentation, including presentation by means of a sound recording, film [or broadcast] of the work.

(3) The playing or showing of the work in public is an act restricted by the copyright in a sound recording, film [or broadcast].

(4) Where copyright in a work is infringed by its being performed, played or shown in public by means of apparatus for receiving visual images or sounds conveyed by electronic means, the person by whom the visual images or sounds are sent, and in the case of a performance the performers, shall not be regarded as responsible for the infringement.

Note: The words in square brackets in subss.(2)(b) and (3) substituted for the former words ", broadcast or cable programme" by the Copyright and Related Rights Regulations 2003 (SI 2003/2498), Sch.1 para.3 with effect from October 31, 2003. For savings and transitional provisions, see Part 3 of those Regulations.

Infringement by communication to the public

[**20.**—(1) The communication to the public of the work is an act restricted by the copyright in—

(a) a literary, dramatic, musical or artistic work,

(b) a sound recording or film, or

(c) a broadcast.

(2) References in this Part to communication to the public are to communication to the public by electronic transmission, and in relation to a work include—

(a) the broadcasting of the work;

(b) the making available to the public of the work by electronic transmission in such a way that members of the public may access it from a place and at a time individually chosen by them.]

Note: Section 20 was substituted by the Copyright and Related Rights Regulations 2003 (SI 2003/2498), reg.6 with effect from October 31, 2003. For savings and transitional provisions, see Part 3 of those Regulations. The former s.20 provided:

Infringement by broadcasting or inclusion in a cable programme service

"**20.** *The broadcasting of the work or its inclusion in a cable programme service is an act restricted by the copyright in—*

(a) *a literary, dramatic, musical or artistic work,*

(b) *a sound recording or film, or*

(c) *a broadcast or cable programme.*"

Infringement by making adaptation or act done in relation to adaptation

21.—(1) The making of an adaptation of the work is an act restricted by the copyright in a literary, dramatic or musical work.

For this purpose an adaptation is made when it is recorded, in writing or otherwise.

(2) The doing of any of the acts specified in sections 17 to 20, or subsection (1) above, in relation to an adaptation of the work is also an act restricted by the copyright in a literary, dramatic or musical work.

For this purpose it is immaterial whether the adaptation has been recorded, in writing or otherwise, at the time the act is done.

(3) In this Part "adaptation"

  (a) in relation to a literary [work, other than a computer program or a database, or in relation to a] dramatic work, means—

    (i) a translation of the work;

    (ii) a version of a dramatic work in which it is converted into a non-dramatic work or, as the case may be, of a non-dramatic work in which it is converted into a dramatic work;

    (iii) a version of the work in which the story or action is conveyed wholly or mainly by means of pictures in a form suitable for reproduction in a book, or in a newspaper, magazine or similar periodical;

  [(ab) in relation to a computer program, means an arrangement or altered version of the program or a translation of it;]

  [(ac) in relation to a database, means an arrangement or altered version of the database or a translation of it;]

  (b) in relation to a musical work, means an arrangement or transcription of the work.

(4) In relation to a computer program a "translation" includes a version of the program in which it is converted into or out of a computer language or code or into a different computer language or code […].

(5) No inference shall be drawn from this section as to what does or does not amount to copying a work.

Notes:

  (1) Subsection (1) is subject to modifications contained in the Copyright (Application to Other Countries) Order 1999 (SI 1999/1751) Sch.5 para.2 with effect from July 22, 1999.

  (2) Subsections (3)(a) and (4) are printed as amended by, and subs.(3)(ab) was inserted by, the Copyright (Computer Programs) Regulations 1992 (SI 1992/3233), with effect from January 1, 1993. For savings and transitional provisions, see reg.12 of those Regulations. Subsection (3)(a) is printed as further amended by, and subs.(3)(ac) was inserted by, the Copyright and Rights in Databases Regulations 1997 (SI 1997/3032), with effect from January 1, 1998. For savings and transitional provisions, see regs 26 to 30 of those Regulations.

Secondary infringement of copyright

Secondary infringement: importing infringing copy

22. The copyright in a work is infringed by a person who, without the licence of the copyright owner, imports into the United Kingdom, otherwise than for his private and domestic use, an article which is, and which he knows or has reason to believe is, an infringing copy of the work.

Secondary infringement: possessing or dealing with infringing copy

23. The copyright in a work is infringed by a person who, without the licence of the copyright owner—

(a) possesses in the course of business,

(b) sells or lets for hire, or offers or exposes for sale or hire,

(c) in the course of a business exhibits in public or distributes, or

(d) distributes otherwise than in the course of a business to such an extent as to affect prejudicially the owner of the copyright,

an article which is, and which he knows or has reason to believe is, an infringing copy of the work.

Secondary infringement: providing means for making infringing copies

24.—(1) Copyright in a work is infringed by a person who, without the licence of the copyright owner—

(a) makes,

(b) imports into the United Kingdom,

(c) possesses in the course of a business, or

(d) sells or lets for hire, or offers or exposes for sale or hire,

an article specifically designed or adapted for making copies of that work, knowing or having reason to believe that it is to be used to make infringing copies.

(2) Copyright in a work is infringed by a person who without the licence of the copyright owner transmits the work by means of a telecommunications system (otherwise than by [communication to the public]), knowing or having reason to believe that infringing copies of the work will be made by means of the reception of the transmission in the United Kingdom or elsewhere.

Note: In subs.(2), the words in square brackets substituted for the former words "broadcasting or inclusion in a cable programme service" by the Copyright and Related Rights Regulations 2003 (SI 2003/2498), Sch.1 para.5 with effect from October 31, 2003. For savings and transitional provisions, see Part 3 of those Regulations.

Secondary infringement: permitting use of premises for infringing performance

25.—(1) Where the copyright in a literary, dramatic or musical work is infringed by a performance at a place of public entertainment, any person who gave permission for that place to be used for the performance is also liable for the infringement unless when he gave permission he believed on reasonable grounds that the performance would not infringe copyright.

(2) In this section "place of public entertainment" includes premises which are occupied mainly for other purposes but are from time to time made available for hire for the purposes of public entertainment.

Secondary infringement: provision of apparatus for infringing performance, &c.

26.—(1) Where copyright in a work is infringed by a public performance of the work, or by the playing or showing of the work in public, by means of apparatus for—

(a) playing sound recordings,

(b) showing films, or

(c) receiving visual images or sounds conveyed by electronic means,

the following persons are also liable for the infringement.

(2) A person who supplied the apparatus, or any substantial part of it, is liable for the infringement if when he supplied the apparatus or part—

(a) he knew or had reason to believe that the apparatus was likely to be so used as to infringe copyright, or

(b) in the case of apparatus whose normal use involves a public performance, playing or showing, he did not believe on reasonable grounds that it would not be so used as to infringe copyright.

(3) An occupier of premises who gave permission for the apparatus to be brought on to the premises is liable for the infringement if when he gave permission he knew or had reason to believe that the apparatus was likely to be so used as to infringe copyright.

(4) A person who supplied a copy of a sound recording or film used to infringe copyright is liable for the infringement if when he supplied it he knew or had reason to believe that what he supplied, or a copy made directly or indirectly from it, was likely to be so used as to infringe copyright.

Infringing copies

Meaning of "infringing copy"

27.—(1) In this Part "infringing copy," in relation to a copyright work, shall be construed in accordance with this section.

(2) An article is an infringing copy if its making constituted an infringement of the copyright in the work in question.

[(3) An article is also an infringing copy if

(a) it has been or is proposed to be imported into the United Kingdom, and

(b) its making in the United Kingdom would have constituted an infringement of the copyright in the work in question, or a breach of an exclusive licence agreement relating to that work.]

(4) Where in any proceedings the question arises whether an article is an infringing copy and it is shown—

(a) that the article is a copy of the work, and

(b) that copyright subsists in the work or has subsisted at any time,

it shall be presumed until the contrary is proved that the article was made at a time when copyright subsisted in the work.

(5) Nothing in subsection (3) shall be construed as applying to an article which may lawfully be imported into the United Kingdom by virtue of any enforceable [EU] Community right within the meaning of section 2(1) of the European Communities Act 1972.

(6) In this Part "infringing copy" includes a copy falling to be treated as an infringing copy by virtue of any of the following provisions—

> [section 28B(7) and (9) (personal copies for private use),]
> [section 29A(3) (copies for text and data analysis for non-commercial research),]
> [[section 31A(5) and (6) (disabled persons: copies of works for personal use),]
> [section 31B(11) (making and supply of accessible copies by authorised bodies),]
> [...]]
> [section 35(5) (recording by educational establishments of broadcasts),]
> [section 36(8) (copying and use of extracts of works by educational establishments),]

[section 42A(5)(b) (copying by librarians: single copies of published works),]

[section 43(5)(b) (copying by librarians or archivists: single copies of unpublished works),]

[...]

section 56(2) (further copies, adaptations, &c. of work in electronic form retained on transfer of principal copy),

[section 61(6)(b) (recordings of folksongs),]

section 63(2) (copies made for purpose of advertising artistic work for sale),

section 68(4) (copies made for purpose of broadcast [...]),

[section 70(2) (recording for the purposes of time-shifting),

section 71(2) (photographs of broadcasts), or]

any provision of an order under section 141 (statutory licence for certain reprographic copying by educational establishments).

Notes:

(1) Subsection (3) is printed as amended by the Copyright and Related Rights Regulations 1996 (SI 1996/2967, which deleted a reference to subs.(3A) (also deleted by those Regulations) with effect from December 1, 1996. For savings and transitional provisions, see Part III of those Regulations.

(2) In subs.(5) word substituted by the Treaty of Lisbon (Changes in Terminology) Order 2011 (SI 2011/1043) art.6(1)(f) with effect from April 22, 2011.

(3) In subs.(6), the entries relating to ss.31A, 31B and 31C inserted by the Copyright (Visually Impaired Persons) Act 2002 (c.33) s.7 with effect from October 31, 2003 (see the Copyright (Visually Impaired Persons) Act 2002 (Commencement) Order 2003 (SI 2003/2499)). The entries relating to ss.70 and 71 inserted and the words "or cable programme" repealed by the Copyright and Related Rights Regulations 2003 (SI 2003/2498), reg.20 and Sch.2 with effect from October 31, 2003. For savings and transitional provisions, see Part 3 of those Regulations.

(4) Entries relating to ss.29A(3), 35(5), 36(8), 42A(5)(b), 43(5)(b), 61(6)(b) inserted, and entries relating to ss.32(5), 35(3), 36(5) and 37(3)(b) repealed, by the Copyright and Rights in Performances (Research, Education, Libraries and Archives) Regulations 2014 (SI 2014/1372), Sch. para.2(b), with effect from June 1, 2014 at 00.02.

(5) Entries relating to s.31A(5) and (6), and s.31B(11), inserted, and entry relating to s.31C(2) repealed, by the Copyright and Rights in Performances (Disability) Regulations 2014 (SI 2014/1384), Sch. para.1, with effect from June 1, 2014 at 00.01.

(6) Entry in italics and square brackets relating to s.28B(7) and (9) was inserted by the Copyright and Rights in Performances (Personal Copies for Private Use) Regulations 2014 (SI 2014/2361), reg.4(1), with effect from October 1, 2014. However, SI 2014/2361 was quashed with prospective effect on July 17, 2015: *The Queen on the application of British Academy of Songwriters, Composers and Authors v Secretary of State for Business, Innovation and Skills* [2015] EWHC 2041 (Admin) at [11], [21]. Accordingly, this consequential amendment has no effect from that date. However, the Court declined to rule as to whether the regulations were void during the period from October 1, 2014 to July 16, 2015. Accordingly the question of whether this amendment is effective during that period remains undecided: see the judgment at [19], [21].

Chapter III

Acts Permitted in Relation to Copyright Works

Introductory

Introductory provisions

28.—(1) The provisions of this Chapter specify acts which may be done in relation to copyright works notwithstanding the subsistence of copyright; they relate only to the question of infringement of copyright and do not affect any other right or obligation restricting the doing of any of the specified acts.

(2) Where it is provided by this Chapter that an act does not infringe copyright, or may be done without infringing copyright, and no particular description of copyright work is mentioned, the act in question does not infringe the copyright in a work of any description.

(3) No inference shall be drawn from the description of any act which may by virtue of this Chapter be done without infringing copyright as to the scope of the acts restricted by the copyright in any description of work.

(4) The provisions of this Chapter are to be construed independently of each other, so that the fact that an act does not fall within one provision does not mean that it is not covered by another provision.

General

Making of temporary copies

[**28A.** Copyright in a literary work, other than a computer program or a database, or in a dramatic, musical or artistic work, the typographical arrangement of a published edition, a sound recording or a film, is not infringed by the making of a temporary copy which is transient or incidental, which is an integral and essential part of a technological process and the sole purpose of which is to enable

  (a) a transmission of the work in a network between third parties by an intermediary; or

  (b) a lawful use of the work;

and which has no independent economic significance.]

Note: Section 28A was inserted by the Copyright and Related Rights Regulations 2003 (SI 2003/2498), reg.8 with effect from October 31, 2003. For savings and transitional provisions, see Part 3 of those Regulations.

[**28B.** [...]]]

Note: The Copyright and Rights in Performance (Personal Copies for Private Use) Regulations 2014 (SI 2014/2361), which introduced s.28B with effect from October 1, 2014, were quashed with prospective effect on July 17, 2015: *The Queen on the application of British Academy of Songwriters, Composers and Authors v Secretary of State for Business, Innovation and Skills* [2015] EWHC 2041 (Admin) at [11], [21]. Accordingly, s.28B has been of no effect from that date. However, the Court declined to rule as to whether the regulations (and therefore s.28B) were void during the period from October 1, 2014 to July 16, 2015. Accordingly the question whether s.28B was effective during that period remains undecided: see the judgment at [19], [21]. Section 28B read as follows:

Personal copies for private use

28B.—*(1) The making of a copy of a work, other than a computer program, by an individual does not infringe copyright in the work provided that the copy—*

  (a) is a copy of—

    (i) individual's own copy of the work, or

    (ii) a personal copy of the work made by the individual,

  (b) is made for the individual's private use, and

  (c) is made for ends which are neither directly nor indirectly commercial.

  (2) In this section "the individual's own copy" is a copy which—

    (a) has been lawfully acquired by the individual on a permanent basis,

(b) is not an infringing copy, and

(c) has not been made under any provision of this Chapter which permits the making of a copy without infringing copyright.

(3) In this section a "personal copy" means a copy made under this section.

(4) For the purposes of subsection (2)(a), a copy "lawfully acquired on a permanent basis"—

(a) includes a copy which has been purchased, obtained by way of a gift, or acquired by means of a download resulting from a purchase or a gift (other than a download of a kind mentioned in paragraph (b)); and

(b) does not include a copy which has been borrowed, rented, broadcast or streamed, or a copy which has been obtained by means of a download enabling no more than temporary access to the copy.

(5) In subsection (1)(b) "private use" includes private use facilitated by the making of a copy—

(a) as a back up copy,

(b) for the purposes of format shifting, or

(c) for the purposes of storage, including in an electronic storage area accessed by means of the internet or similar means which is accessible only by the individual (and the person responsible for the storage area).

(6) Copyright in a work is infringed if an individual transfers a personal copy of the work to another person (otherwise than on a private and temporary basis), except where the transfer is authorised by the copyright owner.

(7) If copyright is infringed as set out in subsection (6), a personal copy which has been transferred is for all purposes subsequently treated as an infringing copy.

(8) Copyright in a work is also infringed if an individual, having made a personal copy of the work, transfers the individual's own copy of the work to another person (otherwise than on a private and temporary basis) and, after that transfer and without the licence of the copyright owner, retains any personal copy.

(9) If copyright is infringed as set out in subsection (8), any retained personal copy is for all purposes subsequently treated as an infringing copy.

(10) To the extent that a term of a contract purports to prevent or restrict the making of a copy which, by virtue of this section, would not infringe copyright, that term is unenforceable."

Research and private study

29.—[(1) Fair dealing with a [...] work for the purposes of research for a non-commercial purpose does not infringe any copyright in the work provided that it is accompanied by a sufficient acknowledgement.]

[(1A) [...]]

[(1B) No acknowledgement is required in connection with fair dealing for the purposes mentioned in subsection (1) where this would be impossible for reasons of practicality or otherwise.]

[(1C) Fair dealing with a [...] work for the purposes of private study does not infringe any copyright in the work.]

(2) [...]

(3) Copying by a person other than the researcher or student himself is not fair dealing if—

[(a) in the case of a librarian, or a person acting on behalf of a librarian, that person does anything which is not permitted under section 42A (copying by librarians: single copies of published works), or]

(b) in any other case, the person doing the copying knows or has reason to believe that it will result in copies of substantially the same material being provided to more than one person at substantially the same time and for substantially the same purpose.

[(4) It is not fair dealing

(a) to convert a computer program expressed in a low level language into a version expressed in a higher level language, or

(b) incidentally in the course of so converting the program, to copy it,

(these being acts permitted if done in accordance with section 50B (decompilation)).]

[(4A) It is not fair dealing to observe, study or test the functioning of a computer program in order to determine the ideas and principles which underlie any element of the program (these acts being permitted if done in accordance with section 50BA (observing, studying and testing)).]

[(4B) To the extent that a term of a contract purports to prevent or restrict the doing of any act which, by virtue of this section, would not infringe copyright, that term is unenforceable.]

(5) [...]

Notes:

(1) Subsection (1) was amended by, and subss.(1A) and (5) inserted by the Copyright and Rights in Databases Regulations 1997 (SI 1997/3032), with effect from January 1, 1998. For savings and transitional provisions, see regs 26 to 30 of those Regulations. The amended subss.(1), (1A) and (5) provided:

"(1) Fair dealing with a literary [work, other than a database, or a] dramatic, musical or artistic work for the purposes of research or private study does not infringe any copyright in the work or, in the case of a published edition, in the typographical arrangement.

[(1A) Fair dealing with a database for the purposes of research or private study does not infringe any copyright in the database provided that the source is indicated.

(5) The doing of anything in relation to a database for the purposes of research for a commercial purpose is not fair dealing with the database.]"

(2) Subsection (4) was inserted by the Copyright (Computer Programs) Regulations 1992 (SI 1992/3233), with effect from January 1, 1993. For savings and transitional provisions, see reg.12 of those Regulations.

(3) Subsection (1) was substituted, subss.(1B), (1C) and (4A) inserted, subss.(1A) and (5) repealed and the words in square brackets in subs.(2) substituted for the former words "mentioned in subsection (1)" by the Copyright and Related Rights Regulations 2003 (SI 2003/2498), reg.9 with effect from October 31, 2003.

(4) In subss.(1), (1C) words "literary, dramatic, musical or artistic" repealed, subs.(2) repealed, subs.(3)(a) substituted, and subs.(4B) inserted, by the Copyright and Rights in Performances (Research, Education, Libraries and Archives) Regulations 2014 (SI 2014/1372), reg.3(1), with effect from June 1, 2014 at 00.02. Subs.(2) formerly read:

"(2) Fair dealing with the typographical arrangement of a published edition for the purposes [of research or private study] does not infringe any copyright in the arrangement."

and subs.(3)(a) formerly read:

"(a) in the case of a librarian, or a person acting on behalf of a librarian, he does anything which regulations under section 40 would not permit to be done under section 38 or 39 (articles or parts of published works: restriction on multiple copies of same material), or"

Copies for text and data analysis for non-commercial research

[29A.—(1) The making of a copy of a work by a person who has lawful access to the work does not infringe copyright in the work provided that—

(a) the copy is made in order that a person who has lawful access to the work may carry out a computational analysis of anything recorded in the work for the sole purpose of research for a non-commercial purpose, and

(b) the copy is accompanied by a sufficient acknowledgement (unless this would be impossible for reasons of practicality or otherwise).

(2) Where a copy of a work has been made under this section, copyright in the work is infringed if—

(a) the copy is transferred to any other person, except where the transfer is authorised by the copyright owner, or

(b) the copy is used for any purpose other than that mentioned in subsection (1)(a), except where the use is authorised by the copyright owner.

(3) If a copy made under this section is subsequently dealt with—

(a) it is to be treated as an infringing copy for the purposes of that dealing, and

(b) if that dealing infringes copyright, it is to be treated as an infringing copy for all subsequent purposes.

(4) In subsection (3) "dealt with" means sold or let for hire, or offered or exposed for sale or hire.

(5) To the extent that a term of a contract purports to prevent or restrict the making of a copy which, by virtue of this section, would not infringe copyright, that term is unenforceable.]

Notes:

Section 29A inserted, by the Copyright and Rights in Performances (Research, Education, Libraries and Archives) Regulations 2014 (SI 2014/1372), reg.3(2), with effect from June 1, 2014 at 00.02.

Criticism, review[, quotation] and news reporting

30.—(1) Fair dealing with a work for the purpose of criticism or review, of that or another work or of a performance of a work, does not infringe any copyright in the work provided that it is accompanied by a sufficient acknowledgement [(unless this would be impossible for reasons of practicality or otherwise)] [and provided that the work has been made available to the public.]

[(1ZA) Copyright in a work is not infringed by the use of a quotation from the work (whether for criticism or review or otherwise) provided that—

(a) the work has been made available to the public,

(b) the use of the quotation is fair dealing with the work,

(c) the extent of the quotation is no more than is required by the specific purpose for which it is used, and

(d) the quotation is accompanied by a sufficient acknowledgement (unless this would be impossible for reasons of practicality or otherwise).]

[(1A) For the purposes of [subsections (1) and (1ZA)]subsection (1) a work has been made available to the public if it has been made available by any means, including—

(a) the issue of copies to the public;

(b) making the work available by means of an electronic retrieval system;

(c) the rental or lending of copies of the work to the public;

(d) the performance, exhibition, playing or showing of the work in public;

(e) the communication to the public of the work,

but in determining generally for the purposes of [those subsections] that subsection whether a work has been made available to the public no account shall be taken of any unauthorised act.]

(2) Fair dealing with a work (other than a photograph) for the purpose of

reporting current events does not infringe any copyright in the work provided that (subject to subsection (3)) it is accompanied by a sufficient acknowledgement.

(3) No acknowledgement is required in connection with the reporting of current events by means of a sound recording, film [or broadcast where this would be impossible for reasons of practicality or otherwise].

[(4) To the extent that a term of a contract purports to prevent or restrict the doing of any act which, by virtue of subsection (1ZA), would not infringe copyright, that term is unenforceable.]

Notes:

(1) The words in square brackets in subs.(1) and subs.(1A) inserted and the words in square brackets in subs.(3) substituted for the former words ", broadcast or cable programme" by the Copyright and Related Rights Regulations 2003 (SI 2003/2498), reg.10 with effect from October 31, 2003. For savings and transitional provisions, see Part 3 of those Regulations.

(2) The Broadcasting Act 1996 s.137(1) provides:

"*(1) Any provision in an agreement is void in so far as it purports to prohibit or restrict relevant dealing with a broadcast in any circumstance where by virtue of section 30(2) of the Copyright, Designs and Patents Act 1988 (fair dealing for the purpose of reporting current events) copyright in the broadcast is not infringed.*"

This provision was brought into effect from October 1, 1996 by virtue of the Broadcasting Act 1996 (Commencement No.1 and Transitional Provisions) Order 1996 (SI 1996/2120) and is printed as amended by the Copyright and Related Rights Regulations 2003 (SI 2003/2498), reg.2 Sch.2, with effect from October 31, 2003.

(3) In heading and subs.(1), words in square brackets inserted, in subs.(1A) words in square brackets substituted for words "subsection (1)" and "that subsection", and subss.(1ZA), (4) inserted, by the Copyright and Rights in Performances (Quotation and Parody) Regulations 2014 (SI 2014/2356), reg.3, with effect from October 1, 2014.

Caricture, parody or pastiche

[**30A.**—(1) Fair dealing with a work for the purposes of caricature, parody or pastiche does not infringe copyright in the work.

(2) To the extent that a term of a contract purports to prevent or restrict the doing of any act which, by virtue of this section, would not infringe copyright, that term is unenforceable.]

Note: Section 30A inserted by the Copyright and Rights in Performances (Quotation and Parody) Regulations 2014 (SI 2014/2356), reg.5(1), with effect from October 1, 2014.

Incidental inclusion of copyright material

31.—(1) Copyright in a work is not infringed by its incidental inclusion in an artistic work, sound recording, film [or broadcast].

(2) Nor is the copyright infringed by the issue to the public of copies, or the playing, showing [or communication to the public], of anything whose making was, by virtue of subsection (1), not an infringement of the copyright.

(3) A musical work, words spoken or sung with music, or so much of a sound recording or broadcast as includes a musical work or such words, shall not be regarded as incidentally included in another work if it is deliberately included.

Note: The words in square brackets in subss.(1) and (3) substituted for the former words ", broadcast or cable programme" and the words in square brackets in subs.(2) substituted for the former words ", broadcasting or inclusion in a cable programme service" by the Copyright and Related Rights Regulations 2003 (SI 2003/2498), Sch.1 paras 3 and 6 with effect from October 31, 2003. For savings and transitional provisions, see Part 3 of those Regulations.

[Disability]

Disabled persons: copies of works for personal use

[**31A.**—(1) This section applies if—

    (a) a disabled person has lawful possession or lawful use of a copy of the whole or part of a work, and

    (b) the person's disability prevents the person from enjoying the work to the same degree as a person who does not have that disability.

(2) The making of an accessible copy of the copy of the work referred to in subsection (1)(a) does not infringe copyright if—

    (a) the copy is made by the disabled person or by a person acting on behalf of the disabled person,

    (b) the copy is made for the disabled person's personal use, and

    (c) the same kind of accessible copies of the work are not commercially available on reasonable terms by or with the authority of the copyright owner.

(3) If a person makes an accessible copy under this section on behalf of a disabled person and charges the disabled person for it, the sum charged must not exceed the cost of making and supplying the copy.

(4) Copyright is infringed by the transfer of an accessible copy of a work made under this section to any person other than—

    (a) a person by or for whom an accessible copy of the work may be made under this section, or

    (b) a person who intends to transfer the copy to a person falling within paragraph (a), except where the transfer is authorised by the copyright owner.

(5) An accessible copy of a work made under this section is to be treated for all purposes as an infringing copy if it is held by a person at a time when the person does not fall within subsection (4)(a) or (b).

(6) If an accessible copy made under this section is subsequently dealt with—

(7) In this section "dealt with" means sold or let for hire or offered or exposed for sale or hire.]

Note: Section 31A substituted, and preceding cross-heading substituted, by the Copyright and Rights in Performances (Disability) Regulations 2014 (SI 2014/1384), reg.2(2), (3), with effect from June 1, 2014 at 00.01. Section 31A (as inserted by SI 2003/2499) formerly read:

"[Visual impairment]

Making a single accessible copy for personal use

[**31A.**—*(1) If a visually impaired person has lawful possession or lawful use of a copy ("the master copy") of the whole or part of—*

    (a) a literary, dramatic, musical or artistic work; or

    (b) a published edition,

which is not accessible to him because of the impairment, it is not an infringement of copyright in the work, or in the typographical arrangement of the published edition, for an accessible copy of the master copy to be made for his personal use.

    (2) Subsection (1) does not apply—

        (a) if the master copy is of a musical work, or part of a musical work, and the making of an accessible copy would involve recording a performance of the work or part of it; or

        (b) if the master copy is of a database, or part of a database, and the making of an accessible copy would infringe copyright in the database.

(3) Subsection (1) does not apply in relation to the making of an accessible copy for a particular visually impaired person if, or to the extent that, copies of the copyright work are commercially available, by or with the authority of the copyright owner, in a form that is accessible to that person.

(4) An accessible copy made under this section must be accompanied by—

    (a) a statement that it is made under this section; and

    (b) a sufficient acknowledgement.

(5) If a person makes an accessible copy on behalf of a visually impaired person under this section and charges for it, the sum charged must not exceed the cost of making and supplying the copy.

(6) If a person holds an accessible copy made under subsection (1) when he is not entitled to have it made under that subsection, the copy is to be treated as an infringing copy, unless he is a person falling within subsection (7)(b).

(7) A person who holds an accessible copy made under subsection (1) may transfer it to—

    (a) a visually impaired person entitled to have the accessible copy made under subsection (1); or

    (b) a person who has lawful possession of the master copy and intends to transfer the accessible copy to a person falling within paragraph (a).

(8) The transfer by a person ("V") of an accessible copy made under subsection (1) to another person ("T") is an infringement of copyright by V unless V has reasonable grounds for believing that T is a person falling within subsection (7)(a) or (b).

(9) If an accessible copy which would be an infringing copy but for this section is subsequently dealt with—

    (a) it is to be treated as an infringing copy for the purposes of that dealing; and

    (b) if that dealing infringes copyright, is to be treated as an infringing copy for all subsequent purposes.

(10) In subsection (9), "dealt with" means sold or let for hire or offered or exposed for sale or hire or included in a broadcast or cable programme service]."

Making and supply of accessible copies by authorised bodies

[31B.—(1) If an authorised body has lawful possession of a copy of the whole or part of a published work, the body may, without infringing copyright, make and supply accessible copies of the work for the personal use of disabled persons.

(2) But subsection (1) does not apply if the same kind of accessible copies of the work are commercially available on reasonable terms by or with the authority of the copyright owner.

(3) If an authorised body has lawful access to or lawful possession of the whole or part of a broadcast or a copy of a broadcast, the body may, without infringing copyright—

    (a) in the case of a broadcast, make a recording of the broadcast, and make and supply accessible copies of the recording or of any work included in the broadcast, and

    (b) in the case of a copy of a broadcast, make and supply accessible copies of that copy or of any work included in the broadcast,

(4) But subsection (3) does not apply if the same kind of accessible copies of the broadcast, or of any work included in it, are commercially available on reasonable terms by or with the authority of the copyright owner.

(5) For the purposes of subsections (1) and (3), supply "for the personal use of disabled persons" includes supply to a person acting on behalf of a disabled person.

(6) An authorised body which is an educational establishment conducted for profit must ensure that any accessible copies which it makes under this section are used only for its educational purposes.

(7) An accessible copy made under this section must be accompanied by—
  (a) a statement that it is made under this section, and
  (b) a sufficient acknowledgement (unless this would be impossible for reasons of practicality or otherwise).

(8) If an accessible copy is made under this section of a work which is in copy-protected electronic form, the accessible copy must, so far as is reasonably practicable, incorporate the same or equally effective copy protection (unless the copyright owner agrees otherwise).

(9) An authorised body which has made an accessible copy of a work under this section may supply it to another authorised body which is entitled to make accessible copies of the work under this section for the purposes of enabling that other body to make accessible copies of the work.

(10) If an authorised body supplies an accessible copy it has made under this section to a person or authorised body as permitted by this section and charges the person or body for it, the sum charged must not exceed the cost of making and supplying the copy.

(11) If an accessible copy made under this section is subsequently dealt with—
  (a) it is to be treated as an infringing copy for the purposes of that dealing, and
  (b) if that dealing infringes copyright, it is to be treated as an infringing copy for all subsequent purposes.

(12) In this section "dealt with" means sold or let for hire or offered or exposed for sale or hire.]

Note: Sections 31B, BA, BB substituted for existing s.31B, by the Copyright and Rights in Performances (Disability) Regulations 2014 (SI 2014/1384), reg.2(4), with effect from June 1, 2014 at 00.01. Section 31B (as inserted by SI 2003/2499) formerly read:

Multiple copies for visually impaired persons

"**[31B.**—*(1) If an approved body has lawful possession of a copy ("the master copy") of the whole or part of—*
  (a) a commercially published literary, dramatic, musical or artistic work; or
  (b) a commercially published edition,
it is not an infringement of copyright in the work, or in the typographical arrangement of the published edition, for the body to make, or supply, accessible copies for the personal use of visually impaired persons to whom the master copy is not accessible because of their impairment.

(2) Subsection (1) does not apply—
  (a) if the master copy is of a musical work, or part of a musical work, and the making of an accessible copy would involve recording a performance of the work or part of it; or
  (b) if the master copy is of a database, or part of a database, and the making of an accessible copy would infringe copyright in the database.

(3) Subsection (1) does not apply in relation to the making of an accessible copy if, or to the extent that, copies of the copyright work are commercially available, by or with the authority of the copyright owner, in a form that is accessible to the same or substantially the same degree.

(4) Subsection (1) does not apply in relation to the supply of an accessible copy to a particular visually impaired person if, or to the extent that, copies of the copyright work are commercially available, by or with the authority of the copyright owner, in a form that is accessible to that person.

(5) An accessible copy made under this section must be accompanied by—

(a) a statement that it is made under this section; and

(b) a sufficient acknowledgement.

(6) If an approved body charges for supplying a copy made under this section, the sum charged must not exceed the cost of making and supplying the copy.

(7) An approved body making copies under this section must, if it is an educational establishment, ensure that the copies will be used only for its educational purposes.

(8) If the master copy is in copy-protected electronic form, any accessible copy made of it under this section must, so far as it is reasonably practicable to do so, incorporate the same, or equally effective, copy protection (unless the copyright owner agrees otherwise).

(9) If an approved body continues to hold an accessible copy made under subsection (1) when it would no longer be entitled to make or supply such a copy under that subsection, the copy is to be treated as an infringing copy.

(10) If an accessible copy which would be an infringing copy but for this section is subsequently dealt with—

(a) it is to be treated as an infringing copy for the purposes of that dealing; and

(b) if that dealing infringes copyright, is to be treated as an infringing copy for all subsequent purposes.

(11) In subsection (10), "dealt with" means sold or let for hire or offered or exposed for sale or hire or included in a broadcast or cable programme service.

(12) "Approved body" means an educational establishment or a body that is not conducted for profit.

(13) "Supplying" includes lending.] "

Making and supply of intermediate copies by authorised bodies

[31BA—(1) An authorised body which is entitled to make an accessible copy of a work under section 31B may, without infringing copyright, make a copy of the work ("an intermediate copy") if this is necessary in order to make the accessible copy.

(2) An authorised body which has made an intermediate copy of a work under this section may supply it to another authorised body which is entitled to make accessible copies of the work under section 31B for the purposes of enabling that other body to make accessible copies of the work.

(3) Copyright is infringed by the transfer of an intermediate copy made under this section to a person other than another authorised body as permitted by subsection (2), except where the transfer is authorised by the copyright owner.

(4) If an authorised body supplies an intermediate copy to an authorised body under subsection (2) and charges the body for it, the sum charged must not exceed the cost of making and supplying the copy.]

Note: Sections 31B, BA, BB substituted for existing s.31B, by the Copyright and Rights in Performances (Disability) Regulations 2014 (SI 2014/1384), reg.2(4), with effect from June 1, 2014 at 00.01.

Accessible and intermediate copies: records and notification

[31BB.—(1) An authorised body must keep a record of—

(a) accessible copies it makes under section 31B,

(b) intermediate copies it makes under section 31BA, and

(c) the persons to whom such copies are supplied.

(2) An authorised body must allow the copyright owner or a person acting for

the copyright owner, on giving reasonable notice, to inspect at any reasonable time—

    (a) records kept under subsection (1), and

    (b) records of copies made under sections 31B and 31C as those sections were in force before the coming into force of these Regulations.

  (3) Within a reasonable time of making an accessible copy under section 31B, an authorised body must—

    (a) notify any body which—

        (i) represents particular copyright owners or owners of copyright in the type of work concerned, and

        (ii) has given notice to the Secretary of State of the copyright owners, or the classes of copyright owner, represented by it, or

    (b) if there is no such body, notify the copyright owner (unless it is not reasonably possible to ascertain the name and address of the copyright owner).]

Note: Sections 31B, 31BA, 31BB substituted for existing s.31B, by the Copyright and Rights in Performances (Disability) Regulations 2014 (SI 2014/1384), reg.2(4), with effect from June 1, 2014 at 00.01.

31C.–31E. [...]

Note: Sections 31C to 31E repealed by the Copyright and Rights in Performances (Disability) Regulations 2014 (SI 2014/1384), Sch. para.8, with effect from June 1, 2014 at 00.01.

Sections 31C to 31E (as inserted by SI 2003/2499) formerly read:

Intermediate copies and records

  "[31C.—(1) An approved body entitled to make accessible copies under section 31B may hold an intermediate copy of the master copy which is necessarily created during the production of the accessible copies, but only—

    (a) if and so long as the approved body continues to be entitled to make accessible copies of that master copy; and

    (b) for the purposes of the production of further accessible copies.

  (2) An intermediate copy which is held in breach of subsection (1) is to be treated as an infringing copy.

  (3) An approved body may lend or transfer the intermediate copy to another approved body which is entitled to make accessible copies of the work or published edition under section 31B.

  (4) The loan or transfer by an approved body ("A") of an intermediate copy to another person ("B") is an infringement of copyright by A unless A has reasonable grounds for believing that B—

    (a) is another approved body which is entitled to make accessible copies of the work or published edition under section 31B; and

    (b) will use the intermediate copy only for the purposes of the production of further accessible copies.

  (5) If an approved body charges for lending or transferring the intermediate copy, the sum charged must not exceed the cost of the loan or transfer.

  (6) An approved body must—

    (a) keep records of accessible copies made under section 31B and of the persons to whom they are supplied;

    (b) keep records of any intermediate copy lent or transferred under this section and of the persons to whom it is lent or transferred; and

    (c) allow the copyright owner or a person acting for him, on giving reasonable notice, to inspect the records at any reasonable time.

  (7) Within a reasonable time of making an accessible copy under section 31B, or

lending or transferring an intermediate copy under this section, the approved body must—

    (a) notify each relevant representative body; or

    (b) if there is no such body, notify the copyright owner.

(8) A relevant representative body is a body which—

    (a) represents particular copyright owners, or owners of copyright in the type of copyright work concerned; and

    (b) has given notice to the Secretary of State of the copyright owners, or the classes of copyright owner, represented by it.

(9) The requirement to notify the copyright owner under subsection (7)(b) does not apply if it is not reasonably possible for the approved body to ascertain the name and address of the copyright owner.]

Licensing schemes

[31D.—*(1) Section 31B does not apply to the making of an accessible copy in a particular form if—*

    (a) a licensing scheme operated by a licensing body is in force under which licences may be granted by the licensing body permitting the making and supply of copies of the copyright work in that form;

    (b) the scheme is not unreasonably restrictive; and

    (c) the scheme and any modification made to it have been notified to the Secretary of State by the licensing body.

(2) A scheme is unreasonably restrictive if it includes a term or condition which—

    (a) purports to prevent or limit the steps that may be taken under section 31B or 31C; or

    (b) has that effect.

(3) But subsection (2) does not apply if—

    (a) the copyright work is no longer published by or with the authority of the copyright owner; and

    (b) there are reasonable grounds for preventing or restricting the making of accessible copies of the work.

(4) If section 31B or 31C is displaced by a licensing scheme, sections 119 to 122 apply in relation to the scheme as if it were one to which those sections applied as a result of section 117.]

Limitations, etc. following infringement of copyright

[31E.—*(1) The Secretary of State may make an order under this section if it appears to him that the making of copies—*

    (a) under section 31B; or

    (b) under a licence granted under a licensing scheme that has been notified under section 31D,

has led to infringement of copyright on a scale which, in the Secretary of State's opinion, would not have occurred if section 31B had not been in force, or the licence had not been granted.

(2) The order may prohibit one or more named approved bodies, or one or more specified categories of approved body, from—

    (a) acting under section 31B; or

    (b) acting under a licence of a description specified in the order.

(3) The order may disapply—

    (a) the provisions of section 31B; or

    (b) the provisions of a licence, or a licensing scheme, of a description specified in the order, *in respect of the making of copies of a description so specified.*

(4) If the Secretary of State proposes to make an order he must, before making it, consult—

   (a) such bodies representing copyright owners as he thinks fit; and

   (b) such bodies representing visually impaired persons as he thinks fit.

(5) If the Secretary of State proposes to make an order which includes a prohibition he must, before making it, consult—

   (a) if the proposed order is to apply to one or more named approved bodies, that body or those bodies;

   (b) if it is to apply to one or more specified categories of approved body, to such bodies representing approved bodies of that category or those categories as he thinks fit.

(6) An approved body which is prohibited by an order from acting under a licence may not apply to the Copyright Tribunal under section 121(1) in respect of a refusal or failure by a licensing body to grant such a licence.]"

Sections 31A to 31BB: interpretation and general

[**31F.**—(1) This section supplements sections 31A to 31BB and includes definitions.

(2) "Disabled person" means a person who has a physical or mental impairment which prevents the person from enjoying a copyright work to the same degree as a person who does not have that impairment, and "disability" is to be construed accordingly.

(3) But a person is not to be regarded as disabled by reason only of an impairment of visual function which can be improved, by the use of corrective lenses, to a level that is normally acceptable for reading without a special level or kind of light.

(4) An "accessible copy" of a copyright work means a version of the work which enables the fuller enjoyment of the work by disabled persons.

(5) An accessible copy—

   (a) may include facilities for navigating around the version of the work, but

   (b) must not include any changes to the work which are not necessary to overcome the problems suffered by the disabled persons for whom the accessible copy is intended.

(6) "Authorised body" means—

   (a) an educational establishment, or

   (b) a body that is not conducted for profit.

(7) The "supply" of a copy includes making it available for use, otherwise than for direct or indirect economic or commercial advantage, on terms that it will or may be returned.

(8) To the extent that a term of a contract purports to prevent or restrict the doing of any act which, by virtue of section 31A, 31B or 31BA, would not infringe copyright, that term is unenforceable.]

Note: Section 31F substituted, subject to savings, by the Copyright and Rights in Performances (Disability) Regulations 2014 (SI 2014/1384), reg.2(5), with effect from June 1, 2014 at 00.01 (for savings see Schedule, para.9). Section 31F (as inserted by SI 2003/2499) formerly read:

Definitions and other supplementary provision for sections 31A to 31E

"[**31F.**—*(1) This section supplements sections 31A to 31E and includes definitions.*

(2) A copy of a copyright work (other than an accessible copy made under section 31A or 31B) is to be taken to be accessible to a visually impaired person only if it is as accessible to him as it would be if he were not visually impaired.

(3) "Accessible copy", in relation to a copyright work, means a version which provides for a visually impaired person improved access to the work.

(4) An accessible copy may include facilities for navigating around the version of the copyright work but may not include—

(a) changes that are not necessary to overcome problems caused by visual impairment; or

(b) changes which infringe the right (provided by section 80) not to have the work subjected to derogatory treatment.

(5) "Approved body" has the meaning given in section 31B(12).

(6) "Lending", in relation to a copy, means making it available for use, otherwise than for direct or indirect economic or commercial advantage, on terms that it will or may be returned.

(7) For the purposes of subsection (6), a loan is not to be treated as being for direct or indirect economic or commercial advantage if a charge is made for the loan which does not exceed the cost of making and supplying the copy.

(8) The definition of "lending" in section 18A does not apply for the purposes of sections 31B and 31C.

(9) "Visually impaired person" means a person—

(a) who is blind;

(b) who has an impairment of visual function which cannot be improved, by the use of corrective lenses, to a level that would normally be acceptable for reading without a special level or kind of light;

(c) who is unable, through physical disability, to hold or manipulate a book; or

(d) who is unable, through physical disability, to focus or move his eyes to the extent that would normally be acceptable for reading.

(10) The Secretary of State may by regulations prescribe—

(a) the form in which; or

(b) the procedure in accordance with which,

any notice required under section 31C(7) or (8), or 31D(1), must be given.

(11) Any power to make regulations or orders is exercisable by statutory instrument subject to annulment in pursuance of a resolution of either House of Parliament.]"

Education

Illustration for instruction

[**32.**—(1) Fair dealing with a work for the sole purpose of illustration for instruction does not infringe copyright in the work provided that the dealing is—

(a) for a non-commercial purpose;

(b) by a person giving or receiving instruction (or preparing for giving or receiving instruction), and

(c) accompanied by a sufficient acknowledgement (unless this would be impossible for reasons of practicality or otherwise).

(2) For the purposes of subsection (1), "giving or receiving instruction" includes setting examination questions, communicating the questions to pupils and answering the questions.

(3) To the extent that a term of a contract purports to prevent or restrict the doing of any act which, by virtue of this section, would not infringe copyright, that term is unenforceable.]

Note: Section 32 substituted by the Copyright and Rights in Performances (Research, Education, Libraries and Archives) Regulations 2014 (SI 2014/1372), reg.4(1), with effect from June 1, 2014 at 00.02. Section 32 (as amended by SI 2003/2498) formerly read:

Education

Things done for purposes of instruction or examination

"**32.**—*[(1) Copyright in a literary, dramatic, musical or artistic work is not infringed by its being copied in the course of instruction or of preparation for instruction, provided the copying—*

(a) *is done by a person giving or receiving instruction,*

(b) *is not done by means of a reprographic process, and*

(c) *is accompanied by a sufficient acknowledgement,*

and provided that the instruction is for a non-commercial purpose.

(2) *Copyright in a sound recording, film or broadcast is not infringed by its being copied by making a film or film sound-track in the course of instruction, or of preparation for instruction, in the making of films or film sound-tracks, provided the copying—*

(a) *is done by a person giving or receiving instruction, and*

(b) *is accompanied by a sufficient acknowledgement,*

and provided that the instruction is for a non-commercial purpose.

(2A) *Copyright in a literary, dramatic, musical or artistic work which has been made available to the public is not infringed by its being copied in the course of instruction or of preparation for instruction, provided the copying—*

(a) *is fair dealing with the work,*

(b) *is done by a person giving or receiving instruction,*

(c) *is not done by means of a reprographic process, and*

(d) *is accompanied by a sufficient acknowledgement.*

(2B) *The provisions of section 30(1A) (works made available to the public) apply for the purposes of subsection (2A) as they apply for the purposes of section 30(1).]*

(3) *Copyright is not infringed by anything done for the purposes of an examination by way of setting the questions, communicating the questions to the candidates or answering the questions[, provided that the questions are accompanied by a sufficient acknowledgement].*

[(3A) No acknowledgement is required in connection with copying as mentioned in subsection (1), (2) or (2A), or in connection with anything done for the purposes mentioned in subsection (3), where this would be impossible for reasons of practicality or otherwise].

(4) *Subsection (3) does not extend to the making of a reprographic copy of a musical work for use by an examination candidate in performing the work.*

(5) *Where a copy which would otherwise be an infringing copy is made in accordance with this section but is subsequently dealt with, it shall be treated as an infringing copy for the purpose of that dealing, and if that dealing infringes copyright for all subsequent purposes.*

[For this purpose "dealt with" means—

(a) *sold or let for hire, offered or exposed for sale or hire; or*

(b) *communicated to the public, unless that communication, by virtue of subsection (3), is not an infringement of copyright.]*"

Anthologies for educational use

33.—(1) The inclusion of a short passage from a published literary or dramatic work in a collection which—

(a) is intended for use in educational establishments and is so described in its title, and in any advertisements issued by or on behalf of the publisher, and

(b) consists mainly of material in which no copyright subsists,

does not infringe the copyright in the work if the work itself is not intended for use in such establishments and the inclusion is accompanied by a sufficient acknowledgement.

(2) Subsection (1) does not authorise the inclusion of more than two excerpts from copyright works by the same author in collections published by the same publisher over any period of five years.

(3) In relation to any given passage the reference in subsection (2) to excerpts from works by the same author—

(a) shall be taken to include excerpts from works by him in collaboration with another, and

(b) if the passage in question is from such a work, shall be taken to include excerpts from works by any of the authors, whether alone or in collaboration with another.

(4) References in this section to the use of a work in an educational establishment are to any use for the educational purposes of such an establishment.

Performing, playing or showing work in course of activities of educational establishment

34.—(1) The performance of a literary, dramatic or musical work before an audience consisting of teachers and pupils at an educational establishment and other persons directly connected with the activities of the establishment—

(a) by a teacher or pupil in the course of the activities of the establishment, or

(b) at the establishment by any person for the purposes of instruction,

is not a public performance for the purposes of infringement of copyright.

(2) The playing or showing of a sound recording, film [or broadcast] before such an audience at an educational establishment for the purposes of instruction is not a playing or showing of the work in public for the purposes of infringement of copyright.

(3) A person is not for this purpose directly connected with the activities of the educational establishment simply because he is the parent of a pupil at the establishment.

Note: The words in square brackets in subs.(2) substituted for the former words ", broadcast or cable programme" by the Copyright and Related Rights Regulations 2003 (SI 2003/2498), Sch.1 para.3 with effect from October 31, 2003. For savings and transitional provisions, see Part 3 of those Regulations.

Recording by educational establishments of broadcasts

[**35.**—(1) A recording of a broadcast, or a copy of such a recording, may be made by or on behalf of an educational establishment for the educational purposes of that establishment without infringing copyright in the broadcast, or in any work included in it, provided that—

(a) the educational purposes are non-commercial, and

(b) the recording or copy is accompanied by a sufficient acknowledgement (unless this would be impossible for reasons of practicality or otherwise).

(2) Copyright is not infringed where a recording of a broadcast or a copy of such a recording, made under subsection (1), is communicated by or on behalf of the educational establishment to its pupils or staff for the non-commercial educational purposes of that establishment.

(3) Subsection (2) only applies to a communication received outside the premises of the establishment if that communication is made by means of a secure electronic network accessible only by the establishment's pupils and staff.

(4) Acts which would otherwise be permitted by this section are not permitted if, or to the extent that, licences are available authorising the acts in question and the educational establishment responsible for those acts knew or ought to have been aware of that fact.

(5) If a copy made under this section is subsequently dealt with—

    (a) it is to be treated as an infringing copy for the purposes of that dealing, and

    (b) if that dealing infringes copyright, it is to be treated as an infringing copy for all subsequent purposes.

(6) In this section "dealt with" means—

    (a) sold or let for hire,

    (b) offered or exposed for sale or hire, or

    (c) communicated otherwise than as permitted by subsection (2).]

Note: Section 35 substituted by the Copyright and Rights in Performances (Research, Education, Libraries and Archives) Regulations 2014 (SI 2014/1372), reg.4(2), with effect from June 1, 2014 at 00.02. Section 35 (as amended by SI 2003/2498) formerly read:

Recording by educational establishments of broadcasts

"35.—*(1) A recording of a broadcast [...], or a copy of such a recording, may be made by or on behalf of an educational establishment for the educational purposes of that establishment without thereby infringing the copyright in the broadcast [...], or in any work included in it, [provided that it is accompanied by a sufficient acknowledgment of the broadcast in that the educational purposes are non-commercial].*

[(1A) Copyright is not infringed where a recording of a broadcast or a copy of such a recording, whose making was by virtue of subsection (1) not an infringement of copyright, is communicated to the public by a person situated within the premises of an educational establishment provided that the communication cannot be received by any person situated outside the premises of that establishment.]

(2) This section does not apply if or to the extent that there is a licensing scheme certified for the purposes of this section under section 143 providing for the grant of licences.

(3) Where a copy which would otherwise be an infringing copy is made in accordance with this section but is subsequently dealt with, it shall be treated as an infringing copy for the purposes of that dealing, and if that dealing infringes copyright for all subsequent purposes.

For this purpose "dealt with" means sold or let for hire [; offered or exposed for sale or hire, or communicated than within the premises of an educational establishment to any person situated outside those premises.]."

Copying and use of extracts of works by educational establishments

[**36.**—(1) The copying of extracts of a relevant work by or on behalf of an educational establishment does not infringe copyright in the work, provided that—

    (a) the copy is made for the purposes of instruction for a non-commercial purpose, and

    (b) the copy is accompanied by a sufficient acknowledgement (unless this would be impossible for reasons of practicality or otherwise).

(2) Copyright is not infringed where a copy of an extract made under subsection (1) is communicated by or on behalf of the educational establishment to its pupils or staff for the purposes of instruction for a non-commercial purpose.

(3) Subsection (2) only applies to a communication received outside the premises of the establishment if that communication is made by means of a secure electronic network accessible only by the establishment's pupils and staff.

(4) In this section "relevant work" means a copyright work other than—

(a) a broadcast, or

(b) an artistic work which is not incorporated into another work.

(5) Not more than 5% of a work may be copied under this section by or on behalf of an educational establishment in any period of 12 months, and for these purposes a work which incorporates another work is to be treated as a single work.

(6) Acts which would otherwise be permitted by this section are not permitted if, or to the extent that, licences are available authorising the acts in question and the educational establishment responsible for those acts knew or ought to have been aware of that fact.

(7) The terms of a licence granted to an educational establishment authorising acts permitted by this section are of no effect so far as they purport to restrict the proportion of a work which may be copied (whether on payment or free of charge) to less than that which would be permitted by this section.

(8) If a copy made under this section is subsequently dealt with—

(a) it is to be treated as an infringing copy for the purposes of that dealing, and

(b) if that dealing infringes copyright, it is to be treated as an infringing copy for all subsequent purposes.

(9) In this section "dealt with" means—

(a) sold or let for hire,

(b) offered or exposed for sale or hire, or

(c) communicated otherwise than as permitted by subsection (2).]

Note: Section 36 substituted by the Copyright and Rights in Performances (Research, Education, Libraries and Archives) Regulations 2014 (SI 2014/1372), reg.4(3), with effect from June 1, 2014 at 00.02. Section 36 (as amended by SI 2003/2498) formerly read:

"Reprographic copying by educational establishments of passages from published works

*"**36.**—(1) Reprographic copies of passages from published literary, dramatic or musical works may, to the extent permitted by this section, be made by or on behalf of an educational establishment for the purposes of instruction without infringing any copyright in the work, [provided that they are accompanied by a sufficient acknowledgement and the instruction is for a non-commercial purpose].*

[(1A) No acknowledgement is required in connection with the making of copies as mentioned in subsection (1) where this would be impossible for reasons of practicality or otherwise.

(1B) Reprographic copies of passages from published editions may, to the extent permitted by this section, be made by or on behalf of an educational establishment for the purposes of instruction without infringing any copyright in the typographical arrangement of the edition.]

(2) Not more than one per cent of any work may be copied by or on behalf of an establishment by virtue of this section in any quarter, that is, in any period 1st January to 31st March, 1st April to 30th June, 1st July to 30th September or 1st October to 31st December.

(3) Copying is not authorised by this section if, or to the extent that, licences are available authorising the copying in question and the person making the copies knew or ought to have been aware of that fact.

(4) The terms of a licence granted to an educational establishment authorising the reprographic copying for the purposes of instruction of passages from published [...] works are of no effect so far as they purport to restrict the proportion of a work which may be copied (whether on payment or free of charge) to less than that which would be permitted under this section.

(5) Where a copy which would otherwise be an infringing copy is made in accordance with this section but is subsequently dealt with, it shall be treated as an infringing copy for the purposes of that dealing, and if that dealing infringes copyright for all subsequent purposes.

For this purpose "dealt with" means sold or let for hire[, offered or exposed for sale or hire or communicated to the public]."

Lending of copies by educational establishments

[**36A.** Copyright in a work is not infringed by the lending of copies of the work by an educational establishment.]

Note: This section was inserted by the Copyright and Related Rights Regulations 1996 (SI 1996/2967), with effect from December 1, 1996. For savings and transitional provisions, see Part III of those Regulations.

37.–40. [...]

Note: Sections 37 to 40 repealed by the Copyright and Rights in Performances (Research, Education, Libraries and Archives) Regulations 2014 (SI 2014/1372), Sch. para.14, with effect from June 1, 2014 at 00.02.

Sections 37 to 40 (as amended by SI 2003/2498) formerly read:

"Libraries and archives

Libraries and archives: introductory

37.—(1) In sections 38 to 43 (copying by librarians and archivists)—

> *(a) references in any provision to a prescribed library or archive are to a library or archive of a description prescribed for the purposes of that provision by regulations made by the Secretary of State; and*
>
> *(b) references in any provision to the prescribed conditions are to the conditions so prescribed.*

(2) The regulations may provide that, where a librarian or archivist is required to be satisfied as to any matter before making or supplying a copy of a work—

> *(a) he may rely on a signed declaration as to that matter by the person requesting the copy, unless he is aware that it is false in a material particular, and*
>
> *(b) in such cases as may be prescribed, he shall not make or supply a copy in the absence of a signed declaration in such form as may be prescribed.*

(3) Where a person requesting a copy makes a declaration which is false in a material particular and is supplied with a copy which would have been an infringing copy if made by him—

> *(a) he is liable for infringement of copyright as if he had made the copy himself, and*
>
> *(b) the copy shall be treated as an infringing copy.*

(4) The regulations may make different provision for different descriptions of libraries or archives and for different purposes.

(5) Regulations shall be made by statutory instrument which shall be subject to annulment in pursuance of a resolution of either House of Parliament.

(6) References in this section, and in sections 38 to 43, to the librarian or archivist include a person acting on his behalf.

Copying by librarians: articles in periodicals

38.—*(1) The librarian of a prescribed library may, if the prescribed conditions are complied with, make and supply a copy of an article in a periodical without infringing any copyright in the text, in any illustrations accompanying the text or in the typographical arrangement.*

(2) The prescribed conditions shall include the following—

  [(a) that copies are supplied only to persons satisfying the librarian that they require them for the purposes of—

    (i) research for a non-commercial purpose, or

    (ii) private study,

and will not use them for any other purpose;]

  (b) that no person is furnished with more than one copy of the same article or with copies of more than one article contained in the same issue of a periodical; and

  (c) that persons to whom copies are supplied are required to pay for them a sum not less than the cost (including a contribution to the general expenses of the library) attributable to their production.

Copying by librarians: parts of published works

39.—*(1) The librarian of a prescribed library may, if the prescribed conditions are complied with, make and supply from a published edition a copy of part of a literary, dramatic or musical work (other than an article in a periodical) without infringing any copyright in the work, in any illustrations accompanying the work or in the typographical arrangement.*

(2) The prescribed conditions shall include the following—

  [(a) that copies are supplied only to persons satisfying the librarian that they require them for the purposes of—

    (i) research for a non-commercial purpose, or

    (ii) private study,

and will not use them for any other purpose;]

  (b) that no person is furnished with more than one copy of the same material or with a copy of more than a reasonable proportion of any work; and

  (c) that persons to whom copies are supplied are required to pay for them a sum not less than the cost (including a contribution to the general expenses of the library) attributable to their production.

Restrictions on production of multiple copies of the same material

40.—*(1) Regulations for the purposes of sections 38 and 39 (copying by librarian of article or part of published work) shall contain provision to the effect that a copy shall be supplied only to a person satisfying the librarian that his requirement is not related to any similar requirement of another person.*

(2) The regulations may provide—

  (a) that requirements shall be regarded as similar if the requirements are

*for copies of substantially the same material at substantially the same
time and for substantially the same purpose; and*

(b) *that requirements of persons shall be regarded as related if those
persons receive instructions to which the material is relevant at the
same time and place."*

Lending of copies by librarians or archives

[40A.—[(1) Copyright in a work of any description is not infringed by the following acts by a public library in relation to a book within the public lending right scheme—

(a) lending the book;

(b) in relation to an audio-book or e-book, copying or issuing a copy of the book as an act incidental to lending it.

(1A) In subsection (1)—

(a) "book", "audio-book" and "e-book" have the meanings given in section 5 of the Public Lending Right Act 1979,

(b) "the public lending right scheme" means the scheme in force under section 1 of that Act,

(c) a book is within the public lending right scheme if it is a book within the meaning of the provisions of the scheme relating to eligibility, whether or not it is in fact eligible, and

(d) "lending" is to be read in accordance with the definition of "lent out" in section 5 of that Act (and section 18A of this Act does not apply).]

(2) Copyright in a work is not infringed by the lending of copies of the work by a [...] library or archive (other than a public library) which is not conducted for profit.]

Notes:

(1) This section was inserted by the Copyright and Related Rights Regulations 1996 (SI 1996/2967), with effect from December 1, 1996. For savings and transitional provisions, see Part III of those Regulations.

(2) Subsections (1) and (1A) substituted for existing subs.(1) by the Digital Economy Act 2010 s.43(7), with effect from June, 30 2014 (see SI 2014/1659). Subs.(1) formerly read:.

Copyright in a work of any description is not infringed by the lending of a book by a public library if the book is within the public lending right scheme.

For this purpose—

(a) *"the public lending right scheme" means the scheme in force under section 1 of the Public Lending Right Act 1979, and*

(b) *a book is within the public lending right scheme if it is a book within the meaning of the provisions of the scheme relating to eligibility whether or not it is in fact eligible."*

(3) In subs.(2) word "prescribed" repealed by the Copyright and Rights in Performances (Research, Education, Libraries and Archives) Regulations 2014 (SI 2014/1372), Sch. para.3, with effect from June 1, 2014 at 00.02.

Libraries and educational establishments etc: making works available through dedicated terminals

[40B.—(1) Copyright in a work is not infringed by an institution specified in subsection (2) communicating the work to the public or making it available to the public by means of a dedicated terminal on its premises, if the conditions in subsection (3) are met.

(2) The institutions are—

(a) a library,

(b) an archive,

(c) a museum, and

(d) an educational establishment.

(3) The conditions are that the work or a copy of the work—

    (a) has been lawfully acquired by the institution,

    (b) is communicated or made available to individual members of the public for the purposes of research or private study, and

    (c) is communicated or made available in compliance with any purchase or licensing terms to which the work is subject.]

Note: Section 40B inserted by the Copyright and Rights in Performances (Research, Education, Libraries and Archives) Regulations 2014 (SI 2014/1372), reg.5(1), with effect from June 1, 2014 at 00.02.

Copying by librarians: supply of single copies to other libraries

[**41.**—(1) A librarian may, if the conditions in subsection (2) are met, make a single copy of the whole or part of a published work and supply it to another library, without infringing copyright in the work.

(2) The conditions are—

    (a) the copy is supplied in response to a request from a library which is not conducted for profit, and

    (b) at the time of making the copy the librarian does not know, or could not reasonably find out, the name and address of a person entitled to authorise the making of a copy of the work.

(3) The condition in subsection (2)(b) does not apply where the request is for a copy of an article in a periodical.

(4) Where a library makes a charge for supplying a copy under this section, the sum charged must be calculated by reference to the costs attributable to the production of the copy.

(5) To the extent that a term of a contract purports to prevent or restrict the doing of any act which, by virtue of this section, would not infringe copyright, that term is unenforceable.]

Note: Sections 41, 42, 42A, 43, 43A substituted for existing ss.41-43 by the Copyright and Rights in Performances (Research, Education, Libraries and Archives) Regulations 2014 (SI 2014/1372), reg.5(2), with effect from June 1, 2014 at 00.02.

Copying by librarians etc: replacement copies of works

[**42.**—(1) A librarian, archivist or curator of a library, archive or museum may, without infringing copyright, make a copy of an item in that institution's permanent collection—

    (a) in order to preserve or replace that item in that collection, or

    (b) where an item in the permanent collection of another library, archive or museum has been lost, destroyed or damaged, in order to replace the item in the collection of that other library, archive or museum,

provided that the conditions in subsections (2) and (3) are met.

(2) The first condition is that the item is—

    (a) included in the part of the collection kept wholly or mainly for the purposes of reference on the institution's premises,

    (b) included in a part of the collection not accessible to the public, or

    (c) available on loan only to other libraries, archives or museums.

(3) The second condition is that it is not reasonably practicable to purchase a copy of the item to achieve either of the purposes mentioned in subsection (1).

(4) The reference in subsection (1)(b) to a library, archive or museum is to a library, archive or museum which is not conducted for profit.

(5) Where an institution makes a charge for supplying a copy to another library, archive or museum under subsection (1)(b), the sum charged must be calculated by reference to the costs attributable to the production of the copy.

(6) In this section "item" means a work or a copy of a work.

(7) To the extent that a term of a contract purports to prevent or restrict the doing of any act which, by virtue of this section, would not infringe copyright, that term is unenforceable.

Note: Sections 41, 42, 42A, 43, 43A substituted for existing ss.41-43 by the Copyright and Rights in Performances (Research, Education, Libraries and Archives) Regulations 2014 (SI 2014/1372), reg.5(2), with effect from June 1, 2014 at 00.02.

Copying by librarians: single copies of published works

[**42A.**—(1) A librarian of a library which is not conducted for profit may, if the conditions in subsection (2) are met, make and supply a single copy of—

  (a) one article in any one issue of a periodical, or

  (b) a reasonable proportion of any other published work,

without infringing copyright in the work.

(2) The conditions are—

  (a) the copy is supplied in response to a request from a person who has provided the librarian with a declaration in writing which includes the information set out in subsection (3), and

  (b) the librarian is not aware that the declaration is false in a material particular.

(3) The information which must be included in the declaration is—

  (a) the name of the person who requires the copy and the material which that person requires,

  (b) a statement that the person has not previously been supplied with a copy of that material by any library,

  (c) a statement that the person requires the copy for the purposes of research for a non-commercial purpose or private study, will use it only for those purposes and will not supply the copy to any other person, and

  (d) a statement that to the best of the person's knowledge, no other person with whom the person works or studies has made, or intends to make, at or about the same time as the person's request, a request for substantially the same material for substantially the same purpose.

(4) Where a library makes a charge for supplying a copy under this section, the sum charged must be calculated by reference to the costs attributable to the production of the copy.

(5) Where a person ("P") makes a declaration under this section that is false in a material particular and is supplied with a copy which would have been an infringing copy if made by P—

  (a) P is liable for infringement of copyright as if P had made the copy, and

  (b) the copy supplied to P is to be treated as an infringing copy for all purposes.

(6) To the extent that a term of a contract purports to prevent or restrict the doing of any act which, by virtue of this section, would not infringe copyright, that term is unenforceable.]

Note: Sections 41, 42, 42A, 43, 43A substituted for existing ss.41–43 by the Copyright and Rights in Performances (Research, Education, Libraries and Archives) Regulations 2014 (SI 2014/1372), reg.5(2), with effect from June 1, 2014 at 00.02.

Copying by librarians or archivists: single copies of unpublished works

[43.—(1) A librarian or archivist may make and supply a single copy of the whole or part of a work without infringing copyright in the work, provided that—

(a) the copy is supplied in response to a request from a person who has provided the librarian or archivist with a declaration in writing which includes the information set out in subsection (2), and

(b) the librarian or archivist is not aware that the declaration is false in a material particular.

(2) The information which must be included in the declaration is—

(a) the name of the person who requires the copy and the material which that person requires,

(b) a statement that the person has not previously been supplied with a copy of that material by any library or archive, and

(c) a statement that the person requires the copy for the purposes of research for a non-commercial purpose or private study, will use it only for those purposes and will not supply the copy to any other person.

(3) But copyright is infringed if—

(a) the work had been published or communicated to the public before the date it was deposited in the library or archive, or

(b) the copyright owner has prohibited the copying of the work,

and at the time of making the copy the librarian or archivist is, or ought to be, aware of that fact.

(4) Where a library or archive makes a charge for supplying a copy under this section, the sum charged must be calculated by reference to the costs attributable to the production of the copy.

(5) Where a person ("P") makes a declaration under this section that is false in a material particular and is supplied with a copy which would have been an infringing copy if made by P—

(a) P is liable for infringement of copyright as if P had made the copy, and

(b) the copy supplied to P is to be treated as an infringing copy for all purposes.]

Note: Sections 41, 42, 42A, 43, 43A substituted for existing ss.41-43 by the Copyright and Rights in Performances (Research, Education, Libraries and Archives) Regulations 2014 (SI 2014/1372), reg.5(2), with effect from June 1, 2014 at 00.02.

Sections 40A to 43: interpretation

[43A.—(1) The following definitions have effect for the purposes of sections 40A to 43.

(2) "Library" means—

(a) a library which is publicly accessible, or

(b) a library of an educational establishment.

(3) "Museum" includes a gallery.

(4) "Conducted for profit", in relation to a library, archive or museum, means a body of that kind which is established or conducted for profit or which forms part of, or is administered by, a body established or conducted for profit.

(5) References to a librarian, archivist or curator include a person acting on behalf of a librarian, archivist or curator.]

Note: Sections 41, 42, 42A, 43, 43A substituted for existing ss.41-43 by the Copyright and Rights in Performances (Research, Education, Libraries and Archives) Regulations 2014 (SI 2014/1372), reg.5(2), with effect from June 1, 2014 at 00.02. Sections 41 to 43 (as amended by SI 2003/2498) formerly read:

Copying by librarians: supply of copies to other libraries

"41.—*(1) The librarian of a prescribed library may, if the prescribed conditions are complied with, make and supply to another prescribed library a copy of—*

(a) *an article in a periodical, or*

(b) *the whole or part of a published edition of a literary, dramatic or musical work,*

without infringing any copyright in the text of the article or, as the case may be, in the work, in any illustrations accompanying it or in the typographical arrangement.

(2) Subsection (1)(b) does not apply if at the time the copy is made the librarian making it knows, or could by reasonable inquiry ascertain, the name and address of a person entitled to authorise the making of the copy.

Copying by librarians or archivists: replacement copies of works

42.—*(1) The librarian or archivist of a prescribed library or archive may, if the prescribed conditions are complied with, make a copy from any item in the permanent collection of the library or archive—*

(a) *in order to preserve or replace that item by placing the copy in its permanent collection in addition to or in place of it, or*

(b) *in order to replace in the permanent collection of another prescribed library or archive an item which has been lost, destroyed or damaged,*

without infringing the copyright in any literary, dramatic or musical work, in any illustrations accompanying such a work or, in the case of a published edition, in the typographical arrangement.

(2) The prescribed conditions shall include provision for restricting the making of copies to cases where it is not reasonably practicable to purchase a copy of the item in question to fulfil that purpose.

Copying by librarians or archivists: certain unpublished works

43.—*(1) The librarian or archivist of a prescribed library or archive may, if the prescribed conditions are complied with, make and supply a copy of the whole or part of a literary, dramatic or musical work from a document in the library or archive without infringing any copyright in the work or any illustrations accompanying it.*

(2) This section does not apply if—

(a) *the work had been published before the document was deposited in the library or archive, or*

(b) *the copyright owner has prohibited copying of the work,*

and at the time the copy is made the librarian or archivist making it is, or ought to be, aware of that fact.

(3) The prescribed conditions shall include the following—

[(a) *that copies are supplied only to persons satisfying the librarian or archivist that they require them for the purposes of—*

(i) *research for a non-commercial purpose, or*

(ii) *private study,*

and will not use them for any other purpose;]

(b) *that no person is furnished with more than one copy of the same material; and*

(c) *that persons to whom copies are supplied are required to pay for them a sum not less than the cost (including a contribution to the general expenses of the library or archive) attributable to their production."*

Copy of work required to be made as condition of export

44. If an article of cultural or historical importance or interest cannot lawfully be exported from the United Kingdom unless a copy of it is made and deposited in an appropriate library or archive, it is not an infringement of copyright to make that copy.

Legal deposit libraries

[44A.—(1) Copyright is not infringed by the copying of a work from the internet by a deposit library or person acting on its behalf if—

  (a) the work is of a description prescribed by regulations under section 10(5) of the 2003 Act,

  (b) its publication on the internet, or a person publishing it there, is connected with the United Kingdom in a manner so prescribed, and

  (c) the copying is done in accordance with any conditions so prescribed.

(2) Copyright is not infringed by the doing of anything in relation to relevant material permitted to be done under regulations under section 7 of the 2003 Act.

(3) The Secretary of State may by regulations make provision excluding, in relation to prescribed activities done in relation to relevant material, the application of such of the provisions of this Chapter as are prescribed.

(4) Regulations under subsection (3) may in particular make provision prescribing activities—

  (a) done for a prescribed purpose,

  (b) done by prescribed descriptions of reader,

  (c) done in relation to prescribed descriptions of relevant material,

  (d) done other than in accordance with prescribed conditions.

(5) Regulations under this section may make different provision for different purposes.

(6) Regulations under this section shall be made by statutory instrument which shall be subject to annulment in pursuance of a resolution of either House of Parliament.

(7) In this section—

  (a) "the 2003 Act" means the Legal Deposit Libraries Act 2003;

  (b) "deposit library", "reader" and "relevant material" have the same meaning as in section 7 of the 2003 Act;

  (c) "prescribed" means prescribed by regulations made by the Secretary of State.]

Note: Section 44A was inserted by the Legal Deposit Libraries Act 2003 s.8 with effect from February 1, 2004 (see the Legal Deposit Libraries Act 2003 (Commencement) Order 2004 (SI 2004/130)).

Orphan works

Permitted uses of orphan works

[44B.—(1) Copyright in an orphan work is not infringed by a relevant body in the circumstances set out in paragraph 1(1) of Schedule ZA1 (subject to paragraph 6 of that Schedule).

(2) "Orphan work" and "relevant body" have the meanings given by that Schedule.]

Note: Section 44B inserted by the Copyright and Rights in Performances (Certain Permitted Uses of Orphan Works) Regulations 2014 (SI 2014/2861), reg.3(1), with effect from October 29, 2014.

Public administration

Parliamentary and judicial proceedings

45.—(1) Copyright is not infringed by anything done for the purposes of parliamentary or judicial proceedings.

(2) Copyright is not infringed by anything done for the purposes of reporting such proceedings; but this shall not be construed as authorising the copying of a work which is itself a published report of the proceedings.

Royal Commissions and statutory inquiries

46.—(1) Copyright is not infringed by anything done for the purposes of the proceedings of a Royal Commission or statutory inquiry.

(2) Copyright is not infringed by anything done for the purpose of reporting any such proceedings held in public; and this shall not be construed as authorising the copying of a work which is itself a published report of the proceedings.

(3) Copyright in a work is not infringed by the issue to the public of copies of the report of a Royal Commission or statutory inquiry containing the work or material from it.

(4) In this section—

"Royal Commission" includes a Commission appointed for Northern Ireland by the Secretary of State in pursuance of the prerogative powers of Her Majesty delegated to him under section 7(2) of the Northern Ireland Constitution Act 1973; and

"statutory inquiry" means an inquiry held or investigation conducted in pursuance of a duty imposed or power conferred by or under an enactment.

Material open to public inspection or on official register

47.—(1) Where material is open to public inspection pursuant to a statutory requirement, or is on a statutory register, any copyright in the material as a literary work is not infringed by the copying of so much of the material as contains factual information of any description, by or with the authority of the appropriate person, for a purpose which does not involve the issuing of copies to the public.

[(2) Where material is open to public inspection pursuant to a statutory requirement, copyright in the material is not infringed by an act to which subsection (3A) applies provided that—

(a) the act is done by or with the authority of the appropriate person,

(b) the purpose of the act is—

(i) to enable the material to be inspected at a more convenient time or place, or

(ii) to otherwise facilitate the exercise of any right for the purpose of which the statutory requirement is imposed, and

(c) in the case of the act specified in subsection (3A)(c), the material is not commercially available to the public by or with the authority of the copyright owner.

(3) Where material which contains information about matters of general scientific, technical, commercial or economic interest is on a statutory register or is open to public inspection pursuant to a statutory requirement, copyright in the material is not infringed by an act to which subsection (3A) applies provided that—

(a) the act is done by or with the authority of the appropriate person,

(b) the purpose of the act is to disseminate that information, and

(c) in the case of the act specified in subsection (3A)(c), the material is not commercially available to the public by or with the authority of the copyright owner.

(3A) This subsection applies to any of the following acts—

(a) copying the material,

(b) issuing copies of the material to the public, and

(c) making the material (or a copy of it) available to the public by electronic transmission in such a way that members of the public may access it from a place and at a time individually chosen by them.]

(4) The Secretary of State may by order provide that subsection (1), (2) or (3) shall, in such cases as may be specified in the order, apply only to copies marked in such manner as may be so specified.

(5) The Secretary of State may by order provide that subsections (1) to (3) apply, to such extent and with such modifications as may be specified in the order—

(a) to material made open to public inspection by—

(i) an international organisation specified in the order, or

(ii) a person so specified who has functions in the United Kingdom under an international agreement to which the United Kingdom is party, or

(b) to a register maintained by an international organisation specified in the order,

as they apply in relation to material open to public inspection pursuant to a statutory requirement or to a statutory register.

(6) In this section—

"appropriate person" means the person required to make the material open to public inspection or, as the case may be, the person maintaining the register;

"statutory register" means a register maintained in pursuance of a statutory requirement; and

"statutory requirement" means a requirement imposed by provision made by or under an enactment.

(7) An order under this section shall be made by statutory instrument which shall be subject to annulment in pursuance of a resolution of either House of Parliament.

Notes:

(1) Subsections (1) to (3) apply, subject to the modifications set out in Copyright (Material Open to Public Inspection) (International Organisations) Order 1989 (SI 1989/1098), art.3, to material made open to public inspection by the European Patent Office under the Convention on the Grant of European Patents and the World Intellectual Property Organisation under the Patent Co-operation Treaty as they apply in relation to material open to public inspection pursuant to a statutory requirement or to a statutory register.

(2) Subsections (2), (3), (3A) substituted for existing subss (2), (3) by the Copyright (Public Administration) Regulations 2014 (SI 2014/1385), reg.2(1), with effect from June 1, 2014. Subss (2), (3) formerly read:

"(2) Where material is open to public inspection pursuant to a statutory requirement, copyright is not infringed by the copying or issuing to the public of copies of the material, by or with the authority of the appropriate person, for the purpose of enabling the material to be inspected at a more convenient time or place or otherwise facilitating the exercise of any right for the purpose of which the requirement is imposed.

(3) Where material which is open to public inspection pursuant to a statutory requirement, or which is on a statutory register, contains information about mat-

ters of general scientific, technical, commercial or economic interest, copyright is not infringed by the copying or issuing to the public of copies of the material, by or with the authority of the appropriate person, for the purpose of disseminating that information."

Material communicated to the Crown in the course of public business

48.—(1) This section applies where a literary, dramatic, musical or artistic work has in the course of public business been communicated to the Crown for any purpose, by or with the licence of the copyright owner and a document or other material thing recording or embodying the work is owned by or in the custody of control of the Crown.

[(2) The Crown may, without infringing copyright in the work, do an act specified in subsection (3) provided that—

(a) the act is done for the purpose for which the work was communicated to the Crown, or any related purpose which could reasonably have been anticipated by the copyright owner, and

(b) the work has not been previously published otherwise than by virtue of this section.

(3) The acts referred to in subsection (2) are—

(a) copying the work,

(b) issuing copies of the work to the public, and

(c) making the work (or a copy of it) available to the public by electronic transmission in such a way that members of the public may access it from a place and at a time individually chosen by them.]

(4) In subsection (1) "public business" includes any activity carried on by the Crown.

(5) This section has effect subject to any agreement to the contrary between the Crown and the copyright owner.

(6) [In this section "the Crown" includes a health service body, as defined in section 60(7) of the National Health Service and Community Care Act 1990, [the National Health Service Commissioning Board, a clinical commissioning group established under section 14D of the National Health Service Act 2006,] [the Care Quality Commission] [, Health Education England][, the Health Research Authority] and a National Health Service trust established under [section 25 of the National Health Service Act 2006, section 18 of the National Health Service (Wales) Act 2006] or the National Health Service (Scotland) Act 1978 [and an NHS foundation trust] [and also includes a health and social services body, as defined in Article 7(6) of the Health and Personal Social Services (N.I.) Order 1991, and a Health and Social Services trust established under that Order]; and the reference in subsection (1) above to public business shall be construed accordingly.]

Notes:

(1) Subsection (6) was initially inserted by the National Health Service and Community Care Act 1990 with effect from April 1, 1991 (National Health Service and Community Care Act 1990 (Commencement No.1) Order 1990 (SI 1990/1329)). In its original form it read as follows:

"(6) In this section "the Crown" includes a health service body, as defined in section 60(7) of the National Health Service and Community Care Act 1990, and a National Health Service trust established under Part I of that Act or the National Health Service (Scotland) Act 1978; and the reference in subsection (1) above to public business shall be construed accordingly."

(2) The words "a Primary Care Trust established under section 18 of the National Health Service Act 2006" inserted as a result of the following amendments. First,

the words "a Primary Care Trust established under section 16A of the National Health Service Act 1977," inserted in that position by the Health Act 1999 (Supplementary, Consequential etc. Provisions) Order 2000 (SI 2000/90), Sch.1 para.22 with effect from February 8, 2000. Secondly, the reference to s.18 of the 2006 Act was substituted for the reference to s.16A of the 1977 Act with effect from March 1, 2007 by the National Health Service (Consequential Provisions) Act 2006 (c.43), Sch.1 para.112.

(3) The words "the Care Quality Commission" inserted as a result of the following amendments. First, the words "the Commission for Health Improvement" inserted in that position by the Health Act 1999 (Supplementary and Consequential Provisions) Order 1999 (SI 1999/2795), art.3 with effect from November 1, 1999. Secondly, the words "the Commission for Social Care Inspection" and "the Commission for Healthcare Audit and Inspection" substituted for those words by the Health and Social Care (Community Health and Standards) Act 2003 (Commission for Healthcare Audit and Inspection and Commission for Social Care Inspection) (Consequential Provisions) Order 2004 (SI 2004/2987), with effect from November 11, 2004. Third, the words "the Care Quality Commission" substituted for those words by para.60 of Sch.5 to the Health and Social Care Act 2008 with effect from April 1, 2009.

(4) The words "section 25 of the National Health Service Act 2006, section 18 of the National Health Service (Wales) Act 2006" substituted for the words "Part I of that Act" by the National Health Service (Consequential Provisions) Act 2006 (c.43), Sch.1 para.112, with effect from March 1, 2007.

(5) The words "and an NHS foundation trust" inserted in that position by the Health and Social Care (Community Health and Standards) Act 2003 (c.43), Sch.4 para.72 with effect from April 1, 2004 (Health and Social Care (Community Health and Standards) Act 2003 Commencement (No.3) Order 2004 (SI 2004/759)).

(6) The words "and also includes a health and social services body, as defined in Article 7(6) of the Health and Personal Social Services (N.I.) Order, and a Health and Social Services trust established under that Order" inserted by the Health and Personal Social Services (NI) Order 1991 (SI 1991/194 (N.I. 1)) with effect from April 1, 1992 (Health and Personal Social Services (1991 Order) (Commencement No.1) Order (Northern Ireland) 1991 (SI 1991/131)).

(7) In subs.(6) first words in square brackets inserted by the Health and Social Care Act 2012 Sch.5 para.44(4)(a) with effect from October 1, 2012.

(8) In subs.(6) the words ", [a Primary Care Trust established under [section 18 of the National Health Service Act 2006]," repealed by the Health and Social Care Act 2012 Sch.5 para.44(4)(b) with effect from April 1, 2013.

(9) Subss (2), (3) substituted by the Copyright (Public Administration) Regulations 2014 (SI 2014/1385), reg.2(2), with effect from June 1, 2014. Subss (2), (3) formerly read:

"(2) The Crown may, for the purpose for which the work was communicated to it, or any related purpose which could reasonably have been anticipated by the copyright owner, copy the work and issue copies of the work to the public without infringing any copyright in the work.

(3) The Crown may not copy a work, or issue copies of a work to the public, by virtue of this section if the work has previously been published otherwise than by virtue of this section."

(10) In subs.(6) words ", the Health Research Authority" inserted by the Care Act 2014, Sch.5, para.25, with effect from January 1, 2015.

(11) In subs.(6) words ", Health Education England" inserted by the Care Act 2014, Sch.5, para.33, with effect from April 1, 2015.

Public records

49. Material which is comprised in public records within the meaning of the Public Records Act 1958, the Public Records (Scotland) Act 1937 or the Public Records Act (Northern Ireland) 1923 [, or in Welsh public records (as defined in the [Government of Wales Act 2006]),] which are open to public inspection in pursuance of that Act, may be copied, and a copy may be supplied to any person, by or with the authority of any officer appointed under that Act, without infringement of copyright."

Notes:

(1) The words in square brackets inserted by the Government of Wales Act 1998

(c.38), s.125, Sch.12, paras 26, 27, with effect from April 1, 1999 (Government of Wales Act 1998 (Commencement No.4) Order 1999 (SI 1999/782)).

(2) The words in the internal square brackets in s.49 substituted by the Government of Wales Act 2006 (c.32), Sch.10 para.24, with effect from May 4, 2007.

Acts done under statutory authority

50.—(1) Where the doing of a particular act is specifically authorised by an Act of Parliament, whenever passed, then, unless the Act provides otherwise, the doing of that act does not infringe copyright.

(2) Subsection (1) applies in relation to an enactment contained in Northern Ireland legislation as it applies in relation to an Act of Parliament.

(3) Nothing in this section shall be construed as excluding any defence of statutory authority otherwise available under or by virtue of any enactment.

[Computer programs: lawful users

Back up copies

50A.—(1) It is not an infringement of copyright for a lawful user of a copy of a computer program to make any back up copy of it which it is necessary for him to have for the purposes of his lawful use.

(2) For the purposes of this section and sections 50BA[, 50BA] and 50C a person is a lawful user of a computer program if (whether under a licence to do any acts restricted by the copyright in the program or otherwise), he has a right to use the program.

(3) Where an act is permitted under this section, it is irrelevant whether or not there exists any term or condition in an agreement which purports to prohibit or restrict the act (such terms being, by virtue of section 296A, void).]

Notes:

(1) This section and the heading preceding it inserted by the Copyright (Computer Programs) Regulations 1992 (SI 1992/3233), with effect from January 1, 1993. For savings and transitional provisions, see regulation 12 of those Regulations.

(2) The words in square brackets in subs.(2) inserted by the Copyright and Related Rights Regulations 2003 (SI 2003/2498), reg.15 with effect from October 31, 2003. For savings and transitional provisions, see Part 3 of those Regulations.

Decompilation

[50B.—(1) It is not an infringement of copyright for a lawful user of a copy of a computer program expressed in a low level language—

(a) to convert it into a version expressed in a higher level language, or

(b) incidentally in the course of so converting the program, to copy it, (that is, to "decompile" it), provided that the conditions in subsection (2) are met.

(2) The conditions are that—

(a) it is necessary to decompile the program to obtain the information necessary to create an independent program which can be operated with the program decompiled or with another program ("the permitted objective"); and

(b) the information so obtained is not used for any purpose other than the permitted objective.

(3) In particular, the conditions in subsection (2) are not met if the lawful user—

(a) has readily available to him the information necessary to achieve the permitted objective;

(b) does not confine the decompiling to such acts as are necessary to achieve the permitted objective;

(c) supplies the information obtained by the decompiling to any person to whom it is not necessary to supply it in order to achieve the permitted objective; or

(d) uses the information to create a program which is substantially similar in its expression to the program decompiled or to do any act restricted by copyright.

(4) Where an act is permitted under this section, it is irrelevant whether or not there exists any term or condition in an agreement which purports to prohibit or restrict the act (such terms being, by virtue of section 296A, void).]

Note: This section was inserted by the Copyright (Computer Programs) Regulations 1992 (SI 1992/3233), with effect from January 1, 1993. For savings and transitional provisions, see reg.12 of those Regulations.

Observing, studying and testing of computer programs

[**50BA.**—(1) It is not an infringement of copyright for a lawful user of a copy of a computer program to observe, study or test the functioning of the program in order to determine the ideas and principles which underlie any element of the program if he does so while performing any of the acts of loading, displaying, running, transmitting or storing the program which he is entitled to do.

(2) Where an act is permitted under this section, it is irrelevant whether or not there exists any term or condition in an agreement which purports to prohibit or restrict the act (such terms being, by virtue of section 296A, void).]

Note: Section 50BA was inserted by the Copyright and Related Rights Regulations 2003 (SI 2003/2498), reg.15 with effect from October 31, 2003. For savings and transitional provisions, see Part 3 of those Regulations.

Other acts permitted to lawful users

[**50C.**—(1) It is not an infringement of copyright for a lawful user of a copy of a computer program to copy or adapt it, provided that the copying or adapting—

(a) is necessary for his lawful use; and

(b) is not prohibited under any term or condition of an agreement regulating the circumstances in which his use is lawful.

(2) It may, in particular, be necessary for the lawful use of a computer program to copy it or adapt it for the purpose of correcting errors in it.

(3) This section does not apply to any copying or adapting permitted under [section 50A, 50B or 50BA].]

Notes:

(1) This section was inserted by the Copyright (Computer Programs) Regulations 1992 (SI 1992/3233), with effect from January 1, 1993. For savings and transitional provisions, see reg.12 of those Regulations.

(2) The words in internal square brackets in subs.(3) substituted for the former words "section 50A or 50B" by the Copyright and Related Rights Regulations 2003 (SI 2003/2498), reg.15 with effect from October 31, 2003. For savings and transitional provisions, see Part 3 of those Regulations.

[Databases: permitted acts

Acts permitted in relation to databases

50D.—(1) It is not an infringement of copyright in a database for a person who has a right to use the database or any part of the database, (whether under a licence to do any of the acts restricted by the copyright in the database or otherwise) to do, in the exercise of that right, anything which is necessary for the purposes of access to and use of the contents of the database or of that part of the database.

(2) Where an act which would otherwise infringe copyright in a database is permitted under this section, it is irrelevant whether or not there exists any term or condition in any agreement which purports to prohibit or restrict the act (such terms being, by virtue of section 296B, void).]

Note: This section and the heading preceding it was inserted by the Copyright and Rights in Databases Regulations 1997 (SI 1997/3032), with effect from January 1, 1998. For savings and transitional provisions, see regs 26 to 30 of those Regulations.

Designs

Design documents and models

51.—(1) It is not an infringement of any copyright in a design document or model recording or embodying a design for anything other than an artistic work or a typeface to make an article to the design or to copy an article made to the design.

(2) Nor is it an infringement of the copyright to issue to the public, or include in a film [or communicate to the public], anything the making of which was, by virtue of subsection (1), not an infringement of that copyright.

(3) In this section—

"design" means the design of [...] the shape or configuration (whether internal or external) of the whole or part of an article, other than surface decoration; and

"design document" means any record of a design, whether in the form of a drawing, a written description, a photograph, data stored in a computer or otherwise.

Notes:

(1) The words in square brackets in subs.(2) substituted for the former words "section 50A or 50B, broadcast or cable programme service" by the Copyright and Related Rights Regulations 2003 (SI 2003/2498), Sch.1 para.8 with effect from October 31, 2003. For savings and transitional provisions, see Part 3 of those Regulations.

(2) In subs.(3), in definition "design" words "any aspect of" repealed by the Intellectual Property Act 2014, s.1(2), with effect from October 1, 2014 (see SI 2014/2330).

Effect of exploitation of design derived from artistic work

52.—(1) This section applies where an artistic work has been exploited, by or with the licence of the copyright owner, by—

(a) making by an industrial process articles falling to be treated for the purposes of this Part as copies of the work, and

(b) marketing such articles, in the United Kingdom or elsewhere.

(2) After the end of the period of 25 years from the end of the calendar year in which such articles are first marketed, the work may be copied by making articles of any description, or doing anything for the purpose of making articles of any description, and anything may be done in relation to articles so made, without infringing copyright in the work.

(3) Where only part of an artistic work is exploited as mentioned in subsection (1), subsection (2) applies only in relation to that part.

(4) The Secretary of State may by order make provision—

(a) as to the circumstances in which an article, or any description of article, is to be regarded for the purposes of this section as made by an industrial process;

(b) excluding from the operation of this section such articles of a primarily literary or artistic character as he thinks fit.

(5) An order shall be made by statutory instrument which shall be subject to annulment in pursuance of a resolution of either House of Parliament.

(6) In this section—

(a) references to articles do not include films; and

(b) references to the marketing of an article are to its being sold or let for hire or offered or exposed for sale or hire.

Note: Section 52 was repealed by the Enterprise and Regulatory Reform Act 2013, s.74(2), but only so far as is necessary for enabling the exercise of any power (arising under or by virtue of that provision) to make provision by regulations, rules or order made by statutory instrument, with effect from April 25, 2013 (see s.103(i) of the Act). Section 52 is prospectively repealed for remaining purposes, with effect from a date to be appointed. Note that of the Enterprise and Regulatory Reform Act 2013, s.74 was prospectively brought into force on April 16, 2020 by the Enterprise and Regulatory Reform Act 2013 (Commencement No.8 and Saving Provisions) Order 2015 (SI 2015/ 641). However, that SI was subsequently revoked by the Enterprise and Regulatory Reform Act 2013 (Commencement No.8 and Saving Provisions) (Revocation) Order 2015 (SI 2015/1558) with effect from July 20, 2015. Consequently s.74 currently remains in force save for the purposes of making regulations, rules or orders.

Things done in reliance on registration of design

53.—(1) The copyright in an artistic work is not infringed by anything done—

(a) in pursuance of an assignment or licence made or granted by a person registered under the Registered Designs Act 1949 as the proprietor of a corresponding design, and

(b) in good faith in reliance on the registration and without notice of any proceedings for the cancellation [or invalidation] of the registration or[, in a case of registration under the 1949 Act,]for rectifying the relevant entry in the register of designs [or, in a case of registration under the Community Design Regulation, that the person registered as the right holder was not the right holder of the design for the purposes of the Regulation];

and this is so notwithstanding that the person registered as the proprietor was not the proprietor of the design for the purposes of the 1949 Act.

(2) In subsection (1) (a) "corresponding design", in relation to an artistic work, means a design within the meaning of the 1949 Act which if applied to an article would produce something which would be treated for the purposes of this Part as a copy of the artistic work.

[(3) In subsection (1), a "corresponding registered Community design", in relation to an artistic work, means a design within the meaning of the Community Design Regulation which if applied to an article would produce something which would be treated for the purposes of this Part as a copy of the artistic work.]

[(4) In this section, "the Community Design Regulation" means Council Regulation (EC) No 6/2002 of December 12, 2001 on Community designs.]

Notes:

(1) In subs.(1)(b) first words in square brackets inserted by the Registered Designs Regulations (SI 2001/3949), Sch.1 para.16 with effect from December 9, 2001.

(2) In subs.(1)(b) second and third words in square brackets inserted, and subs (3), (4) inserted, by the Intellectual Property Act 2014, s.5, with effect from October 1, 2014 (see the Intellectual Property Act 2014 (Commencement No.3 and Transitional Provisions) Order 2014 (SI 2014/2330).

Typefaces

Use of typeface in ordinary course of printing

54.—(1) It is not an infringement of copyright in an artistic work consisting of the design of a typeface—

    (a) to use the typeface in the ordinary course of typing, composing text, typesetting or printing,

    (b) to possess an article for the purpose of such use, or

    (c) to do anything in relation to material produced by such use;

and this is so notwithstanding that an article is used which is an infringing copy of the work.

(2) However, the following provisions of this Part apply in relation to persons making, importing or dealing with articles specifically designed or adapted for producing material in a particular typeface, or possessing such articles for the purpose of dealing with them, as if the production of material as mentioned in subsection (1) did infringe copyright in the artistic work consisting of the design of the typeface—

        section 24 (secondary infringement: making, importing, possessing or dealing with article for making infringing copy),

        sections 99 and 100 (order for delivery up and right of seizure),

        section 107(2) (offence of making or possessing such an article), and

        section 108 (order for delivery up in criminal proceedings).

(3) The references in subsection (2) to "dealing with" an article are to selling, letting for hire, or offering or exposing for sale or hire, exhibiting in public, or distributing.

Articles for producing material in particular typeface

55.—(1) This section applies to the copyright in an artistic work consisting of the design of a typeface where articles specifically designed or adapted for producing materials in that typeface have been marketed by or with the licence of the copyright owner.

(2) After the period of 25 years from the end of the calendar year in which the first such articles are marketed, the work may be copied by making further such articles, or doing anything for the purpose of making such articles, and anything may be done in relation to articles so made, without infringing copyright in the work.

(3) In subsection (1) "marketed" means sold, let for hire or offered or exposed for sale or hire, in the United Kingdom or elsewhere.

Works in electronic form

Transfers of copies of works in electronic form

56.—(1) This section applies where a copy of a work in electronic form has been purchased on terms which, expressly or impliedly or by virtue of any rule of law, allow the purchaser to copy the work, or to adapt it or make copies of an adaptation, in connection with his use of it.

(2) If there are no express terms—

    (a) prohibiting the transfer of the copy by the purchaser, imposing obligations which continue after a transfer, prohibiting the assignment of any licence or terminating any licence on a transfer, or

    (b) providing for the terms on which a transferee may do things which the purchaser was permitted to do, anything which the purchaser was allowed to do may also be done without infringement of copyright by a transferee; but any copy, adaptation or copy of an adaptation made by the purchaser which is not also transferred shall be treated as an infringing copy for all purposes after the transfer.

(3) The same applies where the original purchased copy is no longer usable and what is transferred is a further copy used in its place.

(4) The above provisions also apply on a subsequent transfer, with the substitution for references in subsection (2) to the purchaser of references to the subsequent transferor.

Miscellaneous: literary, dramatic, musical and artistic works

Anonymous or pseudonymous works: acts permitted on assumptions as to expiry of copyright or death of author

57.—(1) Copyright in a literary, dramatic, musical or artistic work is not infringed by an act done at a time when, or in pursuance of arrangements made at a time when—

(a) it is not possible by reasonable inquiry to ascertain the identity of the author, and

(b) it is reasonable to assume—
    (i) that copyright has expired, or
    (ii) that the author died [70 years] or more before the beginning of the calendar year in which the act is done or the arrangements are made.

(2) Subsection (1)(b)(ii) does not apply in relation to—

(a) a work in which Crown copyright subsists, or

(b) a work in which copyright originally vested in an international organisation by virtue of section 168 and in respect of which an Order under that section specifies a copyright period longer than [70 years].

(3) In relation to a work of joint authorship—

(a) the reference in subsection (1) to its being possible to ascertain the identity of the author shall be construed as a reference to its being possible to ascertain the identity of any of the authors, and

(b) the reference in subsection (1)(b)(ii) to the author having died shall be construed as a reference to all the authors having died.

Note: Subsection (1)(b)(ii) and subs.(2)(b) are printed as amended by the Duration of Copyright and Rights in Performances Regulations 1995 (SI 1995/3297), with effect from January 1, 1996. For savings and transitional provisions, see Part III of those Regulations.

Use of notes or recordings of spoken words in certain cases

58.—(1) Where a record of spoken words is made, in writing or otherwise, for the purpose—

(a) of reporting current events, or

(b) of [communicating to the public] the whole or part of the work,

it is not an infringement of any copyright in the words as a literary work to use the record or material taken from it (or to copy the record, or any such material, and use the copy) for that purpose, provided the following conditions are met.

(2) The conditions are that—

(a) the record is a direct record of the spoken words and is not taken from a previous record or from a broadcast [...];

(b) the making of the record was not prohibited by the speaker and, where copyright already subsisted in the work, did not infringe copyright;

    (c) the use made of the record or material taken from it is not of a kind prohibited by or on behalf of the speaker or copyright owner before the record was made; and

    (d) the use is by or with the authority of a person who is lawfully in possession of the record.

Note: The words in square brackets in subs.(1)(b) substituted for the former words "broadcasting or including in a cable programme service" and the words "or cable programme" repealed from subs.(2)(a) by the Copyright and Related Rights Regulations 2003 (SI 2003/2498), Sch.1 para.12 and Sch.2 with effect from October 31, 2003. For savings and transitional provisions, see Part 3 of those Regulations.

Public reading or recitation

59.—(1) The reading or recitation in public by one person of a reasonable extract from a published literary or dramatic work does not infringe any copyright in the work if it is accompanied by a sufficient acknowledgement.

(2) Copyright in a work is not infringed by the making of a sound recording, or the [communication to the public], of a reading or recitation which by virtue of subsection (1) does not infringe copyright in the work, provided that the recording, [or communication to the public] consists mainly of material in relation to which it is not necessary to rely on that subsection.

Note: The words in the first set of square brackets in subs.(2) substituted for the former words "broadcasting or inclusion in a cable programme service" and the words in the second set of square brackets substituted for the former words ", broadcast or cable programme" by the Copyright and Related Rights Regulations 2003 (SI 2003/2498), Sch.1 paras 5, 9 with effect from October 31, 2003. For savings and transitional provisions, see Part 3 of those Regulations.

Abstracts of scientific or technical articles

60.—(1) Where an article on a scientific or technical subject is published in a periodical accompanied by an abstract indicating the contents of the article, it is not an infringement of copyright in the abstract, or in the article, to copy the abstract or issue copies of it to the public.

(2) This section does not apply if or to the extent that there is a licensing scheme certified for the purposes of this section under section 143 providing for the grant of licences.

Recordings of folksongs

61.—(1) A sound recording of a performance of a song may be made for the purpose of including it in an archive maintained by a [body not established or conducted for profit] without infringing any copyright in the words as a literary work or in the accompanying musical work, provided the conditions in subsection (2) below are met.

(2) The conditions are that—

    (a) the words are unpublished and of unknown authorship at the time the recording is made,

    (b) the making of the recording does not infringe any other copyright, and

    (c) its making is not prohibited by any performer.

[(3) A single copy of a sound recording made in reliance on subsection (1) and included in an archive referred to in that subsection may be made and supplied by the archivist without infringing copyright in the recording or the works included in it, provided that—

    (a) the copy is supplied in response to a request from a person who has provided the archivist with a declaration in writing which includes the information set out in subsection (4), and

    (b) the archivist is not aware that the declaration is false in a material particular.

(4) The information which must be included in the declaration is—

    (a) the name of the person who requires the copy and the sound recording which is the subject of the request,

    (b) a statement that the person has not previously been supplied with a copy of that sound recording by any archivist, and

    (c) a statement that the person requires the copy for the purposes of research for a non-commercial purpose or private study, will use it only for those purposes and will not supply the copy to any other person.

(5) Where an archive makes a charge for supplying a copy under this section, the sum charged must be calculated by reference to the costs attributable to the production of the copy.

(6) a person ("P") makes a declaration under this section that is false in a material particular and is supplied with a copy which would have been an infringing copy if made by P—

    (a) P is liable for infringement of copyright as if P had made the copy, and

    (b) the copy supplied to P is to be treated as an infringing copy for all purposes.

(7) In this section references to an archivist include a person acting on behalf of an archivist.]

Notes:

    (1) Subsection (4)(a) was substituted by the Copyright and Related Rights Regulations 2003 (SI 2003/2498), reg.16 with effect from October 31, 2003. For savings and transitional provisions, see Part 3 of those Regulations. The former subs.(4)(a) provided:

        "(a) *that copies are only supplied to persons satisfying the archivist that they require them for purposes of research or private study and will not use them for any other purpose, and".*

    (2) In subs.(1) words in square brackets substituted for "designated body" and subss (3)–(7) substituted for existing subss (3)–(6), by the Copyright and Rights in Performances (Research, Education, Libraries and Archives) Regulations 2014 (SI 2014/1372), reg.7(2), with effect from June 1, 2014 at 00.02. Subss (3)–(6) (as amended by the Copyright and Related Rights Regulations 2003 (SI 2003/2498) formerly read:

"(3) Copies of a sound recording made in reliance on subsection (1) and included in an archive maintained by a designated body may, if the prescribed conditions are met, be made and supplied by the archivist without infringing copyright in the recording or the works included in it.

(4) The prescribed conditions shall include the following—

[(a) that copies are only supplied to persons satisfying the archivist that they require them for the purposes of—

    (i) research for a non-commercial purpose, or

    (ii) private study,

    and will not use them for any other purpose, and]

(b) that no person is furnished with more than one copy of the same recording.

(5) In this section—

(a) "designated" means designated for the purposes of this section by order of the Secretary of State, who shall not designate a body unless satisfied that it is not established or conducted for profit,

(b) "prescribed" means prescribed for the purposes of this section by order of the Secretary of State, and

(c) references to the archivist include a person acting on his behalf.

(6) An order under this section shall be made by statutory instrument which shall be subject to annulment in pursuance of a resolution of either House of Parliament."

Representation of certain artistic works on public display

62.—(1) This section applies to—

(a) buildings, and

(b) sculptures, models for buildings and works of artistic craftsmanship, if permanently situated in a public place or in premises open to the public.

(2) The copyright in such a work is not infringed by—

(a) making a graphic work representing it,

(b) making a photograph or film of it, or

(c) [making a broadcast of] a visual image of it.

(3) Nor is the copyright infringed by the issue to the public of copies, or the [communication to the public], of anything whose making was, by virtue of this section, not an infringement of the copyright.

Note: The words in square brackets in subs.(2) substituted for the former words "broadcasting or including in a cable programme service" and the words in square brackets in subs.(3) substituted for the former words "broadcasting or inclusion in a cable programme service" by the Copyright and Related Rights Regulations 2003 (SI 2003/2498), Sch.1 paras 5, 14 with effect from October 31, 2003. For savings and transitional provisions, see Part 3 of those Regulations.

Advertisement of sale of artistic work

63.—(1) It is not an infringement of copyright in an artistic work to copy it, or to issue copies to the public, for the purpose of advertising the sale of the work.

(2) Where a copy which would otherwise be an infringing copy is made in accordance with this section but is subsequently dealt with for any other purpose, it shall be treated as an infringing copy for the purposes of that dealing, and if that dealing infringes copyright for all subsequent purposes.

For this purpose "dealt with" means sold or let for hire, offered or exposed for sale or hire, exhibited in public[, distributed or communicated to the public].

Note: The words in square brackets in subs.(2) substituted for the former words "or distributed" by the Copyright and Related Rights Regulations 2003 (SI 2003/2498), reg.17 with effect from October 31, 2003. For savings and transitional provisions, see Part 3 of those Regulations.

Making of subsequent works by same artist

64. Where the author of an artistic work is not the copyright owner, he does not infringe the copyright by copying the work in making another artistic work, provided he does not repeat or imitate the main design of the earlier work.

Reconstruction of buildings

65. Anything done for the purposes of reconstructing a building does not infringe any copyright—

(a) in the building, or

(b) in any drawings or plans in accordance with which the building was, by or with the licence of the copyright owner, constructed.

[Miscellaneous: lending of works and playing of sound recordings

Lending to public of copies of certain works

66.—(1) The Secretary of State may by order provide that in such cases as may be specified in the order the lending to the public of copies of literary, dramatic, musical or artistic works, sound recordings or films shall be treated as licensed by the copyright owner subject only to the payment of such reasonable royalty or other payment as may be agreed or determined in default of agreement by the Copyright Tribunal.

(2) No such order shall apply if, or to the extent that; there is a licensing scheme certified for the purposes of this section under section 143 providing for the grant of licences.

(3) An order may make different provision for different cases and may specify cases by reference to any factor relating to the work, the copies lent, the lender or the circumstances of the lending.

(4) An order shall be made by statutory instrument; and no order shall be made unless a draft of it has been laid before and approved by a resolution of each House of Parliament.

(5) Nothing in this section affects any liability under section 23 (secondary infringement: possessing or dealing with infringing copy) in respect of the lending of infringing copies.]

Note: This section and the heading preceding it inserted by the Copyright and Related Rights Regulations 1996 (SI 1996/2967), which replaced the old s.66 and the heading preceding it with effect from December 1, 1996. The old s.66 and heading preceding it provided:

"Miscellaneous: sound recordings, films and computer programs

Rental of sound recordings, films and computer programs

66.—(1) *The Secretary of State may by order provide that in such cases as may be specified in the order the rental to the public of copies of sound recordings, films or computer programs shall be treated as licensed by the copyright owner subject only to the payment of such reasonable royalty or other payment as may be agreed or determined in default of agreement by the Copyright Tribunal.*

(2) *No such order shall apply if, or to the extent that, there is a licensing scheme certified for the purposes of this section under section 143 providing for the grant of licences.*

(3) *An order may make different provision for different cases and may specify cases by reference to any factor relating to the work, the copies rented, the renter or the circumstances of the rental.*

(4) *An order shall be made by statutory instrument; and no order shall be made unless a draft of it has been laid before and approved by a resolution of each House of Parliament.*

(5) *Copyright in a computer program is not infringed by the rental of copies to the public after the end of the period of 50 years from the end of the calendar year in which copies of it were first issued to the public in electronic form.*

(6) *Nothing in this section affects any liability under section 23 (secondary infringement) in respect of the rental of infringing copies."*

For savings and transitional provisions, see Part III of those Regulations.

[Miscellaneous: films and sound recordings

Films: acts permitted on assumptions as to expiry of copyright, &c.

66A.—(1) Copyright in a film is not infringed by an act done at a time when, or in pursuance of arrangements made at a time when—

(a) it is not possible by reasonable inquiry to ascertain the identity of any of the persons referred to in section 13B(2)(a) to (d) (persons by reference to whose life the copyright is ascertained), and

(b) it is reasonable to assume—
    (i) that copyright has expired, or
    (ii) that the last to die of those persons died 70 years or more before the beginning of the calendar year in which the act is done or the arrangements are made.
(2) Subsection (1)(b)(ii) does not apply in relation to—
    (a) a film in which Crown copyright subsists, or
    (b) a film in which copyright originally vested in an international organisation by virtue of section 168 and in respect of which an Order under that section specifies a copyright period longer than 70 years.]

Note: This section and the heading preceding it inserted by the Duration of Copyright and Rights in Performances Regulations 1995 (SI 1995/3297), with effect from January 1, 1996. For savings and transitional provisions, see Part III of those Regulations.

Playing of sound recordings for purposes of clubs, society, &c.

67. [...]

Notes:
(1) Section 67 was omitted by the Copyright, Designs and Patents Act 1988 (Amendment) Regulations 2010 (SI 2010/2694) with effect from January 1, 2011.
The former s.67 provided:

Playing of sound recordings for purposes of clubs, society, &c.

"**67.**—(1) *It is not an infringement of the copyright in a sound recording to play it as part of the activities of, or for the benefit of, a club, society or other organisation if the following conditions are met.*
    (2) *The conditions are—*
        (a) *that the organisation is not established or conducted for profit and its main objects are charitable or are otherwise concerned with the advancement of religion, education or social welfare,*
      [(b) *that the sound recording is played by a person who is acting primarily and directly for the benefit of the organisation and who is not acting with a view to gain,*
        (c) *that the proceeds of any charge for admission to the place where the recording is to be heard are applied solely for the purposes of the organisation, and*
        (d) [...]*"
(2) Subsection (2)(b) was substituted and (c) and (d) added to the old s.67 by the copyright and Related Rights Regulations 2003 (SI 2003/2498) reg.18 with effect from October 31, 2003. The former subs.(2)(b) provided:
    "(b) *that the proceeds of any charge for admission to the place where the recording is to be heard are applied solely for the purposes of the organisation.*"

Miscellaneous: broadcasts

Incidental recording for purposes of broadcast

68.—(1) This section applies where by virtue of a licence or assignment of copyright a person is authorised to broadcast [...]—
    (a) a literary, dramatic or musical work, or an adaptation of such a work,
    (b) an artistic work, or
    (c) a sound recording or film.
(2) He shall by virtue of this section be treated as licensed by the owner of the copyright in the work to do or authorise any of the following for the purposes of the broadcast [...]—

(a) in the case of a literary, dramatic or musical work, or an adaptation of such a work, to make a sound recording or film of the work or adaptation;

(b) in the case of an artistic work, to take a photograph or make a film of the work;

(c) in the case of a sound recording or film, to make a copy of it.

(3) That licence is subject to the condition that the recording, film, photograph or copy in question—

(a) shall not be used for any other purpose, and

(b) shall be destroyed within 28 days of being first used for broadcasting the work [...].

(4) A recording, film, photograph or copy made in accordance with this section shall be treated as an infringing copy—

(a) for the purposes of any use in breach of the condition mentioned in subsection (3)(a), and

(b) for all purposes after that condition or the condition mentioned in subsection (3)(b) is broken.

Note: The words in subss.(1), (2) and (3) referring to cable programmes repealed by the Copyright and Related Rights Regulations 2003 (SI 2003/2498), Sch.2 with effect from October 31, 2003. For savings and transitional provisions, see Part 3 of those Regulations.

Recording for purposes of supervision and control of broadcasts and other services

69.—(1) Copyright is not infringed by the making or use by the British Broadcasting Corporation, for the purpose of maintaining supervision and control over programmes broadcast by them [or included in any on-demand programme service provided by them], of recordings of those programmes.

[(2) Copyright is not infringed by anything done in pursuance of—

[(a) section 167(1) of the Broadcasting Act 1990, section 115(4) or (6) or 117 of the Broadcasting Act 1996 or paragraph 20 of Schedule 12 to the Communications Act 2003;]

(b) a condition which, [by virtue of section 334(1) of the Communications Act 2003] is included in a licence granted under Part I or III of that Act or Part I or II of the Broadcasting Act 1996;

(c) a direction given under section 109(2) of the Broadcasting Act 1990 (power of [OFCOM] to require production of recordings etc).

[(d) section 334(3)[, 368O(1) or (3)] of the Communications Act 2003.]]

[(3) Copyright is not infringed by the use by OFCOM in connection with the performance of any of their functions under the Broadcasting Act 1990, the Broadcasting Act 1996 or the Communications Act 2003 of—

(a) any recording, script or transcript which is provided to them under or by virtue of any provision of those Acts; or

(b) any existing material which is transferred to them by a scheme made under section 30 of the Communications Act 2003.

(4) In subsection (3), 'existing material' means—

(a) any recording, script or transcript which was provided to the Independent Television Commission or the Radio Authority under or by virtue of any provision of the Broadcasting Act 1990 or the Broadcasting Act 1996; and

(b) any recording or transcript which was provided to the Broadcasting Standards Commission under section 115(4) or (6) or 116(5) of the Broadcasting Act 1996.]

[(5) Copyright is not infringed by the use by an appropriate regulatory authority designated under section 368B of the Communications Act 2003, in connection with the performance of any of their functions under that Act, of any recording, script or transcript which is provided to them under or by virtue of any provision of that Act.

(6) In this section "on-demand programme service" has the same meaning as in the Communications Act 2003 (see section 368A of that Act).]

Notes:

(1) The words in square brackets in s.69(1), the words in square brackets internal to s.69(2)(d) and subss.(5) and (6) all inserted by the Audiovisual Media Services Regulations 2009 (SI 2009/2979) reg.12(2)(a), (b) and (c) with effect from December 29, 2009.

(2) As enacted, subss.(2) and (3) provided as follows:

"(2) *Copyright is not infringed by—*

(a) *the making or use of recordings by the Independent Broadcasting Authority for the purposes mentioned in section 4(7) of the Broadcasting Act 1981 (maintenance of supervision and control over programmes and advertisements); or*

(b) *anything done under or in pursuance of provision included in a contract between a programme contractor and the Authority in accordance with section 21 of that Act.*

(3) *Copyright is not infringed by—*

(a) *the making by or with the authority of the Cable Authority, or the use by that Authority, for the purpose of maintaining supervision and control over programmes included in services licensed under Part I of the Cable and Broadcasting Act 1984, of recordings of those programmes; or*

(b) *anything done under or in pursuance of—*

(i) *a notice or direction given under section 16 of the Cable and Broadcasting Act 1984 (power of Cable Authority to require production of recordings); or*

(ii) *a condition included in a licence by virtue of section 35 of that Act (duty of Authority to secure that recordings are available for certain purposes)."*

(3) The original subss.(2) and (3) set out in Note (2) above replaced by s.203(1) and para.50(1) of Sch.20 to the Broadcasting Act 1990 as provided by the Broadcasting Act 1990 (Commencement No. 1 and Transitional Provisions) Order 1990 (SI 1990/2347), with effect from January 1, 1991. The revised subsections provided as follows:

"(2) *Copyright is not infringed by anything done in pursuant of—*

(a) *section 11(1), 95(1), 145(4), (5) or (7), 155(3) or 167(1) of the Broadcasting Act 1990;*

(b) *a condition which, by virtue of section 11(2) or 95(2) of that Act, is included in a licence granted under Part I or III of that Act; or*

(c) *a direction given under section 109(2) of that Act (power of Radio Authority to require production of recordings etc.).*

(3) *Copyright is not infringed by—*

(a) *the use by the Independent Television Commission or the Radio Authority, in connection with the performance of any of their functions under the Broadcasting Act 1990, of any recording, script or transcript which is provided to them under or by virtue of any provision of that Act; or*

(b) *the use by the Broadcasting Complaints Commission or the Broadcasting Standards Council, in connection with any complaint made to them under that Act, of any recording or transcript requested or required to be provided to them, and so provided, under section 145(4) or (7) or section 155(3) of that Act."*

(4) Subsections (2) and (3) as set out in Note (3) above replaced again by section 148 and paragraph 31 of Schedule 10 to the Broadcasting Act 1996 as provided by the

Broadcasting Act 1996 (Commencement No. 1 and Transitional Provisions) Order 1996 (SI 1996/2120), with effect from October 1, 1996, so far as relating to anything done under Parts I or II of the 1996 Act (Schedule 1 to the Regulations). The replacement subsections read as follows:

"(2) *Copyright is not infringed by anything done in pursuant of—*

  (a) *section 11(1), 95(1) or 167(1) of the Broadcasting Act 1990 or section 115(4) or (6), 116(5) or 117 of the Broadcasting Act 1996;*

  (b) *a condition which, by virtue of section 11(2) or 95(2) of the Broadcasting Act 1990, is included in a licence granted under Part I or III of that Act or Part I or II of the Broadcasting Act 1996; or*

  (c) *a direction given under section 109(2) of the Broadcasting Act 1990 (power of Radio Authority to require production of recordings etc).*

  (3) *Copyright is not infringed by—*

  (a) *the use by the Independent Television Commission or the Radio Authority, in connection with the performance of any of their functions under the Broadcasting Act 1990 or the Broadcasting Act 1996, of any recording, script or transcript which is provided to them under or by virtue of any provision of those Acts; or*

  (b) *the use by the Broadcasting Standards Commission, in connection with any complaint made to them under the Broadcasting Act 1996, of any recording or transcript requested or required to be provided to them, and so provided, under section 115(4) or (6) or 116(5) of that Act."*

 (5) Subsection (2)(a) was substituted, the words in square brackets in subs.(2)(b) substituted for the former words "by virtue of ss.11(2) or 95(2) of the Broadcasting Act 1990", the words in square brackets in subs.(2)(c) substituted for the former words "Radio Authority", subs.(2)(d) was inserted and subs.(3) was substituted by the Communications Act 2003 (c.21), Sch.17 para.91 and Sch.19 with effect from December 29, 2003 (Office of Communications Act 2002 (Commencement No. 3) and Communications Act 2003 (Commencement No. 2) Order 2003 (SI 2003/3142)).

Recording for purposes of time-shifting

70.—(1) The making [in domestic premises] for private and domestic use of a recording of a broadcast [...] solely for the purpose of enabling it to be viewed or listened to at a more convenient time does not infringe any copyright in the broadcast [...] or in any work included in it.

[(2) Where a copy which would otherwise be an infringing copy is made in accordance with this section but is subsequently dealt with—

  (a) it shall be treated as an infringing copy for the purposes of that dealing; and

  (b) if that dealing infringes copyright, it shall be treated as an infringing copy for all subsequent purposes.

(3) In subsection (2), "dealt with" means sold or let for hire, offered or exposed for sale or hire or communicated to the public.]

Note: In subs.(1), the words in square brackets inserted and the words "or cable programme" where they appeared both times repealed and subss.(2) and (3) inserted by the Copyright and Related Rights Regulations 2003 (SI 2003/2498), reg.19 and Sch.2 with effect from October 31, 2003. For savings and transitional provisions, see Part 3 of those Regulations.

Photographs of broadcasts

[71.—(1) The making in domestic premises for private and domestic use of a photograph of the whole or any part of an image forming part of a broadcast, or a copy of such a photograph, does not infringe any copyright in the broadcast or in any film included in it.

(2) Where a copy which would otherwise be an infringing copy is made in accordance with this section but is subsequently dealt with—

(a) it shall be treated as an infringing copy for the purposes of that dealing; and

(b) if that dealing infringes copyright, it shall be treated as an infringing copy for all subsequent purposes.

(3) In subsection (2), "dealt with" means sold or let for hire, offered or exposed for sale or hire or communicated to the public.]

Note: Section 71 was substituted by the Copyright and Related Rights Regulations 2003 (SI 2003/2498), reg.20 with effect from October 31, 2003. For savings and transitional provisions, see Part 3 of those Regulations. The former s.71 provided:

Photographs of television broadcasts or cable programmes

"**71.** *The making for private and domestic use of a photograph of the whole or any part of an image forming part of a television broadcast or cable programme, or a copy of such a photograph, does not infringe any copyright in the broadcast or cable programme or in any film included in it.*"

Free public showing or playing of broadcast

72.—(1) The showing or playing in public of a broadcast [...] to an audience who have not paid for admission to the place where the broadcast [...] is to be seen or heard does not infringe any copyright in—

[(a) the broadcast;

(b) any sound recording (except so far as it is an excepted sound recording) included in it; or

(c) any film included in it.]

[(1A) For the purposes of this Part an "excepted sound recording" is a sound recording—

(a) whose author is not the author of the broadcast in which it is included; and

(b) which is a recording of music with or without words spoken or sung.

(1B) Where by virtue of subsection (1) the copyright in a broadcast shown or played in public is not infringed, copyright in any excepted sound recording included in it is not infringed if the playing or showing of that broadcast in public—

(a) [...]

(b) is necessary for the purposes of—

(i) repairing equipment for the reception of broadcasts;

(ii) demonstrating that a repair to such equipment has been carried out; or

(iii) demonstrating such equipment which is being sold or let for hire or offered or exposed for sale or hire.]

(2) The audience shall be treated as having paid for admission to a place—

(a) if they have paid for admission to a place of which that place forms part; or

(b) if goods or services are supplied at that place (or a place of which it forms part)—

(i) at prices which are substantially attributable to the facilities afforded for seeing or hearing the broadcast [...], or

(ii) at prices exceeding those usually charged there and which are partly attributable to those facilities.

(3) The following shall not be regarded as having paid for admission to a place—

(a) persons admitted as residents or inmates of the place;

(b) persons admitted as members of a club or society where the payment is only for membership of the club or society and the provision of facilities for seeing or hearing broadcasts [...] is only incidental to the main purposes of the club or society.

(4) Where the making of the broadcast [...] was an infringement of the copyright in a sound recording or film, the fact that it was heard or seen in public by the reception of the broadcast [...] shall be taken into account in assessing the damages for that infringement.

Notes:

(1) References to cable programmes repealed, subs.(1)(a) and (b) substituted and subs.(1)(c), (1A) and (1B) inserted by the Copyright and Related Rights Regulations 2003 (SI 2003/2498), reg.21 and Sch.2 with effect from October 31, 2003. For savings and transitional provisions, see Part 3 of those Regulations. The former subs.(1)(a) and (b) provided:

"(a) *the broadcast or cable programme, or*

(b) *any sound recording or film included in it.*"

(2) Section 72(1B)(a) was omitted by the Copyright, Designs and Patents Act 1988 (Amendment) Regulations 2010 (SI 2010/2694) with effect from January 1, 2011. It provided:

"(a) *forms part of the activities of an organisation that is not established conducted for profit; or*"

Reception and re-transmission of [wireless broadcast by cable]

[73.—(1) This section applies where a [wireless] broadcast made from a place in the United Kingdom is [received and immediately re-transmitted by cable].

(2) The copyright in the broadcast is not infringed—

(a) if the [re-transmission by cable] is in pursuance of a relevant requirement, or

(b) if and to the extent that the broadcast is made for reception in the area in which [it is re-transmitted by cable] and forms part of a qualifying service.

(3) The copyright in any work included in the broadcast is not infringed if and to the extent that the broadcast is made for reception in the area in which [it is re-transmitted by cable]; but where the making of the broadcast was an infringement of the copyright in the work, the fact that the broadcast was re-transmitted [by cable] shall be taken into account in assessing the damages for that infringement.

(4) Where—

(a) the [re-transmission by cable] is in pursuance of a relevant requirement, but

(b) to any extent, the area in which the [re-transmission by cable takes place] ("the cable area") falls outside the area for reception in which the broadcast is made ("the broadcast area"),

the [re-transmission by cable] (to the extent that it is provided for so much of the cable area as falls outside the broadcast area) of any work included in the broadcast shall, subject to subsection (5), be treated as licensed by the owner of the copyright in the work, subject only to the payment to him by the person making the broadcast of such reasonable royalty or other payment in respect of the [re-transmission by cable of the broadcast] as may be agreed or determined in default of agreement by the Copyright Tribunal.

(5) Subsection (4) does not apply if, or to the extent that, the [re-transmission of the work by cable] is (apart from that subsection) licensed by the owner of the copyright in the work.

(6) In this section "qualifying service" means, subject to subsection (8), any of the following services—

(a) a regional or national Channel 3 service,

(b) Channel 4, Channel 5 and S4C,

[(c) the public teletext service,

(d) S4C Digital, and]

(e) the television broadcasting services and teletext service of the British Broadcasting Corporation;

[and expressions used in this subsection have the same meanings as in Part 3 of the Communications Act 2003.]

[(7) In this section 'relevant requirement' means a requirement imposed by a general condition (within the meaning of Chapter 1 of Part 2 of the Communications Act 2003) the setting of which is authorised under section 64 of that Act (must-carry obligations).]

(8) The Secretary of State may by order amend subsection (6) so as to add any service to, or remove any service from, the definition of "qualifying service".

(9) The Secretary of State may also by order—

(a) provide that in specified cases subsection (3) is to apply in relation to broadcasts of a specified description which are not made as mentioned in that subsection, or

(b) exclude the application of that subsection in relation to broadcasts of a specified description made as mentioned in that subsection.

(10) Where the Secretary of State exercises the power conferred by subsection (9)(b) in relation to broadcasts of any description, the order may also provide for subsection (4) to apply, subject to such modifications as may be specified in the order, in relation to broadcasts of that description.

(11) An order under this section may contain such transitional provision as appears to the Secretary of State to be appropriate.

(12) An order under this section shall be made by statutory instrument which shall be subject to annulment in pursuance of a resolution of either House of Parliament.]

[(13) In this section references to re-transmission by cable include the transmission of microwave energy between terrestrial fixed points.]

Notes:

(1) As enacted, s.73 provided as follows:

Reception and re-transmission of broadcast in cable programme service

"**73.**—(1) *This section applies where a broadcast made from a place in the United Kingdom is, by reception and immediate re-transmission, included in a cable programme service.*

(2) *The copyright in the broadcast is not infringed—*

(a) *if the inclusion is in pursuance of a requirement imposed under section 13(1) of the Cable and Broadcasting Act 1984 (duty of Cable Authority to secure inclusion in cable service of certain programmes), or*

(b) *if and to the extent that the broadcast is made for reception in the area in which the cable programme service is provided and is not a satellite transmission or an encrypted transmission.*

(3) *The copyright in any work included in the broadcast is not infringed—*

(a) *if the inclusion is in pursuance of a requirement imposed under section 13(1) of the Cable and Broadcasting Act 1984 (duty of Cable Authority to secure inclusion in cable service of certain programmes), or*

(b) *if and to the extent that the broadcast is made for reception in the area in which the cable programme service is provided.*

but where the making of the broadcast was an infringement of the copyright in the work, the fact that the broadcast was re-transmitted as a programme in a cable programme service shall be taken into account in assessing the damages for that infringement."

(2) Subsections (2)(a) and (3)(a) of the old s.73 repealed by s.203(3) of and Sch.21 to the Broadcasting Act 1990 with effect from December 1, 1990 by the Broadcasting Act 1990 (Commencement No.1 and Transitional Provisions) Order 1990 (SI 1990/2347).

(3) Section 73 was substituted by the Broadcasting Act 1996 s.138 and Sch.9 with effect from October 1, 1996 (Broadcasting Act 1996 (Commencement No.1 and Transitional Provisions) Order 1996 (SI 1996/2120)).

(4) The substituted s.73 was amended by the Copyright and Related Rights Regulations 2003 (SI 2003/2498), reg.22, with effect from October 31, 2003, as follows:

    (a) in the heading the words in square brackets substituted for the former words "broadcast in cable programme service";

    (b) in subs.(1) the word in the first set of square brackets was inserted and the words in the second set of square brackets substituted for the former words ", by reception and immediate re-transmission, included in a cable programme service";

    (c) in subs.(2)(a), the words in square brackets substituted for the former word "inclusion";

    (d) in subs.(2)(b), the words in square brackets substituted for the former words "the cable programme service is provided";

    (d) in subs.(3) the words in the first set of square brackets substituted for the former words "the cable programme service is provided" and the words in the second set of square brackets were substituted for the former words "as a programme in a cable programme service";

    (e) in subs.(4)(a), the words in square brackets substituted for the former word "inclusion";

    (f) in subs.(4)(b) the words in square brackets substituted for the former words "cable programme service is required";

    (g) in subs.(4) the words in the first set of square brackets (after paragraph (b)) substituted for the former words "inclusion in the cable programme service" and the words in the second set of square brackets substituted for the former words "inclusion of the broadcast in the cable programme service";

    (h) in subs.(5), the words in square brackets substituted for the former words "inclusion of the work in the cable programme service"; and

    (i) subs.(13) was inserted.

For savings and transitional provisions, see Part 3 of those Regulations.

(5) Section 73 was further amended by the Communications Act 2003 (c.21), Sch.17 para.92 with effect from December 29, 2003 (Office of Communications Act 2002 (Commencement No.3) and Communications Act 2003 (Commencement No.2) Order 2003 (SI 2003/3142)) as follows:

    (a) subs.(6)(c) and (d) were substituted;

    (b) the words in square brackets after subs.(6)(e) substituted for the former words "and expressions used in this subsection have the same meaning as in Part I of the Broadcasting Act 1990."; and

    (c) subs.(7) was substituted.

The former subs.(6)(c) and (d) provided:

    "(c) the teletext service referred to in section 49(2) of the Broadcasting Act 1990,

    (d) the service referred to in section 57(1A)(a) of that Act (power of S4C to provide digital service."

The former subs.(7) provided:

    "(7) In this section

"relevant requirement" means a requirement imposed under—

    (a) section 78A of the Broadcasting Act 1990 (inclusion of certain services in local delivery services provided by digital means), or

(b) *paragraph 4 of Part III of Schedule 12 to that Act (inclusion of certain services in diffusion services originally licensed under the Cable and Broadcasting Act 1984)."*

Royalty or other sum payable in pursuance of section 73(4)

[**73A.**—(1) An application to settle the royalty or other sum payable in pursuance of subsection (4) of section 73 (reception and re-transmission of [wireless broadcast by cable]) may be made to the Copyright Tribunal by the copyright owner or the person making the broadcast.

(2) The Tribunal shall consider the matter and make such order as it may determine to be reasonable in the circumstances.

(3) Either party may subsequently apply to the Tribunal to vary the order, and the Tribunal shall consider the matter and make such order confirming or varying the original order as it may determine to be reasonable in the circumstances.

(4) An application under subsection (3) shall not, except with the special leave of the Tribunal, be made within twelve months from the date of the original order or of the order on a previous application under that subsection.

(5) An order under subsection (3) has effect from the date on which it is made or such later date as may be specified by the Tribunal.]

Notes:

(1) Section 73A was inserted by s.138 and Sch.9 to the Broadcasting Act 1996 with effect from October 1, 1996 by virtue of the Broadcasting Act 1996 (Commencement No. 1 and Transitional Provisions) Order 1996 (SI 1996/2120).

(2) The words in square brackets in subs.(1) substituted for the former words "broadcast in cable programme service" by the Copyright and Related Rights Regulations 2003 (SI 2003/2498), reg.22, with effect from October 31, 2003. For savings and transitional provisions, see Part 3 of those Regulations.

Provision of sub-titled copies of broadcast

74. [...]

Note: Section 74 was repealed by the Copyright and Rights in Performances (Disability) Regulations 2014 (SI 2014/1384), Sch. para.8, with effect from June 1, 2014 at 00.01. Section 74 (as amended by the Copyright and Related Rights Regulations 2003 (SI 2003/2498) formerly read:

"(1) A designated body may, for the purpose of providing people who are deaf or hard of hearing, or physically or mentally handicapped in other ways, with copies which are sub-titled or otherwise modified for their special needs, make copies of [...] broadcasts [...] and issue [or lend] copies to the public, without infringing any copyright in the broadcasts [...] or works included in them.

(2) A "designated body" means a body designated for the purposes of this section by order of the Secretary of State, who shall not designate a body unless he is satisfied that it is not established or conducted for profit.

(3) An order under this section shall be made by statutory instrument which shall be subject to annulment in pursuance of a resolution of either House of Parliament.

(4) This section does not apply if, or to the extent that, there is a licensing scheme certified for the purposes of this section under s.143 providing for the grant of licences."

Recording for archival purposes

[**75.**—(1) A recording of a broadcast or a copy of such a recording may be made for the purpose of being placed in an archive maintained by a body which is not established or conducted for profit without infringing any copyright in the broadcast or in any work included in it.

(2) To the extent that a term of a contract purports to prevent or restrict the do-

ing of any act which, by virtue of this section, would not infringe copyright, that term is unenforceable.]

Note: Section 75 substituted by the Copyright and Rights in Performances (Research, Education, Libraries and Archives) Regulations 2014 (SI 2014/1372), reg.8(1), with effect from June 1, 2014 at 00.02. Section 75 (as amended by the Copyright and Related Rights Regulations 2003 (SI 2003/2498)) formerly read:

"**75.**—*(1) A recording of a broadcast [...] of a designated class, or a copy of such a recording, may be made for the purpose of being placed in an archive maintained by a designated body without thereby infringing any copyright in the broadcast [...] or in any work included in it.*

(2) In subsection (1) "designated" means designated for the purposes of this section by order of the Secretary of State, who shall not designate a body unless he is satisfied that it is not established or conducted for profit.

(3) An order under this section shall be made by statutory instrument which shall be subject to annulment in pursuance of a resolution of either House of Parliament."

Adaptations

Adaptations

76. An act which by virtue of this Chapter may be done without infringing copyright in a literary, dramatic or musical work does not, where that work is an adaptation, infringe any copyright in the work from which the adaptation was made.

Note: See also s.176 of and Sch.17 to the Broadcasting Act 1990, which contain provisions relating to the statutory duty to provide information about programmes and the settling of terms of payment by the Copyright Tribunal. The 1988 Act is not amended by these provisions but para.7(1) of Sch.17 provides that the 1988 Act shall have effect as if those provisions were included in Ch.III of Pt I of the 1988 Act. These provisions came into force as provided by The Broadcasting Act 1990 (Commencement No. 1 and Transitional Provisions) Order 1990 (SI 1990/2347).

[CHAPTER 3A

CERTAIN PERMITTED USES OF ORPHAN WORKS

Certain permitted uses of orphan works

76A. Schedule ZA1 makes provision about the use by relevant bodies of orphan works.]

Note: Section 76A inserted by the Copyright and Rights in Performances (Certain Permitted Uses of Orphan Works) Regulations 2014 (SI 2014/2861), reg.3(2), with effect from October 29, 2014.

CHAPTER IV

MORAL RIGHTS

Right to be identified as author or director

Right to be identified as author or director

77.—(1) The author of a copyright literary, dramatic, musical or artistic work, and the director of a copyright film, has the right to be identified as the author or director of the work in the circumstances mentioned in this section; but the right is not infringed unless it has been asserted in accordance with section 78.

(2) The author of a literary work (other than words intended to be sung or spoken with music) or a dramatic work has the right to be identified whenever—

(a) the work is published commercially, performed in public [or communicated to the public]; or

(b) copies of a film or sound recording including the work are issued to the public;

and that right includes the right to be identified whenever any of those events occur in relation to an adaptation of the work as the author of the work from which the adaptation was made.

(3) The author of a musical work, or a literary work consisting of words intended to be sung or spoken with music, has the right to be identified whenever—

(a) the work is published commercially;

(b) copies of a sound recording of the work are issued to the public; or

(c) a film of which the sound-track includes the work is shown in public or copies of such a film are issued to the public;

and that right includes the right to be identified whenever any of those events occur in relation to an adaptation of the work as the author of the work from which the adaptation was made.

(4) The author of an artistic work has the right to be identified whenever—

(a) the work is published commercially or exhibited in public, or a visual image of it is [communicated to the public];

(b) a film including a visual image of the work is shown in public or copies of such a film are issued to the public; or

(c) in the case of a work of architecture in the form of a building or a model for a building, a sculpture or a work of artistic craftsmanship, copies of a graphic work representing it, or of a photograph of it, are issued to the public.

(5) The author of a work of architecture in the form of a building also has the right to be identified on the building as constructed or, where more than one building is constructed to the design, on the first to be constructed.

(6) The director of a film has the right to be identified whenever the film is shown in public, broadcast or included in a cable programme service or copies of the film are issued to the public.

(7) The right of the author or director under this section is—

(a) in the case of commercial publication or the issue to the public of copies of a film or sound recording, to be identified in or on each copy or, if that is not appropriate, in some other manner likely to bring his identity to the notice of a person acquiring a copy,

(b) in the case of identification on a building, to be identified by appropriate means visible to persons entering or approaching the building, and

(c) in any other case, to be identified in a manner likely to bring his identity to the attention of a person seeing or hearing the performance, exhibition, showing [or communication to the public] in question;

and the identification must in each case be clear and reasonably prominent.

(8) If the author or director in asserting his right to be identified specifies a pseudonym, initials or some other particular form of identification, that form shall be used; otherwise any reasonable form of identification may be used.

(9) This section has effect subject to section 79 (exceptions to right).

Note: The words in square brackets in subs.(2)(a) substituted for the former words ", broadcast or included in a cable programme service"; the words in square brackets in subs.(4)(a) substituted for the former words "broadcast or included in a cable programme service"; the words in square brackets in subs.(7)(c) substituted for the former words ", broadcast or cable programme" by the Copyright and Related Rights Regulations 2003 (SI 2003/2498), Sch.1 paras 8, 9, with effect from October 31, 2003. For savings and transitional provisions, see Part 3 of those Regulations.

Requirement that right be asserted

78.—(1) A person does not infringe the right conferred by section 77 (right to be identified as author or director) by doing any of the acts mentioned in that section unless the right has been asserted in accordance with the following provisions so as to bind him in relation to that act.

(2) The right may be asserted generally, or in relation to any specified act or description of acts—

  (a) on an assignment of copyright in the work, by including in the instrument effecting the assignment a statement that the author or director asserts in relation to that work his right to be identified, or

  (b) by instrument in writing signed by the author or director.

(3) The right may also be asserted in relation to the public exhibition of an artistic work—

  (a) by securing that when the author or other first owner of copyright parts with possession of the original, or of a copy made by him or under his direction or control, the author is identified on the original or copy, or on a frame, mount or other thing to which it is attached, or

  (b) by including in a licence by which the author or other first owner of copyright authorises the making of copies of the work a statement signed by or on behalf of the person granting the licence that the author asserts his right to be identified in the event of the public exhibition of a copy made in pursuance of the licence.

(4) The persons bound by an assertion of the right under subsection (2) or (3) are—

  (a) in the case of an assertion under subsection (2)(a), the assignee and anyone claiming through him, whether or not he has notice of the assertion;

  (b) in the case of an assertion under subsection (2)(b), anyone to whose notice the assertion is brought;

  (c) in the case of an assertion under subsection (3)(a), anyone into whose hands that original or copy comes, whether or not the identification is still present or visible;

  (d) in the case of an assertion under subsection (3)(b), the licensee and anyone into whose hands a copy made in pursuance of the licence comes, whether or not he has notice of the assertion.

(5) In an action for infringement of the right the court shall, in considering remedies, take into account any delay in asserting the right.

Exceptions to right

79.—(1) The right conferred by section 77 (right to be identified as author or director) is subject to the following exceptions.

(2) The right does not apply in relation to the following descriptions of work—

  (a) a computer program;

  (b) the design of a typeface;

  (c) any computer-generated work.

(3) The right does not apply to anything done by or with the authority of the copyright owner where copyright in the work originally [vested in the author's or director's employer by virtue of section 11(2) (works produced in the course of employment)].

(4) The right is not infringed by an act which by virtue of any of the following provisions would not infringe copyright in the work—

(a) section 30 (fair dealing for certain purposes), so far as it relates to the reporting of current events by means of a sound recording, film [or broadcast];

(b) section 31 (incidental inclusion of work in an artistic work, sound recording, film [or broadcast]);

(c) [...]

(d) section 45 (parliamentary and judicial proceedings);

(e) section 46(1) or (2) (Royal Commissions and statutory inquiries);

(f) section 51 (use of design documents and models);

(g) *section 52 (effect of exploitation of design derived from artistic work);*

(h) [section 57 or 66A (acts permitted on assumptions as to expiry of copyright, &c.)].

[(4A) The right is also not infringed by any act done for the purposes of an examination which by virtue of any provision of Chapter 3 of Part 1 would not infringe copyright.]

(5) The right does not apply in relation to any work made for the purpose of reporting current events.

(6) The right does not apply in relation to the publication in—

(a) a newspaper, magazine or similar periodical, or

(b) an encyclopaedia, dictionary, yearbook or other collective work of reference,

of a literary, dramatic, musical or artistic work made for the purposes of such publication or made available with the consent of the author for the purposes of such publication.

(7) The right does not apply in relation to—

(a) a work in which Crown copyright or Parliamentary copyright subsists, or

(b) a work in which copyright originally vested in an international organisation by virtue of section 168,

unless the author or director has previously been identified as such in or on published copies of the work.

Notes:

(1) Subsection (4) is printed as amended by the Duration of Copyright and Rights in Performances Regulations 1995 (SI 1995/3297), with effect from January 1, 1996. For savings and transitional provisions, see Part III of those Regulations.

(2) The words in square brackets in subs.(3) substituted for the former words:

"(a) *in the author's employer by virtue of section 11(2) (works produced in course of employment), or*

(b) *in the director's employer by virtue of section9(2)(a) (person to be treated as author of film)."*

(3) The words in square brackets in subs.(4)(a) and (b) substituted for the former words ", broadcast or cable programme" by the Copyright and Related Rights Regulations 2003 (SI 2003/2498), Sch.1 paras 3, 18, with effect from October 31, 2003. For savings and transitional provisions, see Part 3 of those Regulations.

(4) Subs.(4)(c) repealed and subs.(4A) inserted by the Copyright and Rights in Performances (Research, Education, Libraries and Archives) Regulations 2014 (SI 2014/1372), Sch para.4, with effect from June 1, 2014 at 00.02. Subs.(4)(c) formerly read:

"(c) section 32(3) (examination questions);"
   (5) Subs.(4)(g) in italics prospectively repealed by the Enterprise and Regulatory Reform Act 2013 s.74(3)(a), with effect from a date to be appointed.

Right to object to derogatory treatment of work

Right to object to derogatory treatment of work

80.—(1) The author of a copyright literary, dramatic, musical or artistic work, and the director of a copyright film, has the right in the circumstances mentioned in this section not to have his work subjected to derogatory treatment.

   (2) For the purposes of this section—

     (a) "treatment" of a work means any addition to, deletion from or alteration to or adaptation of the work, other than—

        (i) a translation of a literary or dramatic work, or

        (ii) an arrangement or transcription of a musical work involving no more than a change of key or register; and

     (b) the treatment of a work is derogatory if it amounts to distortion or mutilation of the work or is otherwise prejudicial to the honour or reputation of the author or director;

and in the following provisions of this section references to a derogatory treatment of a work shall be construed accordingly.

   (3) In the case of a literary, dramatic or musical work the right is infringed by a person who—

     (a) publishes commercially, performs in public, [or communicates to the public] a derogatory treatment of the work; or

     (b) issues to the public copies of a film or sound recording of, or including, a derogatory treatment of the work.

   (4) In the case of an artistic work the right is infringed by a person who—

     (a) publishes commercially or exhibits in public a derogatory treatment of the work, or [or communicates to the public] a visual image of a derogatory treatment of the work,

     (b) shows in public a film including a visual image of a derogatory treatment of the work or issues to the public copies of such a film, or

     (c) in the case of—

        (i) a work of architecture in the form of a model for a building,

        (ii) a sculpture, or

        (iii) a work of artistic craftsmanship,

issues to the public copies of a graphic work representing, or of a photograph of, a derogatory treatment of the work.

   (5) Subsection (4) does not apply to a work of architecture in the form of a building; but where the author of such a work is identified on the building and it is the subject of derogatory treatment he has the right to require the identification to be removed.

   (6) In the case of a film, the right is infringed by a person who—

     (a) shows in public [or communicates to the public] a derogatory treatment of the film; or

     (b) issues to the public copies of a derogatory treatment of the film [...].

   (7) The right conferred by this section extends to the treatment of parts of a work resulting from a previous treatment by a person other than the author or director, if those parts are attributed to, or are likely to be regarded as the work of, the author or director.

   (8) This section has effect subject to sections 81 and 82 (exceptions to and qualifications of right).

Notes:

(1) Subsection (6) is printed as amended by the Duration of Copyright and Rights in Performances Regulations 1995 (SI 1995/3297), with effect from January 1, 1996, by virtue of which the words:

> "*or who, along with the film, plays in public, broadcasts or includes in a cable programme service, or issues to the public copies of, a derogatory treatment of the film sound-track.*"

omitted from the end of subs.(6).

(2) The words in square brackets in subs.(3)(a) substituted for the former words ", broadcasts or includes in a cable programme service"; the words in square brackets in subs.(4)(a) substituted for the former words "or broadcasts or includes in a cable programme service" and the words in square brackets in subs.(6)(a) substituted for the former words ", broadcasts or includes in a cable programme service" by the Copyright and Related Rights Regulations 2003 (SI 2003/2498), Sch.1 paras 10, 13, with effect from October 31, 2003. For savings and transitional provisions, see Part 3 of those Regulations.

Exceptions to right

81.—(1) The right conferred by section 80 (right to object to derogatory treatment of work) is subject to the following exceptions.

(2) The right does not apply to a computer program or to any computer-generated work.

(3) The right does not apply in relation to any work made for the purpose of reporting current events.

(4) The right does not apply in relation to the publication in—

(a) a newspaper, magazine or similar periodical, or

(b) an encyclopaedia, dictionary, yearbook or other collective work of reference,

of a literary, dramatic, musical or artistic work made for the purposes of such publication or made available with the consent of the author for the purposes of such publication.

Nor does the right apply in relation to any subsequent exploitation elsewhere of such a work without any modification of the published version.

(5) The right is not infringed by an act which by virtue of [section 57 or 66A (acts permitted on assumptions as to expiry of copyright, &c.)] would not infringe copyright.

(6) The right is not infringed by anything done for the purpose of—

(a) avoiding the commission of an offence,

(b) complying with a duty imposed by or under an enactment, or

(c) in the case of the British Broadcasting Corporation, avoiding the inclusion in a programme broadcast by them of anything which offends against good taste or decency or which is likely to encourage or incite to crime or to lead to disorder or to be offensive to public feeling,

provided, where the author or director is identified at the time of the relevant act or has previously been identified in or on published copies of the work, that there is a sufficient disclaimer.

Note: Subsection (5) is printed as amended by the Duration of Copyright and Rights in Performances Regulations 1995 (SI 1995/3297), with effect from January 1, 1996. For savings and transitional provisions, see Part III of those Regulations.

Qualification of right in certain cases

82.—(1) This section applies to—

(a) works in which copyright originally vested in the author's [or director's] employer by virtue of section 11(2) (works produced in course of employment) [...],

(b) works in which Crown copyright or Parliamentary copyright subsists, and

(c) works in which copyright originally vested in an international organisation by virtue of section 168.

(2) The right conferred by section 80 (right to object to derogatory treatment of work) does not apply to anything done in relation to such a work by or with the authority of the copyright owner unless the author or director—

(a) is identified at the time of the relevant act, or

(b) has previously been identified in or on published copies of the work;

and where in such a case the right does apply, it is not infringed if there is a sufficient disclaimer.

Note: The words in square brackets in subs.(1)(a) inserted and the former words "or in the director's employer by virtue of section 9(2)(a) (person to be treated as author of film)" by the Copyright and Related Rights Regulations 2003 (SI 2003/2498), Sch.1 para.18, Sch.2, with effect from October 31, 2003. For savings and transitional provisions, see Part 3 of those Regulations.

Infringement of right by possessing or dealing with infringing article

83.—(1) The right conferred by section 80 (right to object to derogatory treatment of work) is also infringed by a person who—

(a) possesses in the course of a business, or

(b) sells or lets for hire, or offers or exposes for sale or hire, or

(c) in the course of a business exhibits in public or distributes, or

(d) distributes otherwise than in the course of a business so as to affect prejudicially the honour or reputation of the author or director,

an article which is, and which he knows or has reason to believe is, an infringing article.

(2) An "infringing article" means a work or a copy of a work which—

(a) has been subjected to derogatory treatment within the meaning of section 80, and

(b) has been or is likely to be the subject of any of the acts mentioned in that section in circumstances infringing that right.

False attribution of work

False attribution of work

84.—(1) A person has the right in the circumstances mentioned in this section—

(a) not to have a literary, dramatic, musical or artistic work falsely attributed to him as author, and

(b) not to have a film falsely attributed to him as director;

and in this section an "attribution", in relation to such a work, means a statement (express or implied) as to who is the author or director.

(2) The right is infringed by a person who—

(a) issues to the public copies of a work of any of those descriptions in or on which there is a false attribution, or

(b) exhibits in public an artistic work, or a copy of an artistic work, in or on which there is a false attribution.

(3) The right is also infringed by a person who—

(a) in the case of a literary, dramatic or musical work, performs the work in public, [or communicates it to the public] as being the work of a person, or

(b) in the case of a film, shows it in public, [or communicates it to the public] as being directed by a person,

knowing or having reason to believe that the attribution is false.

(4) The right is also infringed by the issue to the public or public display of material containing a false attribution in connection with any of the acts mentioned in subsection (2) or (3).

(5) The right is also infringed by a person who in the course of a business—

(a) possesses or deals with a copy of a work of any of the descriptions mentioned in subsection (1) in or on which there is a false attribution, or

(b) in the case of an artistic work, possesses or deals with the work itself when there is a false attribution in or on it,

knowing or having reason to believe that there is such an attribution and that it is false.

(6) In the case of an artistic work the right is also infringed by a person who in the course of a business—

(a) deals with a work which has been altered after the author parted with possession of it as being the unaltered work of the author, or

(b) deals with a copy of such a work as being a copy of the unaltered work of the author,

knowing or having reason to believe that that is not the case.

(7) References in this section to dealing are to selling or letting for hire, offering or exposing for sale or hire, exhibiting in public, or distributing.

(8) This section applies where, contrary to the fact—

(a) a literary, dramatic or musical work is falsely represented as being an adaptation of the work of a person, or

(b) a copy of an artistic work is falsely represented as being a copy made by the author of the artistic work,

as it applies where the work is falsely attributed to a person as author.

Note: The words in square brackets in subs.(3)(a) and (b) substituted for the former words ", broadcasts it or includes it in a cable programme service" by the Copyright and Related Rights Regulations 2003 (SI 2003/2498), Sch.1 para.10, with effect from October 31, 2003. For savings and transitional provisions, see Part 3 of those Regulations.

Right to privacy of certain photographs and films

Right to privacy of certain photographs and films

85.—(1) A person who for private and domestic purposes commissions the taking of a photograph or the making of a film has, where copyright subsists in the resulting work, the right not to have—

(a) copies of the work issued to the public,

(b) the work exhibited or shown in public, or

(c) the work [communicated to the public]

and, except as mentioned in subsection (2), a person who does or authorises the doing of any of those acts infringes that right.

(2) The right is not infringed by an act which by virtue of any of the following provisions would not infringe copyright in the work—

(a) section 31 (incidental inclusion of work in an artistic work, film [or broadcast]);

(b) section 45 (parliamentary and judicial proceedings);

(c) section 46 (Royal Commissions and statutory inquiries);

(d) section 50 (acts done under statutory authority);

(e) [section 57 or 66A (acts permitted on assumptions as to expiry of copyright, &c.)].

Notes:

(1) Subsection (2) is printed as amended by the Duration of Copyright and Rights in Performances Regulations 1995 (SI 1995/3297), with effect from January 1, 1996. For savings and transitional provisions, see Part III of those Regulations.

(2) The words in square brackets in subs.(1)(a) substituted for the former words "broadcast or included in a cable programme service" and the words in square brackets in subs.(2)(a) substituted for the former words ", broadcast or cable programme" by the Copyright and Related Rights Regulations 2003 (SI 2003/2498), Sch.1 paras 3, 8, with effect from October 31, 2003. For savings and transitional provisions, see Part 3 of those Regulations.

Supplementary

Duration of rights

86.—(1) The rights conferred by section 77 (right to be identified as author or director), section 80 (right to object to derogatory treatment of work) and section 85 (right to privacy of certain photographs and films) continue to subsist so long as copyright subsists in the work.

(2) The right conferred by section 84 (false attribution) continues to subsist until 20 years after a person's death.

Consent and waiver of rights

87.—(1) It is not an infringement of any of the rights conferred by this Chapter to do any act to which the person entitled to the right has consented.

(2) Any of those rights may be waived by instrument in writing signed by the person giving up the right.

(3) A waiver—

(a) may relate to a specific work, to works of a specified description or to works generally, and may relate to existing or future works, and

(b) may be conditional or unconditional and may be expressed to be subject to revocation;

and if made in favour of the owner or prospective owner of the copyright in the work or works to which it relates, it shall be presumed to extend to his licensees and successors in title unless a contrary intention is expressed.

(4) Nothing in this Chapter shall be construed as excluding the operation of the general law of contract or estoppel in relation to an informal waiver or other transaction in relation to any of the rights mentioned in subsection (1).

Application of provisions to joint works

88.—(1) The right conferred by section 77 (right to be identified as author or director) is, in the case of a work of joint authorship, a right of each joint author to be identified as a joint author and must be asserted in accordance with section 78 by each joint author in relation to himself.

(2) The right conferred by section 80 (right to object to derogatory treatment of work) is, in the case of a work of joint authorship, a right of each joint author and his right is satisfied if he consents to the treatment in question.

(3) A waiver under section 87 of those rights by one joint author does not affect the rights of the other joint authors.

(4) The right conferred by section 84 (false attribution) is infringed, in the circumstances mentioned in that section—

(a) by any false statement as to the authorship of a work of joint authorship, and

(b) by the false attribution of joint authorship in relation to a work of sole authorship;

and such a false attribution infringes the right of every person to whom authorship of any description is, whether rightly or wrongly, attributed.

(5) The above provisions also apply (with any necessary adaptations) in relation to a film which was, or is alleged to have been, jointly directed, as they apply to a work which is, or is alleged to be, a work of joint authorship.

A film is "jointly directed" if it is made by the collaboration of two or more directors and the contribution of each director is not distinct from that of the other director or directors.

(6) The right conferred by section 85 (right to privacy of certain photographs and films) is, in the case of a work made in pursuance of a joint commission, a right of each person who commissioned the making of the work, so that—

(a) the right of each is satisfied if he consents to the act in question, and

(b) a waiver under section 87 by one of them does not affect the rights of the others.

Application of provisions to parts of works

89.—(1) The rights conferred by section 77 (right to be identified as author or director) and section 85 (right to privacy of certain photographs and films) apply in relation to the whole or any substantial part of a work.

(2) The rights conferred by section 80 (right to object to derogatory treatment of work) and section 84 (false attribution) apply in relation to the whole or any part of a work.

Chapter V

Dealings with Rights in Copyright Works

Copyright

Assignment and licences

90.—(1) Copyright is transmissible by assignment, by testamentary disposition or by operation of law, as personal or moveable property.

(2) An assignment or other transmission of copyright may be partial, that is, limited so as to apply—

(a) to one or more, but not all, of the things the copyright owner has the exclusive right to do;

(b) to part, but not the whole, of the period for which the copyright is to subsist.

(3) An assignment of copyright is not effective unless it is in writing signed by or on behalf of the assignor.

(4) A licence granted by a copyright owner is binding on every successor in title to his interest in the copyright, except a purchaser in good faith for valuable consideration and without notice (actual or constructive) of the licence or a person deriving title from such a purchaser; and references in this Part to doing anything with, or without, the licence of the copyright owner shall be construed accordingly.

Prospective ownership of copyright

91.—(1) Where by an agreement made in relation to future copyright, and signed by or on behalf of the prospective owner of the copyright, the prospective owner purports to assign the future copyright (wholly or partially) to another person, then if, on the copyright coming into existence, the assignee or another person claiming under him would be entitled as against all other persons to require the copyright to be vested in him, the copyright shall vest in the assignee or his successor in title by virtue of this subsection.

(2) In this Part—

"future copyright" means copyright which will or may come into existence in respect of a future work or class of works or on the occurrence of a future event; and

"prospective owner" shall be construed accordingly, and includes a person who is prospectively entitled to copyright by virtue of such an agreement as is mentioned in subsection (1).

(3) A licence granted by a prospective owner of copyright is binding on every successor in title to his interest (or prospective interest) in the right, except a purchaser in good faith for valuable consideration and without notice (actual or constructive) of the licence or a person deriving title from such a purchaser; and references in this Part to doing anything with, or without, the licence of the copyright owner shall be construed accordingly.

Exclusive licences

92.—(1) In this Part an "exclusive licence" means a licence in writing signed by or on behalf of the copyright owner authorising the licensee to the exclusion of all other persons, including the person granting the licence, to exercise a right which would otherwise be exercisable exclusively by the copyright owner.

(2) The licensee under an exclusive licence has the same rights against a successor in title who is bound by the licence as he has against the person granting the licence.

Copyright to pass under will with unpublished work

93. Where under a bequest (whether specific or general) a person is entitled, beneficially or otherwise, to—

(a) an original document or other material thing recording or embodying a literary, dramatic, musical or artistic work which was not published before the death of the testator, or

(b) an original material thing containing a sound recording or film which was not published before the death of the testator,

the bequest shall, unless a contrary intention is indicated in the testator's will or a codicil to it, be construed as including the copyright in the work in so far as the testator was the owner of the copyright immediately before his death.

Presumption of transfer of rental right in case of film production agreement

[93A.—(1) Where an agreement concerning film production is concluded between an author and a film producer, the author shall be presumed, unless the agreement provides to the contrary, to have transferred to the film producer any rental right in relation to the film arising by virtue of the inclusion of a copy of the author's work in the film.

(2) In this section "author" means an author, or prospective author, of a literary, dramatic, musical or artistic work.

(3) Subsection (1) does not apply to any rental right in relation to the film arising by virtue of the inclusion in the film of the screenplay, the dialogue or music specifically created for and used in the film.

(4) Where this section applies, the absence of signature by or on behalf of the author does not exclude the operation of section 91(1) (effect of purported assignment of future copyright).

(5) The reference in subsection (1) to an agreement concluded between an author and a film producer includes any agreement having effect between those persons, whether made by them directly or through intermediaries.

(6) Section 93B (right to equitable remuneration on transfer of rental right) applies where there is a presumed transfer by virtue of this section as in the case of an actual transfer.]

Note: This section was inserted by the Copyright and Related Rights Regulations 1996 (SI 1996/2967), with effect from December 1, 1996. For savings and transitional provisions, see Pt III of those Regulations.

[Right to equitable remuneration where rental right transferred

Right to equitable remuneration where rental right transferred

93B.—(1) Where an author to whom this section applies has transferred his rental right concerning a sound recording or a film to the producer of the sound recording or film, he retains the right to equitable remuneration for the rental.

The authors to whom this section applies are—

    (a) the author of a literary, dramatic, musical or artistic work, and

    (b) the principal director of a film.

(2) The right to equitable remuneration under this section may not be assigned by the author except to a collecting society for the purpose of enabling it to enforce the right on his behalf.

The right is, however, transmissible by testamentary disposition or by operation of law as personal or moveable property, and it may be assigned or further transmitted by any person into whose hands it passes.

(3) Equitable remuneration under this section is payable by the person for the time being entitled to the rental right, that is, the person to whom the right was transferred or any successor in title of his.

(4) The amount payable by way of equitable remuneration is as agreed by or on behalf of the persons by and to whom it is payable, subject to section 93C (reference to amount to Copyright Tribunal).

(5) An agreement is of no effect in so far as it purports to exclude or restrict the right to equitable remuneration under this section.

(6) References in this section to the transfer of rental right by one person to another include any arrangement having that effect, whether made by them directly or through intermediaries.

(7) In this section a "collecting society" means a society or other organisation which has as its main object, or one of its main objects, the exercise of the right to equitable remuneration under this section on behalf of more than one author.]

Note: This section and the heading preceding it inserted by the Copyright and Related Rights Regulations 1996 (SI 1996/2967), with effect from December 1, 1996. For savings and transitional provisions, see Pt III of those Regulations.

Equitable remuneration: reference of amount to Copyright Tribunal

[**93C.**—(1) In default of agreement as to the amount payable by way of equitable remuneration under section 93B, the person by or to whom it is payable may apply to the Copyright Tribunal to determine the amount payable.

(2) A person to or by whom equitable remuneration is payable under that section may also apply to the Copyright Tribunal—

(a) to vary any agreement as to the amount payable, or

(b) to vary any previous determination of the Tribunal as to that matter;

but except with the special leave of the Tribunal no such application may be made within twelve months from the date of a previous determination.

An order made on an application under this subsection has effect from the date on which it is made or such later date as may be specified by the Tribunal.

(3) On an application under this section the Tribunal shall consider the matter and make such order as to the method of calculating and paying equitable remuneration as it may determine to be reasonable in the circumstances, taking into account the importance of the contribution of the author to the film or sound recording.

(4) Remuneration shall not be considered inequitable merely because it was paid by way of a single payment or at the time of the transfer of the rental right.

(5) An agreement is of no effect in so far as it purports to prevent a person questioning the amount of equitable remuneration or to restrict the powers of the Copyright Tribunal under this section.]

Note: This section was inserted by the Copyright and Related Rights Regulations 1996 (SI 1996/2967), with effect from December 1, 1996. For savings and transitional provisions, see Pt III of those Regulations.

Moral rights

Moral rights not assignable

94. The rights conferred by Chapter IV (moral rights) are not assignable.

Transmission of moral rights on death

95.—(1) On the death of a person entitled to the right conferred by section 77 (right to identification of author or director), section 80 (right to object to derogatory treatment of work) or section 85 (right to privacy of certain photographs and films)

(a) the right passes to such person as he may by testamentary disposition specifically direct,

(b) if there is no such direction but the copyright in the work in question forms part of his estate, the right passes to the person to whom the copyright passes, and

(c) if or to the extent that the right does not pass under paragraph (a) or (b) it is exercisable by his personal representatives.

(2) Where copyright forming part of a person's estate passes in part to one person and in part to another, as for example where a bequest is limited so as to apply—

(a) to one or more, but not all, of the things the copyright owner has the exclusive right to do or authorise, or

(b) to part, but not the whole, of the period for which the copyright is to subsist,

any right which passes with the copyright by virtue of subsection (1) is correspondingly divided.

(3) Where by virtue of subsection (1)(a) or (b) a right becomes exercisable by more than one person—

(a) it may, in the case of the right conferred by section 77 (right to identification of author or director), be asserted by any of them;

(b) it is, in the case of the right conferred by section 80 (right to object to derogatory treatment of work) or section 85 (right to privacy of certain photographs and films), a right exercisable by each of them and is satisfied in relation to any of them if he consents to the treatment or act in question; and

(c) any waiver of the right in accordance with section 87 by one of them does not affect the rights of the others.

(4) A consent or waiver previously given or made binds any person to whom a right passes by virtue of subsection (1).

(5) Any infringement after a person's death of the right conferred by section 84 (false attribution) is actionable by his personal representatives.

(6) Any damages recovered by personal representatives by virtue of this section in respect of an infringement after a person's death shall devolve as part of his estate as if the right of action had subsisted and been vested in him immediately before his death.

Chapter VI

Remedies for Infringement

Rights and remedies of copyright owner

Infringement actionable by copyright owner

96.—(1) An infringement of copyright is actionable by the copyright owner.

(2) In an action for infringement of copyright all such relief by way of damages, injunctions, accounts or otherwise is available to the plaintiff as is available in respect of the infringement of any other property right.

(3) This section has effect subject to the following provisions of this Chapter.

Provisions as to damages in infringement action

97.—(1) Where in an action for infringement of copyright it is shown that at the time of the infringement the defendant did not know, and had no reason to believe, that copyright subsisted in the work to which the action relates, the plaintiff is not entitled to damages against him, but without prejudice to any other remedy.

(2) The court may in an action for infringement of copyright having regard to all the circumstances, and in particular to—

(a) the flagrancy of the infringement, and

(b) any benefit accruing to the defendant by reason of the infringement,

award such additional damages as the justice of the case may require.

Injunctions against service providers

[97A.—(1) The High Court (in Scotland, the Court of Session) shall have power to grant an injunction against a service provider, where that service provider has actual knowledge of another person using their service to infringe copyright.

(2) In determining whether a service provider has actual knowledge for the purpose of this section, a court shall take into account all matters which appear to it in the particular circumstances to be relevant and, amongst other things, shall have regard to—

(a) whether a service provider has received a notice through a means of contact made available in accordance with regulation 6(1)(c) of the

Electronic Commerce (EC Directive) Regulations 2002 (SI 2002/2013); and

   (b) the extent to which any notice includes—

      (i) the full name and address of the sender of the notice;

     (ii) details of the infringement in question.

(3) In this section "service provider" has the meaning given to it by regulation 2 of the Electronic Commerce (EC Directive) Regulations 2002.]

Note: Section 97A was inserted by the Copyright and Related Rights Regulations 2003 (SI 2003/2498), reg.27, with effect from October 31, 2003. For savings and transitional provisions, see Part 3 of those Regulations.

Undertaking to take licence of right in infringement proceedings

98.—(1) If in proceedings for infringement of copyright in respect of which a licence is available as of right under section 144 (powers exercisable in consequence of report of [Competition and Markets Authority]) the defendant undertakes to take a licence on such terms as may be agreed or, in default of agreement, settled by the Copyright Tribunal under that section—

   (a) no injunction shall be granted against him,

   (b) no order for delivery up shall be made under section 99, and

   (c) the amount recoverable against him by way of damages or on an account of profits shall not exceed double the amount which would have been payable by him as licensee if such a licence on those terms had been granted before the earliest infringement.

(2) An undertaking may be given at any time before final order in the proceedings, without any admission of liability.

(3) Nothing in this section affects the remedies available in respect of an infringement committed before licences of right were available.

Note: In subs.(1) words in square brackets substituted for "Competition Commission", subject to transitional provision, by the Enterprise and Regulatory Reform Act 2013 (Competition) (Consequential, Transitional and Saving Provisions) Order 2014 (SI 2014/892) Sch 1 para.56, (for transitional provision see Sch.2) with effect from April 1, 2014.

Order for delivery up

99.—(1) Where a person—

   (a) has an infringing copy of a work in his possession, custody or control in the course of a business, or

   (b) has in his possession, custody or control an article specifically designed or adapted for making copies of a particular copyright work, knowing or having reason to believe that it has been or is to be used to make infringing copies,

the owner of the copyright in the work may apply to the court for an order that the infringing copy or article be delivered up to him or to such other person as the court may direct.

(2) An application shall not be made after the end of the period specified in section 113 (period after which remedy of delivery up not available); and no order shall be made unless the court also makes, or it appears to the court that there are grounds for making, an order under section 114 (order as to disposal of infringing copy or other article).

(3) A person to whom an infringing copy or other article is delivered up in pursuance of an order under this section shall, if an order under section 114 is not made, retain it pending the making of an order, or the decision not to make an order, under that section.

(4) Nothing in this section affects any other power of the court.

Right to seize infringing copies and other articles

100.—(1) An infringing copy of a work which is found exposed or otherwise immediately available for sale or hire, and in respect of which the copyright owner would be entitled to apply for an order under section 99, may be seized and detained by him or a person authorised by him.

The right to seize and detain is exercisable subject to the following conditions and is subject to any decision of the court under section 114.

(2) Before anything is seized under this section notice of the time and place of the proposed seizure must be given to a local police station.

(3) A person may for the purpose of exercising the right conferred by this section enter premises to which the public have access but may not seize anything in the possession, custody or control of a person at a permanent or regular place of business of his, and may not use any force.

(4) At the time when anything is seized under this section there shall be left at the place where it was seized a notice in the prescribed form containing the prescribed particulars as to the person by whom or on whose authority the seizure is made and the grounds on which it is made.

(5) In this section—

"premises" includes land, buildings, moveable structures, vehicles, vessels, aircraft and hovercraft; and

"prescribed" means prescribed by order of the Secretary of State.

(6) An order of the Secretary of State under this section shall be made by statutory instrument which shall be subject to annulment in pursuance of a resolution of either House of Parliament.

Rights and remedies of exclusive licensee

Rights and remedies of exclusive licensee

101.—(1) An exclusive licensee has, except against the copyright owner, the same rights and remedies in respect of matters occurring after the grant of the licence as if the licence had been an assignment.

(2) His rights and remedies are concurrent with those of the copyright owner; and references in the relevant provisions of this Part to the copyright owner shall be construed accordingly.

(3) In an action brought by an exclusive licensee by virtue of this section a defendant may avail himself of any defence which would have been available to him if the action had been brought by the copyright owner.

Certain infringements actionable by a non-exclusive licensee

[**101A.**—(1) A non-exclusive licensee may bring an action for infringement of copyright if—

(a) the infringing act was directly connected to a prior licensed act of the licensee; and

(b) the licence—

(i) is in writing and is signed by or on behalf of the copyright owner; and

(ii) expressly grants the non-exclusive licensee a right of action under this section.

(2) In an action brought under this section, the non-exclusive licensee shall

have the same rights and remedies available to him as the copyright owner would have had if he had brought the action.

(3) The rights granted under this section are concurrent with those of the copyright owner and references in the relevant provisions of this Part to the copyright owner shall be construed accordingly.

(4) In an action brought by a non-exclusive licensee by virtue of this section a defendant may avail himself of any defence which would have been available to him if the action had been brought by the copyright owner.

(5) Subsections (1) to (4) of section 102 shall apply to a non-exclusive licensee who has a right of action by virtue of this section as it applies to an exclusive licensee.

(6) In this section a "non-exclusive licensee" means the holder of a licence authorising the licensee to exercise a right which remains exercisable by the copyright owner.]

Note: Section 101A was inserted by the Copyright and Related Rights Regulations 2003 (SI 2003/2498), reg.28, with effect from October 31, 2003. For savings and transitional provisions, see Part 3 of those Regulations.

Exercise of concurrent rights

102.—(1) Where an action for infringement of copyright brought by the copyright owner or an exclusive licensee relates (wholly or partly) to an infringement in respect of which they have concurrent rights of action, the copyright owner or, as the case may be, the exclusive licensee may not, without the leave of the court, proceed with the action unless the other is either joined as a plaintiff or added as a defendant.

(2) A copyright owner or exclusive licensee who is added as a defendant in pursuance of subsection (1) is not liable for any costs in the action unless he takes part in the proceedings.

(3) The above provisions do not affect the granting of interlocutory relief on an application by a copyright owner or exclusive licensee alone.

(4) Where an action for infringement of copyright is brought which relates (wholly or partly) to an infringement in respect of which the copyright owner and an exclusive licensee have or had concurrent rights of action—

(a) the court shall in assessing damages take into account—
    (i) the terms of the licence, and
    (ii) any pecuniary remedy already awarded or available to either of them in respect of the infringement;

(b) no account of profits shall be directed if an award of damages has been made, or an account of profits has been directed, in favour of the other of them in respect of the infringement; and

(c) the court shall if an account of profits is directed apportion the profits between them as the court considers just, subject to any agreement between them;

and these provisions apply whether or not the copyright owner and the exclusive licensee are both parties to the action.

(5) The copyright owner shall notify any exclusive licensee having concurrent rights before applying for an order under section 99 (order for delivery up) or exercising the right conferred by section 100 (right of seizure); and the court may on the application of the licensee make such order under section 99 or, as the case may be, prohibiting or permitting the exercise by the copyright owner of the right conferred by section 100, as it thinks fit having regard to the terms of the licence.

Remedies for infringement of moral rights

Remedies for infringement of moral rights

103.—(1) An infringement of a right conferred by Chapter IV (moral rights) is actionable as a breach of statutory duty owed to the person entitled to the right.

(2) In proceedings for infringement of the right conferred by section 80 (right to object to derogatory treatment of work) the court may, if it thinks it is an adequate remedy in the circumstances, grant an injunction on terms prohibiting the doing of any act unless a disclaimer is made, in such terms and in such manner as may be approved by the court, dissociating the author or director from the treatment of the work.

Presumptions

Presumptions relevant to literary, dramatic, musical and artistic works

104.—(1) The following presumptions apply in proceedings brought by virtue of this Chapter with respect to a literary, dramatic, musical or artistic work.

(2) Where a name purporting to be that of the author appeared on copies of the work as published or on the work when it was made, the person whose name appeared shall be presumed, until the contrary is proved—

  (a) to be the author of the work;
  (b) to have made it in circumstances not falling within section 11(2), 163, 165 or 168 (works produced in course of employment, Crown copyright, Parliamentary copyright or copyright of certain international organisations).

(3) In the case of a work alleged to be a work of joint authorship, subs.(2) applies in relation to each person alleged to be one of the authors.

(4) Where no name purporting to be that of the author appeared as mentioned in subsection (2) but—

  (a) the work qualifies for copyright protection by virtue of section 155 (qualification by reference to country of first publication), and
  (b) a name purporting to be that of the publisher appeared on copies of the work as first published,

the person whose name appeared shall be presumed, until the contrary is proved, to have been the owner of the copyright at the time of publication.

(5) If the author of the work is dead or the identity of the author cannot be ascertained by reasonable inquiry, it shall be presumed, in the absence of evidence to the contrary—

  (a) that the work is an original work, and
  (b) that the plaintiff's allegations as to what was the first publication of the work and as to the country of first publication are correct.

Presumptions relevant to sound recordings and films

105.—(1) In proceedings brought by virtue of this Chapter with respect to a sound recording, where copies of the recording as issued to the public bear a label or other mark stating—

  (a) that a named person was the owner of copyright in the recording at the date of issue of the copies, or
  (b) that the recording was first published in a specified year or in a specified country,

the label or mark shall be admissible as evidence of the facts stated and shall be presumed to be correct until the contrary is proved.

(2) In proceedings brought by virtue of this Chapter with respect to a film, where copies of the film as issued to the public bear a statement—

   (a) that a named person was the [director or producer] of the film,

   [(aa) that a named person was the principal director, the author of the screenplay, the author of the dialogue or the composer of music specifically created for and used in the film,]

   (b) that a named person was the owner of copyright in the film at the date of issue of the copies, or

   (c) that the film was first published in a specified year or in a specified country,

the statement shall be admissible as evidence of the facts stated and shall be presumed to be correct until the contrary is proved.

(3) In proceedings brought by virtue of this Chapter with respect to a computer program, where copies of the program are issued to the public in electronic form bearing a statement—

   (a) that a named person was the owner of copyright in the program at the date of issue of the copies, or

   (b) that the program was first published in a specified country or that copies of it were first issued to the public in electronic form in a specified year,

the statement shall be admissible as evidence of the facts stated and shall be presumed to be correct until the contrary is proved.

(4) The above presumptions apply equally in proceedings relating to an infringement alleged to have occurred before the date on which the copies were issued to the public.

(5) In proceedings brought by virtue of this Chapter with respect to a film, where the film as shown in public, [or communicated to the public] bears a statement—

   (a) that a named person was the [director or producer] of the film, or

   [(aa) that a named person was the principal director of the film, the author of the screenplay, the author of the dialogue or the composer of music specifically created for and used in the film, or,]

   (b) that a named person was the owner of copyright in the film immediately after it was made,

the statement shall be admissible as evidence of the facts stated and shall be presumed to be correct until the contrary is proved.

This presumption applies equally in proceedings relating to an infringement alleged to have occurred before the date on which the film was shown in public, [or communicated to the public].

[(6) For the purposes of this section, a statement that a person was the director of a film shall be taken, unless a contrary indication appears, as meaning that he was the principal director of the film.]

Notes:

   (1) The heading preceding this section omits a reference to computer programs, which is included in the arrangement of sections at the beginning of the official version of this Act, presumably in error.

   (2) Subsection (2)(aa), was inserted by the Duration of Copyright and Rights in Performances Regulations 1995 (SI 1995/3297), with effect from January 1, 1996. For savings and transitional provisions, see Part III of those Regulations.

   (3) Subsections (2)(a) and (5)(a) were amended, and subss.(5)(aa) and (6) inserted by the Copyright and Related Rights Regulations 1996 (SI 1996/2967), with effect from December 1, 1996.

   (4) The words in the first and fourth set of square brackets in subs.(5) substituted for the former words ", broadcast or included in a cable programme service" by the Copyright and Related Rights Regulations 2003 (SI 2003/2498), Sch.1 para.8,

with effect from October 31, 2003. For savings and transitional provisions, see Part 3 of those Regulations.

Presumptions relevant to works subject to Crown copyright

106. In proceedings brought by virtue of this Chapter with respect to a literary, dramatic or musical work in which Crown copyright subsists, where there appears on printed copies of the work a statement of the year in which the work was first published commercially, that statement shall be admissible as evidence of the fact stated and shall be presumed to be correct in the absence of evidence to the contrary.

Offences

Criminal liability for making or dealing with infringing articles, &c

107.—(1) A person commits an offence who, without the licence of the copyright owner—

(a) makes for sale or hire, or

(b) imports into the United Kingdom otherwise than for his private and domestic use, or

(c) possesses in the course of a business with a view to committing any act infringing the copyright, or

(d) in the course of a business—

    (i) sells or lets for hire, or

    (ii) offers or exposes for sale or hire, or

    (iii) exhibits in public, or

    (iv) distributes, or

(e) distributes otherwise than in the course of a business to such an extent as to affect prejudicially the owner of the copyright,

an article which is, and which he knows or has reason to believe is, an infringing copy of a copyright work.

(2) A person commits an offence who—

(a) makes an article specifically designed or adapted for making copies of a particular copyright work, or

(b) has such an article in his possession,

knowing or having reason to believe that it is to be used to make infringing copies for sale or hire or for use in the course of a business.

[(2A) A person who infringes copyright in a work by communicating the work to the public—

(a) in the course of a business, or

(b) otherwise than in the course of a business to such an extent as to affect prejudicially the owner of the copyright,

commits an offence if he knows or has reason to believe that, by doing so, he is infringing copyright in that work.]

(3) Where copyright is infringed (otherwise than by reception of a [communication to the public])—

(a) by the public performance of a literary, dramatic or musical work, or

(b) by the playing or showing in public of a sound recording or film, any person who caused the work to be so performed, played or shown is guilty of an offence if he knew or had reason to believe that copyright would be infringed.

(4) A person guilty of an offence under subsection (1)(a), (b), (d)(iv) or (e) is liable—

(a) on summary conviction to imprisonment for a term not exceeding six months or [a fine], or both;

(b) on conviction on indictment to a fine or imprisonment for a term not exceeding [ten] years, or both.

[(4A) A person guilty of an offence under subsection (2A) is liable—

(a) on summary conviction to imprisonment for a term not exceeding three months or [a fine], or both;

(b) on conviction on indictment to a fine or imprisonment for a term not exceeding two years, or both.]

(5) A person guilty of any other offence under this section is liable on summary conviction to imprisonment for a term not exceeding [three] months or a fine not exceeding level 5 on the standard scale, or both.

(6) Sections 104 to 106 (presumptions as to various matters connected with copyright) do not apply to proceedings for an offence under this section; but without prejudice to their application in proceedings for an order under section 108.

Notes:

(1) Subsections (2A) and (4A) inserted and the words in square brackets in subs.(3) substituted for the former words "broadcast or cable programme" by the Copyright and Related Rights Regulations 2003 (SI 2003/2498), reg.26 and Sch.1 para.9, with effect from October 31, 2003. For savings and transitional provisions, see Part 3 of those Regulations.

(2) The word in square brackets in subs.(4)(b) was substituted for the former word "two" by the Copyright, etc. and Trade Marks (Offences and Enforcement) Act 2002 (c.25) s.1, with effect from November 20, 2002 (Copyright, etc. and Trade Marks (Offences and Enforcement) Act 2002 (Commencement) Order 2002 (SI 2002/2749)).

(3) The figures in square brackets in subss.(4)(a) and (4A)(a) substituted for the former words "the statutory maximum" by the Digital Economy Act 2010 s.42(2), with effect from June 8, 2010.

(4) In s.107(5) the word "three" was substituted for the word "six" the Copyright, Designs and Patents Act 1988 (Amendment) Regulations 2010 with effect from January 1, 2011.

(5) In subs.(4)(a), (4A)(a) words in square brackets substituted, subject to transitional provisions and savings, by the Legal Aid, Sentencing and Punishment of Offenders Act 2012 (Fines on Summary Conviction) Regulations 2015 (SI 2015/664) Sch.4, para.17(2), with effect from March 12, 2015 (for transitional provisions and savings see the Legal Aid, Sentencing and Punishment of Offenders Act 2012 (Fines on Summary Conviction) Regulations 2015 (SI 2015/664), reg.5(1)). The existing wording, in both places, was "a fine not exceeding £50,000".

Enforcement by local weights and measures authority

[107A.—(1) It is the duty of every local weights and measures authority to enforce within their area the provisions of section 107.

(3) Subsection (1) above does not apply in relation to the enforcement of section 107 in Northern Ireland, but it is the duty of the Department of Economic Development to enforce that section in Northern Ireland.

[(3A) For the investigatory powers available to a local weights and measures authority or the Department of Enterprise, Trade and Investment in Northern Ireland for the purposes of the duties in this section, see Schedule 5 to the Consumer Rights Act 2015.]

(4) Any enactment which authorises the disclosure of information for the purpose of facilitating the enforcement of the Trade Descriptions Act 1968 shall apply as if section 107 were contained in that Act and as if the functions of any person in relation to the enforcement of that section were functions under that Act.

(5) Nothing in this section shall be construed as authorising a local weights and measures authority to bring proceedings in Scotland for an offence.]

Notes:
    (1) Section 107A inserted by s.165 of the Criminal Justice and Public Order Act 1994, with effect from April 6, 2007 (see SI 2007/621).
    (2) Subsection (2) and words in subs.(3) repealed, and subs.(3A) inserted, by the Consumer Rights Act 2015, Sch.6, para.49, with effect from October 1, 2015. Subs.(2) formerly read:

"(2) The following provisions of the Trade Descriptions Act 1968 apply in relation to the enforcement of that section by such an authority as in relation to the enforcement of that Act—
    section 27 (power to make test purchases).
    section 28 (power to enter premises and inspect and seize goods and documents),
    section 29 (obstruction of authorised officers), and
    section 33 (compensation for loss, &c. of goods seized)."
The words in sub.(3) which were repealed read:
"For that purpose the provisions of the Trade Descriptions Act 1968 specified in subsection (2) apply as if for the references to a local weights and measures authority and any officer of such an authority there were substituted references to that Department and any of its officers."

Order for delivery up in criminal proceedings

108.—(1) The court before which proceedings are brought against a person for an offence under section 107 may, if satisfied that at the time of his arrest or charge—
    (a) he had in his possession, custody or control in the course of a business an infringing copy of a copyright work, or
    (b) he had in his possession, custody or control an article specifically designed or adapted for making copies of a particular copyright work, knowing or having reason to believe that it had been or was to be used to make infringing copies,
order that the infringing copy or article be delivered up to the copyright owner or to such other person as the court may direct.

    (2) For this purpose a person shall be treated as charged with an offence—
    (a) in England, Wales and Northern Ireland, when he is orally charged or is served with a summons or indictment;
    (b) in Scotland, when he is cautioned, charged or served with a complaint or indictment.

    (3) An order may be made by the court of its own motion or on the application of the prosecutor (or, in Scotland, the Lord Advocate or procurator-fiscal), and may be made whether or not the person is convicted of the offence, but shall not be made—
    (a) after the end of the period specified in section 113 (period after which remedy of delivery up is not available), or
    (b) if it appears to the court unlikely that any order will be made under section 114 (order as to disposal of infringing copy or other article).

    (4) An appeal lies from an order made under this section by a magistrates' court—
    (a) in England and Wales, to the Crown Court, and
    (b) in Northern Ireland, to the county court;
and in Scotland, where an order has been made under this section, the person from whose possession, custody or control the infringing copy or article has been removed may, without prejudice to any other form of appeal under any rule of law, appeal against that order in the same manner as against sentence.

(5) A person to whom an infringing copy or other article is delivered up in pursuance of an order under this section shall retain it pending the making of an order, or the decision not to make an order, under section 114.

(6) Nothing in this section affects the powers of the court under[section 143 of the Powers of Criminal Courts (Sentencing) Act 2000], [Part II of the Proceeds of Crime (Scotland) Act 1995] or [Article 11 of the Criminal Justice (Northern Ireland) Order 1994] (general provisions as to forfeiture in criminal proceedings).

Notes:

(1) Subsection (6) is printed as amended by the Criminal Procedure (Consequential Provisions) (Scotland) Act 1995, with effect from April 1, 1996 by virtue of that Act, which inserted the words in the second set of square brackets in place of "Chapter II of Part II of the Criminal Justice (Scotland) Act 1995", such words having been inserted into subs.(6) by the Criminal Justice (Scotland) Act 1995 with effect from September 26, 1995 by virtue of the Criminal Justice (Scotland) Act 1995 (Commencement No.1, Transitional Provisions and Savings) Order 1995 (SI 1995/2995).

(2) Subsection (6) is printed as further amended by the Criminal Justice (Northern Ireland) Order 1994 (SI 1994/2795 (N.I. 15)) with effect from January 9, 1995 by virtue of the Criminal Justice (1994 Order) (Commencement) Order (Northern Ireland) 1994 (S.R. 1994 No 446).

(3) The words in the first set of square brackets in subs.(6) substituted for the former words "section 43 of the Powers of Criminal Courts Act 1973" by the Powers of Criminal Courts (Sentencing) Act 2000 (c.6), s.165 and Sch.9 para 115, with effect from August 25, 2000.

Search warrants

109.—(1) Where a justice of the peace (in Scotland, a sheriff or justice of the peace) is satisfied by information on oath given by a constable (in Scotland, by evidence on oath) that there are reasonable grounds for believing—

(a) that an offence under section [107(1), (2) or (2A)] has been or is about to be committed in any premises, and

(b) that evidence that such an offence has been or is about to be committed is in those premises,

he may issue a warrant authorising a constable to enter and search the premises, using such reasonable force as is necessary.

(2) The power conferred by subsection (1) does not, in England and Wales, extend to authorising a search for material of the kinds mentioned in section 9(2) of the Police and Criminal Evidence Act 1984 (certain classes of personal or confidential material).

(3) A warrant under this section—

(a) may authorise persons to accompany any constable executing the warrant, and

(b) remains in force for [three months] from the date of its issue.

(4) In executing a warrant issued under this section a constable may seize an article if he reasonably believes that it is evidence that any offence under section [107(1), (2) or (2A)] has been or is about to be committed.

(5) In this section "premises" includes land, buildings, [fixed or] moveable structures, vehicles, vessels, aircraft and hovercraft.

Notes:

(1) The words in square brackets in subss.(1)(a) and (4) substituted for the former words "107(1) or (2)" by the Copyright and Related Rights Regulations 2003 (SI 2003/2498), reg.26, with effect from October 31, 2003. For savings and transitional provisions, see Part 3 of those Regulations. That former wording had previously been substituted for the original words "107(1)(a), (b), (d)(iv) or (e)" in subss.(1)(a) and "107(1)" in subs.(2) and the words in square brackets in subs.(5)

inserted by the Copyright, etc. and Trade Marks (Offences and Enforcement) Act 2002 (c.25) s.2, with effect from November 20, 2002 (Copyright, etc. and Trade Marks (Offences and Enforcement) Act 2002 (Commencement) Order 2002 (SI 2002/2749)).

(2) The words in square brackets in subs.(3)(b) substituted for the former words "28 days" by the Serious Organised Crime and Police Act 2005 (c.15), Sch.16 para.6, with effect from January 1, 2006.

Offence by body corporate: liability of officers

110.—(1) Where an offence under section 107 committed by a body corporate is proved to have been committed with the consent or connivance of a director, manager, secretary or other similar officer of the body, or a person purporting to act in any such capacity, he as well as the body corporate is guilty of the offence and liable to be proceeded against and punished accordingly.

(2) In relation to a body corporate whose affairs are managed by its members "director" means a member of the body corporate.

Provision for preventing importation of infringing copies

Infringing copies may be treated as prohibited goods

111.—(1) The owner of the copyright in a published literary, dramatic or musical work may give notice in writing to the Commissioners of Customs and Excise—

(a) that he is the owner of the copyright in the work, and

(b) that he requests the Commissioners, for a period specified in the notice, to treat as prohibited goods printed copies of the work which are infringing copies.

(2) The period specified in a notice under subsection (1) shall not exceed five years and shall not extend beyond the period for which copyright is to subsist.

(3) The owner of the copyright in a sound recording or film may give notice in writing to the Commissioners of Customs and Excise—

(a) that he is the owner of the copyright in the work,

(b) that infringing copies of the work are expected to arrive in the United Kingdom at a time and a place specified in the notice, and

(c) that he requests the Commissioners to treat the copies as prohibited goods.

[3A) The Commissioners may treat as prohibited goods only infringing copies of works which arrive in the United Kingdom—

(a) from outside the European Economic Area, or

(b) from within that Area but not having been entered for free circulation.]

[(3B) This section does not apply to goods placed in, or expected to be placed in, one of the situations referred to in Article 1(1), in respect of which an application may be made under Article 5(1) of Council Regulation (EC) No. 1383/2003 concerning customs action against goods suspected of infringing certain intellectual property rights and the measures to be taken against goods found to have infringed such rights.]

(4) When a notice is in force under this section the importation of goods to which the notice relates, otherwise than by a person for his private and domestic use, [subject to subsections (3A) and (3B),] is prohibited; but a person is not by reason of the prohibition liable to any penalty other than forfeiture of the goods.

Notes:

(1) Subsections (3A) and (3B) inserted and subs.(4) is printed as amended by the

Copyright (EC Measures Relating to Pirated Goods and Abolition of Restrictions on the Import of Goods) Regulations 1995 (SI 1995/1445) with effect from July 1, 1995.

(2) Subsection (3B) was substituted by the Goods Infringing Intellectual Property Rights (Customs) Regulations 2004 (SI 2004/1473) with effect from July 1, 2004. Subsection 3B formerly provided—

"(3B) *This section does not apply to goods entered, or expected to be entered, for free circulation, export, re-export or for a suspensive procedure in respect of which an application may be made under Article 3(1) of Council Regulation (EC) No. 3295/94 laying down measures to prohibit the release for free circulation, export, re-export or entry for a suspensive procedure of counterfeit and pirated goods.*"

Power of Commissioners of Customs and Excise to make regulations

112.—(1) The Commissioners of Customs and Excise may make regulations prescribing the form in which notice is to be given under section 111 and requiring a person giving notice—

(a) to furnish the Commissioners with such evidence as may be specified in the regulations, either on giving notice or when the goods are imported, or at both those times, and

(b) to comply with such other conditions as may be specified in the regulations.

(2) The regulations may, in particular, require a person giving such a notice—

(a) to pay such fees in respect of the notice as may be specified by the regulations;

(b) to give such security as may be so specified in respect of any liability or expense which the Commissioners may incur in consequence of the notice by reason of the detention of any article or anything done to an article detained;

(c) to indemnify the Commissioners against any such liability or expense, whether security has been given or not.

(3) The regulations may make different provision as respects different classes of case to which they apply and may include such incidental and supplementary provisions as the Commissioners consider expedient.

(4) Regulations under this section shall be made by statutory instrument which shall be subject to annulment in pursuance of a resolution of either House of Parliament.

(5) [...]

Note: Subsection (5) was repealed by the Commissioners for Revenue and Customs Act 2005 (c.11), Sch.5, with effect from April 18, 2005. The subsection formerly provided:

"(5) *Section 17 of the Customs and Excise Management Act 1979 (general provisions as to Commissioners' receipts) applies to fees paid in pursuance of regulations under this section as to receipts under the enactments relating to customs and excise.*"

Supplementary

Period after which remedy of delivery up not available

113.—(1) An application for an order under section 99 (order for delivery up in civil proceedings) may not be made after the end of the period of six years from the date on which the infringing copy or article in question was made, subject to the following provisions.

(2) If during the whole or any part of that period the copyright owner—

(a) is under a disability, or

(b) is prevented by fraud or concealment from discovering the facts entitling him to apply for an order, an application may be made at any time before the end of the period of six years from the date on which he ceased to be under a disability or, as the case may be, could with reasonable diligence have discovered those facts.

(3) In subsection (2) "disability"—

(a) in England and Wales, has the same meaning as in the Limitation Act 1980;

(b) in Scotland, means legal disability within the meaning of the Prescription and Limitation (Scotland) Act 1973;

(c) in Northern Ireland, has the same meaning as in the Statute of Limitations (Northern Ireland) Act 1958.

(4) An order under section 108 (order for delivery up in criminal proceedings) shall not, in any case, be made after the end of the period of six years from the date on which the infringing copy or article in question was made.

Order as to disposal of infringing copy or other article

114.—(1) An application may be made to the court for an order that an infringing copy or other article delivered up in pursuance of an order under section 99 or 108, or seized and detained in pursuance of the right conferred by section 100, shall be—

(a) forfeited to the copyright owner, or

(b) destroyed or otherwise dealt with as the court may think fit,

or for a decision that no such order should be made.

(2) In considering what order (if any) should be made, the court shall consider whether other remedies available in an action for infringement of copyright would be adequate to compensate the copyright owner and to protect his interests.

(3) Provision shall be made by rules of court as to the service of notice on persons having an interest in the copy or other articles, and any such person is entitled—

(a) to appear in proceedings for an order under this section, whether or not he was served with notice, and

(b) to appeal against any order made, whether or not he appeared;

and an order shall not take effect until the end of the period within which notice of an appeal may be given or, if before the end of that period notice of appeal is duly given, until the final determination or abandonment of the proceedings on the appeal.

(4) Where there is more than one person interested in a copy or other article, the court shall make such order as it thinks just and may (in particular) direct that the article be sold, or otherwise dealt with, and the proceeds divided.

(5) If the court decides that no order should be made under this section, the person in whose possession, custody or control the copy or other article was before being delivered up or seized is entitled to its return.

(6) References in this section to a person having an interest in a copy or other article include any person in whose favour an order could be made in respect of it[—]

[(a) under this section or under section 204 or 231 of this Act;

(b) under section 24D of the Registered Designs Act 1949;

(c) under section 19 of Trade Marks Act 1994 (including that section as applied by regulation 4 of the Community Trade Mark Regulations 2006 (SI 2006/1027)); or

(d) under regulation 1C of the Community Design Regulations 2005 (SI 2005/2339).]

Note: Section 114(6) was amended by the Intellectual Property (Enforcement, etc.) Regulations 2006 (SI 2006/1028), Sch.2 para.7, with effect from April 29, 2006.

Forfeiture of infringing copies, etc.: England and Wales or Northern Ireland

[**114A.**—(1) In England and Wales or Northern Ireland where there have come into the possession of any person in connection with the investigation or prosecution of a relevant offence—

(a) infringing copies of a copyright work, or

(b) articles specifically designed or adapted for making copies of a particular copyright work,

that person may apply under this section for an order for the forfeiture of the infringing copies or articles.

(2) For the purposes of this section "relevant offence" means:

(a) an offence under [section 107(1), (2) or (2A)] (criminal liability for making or dealing with infringing articles, etc.),

(b) an offence under the Trade Descriptions Act 1968 (c. 29),

[(ba) an offence under the Business Protection from Misleading Marketing Regulations 2008,

(bb) an offence under the Consumer Protection from Unfair Trading Regulations 2008, or]

(c) an offence involving dishonesty or deception."

(3) An application under this section may be made—

(a) where proceedings have been brought in any court for a relevant offence relating to some or all of the infringing copies or articles, to that court, or

(b) where no application for the forfeiture of the infringing copies or articles has been made under paragraph (a), by way of complaint to a magistrates' court.

(4) On an application under this section, the court shall make an order for the forfeiture of any infringing copies or articles only if it is satisfied that a relevant offence has been committed in relation to the infringing copies or articles.

(5) A court may infer for the purposes of this section that such an offence has been committed in relation to any infringing copies or articles if it is satisfied that such an offence has been committed in relation to infringing copies or articles which are representative of the infringing copies or articles in question (whether by reason of being of the same design or part of the same consignment or batch or otherwise).

(6) Any person aggrieved by an order made under this section by a magistrates' court, or by a decision of such a court not to make such an order, may appeal against that order or decision—

(a) in England and Wales, to the Crown Court, or

(b) in Northern Ireland, to the county court.

(7) An order under this section may contain such provision as appears to the court to be appropriate for delaying the coming into force of the order pending the making and determination of any appeal (including any application under section 111 of the Magistrates' Courts Act 1980 (c. 43) or Article 146 of the Magistrates' Courts (Northern Ireland) Order 1981 (SI 1981/1675 (N.I. 26)) (statement of case)).

(8) Subject to subsection (9), where any infringing copies or articles are forfeited under this section they shall be destroyed in accordance with such directions as the court may give.

(9) On making an order under this section the court may direct that the infringing copies or articles to which the order relates shall (instead of being destroyed) be forfeited to the owner of the copyright in question or dealt with in such other way as the court considers appropriate.]

Notes:

(1) Section 114A was inserted by the Copyright, etc. and Trade Marks (Offences and Enforcement) Act 2002 (c.25) s.3, with effect from November 20, 2002 (Copyright, etc. and Trade Marks (Offences and Enforcement) Act 2002 (Commencement) Order 2002 (SI 2002/2749)).

(2) The words in square brackets in subs.(2)(a) substituted for the former words "section 107(1) or (2)" by the Copyright and Related Rights Regulations 2003 (SI 2003/2498), reg.26, with effect from October 31, 2003. For savings and transitional provisions, see Part 3 of those Regulations.

(3) In subs.(2) paras (ba) and (bb) inserted by the Consumer Protection from Unfair Trading Regulations 2008 (SI 2008/1277), reg.30(1), Sch.2 para.40, with effect from May 26, 2008.

Forfeiture of infringing copies, etc.: Scotland

[114B.—(1) In Scotland the court may make an order under this section for the forfeiture of any—

(a) infringing copies of a copyright work, or

(b) articles specifically designed or adapted for making copies of a particular copyright work.

(2) An order under this section may be made—

(a) on an application by the procurator-fiscal made in the manner specified in section 134 of the Criminal Procedure (Scotland) Act 1995 (c. 46), or

(b) where a person is convicted of a relevant offence, in addition to any other penalty which the court may impose.

(3) On an application under subsection (2)(a), the court shall make an order for the forfeiture of any infringing copies or articles only if it is satisfied that a relevant offence has been committed in relation to the infringing copies or articles.

(4) The court may infer for the purposes of this section that such an offence has been committed in relation to any infringing copies or articles if it is satisfied that such an offence has been committed in relation to infringing copies or articles which are representative of the infringing copies or articles in question (whether by reason of being of the same design or part of the same consignment or batch or otherwise).

(5) The procurator-fiscal making the application under subsection (2)(a) shall serve on any person appearing to him to be the owner of, or otherwise to have an interest in, the infringing copies or articles to which the application relates a copy of the application, together with a notice giving him the opportunity to appear at the hearing of the application to show cause why the infringing copies or articles should not be forfeited.

(6) Service under subsection (5) shall be carried out, and such service may be proved, in the manner specified for citation of an accused in summary proceedings under the Criminal Procedure (Scotland) Act 1995.

(7) Any person upon whom notice is served under subsection (5) and any other person claiming to be the owner of, or otherwise to have an interest in, infringing copies or articles to which an application under this section relates shall be entitled to appear at the hearing of the application to show cause why the infringing copies or articles should not be forfeited.

(8) The court shall not make an order following an application under subsection (2)(a)—

(a) if any person on whom notice is served under subsection (5) does not appear, unless service of the notice on that person is proved, or

(b) if no notice under subsection (5) has been served, unless the court is satisfied that in the circumstances it was reasonable not to serve such notice.

(9) Where an order for the forfeiture of any infringing copies or articles is made following an application under subsection (2)(a), any person who appeared, or was entitled to appear, to show cause why infringing copies or articles should not be forfeited may, within 21 days of the making of the order, appeal to the High Court by Bill of Suspension.

(10) Section 182(5)(a) to (e) of the Criminal Procedure (Scotland) Act 1995 (c. 46) shall apply to an appeal under subsection (9) as it applies to a stated case under Part 2 of that Act.

(11) An order following an application under subsection (2)(a) shall not take effect—

    (a) until the end of the period of 21 days beginning with the day after the day on which the order is made, or

    (b) if an appeal is made under subsection (9) above within that period, until the appeal is determined or abandoned.

(12) An order under subsection (2)(b) shall not take effect—

    (a) until the end of the period within which an appeal against the order could be brought under the Criminal Procedure (Scotland) Act 1995, or

    (b) if an appeal is made within that period, until the appeal is determined or abandoned.

(13) Subject to subsection (14), infringing copies or articles forfeited under this section shall be destroyed in accordance with such directions as the court may give.

(14) On making an order under this section the court may direct that the infringing copies or articles to which the order relates shall (instead of being destroyed) be forfeited to the owner of the copyright in question or dealt with in such other way as the court considers appropriate.

(15) For the purposes of this section—

["relevant offence"] means—

    (a) an offence under section 107(1), (2) or (2A) (criminal liability for making or dealing with infringing articles, etc),

    (b) an offence under the Trade Descriptions Act 1968,

    (c) an offence under the Business Protection from Misleading Marketing Regulations 2008,

    (d) an offence under the Consumer Protection from Unfair Trading Regulations 2008, or

    (e) any offence involving dishonesty or deception;]

"the court" means—

    (a) in relation to an order made on an application under subsection (2)(a), the sheriff, and

    (b) in relation to an order made under subsection (2)(b), the court which imposed the penalty.]

Notes:

    (1) Section 114B was inserted by the Copyright, etc. and Trade Marks (Offences and Enforcement) Act 2002 (c.25) s.3, with effect from November 20, 2002 (Copyright, etc. and Trade Marks (Offences and Enforcement) Act 2002 (Commencement) Order 2002 (SI 2002/2749)).

    (2) The words in square brackets in subs.(15) substituted for the former words "section 107(1) or (2)" by the Copyright and Related Rights Regulations 2003 (SI 2003/2498), reg.26, with effect from October 31, 2003. For savings and transitional provisions, see Part 3 of those Regulations.

    (3) In subs.(15) the definition of "relevant offence" substituted by the Consumer Protection from Unfair Trading Regulations 2008 (SI 2008/1277), reg.30(1), Sch.2 para.41, with effect from May 26, 2008.

Jurisdiction of county court and sheriff court

115.—(1) In England [and Wales the county court and in] Northern Ireland a county court may entertain proceedings under—

section 99 (order for delivery up of infringing copy or other article),

section 101(5) (order as to exercise of rights by copyright owner where exclusive licensee has concurrent rights), or

section 114 (order as to disposal of infringing copy or other article),

[save that, in Northern Ireland, a county court may entertain such proceedings only] where the value of the infringing copies and other articles in question does not exceed the county court limit for actions in tort.

(2) In Scotland proceedings for an order under any of those provisions may be brought in the sheriff court.

(3) Nothing in this section shall be construed as affecting the jurisdiction of the High Court or, in Scotland, the Court of Session.

Notes:

(1) The reference in subs.(1) to s.101(5) was presumably intended to be a reference to s.102(5). Subsection (1) is printed as amended by the High Court and County Courts Jurisdiction Order 1991 (SI 1991/724).

(2) In subs.(1) words in square brackets substituted for words "Wales and", subject to savings and transitional provisions, by the Crime and Courts Act 2013 Sch.9 para.72, with effect from April 22, 2014 (for savings and transitional provisions see the Crime and Courts Act 2013 (Commencement No.10 and Transitional Provision) Order 2014 (SI 2014/954), arts 2, 3).

Chapter VII

Copyright Licensing

Licensing schemes and licensing bodies

Licensing schemes and licensing bodies

116.—(1) In this Part a "licensing scheme" means a scheme setting out—

(a) the classes of case in which the operator of the scheme, or the person on whose behalf he acts, is willing to grant copyright licences, and

(b) the terms on which licences would be granted in those classes of case;

and for this purpose a "scheme" includes anything in the nature of a scheme, whether described as a scheme or as a tariff or by any other name.

(2) In this Chapter a "licensing body" means a society or other organisation which has as its main object, or one of its main objects, the negotiation or granting, either as owner or prospective owner of copyright or as agent for him, of copyright licences, and whose objects include the granting of licences covering works of more than one author.

(3) In this section "copyright licences" means licences to do, or authorise the doing of, any of the acts restricted by copyright.

(4) References in this Chapter to licences or licensing schemes covering works of more than one author do not include licences or schemes covering only—

(a) a single collective work or collective works of which the authors are the same, or

(b) works made by, or by employees of or commissioned by, a single individual, firm, company or group of companies.

For this purpose a group of companies means a holding company and its subsidiaries, within the meaning of [section 1159 of the Companies Act 2006].

[(5) Schedule A1 confers powers to provide for the regulation of licensing bodies.]

Notes:

(1) The words in square brackets in s.116(4) substituted for the former words "section 736 of the Companies Act 1985" by the Companies Act 2006 (Consequential Amendments, Transitional Provisions and Savings) Order 2009 (SI 2009/1941) art.2(1), Sch.1 para.98(a), with effect from October 1, 2009.

(2) Subsection (5) inserted by the Enterprise and Regulatory Reform Act 2013, s.77(2), with effect from April 25, 2013.

[Orphan works licensing and extended collective licensing]

Power to provide for licensing of orphan works

[116A.—(1) The Secretary of State may by regulations provide for the grant of licences in respect of works that qualify as orphan works under the regulations.

(2) The regulations may—

(a) specify a person or a description of persons authorised to grant licences, or

(b) provide for a person designated in the regulations to specify a person or a description of persons authorised to grant licences.

(3) The regulations must provide that, for a work to qualify as an orphan work, it is a requirement that the owner of copyright in it has not been found after a diligent search made in accordance with the regulations.

(4) The regulations may provide for the granting of licences to do, or authorise the doing of, any act restricted by copyright that would otherwise require the consent of the missing owner.

(5) The regulations must provide for any licence—

(a) to have effect as if granted by the missing owner;

(b) not to give exclusive rights;

(c) not to be granted to a person authorised to grant licences.

(6) The regulations may apply to a work although it is not known whether copyright subsists in it, and references to a missing owner and a right or interest of a missing owner are to be read as including references to a supposed owner and a supposed right or interest.]

Note: Sections 116A to 116D inserted by the Enterprise and Regulatory Reform Act 2013, s.77(3), with effect from April 25, 2013.

Extended collective licensing

[116B.—(1) The Secretary of State may by regulations provide for a licensing body that applies to the Secretary of State under the regulations to be authorised to grant copyright licences in respect of works in which copyright is not owned by the body or a person on whose behalf the body acts.

(2) An authorisation must specify—

(a) the types of work to which it applies, and

(b) the acts restricted by copyright that the licensing body is authorised to license.

(3) The regulations must provide for the copyright owner to have a right to limit or exclude the grant of licences by virtue of the regulations.

(4) The regulations must provide for any licence not to give exclusive rights.

(5) In this section "copyright licences" has the same meaning as in section 116.

(6) Nothing in this section applies in relation to Crown copyright or Parliamentary copyright.]

Note: Sections 116A to 116D inserted by the Enterprise and Regulatory Reform Act 2013, s.77(3) with effect from April 25, 2013.

General provision about licensing under sections 116A and 116B

[**116C.**—(1) This section and section 116D apply to regulations under sections 116A and 116B.

(2) The regulations may provide for a body to be or remain authorised to grant licences only if specified requirements are met, and for a question whether they are met to be determined by a person, and in a manner, specified in the regulations.

(3) The regulations may specify other matters to be taken into account in any decision to be made under the regulations as to whether to authorise a person to grant licences.

(4) The regulations must provide for the treatment of any royalties or other sums paid in respect of a licence, including—

(a) the deduction of administrative costs;

(b) the period for which sums must be held;

(c) the treatment of sums after that period (as bona vacantia or otherwise).

(5) The regulations must provide for circumstances in which an authorisation to grant licences may be withdrawn, and for determining the rights and obligations of any person if an authorisation is withdrawn.

(6) The regulations may include other provision for the purposes of authorisation and licensing, including in particular provision—

(a) for determining the rights and obligations of any person if a work ceases to qualify as an orphan work (or ceases to qualify by reference to any copyright owner), or if a rights owner exercises the right referred to in section 116B(3), while a licence is in force;

(b) about maintenance of registers and access to them;

(c) permitting the use of a work for incidental purposes including an application or search;

(d) for a right conferred by section 77 to be treated as having been asserted in accordance with section 78;

(e) for the payment of fees to cover administrative expenses.]

Note: Sections 116A to 116D inserted by the Enterprise and Regulatory Reform Act 2013, s.77(3) with effect from April 25, 2013.

Regulations under sections 116A and 116B

[**116D.**—(1) The power to make regulations includes power—

(a) to make incidental, supplementary or consequential provision, including provision extending or restricting the jurisdiction of the Copyright Tribunal or conferring powers on it;

(b) to make transitional, transitory or saving provision;

(c) to make different provision for different purposes.

(2) Regulations under any provision may amend this Part, or any other enactment or subordinate legislation passed or made before that provision comes into force, for the purpose of making consequential provision or extending or restricting the jurisdiction of the Copyright Tribunal or conferring powers on it.

(3) Regulations may make provision by reference to guidance issued from time to time by any person.

(4) The power to make regulations is exercisable by statutory instrument.

(5) A statutory instrument containing regulations may not be made unless a draft of the instrument has been laid before and approved by a resolution of each House of Parliament.]

Note: Sections 116A to 116D inserted by the Enterprise and Regulatory Reform Act 2013, s.77(3) with effect from April 25, 2013.

References and applications with respect to licensing schemes

Licensing schemes to which following sections apply

[**117.** Sections 118 to 123 (references and applications with respect to licensing schemes) apply to licensing schemes which are operated by licensing bodies and cover works of more than one author, so far as they relate to licences for—

  (a) copying the work,

  (b) rental or lending of copies of the work to the public,

  (c) performing, showing or playing the work in public, or

  [(d) communicating the work to the public;]

and references in those sections to a licensing scheme shall be construed accordingly.]

Notes:

  (1) This section was substituted by the Copyright and Related Rights Regulations 1996 (SI 1996/2967), which replaced the old s.117 with effect from December 1, 1996. The original wording of s.117 was as follows:

Licensing schemes to which ss. 118 to 123 apply

"**117.** *Sections 118 to 123 (references and applications with respect to licensing schemes) apply to—*

  (a) *licensing schemes operated by licensing bodies in relation to the copyright in literary, dramatic, musical or artistic works or films (or film sound-tracks when accompanying a film) which cover works of more than one author, so far as they relate to licences for—*

    (i) *copying the work,*

    (ii) *performing, playing or showing the work in public, or*

    (iii) *broadcasting the work or including it in a cable programme service;*

  (b) *all licensing schemes in relation to the copyright in sound recordings (other than film sound-tracks when accompanying a film), broadcasts or cable programmes, or the typographical arrangement of published editions; and*

  (c) *all licensing schemes in relation to the copyright in sound recordings, films or computer programs so far as they relate to licences for the rental of copies to the public; or*

  and in those sections "licensing scheme" means a licensing scheme of any of those descriptions."

  (2) Subsection (d) was substituted by the Copyright and Related Rights Regulations 2003 (SI 2003/2498), Sch.1 para.4, with effect from October 31, 2003. For savings and transitional provisions, see Part 3 of those Regulations.

Reference of proposed licensing scheme to tribunal

118.—(1) The terms of a licensing scheme proposed to be operated by a licensing body may be referred to the Copyright Tribunal by an organisation claiming to be representative of persons claiming that they require licences in cases of a description to which the scheme would apply, either generally or in relation to any description of case.

(2) The Tribunal shall first decide whether to entertain the reference, and may decline to do so on the ground that the reference is premature.

(3) If the Tribunal decides to entertain the reference it shall consider the matter referred and make such order, either confirming or varying the proposed scheme, either generally or so far as it relates to cases of the description to which the reference relates, as the Tribunal may determine to be reasonable in the circumstances.

(4) The order may be made so as to be in force indefinitely or for such period as the Tribunal may determine.

Reference of licensing scheme to tribunal

119.—(1) If while a licensing scheme is in operation a dispute arises between the operator of the scheme and—

(a) a person claiming that he requires a licence in a case of a description to which the scheme applies, or

(b) an organisation claiming to be representative of such persons,

that person or organisation may refer the scheme to the Copyright Tribunal in so far as it relates to cases of that description.

(2) A scheme which has been referred to the Tribunal under this section shall remain in operation until proceedings on the reference are concluded.

(3) The Tribunal shall consider the matter in dispute and make such order, either confirming or varying the scheme so far as it relates to cases of the description to which the reference relates, as the Tribunal may determine to be reasonable in the circumstances.

(4) The order may be made so as to be in force indefinitely or for such period as the Tribunal may determine.

Further reference of scheme to tribunal

120.—(1) Where the Copyright Tribunal has on a previous reference of a licensing scheme under [section 118, 119 or 128A], or under this section, made an order with respect to the scheme, then, while the order remains in force—

(a) the operator of the scheme,

(b) a person claiming that he requires a licence in a case of the description to which the order applies, or

(c) an organisation claiming to be representative of such persons,

may refer the scheme again to the Tribunal so far as it relates to cases of that description.

(2) A licensing scheme shall not, except with the special leave of the Tribunal, be referred again to the Tribunal in respect of the same description of cases—

(a) within twelve months from the date of the order on the previous reference, or

(b) if the order was made so as to be in force for 15 months or less, until the last three months before the expiry of the order.

(3) A scheme which has been referred to the Tribunal under this section shall remain in operation until proceedings on the reference are concluded.

(4) The Tribunal shall consider the matter in dispute and make such order, either confirming, varying or further varying the scheme so far as it relates to cases of the description to which the reference relates, as the Tribunal may determine to be reasonable in the circumstances.

(5) The order may be made so as to be in force indefinitely or for such period as the Tribunal may determine.

Note: The words in subs.(1) substituted for the former words "section 118 or 119" by the Copyright and Related Rights Regulations 2003 (SI 2003/2498), reg.21, with effect from October 31, 2003. For savings and transitional provisions, see Part 3 of those Regulations.

Application for grant of licence in connection with licensing scheme

121.—(1) A person who claims, in a case covered by a licensing scheme, that the operator of the scheme has refused to grant him or procure the grant to him of a licence in accordance with the scheme, or has failed to do so within a reasonable time after being asked, may apply to the Copyright Tribunal.

(2) A person who claims, in a case excluded from a licensing scheme, that the operator of the scheme either—

(a) has refused to grant him a licence or procure the grant to him of a licence, or has failed to do so within a reasonable time of being asked, and that in the circumstances it is unreasonable that a licence should not be granted, or

(b) proposes terms for a licence which are unreasonable,

may apply to the Copyright Tribunal.

(3) A case shall be regarded as excluded from a licensing scheme for the purposes of subsection (2) if—

(a) the scheme provides for the grant of licences subject to terms excepting matters from the licence and the case falls within such an exception, or

(b) the case is so similar to those in which licences are granted under the scheme that it is unreasonable that it should not be dealt with in the same way.

(4) If the Tribunal is satisfied that the claim is well-founded, it shall make an order declaring that, in respect of the matters specified in the order, the applicant is entitled to a licence on such terms as the Tribunal may determine to be applicable in accordance with the scheme or, as the case may be, to be reasonable in the circumstances.

(5) The order may be made so as to be in force indefinitely or for such period as the Tribunal may determine.

Application for review of order as to entitlement to licence

122.—(1) Where the Copyright Tribunal has made an order under section 121 that a person is entitled to a licence under a licensing scheme, the operator of the scheme or the original applicant may apply to the Tribunal to review its order.

(2) An application shall not be made, except with the special leave of the Tribunal—

(a) within twelve months from the date of the order, or of the decision on a previous application under this section, or

(b) if the order was made so as to be in force for 15 months or less, or as a result of the decision on a previous application under this section is due to expire within 15 months of that decision, until the last three months before the expiry date.

(3) The Tribunal shall on an application for review confirm or vary its order as the Tribunal may determine to be reasonable having regard to the terms applicable in accordance with the licensing scheme or, as the case may be, the circumstances of the case.

Effect of order of tribunal as to licensing scheme

123.—(1) A licensing scheme which has been confirmed or varied by the Copyright Tribunal—

    (a) under section 118 (reference of terms of proposed scheme), or

    (b) under section 119 or 120 (reference of existing scheme to Tribunal),

shall be in force or, as the case may be, remain in operation, so far as it relates to the description of case in respect of which the order was made, so long as the order remains in force.

    (2) While the order is in force a person who in a case of a class to which the order applies—

    (a) pays to the operator of the scheme any charges payable under the scheme in respect of a licence covering the case in question or, if the amount cannot be ascertained, gives an undertaking to the operator to pay them when ascertained, and

    (b) complies with the other terms applicable to such a licence under the scheme,

shall be in the same position as regards infringement of copyright as if he had at all material times been the holder of a licence granted by the owner of the copyright in question in accordance with the scheme.

    (3) The Tribunal may direct that the order, so far as it varies the amount of charges payable, has effect from a date before that on which it is made, but not earlier than the date on which the reference was made or, if later, on which the scheme came into operation.

    If such a direction is made—

    (a) any necessary repayments, or further payments, shall be made in respect of charges already paid, and

    (b) the reference in subsection (2)(a) to the charges payable under the scheme shall be construed as a reference to the charges so payable by virtue of the order.

    No such direction may be made where subsection (4) below applies.

    (4) An order of the Tribunal under section 119 or 120 made with respect to a scheme which is certified for any purpose under section 143 has effect, so far as it varies the scheme by reducing the charges payable for licences, from the date on which the reference was made to the Tribunal.

    (5) Where the Tribunal has made an order under section 121 (order as to entitlement to licence under licensing scheme) and the order remains in force, the person in whose favour the order is made shall if he—

    (a) pays to the operator of the scheme any charges payable in accordance with the order or, if the amount cannot be ascertained, gives an undertaking to pay the charges when ascertained, and

    (b) complies with the other terms specified in the order,

be in the same position as regards infringement of copyright as if he had at all material times been the holder of a licence granted by the owner of the copyright in question on the terms specified in the order.

References and applications with respect to licensing by licensing bodies

Licences to which following sections apply

    [**124.** Sections 125 to 128 (references and applications with respect to licensing by licensing bodies) apply to licences which are granted by a licensing body otherwise than in pursuance of a licensing scheme and cover works of more than one author, so far as they authorise—

    (a) copying the work,

    (b) rental or lending of copies of the work to the public,

    (c) performing, showing or playing the work in public, or

    [(d) communicating the work to the public;]

and references in those sections to a licence shall be construed accordingly.]

Notes:

   (1) This section was substituted by the Copyright and Related Rights Regulations 1996 (SI 1996/2967), which replaced the old s.124 with effect from December 1, 1996. The original wording of s.124 was as follows:

Licences to which ss. 125 to 128 apply

"124. *Sections 125 to 128 (references and applications with respect to licensing by licensing bodies) apply to the following descriptions of licence granted by a licensing body otherwise than in pursuance of a licensing scheme—*

      (a) *licences relating to the copyright in literary, dramatic, musical or artistic works or films (or film sound-tracks when accompanying a film) which cover works of more than one author, so far as they authorise—*

         (i) *copying the work,*

        (ii) *performing, playing or showing the work in public, or*

       (iii) *broadcasting the work or including it in a cable programme service;*

      (b) *any licence relating to the copyright in a sound recording (other than a film sound-track when accompanying a film), broadcast or cable programme, or the typographical arrangement of a published edition; and*

      (c) *all licences in relation to the copyright in sound recordings, films or computer programs so far as they relate to the rental of copies to the public;*

and in those sections a "licence" means a licence of any of those descriptions."

    For savings and transitional provisions, see Part III of those Regulations.

   (2) Subsection (d) was substituted by the Copyright and Related Rights Regulations 2003 (SI 2003/2498), Sch.1 para.4, with effect from October 31, 2003. For savings and transitional provisions, see Part 3 of those Regulations.

Reference to tribunal of proposed licence

125.—(1) The terms on which a licensing body proposes to grant a licence may be referred to the Copyright Tribunal by the prospective licensee.

   (2) The Tribunal shall first decide whether to entertain the reference, and may decline to do so on the ground that the reference is premature.

   (3) If the Tribunal decides to entertain the reference it shall consider the terms of the proposed licence and make such order, either confirming or varying the terms, as it may determine to be reasonable in the circumstances.

   (4) The order may be made so as to be in force indefinitely or for such period as the Tribunal may determine.

Reference to tribunal of expiring licence

126.—(1) A licensee under a licence which is due to expire, by effluxion of time or as a result of notice given by the licensing body, may apply to the Copyright Tribunal on the ground that it is unreasonable in the circumstances that the licence should cease to be in force.

   (2) Such an application may not be made until the last three months before the licence is due to expire.

   (3) A licence in respect of which a reference has been made to the Tribunal shall remain in operation until proceedings on the reference are concluded.

   (4) If the Tribunal finds the application well-founded, it shall make an order declaring that the licensee shall continue to be entitled to the benefit of the licence on such terms as the Tribunal may determine to be reasonable in the circumstances.

(5) An order of the Tribunal under this section may be made so as to be in force indefinitely or for such period as the Tribunal may determine.

Application for review of order as to licence

127.—(1) Where the Copyright Tribunal has made an order under [section 125, 126 or 128B (where that order did not relate to a licensing scheme)], the licensing body or the person entitled to the benefit of the order may apply to the Tribunal to review its order.

(2) An application shall not be made, except with the special leave of the Tribunal—

(a) within twelve months from the date of the order or of the decision on a previous application under this section, or

(b) if the order was made so as to be in force for 15 months or less, or as a result of the decision on a previous application under this section is due to expire within 15 months of that decision, until the last three months before the expiry date.

(3) The Tribunal shall on an application for review confirm or vary its order as the Tribunal may determine to be reasonable in the circumstances.

Note: The words in subs.(1) substituted for the former words "section 125 or 126" by the Copyright and Related Rights Regulations 2003 (SI 2003/2498), reg.21, with effect from October 31, 2003. For savings and transitional provisions, see Part 3 of those Regulations.

Effect of order of tribunal as to licence

128.—(1) Where the Copyright Tribunal has made an order under section 125 or 126 and the order remains in force, the person entitled to the benefit of the order shall if he—

(a) pays to the licensing body any charges payable in accordance with the order or, if the amount cannot be ascertained, gives an undertaking to pay the charges when ascertained, and

(b) complies with the other terms specified in the order,

be in the same position as regards infringement of copyright as if he had at all material times been the holder of a licence granted by the owner of the copyright in question on the terms specified in the order.

(2) The benefit of the order may be assigned—

(a) in the case of an order under section 125, if assignment is not prohibited under the terms of the Tribunal's order; and

(b) in the case of an order under section 126, if assignment was not prohibited under the terms of the original licence.

(3) The Tribunal may direct that an order under section 125 or 126, or an order under section 127 varying such an order, so far as it varies the amount of charges payable, has effect from a date before that on which it is made, but not earlier than the date on which the reference or application was made or, if later, on which the licence was granted or, as the case may be, was due to expire.

If such a direction is made—

(a) any necessary repayments, or further payments, shall be made in respect of charges already paid, and

(b) the reference in subsection (1)(a) to the charges payable in accordance with the order shall be construed, where the order is varied by a later order, as a reference to the charges so payable by virtue of the later order.

Notification of licence or licensing scheme for excepted sound recordings

128A. [...]

Notes:

(1) Section 128A was omitted by the Copyright, Designs and Patents Act 1988 (Amendment) Regulations 2010 effective from January 1, 2011. It previously provided:

Notification of licence or licensing scheme for excepted sound recordings

"**128A.**—(1) *This section only applies to a proposed licence or licensing scheme that will authorise the playing in public of excepted sound recordings included in broadcasts, in circumstances where by reason of the exclusion of excepted sound recordings from section 72(1), the playing in public of such recordings would otherwise infringe the copyright in them.*

(2) *A licensing body must notify the Secretary of State of the details of any proposed licence or licensing scheme for excepted sound recordings before it comes into operation.*

(3) *A licence or licensing scheme, which has been notified under subsection (2), may not be operated by the licensing body until 28 days have elapsed since that notification.*

(4) *Subject to subsection (5), the Secretary of State shall take into account the matters set out in subsection (6) and then either*

(a) *refer the licence or licensing scheme to the Copyright Tribunal for a determination of whether the licence or licensing scheme is reasonable in the circumstances, or*

(b) *notify the licensing body that he does not intend to refer the licence or licensing scheme to the Tribunal.*

(5) *If the Secretary of State becomes aware—*

(a) *that a licensing body has failed to notify him of a licence or licensing scheme under subsection (2) before it comes into operation; or*

(b) *that a licence or licensing scheme has been operated within 28 days of a notification under subsection (2),*

subsection (4) does not apply, but the Secretary of State may at any time refer the licence or licensing scheme to the Tribunal for a determination of whether the licence or licensing scheme is reasonable in the circumstances, or may notify the licensing body that he does not intend to refer it to the Tribunal.

(6) *The matters referred to in subsection (4) are—*

(a) *whether the terms and conditions of the proposed licence or licensing scheme have taken into account the factors set out in subsection (7);*

(b) *any written representations received by the Secretary of State;*

(c) *previous determinations of the Tribunal;*

(d) *the availability of other schemes, or the granting of other licences, to other persons in similar circumstances, and the terms of those schemes or licences; and*

(e) *the extent to which the licensing body has consulted any person who would be affected by the proposed licence or licensing scheme, or organisations representing such persons, and the steps, if any, it has taken as a result.*

(7) *The factors referred to in subsection (6) are—*

(a) *the extent to which the broadcasts to be shown or played by a potential licensee in circumstances mentioned in subsection (1) are likely to include excepted sound recordings;*

(b) *the size and the nature of the audience that a licence or licensing scheme would permit to hear the excepted sound recordings;*

(c) *what commercial benefit a potential licensee is likely to obtain from playing the excepted sound recordings; and*

(d) *the extent to which the owners of copyright in the excepted sound recordings will receive equitable remuneration, from sources other than the proposed licence or licensing scheme, for the inclusion of their recordings in the broadcasts to be shown or played in public by a potential licensee.*

(8) *A proposed licence or licensing scheme that must be notified to the Secretary of State under subsection (2) may only be referred to the Tribunal under section 118 or 125 before such notification takes place.*

(9) *A proposed licensing scheme that has been notified to the Secretary of State under subsection (2) may only be referred to the Tribunal under section 119 after the Secretary of State has notified the licensing body that he does not intend to refer the licensing scheme to the Tribunal.*

(10) *If a reference made to the Tribunal under section 118 or 125 is permitted under subsection (8) then—*

(a) *the reference shall not be considered premature only because the licence or licensing scheme has not been notified to the Secretary of State under subsection (2); and*

(b) *where the Tribunal decides to entertain the reference, subsection (2) to (5) shall not apply.*

(11) *Nothing in this section shall be taken to prejudice any right to make a reference or application to the Tribunal under sections 120 to 122, 126 or 127.*

(12) *This section applies to modifications to an existing licence or licensing scheme as it applies to a proposed licence or licensing scheme.*

(13) *In this section and in section 128B, any reference to a "licence" means a licence granted by a licensing body otherwise than in pursuance of a licensing scheme and which covers works of more than one author."*

(2) Section 128A was originally inserted by the Copyright and Related Rights Regulations 2003 (SI 2003/2498), reg.21, with effect from October 31, 2003. For savings and transitional provisions, see Part 3 of those Regulations.

References to the Tribunal by the Secretary of State under section 128A

128B. [...]

Notes:

(1) Section 128B was omitted by the Copyright Designs and Patents Act 1988 (Amendment) Regs 2010 (SI 2010/2894) with effect from January 1, 2011. It previously provided:

References to the Tribunal by the Secretary of State under section 128A

"128B.—(1) *The Copyright Tribunal may make appropriate enquiries to establish whether a licence or licensing scheme referred to it by the Secretary of State under section 128A(4)(a) or (5) is reasonable in the circumstances.*

(2) *When considering the matter referred, and after concluding any such enquiries, the Tribunal shall take into account—*

(a) *whether the terms and conditions of the proposed licence or licensing scheme have taken into account the factors set out in section 128A(7); and*

(b) *any other factors it considers relevant,*

and shall then make an order under subsection (3).

(3) *The Tribunal shall make such order—*

(a) *in the case of a licensing scheme, either confirming or varying the proposed scheme, either generally or so far as it relates to cases of any description; or*

(b) *in the case of a licence, either confirming or varying the proposed licence, as the Tribunal may determine to be reasonable in the circumstances.*

(4) *The Tribunal may direct that the order, so far as it reduces the amount of charges payable, has effect from a date before that on which it is made.*

If such a direction is made, any necessary repayments to a licensee shall be made in respect of charges already paid.

(5) *The Tribunal may award simple interest on repayments, at such rate and for such period, ending not later than the date of the order, as it thinks fit."*

(2) Section 128B was originally inserted by the Copyright and Related Rights Regula-

tions 2003 (SI 2003/2498), reg.21, with effect from October 31, 2003. For savings and transitional provisions, see Part 3 of those Regulations.

Factors to be taken into account in certain classes of case

General considerations: unreasonable discrimination

129. In determining what is reasonable on a reference or application under this Chapter relating to a licensing scheme or licence, the Copyright Tribunal shall have regard to—

(a) the availability of other schemes, or the granting of other licences, to other persons in similar circumstances, and

(b) the terms of those schemes or licences,

and shall exercise its powers so as to secure that there is no unreasonable discrimination between licensees, or prospective licensees, under the scheme or licence to which the reference or application relates and licensees under other schemes operated by, or other licences granted by, the same person.

Licences for reprographic copying

130. Where a reference or application is made to the Copyright Tribunal under this Chapter relating to the licensing of reprographic copying of published literary, dramatic, musical or artistic works, or the typographical arrangement of published editions, the Tribunal shall have regard to—

(a) the extent to which published editions of the works in question are otherwise available,

(b) the proportion of the work to be copied, and

(c) the nature of the use to which the copies are likely to be put.

Licences for educational establishments in respect of works included in broadcasts

131.—(1) This section applies to references or applications under this Chapter relating to licences for the recording by or on behalf of educational establishments of broadcasts [...] which include copyright works, or the making of copies of such recordings, for educational purposes.

(2) The Copyright Tribunal shall, in considering what charges (if any) should be paid for a licence, have regard to the extent to which the owners of copyright in the works included in the broadcast [...] have already received, or are entitled to receive, payment in respect of their inclusion.

Note: In subs.(1), the words "or cable programmes" and in subs.(2) the words "or cable programme" repealed by the Copyright and Related Rights Regulations 2003 (SI 2003/2498), Sch.2, with effect from October 31, 2003. For savings and transitional provisions, see Part 3 of those Regulations.

Licences to reflect conditions imposed by promoters of events

132.—(1) This section applies to references or applications under this Chapter in respect of licences relating to sound recordings, films, [or broadcasts] which include, or are to include, any entertainment or other event.

(2) The Copyright Tribunal shall have regard to any conditions imposed by the promoters of the entertainment or other event; and, in particular, the Tribunal shall not hold a refusal or failure to grant a licence to be unreasonable if it could not have been granted consistently with those conditions.

(3) Nothing in this section shall require the Tribunal to have regard to any such conditions in so far as they—

    (a) purport to regulate the charges to be imposed in respect of the grant of licences, or

    (b) relate to payments to be made to the promoters of any event in consideration of the grant of facilities for making the recording, film [or broadcast].

Note: In subs.(1), the words in square brackets substituted for the former words ", broadcasts or cable programmes" and in subs.(3)(b) the words in square brackets substituted for the former words ", broadcast or cable programme" by the Copyright and Related Rights Regulations 2003 (SI 2003/2498), Sch.1 para.3, with effect from October 31, 2003. For savings and transitional provisions, see Part 3 of those Regulations.

Licences to reflect payments in respect of underlying rights

133.—[(1) In considering what charges should be paid for a licence—

    (a) on a reference or application under this Chapter relating to licences for the rental or lending of copies of a work, or

    (b) on an application under section 142 (royalty or other sum payable for lending of certain works),

the Copyright Tribunal shall take into account any reasonable payments which the owner of the copyright in the work is liable to make in consequence of the granting of the licence, or of the acts authorised by the licence, to owners of copyright in works included in that work.]

(2) On any reference or application under this Chapter relating to licensing in respect of the copyright in sound recordings, films [or broadcasts], the Copyright Tribunal shall take into account, in considering what charges should be paid for a licence, any reasonable payments which the copyright owner is liable to make in consequence of the granting of the licence, or of the acts authorised by the licence, in respect of any performance included in the recording, film [or broadcast].

Notes:

    (1) Subsection (1) is printed as amended by the Copyright and Related Rights Regulations 1996 (SI 1996/2967), which replaced the old subs.(1) with effect from 1st December 1996.

        For savings and transitional provisions, see Part III of those Regulations.

    (2) In subs.(2), the words in the first set of square brackets substituted for the former words ", broadcasts or cable programmes" and the words in the second set of square brackets substituted for the former words ", broadcast or cable programme" by the Copyright and Related Rights Regulations 2003 (SI 2003/2498), Sch.1 para.3, with effect from October 31, 2003. For savings and transitional provisions, see Part 3 of those Regulations.

Licences in respect of works included in re-transmissions

134.—(1) [Subject to subsection (3A)] this section applies to references or applications under this Chapter relating to licences to include in a broadcast [...]—

    (a) literary, dramatic, musical or artistic works, or,

    (b) sound recordings or films,

where one broadcast [...] ("the first transmission") is, by reception and immediate re-transmission, to be further broadcast [...] ("the further transmission").

(2) So far as the further transmission is to the same area as the first transmission, the Copyright Tribunal shall, in considering what charges (if any) should be paid for licences for either transmission, have regard to the extent to which the copyright owner has already received, or is entitled to receive, payment for the other transmission which adequately remunerates him in respect of transmissions to that area.

(3) So far as the further transmission is to an area outside that to which the

first transmission was made, the Tribunal shall [...] leave the further transmission out of account in considering what charges (if any) should be paid for licences for the first transmission.

[(3A) This section does not apply in relation to any application under section 73A (royalty or other sum payable in pursuance of section 73(4)).]

(4) [...]

Notes:

(1) Subsection (1) is printed as amended by and subs.(3A) was inserted by s.138 and Sch.9 to the Broadcasting Act 1996 with effect from October 1, 1996 by virtue of the Broadcasting Act 1996 (Commencement No.1 and Transitional Provisions) Order 1996 (SI 1996/2120).

(2) Subsection (4) was repealed by the Broadcasting Act 1990 with effect from December 1, 1990 by virtue of the Broadcasting Act 1990 (Commencement No.1 and Transitional Provisions) Order 1990 (SI 1990/2347). The provision formerly read:

"(4) *If the Tribunal is satisfied that requirements imposed under section 13(1) of the [1984 c. 46.] Cable and Broadcasting Act 1984 (duty of Cable Authority to secure inclusion of certain broadcasts in cable programme services) will result in the further transmission being to areas part of which fall outside the area to which the first transmission is made, the Tribunal shall exercise its powers so as to secure that the charges payable for licences for the first transmission adequately reflect that fact."*

(3) In subs.(1), the words "or cable programme service", "or cable programme" and "or included in a cable programme service" and in subs.(3) the words "(except where subsection (4) applies)" repealed by the Copyright and Related Rights Regulations 2003 (SI 2003/2498), Sch.2, with effect from October 31, 2003. For savings and transitional provisions, see Part 3 of those Regulations.

Mention of specific matters not to exclude other relevant considerations

135. The mention in sections 129 to 134 of specific matters to which the Copyright Tribunal is to have regard in certain classes of case does not affect the Tribunal's general obligation in any case to have regard to all relevant considerations.

[Use as of right of sound recordings in broadcasts and cable programme services

Circumstances in which right available

[135A.—(1) Section 135C applies to the inclusion in a broadcast [...] of any sound recordings if—

(a) a licence to include those recordings in the broadcast [...] could be granted by a licensing body or such a body could procure the grant of a licence to do so,

(b) the condition in subsection (2) or (3) applies, and

(c) the person including those recordings in the broadcast [...] has complied with section 135B.

(2) Where the person including the recordings in the broadcast [...] does not hold a licence to do so, the condition is that the licensing body refuses to grant, or procure the grant of, such a licence, being a licence—

(a) whose terms as to payment for including the recordings in the broadcast [...] would be acceptable to him or comply with an order of the Copyright Tribunal under section 135D relating to such a licence or any scheme under which it would be granted, and

(b) allowing unlimited needletime or such needletime as he has demanded.

(3) Where he holds a licence to include the recordings in the broadcast [...], the condition is that the terms of the licence limit needletime and the licensing body refuses to substitute or procure the substitution of terms allowing unlimited needletime or such needletime as he has demanded, or refuses to do so on terms that fall within subsection (2)(a).

(4) The references in subsection (2) to refusing to grant, or procure the grant of, a licence, and in subsection (3) to refusing to substitute of procure the substitution of terms, include failing to do so within a reasonable time of being asked.

(5) In the group of sections from this section to section 135G—

["broadcast" does not include any broadcast which is a transmission of the kind specified in section 6(1A)(b) or (c)];

"needletime" means the time in any period (whether determined as a number of hours in the period or a proportion of the period, or otherwise) in which any recordings may be included in a broadcast [...];

"sound recording" does not include a film sound track when accompanying a film.

(6) In sections 135B to 135G, "terms of payment" means terms as to payment for including sound recordings in a broadcast [...].]

Notes:

(1) This section and the heading preceding it inserted by s.175 of the Broadcasting Act 1990 with effect from February 1, 1991 by virtue of the Broadcasting Act 1990 (Commencement No.1 and Transitional Provisions) Order 1990 (SI 1990/2347).

(2) The definition of "broadcast" was inserted and the words "or cable programme service" repealed wherever they occurred by the Copyright and Related Rights Regulations 2003 (SI 2003/2498), Sch.1 para.15 and Sch.2, with effect from October 31, 2003. For savings and transitional provisions, see Part 3 of those Regulations.

Notice of intention to exercise right

[135B.—(1) A person intending to avail himself of the right conferred by section 135C must—

(a) give notice to the licensing body of his intention to exercise the right, asking the body to propose terms of payment, and

(b) after receiving the proposal or the expiry of a reasonable period, give reasonable notice to the licensing body of the date on which he proposes to begin exercising that right, and the terms of payment in accordance with which he intends to do so.

(2) Where he has a licence to include the recordings in a broadcast [...], the date specified in a notice under subsection (1)(b) must not be sooner than the date of expiry of that licence except in a case falling within section 135A(3).

(3) Before the person intending to avail himself of the right begins to exercise it, he must—

(a) give reasonable notice to the Copyright Tribunal of his intention to exercise the right, and of the date on which he proposes to begin to do so, and

(b) apply to the Tribunal under section 135D to settle the terms of payment.]

Notes:

(1) This section was inserted by s.175 of the Broadcasting Act 1990 with effect from February 1, 1991 by virtue of the Broadcasting Act 1990 (Commencement No.1 and Transitional Provisions) Order 1990 (SI 1990/2347).

(2) In subs.(2), the words "or cable programme service" repealed by the Copyright

and Related Rights Regulations 2003 (SI 2003/2498), Sch.2, with effect from October 31, 2003. For savings and transitional provisions, see Part 3 of those Regulations.

Conditions for exercise of right

[**135C.**—(1) A person who, on or after the date specified in a notice under section 135B(1)(b), includes in a broadcast [...] any sound recordings in circumstances in which this section applies, and who—

(a) complies with any reasonable condition, notice of which has been given to him by the licensing body, as to inclusion in the broadcast [...] of those recordings,

(b) provides that body with such information about their inclusion in the broadcast [...] as it may reasonably require, and

(c) makes the payments to the licensing body that are required by this section,

shall be in the same position as regards infringement of copyright as if he had at all material times been the holder of a licence granted by the owner of the copyright in question.

(2) Payments are to be made at not less than quarterly intervals in arrears.

(3) The amount of any payment is that determined in accordance with any order of the Copyright Tribunal under section 135D or, if no such order has been made—

(a) in accordance with any proposal for terms of payment made by the licensing body pursuant to a request under section 135B, or

(b) where no proposal has been so made or the amount determined in accordance with the proposal so made is unreasonably high, in accordance with the terms of payment notified to the licensing body under section 135B(1)(b).

(4) Where this section applies to the inclusion in a broadcast [...] of any sound recordings, it does so in place of any licence.]

Notes:

(1) This section was inserted by s.175 of the Broadcasting Act 1990 with effect from February 1, 1991 by virtue of the Broadcasting Act 1990 (Commencement No.1 and Transitional Provisions) Order 1990 (SI 1990/2347).

(2) In subss.(1) and (4) the words "or cable programme service" repealed wherever they occurred by the Copyright and Related Rights Regulations 2003 (SI 2003/2498), Sch.2, with effect from October 31, 2003. For savings and transitional provisions, see Part 3 of those Regulations.

Applications to settle payments

[**135D.**—(1) On an application to settle the terms of payment, the Copyright Tribunal shall consider the matter and make such order as it may determine to be reasonable in the circumstances.

(2) An order under subsection (1) has effect from the date the applicant begins to exercise the right conferred by section 135C and any necessary repayments, or further payments, shall be made in respect of amounts that have fallen due.]

Note: This section was inserted by s.175 of the Broadcasting Act 1990 with effect from February 1, 1991 by virtue of the Broadcasting Act 1990 (Commencement No.1 and Transitional Provisions) Order 1990 (SI 1990/2347).

References etc. about conditions, information and other terms

[**135E.**—(1) A person exercising the right conferred by section 135C, or who has given notice to the Copyright Tribunal of his intention to do so, may refer to the Tribunal—

(a) any question whether any condition as to the inclusion in a broadcast [...] of sound recordings, notice of which has been given to him by the licensing body in question, is a reasonable condition, or

(b) any question whether any information is information which the licensing body can reasonably require him to provide.

(2) On a reference under this section, the Tribunal shall consider the matter and make such order as it may determine to be reasonable in the circumstances.]

Notes:

(1) This section was inserted by s.175 of the Broadcasting Act 1990 with effect from February 1, 1991 by virtue of the Broadcasting Act 1990 (Commencement No.1 and Transitional Provisions) Order 1990 (SI 1990/2347).

(2) In subs.(1)(a), the words "or cable programme service" repealed by the Copyright and Related Rights Regulations 2003 (SI 2003/2498), Sch.2, with effect from October 31, 2003. For savings and transitional provisions, see Part 3 of those Regulations.

Application for review of order

[135F.—(1) A person exercising the right conferred by section 135C or the licensing body may apply to the Copyright Tribunal to review any order under section 135D or 135E.

(2) An application shall not be made, except with the special leave of the Tribunal—

(a) within twelve months from the date of the order, or of the decision on a previous application under this section, or

(b) if the order was made so as to be in force for fifteen months or less, or as a result of a decision on a previous application is due to expire within fifteen months of that decision, until the last three months before the expiry date.

(3) On the application the Tribunal shall consider the matter and make such order confirming or varying the original order as it may determine to be reasonable in the circumstances.

(4) An order under this section has effect from the date on which it is made or such later date as may be specified by the Tribunal.]

Note: This section was inserted by s.175 of the Broadcasting Act 1990 with effect from February 1, 1991 by virtue of the Broadcasting Act 1990 (Commencement No.1 and Transitional Provisions) Order 1990 (SI 1990/2347).

Factors to be taken into account

[135G.—(1) In determining what is reasonable on an application or reference under section 135D or 135E, or on reviewing any order under section 135F, the Copyright Tribunal shall—

(a) have regard to the terms of any orders which it has made in the case of persons in similar circumstances exercising the right conferred by section 135C, and

(b) exercise its powers so as to secure that there is no unreasonable discrimination between persons exercising that right against the same licensing body.

(2) In settling the terms of payment under section 135D, the Tribunal shall not be guided by any order it has made under any enactment other than that section.

(3) Section 134 (factors to be taken into account: retransmissions) applies on

an application or reference under sections 135D to 135F as it applies on an application or reference relating to a licence.]

Note: This section was inserted by s.175 of the Broadcasting Act 1990 with effect from February 1, 1991 by virtue of the Broadcasting Act 1990 (Commencement No.1 and Transitional Provisions) Order 1990 (SI 1990/2347).

Power to amend sections 135A to 135G

[**135H.**—(1) The Secretary of State may by order, subject to such transitional provision as appears to him to be appropriate, amend sections 135A to 135G so as—

    (a) to include in any reference to sound recordings any works of a description specified in the order; or

    (b) to exclude from any reference to a broadcast [...] any broadcast [...] of a description so specified.

(2) An order shall be made by statutory instrument; and no order shall be made unless a draft of it has been laid before and approved by resolution of each House of Parliament.]

Notes:

    (1) This section was inserted by s.139 of the Broadcasting Act 1996 with effect from November 1, 1996 by virtue of the Broadcasting Act 1996 (Commencement No.1 and Transitional Provisions) Order 1996 (SI 1996/2120).

    (2) In subs.(1)(b), the words "or cable programme service" repealed in both places by the Copyright and Related Rights Regulations 2003 (SI 2003/2498), Sch.2, with effect from October 31, 2003. For savings and transitional provisions, see Part 3 of those Regulations.

Implied indemnity in certain schemes and licences for reprographic copying

Implied indemnity in certain schemes and licences for reprographic copying

136.—(1) This section applies to—

    (a) schemes for licensing reprographic copying of published literary, dramatic, musical or artistic works, or the typographical arrangement of published editions, and

    (b) licences granted by licensing bodies for such copying,

where the scheme or licence does not specify the works to which it applies with such particularity as to enable licensees to determine whether a work falls within the scheme or licence by inspection of the scheme or licence and the work.

(2) There is implied—

    (a) in every scheme to which this section applies an undertaking by the operator of the scheme to indemnify a person granted a licence under the scheme, and

    (b) in every licence to which this section applies an undertaking by the licensing body to indemnify the licensee,

against any liability incurred by him by reason of his having infringed copyright by making or authorising the making of reprographic copies of a work in circumstances within the apparent scope of his licence.

(3) The circumstances of a case are within the apparent scope of a licence if—

    (a) it is not apparent from inspection of the licence and the work that it does not fall within the description of works to which the licence applies; and

(b) the licence does not expressly provide that it does not extend to copyright of the description infringed.

(4) In this section "liability" includes liability to pay costs; and this section applies in relation to costs reasonably incurred by a licensee in connection with actual or contemplated proceedings against him for infringement of copyright as it applies to sums which he is liable to pay in respect of such infringement.

(5) A scheme or licence to which this section applies may contain reasonable provision—

(a) with respect to the manner in which, and time within which, claims under the undertaking implied by this section are to be made;

(b) enabling the operator of the scheme or, as the case may be, the licensing body to take over the conduct of any proceedings affecting the amount of his liability to indemnify.

Reprographic copying by educational establishments

Power to extend coverage of scheme or licence

137.—(1) This section applies to—

(a) a licensing scheme to which sections 118 to 123 apply (see section 117) and which is operated by a licensing body, or

(b) a licence to which sections 125 to 128 apply (see section 124),

so far as it provides for the grant of licences, or is a licence, authorising the making by or on behalf of educational establishments for the purposes of instruction of reprographic copies of published literary, dramatic, musical or artistic works, or of the typographical arrangement of published editions.

(2) If it appears to the Secretary of State with respect to a scheme or licence to which this section applies that—

(a) works of a description similar to those covered by the scheme or licence are unreasonably excluded from it, and

(b) making them subject to the scheme or licence would not conflict with the normal exploitation of the works or unreasonably prejudice the legitimate interests of the copyright owners,

he may by order provide that the scheme or licence shall extend to those works.

(3) Where he proposes to make such an order, the Secretary of State shall give notice of the proposal to— ·

(a) the copyright owners,

(b) the licensing body in question, and

(c) such persons or organisations representative of educational establishments, and such other persons or organisations, as the Secretary of State thinks fit.

(4) The notice shall inform those persons of their right to make written or oral representations to the Secretary of State about the proposal within six months from the date of the notice; and if any of them wishes to make oral representations, the Secretary of State shall appoint a person to hear the representations and report to him.

(5) In considering whether to make an order the Secretary of State shall take into account any representations made to him in accordance with subsection (4), and such other matters as appear to him to be relevant.

Variation or discharge of order extending scheme or licence

138.—(1) The owner of the copyright in a work in respect of which an order is in force under section 137 may apply to the Secretary of State for the variation or discharge of the order, stating his reasons for making the application.

(2) The Secretary of State shall not entertain an application made within two years of the making of the original order, or of the making of an order on a previous application under this section, unless it appears to him that the circumstances are exceptional.

(3) On considering the reasons for the application the Secretary of State may confirm the order forthwith; if he does not do so, he shall give notice of the application to—

  (a) the licensing body in question, and

  (b) such persons or organisations representative of educational establishments, and such other persons or organisations, as he thinks fit.

(4) The notice shall inform those persons of their right to make written or oral representations to the Secretary of State about the application within the period of two months from the date of the notice; and if any of them wishes to make oral representations, the Secretary of State shall appoint a person to hear the representations and report to him.

(5) In considering the application the Secretary of State shall take into account the reasons for the application, any representations made to him in accordance with subsection (4), and such other matters as appear to him to be relevant.

(6) The Secretary of State may make such order as he thinks fit confirming or discharging the order (or, as the case may be, the order as previously varied), or varying (or further varying) it so as to exclude works from it.

Appeals against orders

139.—(1) The owner of the copyright in a work which is the subject of an order under section 137 (order extending coverage of scheme or licence) may appeal to the Copyright Tribunal which may confirm or discharge the order, or vary it so as to exclude works from it, as it thinks fit having regard to the considerations mentioned in subsection (2) of that section.

(2) Where the Secretary of State has made an order under section 138 (order confirming, varying or discharging order extending coverage of scheme or licence)—

  (a) the person who applied for the order, or

  (b) any person or organisation representative of educational establishments who was given notice of the application for the order and made representations in accordance with subsection (4) of that section,

may appeal to the Tribunal which may confirm or discharge the order or make any other order which the Secretary of State might have made.

(3) An appeal under this section shall be brought within six weeks of the making of the order or such further period as the Tribunal may allow.

(4) An order under section 137 or 138 shall not come into effect until the end of the period of six weeks from the making of the order or, if an appeal is brought before the end of that period, until the appeal proceedings are disposed of or withdrawn.

(5) If an appeal is brought after the end of that period, any decision of the Tribunal on the appeal does not affect the validity of anything done in reliance on the order appealed against before that decision takes effect.

Inquiry whether new scheme or general licence required

140.—(1) The Secretary of State may appoint a person to inquire into the question whether new provision is required (whether by way of a licensing scheme or general licence) to authorise the making by or on behalf of educational establishments for the purposes of instruction of reprographic copies of—

(a) published literary, dramatic, musical or artistic works, or

(b) the typographical arrangement of published editions,

of a description which appears to the Secretary of State not to be covered by an existing licensing scheme or general licence and not to fall within the power conferred by section 137 (power to extend existing schemes and licences to similar works).

(2) The procedure to be followed in relation to an inquiry shall be such as may be prescribed by regulations made by the Secretary of State.

(3) The regulations shall, in particular, provide for notice to be given to—

(a) persons or organisations appearing to the Secretary of State to represent the owners of copyright in works of that description, and

(b) persons or organisations appearing to the Secretary of State to represent educational establishments,

and for the making of written or oral representations by such persons; but without prejudice to the giving of notice to, and the making of representations by, other persons and organisations.

(4) The person appointed to hold the inquiry shall recommend the making of new provision unless he is satisfied—

(a) that it would be of advantage to educational establishments to be authorised to make reprographic copies of the works in question, and

(b) that making those works subject to a licensing scheme or general licence would not conflict with the normal exploitation of the works or unreasonably prejudice the legitimate interests of the copyright owners.

(5) If he does recommend the making of new provision he shall specify any terms, other than terms as to charges payable, on which authorisation under the new provision should be available.

(6) Regulations under this section shall be made by statutory instrument which shall be subject to annulment in pursuance of a resolution of either House of Parliament.

(7) In this section (and section 141) a "general licence" means a licence granted by a licensing body which covers all works of the description to which it applies.

Statutory licence where recommendation not implemented

141.—(1) The Secretary of State may, within one year of the making of a recommendation under section 140 by order provide that if, or to the extent that, provision has not been made in accordance with the recommendation, the making by or on behalf of an educational establishment, for the purposes of instruction, of reprographic copies of the works to which the recommendation relates shall be treated as licensed by the owners of the copyright in the works.

(2) For that purpose provision shall be regarded as having been made in accordance with the recommendation if—

(a) a certified licensing scheme has been established under which a licence is available to the establishment in question, or

(b) a general licence has been—

(i) granted to or for the benefit of that establishment, or

(ii) referred by or on behalf of that establishment to the Copyright Tribunal under section 125 (reference in terms of proposed licence), or

(iii) offered to or for the benefit of that establishment and refused without such a reference.

and the terms of the scheme or licence accord with the recommendation.

(3) The order shall also provide that any existing licence authorising the making of such copies (not being a licence granted under a certified licensing scheme or a general licence) shall cease to have effect to the extent that it is more restricted or more onerous than the licence provided for by the order.

(4) The order shall provide for the licence to be free of royalty but, as respects other matters, subject to any terms specified in the recommendation and to such other terms as the Secretary of State may think fit.

(5) The order may provide that where a copy which would otherwise be an infringing copy is made in accordance with the licence provided by the order but is subsequently dealt with, it shall be treated as an infringing copy for the purposes of that dealing, and if that dealing infringes copyright for all subsequent purposes.

In this subsection "dealt with" means sold or let for hire, offered or exposed for sale or hire, or exhibited in public.

(6) The order shall not come into force until at least six months after it is made.

(7) An order may be varied from time to time, but not so as to include works other than those to which the recommendation relates or remove any terms specified in the recommendation, and may be revoked.

(8) An order under this section shall be made by statutory instrument which shall be subject to annulment in pursuance of a resolution of either House of Parliament.

(9) In this section a "certified licensing scheme" means a licensing scheme certified for the purposes of this section under section 143.

[Royalty or other sum payable for lending of certain works

Royalty or other sum payable for lending of certain works

142.—(1) An application to settle the royalty or other sum payable in pursuance of section 66 (lending of copies of certain copyright works) may be made to the Copyright Tribunal by the copyright owner or the person claiming to be treated as licensed by him.

(2) The Tribunal shall consider the matter and make such order as it may determine to be reasonable in the circumstances.

(3) Either party may subsequently apply to the Tribunal to vary the order, and the Tribunal shall consider the matter and make such order confirming or varying the original order as it may determine to be reasonable in the circumstances.

(4) An application under subsection (3) shall not, except with the special leave of the Tribunal, be made within twelve months from the date of the original order or of the order on a previous application under that subsection.

(5) An order under subsection (3) has effect from the date on which it is made or such later date as may be specified by the Tribunal.]

Note: This section and the heading preceding it substituted by the Copyright and Related Rights Regulations 1996 (SI 1996/2967), which replaced the old s.142 and heading preceding it with effect from December 1, 1996. The section originally read:

"Royalty or other sum payable for rental of certain works

Royalty or other sum payable for rental of sound recording, film or computer program

142.—(1) *An application to settle the royalty or other sum payable in pursuance of sec-*

tion 66 (rental of sound recordings, films and computer programs) may be made to the Copyright Tribunal by the copyright owner or the person claiming to be treated as licensed by him.

(2) The Tribunal shall consider the matter and make such order as it may determine to be reasonable in the circumstances.

(3) Either party may subsequently apply to the Tribunal to vary the order, and the Tribunal shall consider the matter and make such order confirming or varying the original order as it may determine to be reasonable in the circumstances.

(4) An application under subsection (3) shall not, except with the special leave of the Tribunal, be made within twelve months from the date of the original order or of the order on a previous application under that subsection.

(5) An order under subsection (3) has effect from the date on which it is made or such later date as may be specified by the Tribunal."

For savings and transitional provisions, see Part III of those Regulations.

Certification of licensing schemes

Certification of licensing schemes

143.—(1) A person operating or proposing to operate a licensing scheme may apply to the Secretary of State to certify the scheme for the purposes of—

(a) [...]

(b) section 60 (abstracts of scientific or technical articles),

[(c) section 66 (lending to public of copies of certain works)],

(d) [...] or

(e) section 141 (reprographic copying of published works by educational establishments).

(2) The Secretary of State shall by order made by statutory instrument certify the scheme if he is satisfied that it—

(a) enables the works to which it relates to be identified with sufficient certainty by persons likely to require licences, and

(b) sets out clearly the charges (if any) payable and the other terms on which licences will be granted.

(3) The scheme shall be scheduled to the order and the certification shall come into operation for the purposes of section [...] 60, 66, [...] or 141, as the case may be—

(a) on such date, not less than eight weeks after the order is made, as may be specified in the order, or

(b) if the scheme is the subject of a reference under section 118 (reference of proposed scheme), any later date on which the order of the Copyright Tribunal under that section comes into force or the reference is withdrawn.

(4) A variation of the scheme is not effective unless a corresponding amendment of the order is made; and the Secretary of State shall make such an amendment in the case of a variation ordered by the Copyright Tribunal on a reference under section 118, 119 or 120, and may do so in any other case if he thinks fit.

(5) The order shall be revoked if the scheme ceases to be operated and may be revoked if it appears to the Secretary of State that it is no longer being operated according to its terms.

Notes:

(1) Subsection (1)(c) is printed as amended by the Copyright and Related Rights Regulations 1996 (SI 1996/2967), with effect from December 1, 1996. For savings and transitional provisions, see Part III of those Regulations.

(2) Subsection (1)(a) repealed and in subs.(3) first reference in square brackets re-

pealed by the Copyright and Rights in Performances (Research, Education, Libraries and Archives) Regulations 2014 (SI 2014/1372) Sch. para.5, with effect from
June 1, 2014 at 00.02. Subs.(1)(a) formerly read:
"(a) section 35 (educational recording of broadcasts [...]),"
  (3) Subsection (1)(d) repealed and in subs.(3) second reference in square brackets repealed by the Copyright and Rights in Performances (Disability) Regulations
2014 (SI 2014/1384) Sch. para.2, with effect from June 1, 2014 at 00.01.
Subs.(1)(d) formerly read:
*"(d) section 74 (sub-titled copies of broadcasts [...] for people who are deaf or hard of
hearing), or"*

Powers exercisable in consequence of competition report

Powers exercisable in consequence of report of Competition Commission [Competition and Markets Authority]

144.—[(1) Subsection (1A) applies where whatever needs to be remedied, mitigated or prevented by the Secretary of State, the Office of Fair Trading or (as the case may be) the Competition Commission [or (as the case may be) the Competition and Markets Authority] under section 12(5) of the Competition Act 1980 or section 41(2), 55(2), 66(6), 75(2), 83(2), 138(2), 147(2)[, 147A2] or 160(2) of, or paragraph 5(2) or 10(2) of Schedule 7 to, the Enterprise Act 2002 (powers to take remedial action following references to the [Competition and Markets Authority] in connection with public bodies and certain other persons, mergers or market investigations) consists of or includes—

  (a) conditions in licences granted by the owner of copyright in a work restricting the use of the work by the licensee or the right of the copyright owner to grant other licences; or

  (b) a refusal of a copyright owner to grant licences on reasonable terms.

(1A) The powers conferred by Schedule 8 to the Enterprise Act 2002 include power to cancel or modify those conditions and, instead or in addition, to provide that licences in respect of the copyright shall be available as of right.

(2) The references to anything permitted by Schedule 8 to the Enterprise Act 2002 in section 12(5A) of the Competition Act 1980 and in sections 75(4)(a), 83(4)(a), 84(2)(a), 89(1), 160(4)(a), 161(3)(a) and 164(1) of, and paragraphs 5, 10 and 11 of Schedule 7 to, the Act of 2002 shall be construed accordingly.]

(3) [The Secretary of State [or (as the case may be) the Competition and Markets Authority]] shall only exercise the powers available by virtue of this section if he [or it] is satisfied that to do so does not contravene any Convention relating to copyright to which the United Kingdom is a party.

(4) The terms of a licence available by virtue of this section shall, in default of agreement, be settled by the Copyright Tribunal on an application by the person requiring the licence; and terms so settled shall authorise the licensee to do everything in respect of which a licence is so available.

(5) Where the terms of a licence are settled by the Tribunal, the licence has effect from the date on which the application to the Tribunal was made.

Notes:
  (1) Subsections (1), (1A) and (2) substituted and in subs.(3) the words in the first set
of square brackets substituted for the former words "A Minister" and the words in
the third set of square brackets inserted by the Enterprise Act 2002 (c.40) Sch.25
para.18 with effect from June 20, 2003.
  (2) In heading and subs.(1) words in first internal square brackets and subs.(3) words
in second internal square brackets substituted, subject to transitional provision, by
the Enterprise and Regulatory Reform Act 2013 (Competition) (Consequential,
Transitional and Saving Provisions) Order 2014 (SI 2014/892), Sch.1 para.57 (for
transitional provision see Sch.2), with effect from April 1, 2014.

[Compulsory collective administration of certain rights

Collective exercise of certain rights in relation to cable re-transmission

[**144A.**—(1) This section applies to the right of the owner of copyright in a literary, dramatic, musical or artistic work, sound recording or film to grant or refuse authorisation for cable re-transmission of a [wireless] broadcast from another EEA [...] state in which the work is included.

That right is referred to below as "cable re-transmission right".

(2) Cable re-transmission right may be exercised against a cable operator only through a licensing body.

(3) Where a copyright owner has not transferred management of his cable re-transmission right to a licensing body, the licensing body which manages rights of the same category shall be deemed to be mandated to manage his right.

Where more than one licensing body manages rights of that category, he may choose which of them is deemed to be mandated to manage his right.

(4) A copyright owner to whom subsection (3) applies has the same rights and obligations resulting from any relevant agreement between the cable operator and the licensing body as have copyright owners who have transferred management of their cable re-transmission right to that licensing body.

(5) Any rights to which a copyright owner may be entitled by virtue of subsection (4) must be claimed within the period of three years beginning with the date of the cable re-transmission concerned.

(6) This section does not affect any rights exercisable by the maker of the broadcast, whether in relation to the broadcast or a work included in it.

[(7) In this section—

"cable operator" means a person responsible for cable re-transmission of a wireless broadcast; and

"cable re-transmission" means the reception and immediate re-transmission by cable, including the transmission of microwave energy between terrestrial fixed points, of a wireless broadcast.]]

Notes:

(1) This section and the heading preceding it inserted by the Copyright and Related Rights Regulations 1996 (SI 1996/2967), with effect from December 1, 1996. For savings and transitional provisions, see Part IIIof those Regulations.

(2) The word "wireless" was inserted in subs.(1) and subs.(7) was substituted by the Copyright and Related Rights Regulations 2003 (SI 2003/2498), reg.5 and Sch.1 para.15, with effect from October 31, 2003. For savings and transitional provisions, see Part 3 of those Regulations.

(3) In subs.(1) the word "member" was repealed by the Intellectual Property (Enforcement, etc.) Regulations 2006 (SI 2006/1028), Sch.4, with effect from April 29, 2006.

Chapter VIII

The Copyright Tribunal

The Tribunal

The Copyright Tribunal

145.—(1) The Tribunal established under section 23 of the Copyright Act 1956 is renamed the Copyright Tribunal.

(2) The Tribunal shall consist of a chairman and two deputy chairmen appointed by the Lord Chancellor, after consultation with the Lord Advocate, and

not less than two or more than eight ordinary members appointed by the Secretary of State.

(3) A person is not eligible for appointment as chairman or deputy chairman unless—

[(a) he satisfies the judicial-appointment eligibility condition on a 5-year basis;]

(b) he is an advocate or solicitor in Scotland of at least [5] years' standing;

(c) he is a member of the Bar of Northern Ireland or [solicitor of the Court of Judicature of Northern Ireland] of at least [5 years' standing; or

(d) he has held judicial office.]

Note: Subsection (3) is printed as amended by the Courts and Legal Services Act 1990 with effect from January 1, 1991, by the Tribunals, Courts and Enforcement Act 2007 (c.15) ss.50(6), 148, Sch.10 para.20 with effect from July 21, 2008, and by the Constitutional Reform Act 2005 (c.4) ss.59, 148, Sch.11 para.5 with effect from October 1, 2009.

Membership of the Tribunal

146.—(1) The members of the Copyright Tribunal shall hold and vacate office in accordance with their terms of appointment, subject to the following provisions.

(2) A member of the Tribunal may resign office by notice in writing to the Secretary of State or, in the case of the chairman or a deputy chairman, to the Lord Chancellor.

(3) The Secretary of State or, in the case of the chairman or a deputy chairman, the Lord Chancellor may by notice in writing to the member concerned remove him from office if—

(a) he has become bankrupt or made an arrangement with his creditors or, in Scotland, his estate has been sequestrated or he has executed a trust deed for his creditors or entered into a composition contract, or

(c) he is incapacitated by physical or mental illness,

or if he is in the opinion of the Secretary of State or, as the case may be, the Lord Chancellor otherwise unable or unfit to perform his duties as member.

[(3A) A person who is the chairman or a deputy chairman of the Tribunal shall vacate his office on the day on which he attains the age of 70 years; but this subsection is subject to section 26(4) to (6) of the Judicial Pensions and Retirement Act 1993 (power to authorise continuance in office up to the age of 75 years).]

(4) If a member of the Tribunal is by reason of illness, absence or other reasonable cause for the time being unable to perform the duties of his office, either generally or in relation to particular proceedings, a person may be appointed to discharge his duties for a period not exceeding six months at one time or, as the case may be, in relation to those proceedings.

(5) The appointment shall be made—

(a) in the case of the chairman or deputy chairman, by the Lord Chancellor, who shall appoint a person who would be eligible for appointment to that office, and

(b) in the case of any ordinary member, by the Secretary of State;

and a person so appointed shall have during the period of his appointment, or in relation to the proceedings in question the same powers as the person in whose place he is appointed.

(6) The Lord Chancellor shall consult the Lord Advocate before exercising his powers under this section.

(7) The Lord Chancellor may exercise his powers to remove a person under

subsection (3) or to appoint a person under subsection (4) only with the concurrence of the appropriate senior judge.

(8) The appropriate senior judge is the Lord Chief Justice of England and Wales, unless—

    (a) the person to be removed exercises functions [, or the person to be appointed is to exercise functions,] wholly or mainly in Scotland, in which case it is the Lord President of the Court of Session, or

    (b) the person to be removed exercises functions [, or the person to be appointed is to exercise functions,] wholly or mainly in Northern Ireland, in which case it is the Lord Chief Justice of Northern Ireland.

(9) The Lord Chief Justice of England and Wales may nominate a judicial office holder (as defined in section 109(4) of the Constitutional Reform Act 2005) to exercise his functions under subsection (7) in relation to the appointment of a person under subsection (4).

(10) The Lord President of the Court of Session may nominate a judge of the Court of Session who is a member of the First or Second Division of the Inner House of that Court to exercise his functions under subsection (7) in relation to the appointment of a person under subsection (4).

(11) The Lord Chief Justice of Northern Ireland may nominate any of the following to exercise his functions under subsection (7) in relation to the appointment of a person under subsection (4)—

    (a) the holder of one of the offices listed in Schedule 1 to the Justice (Northern Ireland) Act 2002;

    (b) a Lord Justice of Appeal (as defined in section 88 of that Act).

Notes:

    (1) Subsection (3A) was inserted by the Judicial Pensions and Retirement Act 1993, with effect from March 31, 1995 by virtue of the Judicial Pensions and Retirement Act 1993 (Commencement) Order 1995 (SI 1995/631).

    (2) Subsections (7) to (11) inserted by the Constitutional Reform Act 2005 (c.4), Sch.4 para.199, with effect from April 3, 2006.

    (3) The words in square brackets in s.146(8) inserted by the Lord Chancellor (Transfer of Functions and Supplementary Provisions) (No.2) Order 2006 (SI 2006/1016), Sch.3, with effect from April 3, 2006.

Financial provisions

147.—(1) There shall be paid to the members of the Copyright Tribunal such remuneration (whether by way of salaries or fees), and such allowances, as the Secretary of State with the approval of the Treasury may determine.

(2) The Secretary of State may appoint such staff for the Tribunal as, with the approval of the Treasury as to members and remuneration, he may determine.

(3) The remuneration and allowance of members of the Tribunal, the remuneration of any staff and such other expenses of the Tribunal as the Secretary of State with the approval of the Treasury may determine shall be paid out of money provided by Parliament.

Constitution for purposes of proceedings

148.—(1) For the purposes of any proceedings the Copyright Tribunal shall consist of—

    (a) a chairman, who shall be either the chairman or a deputy chairman of the Tribunal, and

    (b) two or more ordinary members.

(2) If the members of the Tribunal dealing with any matter are not unanimous,

the decision shall be taken by majority vote; and if, in such a case, the votes are equal the chairman shall have a further, casting vote.

(3) Where part of any proceedings before the Tribunal has been heard and one or more members of the Tribunal are unable to continue, the Tribunal shall remain duly constituted for the purpose of those proceedings so long as the number of members is not reduced to less than three.

(4) If the chairman is unable to continue, the chairman of the Tribunal shall—

    (a) appoint one of the remaining members to act as chairman, and

    (b) appoint a suitably qualified person to attend the proceedings and advise the members on any questions of law arising.

(5) A person is "suitably qualified" for the purposes of subsection (4)(b) if he is, or is eligible for appointment as, a deputy chairman of the Tribunal.

Jurisdiction and procedure

Jurisdiction of the Tribunal

149. [The Copyright Tribunal has jurisdiction under this Part] to hear and determine proceedings under—

[(za) section 73 (determination of royalty or other remuneration to be paid with respect to re-transmission of broadcast including work);]

[(zb) section 93C (application to determine amount of equitable remuneration under section 93B);]

    (a) section 118, 119, or 120 (reference of licensing scheme);

    (b) section 121 or 122 (application with respect to entitlement to licence under licensing scheme);

    (c) section 125, 126 or 127 (reference or application with respect to licensing by licensing body:);

[(ca) Section 128B (reference by the Secretary of State under Section 128A);]

[(cc) section 135D or 135E (application or reference with respect to use as of right of sound recordings in broadcasts [...]);]

    (d) section 139 (appeal against order as to coverage of licensing scheme or licence);

    (e) section 142 (application to settle royalty or other sum payable for [lending of certain works]);

    (f) section 144(4) (application to settle terms of copyright licence available as of right).

[(fa) paragraph 7 of Schedule ZA1 (application to determine compensation for use of orphan works).]

Notes:

    (1) Subsection (cc) was inserted by s.175 of the Broadcasting Act 1990 with effect from February 1, 1991 by virtue of the Broadcasting Act 1990 (Commencement No.1 and Transitional Provisions) Order 1990 (SI 1990/2347).

    (2) See A2.i below for Sch.17 to the 1990 Act.

    (3) The opening words of this section and para.(e) were amended by, and para.(zb) inserted by and paras (g) and (h) omitted by the Copyright and Related Rights Regulations 1996 (SI 1996/2967), with effect from December 1, 1996. For savings and transitional provisions, see Part III of those Regulations.

    (4) Subsection (za) was inserted by s.138 and Sch.9 to the Broadcasting Act 1996 with effect from October 1, 1996 by virtue of the Broadcasting Act 1996 (Commencement No.1 and Transitional Provisions) Order 1996 (SI 1996/2120).

    (5) Subsection (ca) was inserted by the Copyright and Related Rights Regulations 2003 (2003/2498), Reg.21(6), with effect from October 31, 2003. For savings and transitional provisions, see Part III of those Regulations.

(6) The words "or cable programme services" repealed from subs.(cc) by the Copyright and Related Rights Regulations 2003 (SI 2003/2498), Sch.2, with effect from October 31, 2003. For savings and transitional provisions, see Part 3 of those Regulations.

(7) Paragraph (fa) inserted by the Copyright and Rights in Performances (Certain Permitted Uses of Orphan Works) Regulations 2014 (SI 2014/2861), reg.3(3), with effect from October 29, 2014.

General power to make rules

150.—(1) The Lord Chancellor may, after consultation with the Lord Advocate, make rules for regulating proceedings before the Copyright Tribunal and, subject to the approval of the Treasury, as to the fees chargeable in respect of such proceedings.

[(2) The rules may apply in relation to the Tribunal, as respects proceedings in England and Wales or Northern Ireland, any of the provisions of Part I the Arbitration Act 1996.]

(3) Provision shall be made by the rules—

(a) prohibiting the Tribunal from entertaining a reference under section 118, 119 or 120 by a representative organisation unless the Tribunal is satisfied that the organisation is reasonably representative of the class of persons which it claims to represent;

(b) specifying the parties to any proceedings and enabling the Tribunal to make a party to the proceedings any person or organisation satisfying the Tribunal that they have a suitable interest in the matter; and

(c) requiring the Tribunal to give the parties to proceedings an opportunity to state their case, in writing or orally as the rules may provide.

(4) The rules may make provision for regulating or prescribing any matters incidental to or consequential upon any appeal from the Tribunal under section 152 (appeal to the court on point of law).

(5) Rules under this section shall be made by statutory instrument which shall be subject to annulment in pursuance of a resolution of either House of Parliament.

Note: Subsection (2) as printed was substituted by the Arbitration Act 1996, with effect from January 31, 1997, by virtue of the Arbitration Act 1996 (Commencement No.1) Order 1996 (SI 1996/3146).

Costs, proof of orders, &c.

151.—(1) The Copyright Tribunal may order that the costs of a party to proceedings before it shall be paid by such other party as the Tribunal may direct; and the Tribunal may tax or settle the amount of the costs, or direct in what manner they are to be taxed.

(2) A document purporting to be a copy of an order of the Tribunal and to be certified by the chairman to be a true copy shall, in any proceedings, be sufficient evidence of the order unless the contrary is proved.

(3) As respects proceedings in Scotland, the Tribunal has the like powers for securing the attendance of witnesses and the production of documents, and with regard to the examination of witnesses on oath, as an arbiter under a submission.

Award of interest

[**151A.**—(1) Any of the following, namely—

(a) a direction under section 123(3) so far as relating to a licence for [communicating a work to the public];

(b) a direction under section 128(3) so far as so relating;

(c) an order under section 135D(1); and

(d) an order under section 135F confirming or varying an order under section 135D(1),

may award simple interest at such rate and for such period, beginning not earlier than the relevant date and ending not later than the date of the order, as the Copyright Tribunal thinks reasonable in the circumstances.

(2) In this section "the relevant date" means—

(a) in relation to a direction under section 123(3), the date on which the reference was made;

(b) in relation to a direction under section 128(3), the date on which the reference or application was made;

(c) in relation to an order [under] section 135D(1), the date on which the first payment under section 135C(2) became due; and

(d) in relation to an order under section 135F, the date on which the application was made.]

Notes:

(1) This section was inserted by s.139(2) of the Broadcasting Act 1996 with effect from November 1, 1996 by virtue of the Broadcasting Act 1996 (Commencement No.1 and Transitional Provisions) Order 1996 (SI 1996/2120).

(2) The word "under" in subs.(2)(c) does not appear in s.139 of the Broadcasting Act 1996.

(3) As to savings and transitional provisions, s.139(3) of the Broadcasting Act 1996 provides:

"(3) *Subsection (2) does not apply in any case where the reference or application to the Copyright Tribunal was or is made before the commencement of this section.*"

(4) In subs.(1)(a), the words in square brackets substituted for the former words "broadcasting a work or including a work in a cable programme service" by the Copyright and Related Rights Regulations 2003 (SI 2003/2498), Sch.1, with effect from October 31, 2003. For savings and transitional provisions, see Part 3 of those Regulations.

Appeals

Appeal to the court on point of law

152.—(1) An appeal lies on any point of law arising from a decision of the Copyright Tribunal to the High Court or, in the case of proceedings of the Tribunal in Scotland, to the Court of Session.

(2) Provision shall be made by rules under section 150 limiting the time within which an appeal may be brought.

(3) Provision may be made by rules under that section—

(a) for suspending, or authorising or requiring the Tribunal to suspend, the operation of orders of the Tribunal in cases where its decision is appealed against;

(b) for modifying in relation to an order of the Tribunal whose operation is suspended the operation of any provision of this Act as to the effect of the order;

(c) for the publication of notices or the taking of other steps for securing that persons affected by the suspension of an order of the Tribunal will be informed of its suspension.

CHAPTER IX

QUALIFICATION FOR AND EXTENT OF COPYRIGHT PROTECTION

Qualification for copyright protection

Qualification for copyright protection

153.—(1) Copyright does not subsist in a work unless the qualification requirements of this Chapter are satisfied as regards—
   (a) the author (see section 154), or
   (b) the country in which the work was first published (see section 155), or
   (c) in the case of a broadcast [...], the country from which the broadcast was made [...] (see section 156).

(2) Subsection (1) does not apply in relation to Crown copyright or Parliamentary copyright (see sections 163 to [166D]) or to copyright subsisting by virtue of section 168 (copyright of certain international organisations).

(3) If the qualification requirements of this Chapter, or section 163, 165 or 168, are once satisfied in respect of a work, copyright does not cease to subsist by reason of any subsequent event.

Notes:
   (1) In subs.(1)(c), the words "or cable programme" and the words "or the cable programme was sent" repealed by the Copyright and Related Rights Regulations 2003 (SI 2003/2498), Sch.2, with effect from October 31, 2003. For savings and transitional provisions, see Part 3 of those Regulations.
   (2) The words in square brackets in s.153(2) substituted by the Government of Wales Act 2006 (c.32), Sch.10 para.25, with effect from May 4, 2007.

Qualification by reference to author

154.—(1) A work qualifies for copyright protection if the author was at the material time a qualifying person, that is—
   (a) a British citizen, [*a national of another EEA state,*] a British Dependent Territories Citizen, a British National (Overseas), a British Overseas Citizen, a British subject or a British protected person within the meaning of the British Nationality Act 1981, or
   (b) an individual domiciled or resident in the United Kingdom or another country to which the relevant provisions of this Part extend, or
   [(b) *an individual domiciled or resident in the United Kingdom or another EEA state or in the Channel Islands, the Isle of Man or Gibraltar or in a country to which the relevant provisions of this Part extend,*]
   (c) a body incorporated under the law of a part of the United Kingdom or of another country to which the relevant provisions of this Part extend.
   [(c) *a body incorporated under the law of a part of the United Kingdom or another EEA state or of the Channel Islands, the Isle of Man or Gibraltar or of a country to which the relevant provisions of this Part extend.*]

(2) Where, or so far as, provision is made by Order under section 159 (application of this Part to countries to which it does not extend), a work also qualifies for copyright protection if at the material time the author was a citizen or subject of, an individual domiciled or resident in, or a body incorporated under the law of, a country to which the Order relates.

(3) A work of joint authorship qualifies for copyright protection if at the material time any of the authors satisfies the requirements of subsection (1) or (2); but

where a work qualifies for copyright protection only under this section, only those authors who satisfy those requirements shall be taken into account for the purposes of—

>   section 11(1) and (2) (first ownership of copyright entitlement of author or author's employer),
>
>   [section 12 (duration of copyright), and section 9(4) (meaning of "unknown authorship") so far as it applies for the purposes of section 12, and]
>
>   section 57 (anonymous or pseudonymous works: acts permitted on assumptions as to expiry of copyright or death of author).

(4) The material time in relation to a literary, dramatic, musical or artistic work is—

> (a) in the case of an unpublished work, when the work was made or, if the making of the work extended over a period, a substantial part of that period;
>
> (b) in the case of a published work, when the work was first published or, if the author had died before that time, immediately before his death.

(5) The material time in relation to other descriptions of work is as follows—

> (a) in the case of a sound recording or film, when it was made;
>
> (b) in the case of a broadcast, when the broadcast was made;
>
> (c) [...]
>
> (d) in the case of the typographical arrangement of a published edition, when the edition was first published.

Notes:

> (1) Subsection (3) is printed as amended by the Duration of Copyright and Rights in Performances Regulations 1995 (SI 1995/3297), with effect from January 1, 1996. For savings and transitional provisions, see Part III of those Regulations.
>
> (2) Subsection (5)(c) was repealed by the Copyright and Related Rights Regulations 2003 (SI 2003/2498), Sch.2, with effect from October 31, 2003. For savings and transitional provisions, see Part 3 of those Regulations.
>
> (3) In subs.(1)(a) words in square brackets prospectively inserted, and subs.(1)(b), (c) in square brackets prospectively substituted for preceding subs.(1)(b), (c), by the Intellectual Property Act 2014, s.22(1), with effect from a date to be appointed.

Qualification by reference to country of first publication

155.—(1) A literary, dramatic, musical or artistic work, a sound recording or film, or the typographical arrangement of a published edition, qualifies for copyright protection if it is first published—

> (a) in the United Kingdom[, *another EEA state, the Channel Islands, the Isle of Man or Gibraltar*], or
>
> (b) in another country [*a country*] to which the relevant provisions of this Part extend.

(2) Where, or so far as, provision is made by Order under section 159 (application of this Part to countries to which it does not extend), such a work also qualifies for copyright protection if it is first published in a country to which the Order relates.

(3) For the purposes of this section, publication in one country shall not be regarded as other than the first publication by reason of simultaneous publication elsewhere; and for this purpose publication elsewhere within the previous 30 days shall be treated as simultaneous.

Note: In subs.(1)(a) words in square brackets prospectively inserted, and in subs.(1)(b) words in square brackets prospectively substituted for "another country", by the Intellectual Property Act 2014, s.22(2), with effect from a date to be appointed.

Qualification by reference to place of transmission

156.—(1) A broadcast qualifies for copyright protection if it is made from [...] a place in—

  (a) the United Kingdom[, *another EEA state, the Channel Islands, the Isle of Man or Gibraltar*], or

  (b) another country [*a country*] to which the relevant provisions of this Part extend.

(2) Where, or so far as, provision is made by Order under section 159 (application of this Part to countries to which it does not extend), a broadcast [...] also qualifies for copyright protection if it is made from [...] a place in a country to which the Order relates.

Notes:

  (1) In subs.(1), the words ", and a cable programme qualifies for copyright protection if it is sent from," and in subs.(2), the words "or cable programme" and "or, as the case may be, sent from" repealed by the Copyright and Related Rights Regulations 2003 (SI 2003/2498), Sch.2, with effect from October 31, 2003. For savings and transitional provisions, see Part 3 of those Regulations.

  (2) In subs.(1)(a) words in square brackets prospectively inserted, and in subs.(1)(b) words in square brackets prospectively substituted for preceding words, by the Intellectual Property Act 2014, s.22(3), with effect from a date to be appointed.

Extent and application of this Part

Countries to which this Part extends

157.—(1) This Part extends to England and Wales, Scotland and Northern Ireland.

(2) Her Majesty may by Order in Council direct that this Part shall extend, subject to such exceptions and modifications as may be specified in the Order, to—

  (a) any of the Channel Islands,

  (b) the Isle of Man, or

  (c) any colony.

(3) That power includes power to extend, subject to such exceptions and modifications as may be specified in the Order, any Order in Council made under the following provisions of this Chapter.

(4) The legislature of a country to which this Part has been extended may modify or add to the provisions of this Part, in their operation as part of the law of that country, as the legislature may consider necessary to adapt the provisions to the circumstances of that country—

  (a) as regards procedure and remedies, or

  (b) as regards works qualifying for copyright protection by virtue of a connection with that country.

(5) Nothing in this section shall be construed as restricting the extent of paragraph 36 of Schedule 1 (transitional provisions: dependent territories where the Copyright Act 1956 or the Copyright Act 1911 remains in force) in relation to the law of a dependent territory to which this Part does not extend.

Countries ceasing to be colonies

158.—(1) The following provisions apply where a country to which this Part has been extended ceases to be a colony of the United Kingdom.

(2) As from the date on which it cases to be a colony it shall cease to be regarded as a country to which this Part extends for the purposes of—

(a) section 160(2)(a) (denial of copyright protection to citizens of countries not giving adequate protection to British works), and

(b) sections 163 and 165 (Crown and Parliamentary copyright).

(3) But it shall continue to be treated as a country to which this Part extends for the purposes of sections 154 to 156 (qualification for copyright protection) until—

(a) an Order in Council is made in respect of that country under section 159 (application of this Part to countries to which it does not extend), or

(b) an Order in Council is made declaring that it shall cease to be so treated by reason of the fact that the provisions of this Part as part of the law of that country have been repealed or amended.

(4) A statutory instrument containing an Order in Council under subsection (3)(b) shall be subject to annulment in pursuance of a resolution of either House of Parliament.

Application of this Part to countries to which it does not extend

159.—(1) Her Majesty may by Order in Council make provision for applying in relation to a country to which this Part does not extend any of the provisions of this Part specified in the Order, so as to secure that those provisions—

(a) apply in relation to persons who are citizens or subjects of that country or are domiciled or resident there, as they apply to persons who are British citizens or are domiciled or resident in the United Kingdom, or

(b) apply in relation to bodies incorporated under the law of that country as they apply in relation to bodies incorporated under the law of a part of the United Kingdom, or

(c) apply in relation to works first published in that country as they apply in relation to works first published in the United Kingdom, or

(d) apply in relation to broadcasts made from [...] that country as they apply in relation to broadcasts made from [...] the United Kingdom.

(2) An Order may make provision for all or any of the matters mentioned in subsection (1) and may—

(a) apply any provisions of this Part subject to such exceptions and modifications as are specified in the Order; and

(b) direct that any provisions of this Part apply either generally or in relation to such classes of works, or other classes of case, as are specified in the Order.

(3) Except in the case of a Convention country or another member State of the European Economic Community, Her Majesty shall not make an Order in Council under this section in relation to a country unless satisfied that provision has been or will be made under the law of that country, in respect of the class of works to which the Order relates, giving adequate protection to the owners of copyright under this Part.

(4) In subsection (3) "Convention country" means a country which is a party to a Convention relating to copyright to which the United Kingdom is also a party.

(5) A statutory instrument containing an Order in Council under this section shall be subject to annulment in pursuance of a resolution of either House of Parliament.

Notes:

(1) In subs.(1)(d), the words "or cable programmes sent from" repealed in both places by the Copyright and Related Rights Regulations 2003 (SI 2003/2498), Sch.2, with effect from October 31, 2003. For savings and transitional provisions, see Part 3 of those Regulations.

(2) Section 159 is prospectively substituted by the Intellectual Property Act 2014, s.22(4), with effect from a date to be appointed. The prospective text is as follows:

Application of this Part to countries to which it does not extend

[159.—*(1) Where a country is a party to the Berne Convention or a member of the World Trade Organisation, this Part, so far as it relates to literary, dramatic, musical and artistic works, films and typographical arrangements of published editions—*

    (a) applies in relation to a citizen or subject of that country or a person domiciled or resident there as it applies in relation to a person who is a British citizen or is domiciled or resident in the United Kingdom,

    (b) applies in relation to a body incorporated under the law of that country as it applies in relation to a body incorporated under the law of a part of the United Kingdom, and

    (c) applies in relation to a work first published in that country as it applies in relation to a work first published in the United Kingdom.

(2) Where a country is a party to the Rome Convention, this Part, so far as it relates to sound recordings and broadcasts—

    (a) applies in relation to that country as mentioned in paragraphs (a), (b) and (c) of subsection (1), and

    (b) applies in relation to a broadcast made from that country as it applies to a broadcast made from the United Kingdom.

(3) Where a country is a party to the WPPT, this Part, so far as relating to sound recordings, applies in relation to that country as mentioned in paragraphs (a), (b) and (c) of subsection (1).

(4) Her Majesty may by Order in Council—

    (a) make provision for the application of this Part to a country by subsection (1), (2) or (3) to be subject to specified restrictions;

    (b) make provision for applying this Part, or any of its provisions, to a specified country;

    (c) make provision for applying this Part, or any of its provisions, to any country of a specified description;

    (d) make provision for the application of legislation to a country under paragraph (b) or (c) to be subject to specified restrictions.

(5) Provision made under subsection (4) may apply generally or in relation to such classes of works, or other classes of case, as are specified.

(6) Her Majesty may not make an Order in Council containing provision under subsection (4)(b) or (c) unless satisfied that provision has been or will be made under the law of the country or countries in question, in respect of the classes to which the provision under subsection (4)(b) or (c) relates, giving adequate protection to the owners of copyright under this Part.

(7) Application under subsection (4)(b) or (c) is in addition to application by subsections (1) to (3).

(8) Provision made under subsection (4)(c) may cover countries that become (or again become) of the specified description after the provision comes into force.

(9) In this section—

    "the Berne Convention" mean any Act of the International Convention for the Protection of Literary and Artistic Works signed at Berne on 9 September 1886;

    "the Rome Convention" means the International Convention for the Protection of Performers, Producers of Phonograms and Broadcasting Organisations done at Rome on 26 October 1961;

"the WPPT" means the World Intellectual Property Organisation Performances and Phonograms Treaty adopted in Geneva on 20 December 1996.

(10) A statutory instrument containing an Order in Council under this section is subject to annulment in pursuance of a resolution of either House of Parliament.]

Denial of copyright protection to citizens of countries not giving adequate protection to British works

160.—(1) If it appears to Her Majesty that the law of a country fails to give adequate protection to British works to which this section applies, or to one or more classes of such works, Her Majesty may make provision by Order in Council in accordance with this section restricting the rights conferred by this Part in relation to works of authors connected with that country.

(2) An Order in Council under this section shall designate the country concerned and provide that, for the purposes specified in the Order, works first published after a date specified in the Order shall not be treated as qualifying for copyright protection by virtue of such publication if at that time the authors are—

(a) citizens or subjects of that country (not domiciled or resident in the United Kingdom or another country to which the relevant provisions of this Part extend), or

(b) bodies incorporated under the law of that country;

and the Order may make such provision for all the purposes of this Part or for such purposes as are specified in the Order, and either generally or in relation to such class of cases as are specified in the Order, having regard to the nature and extent of that failure referred to in subsection (1).

(3) This section applies to literary, dramatic, musical and artistic works, sound recordings and films; and "British works" means works of which the author was a qualifying person at the material time within the meaning of section 154.

(4) A statutory instrument containing an Order in Council under this section shall be subject to annulment in pursuance of a resolution of either House of Parliament.

Supplementary

Territorial waters and the continental shelf

161.—(1) For the purposes of this Part the territorial waters of the United Kingdom shall be treated as part of the United Kingdom.

(2) This Part applies to things done in the United Kingdom sector of the continental shelf on a structure or vessel which is present there for purposes directly connected with the exploration of the sea bed or subsoil or the exploitation of their natural resources as it applies to things done in the United Kingdom.

(3) The United Kingdom sector of the continental shelf means the areas designated by order under section 1(7) of the Continental Shelf Act 1964.

British ships, aircraft and hovercraft

162.—(1) This Part applies to things done on a British ship, aircraft or hovercraft as it applies to things done in the United Kingdom.

(2) In this section—

"British ship" means a ship which is a British ship for the purposes of the [Merchant Shipping Act 1995] otherwise than by virtue of registration in a country outside the United Kingdom; and

"British aircraft" and "British hovercraft" mean an aircraft or hovercraft registered in the United Kingdom.

Note: Subsection (2) is printed as amended by the Merchant Shipping Act 1995.

CHAPTER X

MISCELLANEOUS AND GENERAL

Crown and Parliamentary copyright

Crown copyright

163.—(1) Where a work is made by Her Majesty or by an officer or servant of the Crown in the course of his duties—

(a) the work qualifies for copyright protection notwithstanding section 153(1) (ordinary requirement as to qualification for copyright protection), and

(b) Her Majesty is the first owner of any copyright in the work.

[(1A) ...]

(2) Copyright in such a work is referred to in this Part as "Crown copyright", notwithstanding that it may be, or have been, assigned to another person.

(3) Crown copyright in a literary, dramatic, musical or artistic work continues to subsist—

(a) until the end of the period of 125 years from the end of the calendar year in which the work was made, or

(b) if the work is published commercially before the end of the period of 75 years from the end of the calendar year in which it was made, until the end of the period of 50 years from the end of the calendar year in which it was first so published.

(4) In the case of a work of joint authorship where one or more but not all of the authors are persons falling within subsection (1), this section applies only in relation to those authors and the copyright subsisting by virtue of their contribution to the work.

(5) Except as mentioned above, and subject to any express exclusion elsewhere in this Part, the provisions of this Part apply in relation to Crown copyright as to other copyright.

(6) This section does not apply to a work if, or to the extent that, Parliamentary copyright subsists in the work (see sections 165 and [166D]).

Notes:

(1) Section 163(1A) was omitted and the words in square brackets in s.163(6) substituted by the Government of Wales Act 2006 (c.32), Sch.10 para.26, with effect from May 4, 2007. Subsection (1A) previously read:

"(1A) *For the purposes of this section works made by Her Majesty include any sound recording, film [or live broadcast] of the proceedings of the National Assembly for Wales (including proceedings of a committee of the Assembly or of a subcommittee of such a committee) which is made by or under the direction or control of the Assembly; but a work shall not be regarded as made by or under the direction or control of the Assembly by reason only of its being commissioned by or on behalf of the Assembly.*"

(2) The words in internal square brackets in old subs.(1A) substituted for the former words ", live broadcast or live cable programme" by the Copyright and Related Rights Regulations 2003 (SI 2003/2498), Sch.1, para.11, with effect from October 31, 2003. For savings and transitional provisions, see Part 3 of those Regulations.

Copyright in Acts and Measures

164.—(1) Her Majesty is entitled to copyright in every Act of Parliament [, Act of the Scottish Parliament][, [Measure of the National Assembly for Wales, Act of the National Assembly for Wales,] Act of the Northern Ireland Assembly] or Measure of the General Synod of the Church of England.

(2) The copyright subsists[—]

[(a) in the case of an Act or a Measure of the General Synod of the Church of England, until the end of the period of 50 years from the end of the calendar year in which Royal Assent was given, and

(b) in the case of a Measure of the National Assembly for Wales, until the end of the period of 50 years from the end of the calendar year in which the Measure was approved by Her Majesty in Council.]

(3) References in this Part to Crown copyright (except in section 163) include copyright under this section; and, except as mentioned above, the provisions of this Part apply in relation to copyright under this section as to other Crown copyright.

(4) No other copyright, or right in the nature of copyright, subsists in an Act or Measure.

Notes:

(1) The words in the first set of square brackets in subs.(1) inserted by the Scotland Act 1998, s.125, Sch.8, para.25, with effect from May 6, 1999 (Scotland Act 1998 (Commencement) Order 1998 (SI 1998/3178))

(2) The words "Measure of the National Assembly for Wales, Act of the National Assembly for Wales," in s.164(1) inserted and the words in square brackets in s.164(2) substituted by the Government of Wales Act 2006 (c.32), Sch.10 para.27, with effect from May 4, 2007.

(3) The words in "Act of the Northern Ireland Assembly" inserted by the Northern Ireland Act 1998, s.99, Sch.13, para.8, with effect from December 2, 1999 (Northern Ireland Act 1998 (Commencement No.5) Order 1999 (SI 1999/3209)).

Parliamentary copyright

165.—(1) Where a work is made by or under the direction or control of the House of Commons or the House of Lords—

(a) the work qualifies for copyright protection notwithstanding section 153(1) (ordinary requirement as to qualification for copyright protection), and

(b) the House by whom, or under whose direction or control, the work is made is the first owner of any copyright in the work, and if the work is made by or under the direction or control of both Houses, the two Houses are joint first owners of copyright.

(2) Copyright in such a work is referred to in this Part as "Parliamentary copyright", notwithstanding that it may be, or have been, assigned to another person.

(3) Parliamentary copyright in a literary, dramatic, musical or artistic work continues to subsist until the end of the period of 50 years from the end of the calendar year in which the work was made.

(4) For the purposes of this section, works made by or under the direction or control of the House of Commons or the House of Lords include—

(a) any work made by an officer or employee of that House in the course of his duties, and

(b) any sound recording, film [or live broadcast] of the proceedings of that House;

but a work shall not be regarded as made by or under the direction or control of either House by reason only of its being commissioned by or on behalf of that House.

(5) In the case of a work of joint authorship where one or more but not all of the authors are acting on behalf of, or under the direction or control of, the House of Commons or the House of Lords, this section applies only in relation to those authors and the copyright subsisting by virtue of their contribution to the work.

(6) Except as mentioned above, and subject to any express exclusion elsewhere in this Part, the provisions of this Part apply in relation to Parliamentary copyright as to other copyright.

(7) The provisions of this section also apply, subject to any exceptions or modifications specified by Order in Council, to works made by or under the direction or control of any other legislative body of a country to which this Part extends; and references in this Part to "Parliamentary copyright" shall be construed accordingly.

(8) A statutory instrument containing an Order in Council under subsection (7) shall be subject to annulment in pursuance of a resolution of either House of Parliament.

Copyright in Parliamentary Bills

166.—(1) Copyright in every Bill introduced into Parliament belongs, in accordance with the following provisions, to one or both of the Houses of Parliament.

(2) Copyright in a public Bill belongs in the first instance to the House into which the Bill is introduced, and after the Bill has been carried to the second House to both Houses jointly, and subsists from the time when the text of the Bill is handed in to the House in which it is introduced.

(3) Copyright in a private Bill belongs to both Houses jointly and subsists from the time when a copy of the Bill is first deposited in either House.

(4) Copyright in a personal Bill belongs in the first instance to the House of Lords, and after the Bill has been carried to the House of Commons to both Houses jointly, and subsists from the time when it is given a First Reading in the House of Lords.

(5) Copyright under this section ceases—
    (a) on Royal Assent, or
    (b) if the Bill does not receive Royal Assent, on the withdrawal or rejection of the Bill or the end of the Session.

Provided that, copyright in a Bill continues to subsist notwithstanding its rejection in any Session by the House of Lords if, by virtue of the Parliament Acts 1911 and 1949, it remains possible for it to be presented for Royal Assent in that Session.

(6) References in this Part to Parliamentary copyright (except in section 165) include copyright under this section; and, except as mentioned above, the provisions of this Part apply in relation to copyright under this section as to other Parliamentary copyright.

(7) No other copyright, or right in the nature of copyright, subsists in a Bill after copyright has once subsisted under this section; but without prejudice to the subsequent operation of this section in relation to a Bill which, not having passed in one Session, is reintroduced in a subsequent Session.

Copyright in Bills of the Scottish Parliament.

[**166A.**—(1) Copyright in every Bill introduced into the Scottish Parliament belongs to the Scottish Parliamentary Corporate Body.

(2) Copyright under this section subsists from the time when the text of the Bill is handed in to the Parliament for introduction—

(a) until the Bill receives Royal Assent, or

(b) if the Bill does not receive Royal Assent, until it is withdrawn or rejected or no further parliamentary proceedings may be taken in respect of it.

(3) References in this Part to Parliamentary copyright (except in section 165) include copyright under this section; and, except as mentioned above, the provisions of this Part apply in relation to copyright under this section as to other Parliamentary copyright.

(4) No other copyright, or right in the nature of copyright, subsists in a Bill after copyright has once subsisted under this section; but without prejudice to the subsequent operation of this section in relation to a Bill which, not having received Royal Assent, is later reintroduced into the Parliament.]

Note: This section was inserted by the Scotland Act 1998, s.125, Sch.8, para.25, with effect from May 6, 1999 (Scotland Act 1998 (Commencement) Order 1998 (SI 1998/3178)).

Copyright in Bills of the Northern Ireland Assembly.

[**166B.**—(1) Copyright in every Bill introduced into the Northern Ireland Assembly belongs to the Northern Ireland Assembly Commission.

(2) Copyright under this section subsists from the time when the text of the Bill is handed in to the Assembly for introduction—

(a) until the Bill receives Royal Assent, or

(b) if the Bill does not receive Royal Assent, until it is withdrawn or rejected or no further proceedings of the Assembly may be taken in respect of it.

(3) References in this Part to Parliamentary copyright (except in section 165) include copyright under this section; and, except as mentioned above, the provisions of this Part apply in relation to copyright under this section as to other Parliamentary copyright.

(4) No other copyright, or right in the nature of copyright, subsists in a Bill after copyright has once subsisted under this section; but without prejudice to the subsequent operation of this section in relation to a Bill which, not having received Royal Assent, is later reintroduced into the Assembly.]

Note: This section was inserted by the Northern Ireland Act 1998, s.99, Sch.13, para.8, with effect from December 2, 1999 (Northern Ireland Act 1998 (Commencement No.5) Order 1999 (SI 1999/3209)).

Copyright in proposed Measures of the National Assembly for Wales

[**166C.**—(1) Copyright in every proposed Assembly Measure introduced into the National Assembly for Wales belongs to the National Assembly for Wales Commission.

(2) Copyright under this section subsists from the time when the text of the proposed Assembly Measure is handed in to the Assembly for introduction—

(a) until the proposed Assembly Measure is approved by Her Majesty in Council, or

(b) if the proposed Assembly Measure is not approved by Her Majesty in Council, until it is withdrawn or rejected or no further proceedings of the Assembly may be taken in respect of it.

(3) References in this Part to Parliamentary copyright (except in section 165) include copyright under this section; and, except as mentioned above, the provisions of this Part apply in relation to copyright under this section as to other Parliamentary copyright.

(4) No other copyright, or right in the nature of copyright, subsists in a

proposed Assembly Measure after copyright has once subsisted under this section; but without prejudice to the subsequent operation of this section in relation to a proposed Assembly Measure which, not having been approved by Her Majesty in Council, is later reintroduced into the Assembly.]

Note: This section was inserted by the Government of Wales Act 2006 c. 32 Sch.10 para.28, with effect from May 4, 2007.

Copyright in Bills of the National Assembly for Wales

[166D.—(1) Copyright in every Bill introduced into the National Assembly for Wales belongs to the National Assembly for Wales Commission.

(2) Copyright under this section subsists from the time when the text of the Bill is handed in to the Assembly for introduction—

(a) until the Bill receives Royal Assent, or

(b) if the Bill does not receive Royal Assent, until it is withdrawn or rejected or no further proceedings of the Assembly may be taken in respect of it.

(3) References in this Part to Parliamentary copyright (except in section 165) include copyright under this section; and, except as mentioned above, the provisions of this Part apply in relation to copyright under this section as to other Parliamentary copyright.

(4) No other copyright, or right in the nature of copyright, subsists in a Bill after copyright has once subsisted under this section; but without prejudice to the subsequent operation of this section in relation to a Bill which, not having received Royal Assent, is later reintroduced into the Assembly.]

Note: This section was inserted by the Government of Wales Act 2006 c. 32 Sch.10 para.28, with effect from May 4, 2007.

Houses of Parliament: supplementary provisions with respect to copyright

167.—(1) For the purposes of holding, dealing with and enforcing copyright, and in connection with all legal proceedings relating to copyright, each House of Parliament shall be treated as having the legal capacities of a body corporate, which shall not be affected by a prorogation or dissolution.

(2) The functions of the House of Commons as owner of copyright shall be exercised by the Speaker on behalf of the House; and if so authorised by the Speaker, or in case of a vacancy in the office of Speaker, those functions may be discharged by the Chairman of Ways and Means or a Deputy Chairman.

(3) For this purpose a person who on the dissolution of Parliament was Speaker of the House of Commons, Chairman of Ways and Means or a Deputy Chairman may continue to act until the corresponding appointment is made in the next Session of Parliament.

(4) The functions of the House of Lords as owner of copyright shall be exercised by the Clerk of the Parliaments on behalf of the House, and if so authorised by him, or in case of a vacancy in the office of Clerk of the Parliaments, those functions may be discharged by the Clerk Assistant or the Reading Clerk.

(5) Legal proceedings relating to copyright—

(a) shall be brought by or against the House of Commons in the name of "The Speaker of the House of Commons"; and

(b) shall be brought by or against the House of Lords in the name of "The Clerk of the Parliaments".

Other miscellaneous provisions

Copyright vesting in certain international organisations

168.—(1) Where an original literary, dramatic, musical or artistic work—

    (a) is made by an officer or employee of, or is published by, an international organisation to which this section applies, and

    (b) does not qualify for copyright protection under section 154 (qualification by reference to author) or section 155 (qualification by reference to country of first publication),

copyright nevertheless subsists in the work by virtue of this section and the organisation is first owner of that copyright.

(2) The international organisations to which this section applies are those as to which Her Majesty has by Order in Council declared that it is expedient that this section should apply.

(3) Copyright of which an international organisation is first owner by virtue of this section continues to subsist until the end of the period of 50 years from the end of the calendar year in which the work was made or such longer period as may be specified by Her Majesty by Order in Council for the purpose of complying with the international obligations of the United Kingdom.

(4) An international organisation to which this section applies shall be deemed to have, and to have had at all material times, the legal capacities of a body corporate for the purpose of holding, dealing with and enforcing copyright and in connection with all legal proceedings relating to copyright.

(5) A statutory instrument containing an Order in Council under this section shall be subject to annulment in pursuance of a resolution of either House of Parliament.

Folklore, &c.: anonymous unpublished works

169.—(1) Where in the case of an unpublished literary, dramatic, musical or artistic work of unknown authorship there is evidence that the author (or, in the case of a joint work, any of the authors) was a qualifying individual by connection with a country outside the United Kingdom, it shall be presumed until the contrary is proved that he was such a qualifying individual and that copyright accordingly subsists in the work, subject to the provisions of this Part.

(2) If under the law of that country a body is appointed to protect and enforce copyright in such works, Her Majesty may by Order in Council designate that body for the purposes of this section.

(3) A body so designated shall be recognised in the United Kingdom as having authority to do in place of the copyright owner anything, other than assign copyright, which it is empowered to do under the law of that country; and it may, in particular, bring proceedings in its own name.

(4) A statutory instrument containing an Order in Council under this section shall be subject to annulment in pursuance of a resolution of either House of Parliament.

(5) In subsection (1) a "qualifying individual" means an individual who at the material time (within the meaning of section 154) was a person whose works qualified under that section for copyright protection.

(6) This section does not apply if there has been an assignment of copyright in the work by the author of which notice has been given to the designated body, and nothing in this section affects the validity of an assignment of copyright made, or licence granted, by the author or a person lawfully claiming under him.

Transitional provisions and savings

Transitional provisions and savings

170.—(1) Schedule 1 contains transitional provisions and savings relating to works made, and acts or events occurring, before the commencement of this Part, and otherwise with respect to the operation of the provisions of this Part.

(2) The Secretary of State may by regulations amend Schedule 1 to reduce the duration of copyright in existing works which are unpublished, other than photographs or films.

(3) The regulations may provide for the copyright to expire—

(a) with the end of the term of protection of copyright laid down by Directive 2006/116/EC or at any later time;

(b) subject to that, on the commencement of the regulations or at any later time.

(4) "Existing works" has the same meaning as in Schedule 1.

(5) Regulations under subsection (2) may—

(a) make different provision for different purposes;

(b) make supplementary or transitional provision;

(c) make consequential provision, including provision amending any enactment or subordinate legislation passed or made before that subsection comes into force.

(6) The power to make regulations under subsection (2) is exercisable by statutory instrument.

(7) A statutory instrument containing regulations under subsection (2) may not be made unless a draft of the instrument has been laid before and approved by resolution of each House of Parliament."

Note: Section 170 renumbered as s.170(1) and subss (2)–(7) inserted by the Enterprise and Regulatory Reform Act 2013 s.76, with effect from April 25, 2013.

Rights and privileges under other enactments or the common law

171.—(1) Nothing in this Part affects—

(a) any right or privilege of any person under any enactment (except where the enactment is expressly repealed, amended or modified by this Act);

(b) any right or privilege of the Crown subsisting otherwise than under an enactment;

(c) any right or privilege of either House of Parliament;

(d) the right of the Crown or any person deriving title from the Crown to sell, use or otherwise deal with articles forfeited under the laws relating to customs and excise;

(e) the operation of any rule of equity relating to breaches of trust or confidence.

(2) Subject to those savings, no copyright or right in the nature of copyright shall subsist otherwise than by virtue of this Part or some other enactment in that behalf.

(3) Nothing in this Part affects any rule of law preventing or restricting the enforcement of copyright, on grounds of public interest or otherwise.

(4) Nothing in this Part affects any right of action or other remedy, whether civil or criminal, available otherwise than under this Part in respect of acts infringing any of the rights conferred by Chapter IV (moral rights).

(5) The savings in subsection (1) have effect subject to section 164(4) and section 166(7) (copyright in Acts, Measures and Bills: exclusion of other rights in the nature of copyright).

Interpretation

General provisions as to construction

172.—(1) This Part restates and amends the law of copyright, that is, the provisions of the Copyright Act 1956, as amended.

(2) A provision of this Part which corresponds to a provision of the previous law shall not be construed as departing from the previous law merely because of a change of expression.

(3) Decisions under the previous law may be referred to for the purpose of establishing whether a provision of this Part departs from the previous law, or otherwise for establishing the true construction of this Part.

Meaning of EEA and related expressions

[**172A.**—[(1) In this Part—
  "the EEA" means the European Economic Area; and
  "EEA state" means a member State, Iceland, Liechtenstein or Norway.]

(2) References in this Part to a person being [a national of an EEA State] shall be construed in relation to a body corporate as references to its being incorporated under the law of an EEA state.

(3) [...]]]

Notes:

(1) This section was inserted by the Duration of Copyright and Rights in Performances Regulations 1995 (SI 1995/3297), with effect from January 1, 1996.

(2) This section is printed as amended by the Copyright and Related Rights Regulations 1996 (SI 1996/2967), which added the definition of "The EEA" with effect from December 1, 1996.

(3) Subsection (1) was substituted, in subs.(2) the words in square brackets substituted for the former words "an EEA national" and subs.(3) was repealed by the Intellectual Property (Enforcement, etc.) Regulations 2006 (SI 2006/1028), Sch.2 para.8 and Sch.4, with effect from April 29, 2006. Subsection (3) formerly read:

  "(3) *The "EEA Agreement" means the Agreement on the European Economic Area signed at Oporto on 2nd May 1992, as adjusted by the Protocol signed at Brussels on 17th March 1993.*"

Construction of references to copyright owner

173.—(1) Where different persons are (whether in consequence of a partial assignment or otherwise) entitled to different aspects of copyright in a work, the copyright owner for any purpose of this Part is the person who is entitled to the aspect of copyright relevant for that purpose.

(2) Where copyright (or any aspect of copyright) is owned by more than one person jointly, references in this Part to the copyright owner are to all the owners, so that, in particular, any requirement of the licence of the copyright owner requires the licence of all of them.

Meaning of "educational establishment" and related expressions

174.—(1) The expression "educational establishment" in a provision of this Part means—
  (a) any school, and
  (b) any other description of educational establishment specified for the purposes of this Part, or that provision, by order of the Secretary of State.

(2) The Secretary of State may by order provide that the provisions of this

Part relating to educational establishments shall apply, with such modifications and adaptations as may be specified in the order, in relation to teachers who are employed by a [local authority (as defined in section 579(1) of the Education Act 1996) or (in Northern Ireland) a local education authority,] to give instruction elsewhere to pupils who are unable to attend an educational establishment.

(3) In subsection (1)(a)"school" —

(a) in relation to England and Wales, has the same meaning as in the [Education Act 1996];

(b) in relation to Scotland, has the same meaning as in the Education (Scotland) Act 1962, except that it includes an approved school within the meaning of the Social Work (Scotland) Act 1968; and

(c) in relation to Northern Ireland, has the same meaning as in the Education and Libraries (Northern Ireland) Order 1986.

(4) An order under subsection (1)(b) may specify a description of educational establishment by reference to the instruments from time to time in force under any enactment specified in the order.

(5) In relation to an educational establishment the expressions "teacher" and "pupil" in this Part include, respectively, any person who gives and any person who receives instruction.

(6) References in this Part to anything being done "on behalf of" an educational establishment are to its being done for the purposes of that establishment by any person.

(7) An order under this section shall be made by statutory instrument which shall be subject to annulment in pursuance of a resolution of either House of Parliament.

Notes:

(1) Subsection (3)(a) is printed as amended by the Education Act 1996 with effect from November 1, 1996, by virtue of the Education Act 1996 (Commencement No.1) Order 1996 (SI 1996/2904).

(2) The words in square brackets in subs.(2) substituted for the former words "local education authority" by the Local Education Authorities and Children's Services Authorities (Integration of Functions) Order 2010 (SI 2010/1158) Sch.2 para.36 with effect from May 5, 2010.

Meaning of publication and commercial publication

175.—(1) In this Part "publication", in relation to a work—

(a) means the issue of copies to the public, and

(b) includes, in the case of a literary, dramatic, musical or artistic work, making it available to the public by means of an electronic retrieval system;

and related expressions shall be construed accordingly.

(2) In this Part "commercial publication", in relation to a literary, dramatic, musical or artistic work means—

(a) issuing copies of the work to the public at a time when copies made in advance of the receipt of orders are generally available to the public, or

(b) making the work available to the public by means of an electronic retrieval system; and related expressions shall be construed accordingly.

(3) In the case of a work of architecture in the form of a building, or an artistic work incorporated in a building, construction of the building shall be treated as equivalent to publication of the work.

(4) The following do not constitute publication for the purposes of this Part and references to commercial publication shall be construed accordingly—

   (a) in the case of a literary, dramatic or musical work—
      (i) the performance of the work, or
      (ii) the [communication to the public of the work] (otherwise than for the purposes of an electronic retrieval system);
   (b) in the case of an artistic work—
      (i) the exhibition of the work,
      (ii) the issue to the public of copies of a graphic work representing, or of photographs of, a work of architecture in the form of a building or a model for a building, a sculpture or a work of artistic craftsmanship.
      (iii) the issue to the public of copies of a film including the work, or
      (iv) the [communication to the public of the work] (otherwise than for the purposes of an electronic retrieval system);
   (c) in the case of a sound recording or film—
      (i) the work being played or shown in public, or
      (ii) the [communication to the public of the work].

(5) References in this Part to publication or commercial publication do not include publication which is merely colourable and not intended to satisfy the reasonable requirements of the public.

(6) No account shall be taken for the purposes of this section of any unauthorised act.

Note: The words in square brackets in subs.(4)(a)(ii), (b)(iv) and (c)(ii) substituted for the former words "broadcasting of the work or its inclusion in a cable programme service" by the Copyright and Related Rights Regulations 2003 (SI 2003/2498), Sch.1, para.6, with effect from October 31, 2003. For savings and transitional provisions, see Part 3 of those Regulations.

Requirement of signature: application in relation to body corporate

176.—(1) The requirement in the following provisions that an instrument be signed by or on behalf of a person is also satisfied in the case of a body corporate by the affixing of its seal—
    section 78(3)(b) (assertion by licensor of right to identification of author in case of public exhibition of copy made in pursuance of the licence),
    section 90(3) (assignment of copyright),
    section 91(1) (assignment of future copyright),
    section 92(1) (grant of exclusive licence).

(2) The requirement in the following provisions that an instrument be signed by a person is satisfied in the case of a body corporate by signature on behalf of the body or by the affixing of its seal—
    section 78(2)(b) (assertion by instrument in writing of right to have author identified),
    section 87(2) (waiver of moral rights).

Adaptation of expressions for Scotland

177. In the application of this Part to Scotland—
    "account of profits" means accounting and payment of profits;
    "accounts" means count, reckoning and payment;
    "assignment" means assignation;
    "costs" means expenses;
    "defendant" means defender;
    "delivery up" means delivery;

"estoppel" means personal bar;
"injunction" means interdict;
"interlocutory relief" means interim remedy; and
"plaintiff" means pursuer.

Minor definitions

178. In this Part—

"article", in the context of an article in a periodical, includes an item of any description;

"business" includes a trade or profession;

"collective work" means—

(a) a work of joint authorship, or

(b) a work in which there are distinct contributions by different authors or in which works or parts of works of different authors are incorporated;

"computer-generated", in relation to a work, means that the work is generated by computer in circumstances such that there is no human author of the work;

"country" includes any territory;

"the Crown" includes the Crown in right [of the Scottish Administration [, of the Welsh [...] Government] or of] Her Majesty's Government in Northern Ireland or in any country outside the United Kingdom to which this Part extends;

"electronic" means actuated by electric, magnetic, electro-magnetic, electro-chemical or electro-mechanical energy, and "in electronic form" means in a form usable only by electronic means;

"employed", "employee", "employer" and "employment" refer to employment under a contract of service or of apprenticeship;

"facsimile copy" includes a copy which is reduced or enlarged in scale;

"international organisation" means an organisation the members of which include one or more states;

"judicial proceedings" includes proceedings before any court, tribunal or person having authority to decide any matter affecting a person's legal rights or liabilities;

"parliamentary proceedings" includes proceedings of the Northern Ireland Assembly [...] [of the Scottish Parliament] or of the European Parliament [and Assembly proceedings within the meaning of section 1(5) of the Government of Wales Act 2006];

["private study" does not include any study which is directly or indirectly for a commercial purpose;]

["producer", in relation to a sound recording or a film, means the person by whom the arrangements necessary for the making of the sound recording or film are undertaken;]

["public library" means a library administered by or on behalf of—

(a) in England and Wales, a library authority within the meaning of the Public Libraries and Museums Act 1964;

(b) in Scotland, a statutory library authority within the meaning of the Public Libraries (Scotland) Act 1955;

(c) in Northern Ireland, an Education and Library Board within the meaning of the Education and Libraries (Northern Ireland) Order 1986;]

["rental right" means the right of a copyright owner to authorise or prohibit the rental of copies of the work (see section 18A);]

"reprographic copy" and "reprographic copying" refer to copying by means
of a reprographic process;

"reprographic process" means a process—

(a) for making facsimile copies, or

(b) involving the use of an appliance for making multiple copies,

and includes, in relation to a work held in electronic form, any copying by
electronic means, but does not include the making of a film or sound recording;

"sufficient acknowledgement" means an acknowledgement identifying the
work in question by its title or other description, and identifying the
author unless—

(a) in the case of a published work, it is published anonymously;

(b) in the case of an unpublished work, it is not possible for a
person to ascertain the identity of the author by reasonable inquiry;

"sufficient disclaimer", in relation to an act capable of infringing the right
conferred by section 80 (right to object to derogatory treatment of
work), means a clear and reasonably prominent indication—

(a) given at the time of the act, and

(b) if the author or director is then identified, appearing along
with identification,

that the work has been subjected to treatment to which the author or director has not consented;

"telecommunications system" means a system for conveying visual images, sounds or other information by electronic means;

"typeface" includes an ornamental motif used in printing;

"unauthorised", as regards anything done in relation to a work, means done
otherwise than—

(a) by or with the licence of the copyright owner, or

(b) if copyright does not subsist in the work, by or with the
licence of the author or, in a case where section 11(2) would
have applied, the author's employer or, in either case, persons
lawfully claiming under him, or

(c) in pursuance of section 48 (copying, &c. of certain material by the Crown);

["wireless broadcast" means a broadcast by means of wireless telegraphy;]

"wireless telegraphy" means the sending of electro-magnetic energy over
paths not provided by a material substance constructed or arranged
for that purpose [but does not include the transmission of microwave
energy between terrestrial fixed points];

"writing" includes any form of notation or code, whether by hand or
otherwise and regardless of the method by which, or medium in or on
which, it is recorded, and "written" shall be construed accordingly.

Notes:

(1) The definition of "wireless telegraphy" is printed as amended by the Copyright
and Related Rights Regulations 1996 (SI 1996/2967), with effect from December
1, 1996. For savings and transitional provisions, see Part III of those Regulations.

(2) The definition of "rental" was deleted, and those of "public library", "producer"
and "rental right" inserted by the Copyright and Related Rights Regulations 1996
(SI 1996/2967), with effect from December 1, 1996.

(3) The words in square brackets in the definition of "the Crown" and in the second set of square brackets in the definition of "parliamentary proceedings" inserted by the Scotland Act 1998, s.125, Sch.8, para.25, with effect from May 6, 1999 (Scotland Act 1998 (Commencement) Order 1998 (SI 1998/3178)).

(4) The words "or the new Northern Ireland Assembly" omitted from the definition of "parliamentary proceedings" repealed by the Northern Ireland Act 1998, s.99, Sch.13, para.8, with effect from December 2, 1999 (Northern Ireland Act 1998 (Commencement No.5) Order 1999 (SI 1999/3209)), those words having previously been inserted by the Northern Ireland (Elections) Act 1998.

(5) The definitions of "private study" and "wireless broadcast" inserted by the Copyright and Related Rights Regulations 2003 (SI 2003/2498), Sch.1, para.15, with effect from October 31, 2003. For savings and transitional provisions, see Part 3 of those Regulations.

(6) The words in the internal square brackets in the definition of "the Crown" and the words in square brackets at the end of the definition of "parliamentary proceedings" inserted by the Government of Wales Act 2006 (c.32), Sch.10 para.29, with effect from May 4, 2007.

(7) In definition "the Crown", word "Assembly" repealed by the Government of Wales Act 2006, Sch.10 para.29, with effect from February 17, 2015 (commenced by an amendment).

Index of defined expressions

179. The following Table shows provisions defining or otherwise explaining expressions used in this Part (other than provisions defining or explaining an expression used only in the same section—

[accessible copy (in sections 31A to 31F)	section 31F(4)]
account of profits and accounts (in Scotland)	section 177
acts restricted by copyright	section 16(1)
adaptation	section 21(3)
[...]	[...]
[archivist (in sections 40A to 43)	section 43A(5),]
article (in a periodical)	section 178
artistic work	section 4(1)
assignment (in Scotland)	section 177
author	sections 9 and 10(3)
[authorised body (in sections 31B to 31BB)	section 31F(6)]
broadcast (and related expressions)	section 6
building	section 4(2)
business	section 178
collective work	section 178
commencement (in Schedule 1)	paragraph 1(2) of that Schedule
commercial publication	section 175
[communication to the public	section 20]
computer-generated	section 178
[conducted for profit (in sections 40A to 43)	section 43A(4),]
copy and copying	section 17
copyright (in Schedule 1)	paragraph 2(2) of that Schedule
copyright owner	sections 101(2) and 173
Copyright Tribunal	section 145
copyright work	section 1(2)

costs (in Scotland)	section 177
country	section 178
[country of origin	section 15A]
the Crown	section 178
Crown copyright	sections 163(2) and 164(3)
[curator (in sections 40A to 43)	section 43A(5),]
[database	section 3A(1)]
defendant (in Scotland)	section 177
delivery up (in Scotland)	section 177
[disabled person (in sections 31A to 31F)	section 31F(2) and (3)]
dramatic work	section 3(1)
the EEA, EEA state and national of an EEA state	section 172A]
educational establishment	sections 174(1) to (4)
electronic and electronic form	section 178
employed, employee, employer and employment	section 178
exclusive licence	section 92(1)
existing works (in Schedule 1)	paragraph 1(3) of that Schedule
facsimile copy	section 178
film	[section 5B]
future copyright	section 91(2)
general licence (in sections 140 and 141)	section 140(7)
graphic work	section 4(2)
infringing copy	section 27
injunction (in Scotland)	section 177
interlocutory relief (in Scotland)	section 177
international organisation	section 178
issue of copies to the public	[section 18]
joint authorship (work of)	section 10(1) and (2)
judicial proceedings	section 178
[lawful user (in sections 50A to 50C)	section 50A(2)]
[lending	section 18A(2) to (6)]
[librarian (in sections 40A to 43)	section 43A(5),]
[library (in sections 40A to 43)	section 43A(2),]
licence (in sections 125 to 128)	section 124
licence of copyright owner	sections 90(4), 91(3) and 173
licensing body (in Chapter VII)	section 116(2)
licensing scheme (generally)	section 116(1)
licensing scheme (in sections 118 to 121)	section 117
literary work	section 3(1)
made (in relation to a literary, dramatic or musical work)	section 3(2)
[museum (in sections 40A to 43)	section 43A(3),]
musical work	section 3(1)
[needletime	section 135A]

the new copyright provisions (in Schedule 1)	paragraph 1(1) of that Schedule
the 1911 Act (in Schedule 1)	paragraph 1(1) of that Schedule
the 1956 Act (in Schedule 1)	paragraph 1(1) of that Schedule
on behalf of (in relation to an educational establishment)	section 174(5)
[original (in relation to a database)	section 3A(2)]
Parliamentary copyright	sections 165(2) and (7), [166(6) [, 166A(3) [166B(3) 166C(3) and 166D(3)]]]
Parliamentary proceedings	section 178
performance	section 19(2)
photograph	section 4(2)
plaintiff (in Scotland)	section 177
[...]	[...]
[private study	section 178]
[producer (in relation to a sound recording or film)	section 178]
programme (in the context of broadcasting)	section 6(3)
prospective owner (of copyright)	section 91(2)
publication and related expressions	section 175
[public library	section 178]
published edition (in the context of copyright in the typographical arrangement)	section 8
pupil	section 174(5)
rental	[section 18A(2) to (6)]
[rental right	section 178]
reprographic copies and reprographic copying	section 178
reprographic process	section 178
sculpture	section 4(2)
signed	section 176
sound recording	[sections 5A and 135A]
sufficient acknowledgement	section 178
sufficient disclaimer	section 178
[supply (in sections 31B to 31BB)	section 31F(7)]
teacher	section 174(5)
telecommunications system	section 178
[terms of payment	section 135A]
typeface	section 178
unauthorised (as regards things done in relation to a work)	section 178
unknown (in relation to the author of a work)	section 9(5)
unknown authorship (work of)	section 9(4)
[...]	[...]

[wireless broadcast	section 178]
wireless telegraphy	section 178
work (in Schedule 1)	paragraph 2(1) of that Schedule
work of more than one author (in Chapter VII)	section 116(4)
writing and written	section 178

Notes:

(1) The references to "needletime" and "terms of payment" inserted by, and the reference to "sound recording" amended by the addition of a reference to s.135A by s.175 of the Broadcasting Act 1990 with effect from February 1, 1991 by virtue of the Broadcasting Act 1990 (Commencement No.1 and Transitional Provisions) Order 1990 (SI 1990/2347).

(2) The reference to "lawful user" was added by the Copyright (Computer Programs) Regulations 1992 (SI 1992/3233), with effect from January 1, 1993.

(3) The references to "film" and "sound recording" were amended by the alteration of the reference to ss.5 to 5A, and the references to "country of origin" and "EEA national and EEA state" inserted by the Duration of Copyright and Rights in Performance Regulations 1995 (SI 1995/3297), with effect from January 1, 1996; the reference to "EEA" being subsequently added by the Copyright and Related Rights Regulations 1996 (SI 1996/2967), with effect from December 1, 1996.

(4) The references to "issue of copies to the public" and "rental" were amended by, and the references to "lending", "producer (in relation to a sound recording or film)", "public library" and "rental right" inserted by the Copyright and Related Rights Regulations 1996 (SI 1996/2967), with effect from December 1, 1996.

(5) The references to "database" and "original (in relation to a database)" inserted by the Copyright and Rights in Databases Regulations 1997 (SI 1997/3032), with effect from January 1, 1998.

(6) The entry for "cable programme" was repealed and the entries for "communication to the public", "private study" and "wireless broadcast" inserted by the Copyright and Related Rights Regulations 2003 (SI 2003/2498), Sch.1, para.15, Sch.2 with effect from October 31, 2003. For savings and transitional provisions, see Part 3 of those Regulations. The former entry for "cable programme" provided:

> *"cable programme, cable programme service (and related expressions)*
> *section 7"*

(7) The words in the first (outer) pair of square brackets in the entry "Parliamentary copyright" substituted by the Scotland Act 1998, s.125, Sch.8, para.25, with effect from May 6, 1999 (Scotland Act 1998 (Commencement) Order 1998 (SI 1998/3178)) and the words in the second (inner) pair of square brackets in that entry substituted by the Northern Ireland Act 1998, s.99, Sch.13, para.8, with effect from December 2, 1999 (Northern Ireland Act 1998 (Commencement No.5) Order 1999 (SI 1999/3209)).

(8) Section 179 was amended by the Intellectual Property (Enforcement, etc.) Regulations 2006 (SI 2006/1028), Sch.2 para.9, with effect from April 29, 2006.

(9) The definition of "Parliamentary copyright" was further amended by the Government of Wales Act 2006 (c.32), Sch.10 para.30, with effect from May 4, 2007.

(10) In table, entries relating to "archivist" and "librarian" substituted, entries relating to "conducted for profit", "curator", "library", "museum" inserted, and entries relating to "prescribed conditions" and "prescribed library or archive" repealed, by the Copyright and Rights in Performances (Research, Education, Libraries and Archives) Regulations 2014 (SI 2014/1372), Sch. para.6, with effect from June 1, 2014 at 00.02.

(11) In table, entry relating to "accessible copy" substituted, entries relating to "authorised body", "disabled person", "supply" inserted, and entries relating to "approved body" and "visually impaired person" repealed, by the Copyright and Rights in Performances (Disability) Regulations 2014 (SI 2014/1384), Sch. para.3, with effect from June 1, 2014 at 00.01.

PART II

RIGHTS IN PERFORMANCES

[CHAPTER 1

INTRODUCTORY]

Rights conferred on performers and persons having recording rights

180.—(1) [Chapter 2 of this Part (economic rights)] confers rights—

(a) on a performer, by requiring his consent to the exploitation of his performances (see sections 181 to 184), and

(b) on a person having recording rights in relation to a performance, in relation to recordings made without his consent or that of the performer (see sections 185 to 188),

and creates offences in relation to dealing with or using illicit recordings and certain other related acts (see sections 198 and 201).

[(1A) Rights are also conferred on a performer by the following provisions of Chapter 3 of this Part (moral rights)—

(a) section 205C (right to be identified);

(b) section 205F (right to object to derogatory treatment of performance).]

(2) In this Part—

"performance" means—

(a) a dramatic performance (which includes dance and mime),

(b) a musical performance,

(c) a reading or recitation of a literary work, or

(d) a performance of a variety act or any similar presentation,

which is, or so far as it is, a live performance given by one or more individuals; and

"recording", in relation to a performance, means a film or sound recording—

(a) made directly from the live performance.

(b) made from a broadcast of [...] the performance, or

(c) made, directly or indirectly, from another recording of the performance.

(3) The rights conferred by this Part apply in relation to performances taking place before the commencement of this Part; but no other act done before commencement, or in pursuance of arrangements made before commencement, shall be regarded as infringing those rights.

(4) The rights conferred by this Part are independent of—

(a) any copyright in, or moral rights relating to, any work performed or any film or sound recording of, or broadcast including [...] the performance, and

(b) any other right or obligation arising otherwise than under this Part.

Notes:

(1) The words ", or cable programme including," in the definition of "recording" in subs.(2) and the words "or cable programme" in subs.(4)(a) repealed by the Copyright and Related Rights Regulations 2003 (SI 2003/2498), Sch.2 with effect from October 31, 2003. For savings and transitional provisions, see Part 3 of those Regulations.

(2) The words in square brackets at the beginning of subs.(1) substituted for the for-

mer words "This Part" and subs.(1A) was inserted by the Performances (Moral Rights, etc.) Regulations 2006 (SI 2006/18), reg.5, with effect from February 1, 2006.

Qualifying performances

181. A performance is a qualifying performance for the purposes of the provisions of this Part relating to performers' rights if it is given by a qualifying individual (as defined in section 206) or takes place in a qualifying country (as so defined).

Note Sections 180 and 181 became Chapter 1 of Part 2, the existing cross-headings before ss.180 and 181 omitted and the cross-heading before s.180 was inserted by the Performances (Moral Rights, etc.) Regulations 2006 (SI 2006/18), reg.4(2), (3), with effect from February 1, 2006.

[Chapter 2

Economic Rights

Performers' rights]

Consent required for recording, &c. of live performance

[182.—(1) A performer's rights are infringed by a person who, without his consent—

   (a) makes a recording of the whole or any substantial part of a qualifying performance directly from the live performance,

   (b) broadcasts live [...] the whole or any substantial part of a qualifying performance,

   (c) makes a recording of the whole or any substantial part of a qualifying performance directly from a broadcast of [...] the live performance [or, where copyright in the sound recording has expired pursuant to section 191HA(4), from a person who plays the sound recording in public or communicates the sound recording to the public].

[...]

(3) In an action for infringement of a performer's rights brought by virtue of this section damages shall not be awarded against a defendant who shows that at the time of the infringement he believed on reasonable grounds that consent had been given.]

Notes:

   (1) This section was substituted by the Copyright and Related Rights Regulations 1996 (SI 1996/2967), which replaced the old section 182 with effect from December 1, 1996. The section originally read:

Consent required for recording or live transmission of performance

"**182.**—(1) *A performer's rights are infringed by a person who, without his consent—*

   (a) *makes, otherwise than for his private and domestic use, a recording of the whole or any substantial part of a qualifying performance, or*

   (b) *broadcast live, or includes live in a cable programme service, the whole or any substantial part of a qualifying performance.*

   (3) *In an action for infringement of a performer's rights brought by virtue of this section damages shall not be awarded against a defendant who shows that at the time of the infringement he believed on reasonable grounds that consent had been given.*"

For savings and transitional provisions, see Part III of those Regulations.

(2) The words ", or includes live in a cable programme service," in subs.(1)(b), the words ", or cable programme including," in subs.(1)(c) and subs.(2) repealed by the Copyright and Related Rights Regulations 2003 (SI 2003/2498), Sch.2 with effect from October 31, 2003. For savings and transitional provisions, see Part 3 of those Regulations. The former subs.(2) provided:

"(2) *A performer's rights are not infringed by the making of any such recording by a person for his private and domestic use.*"

(3) In subs.(1)(c) words in square brackets inserted, subject to savings, transitional and review provisions, by the Copyright and Duration of Rights in Performances Regulations 2013 (SI 2013/1782), reg.7 with effect from November 1, 2013 (for savings, transitional and review provisions see regs 11–27).

Consent required for copying of recording

[**182A.**—(1) A performer's rights are infringed by a person who, without his consent, makes [...] a copy of a recording of the whole or any substantial part of a qualifying performance.

[(1A) In subsection (1) making a copy of a recording includes making a copy which is transient or is incidental to some other use of the original recording.]

(2) It is immaterial whether the copy is made directly or indirectly.

(3) The right of a performer under this section to authorise or prohibit the making of such copies is referred to in [this Chapter] as "reproduction right".]

Notes:

(1) This section was inserted by the Copyright and Related Rights Regulations 1996 (SI 1996/2967), with effect from December 1, 1996. For savings and transitional provisions, see Part III of those Regulations.

(2) The words ", otherwise than for his private and domestic use," in subs.(1) repealed by the Copyright and Related Rights Regulations 2003 (SI 2003/2498), Sch.2 with effect from October 31, 2003. For savings and transitional provisions, see Part 3 of those Regulations.

(3) Section (1A) was inserted by the Copyright and Related Rights Regulations 2003 (SI 2003/2498), Reg.8 with effect from October 31, 2003. For savings and transitional provisions, see Part 3 of those Regulations.

(4) In subs.(3) the words "this Chapter" substituted for the former words "this Part" by the Performances (Moral Rights, etc.) Regulations 2006 (SI 2006/18), Sch. para.8, with effect from February 1, 2006.

Consent required for issue of copies to public

[**182B.**—(1) A performer's rights are infringed by a person who, without his consent, issues to the public copies of a recording of the whole or any substantial part of a qualifying performance.

(2) References in this Part to the issue to the public of copies of a recording are to—

(a) the act of putting into circulation in the EEA copies not previously put into circulation in the EEA by or with the consent of the performer, or

(b) the act of putting into circulation outside the EEA copies not previously put into circulation in the EEA or elsewhere.

(3) References in this Part to the issue to the public of copies of a recording do not include—

(a) any subsequent distribution, sale, hiring or loan of copies previously put into circulation (but see section 182C: consent required for rental or lending), or

(b) any subsequent importation of such copies into the United Kingdom or another EEA state,

except so far as paragraph (a) of subsection (2) applies to putting into circulation in the EEA copies previously put into circulation outside the EEA.

(4) References in this Part to the issue of copies of a recording of a performance include the issue of the original recording of the live performance.

(5) The right of a performer under this section to authorise or prohibit the issue of copies to the public is referred to in [this Chapter] as "distribution right".]

Notes:

   (1) This section was inserted by the Copyright and Related Rights Regulations 1996 (SI 1996/2967), with effect from December 1, 1996. For savings and transitional provisions, see Part III of those Regulations.

   (2) In subs.(5) the words "this Chapter" substituted for the former words "this Part" by the Performances (Moral Rights, etc.) Regulations 2006 (SI 2006/18), Sch. para.8, with effect from February 1, 2006.

Consent required for rental or lending of copies to public

[**182C.**—(1) A performer's rights are infringed by a person who, without his consent, rents or lends to the public copies of a recording of the whole or any substantial part of a qualifying performance.

(2) In [this Chapter], subject to the following provisions of this section—

   (a) "rental" means making a copy of a recording available for use, on terms that it will or may be returned, for direct or indirect economic or commercial advantage, and

   (b) "lending" means making a copy of a recording available for use, on terms that it will or may be returned, otherwise than for direct or indirect economic or commercial advantage, through an establishment which is accessible to the public.

(3) The expressions "rental" and "lending" do not include—

   (a) making available for the purpose of public performance, playing or showing in public [or communication to the public];

   (b) making available for the purpose of exhibition in public; or

   (c) making available for on-the-spot reference use.

(4) The expression "lending" does not include making available between establishments which are accessible to the public.

(5) Where lending by an establishment accessible to the public gives rise to a payment the amount of which does not go beyond what is necessary to cover the operating costs of the establishment, there is no direct or indirect economic or commercial advantage for the purposes of this section.

(6) References in [this Chapter] to the rental or lending of copies of a recording of a performance include the rental or lending of the original recording of the live performance.

(7) In [this Chapter]—

   "rental right" means the right of a performer under this section to authorise or prohibit the rental of copies to the public, and

   "lending right" means the right of a performer under this section to authorise or prohibit the lending of copies to the public.]

Notes:

   (1) This section was inserted by the Copyright and Related Rights Regulations 1996 (SI 1996/2967), with effect from December 1, 1996. For savings and transitional provisions, see Part III of those Regulations.

   (2) The words in square brackets in subs.(3)(a) substituted for the former words ", broadcasting or inclusion in a cable programme service" by the Copyright and Related Rights Regulations 2003 (SI 2003/2498), Sch.1, para.6 with effect from October 31, 2003. For savings and transitional provisions, see Part 3 of those Regulations.

   (3) In subs.(2), (6) and (7) the words "this Chapter" substituted for the former words

"this Part" by the Performances (Moral Rights, etc.) Regulations 2006 (SI 2006/18), Sch. para.8, with effect from February 1, 2006.

Consent required for making available to the public

[182CA.—(1) A performer's rights are infringed by a person who, without his consent, makes available to the public a recording of the whole or any substantial part of a qualifying performance by electronic transmission in such a way that members of the public may access the recording from a place and at a time individually chosen by them.

(2) The right of a performer under this section to authorise or prohibit the making available to the public of a recording is referred to in [this Chapter] as "making available right".]

Notes:

(1) This section was inserted by the Copyright and Related Rights Regulations 2003 (SI 2003/2498), reg.7 with effect from October 31, 2003. For savings and transitional provisions, see Part 3 of those Regulations.

(2) In subs.(2) the words "this Chapter" substituted for the former words "this Part" by the Performances (Moral Rights, etc.) Regulations 2006 (SI 2006/18), Sch. para.8, with effect from February 1, 2006.

Right to equitable remuneration for exploitation of sound recording

[182D.—(1) Where a commercially published sound recording of the whole or any substantial part of a qualifying performance—

(a) is played in public, or

[(b) is communicated to the public otherwise than by its being made available to the public in the way mentioned in section 182CA(1),]

the performer is entitled to equitable remuneration from the owner of the copyright in the sound recording [or, where copyright in the sound recording has expired pursuant to section 191HA(4),from a person who plays the sound recording in public or communicates the sound recording to the public].

[(1A) In subsection (1), the reference to publication of a sound recording includes making it available to the public by electronic transmission in such a way that members of the public may access it from a place and at a time individually chosen by them.]

(2) The right to equitable remuneration under this section may not be assigned by the performer except to a collecting society for the purpose of enabling it to enforce the right on his behalf.

The right is, however, transmissible by testamentary disposition or by operation of law as personal or moveable property; and it may be assigned or further transmitted by any person into whose hands it passes.

(3) The amount payable by way of equitable remuneration is as agreed by or on behalf of the persons by and to whom it is payable, subject to the following provisions.

(4) In default of agreement as to the amount payable by way of equitable remuneration, the person by or to whom it is payable may apply to the Copyright Tribunal to determine the amount payable.

(5) A person to or by whom equitable remuneration is payable may also apply to the Copyright Tribunal—

(a) to vary any agreement as to the amount payable, or

(b) to vary any previous determination of the Tribunal as to that matter;

but except with the special leave of the Tribunal no such application may be made within twelve months from the date of a previous determination.

An order made on an application under this subsection has effect from the date on which it is made or such later date as may be specified by the Tribunal.

(6) On an application under this section the Tribunal shall consider the matter and make such order as to the method of calculating and paying equitable remuneration as it may determine to be reasonable in the circumstances, taking into account the importance of the contribution of the performer to the sound recording.

(7) An agreement is of no effect in so far as it purports—

(a) to exclude or restrict the right to equitable remuneration under this section, or

(b) to prevent a person questioning the amount of equitable remuneration or to restrict the powers of the Copyright Tribunal under this section.

[(8) In this section "collecting society" means a society or other organisation which has as its main object, or one of its main objects, the exercise of the right to equitable remuneration on behalf of more than one performer.]]

Notes:

(1) This section was inserted by the Copyright and Related Rights Regulations 1996 (SI 1996/2967), with effect from December 1, 1996. For savings and transitional provisions, see Part III of those Regulations.

(2) Subsection (1)(b) was substituted by the Copyright and Related Rights Regulations 2003 (SI 2003/2498), reg.7 with effect from October 31, 2003. For savings and transitional provisions, see Part 3 of those Regulations. The former subs.(1)(b) provided:

"(b *is included in a broadcast or cable programme service,*"

(3) Subsection (1A) and (8) inserted by the Performances (Moral Rights, etc.) Regulations 2006 (SI 2006/18), Sch. para.3, with effect from February 1, 2006.

(4) In subs.(1)(b) words in square brackets inserted by the Copyright and Duration of Rights in Performances Regulations 2013 (SI 2013/1782), reg.7, with effect from November 1, 2013.

Infringement of performer's rights by use of recording made without consent

183. A performer's rights are infringed by a person who, without his consent—

(a) shows or plays in public the whole or any substantial part of a qualifying performance, or

(b) [communicates to the public] the whole or any substantial part of a qualifying performance,

by means of a recording which was, and which that person knows or has reason to believe was, made without the performer's consent.

Note: The words in square brackets in subs.(b) substituted for the former words "broadcasts or includes in a cable programme service" by the Copyright and Related Rights Regulations 2003 (SI 2003/2498), Sch.1, para.13 with effect from October 31, 2003. For savings and transitional provisions, see Part 3 of those Regulations.

Infringement of performer's rights by importing, possessing or dealing with illicit recording

184.—(1) A performer's rights are infringed by a person who, without his consent—

(a) imports into the United Kingdom otherwise than for his private and domestic use, or

(b) in the course of a business possesses, sells or lets for hire, offers or exposes for sale or hire, or distributes,

a recording of a qualifying performance which is, and which that person knows or has reason to believe is, an illicit recording.

(2) Where in an action for infringement of a performer's rights brought by virtue of this section a defendant shows that the illicit recording was innocently acquired by him or a predecessor in title of his, the only remedy available against him in respect of the infringement is damages not exceeding a reasonable payment in respect of the act complained of.

(3) In subsection (2) "innocently acquired" means that the person acquiring the recording did not know and had no reason to believe that it was an illicit recording.

Rights of person having recording rights

Exclusive recording contracts and persons having recording rights

185.—(1) In [this Chapter] an "exclusive recording contract" means a contract between a performer and another person under which that person is entitled to the exclusion of all other persons (including the performer) to make recordings of one or more of his performances with a view to their commercial exploitation.

(2) References in this Part to a "person having recording rights", in relation to a performance, are (subject to subsection (3)) to a person—

(a) who is party to and has the benefit of an exclusive recording contract to which the performance is subject, or

(b) to whom the benefit of such a contract has been assigned,

and who is a qualifying person.

(3) If a performance is subject to an exclusive recording contract but the person mentioned in subsection (2) is not a qualifying person, references in [this Chapter] to a "person having recording rights" in relation to the performance are to any person—

(a) who is licensed by such a person to make recordings of the performance with a view to their commercial exploitation, or

(b) to whom the benefit of such a licence has been assigned,

and who is a qualifying person.

(4) In this section "with a view to commercial exploitation" means with a view to the recordings being sold or let for hire, or shown or played in public.

Note: In subs.(1) to (3) the words "this Chapter" substituted for the former words "this Part" by the Performances (Moral Rights, etc.) Regulations 2006 (SI 2006/18), Sch. para.8, with effect from February 1, 2006.

Consent required for recording of performance subject to exclusive contract

186.—(1) A person infringes the rights of a person having recording rights in relation to a performance who, without his consent or that of the performer, makes a recording of the whole or any substantial part of the performance [...].

(2) In an action for infringement of those rights brought by virtue of this section damages shall not be awarded against a defendant who shows that at the time of the infringement he believed on reasonable grounds that consent had been given.

Note: The words ", otherwise that for his private and domestic use" repealed from subs.(1) by the Copyright and Related Rights Regulations 2003 (SI 2003/2498), Sch.2 with effect from October 31, 2003. For savings and transitional provisions, see Part 3 of those Regulations.

Infringement of recording rights by use of recording made without consent

187.—(1) A person infringes the rights of a person having recording rights in relation to a performance who, without his consent or, in the case of a qualifying performance, that of the performer—

(a) shows or plays in public the whole or any substantial part of the performance, or

(b) [communicates to the public] the whole or any substantial part of the performance,

by means of a recording which was, and which that person knows or has reason to believe was, made without the appropriate consent.

(2) The reference in subsection (1) to "the appropriate consent" is to the consent of—

(a) the performer, or

(b) the person who at the time the consent was given had recording rights in relation to the performance (or, if there was more than one such person, of all of them).

Note: The words in square brackets in subs.(1)(b) substituted for the former words "broadcasts or includes in a cable programme service" by the Copyright and Related Rights Regulations 2003 (SI 2003/2498), Sch.1, para.13 with effect from October 31, 2003. For savings and transitional provisions, see Part 3 of those Regulations.

Infringement of recording rights by importing, possessing or dealing with illicit recording

188.—(1) A person infringes the rights of a person having recording rights in relation to a performance who, without his consent or, in the case of a qualifying performance, that of the performer—

(a) imports into the United Kingdom otherwise than for his private and domestic use, or

(b) in the course of a business possesses, sells or lets for hire, offers or exposes for sale or hire, or distributes,

a recording of the performance which is, and which that person knows or has reason to believe is, an illicit recording.

(2) Where in an action for infringement of those rights brought by virtue of this section a defendant shows that the illicit recording was innocently acquired by him or a predecessor in title of his, the only remedy available against him in respect of the infringement is damages not exceeding a reasonable payment in respect of the act complained of.

(3) In subsection (2) "innocently acquired" means that the person acquiring the recording did not know and had no reason to believe that it was an illicit recording.

Exceptions to rights conferred

Acts permitted notwithstanding rights conferred by [this Chapter]

189. The provisions of Schedule 2 specify acts which may be done notwithstanding the rights conferred by [this Chapter], being acts which correspond broadly to certain of those specified in Chapter III of Part I (acts permitted notwithstanding copyright).

Note: In s.189 and the heading preceding it the words "this Chapter" substituted in each place for the former words "this Part" by the Performances (Moral Rights, etc.) Regulations 2006 (SI 2006/18), Sch. para.8, with effect from February 1, 2006.

Power of tribunal to give consent on behalf of performer in certain cases

190.—[(1) The Copyright Tribunal may, on the application of a person wishing to make a copy of a recording of a performance, give consent in a case where the identity or whereabouts of the person entitled to the reproduction right cannot be ascertained by reasonable inquiry.]

(2) Consent given by the Tribunal has effect as consent of [the person entitled to the reproduction right] for the purposes of—

(a) the provisions of [this Chapter] relating to performers' rights, and

(b) section 198(3)(a) (criminal liability: sufficient consent in relation to qualifying performances),

and may be given subject to any conditions specified in the Tribunal's order.

(3) The Tribunal shall not give consent under subsection (1)(a) except after the service or publication of such notices as may be required by rules made under section 150 (general procedural rules) or as the Tribunal may in any particular case direct.

(4) [...]

(5) In any case the Tribunal shall take into account the following factors—

(a) whether the original recording was made with the performer's consent and is lawfully in the possession or control of the person proposing to make the further recording;

(b) whether the making of the further recording is consistent with the obligations of the parties to the arrangements under which, or is otherwise consistent with the purposes for which, the original recording was made.

(6) Where the Tribunal gives consent under this section it shall, in default of agreement between the applicant and [the person entitled to the reproduction right], make such order as it thinks fit as to the payment to be made to [that person] in consideration of consent being given.

Notes:

(1) Subsection (1) was inserted, subss.(2) and (6) were amended and subs.(4) deleted by the Copyright and Related Rights Regulations 1996 (SI 1996/2967), with effect from December 1, 1996. The old subss.(1) and (4) provided:

"(1) *The Copyright Tribunal may, on the application of a person wishing to make a recording from a previous recording of a performance, give consent in a case where—*

(a) *the identity or whereabouts of a performer cannot be ascertained by reasonable enquiry, or*

(b) *a performer unreasonably withholds his consent.*

(4) *The Tribunal shall not give consent under subsection (1)(b) unless satisfied that the performer's reasons for withholding consent do not include the protection of any legitimate interest of his; but it shall be for the performer to show what his reasons are for withholding consent, and in default of evidence as to his reasons the Tribunal may draw such inferences as it thinks fit.*"

For savings and transitional provisions, see Part III of those Regulations.

(2) In subs.(2)(a) the words "this Chapter" substituted for the former words "this Part" by the Performances (Moral Rights, etc.) Regulations 2006 (SI 2006/18), Sch. para.8, with effect from February 1, 2006.

[Duration of rights]

Duration of rights

[**191.**—(1) The following provisions have effect with respect to the duration of the rights conferred by [this Chapter].

(2) The rights conferred by [this Chapter] in relation to a performance expire—

(a) at the end of the period of 50 years from the end of the calender year in which the performance takes place, or

(b) if during that period a recording of the performances[, other than a sound recording,] is released, 50 years from the end of the calendar year in which it is released, [or]
(c) if during that period a sound recording of the performance is released, 70 years from the end of the calendar year in which it is released.]
subject as follows.

(3) For the purposes of subsection (2) a recording is "released" when it is first published, played or shown in public [or communicated to the public]; but in determining whether a recording has been released no account shall be taken of any unauthorised act.

(4) Where a performer is not a national of an EEA state, the duration of the rights conferred by [this Chapter] in relation to his performance is that to which the performance is entitled in the country of which he is a national, provided that does not exceed the period which would apply under subsections (2) and (3).

(5) If or to the extent that the application of subsection (4) would be at variance with an international obligation to which the United Kingdom became subject prior to 29th October 1993, the duration of the rights conferred by [this Chapter] shall be as specified in subsections (2) and (3).]

Notes:

(1) The heading preceding this section was amended by the Copyright and Related Rights Regulations 1996 (SI 1996/2967), with effect from December 1, 1996. For savings and transitional provisions, see Part III of theose Regulations.
(2) This section was inserted by the Duration of Copyright and Rights in Performances Regulations 1995 (SI 1995/3297), which replaced the old s.191 with effect from January 1, 1996.
The old s.191 and heading preceding it provided:

"Duration and transmission of rights; consent

191. *The rights conferred by this Part continue to subsist in relation to a performance until the end of the period of 50 years from the end of the calendar year in which the performance takes place."*

For savings and transitional provisions, see Part III of those Regulations.
(3) The words in square brackets in subs.(3) substituted for the former words ", broadcast or included in a cable programme service" by the Copyright and Related Rights Regulations 2003 (SI 2003/2498), Sch.1, para.8 with effect from October 31, 2003. For savings and transitional provisions, see Part 3 of those Regulations.
(4) In subss.(1), (2), (4) and (5) the words "this Chapter" substituted for the former words "this Part" by the Performances (Moral Rights, etc.) Regulations 2006 (SI 2006/18), Sch. para.8, with effect from February 1, 2006.
(5) In subs.(2)(b) words in square brackets inserted, and subs.(2)(c) inserted, subject to savings, transitional and review provisions, by the Copyright and Duration of Rights in Performances Regulations 2013 (SI 2013/1782), reg.8, with effect from November 1, 2013 (for savings, transitional and review provisions see regs 11–7).

[Performers' property rights

Performers' property rights

191A.—(1) The following rights conferred by [this Chapter] on a performer—
reproduction right (section 182A),
distribution right (section 182B),
rental right and lending right (section 182C),
[making available right (section 182CA),]
are property rights ("a [...] performer's property rights").
(2) References in [this Chapter] to the consent of the performer shall be

construed in relation to a performer's property rights as references to the consent of the rights owner.

(3) Where different persons are (whether in consequence of a partial assignment or otherwise) entitled to different aspects of a performer's property rights in relation to a performance, the rights owner for any purpose of [this Chapter] is the person who is entitled to the aspect of those rights relevant for that purpose.

(4) Where a performer's property rights (or any aspect of them) is owned by more than one person jointly, references in [this Chapter] to the rights owner are to all the owners, so that, in particular, any requirement of the licence of the rights owner requires the licence of all of them.]

Notes:

(1) This section and the heading preceding it inserted by the Copyright and Related Rights Regulations 1996 (SI 1996/2967), with effect from December 1, 1996. For savings and transitional provisions, see Part III of those Regulations.
(2) The words in square brackets in subs.(1) inserted by the Copyright and Related Rights Regulations 2003 (SI 2003/2498), reg.7 with effect from October 31, 2003. For savings and transitional provisions, see Part 3 of those Regulations.
(3) In subs.(1) to (4) the words "this Chapter" substituted for the former words "this Part" by the Performances (Moral Rights, etc.) Regulations 2006 (SI 2006/18), Sch. para.8, with effect from February 1, 2006.
(4) In subs.(1) the word "a" formerly appearing before the words "performers' property rights" was omitted by the Performances (Moral Rights, etc.) Regulations 2006 (SI 2006/18), Sch. para.4, with effect from February 1, 2006.

Assignment and licences

[191B.—(1) A performer's property rights are transmissible by assignment, by testamentary disposition or by operation of law, as personal or moveable property.

(2) An assignment or other transmission of a performer's property rights may be partial, that is, limited so as to apply—

(a) to one or more, but not all, of the things requiring the consent of the rights owner;

(b) to part, but not the whole, of the period for which the rights are to subsist.

(3) An assignment of a performer's property rights is not effective unless it is in writing signed by or on behalf of the assignor.

(4) A licence granted by the owner of a performer's property rights is binding on every successor in title to his interest in the rights, except a purchaser in good faith for valuable consideration and without notice (actual or constructive) of the licence or a person deriving title from such a purchaser; and references in [this Chapter] to doing anything with, or without, the licence of the rights owner shall be construed accordingly.]

Notes:

(1) This section was inserted by the Copyright and Related Rights Regulations 1996 (SI 1996/2967), with effect from December 1, 1996. For savings and transitional provisions, see Part III of those Regulations.
(2) In subs.(4) the words "this Chapter" substituted for the former words "this Part" by the Performances (Moral Rights, etc.) Regulations 2006 (SI 2006/18), Sch. para.8, with effect from February 1, 2006.

Prospective ownership of a performer's property rights

[191C.—(1) This section applies where by an agreement made in relation to a future recording of a performance, and signed by or on behalf of the performer, the performer purports to assign his performer's property rights (wholly or partially) to another person.

(2) If on the rights coming into existence the assignee or another person claiming under him would be entitled as against all other persons to require the rights to be vested in him, they shall vest in the assignee or his successor in title by virtue of this subsection.

(3) A licence granted by a prospective owner of a performer's property rights is binding on every successor in title to his interest (or prospective interest) in the rights, except a purchaser in good faith for valuable consideration and without notice (actual or constructive) of the licence or a person deriving title from such a purchaser.

References in [this Chapter] to doing anything with, or without, the licence of the rights owner shall be construed accordingly.

(4) In subsection (3) "prospective owner" in relation to a performer's property rights means a person who is prospectively entitled to those rights by virtue of such an agreement as is mentioned in subsection (1).]

Notes:

(1) This section was inserted by the Copyright and Related Rights Regulations 1996 (SI 1996/2967), with effect from December 1, 1996. For savings and transitional provisions, see Part III of those Regulations.

(2) In subs.(3) the words "this Chapter" substituted for the former words "this Part" by the Performances (Moral Rights, etc.) Regulations 2006 (SI 2006/18), Sch. para.8, with effect from February 1, 2006.

Exclusive licences

[191D.—(1) In [this Chapter] an "exclusive licence" means a licence in writing signed by or on behalf of the owner of a performer's property rights authorising the licensee to the exclusion of all other persons, including the person granting the licence, to do anything requiring the consent of the rights owner.

(2) The licensee under an exclusive licence has the same rights against a successor in title who is bound by the licence as he has against the person granting the licence.]

Notes:

(1) This section was inserted by the Copyright and Related Rights Regulations 1996 (SI 1996/2967), with effect from December 1, 1996. For savings and transitional provisions, see Part III of those Regulations.

(2) In subs.(1) the words "this Chapter" substituted for the former words "this Part" by the Performances (Moral Rights, etc.) Regulations 2006 (SI 2006/18), Sch. para.8, with effect from February 1, 2006.

Performer's property right to pass under will with unpublished original recording

[191E. Where under a bequest (whether general or specific) a person is entitled beneficially or otherwise to any material thing containing an original recording of a performance which was not published before the death of the testator, the bequest shall, unless a contrary intention is indicated in the testator's will or a codicil to it, be construed as including any performer's rights in relation to the recording to which the testator was entitled immediately before his death.]

Note: This section was inserted by the Copyright and Related Rights Regulations 1996 (SI 1996/2967), with effect from December 1, 1996. For savings and transitional provisions, see Part III of those Regulations.

Presumption of transfer of rental right in case of film production agreement

[191F.—(1) Where an agreement concerning film production is concluded between a performer and a film producer, the performer shall be presumed, unless the agreement provides to the contrary, to have transferred to the film producer any rental right in relation to the film arising from the inclusion of a recording of his performance in the film.

(2) Where this section applies, the absence of signature by or on behalf of the performer does not exclude the operation of section 191C (effect of purported assignment of future rights).

(3) The reference in subsection (1) to an agreement concluded between a performer and a film producer includes any agreement having effect between those persons, whether made by them directly or though intermediaries.

(4) Section 191G (right to equitable remuneration on transfer of rental right) applies where there is a presumed transfer by virtue of this section as in the case of an actual transfer.]

Note: This section was inserted by the Copyright and Related Rights Regulations 1996 (SI 1996/2967), with effect from December 1, 1996. For savings and transitional provisions, see Part III of those Regulations.

Right to equitable remuneration where rental right transferred

[191G.—(1) Where a performer has transferred his rental right concerning a sound recording or a film to the producer of the sound recording or film, he retains the right to equitable remuneration for the rental.

The reference above to the transfer of rental right by one person to another includes any arrangement having that effect, whether made by them directly or through intermediaries.

(2) The right to equitable remuneration under this section may not be assigned by the performer except to a collecting society for the purpose of enabling it to enforce the right on his behalf.

The right is, however, transmissible by testamentary disposition or by operation of law as personal or moveable property; and it may be assigned or further transmitted by any person into whose hands it passes.

(3) Equitable remuneration under this section is payable by the person for the time being entitled to the rental right, that is, the person to whom the right was transferred or any successor in title of his.

(4) The amount payable by way of equitable remuneration is as agreed by or on behalf of the persons by and to whom it is payable, subject to section 191H (reference of amount to Copyright Tribunal).

(5) An agreement is of no effect in so far as it purports to exclude or restrict the right to equitable remuneration under this section.

(6) In this section a "collecting society" means a society or other organisation which has as its main object, or one of its main objects, the exercise of the right to equitable remuneration on behalf of more than one performer.]

Note: This section was inserted by the Copyright and Related Rights Regulations 1996 (SI 1996/2967), with effect from December 1 1996. For savings and transitional provisions, see Part III of those Regulations.

Equitable remuneration: reference of amount to Copyright Tribunal

[191H.—(1) In default of agreement as to the amount payable by way of equitable remuneration under section 191G, the person by or to whom it is payable may also apply to the Copyright Tribunal to determine the amount payable.

(2) A person to or by whom equitable remuneration is payable may also apply to the Copyright Tribunal—

(a) to vary any agreement as to the amount payable, or

(b) to vary any previous determination of the Tribunal as to that matter;
but except with the special leave of the Tribunal no such application may be
made within twelve months from the date of a previous determination.

An order made on an application under this subsection has effect from the date
on which it is made or such later date as may be specified by the Tribunal.

(3) On an application under this section the Tribunal shall consider the matter
and make such order as to the method of calculating and paying equitable remuneration as it may determine to be reasonable in the circumstances, taking into
account the importance of the contribution of the performer to the film or sound
recording.

(4) Remuneration shall not be considered inequitable merely because it was
paid by way of a single payment or at the time of the transfer of the rental right.

(5) An agreement is of no effect in so far as it purports to prevent a person
questioning the amount of equitable remuneration or to restrict the powers of the
Copyright Tribunal under this section.]

Note: This section was inserted by the Copyright and Related Rights Regulations 1996
(SI 1996/2967), with effect from December 1, 1996. For savings and transitional provisions, see Part III of those Regulations.

Assignment of performer's property rights in a sound recording

[**191HA.**—(1) This section applies where a performer has [by an agreement]
assigned the following rights concerning a sound recording to the producer of the
sound recording—

(a) reproduction, distribution and making available rights, or

(b) performer's property rights.

(2) If, at the end of the 50-year period, the producer has failed to meet one or
both of the following conditions, the performer may give a notice in writing to
the producer of the performer's intention to terminate the agreement—

(a) condition 1 is to issue to the public copies of the sound recording in sufficient quantities;

(b) condition 2 is to make the sound recording available to the public by
electronic transmission in such a way that a member of the public may
access the recording from a place and at a time chosen by him or her.

(3) If, at any time after the end of the 50-year period, the producer, having met
one or both of the conditions referred to in subsection (2), fails to do so, the
performer may give a notice in writing to the producer of the performer's intention to terminate the agreement.

(4) If at the end of the period of 12 months beginning with the date of the notice, the producer has not met the conditions referred to in subsection (2), the
agreement terminates and the copyright in the sound recording expires with immediate effect.

(5) An agreement is of no effect in so far as it purports to exclude or restrict
the right to give a notice under subsection (2) or (3).

(6) A reference in this section to the assignment of rights includes any arrangement having that effect, whether made directly between the parties or
through intermediaries.

(7) In this section—

"50-year period" means

(a) where the sound recording is published during the initial
period, the period of 50 years from the end of the calendar year
in which the sound recording is first published, or

(b) where during the initial period the sound recording is not published but is made available to the public by being played in public or communicated to the public, the period of 50 years from the end of the calendar year in which it was first made available to the public, but in determining whether a sound recording has been published, played in public or communicated to the public, no account shall be taken of any unauthorised act,

"initial period" means the period beginning on the date the recording is made and ending 50 years from the end of the calendar year in which the sound recording is made,

"producer" means the person for the time being entitled to the copyright in the sound recording,

"sufficient quantities" means such quantity as to satisfy the reasonable requirements of the public for copies of the sound recording,

"unauthorised act" has the same meaning as in section 178.]

Notes:

(1) Sections 191HA and 191HB inserted, subject to savings, transitional and review provisions, by the Copyright and Duration of Rights in Performances Regulations 2013 (SI 2013/1782), reg.9, with effect from November 1, 2013 (for savings, transitional and review provisions see regs 11–27).

(2) In subs.(1) words in square brackets inserted by the Copyright and Duration of Rights in Performances (Amendment) Regulations 2014 (SI 2014/434), reg.4, with effect from April 6, 2014.

Payment in consideration of assignment

[**191HB.**—(1) A performer who, under an agreement relating to the assignment of rights referred to in section 191HA(1) (an "assignment agreement"), is entitled to a non-recurring payment in consideration of the assignment, is entitled to an annual payment for each relevant period from—

(a) the producer, or

(b) where the producer has granted an exclusive licence of the copyright in the sound recording, the licensee under the exclusive licence (the "exclusive licensee").

(2) In this section, "relevant period" means—

(a) the period of 12 months beginning at the end of the 50-year period, and

(b) each subsequent period of 12 months beginning with the end of the previous period, until the date on which copyright in the sound recording expires.

(3) The producer or, where relevant, the exclusive licensee gives e__ect to the entitlement under subsection (1) by remitting to a collecting society for distribution to the performer in accordance with its rules an amount for each relevant period equal to 20% of the gross revenue received during that period in respect of—

(a) the reproduction and issue to the public of copies of the sound recording, and

(b) the making available to the public of the sound recording by electronic transmission in such a way that members of the public may access it from a place and at a time individually chosen by them.

(4) The amount required to be remitted under subsection (3) is payable within 6 months of the end of each relevant period and is recoverable by the collecting society as a debt.

(5) Subsection (6) applies where—

(a) the performer makes a written request to the producer or, where relevant, the exclusive licensee for information in that person's possession or under that person's control to enable the performer—

       (i) to ascertain the amount of the annual payment to which the performer is entitled under subsection (1), or

      (ii) to secure its distribution by the collecting society, and

   (b) the producer or, where relevant, the exclusive licensee does not supply the information within the period of 90 days beginning with the date of the request.

(6) The performer may apply to the county court, or in Scotland to the sheriff, for an order requiring the producer or, where relevant, the exclusive licensee to supply the information.

(7) An agreement is of no effect in so far as it purports to exclude or restrict the entitlement under subsection (1).

(8) In the event of any dispute as to the amount required to be remitted under subsection (3), the performer may apply to the Copyright Tribunal to determine the amount payable.

(9) Where a performer is entitled under an assignment agreement to recurring payments in consideration of the assignment, the payments must, from the end of the 50-year period, be made in full, regardless of any provision in the agreement which entitles the producer to withhold or deduct sums from the amounts payable.

(10) In this section—

    "producer" and "50-year period" each has the same meaning as in section 191HA,

    "exclusive licence" has the same meaning as in section 92, and

    "collecting society" has the same meaning as in section 191G.]

Note: Sections 191HA and 191HB inserted, subject to savings, transitional and review provisions, by the Copyright and Duration of Rights in Performances Regulations 2013 (SI 2013/1782), reg.9, with effect from November 1, 2013 (for savings, transitional and review provisions see regs 11–27).

Infringement actionable by rights owner

[191I.—(1) An infringement of a performer's property rights is actionable by the rights owner.

(2) In an action for infringement of a performer's property rights all such relief by way of damages, injunctions, accounts or otherwise is available to the plaintiff as is available in respect of the infringement of any other property right.

(3) This section has effect subject to the following provisions of [this Chapter].]

Notes:

(1) This section was inserted by the Copyright and Related Rights Regulations 1996 (SI 1996/2967), with effect from December 1, 1996. For savings and transitional provisions, see Part III of those Regulations.

(2) In subs.(3) the words "this Chapter" substituted for the former words "this Part" by the Performances (Moral Rights, etc.) Regulations 2006 (SI 2006/18), Sch. para.8, with effect from February 1, 2006.

Provisions as to damages in infringement action

[191J.—(1) Where in an action for infringement of a performer's property rights it is shown that at the time of the infringement the defendant did not know, and had no reason to believe, that the rights subsisted in the recording to which the action relates, the plaintiff is not entitled to damages against him, but without prejudice to any other remedy.

(2) The court may in an action for infringement of a performer's property rights having regard to all the circumstances, and in particular to—

(a) the flagrancy of the infringement, and

(b) any benefit accruing to the defendant by reason of the infringement,

award such additional damages as the justice of the case may require.]

Note: This section was inserted by the Copyright and Related Rights Regulations 1996 (SI 1996/2967), with effect from December 1, 1996. For savings and transitional provisions, see Part III of those Regulations.

Injunctions against service providers

[191JA.—(1) The High Court (in Scotland, the Court of Session) shall have power to grant an injunction against a service provider, where that service provider has actual knowledge of another person using their service to infringe a performer's property right.

(2) In determining whether a service provider has actual knowledge for the purpose of this section, a court shall take into account all matters which appear to it in the particular circumstances to be relevant and, amongst other things, shall have regard to—

(a) whether a service provider has received a notice through a means of contact made available in accordance with regulation 6(1)(c) of the Electronic Commerce (EC Directive) Regulations 2002 (SI 2002/2013); and

(b) the extent to which any notice includes—

(i) the full name and address of the sender of the notice;

(ii) details of the infringement in question.

(3) In this section "service provider" has the meaning given to it by regulation 2 of the Electronic Commerce (EC Directive) Regulations 2002.

(4) Section 177 applies in respect of this section as it applies in respect of Part 1.]

Note: This section was inserted by Copyright and Related Rights Regulations 2003 (SI 2003/2498), reg.27 with effect from October 31, 2003. For savings and transitional provisions, see Part 3 of those Regulations.

Undertaking to take licence of right in infringement proceedings

[191K.—(1) If in proceedings for infringement of a performer's property rights in respect of which a licence is available as of right under paragraph 17 of Schedule 2A (powers exercisable in consequence of competition report) the defendant undertakes to take a licence on such terms as may be agreed or, in default of agreement, settled by the Copyright Tribunal under that paragraph—

(a) no injunction shall be granted against him,

(b) no order for delivery up shall be made under section 195, and

(c) the amount recoverable against him by way of damages or on an account of profits shall not exceed double the amount which would have been payable by him as licensee if such a licence on those terms had been granted before the earliest infringement.

(2) An undertaking may be given at any time before final order in the proceedings, without any admission of liability.

(3) Nothing in this section affects the remedies available in respect of an infringement committed before licences of right were available.]

Note: This section was inserted by the Copyright and Related Rights Regulations 1996 (SI 1996/2967), with effect from December 1, 1996. For savings and transitional provisions, see Part III of those Regulations.

Rights and remedies for exclusive licensee

[191L.—(1) An exclusive licensee has, except against the owner of a performer's property rights, the same rights and remedies in respect of matters occurring after the grant of the licence as if the licence had been an assignment.

(2) His rights and remedies are concurrent with those of the rights owner; and references in the relevant provisions of [this Chapter] to the rights owner shall be construed accordingly.

(3) In an action brought by an exclusive licensee by virtue of this section a defendant may avail himself of any defence which would have been available to him if the action had been brought by the rights owner.]

Notes:

(1) This section was inserted by the Copyright and Related Rights Regulations 1996 (SI 1996/2967), with effect from December 1, 1996. For savings and transitional provisions, see Part III of those Regulations.
(2) In subs.(2) the words "this Chapter" substituted for the former words "this Part" by the Performances (Moral Rights, etc.) Regulations 2006 (SI 2006/18), Sch. para.8, with effect from February 1, 2006.

Exercise of concurrent rights

[191M.—(1) Where an action for infringement of a performer's property rights brought by the rights owner or an exclusive licensee relates (wholly or partly) to an infringement in respect of which they have concurrent rights of action, the rights owner or, as the case may be, the exclusive licensee may not, without the leave of the court, proceed with the action unless the other is either joined as plaintiff or added as a defendant.

(2) A rights owner or exclusive licensee who is added as a defendant in pursuance of subsection (1) is not liable for any costs in the action unless he takes part in the proceedings.

(3) The above provisions do not affect the granting of interlocutory relief on an application by the rights owner or exclusive licensee alone.

(4) Where an action for infringement of a performer's property rights is brought which relates (wholly or partly) to an infringement in respect of which the rights owner and an exclusive licensee have or had concurrent rights of action—

(a) the court shall in assessing damages take into account—
  (i) the terms of the licence, and
  (ii) any pecuniary remedy already awarded or available to either of them in respect of the infringement;
(b) no account of profits shall be directed if an award of damages has been made, or an account of profits has been directed, in favour of the other of them in respect of the infringement; and
(c) the court shall if an account of profits is directed apportion the profits between them as the court considers just, subject to any agreement between them;

and these provisions apply whether or not the rights owner and the exclusive licensee are both parties to the action.

(5) The owner of a performer's property rights shall notify any exclusive licensee having concurrent rights before applying for an order under section 195 (order for delivery up) or exercising the right conferred by section 196 (right of seizure); and the court may on the application of the licensee make such order under section 195 or, as the case may be, prohibiting or permitting the exercise by the rights owner of the right conferred by section 196, as it thinks fit having regard to the terms of the licence.]

Note: This section was inserted by the Copyright and Related Rights Regulations 1996

(SI 1996/2967), with effect from December 1, 1996. For savings and transitional provisions, see Part III of those Regulations.

Transmission of rights

192. [...]

Note: Section 192 was replaced with ss.192A and 192B by the Copyright and Related Rights Regulations 1996 (SI 1996/2967) with effect from December 1, 1996. The old s.192 provided:

Transmission of rights

"**192.**—(1) *The rights conferred by this Part are not assignable or transmissible, except to the extent that performers' rights are transmissible in accordance with the following provisions.*

(2) *On the death of a person entitled to performer's rights—*

(a) *the rights pass to such person as he may by testamentary disposition specifically direct, and*

(b) *if or to the extent that there is no such direction, the rights are exercisable by his personal representatives;*

and references in this Part to the performer, in the context of the person having performers' rights, shall be construed as references to the person for the time being entitled to exercise those rights.

(3) *Where by virtue of subsection (2)(a) a right becomes exercisable by more than one person, it is exercisable by each of them independently of the other or others.*

(4) *The above provisions do not affect section 185(2)(b) or (3)(b), so far as those provisions confer rights under this Part on a person to whom the benefit of a contract or licence is assigned.*

(5) *Any damages recovered by personal representatives by virtue of this section in respect of an infringement after a person's death shall devolve as part of his estate as if the right of action had subsisted and been vested in him immediately before his death.*"

[Non property rights

Performers' non-property rights

192A.—(1) The rights conferred on a performer by—

section 182 (consent required for recording, &c. of live performance),

section 183 (infringement of performer's rights by use of recording made without consent), [...]

section 184 (infringement of performer's rights importing, possessing or dealing with illicit recording),

[section 191HA (assignment of performer's property rights in a sound recording), and

section 191HB (payment in consideration of assignment),]

are not assignable or transmissible, except to the following extent.

They are referred to in [this Chapter] as "[...] performer's non-property rights".

(2) On the death of a person entitled to any such right—

(a) the right passes to such person as he may by testamentary disposition specifically direct, and

(b) if or to the extent that there is no such direction, the right is exercisable by his personal representatives.

(3) References in [this Chapter] to the performer, in the context of the person

having any such right, shall be construed as references to the person for the time being entitled to exercise those rights.

(4) Where by virtue of subsection (2)(a) a right becomes exercisable by more than one person, it is exercisable by each of them independently of the other or others.

(5) Any damages recovered by personal representatives by virtue of this section in respect of an infringement after a person's death shall devolve as part of his estate as if the right of action had subsisted and been vested in him immediately before his death.]

Notes:
  (1) Sections 192A and 192B and the heading preceding the sections inserted by the Copyright and Related Rights Regulations 1996 (SI 1996/2967) and replaced the old s.192 with effect from December 1, 1996.
  (2) In subs.(1) the word "a" formerly appearing before the words "performers' non-property rights" was omitted by the Performances (Moral Rights, etc.) Regulations 2006 (SI 2006/18), Sch. para.5, with effect from February 1, 2006.
  (3) In s.192A(1) and (3) the words "this Chapter" substituted for the former words "this Part" by the Performances (Moral Rights, etc.) Regulations 2006 (SI 2006/18), Sch. para.8, with effect from February 1, 2006
  (4) In subs.(1) word "and" repealed and entries relating to sections 191HA and 191HB inserted, subject to savings, transitional and review provisions, by the Copyright and Duration of Rights in Performances Regulations 2013 (SI 2013/1782), reg.10, with effect from November 1, 2013 (for savings, transitional and review provisions see regs 11–27).

Transmissibility of rights of person having recording rights

[192B.—(1) The rights conferred by [this Chapter] on a person having recording rights are not assignable or transmissible.

(2) This does not affect section 185(2)(b) or (3)(b), so far as those provisions confer rights under [this Chapter] on a person to whom the benefit of a contract or licence is assigned.]

Notes:
  (1) Sections 192A and 192B and the heading preceding them inserted by the Copyright and Related Rights Regulations 1996 (SI 1996/2967), replaced the old s.192 with effect from December 1, 1996.
     For savings and transitional provisions, see Part III of those Regulations.
  (2) In subs.(1) and (2) the words "this Chapter" substituted for the former words "this Part" by the Performances (Moral Rights, etc.) Regulations 2006 (SI 2006/18), Sch. para.8, with effect from February 1, 2006.

Consent

193.—(1) Consent for the purposes of [this Chapter] [by a person having a performer's non-property rights, or by a person having recording rights,] may be given in relation to a specific performance, a specified description of performances or performances generally, and may relate to past or future performances.

(2) A person having recording rights in a performance is bound by any consent given by a person through whom he derives his rights under the exclusive recording contract or licence in question, in the same way as if the consent had been given by him.

(3) Where [a performer's non-property right] passes to another person, any consent binding on the person previously entitled binds the person to whom the right passes in the same way as if the consent had been given by him.

Notes:
  (1) Subsections (1) and (3) are printed as amended by the Copyright and Related

Rights Regulations 1996 (SI 1996/2967), with effect from December 1, 1996. For savings and transitional provisions, see Part III of thesoe Regulations.

(2) In subs.(1) the words "this Chapter" substituted for the former words "this Part" by the Performances (Moral Rights, etc.) Regulations 2006 (SI 2006/18), Sch. para.8, with effect from February 1, 2006.

Remedies for infringement

Infringement actionable as breach of statutory duty

194. An infringement of [—

(a) a performer's non-property rights, or

(b) any right conferred by [this Chapter] on a person having recording rights,]

is actionable by the person entitled to the right as a breach of statutory duty.

Notes:

(1) Section 194 is printed as amended by the Copyright and Related Rights Regulations 1996 (SI 1996/2967), with effect from December 1, 1996, which also deleted the heading before the section: *"Remedies for infringement"*. For savings and transitional provisions, see Part III of those Regulations.

(2) In subs.(b) the words "this Chapter" substituted for the former words "this Part" by the Performances (Moral Rights, etc.) Regulations 2006 (SI 2006/18), Sch. para.8, with effect from February 1, 2006.

[Delivery up or seizure of illicit recordings]

Order for delivery up

195.—(1) Where a person has in his possession, custody or control in the course of a business an illicit recording of a performance, a person having performer's rights or recording rights in relation to the performance under [this Chapter] may apply to the court for an order that the recording be delivered up to him or to such other person as the court may direct.

(2) An application shall not be made after the end of the period specified in section 203; and no order shall be made unless the court also makes, or it appears to the court that there are grounds for making, an order under section 204 (order as to disposal of illicit recording).

(3) A person to whom a recording is delivered up in pursuance of an order under this section shall, if an order under section 204 is not made, retain it pending the making of an order, or the decision not to make an order, under that section.

(4) Nothing in this section affects any other power of the court.

Notes:

(1) The heading preceding this section was inserted by the Copyright and Related Rights Regulations 1996 (SI 1996/2967), with effect from December 1, 1996.

(2) In subs.(1) the words "this Chapter" substituted for the former words "this Part" by the Performances (Moral Rights, etc.) Regulations 2006 (SI 2006/18), Sch. para.8, with effect from February 1, 2006.

Right to seize illicit recordings

196.—(1) An illicit recording of a performance which is found exposed or otherwise immediately available for sale or hire, and in respect of which a person would be entitled to apply for an order under section 195, may be seized and detained by him or a person authorised by him.

The right to seize and detain is exercisable subject to the following conditions and is subject to any decision of the court under section 204 (order as to disposal of illicit recording).

(2) Before anything is seized under this section notice of the time and place of the proposed seizure must be given to a local police station.

(3) A person may for the purpose of exercising the right conferred by this section enter premises to which the public have access but may not seize anything in the possession, custody or control of a person at a permanent or regular place of business of his and may not use any force.

(4) At the time when anything is seized under this section there shall be left at the place where it was seized a notice in the prescribed form containing the prescribed particulars as to the person by whom or on whose authority the seizure is made and the grounds on which it is made.

(5) In this section—

"premises" includes land, buildings, fixed or moveable structures, vehicles, vessels, aircraft and hovercraft; and

"prescribed" means prescribed by order of the Secretary of State.

(6) An order of the Secretary of State under this section shall be made by statutory instrument which shall be subject to annulment in pursuance of a resolution of either House of Parliament.

Meaning of "illicit recording"

197.—(1) In [this Chapter] "illicit recording", in relation to a performance, shall be construed in accordance with this section.

(2) For the purposes of a performer's rights, a recording of the whole or any substantial part of a performance of his is an illicit recording if it is made, otherwise than for private purposes, without his consent.

(3) For the purposes of the rights of a person having recording rights, a recording of the whole or any substantial part of a performance subject to the exclusive recording contract is an illicit recording if it is made, otherwise than for private purposes, without his consent or that of the performer.

(4) For the purposes of sections 198 and 199 (offences and orders for delivery up in criminal proceedings), a recording is an illicit recording if it is an illicit recording for the purposes mentioned in subsection (2) or subsection (3).

(5) In [this Chapter] "illicit recording" includes a recording falling to be treated as an illicit recording by virtue of any of the following provisions of Schedule 2—

[*paragraph 1B(5) and (7) (personal copies of recordings for private use),*]

[paragraph 1D(3) (copies for text and data analysis for non-commercial research),]

[...]

[paragraph 3A(5) or (6) or 3B(10) (accessible copies of recordings made for disabled persons)]

[paragraph 6(5) (recording by educational establishments of broadcasts),]

[paragraph 6ZA(7) (copying and use of extracts of recordings by educational establishments),]

[paragraph 6F(5)(b) (copying by librarians: single copies of published recordings),]

[paragraph 6G(5)(b) (copying by librarians or archivists: single copies of unpublished recordings),]

paragraph 12(2) (recordings of performance in electronic form retained on transfer of principal recording),

[paragraph 14(6)(b) (recordings of folksongs),]
paragraph 16(3) (recordings made for purposes of broadcast [...]),
[paragraph 17A(2) (recording for the purposes of time-shifting),or
paragraph 17B(2) (photographs of broadcasts),]
but otherwise does not include a recording made in accordance with any of the provisions of that Schedule.

(6) It is immaterial for the purposes of this section where the recording was made.

Notes:

(1) In subs.(5), the words "or cable programme" repealed and the entries for paragraphs 17A(2) and 17B(2) inserted by the Copyright and Related Rights Regulations 2003 (SI 2003/2498), reg.20 and Sch.2, with effect from October 31, 2003. For savings and transitional provisions, see Part 3 of those Regulations.

(2) In subs.(1) and (5) the words "this Chapter" substituted for the former words "this Part" by the Performances (Moral Rights, etc.) Regulations 2006 (SI 2006/18), Sch. para.8, with effect from February 1, 2006.

(3) In subs.(5) entries relating to paras 1D(3), 6ZA(7), 6F(5)(b), 6G(5)(b), 14(6)(b) inserted, entry relating to para.4(3) repealed, and entry relating to para.6(5) substituted, by the Copyright and Rights in Performances (Research, Education, Libraries and Archives) Regulations 2014 (SI 2014/1372), Sch. para.7, with effect from June 1, 2014 at 00.02.

(4) In subs.(5) entry relating to para.3A(5) or (6) or 3B(10) inserted by the Copyright and Rights in Performances (Disability) Regulations 2014 (SI 2014/1384), Sch. para.4, with effect from June 1, 2014 at 00.01.

(5) In subs.(5) entry relating to para.1B(5) and (7) inserted by the Copyright and Rights in Performances (Personal Copies for Private Use) Regulations 2014 (SI 2014/2361), reg.4(2), with effect from October 1, 2014. However, SI 2014/2361 was quashed with prospective effect on July 17, 2015: The Queen on the application of British Academy of Songwriters, Composers and Authors v Secretary of State for Business, Innovation and Skills [2015] EWHC 2041 (Admin) at [11], [21]. Accordingly, this consequential amendment has no effect from that date. However, the Court declined to rule as to whether the regulations were void during the period from October 1, 2014 to July 16, 2015. Accordingly the question of whether this amendment is effective during that period remains undecided: see the judgment at [19], [21].

Presumptions relevant to recordings of performances

[197A.—(1) In proceedings brought by virtue of this Part with respect to the rights in a performance, where copies of a recording of the performance as issued to the public bear a statement that a named person was the performer, the statement shall be admissible as evidence of the fact stated and shall be presumed to be correct until the contrary is proved.

(2) Subsection (1) does not apply to proceedings for an offence under section 198 (criminal liability for making etc. illicit recordings); but without prejudice to its application in proceedings for an order under section 199 (order for delivery up in criminal proceedings).]

Note: Section 197A was inserted by the Intellectual Property (Enforcement, etc.) Regulations 2006 (SI 2006/1028), Sch.2 para.10, with effect from April 29, 2006.

Offences

Criminal liability for making, dealing with or using illicit recordings

198.—(1) A person commits an offence who without sufficient consent—
(a) makes for sale or hire, or
(b) imports into the United Kingdom otherwise than for his private and domestic use, or

(c) possesses in the course of a business with a view to committing any act infringing the rights conferred by [this Chapter], or

(d) in the course of a business—

   (i) sells or lets for hire, or

   (ii) offers or exposes for sale or hire, or

   (iii) distributes,

a recording which is, and which he knows or has reason to believe is, an illicit recording.

[(1A) A person who infringes a performer's making available right—

(a) in the course of a business, or

(b) otherwise than in the course of a business to such an extent as to affect prejudicially the owner of the making available right,

commits an offence if he knows or has reason to believe that, by doing so, he is infringing the making available right in the recording.]

(2) A person commits an offence who causes a recording of a performance made without sufficient consent to be—

(a) shown or played in public, or

[(b) communicated to the public,]

thereby infringing any of the rights conferred by [this Chapter], if he knows or has reason to believe that those rights are thereby infringed.

(3) In subsections (1) and (2) "sufficient consent" means—

(a) in the case of a qualifying performance, the consent of the performer, and

(b) in the case of a non-qualifying performance subject to an exclusive recording contract—

   (i) for the purposes of subsection (1)(a) (making of recording), the consent of the performer or the person having recording rights, and

   (ii) for the purposes of subsection (1)(b), (c) and (d) and subsection (2) (dealing with or using recording), the consent of the person having recording rights.

The references in this subsection to the person having recording rights are to the person having those rights at the time the consent is given or, if there is more than one such person, to all of them.

(4) No offence is committed under subsection (1) or (2) by the commission of an act which by virtue of any provision of Schedule 2 may be done without infringing the rights conferred by [this Chapter].

(5) A person guilty of an offence under subsection (1)(a), (b) or (d)(iii) is liable—

(a) on summary conviction to imprisonment for a term not exceeding six months or [a fine], or both;

(b) on conviction on indictment to a fine or imprisonment for a term not exceeding [ten] years, or both.

[(5A) A person guilty of an offence under subsection (1A) is liable—

(a) on summary conviction to imprisonment for a term not exceeding three months or [a fine], or both;

(b) on conviction on indictment to a fine or imprisonment for a term not exceeding two years, or both.]

(6) A person guilty of any other offence under this section is liable on summary conviction to a fine not exceeding level 5 on the standard scale or imprisonment for a term not exceeding six months, or both.

Notes:

(1) The word in square brackets in subs.(5)(b) was substituted for the former word

"two" by the Copyright, etc. and Trade Marks (Offences and Enforcement) Act 2002 (c.25), s.1, with effect from November 20, 2002 (Copyright, etc. and Trade Marks (Offences and Enforcement) Act 2002 (Commencement) Order 2002 (SI 2002/2749)).

(2) Subsection (2A) and (5A) inserted and subs.(2)(b) was substituted by reg.26 of para.4(5) of Sch.1 to the Copyright and Related Rights Regulations 2003 (SI 2003/2498).

(3) In subs.(1)(c), (2) and (4) the words "this Chapter" substituted for the former words "this Part" by the Performances (Moral Rights, etc.) Regulations 2006 (SI 2006/18), Sch. para.8, with effect from February 1, 2006.

(4) The figures in square brackets in subss.(5)(a) and (5A)(a) substituted for the former words "the statutory maximum" by the Digital Economy Act 2010 s.42(3), with effect from June 8, 2010.

(5) In subs.(5)(a), (5A)(a) words in square brackets substituted, subject to transitional provisions and savings, by the Legal Aid, Sentencing and Punishment of Offenders Act 2012 (Fines on Summary Conviction) Regulations 2015 (SI 2015/664), Sch.4 para.17(3), with effect from March 12, 2015 (for transitional provisions and savings see SI 2015/664, reg.5(1)). The existing wording, in both places, was "a fine not exceeding £50,000".

Enforcement by local weights and measures authority

[198A.—(1) It is the duty of every local weights and measures authority to enforce within their area the provisions of section 198.

(3) Subsection (1) above does not apply in relation to the enforcement of section 198 in Northern Ireland, but it is the duty of the Department of Economic Development to enforce that section in Northern Ireland.

[(3A) For the investigatory powers available to a local weights and measures authority or the Department of Enterprise, Trade and Investment in Northern Ireland for the purposes of the duties in this section, see Schedule 5 to the Consumer Rights Act 2015.]

(4) Any enactment which authorises the disclosure of information for the purpose of facilitating the enforcement of the Trade Descriptions Act 1968 shall apply as if section 198 were contained in that Act and as if the functions of any person in relation to the enforcement of that section were functions under that Act.

(5) Nothing in this section shall be construed as authorising a local weights and measures authority to bring proceedings in Scotland for an offence.]

Note: Subsection (2) and words in subs.(3) repealed, and subs.(3A) inserted, by the Consumer Rights Act 2015, Sch.6 para.50, with effect from October 1, 2015 subject to transitional provisions and savings specified in SI 2015/1630, art.8. Subs.(2) previously read:

"(2) The following provisions of the Trade Descriptions Act 1968 apply in relation to the enforcement of that section by such an authority as in relation to the enforcement of that Act—

section 27 (power to make test purchases),

section 28 (power to enter premises and inspect and seize goods and documents),

section 29 (obstruction of authorised officers), and

section 33 (compensation for loss, &c. of goods seized)."

The words repealed in subs.(3) read:

"For that purpose the provisions of the Trade Descriptions Act 1968 specified in subsection (2) apply as if for the references to a local weights and measures authority and any officer of such an authority there were substituted references to that Department and any of its officers."

Order for delivery up in criminal proceedings

199.—(1) The court before which proceedings are brought against a person for an offence under section 198 may, if satisfied that at the time of his arrest or charge he had in his possession, custody or control in the course of a business an illicit recording of a performance, order that it be delivered up to a person having performers' rights or recording rights in relation to the performance or to such other person as the court may direct.

(2) For this purpose a person shall be treated as charged with an offence—

   (a) in England, Wales and Northern Ireland, when he is orally charged or is served with a summons or indictment;

   (b) in Scotland, when he is cautioned, charged or served with a complaint or indictment.

(3) An order may be made by the court of its own motion or on the application of the prosecutor (or, in Scotland, the Lord Advocate or procurator-fiscal), and may be made whether or not the person is convicted of the offence, but shall not be made—

   (a) after the end of the period specified in section 203 (period after which remedy of delivery up not available), or

   (b) if it appears to the court unlikely that any order will be made under section 204 (order as to disposal of illicit recording).

(4) An appeal lies from an order made under this section by a magistrates' court—

   (a) in England and Wales, to the Crown Court, and

   (b) in Northern Ireland, to the county court;

and in Scotland, where an order has been made under this section, the person from whose possession, custody or control the illicit recording has been removed may, without prejudice to any other form of appeal under any rule of law, appeal against that order in the same manner as against sentence.

(5) A person to whom an illicit recording is delivered up in pursuance of an order under this section shall retain it pending the making of an order, or the decision not to make an order, under section 204.

(6) Nothing in this section affects the powers of the court under [section 143 of the Powers of Criminal Courts (Sentencing) Act 2000], [Part II of the Proceeds of Crime (Scotland) Act 1995] or [Article 11 of the Criminal Justice (Northern Ireland) Order 1994] (general provisions as to forfeiture in criminal proceedings).

Notes:

  (1) The official version of this Act has the word "in" twice at the start of subs.(6), presumably in error.

  (2) In subs.(6), the words in the first set of square brackets substituted for the former words "section 43 of the Powers of Criminal Courts Act 1973" by the Powers of Criminal Courts (Sentencing) Act 2000 (c.6), s.165 and Sch.9, para 116, with effect from August 25, 2000. Subsection (6) had previously been amended by the Criminal Procedure (Consequential Provisions) (Scotland) Act 1995, with effect from April 1, 1996 by virtue of that Act, which inserted the words in the first set of square brackets in place of "Chapter II of Part II of the Criminal Justice (Scotland) Act 1995", such words having been inserted into Subsection (6) by the Criminal Justice (Scotland) Act 1995 with effect from September 26, 1995 by virtue of the Criminal Justice (Scotland) Act 1995 (Commencement No.1 Transitional Provisions and Savings) Order 1995 (SI 1995/2995).

  (3) Subsection (6) is printed as further amended by the Criminal Justice (Northern Ireland) Order 1994 (SI 1994/2795 (N.I.15)) with effect from January 9, 1995 by virtue of the Criminal Justice (1994 Order) (Commencement) Order (Northern Ireland) 1994 (SI 1994/446).

Search warrants

200.—(1) Where a justice of the peace (in Scotland, a sheriff or justice of the peace) is satisfied by information on oath given by a constable (in Scotland, by evidence on oath) that there are reasonable grounds for believing—

(a) that an offence under [section 198(1) or (1A)] (offences of making, importing [, possessing, selling etc.] or distributing illicit recordings) has been or is about to be committed in any premises, and

(b) that evidence that such an offence has been or is about to be committed is in those premises,

he may issue a warrant authorising a constable to enter and search the premises, using such reasonable force as is necessary.

(2) The power conferred by subsection (1) does not, in England and Wales, extend to authorising a search for material of the kinds mentioned in section 9(2) of the Police and Criminal Evidence Act 1984 (certain classes of personal or confidential material).

(3) A warrant under subsection (1)—

(a) may authorise persons to accompany any constable executing the warrant, and

(b) remains in force for [three months] from the date of its issue.

[(3A) In executing a warrant issued under subsection (1) a constable may seize an article if he reasonably believes that it is evidence that any offence under section 198(1) or (1A) has been or is about to be committed.]

(4) In this section "premises" includes land, buildings, fixed or moveable structures, vehicles, vessels, aircraft and hovercraft.

Notes:

(1) In subs.(1)(a), the words in square brackets substituted for the former words "section 198(1)" by the Copyright and Related Rights Regulations 2003 (SI 2003/2498), reg.26 with effect from October 31, 2003. For savings and transitional provisions, see Part 3 of those Regulations. The words "198(1)" were previously substituted for the original words "198(1)(a), (b) or (d)(iii)" by the Copyright, etc. and Trade Marks (Offences and Enforcement) Act 2002 (c.25), s.2, with effect from November 20, 2002 (Copyright, etc. and Trade Marks (Offences and Enforcement) Act 2002 (Commencement) Order 2002 (SI 2002/2749)).

(2) Subsection (3A) was inserted by the Copyright, etc. and Trade Marks (Offences and Enforcement) Act 2002 (c.25), s.2, with effect from November 20, 2002 (Copyright, etc. and Trade Marks (Offences and Enforcement) Act 2002 (Commencement) Order 2002 (SI 2002/2749)).

(3) The words in square brackets in subs.(3)(b) substituted for the former words "28 days" by the Serious Organised Crime and Police Act 2005 (c.15), Sch.16 para.6, with effect from January 1, 2006.

False representation of authority to give consent

201.—(1) It is an offence for a person to represent falsely that he is authorised by any person to give consent for the purposes of [this Chapter] in relation to a performance, unless he believes on reasonable grounds that he is so authorised.

(2) A person guilty of an offence under this section is liable on summary conviction to imprisonment for a term not exceeding six months or a fine not exceeding level 5 on the standard scale or both.

Note: In subs.(1) the words "this Chapter" substituted for the former words "this Part" by the Performances (Moral Rights, etc.) Regulations 2006 (SI 2006/18), Sch. para.8, with effect from February 1, 2006.

Offence by body corporate: liability of officers

202.—(1) Where an offence under [this Chapter] committed by a body corporate is proved to have been committed with the consent or connivance of a director, manager, secretary or other similar officer of the body, or a person purporting to act in any such capacity, he as well as the body corporate is guilty of the offence and liable to be proceeded against and punished accordingly.

(2) In relation to a body corporate whose affairs are managed by its members "director" means a member of the body corporate.

Note: In s.202(1) the words "this Chapter" substituted for the former words "this Part" by the Performances (Moral Rights, etc.) Regulations 2006 (SI 2006/18), Sch. para.8, with effect from February 1, 2006.

Supplementary provisions with respect to delivery up and seizure

Period after which remedy of delivery up not available

203.—(1) An application for an order under section 195 (order for delivery up in civil proceedings) may not be made after the end of the period of six years from the date on which the illicit recording in question was made, subject to the following provisions.

(2) If during the whole or any part of that period a person entitled to apply for an order—

(a) is under a disability, or

(b) is prevented by fraud or concealment from discovering the facts entitling him to apply,

an application may be made by him at any time before the end of the period of six years from the date on which he ceased to be under a disability or, as the case may be, could with reasonable diligence have discovered those facts.

(3) In subsection (2) "disability"—

(a) in England and Wales, has the same meaning as in the Limitation Act 1980;

(b) in Scotland, means legal disability within the meaning of the Prescription and Limitations (Scotland) Act 1973;

(c) in Northern Ireland, has the same meaning as in the Statute of Limitation (Northern Ireland) 1958.

(4) An order under section 199 (order for delivery up in criminal proceedings) shall not, in any case, be made after the end of the period of six years from the date on which the illicit recording in question was made.

Order as to disposal of illicit recording

204.—(1) An application may be made to the court for an order that an illicit recording of a performance delivered up in pursuance of an order under section 195 or 199, or seized and detained in pursuance of the right conferred by section 196, shall be—

(a) forfeited to such person having performer's rights or recording rights in relation to the performance as the court may direct, or

(b) destroyed or otherwise dealt with as the court may think fit,

or for a decision that no such order should be made.

(2) In considering what order (if any) should be made, the court shall consider whether other remedies available in an action for infringement of the rights conferred by [this Chapter] would be adequate to compensate the person or persons entitled to the rights and to protect their interests.

(3) Provision shall be made by rules of court as to the service of notice on persons having an interest in the recording, and any such person is entitled—

(a) to appear in proceedings for an order under this section, whether or not he was served with notice, and

(b) to appeal against any order made, whether or not he appeared;

and an order shall not take effect until the end of the period within which notice of an appeal may be given or, if before the end of that period notice of appeal is duly given, until the final determination or abandonment of the proceedings on the appeal.

(4) Where there is more than one person interested in a recording, the court shall make such order as it thinks just and may (in particular) direct that the recording be sold, or otherwise dealt with, and the proceeds divided.

(5) If the court decides that no order should be made under this section, the person in whose possession, custody or control the recording was before being delivered up or seized is entitled to its return.

(6) References in this section to a person having an interest in a recording include any person in whose favour an order could be made in respect of the recording

[(a) under this section or under section 114 or 231 of this Act;

(b) under section 24D of the Registered Designs Act 1949;

(c) under section 19 of Trade Marks Act 1994 (including that section as applied by regulation 4 of the Community Trade Mark Regulations 2006 (SI 2006/1027)); or

(d) under regulation 1C of the Community Design Regulations 2005 (SI 2005/2339).]

Notes:

(1) Subsection (6) is printed as amended by the Trade Marks Act 1994 with effect from October 31, 1994 by virtue of the Trade Marks Act 1994 (Commencement) Order 1994 (SI 1994/2550).

(2) In subs.(2) the words "this Chapter" substituted for the former words "this Part" by the Performances (Moral Rights, etc.) Regulations 2006 (SI 2006/18), Sch. para.8, with effect from February 1, 2006.

(3) The words in square brackets in subs.(6) substituted by the Intellectual Property (Enforcement, etc.) Regulations 2006 (SI 2006/1028), Sch.2 para.11, with effect from April 29, 2006.

Forfeiture of illicit recordings: England and Wales or Northern Ireland

[204A.—(1) In England and Wales or Northern Ireland where illicit recordings of a performance have come into the possession of any person in connection with the investigation or prosecution of a relevant offence, that person may apply under this section for an order for the forfeiture of the illicit recordings.

(2) For the purposes of this section "relevant offence" means—

(a) an offence under [section 198(1) or (1A)] (criminal liability for making or dealing with illicit recordings),

(b) an offence under the Trade Descriptions Act 1968 (c. 29),

[(ba) an offence under the Business Protection from Misleading Marketing Regulations 2008,

(bb) an offence under the Consumer Protection from Unfair Trading Regulations 2008, or]

(c) an offence involving dishonesty or deception.

(3) An application under this section may be made—

(a) where proceedings have been brought in any court for a relevant offence relating to some or all of the illicit recordings, to that court, or

(b) where no application for the forfeiture of the illicit recordings has been made under paragraph (a), by way of complaint to a magistrates' court.

(4) On an application under this section, the court shall make an order for the forfeiture of any illicit recordings only if it is satisfied that a relevant offence has been committed in relation to the illicit recordings.

(5) A court may infer for the purposes of this section that such an offence has

been committed in relation to any illicit recordings if it is satisfied that such an offence has been committed in relation to illicit recordings which are representative of the illicit recordings in question (whether by reason of being part of the same consignment or batch or otherwise).

(6) Any person aggrieved by an order made under this section by a magistrates' court, or by a decision of such a court not to make such an order, may appeal against that order or decision—

(a) in England and Wales, to the Crown Court, or

(b) in Northern Ireland, to the county court.

(7) An order under this section may contain such provision as appears to the court to be appropriate for delaying the coming into force of the order pending the making and determination of any appeal (including any application under section 111 of the Magistrates' Courts Act 1980 (c. 43) or Article 146 of the Magistrates' Courts (Northern Ireland) Order 1981 (SI 1987/1675 (N.I. 26)) (statement of case)).

(8) Subject to subsection (9), where any illicit recordings are forfeited under this section they shall be destroyed in accordance with such directions as the court may give.

(9) On making an order under this section the court may direct that the illicit recordings to which the order relates shall (instead of being destroyed) be forfeited to the person having the performers' rights or recording rights in question or dealt with in such other way as the court considers appropriate.]

Notes:

(1) Section 204A was inserted by the Copyright, etc. and Trade Marks (Offences and Enforcement) Act 2002 (c.25), s.4, with effect from November 20, 2002 (Copyright, etc. and Trade Marks (Offences and Enforcement) Act 2002 (Commencement) Order 2002 (SI 2002/2749)).

(2) The words in square brackets in subs.(2)(a) substituted for the former words "section 198(1)" by the Copyright and Related Rights Regulations 2003 (SI 2003/2498), reg.26, with effect from October 31, 2003. For savings and transitional provisions, see Part 3 of those Regulations.

(3) In subs.(2) paras (ba) and (bb) inserted by the Consumer Protection from Unfair Trading Regulations 2008 (SI 2008/1277), reg.30(1), Sch.2, para.42, with effect from May 26, 2008.

Forfeiture: Scotland

[204B.—(1) In Scotland the court may make an order under this section for the forfeiture of any illicit recordings.

(2) An order under this section may be made—

(a) on an application by the procurator-fiscal made in the manner specified in section 134 of the Criminal Procedure (Scotland) Act 1995 (c. 46), or

(b) where a person is convicted of a relevant offence, in addition to any other penalty which the court may impose.

(3) On an application under subsection (2)(a), the court shall make an order for the forfeiture of any illicit recordings only if it is satisfied that a relevant offence has been committed in relation to the illicit recordings.

(4) The court may infer for the purposes of this section that such an offence has been committed in relation to any illicit recordings if it is satisfied that such an offence has been committed in relation to illicit recordings which are representative of the illicit recordings in question (whether by reason of being part of the same consignment or batch or otherwise).

(5) The procurator-fiscal making the application under subsection (2)(a) shall serve on any person appearing to him to be the owner of, or otherwise to have an interest in, the illicit recordings to which the application relates a copy of the ap-

plication, together with a notice giving him the opportunity to appear at the hearing of the application to show cause why the illicit recordings should not be forfeited.

(6) Service under subsection (5) shall be carried out, and such service may be proved, in the manner specified for citation of an accused in summary proceedings under the Criminal Procedure (Scotland) Act 1995.

(7) Any person upon whom notice is served under subsection (5) and any other person claiming to be the owner of, or otherwise to have an interest in, illicit recordings to which an application under this section relates shall be entitled to appear at the hearing of the application to show cause why the illicit recordings should not be forfeited.

(8) The court shall not make an order following an application under subsection (2)(a)—

(a) if any person on whom notice is served under subsection (5) does not appear, unless service of the notice on that person is proved, or

(b) if no notice under subsection (5) has been served, unless the court is satisfied that in the circumstances it was reasonable not to serve such notice.

(9) Where an order for the forfeiture of any illicit recordings is made following an application under subsection (2)(a), any person who appeared, or was entitled to appear, to show cause why the illicit recordings should not be forfeited may, within 21 days of the making of the order, appeal to the High Court by Bill of Suspension.

(10) Section 182(5)(a) to (e) of the Criminal Procedure (Scotland) Act 1995 shall apply to an appeal under subsection (9) as it applies to a stated case under Part 2 of that Act.

(11) An order following an application under subsection (2)(a) shall not take effect—

(a) until the end of the period of 21 days beginning with the day after the day on which the order is made, or

(b) if an appeal is made under subsection (9) above within that period, until the appeal is determined or abandoned.

(12) An order under subsection (2)(b) shall not take effect—

(a) until the end of the period within which an appeal against the order could be brought under the Criminal Procedure (Scotland) Act 1995 (c. 46), or

(b) if an appeal is made within that period, until the appeal is determined or abandoned.

(13) Subject to subsection (14), illicit recordings forfeited under this section shall be destroyed in accordance with such directions as the court may give.

(14) On making an order under this section the court may direct that the illicit recordings to which the order relates shall (instead of being destroyed) be forfeited to the person having the performers' rights or recording rights in question or dealt with in such other way as the court considers appropriate.

(15) For the purposes of this section—

["relevant offence" means—

(a) an offence under section 198(1) or (1A) (criminal liability for making or dealing with illicit recordings),

(b) an offence under the Trade Descriptions Act 1968,

(c) an offence under the Business Protection from Misleading Marketing Regulations 2008,

(d) an offence under the Consumer Protection from Unfair Trading Regulations 2008, or

(e) any offence involving dishonesty or deception;"]

"the court" means—
> (a) in relation to an order made on an application under subsection (2)(a), the sheriff, and
> (b) in relation to an order made under subsection (2)(b), the court which imposed the penalty.]

Notes:

(1) Section 204B was inserted by the Copyright, etc. and Trade Marks (Offences and Enforcement) Act 2002 (c.25), s.4, with effect from November 20, 2002 (Copyright, etc. and Trade Marks (Offences and Enforcement) Act 2002 (Commencement) Order 2002 (SI 2002/2749)).

(2) In subs.(15) the definition of "relevant offence" substituted by the Consumer Protection from Unfair Trading Regulations 2008 (SI 2008/1277), reg.30(1), Sch.2, para.43, with effect from May 26, 2008.

Jurisdiction of county court and sheriff court

205.—(1) In England [and Wales the county court and in] and Northern Ireland a county court may entertain proceedings under—

> section 195 (order for delivery up of illicit recording), or

> section 204 (order as to disposal of illicit recording),

[save that, in Northern Ireland, a county court may entertain such proceedings only] where the value of the illicit recordings in question does not exceed the county court limit for actions in tort.

(2) In Scotland proceedings for an order under either of those provisions may be brought in the sheriff court.

(3) Nothing in this section shall be construed as affecting the jurisdiction of the High Court or, in Scotland, the Court of Session.

Notes:

(1) Subsection (1) is printed as amended by the High Court and County Courts Jurisdiction Order 1991 (SI 1991/724).

(2) In subs.(1) words in square brackets substituted for words ", Wales and", subject to savings and transitional provisions, by the Crime and Courts Act 2013, Sch.9(3) para.72, with effect from April 22, 2014 (for savings and transitional provisions, see Sch.8 of the Act and the Crime and Courts Act 2013 (Commencement No.10 and Transitional Provision) Order 2014 (SI 2014/954), arts 2(c), 3).

[Licensing of performers' [...] rights

Licensing of performers' [...] rights

205A. The provisions of Schedule 2A have effect with respect to the licensing of performers' [...] rights.]

Notes:

(1) This section and the heading preceding it inserted by the Copyright and Related Rights Regulations 1996 (SI 1996/2967), with effect from December 1, 1996. For savings and transitional provisions, see Part III of those Regulations.

(2) In s.205A and the preceding heading, the word "property" repealed by the Enterprise and Regulatory Reform Act 2013, Sch.22 para.6, with effect from April 25, 2013.

[Jurisdiction of Copyright Tribunal

Jurisdiction of Copyright Tribunal

205B.—(1) The Copyright Tribunal has jurisdiction under [this Chapter] to hear and determine proceedings under—

    (a) section 182D (amount of equitable remuneration for exploitation of commercial sound recording);

    (b) section 190 (application to give consent on behalf of owner of reproduction right);

    (c) section 191H (amount of equitable remuneration on transfer of rental right);

[(cc) paragraph 19 of Schedule 2 (determination of royalty or other remuneration to be paid with respect to re-transmission of broadcast including performance or recording);]

    (d) paragraph 3, 4 or 5 of Schedule 2A (reference of licensing scheme);

    (e) paragraph 6 or 7 of that Schedule (application with respect to licence under licensing scheme);

    (f) paragraph 10, 11 or 12 of that Schedule (reference or application with respect to licensing by licensing body);

    (g) paragraph 15 of that Schedule (application to settle royalty for certain lending);

    (h) paragraph 17 of that Schedule (application to settle terms of licence available as of right).

(2) The provisions of Chapter VIII of Part I (general provisions relating to the Copyright Tribunal) apply in relation to the Tribunal when exercising any jurisdiction under [this Chapter].

(3) Provision shall be made by rules under section 150 prohibiting the Tribunal from entertaining a reference under paragraph 3, 4 or 5 of Schedule 2A (reference of licensing scheme) by a representative organisation unless the Tribunal is satisfied that the organisation is reasonably representative of the class of persons which it claims to represent.]

Notes:

    (1) This section and the heading preceding it inserted by the Copyright and Related Rights Regulations 1996 (SI 1996/2967), with effect from December 1, 1996. For savings and transitional provisions, see Part III of those Regulations.

    (2) Subsection (1)(cc) was inserted by s.138 and Sch.9 to the Broadcasting Act 1996 with effect from October 1, 1996 by virtue of the Broadcasting Act 1996 (Commencement No.1 and Transitional Provisions) Order 1996 (SI 1996/2120).

    (3) In subs.(1) and (2) the words "this Chapter" substituted for the former words "this Part" by the Performances (Moral Rights, etc.) Regulations 2006 (SI 2006/18), Sch. para.8, with effect from February 1, 2006.

Note: Sections 182 to 205B became Chapter 2 of Part 2 and the cross-heading before s.182 was inserted by the Performances (Moral Rights, etc.) Regulations 2006 (SI 2006/18), reg.4(4), (5), with effect from February 1, 2006.

[Chapter 3

Moral Rights

Right to be identified as performer

Right to be identified as performer

205C.—(1) Whenever a person—

    (a) produces or puts on a qualifying performance that is given in public,

    (b) broadcasts live a qualifying performance,

    (c) communicates to the public a sound recording of a qualifying performance, or

(d) issues to the public copies of such a recording,
the performer has the right to be identified as such.

(2) The right of the performer under this section is—

(a) in the case of a performance that is given in public, to be identified in any programme accompanying the performance or in some other manner likely to bring his identity to the notice of a person seeing or hearing the performance,

(b) in the case of a performance that is broadcast, to be identified in a manner likely to bring his identity to the notice of a person seeing or hearing the broadcast,

(c) in the case of a sound recording that is communicated to the public, to be identified in a manner likely to bring his identity to the notice of a person hearing the communication,

(d) in the case of a sound recording that is issued to the public, to be identified in or on each copy or, if that is not appropriate, in some other manner likely to bring his identity to the notice of a person acquiring a copy,

or (in any of the above cases) to be identified in such other manner as may be agreed between the performer and the person mentioned in subsection (1).

(3) The right conferred by this section in relation to a performance given by a group (or so much of a performance as is given by a group) is not infringed—

(a) in a case falling within paragraph (a), (b) or (c) of subsection (2), or

(b) in a case falling within paragraph (d) of that subsection in which it is not reasonably practicable for each member of the group to be identified,

if the group itself is identified as specified in subsection (2).

(4) In this section "group" means two or more performers who have a particular name by which they may be identified collectively.

(5) If the assertion under section 205D specifies a pseudonym, initials or some other particular form of identification, that form shall be used; otherwise any reasonable form of identification may be used.

(6) This section has effect subject to section 205E (exceptions to right).

Requirement that right be asserted

205D.—(1) A person does not infringe the right conferred by section 205C (right to be identified as performer) by doing any of the acts mentioned in that section unless the right has been asserted in accordance with the following provisions so as to bind him in relation to that act.

(2) The right may be asserted generally, or in relation to any specified act or description of acts—

(a) by instrument in writing signed by or on behalf of the performer, or

(b) on an assignment of a performer's property rights, by including in the instrument effecting the assignment a statement that the performer asserts in relation to the performance his right to be identified.

(3) The persons bound by an assertion of the right under subsection (2) are—

(a) in the case of an assertion under subsection (2)(a), anyone to whose notice the assertion is brought;

(b) in the case of an assertion under subsection (2)(b), the assignee and anyone claiming through him, whether or not he has notice of the assertion.

(4) In an action for infringement of the right the court shall, in considering remedies, take into account any delay in asserting the right.

Exceptions to right

205E.—(1) The right conferred by section 205C (right to be identified as performer) is subject to the following exceptions.

(2) The right does not apply where it is not reasonably practicable to identify the performer (or, where identification of a group is permitted by virtue of section 205C(3), the group).

(3) The right does not apply in relation to any performance given for the purposes of reporting current events.

(4) The right does not apply in relation to any performance given for the purposes of advertising any goods or services.

(5) The right is not infringed by an act which by virtue of any of the following provisions of Schedule 2 would not infringe any of the rights conferred by Chapter 2—

(a) paragraph 2(1A) (news reporting);
(b) paragraph 3 (incidental inclusion of a performance or recording);
(c) paragraph 4(2) (things done for the purposes of examination);
(d) paragraph 8 (parliamentary and judicial proceedings);
(e) paragraph 9 (Royal Commissions and statutory inquiries).

Right to object to derogatory treatment

Right to object to derogatory treatment of performance

205F.—(1) The performer of a qualifying performance has a right which is infringed if—

(a) the performance is broadcast live, or
(b) by means of a sound recording the performance is played in public or communicated to the public, with any distortion, mutilation or other modification that is prejudicial to the reputation of the performer.

(2) This section has effect subject to section 205G (exceptions to right).

Exceptions to right

205G.—(1) The right conferred by section 205F (right to object to derogatory treatment of performance) is subject to the following exceptions.

(2) The right does not apply in relation to any performance given for the purposes of reporting current events.

(3) The right is not infringed by modifications made to a performance which are consistent with normal editorial or production practice.

(4) Subject to subsection (5), the right is not infringed by anything done for the purpose of—

(a) avoiding the commission of an offence,
(b) complying with a duty imposed by or under an enactment, or
(c) in the case of the British Broadcasting Corporation, avoiding the inclusion in a programme broadcast by them of anything which offends against good taste or decency or which is likely to encourage or incite crime or lead to disorder or to be offensive to public feeling.

(5) Where—

(a) the performer is identified in a manner likely to bring his identity to the notice of a person seeing or hearing the performance as modified by the act in question; or
(b) he has previously been identified in or on copies of a sound recording issued to the public, subsection (4) applies only if there is sufficient disclaimer.

(6) In subsection (5) "sufficient disclaimer", in relation to an act capable of infringing the right, means a clear and reasonably prominent indication—

(a) given in a manner likely to bring it to the notice of a person seeing or hearing the performance as modified by the act in question, and

(b) if the performer is identified at the time of the act, appearing along with the identification, that the modifications were made without the performer's consent.

Infringement of right by possessing or dealing with infringing article

205H.—(1) The right conferred by section 205F (right to object to derogatory treatment of performance) is also infringed by a person who—

(a) possesses in the course of business, or

(b) sells or lets for hire, or offers or exposes for sale or hire, or

(c) distributes, an article which is, and which he knows or has reason to believe is, an infringing article.

(2) An "infringing article" means a sound recording of a qualifying performance with any distortion, mutilation or other modification that is prejudicial to the reputation of the performer.

Supplementary

Duration of rights

205I.—(1) A performer's rights under this Chapter in relation to a performance subsist so long as that performer's rights under Chapter 2 subsist in relation to the performance.

(2) In subsection (1) "performer's rights" includes rights of a performer that are vested in a successor of his.

Consent and waiver of rights

205J.—(1) It is not an infringement of the rights conferred by this Chapter to do any act to which consent has been given by or on behalf of the person entitled to the right.

(2) Any of those rights may be waived by instrument in writing signed by or on behalf of the person giving up the right.

(3) A waiver—

(a) may relate to a specific performance, to performances of a specified description or to performances generally, and may relate to existing or future performances, and

(b) may be conditional or unconditional and may be expressed to be subject to revocation, and if made in favour of the owner or prospective owner of a performer's property rights in the performance or performances to which it relates, it shall be presumed to extend to his licensees and successors in title unless a contrary intention is expressed.

(4) Nothing in this Chapter shall be construed as excluding the operation of the general law of contract or estoppel in relation to an informal waiver or other transaction in relation to either of the rights conferred by this Chapter.

Application of provisions to parts of performances

205K.—(1) The right conferred by section 205C (right to be identified as performer) applies in relation to the whole or any substantial part of a performance.

(2) The right conferred by section 205F (right to object to derogatory treatment of performance) applies in relation to the whole or any part of a performance.

Moral rights not assignable

205L. The rights conferred by this Chapter are not assignable.

Transmission of moral rights on death

205M.—(1) On the death of a person entitled to a right conferred by this Chapter—

    (a) the right passes to such person as he may by testamentary disposition specifically direct,

    (b) if there is no such direction but the performer's property rights in respect of the performance in question form part of his estate, the right passes to the person to whom the property rights pass,

    (c) if or to the extent that the right does not pass under paragraph (a) or (b) it is exercisable by his personal representatives.

(2) Where a performer's property rights pass in part to one person and in part to another, as for example where a bequest is limited so as to apply—

    (a) to one or more, but not all, of the things to which the owner has the right to consent, or

    (b) to part, but not the whole, of the period for which the rights subsist, any right which by virtue of subsection (1) passes with the performer's property rights is correspondingly divided.

(3) Where by virtue of subsection (1)(a) or (1)(b) a right becomes exercisable by more than one person—

    (a) it is, in the case of the right conferred by section 205F (right to object to derogatory treatment of performance), a right exercisable by each of them and is satisfied in relation to any of them if he consents to the treatment or act in question, and

    (b) any waiver of the right in accordance with section 205J by one of them does not affect the rights of the others.

(4) A consent or waiver previously given or made binds any person to whom a right passes by virtue of subsection (1).

(5) Any damages recovered by personal representatives by virtue of this section in respect of an infringement after a person's death shall devolve as part of his estate as if the right of action had subsisted and been vested in him immediately before his death.

Remedies for infringement of moral rights

205N.—(1) An infringement of a right conferred by this Chapter is actionable as a breach of statutory duty owed to the person entitled to the right.

(2) Where—

    (a) there is an infringement of a right conferred by this Chapter,

    (b) a person falsely claiming to act on behalf of a performer consented to the relevant conduct or purported to waive the right, and

    (c) there would have been no infringement if he had been so acting, that person shall be liable, jointly and severally with any person liable in respect of the infringement by virtue of subsection (1), as if he himself had infringed the right.

(3) Where proceedings for infringement of the right conferred on a performer by this Chapter, it shall be a defence to prove—

    (a) that a person claiming to act on behalf of the performer consented to the defendant's conduct or purported to waive the right, and

    (b) that the defendant reasonably believed that the person was acting on behalf of the performer.

(4) In proceedings for infringement of the right conferred by section 205F the court may, if it thinks it an adequate remedy in the circumstances, grant an injunction on terms prohibiting the doing of any act unless a disclaimer is made, in such terms and in such manner as may be approved by the court, dissociating the performer from the broadcast or sound recording of the performance.]

Note: Sections 205C to 205N inserted by the Performances (Moral Rights, etc.) Regulations 2006 (SI 2006/18), reg.6; those sections became Chapter 3 of Part 2 and the cross heading for that Chapter was inserted by reg.4(6) of those Regulations, both with effect from February 1, 2006.

[CHAPTER 4

QUALIFICATION FOR PROTECTION, EXTENT AND INTERPRETATION]

Qualification for protection and extent

Qualifying countries, individuals and persons

206.—(1) In this Part—
    "qualifying country" means—
        (a) the United Kingdom,
        [(b) another member State of the European Economic Community]
        [(b) *another EEA state,*]
        [(ba) *the Channel Islands, the Isle of Man or Gibraltar,*]
        [(bb) *a country which is a party to the Rome Convention,*]
            or
        (c) to the extent that an Order under section 208 so provides, a country designated under that section as enjoying reciprocal protection;
    "qualifying individual" means a citizen or subject of, or an individual resident in, a qualifying country; and
    "qualifying person" means a qualifying individual or a body corporate or other body having legal personality which—
        (a) is formed under the law of a part of the United Kingdom or another qualifying country, and
        (b) has in any qualifying country a place of business at which substantial business activity is carried on.

(2) The reference in the definition of "qualifying individual" to a person's being a citizen or subject of a qualifying country shall be construed—
    (a) in relation to the United Kingdom, as a reference to his being a British citizen, and
    (b) in relation to a colony of the United Kingdom, as a reference to his being a British Dependent Territories' citizen by connection with that colony.

(3) In determining for the purpose of the definition of "qualifying person" whether substantial business activity is carried on at a place of business in any country, no account shall be taken of dealings in goods which are at all material times outside that country.

[(4) *Her Majesty may by Order in Council—*
    (a) *make provision for the application of this Part to a country by virtue of paragraph (bb) or (c) of the definition of "qualifying country" in subsection (1) to be subject to specified restrictions;*

(b) *amend the definition of "qualifying country" in subsection (1) so as to add a country which is not a party to the Rome Convention;*

(c) *make provision for the application of this Part to a country added under paragraph (b) to be subject to specified restrictions.*

(5) *A statutory instrument containing an Order in Council under this section is subject to annulment in pursuance of a resolution of either House of Parliament.*]

[(6) *In this section, "the Rome Convention" means the International Convention for the Protection of Performers, Producers of Phonograms and Broadcasting Organisations done at Rome on 26 October 1961.*]

Note: Subsection (1)(b) in square brackets in italics prospectively substituted for preceding subs.(1)(b), subs.(1)(ba), (bb) prospectively inserted, and subss (4)–(6) prospectively inserted, by the Intellectual Property Act 2014, s.22(5), (6), (7), with effect from a date to be appointed.

Countries to which this Part extends

207. This Part extends to England and Wales, Scotland and Northern Ireland.

Countries enjoying reciprocal protection

208.—(1) Her Majesty may by Order in Council designate as enjoying reciprocal protection under this Part—

(a) a Convention country, or

(b) a country as to which Her Majesty is satisfied that provision has been or will be made under its law giving adequate protection for British performances.

(2) A "Convention country" means a country which is a party to a Convention relating to performers' rights to which the United Kingdom is also a party.

(3) A "British performance" means a performance—

(a) given by an individual who is a British citizen or resident in the United Kingdom, or

(b) taking place in the United Kingdom.

(4) If the law of that country provides adequate protection only for certain descriptions of performance, an Order under subsection (1)(b) designating that country shall contain provision limiting to a corresponding extent the protection afforded by this Part in relation to performances connected with that country.

(5) The power conferred by subsection (1)(b) is exercisable in relation to *any of the Channel Islands, the Isle of Man or* any colony of the United Kingdom, as in relation to a foreign country.

(6) A statutory instrument containing an Order in Council under this section shall be subject to annulment in pursuance of a resolution of either House of Parliament.

Note: In subs.(5) words in italics prospectively repealed by the Intellectual Property Act 2014, s.22(8), with effect from a date to be appointed.

Territorial waters and the continental shelf

209.—(1) For the purposes of this Part the territorial waters of the United Kingdom shall be treated as part of the United Kingdom.

(2) This Part applies to things done in the United Kingdom sector of the continental shelf on a structure or vessel which is present there for purposes directly connected with the exploration of the sea bed or subsoil or the exploitation of their natural resources as it applies to things done in the United Kingdom.

(3) The United Kingdom sector of the continental shelf means the areas designated by order under section 1(7) of the Continental Shelf Act 1964.

British ships, aircraft and hovercraft

210.—(1) This Part applies to things done on a British ship, aircraft or hovercraft as it applies to things done in the United Kingdom.

(2) In this section—

"British ship" means a ship which is a British ship for the purposes of the [Merchant Shipping Act 1995] otherwise than by virtue of registration in a country outside the United Kingdom; and

"British aircraft" and "British hovercraft" mean an aircraft or hovercraft registered in the United Kingdom.

Note: Subsection (2) is printed as amended by the Merchant Shipping Act 1995.

Requirement of signature: application in relation to body corporate

[210A.—(1) The requirement in the following provisions that an instrument be signed by or on behalf of a person is also satisfied in the case of a body corporate by the affixing of its seal—

section 191B(3) (assignment of performer's property rights);

section 191C(1) (assignment of future performer's property rights);

section 191D(1) (grant of exclusive licence).

(2) The requirement in the following provisions that an instrument be signed by a person is also satisfied in the case of a body corporate by signature on behalf of the body or by the affixing of its seal—

section 205D(2)(a) (assertion of performer's moral rights);

section 205J(2) (waiver of performer's moral rights).]

Note: Section 210A was inserted by the Performances (Moral Rights, etc.) Regulations 2006 (SI 2006/18), reg.7, with effect from February 1, 2006.

Interpretation

Expressions having same meaning as in copyright provisions

211.—(1) The following expressions have the same meaning in this Part as in Part I (copyright)—

[assignment (in Scotland),]

broadcast,

business,

[communication to the public,]

country,

defendant (in Scotland),

delivery up (in Scotland),

[the EEA,]

[EEA State,]

film,

[injunction (in Scotland)]

literary work,

published,

[signed,]

[sound recording, and]

[wireless broadcast.]
(2) [The provisions of—
  (a) section 5B(2) and (3) (supplementary provisions relating to films), and
  (b) section 6(3) to (5A) and section 19(4) (supplementary provisions relating to broadcasting),
apply] for the purposes of this Part, and in relation to an infringement of the rights conferred by this Part, as they apply for the purposes of Part I and in relation to an infringement of copyright.

Notes:

(1) Subsection (1) is printed as amended by the Duration of Copyright and Rights in Performances Regulations 1995 (SI 1995/3297), which added "EEA national" with effect from January 1, 1996.
(2) In subs.(1), the entries for "communication to the public", "injunction (Scotland)" and "wireless broadcast" inserted, the entry for "sound recording" amended and the entries for "cable programme" and "cable programme service" repealed by the Copyright and Related Rights Regulations 2003 (SI 2003/2498), Sch.1, para.15, Sch.2, with effect from October 31, 2003. For savings and transitional provisions, see Part 3 of those Regulations.
(3) In subs.(2) the words in square brackets substituted for the former words "6(3) to (5), section 7(5) and 19(4)" and the words "and cable programme services" repealed by the Copyright and Related Rights Regulations 2003 (SI 2003/2498), Sch.1, para.15, Sch.2, with effect from October 31, 2003. For savings and transitional provisions, see Part 3 of those Regulations.
(4) The expressions "assignment (in Scotland)," and "signed," inserted into subs.(1) and the words in square brackets in subs.(2) substituted by the Performances (Moral Rights, etc.) Regulations 2006 (SI 2006/18), Sch. para.6, with effect from February 1, 2006. Also in subs.(1) the expressions "the EEA" and "EEA State" substituted for the former expression "EEA national" by the Intellectual Property (Enforcement, etc.) Regulations 2006 (SI 2006/1028), Sch.2 para.12, with effect from April 29, 2006.

Index of defined expressions

212. The following Table shows provisions defining or otherwise explaining expressions used in this Part (other than provisions defining or explaining an expression used only in the same section)—

[accessible copy (in paragraphs 3A to 3E of Schedule 2)	paragraph 3E(4) of Schedule 2]
[assignment (in Scotland)	section 211(1) (and section 177);]
broadcast (and related expressions)	section 211(1) (and section 6)
business	section 211(1) (and section 178)
[communication to the public	section 211(1) (and section 20)]
[consent of performer (in relation to performer's property rights)	section 191A(2)]
country	section 211(1) (and section 178)
defendant (in Scotland)	section 211(1) (and section 177)
delivery up (in Scotland)	section 211(1) (and section 177)
[disabled person (in paragraphs 3A to 3E of Schedule 2)	paragraph 3E(2) and (3) of Schedule 2]
[distribution right	section 182B(5)]

[the EEA and EEA State	section 211(1) (and section 172A)]
exclusive recording contract	section 185(1)
film	section 211(1) (and [section 5B])
[group	section 205C(4);]
illicit recording	section 197
[injunction (in Scotland)	section 211(1) (and section 177)]
[issue to the public	section 182B;]
[lending right	section 182C(7)]
literary work	section 211(1) (and section 3(1))
[making available right	section 182CA]
performance	section 180(2)
[performer's non-property rights	section 192A(1)]
[performer's property rights	section 191A(1)]
published	section 211(1) (and section 175)
qualifying country	section 206(1)
qualifying individual	section 206(1) and (2)
qualifying performance	section 181
qualifying person	section 206(1) and (3)
recording (of a performance)	section 180(2)
recording rights (person having)	section 185(2) and (3)
[rental right	section 182C(7)]
[reproduction right	section 182A(3)]
[rights owner (in relation to performer's property rights)	section 191A(3) and (4)]
[signed	section 211(1) (and section 176);]
sound recording	section 211(1) (and [section 5A]).
[wireless broadcast	section 211(1) (and section 178).]

Notes:

(1) The references to "film" and "sound recording" amended by, and the reference to "EEA national" was inserted by the Duration of Copyright and Rights in Performances Regulations 1995 (SI 1995/3297), with effect from January 1, 1996.

(2) The references to "consent of performer (in relation to performer's property rights)", "distribution right", "lending right", "performer's non-property rights", "performer's property rights", "rental right", "reproduction right", and "rights owner (in relation to performers' property rights)" inserted by the Copyright and Related Rights Regulations 1996 (SI 1996/2967), with effect from December 1, 1996.

(3) The entries for "communication to the public", "injunction (Scotland)" and "making available right" inserted and the entry for "cable programme" repealed by the Copyright and Related Rights Regulations 2003 (SI 2003/2498), Sch.1, para.15, Sch.2, with effect from October 31, 2003. For savings and transitional provisions, see Part 3 of those Regulations. The former entry for "cable programme" provided:

cable programme, cable programme service   *section 211(1) (and section 7)*
(and related expressions)

(4) The expressions "assignment (in Scotland)" "group", "issue to the public", "signed" and "wireless broadcast" inserted into s.212 by the Performances (Moral Rights, etc.) Regulations 2006 (SI 2006/18), Sch. para.7, with effect from February 1, 2006. Also in s.212 the expression "the EEA and EEA State" was substituted for the former expression "EEA national" by the Intellectual Property (Enforcement, etc.) Regulations 2006 (SI 2006/1028), Sch.2 para.13, with effect from April 29, 2006.

(5) In the table, entries relating to "accessible copy " and "disabled person" inserted by the Copyright and Rights in Performances (Disability) Regulations 2014 (SI 2014/1384), Sch. para.5, with effect from June 1, 2014 at 00.01.

Note: Sections 206 to 212 became Chapter 4 and the cross heading before s.206 was inserted by the Performances (Moral Rights, etc.) Regulations 2006 (SI 2006/18), reg.4(7), with effect from February 1, 2006.

[Supplementary

Power to amend in consequence of changes to international law

[212A.—(1) The Secretary of State may by order amend this Part in consequence of changes to international law in the area of performance rights.

(2) An order under this section must be made by statutory instrument; and no order may be made unless a draft of it has been laid before and approved by a resolution of each House of Parliament.]

Note: Section 212A is prospectively inserted, by the Intellectual Property Act 2014, s.22(9), with effect from a date to be appointed.

Part III

Design Right

Chapter I

Design Right in Original Designs

Introductory

Design right

213.—(1) Design right is a property right which subsists in accordance with this Part in an original design.

(2) In this Part "design" means the design of [...] the shape or configuration (whether internal or external) of the whole or part of an article.

(3) Design right does not subsist in—

  (a) a method or principle of construction,

  (b) features of shape or configuration of an article which—

      (i) enable the article to be connected to, or placed in, around or against, another article so that either article may perform its function, or

      (ii) are dependent upon the appearance of another article of which the article is intended by the designer to form an integral part, or

  (c) surface decoration.

(4) A design is not "original" for the purposes of this Part if it is commonplace

[in a qualifying country] in the design field in question at the time of its creation[; and "qualifying country" has the meaning given in section 217(3)].

(5) Design right subsists in a design only if the design qualifies for design right protection by reference to—

(a) the designer or the person by whom [the designer was employed] (see sections 218 and 219), or

(b) the person by whom and country in which articles made to the design were first marketed (see section 220),

or in accordance with any Order under section 221 (power to make further provision with respect to qualification).

[(5A) Design right does not subsist in a design which consists of or contains a controlled representation within the meaning of the Olympic Symbol etc. (Protection) Act 1995.]

(6) Design right does not subsist unless and until the design has been recorded in a design document or an article has been made to the design.

(7) Design right does not subsist in a design which was so recorded, or to which an article was made, before the commencement of this Part.

Notes:

(1) Subsection (5A) was inserted by the Olympic Symbol etc.(Protection) Act 1995 with effect from September 20, 1995 by virtue of the Olympic Symbol etc. (Protection) Act 1995 (Commencement) Order 1995 (SI 1995/2472). It has effect in relation to designs created on or after that date (section 14(2) of the 1995 Act); for such purposes a design is created on the first day on which (a) it is recorded in a design document or (b) an article is made to it.

(2) In subs.(2) words "of any aspect" repealed, in subs.(4) words in square brackets inserted, subject to savings, and in subs (5) words in square brackets substituted for words "the design was commissioned or the designer employed", subject to savings, by the Intellectual Property Act 2014, ss 1(3), 2(2)(a), with effect from October 1, 2014 (see the Intellectual Property Act 2014 (Commencement No.3 and Transitional Provisions) Order 2014 (SI 2014/2330) (for savings see regs 1(4) and 2(3) thereof).

The designer

214.—(1) In this Part the "designer", in relation to a design, means the person who creates it.

(2) In the case of a computer-generated design the person by whom the arrangements necessary for the creation of the design are undertaken shall be taken to be the designer.

Ownership of design right

215.—(1) The designer is the first owner of any design right in any design which is not created [...] the course of employment.

(2) [...]

(3) Where [...] a design is created by an employee in the course of his employment, his employer is the first owner of any design right in the design.

(4) If a design qualifies for design right protection by virtue of section 220 (qualification by reference to first marketing of articles made to the design), the above rules do not apply and the person by whom the articles in question are marketed is the first owner of the design right.

Note: In subs.(1) words "in pursuance of a commission or" repealed, in subs.(3) words ", in a case not falling within subsection (2)" repealed, and subs.(2) repealed, subject to savings, by the Intellectual Property Act 2014, s.2(1), with effect from October 1, 2014 (see SI 2014/2330) (for savings see reg. 2(3) thereof). Subs.(2) formerly read:

"(2) Where a design is created in pursuance of a commission, the person commissioning the design is the first owner of any design right in it."

Duration of design right

216.—(1) Design right expires—

    (a) fifteen years from the end of the calendar year in which the design was first recorded in a design document or an article was first made to the design, whichever first occurred, or

    (b) if articles made to the design are made available for sale or hire within five years from the end of that calendar year, ten years from the end of the calendar year in which that first occurred.

(2) The reference in subsection (1) to articles being made available for sale or hire is to their being made so available anywhere in the world by or with the licence of the design right owner.

Qualification for design right protection

Qualifying individuals and qualifying persons

217.—(1) In this Part—

    [...]

    ["qualifying person" means—

        (a) an individual habitually resident in a qualifying country, or

        (b) a body corporate or other body having legal personality which—

            (i) is formed under the law of a part of the United Kingdom or another qualifying country, and

            (ii) has in any qualifying country a place of business at which substantial business activity is carried on.]

(2) References in this Part to a qualifying person include the Crown and the government of any other qualifying country.

(3) In this section "qualifying country" means—

    (a) the United Kingdom,

    (b) a country to which this Part extends by virtue of an Order under section 255,

    (c) another member State of the European Economic Community, or

    (d) to the extent that an Order under section 256 so provides, a country designated under that section as enjoying reciprocal protection.

(4) [...]

(5) In determining for the purpose of the definition of "qualifying person" whether substantial business activity is carried on at a place of business in any country, no account shall be taken of dealings in goods which are at all material times outside that country.

Note: In subs.(1), definition "qualifying individual" repealed and definition "qualifying person" substituted, and subs.(4) repealed, subject to savings, by the Intellectual Property Act 2014, s.3(1), (2), with effect from October 1, 2014 (for savings see reg. 3(6) thereof). Definitions "qualifying individual" and "qualifying person" formerly read:

    " "qualifying individual" means a citizen or subject of, or an individual habitually resident in, a qualifying country, and

    "qualifying person" means a qualifying individual or a body corporate or other body having legal personality which—

        (a) is formed under the law of a part of the United Kingdom or another qualifying country, and

(b) has in any qualifying country a place of business at which substantial business activity is carried on."

Subs.(4) formerly read:

"(4) the reference in the definition of "qualifying individual" to a person's being a citizen or subject of a qualifying country shall be construed—

(a) in relation to the United Kingdom, as a reference to his being a British citizen, and

(b) in relation to a colony of the United Kingdom, as a reference to his being a British Dependent Territories' citizen by connection with that colony."

Qualification by reference to designer

218.—(1) This section applies to a design which is not created [...] in the course of employment.

(2) A design to which this section applies qualifies for design right protection if the designer is [...] qualifying person.

(3) A joint design to which this section applies qualifies for design right protection if any of the designers is [...] a qualifying person.

(4) Where a joint design qualifies for design right protection under this section, only those designers who are [...] qualifying persons are entitled to design right under section 215(1) (first ownership of design right: entitlement of designer).

Note: In subss (1)–(4), words "in pursuance of a commission", "a qualifying individual or, in the case of a computer-generated design," , "a qualifying individual or, as the case may be,", "qualifying individuals or" repealed, subject to savings, by the Intellectual Property Act 2014, ss.2(2), 3(3), with effect from October 1, 2014 (see SI 2014/2330) (for savings see regs 2(3), 3(6) thereof).

Qualification by reference to commissioner or employer

219.—(1) A design qualifies for design right protection if it is created [in the course of employment with] in pursuance of a commission from, or in the course of employment with, a qualifying person.

(2) In the case of [...] joint commission or joint employment a design qualifies for design right protection if any of the commissioners or employers is a qualifying person.

(3) Where a design which is [...] created in the course of joint employment qualifies for design right protection under this section, only those [...] employers who are qualifying persons are entitled to design right under section 215(2) or (3) (first ownership of design right: entitlement of [...] employer).

Note: In subs.(1) words in square brackets substituted for words "in pursuance of a commission from, or in the course of employment with,", and in subss (2), (3) words "a joint commission or", "jointly commissioned or", "commissioners or", "commissioner or" repealed, subject to savings, by the Intellectual Property Act 2014, ss 2(2), with effect from October 1, 2014 (see SI 2014/2330) (for savings see reg.2(3) thereof).

Qualification by reference to first marketing

220.—(1) A design which does not qualify for design right protection under section 218 or 219 (qualification by reference to designer [...] or employer) qualifies for design right protection if the first marketing of articles made to the design—

(a) is by a qualifying person [...], and

(b) takes place in the United Kingdom, another country to which this Part extends by virtue of an Order under section 255, or another member State of the European Economic Community.

(2) If the first marketing of articles made to the design is done jointly by two or more persons, the design qualifies for design right protection if any of those persons meets the [requirement] specified in subsection (1)(a).

(3) In such a case only the persons who meet [that requirement] are entitled to design right under section 215(4) (first ownership of design right: entitlement of first marketer of articles made to the design).

(4) [...]

Note: In subs.(1) words ", commissioner or", "who is exclusively authorised to put such articles on the market in the United Kingdom" repealed, in subs.(2) words in square brackets substituted, and subs.(4) repealed, subject to savings, by the Intellectual Property Act 2014, ss 2(2), 3(4), with effect from October 1, 2014 (see SI 2014/2330) (for savings see regs 2(3), 3(6) thereof). Subs.(4) formerly read:

"(4) In subsection (1)(a) "exclusively authorised" refers—

(a) to authorisation by the person who would have been __rst owner of design right as designer, commissioner of the design or employer of the designer if he had been a qualifying person, or by a person lawfully claiming under such a person, and

(b) to exclusivity capable of being enforced by legal proceedings in the United Kingdom."

Power to make further provision as to qualification

221.—(1) Her Majesty may, with a view to fulfilling an international obligation of the United Kingdom, by Order in Council provide that a design qualifies for design right protection if such requirements as are specified in the Order are met.

(2) An Order may make different provision for different descriptions of design or article; and may make such consequential modifications of the operation of section 215 (ownership of design right) and sections 218 to 220 (other means of qualification) as appear to Her Majesty to be appropriate.

(3) A statutory instrument containing an Order in Council under this section shall be subject to annulment in pursuance of a resolution of either House of Parliament.

Dealings with design right

Assignment and licences

222.—(1) Design right is transmissible by assignment, by testamentary disposition or by operation of law, as personal or moveable property.

(2) An assignment or other transmission of design right may be partial, that is, limited so as to apply—

    (a) to one or more, but not all, of the things the design right owner has the exclusive right to do;

    (b) to part, but not the whole, of the period for which the right is to subsist.

(3) An assignment of design right is not effective unless it is in writing signed by or on behalf of the assignor.

(4) A licence granted by the owner of design right is binding on every successor in title to his interest in the right, except a purchaser in good faith for valuable consideration and without notice (actual or constructive) of the licence or a person deriving title from such a purchaser; and references in this Part to doing anything with, or without, the licence of the design right owner shall be construed accordingly.

Prospective ownership of design right

223.—(1) Where by an agreement made in relation to future design right, and signed by or on behalf of the prospective owner of the design right, the prospective owner purports to assign the future design right (wholly or partially) to another person, then if, on the right coming into existence, the assignee or another person claiming under him would be entitled as against all other persons to require the right to be vested in him, the right shall vest in him by virtue of this section.

(2) In this section—

"future design right" means design right which will or may come into existence in respect of a future design or class of designs or on the occurrence of a future event; and

"prospective owner" shall be construed accordingly, and includes a person who is prospectively entitled to design right by virtue of such an agreement as is mentioned in subsection (1).

(3) A licence granted by a prospective owner of design right is binding on every successor in title to his interest (or prospective interest) in the right, except a purchaser in good faith for valuable consideration and without notice (actual or constructive) of the licence or a person deriving title from such a purchaser; and references in this Part to doing anything with, or without, the licence of the design right owner shall be construed accordingly.

Assignment of right in registered design presumed to carry with it design right

224. Where a design consisting of a design in which design right subsists is registered under the Registered Designs Act 1949 and the proprietor of the registered design is also the design right owner, an assignment of the right in the registered design shall be taken to be also an assignment of the design right, unless a contrary intention appears.

Exclusive licences

225.—(1) In this Part an "exclusive licence" means a licence in writing signed by or on behalf of the design right owner authorising the licensee to the exclusion of all other persons, including the person granting the licence, to exercise a right which would otherwise be exercisable exclusively by the design right owner.

(2) The licensee under an exclusive licence has the same rights against any successor in title who is bound by the licence as he has against the person granting the licence.

CHAPTER II

RIGHTS OF DESIGN RIGHT OWNER AND REMEDIES

Infringement of design right

Primary infringement of design right

226.—(1) The owner of design right in a design has the exclusive right to reproduce the design for commercial purposes—

(a) by making articles to that design, or

(b) by making a design document recording the design for the purpose of enabling such articles to be made.

(2) Reproduction of a design by making articles to the design means copying the design so as to produce articles exactly or substantially to that design, and references in this Part to making articles to a design shall be construed accordingly.

(3) Design right is infringed by a person who without the licence of the design right owner does, or authorises another to do, anything which by virtue of this section is the exclusive right of the design right owner.

(4) For the purposes of this section reproduction may be direct or indirect, and it is immaterial whether any intervening acts themselves infringe the design right.

(5) This section has effect subject to the provisions of Chapter III (exceptions to rights of design right owner).

Secondary infringement: importing or dealing with infringing article

227.—(1) Design right is infringed by a person who, without the licence of the design right owner—

(a) imports into the United Kingdom for commercial purposes, or

(b) has in his possession for commercial purposes, or

(c) sells, lets for hire, or offers or exposes for sale or hire, in the course of a business,

an article which is, and which he knows or has reason to believe is, an infringing article.

(2) This section has effect subject to the provisions of Chapter III (exceptions to rights of design right owner).

Meaning of "infringing article"

228.—(1) In this Part "infringing article", in relation to a design, shall be construed in accordance with this section.

(2) An article is an infringing article if its making to that design was an infringement of design right in the design.

(3) An article is also an infringing article if—

(a) it has been or is proposed to be imported into the United Kingdom, and

(b) its making to that design in the United Kingdom would have been an infringement of design right in the design or a breach of an exclusive licence agreement relating to the design.

(4) Where it is shown that an article is made to a design in which design right subsists or has subsisted at any time, it shall be presumed until the contrary is proved that the article was made at a time when design right subsisted.

(5) Nothing in subsection (3) shall be construed as applying to an article which may lawfully be imported into the United Kingdom by virtue of any enforceable [EU] right within the meaning of section 2(1) of the European Communities Act 1972.

(6) The expression "infringing article" does not include a design document, notwithstanding that its making was or would have been an infringement of design right.

Note: In subs.(5) the expression "EU" was substituted for the word "Community" by the Treaty of Lisbon (Changes in Terminology) Order 2011 (SI 2011/1043) art.6(1)(f) with effect from April 22, 2011.

Remedies for infringement

Rights and remedies of design right owner

229.—(1) An infringement of design right is actionable by the design right owner.

(2) In an action for infringement of design right all such relief by way of damages, injunctions, accounts or otherwise is available to the plaintiff as is available in respect of the infringement of any other property right.

(3) The court may in an action for infringement of design right, having regard to all the circumstances and in particular to—

(a) the flagrancy of the infringement, and

(b) any benefit accruing to the defendant by reason of the infringement,

award such additional damages as the justice of the case may require.

(4) This section has effect subject to section 233 (innocent infringement).

Order for delivery up

230.—(1) Where a person—

(a) has in his possession, custody or control for commercial purposes an infringing article, or

(b) has in his possession, custody or control anything specifically designed or adapted for making articles to a particular design, knowing or having reason to believe that it has been or is to be used to make an infringing article,

the owner of the design right in the design in question may apply to the court for an order that the infringing article or other thing be delivered up to him or to such other person as the court may direct.

(2) An application shall not be made after the end of the period specified in the following provisions of this section; and no order shall be made unless the court also makes, or it appears to the court that there are grounds for making, an order under section 231 (order as to disposal of infringing article, &c.).

(3) An application for an order under this section may not be made after the end of the period of six years from the date on which the article or thing in question was made, subject to subsection (4).

(4) If during the whole or any part of that period the design right owner—

(a) is under a disability, or

(b) is prevented by fraud or concealment from discovering the facts entitling him to apply for an order,

an application may be made at any time before the end of the period of six years from the date on which he ceased to be under a disability or, as the case may be, could with reasonable diligence have discovered those facts.

(5) In subsection (4) "disability"—

(a) in England and Wales, has the same meaning as in the Limitation Act 1980;

(b) in Scotland, means legal disability within the meaning of the Prescription and Limitation (Scotland) Act 1973;

(c) in Northern Ireland, has the same meaning as in the Statute of Limitations (Northern Ireland) 1958.

(6) A person to whom an infringing article or other thing is delivered up in pursuance of an order under this section shall, if an order under section 231 is not made, retain it pending the making of an order, or the decision not to make an order, under that section.

(7) Nothing in this section affects any other power of the court.

Order as to disposal of infringing articles, &c.

231.—(1) An application may be made to the court for an order that an infringing article or other thing delivered up in pursuance of an order under section 230 shall be—

(a) forfeited to the design right owner, or

(b) destroyed or otherwise dealt with as the court may think fit, or for a decision that no such order should be made.

(2) In considering what order (if any) should be made, the court shall consider whether other remedies available in an action for infringement of design right would be adequate to compensate the design right owner and to protect his interests.

(3) Provision shall be made by rules of court as to the service of notice on persons having an interest in the article or other thing, and any such person is entitled—

(a) to appear in proceedings for an order under this section, whether or not he was served with notice, and

(b) to appeal against any order made, whether or not he appeared;

and an order shall not take effect until the end of the period within which notice of an appeal may be given or, if before the end of that period notice of appeal is duly given, until the final determination or abandonment of the proceedings on the appeal.

(4) Where there is more than one person interested in an article or other thing, the court shall make such order as it thinks just and may (in particular) direct that the thing be sold, or otherwise dealt with, and the proceeds divided.

(5) If the court decides that no order should be made under this section, the person in whose possession, custody or control the article or other thing was before being delivered up [...] is entitled to its return.

(6) References in this section to a person having an interest in an article or other thing include any person in whose favour an order could be made in respect of it[—]

(a) under this section or under section 114 or 204 of this Act;

(b) under section 24 of the Registered Designs Act 1949;

(c) under section 19 of the Trade Marks Act 1994 (including that section as applied by regulation 4 of the Community Trade Mark Regulations 2006 (SI 2006/1027)); or

(d) under regulation 1C of the Community Design Regulations 2005 (SI 2005/2339).]

Note: The words "or siezed" repealed in subs.(5) and in subs.(6) the words in square brackets substituted by the Intellectual Property (Enforcement, etc.) Regulations 2006 (SI 2006/1028), Sch.2 para.14 and Sch.4, with effect from April 29, 2006.

Jurisdiction of county court and sheriff court

232.—(1) In England [and Wales the county court and in] Northern Ireland a county court may entertain proceedings under—

section 230 (order for delivery up of infringing article, &c.),

section 231 (order as to disposal of infringing article, &c.), or

section 235(5) (application by exclusive licensee having concurrent rights),

[save that, in Northern Ireland, a county court may entertain such proceedings only] where the value of the infringing articles and other things in question does not exceed the county court limit for actions in tort.

(2) In Scotland proceedings for an order under any of those provisions may be brought in the sheriff court.

(3) Nothing in this section shall be construed as affecting the jurisdiction of the High Court or, in Scotland, the Court of Session.

Notes:

(1) Subsection (1) is printed as amended by the High Court and County Courts Jurisdiction Order 1991 (SI 1991/724).

(2) In subs.(1) words in square brackets substituted for words ", Wales and", subject to savings and transitional provisions, by the Crime and Courts Act 2013, Sch.9(3) para.72, with effect from April 22, 2014 (for savings and transitional provisions, see Sch.8 of the Act and SI 2014/954, arts 2(c), 3).

Innocent infringement

233.—(1) Where in an action for infringement of design right brought by virtue of section 226 (primary infringement) it is shown that at the time of the infringement the defendant did not know, and had no reason to believe, that design right subsisted in the design to which the action relates, the plaintiff is not entitled to damages against him, but without prejudice to any other remedy.

(2) Where in an action for infringement of design right brought by virtue of section 227 (secondary infringement) a defendant shows that the infringing article was innocently acquired by him or a predecessor in title of his, the only remedy available against him in respect of the infringement is damages not exceeding a reasonable royalty in respect of the act complained of.

(3) In subsection (2) "innocently acquired" means that the person acquiring the article did not know and had no reason to believe that it was an infringing article.

Rights and remedies of exclusive licensee

234.—(1) An exclusive licensee has, except against the design right owner, the same rights and remedies in respect of matters occurring after the grant of the licence as if the licence had been an assignment.

(2) His rights and remedies are concurrent with those of the design right owner; and references in the relevant provisions of this Part to the design right owner shall be construed accordingly.

(3) In an action brought by an exclusive licensee by virtue of this section a defendant may avail himself of any defence which would have been available to him if the action had been brought by the design right owner.

Exercise of concurrent rights

235.—(1) Where an action for infringement of design right brought by the design right owner or an exclusive licensee relates (wholly or partly) to an infringement in respect of which they have concurrent rights of action, the design right owner or, as the case may be, the exclusive licensee may not, without the leave of the court, proceed with the action unless the other is either joined as a plaintiff or added as a defendant.

(2) A design right owner or exclusive licensee who is added as a defendant in pursuance of subsection (1) is not liable for any costs in the action unless he takes part in the proceedings.

(3) The above provisions do not affect the granting of interlocutory relief on the application of the design right owner or an exclusive licensee.

(4) Where an action for infringement of design right is brought which relates (wholly or partly) to an infringement in respect of which the design right owner and an exclusive licensee have concurrent rights of action—

    (a) the court shall, in assessing damages, take into account—

        (i) the terms of the licence, and

        (ii) any pecuniary remedy already awarded or available to either of them in respect of the infringement;

    (b) no account of profits shall be directed if an award of damages has been made, or an account of profits has been directed, in favour of the other of them in respect of the infringement; and

    (c) the court shall if an account of profits is directed apportion the profits be-
tween them as the court considers just, subject to any agreement between them;

and these provisions apply whether or not the design right owner and the
exclusive licensee are both parties to the action.

(5) The design right owner shall notify any exclusive licensee having concurrent rights before applying for an order under section 230 (order for delivery up
of infringing article, &c.); and the court may on the application of the licensee
make such order under that section as it thinks fit having regard to the terms of
the licence.

Chapter III

Exceptions to Rights of Design Right Owners

Infringement of copyright

Infringement of copyright

236. Where copyright subsists in a work which consists of or includes a design
in which design right subsists, it is not an infringement of design right in the
design to do anything which is an infringement of the copyright in that work.

Availability of licences of right

Licences available in last five years of design right

237.—(1) Any person is entitled as of right to a licence to do in the last five
years of the design right term anything which would otherwise infringe the design
right.

(2) The terms of the licence shall, in default of agreement, be settled by the
comptroller.

(3) The Secretary of State may if it appears to him necessary in order to—

    (a) comply with an international obligation of the United Kingdom, or

    (b) secure or maintain reciprocal protection for British designs in other
        countries,

by order exclude from the operation of subsection (1) designs of a description
specified in the order or designs applied to articles of a description so specified.

(4) An order shall be made by statutory instrument; and no order shall be
made unless a draft of it has been laid before and approved by a resolution of
each House of Parliament.

Powers exercisable for protection of the public interest

238.—[(1) Subsection (1A) applies where whatever needs to be remedied,
mitigated or prevented by the Secretary of State [or (as the case may be) the
Competition and Markets Authority] under section 12(5) of the Competition Act
1980 or section 41(2), 55(2), 66(6), 75(2), 83(2), 138(2), 147(2)[, 147A(2)] or
160(2) of, or paragraph 5(2) or 10(2) of Schedule 7 to, the Enterprise Act 2002
(powers to take remedial action following references to the [Competition and
Markets Authority] in connection with public bodies and certain other persons,
mergers or market investigations etc.) consists of or includes—

    (a) conditions in licences granted by a design right owner restricting the use
        of the design by the licensee or the right of the design right owner to
        grant other licences, or

(b) a refusal of a design right owner to grant licences on reasonable terms.

(1A) The powers conferred by Schedule 8 to the Enterprise Act 2002 include power to cancel or modify those conditions and, instead or in addition, to provide that licences in respect of the design right shall be available as of right.

(2) The references to anything permitted by Schedule 8 to the Enterprise Act 2002 in section 12(5A) of the Competition Act 1980 and in sections 75(4)(a), 83(4)(a), 84(2)(a), 89(1), 160(4)(a), 161(3)(a) and 164(1) of, and paragraphs 5, 10 and 11 of Schedule 7 to, the Act of 2002 shall be construed accordingly.]

(3) The terms of a licence available by virtue of this section shall, in default of agreement, be settled by the comptroller.

Notes:

(1) Subsections (1) and (2) substituted by the Enterprise Act 2002 (c.40), Sch.25, para.18 with effect from June 20, 2003. subss.(1) and (2) formerly provided:

"*(1) Where the matters specified in a report of the Monopolies and Mergers Commission as being those which in the Commission's opinion operate, may be expected to operate or have operated against the public interest include—*

(a) *conditions in licences granted by a design right owner restricting the use of the design by the licensee or the right of the design right owner to grant other licences, or*

(b) *a refusal of a design right owner to grant licences on reasonable terms,*

the powers conferred by Part I of Schedule 8 to the Fair Trading Act 1973 (powers exercisable for purpose of remedying or preventing adverse effects specified in report of Commission) include power to cancel or modify those conditions and, instead or in addition, to provide that licences in respect of the design right shall be available as of right.

(2) The references in sections 56(2) and 73(2) of that Act, and [section] 12(5) of the Competition Act 1980, to the powers specified in that Part of that Schedule shall be construed accordingly."

(2) The word in square brackets in the former subs.(2) was substituted for the original words "sections 10(2)(b) and" by the Competition Act 1998 (Transitional, Consequential and Supplemental Provisions) Order 2000 (SI 2000/311), with effect from March 1, 2000.

(3) In subs.(1) words in square brackets substituted, subject to transitional provision, by the Enterprise and Regulatory Reform Act 2013 (Competition) (Consequential, Transitional and Saving Provisions) Order 2014 (SI 2014/892; for transitional provision see Sch.2), Sch.1 para.58, with effect from April 1, 2014.

Undertaking to take licence of right in infringement proceedings

239.—(1) If in proceedings for infringement of design right in a design in respect of which a licence is available as of right under section 237 or 238 the defendant undertakes to take a licence on such terms as may be agreed or, in default of agreement, settled by the comptroller under that section—

(a) no injunction shall be granted against him,

(b) no order for delivery up shall be made under section 230, and

(c) the amount recoverable against him by way of damages or on an account of profits shall not exceed double the amount which would have been payable by him as licensee if such a licence on those terms had been granted before the earliest infringement.

(2) An undertaking may be given at any time before final order in the proceedings, without any admission of liability.

(3) Nothing in this section affects the remedies available in respect of an infringement committed before licences of right were available.

Crown use of designs

Crown use of designs

240.—(1) A government department, or a person authorized in writing by a government department, may without the licence of the design right owner—
  (a) do anything for the purpose of supplying articles for the services of the Crown, or
  (b) dispose of articles no longer required for the services of the Crown;
and nothing done by virtue of this section infringes the design right.

(2) References in this Part to "the services of the Crown" are to—
  (a) the defence of the realm,
  (b) foreign defence purposes, and
  (c) health service purposes.

(3) The reference to the supply of articles for "foreign defence purposes" is to their supply—
  (a) for the defence of a country outside the realm in pursuance of an agreement or arrangement to which the government of that country and Her Majesty's Government in the United Kingdom are parties; or
  (b) for use by armed forces operating in pursuance of a resolution of the United Nations or one of its organs.

(4) The reference to the supply of articles for "health service purposes" are to their supply for the purposes of providing—
  [(za) primary medical services or primary dental services under [the National Health Service Act 2006 or the National Health Service (Wales) Act 2006,] [or primary medical services under Part 1 of the National Health Service (Scotland) Act 1978];]]
  [(a) pharmaceutical services, general medical services or general dental services under—
      (i) [Chapter 1 of Part 7 of the National Health Service Act 2006, or Chapter 1 of Part 7 of the National Health Service (Wales) Act 2006 (in the case of pharmaceutical services),]
      (ii) Part II of the National Health Service (Scotland) Act 1978 [(in the case of pharmaceutical services or general dental services)], or
      (iii) the corresponding provisions of the law in force in Northern Ireland; or
  (b) personal medical services [...] in accordance with arrangements made under—
      (i) [...]
      (ii) section 17C of the 1978 Act [(in the case of personal dental services)], or
      (iii) the corresponding provisions of the law in force in Northern Ireland.]
  [(c) local pharmaceutical services provided under [the National Health Service Act 2006 or the National Health Service (Wales) Act 2006.]]

(5) In this Part—
  "Crown use", in relation to a design, means the doing of anything by virtue of this section which would otherwise be an infringement of design right in the design; and
  "the government department concerned", in relation to such use, means the government department by whom or on whose authority the act was done.

(6) The authority of a government department in respect of Crown use of a design may be given to a person either before or after the use and whether or not he is authorized, directly or indirectly, by the design right owner to do anything in relation to the design.

(7) A person acquiring anything sold in the exercise of powers conferred by this section, and any person claiming under him, may deal with it in the same manner as if the design right were held on behalf of the Crown.

Notes:

(1) The power conferred by subs.(1) on a government department or a person authorised in writing by a government department, insofar as it can be exercised for the purpose of a visiting force or headquarters, is modified by the Visiting Forces and International Headquarters (Application of Law) Order 1999 (SI 1999/1736) with effect from June 23, 2003. Schedule 4 para.3 of that order provides:

> *Use of articles without the licence of the design rights owner*
> **"3.**—(1) *Subject to sub-paragraph (2), the power conferred by section 240(1) of the Copyright, Designs and Patents Act 1988 on a government department, or person authorised in writing by a government department, in relation to the use of articles without the licence of the design rights owner for the services of the Crown shall be exercisable for the purposes of a visiting force or headquarters to the extent that it would be exercisable if the visiting force or headquarters were a part of any of the home forces.*
>
> (2) *Sub-paragraph (1) shall not have effect to authorise the doing of anything in relation to a design right which is for foreign defence purposes or health service purposes within the meaning of section 240(3) and (4) of the Copyright, Designs and Patents Act 1988.*
>
> (3) *In relation to the exercise of the powers conferred by sub-paragraph (1), section 240(5) to (7) and sections 241 to 243 shall have effect with any reference in those provisions to Crown use of a design right being construed as a reference to the use of a design right for the purposes of a visiting force or headquarters."*

(2) Subsection (4)(za) was inserted and subs.(4)(b)(i) repealed by the Health and Social Care (Community Standards) Act 2003 (c.43), Sch.11, para.52 and Sch.14, Pt 4, with effect from April 1, 2004. Subsection (4)(b)(i) formerly provided:

> *"section 28C of the 1977 Act"*

(3) Subsection (4)(a) and (b) substituted by the National Health Service (Primary Care) Act 1997, s.41(10), Sch.2, para.63, with effect from April 1, 1998 in place of the following text:

> "(a) *pharmaceutical services,*
> (b) *general medical services, or*
> (c) *general dental services,*
>
>   *that is, services of those kinds under Part II of the National Health Service Act 1977, Part II of the National Health Service (Scotland) Act 1978 or the corresponding provisions of the law in force in Northern Ireland."*

(4) Subsection (4)(c) was inserted by the Health and Social Care Act 2001 (c.15), s.67, Sch.5 para.7 with effect from July 1, 2002.

(5) The words in the second set of square brackets in subs.(4)(za), and in the square brackets in subs.(4)(a)(ii) and (b)(ii) inserted by the Primary Medical Services (Scotland) Act 2004 (Consequential Modifications) Order 2004 (SI 2004/957), Sch.1 para.5, with effect from April 1, 2004.

(6) The words in the first set of square brackets in subs.(4)(za), in the square brackets in subs.(4)(a)(i) and in the internal square brackets in subs.(4)(c) substituted by the National Health Service (Consequential Provisions) Act 2006 (c.43), Sch.1 para.113, with effect from March 1, 2007.

Settlement of terms for Crown use

241.—(1) Where Crown use is made of a design, the government department concerned shall—

  (a) notify the design right owner as soon as practicable, and

    (b) give him such information as to the extent of the use as he may from time to time require,

unless it appears to the department that it would be contrary to the public interest to do so or the identity of the design right owner cannot be ascertained on reasonable inquiry.

(2) Crown use of a design shall be on such terms as, either before or after the use, are agreed between the government department concerned and the design right owner with the approval of the Treasury or, in default of agreement, are determined by the court.

In the application of this subsection to Northern Ireland the reference to the Treasury shall, where the government department referred to in that subsection is a Northern Ireland department, be construed as a reference to the Department of Finance and Personnel.

[In the application of this subsection to Scotland, where the government department referred to in that subsection is any part of the Scottish Administration, the words "with the approval of the Treasury" are omitted.]

(3) Where the identity of the design right owner cannot be ascertained on reasonable inquiry, the government department concerned may apply to the court who may order that no royalty or other sum shall be payable in respect of Crown use of the design until the owner agrees terms with the department or refers the matter to the court for determination.

Notes:

    (1) The words in square brackets in subs.(2) inserted by the Scotland Act 1998 (Consequential Modifications) (No.2) Order 1999 (SI 1999/1820), with effect from July 1, 1999.
    (2) See also the note in relation to "Crown use of designs" (s.240) concerning the Visiting Forces and International Headquarters (Application of Law) Order 1999 (SI 1999/1736).

Rights of third parties in case of Crown use

242.—(1) The provisions of any licence, assignment or agreement made between the design right owner (or anyone deriving title from him or from whom he derives title) and any person other than a government department are of no effect in relation to Crown use of a design, or any act incidental to Crown use, so far as they—

    (a) restrict or regulate anything done in relation to the design, or the use of any model, document or other information relating to it, or
    (b) provide for the making of payments in respect of, or calculated by reference to such use;

and the copying or issuing to the public of copies of any such model or document in connection with the thing done, or any such use, shall be deemed not to be an infringement of any copyright in the model or document.

(2) Subsection (1) shall not be construed as authorising the disclosure of any such model, document or information in contravention of the licence, assignment or agreement.

(3) Where an exclusive licence is in force in respect of the design—

    (a) if the licence was granted for royalties—
        (i) any agreement between the design right owner and a government department under section 241 (settlement of terms for Crown use) requires the consent of the licensee, and
        (ii) the licensee is entitled to recover from the design right owner such part of the payment for Crown use as may be agreed between them or, in default of agreement, determined by the court;

(b) if the licence was granted otherwise than for royalties—
  (i) section 241 applies in relation to anything done which but for section 240 (Crown use) and subsection (1) above would be an infringement of the rights of the licensee with the substitution for references to the design right owner of references to the licensee, and
  (ii) section 241 does not apply in relation to anything done by the licensee by virtue of an authority given under section 240.

(4) Where the design right has been assigned to the design right owner in consideration of royalties—
  (a) section 241 applies in relation to Crown use of the design as if the references to the design right owner included the assignor, and any payment for Crown use shall be divided between them in such proportion as may be agreed or, in default of agreement, determined by the court; and
  (b) section 241 applies in relation to any act incidental to Crown use as it applies in relation to Crown use of the design.

(5) Where any model, document or other information relating to a design is used in connection with Crown use of the design, or any act incidental to Crown use, section 241 applies to the use of the model, document or other information with the substitution for the references to the design right owner of references to the person entitled to the benefit of any provision of an agreement rendered inoperative by subsection (1) above.

(6) In this section—
  "act incidental to Crown use" means anything done for the services of the Crown to the order of a government department by the design right owner in respect of a design;
  "payment for Crown use" means such amount as is payable by the government department concerned by virtue of section 241; and
  "royalties" includes any benefit determined by reference to the use of the design.

Note: See the note in relation to "Crown use of designs" (s.240) concerning the Visiting Forces and International Headquarters (Application of Law) Order 1999 (SI 1999/1736).

Crown use: compensation for loss of profit

243.—(1) Where Crown use is made of a design, the government department concerned shall pay—
  (a) to the design right owner, or
  (b) if there is an exclusive licence in force in respect of the design, to the exclusive licensee,
compensation for any loss resulting from his not being awarded a contract to supply the articles made to the design.

(2) Compensation is payable only to the extent that such a contract could have been fulfilled from his existing manufacturing capacity; but is payable notwithstanding the existence of circumstances rendering him ineligible for the award of such a contract.

(3) In determining the loss, regard shall be had to the profit which would have been made on such a contract and to the extent to which any manufacturing capacity was under-used.

(4) No compensation is payable in respect of any failure to secure contracts for the supply of articles made to the design otherwise than for the services of the Crown.

(5) The amount payable shall, if not agreed between the design right owner or licensee and the government department concerned with the approval of the Treasury, be determined by the court on a reference under section 252; and it is in addition to any amount payable under section 241 or 242.

(6) In the application of this section to Northern Ireland, the reference in subsection (5) to the Treasury shall, where the government department concerned is a Northern Ireland department, be construed as a reference to the Department of Finance and Personnel.

[(7) In the application of this section to Scotland, where the government department referred to in subsection (5) is any part of the Scottish Administration, the words "with the approval of the Treasury" in that subsection are omitted.]

Notes:

(1) Subsection (7) was inserted by the Scotland Act 1998 (Consequential Modifications) (No.2) Order 1999 (SI 1999/1820), with effect from July 1, 1999.

(2) See also the note in relation to Crown use of designs (s.240) concerning the Visiting Forces and International Headquarters (Application of Law) Order 1999 (SI 1999/1736).

Special provision for Crown use during emergency

244.—(1) During a period of emergency the powers exercisable in relation to a design by virtue of section 240 (Crown use) include power to do any act which would otherwise be an infringement of design right for any purpose which appears to the government department concerned necessary or expedient—

(a) for the efficient prosecution of any war in which Her Majesty may be engaged;

(b) for the maintenance of supplies and services essential to the life of the community;

(c) for securing a sufficiency of supplies and services essential to the wellbeing of the community;

(d) for promoting the productivity of industry, commerce and agriculture;

(e) for fostering and directing exports and reducing imports, or imports of any classes, from all or any countries and for redressing the balance of trade;

(f) generally for ensuring that the whole resources of the community are available for use, and are used, in a manner best calculated to serve the interests of the community; or

(g) for assisting the relief of suffering and the restoration and distribution of essential supplies and services in any country outside the United Kingdom which is in grave distress as the result of war.

(2) References in this Part to the services of the Crown include, as respects a period of emergency, those purposes; and references to "Crown use" include any act which would apart from this section be an infringement of design right.

(3) In this section "period of emergency" means a period beginning with such date as may be declared by Order in Council to be the beginning, and ending with such date as may be so declared to be the end, of a period of emergency for the purposes of this section.

(4) No Order in Council under this section shall be submitted to Her Majesty unless a draft of it has been laid before and approved by a resolution of each House of Parliament.

[Miscellaneous

Exception for private acts, experiments and teaching

[244A. Design right is not infringed by—
  (a) an act which is done privately and for purposes which are not commercial;
  (b) an act which is done for experimental purposes; or
  (c) an act of reproduction for teaching purposes or for the purpose of making citations provided that—
     (i) the act of reproduction is compatible with fair trade practice and does not unduly prejudice the normal exploitation of the design, and
     (ii) mention is made of the source.

Note: Sections 244A and 244B inserted by the Intellectual Property Act 2014, s.4, with effect from October 1, 2014.

Exception for overseas ships and aircraft

[244B. Design right is not infringed by—
(a) the use of equipment on ships or aircraft which are registered in another country but which are temporarily in the United Kingdom;
(b) the importation into the United Kingdom of spare parts or accessories for the purpose of repairing such ships or aircraft; or
(c) the carrying out of repairs on such ships or aircraft.]

Note: Sections 244A and 244B inserted by the Intellectual Property Act 2014, s.4, with effect from October 1, 2014 (see SI 2014/2330).

General

Power to provide for further exceptions

245.— (1) The Secretary of State may if it appears to him necessary in order to—
  (a) comply with an international obligation of the United Kingdom, or
  (b) secure or maintain reciprocal protection for British designs in other countries,
by order provide that acts of a description specified in the order do not infringe design right.

(2) An order may make different provision for different descriptions of design or article.

(3) An order shall be made by statutory instrument and no order shall be made unless a draft of it has been laid before and approved by a resolution of each House of Parliament.

CHAPTER IV

JURISDICTION OF THE COMPTROLLER AND THE COURT

Jurisdiction of the comptroller

Jurisdiction to decide matters relating to design right

246.—(1) A party to a dispute as to any of the following matters may refer the dispute to the comptroller for his decision—

    (a) the subsistence of design right,

    (b) the term of design right, or

    (c) the identity of the person in whom design right first vested;

and the comptroller's decision on the reference is binding on the parties to the dispute.

(2) No other court or tribunal shall decide any such matter except—

    (a) on a reference or appeal from the comptroller,

    (b) in infringement or other proceedings in which the issue arises incidentally, or

    (c) in proceedings brought with the agreement of the parties or the leave of the comptroller.

(3) The comptroller has jurisdiction to decide any incidental question of fact or law arising in the course of a reference under this section.

Application to settle terms of licence of right

247.—(1) A person requiring a licence which is available as of right by virtue of—

    (a) section 237 (licence available in the last five years of design right), or

    (b) an order under section 238 (licence made available in the public interest),

may apply to the comptroller to settle the terms of the licence.

(2) No application for the settlement of the terms of a licence available by virtue of section 237 may be made earlier than one year before the earliest date on which which the licence may take effect under that section.

(3) The terms of a licence settled by the comptroller shall authorise the licensee to do—

    (a) in the case of licence available by virtue of section 237, everything which would be an infringement of the design right in the absence of a licence;

    (b) in the case of a licence available by virtue of section 238, everything in respect of which a licence is so available.

(4) In settling the terms of a licence the comptroller shall have regard to such factors as may be prescribed by the Secretary of State by order made by statutory instrument.

(5) No such order shall be made unless a draft of it has been laid before and approved by a resolution of each House of Parliament.

(6) Where the terms of a licence are settled by the comptroller, the licence has effect—

    (a) in the case of an application in respect of a licence available by virtue of section 237 made before the earliest date on which the licence may take effect under that section, from that date;

    (b) in any other case, from the date on which the application to the comptroller was made.

Settlement of terms where design right owner unknown

248.—(1) This section applies where a person making an application under section 247 (settlement of terms of licence of right) is unable on reasonable inquiry to discover the identity of the design right owner.

(2) The comptroller may in settling the terms of the licence order that the licence shall be free of any obligation as to royalties or other payments.

(3) If such an order is made the design right owner may apply to the comptroller to vary the terms of the licence with effect from the date on which his application is made.

(4) If the terms of a licence are settled by the comptroller and it is subsequently established that a licence was not available as of right, the licensee shall not be liable in damages for, or for an account of profits in respect of, anything done before he was aware of any claim by the design right owner that a licence was not available.

Appeals as to terms of licence of right

249.—(1) An appeal lies from any decision of the comptroller under section 247 or 248 (settlement of terms of licence of right) to [a person appointed under section 27A of the Registered Designs Act 1949].

[*(1A) In subsection (1) "the court" means—*

(a) *in England and Wales or Northern Ireland, the High Court;*

(b) *in Scotland, theCourt of Session.*]

(2) [...].

Notes:

(1) In subs.(1) words in square brackets substituted for the words "the Appeal Tribunal constituted under section 28 of the Registered Designs Act 1949", and subs.(2) repealed by the Intellectual Property Act 2014, s.10(7), with effect from April 6, 2015 (see SI 2015/165). Subs.(2) formerly read:

"(2) Section 28 of that Act applies to appeals from the comptroller under this section as it applies to appeals from the registrar under that Act; but rules made under that section may make different provision for appeals under this section."

(2) Subs.(1A) was prospectively inserted by the Tribunals, Courts and Enforcement Act 2007 s.143(3), with effect from a date to be appointed.

Opinions service

[**249A.** The descriptions of designs which may be specified in regulations under subsection (1)(b) of section 28A of the Registered Designs Act 1949 (requests to the comptroller for opinions on designs) include, in particular—

(a) designs in which design right subsists in accordance with this Part, and

(b) designs in relation to which there is a question whether design right so subsists.]

Note: Section 249A inserted by the Intellectual Property Act 2014, s.11, with effect from October 1, 2014 (see SI 2014/2330).

Rules

250.—(1) The Secretary of State may make rules for regulating the procedure to be followed in connection with any proceeding before the comptroller under this Part.

(2) Rules may, in particular, make provision—

(a) prescribing forms;

(b) requiring fees to be paid;

(c) authorising the rectification of irregularities of procedure;

(d) regulating the mode of giving evidence and empowering the comptroller to compel the attendance of witnesses and the discovery of and production of documents;

(e) providing for the appointment of advisers to assist the comptroller in proceedings before him;

(f) prescribing time limits for doing anything required to be done (and providing for the alteration of any such limit); and

(g) empowering the comptroller to award costs and to direct how, to what party and from what parties, costs are to be paid.

(3) Rules prescribing fees require the consent of the Treasury.

(4) The remuneration of an adviser appointed to assist the comptroller shall be determined by the Secretary of State with the consent of the Treasury and shall be defrayed out of money provided by Parliament.

(5) Rules shall be made by statutory instrument which shall be subject to annulment in pursuance of a resolution of either House of Parliament.

Jurisdiction of the court

References and appeals on design right matters

251.—(1) In any proceedings before him under section 246 (reference of matter relating to design right), the comptroller may at any time order the whole proceedings or any question or issue (whether of fact of law) to be referred, on such terms as he may direct, to the High Court or, in Scotland, the Court of Session.

(2) The comptroller shall make such an order if the parties to the proceedings agree that he should do so.

(3) On a reference under this section the court may exercise any power available to the comptroller by virtue of this Part as respects the matter referred to it and, following its determination, may refer any matter back to the comptroller.

(4) An appeal lies from any decision of the comptroller in proceedings before him under section 246 (decisions on matters relating to design right) to[—

    (a)] the High Court or, in Scotland, the Court of Session[, or

    (b) a person appointed under section 27A of the Registered Designs Act 1949.]

Note: In subs.(4), para (a) numbered as such, and para.(b) inserted, by the Intellectual Property Act 2014, s.10(8), with effect from April 6, 2015 (see SI 2015/165).

Reference of disputes relating to Crown use

252.—(1) A dispute as to any matter which falls to be determined by the court in default of agreement under—

    (a) section 241 (settlement of terms for Crown use),

    (b) section 242 (rights of third parties in case of Crown use), or

    (c) section 243 (Crown use: compensation for loss of profit),

may be referred to the court by any party to the dispute.

(2) In determining a dispute between a government department and any person as to the terms for Crown use of a design the court shall have regard to—

    (a) any sums which that person or a person from whom he derives title has received or is entitled to receive, directly or indirectly, from any government department in respect of the design; and

    (b) whether that person or a person from whom he derives title has in the court's opinion without reasonable cause failed to comply with a request of the department for the use of the design on reasonable terms.

(3) One of two or more joint owners of design right may, without the concurrence of the others, refer a dispute to the court under this section, but shall not do so unless the others are made parties, and none of those others is liable for any costs unless he takes part in the proceedings.

(4) Where the consent of an exclusive licensee is required by section 242(3)(a)(i) to the settlement by agreement of the terms for Crown use of a design, a determination by the court of the amount of any payment to be made for such use is of no effect unless the licensee has been notified of the reference and given an opportunity to be heard.

(5) On the reference of a dispute as to the amount recoverable as mentioned in section 242(3)(a)(ii) (right of exclusive licensee to recover part of amount payable to design right owner) the court shall determine what is just having regard to any expenditure incurred by the licensee—

(a) in developing the design, or

(b) in making payments to the design right owner in consideration of the licence (other than royalties or other payments determined by reference to the use of the design).

(6) In this section "the court" means—

(a) in England and Wales, the High [Court] having jurisdiction by virtue of an order under section 287 of this Act,

(b) in Scotland, the Court of Session, and

(c) in Northern Ireland, the High Court.

Note: In subs.(6)(a) word in square brackets substituted for words "Court or any patents county court", subject to savings and transitional provisions, by the Crime and Courts Act 2013, s.30(2), with effect from October 1, 2013 (for savings and transitional provisions see Sch.8 of the Act and SI 2013/1725).

CHAPTER V

MISCELLANEOUS AND GENERAL

Miscellaneous

Remedy for groundless threats of infringement proceedings

253.—(1) Where a person threatens another person with proceedings for infringement of design right, a person aggrieved by the threats may bring an action against him claiming—

(a) a declaration to the effect that the threats are unjustifiable;

(b) an injunction against the continuance of the threats;

(c) damages in respect of any loss which he has sustained by the threats.

(2) If the plaintiff proves that the threats were made and that he is a person aggrieved by them, he is entitled to the relief claimed unless the defendant shows that the acts in respect of which proceedings were threatened did constitute, or if done would have constituted, an infringement of the design right concerned.

(3) Proceedings may not be brought under this section in respect of a threat to bring proceedings for an infringement alleged to consist of making or importing anything.

(4) Mere notification that a design is protected by design right does not constitute a threat of proceedings for the purposes of this section.

Licensee under licence of right not to claim connection with design right owner

254.—(1) A person who has a licence in respect of a design by virtue of section 237 or 238 (licence of right) shall not, without the consent of the design right owner—

(a) apply to goods which he is marketing, or proposes to market, in reliance on that licence a trade description indicating that he is the licensee of the design right owner, or

(b) use any such trade description in an advertisement in relation to such goods.

(2) A contravention of subsection (1) is actionable by the design right owner.

(3) In this section "trade description", the reference to applying a trade description to goods and "advertisement" have the same meaning as in the Trade Descriptions Act 1968.

Extent of operation of this Part

Countries to which this Part extends

255.—(1) This Part extends to England and Wales, Scotland and Northern Ireland.

(2) Her Majesty may by Order in Council direct that this Part shall extend, subject to such exceptions and modifications as may be specified in the Order to—

(a) any of the Channel Islands,

(b) the Isle of Man, or

(c) any colony.

(3) That power includes power to extend, subject to such exceptions and modifications as may be specified in the Order, any Order in Council made under section 221 (further provision as to qualification for design right protection) or section 256 (countries enjoying reciprocal protection).

(4) The legislature of a country to which this Part has been extended may modify or add to the provisions of this Part, in their operation as part of the law of that country, as the legislature may consider necessary to adapt the provisions to the circumstances of that country; but not so as to deny design right protection in a case where it would otherwise exist.

(5) Where a country to which this Part extends ceases to be a colony of the United Kingdom, it shall continue to be treated as such a country for the purposes of this Part until—

(a) an Order in Council is made under section 256 designating it as a country enjoying reciprocal protection, or

(b) an Order in Council is made declaring that it shall cease to be so treated by reason of the fact that the provisions of this Part as part of the law of that country have been amended or repealed.

(6) A statutory instrument containing an Order in Council under subsection (5)(b) shall be subject to annulment in pursuance of a resolution of either House of Parliament.

Countries enjoying reciprocal protection

256.—(1) Her Majesty may, if it appears to Her that the law of a country provides adequate protection for British designs, by Order in Council designate that country as one enjoying reciprocal protection under this Part.

(2) If the law of a country provides adequate protection only for certain classes of British design, or only for designs applied to certain classes of article, any Order designating that country shall contain provision limiting, to a corresponding extent, the protection afforded by this Part in relation to designs connected with that country.

(3) An Order under this section shall be subject to annulment in pursuance of a resolution of either House of Parliament.

Territorial waters and the continental shelf

257.—(1) For the purposes of this Part the territorial waters of the United Kingdom shall be treated as part of the United Kingdom.

(2) This Part applies to things done in the United Kingdom sector of the continental shelf on a structure or vessel which is present there for purposes directly connected with the exploration of the sea bed or subsoil or the exploitation of their natural resources as it applies to things done in the United Kingdom.

(3) The United Kingdom sector of the continental shelf means the areas designated by order under section 1(7) of the Continental Shelf Act 1964.

Interpretation

Construction of references to design right owner

258.—(1) Where different persons are (whether in consequence of a partial assignment or otherwise) entitled to different aspects of design right in a work, the design right owner for any purpose of this Part is the person who is entitled to the right in the respect relevant for that purpose.

(2) Where design right (or any aspect of design right) is owned by more than one person jointly, references in this Part to the design right owner are to all the owners, so that, in particular, any requirement of the licence of the design right owner requires the licence of all of them.

Joint designs

259.—(1) In this Part a "joint design" means a design produced by the collaboration of two or more designers in which the contribution of each is not distinct from that of the other or others.

(2) References in this Part to the designer of a design shall, except as otherwise provided, be construed in relation to a joint design as references to all the designers of the design.

Application of provisions to articles in kit form

260.—(1) The provisions of this Part apply in relation to a kit, that is, a complete or substantially complete set of components intended to be assembled into an article, as they apply in relation to the assembled article.

(2) Subsection (1) does not affect the question whether design right subsists in any aspect of the design of the components of a kit as opposed to the design of the assembled article.

Requirement of signature: application in relation to body corporate

261. The requirement in the following provisions that an instrument be signed by or on behalf of a person is also satisfied in the case of a body corporate by the affixing of its seal—

    section 222(3) (assignment of design right),
    section 223(1) (assignment of future design right),
    section 225(1) (grant of exclusive licence).

Adaptation of expressions in relation to Scotland

262. In the application of this Part to Scotland—
    "account of profits" means accounting and payment of profits;
    "accounts" means count, reckoning and payment;
    "assignment" means assignation;
    "costs" means expenses;
    "defendant" means defender;

"delivery up" means delivery;

"injunction" means interdict;

"interlocutory relief" means interim remedy; and

"plaintiff" means pursuer.

Minor definitions

263.—(1) In this Part—

"British design" means a design which qualifies for design right protection by reason of a connection with the United Kingdom of the designer or the person by whom [...] the designer is employed;

"business" includes a trade or profession;

[...] ;

"computer-generated", in relation to a design, means that the design is generated by computer in circumstances such that there is no human designer,

"country" includes any territory;

"the Crown" includes the Crown in right of Her Majesty's Government in Northern Ireland [and the Crown in right of the Scottish Administration] [and the Crown in right of the Welsh [...] Government];

"design document" means any record of a design, whether in the form of a drawing, a written description, a photograph, data stored in a computer or otherwise;

"employee", "employment" and "employer" refer to employment under a contract of service or of apprenticeship;

"government department" includes a Northern Ireland department [and any part of the Scottish Administration] [and any part of the Welsh Assembly Government].

(2) References in this Part to "marketing", in relation to an article, are to its being sold or let for hire, or offered or exposed for sale or hire, in the course of a business, and related expressions shall be construed accordingly; but no account shall be taken for the purposes of this Part of marketing which is merely colourable and not intended to satisfy the reasonable requirements of the public.

(3) References in this Part to an act being done in relation to an article for "commercial purposes" are to its being done with a view to the article in question being sold or hired in the course of a business.

Notes:

(1) The words in square brackets in the definitions of "the Crown" and "government department" inserted by the Scotland Act 1998 (Consequential Modifications) (No.2) Order 1999 (SI 1999/1820), art.4, Sch.2, para.93, with effect from July 1, 1999. Note also that by art.2 of that Order references in enactments passed prior to July 1, 1999 (save those listed in Sch.1 to the Order) to government departments or parts or officers thereof are to be read, so far as the effect of the Scotland Act 1998 makes it necessary or expedient to do so, as including or being a reference to, or to any corresponding part or member of staff of, the Scottish Administration.

(2) The words in the second set of square brackets in the definitions of "the Crown" and "government department" inserted by the Government of Wales Act 2006 (c.32), Sch.10 para.31, with effect from May 4, 2007.

(3) In subs.(1), in definition "British design" words omitted repealed, and definition "commission" repealed, subject to savings, by the Intellectual Property Act 2014, ss.2(2)(i), (j), with effect from October 1, 2014 (see SI 2014/2330) (for savings see reg.2(3) thereof).

(4) In definition "the Crown" word omitted repealed by the Government of Wales Act 2006, Sch.10 para.31, with effect from February 17, 2015 (commenced by an amendment).

Index of defined expressions

264. The following Table shows provisions defining or otherwise explaining expressions used in this Part (other than provisions defining or explaining an expression used only in the same section)—

account of profits and accounts (in Scotland)	section 262
assignment (in Scotland)	section 262
British designs	section 263(1)
business	section 263(1)
commercial purposes	section 263(3)
[...]	[...]
the comptroller	section 263(1)
computer-generated	section 263(1)
costs (in Scotland)	section 262
country	section 263(1)
the Crown	section 263(1)
Crown use	sections 240(5) and 244(2)
defendant (in Scotland)	section 262
delivery up (in Scotland)	section 262
design	section 213(2)
design document	section 263(1)
designer	sections 214 and 259(2)
design right	section 213(1)
design right owner	sections 234(2) and 258
employee, employment and employer	section 263(1)
exclusive licence	section 225(1)
government department	section 263(1)
government department concerned (in relation to Crown use)	section 240(5)
infringing article	section 228
injunction (in Scotland)	section 262
interlocutory relief (in Scotland)	section 262
joint design	section 259(1)
licence (of the design right owner)	sections 222(4), 223(3) and 258
making articles to a design	section 226(2)
marketing (and related expressions)	section 263(2)
original	section 213(4)
plaintiff (in Scotland)	section 262
[...]	[...]
qualifying person	section 217(1) and (2)
signed	section 261

Note: Definitions "commission" and "qualifying individual" repealed, subject to savings, by the Intellectual Property Act 2014, ss.2(2)(k), 3(5), with effect from October 1, 2014 (see SI 2014/2330) (for savings see regs 2(3), 3(6) thereof).

Amendments of the Registered Designs Act 1949

Registrable designs

265. [...]

Notes:

(1) This section was repealed by the Registered Designs Regulations 2001 (SI 2001/ 3949), reg.9, Sch.2, with effect from December 9, 2001. The section formerly provided:

Registrable designs

"**265.**—(1) *For section 1 of the Registered Designs Act 1949 (designs registrable under that Act) substitute*—[amendment not re-printed here; see note (2), below.]

(2) *The above amendment does not apply in relation to applications for registration made before the commencement of this Part; but the provisions of section 266 apply with respect to the right in certain designs registered in pursuance of such an application.*"

(2) The Registered Designs Act 1949 as amended by this Act is printed in italics at section B8.i, below. The 1949 Act was subsequently amended by the Registered Design Regulations 2001 (SI 2001/3949).

Provisions with respect to certain designs registered in pursuance of application made before commencement

266.—(1) Where a design is registered under the Registered Designs Act 1949 in pursuance of an application made after 12th January 1988 and before the commencement of this Part which could not have been registered under section 1 of that Act as substituted by section 265 above—

(a) the right in the registered design expires ten years after the commencement of this Part, if it does not expire earlier in accordance with the 1949 Act, and

(b) any person is, after the commencement of this Part, entitled as of right to a licence to do anything which would otherwise infringe the right in the registered design.

(2) The terms of a licence available by virtue of this section shall, in default of agreement, be settled by the registrar on an application by the person requiring the licence; and the terms so settled shall authorise the licensee to do everything which would be an infringement of the right in the registered design in the absence of a licence.

(3) In settling the terms of a licence the registrar shall have regard to such factors as may be prescribed by the Secretary of State by order made by statutory instrument.

No such order shall be made unless a draft of it has been laid before and approved by a resolution of each House of Parliament.

(4) Where the terms of a licence are settled by the registrar, the licence has effect from the date on which the application to the registrar was made.

(5) Section 11B of the 1949 Act (undertaking to take licence of right in infringement proceedings), as inserted by section 270 below, applies where a licence is available as of right under this section, as it applies where a licence is available as of right under section 11A of that Act.

(6) Where a licence is available as of right under this section, a person to whom the licence was granted before the commencement of this Part may apply to the registrar for an order adjusting the terms of that licence.

(7) An appeal lies from any decision of the registrar under this section.

(8) This section shall be construed as one with the Registered Designs Act 1949.

Authorship and first ownership of designs

267.—(1) Section 2 of the Registered Designs Act 1949 (proprietorship of designs) is amended as follows—[*amendment not re-printed here; see note below.*]

(4) The amendments made by this section do not apply in relation to an application for registration made before the commencement of this Part.

Note: The Registered Designs Act 1949 as amended by this Act is printed in italics at section B8.i, below. The 1949 Act was subsequently amended by the Registered Design Regulations 2001 (SI 2001/3949).

Right given by registration of design

268. [...]

Notes:

(1) Section 268 was repealed by the Registered Designs Regulations 2001 (SI 2001/3949), reg.9, Sch.2, with effect from December 9, 2001. This section formerly provided:

Right given by registration of design

"**268.**—(1) *For section 7 of the Registered Designs Act 1949 (right given by registration) substitute*—[amendment not reprinted here; see note (2), below]

　　(2) *The above amendment does not apply in relation to a design registered in pursuance of an application made before the commencement of this Part.*"

(2) The Registered Designs Act 1949 as amended by this Act is printed in italics section B8.i, below. The 1949 Act was subsequently amended by the Registered Design Regulations 2001 (SI 2001/3949).

Duration of right in registered design

269.—(1) For section 8 of the Registered Designs Act 1949 (period of right) substitute—[*amendment not reprinted here; see note below*]

(2) The above amendment does not apply in relation to the right in a design registered in pursuance of an application made before the commencement of this Part.

Note: The Registered Designs Act 1949 as amended by this Act is printed in italics at section B8.i, below. The 1949 Act was subsequently amended by the Registered Design Regulations 2001 (SI 2001/3949).

Powers exercisable for protection of the public interest

270. In the Registered Designs Act 1949 after section 11 insert—[*amendment not reprinted here; see note below*]

Note: The Registered Designs Act 1949 as amended by this Act is printed in italics at section B8.i, below. The 1949 Act was subsequently amended by the Registered Design Regulations 2001 (SI 2001/3949).

Crown use: compensation for loss of profit

271.—(1) In Schedule 1 to the Registered Designs Act 1949 (Crown use), after paragraph 2 insert—[*amendment not reprinted here; see note below*]

(2) In paragraph 3 of that Schedule (reference of disputes as to Crown use), for sub-paragraph (1) substitute—[*amendment not reprinted here; see note below*]

(3) The above amendments apply in relation to any Crown use of a registered design after the commencement of this section, even if the terms for such use were settled before commencement.

Note: The Registered Designs Act 1949 as amended by this Act is printed in italics at section B8.i, below. The 1949 Act was subsequently amended by the Registered Design Regulations 2001 (SI 2001/3949).

Minor and consequential amendments

272. The Registered Design Act 1949 is further amended in accordance with Schedule 3 which contains minor amendments and amendments consequential upon the provisions of this Act.

Supplementary

Text of Registered Designs Act 1949 as amended

273. Schedule 4 contains the text of the Registered Designs Act 1949 as amended.

Note: The Registered Designs Act 1949 as amended by this Act is printed in italics at section B8.i, below. The 1949 Act was subsequently amended by the Registered Design Regulations 2001 (SI 2001/3949).

Part V

Patent Agents and Trade Mark Agents

Patent agents

Persons permitted to carry on business of a patent agent

274.—(1) Any individual, partnership or body corporate may, subject to the following provisions of this Part [and to the Legal Services Act 2007], carry on the business of acting as agent for others for the purpose of—

(a) applying for or obtaining patents, in the United Kingdom or elsewhere, or

(b) conducting proceedings before the comptroller relating to applications for, or otherwise in connection with, patents.

(2) This does not affect any restriction under the European Patent Convention as to who may act on behalf of another for any purpose relating to European patents.

Note: In subs.(1) words in square brackets inserted by the Legal Services Act 2007, s.185(2), with effect from January 1, 2010.

The register of patent attorneys

[275.—(1) There is to continue to be a register of persons who act as agent for others for the purpose of applying for or obtaining patents.

(2) In this Part a registered patent attorney means an individual whose name is entered on the register kept under this section.

(3) The register is to be kept by the Chartered Institute of Patent Attorneys.

(4) The Secretary of State may, by order, amend subsection (3) so as to require the register to be kept by the person specified in the order.

(5) Before making an order under subsection (4), the Secretary of State must consult the Legal Services Board.

(6) An order under this section must be made by statutory instrument.

(7) An order under this section may not be made unless a draft of it has been laid before, and approved by a resolution of, each House of Parliament.]

Note: This section and s.275A substituted for original s.275 by the Legal Services Act 2007 s.185(3), with effect from January 1, 2010.

Regulation of patent attorneys

[**275A.**—(1) The person who keeps the register under section 275 may make regulations which regulate—
  (a) the keeping of the register and the registration of persons;
  (b) the carrying on of patent attorney work by registered persons.

(2) Those regulations may, amongst other things, make—
  (a) provision as to the educational and training qualifications, and other requirements, which must be satisfied before an individual may be registered or for an individual to remain registered;
  (b) provision as to the requirements which must be met by a body (corporate or unincorporate) before it may be registered, or for it to remain registered, including provision as to the management and control of the body;
  (c) provision as to the educational, training and other requirements to be met by regulated persons;
  (d) provision regulating the practice, conduct and discipline of registered persons or regulated persons;
  (e) provision authorising in such cases as may be specified in the regulations the erasure from the register of the name of any person registered in it, or the suspension of a person's registration;
  (f) provision requiring the payment of such fees as may be specified in or determined in accordance with the regulations;
  (g) provision requiring the payment of such fees as may be specified in or determined in accordance with the regulations;
  (h) provision about the keeping by registered persons or regulated persons of records and accounts;
  (i) provision for reviews of or appeals against decisions made under the regulations;
  (j) provision as to the indemnification of registered persons or regulated persons against losses arising from claims in respect of civil liability incurred by them.

(3) Regulations under this section may make different provision for different purposes.

(4) Regulations under this section which are not regulatory arrangements within the meaning of the Legal Services Act 2007 are to be treated as such arrangements for the purposes of that Act.

(5) Before the appointed day, regulations under this section may be made only with the approval of the Secretary of State.

(6) The powers conferred to make regulations under this section are not to be taken to prejudice—
  (a) any other power which the person who keeps the register may have to

make rules or regulations (however they may be described and whether they are made under an enactment or otherwise);

(b) any rules or regulations made by that person under any such power.

(7) In this section—

"appointed day" means the day appointed for the coming into force of paragraph 1 of Schedule 4 to the Legal Services Act 2007;

"manager", in relation to a body, has the same meaning as in the Legal Services Act 2007 (see section 207);

"patent attorney work" means work done in the course of carrying on the business of acting as agent for others for the purpose of—

(a) applying for or obtaining patents, in the United Kingdom or elsewhere, or

(b) conducting proceedings before the comptroller relating to applications for, or otherwise in connection with, patents;

"registered person" means—

(a) a registered patent attorney, or

(b) a body (corporate or unincorporate) registered in the register kept under section 275;

"regulated person" means a person who is not a registered person but is a manager or employee of a body which is a registered person.]

Note: This section and new s.275 substituted for original s.275 by the Legal Services Act 2007 s.185(3), with effect from January 1, 2010.

Persons entitled to describe themselves as patent agents

276.—(1) An individual who is not a [registered patent attorney] shall not.

(a) carry on a business (otherwise than in partnership) under any name or other description which contains the words "patent agent" or "patent attorney"; or

(b) in the course of a business otherwise describe himself, or permit himself to be described, as a "patent agent" or "patent attorney".

(2) A partnership [or other unincorporated body] shall not.

(a) carry on a business under any name or other description which contains the words "patent agent" or "patent attorney"; or

(b) in the course of a business otherwise describe itself, or permit itself to be described as, a firm of "patent agents" or "patent attorneys", unless [the partnership or other body is registered in the register kept under section 275.]

(3) A body corporate shall not:

(a) carry on a business (otherwise than in partnership) under any name or other description which contains the words "patent agent" or "patent attorney"; or

(b) in the course of a business otherwise describe itself, or permit itself to be described as, a "patent agent" or "patent attorney", unless [the body corporate is registered in the register kept under section 275.]

(4) Subsection (3) does not apply to a company which began to carry on business as a patent agent before 17th November 1917 if the name of a director or the manager of the company who is a registered patent [attorney] is mentioned as being so registered in all professional advertisements, circulars or letters issued by or with the company's consent on which its name appears.

(5) Where this section would be contravened by the use of the words "patent agent" or "patent attorney" in reference to an individual, partnership or body

corporate, it is equally contravened by the use of other expressions in reference to that person, or his business or place of business, which are likely to be understood as indicating that he is entitled to be described as a "patent agent" or "patent attorney".

(6) A person who contravenes this section commits an offence and is liable on summary conviction to a fine not exceeding level 5 on the standard scale; and proceedings for such an offence may be begun at any time within a year from the date of the offence.

(7) This section has effect subject to:

    (a) section 277 (persons entitled to describe themselves as European patent attorneys, &c), and

    (b) section 278(1) (use of term "patent attorney" in reference to solicitors)."

Note: In subss.(1)–(4) words in square brackets substituted for preceding words in italics, and in subs.(2) words in square brackets inserted by the Legal Services Act 2007 ss.185(4), 208(1), Sch.21 paras 75, 76, with effect from January 1, 2010.

Persons entitled to describe themselves as European patent attorneys, &c.

277.—(1) The term "European patent attorney" or "European patent agent" may be used in the following cases without any contravention of section 276.

(2) An individual who is on the European list may—

    (a) carry on business under a name or other description which contains the words "European patent attorney" or "European patent agent", or

    (b) otherwise describe himself, or permit himself to be described as a "European patent attorney" or "European patent agent".

(3) A partnership of which not less than the prescribed number or proportion of partners is on the European list may—

    (a) carry on a business under a name or other description which contains the words "European patent attorneys" or "European patent agents", or

    (b) otherwise describe itself, or permit itself to be described, as a firm which carries on the business of a "European patent attorney" or "European patent agent".

(4) A body corporate of which not less than the prescribed number or proportion of directors is on the European list may—

    (a) carry on a business under a name or other description which contains the words "European patent attorney" or "European patent agent", or

    (b) otherwise describe itself, or permit itself to be described as, a company which carries on the business of a "European patent attorney" or "European patent agent".

(5) Where the term "European patent attorney" or "European patent agent" may, in accordance with this section, be used in reference to an individual, partnership or body corporate, it is equally permissible to use other expressions in reference to that person, or to his business or place of business, which are likely to be understood as indicating that he is entitled to be described as a "European patent attorney" or "European patent agent".

Use of the term "patent attorney": supplementary provisions

278.—(1) The term "patent attorney" may be used in reference to a solicitor, and a firm of solicitors may be described as a firm of "patent attorneys", without any contravention of section 276.

(2) No offence is committed under the enactments restricting the use of certain expressions in reference to persons not qualified to act as solicitors—

    (a) by the use of the term "patent attorney" in reference to a registered patent agent, or

    (b) by the use of the term "European patent attorney" in reference to a person on the European list.

(3) The enactments referred to in subsection (2) are section 21 of the Solicitors Act 1974, section 31 of the Solicitors (Scotland) Act 1980 and Article 22 of the Solicitors (Northern Ireland) Order 1976.

Power to prescribe conditions, &c. for mixed partnerships and bodies corporate

279. [...]

Note: Section 279 was repealed by the Legal Services Act 2007 ss.185(5), 210, Sch.23, with effect from January 1, 2010. It formerly provided:

Power to prescribe conditions, &c. for mixed partnerships and bodies corporate

"279.—(1) *The Secretary of State may make rules—*

    (a) *prescribing the conditions to be satisfied for the purposes of section 276 (persons entitled to describe themselves as patent agents) in relation to a partnership where not all the partners are qualified persons or a body corporate where not all the directors are qualified persons, and*

    (b) *imposing requirements to be complied with by such partnerships and bodies corporate.*

  (2) *The rules may, in particular—*

    (a) *prescribe conditions as to the number or proportion of partners or directors who must be qualified persons;*

    (b) *impose requirements as to—*

        (i) *the identification of qualified and unqualified persons in professional advertisements, circulars or letters issued by or with the consent of the partnership or body corporate and which relate to it or to its business; and*

        (ii) *the manner in which a partnership or body corporate is to organise its affairs so as to secure that qualified persons exercise a sufficient degree of control over the activities of unqualified persons.*

  (3) *Contravention of a requirement imposed by the rules is an offence for which a person is liable on summary conviction to a fine not exceeding level 5 on the standard scale.*

  (4) *The Secretary of State may make rules prescribing for the purposes of section 277 the number or proportion of partners of a partnership of directors of a body corporate who must be qualified persons in order for the partnership or body to take advantage of that section.*

  (5) *In this section "qualified person"—*

    (a) *in subsections (1) and (2), means a person who is a registered patent agent, and*

    (b) *in subsection (4), means a person who is on the European list.*

  (6) *Rules under this section shall be made by statutory instrument which shall be subject to annulment in pursuance of a resolution of either House of Parliament.*"

Privilege for communications with patent agents

280.—(1) This section applies to communications as to any matter relating to [—]

    [(a) the protection of any invention, design, technical information, [or trade mark], or as to any matter involving passing off , and

(b) documents, material or information relating to any matter mentioned in paragraph (a).]

[(2) Where a patent attorney acts for a client in relation to a matter mentioned in subsection (1), any communication, document, material or information to which this section applies is privileged from disclosure in like manner as if the patent attorney had at all material times been acting as the client's solicitor.]

(3) In subsection (2) "patent [attorney]" means:

(a) a registered patent [attorney] or a person who is on the European list,

(b) a partnership entitled to describe itself as a firm of patent [attorneys] or as a firm carrying on the business of a European patent attorney, or

[(ba) an unincorporated body (other than a partnership) entitled to describe itself as a patent attorney, or]

(c) a body corporate entitled to describe itself as a patent [attorney] or as a company carrying on the business of a European patent attorney.

(4) [...]

Notes:

(1) Subsection (1) is printed as amended by the Trade Marks Act 1994 (c.26) Sch.4 para.8(3) and the words in square brackets were amended by the Legal Services Act 2007 Sch.21 para.77, with effect from January 1, 2010.

(2) Subsection (2) was substituted by the Legal Services Act 2007 Sch.21, para.77, with effect from January 1, 2010. Subsection (2) formerly read:

"(2) *Any such communication:*

(a) *between a person and his patent agent, or*

(b) *for the purpose of obtaining, or in response to a request for; information which a person is seeking for the purpose of instructing his patent agent, is privileged from disclosure in legal proceedings in England, Wales or Northern Ireland in the same way as a communication between a person and his solicitor or, as the case may be, a communication for the purpose of obtaining, or in response to a request for, information which a person seeks for the purpose of instructing his solicitor.*"

(3) In subs.(3), the words in square brackets substituted for the former words "agent" or "agents" and subs. (3)(ba) was inserted by the Legal Services Act 2007 ss.185(6), Sch.21 para.77, with effect from January 1, 2010.

(4) Subsection (4) was repealed by the Legal Services Act 2007 Sch.21 para.77, with effect from January 1, 2010. Subsection (4) formerly read:

"(4) *It is hereby declared that in Scotland the rules of law which confer privilege from disclosure in legal proceedings in respect of communications extend to such communications as are mentioned in this section.*"

Power of comptroller to refuse to deal with certain agents

281.—(1) This section applies to business under the Patents Act 1949, the Registered Designs Act 1949 or the Patents Act 1977.

(2) The Secretary of State may make rules authorising the comptroller to refuse to recognise as agent in respect of any business to which this section applies

(a) a person who has been convicted of an offence under section 88 of the Patents Act 1949, section 114 of the Patents Act 1977 or section 276 of this Act;

(b) [a person] whose name has been erased from and not restored to, or who is suspended from, the register of patent [attorneys] on the ground of misconduct;

(c) a person who is found by the Secretary of State to have been guilty of such conduct as would, in the case of [a person] registered in the register of patent [attorneys], render [the person] liable to have [the persons] name erased from the register on the ground of misconduct;

(d) a partnership or body corporate of which one of the partners or directors is a person whom the comptroller could refuse to recognise under paragraph (a), (b) or (c) above.

(3) The rules may contain such incidental and supplementary provisions as appear to the Secretary of State to be appropriate and may, in particular, prescribe circumstances in which a person is or is not to be taken to have been guilty of misconduct.

(4) Rules made under this section shall be made by statutory instrument which shall be subject to annulment in pursuance of a resolution of either House of Parliament.

(5) The comptroller shall refuse to recognise as agent in respect of any business to which this section applies a person who neither resides nor has a place of business in the United Kingdom, the Isle of Man or another member State of the European Economic Community.

Note: In subs.(2)(b) and (c) the words "attorneys" in square brackets substituted for the former words "agents" by the Legal Services Act 2007 ss.208(1), 210, Sch.21 paras 75, 78, Sch.23, with effect from January 1, 2010.

Trade mark agents

282.–284. [...]

Note: Sections 282 to 284 repealed by the Trade Marks Act 1994 (c.26), Sch.5.

Supplementary

Offences committed by partnerships and bodies corporate

285.—(1) Proceedings for an offence under this Part alleged to have been committed by a partnership shall be brought in the name of the partnership and not in that of the partners; but without prejudice to any liability of theirs under subsection (4) below.

(2) The following provisions apply for the purposes of such proceedings as in relation to a body corporate—

(a) any rules of court relating to the service of documents;

(b) in England, Wales or Northern Ireland, Schedule 3 to the Magistrates' Courts Act 1980 or Schedule 4 to the Magistrates' Courts (Northern Ireland) Order 1981 (procedure on charge of offence).

(3) A fine imposed on a partnership on its conviction in such proceedings shall be paid out of the partnership assets.

(4) Where a partnership is guilty of an offence under this Part, every partner, other than a partner who is proved to have been ignorant of or to have attempted to prevent the commission of the offence, is also guilty of the offence and liable to be proceeded against and punished accordingly.

(5) Where an offence under this Part committed by a body corporate is proved to have been committed with the consent or connivance of a director, manager, secretary or other similar officer of the body, or a person purporting to act in any such capacity, he as well as the body corporate is guilty of the offence and liable to be proceeded against and punished accordingly.

Interpretation

286. In this Part—

"the comptroller" means the Comptroller-General of Patents, Designs and Trade Marks;

"director", in relation to a body corporate whose affairs are managed by its members, means any member of the body corporate;

"the European list" means the list of professional representatives maintained by the European Patent Office in pursuance of the European Patent Convention;

["registered patent attorney"] has the meaning given by [section 275(2)].

Notes:

(1) The definition of "registered trade mark agent" was deleted by the Trade Marks Act 1994 (c.26) Sch.5.

(2) The definition of "registered patent agent" was amended to "registered patent attorney" by the Legal Services Act 2007 Sch.21 para.79(b), with effect from January 1, 2010.

PART VI

PATENTS

Patents county courts

287.–289. [*Sections 287 to 289 repealed, subject to savings and transitional provisions, by the Crime and Courts Act 2013 Sch.9, para.30(3), with effect from October 1, 2013 (for savings and transitional provisions see Sch.8 of the Act and SI 2013/1715).*]

Limitation of costs where pecuniary claim could have been brought in patents county court

290.—(1) Where an action is commenced in the High Court which could have been commenced in a patents county court and in which a claim for a pecuniary remedy is made, then, subject to the provisions of this section, if the plaintiff recovers less than the prescribed amount, he is not entitled to recover any more costs than those to which he would have been entitled if the action had been brought in the county court.

(2) For this purpose a plaintiff shall be treated as recovering the full amount recoverable in respect of his claim without regard to any deduction made in respect of matters not falling to be taken into account in determining whether the action could have been commenced in a patents county court.

(3) This section does not affect any question as to costs if it appears to the High Court that there was reasonable ground for supposing the amount recoverable in respect of the plaintiff's claim to be in excess of the prescribed amount.

(4) The High Court, if satisfied that there was sufficient reason for bringing the action in the High Court, may make an order allowing the costs or any part of the costs on the High Court scale or on such one of the county court scales as it may direct.

(5) This section does not apply to proceedings brought by the Crown.

(6) In this section "the prescribed amount" means such amount as may be prescribed by Her Majesty for the purposes of this section by Order in Council.

(7) No recommendation shall be made to Her Majesty to make an Order under this section unless a draft of the Order has been laid before and approved by a resolution of each House of Parliament.

Note: Section 290 was prospectively repealed by the Courts and Legal Services Act 1990, s.125(7), Sch.20, but has not been brought into force as at date of publication.

291. [*Section 291 repealed, subject to savings and transitional provisions, by* *the Crime and Courts Act 2013 Sch.9 para.30(3), with effect from October 1, 2013 (for savings and transitional provisions see Sch.8 of the Act and SI 2013/ 1715).*]

292. [*Section 292 repealed by the Legal Services Act 2007 Sch.23 para.1. with effect from January 1, 2010.*]

Licences of right in respect of certain patents

Restriction of acts authorised by certain licences

293. In paragraph 4(2)(c) of Schedule 1 to the Patents Act 1977 (licences to be available as of right where term of existing patent extended), at the end insert," but subject to paragraph 4A below", and after that paragraph insert—

"**4A.**—(1) If the proprietor of a patent for an invention which is a product files a declaration with the Patent Office in accordance with this paragraph, the licences to which persons are entitled by virtue of paragraph 4(2)(c) above shall not extend to a use of the product which is excepted by or under this paragraph.

(2) Pharmaceutical use is excepted, that is—

    (a) use as a medicinal product within the meaning of the Medicines Act 1968, and

    (b) the doing of any other act mentioned in section 60(1)(a) above with a view to such use.

(3) The Secretary of State may by order except such other uses as he thinks fit; and an order may—

    (a) specify as an excepted use any act mentioned in section 60(1)(a) above, and

    (b) make different provision with respect to acts done in different circumstances or for different purposes.

(4) For the purposes of this paragraph the question what uses are excepted, so far as that depends on—

    (a) orders under section 130 of the Medicines Act 1968 (meaning of "medicinal product"), or

    (b) orders under sub-paragraph (3) above,

shall be determined in relation to a patent at the beginning of the sixteenth year of the patent.

(5) A declaration under this paragraph shall be in the prescribed form and shall be filed in the prescribed manner and within the prescribed time limits.

(6) A declaration may not be filed—

    (a) in respect of a patent which has at the commencement of section 293 of the Copyright, Designs and Patents Act 1988 passed the end of its fifteenth year; or

    (b) if at the date of filling there is—

        (i) an existing licence for any description of excepted use of the product, or

        (ii) an outstanding application under section 46(3)(a) or (b) above for the settlement by the comptroller of the terms of a licence for any description of excepted use of the product,

and, in either case, the licence took or is to take effect at or after the end of the sixteenth year of the patent.

(7) Where a declaration has been filed under this paragraph in respect of a patent—

    (a) section 46(3)(c) above (restriction of remedies for infringement where licences available as of right) does not apply to an infringement of the patent in so far as it consists of the excepted use of the product after the filing of the declaration; and

    (b) section 46(3)(d) above (abatement of renewal fee if licences available as of right) does not apply to the patent."

When application may be made for settlement of terms of licence

294. In Schedule 1 to the Patents Act 1977, after the paragraph inserted by section 293 above, insert—

"**4B.**—(1) An application under section 46(3)(a) or (b) above for the settlement by the comptroller of the terms on which a person is entitled to a licence by virtue of paragraph 4(2)(c) above is ineffective if made before the beginning of the sixteenth year of the patent.

(2) This paragraph applies to applications made after the commencement of section 294 of the Copyright, Designs and Patents Act 1988 and to any application made before the commencement of that section in respect of a patent which has not at the commencement of that section passed the end of its fifteenth year."

Patents: miscellaneous amendments

Patents: miscellaneous amendments

295. The Patents Act 1949 and the Patents Act 1977 are amended in accordance with Schedule 5.

PART VII

MISCELLANEOUS AND GENERAL

[Circumvention of protection measures

Circumvention of technical devices applied to computer programs

296.—(1) This section applies where—
- (a) a technical device has been applied to a computer program; and
- (b) a person (A) knowing or having reason to believe that it will be used to make infringing copies—
  - (i) manufactures for sale or hire, imports, distributes, sells or lets for hire, offers or exposes for sale or hire, advertises for sale or hire or has in his possession for commercial purposes any means the sole intended purpose of which is to facilitate the unauthorised removal or circumvention of the technical device; or
  - (ii) publishes information intended to enable or assist persons to remove or circumvent the technical device.

(2) The following persons have the same rights against A as a copyright owner has in respect of an infringement of copyright—
- (a) a person—
  - (i) issuing to the public copies of, or
  - (ii) communicating to the public,

the computer program to which the technical device has been applied;
- (b) the copyright owner or his exclusive licensee, if he is not the person specified in paragraph (a);
- (c) the owner or exclusive licensee of any intellectual property right in the technical device applied to the computer program.

(3) The rights conferred by subsection (2) are concurrent, and sections 101(3) and 102(1) to (4) apply, in proceedings under this section, in relation to persons with concurrent rights as they apply, in proceedings mentioned in those provisions, in relation to a copyright owner and exclusive licensee with concurrent rights.

(4) Further, the persons in subsection (2) have the same rights under section

99 or 100 (delivery up or seizure of certain articles) in relation to any such means as is referred to in subsection (1) which a person has in his possession, custody or control with the intention that it should be used to facilitate the unauthorised removal or circumvention of any technical device which has been applied to a computer program, as a copyright owner has in relation to an infringing copy.

(5) The rights conferred by subsection (4) are concurrent, and section 102(5) shall apply, as respects anything done under section 99 or 100 by virtue of subsection (4), in relation to persons with concurrent rights as it applies, as respects anything done under section 99 or 100, in relation to a copyright owner and exclusive licensee with concurrent rights.

(6) In this section references to a technical device in relation to a computer program are to any device intended to prevent or restrict acts that are not authorised by the copyright owner of that computer program and are restricted by copyright.

(7) The following provisions apply in relation to proceedings under this section as in relation to proceedings under Part 1 (copyright)—

(a) sections 104 to 106 of this Act (presumptions as to certain matters relating to copyright); and

(b) section 72 of the [Senior Courts Act 1981], section 15 of the Law Reform (Miscellaneous Provisions) (Scotland) Act 1985 and section 94A of the Judicature (Northern Ireland) Act 1978 (withdrawal of privilege against self-incrimination in certain proceedings relating to intellectual property);

and section 114 of this Act applies, with the necessary modifications, in relation to the disposal of anything delivered up or seized by virtue of subsection (4).

(8) Expressions used in this section which are defined for the purposes of Part 1 of this Act (copyright) have the same meaning as in that Part.]

Notes:

(1) This section was substituted by the Copyright and Related Rights Regulations 2003 (SI 2003/2498), reg.24 with effect from October 31, 2003. For savings and transitional provisions, see Part 3 of those Regulations. The former s.296 provided:

Devices designed to circumvent copy-protection

"**296.**—(1) *This section applies where copies of a copyright work are issued to the public, by or with the licence of the copyright owner, in an electronic form which is copy-protected.*

(2) *The person issuing the copies to the public has the same rights against a person who, knowing or having reason to believe that it will be sued to make infringing copies—*

(a) *makes, imports, sells or lets for hire, offers or exposes for sale or hire, or advertises for sale or hire, any device or means specifically designed or adapted to circumvent the form of copy-protection employed, or*

(b) *publishes information intended to enable or assist persons to circumvent that form of copy-protection,*

as a copyright owner has in respect of an infringement of copyright.

[(2A) *Where the copies being issued to the public as mentioned in subsection (1) are copies of a computer program, subsection (2) applies as if for the words "or advertises for sale or hire" there were substituted "advertises for sale or hire or possesses in the course of a business".]*

(3) *Further, he has the same rights under section 99 or 100 (delivery up or seizure of certain articles) in relation to any such device or means which a person has in his possession, custody or control with the intention that it should be used to make infringing copies of copyright works, as a copyright owner has in relation to an infringing copy.*

(4) *References in this section to copy-protection include any device or means intended to prevent or restrict copying of a work or to impair the quality of copies made.*

(5) *Expressions used in this section which are defined for the purposes of Part I of this Act (copyright) have the same meaning as in that Part.*

(6) *The following provisions apply in relation to proceedings under this section as in relation to proceedings under Part I (copyright)—*

    (a) *section 104 to 106 of this Act (presumptions as to certain matters relating to copyright), and*

    (b) *section 72 of the Supreme Court Act 1981, section 15 of the Law Reform (Miscellaneous Provisions) (Scotland) Act 1985 and section 94A of the Judicature (Northern Ireland) Act 1978 (withdrawal of privilege against self-incrimination in certain proceedings relating to intellectual property);*

and section 114 of this Act applies, with the necessary modifications, in relation to the disposal of anything delivered up or seized by virtue of subsection (3) above."

(2) In s.296(7)(b), the words "Senior Courts Act 1981" substituted for the former words "Supreme Court Act 1981" by the Constitutional Reform Act 2005 Sch.11 para.1, with effect from October 1, 2009.

Circumvention of technological measures

[296ZA.—(1) This section applies where—

    (a) effective technological measures have been applied to a copyright work other than a computer program; and

    (b) a person (B) does anything which circumvents those measures knowing, or with reasonable grounds to know, that he is pursuing that objective.

(2) This section does not apply where a person, for the purposes of research into cryptography, does anything which circumvents effective technological measures unless in so doing, or in issuing information derived from that research, he affects prejudicially the rights of the copyright owner.

(3) The following persons have the same rights against B as a copyright owner has in respect of an infringement of copyright—

    (a) a person—

        (i) issuing to the public copies of, or

        (ii) communicating to the public,

the work to which effective technological measures have been applied; and

    (b) the copyright owner or his exclusive licensee, if he is not the person specified in paragraph (a).

(4) The rights conferred by subsection (3) are concurrent, and sections 101(3) and 102(1) to (4) apply, in proceedings under this section, in relation to persons with concurrent rights as they apply, in proceedings mentioned in those provisions, in relation to a copyright owner and exclusive licensee with concurrent rights.

(5) The following provisions apply in relation to proceedings under this section as in relation to proceedings under Part 1 (copyright)—

    (a) sections 104 to 106 of this Act (presumptions as to certain matters relating to copyright); and

    (b) section 72 of the [Senior Courts Act 1981], section 15 of the Law Reform (Miscellaneous Provisions) (Scotland) Act 1985 and section 94A of the Judicature (Northern Ireland) Act 1978 (withdrawal of privilege against self-incrimination in certain proceedings relating to intellectual property).

(6) Subsections (1) to (4) and (5)(b) and any other provision of this Act as it has effect for the purposes of those subsections apply, with any necessary adaptations, to rights in performances, publication right and database right.

(7) The provisions of regulation 22 (presumptions relevant to database right) of the Copyright and Rights in Databases Regulations 1997 (SI 1997/3032) apply in proceedings brought by virtue of this section in relation to database right.]

Notes:

(1) This section was inserted by the Copyright and Related Rights Regulations 2003 (SI 2003/2498), reg.24 with effect from October 31, 2003. For savings and transitional provisions, see Part 3 of those Regulations.

(2) In subs.(6)(b) the words "Senior Courts Act 1981" substituted for the former words "Supreme Court Act 1981" by the Constitutional Reform Act 2005 (c.4), Sch.11 para.1, from October 1, 2009.

Devices and services designed to circumvent technological measures

[296ZB.—(1) A person commits an offence if he—

(a) manufactures for sale or hire, or

(b) imports otherwise than for his private and domestic use, or

(c) in the course of a business—

    (i) sells or lets for hire, or

    (ii) offers or exposes for sale or hire, or

    (iii) advertises for sale or hire, or

    (iv) possesses, or

    (v) distributes, or

(d) distributes otherwise than in the course of a business to such an extent as to affect prejudicially the copyright owner,

any device, product or component which is primarily designed, produced, or adapted for the purpose of enabling or facilitating the circumvention of effective technological measures.

(2) A person commits an offence if he provides, promotes, advertises or markets—

(a) in the course of a business, or

(b) otherwise than in the course of a business to such an extent as to affect prejudicially the copyright owner,

a service the purpose of which is to enable or facilitate the circumvention of effective technological measures.

(3) Subsections (1) and (2) do not make unlawful anything done by, or on behalf of, law enforcement agencies or any of the intelligence services—

(a) in the interests of national security; or

(b) for the purpose of the prevention or detection of crime, the investigation of an offence, or the conduct of a prosecution,

and in this subsection "intelligence services" has the meaning given in section 81 of the Regulation of Investigatory Powers Act 2000.

(4) A person guilty of an offence under subsection (1) or (2) is liable—

(a) on summary conviction, to imprisonment for a term not exceeding three months, or to a fine not exceeding the statutory maximum, or both;

(b) on conviction on indictment to a fine or imprisonment for a term not exceeding two years, or both.

(5) It is a defence to any prosecution for an offence under this section for the defendant to prove that he did not know, and had no reasonable ground for believing, that—

(a) the device, product or component; or

(b) the service,

enabled or facilitated the circumvention of effective technological measures.]

Note: This section was inserted by the Copyright and Related Rights Regulations 2003

(SI 2003/2498), reg.24 with effect from October 31, 2003. For savings and transitional provisions, see Part 3 of those Regulations.

Devices and services designed to circumvent technological measures: search warrants and forfeiture

[296ZC.—(1) The provisions of sections 297B (search warrants), 297C (forfeiture of unauthorised decoders: England and Wales or Northern Ireland) and 297D (forfeiture of unauthorised decoders: Scotland) apply to offences under section 296ZB with the following modifications.

(2) In section 297B the reference to an offence under section 297A(1) shall be construed as a reference to an offence under section 296ZB(1) or (2).

(3) In sections 297C(2)(a) and 297D(15) the references to an offence under section 297A(1) shall be construed as a reference to an offence under section 296ZB(1).

(4) In sections 297C and 297D references to unauthorised decoders shall be construed as references to devices, products or components for the purpose of circumventing effective technological measures.]

Note: This section was inserted by the Copyright and Related Rights Regulations 2003 (SI 2003/2498), reg.24 with effect from October 31, 2003. For savings and transitional provisions, see Part 3 of those Regulations.

Rights and remedies in respect of devices and services designed to circumvent technological measures

[296ZD.—(1) This section applies where—
  (a) effective technological measures have been applied to a copyright work other than a computer program; and
  (b) a person (C) manufactures, imports, distributes, sells or lets for hire, offers or exposes for sale or hire, advertises for sale or hire, or has in his possession for commercial purposes any device, product or component, or provides services which—
      (i) are promoted, advertised or marketed for the purpose of the circumvention of, or
      (ii) have only a limited commercially significant purpose or use other than to circumvent, or
      (iii) are primarily designed, produced, adapted or performed for the purpose of enabling or facilitating the circumvention of,
those measures.

(2) The following persons have the same rights against C as a copyright owner has in respect of an infringement of copyright—
  (a) a person—
      (i) issuing to the public copies of, or
      (ii) communicating to the public,
the work to which effective technological measures have been applied;
  (b) the copyright owner or his exclusive licensee, if he is not the person specified in paragraph (a); and
  (c) the owner or exclusive licensee of any intellectual property right in the effective technological measures applied to the work.

(3) The rights conferred by subsection (2) are concurrent, and sections 101(3) and 102(1) to (4) apply, in proceedings under this section, in relation to persons with concurrent rights as they apply, in proceedings mentioned in those provisions, in relation to a copyright owner and exclusive licensee with concurrent rights.

(4) Further, the persons in subsection (2) have the same rights under section 99 or 100 (delivery up or seizure of certain articles) in relation to any such device, product or component which a person has in his possession, custody or control with the intention that it should be used to circumvent effective technological measures, as a copyright owner has in relation to any infringing copy.

(5) The rights conferred by subsection (4) are concurrent, and section 102(5) shall apply, as respects anything done under section 99 or 100 by virtue of subsection (4), in relation to persons with concurrent rights as it applies, as respects anything done under section 99 or 100, in relation to a copyright owner and exclusive licensee with concurrent rights.

(6) The following provisions apply in relation to proceedings under this section as in relation to proceedings under Part 1 (copyright)—

(a) sections 104 to 106 of this Act (presumptions as to certain matters relating to copyright); and

(b) section 72 of the [Senior Courts Act 1981], section 15 of the Law Reform (Miscellaneous Provisions) (Scotland) Act 1985 and section 94A of the Judicature (Northern Ireland) Act 1978 (withdrawal of privilege against self-incrimination in certain proceedings relating to intellectual property);

and section 114 of this Act applies, with the necessary modifications, in relation to the disposal of anything delivered up or seized by virtue of subsection (4).

(7) In section 97(1) (innocent infringement of copyright) as it applies to proceedings for infringement of the rights conferred by this section, the reference to the defendant not knowing or having reason to believe that copyright subsisted in the work shall be construed as a reference to his not knowing or having reason to believe that his acts enabled or facilitated an infringement of copyright.

(8) Subsections (1) to (5), (6)(b) and (7) and any other provision of this Act as it has effect for the purposes of those subsections apply, with any necessary adaptations, to rights in performances, publication right and database right.

(9) The provisions of regulation 22 (presumptions relevant to database right) of the Copyright and Rights in Databases Regulations 1997 (SI 1997/3032) apply in proceedings brought by virtue of this section in relation to database right.]

Notes:

(1) This section was inserted by the Copyright and Related Rights Regulations 2003 (SI 2003/2498), reg.24 with effect from October 31, 2003. For savings and transitional provisions, see Part 3 of those Regulations.

(2) In subs.(6)(b) the words in square brackets substituted for the former words "Supreme Court Act 1981" by the Constitutional Reform Act 2005 Sch.11 para.1, with effect from October 1, 2009.

Remedy where effective technological measures prevent permitted acts

[**296ZE.**—(1) In this section—

"permitted act" means an act which may be done in relation to copyright works, notwithstanding the subsistence of copyright, by virtue of a provision of this Act listed in Part 1 of Schedule 5A;

"voluntary measure or agreement" means—

(a) any measure taken voluntarily by a copyright owner, his exclusive licensee or a person issuing copies of, or communicating to the public, a work other than a computer program, or

(b) any agreement between a copyright owner, his exclusive licensee or a person issuing copies of, or communicating to the public, a work other than a computer program and another party, the effect of which is to enable a person to carry out a permitted act.

(2) Where the application of any effective technological measure to a copyright work other than a computer program prevents a person from carrying out a permitted act in relation to that work then that person or a person being a representative of a class of persons prevented from carrying out a permitted act may issue a notice of complaint to the Secretary of State.

(3) Following receipt of a notice of complaint, the Secretary of State may give to the owner of that copyright work or an exclusive licensee such directions as appear to the Secretary of State to be requisite or expedient for the purpose of—

    (a) establishing whether any voluntary measure or agreement relevant to the copyright work the subject of the complaint subsists; or

    (b) (where it is established there is no subsisting voluntary measure or agreement) ensuring that the owner or exclusive licensee of that copyright work makes available to the complainant the means of carrying out the permitted act the subject of the complaint to the extent necessary to so benefit from that permitted act.

(4) The Secretary of State may also give directions—

    (a) as to the form and manner in which a notice of complaint in subsection (2) may be delivered to him;

    (b) as to the form and manner in which evidence of any voluntary measure or agreement may be delivered to him; and

    (c) generally as to the procedure to be followed in relation to a complaint made under this section;

and shall publish directions given under this subsection in such manner as in his opinion will secure adequate publicity for them.

(5) It shall be the duty of any person to whom a direction is given under subsection (3)(a) or (b) to give effect to that direction.

(6) The obligation to comply with a direction given under subsection(3)(b) is a duty owed to the complainant or, where the complaint is made by a representative of a class of persons, to that representative and to each person in the class represented; and a breach of the duty is actionable accordingly (subject to the defences and other incidents applying to actions for breach of statutory duty).

(7) Any direction under this section may be varied or revoked by a subsequent direction under this section.

(8) Any direction given under this section shall be in writing.

(9) This section does not apply to copyright works made available to the public on agreed contractual terms in such a way that members of the public may access them from a place and at a time individually chosen by them.

(10) This section applies only where a complainant has lawful access to the protected copyright work, or where the complainant is a representative of a class of persons, where the class of persons have lawful access to the work.

(11) Subsections (1) to (10) apply with any necessary adaptations to—

    (a) rights in performances, and in this context the expression "permitted act" refers to an act that may be done by virtue of a provision of this Act listed in Part 2 of Schedule 5A;

    (b) database right, and in this context the expression "permitted act" refers to an act that may be done by virtue of a provision of this Act listed in Part 3 of Schedule 5A; and

    (c) publication right.]

Note: This section was inserted by the Copyright and Related Rights Regulations 2003 (SI 2003/2498), reg.24 with effect from October 31, 2003. For savings and transitional provisions, see Part 3 of those Regulations.

296ZEA. [...]

Note: The Copyright and Rights in Performances (Personal Copies for Private Use) Regulations 2014 (SI 2014/2361), which introduced ss.28B and 296ZEA with effect from October 1, 2014, were quashed with prospective effect on July 17, 2015: *The Queen on the application of British Academy of Songwriters, Composers and Authors v Secretary of State for Business, Innovation and Skills* [2015] EWHC 2041 (Admin) at [11], [21]. Accordingly, ss.28B and 296ZEA have been of no effect from that date. However, the Court declined to rule as to whether the regulations (and therefore ss.28B and 296ZEA) were void during the period from October 1, 2014 to July 16, 2015. Accordingly the question whether ss.28B and 296ZEA were effective during that period remains undecided: see the judgment at [19], [21]. Section 296ZEA read as follows:

Remedy where restrictive measures prevent or restrict personal copying

"296ZEA.—*(1) This section applies where an individual is prevented from making a personal copy of a copyright work, or is restricted in the number of personal copies of it which may be made, because of a restrictive measure applied by or on behalf of the copyright owner.*

(2) That individual, or a person being a representative of a class of such individuals, may issue a notice of complaint to the Secretary of State.

(3) Following receipt of a notice of complaint, the Secretary of State may give to the owner of that copyright work or an exclusive licensee such directions as appear to the Secretary of State to be requisite or expedient for the purpose of—

(a) *establishing whether any voluntary measure or agreement relevant to the copyright work subsists, or*

(b) *where it is established there is no subsisting voluntary measure or agreement) ensuring that the owner or exclusive licensee of that copyright work makes available to the complainant or the class of individuals represented by the complainant the means of benefiting from section 28B to the extent necessary to benefit from that section.*

(4) In deciding whether to give such directions, the Secretary of State must consider whether the restrictive measure unreasonably prevents or restricts the making of personal copies, in particular having regard to—

(a) *the right of the copyright owner to adopt adequate measures limiting the number of personal copies which may be made, and*

(b) *whether other copies of the work are commercially available on reasonable terms by or with the authority of the copyright owner in a form which does not prevent or unreasonably restrict the making of personal copies.*

(5) The Secretary of State may also give directions—

(a) *as to the form and manner in which a notice of complaint in subsection (2) may be delivered,*

(b) *as to the form and manner in which evidence of any voluntary measure or agreement may be delivered, and*

(c) *generally as to the procedure to be followed in relation to a complaint made under this section, and shall publish directions given under this subsection in such manner as the Secretary of State thinks will secure adequate publicity for them.*

(6) Subsections (5) to (8) of section 296ZE—

(a) *apply to directions under subsection (3)(a) or (b) as they apply to directions under section 296ZE(3)(a) or (b), and*

(b) *apply to directions under subsection (5) as they apply to directions under section 296ZE(4).*

(7) This section does not apply to copyright works made available to the pub-

lic on agreed contractual terms in such a way that members of the public may access them from a place and at a time individually chosen by them.

(8) In this section—

"*restrictive measure*" *means any technology, device or component designed, in the normal course of its operation, to protect the rights of copyright owners, which has the effect of preventing a copyright work from being copied (in whole or in part) or restricting the number of copies which may be made;*

"*personal copy*" *means a copy of a copyright work which may be made under section 28B;*

"*voluntary measure or agreement*" *has the same meaning as in section 296ZE, except that the reference to carrying out a permitted act is to be read as a reference to making a personal copy. (9) Subsections (1) to (8) apply with any necessary adaptations to—*

(a) rights in performances, and in this context "personal copy" refers to a copy of a recording of a performance which may be made under paragraph 1B of Schedule 2 without infringing the rights conferred by Chapter 2 of Part II (rights in performances), and

(b) publication right."

Interpretation of sections 296ZA to [296ZE]

[**296ZF.**—(1) In sections 296ZA to 296ZE, "technological measures" are any technology, device or component which is designed, in the normal course of its operation, to protect a copyright work other than a computer program.

(2) Such measures are "effective" if the use of the work is controlled by the copyright owner through—

(a) an access control or protection process such as encryption, scrambling or other transformation of the work, or

(b) a copy control mechanism,

which achieves the intended protection.

(3) In this section, the reference to—

(a) protection of a work is to the prevention or restriction of acts that are not authorised by the copyright owner of that work and are restricted by copyright; and

(b) use of a work does not extend to any use of the work that is outside the scope of the acts restricted by copyright.

(4) Expressions used in sections 296ZA to [296ZE] which are defined for the purposes of Part 1 of this Act (copyright) have the same meaning as in that Part.]

Notes:

(1) This section was inserted by the Copyright and Related Rights Regulations 2003 (SI 2003/2498), reg.24 with effect from October 31, 2003. For savings and transitional provisions, see Part 3 of those Regulations.

(2) In heading and subs.(4) "296ZEA" was substituted for "296ZE" by the Copyright and Rights in Performances (Personal Copies for Private Use) Regulations 2014 (SI 2014/2361), reg.4(3), with effect from October 1, 2014. However, SI 2014/2361 was quashed with prospective effect on July 17, 2015: *The Queen on the application of British Academy of Songwriters, Composers and Authors v Secretary of State for Business, Innovation and Skills* [2015] EWHC 2041 (Admin) at [11], [21]. Accordingly, this consequential amendment has no effect from that date. However, the Court declined to rule as to whether the regulations were void during the period from October 1, 2014 to July 16, 2015. Accordingly the question of whether this amendment is effective during that period remains undecided: see the judgment at [19], [21].

Electronic rights management information

[**296ZG.**—(1) This section applies where a person (D), knowingly and without authority, removes or alters electronic rights management information which—

(a) is associated with a copy of a copyright work, or

(b) appears in connection with the communication to the public of a copyright work, and where D knows, or has reason to believe, that by so doing he is inducing, enabling, facilitating or concealing an infringement of copyright.

(2) This section also applies where a person (E), knowingly and without authority, distributes, imports for distribution or communicates to the public copies of a copyright work from which electronic rights management information—

(a) associated with the copies, or

(b) appearing in connection with the communication to the public of the work, has been removed or altered without authority and where E knows, or has reason to believe, that by so doing he is inducing, enabling, facilitating or concealing an infringement of copyright.

(3) A person issuing to the public copies of, or communicating, the work to the public, has the same rights against D and E as a copyright owner has in respect of an infringement of copyright.

(4) The copyright owner or his exclusive licensee, if he is not the person issuing to the public copies of, or communicating, the work to the public, also has the same rights against D and E as he has in respect of an infringement of copyright.

(5) The rights conferred by subsections (3) and (4) are concurrent, and sections 101(3) and 102(1) to (4) apply, in proceedings under this section, in relation to persons with concurrent rights as they apply, in proceedings mentioned in those provisions, in relation to a copyright owner and exclusive licensee with concurrent rights.

(6) The following provisions apply in relation to proceedings under this section as in relation to proceedings under Part 1 (copyright)—

(a) sections 104 to 106 of this Act (presumptions as to certain matters relating to copyright); and

(b) section 72 of the [Senior Courts Act 1981], section 15 of the Law Reform (Miscellaneous Provisions) (Scotland) Act 1985 and section 94A of the Judicature (Northern Ireland) Act 1978 (withdrawal of privilege against self-incrimination in certain proceedings relating to intellectual property).

(7) In this section—

(a) expressions which are defined for the purposes of Part 1 of this Act (copyright) have the same meaning as in that Part; and

(b) "rights management information" means any information provided by the copyright owner or the holder of any right under copyright which identifies the work, the author, the copyright owner or the holder of any intellectual property rights, or information about the terms and conditions of use of the work, and any numbers or codes that represent such information.

(8) Subsections (1) to (5) and (6)(b), and any other provision of this Act as it has effect for the purposes of those subsections, apply, with any necessary adaptations, to rights in performances, publication right and database right.

(9) The provisions of regulation 22 (presumptions relevant to database right) of the Copyright and Rights in Databases Regulations 1997 (SI 1997/3032) apply in proceedings brought by virtue of this section in relation to database right.]

Notes:
(1) Section 296ZG was inserted by the Copyright and Related Rights Regulations 2003 (SI 2003/2498), Pt 2 reg.25, subject to the savings specified reg.32.
(2) In subs.(6)(b) the words in square brackets substituted for the former words "Supreme Court Act 1981" by the Constitutional Reform Act 2005 Sch.11 para.1, with effect from October 1, 2009.

[Computer programs

Avoidance of certain terms

296A.—(1) Where a person has the use of a computer program under an agreement, any term or condition in the agreement shall be void in so far as it purports to prohibit or restrict—

(a) the making of any back up copy of the program which it is necessary for him to have for the purposes of the agreed use;

(b) where the conditions in section 50B(2) are met, the decompiling of the program; or

[(c) the observing, studying or testing of the functioning of the program in accordance with section 50BA.]

(2) In this section, decompile, in relation to a computer program, has the same meaning as in section 50B.]

Notes:
(1) This section and the heading preceding it inserted by the Copyright (Computer Programs) Regulations 1992 (SI 1992/3233), with effect from January 1, 1993. For savings and transitional provisions, see regulation 12 of those Regulations
(2) Subsection (1)(c) was substituted by the Copyright and Related Rights Regulations 2003 (SI 2003/2498), reg.15 with effect from October 31, 2003. For savings and transitional provisions, see Part 3 of those Regulations. The former subs.(1)(c) provided:

"(c) *the use of any device or means to observe, study or test the functioning of the program in order to understand the ideas and principles which underlie any element of the program.*"

[Databases

Avoidance of certain terms relating to databases

296B. Where under an agreement a person has a right to use a database or part of a database, any term or condition in the agreement shall be void in so far as it purports to prohibit or restrict the performance of any act which would but for section 50D infringe copyright in the database.]

Note: This section and the heading preceding it inserted by the Copyright and Rights in Databases Regulations 1997 (SI 1997/3032), with effect from January 1, 1998. For savings and transitional provisions, see regulations 26 to 30 of those Regulations.

Fraudulent reception of transmissions

Offence of fraudulently receiving programmes

297.—(1) A person who dishonestly receives a programme included in a broadcasting [...] service provided from a place in the United Kingdom with intent to avoid payment of any charge applicable to the reception of the programme commits an offence and is liable on summary conviction to a fine not exceeding level 5 on the standard scale.

(2) Where an offence under this section committed by a body corporate is proved to have been committed with the consent or connivance of a director, manager, secretary or other similar officer of the body, or a person purporting to act in any such capacity, he as well as the body corporate is guilty of the offence and liable to be proceeded against and punished accordingly.

In relation to a body corporate whose affairs are managed by its members "director" means a member of the body corporate.

Note: In subs.(1), the words "or cable programme" repealed by the Copyright and Related Rights Regulations 2003 (SI 2003/2498), Sch.2 with effect from October 31, 2003. For savings and transitional provisions, see Part 3 of those Regulations.

Unauthorised decoders.

[**297A.**—(1) A person commits an offence if he—

(a) makes, imports, distributes, sells or lets for hire or offers or exposes for sale or hire any unauthorised decoder;

(b) has in his possession for commercial purposes any unauthorised decoder;

(c) installs, maintains or replaces for commercial purposes any unauthorised decoder; or

(d) advertises any unauthorised decoder for sale or hire or otherwise promotes any unauthorised decoder by means of commercial communications.

(2) A person guilty of an offence under subsection (1) is liable—

[(a) on summary conviction, to imprisonment for a term not exceeding six months, or to a fine not exceeding the statutory maximum, or to both;]

(b) on conviction on indictment, to imprisonment for a term not exceeding [ten] years, or to a fine, or to both.

(3) It is a defence to any prosecution for an offence under this section for the defendant to prove that he did not know, and had no reasonable ground for believing, that the decoder was an unauthorised decoder.

(4) In this section—

"apparatus" includes any device, component or electronic data (including software);

"conditional access technology" means any technical measure or arrangement whereby access to encrypted transmissions in an intelligible form is made conditional on prior individual authorisation;

"decoder" means any apparatus which is designed or adapted to enable (whether on its own or with any other apparatus) an encrypted transmission to be decoded;

"encrypted" includes subjected to scrambling or the operation of cryptographic envelopes, electronic locks, passwords or any other analogous application;

"transmission" means—

(a) any programme included in a broadcasting [...] service which is provided from a place in the United Kingdom or any other member State; or

(b) an information society service (within the meaning of Directive 98/34/EC of the European Parliament and of the Council of 22nd June 1998, as amended by Directive 98/48/EC of the European Parliament and of the Council of 20th July 1998) which is provided from a place in the United Kingdom or any other member State; and

"unauthorised", in relation to a decoder, means that the decoder is designed or adapted to enable an encrypted transmission, or any service of which it forms part, to be accessed in an intelligible form without payment of the fee (however imposed) which the person making the transmission, or on whose behalf it is made, charges for accessing the transmission or service (whether by the circumvention of any conditional access technology related to the transmission or service or by any other means).]

Notes:

(1) Subsection (2)(a) was substituted and the figure in square brackets in subs.(2)(b) was substituted for the former figure "two" by the Copyright, etc. and Trade Marks (Offences and Enforcement) Act 2002 (c.25), s.1, with effect from November 20, 2002 (Copyright, etc. and Trade Marks (Offences and Enforcement) Act 2002 (Commencement) Order 2002 (SI 2002/2749)).

(2) The words "or cable programme" repealed from subs.(4) by the Copyright and Related Rights Regulations 2003 (SI 2003/2498), Sch.2 with effect from October 31, 2003. For savings and transitional provisions, see Part 3 of those Regulations.

(3) This section was substituted by Conditional Access (Unauthorised Decoders) Regulations 2000 (SI 2001/1175), reg.2, with effect from May 28, 2000. The section formerly provided:

Unauthorised decoders

"**297A.**—[(1) *A person who makes, imports, sells or lets for hire, offers or exposes for sale or hire, or advertises for sale or hire, any unauthorised decoder shall be guilty of an offence and liable—*

      (a) *on summary conviction, to a fine not exceeding the statutory maximum;*

      (b) *on conviction on indictment, to imprisonment for a term not exceeding two years, or to a fine, or to both.]*

    (2) *It is a defence to any prosecution for an offence under this section for the defendant to prove that he did not know, and had no reasonable ground for knowing, that the decoder was an unauthorised decoder.*

    (3) *In this section—*

    "apparatus" includes any device, component or electronic data;

    "decoder" means any apparatus which is designed or adapted to enable (whether on its own or with any other apparatus) an encrypted transmission to be decoded;

    "transmission" means any programme included in a broadcasting or cable programme service which is provided from a place in the United Kingdom; and

    "unauthorised," in relation to a decoder, means a decoder which will enable encrypted transmissions to be viewed in decoded form without payment of the fee (however imposed) which the person making the transmission, or on whose behalf it is made, charges for viewing those transmissions, or viewing any service of which they form part."

(4) The original section was inserted by s.179 of the Broadcasting Act 1990 by virtue of the Broadcasting Act 1990 (Commencement No.1 and Transitional Provisions) Order 1990 (SI 1990/2347).

(5) Subsection (1) was amended by s.140(1) of the Broadcasting Act 1996 with effect from October 1, 1996 by virtue of the Broadcasting Act 1996 (Commencement No.1 and Transitional Provisions) Order 1996 (SI 1996/2120).

Search warrants

[**297B.**—(1) Where a justice of the peace (in Scotland, a sheriff or justice of the peace) is satisfied by information on oath given by a constable (in Scotland, by evidence on oath) that there are reasonable grounds for believing—

  (a) that an offence under section 297A(1) has been or is about to be committed in any premises, and

  (b) that evidence that such an offence has been or is about to be committed is in those premises, he may issue a warrant authorising a constable to enter and search the premises, using such reasonable force as is necessary.

(2) The power conferred by subsection (1) does not, in England and Wales, extend to authorising a search for material of the kinds mentioned in section 9(2) of the Police and Criminal Evidence Act 1984 (c. 60) (certain classes of personal or confidential material).

(3) A warrant under subsection (1)—

    (a) may authorise persons to accompany any constable executing the warrant, and

    (b) remains in force for [three months] from the date of its issue.

(4) In executing a warrant issued under subsection (1) a constable may seize an article if he reasonably believes that it is evidence that any offence under section 297A(1) has been or is about to be committed.

(5) In this section "premises" includes land, buildings, fixed or moveable structures, vehicles, vessels, aircraft and hovercraft.]

Notes:

    (1) This section was inserted by the Copyright, etc. and Trade Marks (Offences and Enforcement) Act 2002 (c.25), s.2, with effect from November 20, 2002 (Copyright, etc. and Trade Marks (Offences and Enforcement) Act 2002 (Commencement) Order 2002 (SI 2002/2749)).

    (2) The words in square brackets in subs.(3)(b) substituted for the former words "28 days" by the Serious Organised Crime and Police Act 2005 (c.15), Sch.16 para.6, with effect from January 1, 2006.

Forfeiture of unauthorised decoders: England and Wales or Northern Ireland

[**297C.**—(1) In England and Wales or Northern Ireland where unauthorised decoders have come into the possession of any person in connection with the investigation or prosecution of a relevant offence, that person may apply under this section for an order for the forfeiture of the unauthorised decoders.

(2) For the purposes of this section "relevant offence" means.

    (a) an offence under [section 198(1) or (1A)] (criminal liability for making or dealing with illicit recordings),

    (b) an offence under the Trade Descriptions Act 1968 (c.29),

    [(ba) an offence under the Business Protection from Misleading Marketing Regulations 2008,

    (bb) an offence under the Consumer Protection from Unfair Trading Regulations 2008, or]

    (c) an offence involving dishonesty or deception.

(3) An application under this section may be made—

    (a) where proceedings have been brought in any court for a relevant offence relating to some or all of the unauthorised decoders, to that court, or

    (b) where no application for the forfeiture of the unauthorised decoders has been made under paragraph (a), by way of complaint to a magistrates' court.

(4) On an application under this section, the court shall make an order for the forfeiture of any unauthorised decoders only if it is satisfied that a relevant offence has been committed in relation to the unauthorised decoders.

(5) A court may infer for the purposes of this section that such an offence has been committed in relation to any unauthorised decoders if it is satisfied that such an offence has been committed in relation to unauthorised decoders which are representative of the unauthorised decoders in question (whether by reason of being of the same design or part of the same consignment or batch or otherwise).

(6) Any person aggrieved by an order made under this section by a magistrates' court, or by a decision of such a court not to make such an order, may appeal against that order or decision—

(a) in England and Wales, to the Crown Court, or

(b) in Northern Ireland, to the county court.

(7) An order under this section may contain such provision as appears to the court to be appropriate for delaying the coming into force of the order pending the making and determination of any appeal (including any application under section 111 of the Magistrates' Courts Act 1980 (c. 43) or Article 146 of the Magistrates' Courts (Northern Ireland) Order 1981 (SI 1981/1675 (N.I. 26)) (statement of case)).

(8) Subject to subsection (9), where any unauthorised decoders are forfeited under this section they shall be destroyed in accordance with such directions as the court may give.

(9) On making an order under this section the court may direct that the unauthorised decoders to which the order relates shall (instead of being destroyed) be forfeited to a person who has rights or remedies under section 298 in relation to the unauthorised decoders in question, or dealt with in such other way as the court considers appropriate.]

Notes:

(1) This section was inserted by the Copyright, etc. and Trade Marks (Offences and Enforcement) Act 2002 (c.25), s.5, with effect from November 20, 2002 (Copyright, etc. and Trade Marks (Offences and Enforcement) Act 2002 (Commencement) Order 2002 (SI 2002/2749)).

(2) In subs.(2) paras (ba) and (bb) inserted by the Consumer Protection from Unfair Trading Regulations 2008 (SI 2008/1277), reg.30(1), Sch.2, para.44, with effect from May 26, 2008.

Forfeiture of unauthorised decoders: Scotland

[297D.—(1) In Scotland the court may make an order under this section for the forfeiture of unauthorised decoders.

(2) An order under this section may be made—

(a) on an application by the procurator-fiscal made in the manner specified in section 134 of the Criminal Procedure (Scotland) Act 1995 (c. 46), or

(b) where a person is convicted of a relevant offence, in addition to any other penalty which the court may impose.

(3) On an application under subsection (2)(a), the court shall make an order for the forfeiture of any unauthorised decoders only if it is satisfied that a relevant offence has been committed in relation to the unauthorised decoders.

(4) The court may infer for the purposes of this section that such an offence has been committed in relation to any unauthorised decoders if it is satisfied that such an offence has been committed in relation to unauthorised decoders which are representative of the unauthorised decoders in question (whether by reason of being of the same design or part of the same consignment or batch or otherwise).

(5) The procurator-fiscal making the application under subsection (2)(a) shall serve on any person appearing to him to be the owner of, or otherwise to have an interest in, the unauthorised decoders to which the application relates a copy of the application, together with a notice giving him the opportunity to appear at the hearing of the application to show cause why the unauthorised decoders should not be forfeited.

(6) Service under subsection (5) shall be carried out, and such service may be proved, in the manner specified for citation of an accused in summary proceedings under the Criminal Procedure (Scotland) Act 1995 (c. 46).

(7) Any person upon whom notice is served under subsection (5) and any other person claiming to be the owner of, or otherwise to have an interest in, unauthorised decoders to which an application under this section relates shall be entitled to appear at the hearing of the application to show cause why the unauthorised decoders should not be forfeited.

(8) The court shall not make an order following an application under subsection (2)(a)—

    (a) if any person on whom notice is served under subsection (5) does not appear, unless service of the notice on that person is proved, or

    (b) if no notice under subsection (5) has been served, unless the court is satisfied that in the circumstances it was reasonable not to serve such notice.

(9) Where an order for the forfeiture of any unauthorised decoders is made following an application under subsection (2)(a), any person who appeared, or was entitled to appear, to show cause why the unauthorised decoders should not be forfeited may, within 21 days of the making of the order, appeal to the High Court by Bill of Suspension.

(10) Section 182(5)(a) to (e) of the Criminal Procedure (Scotland) Act 1995 shall apply to an appeal under subsection (9) as it applies to a stated case under Part 2 of that Act.

(11) An order following an application under subsection (2)(a) shall not take effect—

    (a) until the end of the period of 21 days beginning with the day after the day on which the order is made, or

    (b) if an appeal is made under subsection (9) above within that period, until the appeal is determined or abandoned.

(12) An order under subsection (2)(b) shall not take effect—

    (a) until the end of the period within which an appeal against the order could be brought under the Criminal Procedure (Scotland) Act 1995 (c. 46), or

    (b) if an appeal is made within that period, until the appeal is determined or abandoned.

(13) Subject to subsection (14), where any unauthorised decoders are forfeited under this section they shall be destroyed in accordance with such directions as the court may give.

(14) On making an order under this section the court may direct that the unauthorised decoders to which the order relates shall (instead of being destroyed) be forfeited to a person who has rights or remedies under section 298 in relation to the unauthorised decoders in question, or dealt with in such other way as the court considers appropriate.

(15) For the purposes of this section—

    "["relevant offence" means—

        (a) an offence under section 297A(1) (criminal liability for making, importing, etc unauthorised decoders),

        (b) an offence under the Trade Descriptions Act 1968,

        (c) an offence under the Business Protection from Misleading Marketing Regulations 2008,

        (d) an offence under the Consumer Protection from Unfair Trading Regulations 2008, or

        (e) any offence involving dishonesty or deception.]

    "["the court" means—

        (a) in relation to an order made on an application under subsection (2)(a), the sheriff, and

        (b) in relation to an order made under subsection (2)(b), the court which imposed the penalty.

Notes:

(1) This section was inserted by the Copyright, etc. and Trade Marks (Offences and Enforcement) Act 2002 (c.25), s.5, with effect from November 20, 2002 (Copyright, etc. and Trade Marks (Offences and Enforcement) Act 2002 (Commencement) Order 2002 (SI 2002/2749)).

(2) In subs.(15) the definition of "relevant offence" substituted by the Consumer Protection from Unfair Trading Regulations 2008 (SI 2008/1277), reg.30(1), Sch.2, para.45, with effect from May 26, 2008.

Rights and remedies in respect of apparatus, &c. for unauthorised reception of transmissions

[**298.**—(1) A person who—

(a) makes charges for the reception of programmes included in a broadcasting [...] service provided from a place in the United Kingdom or any other member State,

(b) sends encrypted transmissions of any other description from a place in the United Kingdom or any other member State, or

(c) provides conditional access services from a place in the United Kingdom or any other member State,

is entitled to the following rights and remedies.

(2) He has the same rights and remedies against a person—

(a) who—

(i) makes, imports, distributes, sells or lets for hire, offers or exposes for sale or hire, or advertises for sale or hire,

(ii) has in his possession for commercial purposes, or

(iii) installs, maintains or replaces for commercial purposes,

any apparatus designed or adapted to enable or assist persons to access the programmes or other transmissions or circumvent conditional access technology related to the programmes or other transmissions when they are not entitled to do so, or

(b) who publishes or otherwise promotes by means of commercial communications any information which is calculated to enable or assist persons to access the programmes or other transmissions or circumvent conditional access technology related to the programmes or other transmissions when they are not entitled to do so,

as a copyright owner has in respect of an infringement of copyright.

(3) Further, he has the same rights under section 99 or 100 (delivery up or seizure of certain articles) in relation to any such apparatus as a copyright owner has in relation to an infringing copy.

(4) Section 72 of the [Senior Courts Act 1981], section 15 of the Law Reform (Miscellaneous Provisions) (Scotland) Act 1985 and section 94A of the Judicature (Northern Ireland) Act 1978 (withdrawal of privilege against self-incrimination in certain proceedings relating to intellectual property) apply to proceedings under this section as to proceedings under Part I of this Act (copyright).

(5) In section 97(1) (innocent infringement of copyright) as it applies to proceedings for infringement of the rights conferred by this section, the reference to the defendant not knowing or having reason to believe that copyright subsisted in the work shall be construed as a reference to his not knowing or having reason to believe that his acts infringed the rights conferred by this section.

(6) Section 114 applies, with the necessary modifications, in relation to the disposal of anything delivered up or seized by virtue of subsection (3) above.

(7) In this section "apparatus", "conditional access technology" and "en-

crypted" have the same meanings as in section 297A, "transmission" includes transmissions as defined in that section and "conditional access services" means services comprising the provision of conditional access technology.]

Notes:

(1) The words "or cable programme" repealed from subs.(1)(a) by the Copyright and Related Rights Regulations 2003 (SI 2003/2498), Sch.2 with effect from October 31, 2003. For savings and transitional provisions, see Part 3 of those Regulations.

(2) In subsection (4) the words in square brackets substituted for the former words "Supreme Court Act 1981" by the Constitutional Reform Act 2005 Sch.11 para.1, with effect from October 1, 2009.

(3) This section was substituted by Conditional Access (Unauthorised Decoders) Regulations 2000 (SI 2001/1175), reg.2, with effect from May 28, 2000. The section formerly provided:

Rights and remedies in respect of apparatus, &c. for unauthorised reception of transmissions

"**298.**—(1) *A person who—*

(a) *makes charges for the reception of programmes included in a broadcasting or cable programme service provided from a place in the United Kingdom, or*

(b) *sends encrypted transmissions of any other description from a place in the United Kingdom,*

is entitled to the following rights and remedies.

(2) *He has the same rights and remedies against a person who—*

(a) *makes, imports or sells or lets for hire [, offers or exposes for sale or hire, or advertises for sale or hire,] any apparatus or device designed or adapted to enable or assist persons to receive the programmes or other transmissions when they are not entitled to do so, or*

(b) *publishes any information which is calculated to enable or assist persons to receive the programmes or other transmissions when they are not entitled to do so,*

as a copyright owner has in respect of an infringement of copyright.

(3) *Further, he has the same rights under section 99 or 100 (delivery up or seizure of certain articles) in relation to any such apparatus or device as a copyright owner has in relation to an infringing copy.*

(4) *Section 72 of the Supreme Court Act 1981, section 15 of the Law Reform (Miscellaneous Provisions) (Scotland) Act 1985 and section 94A of the Judicature (Northern Ireland) Act 1978 (withdrawal of privilege against self-incrimination in certain proceedings relating to intellectual property) apply to proceedings under this section as to proceedings under Part I of this Act (copyright).*

(5) *In section 97(1) (innocent infringement of copyright) as it applies to proceedings for infringement of the rights conferred by this section, the reference to the defendant not knowing or having reason to believe that copyright subsisted in the work shall be construed as a reference to his not knowing or having reason to believe that his acts infringed the rights conferred by this section.*

(6) *Section 114 of this Act applies, with the necessary modifications, in relation to the disposal of anything delivered up or seized by virtue of subsection (3) above.*"

Supplementary provisions as to fraudulent reception

299.—(1) Her Majesty may by Order in Council—

(a) provide that section 297 applies in relation to programmes included in services provided from a country or territory outside the United Kingdom, and

(b) provide that section 298 applies in relation to such programmes and to encrypted transmissions sent from such a country or territory.

(2) [...]

(3) A statutory instrument containing an Order in Council under subsection (1) shall be subject to annulment in pursuance of a resolution of either House of Parliament.

(4) Where sections 297 and 298 apply in relation to a broadcasting service [...], they also apply to any service run for the person providing that service, or a person providing programmes for that service, which consists wholly or mainly in the sending by means of a telecommunications system of sounds or visual images, or both.

(5) In sections 297 [, 297A] and 298, and this section, "programme" [and "broadcasting]", and related expressions, have the same meaning as in Part I (copyright).

Notes:

   (1) Subsection (2) was repealed by ss.179(2) and 203(3) of and Sch.21 to the Broadcasting Act 1990, and the words in square brackets subs.(5) inserted by s.179(2) of that Act, as provided by the Broadcasting Act 1990 (Commencement No.1 and Transitional Provisions) Order 1990 (SI 1990/2347).

   (2) In subs.(4), the words "or cable programme service" repealed and in subs.(5) the words in square brackets substituted for the former words ", "broadcasting" and "cable programme service" by the Copyright and Related Rights Regulations 2003 (SI 2003/2498), Sch.1, para.3, Sch.2 with effect from October 31, 2003. For savings and transitional provisions, see Part 3 of those Regulations.

300. [...]

Note: Section 300 related to fraudulent application or use of a trade mark and was repealed by the Trade Marks Act 1994. The provision as it formerly read is not reprinted here.

Provisions for the benefit of the Hospital for Sick Children

Provisions for the benefit of the Hospital for Sick Children

301. The provisions of Schedule 6 have effect for conferring on trustees for the benefit of the Hospital for Sick Children, Great Ormond Street, London, a right to a royalty in respect of the public performance, commercial publication, [or communication to the public] of the play "Peter Pan" by Sir James Matthew Barrie, or of any adaptation of that work, notwithstanding that copyright in the work expired on December 31, 1987.

Note: The words in square brackets substituted for the former words ", broadcasting or inclusion in a cable programme service" by the Copyright and Related Rights Regulations 2003 (SI 2003/2498), Sch.1, para.6 with effect from October 31, 2003. For savings and transitional provisions, see Part 3 of those Regulations.

Financial assistance for certain international bodies

Financial assistance for certain international bodies

302.—(1) The Secretary of State may give financial assistance, in the form of grants, loans or guarantees to—

   (a) any international organisation having functions relating to trade marks or other intellectual property, or

   (b) any [EU] institution or other body established under any of the Community Treaties having any such functions,

with a view to the establishment or maintenance by that organisation, institution or body of premises in the United Kingdom.

(2) Any expenditure of the Secretary of State under this section shall be defrayed out of money provided by Parliament; and any sums received by the Secretary of State in consequence of this section shall be paid into the Consolidated Fund.

Note: In subs.(1)(b) the expression "EU" was substituted for the word "Community" by the Treaty of Lisbon (Changes in Terminology) Order 2011 (SI 2011/1043) art.6(1)(c) with effect from April 22, 2011.

General

Consequential amendments and repeals

303.—(1) The enactments specified in Schedule 7 are amended in accordance with that Schedule, the amendments being consequential on the provisions of this Act.

(2) The enactments specified in Schedule 8 are repealed to the extent specified.

Extent

304.—(1) Provision as to the extent of Part I (copyright), Part II (rights in performances) and Part III (design right) is to be found in sections 157, 207 and 255 respectively; the extent of the other provisions of this Act is as follows.

(2) Parts IV to VII extend to England and Wales, Scotland and Northern Ireland, except that—

(a) sections 287 to 292 (patents county courts) extend to England and Wales only,

(b) the proper law of the trust created by Schedule 6 (provisions for the benefit of the Hospital for Sick Children) is the law of England and Wales, and

(c) the amendments and repeals in Schedules 7 and 8 have the same extent as the enactments amended or repealed.

(3) The following provisions extend to the Isle of Man subject to any modifications contained in an Order made by Her Majesty in Council—

(a) sections 293 and 294 (patents: licences of right), and

(b) paragraphs 24 and 29 of Schedule 5 (patents: effect of filing international application for patent and power to extend time limits).

(4) Her Majesty may by Order in Council direct that the following provisions extend to the Isle of Man, with such exceptions and modifications as may be specified in the Order—

(a) Part IV (registered designs),

(b) Part V (patent agents),

(c) the provisions of Schedule 5 (patents: miscellaneous amendments) not mentioned in subsection (3) above,

(d) sections 297 to 299 (fraudulent reception of transmissions), and

(e) section 300 (fraudulent application or use of trade mark).

(5) Her Majesty may by Order in Council direct that sections 297 to 299 (fraudulent reception of transmissions) extend to any of the Channel Islands, with such exceptions and modifications as may be specified in the Order.

(6) Any power conferred by this Act to make provision by Order in Council for or in connection with the extent of provisions of this Act to a country outside the United Kingdom includes power to extend to that country, subject to any modifications specified in the Order, any provision of this Act which amends or repeals an enactment extending to that country.

Commencement

305.—(1) The following provisions of this Act come into force on Royal Assent—

> paragraphs 24 and 29 of Schedule 5 (patents: effect of filing international application for patent and power to extend time limits);
>
> section 301 and Schedule 6 (provisions for the benefit of the Hospital for Sick Children).

(2) Sections 293 and 294 (licences of right) come into force at the end of the period of two months beginning with the passing of this Act.

(3) The other provisions of this Act come into force on such day as the Secretary of State may appoint by order made by statutory instrument, and different days may be appointed for different provisions and different purposes.

Short title

306. This Act may be cited as the Copyright, Designs and Patents Act 1988.

SCHEDULES

[SCHEDULE ZA1

CERTAIN PERMITTED USES OF ORPHAN WORKS

PART 1 GENERAL PROVISIONS

Certain permitted uses of orphan works by relevant bodies

1.—(1) A relevant body does not infringe the copyright in a relevant work in its collection which is an orphan work by—

(a) making the orphan work available to the public; or

(b) reproducing the orphan work for the purposes of digitisation, making available, indexing, cataloguing, preservation or restoration.

(2) A relevant body does not infringe the rights conferred by Chapter 2 of Part 2 by doing either of the following in relation to a relevant work in its collection which is an orphan work—

(a) making the orphan work available to the public; or

(b) reproducing the orphan work for the purposes of digitisation, making available, indexing, cataloguing, preservation or restoration.

(3) A relevant body does not commit an offence under section 107 or 198 by using an orphan work in a way which, by virtue of this Schedule, does not infringe copyright or the rights conferred by Chapter 2 of Part 2.

(4) This paragraph is subject to paragraph 6 (further requirements for use of orphan works).

Meaning of "relevant body", "relevant work" and "rightholder"

2.—(1) In this Schedule "relevant body" means—

(a) a publicly accessible library, educational establishment or museum,

(b) an archive,

(c) a film or audio heritage institution, or

(d) a public service broadcasting organisation.

(2) Subject to sub-paragraph (4), in this Schedule "relevant work" means a work to which sub-paragraph (3) applies which is—

(a) a work in the form of a book, journal, newspaper, magazine or other writing which is contained in the collection of a publicly accessible library, educational establishment or museum, an archive or a film or audio heritage institution;

(b) a cinematographic or audiovisual work or a sound recording which is contained in the collection of a publicly accessible library, educational establishment or museum, an archive or a film or audio heritage institution; or

(c) a cinematographic or audiovisual work or a sound recording which was commissioned for exclusive exploitation by, or produced by, one or more public service broadcasting organisations on or before 31 December 2002 and is contained in the archives of that organisation or one or more of those organisations.

(3) This sub-paragraph applies to a work if—

(a) it is protected by copyright or rights conferred by Chapter 2 of Part 2, and

(b) the first publication or first broadcast of the work was in a member State.

(4) In this Schedule "relevant work" also includes a work listed in any of paragraphs (a) to (c) of sub-paragraph (2) which—

(a) is protected by copyright or rights conferred by Chapter 2 of Part 2, and

(b) has never been published or broadcast, but

(c) has been made publicly accessible by a relevant body with the consent of the rightholders, as long as it is reasonable to assume that the rightholders would not oppose the use of the work as mentioned in paragraph 1(1) or (2).

(5) References in this Schedule to a relevant work include—

(a) a work that is embedded or incorporated in, or constitutes an integral part of, a relevant work, and

(b) a performance in relation to which rights are conferred by Chapter 2 of Part 2 and which is embedded or incorporated in, or constitutes an integral part of, a relevant work.

(6) In this Schedule "rightholder" in relation to a relevant work means—

(a) an owner of the copyright in the work,

(b) a licensee under an exclusive licence in relation to the work,

(c) a person with rights under Chapter 2 of Part 2 in relation to a performance recorded by the work, or

(d) a licensee under an exclusive licence in relation to those rights.

(7) In the application of sub-paragraph (6) to a performance by virtue of sub-paragraph (5), the reference in sub-paragraph (6)(c) to a performance recorded by the work is to be read as a reference to the performance.

(8) In this paragraph "public service broadcasting organisation" includes a public service broadcaster within the meaning of section 264 of the Communications Act 2003(4).

Meaning of "orphan work"

3.—(1) For the purposes of this Schedule a relevant work is an orphan work if—

(a) there is a single rightholder in the work and the rightholder has not been identified or located, or

(b) there is more than one rightholder in the work and none of the rightholders has been identified or located, despite a diligent search for the rightholder or rightholders having been carried out and recorded in accordance with paragraph 5.

(2) Subject as follows, a relevant work with more than one rightholder is also an orphan work for the purposes of this Schedule if—

(a) one or more of the rightholders has been identified or located, and

(b) one or more of the rightholders has not been identified or located despite a diligent search for the rightholder or rightholders having been carried out and recorded in accordance with paragraph 5.

Mutual recognition of orphan work status

4. A relevant work which is designated as an orphan work in another member State is an orphan work for the purposes of this Schedule.

Diligent searches

5.—(1) For the purposes of establishing whether a relevant work is an orphan work, a relevant body must ensure that a diligent search is carried out in good faith in respect of the work by consulting the appropriate sources for the category of work in question.

(2) The relevant body must carry out the diligent search prior to the use of the relevant work.

(3) The sources that are appropriate for each category of relevant work must as a minimum include—

(a) the relevant databases maintained by the Office for Harmonization in the Internal Market; and

(b) where there is no record that the relevant work is an orphan work in the databases referred to in paragraph (a), the relevant sources listed in Part 2 of this Schedule for that category.

(4) The Comptroller-General of Patents, Designs and Trade Marks may issue guidance on the appropriate sources to be consulted under this paragraph for any particular category of work.

(5) Subject to sub-paragraphs (6) to (8), a search of the sources mentioned in sub-paragraph (3)(b) must be carried out in the member State in which the relevant work was first published or broadcast.

(6) If the relevant work is a cinematographic or audiovisual work and the producer of the work has his or her headquarters or habitual residence in a member State, the search must be carried out in the member State of the headquarters or habitual residence.

(7) If the relevant work falls within paragraph 2(4), the search must be carried out in the member State where the organisation that made the work publicly accessible with the consent of the rightholders is established.

(8) If there is evidence to suggest that relevant information on rightholders is to be found in other countries, a relevant body carrying out a search in accordance with sub-paragraph (3)(b) must also consult the sources of information available in those other countries.

(9) A relevant body that makes use of orphan works in accordance with this Schedule must maintain records of its diligent searches and must provide the following information to the Office for Harmonization in the Internal Market—

(a) the results of the diligent searches which the relevant body has carried out and which first established that a work is an orphan work;

(b) the use that the relevant body makes of the orphan works;

(c) any change, pursuant to paragraph 7, of the orphan work status of a relevant work that the relevant body has used and in respect of which the relevant body has been supplied with evidence by a rightholder in accordance with paragraph 7(2); and

(d) the contact information for the relevant body.

Further requirements for use of orphan works

6. This Schedule does not prevent the use by a relevant body of an orphan work as mentioned in paragraph 1 from infringing copyright or the rights conferred by Chapter 2 of Part 2 if—

(a) the revenues generated in the course of the use of the orphan work are used otherwise than for the exclusive purpose of covering the costs of the relevant body in digitising orphan works and making them available to the public;

(b) the relevant body uses the orphan work in order to achieve aims which are not related to its public-interest mission (and the aims which are to be treated as related to its public interest mission include, in particular, the preservation of, the restoration of, and the provision of cultural and educational access to, works contained in its collection);

(c) any rightholder who has been identified or located has, in relation to the rightholder's rights, not authorised the relevant body's use of the orphan work as mentioned in paragraph 1; or

(d) the relevant body fails, in the course of the permitted use of the orphan work, to acknowledge the name of any author of or other rightholder in the work who has been identified.

End of orphan work status

7.—(1) This paragraph applies to a rightholder who has not been identified or located in relation to a relevant work.

(2) A rightholder may put an end to the orphan work status of a relevant work by providing evidence of his or her ownership of the rights to the Office for Harmonization in the

Internal Market or to the relevant body which carried out the diligent search which first established that the relevant work is an orphan work.

(3) A relevant body that is using or has used the orphan work must within a reasonable period provide the rightholder with fair compensation for that body's use of the relevant work together with information on how the fair compensation has been calculated.

(4) If a relevant body and the rightholder cannot agree on the amount of compensation payable, either of them may apply to the Copyright Tribunal to determine the amount.

PART 2 SOURCES TO BE SEARCHED DURING DILIGENT SEARCH

Category of relevant work	Sources to be searched
1. Published books	(a) legal deposit, library catalogues and authority files maintained by libraries and other institutions; (b) the publishers' and authors' associations in the country in question; (c) existing databases and registries, WATCH (Writers, Artists and their Copyright Holders), the ISBN (International Standard Book Number) and databases listing books in print; (d) the databases of the relevant collecting societies, including reproduction rights organisations; (e) sources that integrate multiple databases and registries, including VIAF (Virtual International Authority Files) and AR-ROW (Accessible Registries of Rights Information and Orphan Works).
2. Newspapers, magazines, journals and periodicals	(a) the ISSN (International Standard Serial Number) for periodical publications; (b) indexes and catalogues from library holdings and collections; (c) legal deposit; (d) the publishers' associations and the authors' and journalists' associations in the country in question; (e) the databases of relevant collecting societies including reproduction rights organisations.
3. Visual works, including fine art, photography, illustration, design, architecture, sketches of the latter works and other such works that are contained in books, journals, newspapers and magazines or other works	(a) the sources referred to in paragraphs 1 and 2; (b) the databases of the relevant collecting societies, in particular for visual arts, and including reproduction rights organisations; (c) the databases of picture agencies, where applicable.

4. Audiovisual works and sound recordings

(a) legal deposit;
(b) the producers' associations in the country in question;
(c) databases of film or audio heritage institutions and national libraries;
(d) databases with relevant standards and identifiers such as ISAN (International Standard Audiovisual Number) for audiovisual material, ISWC (International Standard Music Work Code) for musical works and ISRC (International Standard Recording Code) for sound recordings;
(e) the databases of the relevant collecting societies, in particular for authors, performers, sound recording producers and audiovisual producers;
(f) credits and other information appearing on the work's packaging;
(g) databases of other relevant associations representing a specific category of rightholders.

5. Relevant works which have not been published or broadcast

Those sources that are listed in paragraphs 1 to 4 above which are appropriate to a relevant work which is unpublished.]

Note: Schedule ZA1 inserted by the Copyright and Rights in Performances (Certain Permitted Uses of Orphan Works) Regulations 2014 (SI 2014/2861), Sch para.1, with effect from October 29, 2014.

SCHEDULE A1

REGULATION OF LICENSING BODIES

CODES OF PRACTICE

1.—(1) The Secretary of State may by regulations make provision for a licensing body to be required to adopt a code of practice that complies with criteria specified in the regulations.

(2) The regulations may provide that, if a licensing body fails to adopt such a code of practice, any code of practice that is approved for the purposes of that licensing body by the Secretary of State, or by a person designated by the Secretary of State under the regulations, has effect as a code of practice adopted by the body.

(3) The regulations must provide that a code is not to be approved for the purposes of provision under sub-paragraph (2) unless it complies with criteria specified in the regulations.

2. Regulations under paragraph 1 may make provision as to conditions that are to be satisfied, and procedures that are to be followed—

(a) before a licensing body is required to adopt a code of practice as described in paragraph 1(1);

(b) before a code of practice has effect as one adopted by a licensing body as described in paragraph 1(2).

LICENSING CODE OMBUDSMAN

3.—(1) The Secretary of State may by regulations make provision—

(a) for the appointment of a person (the "licensing code ombudsman") to investigate and determine disputes about a licensing body's compliance with its code of practice;

(b) for the reference of disputes to the licensing code ombudsman;

(c) for the investigation and determination of a dispute so referred.

(2) Provision made under this paragraph may in particular include provision—

(a) about eligibility for appointment as the licensing code ombudsman;

(b) about the disputes to be referred to the licensing code ombudsman;

(c) requiring any person to provide information, documents or assistance to the licensing code ombudsman for the purposes of an investigation or determination;

(d) requiring a licensing body to comply with a determination of the licensing code ombudsman;

(e) about the payment of expenses and allowances to the licensing code ombudsman.

CODE REVIEWER

4.—(1) The Secretary of State may by regulations make provision—

(a) for the appointment by the Secretary of State of a person (the "code reviewer") to review and report to the Secretary of State on—

(i) the codes of practice adopted by licensing bodies, and

(ii) compliance with the codes of practice;

(b) for the carrying out of a review and the making of a report by that person.

(2) The regulations must provide for the Secretary of State, before appointing a person as the code reviewer, to consult persons whom the Secretary of State considers represent the interests of licensing bodies, licensees, members of licensing bodies, and the Intellectual Property Office.

(3) regulations may, in particular, make provision—

(a) requiring any person to provide information, documents or assistance to the code reviewer for the purposes of a review or report;

(b) about the payment of expenses and allowances to the code reviewer.

(4) In this paragraph "member", in relation to a licensing body, means a person on whose behalf the body is authorised to negotiate or grant licences.

SANCTIONS

5.—(1) The Secretary of State may by regulations provide for the consequences of a failure by a licensing body to comply with—

(a) a requirement to adopt a code of practice under provision within paragraph 1(1);

(b) a code of practice that has been adopted by the body in accordance with a requirement under provision within paragraph 1(1), or that has e—ect as one adopted by the body under provision within paragraph 1(2);

(c) a requirement imposed on the body under any other provision made under this Schedule;

(d) an authorisation under regulations under section 116A or 116B;

(e) a requirement imposed by regulations under section 116A or 116B;

(f) an authorisation under regulations under paragraph 1A or 1B of Schedule 2A;

(g) a requirement imposed by regulations under paragraph 1A or 1B of that Schedule.

(2) The regulations may in particular provide for—

(a) the imposition of financial penalties or other sanctions;

(b) the imposition of sanctions on a director, manager or similar officer of a licensing body or, where the body's affairs are managed by its members, on a member.

(3) The regulations must include provision—

(a) for determining whether there has been a failure to comply with a requirement or code of practice for the purposes of any provision made under subparagraph (1);

(b) for determining any sanction that may be imposed in respect of the failure to comply;

(c) for an appeal against a determination within paragraph (a) or (b).

(4) A financial penalty imposed under sub-paragraph (2) must not be greater than £50,000.

(5) The regulations may provide for a determination within subparagraph (3)(a) or (3)(b) to be made by the Secretary of State or by a person designated by the Secretary of State under the regulations.

(6) The regulations may make provision for requiring a person to give the person by whom a determination within sub-paragraph (3)(a) falls to be made (the "adjudicator") any information that the adjudicator reasonably requires for the purpose of making that determination.

FEES

6.—(1) The Secretary of State may by regulations require a licensing body to which regulations under any other paragraph of this Schedule apply to pay fees to the Secretary of State.

(2) The aggregate amount of fees payable under the regulations must not be more than the cost to the Secretary of State of administering the operation of regulations under this Schedule.

General

7.—(1) The power to make regulations under this Schedule includes in particular power—

(a) to make incidental, supplementary or consequential provision, including provision extending or restricting the jurisdiction of the Copyright Tribunal or conferring powers on it;

(b) to make provision for bodies of a particular description, or carrying out activities of a particular description, not to be treated as licensing bodies for the purposes of requirements imposed under regulations under this Schedule;

(c) to make provision that applies only in respect of licensing bodies of a particular description, or only in respect of activities of a particular description;

(d) otherwise to make different provision for different purposes.

(2) Regulations under a paragraph of this Schedule may amend Part 1 or Part 2, or any other enactment or subordinate legislation passed or made before the paragraph in question comes into force, for the purpose of making consequential provision or extending or restricting the jurisdiction of the Copyright Tribunal or conferring powers on it.

(3) The power to make regulations is exercisable by statutory instrument.

(4) A statutory instrument containing regulations may not be made unless a draft of the instrument has been laid before and approved by a resolution of each House of Parliament.

8. References in this Schedule to a licensing body are to a body that is a licensing body for the purposes of Chapter 7 of Part 1 or Chapter 2 of Part 2, and references to licensees are to be construed accordingly.

Note: Schedule A1 inserted by the Enterprise and Regulatory Reform Act 2013, Sch.22(1) para.1, with effect from April 25, 2013.

Section 170.   SCHEDULE 1

Copyright: Transitional Provisions and Savings

Introductory

1.—(1) In this Schedule—

"the 1911 Act" means the Copyright Act 1911,

"the 1956 Act" means the Copyright Act 1956, and

"the new copyright provisions" means the provisions of this Act relating to copyright, that is, Part I (including this Schedule) and Schedules 3, 7 and 8 so far as they make amendments or repeals consequential on the provisions of Part I.

(2) References in this Schedule to "commencement", without more, are to the date on which the new copyright provisions come into force.

(3) References in this Schedule to "existing works" are to works made before commencement; and for this purpose a work of which the making extended over a period shall be taken to have been made when its making was completed.

2.—(1) In relation to the 1956 Act, references in this Schedule to a work include any work or other subject-matter within the meaning of that Act.

(2) In relation to the 1911 Act—

(a) references in this Schedule to copyright include the right conferred by section 24 of that Act in substitution for a right subsisting immediately before the commencement of that Act;

(b) references in this Schedule to copyright in a sound recording are to the copyright under that Act in records embodying the recording; and

(c) references in this Schedule to copyright in a film are to any copyright under that Act in the film (so far as it constituted a dramatic work for the purposes of that Act) or in photographs forming part of the film.

General principles: continuity of the law

3. The new copyright provisions apply in relation to things existing at commencement as they apply in relation to things coming into existence after commencement, subject to any express provision to the contrary.

4.—(1) The provisions of this paragraph have effect for securing the continuity of the law so far as the new copyright provisions re-enact (with or without modification) earlier provisions.

(2) A reference in an enactment, instrument or other document to copyright, or to a work or other subject-matter in which copyright subsists, which apart from this Act would be construed as referring to copyright under the 1956 Act shall be construed, so far as may be required for continuing its effect, as being, or as the case may require, including, a reference to copyright under this Act or to works in which copyright subsists under this Act.

(3) Anything done (including subordinate legislation made), or having effect as done, under or for the purposes of a provision repealed by this Act has effect as if done under or for the purposes of the corresponding provision of the new copyright provisions.

(4) References (expressed or implied) in this Act or any other enactment, instrument or document to any of the new copyright provisions shall, so far as the context permits, be construed as including, in relation to times, circumstances and purposes before commencement, a reference to corresponding earlier provisions.

(5) A reference (express or implied) in an enactment, instrument or other document to a provision repealed by this Act shall be construed, so far as may be required for continuing its effect, as a reference to the corresponding provision of this Act.

(6) The provisions of this paragraph have effect subject to any specific transitional provision or saving and to any express amendment made by this Act.

Subsistence of copyright

5.—(1) Copyright subsists in an existing work after commencement only if copyright subsisted in it immediately before commencement.

(2) Sub-paragraph (1) does not prevent an existing work qualifying for copyright protection after commencement—

   (a) under section 155 (qualification by virtue of first publication), or

   (b) by virtue of an Order under section 159 (application of Part I to countries to which it does not extend).

6.—(1) Copyright shall not subsist by virtue of this Act in an artistic work made before June 1, 1957 which at the time when the work was made constituted a design capable of registration under the Registered Designs Act 1949 or under the enactments repealed by that Act, and was used, or intended to be used, as a model or pattern to be multiplied by an industrial process.

(2) For this purpose a design shall be deemed to be used as a model or pattern to be multiplied by any industrial process—

   (a) when the design is reproduced or is intended to be reproduced on more than 50 single articles, unless all the articles in which the design is reproduced or is intended to be reproduced together from only a single set of articles as defined in section 44(1) of the Registered Designs Act 1949, or

   (b) when the design is to be applied to—

      (i) printed paper hangings,

      (ii) carpets, floor cloths or oil cloths, manufactured or sold in lengths or pieces,

      (iii) textile piece goods, or textile goods manufactured or sold in lengths or pieces, or

      (iv) lace, not made by hand.

7.—(1) No copyright subsists in a film, as such, made before June 1, 1957.

(2) Where a film made before that date was an original dramatic work within the meaning of the 1911 Act, the new copyright provisions have effect in relation to the film as if it was an original dramatic work within the meaning of Part I.

(3) The new copyright provisions have effect in relation to photographs forming part of a film made before June 1, 1957 as they have effect in relation to photographs not forming part of a film.

8.—(1) A film sound-track to which section 13(9) of the 1956 Act applied before commencement (film to be taken to include sounds in associated sound-track) shall be treated for the purposes of the new copyright provisions not as part of the film, but as a sound recording.

(2) However—

(a) copyright subsists in the sound recording only if copyright subsisted in the film immediately before commencement, and it continues to subsist until copyright in the film expires;

(b) the author and first owner of copyright in the film shall be treated as having been author and first owner of the copyright in the sound recording; and

(c) anything done before commencement under or in relation to the copyright in the film continues to have effect in relation to the sound recording as in relation to the film.

[**9.** No copyright subsists in—

(a) a wireless broadcast made before 1st June 1957, or

(b) a broadcast by cable made before 1st January 1985;

and any such broadcast shall be disregarded for the purposes of section 14(5) (duration of copyright in repeats).]

Note: Paragraph 9 was substituted by the Copyright and Related Rights Regulations 2003 (SI 2003/2498), Sch.1 para.16 with effect from October 31, 2003. For savings and transitional provisions, see Part 3 of those Regulations. Paragraph 9 formerly provided:

> "**9.** *No copyright subsists in—*
>
> (a) *a broadcast made before 1st June 1957, or*
>
> (b) *a cable programme included in a cable programme service before 1st January 1985;*
>
> *and any such broadcast or cable programme shall be disregarded for the purposes of [section 14(5)] (duration of copyright in repeats)."*

Authorship of work

10. The question who was the author of an existing work shall be determined in accordance with the new copyright provisions for the purposes of the rights conferred by Chapter IV of Part I (moral rights), and for all other purposes shall be determined in accordance with the law in force at the time the work was made.

Note: As to any question arising in relation to the identity of the author of pre-1989 photographs for the purposes of reg.15, 16 or 19(2)(b) of the Duration of Copyright and Rights in Performances Regulations 1995 (SI 1995/3297), reg.19 of the Copyright and Related Rights Regulations 1996 (SI 1996/2967), provides:

> "Any question arising, in relation to photographs which were existing works within the meaning of Schedule 1, as to who is to be regarded as the author for the purposes of—
>
> (a) regulations15 and 16 of the Duration of Copyright and Rights in Performances Regulations 1995 (duration of copyright: application of new provisions subject to general saving), or
>
> (b) regulation 19(2)(b) of those Regulations (ownership of revived copyright),
>
> is to be determined in accordance with section 9 as in force on the commencement of those Regulations (and not, by virtue of paragraph 10 of Schedule 1, in accordance with the law in force at the time when the work was made)."

First ownership of copyright

11.—(1) The question who was first owner of copyright in an existing work shall be determined in accordance with the law in force at the time the work was made.

(2) Where before commencement a person commissioned the making of a work in circumstances falling within—

(a) section 4(3) of the 1956 Act or paragraph (a) of the proviso to section 5(1) of the 1911 Act (photographs, portraits and engravings), or

(b) the proviso to section 12(4) of the 1956 Act (sound recordings),

these provisions apply to determine first ownership of copyright in any work made in pursuance of the commission after commencement.

Duration of copyright in existing works

12.—(1) The following provisions have effect with respect to the duration of copyright in existing works.

The question which provision applies to a work shall be determined by reference to the facts immediately before commencement; and expressions used in this paragraph which were defined for the purposes of the 1956 Act have the same meaning as in that Act.

(2) Copyright in the following descriptions of work continues to subsist until the date on which it would have expired under the 1956 Act—

    (a) literary, dramatic or musical works in relation to which the period of 50 years mentioned in the proviso to section 2(3) of the 1956 Act (duration of copyright in works made available to the public after the death of the author) has begun to run;

    (b) engravings in relation to which the period of 50 years mentioned in the proviso to section 3(4) of the 1956 Act (duration of copyright in works published after the death of the author) has begun to run;

    (c) published photographs and photographs taken before 1st June 1957;

    (d) published sound recordings and sound recordings made before 1st June 1957;

    (e) published films and films falling within section 13(3)(a) of the 1956 Act (films registered under former enactments relating to registration of films).

(3) Copyright in anonymous or pseudonymous literary, dramatic, musical or artistic works (other than photographs) continues to subsist—

    (a) if the work is published, until the date on which it would have expired in accordance with the 1956 Act, and

    (b) if the work is unpublished, until the end of the period of 50 years from the end of the calendar year in which the new copyright provisions come into force or, if during that period the work is first made available to the public within the meaning of [section 12(3)] (duration of copyright in works of unknown authorship), the date on which copyright expires in accordance with that provision;

unless, in any case, the identity of the author becomes known before that date, in which case [section 12(2)] applies (general rule: life of the author [plus 70] years).

(4) Copyright in the following descriptions of work continues to subsist until the end of the period of 50 years from the end of the calendar year in which the new copyright provisions come into force—

    (a) literary, dramatic and musical works of which the author has died and in relation to which none of the acts mentioned in paragraphs (a) to (e) of the proviso to section 2(3) of the 1956 Act has been done;

    (b) unpublished engravings of which the author has died;

    (c) unpublished photographs taken on or after 1st June 1957.

(5) Copyright in the following descriptions of work continues to subsist until the end of the period of 50 years from the end of the calendar year in which the new copyright provisions come into force—

    (a) unpublished sound recordings made on or after 1st June 1957;

    (b) films not falling within sub-paragraph (2)(e) above,

unless the recording or film is published before the end of that period in which case copyright in it shall continue until the end of the period of 50 years from the end of the calendar year in which the recording or film is published.

(6) Copyright in any other description of existing work continues to subsist until the date on which copyright in that description of work expires in accordance with sections 12 to 15 of this Act.

(7) The above provisions do not apply to works subject to Crown or Parliamentary copyright (see paragraphs 41 to 43 below).

Note: The words in the first set of square brackets in subparagraph (3) substituted for the former words "section 12(2)", the words in the second set of square brackets for the former words "section 12(1)" and the words in the third set of square brackets for the former words "plus 50" by the Copyright and Related Rights Regulations 2003 (SI 2003/2498), Sch.1, para.18 with effect from October 31, 2003. For savings and transitional provisions, see Part 3 of those Regulations.

Perpetual copyright under the Copyright Act 1775

13.—(1) The rights conferred on universities and colleges by the Copyright Act 1775 shall continue to subsist until the end of the period of 50 years from the end of the calendar year in which the new copyright provisions come into force and shall then expire.

(2) The provisions of the following Chapters of Part I—

Chapter III (acts permitted in relation to copyright works),

Chapter VI (remedies for infringement),

Chapter VII (provisions with respect to copyright licensing), and

Chapter VIII (the Copyright Tribunal),

apply in relation to those rights as they apply in relation to copyright under this Act.

Acts infringing copyright

14.—(1) The provisions of Chapters II and III of Part I as to the acts constituting an infringement of copyright apply only in relation to acts done after commencement; the provisions of the 1956 Act continue to apply in relation to acts done before commencement.

(2) So much of section 18(2) as extends the restricted act of issuing copies to the public to include the rental to the public of copies of sound recordings, films or computer programs does not apply in relation to a copy of a sound recording, film or computer programs does not apply in relation to a copy of a sound recording, film or computer program acquired by any person before commencement for the purpose of renting it to the public.

(3) For the purposes of section 27 (meaning of "infringing copy") the question whether the making of an article constituted an infringement of copyright, or would have done if the article had been made in the United Kingdom, shall be determined—

(a) in relation to an article made on or after 1st June 1957 and before commencement, by reference to the 1956 Act, and

(b) in relation to an article made before 1st June 1957, by reference to the 1911 Act.

(4) For the purposes of the application of sections 31(2), 51(2) and 62(3) (subsequent exploitation of things whose making was, by virtue of an earlier provision of the section, not an infringement of copyright) to things made before commencement, it shall be assumed that the new copyright provisions were in force at all material times.

(5) Section 55 (articles for producing material in a particular typeface) applies where articles have been marketed as mentioned in subsection (1) before commencement with the substitution for the period mentioned in subsection (2) of the period of 25 years from the end of the calendar year in which the new copyright provisions come into force.

(6) Section 56 (transfer of copies, adaptations, &c. of work in electronic form) does not apply in relation to a copy purchased before commencement.

(7) In section 65 (reconstruction of buildings) the reference to the owner of the copyright in the drawings or plans is, in relation to buildings constructed before commencement, to the person who at the time of the construction was the owner of the copyright in the drawings or plans under the 1956 Act, the 1911 Act or any enactment repealed by the 1911 Act.

15.—(1) Section 57 (anonymous or pseudonymous works: acts permitted on assumptions as to expiry of copyright or death of author) has effect in relation to existing works subject to the following provisions.

(2) Subsection (1)(b)(i) (assumption as to expiry of copyright) does not apply in relation to—

(a) photographs, or

(b) the rights mentioned in paragraph 13 above (rights conferred by the Copyright Act 1775).

(3) [...]

Note: Sub-paragraph (3) was repealed by the Copyright and Related Rights Regulations 2003 (SI 2003/2498), Sch.1 para.16, Sch.2, with effect from October 31, 2003. For savings and transitional provisions, see Part 3 of those Regulations. It formerly provided:

"(3) *Subsection (1)(b)(ii) (assumption as to death of author) applies only—*

(a) *where paragraph 12(3)(b) above applies (unpublished anonymous or pseudonymous works), after the end of the period of 50 years from the end of the calendar year in which the new copyright provisions come into force, or*

(b) *where paragraph 12(6) above applies (cases in which the duration of copyright is the same under the new copyright provisions as under the previous law)."*

16. The following provisions of section 7 of the 1956 Act continue to apply in relation to existing works—

   (a) subsection (6) (copying of unpublished works from manuscript or copy in library, museum or other institution);

   (b) subsection (7) (publication of work containing material to which subsection (6) applies), except paragraph (a) (duty to give notice of intended publication);

   (c) subsection (8) (subsequent broadcasting, performance, &c. of material published in accordance with subsection (7));

and subsection (9)(d) (illustrations) continues to apply for the purposes of those provisions.

17. Where in the case of a dramatic or musical work made before 1st July 1912, the right conferred by the 1911 Act did not include the sole right to perform the work in public, the acts restricted by the copyright shall be treated as not including—

   (a) performing the work in public,

   [(b) communicating the work to the public, or]

   (c) doing any of the above in relation to an adaptation of the work;

and where the right conferred by the 1911 Act consisted only of the sole right to perform the work in public, the acts restricted by the copyright shall be treated as consisting only of those acts.

Note: Subparagraph (b) was substituted by the Copyright and Related Rights Regulations 2003 (SI 2003/2498), Sch.1 para.4, with effect from October 31, 2003. For savings and transitional provisions, see Part 3 of those Regulations. It formerly provided:

   "(b) *broadcasting the work or including it in a cable programme service, or*".

18. Where a work made before 1st July 1912 consists of an essay, article or portion forming part of and first published in a review, magazine or other periodical or work of a like nature, the copyright is subject to any right of publishing the essay, article, or portion in a separate form to which the author was entitled at the commencement of the 1911 Act, or would if that Act had not been passed, have become entitled under section 18 of the Copyright Act 1842.

Designs

19.—(1) Section 51 (exclusion of copyright protection in relation to works recorded or embodied in design document or models) does not apply for ten years after commencement in relation to a design recorded or embodied in a design document or model before commencement.

   (2) During those ten years the following provisions of Part III (design right) apply to any relevant copyright as in relation to design right—

   (a) sections 237 to 239 (availability of licences of right), and

   (b) sections 247 and 248 (application to comptroller to settle terms of licence of right)

   (3) In section 237 as it applies by virtue of this paragraph, for the reference in subsection (1) to the last five years of the design right term there shall be substituted a reference to the last five years of the period of ten years referred to in sub-paragraph (1) above, or to so much of those last five years during which copyright subsists.

   (4) In section 239 as it applies by virtue of this paragraph, for the reference in subsection (1)(b) to section 230 there shall be substituted a reference to section 99.

   (5) Where a licence of right is available by virtue of this paragraph, a person to whom a licence was granted before commencement may apply to the comptroller for an order adjusting the terms of that licence.

   (6) The provisions of sections 249 and 250 (appeals and rules) apply in relation to proceedings brought under or by virtue of this paragraph as to proceedings under Part III.

   (7) A licence granted by virtue of this paragraph shall relate only to acts which would be permitted by section 51 if the design document or model had been made after commencement.

   (8) Section 100 (right to seize infringing copies, &c.) does not apply during the period of ten years referred to in sub-paragraph (1) in relation to anything to which it would not apply if the design in question had been first recorded or embodied in a design document or model after commencement.

(9) Nothing in this paragraph affects the operation of any rule of law preventing or restricting the enforcement of copyright in relation to a design.

20.—(1) *Where section 10 of the 1956 Act (effect of industrial application of design corresponding to artistic work) applied in relation to an artistic work at any time before commencement, section 52(2) of this Act applies with the substitution for the period of 25 years mentioned there of the relevant period of 15 years as defined in section 10(3) of the 1956 Act.*

(2) *Except as provided in sub-paragraph (1), section 52 applies only where articles are marketed as mentioned in subsection (1)(b) after commencement.*

Notes:

   (1) Paragraph 20 is prospectively repealed by the Enterprise and Regulatory Reform Act 2013, s.74(3)(b), with effect from a date to be appointed .

   (2) SI 2015/641 which brought into force s.74 on April 6, 2020 was revoked by SI 2015/1558.

Abolition of statutory recording licence

21. Section 8 of the 1956 Act (statutory licence to copy records sold by retail) continues to apply where notice under subsection (1)(b) of that section was given before the repeal of that section by this Act, but only in respect of the making of records—

   (a) within one year of the repeal coming into force, and

   (b) up to the number stated in the notice as intended to be sold.

Moral rights

22.—(1) No act done before commencement is actionable by virtue of any provision of Chapter IV of Part I (moral rights).

(2) Section 43 of the 1956 Act (false attribution of authorship) continues to apply in relation to acts done before commencement.

23.—(1) The following provisions have effect with respect to the rights conferred by—

   (a) section 77 (right to be identified as author or director), and

   (b) section 80 (right to object to derogatory treatment of work).

(2) The rights do not apply—

   (a) in relation to a literary, dramatic, musical and artistic work of which the author died before commencement, or

   (b) in relation to a film made before commencement.

(3) The rights in relation to an existing literary, dramatic, musical or artistic work do not apply—

   (a) where copyright first vested in the author, to anything which by virtue of an assignment of copyright made or licence granted before commencement may be done without infringing copyright;

   (b) where copyright first vested in a person other than the author, to anything done by or with the licence of the copyright owner.

(4) The rights do not apply to anything done in relation to a record made in pursuance of section 8 of the 1956 Act (statutory recording licence).

24. The right conferred by section 85 (right to privacy of certain photographs and films) does not apply to photographs taken or films made before commencement.

Assignments and licences

25.—(1) Any document made or event occurring before commencement which had any operation—

   (a) affecting the ownership of the copyright in an existing work, or

   (b) creating, transferring or terminating an interest, right or licence in respect of the copyright in an existing work,

has the corresponding operation in relation to copyright in the work under this Act.

(2) Expressions used in such a document shall be construed in accordance with their effect immediately before commencement.

26.—(1) Section 91(1) of this Act (assignment of future copyright: statutory vesting of legal interest on copyright coming into existence) does not apply in relation to an agreement made before 1st June 1957.

(2) The repeal by this Act of section 37(2) of the 1956 Act (assignment of future copyright: devolution of right where assignee dies before copyright comes into existence) does not affect the operation of that provision in relation to an agreement made before commencement.

27.—(1) Where the author of a literary, dramatic, musical or artistic work was the first owner of the copyright in it, no assignment of the copyright and no grant of any interest in it, made by him (otherwise than by will) after the passing of the 1911 Act and before 1st June 1957, shall be operative to vest in the assignee or grantee any rights with respect to the copyright in the work beyond the expiration of 25 years from the death of the author.

(2) The reversionary interest in the copyright expectant on the termination of that period may after commencement be assigned by the author during his life but in the absence of any assignment shall, on his death, devolve on his legal personal representatives as part of his estate.

(3) Nothing in this paragraph affects—

   (a) an assignment of the reversionary interest by a person to whom it has assigned,

   (b) an assignment of the reversionary interest after the death of the author by his personal representatives or any person becoming entitled to it, or

   (c) any assignment of the copyright after the reversionary interest has fallen in.

(4) Nothing in this paragraph applies to the assignment of the copyright in a collective work or a licence to publish a work or part of a work as part of a collective work.

(5) In sub-paragraph (4) "collective work" means—

   (a) any encyclopaedia, dictionary, yearbook, or similar work;

   (b) a newspaper, review, magazine, or similar periodical; and

   (c) any work written in distinct parts by different authors, or in which works or parts of works of different authors are incorporated.

28.—(1) This paragraph applies where copyright subsists in a literary, dramatic, musical or artistic work made before 1st July 1912 in relation to which the author, before the commencement of the 1911 Act, made such an assignment or grant as was mentioned in paragraph (a) of the proviso to section 24(1) of that Act (assignment or grant of copyright or performing right for full term of the right under the previous law).

(2) If before commencement any event has occurred or notice has been given which by virtue of paragraph 38 of Schedule 7 to the 1956 Act had any operation in relation to copyright in the work under that Act, the event or notice has the corresponding operation in relation to copyright under this Act.

(3) Any right which immediately before commencement would by virtue of paragraph 38(3) of that Schedule have been exercisable in relation to the work, or copyright in it, is exercisable in relation to the work or copyright in it under this Act.

(4) If in accordance with paragraph 38(4) of that Schedule copyright would, on a date after the commencement of the 1956 Act, have reverted to the author or his personal representatives and that date falls after the commencement of the new copyright provisions—

   (a) the copyright in the work shall revert to the author or his personal representatives, as the case may be, and

   (b) any interest of any other person in the copyright which subsists on that date by virtue of any document made before the commencement of the 1911 Act shall thereupon determine.

29. Section 92(2) of this Act (rights of exclusive licensee against successors in title of person granting licence) does not apply in relation to an exclusive licence granted before commencement.

Bequests

30.—(1) Section 93 of this Act (copyright to pass under will with original document or other material thing embodying unpublished work)—

   (a) does not apply where the testator died before 1st June 1957, and

   (b) where the testator died on or after that date and before commencement, applies only in relation to an original document embodying a work.

(2) In the case of an author who died before 1st June 1957, the ownership after his death of a manuscript of his, where such ownership has been acquired under a testamentary disposition made by him and the manuscript is of a work which has not been published or performed in public, is prima facie proof of the copyright being with the owner of the manuscript.

Remedies for infringement

31.—(1) Sections 96 and 97 of this Act (remedies for infringement) apply only in relation to an infringement of copyright committed after commencement; section 17 of the 1956 Act continues to apply in relation to infringement committed before commencement.

(2) Sections 99 and 100 of this Act (delivery up or seizure of infringing copies, &c.) apply to infringing copies and other articles made before or after commencement; section 18 of the 1956 Act, and section 7 of the 1911 Act, (conversion damages, &c.), do not apply after commencement except for the purposes of proceedings begun commencement.

(3) Sections 101 to 102 of this Act (rights and remedies of exclusive licensee) apply where sections 96 to 100 of this Act apply, section 19 of the 1956 Act continues to apply where section 17 or 18 of that Act applies.

(4) Sections 104 to 106 of this Act (presumptions) apply only in proceedings brought by virtue of this Act; section 20 of the 1956 Act continues to apply in proceedings brought by virtue of that Act.

32. Sections 101 and 102 of this Act (rights and remedies of exclusive licensee) do not apply to a licence granted before 1st June 1957.

33.—(1) The provisions of section 107 of this Act (criminal liability for making or dealing with infringing articles, &c.) apply only in relation to acts done after commencement; section 21 of the 1956 Act (penalties and summary proceedings in respect of dealings which infringe copyright) continues to apply in relation to acts done before commencement.

(2) Section 109 of this Act (search warrants) applies in relation to offences committed before commencement in relation to which section 21A or 21B of the 1956 Act applied; sections 21A and 21B continue to apply in relation to warrants issued before commencement.

Copyright Tribunal: proceedings pending on commencement

34.—(1) The Lord Chancellor may, after consultation with the Lord Advocate, by rules make such provision as he considers necessary or expedient with respect to proceedings pending under Part IV of the 1956 Act immediately before commencement.

(2) Rules under this paragraph shall be made by statutory instrument which shall be subject to annulment in pursuance of a resolution of either House of Parliament.

Qualification for copyright protection

35. Every work in which copyright subsisted under the 1956 Act immediately before commencement shall be deemed to satisfy the requirements of Part I of this Act as to qualification for copyright protection.

Dependent territories

36.—(1) The 1911 Act shall remain in force as part of the law of any dependent territory in which it was in force immediately before commencement until—

(a) the new copyright provisions come into force in that territory by virtue of an Order under section 157 of this Act (power to extend new copyright provisions), or

(b) in the case of any of the Channel Islands, the Act is repealed by Order under sub-paragraph (3) below.

(2) An Order in Council in force immediately before commencement which extends to any dependent territory any provisions of the 1956 Act shall remain in force as part of the law of that territory until—

(a) the new copyright provisions come into force in that territory by virtue of an Order under section 157 of this Act (power to extend new copyright provisions), or

(b) in the case of the Isle of Man, the Order is revoked by Order under sub-paragraph (3) below;

and while it remains in force such an Order may be varied under the provisions of the 1956 Act under which it was made.

(3) If it appears to Her Majesty that provision with respect to copyright has been made in the law of any of the Channel Islands or the Isle of Man otherwise than by extending the provisions of Part I of this Act, Her Majesty may by Order in Council repeal the 1911 Act as it has effect as part of the law of that territory or, as the case may be, revoke the Order extending the 1956 Act there.

(4) A dependent territory in which the 1911 or 1956 Act remains in force shall be treated, in the law of the countries to which Part I extends, as a country to which that Part extends; and those countries shall be treated in the law of such a territory as countries to which the 1911 Act or, as the case may be, the 1956 Act extends.

(5) If a country in which the 1911 or 1956 Act is in force ceases to be a colony of the United Kingdom, section 158 of this Act (consequences of country ceasing to be colony) applies with the substitution for the reference in subsection (3)(b) to the provisions of Part I of this Act of a reference to the provisions of the 1911 or 1956 Act, as the case may be.

(6) In this paragraph "dependent territory" means any of the Channel Islands, the Isle of Man or any colony.

Note: This paragraph is subject to the modification contained in the British Overseas Territories Act 2002 (c.8) s.1(2) which provides:

"(2) In any other enactment passed or made before the commencement of this section (including an enactment comprised in subordinate legislation), any reference to a dependent territory within the meaning of the British Nationality Act 1981 shall be read as a reference to a British overseas territory."

37.—(1) This paragraph applies to a country which immediately before commencement was not a dependent territory within the meaning of paragraph 36 above but—

(a) was a country to which the 1956 Act extended, or

(b) was treated as such a country by virtue of paragraph 39(2) of Schedule 7 to that Act (countries to which the 1911 Act extended or was treated as extending);

and Her Majesty may by Order in Council conclusively declare for the purposes of this paragraph whether a country was such a country or was so treated.

(2) A country to which this paragraph applies shall be treated as a country to which Part I extends for the purposes of sections 154 to 156 (qualification for copyright protection) until—

(a) an Order in Council is made in respect of that country under section 159 (application of Part I to countries to which it does not extend), or

(b) an Order in Council is made declaring that it shall cease to be so treated by reason of the fact that the provisions of the 1956 Act or, as the case may be, the 1911 Act, which extended there as part of the law of that country have been repealed or amended.

(3) A statutory instrument containing an Order in Council under this paragraph shall be subject to annulment in pursuance of a resolution of either House of Parliament.

Note: See the note regarding the British Overseas Territories Act 2002 (c.8) which follows para.36 above.

Territorial waters and the continental shelf

38. Section 161 of this Act (application of Part I to things done in territorial waters or the United Kingdom sector of the continental shelf) does not apply in relation to anything done before commencement.

British ships, aircraft and hovercraft

39. Section 162 (British ships, aircraft and hovercraft) does not apply in relation to anything done before commencement.

Crown copyright

40.—(1) Section 163 of this Act (general provisions as to Crown copyright) applies to an existing work if—

(a) section 39 of the 1956 Act applied to the work immediately before commencement, and

(b) the work is not one to which section 164, 165 or 166 applies (copyright in Acts, Measures and Bills and Parliamentary copyright: see paragraphs 42 and 43 below).

(2) Section 163(1)(b) (first ownership of copyright) has effect subject to any agreement entered into before commencement under section 39(6) of the 1956 Act.

41.—(1) The following provisions have effect with respect to the duration of copyright in existing works to which section 163 (Crown copyright) applies.

The question which provision applies to a work shall be determined by reference to the facts immediately before commencement, and expressions used in this paragraph, which were defined for the purposes of the 1956 Act have the same meaning as in that Act.

(2) Copyright in the following descriptions of work continues to subsist until the date on which it would have expired in accordance with the 1956 Act—

(a) published literary, dramatic or musical works;

(b) artistic works other than engraving or photographs;

(c) published engravings;

(d) published photographs and photographs taken before 1st June 1957;

(e) published sound recordings and sound recordings made before 1st June 1957;

(f) published films and films falling within section 13(3)(a) of the 1956 Act (films registered under former enactments relating to registration of films).

(3) Copyright in unpublished literary, dramatic or musical works continues to subsist until—

(a) the date on which copyright expires in accordance with section 163(3), or

(b) the end of the period of 50 years from the end of the calendar year in which the new copyright provisions come into force,

whichever is the later.

(4) Copyright in the following descriptions of work continues to subsist until the end of the period of 50 years from the end of the calendar year in which the new copyright provisions come into force—

(a) unpublished engravings;

(b) unpublished photographs taken on or after 1st June 1957.

(5) Copyright in a film or sound recording not falling within sub-paragraph (2) above continues to subsist until the end of the period of 50 years from the end of the calendar year in which the new copyright provisions come into force, unless the film or recording is published before the end of that period, in which case copyright expires 50 years from the end of the calendar year in which it is published.

42.—(1) Section 164 (copyright in Acts and Measures) applies to existing Acts of Parliament and Measures of the General Synod of the Church of England.

(2) References in that section to Measures of the General Synod of the Church of England include Church Assembly Measures.

Parliamentary copyright

43.—(1) Section 165 of this Act (general provisions as to Parliamentary copyright) applies to existing unpublished literary, dramatic, musical or artistic works, but does not otherwise apply to existing works.

(2) Section 166 (copyright in Parliamentary Bills) does not apply—

(a) to a public Bill which was introduced into Parliament and published before commencement,

(b) to a private Bill of which a copy was deposited in either House before commencement, or

(c) to a personal Bill which was given a First Reading in the House of Lords before commencement.

Copyright vesting in certain international organisations

44.—(1) Any work in which immediately before commencement copyright subsisted by virtue of section 33 of the 1956 Act shall be deemed to satisfy the requirements of section 168(1); but otherwise section 168 does not apply to works made or, as the case may be, published before commencement.

(2) Copyright in any such work which is unpublished continues to subsist until the date

on which it would have expired in accordance with the 1956 Act, or the end of the period of 50 years from the end of the calendar year in which the new copyright provisions come into force, whichever is the earlier.

Meaning of "publication"

45. Section 175(3) (construction of building treated as equivalent to publication) applies only where the construction of the building began after commencement.

Meaning of "unauthorised"

46. For the purposes of the application of the definition in section 178 (minor definitions) of the expression "unauthorised" in relation to things done before commencement—

(a) paragraph (a) applies in relation to things done before 1st June 1957 as if the reference to the licence of the copyright owner were a reference to his consent or acquiescence;

(b) paragraph (b) applies with the substitution for the words from "or, in a case" to the end of the words "or any person lawfully claiming under him"; and

(c) paragraph (c) shall be disregarded.

Section 189.   SCHEDULE 2

RIGHTS IN PERFORMANCES: PERMITTED ACTS

Introductory

1.—(1) The provisions of this Schedule specify acts which may be done in relation to a performance or recording notwithstanding the rights conferred by this Chapter; they relate only to the question of infringement of those rights and do not affect any other right or obligation restricting the doing of any of the specified acts.

(2) No inference shall be drawn from the description of any act which may by virtue of this Schedule be done without infringing the rights conferred by this Chapter as to the scope of those rights.

(3) The provisions of this Schedule are to be construed independently of each other, so that the fact an act does not fall within one provision does not mean that it is not covered by another provision.

[Making of temporary copies

1A. The rights conferred by this Chapter are not infringed by the making of a temporary copy of a recording of a performance which is transient or incidental, which is an integral and essential part of a technological process and the sole purpose of which is to enable—

(a) a transmission of the recording in a network between third parties by an intermediary; or

(b) a lawful use of the recording;

and which has no independent economic significance.]

Note: Paragraph 1A was inserted by the Copyright and Related Rights Regulations 2003 (SI 2003/2498), reg.8, with effect from October 31, 2003. For savings and transitional provisions, see Part 3 of those Regulations.

1B. [...]

Note: The Copyright and Rights in Performances (Personal Copies for Private Use) Regulations 2014 (SI 2014/2361), which introduced Sch.2 para.1B with effect from October 1, 2014, were quashed with prospective effect on July 17, 2015: *The Queen on the application of British Academy of Songwriters, Composers and Authors v Secretary of State for Business, Innovation and Skills* [2015] EWHC 2041 (Admin) at [11], [21]. Accordingly, Sch.2 para.1B has been of no effect from that date. However, the Court declined to rule as to whether the Regulations (and therefore Sch.2 para.1B) were void during the period from October 1, 2014 to July 16, 2015. Accordingly the question whether Sch.2 para.1B was effective during that period remains undecided: see the judgment at [19], [21]. Schedule 2 para.1B read as follows:

Personal copies of recordings for private use

"1B.—*(1) The making of a copy of a recording of a performance by an individual does not infringe the rights conferred by this Chapter provided that the copy—*

    (a) *is a copy of—*

        (i) *the individual's own copy of the recording, or*

        (ii) *a personal copy of the recording made by the individual,*

    (b) *is made for the individual's private use, and*

    (c) *is made for ends which are neither directly nor indirectly commercial.*

(2) In this paragraph "the individual's own copy" is a copy of a recording which—

    (a) *has been lawfully acquired by the individual on a permanent basis,*

    (b) *is not an illicit recording, and*

    (c) *has not been made under any provision of this Schedule which permits the making of a copy without infringing the rights conferred by this Chapter.*

(3) In this paragraph a "personal copy" means a copy made under this paragraph.

(4) The rights conferred by this Chapter in a recording are infringed if an individual transfers a personal copy of the recording to another person (otherwise than on a private and temporary basis), except where the transfer is authorised by the rights owner.

(5) If the rights conferred by this Chapter are infringed as set out in sub-paragraph (4), a personal copy which has been transferred is for all purposes subsequently treated as an illicit recording.

(6) The rights conferred by this Chapter in a recording are also infringed if an individual, having made a personal copy of the recording, transfers the individual's own copy of the recording to another person (otherwise than on a private and temporary basis) and, after that transfer and without the consent of the rights owner, retains any personal copy.

(7) If the rights conferred by this Chapter are infringed as set out in sub-paragraph (6), any retained personal copy is for all purposes subsequently treated as an illicit recording.

(8) To the extent that a term of a contract purports to prevent or restrict the making of a copy which, by virtue of this paragraph, would not infringe any right conferred by this Chapter, that term is unenforceable.

(9) Expressions used but not defined in this paragraph have the same meaning as in section 28B."

[Research and private study

1C.—(1) Fair dealing with a performance or a recording of a performance for the purposes of research for a non-commercial purpose does not infringe the rights conferred by this Chapter.

(2) Fair dealing with a performance or recording of a performance for the purposes of private study does not infringe the rights conferred by this Chapter.

(3) Copying of a recording by a person other than the researcher or student is not fair dealing if—

    (a) in the case of a librarian, or a person acting on behalf of a librarian, that person does anything which is not permitted under paragraph 6F (copying by librarians: single copies of published recordings), or

    (b) in any other case, the person doing the copying knows or has reason to believe that it will result in copies of substantially the same material being provided to more than one person at substantially the same time and for substantially the same purpose.

(4) To the extent that a term of a contract purports to prevent or restrict the doing of any act which, by virtue of this paragraph, would not infringe any right conferred by this Chapter, that term is unenforceable.

(5) Expressions used in this paragraph have the same meaning as in section 29.]

[Copies for text and data analysis for non-commercial research

1D.—(1) The making of a copy of a recording of a performance by a person who has lawful access to the recording does not infringe any rights conferred by this Chapter provided that the copy is made in order that a person who has lawful access to the recording may carry out a computational analysis of anything recorded in the recording for the sole purpose of research for a non-commercial purpose.

(2) Where a copy of a recording has been made under this paragraph, the rights conferred by this Chapter are infringed if—

    (a) the copy is transferred to any other person, except where the transfer is authorised by the rights owner, or

    (b) the copy is used for any purpose other than that mentioned in sub-paragraph (1), except where the use is authorised by the rights owner.

(3) If a copy of a recording made under this paragraph is subsequently dealt with—

    (a) it is to be treated as an illicit recording for the purposes of that dealing, and

    (b) if that dealing infringes any right conferred by this Chapter, it is to be treated as an illicit recording for all subsequent purposes.

(4) To the extent that a term of a contract purports to prevent or restrict the making of a copy which, by virtue of this paragraph, would not infringe any right conferred by this Chapter, that term is unenforceable.

(5) Expressions used in this paragraph have the same meaning as in section 29A.]

Note: Paragraphs 1C and 1D inserted by the Copyright and Rights in Performances (Research, Education, Libraries and Archives) Regulations 2014 (SI 2014/1372), reg.3(3), with effect from June 1, 2014 at 00.02.

Criticism, reviews and news reporting

2.—[(1) Fair dealing with a performance or recording for the purpose of criticism or review, of that or another performance or recording, or of a work, does not infringe any of the rights conferred by this Chapter provided that the performance or recording has been made available to the public.

[(1ZA) The rights conferred by this Chapter in a performance or a recording of a performance are not infringed by the use of a quotation from the performance or recording (whether for criticism or review or otherwise) provided that—

    (a) the performance or recording has been made available to the public,

    (b) the use of the quotation is fair dealing with the performance or recording, and

    (c) the extent of the quotation is no more than is required by the specific purpose for which it is used.]

(1A) Fair dealing with a performance or recording for the purpose of reporting current events does not infringe any of the rights conferred by this Chapter.]

[(1B) To the extent that a term of a contract purports to prevent or restrict the doing of any act which, by virtue of sub-paragraph (1ZA), would not infringe any right conferred by this Chapter, that term is unenforceable.]

(2) Expressions used in this paragraph have the same meaning as in section 30.

Notes:

    (1) Paragraph 2(1) was substituted and subpara.(1A) inserted by the Copyright and Related Rights Regulations 2003 (SI 2003/2498), reg.10, with effect from October 31, 2003. For savings and transitional provisions, see Part 3 of those Regulations. The former paragraph 2(1) provided:

        "(1) Fair dealing with a performance or recording—

        (a) *for the purpose of criticism or review, of that or another performance or recording, or of a work, or*

        (b) *for the purpose of reporting current events,*

        does not infringe any of the rights conferred by Part II."

    (2) Subparagraphs (1ZA) and (1B) inserted by the Copyright and Rights in Performances (Quotation and Parody) Regulations 2014 (SI 2014/2356), reg.4(3), with effect from October 1, 2014.

[2A.—(1) Fair dealing with a performance or a recording of a performance for the purposes of caricature, parody or pastiche does not infringe the rights conferred by this Chapter in the performance or recording.

(2) To the extent that a term of a contract purports to prevent or restrict the doing of any act which, by virtue of this paragraph, would not infringe any right conferred by this Chapter, that term is unenforceable.

(3) Expressions used in this paragraph have the same meaning as in section 30A.]

Note: Paragraph 2A inserted by the Copyright and Rights in Performances (Quotation and Parody) Regulations 2014 (SI 2014/2356), reg.5(2), with effect from October 1, 2014.

Incidental inclusion of performance or recording

3.—(1) The rights conferred by this Chapter are not infringed by the incidental inclusion of a performance or recording in a sound recording, film, [or broadcast].

(2) Nor are those rights infringed by anything done in relation to copies of, or the playing, showing, [or communication to the public] of, anything whose making was, by virtue of sub-paragraph (1), not an infringement of those rights.

(3) A performance or recording so far as it consists of music, or words spoken or sung with music, shall not be regarded as incidentally included in a sound recording, [or broadcast] if it is deliberately included.

(4) Expressions used in this paragraph have the same meaning as in section 31.

Note: The words in square brackets in sub-paras (1) and (3) substituted for the former words ", broadcast or cable programme" and the words in square brackets in sub-para.(2) substituted for the former words ", broadcasting or inclusion in a cable programme service" by the Copyright and Related Rights Regulations 2003 (SI 2003/2498), Sch.1 paras 3, 6, with effect from October 31, 2003. For savings and transitional provisions, see Part 3 of those Regulations.

[Disabled persons: copies of recordings for personal use

3A.—(1) This paragraph applies if—
   (a) a disabled person has lawful possession or lawful use of a copy of the whole or part of a recording of a performance, and
   (b) the person's disability prevents the person from enjoying the recording to the same degree as a person who does not have that disability.

(2) The making of an accessible copy of the copy of the recording referred to in sub-paragraph (1)(a) does not infringe the rights conferred by this Chapter if—
   (a) the copy is made by the disabled person or by a person acting on behalf of the disabled person,
   (b) the copy is made for the disabled person's personal use, and
   (c) the same kind of accessible copies of the recording are not commercially available on reasonable terms by or with the authority of the rights owner.

(3) If a person makes an accessible copy under this paragraph on behalf of a disabled person and charges the disabled person for it, the sum charged must not exceed the cost of making and supplying the copy.

(4) The rights conferred by this Chapter are infringed by the transfer of an accessible copy of a recording made under this paragraph to any person other than—
   (a) a person by or for whom an accessible copy of the recording may be made under this paragraph, or
   (b) a person who intends to transfer the copy to a person falling within paragraph (a), except where the transfer is authorised by the rights owner.

(5) An accessible copy of a recording made under this paragraph is to be treated for all purposes as an illicit recording if it is held by a person at a time when the person does not fall within sub-paragraph (4)(a) or (b).

(6) If an accessible copy of a recording made under this paragraph is subsequently dealt with—
   (a) it is to be treated as an illicit recording for the purposes of that dealing, and
   (b) if that dealing infringes any right conferred by this Chapter, it is to be treated as an illicit recording for all subsequent purposes.]

Note: Paragraphs 3A to 3E inserted by the Copyright and Rights in Performances (Disability) Regulations 2014 (SI 2014/1384), reg.3, with effect from June 1, 2014 at 00.01.

[Making and supply of accessible copies by authorised bodies

3B.—(1) If an authorised body has lawful possession of or lawful access to a copy of the whole or part of a recording of a performance (including a recording of a performance included in a broadcast), the body may, without infringing the rights conferred by this Chapter, make and supply accessible copies of the recording for the personal use of disabled persons.

(2) If an authorised body has lawful access to the whole or part of a broadcast, the body may, without infringing the rights conferred by this Chapter, make a recording of the

broadcast, and make and supply accessible copies of the recording, for the personal use of disabled persons.

(3) But sub-paragraphs (1) and (2) do not apply if the same kind of accessible copies of the recording, or of the broadcast, are commercially available on reasonable terms by or with the consent of the rights owner.

(4) For the purposes of sub-paragraphs (1) and (2), supply "for the personal use of disabled persons" includes supply to a person acting on behalf of a disabled person.

(5) An authorised body which is an educational establishment conducted for profit must ensure that any accessible copies which it makes under this paragraph are used only for its educational purposes.

(6) An accessible copy made under this paragraph must be accompanied by a statement that it is made under this paragraph, unless it is accompanied by an equivalent statement in accordance with section 31B(7).

(7) If an accessible copy is made under this paragraph of a recording which is in copy-protected electronic form, the accessible copy must, so far as is reasonably practicable, incorporate the same or equally effective copy protection (unless the rights owner agrees otherwise).

(8) An authorised body which has made an accessible copy of a recording under this paragraph may supply it to another authorised body which is entitled to make accessible copies of the recording under this paragraph for the purposes of enabling that other body to make accessible copies of the recording.

(9) If an authorised body supplies an accessible copy it has made under this paragraph to a person or authorised body as permitted by this paragraph and charges the person or body for it, the sum charged must not exceed the cost of making and supplying the copy.

(10) If an accessible copy of a recording made under this paragraph is subsequently dealt with—

(a) it is to be treated as an illicit recording for the purposes of that dealing, and

(b) if that dealing infringes any right conferred by this Chapter, it is to be treated as an illicit recording for all subsequent purposes.]

Note: Paragraphs 3A to 3E inserted by the Copyright and Rights in Performances (Disability) Regulations 2014 (SI 2014/1384), reg.3, with effect from June 1, 2014 at 00.01.

[Making and supply of intermediate copies by authorised bodies

3C.—(1) An authorised body which is entitled to make an accessible copy of a recording of a performance under paragraph 3B may, without infringing the rights conferred by this Chapter, make a copy of the recording ("an intermediate copy") if this is necessary in order to make the accessible copy.

(2) An authorised body which has made an intermediate copy of a recording under this paragraph may supply it to another authorised body which is entitled to make accessible copies of the recording under paragraph 3B for the purposes of enabling that other body to make accessible copies of the recording.

(3) The rights conferred by this Chapter are infringed by the transfer of an intermediate copy made under this paragraph to a person other than another authorised body as permitted by sub-paragraph (2), except where the transfer is authorised by the rights owner.

(4) If an authorised body supplies an intermediate copy to an authorised body under sub-paragraph (2) and charges the body for it, the sum charged must not exceed the cost of making and supplying the copy.]

Note: Paragraphs 3A to 3E inserted by the Copyright and Rights in Performances (Disability) Regulations 2014 (SI 2014/1384), reg.3, with effect from June 1, 2014 at 00.01.

[Accessible and intermediate copies: records

3D.—(1) An authorised body must keep a record of—

(a) accessible copies it makes under paragraph 3B,

(b) intermediate copies it makes under paragraph 3C, and

(c) the persons to whom such copies are supplied.

(2) An authorised body must allow the rights owner or a person acting for the rights owner, on giving reasonable notice, to inspect the records at any reasonable time.]

Note: Paragraphs 3A to 3E inserted by the Copyright and Rights in Performances (Disability) Regulations 2014 (SI 2014/1384), reg.3, with effect from June 1, 2014 at 00.01.

[Paragraphs 3A to 3D: interpretation and general

3E.—(1) This paragraph supplements paragraphs 3A to 3D and includes definitions.

(2) "Disabled person" means a person who has a physical or mental impairment which prevents the person from enjoying a recording of a performance to the same degree as a person who does not have that impairment, and "disability" is to be construed accordingly.

(3) But a person is not to be regarded as disabled by reason only of an impairment of visual function which can be improved, by the use of corrective lenses, to a level that is normally acceptable for reading without a special level or kind of light.

(4) An "accessible copy" of a recording of a performance means a version of the recording which enables the fuller enjoyment of the recording by disabled persons.

(5) An accessible copy—

  (a) may include facilities for navigating around the version of the recording, but

  (b) must not include any changes to the recording which are not necessary to overcome the problems suffered by the disabled persons for whom the accessible copy is intended.

(6) To the extent that a term of a contract purports to prevent or restrict the doing of any act which, by virtue of paragraph 3A, 3B or 3C, would not infringe any right conferred by this Chapter, that term is unenforceable.

(7) "Authorised body" and "supply" have the meaning given in section 31F, and other expressions used in paragraphs 3A to 3D but not defined in this paragraph have the same meaning as in sections 31A to 31BB.]

Note: Paragraphs 3A to 3E inserted by the Copyright and Rights in Performances (Disability) Regulations 2014 (SI 2014/1384), reg.3, with effect from June 1, 2014 at 00.01.

[Illustration for instruction

4.—(1) Fair dealing with a performance or a recording of a performance for the sole purpose of illustration for instruction does not infringe the rights conferred by this Chapter provided that the dealing is—

  (a) for a non-commercial purpose, and

  (b) by a person giving or receiving instruction (or preparing for giving or receiving instruction).

(2) To the extent that a term of a contract purports to prevent or restrict the doing of any act which, by virtue of this paragraph, would not infringe any right conferred by this Chapter, that term is unenforceable.

(3) Expressions used in this paragraph have the same meaning as in section 32.]

Note: Paragraph 4 substituted by the Copyright and Rights in Performances (Research, Education, Libraries and Archives) Regulations 2014 (SI 2014/1372), reg.4(4), with effect from June 1, 2014 at 00.02. Para.4 (as amended by SI 2003/2498) formerly read:

"Things done for purposes of instruction or examination

4.—*(1) The rights conferred by this Chapter are not infringed by the copying of a recording of a performance in the course of instruction, or of preparation for instruction, in the making of films or film sound-tracks, provided the copying is done by a person giving or receiving instruction [and the instruction is for a non-commercial purpose].*

(2) The rights conferred by this Chapter are not infringed—

  (a) by the copying of a recording of a performance for the purposes of setting or answering the questions in an examination, or

  (b) by anything done for the purposes of an examination by way of communicating the questions to the candidates.

(3) Where a recording which would otherwise be an illicit recording is made in accordance with this paragraph but is subsequently dealt with, it shall be treated as an illicit recording for the purposes of that dealing, and if that dealing infringes any right conferred by this Chapter for all subsequent purposes.

[For this purpose "dealt with" means—

(a) sold or let for hire, offered or exposed for sale or hire; or

(b) communicated to the public, unless that communication, by virtue of sub-paragraph (2)(b), is not an infringement of the rights conferred by this Chapter.]

(4) Expressions used in this paragraph have the same meaning as in section 32."

Playing or showing sound recording, film, [or broadcast] at educational establishment

5.—(1) The playing or showing of a sound recording, film, [or broadcast] at an educational establishment for the purposes of instruction before an audience consisting of teachers and pupils at the establishment and other persons directly connected with the activities of the establishment is not a playing or showing of a performance in public for the purposes of infringement of the right conferred by this Chapter.

(2) A person is not for this purpose directly connected with the activities of the educational establishment simply because he is the parent of a pupil at the establishment.

(3) Expressions used in this paragraph have the same meaning as in section 34 and any provision made under section 174(2) with respect to the application of that section also applies for the purposes of this paragraph.

Note: The words in square brackets in the heading substituted for the former words "broadcast or cable programme" and the words in square brackets in sub-para.(1) substituted for the former words ", broadcast or cable programme" by the Copyright and Related Rights Regulations 2003 (SI 2003/2498), Sch.1 para.3, with effect from October 31, 2003. For savings and transitional provisions, see Part 3 of those Regulations.

[Recording by educational establishments of broadcasts

6.—(1) A recording of a broadcast, or a copy of such a recording, may be made by or on behalf of an educational establishment for the educational purposes of that establishment without infringing any of the rights conferred by this Chapter in relation to any performance or recording included in it, provided that the educational purposes are non-commercial.

(2) The rights conferred by this Chapter are not infringed where a recording of a broadcast or a copy of such a recording, made under sub-paragraph (1), is communicated by or on behalf of the educational establishment to its pupils or staff for the non-commercial educational purposes of that establishment.

(3) Sub-paragraph (2) only applies to a communication received outside the premises of the establishment if that communication is made by means of a secure electronic network accessible only by the establishment's pupils and staff.

(4) Acts which would otherwise be permitted by this paragraph are not permitted if, or to the extent that, licences are available authorising the acts in question and the educational establishment responsible for those acts knew or ought to have been aware of that fact.

(5) If a recording made under this paragraph is subsequently dealt with—

(a) it is to be treated as an illicit recording for the purposes of that dealing, and

(b) if that dealing infringes any right conferred by this Chapter, it is to be treated as an illicit recording for all subsequent purposes.

(6) In this paragraph "dealt with" means—

(a) sold or let for hire,

(b) offered or exposed for sale or hire, or

(c) communicated otherwise than as permitted by sub-paragraph (2).

(7) Expressions used in this paragraph (other than "dealt with") have the same meaning as in section 35 and any provision made under section 174(2) with respect to the application of that section also applies for the purposes of this paragraph.]

Note: Paragraph 6 substituted for existing para.6 by the Copyright and Rights in Performances (Research, Education, Libraries and Archives) Regulations 2014 (SI 2014/1372), reg.4(5), with effect from June 1, 2014 at 00.02.

Paragraph 6 (as amended by SI 2003/2498) formerly read:

"Recording of broadcasts by educational establishments

6.—*(1) A recording of a broadcast [...], or a copy of such a recording, may be made by or on behalf of an educational establishment for the educational purposes of that estab-lish-*

ment without thereby infringing any of the rights conferred by this Chapter in relation to any performance or recording included in it [, provided that the educational purposes are non-commercial].

[(1A) The rights conferred by this Chapter are not infringed where a recording of a broadcast or a copy of such a recording, whose making was by virtue of sub-paragraph (1) not an infringement of such rights, is communicated to the public by a person situated within the premises of an educational establishment provided that the communication cannot be received by any person situated outside the premises of that establishment.

(1B) This paragraph does not apply if or to the extent that there is a licensing scheme certified for the purposes of this paragraph under paragraph 16 of Schedule 2A providing for the grant of licences.]

(2) Where a recording which would otherwise be an illicit recording is made in accordance with this paragraph but is subsequently dealt with, it shall be treated as an illicit recording for the purposes of that dealing, and if that dealing infringes any right conferred by this Chapter for all subsequent purposes.

For this purpose "dealt with" means sold or let for hire [, offered or exposed for sale or hire, or communicated from within the premises of an educational establishment to any person situated outside those premises].

(3) Expressions used in this paragraph have the same meaning as in section 35 and any provision made under section 174(2) with respect to the application of that section also applies for the purposes of this paragraph."

[Copying and use of extracts of recordings by educational establishments

6ZA.—(1) The copying of extracts of a recording of a performance by or on behalf of an educational establishment does not infringe any of the rights conferred by this Chapter in the recording provided that the copy is made for the purposes of instruction for a non-commercial purpose.

(2) The rights conferred by this Chapter are not infringed where an extract of a recording of a performance, made under sub-paragraph (1), is communicated by or on behalf of the educational establishment to its pupils or staff for the purposes of instruction for a non-commercial purpose.

(3) Sub-paragraph (2) only applies to a communication received outside the premises of the establishment if that communication is made by means of a secure electronic network accessible only by the establishment's pupils and staff.

(4) Not more than 5% of a recording may be copied under this paragraph by or on behalf of an educational establishment in any period of 12 months.

(5) Acts which would otherwise be permitted by this paragraph are not permitted if, or to the extent that, licences are available authorising the acts in question and the educational establishment responsible for those acts knew or ought to have been aware of that fact.

(6) The terms of a licence granted to an educational establishment authorising acts permitted by this paragraph are of no effect so far as they purport to restrict the proportion of a recording which may be copied (whether on payment or free of charge) to less than that which would be permitted by this paragraph.

(7) If a recording made under this paragraph is subsequently dealt with—
    (a) it is to be treated as an illicit recording for the purposes of that dealing, and
    (b) if that dealing infringes any right conferred by this Chapter, it is to be treated as an illicit recording for all subsequent purposes.

(8) In this paragraph "dealt with" means—
    (a) sold or let for hire,
    (b) offered or exposed for sale or hire, or
    (c) communicated otherwise than as permitted by sub-paragraph (2).

(9) Expressions used in this paragraph (other than "dealt with") have the same meaning as in section 36 and any provision made under section 174(2) with respect to the application of that section also applies for the purposes of this paragraph.]

Note: Paragraph 6ZA substituted for existing para.6 by the Copyright and Rights in Performances (Research, Education, Libraries and Archives) Regulations 2014 (SI 2014/1372), reg.4(5), with effect from June 1, 2014 at 00.02.

[Lending of copies by educational establishments

6A.—(1) The rights conferred by this Chapter are not infringed by the lending of copies of a recording of a performance by an educational establishment.

(2) Expressions used in this paragraph have the same meaning as in section 36A; and any provision with respect to the application of that section made under section 174(2) (instruction given elsewhere than an educational establishment) applies also for the purposes of this paragraph.]

Note: This paragraph was inserted by the Copyright and Related Rights Regulations 1996 (SI 1996/2967), with effect from December 1, 1996. For savings and transitional provisions, see Part III of those Regulations.

[Lending of copies by libraries or archives

6B.—[(1A) The rights conferred by this Chapter are not infringed by the following acts by a public library in relation to a book within the public lending right scheme—

(a) lending the book;

(b) in relation to an audio-book or e-book, copying or issuing a copy of the book as an act incidental to lending it.

(A2) Expressions used in sub-paragraph (A1) have the same meaning as in section 40A(1).]

(1) The rights conferred by this Chapter are not infringed by the lending of copies of a recording of a performance by a [...] library or archive (other than a public library) which is not conducted for profit.

(2) [...]

Notes:

(1) This paragraph was inserted by the Copyright and Related Rights Regulations 1996 (SI 1996/2967), with effect from December 1, 1996. For savings and transitional provisions, see Part III of those Regulations.

(2) Subparagraphs (A1), (A2) inserted by the Digital Economy Act 2010, s.43(8), with effect from June 30, 2014 (see SI 2014/1659).

(3) In subpara.(1) word "prescribed" repealed, and subpara.(2) repealed, by the Copyright and Rights in Performances (Research, Education, Libraries and Archives) Regulations 2014 (SI 2014/1372), Sch para.8, with effect from June 1, 2014 at 00.02.

Subparagraph (2) formerly read:

"(2) Expressions used in this paragraph have the same meaning as in section 40A(2); and any provision under section 37 prescribing libraries or archives for the purposes of that section applies also for the purposes of this paragraph."

[Libraries and educational establishments etc: making recordings of performances available through dedicated terminals

6C.—(1) The rights conferred by this Chapter in a recording of a performance are not infringed by an institution specified in sub-paragraph (2) communicating the recording to the public or making it available to the public by means of a dedicated terminal on its premises, if the conditions in sub-paragraph (3) are met.

(2) The institutions are—

(a) a library,

(b) an archive,

(c) a museum, and

(d) an educational establishment.

(3) The conditions are that the recording or a copy of the recording—

(a) has been lawfully acquired by the institution,

(b) is communicated or made available to individual members of the public for the purposes of research or private study, and

(c) is communicated or made available in compliance with any purchase or licensing terms to which the recording is subject.]

Note: Paragraphs 6C to 6H inserted by the Copyright and Rights in Performances (Research,

Education, Libraries and Archives) Regulations 2014 (SI 2014/1372), reg.6, with effect from June 1, 2014 at 00.02.

[Copying by librarians: supply of single copies to other libraries

6D.—(1) A librarian may, if the conditions in sub-paragraph (2) are met, make a single copy of the whole or part of a published recording of a performance and supply it to another library, without infringing any rights conferred by this Chapter in the recording.

(2) The conditions are—

    (a) the copy is supplied in response to a request from a library which is not conducted for profit, and

    (b) at the time of making the copy the librarian does not know, or could not reasonably find out, the name and address of a person entitled to authorise the making of a copy of the recording.

(3) Where a library makes a charge for supplying a copy under this paragraph, the sum charged must be calculated by reference to the costs attributable to the production of the copy.

(4) To the extent that a term of a contract purports to prevent or restrict the doing of any act which, by virtue of this paragraph, would not infringe any right conferred by this Chapter, that term is unenforceable.]

Note: Paragraphs 6C to 6H inserted by the Copyright and Rights in Performances (Research, Education, Libraries and Archives) Regulations 2014 (SI 2014/1372), reg.6, with effect from June 1, 2014 at 00.02.

[Copying by librarians etc: replacement copies of recordings

6E.—(1) A librarian, archivist or curator of a library, archive or museum may, without infringing any rights conferred by this Chapter, make a copy of a recording of a performance in that institution's permanent collection—

    (a) in order to preserve or replace that recording in that collection, or

    (b) where a recording in the permanent collection of another library, archive or museum has been lost, destroyed or damaged, in order to replace the recording in the collection of that other library, archive or museum,

provided that the conditions in sub-paragraphs (2) and (3) are met.

(2) The first condition is that the recording is—

    (a) included in the part of the collection kept wholly or mainly for the purposes of reference on the institution's premises,

    (b) included in a part of the collection not accessible to the public, or

    (c) available on loan only to other libraries, archives or museums.

(3) The second condition is that it is not reasonably practicable to purchase a copy of the recording to achieve either of the purposes mentioned in sub-paragraph (1).

(4) The reference in sub-paragraph (1)(b) to a library, archive or museum is to a library, archive or museum which is not conducted for profit.

(5) Where an institution makes a charge for supplying a copy to another library, archive or museum under sub-paragraph (1)(b), the sum charged must be calculated by reference to the costs attributable to the production of the copy.

(6) To the extent that a term of a contract purports to prevent or restrict the doing of any act which, by virtue of this paragraph, would not infringe any right conferred by this Chapter, that term is unenforceable.]

Note: Paragraphs 6C to 6H inserted by the Copyright and Rights in Performances (Research, Education, Libraries and Archives) Regulations 2014 (SI 2014/1372), reg.6, with effect from June 1, 2014 at 00.02.

[Copying by librarians: single copies of published recordings

6F.—(1) A librarian of a library which is not conducted for profit may, if the conditions in sub-paragraph (2) are met, make and supply a single copy of a reasonable proportion of a published recording without infringing any of the rights in the recording conferred by this Chapter.

(2) The conditions are—

    (a) the copy is supplied in response to a request from a person who has provided the librarian with a declaration in writing which includes the information set out in sub-paragraph (3), and

    (b) the librarian is not aware that the declaration is false in a material particular.

(3) The information which must be included in the declaration is—

    (a) the name of the person who requires the copy and the material which that person requires,

    (b) a statement that the person has not previously been supplied with a copy of that material by any library,

    (c) a statement that the person requires the copy for the purposes of research for a non-commercial purpose or private study, will use it only for those purposes and will not supply the copy to any other person, and

    (d) a statement that to the best of the person's knowledge, no other person with whom the person works or studies has made, or intends to make, at or about the same time as the person's request, a request for substantially the same material for substantially the same purpose.

(4) Where a library makes a charge for supplying a copy under this paragraph, the sum charged must be calculated by reference to the costs attributable to the production of the copy.

(5) Where a person ("P") makes a declaration under this paragraph that is false in a material particular and is supplied with a copy of a recording which would have been an illicit recording if made by P—

    (a) P is liable for infringement of the rights conferred by this Chapter as if P had made the copy, and

    (b) the copy supplied to P is to be treated as an illicit recording for all purposes.

(6) To the extent that a term of a contract purports to prevent or restrict the doing of any act which, by virtue of this paragraph, would not infringe any right conferred by this Chapter, that term is unenforceable.]

Note: Paragraphs 6C to 6H inserted by the Copyright and Rights in Performances (Research, Education, Libraries and Archives) Regulations 2014 (SI 2014/1372), reg.6, with effect from June 1, 2014 at 00.02.

[Copying by librarians or archivists: single copies of unpublished recordings

6G.—(1) A librarian or archivist may make and supply a single copy of the whole or part of a recording without infringing any of the rights conferred by this Chapter in the recording, provided that—

    (a) the copy is supplied in response to a request from a person who has provided the librarian or archivist with a declaration in writing which includes the information set out in sub-paragraph (2), and

    (b) the librarian or archivist is not aware that the declaration is false in a material particular.

(2) The information which must be included in the declaration is—

    (a) the name of the person who requires the copy and the material which that person requires,

    (b) a statement that the person has not previously been supplied with a copy of that material by any library or archive, and

    (c) a statement that the person requires the copy for the purposes of research for a non-commercial purpose or private study, will use it only for those purposes and will not supply the copy to any other person.

(3) But the rights conferred by this Chapter are infringed if—

    (a) the recording had been published or communicated to the public before the date it was deposited in the library or archive, or

    (b) the rights owner has prohibited the copying of the recording,

and at the time of making the copy the librarian or archivist is, or ought to be, aware of that fact.

(4) Where a library or archive makes a charge for supplying a copy under this paragraph, the sum charged must be calculated by reference to the costs attributable to the production of the copy.

(5) Where a person ("P") makes a declaration under this paragraph that is false in a material particular and is supplied with a copy of a recording which would have been an illicit recording if made by P—

(a) P is liable for infringement of the rights conferred by this Chapter as if P had made the copy, and

(b) the copy supplied to P is to be treated as an illicit recording for all purposes.]

Note: Paragraphs 6C to 6H inserted by the Copyright and Rights in Performances (Research, Education, Libraries and Archives) Regulations 2014 (SI 2014/1372), reg.6, with effect from June 1, 2014 at 00.02.

[Paragraphs 6B to 6G: interpretation

6H. Expressions used in paragraphs 6B to 6G have the same meaning as in sections 40A to 43.]

Note: Paragraphs 6C to 6H inserted by the Copyright and Rights in Performances (Research, Education, Libraries and Archives) Regulations 2014 (SI 2014/1372), reg.6, with effect from June 1, 2014 at 00.02.

[Certain permitted uses of orphan works

6I.—(1) The rights conferred by this Chapter are not infringed by a relevant body in the circumstances set out in paragraph 1(2) of Schedule ZA1 (subject to paragraph 6 of that Schedule).

(2) "Relevant body" has the meaning given by that Schedule.]

Note: Paragraph 6I inserted by the Copyright and Rights in Performances (Certain Permitted Uses of Orphan Works) Regulations 2014 (SI 2014/2861), reg.3(4), with effect from October 29, 2014.

Copy of work required to be made as condition of export

7.—(1) If an article of cultural or historical importance or interest cannot lawfully be exported from the United Kingdom unless a copy of it is made and deposited in an appropriate library or archive, it is not an infringement of any right conferred by this Chapter to make that copy.

(2) Expressions used in this paragraph have the same meaning as in section 44.

Parliamentary and judicial proceedings

8.—(1) The rights conferred by this Chapter are not infringed by anything done for the purposes of parliamentary or judicial proceedings or for the purpose of reporting such proceedings.

(2) Expressions used in this paragraph have the same meaning as in section 45.

Royal Commissions and statutory inquiries

9.—(1) The rights conferred by this Chapter are not infringed by anything done for the purposes of the proceedings of a Royal Commission or statutory inquiry or for the purpose of reporting any such proceedings held in public.

(2) Expressions used in this paragraph have the same meaning as in section 46.

Public records

10.—(1) Material which is comprised in public records within the meaning of the Public Records (Scotland) Act 1937 or the Public Records Act 1958, the Public Records Act (Northern Ireland) 1923 [, or in Welsh public records (as defined in [the Government of Wales Act 2006]),] which are open to public inspection in pursuance of that Act, may be copied, and a copy may be supplied to any person, by or with the authority of any officer appointed under that Act, without infringing any rights conferred by Part II.

(2) Expressions used in this paragraph have the same meaning as in section 49.

Note: The words in the internal square brackets substituted by the Government of Wales Act 2006 (c.32), Sch.10 para.32, with effect from May 4, 2007.

Acts done under statutory authority

11.—(1) Where the doing of a particular act is specifically authorised by an Act of Parliament, whenever passed, then, unless the Act provides otherwise, the doing of that act does not infringe the rights conferred by this Chapter.

(2) Sub-paragraph (1) applies in relation to an enactment contained in Northern Ireland legislation as it applies to an Act of Parliament.

(3) Nothing in this paragraph shall be construed as excluding any defence of statutory authority otherwise available under or by virtue of any enactment.

(4) Expressions used in this paragraph have the same meaning as in section 50.

Transfer of copies of works in electronic form

12.—(1) This paragraph applies where a recording of a performance in electronic form has been purchased on terms which, expressly or impliedly or by virtue of any rule of law, allow the purchaser to make further recordings in connection with his use of the recording.

(2) If there are no express terms—

(a) prohibiting the transfer of the recording by the purchaser, imposing obligations which continue after a transfer, prohibiting the assignment of any consent or terminating any consent on a transfer, or

(b) providing for the terms on which a transferee may do the things which the purchaser was permitted to do,

anything which the purchaser was allowed to do may also be done by a transferee without infringement of the rights conferred by this Chapter, but any recording made by the purchaser which is not also transferred shall be treated as an illicit recording for all purposes after the transfer.

(3) The same applies where the original purchased recording is no longer usable and what is transferred is a further copy used in its place.

(4) The above provisions also apply on a subsequent transfer, with the substitution for references in sub-paragraph (2) to the purchaser of references to the subsequent transferor.

(5) This paragraph does not apply in relation to a recording purchased before the commencement of this Chapter.

(6) Expressions used in this paragraph have the same meaning as in section 56.

Note: In para.12(2) the words "this Chapter" substituted for the former words "this Part" by the Performances (Moral Rights, etc.) Regulations 2006 (SI 2006/18), Sch. para.8, with effect from February 1, 2006.

Use of recordings of spoken works in certain cases

13.—(1) Where a recording of the reading or recitation of a literary work is made for the purpose—

(a) of reporting current events, or

(b) of [communicating to the public] the whole or part of the reading or recitation,

it is not an infringement of the rights conferred by this Chapter to use the recording (or to copy the recording and use the copy) for that purpose, provided the following conditions are met.

(2) The conditions are that—

(a) the recording is a direct recording of the reading or recitation and is not taken from a previous recording or from a broadcast [...];

(b) the making of the recording was not prohibited by or on behalf of the person giving the reading or recitation;

(c) the use made of the recording is not of a kind prohibited by or on behalf of that person before the recording was made; and

(d) the use is by or with the authority of a person who is lawfully in possession of the recording.

(3) Expressions used in this paragraph have the same meaning as in section 58.

Note: In sub-para.(1), the words in square brackets substituted for the former words "broadcasting or including in a cable programme service" and in sub-para.(2) the words "or cable programme" repealed by the Copyright and Related Rights Regulations 2003 (SI 2003/2498), Sch.1, para.12, Sch.2, with effect from October 31, 2003. For savings and transitional provisions, see Part 3 of those Regulations.

Recordings of folksongs

14.—(1) A recording of a performance of a song may be made for the purpose of including it in an archive maintained by a [body not established or conducted for profit] without infringing any of the rights conferred by [this Chapter], provided the conditions in sub-paragraph (2) below are met.

(2) The conditions are that—

(a) the words are unpublished and of unknown authorship at the time the recording is made,

(b) the making of the recording does not infringe any copyright, and

(c) its making is not prohibited by any performer.

[(3) A single copy of a recording made in reliance on sub-paragraph (1) and included in an archive referred to in that sub-paragraph may be made and supplied by the archivist without infringing any right conferred by this Chapter, provided that—

(a) the copy is supplied in response to a request from a person who has provided the archivist with a declaration in writing which includes the information set out in sub-paragraph (4), and

(a) the archivist is not aware that the declaration is false in a material particular.

(4) The information which must be included in the declaration is—

(a) the name of the person who requires the copy and the recording which is the subject of the request,

(b) a statement that the person has not previously been supplied with a copy of that recording by any archivist, and

(c) a statement that the person requires the copy for the purposes of research for a non-commercial purpose or private study, will use it only for those purposes and will not supply the copy to any other person.

(5) Where an archive makes a charge for supplying a copy under this paragraph, the sum charged must be calculated by reference to the costs attributable to the production of the copy.

(6) Where a person ("P") makes a declaration under this paragraph that is false in a material particular and is supplied with a copy of a recording which would have been an illicit recording if made by P—

(a) P is liable for infringement of the rights conferred by this Chapter as if P had made the copy, and

(b) the copy supplied to P is to be treated as an illicit recording for all purposes.

(7) In this paragraph references to an archivist include a person acting on behalf of an archivist.

(8) Expressions used in this paragraph have the same meaning as in section 61.]

Notes:

(1) In subpara.(1) second words substituted by the Performances (Moral Rights, etc.) Regulations 2006 (SI 2006/18), Sch.1 para.9.

(2) In subpara.(1) first words in square brackets substituted, and subparas (3)–(8) substituted for existing subparas (3), (4), by the Copyright and Rights in Performances (Research, Education, Libraries and Archives) Regulations 2014 (SI 2014/1372), reg.7, with effect from June 1, 2014 at 00.02.

Subpara.(1) formerly read:

"(1) A recording of a performance of a song may be made for the purpose of including it in an archive maintained by a designated body without infringing any of the rights conferred by this Chapter, provided the conditions in sub-paragraph (2) below are met."

Subparas (3), (4) formerly read:

"(3) Copies of a recording made in reliance on sub-paragraph (1) and included in an archive maintained by a designated body may, if the prescribed conditions are met, be made and supplied by the archivist without infringing any of the rights conferred by this Chapter.

(4) In this paragraph—

"designated body" means a body designated for the purposes of section 61, and

"the prescribed conditions" means the conditions prescribed for the purposes of subsection (3) of that section;

and other expressions used in this paragraph have the same meaning as in that section."

[Lending of certain recordings

14A.—(1) The Secretary of State may by order provide that in such cases as may be specified in the order the lending to the public of copies of films or sound recordings shall be treated as licensed by the performer subject only to the payment of such reasonable royalty or other payment as may be agreed or determined in default of agreement by the Copyright Tribunal.

(2) No such order shall apply if, or to the extent that, there is a licensing scheme certified for the purposes of this paragraph under paragraph 16 of Schedule 2A providing for the grant of licences.

(3) An order may make different provision for different cases and may specify cases by reference to any factor relating to the work, the copies lent, the lender or the circumstances of the lending.

(4) An order shall be made by statutory instrument; and no order shall be made unless a draft of it has been laid before and approved by a resolution of each House of Parliament.

(5) Nothing in this section affects any liability under section 184(1)(b) (secondary infringement: possessing or dealing with illicit recording) in respect of the lending of illicit recordings.

(6) Expressions used in this paragraph have the same meaning as in section 66.]

Note: This paragraph was inserted by the Copyright and Related Rights Regulations 1996 (SI 1996/2967), with effect from December 1, 1996. For savings and transitional provisions, see Part III of those Regulations.

Playing of sound recordings for purposes of club, society, &c.

15. [...]

Notes:

(1) Paragraph 15 was omitted by the Copyright, Designs and Patents Act 1988 (Amendment) Regs 2010/2694 with effect from January 1, 2011. The paragraph previously read as follows:

"**15.**—(1) *It is not an infringement of any right conferred by this Chapter to play a sound recording as part of the activities of, or for the benefit of, a club, society or other organisation if the following conditions are met.*

(2) *The conditions are—*

    (a) *that the organisation is not established or conducted for profit and its main objects are charitable or are otherwise concerned with the advancement of religion, education or social welfare,*

    [(b) *that the sound recording is played by a person who is acting primarily and directly for the benefit of the organisation and who is not acting with a view to gain,*

    (c) *that the proceeds of any charge for admission to the place where the recording is to be heard are applied solely for the purposes of the organisation, and*

    (d) *that the proceeds from any goods or services sold by, or on behalf of, the organisation—*

        (i) *in the place where the sound recording is heard, and*

        (ii) *on the occasion when the sound recording is played, are applied solely for the purposes of the organisation.*]

(3) *Expressions used in this paragraph have the same meaning as in section 67.*"

(2) Sub-paragraph (2)(b) was substituted and (c) and (d) inserted by the Copyright and Related Rights Regulations 2003 (SI 2003/2498), reg.18, with effect from October 31, 2003. For savings and transitional provisions, see Part 3 of those Regulations. Sub-paragraph (2)(b) formerly provided:

"(b) *that the proceeds of any charge for admission to the place where the recording is to be heard are applied solely for the purposes of the organisation.*"

Incidental recording for purposes of broadcast

16.—(1) A person who proposes to broadcast a recording of a performance [...] in circumstances not infringing the rights conferred by this Chapter shall be treated as having consent for the purposes of that Chapter for the making of a further recording for the purposes of the broadcast [...].

(2) That consent is subject to the condition that the further recording—

    (a) shall not be used for any other purpose, and

    (b) shall be destroyed within 28 days of being first used for broadcasting the performance [...].

(3) A recording made in accordance with this paragraph shall be treated as an illicit recording—

    (a) for the purposes of any use in breach of the condition mentioned in sub-paragraph (2)(a), and

    (b) for all purposes after that condition or the condition mentioned in sub-paragraph (2)(b) is broken.

(4) Expressions used in this paragraph have the same meaning as in section 68.

Notes:

    (1) The words ", or include a recording of a performance in a cable programme service," and "or cable programme" in sub-para.(1) and the words "or including it in a cable programme service" in sub-para.(2)(b) repealed by the Copyright and Related Rights Regulations 2003 (SI 2003/2498), Sch.2, with effect from October 31, 2003. For savings and transitional provisions, see Part 3 of those Regulations.

    (2) In para.16(1) the words "this Chapter" substituted for the former words "that Part" by the Performances (Moral Rights, etc.) Regulations 2006 (SI 2006/18), Sch. para.10, with effect from February 1, 2006.

Recordings for purposes of supervision and control of broadcasts and [other services]

17.—(1) The rights conferred by this Chapter are not infringed by the making or use by the British Broadcasting Corporation, for the purpose of maintaining supervision and control over programmes broadcast by them, [or included in any on-demand programme service provided by them] of recordings of those programmes.

[(2) The rights conferred by this Chapter are not infringed by anything done in pursuance of—

    [(a) section 167(1) of the Broadcasting Act 1990, section 115(4) or (6) or 117 of the Broadcasting Act 1996 or paragraph 20 of Schedule 12 to the Communications Act 2003;]

    (b) a condition which, [by virtue of section 334(1) of the Communications Act 2003], is included in a licence granted under Part I or III of that Act or Part I or II of the Broadcasting Act 1996; or

    (c) a direction given under section 109(2) of the Broadcasting Act 1990 (power of [OFCOM] to require production of recordings etc.).

    [(d) section 334(3) [, 368O(1) or (3)] of the Communications Act 2003.]

[(3) The rights conferred by this Chapter are not infringed by the use by OFCOM in connection with the performance of any of their functions under the Broadcasting Act 1990, the Broadcasting Act 1996 or the Communications Act 2003 of—

    (a) any recording, script or transcript which is provided to them under or by virtue of any provision of those Acts; or

    (b) any existing material which is transferred to them by a scheme made under section 30 of the Communications Act 2003.

(4) In subsection (3), 'existing material' means—

    (a) any recording, script or transcript which was provided to the Independent Television Commission or the Radio Authority under or by virtue of any provision of the Broadcasting Act 1990 or the Broadcasting Act 1996; and

    (b) any recording or transcript which was provided to the Broadcasting Standards Commission under section 115(4) or (6) or 116(5) of the Broadcasting Act 1996.]

[(5) The rights conferred by this Chapter are not infringed by the use by the appropriate regulatory authority designated under section 368B of the Communications Act 2003, in connection with the performance of any of their functions under that Act, of any recording, script or transcript which is provided to them under or by virtue of any provision of that Act.

(6) In this paragraph "on-demand programme service" has the same meaning as in the Communications Act 2003 (see section 368A of that Act).]

Notes:

(1) The words in square brackets in the heading substituted for the former words "and cable programmes" by the Copyright and Related Rights Regs 2003 (SI 2003/2498) Sch.1, para.2(1) with effect from October 31, 2003. For savings and transitional provisions, see Part 3 of those Regulations. Sub-paragraph (2)(a) was substituted, the words in square brackets in sub-para.(2)(b) substituted for the former words ", by virtue of section 11(2) or 95(2) of the Broadcasting Act 1990,", the words in square brackets in sub-para.(2)(c) substituted for the former words "Radio Authority", sub-para.(2)(d) was inserted and sub-para.(3) was substituted by the Communications Act 2003 (c.21), Sch.17, para.93 and Sch.19 with eect from December 29, 2003 (Oce of Communications Act 2002 (Commencement No.3) and Communications Act 2003 (Commencement No.2) Order 2003 (SI 2003/3142)). Subparagraphs (2)(a) and (3) formerly provided:

"(2)(a) *Section 11(1), 95(1), or 167(1) of the Broadcasting Act 1990 or section 115(4) or (6), 116(5) or 117 of the Broadcasting Act 1996;*

(3) *The rights conferred by Part II are not infringed by—*

(a) *the use by the Independent Television Commission or the Radio Authority, in connection with the performance of any of their functions under the Broadcasting Act 1990 or the Broadcasting Act 1996, of any recording, script or transcript which is provided to them under or by virtue of any provision of those Acts; or*

(b) *the use by the Broadcasting Standards Commission, in connection with any complaint made to them under the Broadcasting Act 1996, of any recording or transcript requested or required to be provided to them, and so provided, under section 115(4) or (6) or 116(5) of that Act.]"*

(2) Sub-paragraphs (2) and (3) inserted by s.148 and para.32 of Sch.10 to the Broadcasting Act 1996 as provided by the Broadcasting Act 1996 (Commencement No.1 and Transitional Provisions) Order 1996 (SI 1996/2120), which replaced the previous sub-paras (2) and (3) with effect from October 1, 1996, except so far as relating to anything done in pursuance of section 115(4) or (6), 116(5) or 117 of the 1996 Act (Schedule 1 to the Regulations). The previous sub-paras (2) and (3) provided:

"(2) *The rights conferred by Part II are not infringed by anything done in pursuance of—*

(a) *section 11(1), 95(1), 145(4), (5) or (7), 155(3) or 167(1) of the Broadcasting Act 1990;*

(b) *a condition which, by virtue of section 11(2) or 95(2) of that Act, is included in a licence granted under Part I or III of that Act; or*

(c) *a direction given under section 109(2) of that Act (power of Radio Authority to require production of recordings etc.).*

(3) *The rights conferred by Part II are not infringed by—*

(a) *the use by the Independent Television Commission or the Radio Authority, in connection with the performance of any of their functions under the Broadcasting Act 1990, of any recording, script or transcript which is provided to them under or by virtue of any provision of that Act; or*

(b) *the use by the Broadcasting Complaints Commission or the Broadcasting Standards Council, in connection with any complaint made to them under that Act, of any recording or transcript requested or required to be provided to them, and so provided, under section 145(4) or (7) or section 155(3) of that Act."*

(3) The previous sub-paras (2) and (3) set out in Note (2) above inserted by s.203(1) and para.50(1) of Schedule 20 to the Broadcasting Act 1990 as provided by the Broadcasting Act 1990 (Commencement No.1 and Transitional Provisions) Order 1990 (SI 1990/2347), in place of the original sub-paras (2) and (3) with effect from January 1, 1991. The original sub-paras (2) and (3) provided:

"(2) *The rights conferred by Part II are not infringed by—*

(a) *the making or use of recordings by the Independent Broadcasting Authority for the purposes mentioned in section 4(7) of the Broadcasting Act 1981 (maintenance of supervision and control over programmes and advertisements); or*

(b) *anything done under or in pursuance of provision included in a contract be-tween a programme contractor and the Authority in accordance with section 21 of that Act.*

(3) *The rights conferred by Part II are not infringed by—*

(a) *the making by or with the authority of the Cable Authority, or the use by that Authority, for the purpose of maintaining supervision and control over programmes included in services licensed under Part I of the Cable and Broadcasting Act 1984, of recordings of those programmes; or*

(b) *anything done under or in pursuance of—*

(i) *a notice or direction given under section 16 of the Cable and Broadcast-ing Act 1984 (power of Cable Authority to require production of record-ings); or*

(ii) *a condition included in a licence by virtue of section 35 of that Act (duty of Authority to secure that recordings are available for certain purposes).*

(4) *Expressions used in this paragraph have the same meaning as in section 69."*

(4) The words in square brackets in para.17(1), (2)(d) and para.17(5) and (6) inserted by the Audiovisual Media Services Regulations 2009 (SI 2009/2979) reg.12, with effect from December 19, 2009.

[Recording for the purposes of time-shifting

17A.—(1) The making in domestic premises for private and domestic use of a recording of a broadcast solely for the purpose of enabling it to be viewed or listened to at a more convenient time does not infringe any right conferred by this Chapter in relation to a per-formance or recording included in the broadcast.

(2) Where a recording which would otherwise be an illicit recording is made in accor-dance with this paragraph but is subsequently dealt with—

(a) it shall be treated as an illicit recording for the purposes of that dealing; and

(b) if that dealing infringes any right conferred by this Chapter, it shall be treated as an illicit recording for all subsequent purposes.

(3) In sub-paragraph (2), "dealt with" means sold or let for hire, offered or exposed for sale or hire or communicated to the public.

(4) Expressions used in this paragraph have the same meaning as in section 70.]

Note: This paragraph was inserted by the Copyright and Related Rights Regulations 2003 (SI 2003/2498), reg.19, with effect from October 31, 2003. For savings and transitional provisions, see Part 3 of those Regulations.

[Photographs of broadcasts

17B.—(1) The making in domestic premises for private and domestic use of a photograph of the whole or any part of an image forming part of a broadcast, or a copy of such a photograph, does not infringe any right conferred by this Chapter in relation to a performance or recording included in the broadcast.

(2) Where a recording which would otherwise be an illicit recording is made in accor-dance with this paragraph but is subsequently dealt with—

(a) it shall be treated as an illicit recording for the purposes of that dealing; and

(b) if that dealing infringes any right conferred by this Chapter, it shall be treated as an illicit recording for all subsequent purposes.

(3) In sub-paragraph (2), "dealt with" means sold or let for hire, offered or exposed for sale or hire or communicated to the public.

(4) Expressions used in this paragraph have the same meaning as in section 71.]

Note: This paragraph was inserted by the Copyright and Related Rights Regulations 2003 (SI 2003/2498), reg.20, with effect from October 31, 2003. For savings and transitional provisions, see Part 3 of those Regulations.

Free public showing or playing of broadcast

18.—(1) The showing or playing in public of a broadcast [...] to an audience who have not paid for admission to the place where the broadcast [...] is to be seen or heard does not infringe any right conferred by this Chapter in relation to a performance or recording included in—

    (a) [...]

    (b) any sound recording [(except so far as it is an excepted sound recording)] or film which is played or shown in public by reception of the broadcast [...].

[(1A) The showing or playing in public of a broadcast to an audience who have not paid for admission to the place where the broadcast is to be seen or heard does not infringe any right conferred by this Chapter in relation to a performance or recording included in any excepted sound recording which is played in public by reception of the broadcast, if the playing or showing of that broadcast in public—

    (a) [...]

    (b) is necessary for the purposes of—

        (i) repairing equipment for the reception of broadcasts;

        (ii) demonstrating that a repair to such equipment has been carried out; or

        (iii) demonstrating such equipment which is being sold or let for hire or offered or exposed for sale or hire.]

(2) The audience shall be treated as having paid for admission to a place—

    (a) if they have paid for admission to a place of which that place forms part; or

    (b) if goods or services are supplied at that place (or a place of which it forms part)—

        (i) at prices which are substantially attributable to the facilities afforded for seeing or hearing the broadcast [...], or

        (ii) at prices exceeding those usually charged there and which are partly attributable to those facilities.

(3) The following shall not be regarded as having paid for admission to a place—

    (a) persons admitted as residents or inmates of the place;

    (b) persons admitted as members of a club or society where the payment is only for membership of the club or society and the provision of facilities for seeing or hearing broadcasts [...] is only incidental to the main purposes of the club or society.

(4) Where the making of the broadcast [...] was an infringement of the rights conferred by this Chapter in relation to a performance or recording, the fact that it was heard or seen in public by the reception of the broadcast [...] shall be taken into account in assessing the damages for that infringement.

(5) Expressions used in this paragraph have the same meaning as in section 72.

Notes:

    (1) The words in square brackets in sub-para.(1) and sub-para.(1A) inserted and the references to "cable programmes" wherever located where repealed by the Copyright and Related Rights Regulations 2003 (SI 2003/2498), reg.21, Sch.2, with effect from October 31, 2003. For savings and transitional provisions, see Part 3 of those Regulations.

    (2) Paragraph (a) was omitted by the Copyright, Designs and Patents Act 1988 (Amendment) Regs 2010/2694 with effect from January 1, 2011. The paragraph previously read as follows:

    "(a) *forms part of the activities of an organisation that is not established or conducted for profit; or*".

Reception and re-transmission of wireless broadcast by cable

[**19.**—(1) This paragraph applies where a [wireless] broadcast made from a place in the United Kingdom is [received and immediately re-transmitted by cable].

(2) The rights conferred by this Chapter in relation to a performance or recording included in the broadcast are not infringed if and to the extent that the broadcast is made for reception in the area in which [it is re-transmitted by cable]; but where the making of the broadcast was an infringement of those rights, the fact that the broadcast was re-transmitted [by cable] shall be taken into account in assessing the damages for that infringement.

    (3) Where—

    (a) the [re-transmission by cable] is in pursuance of a relevant requirement, but

(b) to any extent, the area in which the [re-transmission by cable takes place] ("the cable area") falls outside the area for reception in which the broadcast is made ("the broadcast area"),

the [re-transmission by cable] (to the extent that it is provided for so much of the cable area as falls outside the broadcast area) of any performance or recording included in the broadcast shall, subject to sub-paragraph (4), be treated as licensed by the owner of the rights conferred by this Chapter in relation to the performance or recording, subject only to the payment to him by the person making the broadcast of such reasonable royalty or other payment in respect of the [re-transmission by cable of the broadcast] as may be agreed or determined in default of agreement by the Copyright Tribunal.

(4) Sub-paragraph (3) does not apply if, or to the extent that, the [re-transmission of the performance or recording by cable] is (apart from that sub-paragraph) licensed by the owner of the rights conferred by this Chapter in relation to the performance or recording.

(5) The Secretary of State may by order—

(a) provide that in specified cases sub-paragraph (2) is to apply in relation to broadcasts of a specified description which are not made as mentioned in that sub-paragraph, or

(b) exclude the application of that sub-paragraph in relation to broadcasts of a specified description made as mentioned in that sub-paragraph.

(6) Where the Secretary of State exercises the power conferred by sub-paragraph (5)(b) in relation to broadcasts of any description, the order may also provide for sub-paragraph (3) to apply, subject to such modifications as may be specified in the order, in relation to broadcasts of that description.

(7) An order under this paragraph may contain such transitional provision as appears to the Secretary of State to be appropriate.

(8) An order under this paragraph shall be made by statutory instrument which shall be subject to annulment in pursuance of a resolution of either House of Parliament.

(9) Expressions used in this paragraph have the same meaning as in section 73.]

Notes:

(1) The following amendments were made by the Copyright and Related Rights Regulations 2003 (SI 2003/2498), reg.22, with effect from October 31, 2003. For savings and transitional provisions, see Part 3 of those Regulations.

(a) in the heading, the words wireless broadcast by cable substituted for the former words "broadcast and cable programmes Services";

(b) in sub-para.(1), the word "wireless" was inserted and the words in square brackets substituted for the former words ", by reception and immediate re-transmission, included in a cable programme service";

(c) in sub-para.(2), the words in the first set of square brackets substituted for the former words "the cable programme service is provided" and the words in the second set of square brackets substituted for the former words "as a programme in a cable programme service";

(d) in sub-para.(3), the words in the first set of square brackets substituted for the former words "inclusion", the words in the second set of square brackets substituted for the former words "cable programme service is provided", the words in the third set of square brackets substituted for the former words "inclusion in the cable programme service" and the words in the fourth set of square brackets substituted for the former words "inclusion of the broadcast in the cable programme";

(e) in sub-para.(4), the words in square brackets substituted for the former words "inclusion of the work in the cable programme service".

(2) Paragraph 19 was substituted and paragraph 19A was inserted by s.138 of and Sch.9 to the Broadcasting Act 1996, which replaced the old para.19 with effect from October 1, 1996 by virtue of the Broadcasting Act 1996 (Commencement No.1 and Transitional Provisions) Order 1996 (SI 1996/2120). The old para.19 provided:

"**19.**—(1) *This paragraph applies where a broadcast made from a place in the United Kingdom is, by reception and immediate re-transmission, included in a cable programme service.*

(2) *The rights conferred by Part II in relation to a performance or recording included in the broadcast are not infringed—*

(a) *[...]*

(b) *if and to the extent that the broadcast is made for reception in the area in which the cable programme service is provided;*

but where the making of the broadcast was an infringement of those rights, the fact that the broadcast was re-transmitted as a programme in a cable programme service shall be taken into account in assessing the damages for that infringement.

(3) *Expressions used in this paragraph have the same meaning as in section 73."*

(3) Sub-paragraph (2)(a) of the old para.19 set out in Note (2) above was repealed by s.203(3) of and Sch.21 to the Broadcasting Act 1990 as provided by The Broadcasting Act 1990 (Commencement No.1 and Transitional Provisions) Order 1990 (SI 1990/2347).

[19A.—(1) An application to settle the royalty or other sum payable in pursuance of sub-paragraph (3) of paragraph 19 may be made to the Copyright Tribunal by the owner of the rights conferred by this Chapter or the person making the broadcast.

(2) The Tribunal shall consider the matter and make such order as it may determine to be reasonable in the circumstances.

(3) Either party may subsequently apply to the Tribunal to vary the order, and the Tribunal shall consider the matter and make such order confirming or varying the original order as it may determine to be reasonable in the circumstances.

(4) An application under sub-paragraph (3) shall not, except with the special leave of the Tribunal, be made within twelve months from the date of the original order or of the order on a previous application under that sub-paragraph.

(5) An order under sub-paragraph (3) has effect from the date on which it is made or such later date as may be specified by the Tribunal.]

Note: Paragraph 19 was substituted and paragraph 19A was inserted by s.138 of and Sch.9 to the Broadcasting Act 1996, which replaced the old para.19 with effect from October 1, 1996 by virtue of the Broadcasting Act 1996 (Commencement No.1 and Transitional Provisions) Order 1996 (SI 1996/2120).

Provision of sub-titled copies of broadcast

20. *[Repealed by the Copyright and Rights in Performances (Disability) Regulations 2014 (SI 2014/1384), Schedule, para.8, with effect from June 1, 2014 at 00.01.]*

Note: Paragraph 20 (as amended by SI 2003/2498) formerly read:

"Provision of sub-titled copies of broadcast

20.—*(1) A designated body may, for the purpose of providing people who are deaf or hard of hearing, or physically or mentally handicapped in other ways, with copies which are sub-titled or otherwise modified for their special needs, make recordings of [broadcasts and copies of such recordings, and issue or lend copies to the public,] without infringing any right conferred by this Chapter in relation to a performance or recording included in the broadcast [...].*

(1A) This paragraph does not apply if, or to the extent that, there is a licensing scheme certified for the purposes of this paragraph under paragraph 16 of Schedule 2A providing for the grant of licences.]

(2) In this paragraph "designated body" means a body designated for the purposes of section 74 and other expressions used in this paragraph have the same meaning as in that section."

[Recording of broadcast for archival purposes

21.—(1) A recording of a broadcast or a copy of such a recording may be made for the purpose of being placed in an archive maintained by a body which is not established or conducted for profit without infringing any right conferred by this Chapter in relation to a performance or recording included in the broadcast.

(2) To the extent that a term of a contract purports to prevent or restrict the doing of any act which, by virtue of this paragraph, would not infringe any right conferred by this Chapter, that term is unenforceable.

(3) Expressions used in this paragraph have the same meaning as in section 75.]

Note: Paragraph 21 substituted by the Copyright and Rights in Performances (Research, Education, Libraries and Archives) Regulations 2014 (SI 2014/1372), reg.8(2), with effect from June 1, 2014 at 00.02. Para.21 (as amended by SI 2003/2498, 2006/18) formerly read:

"**21.**—*(1) A recording of a broadcast [...] of a designated class, or a copy of such a recording, may be made for the purpose of being placed in an archive maintained by a designated body without thereby infringing any right conferred by this Chapter in relation to a performance or recording included in the broadcast [...].*

(2) In this paragraph "designated class" and "designated body" means a class or body designated for the purposes of section 75 and other expressions used in this paragraph have the same meaning as in that section."

[SCHEDULE 2A

LICENSING OF PERFORMERS' [...] RIGHTS

Licensing schemes and licensing bodies

1.—(1) In this Chapter a "licensing scheme" means a scheme setting out—

(a) the classes of case in which the operator of the scheme, or the person on whose behalf he acts, is willing to grant performers' property right licences, and

(b) the terms on which licences would be granted in those classes of case,

and for this purpose a "scheme" includes anything in the nature of a scheme, whether described as a scheme or as a tariff or by any other name.

(2) In this Chapter a "licensing body" means a society or other organisation which has as its main object, or one of its main objects, the negotiating or granting, whether as owner or prospective owner of a performer's property rights or as agent for him, of performers' property right licences, and whose objects include the granting of licences covering the performances of more than one performer.

(3) In this paragraph "performers' property right licences" means licences to do, or authorise the doing of, any of the things for which consent is required under section 182A, [182B, 182C or 182CA].

(4) References in this Chapter to licences or licensing schemes covering the performances of more than one performer do not include licences or schemes covering only—

(a) performances recorded in a single recording,

(b) performances recorded in more than one recording where

(i) the performers giving the performances are the same, or

(ii) the recordings are made by, or by employees of or commissioned by, a single individual, firm, company or group of companies.

For this purpose a group of companies means a holding company and its subsidiaries within the meaning of [section 1159 of the Companies Act 2006].

[(5) Schedule A1 confers powers to provide for the regulation of licensing bodies.]

Notes:

(1) In schedule heading, word "property" repealed by the Enterprise and Regulatory Reform Act 2013, Sch.22 para.3, with effect from April 25, 2013.

(2) In sub-para.(3), the words in square brackets substituted for the former words "182B or 182C" by the Copyright and Related Rights Regulations 2003 (SI 2003/2498), reg.7, with effect from October 31, 2003. For savings and transitional provisions, see Part 3 of those Regulations.

(3) The words in square brackets in subs.(4) substituted for the former words "section 736 of the Companies Act 1985" by the Companies Act 2006 (Consequential Amendments, Transitional Provisions and Savings) Order 2009 (SI 2009/1941) Sch.1 para.98(b), with effect from October 1, 2009.

(4) Sub-paragraph (5) inserted by the Enterprise and Regulatory Reform Act 2013, Sch.22, para.4, with effect from April 25, 2013.

[1A.—(1) The Secretary of State may by regulations provide for the grant of licences to do, or authorise the doing of, acts to which section 182, 182A, 182B, 182C, 182CA, 183 or 184 applies in respect of a performance, where—

(a) the performer's consent would otherwise be required under that section, but

(b) the right to authorise or prohibit the act qualifies as an orphan right under the regulations.

(2) The regulations may—

(a) specify a person or a description of persons authorised to grant licences, or

(b) provide for a person designated in the regulations to specify a person or a description of persons authorised to grant licences.

(3) The regulations must provide that, for a right to qualify as an orphan right, it is a requirement that the owner of the right has not been found after a diligent search made in accordance with the regulations.

(4) The regulations must provide for any licence—

(a) to have effect as if granted by the missing owner;

(b) not to give exclusive rights;

(c) not to be granted to a person authorised to grant licences.

(5) The regulations may apply in a case where it is not known whether a performer's right subsists, and references to a right, to a missing owner and to an interest of a missing owner are to be read as including references to a supposed right, owner or interest.]

Note: Paragrpahs 1A and 1B inserted by the Enterprise and Regulatory Reform Act 2013, Sch.22 para.5, with effect from April 25, 2013.

[1B.—(1) The Secretary of State may by regulations provide for a licensing body that applies to the Secretary of State under the regulations to be authorised to grant licences to do, or authorise the doing of, acts to which section 182, 182A, 182B, 182C, 182CA, 183 or 184 applies in respect of a performance, where the right to authorise or prohibit the act is not owned by the body or a person on whose behalf the body acts.

(2) An authorisation must specify the acts to which any of those sections applies that the licensing body is authorised to license.

(3) The regulations must provide for the rights owner to have a right to limit or exclude the grant of licences by virtue of the regulations.

(4) The regulations must provide for any licence not to give exclusive rights.]

Note: Paragrpahs 1A and 1B inserted by the Enterprise and Regulatory Reform Act 2013, Sch.22 para.5, with effect from April 25, 2013.

References and applications with respect to licensing schemes

2. Paragraphs 3 to 8 (references and applications with respect to licensing schemes) apply to licensing schemes operated by licensing bodies in relation to a performer's property rights which cover the performances of more than one performer, so far as they relate to licences for—

(a) copying a recording of the whole or any substantial part of a qualifying performance, [...]

[(aa) making such a recording available to the public in the way mentioned in section 182CA(1), or.]

(b) renting or lending copies of a recording to the public;

and in those paragraphs "licensing scheme" means a licensing scheme of any of those descriptions.

Notes:

(1) Sub-paragraph (aa) was inserted and the word "or" repealed from the end of sub-para(a) by the Copyright and Related Rights Regulations 2003 (SI 2003/2498), reg.7, with effect from October 31, 2003. For savings and transitional provisions, see Part 3 of those Regulations.

(2) In para.1(1) and (2) the words "this Chapter" subsituted for the former words "Part 2" (or "Part II") by the Performances (Moral Rights, etc.) Regulations 2006 (SI 2006/18), Sch, para.9, with effect from February 1, 2006.

(3) In para.1(4) the words "this Chapter" substituted by the former words "this Part" by the Performances (Moral Rights, etc.) Regulations 2006 (SI 2006/18), Sch. para.8, with effect from February 1, 2006.

Reference of proposed licensing scheme to tribunal

3.—(1) The terms of a licensing scheme proposed to be operated by a licensing body may be referred to the Copyright Tribunal by an organisation claiming to be representative of persons claiming that they require licences in cases of a description to which the scheme would apply, either generally or in relation to any description of case.

(2) The Tribunal shall first decide whether to entertain the reference, and may decline to do so on the ground that the reference is premature.

(3) If the Tribunal decides to entertain the reference it shall consider the matter referred and make such order, either confirming or varying the proposed scheme, either generally or so far as it relates to cases of the description to which the reference relates, as the Tribunal may determine to be reasonable in the circumstances.

(4) The order may be made so as to be in force indefinitely or for such period as the Tribunal may determine.

Reference of licensing scheme to tribunal

4.—(1) If while a licensing scheme is in operation a dispute arises between the operator of the scheme and—

(a) a person claiming that he requires a licence in a case of a description to which the scheme applies, or

(b) an organisation claiming to be representative of such persons,

that person or organisation may refer the scheme to the Copyright Tribunal in so far as it relates to cases of that description.

(2) A scheme which has been referred to the Tribunal under this paragraph shall remain in operation until proceedings on the reference are concluded.

(3) The Tribunal shall consider the matter in dispute and make such order, either confirming or varying the scheme so far as it relates to cases of the description to which the reference relates, as the Tribunal may determine to be reasonable in the circumstances.

(4) The order may be made so as to be in force indefinitely or for such period as the Tribunal may determine.

Further reference of scheme to tribunal

5.—(1) Where the Copyright Tribunal has on a previous reference of a licensing scheme under paragraph 3 or 4, or under this paragraph, made an order with respect to the scheme, then, while the order remains in force—

(a) the operator of the scheme,

(b) a person claiming that he requires a licence in a case of the description to which the order applies, or

(c) an organisation claiming to be representative of such persons,

may refer the scheme again to the Tribunal so far as it relates to cases of that description.

(2) A licensing scheme shall not, except with the special leave of the Tribunal, be referred again to the Tribunal in respect of the same description of cases—

(a) within twelve months from the date of the order on the previous reference, or

(b) if the order was made so as to be in force for 15 months or less, until the last three months before the expiry of the order.

(3) A scheme which has been referred to the Tribunal under this paragraph shall remain in operation until proceedings on the reference are concluded.

(4) The Tribunal shall consider the matter in dispute and make such order, either confirming, varying or further varying the scheme so far as it relates to cases of the description to which the reference relates, as the Tribunal may determine to be reasonable in the circumstances.

(5) The order may be made so as to be in force indefinitely or for such period as the Tribunal may determine.

Application for grant of licence in connection with licensing scheme

6.—(1) A person who claims, in a case covered by a licensing scheme, that the operator of the scheme has refused to grant him or procure the grant to him of a licence in accordance with the scheme, or has failed to do so within a reasonable time after being asked, may apply to the Copyright Tribunal.

(2) A person who claims, in a case excluded from a licensing scheme, that the operator of the scheme either—

(a) has refused to grant him a licence or procure the grant to him of a licence, or has failed to do so within a reasonable time of being asked, and that in the circumstances it is unreasonable that a licence should not be granted, or

(b) proposes terms for a licence which are unreasonable,

may apply to the Copyright Tribunal.

(3) A case shall be regarded as excluded from a licensing scheme for the purposes of sub-paragraph (2) if—

(a) the scheme provides for the grant of licences subject to terms excepting matters from the licence and the case falls within such an exception, or

(b) the case is so similar to those in which licences are granted under the scheme that it is unreasonable that it should not be dealt with in the same way.

(4) If the Tribunal is satisfied that the claim is well-founded, it shall make an order declaring that, in respect of the matters specified in the order, the applicant is entitled to a licence on such terms as the Tribunal may determine to be applicable in accordance with the scheme or, as the case may be, to be reasonable in the circumstances.

(5) The order may be made so as to be in force indefinitely or for such period as the Tribunal may determine.

Application for review of order as to entitlement to licence

7.—(1) Where the Copyright Tribunal has made an order under paragraph 6 that a person is entitled to a licence under a licensing scheme, the operator of the scheme or the original applicant may apply to the Tribunal to review its order.

(2) An application shall not be made, except with the special leave of the Tribunal—

(a) within twelve months from the date of the order, or of the decision on a previous application under this paragraph, or

(b) if the order was made so as to be in force for 15 months or less, or as a result of the decision on a previous application under this paragraph is due to expire within 15 months of that decision, until the last three months before the expiry date.

(3) The Tribunal shall on an application for review confirm or vary its order as the Tribunal may determine to be reasonable having regard to the terms applicable in accordance with the licensing scheme or, as the case may be, the circumstances of the case.

Effect of order of tribunal as to licensing scheme

8.—(1) A licensing scheme which has been confirmed or varied by the Copyright Tribunal—

(a) under paragraph 3 (reference of terms of proposed scheme), or

(b) under paragraph 4 or 5 (reference of existing scheme to Tribunal),

shall be in force or, as the case may be, remain in operation, so far as it relates to the description of case in respect of which the order was made, so long as the order remains in force.

(2) While the order is in force a person who in a case of a class to which the order applies—

(a) pays to the operator of the scheme any charges payable under the scheme in respect of a licence covering the case in question or, if the amount cannot be ascertained, gives an undertaking to the operator to pay them when ascertained, and

(b) complies with the other terms applicable to such a licence under the scheme,

shall be in the same position as regards infringement of performers' property rights as if he had at all material times been the holder of a licence granted by the rights owner in question in accordance with the scheme.

(3) The Tribunal may direct that the order, so far as it varies the amount of charges payable, has effect from a date before that on which it is made, but not earlier than the date on which the reference was made or, if later, on which the scheme came into operation.

If such a direction is made—

(a) any necessary repayments, or further payments, shall be made in respect of charges already paid, and

(b) the reference in sub-paragraph (2)(a) to the charges payable under the scheme shall be construed as a reference to the charges so payable by virtue of the order.

No such direction may be made where sub-paragraph (4) below applies.

(4) An order of the Tribunal under paragraph 4 or 5 made with respect to a scheme which is certified for any purpose under paragraph 16 has effect, so far as it varies the scheme by reducing the charges payable for licences, from the date on which the reference was made to the Tribunal.

(5) Where the Tribunal has made an order under paragraph 6 (order as to entitlement to licence under licensing scheme) and the order remains in force, the person in whose favour the order is made shall if he—

(a) pays to the operator of the scheme any charges payable in accordance with the order or, if the amount cannot be ascertained, gives an undertaking to pay the charges when ascertained, and

(b) complies with the other terms specified in the order,

be in the same position as regards infringement of performers' property rights as if he had at all material times been the holder of a licence granted by the rights owner in question on the terms specified in the order.

References and applications with respect to licensing by licensing bodies

9. Paragraphs 10 to 13 (references and applications with respect to licensing by licensing bodies) apply to licences relating to a performer's property rights which cover the performance of more than one performer granted by a licensing body otherwise than in pursuance of a licensing scheme, so far as the licences authorise—

(a) copying a recording of the whole or any substantial part of a qualifying performance, [...]

[(aa) making such a recording available to the public in the way mentioned in section 182CA(1), or.]

(b) renting or lending copies of a recording to the public;

and references in those paragraphs to a licence shall be construed accordingly.

Note: Sub-paragraph (aa) was inserted and the word "or" repealed from the end of sub-para(a) by the Copyright and Related Rights Regulations 2003 (SI 2003/2498), reg.7, with effect from October 31, 2003. For savings and transitional provisions, see Part 3 of those Regulations.

Reference to tribunal of proposed licence

10.—(1) The terms on which a licensing body proposes to grant a licence may be referred to the Copyright Tribunal by the prospective licensee.

(2) The Tribunal shall first decide whether to entertain the reference, and may decline to do so on the ground that the reference is premature.

(3) If the Tribunal decides to entertain the reference it shall consider the terms of the proposed licence and make such order, either confirming or varying the terms as it may determine to be reasonable in the circumstances.

(4) The order may be made so as to be in force indefinitely or for such period as the Tribunal may determine.

Reference to tribunal of expiring licence

11.—(1) A licensee under a licence which is due to expire, by effluxion of time or as a result of notice given by the licensing body, may apply to the Copyright Tribunal on the ground that it is unreasonable in the circumstances that the licence should cease to be in force.

(2) Such an application may not be made until the last three months before the licence is due to expire.

(3) A licence in respect of which a reference has been made to the Tribunal shall remain in operation until proceedings on the reference are concluded.

(4) If the Tribunal finds the application well-founded, it shall make an order declaring that the licensee shall continue to be entitled to the benefit of the licence on such terms as the Tribunal may determine to be reasonable in the circumstances.

(5) An order of the Tribunal under this paragraph may be made so as to be in force indefinitely or for such period as the Tribunal may determine.

Application for review of order as to licence

12.—(1) Where the Copyright Tribunal has made an order under paragraph 10 or 11, the licensing body or the person entitled to the benefit of the order may apply to the Tribunal to review its order.

(2) An application shall not be made, except with the special leave of the Tribunal—

(a) within twelve months from the date of the order or of the decision on a previous application under this paragraph, or

(b) if the order was made so as to be in force for 15 months or less, or as a result of the decision on a previous application under this paragraph is due to expire within 15 months of that decision, until the last three months before the expiry date.

(3) The Tribunal shall on an application for review confirm or vary its order as the Tribunal may determine to be reasonable in the circumstances.

Effect of order of tribunal as to licence

13.—(1) Where the Copyright Tribunal has made an order under paragraph 10 or 11 and the order remains in force, the person entitled to the benefit of the order shall if he—

(a) pays to the licensing body any charges payable in accordance with the order or, if the amount cannot be ascertained, gives an undertaking to pay the charges when ascertained, and

(b) complies with the other terms specified in the order,

be in the same position as regards infringement of performers' property rights as if he had at all material times been the holder of a licence granted by the rights owner in question on the terms specified in the order.

(2) The benefit of the order may be assigned—

(a) in the case of an order under paragraph 10, if assignment is not prohibited under the terms of the Tribunal's order; and

(b) in the case of an order under paragraph 11, if assignment was not prohibited under the terms of the original licence.

(3) The Tribunal may direct that an order under paragraph 10 or 11, or an order under paragraph 12 varying such an order, so far as it varies the amount of charges payable, has effect from a date before that on which it is made, but not earlier than the date on which the reference or application was made or, if later, on which the licence was granted or, as the case may be, was due to expire.

If such a direction is made—

(a) any necessary repayments, or further payments, shall be made in respect of charges already paid, and

(b) the reference in sub-paragraph (1)(a) to the charges payable in accordance with the order shall be construed, where the order is varied by a later order, as a reference to the charges so payable by virtue of the later order.

General considerations: unreasonable discrimination

14.—(1) In determining what is reasonable on a reference or application under this Schedule relating to a licensing scheme or licence, the Copyright Tribunal shall have regard to—

(a) the availability of other schemes, or the granting of other licences, to other persons in similar circumstances, and

(b) the terms of those schemes or licences,

and shall exercise its powers so as to secure that there is no unreasonable discrimination between licensees, or prospective licensees, under the scheme or licence to which the reference or application relates and licensees under other schemes operated by, or other licences granted by, the same person.

(2) This does not affect the Tribunal's general obligation in any case to have regard to all relevant circumstances.

Application to settle royalty or other sum payable for lending

15.—(1) An application to settle the royalty or other sum payable in pursuance of paragraph 14A of Schedule 2 (lending of certain recordings) may be made to the Copyright Tribunal by the owner of a performer's property rights or the person claiming to be treated as licensed by him.

(2) The Tribunal shall consider the matter and make such order as it may determine to be reasonable in the circumstances.

(3) Either party may subsequently apply to the Tribunal to vary the order, and the Tribunal shall consider the matter and make such order confirming or varying the original order as it may determine to be reasonable in the circumstances.

(4) An application under sub-paragraph (3) shall not, except with the special leave of the Tribunal, be made within twelve months from the date of the original order or of the order on a previous application under that sub-paragraph.

(5) An order under sub-paragraph (3) has effect from the date on which it is made or such later date as may be specified by the Tribunal.

Certification of licensing schemes

16.—(1) A person operating or proposing to operate a licensing scheme may apply to the Secretary of State to certify the scheme for the purposes of [paragraph [...], 14A or 20 of Schedule 2 ([...] lending of certain recordings [...]).]

(2) The Secretary of State shall by order made by statutory instrument certify the scheme if he is satisfied that it—

(a) enables the works to which it relates to be identified with sufficient certainty by persons likely to require licences, and

(b) sets out clearly the charges (if any) payable and the other terms on which licences will be granted.

(3) The scheme shall be scheduled to the other and the certification shall come into operation for the purposes of [the relevant paragraph] of Schedule 2—

(a) on such date, not less than eight weeks after the order is made, as may be specified in the order, or

(b) if the scheme is the subject of a reference under paragraph 3 (reference of proposed scheme), any later date on which the order of the Copyright Tribunal under that paragraph comes into force or the reference is withdrawn.

(4) A variation of the scheme is not effective unless a corresponding amendment of the order is made; and the Secretary of State shall make such an amendment in the case of a variation ordered by the Copyright Tribunal on a reference under paragraph 3, 4 or 5, and may do so in any other case if he thinks fit.

(5) The order shall be revoked if the scheme ceases to be operated and may be revoked if it appears to the Secretary of State that it is no longer being operated according to its terms.

Notes:

(1) In sub-para.(1), the words in square brackets substituted for the former words "para.14A of Sch.2 (lending of certain recordings)" and the words in sub-para.(3), the words in square brackets substituted for the former words "para.14A" by the Copyright and Related Rights Regulations 2003 (SI 2003/2498), Sch.1, para.17, with effect from October 31, 2003. For savings and transitional provisions, see Part 3 of those Regulations.

(2) In subs.(1) figure "6," and words "recording of broadcasts by educational establishments," repealed by the Copyright and Rights in Performances (Research, Education, Libraries and Archives) Regulations 2014 (SI 2014/1372), Sch para.9, with effect from June 1, 2014 at 00.02.

(3) In subs.(1) words ", provision of sub-titled copies of broadcast" repealed by the Copyright and Rights in Performances (Disability) Regulations 2014 (SI 2014/1384), Sch. para.6, with effect from June 1, 2014 at 00.01.

Powers exercisable in consequence of competition report

17.—[(1) Sub-paragraph (1A) applies where whatever needs to be remedied, mitigated or prevented by the Secretary of State, the Competition Commission or (as the case may be) the Office of Fair Trading under section 12(5) of the Competition Act 1980 or section 41(2), 55(2), 66(6), 75(2), 83(2), 138(2), 147(2) or 160(2) of, or paragraph 5(2) or 10(2) of Schedule 7 to, the Enterprise Act 2002 (powers to take remedial action following references to the Commission in connection with public bodies and certain other persons, mergers or market investigations etc.) consists of or includes—

(a) conditions in licences granted by the owner of a performer's property rights restricting the use to which a recording may be put by the licensee or the right of the owner to grant other licenses, or

(b) a refusal of an owner of a performer's property rights to grant licences on reasonable terms.

(1A) The powers conferred by Schedule 8 to the Enterprise Act 2002 include power to cancel or modify those conditions and, instead or in addition, to provide that licences in respect of the performer's property rights shall be available as of right.

(2) The references to anything permitted by Schedule 8 to the Enterprise Act 2002 in section 12(5A) of the Competition Act 1980 and in sections 75(4)(a), 83(4)(a), 84(2)(a), 89(1), 160(4)(a), 161(3)(a) and 164(1) of, and paragraphs 5, 10 and 11 of Schedule 7 to, the Act of 2002 shall be construed accordingly.]

(3) [The Secretary of State, the Competition Commission or (as the case may be) the Office of Fair Trading] shall only exercise the powers available by virtue of this paragraph if he [or it] is satisfied that to do so does not contravene any Convention relating to performers' rights to which the United Kingdom is a party.

(4) The terms of a licence available by virtue of this paragraph shall, in default of agreement, be settled by the Copyright Tribunal on an application by the person requiring the licence; and terms so settled shall authorise the licensee to do everything in respect of which a licence is so available.

(5) Where the terms of a licence are settled by the Tribunal, the licence has effect from the date on which the application to the Tribunal was made.]

Notes:

(1) Sub-paragraphs (1) and (2) substituted and in sub-para.(3) the words in the first set of square brackets substituted for the former words "A Minister" and the words in the second set of square brackets inserted by the Enterprise Act 2002 (c.40), Sch.25, para.18 with effect from June 20, 2003. Subsections (1) and (2) formerly provided:

"*(1) Where the matters specified in a report of the [Competition Commission] as being those which in the Commission's opinion operate, may be expected to operate or have operated against the public interest include—*

(a) *conditions in licences granted by the owner of a performer's property rights restricting the use to which a recording may be put by the licensee or the right of the owner to grant other licences, or*

(b) *a refusal of an owner of a performer's property rights to grant licences on reasonable terms,*

the powers conferred by Part I of Schedule 8 to the Fair Trading Act 1973 (powers exercisable for purpose of remedying or preventing adverse effects specified in report of Commission) include power to cancel or modify those conditions and, instead or in addition, to provide that licences in respect of the performer's property rights shall be available as of right.

(2) The references in sections 56(2) and 73(2) of that Act, and [section 12(5)] of the Competition Act 1980, to the powers specified in that Part of that Schedule shall be construed accordingly."

(2) The words in square brackets in the former sub-para.(1) substituted for the original words "Monopolies and Mergers Commission" by the Competition Act 1998 (Competition Commission) Transitional, Consequential and Supplemental Provisions Order 1999 (SI 1999/506), art.23, with effect from April 1, 1999.

(3) The words in square brackets in the former sub-para.(2) substituted for the original words "sections 10(2)(b) and 12(5)" by the Competition Act 1998 (Transitional, Consequential and Supplemental Provisions) Order 2000 (SI 2000/311), with effect from March 1, 2000.

Note: This Schedule was inserted by the Copyright and Related Rights Regulations 1996 (SI 1996/2967), with effect from December 1, 1996. For savings and transitional provisions, see Part III of those Regulations.

Section 272.   SCHEDULE 3

[...]

Note: Schedule 3 makes minor and consequential amendments of the Registered Designs Act 1949. That Act is printed as amended at B8.i, below.

Section 273.   SCHEDULE 4
[...]

Note: Schedule 4 prints the Registered Designs Act 1949 as amended. That Act is reprinted at B8.1, below.

Section 295.   SCHEDULE 5
[...]

Note: Schedule 5 makes miscellaneous amendments to the Patents Act 1949 and the Patents Act 1977 and is not reprinted.

Section 296ZE.   [SCHEDULE 5A

PERMITTED ACTS TO WHICH SECTION 296ZE APPLIES

PART 1

COPYRIGHT EXCEPTIONS

section 29 (research and private study)
[section 29A (copies for text and data analysis for non-commercial research)]
[section 31A [(disabled persons: copies of works for personal use)]
section 31B [(making and supply of accessible copies by authorised bodies)]
[section 31BA (making and supply of intermediate copies by authorised bodies)]]]
[section 32 (illustration for instruction)]
section 35 (recording by educational establishments of broadcasts)
section 36 (reprographic copying by educational establishments of passages from
     published works)
[section 36 (copying and use of extracts of works by educational establishments)]
[section 41 (copying by librarians: supply of single copies to other libraries)]
section 42 (copying by librarians etc: replacement copies of works)
section 42A (copying by librarians: single copies of published works)
section 43 (copying by librarians or archivists: single copies of unpublished
     works)]
[...]
section 44 (copy of work required to be made as condition of export)
section 45 (Parliamentary and judicial proceedings)
section 46 (Royal Commissions and statutory inquiries)
section 47 (material open to public inspection or on official register)
section 48 (material communicated to the Crown in the course of public business)
section 49 (public records)
section 50 (acts done under statutory authority)
section 61 (recordings of folksongs)
section 68 (incidental recording for purposes of broadcast)
section 69 (recording for purposes of supervision and control of broadcasts)
section 70 (recording for purposes of time-shifting)
section 71 (photographs of broadcasts)
[...]
[section 75 (recording of broadcast for archival purposes)]
[...]

Note: Amended by the Copyright and Rights in Performances (Research, Education, Libraries and Archives) Regulations 2014 (SI 2014/1372), Sch. para.10(2), with effect from June 1, 2014 at 00.02. Further amended by the Copyright and Rights in Performances (Disability) Regulations 2014 (SI 2014/1384), Sch para.7(2), with effect from June 1, 2014 at 00.01.

PART 2

RIGHTS IN PERFORMANCES EXCEPTIONS

[paragraph 1C of Schedule 2 (research and private study)]

[paragraph 1D of Schedule 2 (copies for text and data analysis for non-commercial research)]
[paragraph 3A of Schedule 2 (disabled persons: copies of recordings for personal use)]
[paragraph 3B of Schedule 2 (making and supply of accessible copies by authorised bodies)]
[paragraph 3C of Schedule 2 (making and supply of intermediate copies by authorised bodies)]
[paragraph 4 of Schedule 2 (illustration for instruction)]
[paragraph 6 of Schedule 2 (recording by educational establishments of broadcasts)]
[paragraph 6ZA of Schedule 2 (copying and use of extracts of recordings by educational establishments)]
[paragraph 6D of Schedule 2 (copying by librarians: supply of single copies to other libraries)]
[paragraph 6E of Schedule 2 (copying by librarians etc: replacement copies of recordings)]
[paragraph 6F of Schedule 2 (copying by librarians: single copies of published recordings)]
[paragraph 6G of Schedule 2 (copying by librarians or archivists: single copies of unpublished recordings)]
paragraph 7 of Schedule 2 (copy of work required to be made as condition of export)
paragraph 8 of Schedule 2 (Parliamentary and judicial proceedings)
paragraph 9 of Schedule 2 (Royal Commissions and statutory inquiries)
paragraph 10 of Schedule 2 (public records)
paragraph 11 of Schedule 2 (acts done under statutory authority)
paragraph 14 of Schedule 2 (recordings of folksongs)
paragraph 16 of Schedule 2 (incidental recording for purposes of broadcast)
paragraph 17 of Schedule 2 (recordings for purposes of supervision and control of broadcasts)
paragraph 17A of Schedule 2 (recording for the purposes of time-shifting)
paragraph 17B of Schedule 2 (photographs of broadcasts)
[...]
paragraph 21 of Schedule 2 (recording of broadcast for archival purposes)

Note: Amended by the Copyright and Rights in Performances (Research, Education, Libraries and Archives) Regulations 2014 (SI 2014/1372), Sch. para.10(3), with effect from June 1, 2014 at 00.02. Further amended by the Copyright and Rights in Performances (Disability) Regulations 2014 (SI 2014/1384), Sch. para.7(3), with effect from June 1, 2014 at 00.01.

PART 3

DATABASE RIGHT EXCEPTIONS

Regulation 20 of and Schedule 1 to the Copyright and Rights in Databases Regulations 1997 (SI 1997/3032)]

Note: Schedule 5A was inserted by the Copyright and Related Rights Regulations 2003 (SI 2003/2498), Sch.3, with effect from October 31, 2003. For savings and transitional provisions, see Part 3 of those Regulations.

Section 301.　　　　　　　　　　SCHEDULE 6

PROVISIONS FOR THE BENEFIT OF THE HOSPITAL FOR SICK CHILDREN

Interpretation

1.—(1) In this Schedule—
　　"the Hospital" means The Hospital for Sick Children, Great Ormond Street, London,
　　"the trustees" means the special trustees appointed for the Hospital under the National Health Service Act 1977 [or the National Health Service Act 2006]; and
　　"the work" means the play "Peter Pan" by Sir James Matthew Barrie.
　　(2) Expressions used in this Schedule which are defined for the purposes of Part I of this Act (copyright) have the same meaning as in that Part.

Note: The words in square brackets in the definition of "the trustees" in Sch.6 para.1(1) inserted by the National Health Service (Consequential Provisions) Act 2006 (c.43), Sch.1 para.114, with effect from March 1, 2007.

Entitlement to royalty

2.—(1) The trustees are entitled, subject to the following provisions of this Schedule, to a royalty in respect of any public performance, commercial publication, [or communication to the public] of the whole or any substantial part of the work or an adaptation of it.

(2) Where the trustees are or would be entitled to a royalty, another form of remuneration may be agreed.

Note: The words in square brackets in sub-para.(1) substituted for the former words ", broadcasting or inclusion in a cable programme service" by the Copyright and Related Rights Regulations 2003 (SI 2003/2498), Sch.1, para.6, with effect from October 31, 2003. For savings and transitional provisions, see Part 3 of those Regulations.

Exceptions

3. No royalty is payable in respect of—
    (a) anything which immediately before copyright in the work expired on 31st December 1987 could lawfully have been done without the licence, or further licence, of the trustees as copyright owners, or
    (b) anything which if copyright still subsisted in the work could, by virtue of any provision of Chapter III of Part I of this Act (acts permitted notwithstanding copyright), be done without infringing copyright.

Saving

4. No royalty is payable in respect of anything done in pursuance of arrangements made before the passing of this Act.

Procedure for determining amount payable

5.—(1) In default of agreement application may be made to the Copyright Tribunal which shall consider the matter and make such order regarding the royalty or other remuneration to be paid as it may determine to be reasonable in the circumstances.

(2) Application may subsequently be made to the Tribunal to vary its order, and the Tribunal shall consider the matter and make such order confirming or varying the original order as it may determine to be reasonable in the circumstances.

(3) An application for variation shall not, except with the special leave of the Tribunal, be made within twelve months from the date of the original order or of the order on a previous application for variation.

(4) A variation order has effect from the date on which it is made or such later date as may be specified by the Tribunal.

[(5) The provisions of Chapter VIII of Part I (general provisions relating to the Copyright Tribunal) apply in relation to the Tribunal when exercising any jurisdiction under this paragraph.]

Note: Sub-paragraph (5) was inserted by the Copyright and Related Rights Regulations 1996 (SI 1996/2967), with effect from December 1, 1996. For savings and transitional provisions, see Part III of those Regulations.

Sums received to be held on trust

6. The sums received by the trustees by virtue of this Schedule, after deduction of any relevant expenses, shall be held by them on trust for the purposes of the Hospital.

Right only for the benefit of the Hospital

7.—(1) The right of the trustees under this Schedule may not be assigned and shall cease if the trustees purport to assign or charge it.

(2) The right may not be the subject of an order under [section 213 of the National Health Service Act 2006 or section 161 of the National Health Service (Wales) Act 2006] (transfers of trust property by order of the Secretary of State) and shall cease if the Hospital ceases to have a separate identity or ceases to have purposes which include the care of sick children.

(3) Any power of Her Majesty, the court (within the meaning of [the Charities Act 2011]) or any other person to alter the trusts of a charity is not exercisable in relation to the trust created by this Schedule.

Notes:
    (1) The reference to the Charities Act 2011 was substituted, subject to savings and

transitional provisions, for the reference to the Charities Act 1993 by the Charities Act 2011 Sch.7 para.52 with effect from March 14, 2012 (for savings and transitional provisions, see Sch.8 of the Act).

(2) The words in square brackets in Sch.6 para.7(2) substituted by the National Health Service (Consequential Provisions) Act 2006 (c.43), Sch.1 para.114, with effect from March 1, 2007.

Section 303(1).   SCHEDULE 7

CONSEQUENTIAL AMENDMENTS: GENERAL

British Mercantile Marine Uniform Act 1919 (c. 62)

1. For section 2 of the British Mercantile Marine Uniform Act 1919 (copyright in distinctive marks of uniform) substitute—

Right in registered design of distinctive marks of uniform

"**2.** The right of the Secretary of State in any design forming part of the British mercantile marine uniform which is registered under the Registered Designs Act 1949 is not limited to the period prescribed by section 8 of that Act but shall continue to subsist so long as the design remains on the register.".

Chartered Associations (Protection of Names and Uniforms) Act 1925 (c. 26)

2. In section 1(5) of the Chartered Associations (Protection of Names and Uniforms) Act 1926 for "the copyright in respect thereof" substitute "the right in the registered design".

Patents, Designs, Copyright and Trade Marks (Emergency) Act 1939 (c. 107)

3.—(1) The Patents, Designs, Copyright and Trade Marks (Emergency) Act 1939 is amended as follows.

(2) In section 1 (effect of licence where owner is enemy or enemy subject)—

   (a) in subsection (1) after "a copyright" and "the copyright" insert "or design right";

   (b) in subsection (2) after "the copyright" insert "or design right" and for "or copyright" substitute, "copyright or design right".

(3) In section 2 (power of comptroller to grant licences)—

   (a) in subsection (1) after "a copyright", "the copyright" (twice) and "the said copyright" insert "or design right" and for "or copyright" (twice) substitute, ",copyright or design right";

   (b) in subsections (2) and (3) for ", or copyright" substitute ", copyright or design right";

   (c) in subsection (4) and in subsection (5) (twice), after "the copyright" insert "or design right";

   (d) in subsection (8)(c) for "or work in which copyright subsists" substitute "work in which copyright subsists or design in which design right subsists".

(4) In section 5 (effect of war on international arrangements)—

   (a) in subsection (1) for "section twenty-nine of the Copyright Act 1911" substitute "section 159 or 256 of the Copyright, Designs and Patents Act 1988 (countries enjoying reciprocal copyright or design right protection)";

   (b) in subsection (2) after "copyright" (four times) insert "or design right" and for "the Copyright Act 1911" (twice) substitute "Part I or III of the Copyright, Designs and Patents Act 1988".

(5) In section 10(1) (interpretation) omit the definition of "copyright", and for the definitions of "design", "invention", "patent" and "patentee" substitute—

     "'design' has in reference to a registered design the same meaning as in the Registered Designs Act 1949, and in reference to design right the same meaning as in Part III of the Copyright, Designs and Patents Act 1988;

     'invention' and 'patent' have the same meaning as in the Patents Act 1977.".

Crown Proceedings Act 1947 (c. 44)

4.—(1) In the Crown Proceedings Act 1947 for section 3 (provisions as to industrial property) substitute—

Infringement of intellectual property rights

"**3.**—(1) Civil proceedings lie against the Crown for an infringement committed by a servant or agent of the Crown, with the authority of the Crown, of—

(a) a patent,

(b) a registered trade mark or registered service mark,

(c) the right in a registered design,

(d) design right, or

(e) copyright;

but save as provided by this subsection no proceedings lie against the Crown by virtue of this Act in respect of an infringement of any of those rights.

(2) Nothing in this section, or any other provision of this Act, shall be construed as affecting—

(a) the rights of a government department under section 55 of the Patents Act 1977, Schedule 1 to the Registered Designs Act 1949 or section 240 of the Copyright, Designs and Patents Act 1988 (Crown use of patents and designs),

(b) the rights of the Secretary of State under section 22 of the Patents Act 1977 or section 5 of the Registered Designs Act 1949 (security of information prejudicial to defence or public safety).".

(2) In the application of sub-paragraph (1) to Northern Ireland—

(a) the reference to the Crown Proceedings Act 1947 is to that Act as it applies to the Crown in right of Her Majesty's Government in Northern Ireland, as well as to the Crown in right of Her Majesty's Government in the United Kingdom, and

(b) in the substituted section 3 as it applies in relation to the Crown in right of Her Majesty's Government in Northern Ireland, subsection (2)(b) shall be omitted.

Patents Act 1949 (c. 87)

5. In section 47 of the Patents Act 1949 (rights of third parties in respect of Crown use of patent), in the closing words of subsection (1) (which relate to the use of models or documents), after "copyright" insert "or design right".

Public Libraries (Scotland) Act 1955 (c. 27)

6. […]

Note: This paragraph was repealed by the Copyright and Related Rights Regulations 1996 (SI 1996/2967), with effect from December 1, 1996. The paragraph formerly read:

"Public Libraries (Scotland) Act 1955 (c. 27)

6. *In section 4 of the Public Libraries (Scotland) Act 1955 (extension of lending power of public libraries), make the existing provision subsection (1) and after it add—*

"(2) *The provisions of Part I of the Copyright, Designs and Patents Act 1988 (copyright) relating to the rental of copies of sound recordings, films and computer programs apply to any lending by a statutory library authority of copies of such works, whether or not a charge is made for that facility.".*"

For savings and transitional provisions, see Part III of those Regulations.

London County Council (General Powers) Act 1958 (c. xxi)

7. In section 36 of the London County Council (General Powers) Act 1958 (power as to libraries: provision and repair of things other than books) for subsection (5) substitute—

"(5) Nothing in this section shall be construed as authorising an infringement of copyright.".

Public Libraries and Museums Act 1964 (c. 75)

8. […]

Note: This paragraph was repealed by the Copyright and Related Rights Regulations 1996 (SI 1996/2967), with effect from December 1, 1996. The paragraph formerly read:

"Public Libraries and Museums Act 1964 (c. 75)"

8. *In section 8 of the Public Libraries and Museums Act 1964 (restrictions on charges for library facilities), after section (5) add—*

"(6) *The provisions of Part I of the Copyright, Designs and Patents Act 1988 (copyright) relating to the rental of copies of sound recordings, films and computer programs apply to any lending by a library authority of copies of such works, whether or not a charge is made for that facility.".".*

For savings and transitional provisions, see Part III of those Regulations

Marine, &c., Broadcasting (Offences) Act 1967 (c. 41)

9. [...]

Note: Schedule 7 para.9 was repealed by the Wireless Telegraphy Act 2006 (c.36), Sch.9 Pt 1, with effect from February 8, 2007. The paragraph formerly read:

"Marine, &c., Broadcasting (Offences) Act 1967 (c. 41)"

9. *In section 5 of the Marine, &c., Broadcasting (Offences) Act 1967 (provision of material for broadcasting by pirate radio stations)—*

(a) *in subsection (3)(a) for the words from "cinematograph film" to "in the record" substitute "film or sound recording with intent that a broadcast of it"; and*

(b) *in subsection (6) for the words from "and references" to the end substitute "and "film", "sound recording", "literary, dramatic or musical work" and "artistic work" have the same meaning as in Part I of the Copyright, Designs and Patents Act 1988 (copyright)".".*

Medicines Act 1968 (c. 67)

10.—(1) Section 92 of the Medicines Act 1968 (scope of provisions restricting promotion of sales of medicinal products) is amended as follows.

(2) In subsection (1) (meaning of "advertisement") for the words from "or by the exhibition" to "service" substitute "or by means of a photograph, film, sound recording, broadcast or cable programme,".

(3) [...]

Note: Subparagraph (3) was repealed by the Copyright and Related Rights Regulations 2003 (SI 2003/2498), Sch.2, with effect from October 31, 2003. For savings and transitional provisions, see Part 3 of those Regulations. Subparagraph (3) formerly provided:

"(3) *In subsection (2) (exception for the spoken word)—*

(a) *in paragraph (a) omit the words from "or embodied" to "film"; and*

(b) *in paragraph (b) for the words from "by way of" to the end substitute "or included in a cable programme service".*

(4) *For subsection (6) substitute—*

"(6) *In this section 'film', 'sound recording', 'broadcast', 'cable programme', 'cable programme service', and related expressions, have the same meaning as in Part I of the Copyright, Designs and Patents Act 1988 (copyright).".".*

Post Office Act 1969 (c. 48)

11. In Schedule 10 to the Post Office Act 1969 (special transitional provisions relating to use of patents and registered designs), in the closing words of paragraphs 8(1) and 18(1) (which relate to the use of models and documents), after "copyright" insert "or design right".

Merchant Shipping Act 1970 (c. 36)

12. *In section 87 of the Merchant Shipping Act 1970 (merchant navy uniform), for subsection (4) substitute—*

"(4) *Where any design forming part of the merchant navy uniform has beenregistered under the Registered Designs Act 1949 and the Secretary of State is the proprietor of the design, his right in the design is not limited to the period prescribed by section 8 of that Act but shall continue to subsist so long as the design remains registered.".*

Note: Section 87 of the Merchant Shipping Act 1970 was repealed by the Merchant Shipping (Registration, etc.) Act 1993, s.8(4), Sch.5.

Taxes Management Act 1970 (c. 9)

13. In section 16 of the Taxes Management Act 1970 (returns to be made in respect of certain payments)—

    (a) in subsection (1)(c), and

    (b) in subsection (2)(b),

for "or public lending right" substitute ", public lending right, right in a registered design or design right".

Tribunals and Inquiries Act 1971 (c. 62)

14. [...]

Note: Paragraph 14 was repealed by the Tribunals and Inquiries Act 1992, s.18(2), Sch.4. The paragraph previously read:

"Tribunals and Inquiries Act 1971 (c. 62)

14. *In Part I of Schedule 1 to the Tribunals and Inquiries Act 1971 (tribunals under direct supervision of Council on Tribunals) renumber the entry inserted by the Data Protection Act 1984 as "5B" and before it insert—*
Copyright. 5A The Copyright Tribunal."

Fair Trading Act 1973 (c. 41)

15. [...]

Note: Paragraph 15 was repealed by the Enterprise Act 2002 (c.40), Sch.26 with effect from June 20, 2003 (Enterprise Act 2002 (Commencement No.3, Transitional and Transitory Provisions and Savings) Order 2003 (SI 2003/1397)). The paragraph formerly provided:

"15. *In Schedule 4 to the Fair Trading Act 1973 (excluded services), for paragraph 10 (services of patent agents) substitute—*

"10. *The services of registered patent agents (within the meaning of Part V of the Copyright, Designs and Patents Act 1988) in their capacity as such.";*

and in paragraph 10A (services of European patent attorneys) for " section 84(7) of the Patents Act 1977" substitute " Part V of the Copyright, Designs and Patents Act 1988"."

House of Commons Disqualification Act 1975 (c. 24)

16. In Part II of Schedule 1 to the House of Commons Disqualification Act 1975 (bodies of which all members are disqualified), at the appropriate place insert "The Copyright Tribunal".

Northern Ireland Assembly Disqualification Act 1975 (c. 25)

17. In Part II of Schedule 1 to the Northern Ireland Assembly Disqualification Act 1975 (bodies of which all members are disqualified), at the appropriate place insert "The Copyright Tribunal".

Restrictive Trade Practices Act 1976 (c. 34)

18.—(1) The Restrictive Trade Practices Act 1976 is amended as follows.

(2) In Schedule 1 (excluded services) for paragraph 10 (services of patent agents) substitute—

"10. The services of registered patent agents (within the meaning of Part V of the Copyright, Designs and Patents Act 1988) in their capacity as such.];"

and in paragraph 10A (services of European patent attorneys) for "section 84(7) of the Patents Act 1977" substitute "Part V of the Copyright, Designs and Patents Act 1988".

(3) In Schedule 3 (excepted agreements), after paragraph 5A insert—

[Design right

5B.—(1) This Act does not apply to—

(a) a licence granted by the owner or a licensee of any design right,

(b) an assignment of design right, or

(c) an agreement for such a licence or assignment,

if the licence, assignment or agreement is one under which no such restrictions as are described in section 6(1) above are accepted, or no such information provisions as are described in section 7(1) above are made, except in respect of articles made to the design; but subject to the following provisions.

(2) Sub-paragraph (1) does not exclude a licence, assignment or agreement which is a design pooling agreement or is granted or made (directly or indirectly) in pursuance of a design pooling agreement.

(3) In this paragraph a 'design pooling agreement' means an agreement—

(a) to which the parties are or include at least three persons (the "principal parties") each of whom has an interest in one or more design rights, and

(b) by which each principal party agrees, in respect of design right in which he has, or may during the currency of the agreement acquire, an interest to grant an interest (directly or indirectly) to one or more of the other principal parties, or to one or more of those parties and to other persons.

(4) In this paragraph—

'assignment', in Scotland, means assignation; and

'interest' means an interest as owner or licensee of design right.

(5) This paragraph applies to an interest held by or granted to more than one person jointly as it they were one person.

(6) References in this paragraph to the granting of an interest to a person indirectly are to its being granted to a third person for the purpose of enabling him to make a grant to the person in question].

Resale Prices Act 1976 (c. 53)

19. In section 10(4) of the Resale Prices Act 1976 (patented articles: articles to be treated in same way), in paragraph (a) after "protected" insert "by design right or".

Patents Act 1977 (c. 37)

20. In section 57 of the Patents Act 1977 (rights of third parties in respect of Crown use of patent), in the closing words of subsection (1) (which relate to the use of models or documents), after "copyright" insert "or design right".

21. In section 105 of the Patents Act 1977 (privilege in Scotland for communications relating to patent proceedings), omit "within the meaning of section 104 above", make the existing text subsection (1) and after it insert—

"(2) in this section—

"patent proceedings" means proceedings under this Act or any of the relevant conventions, before the court, the comptroller or the relevant convention court, whether contested or uncontested and including an application for a patent; and

"the relevant conventions" means the European Patent Convention, the Community Patent Convention and the Patent Co-operation Treaty.".

22. In section 123(7) of the Patents Act 1977 (publication of case reports by the comptroller)—

(a) for "and registered designs" substitute "registered designs or design right",

(b) for "and copyright" substitute ", copyright and design right".

23. In section 130(1) of the Patents Act 1977 (interpretation), in the definition of "court", for paragraph (a) substitute—

"(a) as respects England and Wales, the High Court or any patents county court having jurisdiction by virtue of an order under section 287 of the Copyright, Designs and Patents Act 1988;".

Unfair Contract Terms Act 1977 (c. 50)

24. In paragraph 1 of Schedule 1 to the Unfair Contract Terms Act 1977 (scope of main provisions: excluded contracts), in paragraph (c) (contracts relating to grant or transfer of interest in intellectual property) after "copyright" insert "or design right".

Judicature (Northern Ireland) Act 1978 (c. 23)

25. In section 94A of the Judicature (Northern Ireland) Act 1978 (withdrawal of privilege against self-incrimination in certain proceedings relating to intellectual property), in subsection (5) (meaning of "intellectual property") after "copyright" insert "or design right".

Capital Gains Tax Act 1979 (c. 14)

26. [...]

Note: Paragraph 26 was repealed by the Taxation of Chargeable Gains Act 1992, section 290, Schedule 12. The paragraph formerly provided:

"Capital Gains Tax Act 1979 (c. 14)

26. *In section 18(4) of the Capital Gains Tax Act 1979 (situation of certain assets for purposes of Act), for paragraph (h) (intellectual property) substitute—*

"(ha) *patents, trade marks, service marks and registered designs are situated where they are registered, and if registered in more than one register, where each register is situated, and rights or licences to use a patent, trade mark, service mark or registered design are situated in the United Kingdom if they or any right derived from them are exercisable in the United Kingdom,*

(hb) *copyright, design right and franchises, and rights or licences to use any copyright work or design in which design right subsists, are situated in the United Kingdom if they or any right derived from them are exercisable in the United Kingdom,"."*

British Telecommunications Act 1981 (c. 38)

27. [...]

Note: Paragraph 27 was repealed by the Communications Act 2003 (c.21), Sch.19 with effect from December 29, 2003 (Office of Communications Act 2002 (Commencement No.3) and Communications Act 2003 (Commencement No.2) Order 2003 (SI 2003/3142)). This paragraph formerly provided:

"27. *In Schedule 5 to the British Telecommunications Act 1981 (special transitional provisions relating to use of patents and registered designs), in the closing words of paragraphs 9(1) and 19(1) (which relate to the use of models and documents), after "copyright" insert "or design right"."*

[Senior Courts Act 1981] (c. 54)

28.—(1) The [Senior Courts Act 1981] is amended as follows.

(2) In section 72 (withdrawal of privilege against self-incrimination in certain proceedings relating to intellectual property), in subsection (5) (meaning of "intellectual property") after "copyright" insert ", design right".

(3) In Schedule 1 (distribution of business in the High Court), in paragraph 1(i) (business assigned to the Chancery Division: causes and matters relating to certain intellectual property) for "or copyright" substitute ", copyright or design right".

Note: In para.28 and the heading preceding it the words in square brackets substituted for the former words "Supreme Court Act 1981" by the Constitutional Reform Act 2005 Sch.11 para.1, with effect from October 1, 2009.

Broadcasting Act 1981 (c. 68)

29. [...]

Note: Paragraph 29 was repealed by s.203(3) of and Sch.21 to the Broadcasting Act 1990 as provided by the Broadcasting Act 1990 (Commencement No.1 and Transitional Provisions) Order (SI 1990/2347). The paragraph formerly read:

"Broadcasting Act 1981 (c. 68)

29.—(1) *The Broadcasting Act 1981 is amended as follows.*

(2) *In section 4 (general duties of IBA as regards programmes) for subsection (7) substitute—*

"(7) For the purpose of maintaining supervision and control over the programmes (including advertisements) broadcast by them the Authority may make and use recordings of those programmes or any part of them.".

(3) In section 20(9), omit paragraph (a)."

Cable and Broadcasting Act 1984 (c. 46)

30. [...]

Note: Paragraph 30 was repealed by s.203(3) of and Sch.21 to the Broadcasting Act 1990 as provided by the Broadcasting Act 1990 (Commencement No.1 and Transitional Provisions) Order (SI 1990/2347). The paragraph formerly read:

"Cable and Broadcasting Act 1984 (c. 46)

30. *The Cable and Broadcasting Act 1984 is amended as follows.*

(2) In section 8, omit subsection (8).

(3) In section 49 (power of Secretary of State to give directions in the public interest), for subsection (7) substitute—

> *"(7) For the purposes of this section the place from which a broadcast is made is, in the case of a satellite transmission, the place from which the signals carrying the broadcast are transmitted to the satellite.".*

(4) In section 56(2) (interpretation) omit the definition of "the 1956 Act"."

Companies Act 1985 (c. 6)

31.—*(1) Part XII of the Companies Act 1985 (registration of charges) is amended as follows.*

(2) In section 396 (registration of charges in England and Wales: charges which must be registered), in subsection (1)(j) for the words from "on a patent" to the end substitute "or on any intellectual property", and after subsection (3) insert—

> *"(3A) The following are 'intellectual property' for the purposes of this section—*
>
> > *(a) any patent, trade mark, service mark, registered design, copyright or design right;*
> >
> > *(b) any licence under or in respect of any such right."*

(3) In section 410 (registration of charges in Scotland: charges which must be registered), in subsection (3)(c) (incorporeal moveable property) after sub-paragraph (vi) insert—

> > *"(vii) a registered design or a licence in respect of such a design,*
> >
> > *(viii) a design right or a licence under a design right,".*

Note: Paragraph 31 is prospectively repealed by the Companies Act 1989 s.212, Sch.24 on a day to be appointed. Consequential amendments to Part XII of the Companies Act 1985 are made by the Companies Act 1989.

Law Reform (Miscellaneous Provisions) (Scotland) Act 1985 (c. 73)

32. In section 15 of the Law Reform (Miscellaneous Provisions) (Scotland) Act 1985 (withdrawal of privilege against self-incrimination in certain proceedings relating to intellectual property), in subsection (5) (meaning of "intellectual property") after "copyright" insert "or design right".

Atomic Energy Authority Act 1986 (c. 3)

33. In section 8(2) of the Atomic Energy Authority Act 1986 (powers of Authority as to exploitation of research: meaning of "intellectual property"), after "copyrights" insert ", design rights".

Education and Libraries (Northern Ireland) Order 1986 (SI 1986/594 (N.I.3))

34. [...]

Note: This paragraph was repealed by the Copyright and Related Rights Regulations 1996 (SI 1996/2967), with effect from December 1, 1996. For savings and transitional provisions, see Part III of those Regulations. The paragraph formerly read:

"Education and Libraries (Northern Ireland) Order 1986 (SI 1986/594 (N.I.3))

34. *In Article 77 of the Education and Libraries (Northern Ireland) Order 1986 (charges for library services), after paragraph (2) add—*

"(3) The provisions of Part I of the Copyright, Designs and Patents Act 1988 (copyright) relating to the rental of copies of sound recordings, films and computer programs apply to any lending by a board of copies of such works, whether or not a charge is made for that facility.".."

Companies (Northern Ireland) Order 1986 (SI 1986/1032 (N.I.6)

35. [...]

Note: Paragraph 35 was repealed by the Companies Act 2006 (Consequential Amendments, Transitional Provisions and Savings) Order 2009 (SI 2009/1941) Sch.2 with effect from October 1, 2009. The paragraph previously read:

"Companies (Northern Ireland) Order 1986 (SI 1986/1032 (N.I.6)

35. *In Article 403 of the Companies (Northern Ireland) Order 1986 (registration of charges: charges which must be registered), in paragraph (1)(j) for the words from "on a patent" to the end substitute "or on any intellectual property", and after paragraph (3) insert—*

> *"(3A) The following are "intellectual property" for the purposes of this Article—*
>
> > (a) *any patent, trade mark, service mark, registered design, copyright or design right;*
> >
> > (b) *any licence under or in respect of any such right.".*

Income and Corporation Taxes Act 1988 (c. 1)

36.—(1) The Income and Corporation Taxes Act 1988 is amended as follows.

(2) In section 83 (fees and expenses deductible in computing profits and gains of trade) for "the extension of the period of copyright in a design" substitute "an extension of the period for which the right in a registered design subsists".

(3) [...]

(4)–(6) [...]

(7) In section 821 (payments made under deduction of tax before passing of Act imposing income tax for that year), in subsection (3) (payments subject to adjustment) after paragraph (a) insert—

> "(aa) any payment for or in respect of a right in a design to which section 537B applies; and".

(8) In Schedule 19 (apportionment of income of close companies), in paragraph 10(4) (cessation or liquidation: debts taken into account although creditor is participator or associate), in paragraph (c) (payments for use of certain property) for the words from "tangible property" to "extend)" substitute—

> "—
>
> > (i) tangible property,
> >
> > (ii) copyright in a literary, dramatic, musical or artistic work within the meaning of Part I of the Copyright, Designs and Patents Act 1988 (or any similar right under the law of a country to which that Part does not extend), or
> >
> > (iii) design right,".

(9) In Schedule 25 (taxation of UK-controlled foreign companies: exempt activities), in paragraph 9(1)(a) (investment business: holding of property) for "patents or copyrights" substitute "or intellectual property" and after that sub-paragraph insert—

> "(1A) In sub-paragraph (1)(a) above 'intellectual property' means patents, registered designs, copyright and design right (or any similar rights under the law of a country outside the United Kingdom).".."

Notes:

> (1) Schedule 7 para.36(3) was repealed by the Income Tax (Trading & Other Income) Act 2005 (c.5), Sch.3, with effect from April 6, 2005. Paragraph 36(3) formerly provided:

"(3) *In section 103 (charge on receipts after discontinuance of trade, profession or vocation), in subsection (3) (sums to which the section does not apply), after paragraph (b) insert—*

"(bb) *a lump sum paid to the personal representatives of the designer of a design in which design right subsists as consideration for the assignment by them, wholly or partially, of that right,*"."

(2) Schedule 7 sub-paras 36(4)–(6) repealed by the Income Tax Act 2007 Sch.3(1) para.1 with effect from April 6, 2007: for income tax purposes, for the tax year 2007–08 and subsequent tax years and for corporation tax purposes for accounting periods ending after April 5, 2007. For savings and transitional provisions, see s.1030(1) and Sch.2 of the Act. For the text of paragraph 36(4)–(6) see *Copinger*, 16th edn, Vol 2, pp.286–287.

Section 303(2).   SCHEDULE 8

REPEALS

Chapter	Short title	Extent of repeal
1939 c. 107.	Patents, Designs, Copyright and Trade Marks (Emergency) Act 1939	In section 10(1), the definition of "copyright".
1945 c. 16.	Limitation (Enemies and War Prisoners) Act 1945.	In sections 2(1) and 4(a), the reference to section 10 of the Copyright Act 1911.
1949 c. 88.	Registered Designs Act 1949	In section 3(2), the words "or original". Section 5(5). In section 11(2), the words "or original". In section 14(3), the words "or the Isle of Man". Section 32. Section 33(2). Section 37(1). Section 38. In section 44(1), the definitions of "copyright" and "Journal". In section 45, paragraphs (1) and (2). In section 46, paragraphs (1) and (2). Section 48(1). In Schedule 1, in paragraph 3(1), the words "in such manner as may be prescribed by rules of court". Schedule 2.
1956 c. 74.	Copyright Act 1956.	The whole Act.
1957 c. 6.	Ghana Independence Act 1957.	In Schedule 2, paragraph 12.
1957 c. 60.	Federation of Malaya Independence Act 1957.	In Schedule 1, paragraphs 14 and 15.
1958 c. 44.	Dramatic and Musical Performers' Protection Act 1958.	The whole Act.
1958 c. 51.	Public Records Act 1958.	Section 11. Schedule 3.
1960 c. 52.	Cyprus Independence Act 1960.	In the Schedule, paragraph 13.
1960 c. 55.	Nigeria Independence Act 1960.	In Schedule 2, paragraphs 12 and 13.
1961 c. 1.	Tanganyika Independence Act 1961.	In Schedule 2, paragraphs 13 and 14.

Chapter	Short title	Extent of repeal
1961 c. 16.	Sierra Leone Independence Act 1961.	In Schedule 3, paragraphs 13 and 14.
1961 c. 25.	Patents and Designs (Renewals, Extensions and Fees) Act 1961.	The whole Act.
1962 c. 40.	Jamaica Independence Act 1962.	In Schedule 2, paragraph 13.
1962 c. 54.	Trinidad and Tobago Independence Act 1962.	In Schedule 2, paragraph 13.
1963 c. 53.	Performers' Protection Act 1963.	The whole Act.
1964 c. 46.	Malawi Independence Act 1964.	In Schedule 2, paragraph 13.
1964 c. 65.	Zambia Independence Act 1964.	In Schedule 1, paragraph 9.
1964 c. 86.	Malta Independence Act 1964.	*In* Schedule 1, paragraph 11.
1964 c. 93.	Gambia Independence Act 1964.	In Schedule 2, paragraph 12.
1966 c. 24.	Lesotho Independence Act 1966.	In the Schedule, paragraph 9.
1966 c. 37.	Barbados Independence Act 1966.	In Schedule 2, paragraph 12.
1966 c. 80.	Criminal Justice Act 1967.	In parts I and IV of Schedule 3, the entries relating to the Registered Designs Act 1949.
1968 c. 56.	Swaziland Independence Act 1968.	In the Schedule, paragraph 9.
1968 c. 67.	Medicines Act 1968.	In section 92(2)(a), the words from "or embodied" to "film". Section 98.
1968 c. 68.	Design Copyright Act 1968.	The whole Act.
1971 c. 4.	Copyright (Amendment) Act 1971.	The whole Act.
1971 c. 23.	Courts Act 1974.	In Schedule 9, the entry relating to the Copyright Act 1956.
1971 c. 62.	Tribunals and Inquiries Act 1971.	In Schedule 1, paragraph 24.
1972 c. 32.	Performers' Protection Act 1972.	The whole Act.
1975 c. 24.	House of Commons Disqualification Act 1975.	In Part II of Schedule 1, the entry relating to the Performing Right Tribunal.
1975 c. 25.	Northern Ireland Assembly Disqualification Act 1975.	In Part II of Schedule 1, the entry relating to the Performing Right Tribunal.
1977 c. 37.	Patents Act 1977.	Section 14(4) and (8). In section 28(3), paragraph (b) and the word "and" preceding it. Section 28(5) to (9). Section 49(3). Section 72(3). Sections 84 and 85. Section 88. Section 104. In section 105, the words "within the meaning of section 104 above". Sections 114 and 115. Section 123(2)(k). In section 130(1), the definition of "patent agent". In section 130(7), the words "88(6) and (7),". In Schedule 5, paragraphs 1 and 2, in paragraph 3 the words "and 44(1)" and "in each case", and paragraphs 7 and 8.
1979 c. 2.	Cutoms and Excise Management Act 1979.	In schedule 4, the entry relating to the Copyright Act 1956.

Chapter	Short title	Extent of repeal
1980 c. 21.	Competition Act 1980.	Section 14.
1981 c. 68.	Broadcasting Act 1981.	Section 20(9)(a).
1982 c. 35.	Copyright Act 1956 (Amendment) Act 1982.	The whole Act.
1983 c. 42.	Copyright (Amendment) Act 1983.	The whole Act.
1984 c. 46.	Cable and Broadcasting Act 1984.	Section 8(8). Section 16(4) and (5). Sections 22 to 24. Section 35(2) and (3). Sections 53 and 54. In section 56(2), the definition of "the 1956 Act". In Schedule 5, paragraphs 6, 7, 13 and 23.
1985 c. 21.	Films Act 1985.	Section 7(2).
1985 c. 41.	Copyright (Computer Software) Amendment Act 1985.	The whole Act.
1985 c. 61.	Administration of Justice Act 1985.	Section 60.
1986 c. 39.	Patents, Designs and Marks Act 1986.	In Schedule 2, paragraphs 1(2)(a), in paragraph 1(2)(k) the words "subsection (1)(j) of section 396 and" and in paragraph 1(2)(1) the words "subsection (2)(i) of section 93".
1988 c. 1.	Income and Corporation Taxes Act 1988.	In Schedule 29, paragraph 5.

Notes:

(1) Although it did not amend Sch.8, para.11(7) of the Copyright and Related Rights Regulations 1996 (SI 1996/2967), repealed the following provisions:

s.4(2) of the Public Libraries (Scotland) Act 1955;

s.8(6) of the Public Libraries and Museums Act 1964;

Article 77(3) of the Education and Libraries (Northern Ireland) Order 1986 (SI 1986/594 (N.I.3)).

with effect from December 1, 1996. For savings and transitional provisions, see Part III of those Regulations.

(2) The entry relating to the Malta Independence Act 1964 was repealed by the Statute Law (Repeals) Act 1993.

A2. Broadcasting Act 1990

A2.i The Broadcasting Act 1990

Part IX

Duty to provide advance information about programmes

176.—(1) A person providing a programme service to which this section applies must make available in accordance with this section information relating to the programmes to be included in the service to any person (referred to in this section and Schedule 17 to this Act as "the publisher") wishing to publish in the United Kingdom any such information.

(2) The duty imposed by subsection (1) is to make available information as to the titles of the programmes which are to be, or may be, included in the service on any date, and the time of their inclusion, to any publisher who has asked the person providing the programme service to make such information available to him and reasonably requires it.

(3) Information to be made available to a publisher under this section is to be made available as soon after it has been prepared as is reasonably practicable but, in any event—

(a) not later than when it is made available to any other publisher, and

(b) in the case of information in respect of all the programmes to be included in the service in any period of seven days, not later than the beginning of the preceding period of fourteen days, or such other number of days as may be prescribed by the Secretary of State by order.

(4) An order under subsection (3) shall be subject to annulment in pursuance of a resolution of either House of Parliament.

(5) The duty imposed by subsection (1) is not satisfied by providing the information on terms, other than terms as to copyright, prohibiting or restricting publication in the United Kingdom by the publisher.

(6) Schedule 17 applies to any information or future information which the person providing a programme service to which this section applies is or may be required to make available under this section.

(7) For the purposes of this section and that Schedule, the following table shows the programme services to which the section and Schedule apply and the persons who provide them or are to be treated as providing them.

Programme service	Provider of service
Services other than services under the Act	
Television and national radio services provided by the BBC for reception in the United Kingdom	The BBC
Services under the Act	
Television programme services subject to [regulation by OFCOM]	The person licensed to provide the service
[The public television services of the Welsh Authority (within the meaning of Part 2 of Schedule 12 to the Communications Act 2003)]	The Authority

Programme service	Provider of service
Any national service (see [section 126(1)]) subject to regulation by [OF-COM] [, any simulcast radio service (within the meaning of Part II of the Broadcasting Act 1996), and any national digital sound programme service (within the meaning of that Part of that Act) subject to regulation by [OFCOM]].	The person licensed to provide the service
Services provided during interim period only	
Television broadcasting services provided by the Independent Commission in accordance with Schedule 11, other than Channel 4	The programme contractor
Channel 4, as so provided	The body corporate referred to in section 12(2) of the Broadcasting Act 1981

(8) This section does not require any information to be given about any advertisement.

Note: Subsection (7) is printed as amended by para.10 of Sch.10 to the Broadcasting Act 1996 with effect from October 1, 1996 by virtue of the Broadcasting Act 1996 (Commencement No.1 and Transitional Provisions) Order 1996 (SI 1996/2120); and is further amended by the Communications Act 2003 (c.21), Sch.15 para.60 with effect from December 29, 2003 (Office of Communications Act 2002 (Commencement No.3) and Communications Act 2003 (Commencement No.2) Order 2003 (SI 2003/3142)).

Section 176   SCHEDULE 17

INFORMATION ABOUT PROGRAMMES: COPYRIGHT

PART I

COPYRIGHT LICENSING

1.—(1) This paragraph applies where the person providing a programme service has assigned to another the copyright in works containing information to which this Schedule applies.

(2) The person providing the programme service, not the assignee, is to be treated as the owner of the copyright for the purposes of licensing any act restricted by the copyright on or after the day on which this paragraph comes into force.

(3) Where the assignment by the person providing the programme service occurred before 29th September 1989 then, in relation to any act restricted by the copyright so assigned—

(a) sub-paragraph (2) does not have effect, and
(b) references below in this Schedule to the person providing the programme service are to the assignee.

PART II

USE OF INFORMATION AS OF RIGHT

Circumstances in which right available

2.—(1) Paragraph 4 applies to any act restricted by the copyright in works containing information to which this Schedule applies done by the publisher if—

A2 BROADCASTING ACT 1990

(a) a licence to do the act could be granted by the person providing the programme service but no such licence is held by the publisher.

(b) the person providing the programme service refuses to grant to the publisher a licence to do the act, being a licence of such duration, and of which the terms as to payment for doing the act are such, as would be acceptable to the publisher, and

(c) the publisher has complied with paragraph 3.

(2) The reference in sub-paragraph (1) to refusing to grant a licence includes failing to do so within a reasonable time of being asked.

(3) References below in this Schedule to the terms of payment are to the terms as to payment for doing any act restricted by the copyright in works containing information to which this Schedule applies.

Notice of intention to exercise right

3.—(1) A publisher intending to avail himself of the right conferred by paragraph 4 must—

(a) give notice of his intention to the person providing the programme service, asking that person to propose terms of payment, and

(b) after receiving the proposal or the expiry of a reasonable time, give reasonable notice to the person providing the programme service of the date on which he proposes to begin exercising the right and the terms of payment in accordance with which he intends to do so.

(2) Before exercising the right the publisher must—

(a) give reasonable notice to the Copyright Tribunal of his intention to exercise the right and of the date on which he proposes to begin to do so, and

(b) apply to the Tribunal under paragraph 5 to settle the terms of payment.

Conditions for exercise of right

4.—(1) Where the publisher, on or after the date specified in a notice under paragraph 3(1)(b), does any act in circumstances in which this paragraph applies, he shall, if he makes the payments required by this paragraph, be in the same position as regards infringement of copyright as if he had at all material times been the holder of a licence to do so granted by the person providing the programme service.

(2) Payments are to be made at not less than quarterly intervals in arrears.

(3) The amount of any payment is that determined in accordance with any order of the Copyright Tribunal under paragraph 5 or, if no such order has been made—

(a) in accordance with any proposal for terms of payment made by the person providing the programme service pursuant to a request under paragraph 3(1)(a), or

(b) where no proposal has been so made or the amount determined in accordance with the proposal so made appears to the publisher to be unreasonably high, in accordance with the terms of payment notified under paragraph 3(1)(b).

Applications to settle payments

5.—(1) On an application to settle the terms of payment, the Copyright Tribunal shall consider the matter and make such order as it may determine to be reasonable in the circumstances.

(2) An order under sub-paragraph (1) has effect from the date the applicant begins to exercise the right conferred by paragraph 4 and any necessary repayments, or further payments, shall be made in respect of amounts that have fallen due.

Application for review of order

6.—(1) A person exercising the right conferred by paragraph 4, or the person providing the programme service, may apply to the Tribunal to review any order under paragraph 5.

(2) An application under sub-paragraph (1) shall not be made, except with the special leave of the Tribunal—

(a) within twelve months from the date of the order, or of the decision on a previous application under this paragraph, or

(b) if the order was made so as to be in force for fifteen months or less, or as a result of a decision on a previous application is due to expire within fifteen months of that decision, until the last three months before the expiry date.

(3) On the application the Tribunal shall consider the matter and make such order confirming or varying the original order as it may determine to be reasonable in the circumstances.

(4) An order under this paragraph has effect from the date on which it is made or such later date as may be specified by the Tribunal.

PART III

Supplementary

7.—(1) This Schedule and the Copyright, Designs and Patents Act 1988 shall have effect as if the Schedule were included in Chapter III of Part I of that Act, and that Act shall have effect as if proceedings under this Schedule were listed in section 149 of that Act (jurisdiction of the Copyright Tribunal).

(2) References in this Schedule to anything done by the publisher include anything done on his behalf.

(3) References in this Schedule to works include future works, and references to the copyright in works include future copyright.

Note: Section 176 of and Schedule 17 to the Broadcasting Act 1990 contain provisions relating to the statutory duty to provide information about programmes and the settling of terms of payment by the Copyright Tribunal. The 1988 Act is not amended by those provisions but note paragraph 7(1) of Schedule 17, above. those provisions are in force by virtue of the Broadcasting Act 1990 (Commencement No.1 and Transitional Provisions) Order 1990 (SI 1990/2347).

A2.ii The Broadcasting Act 1990 (Commencement No. 1 and Transitional Provisions) Order 1990

(SI 1990/2347)

Made   *27th November 1990*

Note: This Order was made by David Waddington, one of Her Majesty's Principal Secretaries of State, Home Office.

In exercise of the powers conferred upon me by sections 200 and 204(2) of the Broadcasting Act 1990[1], I hereby make the following Order:

1.—(1) This Order may be cited as the Broadcasting Act 1990 (Commencement No. 1 and Transitional Provisions) Order 1990.

(2) In this Order "the 1990 Act" means the Broadcasting Act 1990.

2. The provisions of the 1990 Act which are specified in Schedule 1 to this Order shall come into force on 1st December 1990.

3.—(1) Subject to paragraphs (2) and (3) below, the provisions of the 1990 Act which are specified in Schedule 2 to this Order shall come into force on 1st January 1991.

(2) Paragraph (1) above and Schedule 2 to this Order shall not apply so as to bring into force the replacement of the reference to the Independent Broadcasting Authority by the amendment made by paragraph 36 of Schedule 20 to the 1990 Act until such time as that Authority is dissolved by order under section 127(3) of the 1990 Act.

(3) Paragraph (1) above and Schedule 2 to this Order shall not apply so as to

---

[1] c.42.

bring into force the repeal by Schedule 21 to the 1990 Act of those provisions of the Broadcasting Act 1981[2] and the Cable and Broadcasting Act 1984,[3] together with the entries in the said Schedule 21 in respect of paragraph 81 of Schedule 4 to and paragraphs 8(1) and (3) and 30 of Schedule 5 to the Telecommunications Act 1984,[4] the Companies Consolidation (Consequential Provisions) Act 1985,[5] the Finance Act 1986,[6] the Broadcasting Act 1987,[7] the Education Reform Act 1988,[8] sections 73 and 134(4) of, paragraph 19 of Schedule 2 to, and paragraph 29 of Schedule 7 to the Copyright, Designs and Patents Act 1988[9] and the Finance Act 1989,[10] which continue to have effect under or by virtue of sections 127 to 129 and 134 of, and Schedules 9 to 12 to, the 1990 Act.

4. Section 175 of the 1990 Act shall come into force on 1st February 1991.

5. Section 176 of, and Schedule 17 to, the 1990 Act shall come into force on 1st March 1991 except that for the purpose of enabling publication of information about programmes to be included in a programme service on or after that date, those provisions shall come into force on 1st January 1991.

6. The following provisions shall come into force on 1st April 1991; those provisions are:
    (a) section 180 of, and Schedule 18 to, the 1990 Act; and
    (b) the entries in Schedule 21 to the 1990 Act relating to the appeal of—
          (i) the Wireless Telegraphy (Blind Persons) Act 1955[11]; and
          (ii) the Wireless Telegraphy Act 1967.[12]

7. (1) Subject to paragraph (2) below, the provisions of the 1990 Act which are specified in Schedule 3 to this Order shall come into force on 1st January 1993.

(2) For the purposes of enabling conditions of the type specified in sections 34(2), 35(1) and 185(3) of the 1990 Act to be included in a Channel 3 or Channel 5 licence or licence to provide Channel 4, sections 34, 35 and 185 of that Act shall come into force on 1st January 1991.

Article 2   SCHEDULE 1

PROVISIONS OF THE 1990 ACT COMING INTO FORCE ON 1ST DECEMBER 1990

Section 1
Section 2, except subsection (1)
Sections 3 to 9
Section 11
Section 43
Sections 45 to 47
Section 71
Section 83

---

[2] c.68.
[3] c.46.
[4] c.12.
[5] c.9.
[6] c.41.
[7] c.10.
[8] c.40.
[9] c.48.
[10] c.26.
[11] c.7.
[12] c.72.

Sections 126 and 127
Sections 130 to 133
Section 141
Sections 198 to 202
In section 203, subsections (3) and (4)
Section 204
Schedules 1 and 2
Schedules 8 and 9
In Schedule 21, the entry relating to the repeal of the Cable and Broadcasting Act 1984[13] to the extent that the repeal concerns paragraphs (a) and (b) of section 8(1) of that Act.
Paragraphs 1 to 3 of Schedule 22

Article 3   SCHEDULE 2

PROVISIONS OF THE 1990 ACT COMING INTO FORCE ON 1ST JANUARY 1991, SUBJECT TO THE PROVISIONS OF ARTICLE 3 OF THIS ORDER

Section 2(1)
Section 10
Sections 12 to 22
Section 26
Sections 28 to 33
Sections 36 to 42
Section 44
Sections 48 to 70
Sections 72 to 82
Sections 84 to 125
Sections 128 and 129
Sections 134 to 140
Sections 142 to 174
Sections 177 to 179
Sections 181 to 184
Section 186
Sections 188 to 197
In section 203, subsections (1) and (2)
Schedules 4 to 7, 10 to 16 and 19
In Schedule 20, paragraphs 1 to 36 and 38 to 54
In Schedule 21, all of the entries except those relating to:
(a) the Wireless Telegraphy (Blind Persons) Act 1955[14];
(b) the Wireless Telegraphy Act 1967[15];
(c) the entries in Part II of Schedule 1 to the House of Commons Disqualification Act 1975[16] relating to the Cable Authority and the Independent Broadcasting Authority; and
(d) the Northern Ireland Assembly Disqualification Act 1975[17];
In Schedule 22, paragraphs 4 to 7

Article 7   SCHEDULE 3

PROVISIONS OF THE 1990 ACT COMING INTO FORCE ON 1ST JANUARY 1993, SUBJECT TO THE PROVISIONS OF ARTICLE 7 OF THIS ORDER

Sections 23 to 25

---

[13] c.46.
[14] c.7.
[15] c.72.
[16] c.24.
[17] c.25.

Section 27
Sections 34 and 35
Section 185
Section 187
Schedule 3
In Schedule 20, paragraph 37

A3. Regulations amending CDPA 1988 and transitional provisions

A3.i The Copyright (Computer Programs) Regulations 1992

(SI 1992/3233)

Made	*16th December 1992*
Coming into force	*1st January 1993*

Whereas a draft of the following Regulations has been approved by resolution of each House of Parliament:

Now, therefore, the Secretary of State, being a Minister designated for the purposes of section 2(2) of the European Communities Act 1972 in relation to measures relating to the protection of copyright of computer programs, in exercise of powers conferred by section 2(2) and (4) of the said Act of 1972, hereby makes the following Regulations:—

Citation, commencement and extent

1.—(1) These Regulations may be cited as the Copyright (Computer Programs) Regulations 1992 and shall come into force on 1st January 1993.

(2) These Regulations extend to Northern Ireland.

2. The Copyright, Designs and Patents Act 1988 shall be amended as follows.

Amendments of Part I (copyright) and of Part VII (miscellaneous and general) of the Copyright, Designs and Patents Act 1988

3.–11. [...]

Note: The amendments have been printed in the main body of the Act and regs 3 to 11 are not reprinted.

Transitional provisions and savings

Computer programs created before 1st January 1993

12.—(1) Subject to paragraph (2), the amendments of the Copyright, Designs and Patents Act 1988 made by these Regulations apply in relation to computer programs created before 1st January 1993 as they apply to computer programs created on or after that date.

(2) Nothing in these Regulations affects any agreement or any term or condition of an agreement where the agreement, term or condition is entered into before 1st January 1993.

A3.ii The Duration of Copyright and Rights in Performances Regulations 1995

(SI 1995/3297)

Made	*19th December 1995*
Coming into force	*1st January 1996*

ARRANGEMENT OF REGULATIONS

Whereas a draft of the following Regulations has been approved by resolution of each house of Parliament:

Now, therefore, the Secretary of State, being a Minister designated for the purposes of section 2(2) of the European Communities Act 1972 in relation to measures relating to the protection of copyright and rights in performances, in exercise of powers conferred by section 2(2) and (4) of the said Act of 1972, hereby makes the following Regulations—

Part I

Introductory Provisions

Citation, commencement and extent

1.—(1) These Regulations may be cited as the Duration of Copyright and Rights in Performances Regulations 1995.

(2) These Regulations come into force on 1st January 1996.

(3) These Regulations extend to the whole of the United Kingdom.

Interpretation

2. In these Regulations—

"EEA Agreement" means the Agreement on the European Economic Area signed at Oporto on 2nd May 1992, as adjusted by the Protocol signed at Brussels on 17th March 1993; and

"EEA state" means a member State, Iceland, Liechtenstein or Norway.

Note: In reg.2 the definition of "EEA state" was substituted by the Intellectual Property (Enforcement, etc.) Regulations 2006 (SI 2006/1028), Sch.3 para.1, with effect from April 29, 2006.

Implementation of Directive, &c.

3. These Regulations make provision for the purpose of implementing—

(a) the main provisions of Council Directive No. 93/98/EEC of 29th October 1993 harmonizing the term of protection of copyright and certain related rights; and

(b) certain obligations of the United Kingdom created by or arising under the EEA Agreement so far as relevant to the implementation of that Directive.

Scheme of the regulations

4. The Copyright, Designs and Patents Act 1988 is amended in accordance with the provisions of Part II of these Regulations, subject to the savings and transitional provisions in Part III of these Regulations.

Part II

Amendments of the Copyright, Designs and Patents Act 1988

5.–11. […]

Note: The amendments have been printed in the main body of the Act and this Part is not reprinted.

Part III

Savings and Transitional Provisions

Introductory

Introductory

12.—(1) References in this Part to "commencement", without more, are to the date on which these Regulations come into force.

(2) In this Part—

"the 1988 Act" means the Copyright, Designs and Patents Act 1988;

"the 1988 provisions" means the provisions of that Act as they stood immediately before commencement (including the provisions of Schedule 1 to that Act continuing the effect of earlier enactments); and

"the new provisions" means the provisions of that Act as amended by these Regulations.

(3) Expressions used in this Part which are defined for the purposes of Part I or II of the 1988 Act, in particular references to the copyright owner, have the same meaning as in that part.

Films not protected as such

13. In relation to a film in which copyright does not or did not subsist as such but which is or was protected—

(a) as an original dramatic work, or

(b) by virtue of the protection of the photographs forming part of the film,

references in the new provisions, and in this Part, to copyright in a film are to any copyright in the film as an original dramatic work or, as the case may be, in photographs forming part of the film.

Copyright

Copyright: interpretation

14.—(1) In the provisions of this Part relating to copyright—

(a) "existing", in relation to a work, means made before commencement; and

(b) "existing copyright work" means a work in which copyright subsisted immediately before commencement.

(2) For the purposes of those provisions a work of which the making extended over a period shall be taken to have been made when its making was completed.

(3) References in those provisions to "moral rights" are to the rights conferred by Chapter IV of Part I of the 1988 Act.

Duration of copyright: general saving

15.—(1) Copyright in an existing copyright work shall continue to subsist until the date on which it would have expired under the 1988 provisions if that date is later than the date on which copyright would expire under the new provisions.

(2) Where paragraph (1) has effect, section 57 of the 1988 Act (anonymous or pseudonymous works: acts permitted on assumptions as to expiry of copyright or death of author) applies as it applied immediately before commencement (that is, without the amendments made by Regulation 5(2)).

Duration of copyright: application of new provisions

16. The new provisions relating to duration of copyright apply—

(a) to copyright works made after commencement;

(b) to existing works which first qualify for copyright protection after commencement;

(c) to existing copyright works, subject to Regulation 15 (general saving for any longer period applicable under 1988 provisions); and

(d) to existing works in which copyright expired before 31st December 1995 but which were on 1st July 1995 protected in another EEA state under legislation relating to copyright or related rights.

Extended and revived copyright

17. In the following provisions of this part—

"extended copyright" means any copyright which subsists by virtue of the new provisions after the date on which it would have expired under the 1988 provisions; and

"revived copyright" means any copyright which subsists by virtue of the new provisions after having expired under the 1988 provisions or any earlier enactment relating to copyright.

Ownership of extended copyright

18.—(1) The person who is the owner of the copyright in a work immediately before commencement is as from commencement the owner of any extended copyright in the work, subject as follows.

(2) If he is entitled to copyright for a period less than the whole of the copyright period under the 1988 provisions, any extended copyright is part of the reversionary interest expectant on the termination of that period.

Ownership of revived copyright

19.—(1) The person who was the owner of the copyright in a work immediately before it expired (the "former copyright owner") is as from commencement the owner of any revived copyright in the work, subject as follows.

(2) If the former copyright owner has died before commencement, or in the case of a legal person has ceased to exist before commencement, the revived copyright shall vest—

(a) in the case of a film, in the principal director of the film or his personal representatives, and

(b) in any other case, in the author of the work or his personal representatives.

(3) Where revived copyright vests in personal representatives by virtue of paragraph (2), it shall be held by them for the benefit of the person who would have been entitled to it had it been vested in the principal director or author immediately before his death and had devolved as part of his estate.

Prospective ownership of extended or revived copyright

20.—(1) Where by an agreement made before commencement in relation to extended or revived copyright, and signed by or on behalf of the prospective owner of the copyright, the prospective owner purports to assign the extended or revived copyright (wholly or partially) to another person, then if, on commencement the assignee or another person claiming under him would be entitled as against al other persons to require the copyright to be vested in him, the copyright shall vest in the assignee or his successor in title by virtue of this paragraph.

(2) A licence granted by a prospective owner of extended or revived copyright is binding on every successor in title to his interest (or prospective interest) in the right, except a purchaser in good faith for valuable consideration and without notice (actual or constructive) of the licence or a person deriving title from such a purchaser; and references in Part I of the 1988 Act to doing anything with, or without, the licence of the copyright owner shall be construed accordingly.

(3) In paragraph (2) "prospective owner" includes a person who is prospectively entitled to extended or revived copyright by virtue of such an agreement as is mentioned in paragraph (1).

Extended copyright: existing licences, agreement, &c.

21.—(1) Any copyright licence, any term or condition of an agreement relating to the exploitation of a copyright work, or any waiver or assertion of moral rights, which—

> (a) subsists immediately before commencement in relation to an existing copyright work, and
>
> (b) is not to expire before the end of the copyright period under the 1988 provisions,

shall continue to have effect during the period of any extended copyright, subject to any agreement to the contrary.

(2) Any copyright licence, or term or condition relating to the exploitation of a copyright work, imposed by order of the Copyright Tribunal which—

> (a) subsists immediately before commencement in relation to an existing copyright work, and
>
> (b) is not to expire before the end of the copyright period under the 1988 provisions,

shall continue to have effect during the period of any extended copyright, subject to any further order of the Tribunal.

Revived copyright: exercise of moral rights

22.—(1) The following provisions have effect with respect to the exercise of moral rights in relation to a work in which there is revived copyright.

(2) Any waiver or assertion of moral rights which subsisted immediately before the expiry of copyright shall continue to have effect during the period of revived copyright.

(3) Moral rights are exercisable after commencement by the author of a work or, as the case may be, the director of a film in which revived copyright subsists, as with any other copyright work.

(4) Where the author or director died before commencement—

> (a) the rights conferred by—
>
> section 77 (right to identification as author or director),
>
> section 80 (right to object to derogatory treatment of work), or
>
> section 85 (right to privacy of certain photographs and films),

are exercisable after commencement by his personal representatives, and

> (b) any infringement after commencement of the right conferred by Section 84 (false attribution) is actionable by his personal representatives.

(5) Any damages recovered by personal representatives by virtue of this Regulation in respect of an infringement after a person's death shall devolve as part of his estate as if the right of action had subsisted and been vested in him immediately before his death.

(6) Nothing in these Regulations shall be construed as causing a moral right to be exercisable if, or to the extent that, the right was excluded by virtue of paragraph 23 or 24 of Schedule 1 on the commencement of the 1988 Act or would have been so excluded if copyright had not previously expired.

Revived copyright: saving for acts of exploitation when work in public domain, &c.

23.—(1) No act done before commencement shall be regarded as infringing revived copyright in a work.

(2) It is not an infringement of revived copyright in a work—

> (a) to do anything after commencement in pursuance of arrangements made before 1st January 1995 at a time when copyright did not subsist in the work, or

(b) to issue to the public after commencement copies of the work made before 1st July 1995 at a time when copyright did not subsist in the work.

(3) It is not an infringement of revived copyright in a work to do anything after commencement in relation to a literary, dramatic, musical or artistic work or a film made before commencement, which contains a copy of that work or is an adaptation of that work if—

(a) the copy or adaptation was made before 1st July 1995 at a time when copyright did not subsist in the work in which revived copyright subsists, or

(b) the copy or adaptation was made in pursuance of arrangements made before 1st July 1995 at a time when copyright did not subsist in the work in which revived copyright subsists.

(4) It is not an infringement of revived copyright in a work to do after commencement anything which is a restricted act in relation to the work if the act is done at a time when, or is done in pursuance of arrangements made at a time when, the name and address of a person entitled to authorise the act cannot by reasonable inquiry be ascertained.

(5) In this Regulation "arrangements" means arrangements for the exploitation of the work in question.

(6) It is not an infringement of any moral right to do anything which by virtue of this Regulation is not an infringement of copyright.

Revived copyright: use as of right subject to reasonable royalty

24.—(1) In the case of a work in which revived copyright subsists any acts restricted by the copyright shall be treated as licensed by the copyright owner, subject only to the payment of such reasonable royalty or other remuneration as may be agreed or determined in default of agreement by the Copyright Tribunal.

(2) A person intending to avail himself of the right conferred by this Regulation must give reasonable notice of his intention to the copyright owner, stating when he intends to begin to do the acts.

(3) If he does not give such notice, his acts shall not be treated as licensed.

(4) If he does give such notice, his acts shall be treated as licensed and a reasonable royalty or other remuneration shall be payable in respect of them despite the fact that its amount is not agreed or determined until later.

(5) This Regulation does not apply if or to the extent that a licence to do the acts could be granted by a licensing body (within the meaning of section 116(2) of the 1988 Act), whether or not under a licensing scheme.

(6) No royalty or other remuneration is payable by virtue of this Regulation in respect of anything for which a royalty or other remuneration is payable under Schedule 6 to the 1988 Act.

Revived copyright: application to Copyright Tribunal

25.—(1) An application to settle the royalty or other remuneration payable in pursuance of Regulation 24 may be made to the Copyright Tribunal by the copyright owner or the person claiming to be treated as licensed by him.

(2) The Tribunal shall consider the matter and make such order as it may determine to be reasonable in the circumstances.

(3) Either party may subsequently apply to the Tribunal to vary the order, and the Tribunal shall consider the matter and make such order confirming or varying the original order as it may determine to be reasonable in the circumstances.

(4) An application under paragraph (3) shall not, except with the special leave of the Tribunal, be made within twelve months from the date of the original order or of the order on a previous application under that paragraph.

(5) An order under paragraph (3) has effect from the date on which it is made or such later date as may be specified by the Tribunal.

Film sound tracks: application of new provisions

26.—(1) The new provisions relating to the treatment of film sound tracks apply to existing sound tracks as from commencement.

(2) The owner of any copyright in a film has as from commencement corresponding rights as copyright owner in any existing sound track treated as part of the film, but without prejudice to any rights of the owner of the copyright in the sound track as a sound recording.

(3) Anything done before commencement under or in relation to the copyright in the sound recording continues to have effect and shall have effect, so far as concerns the sound track, in relation to the film as in relation to the sound recording.

(4) It is not an infringement of the copyright in the film (or of any moral right in the film) to do anything after commencement in pursuance of arrangements for the exploitation of the sound recording made before commencement.

Rights in performances

Rights in performances: interpretation

27.—(1) In the provisions of this Part relating to rights in performances—
- (a) "existing", in relation to a performance, means given before commencement; and
- (b) "existing protected performance" means a performance in relation to which rights under Part II of the 1988 Act (rights in performances) subsisted immediately before commencement.

(2) References in this Part to performers' rights are to the rights given by section 180(1)(a) of the 1988 Act and references to recording rights are to the rights given by section 180(1)(b) of that Act.

Duration of rights in performances: general saving

28. Any rights under Part II of the 1988 Act in an existing protected performance shall continue to subsist until the date on which they would have expired under the 1988 provisions if that date is later than the date on which the rights would expire under the new provisions.

Duration of rights in performances; application of new provisions

29. The new provisions relating to the duration of rights under Part II of the 1988 Act apply—
- (a) to performances taking place after commencement;
- (b) to existing performances which first qualify for protection under Part II of the 1988 Act after commencement;
- (c) to existing protected performances, subject to Regulation 28 (general saving for any longer period applicable under 1988 provisions); and
- (d) to existing performances—
  - (i) in which rights under Part II of the 1988 Act expired after the commencement of that Part and before 31st December 1995, or
  - (ii) which were protected by earlier enactments relating to the protection of performers and in which rights under that Part did not arise by reason only that the performance was given at a date

such that the rights would have ceased to subsist before the commencement of that Part,

but which were on 1st July 1995 protected in another EEA state under legislation relating to copyright or related rights.

Extended and revived performance rights

30. In the following provisions of this Part—

"extended performance rights" mean rights under Part II of the 1988 Act which subsist by virtue of the new provisions after the date on which they would have expired under the 1988 provisions; and

"revived performance rights" means rights under Part II of the 1988 Act which subsist by virtue of the new provisions—

(a) after having expired under the 1988 provisions, or

(b) in relation to a performance which was protected by earlier enactments relating to the protection of performers and in which rights under that Part did not arise by reason only that the performance was given at a date such that the rights would have ceased to subsist before the commencement of that Part.

References in the following provisions of this Part to "revived pre-1988 rights" are to revived performance rights within paragraph (b) of the above definition.

Entitlement to extended or revived performance rights

31.—(1) Any extended performance rights are exercisable as from commencement by the person who has entitled to exercise those rights immediately before commencement, that is—

(a) in the case of performers' rights, the performer or (if he has died) the person entitled by virtue of section 192(2) of the 1988 Act to exercise those rights;

(b) in the case of recording rights, the person who was within the meaning of section 185 of the 1988 Act the person having those rights.

(2) Any revived performance rights are exercisable as from commencement—

(a) in the case of rights which expired after the commencement of the 1988 Act, by the person who was entitled to exercise those rights immediately before they expired;

(b) in the case of revived pre-1988 performers' rights, by the performer or his personal representatives;

(c) in the case of revived pre-1988 recording rights, by the person who would have been the person having those rights immediately before the commencement of the 1988 Act or, if earlier, immediately before the death of the performer, applying the provisions of section 185 of that Act to the circumstances then obtaining.

(3) Any remuneration or damages received by a person's personal representatives by virtue of a right conferred on them by paragraph (1) or (2) shall devolve as part of that person's estate as if the right had subsisted and been vested in him immediately before his death.

Extended performance rights: existing consents, agreement, &c.

32. Any consent, or any term or condition of an agreement, relating to the exploitation of an existing protected performance which—

(a) subsists immediately before commencement, and

(b) is not to expire before the end of the period for which rights under Part II of the 1988 Act subsist in relation to that performance,

A3 REGULATIONS AMENDING CDPA 1988

shall continue to subsist during the period of any extended performance rights, subject to any agreement to the contrary.

Revived performance rights: saving for acts of exploitation when performance in public domain, &c.

33.—(1) No act done before commencement shall be regarded as infringing revived performance rights in a performance.

(2) It is not an infringement of revived performance rights in a performance—

(a) to do anything after commencement in pursuance of arrangements made before 1st January 1995 at a time when the performance was not protected, or

(b) to issue to the public after commencement a recording of a performance made before 1st July 1995 at a time when the performance was not protected.

(3) It is not an infringement of revived performance rights in a performance to do anything after commencement in relation to a sound recording or film made before commencement, or made in pursuance of arrangements made before commencement which contains a recording of the performance if—

(a) the recording of the performance was made before 1st July 1995 at a time when the performance was not protected, or

(b) the recording of the performance was made in pursuance of arrangements made before 1st July 1995 at a time when the performance was not protected.

(4) It is not an infringement of revived performance rights in a performance to do after commencement anything at a time when, or in pursuance of arrangements made at a time when, the name and address of a person entitled to authorise the act cannot by reasonable inquiry be ascertained.

(5) In this Regulation "arrangements" mean arrangements for the exploitation of the performance in question.

(6) References in this Regulation to a performance being protected are—

(a) in relation to the period after the commencement of the 1988 Act, to rights under Part II of that Act subsisting in relation to the performance, and

(b) in relation to earlier periods, to the consent of the performer being required under earlier enactments relating to the protection of performers.

Revived performance rights: use as of right subject to reasonable remuneration

34.—(1) In the case of a performance in which revived performance rights subsist any acts which require the consent of any person under Part II of the 1988 Act (the "rights owner") shall be treated as having that consent, subject only to the payment of such reasonable remuneration as may be agreed or determined in default of agreement by the Copyright Tribunal.

(2) A person intending to avail himself of the right conferred by this Regulation must give reasonable notice of his intention to the rights owner, stating when he intends to begin to do the acts.

(3) If he does not give such notice, his acts shall not be treated as having consent.

(4) If he does give such notice, his acts shall be treated as having consent and reasonable remuneration shall be payable in respect of them despite the fact that its amount is not agreed or determined until later.

Revived performance rights: application to Copyright Tribunal

35.—(1) An application to settle the remuneration payable in pursuance of Regulation 34 may be made to the Copyright Tribunal by the rights owner or the person claiming to be treated as having his consent.

(2) The Tribunal shall consider the matter and make such order as it may determine to be reasonable in the circumstances.

(3) Either party may subsequently apply to the Tribunal to vary the order, and the Tribunal shall consider the matter and make such order confirming or varying the original order as it may determine to be reasonable in the circumstances.

(4) An application under paragraph (3) shall not, except with the special leave of the Tribunal, be made within twelve months from the date of the original order or of the order on a previous application under that paragraph.

(5) An order under paragraph (3) has effect from the date on which it is made or such later date as may be specified by the Tribunal.

Supplementary

Construction of references to EEA states

36.—(1) For the purpose of the new provisions relating to the term of copyright protection applicable to a work of which the country of origin is not an EEA state and of which the author is not a national of an EEA state—

(a) a work first published before 1st July 1995 shall be treated as published in an EEA state if it was on that date regarded under the law of the United Kingdom or another EEA state as having been published in that state;

(b) an unpublished film made before 1st July 1995 shall be treated as originating in an EEA state if it was on that date regarded under the law of the United Kingdom or another EEA state as a film whose maker had his headquarters in, or was domiciled or resident in, that state; and

(c) the author of a work made before 1st July 1995 shall be treated as an EEA national if he was on that date regarded under the law of the United Kingdom or another EEA state as a national of that state.

The references above to the law of another EEA state are to the law of that state having effect for the purposes of rights corresponding to those provided for in Part I of the 1988 Act.

(2) For the purposes of the new provisions relating to the term of protection applicable to a performance where the performer is not a national of an EEA state, the performer of a performance given before 1st July 1995 shall be treated as an EEA national if he was on that date regarded under the law of the United Kingdom or another EEA state as a national of that state.

The reference above to the law of another EEA state is to the law of that state having effect for the purposes of rights corresponding to those provided for in Part II of the 1988 Act.

(3) In this Regulation "another EEA state" means an EEA state other than the United Kingdom.

A3.iii The Copyright and Related Rights Regulations 1996

(SI 1996/2967)

Made   *26th November 1996*
Coming into force   *1st December 1996*

Whereas a draft of the following Regulations has been approved by resolution of each House of Parliament:

Now, therefore, the Secretary of State, being a Minister designated for the purposes of section 2(2) of the European Communities Act 1972 in relation to measures relating to the protection of copyright and rights in performances, in exercise of powers conferred by section 2(2) and (4) of the said Act of 1972, hereby makes the following Regulations—

Part I

Introductory Provisions

Citation, commencement and extent

1.—(1) These Regulations may be cited as the Copyright and Related Rights Regulations 1996.

(2) These Regulations come into force on 1st December 1996.

(3) These Regulations extend to the whole of the United Kingdom.

Interpretation

2. In these Regulations—

"EEA Agreement" means the Agreement on the European Economic Area signed at Oporto on 2nd May 1992, as adjusted by the Protocol signed at Brussels on 17th March 1993; and "EEA state" means a member State, Iceland, Liechtenstein or Norway.

Note: In reg.2 the definition of "EEA state" was substituted by the Intellectual Property (Enforcement, etc.) Regulations 2006 (SI 2006/1028), Sch.3 para.1, with effect from April 29, 2006.

Implementation of Directives, &c.

3. These Regulations make provision for the purpose of implementing—

(a) Council Directive No. 92/100/EEC of 19 November 1992 on rental right and lending right and on certain rights related to copyright in the field of intellectual property;

(b) Council Directive No. 93/83/EEC of 27 September 1993 on the coordination of certain rules concerning copyright and rights related to copyright applicable to satellite broadcasting and cable retransmission;

(c) the provisions of Council Directive No. 93/98/EEC of 29 October 1993 harmonizing the term of protection of copyright and certain related rights, so far as not implemented by the Duration of Copyright and Rights in Performances Regulations 1995; and

(d) certain obligations of the United Kingdom created by or arising under the EEA Agreement so far as relevant to the implementation of those Directives.

Scheme of the regulations

4. The Copyright, Designs and Patents Act 1988 is amended in accordance with the provisions of Part II of these Regulations, subject to the savings and transitional provisions in Part III of these Regulations.

PART II

AMENDMENTS OF THE COPYRIGHT, DESIGNS AND PATENTS ACT 1988

5.–15. […]

Note: Other than in respect of the regulations set out below, the amendments have been printed in the main body of the Act and are not repeated here.

Publication right

Publication right

16.—(1) A person who after the expiry of copyright protection, publishes for the first time a previously unpublished work has, in accordance with the following provisions, a property right ("publication right") equivalent to copyright.

(2) For this purpose publication includes any [making available] to the public, in particular—

(a) the issue of copies to the public;

(b) making the work available by means of an electronic retrieval system;

(c) the rental or lending of copies of the work to the public;

(d) the performance, exhibition or showing of the work in public; or

[(e) communicating the work to the public.]

(3) No account shall be taken for this purpose of any unauthorised act.

In relation to a time when there is no copyright in the work, an unauthorised act means an act done without the consent of the owner of the physical medium in which the work is embodied or on which it is recorded.

(4) A work qualifies for publication right protection only if—

(a) first publication is in the European Economic Area, and

(b) the publisher of the work is at the time of first publication a national of an EEA state.

Where two or more persons jointly publish the work, it is sufficient for the purposes of paragraph (b) if any of them is a national of an EEA state.

(5) No publication right arises from the publication of a work in which Crown copyright or Parliamentary copyright subsisted.

(6) Publication right expires at the end of the period of 25 years from the end of the calendar year in which the work was first published.

(7) In this regulation [and regulation 17A] a "work" means a literary, dramatic, musical or artistic work or a film.

(8) Expressions used in this regulation (other than "publication") have the same meaning as in Part I.

Notes:

(1) The words in square brackets in reg.16(2) substituted for the former word "communication" and reg.16(2)(e) was substituted by the Copyright and Related Rights Regulations 2003 (SI 2003/2498), Sch.1, para.27 with effect from October 31, 2003. For savings and transitional provisions, see Part 3 of those Regulations.

(2) In reg.16(7) the words in square brackets inserted by the Intellectual Property (Enforcement, etc.) Regulations 2006 (SI 2006/1028), Sch.3 para.4, with effect from April 29, 2006.

Application of copyright provisions to publication right

17.—(1) The substantive provisions of Part I relating to copyright (but not moral rights in copyright works), that is, the relevant provisions of—

Chapter II (rights of copyright owner),

Chapter III (acts permitted in relation to copyright works),

Chapter V (dealings with rights in copyright works),

Chapter VI (remedies for infringement), and

Chapter VII (copyright licensing),

apply in relation to publication right as in relation to copyright, subject to the following exceptions and modifications.

(2) The following provisions do not apply—

(a) in Chapter III (acts permitted in relation to copyright works), sections 57, 64, 66A and 67;

(b) in Chapter VI (remedies for infringement), sections 104 to 106;

(c) in Chapter VII (copyright licensing), section 116(4).

(3) The following provisions have effect with the modifications indicated—

(a) in section 107(4) and (5) (offences of making or dealing in infringing articles, &c.), the maximum punishment on summary conviction is imprisonment for a term not exceeding three months or a fine not exceeding level 5 on the standard scale, or both;

(b) in sections 116(2), 117 and 124 for "works of more than one author" substitute "works of more than one publisher".

(4) The other relevant provisions of Part I, that is—
    in Chapter I, provisions defining expressions used generally in Part I,
        Chapter VIII (the Copyright Tribunal),
    in Chapter IX—
        section 161 (territorial waters and the continental shelf), and
        section 162 (British ships, aircraft and hovercraft), and
    in Chapter X—
        section 171(1) and (3) (savings for other rules of law &c.), and
        sections 172 to 179 (general interpretation provisions),
apply, with any necessary adaptations, for the purposes of supplementing the
substantive provisions of that Part as applied by this regulation.

(5) Except where the context otherwise requires, any other enactment relating
to copyright (whether passed or made before or after these regulations) applies in
relation to publication right as in relation to copyright.

In this paragraph "enactment" includes an enactment contained in subordinate
legislation within the meaning of the Interpretation Act 1978.

Presumptions relevant to works subject to publication right

[17A. In proceedings brought by virtue of Chapter 6 of Part 1 of the Copyright,
Designs and Patents Act 1988, as applied to publication right by regulation 17,
with respect to a work, where copies of the work as issued to the public bear a
statement that a named person was the owner of publication right in the work at
the date of issue of the copies, the statement shall be admissible as evidence of
the fact stated and shall be presumed to be correct until the contrary is proved.]

Application of presumptions in relation to an order for delivery up in criminal proceedings

[17B. Regulation 17A does not apply to proceedings for an offence under section 107 of the Copyright, Designs and Patents Act 1988 as applied and modified
by regulation 17 in relation to publication right; but without prejudice to its application in proceedings for an order under section 108 of the Copyright, Designs
and Patents Act 1988 as that section applies to publication right by virtue of
regulation 17.]

Note: Regulations 17A and 17B inserted by the Intellectual Property (Enforcement,
etc.) Regulations 2006 (SI 2006/1028) Sch.3 para.5, with effect from April 29, 2006.

Authorship of films and certain photographs

Clarification of transitional provisions relating to pre-1989 photographs

19. Any question arising, in relation to photographs which were existing works
within the meaning of Schedule 1, as to who is to be regarded as the author for
the purposes of—
    (a) regulations 15 and 16 of the Duration of Copyright and Rights in Perfor-
        mances Regulations 1995 (duration of copyright: application of new
        provisions subject to general saving), or
    (b) regulation 19(2)(b) of those regulations (ownership of revived copy-
        right),
is to be determined in accordance with section 9 as in force on the commencement of those regulations (and not, by virtue of paragraph 10 of Schedule 1, in
accordance with the law in force at the time when the work was made).

A3 REGULATIONS AMENDING CDPA 1988

Part III

Transitional Provisions and Savings

General provisions

Introductory

25.—(1) In this Part—

"commencement" means the commencement of these Regulations; and

"existing", in relation to a work or performance, means made or given before commencement.

(2) For the purposes of this Part a work of which the making extended over a period shall be taken to have been made when its making was completed.

(3) In this Part a "new right" means a right arising by virtue of these Regulations, in relation to a copyright work or a qualifying performance, to authorise or prohibit an act.

The expression does not include—

(a) a right corresponding to a right which existed immediately before commencement, or

(b) a right to remuneration arising by virtue of these Regulations.

(4) Expressions used in this Part have the same meaning in relation to copyright as they have in Part I of the Copyright, Designs and Patents Act 1988 and in relation to performances as in Part II of that Act.

General rules

26.—(1) Subject to anything in regulations 28 to 36 (special transitional provisions and savings), these regulations apply to copyright works made, and to performances given, before or after commencement.

(2) No act done before commencement shall be regarded as an infringement of any new right, or as giving rise to any right to remuneration arising by virtue of these Regulations.

Saving for certain existing agreements

27.—(1) Except as otherwise expressly provided, nothing in these Regulations affects an agreement made before 19th November 1992.

(2) No act done in pursuance of any such agreement after commencement shall be regarded as an infringement of any new right.

Special provisions

Broadcasts

28. The provisions of—

regulation 5 (place where broadcast treated as made) and

regulation 6 (safeguards in relation to certain satellite broadcasts),

have effect in relation to broadcasts made after commencement.

Satellite broadcasting: international co-production agreements

29.—(1) This regulation applies to an agreement concluded before 1st January 1995—

(a) between two or more co-producers of a film, one of whom is a national of an EEA state, and

(b) the provisions of which grant to the parties exclusive rights to exploit all communication to the public of the film in separate geographical areas.

(2) Where such an agreement giving such exclusive exploitation rights in relation to the United Kingdom does not expressly or by implication address satellite broadcasting from the United Kingdom, the person to whom those exclusive rights have been granted shall not make any such broadcast without the consent of any other party to the agreement whose language-related exploitation rights would be adversely affected by that broadcast.

New rights: exercise of rights in relation to performances

30.—(1) Any new right conferred by these Regulations in relation to a qualifying performance is exercisable as from commencement by the performer or (if he has died) by the person who immediately before commencement was entitled by virtue of section 192(2) to exercise the rights conferred on the performer by Part II in relation to that performance.

(2) Any remuneration or damages received by a person's personal representatives by virtue of a right conferred on them by paragraph (1) shall devolve as part of that person's estate as if the right had subsisted and been vested in him immediately before his death.

New rights: effect of pre-commencement authorisation of copying

31. Where before commencement—
(a) the owner or prospective owner of copyright in a literary, dramatic, musical or artistic work has authorised a person to make a copy of the work, or
(b) the owner or prospective owner of performers' rights in a performance has authorised a person to make a copy of a recording of the performance,

any new right in relation to that copy shall vest on commencement in the person so authorised, subject to any agreement to the contrary.

New rights: effect of pre-commencement film production agreement

32.—(1) Sections 93A and 191F (presumption of transfer of rental right in case of production agreement) apply in relation to an agreement concluded before commencement.

As section 93A so applies, the restriction in subsection (3) of that section shall be omitted (exclusion of presumption in relation to screenplay, dialogue or music specifically created for the film).

(2) Sections 93B and 191G (right to equitable remuneration where rental right transferred) have effect accordingly, but subject to regulation 33 (right to equitable remuneration applicable to rental after 1st April 1997).

Right to equitable remuneration applicable to rental after 1st April 1997

33. No right to equitable remuneration under section 93B or 191G (right to equitable remuneration where rental right transferred) arises—
(a) in respect of any rental of a sound recording or film before 1st April 1997, or
(b) in respect of any rental after that date of a sound recording or film made in pursuance of an agreement entered into before 1st July 1994, unless the author or performer (or a successor in title of his) has before 1st January 1997 notified the person by whom the remuneration would be payable that he intends to exercise that right.

Savings for existing stocks

34.—(1) Any new right in relation to a copyright work does not apply to a copy of the work acquired by a person before commencement for the purpose of renting or lending it to the public.

(2) Any new right in relation to a qualifying performance does not apply to a copy of a recording of the performance acquired by a person before commencement for the purpose of renting or lending it to the public.

Lending of copies by libraries or archives

35. Until the making of regulations under section 37 of the Copyright, Designs and Patents Act 1988 for the purposes of section 40A(2) of that Act (lending of copies by libraries or archives), the reference in section 40A(2) (and in paragraph 6B of Schedule 2) to a prescribed library or archive shall be construed as a reference to any library or archive in the United Kingdom prescribed by paragraphs 2 to 6 of Part A of Schedule I to the Copyright (Librarians and Archivists) (Copying of Copyright Material) Regulations 1989.

Authorship of films

36.—(1) Regulation 18 (authorship of films) applies as from commencement in relation to films made on or after 1st July 1994.

(2) It is not an infringement of any right which the principal director has by virtue of these Regulations to do anything after commencement in pursuance of arrangements for the exploitation of the film made before 19th November 1992.

This does not affect any right of his to equitable remuneration under section 93B.

A3.iv The Copyright and Rights in Databases Regulations 1997

(SI 1997/3032)

Made   *18th December 1997*
Coming into force   *1st January 1998*

ARRANGEMENT OF REGULATIONS

PART I

INTRODUCTORY PROVISIONS

PART II

AMENDMENT OF THE COPYRIGHT, DESIGNS AND PATENTS ACT 1988

[The amendments have been printed in the main body of the Act and this Part is not reprinted.]

PART III

Database Right

PART IV

SAVINGS AND TRANSITIONAL PROVISIONS

Whereas a draft of the following Regulations has been approved by a resolution of each House of Parliament:

Now, therefore, the Secretary of State, being a Minister designated for the purposes of section 2(2) of the European Communities Act 1972 in relation to measures relating to copyright and measures relating to the prevention of unauthorised extraction of the contents of a database and of unauthorised re-utilisation of those contents, in exercise of the powers conferred by section 2(2) and (4) of that Act, hereby makes the following Regulations—

PART I

INTRODUCTORY PROVISIONS

Citation, commencement and extent

1.—(1) These Regulations may be cited as the Copyright and Rights in Databases Regulations 1997.

(2) These Regulations come into force on 1st January 1998.

(3) These Regulations extend to the whole of the United Kingdom.

Implementation of Directive

2.—(1) These Regulations make provision for the purpose of implementing—

(a) Council Directive No. 96/9/EC of 14 March 1996 on the legal protection of databases, [...]

(b) certain obligations of the United Kingdom created by or arising under the EEA Agreement so far as relating to the implementation of that Directive [, and]

[(c) an Agreement in the form of an exchange of letters between the United Kingdom of Great Britain and Northern Ireland on behalf of the Isle of Man and the European Community extending to the Isle of Man the legal protection of databases as provided for in Chapter III of that Directive.]

(2) In this Regulation "the EEA Agreement" means the Agreement on the European Economic Area signed at Oporto on 2nd May 1992, as adjusted by the Protocol signed at Brussels on 17th March 1993.

Note: The word "and" in reg.2(1)(a) was deleted and the words in square brackets at the end of reg.2(1)(b) and (c) inserted by the Copyright and Rights in Databases (Amendment) Regulations 2003 (SI 2003/2501), reg.3 with effect from November 1, 2003.

Interpretation

3. In these Regulations "the 1988 Act" means the Copyright, Designs and Patents Act 1988.

Scheme of the Regulations

4.—(1) The 1988 Act is amended in accordance with the provisions of Part II of these Regulations, subject to the savings and transitional provisions in Part IV of these Regulations.

(2) Part III of these Regulations has effect subject to those savings and transitional provisions.

Part II

Amendment of the Copyright, Designs and Patents Act 1988

5.–11. [...]

General Note:

The amendments have been printed in the main body of the Act and this Part is not reprinted.

Part III

Database Right

Interpretation

12.—(1) In this part—

"database" has the meaning given by section 3A(1) of the 1988 Act (as inserted by Regulation 6);

"extraction", in relation to any contents of a database, means the permanent or temporary transfer of those contents to another medium by any means or in any form;

"insubstantial", in relation to part of the contents of a database, shall be construed subject to Regulation 16(2);

"investment" includes any investment, whether of financial, human or technical resources;

"jointly", in relation to the making of a database, shall be construed in accordance with Regulation 14(6);

"lawful user", in relation to a database, means any person who (whether under a licence to do any of the acts restricted by any database right in the database or otherwise) has a right to use the database;

"maker", in relation to a database, shall be construed in accordance with Regulation 14;

"re-utilisation", in relation to any contents of a database, means making those contents available to the public by any means;

"substantial", in relation to any investment, extraction or "re-utilisation", means substantial in terms of quantity or quality or a combination of both.

(2) The making of a copy of a database available for use, on terms that it will or may be returned, otherwise than for direct or indirect economic or commercial advantage, through an establishment which is accessible to the public shall not be taken for the purposes of this Part to constitute extraction or re-utilisation of the contents of the database.

(3) Where the making of a copy of a database available through an establishment which is accessible to the public gives rise to a payment the amount of which does not go beyond what is necessary to cover the costs of the establishment, there is no direct or indirect economic or commercial advantage for the purposes of paragraph (2).

(4) Paragraph (2) does not apply to the making of a copy of a database available for on-the-spot reference use.

(5) Where a copy of a database has been sold within the EEA [or the Isle of Man] by, or with the consent of, the owner of the database right in the database, the further sale within the EEA [or the Isle of Man] of that copy shall not be taken for the purposes of this Part to constitute extraction or re-utilisation of the contents of the database.

Note: The words in square brackets in reg.12(5) inserted by the Copyright and Rights in Databases (Amendment) Regulations 2003 (SI 2003/2501), reg.4 with effect from November 1, 2003.

Database right

13.—(1) A property right ("database right") subsists, in accordance with this Part, in a database if there has been a substantial investment in obtaining, verifying or presenting the contents of the database.

(2) For the purposes of paragraph (1) it is immaterial whether or not the database or any of its contents is a copyright work, within the meaning of Part I of the 1988 Act.

(3) This Regulation has effect subject to Regulation 18.

The maker of a database

14.—(1) Subject to paragraphs (2) to (4), the person who takes the initiative in obtaining, verifying or presenting the contents of a database and assumes the risk of investing in that obtaining, verification or presentation shall be regarded as the maker of, and as having made, the database.

(2) Where a database is made by an employee in the course of his employment, his employer shall be regarded as the maker of the database, subject to any agreement to the contrary.

(3) Subject to paragraph (4), where a database is made by Her Majesty or by an officer or servant of the Crown in the course of his duties, Her Majesty shall be regarded as the maker of the database.

(4) Where a database is made by or under the direction or control of the House of Commons or the House of Lords—

    (a) the House by whom, or under whose direction or control, the database is made shall be regarded as the maker of the database, and

    (b) if the database is made by or under the direction or control of both Houses, the two Houses shall be regarded as the joint makers of the database.

[(4A) Where a database is made by or under the direction or control of the

Scottish Parliament, the Scottish Parliamentary Corporate Body shall be regarded as the maker of the database.]

(5) For the purposes of this Part a database is made jointly if two or more persons acting together in collaboration take the initiative in obtaining, verifying or presenting the contents of the database and assume the risk of investing in that obtaining, verification or presentation.

(6) References in this Part to the maker of a database shall, except as otherwise provided, be construed, in relation to a database which is made jointly, as references to all the makers of the database.

Note: Regulation 14(4A) was inserted by the Scotland Act 1998 (Consequential Modifications) (No.1) Order 1999 (SI 1999/1042) with effect from May 6, 1999.

First ownership of database right

15. The maker of a database is the first owner of database right in it.

Acts infringing database right

16.—(1) Subject to the provisions of this Part, a person infringes database right in a database if, without the consent of the owner of the right, he extracts or re-utilises all or a substantial part of the contents of the database.

(2) For the purposes of this Part, the repeated and systematic extraction or re-utilisation of insubstantial parts of the contents of a database may amount to the extraction of re-utilisation of a substantial part of those contents.

Term of protection

17.—(1) Database right in a database expires at the end of the period of fifteen years from the end of the calendar year in which the making of the database was completed.

(2) Where a database is made available to the public before the end of the period referred to in paragraph (1), database right in the database shall expire fifteen years from the end of the calendar year in which the database was first made available to the public.

(3) Any substantial change to the contents of a database, including a substantial change resulting from the accumulation of successive additions, deletions or alterations, which would result in the database being considered to be a substantial new investment shall qualify the database resulting from that investment for its own term of protection.

(4) This Regulation has effect subject to Regulation 30.

Qualification for database right

18.—(1) Database right does not subsist in a database unless, at the material time, its maker, or if it was made jointly, one or more of its makers, was—

    (a) an individual who was a national of an EEA state or habitually resident within the EEA,

    (b) a body which was incorporated under the law of an EEA state and which, at that time, satisfied one of the conditions in paragraph (2), [...]

    (c) a partnership or other unincorporated body which was formed under the law of an EEA state and which, at that time, satisfied the condition in paragraph (2)(a),

  [(d) an individual who was habitually resident within the Isle of Man,

    (e) a body which was incorporated under the law of the Isle of Man and which, at that time, satisfied one of the conditions in paragraph (2A), or

    (f) a partnership or other unincorporated body which was formed under the law of the Isle of Man and which, at that time, satisfied the condition in paragraph (2A)(a).]

(2) The conditions mentioned in paragraphs (1)(b) and (c) are—

    (a) that the body has its central administration or principal place of business within the EEA, or

    (b) that the body has its registered office within the EEA and the body's operations are linked on an ongoing basis with the economy of an EEA state.

[(2A) The conditions mentioned in paragraphs (1)(e) and (f) are—

    (a) that the body has its central administration or principal place of business within the Isle of Man, or

    (b) that the body has its registered office within the Isle of Man and the body's operations are linked on an ongoing basis with the economy of the Isle of Man.]

(3) Paragraph (1) does not apply in any case falling within Regulation 14(4).

(4) In this Regulation—

    (a) "EEA" and "EEA state" have the meaning given by section 172A of the 1988 Act;

    (b) "the material time" means the time when the database was made, or if the making extended over a period, a substantial part of that period.

Note: Regulation 18(1)(d), (e), (f) and (2A) inserted and reg.18(1)(b) amended by the deletion of the word "a" by the Copyright and Rights in Databases (Amendment) Regulations 2003 (SI 2003/2501), reg.6 with effect from November 1, 2003.

Avoidance of certain terms affecting lawful users

19.—(1) A lawful user of a database which has been made available to the public in any manner shall be entitled to extract or re-utilise insubstantial parts of the contents of the database for any purpose.

(2) Where under an agreement a person has a right to use a database, or part of a database, which has been made available to the public in any manner, any term or condition in the agreement shall be void in so far as it purports to prevent that person from extracting or re-utilising insubstantial parts of the contents of the database, or of that part of the database, for any purpose.

Exceptions to database right

20.—(1) Database right in a database which has been made available to the public in any manner is not infringed by fair dealing with a substantial part of its contents if—

    (a) that part is extracted from the database by a person who is apart from this paragraph a lawful user of the database,

    (b) it is extracted for the purpose of illustration for teaching or research and not for any commercial purpose, and

    (c) the source is indicated.

(2) The provisions of Schedule 1 specify other acts which may be done in relation to a database notwithstanding the existence of database right.

Exceptions to database right: deposit libraries

[20A.—(1) Database right in a database is not infringed by the copying of a work from the internet by a deposit library or person acting on its behalf if—

    (a) the work is of a description prescribed by regulations under section 10(5) of the 2003 Act,

    (b) its publication on the internet, or a person publishing it there, is connected with the United Kingdom in a manner so prescribed, and

    (c) the copying is done in accordance with any conditions so prescribed.

(2) Database right in a database is not infringed by the doing of anything in relation to relevant material permitted to be done under regulations under section 7 of the 2003 Act.

(3) Regulations under section 44A(3) of the 1988 Act exclude the application of paragraph (2) in relation to prescribed activities in relation to relevant material as (and to the extent that) they exclude the application of section 44A(2) of that Act in relation to those activities.

(4) In this Regulation—

    (a) "the 2003 Act" means the Legal Deposit Libraries Act 2003;

    (b) "deposit library" and "relevant material" have the same meaning as in section 7 of the 2003 Act."]

Note: This regulation was inserted by the Legal Deposit Libraries Act 2003 (c.8), s.8 with effect from February 1, 2004 (Legal Deposit Libraries Act 2003 (Commencement) Order 2004 (SI 2004/130)).

Acts permitted on assumption as to expiry of database right

21.—(1) Database right in a database is not infringed by the extraction or re-utilisation of a substantial part of the contents of the database at a time when, or in pursuance of arrangements made at a time when—

    (a) it is not possible by reasonable inquiry to ascertain the identity of the maker, and

    (b) it is reasonable to assume that database right has expired.

(2) In the case of a database alleged to have been made jointly, paragraph (1) applies in relation to each person alleged to be one of the makers.

Presumptions relevant to database right

22.—(1) The following presumptions apply in proceedings brought by virtue of this Part of these Regulations with respect to a database.

(2) Where a name purporting to be that of the maker appeared on copies of the database as published, or on the database when it was made, the person whose name appeared shall be presumed, until the contrary is proved—

    (a) to be the maker of the database, and

    (b) to have made it in circumstances not falling within Regulation 14(2) to (4).

(3) Where copies of the database as published bear a label or a mark stating—

    (a) that a named person was the maker of the database, or

    (b) that the database was first published in a specified year,

the label or mark shall be admissible as evidence of the facts stated and shall be presumed to be correct until the contrary is proved.

(4) In the case of a database alleged to have been made jointly, paragraphs (2) and (3), so far as is applicable, apply in relation to each person alleged to be one of the makers.

Application of copyright provisions to database right

23. The following provisions of the 1988 Act apply in relation to database right and databases in which that right subsists as they apply in relation to copyright and copyright works—

    sections 90 to 93 (dealing with rights in copyright works)

sections 96 to 102 (rights and remedies of copyright owner and exclusive
   licensee)
sections 113 and 114 (supplementary provisions relating to delivery up)
section 115 (jurisdiction of county court and sheriff court).

Note: Regulation 23 was substituted by the Intellectual Property (Enforcement, etc.)
Regulations 2006 (SI 2006/1028), Sch.3 para.6, with effect from April 29, 2006.

Licensing of database right

24. The provisions of Schedule 2 have effect with respect to the licensing of
database right.

Database right: jurisdiction of Copyright Tribunal

25.—(1) The Copyright Tribunal has jurisdiction under this Part to hear and
determine proceedings under the following provisions of Schedule 2—
   (a) paragraph 3, 4 or 5 (reference of licensing scheme);
   (b) paragraph 6 or 7 (application with respect to licence under licensing
       scheme);
   (c) paragraph 10, 11 or 12 (reference or application with respect to licence
       by licensing body).
   (2) The provisions of Chapter VIII of Part I of the 1988 Act (general provisions relating to the Copyright Tribunal) apply in relation to the Tribunal when
exercising any jurisdiction under this Part.
   (3) Provision shall be made by rules under section 150 of the 1988 Act
prohibiting the Tribunal from entertaining a reference under paragraph 3, 4 or 5
of Schedule 2 (reference of licensing scheme) by a representative organisation
unless the Tribunal is satisfied that the organisation is reasonably representative
of the class of persons which it claims to represent.

PART IV

SAVINGS AND TRANSITIONAL PROVISIONS

Introductory

[26. Expressions used in this Part which are defined for the purposes of Part I
of the 1988 Act have the same meaning as in that Part.]

Note: Regulation 26 was substituted by the Copyright and Rights in Databases (Amendment) Regulations 2003 (SI 2003/2501), reg.6 with effect from November 1, 2003.

General rule

27. Subject to regs 28 and 29, these Regulations apply to databases made before
or after [1st January 1998].

Note: The date in square brackets was substituted for the former word "commencement" by the Copyright and Rights in Databases (Amendment) Regulations 2003 (SI
2003/2501), reg.7 with effect from November 1, 2003.

General savings

[28.—(1) Nothing in these Regulations affects any agreement made before 1st
January 1998.
   (2) Nothing in these Regulations affects any agreement made after 31st
December 1997 and before 1st November 2003 in so far as the effect would only

arise as a result of the amendment of these Regulations by the Copyright and Rights in Databases (Amendment) Regulations 2003.

(3) No act done in respect of any database, in which database right subsists by virtue of the maker of the database (or one or more of its makers) falling within one of the provisions contained in Regulations 14(4) and 18(1)(a), (b) and (c),—

(a) before 1st January 1998, or

(b) after 31st December 1997, in pursuance of an agreement made before 1st January 1998,

shall be regarded as an infringement of database right in the database.

(4) No act done in respect of any database, in which database right subsists by virtue of its maker (or one or more of its makers) falling within one of the provisions contained in Regulation 18(1)(d), (e) and (f),—

(a) before 1st November 2003, or

(b) after 31st October 2003, in pursuance of an agreement made before 1st November 2003,

shall be regarded as an infringement of database right in the database.]

Note: This regulation was substituted by the Copyright and Rights in Databases (Amendment) Regulations 2003 (SI 2003/2501), reg.8 with effect from November 1, 2003.

Saving for copyright in certain existing databases

29.—(1) Where a database—

(a) was created on or before 27th March 1996, and

(b) is a copyright work immediately before [1st January 1998],

copyright shall continue to subsist in the database for the remainder of its copyright term.

(2) In this Regulation "copyright term" means the period of the duration of copyright under section 12 of the 1988 Act (duration of copyright in literary, dramatic, musical or artistic works).

Note: The date in square brackets was substituted for the former word "commencement" by the Copyright and Rights in Databases (Amendment) Regulations 2003 (SI 2003/2501), reg.9 with effect from November 1, 2003.

Database right: term applicable to certain existing databases

[30. Where—

(a) the making of any database is completed on or after 1st January 1983, and before 1st January 1998, and

(b) either—

    (i) the database is a database in which database right subsists by virtue of the maker of the database (or one or more of its makers) falling within one of the provisions contained in Regulations 14(4) and 18(1)(a), (b) and (c) and database right begins to subsist in the database on 1st January 1998, or

    (ii) the database is a database in which database right subsists by virtue of its maker (or one or more of its makers) falling within one of the provisions contained in Regulation 18(1)(d), (e) and (f) and database right begins to subsist in the database on 1st November 2003,

then database right shall subsist in the database for a period of fifteen years beginning with 1st January 1998.]

Note: This regulation was substituted by the Copyright and Rights in Databases

(Amendment) Regulations 2003 (SI 2003/2501), reg.10 with effect from November 1, 2003.

Regulation 20 (2)   SCHEDULE I

EXCEPTIONS TO DATABASE RIGHT FOR PUBLIC ADMINISTRATION

Parliamentary and judicial proceedings

1. Database right in a database is not infringed by anything done for the purposes of parliamentary or judicial proceedings or for the purposes of reporting such proceedings.

Royal Commissions and statutory inquiries

2.—(1) Database right in a database is not infringed by anything done for—

(a) the purposes of the proceedings of a Royal Commission or statutory inquiry, or

(b) the purpose of reporting any such proceedings held in public.

(2) Database right in a database is not infringed by the issue to the public of copies of the report of a Royal Commission or statutory inquiry containing the contents of the database.

(3) In this paragraph "Royal Commission" and "statutory inquiry" have the same meaning as in section 46 of the 1988 Act.

Material open to public inspection or on official register

3.—(1) Where the contents of a database are open to public inspection pursuant to a statutory requirement, or are on a statutory register, database right in the database is not infringed by the extraction of all or a substantial part of the contents containing factual information of any description, by or with the authority of the appropriate person, for a purpose which does not involve re-utilisation of all or a substantial part of the contents.

(2) Where the contents of a database are open to public inspection pursuant to a statutory requirement, database right in the database is not infringed by the extraction or re-utilisation of all or a substantial part of the contents, by or with the authority of the appropriate person, for the purpose of enabling the contents to be inspected at a more convenient time or place or otherwise facilitating the exercise of any right for the purpose of which the requirement is imposed.

(3) Where the contents of a database which is open to public inspection pursuant to a statutory requirement, or which is on a statutory register, contain information about matters of general scientific, technical, commercial or economic interest, database right in the database is not infringed by the extraction or re-utilisation of all or a substantial part of the contents, by or with the authority of the appropriate person, for the purpose of disseminating that information.

(4) In this paragraph—

"appropriate person" means the person required to make the contents of the database open to public inspection or, as the case may be, the person maintaining the register;

"statutory register" means a register maintained in pursuance of a statutory requirement; and

"statutory requirement" means a requirement imposed by provision made by or under an enactment.

[(5) In sub-paragraph (4) the reference to an enactment includes any enactment contained in Part 3 of the Regulatory Reform (Scotland) Act 2014.]

Note: Subsection (5) inserted by the Regulatory Reform (Scotland) Act 2014 (Consequential Modifications) Order 2015 (SI 2015/374), art.10(2), with effect from February 26, 2015.

Material communicated to the Crown in the course of public business

4.—(1) This paragraph applies where the contents of a database have in the course of public business been communicated to the Crown for any purpose, by or with the licence of the owner of the database right and a document or other material thing recording or embodying the contents of the database is owned by or in the custody or control of the Crown.

(2) The Crown may, for the purpose for which the contents of the database were communicated to it, or any related purpose which could reasonably have been anticipated by the owner of the database right in the database, extract or re-utilise all or a substantial part of the contents without infringing database right in the database.

(3) The Crown may not re-utilise the contents of a database by virtue of this paragraph if the contents have previously been published otherwise than by virtue of this paragraph.

(4) In sub-paragraph (1) "public business" includes any activity carried on by the Crown.

(5) This paragraph has effect subject to any agreement to the contrary between the Crown and the owner of the database right in the database.

Public records

5. The contents of a database which are comprised in public records within the meaning of the Public Records Act 1958, the Public Records (Scotland) Act 1937 or the Public Records Act (Ireland) 1923 which are open to public inspection in pursuance of that Act, may be re-utilised by or with the authority of any officer appointed under that Act, without infringement of database right in the database.

Acts done under statutory authority

6.—(1) Where the doing of a particular act is specifically authorised by an Act of Parliament, whenever passed, then, unless the Act provides otherwise, the doing of that act does not infringe database right in a database.

(2) Sub-paragraph (1) applies in relation to an enactment contained in Northern Ireland legislation as it applies in relation to an Act of Parliament.

[(2A) Sub-paragraph (1) applies in relation to an enactment contained in Part 3 of the Regulatory Reform (Scotland) Act 2014 as it applies in relation to an Act of Parliament.]

(3) Nothing in this paragraph shall be construed as excluding any defence of statutory authority otherwise available under or by virtue of any enactment [or other statutory provision].

Note: Subsection (2A) inserted, and in subs.(3) words in square brackets inserted, by the Regulatory Reform (Scotland) Act 2014 (Consequential Modifications) Order 2015 (SI 2015/374), art.10(3), (4), with effect from February 26, 2015.

Regulation 24   SCHEDULE 2

LICENSING OF DATABASE RIGHT

Licensing scheme and licensing bodies

1.—(1) In this Schedule a "licensing scheme" means a scheme setting out—
  (a) the classes of case in which the operator of the scheme, or the person on whose behalf he acts, is willing to grant database right licences, and
  (b) the terms on which licences would be granted in those classes of case;
     and for this purpose a "scheme" includes anything in the nature of a scheme, whether described as a scheme or as a tariff or by any other name.

(2) In this Schedule a "licensing body" means a society or other organisation which has as its main object, or one of its main objects, the negotiating or granting, whether as owner or prospective owner of a database right or as agent for him, of database right licences, and whose objects include the granting of licences covering the databases of more than one maker.

(3) In this paragraph "database right licences" means licences to do, or authorise the doing of, any of the things for which consent is required under Regulation 16.

2. Paragraphs 3 to 8 apply to licensing schemes which are operated by licensing bodies and cover databases of more than one maker so far as they relate to licences for extracting or re-utilising all or a substantial part of the contents of a database; and references in those paragraphs to a licensing scheme shall be construed accordingly.

Reference of proposed licensing scheme to tribunal

3.—(1) The terms of a licensing scheme proposed to be operated by a licensing body may be referred to the Copyright Tribunal by an organisation claiming to be representative of persons claiming that they require licences in cases of a description to which the scheme would apply, either generally or in relation to any description of case.

(2) The Tribunal shall first decide whether to entertain the reference, and may decline to do so on the ground that the reference is premature.

(3) If the Tribunal decides to entertain the reference it shall consider the matter referred and make such order, either confirming or varying the proposed scheme, either generally or so far as it relates to cases of the description to which the reference relates, as the Tribunal may determine to be reasonable in the circumstances.

(4) The order may be made so as to be in force indefinitely or for such period as the Tribunal may determine.

Reference of licensing scheme to tribunal

4.—(1) If while a licensing scheme is in operation a dispute arises between the operator of the scheme and—

(a) a person claiming that he requires a licence in a case of a description to which the scheme applies, or

(b) an organisation claiming to be representative of such persons,

that person or organisation may refer the scheme to the Copyright Tribunal in so far as it relates to cases of that description.

(2) A scheme which has been referred to the Tribunal under this paragraph shall remain in operation until proceedings on the reference are concluded.

(3) The Tribunal shall consider the matter in dispute and make such order, either confirming or varying the scheme so far as it relates to cases of the description to which the reference relates, as the Tribunal may determine to be reasonable in the circumstances.

(4) The order may be made so as to be in force indefinitely or for such period as the Tribunal may determine.

Further reference of scheme to tribunal

5.—(1) Where the Copyright Tribunal has on a previous reference of a licensing scheme under paragraph 3 or 4, or under this paragraph, made an order with respect to the scheme, then, while the order remains in force—

(a) the operator of the scheme,

(b) a person claiming that he requires a licence in a case of the description to which the order applies, or

(c) an organisation claiming to be representative of such persons,

may refer the scheme again to the Tribunal so far as it relates to cases of that description.

(2) A licensing scheme shall not, except with the special leave of the Tribunal, be referred again to the Tribunal in respect of the same description of cases—

(a) within twelve months from the date of the order on the previous reference, or

(b) if the order was made so as to be in force for 15 months or less, until the last three months before the expiry of the order.

(3) A scheme which has been referred to the Tribunal under this section shall remain in operation until proceedings on the reference are concluded.

(4) The Tribunal shall consider the matter in dispute and make such order, either confirming, varying or further varying the scheme so far as it relates to cases of the description to which the reference relates, as the Tribunal may determine to be reasonable in the circumstances.

(5) The order may be made so as to be in force indefinitely or for such period as the Tribunal may determine.

Application for grant of licence in connection with licensing scheme

6.—(1) A person who claims, in a case covered by a licensing scheme, that the operator of the scheme has refused to grant him or procure the grant to him of a licence in accordance with the scheme, or has failed to do so within a reasonable time after being asked, may apply to the Copyright Tribunal.

(2) A person who claims, in a case excluded from a licensing scheme, that the operator of the scheme either—

    (a) has refused to grant him a licence or procure the grant to him of a licence, or has failed to do so within a reasonable time of being asked, and that in the circumstances it is unreasonable that a licence should not be granted, or

    (b) proposes terms for a licence which are unreasonable,

may apply to the Copyright Tribunal.

(3) A case shall be regarded as excluded from a licensing scheme for the purposes of sub-paragraph (2) if—

    (a) the scheme provides for the grant of licences subject to terms excepting matters from the licence and the case falls within such an exception, or

    (b) the case is so similar to those in which licences are granted under the scheme that it is unreasonable that it should not be dealt with in the same way.

(4) If the Tribunal is satisfied that the claim is well-founded, it shall make an order declaring that, in respect of the matters specified in the order, the applicant is entitled to a licence on such terms as the Tribunal may determine to be applicable in accordance with the scheme or, as the case may be, to be reasonable in the circumstances.

(5) The order may be made so as to be in force indefinitely or for such period as the Tribunal may determine.

Application for review of order as to entitlement to licence

7.—(1) Where the Copyright Tribunal has made an order under paragraph 6 that a person is entitled to a licence under a licensing scheme, the operator of the scheme or the original applicant may apply to the Tribunal to review its order.

(2) An application shall not be made, except with the special leave of the Tribunal—

    (a) within twelve months from the date of the order, or of the decision on a previous application under this section, or

    (b) if the order was made so as to be in force for 15 months or less, or as a result of the decision on a previous application under this section is due to expire within 15 months of that decision, until the last three months before the expiry date.

(3) The Tribunal shall on an application for review confirm or vary its order as the Tribunal may determine to be reasonable having regard to the terms applicable in accordance with the licensing scheme or, as the case may be, the circumstances of the case.

Effect of order of tribunal as to licensing scheme

8.—(1) A licensing scheme which has been confirmed or varied by the Copyright Tribunal—

    (a) under paragraph 3 (reference of terms of proposed scheme), or

    (b) under paragraph 4 or 5 (reference of existing scheme to Tribunal),

shall be in force or, as the case may be, remain in operation, so far as it relates to the description of case in respect of which the order was made, so long as the order remains in force.

(2) While the order is in force a person who in a case of a class to which the order applies—

    (a) pays to the operator of the scheme any charges payable under the scheme in respect of a licence covering the case in question or, if the amount cannot be ascertained, gives an undertaking to the operator to pay them when ascertained, and

    (b) complies with the other terms applicable to such a licence under the scheme,

shall be in the same position as regards infringement of database right as if he had at all material times been the holder of a licence granted by the owner of the database right in question in accordance with the scheme.

(3) The Tribunal may direct that the order, so far as it varies the amount of charges payable, has effect from a date before that on which it is made, but not earlier than the date on which the reference was made or, if later, on which the scheme came into operation.

If such a direction is made—

    (a) any necessary repayments, or further payments, shall be made in respect of charges already paid, and

(b) the reference in sub-paragraph (2)(a) to the charges payable under the scheme shall be construed as a reference to the charges so payable by virtue of the order.

No such direction may be made where sub-paragraph (4) below applies.

(4) Where the Tribunal has made an order under paragraph 6 (order as to entitlement to licence under licensing scheme) and the order remains in force, the person in whose favour the order is made shall if he—

(a) pays to the operator of the scheme any charges payable in accordance with the order or, if the amount cannot be ascertained, gives an undertaking to pay the charges when ascertained, and

(b) complies with the other terms specified in the order,

be in the same position as regards infringement of database right as if he had at all material times been the holder of a licence granted by the owner of the database right in question on the terms specified in the order.

References and applications with respect to licences by licensing bodies

9. Paragraphs 10 to 13 (references and applications with respect to licensing by licensing bodies) apply to licences relating to database right which cover databases of more than one maker granted by a licensing body otherwise than in pursuance of a licensing scheme, so far as the licences authorise extracting or re-utilising all or a substantial part of the contents of a database and references in those paragraphs to a licence shall be construed accordingly.

Reference to tribunal of proposed licence

10.—(1) The terms on which a licensing body proposes to grant a licence may be referred to the Copyright Tribunal by the prospective licensee.

(2) The Tribunal shall first decide whether to entertain the reference, and may decline to do so on the ground that the reference is premature.

(3) If the Tribunal decides to entertain the reference it shall consider the terms of the proposed licence and make such order, either confirming or varying the terms, as it may determine to be reasonable in the circumstances.

(4) The order may be made so as to be in force indefinitely or for such period as the Tribunal may determine.

Reference to tribunal of expiring licence

11.—(1) A licensee under a licence which is due to expire, by effluxion of time or as a result of notice given by the licensing body, may apply to the Copyright Tribunal on the ground that it is unreasonable in the circumstances that the licence should cease to be in force.

(2) Such an application may not be made until the last three months before the licence is due to expire.

(3) A licence in respect of which a reference has been made to the Tribunal shall remain in operation until proceedings on the reference are concluded.

(4) If the Tribunal finds the application well-founded, it shall make an order declaring that the licensee shall continue to be entitled to the benefit of the licence on such terms as the Tribunal may determine to be reasonable in the circumstances.

(5) An order of the Tribunal under this section may be made so as to be in force indefinitely or for such period as the Tribunal may determine.

Application for review of order as to licence

12.—(1) Where the Copyright Tribunal has made an order under paragraph 10 or 11, the licensing body or the person entitled to the benefit of the order may apply to the Tribunal to review its order.

(2) An application shall not be made, except with the special leave of the Tribunal—

(a) within twelve months from the date of the order or of the decision on a previous application under this paragraph or

(b) if the order was made so as to be in force for 15 months or less, or as a result of the decision on a previous application under this section is due to expire within 15 months of that decision, until the last three months before the expiry date.

(3) The Tribunal shall on an application for review confirm or vary its order as the Tribunal may determine to be reasonable in the circumstances.

Effect of order of tribunal as to licence

13.—(1) Where the Copyright Tribunal has made an order under paragraph 10 or 11 and the order remains in force, the person entitled to the benefit of the order shall if he—

    (a) pays to the licensing body any charges payable in accordance with the order or, if the amount cannot be ascertained, gives an undertaking to pay the charges when ascertained, and

    (b) complies with the other terms specified in the order,

be in the same position as regards infringement of database right as if he had at all material times been the holder of a licence granted by the owner of the database right in question on the terms specified in the order.

(2) The benefit of the order may be assigned—

    (a) in the case of an order under paragraph 10, if assignment is not prohibited under the terms of the Tribunal's order; and

    (b) in the case of an order under paragraph 11, if assignment was not prohibited under the terms of the original licence.

(3) The Tribunal may direct that an order under paragraph 10 or 11, or an order under paragraph 12 varying such an order, so far as it varies the amount of charges payable, has effect from a date before that on which it is made, but not earlier than the date on which the reference or application was made or, if later, on which the licence was granted or, as the case may be, was due to expire.

If such a direction is made—

    (a) any necessary repayments, or further payments, shall be made in respect of charges already paid, and

    (b) the reference in sub-paragraph (1)(a) to the charges payable in accordance with the order shall be construed, where the order is varied by a later order, as a reference to the charges so payable by virtue of the later order.

General considerations: unreasonable discrimination

14. In determining what is reasonable on a reference or application under this Schedule relating to a licensing scheme or licence, the Copyright Tribunal shall have regard to—

    (a) the availability of other schemes, or the granting of other licences, to other persons in similar circumstances, and

    (b) the terms of those schemes or licences,

and shall exercise its powers so as to secure that there is no unreasonable discrimination between licensees, or prospective licensees, under the scheme or licence to which the reference or application relates and licensees under other schemes operated by, or other licences granted by, the same person.

Powers exercisable in consequence of competition report

15.—[(1) Sub-paragraph (1A) applies where whatever needs to be remedied, mitigated or prevented by the Secretary of State [or (as the case may be) the Competition and Markets Authority] under section 12(5) of the Competition Act 1980 or section 41(2), 55(2), 66(6), 75(2), 83(2), 138(2), 147(2)[, 147A(2)] or 160(2) of, or paragraph 5(2) or 10(2) of Schedule 7 to, the Enterprise Act 2002 (powers to take remedial action following references [to the chair of the Competition and Markets Authority for the constitution of a group] to the Commission in connection with public bodies and certain other persons, mergers or market investigations) or article 12(7) of, or paragraph 5(2) or 10(2) of Schedule 2 to, the Enterprise Act 2002 (Protection of Legitimate Interests) Order 2003 (power to take remedial action following references [to the chair of the Competition and Markets Authority for the constitution of a group] in connection with European mergers) consists of or includes—

    (a) conditions in licences granted by the owner of database right in a database restricting the use of the database by the licensee or the right of the owner of the database right to grant other licences; or

    (b) a refusal of an owner of database right to grant licences on reasonable terms.

(1A) The powers conferred by Schedule 8 to the Enterprise Act 2002 include power to cancel or modify those conditions and, instead or in addition, to provide that licences in respect of the database right shall be available as of right.

(2) The references to anything permitted by Schedule 8 to the Enterprise Act 2002 in section 12(5A) of the Competition Act 1980 and in sections 75(4)(a), 83(4)(a), 84(2)(a), 89(1), 160(4)(a), 161(3)(a) and 164(1) of, and paragraphs 5, 10 and 11 of Schedule 7 to, the Act of 2002 and paragraphs 5, 10 and 11 of Schedule 2 to the Enterprise Act 2002 (Protection of Legitimate Interests) Order 2003 shall be construed accordingly.]

(3) The terms of a licence available by virtue of this paragraph shall, in default of agreement, be settled by the Copyright Tribunal on an application by the person requiring the licence; and terms so settled shall authorise the licensee to do everything in respect of which a licence is so available.

(4) Where the terms of a licence are settled by the Tribunal, the licence has effect from the date on which the application to the Tribunal was made.

Notes:

(1) Sub-paragraph (2) substituted and subpara.(1A) inserted by the Enterprise Act 2002 (Consequential and Supplemental Provisions) Order 2003 (SI 2003/1398), Sch.1 para.31 with effect from June 20, 2003.

(2) In subpara.(1) words in square brackets substituted or inserted, subject to transitional provisions and savings, by the Enterprise and Regulatory Reform Act 2013 (Competition) (Consequential, Transitional and Saving Provisions) (No. 2) Order 2014 (SI 2014/549), Sch.1 para.27, with effect from April 1, 2014 (for transitional provisions and savings see art.3 thereof). Sub-para.1 (as substituted by SI 2003/1398) formerly read:

"[(1A) Sub-paragraph (1A) applies where whatever needs to be remedied, mitigated or prevented by the Secretary of State, the Office of Fair Trading or (as the case may be) the Competition Commission under section 12(5) of the Competition Act 1980 or section 41(2), 55(2), 66(6), 75(2), 83(2), 138(2), 147(2) or 160(2) of, or paragraph 5(2) or 10(2) of Schedule 7 to, the Enterprise Act 2002 (powers to take remedial action following references to the Commission in connection with public bodies and certain other persons, mergers or market investigations) or article 12(7) of, or paragraph 5(2) or 10(2) of Schedule 2 to, the Enterprise Act 2002 (Protection of Legitimate Interests) Order 2003 (power to take remedial action following references to the Commission in connection with European mergers) consists of or includes—

(a) conditions in licences granted by the owner of database right in a database restricting the use of the database by the licensee or the right of the owner of the database right to grant other licences; or

(b) a refusal of an owner of database right to grant licences on reasonable terms."

A3.v The Copyright and Related Rights Regulations 2003

(SI 2003/2498)

Made	*27th September 2003*
Laid before Parliament	*3rd October 2003*
Coming into force	*31st October 2003*

ARRANGEMENT OF REGULATIONS

PART 1

INTRODUCTORY PROVISIONS

1.   Citation and commencement
2.   Consequential amendments and repeals

PART 2

AMENDMENTS OF THE COPYRIGHT, DESIGNS AND PATENTS ACT 1988

3.   Introductory

[The amendments have been printed in the main body of the Act and have not been reproduced here.]

Part 3

Savings and transitional provisions

General provisions

Special provisions

The Secretary of State, being a Minister designated for the purposes of section 2(2) of the European Communities Act 1972, in relation to measures relating to copyright and to rights in performances and also in relation to measures relating to the prevention of unauthorised extraction of the contents of a database, and of unauthorised reutilisation of those contents, in exercise of the powers conferred on her by that section, hereby makes the following Regulations:

Part 1

Introductory Provisions

Citation and commencement

1. These Regulations may be cited as the Copyright and Related Rights Regulations 2003 and shall come into force on 31st October 2003.

Consequential amendments and repeals

2.—(1) Schedule 1 (consequential amendments) shall have effect.

(2) Schedule 2 (repeals) shall have effect.

Part 2

Amendments of the Copyright, Designs and Patents Act 1988

Introductory

3. The Copyright, Designs and Patents Act 1988 shall be amended as follows and, except where otherwise indicated, any reference in this Part to a section or paragraph is a reference to a section or paragraph of that Act and reference to a Schedule is to a Schedule to that Act.

4. [...]

Note: The amendments have been printed in the main body of the Act and have not been reproduced here.

Part 3

Savings and Transitional Provisions

General Provisions

Introductory

30.—(1) In this Part—

"commencement" means the date upon which these regulationscome into force;

"extended copyright" means any copyright in sound recordings which subsists by virtue of section 13A of the 1988 Act (as amended by regulation 29) after the date on which it would have expired under the 1988 provisions;

"prospective owner" includes a person who is prospectively entitled to extended copyright in a sound recording by virtue of such an agreement as is mentioned in regulation 37(1);

"the 1988 Act" means the Copyright, Designs and Patents Act 1988; and

"the 1988 provisions" means the provisions of the 1988 Act as they stood immediately before commencement (including the provisions of Schedule 1 to that Act continuing the effect of earlier enactments).

(2) Expressions used in this Part which are defined for the purposes of Part 1 or 2 of the 1988 Act have the same meaning as in that Part.

General rules

31.—(1) Subject to regulation 32, these Regulations apply to—

(a) copyright works made,

(b) performances given,

(c) databases, in which database right vests, made, and

(d) works, in which publication right vests, first published, before or after commencement.

(2) No act done before commencement shall be regarded as an infringement of any new or extended right arising by virtue of these Regulations.

Savings for certain existing agreements

32.—(1) Nothing in these Regulations affects any agreement made before 22nd December 2002.

(2) No act done after commencement, in pursuance of an agreement made before 22nd December 2002, shall be regarded as an infringement of any new or extended right arising by virtue of these Regulations.

Special provisions

Permitted acts

33. The provisions of Chapter 3 of Part 1 (acts permitted in relation to copyright works) and Schedule 2 (rights in performances: permitted acts) in the 1988 provisions shall continue to apply to anything done after commencement in completion of an act begun before commencement which was permitted by those provisions.

Performers' rights: making available to the public

34.—(1) Those parts of section 182D in the 1988 provisions which confer a right to equitable remuneration in relation to the making available to the public in the way mentioned in section 182CA(1) (regulation 7) of a commercially published sound recording shall cease to apply on commencement.

(2) Any assignment made before commencement under the provisions of section 182D(2) shall, on commencement, cease to apply insofar as it relates to the new making available to the public right conferred by section 182CA (regulation 7).

Exercise of rights in relation to performances

35.—(1) The new right conferred by section 182CA (consent required for making available to the public) (in regulation 7) is exercisable as from commencement by the performer or (if he has died) by the person who immediately before commencement was entitled by virtue of section 192A(2) to exercise the rights conferred on the performer by Part 2 in relation to that performance.

(2) Any damages received by a person's personal representatives by virtue of the right conferred by paragraph (1) shall devolve as part of that person's estate as if the right had subsisted and been vested in him immediately before his death.

Ownership of extended copyright in sound recordings

36. The person who is the owner of the copyright in a sound recording immediately before commencement is as from commencement the owner of any extended copyright in that sound recording.

Prospective ownership of extended copyright in sound recordings

37.—(1) Where by an agreement made before commencement in relation to extended copyright in a sound recording, and signed by or on behalf of the prospective owner of the copyright, the prospective owner purports to assign the extended copyright (wholly or partially) to another person, then, if on commencement the assignee or another person claiming under him would be entitled as against all other persons to require the copyright to be vested in him, the copyright shall vest in the assignee or his successor in title by virtue of this paragraph.

(2) A licence granted by a prospective owner of extended copyright in a sound recording is binding on every successor in title to his interest (or prospective interest) in the right, except a purchaser in good faith for valuable consideration and without notice (actual or constructive) of the licence or a person deriving title from such a purchaser; and references in Part 1 of the 1988 Act to doing anything with, or without, the licence of the copyright owner shall be construed accordingly.

Extended copyright in sound recordings: existing licences, agreements, etc.

38.—(1) Any copyright licence or any term or condition of an agreement relating to the exploitation of a sound recording which—

(a) subsists immediately before commencement in relation to an existing sound recording, and

(b) is not to expire before the end of the copyright period under the 1988 provisions,

shall continue to have effect during the period of any extended copyright in that sound recording, subject to any agreement to the contrary.

(2) Any copyright licence, or term or condition relating to the exploitation of a sound recording, imposed by order of the Copyright Tribunal which—

(a) subsists immediately before commencement in relation to an existing sound recording, and

(b) is not to expire before the end of the copyright period under the 1988 provisions,

shall continue to have effect during the period of any extended copyright, subject to any further order of the Tribunal.

Duration of copyright in sound recordings: general saving

39. Copyright in an existing sound recording shall continue to subsist until the date it would have expired under Regulation 15 of the Duration of Copyright and Rights in Performances Regulations 1995(SI 1995/3297) if that date is later than the date on which copyright would expire under the provisions of section 13A of the 1988 Act as amended by regulation 29.

Sanctions and remedies

40.—(1) Section 296 in the 1988 provisions (devices designed to circumvent copy-protection) shall continue to apply to acts done in relation to computer programs or other works prior to commencement.

(2) Section 296 as substituted by regulation 24(1) (circumvention of technical devices applied to computer programs), and sections 296ZA (circumvention of technological measures) and 296ZD (rights and remedies in respect of devices designed to circumvent technological measures), introduced by regulation 24(1), shall apply to acts done in relation to computer programs or other works on or after commencement.

(3) Sections 107(2A), 198(1A) and 296ZB(1) and (2) (offences) do not have effect in relation to any act committed before commencement.

A3.vi The Copyright and Duration of Rights in Performances Regulations 2013

(SI 2013/1782)

Made	*17th July 2013*
Laid before Parliament	*18th July 2013*
Coming into force	*1st November 2013*

The Secretary of State, being a Minister designated for the purposes of section 2(2) of the European Communities Act 1972 in relation to measures relating to copyright and rights in performances, in exercise of powers conferred by that section and section 78 of the Enterprise and Regulatory Reform Act 2013, makes the following Regulations:

PART 1

INTRODUCTORY PROVISIONS

Citation and commencement

1. These Regulations may be cited as the Copyright and Duration of Rights in Performances Regulations 2013 and come into force on 1st November 2013.

Consequential amendments and repeals

2. In these Regulations "the Act" means the Copyright, Designs and Patents Act 1988.

Scheme of the Regulations

3. The Act is amended in accordance with the provisions of Part 2 of these

Regulations, subject to the savings and transitional provisions in Part 3 of these Regulations.

Note: Regulations 4 to 10 amend the Copyright, Designs and Patents Act 1988 and are not reproduced here. For the amendments to the Act, see A1 above.

PART 3

SAVINGS, TRANSITIONAL AND REVIEW PROVISIONS

INTRODUCTORY

Introductory

11.—(1) References in this Part to "commencement", without more, are to the date on which these Regulations come into force.

(2) In this Part—

"the 1988 provisions" means the provisions of the Act as they stood immediately before commencement (including the provisions of Schedule 1 to the Act continuing the effect of earlier enactments); and

"the new provisions" means the provisions of the Act as amended by these Regulations.

(3) Expressions used in this Part which are defined for the purposes of Part 1 or Part 2 of the Act have the same meaning as in that Part.

COPYRIGHT

Copyright: interpretation

12.—(1) In the provisions of this Part relating to copyright—

(a) "existing" in relation to a work, means made before commencement; and

(b) "existing copyright work" means a work in which copyright subsisted immediately before commencement.

(2) For the purposes of those provisions a work of which the making extended over a period shall be taken to have been made when its making was completed.

(3) References in those provisions to "moral rights" are to the rights conferred by Chapter IV of Part I of the Act.

Duration of copyright: general saving

13. Copyright in an existing copyright work shall continue to subsist until the date on which it would have expired under the 1988 provisions if that date is later than the date on which copyright would expire under the new provisions.

Duration of copyright: application of new provisions

14. The new provisions relating to duration of copyright in sound recordings and works comprised in works of co-authorship apply—

(a) to sound recordings and works of co-authorship made after commencement;

(b) to existing sound recordings and works of co-authorship which ⎯rst qualify for copyright protection after commencement;

(c) to existing sound recordings in which copyright subsisted immediately before commencement;

(d) to works of co-authorship of which either or both the musical work and the literary work were existing copyright works; and

(e) to works of co-authorship of which the musical work or the literary work were on commencement protected as copyright works in another EEA state under legislation relating to copyright or related rights.

Extended and revived copyright

15. In the following provisions of this Part—

(a) "extended copyright" means any copyright which subsists by virtue of the new provisions after the date on which it would have expired under the 1988 provisions; and

(b) "revived copyright" means any copyright in a musical or literary work comprised in a work of co-authorship which subsists by virtue of the new provisions after having expired under the 1988 provisions or any earlier enactment relating to copyright.

Ownership of extended copyright

16.—(1) The person who is the owner of the copyright in a sound recording or in a work comprised in a work of co-authorship immediately before commencement is as from commencement the owner of any extended copyright in the sound recording or work, subject as follows.

(2) If he or she is entitled to copyright for a period less than the whole of the copyright period under the 1988 provisions, any extended copyright is part of the reversionary interest expectant on the termination of that period.

Ownership of revived copyright in works of co-authorship

17.—(1) The person who was the owner of the copyright in a musical or literary work comprised in the work of co-authorship immediately before it expired (the "former copyright owner") is as from commencement the owner of any revived copyright in the work, subject as follows.

(2) If the former copyright owner has died before commencement, or in the case of a legal person has ceased to exist before commencement, the revived copyright shall vest in the author of the work or his or her personal representatives.
(3) Where revived copyright vests in personal representatives by virtue of paragraph (2), it shall be held by them for the benefit of the person who would have been entitled to it had it been vested in the author immediately before his or her death and had devolved as part of his or her estate.

Prospective ownership of extended or revived copyright

18.—(1) Where by an agreement made before commencement in relation to extended or revived copyright, and signed by or on behalf of the prospective owner of the copyright, the prospective owner purports to assign the extended or revived copyright (wholly or partially) to another person, then if, on commencement the assignee or another person claiming under the assignee would be entitled as against all other persons to require the copyright to be vested in him or her, the copyright shall vest in the assignee or his or her successor in title by virtue of this paragraph.

(2) A licence granted by a prospective owner of extended or revived copyright is binding on every successor in title to the prospective owner's interest (or prospective interest) in the right, except a purchaser in good faith for valuable consideration and without notice (actual or constructive) of the licence or a person

deriving title from such a purchaser and references in Part 1 of the Act to do anything with, or without, the licence of the copyright owner shall be construed accordingly.

(3) In paragraph (2) "prospective owner" includes a person who is prospectively entitled to extended or revived copyright by virtue of such an agreement as is mentioned in paragraph (1).

Extended copyright: existing licences, agreements, &c

19.—(1) Subject to sections 191HA(5) and 191HB(7) and (9), any copyright licence, any term or condition of an agreement relating to the exploitation of a copyright work, or any waiver or assertion of moral rights, which—

    (a) subsists immediately before commencement in relation to an existing copyright work, and

    (b) is not to expire before the end of the copyright period under the 1988 provisions, shall continue to have effect during the period of any extended copyright, subject to any agreement to the contrary.

(2) Any copyright licence, or term or condition relating to the exploitation of a copyright work, imposed by order of the Copyright Tribunal which—

    (a) subsists immediately before commencement in relation to an existing copyright work, and

    (b) is not to expire before the end of the copyright period under the 1988 provisions, shall continue to have effect during the period of any extended copyright, subject to any further order of the Tribunal.

Revived copyright: exercise of moral rights

20.—(1) The following provisions have e_ect with respect to the exercise of moral rights in relation to a work comprised in a work of co-authorship in which there is revived copyright.

(2) Any waiver or assertion of moral rights which subsisted immediately before the expiry of copyright shall continue to have e_ect during the period of revived copyright.

(3) Moral rights are exercisable after commencement by the author of a work as with any other copyright work.

(4) Where the author died before commencement—

    (a) the rights conferred by—

        (i) section 77 (right to identification as author or director); or

        (ii) section 80 (right to object to derogatory treatment of work), are exercisable after commencement by his personal representatives, and

    (b) any infringement after commencement of the right conferred by section 84 (false attribution) is actionable by his personal representatives.

(5) Any damages recovered by personal representatives by virtue of this regulation in respect of an infringement after a person's death shall devolve as part of his or her estate as if the right of action had subsisted and been vested in him or her immediately before his or her death.

(6) Nothing in these Regulations shall be construed as causing a moral right to be exercisable if, or to the extent that, the right was excluded by virtue of paragraph 23 of Schedule 1 on the commencement of the Act or would have been so excluded if copyright had not previously expired.

Revived copyright: saving for acts of exploitation when work in public domain, &c

21.—(1) No act done before commencement shall be regarded as infringing revived copyright in a work.

(2) It is not an infringement of revived copyright in a work—

   (a) to do anything after commencement in pursuance of arrangements made before commencement at a time when copyright did not subsist in the work, or

   (b) to issue to the public after commencement copies of the work made before commencement at a time when copyright did not subsist in the work.

(3) It is not an infringement of revived copyright in a work to do anything after commencement in relation to a literary, dramatic or musical work or a film made before commencement or made in pursuance of arrangements made before commencement, which contains a copy of that work or is an adaptation of that work if—

   (a) the copy or adaptation was made before commencement at a time when copyright did not subsist in the work in which revived copyright subsists, or

   (b) the copy or adaptation was made in pursuance of arrangements made before commencement at a time when copyright did not subsist in the work in which revived copyright subsists.

(4) It is not an infringement of revived copyright in a work to do after commencement anything which is a restricted act in relation to the work if the act is done at a time when, or is done in pursuance of arrangements made at a time when, the name and address of a person entitled to authorise the act cannot by reasonable inquiry be ascertained.

(5) In this regulation "arrangements" means arrangements for the exploitation of the work in question.

(6) It is not an infringement of any moral right to do anything which by virtue of this regulation is not an infringement of copyright.

RIGHTS IN PERFORMANCES

Rights in performances: interpretation

22.—(1) In the provisions of this Part relating to rights in performances—

   "existing protected performance" means a performance in a sound recording in relation to which rights under Part II of the Act (rights in performances) subsisted immediately before commencement,

   "a new right" means a right arising by virtue of regulation 9 in relation to an assignment of a performer's property rights in a sound recording. References in this Part to performers' rights are to the rights given by section 180(1)(a) of the Act.

Rights in performances: application of new provisions

23. The new provisions relating to the duration of performers' rights in sound recordings and rights in relation to an assignment of performers' rights in a sound recording apply—

   (a) to performances taking place after commencement;

   (b) to existing performances which first qualify for protection under Part II of the 1988 Act after commencement; and

   (c) to existing protected performances.

Extended performance rights

24. In the following provisions of this Part "extended performance rights" means rights under Part II of the Act which subsist by virtue of the new provisions after the date on which they would have expired under the 1988 provisions.

Entitlement to extended performance rights and new rights

25.—(1) Any extended performance rights and any new rights are exercisable as from commencement by the performer or (if he or she has died) the person entitled to exercise those rights by virtue of section 191B(1) or 192A of the Act.

(2) Any remuneration or damages received by a person's personal representatives by virtue of a right conferred on them by paragraph (1) shall devolve as part of that person's estate as if the right had subsisted and been vested in him or her immediately before his or her death.

Extended performance rights: existing consents, agreements, etc.

26. Subject to the provisions of sections 191HA(5) and 191HB(7) and (9), any consent, or any term or condition of an agreement, relating to the exploitation of an existing protected performance which—

(a) subsists immediately before commencement, and

(b) is not to expire before the end of the period for which rights under Part II of the Act subsist in relation to that performance, shall continue to subsist during the period of any extended performance rights, subject to any agreement to the contrary.

Review

27.—(1) Before the end of each review period, the Secretary of State must—

(a) carry out a review of regulations 4 to 26,

(b) set out the conclusions of the review in a report, and

(c) lay the report before Parliament.

(2) In carrying out the review the Secretary of State must, so far as is reasonable, have regard to how the Directive (which is implemented by means of regulations 4 to 26) is implemented in other Member States and must in particular—

(a) consider whether and if so, to what extent certain producers should be subject to the obligation to pay the annual payment referred to in section 191HB of the Act (as inserted by regulation 9) having regard to the provisions of Recital (12) of the Directive, and

(b) consider whether to implement the provision set out in Article 10a, paragraph 2 of Directive 2006/116/EC as inserted by Article 1(4) of the Directive.

(3) The report must in particular—

(a) set out the objectives intended to be achieved by the regulatory system established by those regulations,

(b) assess the extent to which those objectives are achieved, and

(c) assess whether those objectives remain appropriate and, if so, the extent to which they could be achieved with a system that imposes less regulation.

(4) In this Regulation—

"Directive" means Directive 2011/77/EU of the European Parliament and of the Council of 27th September 2011 amending Directive 2006/116/EC on the term of protection of copyright and related rights;

"Review period" means—

(a) the period of five years beginning with the day on which regulations 4 to 26 come into force, and

(b) subject to paragraph (5), each successive period of five years.

(5) If a report under this regulation is laid before Parliament before the last day of the review period to which it relates, the following review period is to begin with the day on which that report is laid.

Note: Regulations 4 to 10 amend the Copyright, Designs and Patents Act 1988. The amendments are referred to in the appropriate places in the text of the Act.

A3.vii Copyright and Rights in Performances (Disability) Regulations 2014

(2014/1384)

Made *19th May 2014*

The Secretary of State is a Minister designated for the purposes of section 2(2) of the European Communities Act 1972[1] in relation to matters relating to copyright and rights in performances[2]. In accordance with paragraph 2(2) of Schedule 2 to that Act, a draft of this instrument was laid before Parliament and approved by a resolution of each House of Parliament. The Secretary of State, in exercise of the powers conferred by section 2(2) of that Act makes the following Regulations:

Citation, commencement and interpretation

1.—(1) These Regulations may be cited as the Copyright and Rights in Performances (Disability) Regulations 2014 and come into force at 00.01 on 1st June 2014.

(2) In these Regulations "the 1988 Act" means the Copyright, Designs and Patents Act 1988.

SCHEDULE 1

CONSEQUENTIAL AMENDMENTS, REPEALS, REVOCATION AND SAVING PROVISIONS

Saving provisions
9. Section 31F of the 1988 Act, as in force immediately before the commencement of these Regulations, continues to have effect for the purposes of regulation 26 of the Legal Deposit Libraries (Non-Print Works) Regulations 2013 (reader access to relevant material: visually impaired persons)[3].

---

[1] Section 2(2) was amended by the Legislative and Regulatory Reform Act 2006 (c.51), section 27(1) and the European Union (Amendment) Act 2008 (c.7), section 3(3) and Part 1 of the Schedule.
[2] S.I. 1992/707 and S.I.1993/595.
[3] S.I. 2013/777.

A4. Regulations made under CDPA 1988 relating to Copyright, Performances and Fraudulent Reception

A4.i The Copyright and Rights in Performances (Notice of Seizure) Order 1989

(SI 1989/1006)

Made	*13th June 1989*
Laid before Parliament	*26th June 1989*
Coming into force	*1st August 1989*

The Secretary of State, in exercise of the powers conferred upon him by section 100(4) and (5) and section 196(4) and (5) of the Copyright, Designs and Patents Act 1988 ("the Act"), hereby makes the following Order—

1. This Order may be cited as the Copyright and Rights in Performances (Notice of Seizure) Order 1989 and shall come into force on 1st August 1989.

2. The form set out in the Schedule to this Order is hereby prescribed for the notice required under section 100(4) and section 196(4), respectively, of the Act.

Article 2   SCHEDULE

THE COPYRIGHT AND RIGHTS IN PERFORMANCES (NOTICE OF SEIZURE) ORDER 1989

NOTICE OF SEIZURE

To Whom it May Concern

1. Goods in which you were trading have been seized. This notice tells you who carried out the seizure, the legal grounds on which this has been done and the goods which have been seized and detained. As required by the Copyright, Designs and patents Act 1988, notice of the proposed seizure was given to the police station at (state address).

Person carrying out seizure

2. (State name and address)

*acting on the authority of (state name and address).

Legal grounds for seizure and detention

3. This action has been taken under *section 100/ section 196 of the Act which (subject to certain conditions) permits a copyright owner, or a person having performing rights or recording rights, to seize and detain infringing copies or illicit recordings found exposed or immediately available for sale or hire, or to authorise such seizure. The right to seize and detain is subject to a decision of the court under *section 114/ section 204 of the Act (order as to disposal of goods seized and detained).

Nature of the goods seized and detained

4. *Infringing copies of works (within the meaning of section 27 of the Act)—(specify all articles seized)

Illicit recordings (within the meaning of section 197 of the Act)—(specify all articles seized)

Signed...................Date...................

*Delete as necessary

A4.ii The Copyright (Recordings of Folksongs for Archives) (Designated Bodies) Order 1989

(SI 1989/1012)

Made	*13th June 1989*

Laid before Parliament   *26th June 1989*
Coming into force   *1st August 1989*

The Secretary of State, in exercise of the powers conferred upon him by section 61 of the Copyright, Designs and Patents Act 1988 ("the Act"), and upon being satisfied that the bodies designated by this Order are not established or conducted for profit, hereby makes the following Order—

1. This Order may be cited as the Copyright (Recordings of Folksongs for Archives) (Designated Bodies) Order 1989 and shall come into force on 1st August 1989.

2. Each of the bodies specified in the Schedule to this Order is designated as a body for the purposes of section 61 of the Act.

3.—(1) For the purposes of section 61(3) of the Act the conditions specified in paragraph (2) of this article are prescribed as the conditions which must be met for the making and supply, by the archivist of an archive maintained by a body designated by this Order, of a copy of a sound recording made in reliance on section 61(1) of the Act and included in such archive.

(2) The prescribed conditions are—
  (a) that the person requiring a copy satisfies the archivist that he requires it for purposes of research [for a non-commercial purpose] or private study and will not use it for any other purpose, and
  (b) that no person is furnished with more than one copy of the same recording.

Note: The words in square brackets in reg.3(2)(a) inserted by the Copyright and Related Rights Regulations 2003 (SI 2003/2498), Sch.1 para.24 with effect from October 31, 2003. For savings and transitional provisions, see Part 3 of those Regulations.

Article 2   SCHEDULE
1. The Archive of Traditional Welsh Music, University College of North Wales.
2. The Centre for English Cultural Tradition and Language.
3. The Charles Parker Archive Trust (1982).
4. The European Centre for Traditional and Regional Cultures.
5. The Folklore Society.
6. The Institute of Folklore Studies in Britain and Canada.
7. The National Museum of Wales, Welsh Folk Museum.
8. The National Sound Archive, the British Library.
9. The North West Sound Archive.
10. The Sound Archives, British Broadcasting Corporation.
11. Ulster Folk and Transport Museum.
12. The Vaughan Williams Memorial Library, English Folk Dance and Song Society.

A4.iii The Copyright (Sub-titling of Broadcasts and Cable Programmes) (Designated Body) Order 1989

(SI 1989/1013)

Made   *13th June 1989*
Laid before Parliament   *26th June 1989*
Coming into force   *1st August 1989*

The Secretary of State, in exercise of the powers conferred upon him by section 74 of the Copyright, Designs and Patents Act 1988 ("the Act"), and upon being satisfied that the body designated by this Order is not established or conducted for profit, hereby makes the following Order—

1. *This Order may be cited as the Copyright (Sub-titling of Broadcasts and Cable Programmes) (Designated Body) Order 1989 and shall come into force on 1st August 1989.*

2. *The National Subtitling Library for Deaf People is designated as a body for the purposes of section 74 of the Act.*

Note: Lapsed on the repeal of the Copyright, Designs and Patents Act 1988, s.74, with effect from June 1, 2014 at 00.01 (see s.74 of the 1988 Act above, and the Copyright and Rights in Performances (Disability) Regulations 2014 (SI 2014/1384), Sch. para.8).

A4.iv The Copyright (Application of Provisions relating to Educational Establishments to Teachers) (No.2) Order 1989

(SI 1989/1067)

Made	*26th June 1989*
Laid before Parliament	*4th July 1989*
Coming into force	*1st August 1989*

The Secretary of State, in exercise of the powers conferred upon him by section 174(2) of the Copyright, Designs and Patents Act 1988 ("the Act"), hereby makes the following Order—

1. This Order may be cited as the Copyright (Application of Provisions relating to Educational Establishments to Teachers) (No. 2) Order 1989 and shall come into force on 1st August 1989.

2. Sections 35 and 36 of the Act ([recording by educational establishments of broadcasts and copying and use of extracts by educational establishments]) and sections 137 to 141 of the Act (which provide for reprographic copying of works under licence) shall apply in relation to teachers who are employed by a [local authority (within the meaning of the Education Act 1996) or, in Northern Ireland, a local education authority] to give instruction elsewhere to pupils who are unable to attend an educational establishment.

3. The Copyright (Application of Provisions relating to Educational Establishments to Teachers) Order 1989 is hereby revoked.

Notes:

(1) The words "and cable programmes" repealed from reg.2 by the Copyright and Related Rights Regulations 2003 (SI 2003/2498), Sch.2 with effect from October 31, 2003. For savings and transitional provisions, see Pt 3 of those Regulations.

(2) In art.2, second words in square brackets substituted for words "local education authority" by the Local Education Authorities and Children's Services Authorities (Integration of Functions) (Local and Subordinate Legislation) Order 2010 (SI 2010/1172) art.4, Sch.3 para.15 with effect from May 5, 2010.

(3) In art.2, first words in square brackets substituted for words "which provide for educational use of recordings of broadcasts [...] and copying of passages from published works in which copyright subsists" by the Copyright and Rights in Performances (Research, Education, Libraries and Archives) Regulations 2014 (SI 2014/1372), Sch. para.13, with effect from June 1, 2014 at 00.02.

(4) This Order was made on June 13, 1989, but was not laid before Parliament.

A4.v The Copyright (Material Open to Public Inspection) (International Organisations) Order 1989

(SI 1989/1098)

Made	*29th June 1989*

Laid before Parliament   *10th July 1989*

Coming into force 1st August 1989   *1st August 1989*

The Secretary of State, in exercise of the powers conferred upon him by section 47(5) of the Copyright, Designs and Patents Act 1988,[1] hereby makes the following Order—

1. This Order may be cited as the Copyright (Material Open to Public Inspection) (International Organisations) Order 1989 and shall come into force on 1st August 1989.

2. Subsections (1) to (3) of section 47 of the Copyright, Designs and Patents Act 1988 apply, subject to the modifications set out in article 3 below, to material made open to public inspection by—

(a) the European Patent Office under the Convention on the Grant of European Patents[2] and

(b) the World Intellectual Property Organisation under the Patent Co-operation Treaty[3]

as they apply in relation to material open to public inspection pursuant to a statutory requirement or to a statutory register.

3. Subsections (1) to (3) of the said section 47 shall be modified by the substitution for the words "the appropriate person", in each place where they occur, of the words "the Comptroller-General of Patents, Designs and Trade Marks".

A4.vi The Copyright (Material Open to Public Inspection) (Marking of Copies of Maps) Order 1989

(SI 1989/1099)

Made   ·   *29th June 1989*

Laid before Parliament   *10th July 1989*

Coming into force   *1st August 1989*

The Secretary of State, in exercise of the powers conferred upon him by section 47(4) of the Copyright, Designs and Patents Act 1988, hereby makes the following Order—

1. This Order may be cited as the Copyright (Material Open to Public Inspection) (Marking of Copies of Maps) Order 1989 and shall come into force on 1st August 1989.

2. Subsections (2) and (3) of section 47 of the Copyright, Designs and Patents Act 1988 shall, in the case of a map which is open to public inspection pursuant to a statutory requirement, or is on a statutory register, apply only to copies of the map marked in the following manner—

> "This copy has been made by or with the authority of [insert the name of the person required to make the map open to public inspection or the person maintaining the register] pursuant to section 47 of the Copyright, Designs and Patents Act 1988 ("the Act"). Unless the act provides a relevant exception to copyright, the copy must not be copied without the prior permission of the copyright owner."

---

[1] c.48.

[2] Cmnd.8510.

[3] Cmnd.7340.

A4.vii The Copyright (Librarians and Archivists) (Copying of Copyright Material) Regulations 1989

(SI 1989/1212)

Made	*14th July 1989*
Laid before Parliament	*18th July 1989*
Coming into force 1st August 1989	*1st August 1989*

The Secretary of State, in exercise of the powers conferred upon him by sections 37(1), (2) and (4) and 38 to 43 of the Copyright, Designs and Patents Act 1988,[1] hereby makes the following Regulations—

Citation and commencement

1. These Regulations may be cited as the Copyright (Librarians and Archivists) (Copying of Copyright Material) Regulations 1989 and shall come into force on 1st August 1989.

Interpretation

2. In these Regulations—

"the Act" means the Copyright, Designs and Patents Act 1988;

"the archivist" means the archivist of a prescribed archive;

"the librarian" means the librarian of a prescribed library;

"prescribed archive" means an archive of the descriptions specified in paragraph (4) of regulation 3 below;

"prescribed library" means a library of the descriptions specified in paragraphs (1), (2) and (3) of regulation 3 below.

Description of libraries and archives

3.—(1) The descriptions of libraries specified in Part A of Schedule 1 to these Regulations are prescribed for the purposes of section 38 and 39 of the Act:

Provided that any library conducted for profit shall not be a prescribed library for the purposes of those sections.

(2) All libraries in the United Kingdom are prescribed for the purposes of sections 41, 42 and 43 of the Act as libraries the librarians of which may make and supply copies of any material to which those sections relate.

(3) Any library of a description specified in Part A of Schedule 1 to these Regulations which is not conducted for profit and any library of the description specified in Part B of that Schedule which is not conducted for profit are prescribed for the purposes of sections 41 and 42 of the Act as libraries for which copies of any material to which those sections relate may be made and supplied by the librarian of a prescribed library.

(4) All archives in the United Kingdom are prescribed for the purposes of sections 42 and 43 of the Act as archives which may make and supply copies of any material to which those sections relate and any archive within the United Kingdom which is not conducted for profit is prescribed for the purposes of section 42 of the Act as an archive for which copies of any material to which that section relates may be made and supplied by the archivist of a prescribed archive.

(5) In this regulation "conducted for profit", in relation to a library or archive, means a library or archive which is established or conducted for profit or which forms part of, or is administered by, a body established or conducted for profit.

---

[1] c.48.

Copying by librarian of article or part of published work

4.—(1) For the purposes of sections 38 and 39 of the Act the conditions specified in paragraph (2) of this regulation are prescribed as the conditions which
must be complied with when the librarian of a prescribed library makes and supplies a copy of any article in a periodical or, as the case may be, of a part of a literary, dramatic or musical work from a published edition to a person requiring
the copy.

(2) The prescribed conditions are—

(a) that no copy of any article or any part of a work shall be supplied to the
person requiring the same unless—

(i) he satisfies the librarian that he requires the copy for purposes of
research [for a non-commercial purpose] or private study and
will not use it for any other purpose; and

(ii) he has delivered to the librarian a declaration in writing, in relation to that article or part of a work, substantially in accordance
with Form A in Schedule 2 to these Regulations and signed in
the manner therein indicated;

(b) that the librarian is satisfied that the requirement of such person and that
of any other person—

(i) are not similar, that is to say, the requirements are not for copies
of substantially the same article or part of a work at substantially
the same time and for substantially the same purpose; and

(ii) are not related, that is to say, he and that person do not receive
instruction to which the article or part of the work is relevant at
the same time and place;

(c) that such person is not furnished—

(i) in the case of an article, with more than one copy of the article or
more than one article contained in the same issue of a periodical;
or

(ii) in the case of a part of a published work, with more than one
copy of the same material or with a copy of more than a reasonable proportion of any work; and

(d) that such person is required to pay for the copy a sum not less than the
cost (including a contribution to the general expenses of the library) attributable to its production.

(3) Unless the librarian is aware that the signed declaration delivered to him
pursuant to paragraph (2)(a)(ii) above is false in a material particular, he may rely
on it as to the matter he is required to be satisfied on under paragraph (2)(a)(i)
above before making or supplying the copy.

Note: The words in square brackets in reg.4(2)(a)(i) inserted by the Copyright and Related Rights Regulations 2003 (SI 2003/2498), Sch.1 para.26 with effect from October 31,
2003. For savings and transitional provisions, see Part 3 of those Regulations.

Copying by librarian to supply other libraries

5.—(1) For the purposes of section 41 of the Act the conditions specified in
paragraph (2) of this regulation are prescribed as the conditions which must be
complied with when the librarian of a prescribed library makes and supplies to
another prescribed library a copy of any article in a periodical or, as the case may
be, of the whole or part of a published edition of a literary, dramatic or musical
work required by that other prescribed library.

(2) The prescribed conditions are—

(a) that the other prescribed library is not furnished with more than one
copy of the article or of the whole or part of the published edition; or

(b) that, where the requirement is for a copy of more than one article in the same issue of a periodical, or for a copy of the whole or part of a published edition, the other prescribed library furnishes a written statement to the effect that it is a prescribed library and that it does not know, and could not by reasonable inquiry ascertain, the name and address of a person entitled to authorise the making of the copy; and

(c) that the other prescribed library shall be required to pay for the copy a sum [equivalent to but not exceeding] the cost (including a contribution to the general expenses of the library) attributable to its production.

Note: The words in square brackets in reg.5(2)(c) substituted for the former words "not less than" by the Copyright and Related Rights Regulations 2003 (SI 2003/2498), Sch.1 para.26 with effect from October 31, 2003. For savings and transitional provisions, see Part 3 of those Regulations.

Copying by librarian or archivist for the purposes of replacing items in a permanent collection

6.—(1) For the purposes of section 42 of the Act the conditions specified in paragraph (2) of this regulation are prescribed as the conditions which must be complied with before the librarian or, as the case may be, the archivist makes a copy from any item in the permanent collection of the library or archive in order to preserve or replace that item in the permanent collection of that library or archive or in the permanent collection of another prescribed library or archive.

(2) The prescribed conditions are—

(a) that the item in question is an item in the part of the permanent collection maintained by the library or archive wholly or mainly for the purposes of reference on the premises of the library or archive, or is an item in the permanent collection of the library or archive which is available on loan only to other libraries or archives;

(b) that it is not reasonably practicable for the librarian or archivist to purchase a copy of that item to fulfil the purpose under section 42(1)(a) or (b) of the Act;

(c) that the other prescribed library or archive furnishes a written statement to the effect that the item has been lost, destroyed or damaged and that it is not reasonably practicable for it to purchase a copy of that item, and that if a copy is supplied it will only be used to fulfil the purpose under section 42(1)(b) of the Act; and

(d) that the other prescribed library or archive shall be required to pay for the copy a sum [equivalent to but not exceeding] the cost (including a contribution to the general expenses of the library or archive) attributable to its production.

Note: The words in square brackets in reg.6(2)(d) substituted for the former words "not less than" by the Copyright and Related Rights Regulations 2003 (SI 2003/2498), Sch.1 para.26 with effect from October 31, 2003. For savings and transitional provisions, see Part 3 of those Regulations.

Copying by librarian or archivist of certain unpublished works

7.—(1) For the purposes of section 43 of the Act the conditions specified in paragraph (2) of this regulation are prescribed as the conditions which must be complied with in the circumstances in which that section applies when the librarian or, as the case may be, the archivist makes and supplies a copy of the whole or part of a literary, dramatic or musical work from a document in the library or archive to a person requiring the copy.

(2) The prescribed conditions are—

(a) that no copy of the whole or part of the work shall be supplied to the person requiring the same unless—

(i) he satisfies the librarian or archivist that he requires the copy for purposes of research [for a non-commercial purpose] or private study and will not use it for any other purpose; and

(ii) he has delivered to the librarian or, as the case may be, the archivist a declaration in writing, in relation to that work, substantially in accordance with Form B in Schedule 2 to these Regulations and signed in the manner therein indicated;

(b) that such person is not furnished with more than one copy of the same material; and

(c) that such person is required to pay for the copy a sum not less than the cost (including a contribution to the general expenses of the library or archive) attributable to its production.

(3) Unless the librarian or archivist is aware that the signed declaration delivered to him pursuant to paragraph (2)(a)(ii) above is false in a material particular, he may rely on it as to the matter he is required to be satisfied on under paragraph (2)(a)(i) above before making or supplying the copy.

Note: The words in square brackets in reg.7(2)(a)(i) inserted by the Copyright and Related Rights Regulations 2003 (SI 2003/2498), Sch.1 para.26 with effect from October 31, 2003. For savings and transitional provisions, see Part 3 of those Regulations.

Revocations

8. The Regulations mentioned in Schedule 3 to these Regulations are hereby revoked.

Regulation 3   SCHEDULE 1

Regulation 3(1) and (3)   PART A

1. Any library administered by—

(a) a library authority within the meaning of the Public Libraries and Museums Act 1964[2] in relation to England and Wales;

(b) a statutory library authority within the meaning of the Public Libraries (Scotland) Act 1955,[3] in relation to Scotland;

(c) an Education and Library Board within the meaning of the Education and Libraries (Northern Ireland) Order 1986,[4] in relation to Northern Ireland.

2. The British Library, the National Library of Wales, the National Library of Scotland, the Bodleian Library, Oxford and the University Library, Cambridge.

3. Any library of a school within the meaning of section 174 of the Act and any library of a description of educational establishment specified under that section in the Copyright (Educational Establishments) (No. 2) Order 1989.[5]

4. Any parliamentary library or library administered as part of a government department, including a Northern Ireland department, [or as part of the Scottish Administration] or any library conducted for or administered by an agency which is administered by a Minister of the Crown.

5. Any library administered by—

(a) in England and Wales, a local authority within the meaning of the Local Govern-

---

[2] c.75.
[3] c.27.
[4] SI 1986/594 (N.I.3).
[5] SI 1989/1068.

ment Act 1972,[6] the Common Council of the City of London or the Council of the Isles of Scilly;

(b) in Scotland, a local authority within the meaning of the Local Government (Scotland) Act 1973[7];

(c) in Northern Ireland, a district council established under the Local Government Act (Northern Ireland) 1972.[8]

6. Any other library conducted for the purpose of facilitating or encouraging the study of bibliography, education, fine arts, history, languages, law, literature, medicine, music, philosophy, religion, science (including natural and social science) or technology, or administered by any establishment or organisation which is conducted wholly or mainly for such a purpose.

Note: The words in square brackets in para.4 inserted by the Scotland Act 1998 (Consequential Modifications) (No.1) Order 1999 (SI 1999/1042) with effect from May 6, 1999.

REGULATION 3(3)   PART B

Any library outside the United Kingdom which is conducted wholly or mainly for the purpose of facilitating or encouraging the study of bibliography, education, fine arts, history, languages, law, literature, medicine, music, philosophy, religion, science (including natural and social science) or technology.

Regulations 4 and 7   SCHEDULE 2

FORM A

DECLARATION. COPY OF ARTICLE OR PART OF PUBLISHED WORK

To:

The Librarian of....................Library [Address of Library]

1. Please supply me with a copy of:

*the article in the periodical, the particulars of which are [   ]

*the part of the published work, the particulars of which are [   ]

required by me for the purposes of research or private study.

2. I declare that—

(a) I have not previously been supplied with a copy of the same material by you or any other librarian;

(b) I will not use the copy except for research [for a non-commercial purpose] or private study and will not supply a copy of it to any other person; and

(c) to the best of my knowledge no other person with whom I work or study has made or intends to make, at or about the same time as this request, a request for substantially the same material for substantially the same purpose.

3. I understand that if the declaration is false in a material particular the copy supplied to me by you will be an infringing copy and that I shall be liable for infringement of copyright as if I had made the copy myself.

† Signature ....

Date ....

Name ....

Address ....

....

....

*Delete whichever is inappropriate

A4 REGULATIONS MADE UNDER CDPA 1988

---

[6] c.70.

[7] c.65.

[8] c.9 (N.I.).

† This must be the personal signature of the person making the request. A stamped or typewritten signature, or the signature of an agent, is NOT acceptable. *Note:* The official version of FORM A has no paragraph numbered "1". It is assumed that the paragraph starting "Please supply" was intended to be so numbered.

FORM B

Declaration: Copy of Whole or Part of Unpublished Work

To:

The *Librarian/ Archivist of .... *Library/ Archive

[Address of Library/ Archive]

1. Please supply me with a copy of:

the *whole/ following part [particulars of part] of the [particulars of the unpublished work] required by me for the purposes of research or private study.

2. I declare that—

(a) I have not previously been supplied with a copy of the same material by you or any other librarian or archivist;

(b) I will not use the copy except for research [for a non-commercial purpose] or private study and will not supply a copy of it to any other person; and

(c) to the best of my knowledge the work had not been published before the document was deposited in your *library/ archive and the copyright owner has not prohibited copying of the work.

3. I understand that if the declaration is false in a material particular the copy supplied to me by you will be an infringing copy and that I shall be liable for infringement of copyright as if I had made the copy myself.

†Signature ....

Date ....

Name ....

Address ....

....

....

*Delete whichever is inappropriate

† This must be the personal signature of the person making the request. A stamped or typewritten signature, or the signature of an agent, is NOT acceptable. *Note:* The official version of FORM B has no paragraph numbered "1". It is assumed that the paragraph starting "Please supply" was intended to be so numbered.

Regulation 8 SCHEDULE 3

Revocations

Number	Title
SI 1957/868	The Copyright (Libraries) Regulations 1957
SI 1989/1009	The Copyright (Copying by Librarians and Archivists) Regulations 1989
SI 1989/1069	The Copyright (Copying by Librarians and Archivists) (Amendment) Regulations 1989

Notes:

(1) The words in square brackets in para.(2) of Forms A and B inserted by the Copyright and Related Rights Regulations 2003 (SI 2003/2498), Sch.1 para.26 with effect from October 31, 2003. For savings and transitional provisions, see Part 3 of those Regulations.

(2) The last two Orders were defective and revoked before they came into force.

A4.viii The Copyright, Designs and Patents Act 1988 (Guernsey) Order 1989

(SI 1989/1997)

Made	*1st November 1989*
Coming into force	*1st December 1989*

At the Court at Buckingham Palace, the 1st day of November 1989

Present.

The Queen's Most Excellent Majesty in Council

Her Majesty, in pursuance of section 304(5) of the Copyright, Designs and Patents Act 1988, is pleased, by and with the advice of Her Privy Council, to order, and it is hereby ordered, as follows:

1. This Order may be cited as the Copyright, Designs and Patents Act 1988 (Guernsey) Order 1989 and shall come into force on 1st December 1989.

2. Sections 297 to 299 of the Copyright, Designs and Patents Act 1988 (fraudulent reception of transmissions) shall extend to the Bailiwick of Guernsey with the exceptions and modifications specified in the Schedule to this Order.

Article 2 SCHEDULE

EXCEPTIONS AND MODIFICATIONS IN THE EXTENSION OF SECTIONS 297 TO 299 OF THE COPYRIGHT, DESIGNS AND PATENTS ACT 1988 TO THE BAILIWICK OF GUERNSEY

1. Any reference to an enactment shall be construed, unless the contrary intention appears, as a reference to it as it has effect in the Bailiwick of Guernsey.

2. In section 297(1), after "United Kingdom" there shall be inserted "or Bailiwick of Guernsey".

3. In section 298—

(a) in subsection (1)(a) and (b), after "United Kingdom" there shall be inserted "or Bailiwick of Guernsey";

(b) in subsection (3), for "99 or 100 (delivery up or seizure of certain articles)" there shall be substituted "7 of the Copyright Act 1911 (rights of owner against persons possessing or dealing with infringing copies etc.)", and

(c) for subsections (4) to (6) there shall be substituted the following subsection:

"(4) In section 8 of the Copyright Act 1911 (exemption of innocent infringer from liability to pay damages etc.) as it applies to proceedings for infringement of the rights conferred by this section, the references to the defendant not being aware of the existence of the copyright in the work, and to his not being aware and having no reasonable ground for suspecting that copyright subsisted in the work, shall be construed respectively as references to his not being aware, and to his not being aware and having no reasonable ground for suspecting, that his acts infringed the rights conferred by this section."

4. In section 299—

(a) in subsection (1)(a), after "United Kingdom" there shall be inserted "and Bailiwick of Guernsey";

(b) in subsection (2), for "United Kingdom" whenever occurring there shall be substituted "Bailiwick of Guernsey";

(c) subsection (3) shall be omitted, and

(d) in subsection (5), for "(copyright)" there shall be substituted "of this Act as it has effect in England and Wales.".

A4.ix The Fraudulent Reception of Transmissions (Guernsey) Order 1989

(SI 1989/2003)

Made *1st November 1989*

Laid before Parliament   *8th November 1989*
Coming into force   *1st December 1989*

At the Court at Buckingham Palace, the 1st day of November 1989

Present,

The Queen's Most Excellent Majesty in Council

Whereas it appears to Her Majesty that provision will be made under the laws of the Bailiwick of Guernsey giving adequate protection to persons making charges for programmes included in broadcasting or cable programme services provided from the United Kingdom and for encrypted transmissions sent from the United Kingdom:

Now, therefore, Her Majesty, by virtue of the authority conferred upon Her by section 299(1) of the Copyright, Designs and Patents Act 1988, is pleased, by and with the advice of Her Privy Council, to order, and it is hereby ordered, as follows:

1. This Order may be cited as the Fraudulent Reception of Transmissions (Guernsey) Order 1989 and shall come into force on 1st December 1989.

2. Section 297 of the Copyright, Designs and Patents Act 1988 applies in relation to programmes included in broadcasting or cable programme services provided from a place in the Bailiwick of Guernsey, and section 298 of the said Act applies in relation to such programmes and to encrypted transmissions of any other description provided or sent from a place in the Bailiwick of Guernsey.

A4.x Act of Sederunt (Summary Applications, Statutory Applications and Appeals etc. Rules) 1999

(SI 1999/929)

Made   *19th March 1999*
Coming into force   *1st July 1999*

ARRANGEMENT OF REGULATIONS

CHAPTER 1

GENERAL

CHAPTER 3

RULES ON APPLICATIONS UNDER SPECIFIC STATUTES

PART V

COPYRIGHT, DESIGNS AND TRADE MARKS

The Lords of Council and Session, under and by virtue of the powers conferred on them by Schedule 1, paragraphs 24(1), 28D and 28(2), Schedule 2, paragraph 7 and Schedule 3, paragraph 13(3) to the Betting Gaming and Lotteries Act 1963, Schedule 2, paragraphs 33(1), 34(1), 45 and 47, and

Schedule 9, paragraph 15 to the Gaming Act 1968, section 32 of the Sheriff Courts (Scotland) Act 1971, sections 66(5A) and 75 of the Sex Discrimination Act 1975, section 39(9) of the Licensing (Scotland) Act 1976, Schedule 3, paragraph 12 to the Lotteries and Amusements Act 1976, sections 136, 139, 146, 147, 152, 153, 182(3) and 185 of the Representation of the People Act 1983, sections 114(3), 204(3) and 231(3) of the Copyright, Designs and Patents Act 1988, section 19(3) of the Trade Marks Act 1994, section 46 of the Drug Trafficking Act 1994, Regulation 5(3) of the Olympics Association Right (Infringement Proceedings) Regulations 1995, and sections 31(5) and 48 of, and Schedule 1, paragraph 11 to, the Proceeds of Crime (Scotland) Act 1995 and of all other powers enabling them in that behalf, having approved draft rules submitted to them by the Sheriff Court Rules Council in accordance with section 34 of the Sheriff Courts (Scotland) Act 1971, do hereby enact and declare:

CHAPTER 1

GENERAL

Citation and commencement

1.1—(1) This Act of Sederunt may be cited as the Act of Sederunt (Summary Applications, Statutory Applications and Appeals etc. Rules) 1999 and shall come into force on 1st July 1999.

(2) This Act of Sederunt shall be inserted in the Books of Sederunt.

Interpretation

1.2—(1) In this Act of Sederunt, unless the context otherwise requires—

[" the 2004 Act" means the Vulnerable Witnesses (Scotland) Act 2004;]

[" enactment" includes an enactment comprised in, or in an instrument made under, an Act of the Scottish Parliament;]

"Ordinary Cause Rules" means the First Schedule to the Sheriff Courts (Scotland) Act 1907;

"sheriff clerk" includes sheriff clerk depute; and

"summary application" has the meaning given by section 3(p) of the Sheriff Courts (Scotland) Act 1907.

(2) Unless the context otherwise requires, any reference in this Act of Sederunt to a specified Chapter, Part or rule shall be construed as a reference to the Chapter, Part or rule bearing that number in this Act of Sederunt, and a reference to a specified paragraph, sub-paragraph or head shall be construed as a reference to the paragraph, sub-paragraph or head so numbered or lettered in the provision in which that reference occurs.

(3) Any reference in this Act of Sederunt to a numbered Form shall, unless the context otherwise requires, be construed as a reference to the Form so numbered in Schedule 1 to this Act of Sederunt and includes a form substantially to the same effect with such variation as circumstances may require.

[(4) In this Act of Sederunt, references to a solicitor include a reference to a member of a body which has made a successful application under section 25 of the Law Reform (Miscellaneous Provisions) (Scotland) Act 1990 but only to the extent that the member is exercising rights acquired by virtue of section 27 of that Act.]

Notes:

(1) In r.1.2(1), the definition of "enactment" was inserted by the Act of Sederunt (Ordinary Cause, Summary Application, Summary Cause and Small Claim Rules)

Amendment (Miscellaneous) 2007 (SSI 2007/6) r.3(2) with effect from January 29, 2007 and the definition of "the 2004 Act" was inserted by the Act of Sederunt (Ordinary Cause, Summary Application, Summary Cause and Small Claim Rules) Amendment (Vulnerable Witnesses (Scotland) Act 2004) 2007 (SSI 2007/463) r.3(2) with effect from November 1, 2007.

(2) Rule 1.2(4) was inserted by the Act of Sederunt (Sheriff Court Rules Amendment) (ss.25 to 29 of the Law Reform (Miscellaneous Provisions) (Scotland) Act 1990) 2009 (SI 2009/164) r.3 with effect from May 20, 2009.

Revocation

1.3 The Acts of Sederunt mentioned in column (1) of Schedule 2 to this Act of Sederunt are revoked to the extent specified in column (3) of that Schedule.

Application

1.4 Unless otherwise provided in this Act of Sederunt or in any other enactment, any application or appeal to the sheriff shall be by way of summary application and the provisions of Chapter 2 of this Act of Sederunt shall apply accordingly.

CHAPTER 3

RULES ON APPLICATIONS UNDER SPECIFIC STATUTES

PART V

COPYRIGHT, DESIGNS AND TRADE MARKS

Interpretation

3.5.1 In this Part—

"the 1988 Act" means the Copyright, Designs and Patents Act 1988;

"the 1994 Act" means the Trade Marks Act 1994; and

"the 1995 Regulations" means the Olympics Association Right (Infringement Proceedings) Regulations 1995.

Orders for delivery up, forfeiture, destruction or other disposal

3.5.2 An application to the sheriff made under sections 99, 114, 195, 204, 230, 231 or 298 of the 1988 Act, under sections 16 or 19 of the 1994 Act or under Regulation 3 or 5 of the 1995 Regulations, shall be made—

(a) by motion or incidental application, as the case may be, where proceedings have been commenced; or

(b) by summary application where no proceedings have been commenced.

Service of notice on interested persons

3.5.3 Where an application has been made under section 114, 204, 231 or 298 of the 1988 Act, section 19 of the 1994 Act or Regulation 5 of the 1995 Regulations—

(a) the application shall—

(i) specify the name and address of any person known or believed by the applicant to have an interest in the subject matter of the application; or

(ii) state that to the best of the applicant's knowledge and belief no other person has such an interest; and

(b) the sheriff shall order that there be intimated to any person who has such an interest, a copy of the pleadings and any motion, incidental application or summary application, as the case may be.

Procedure where leave of court required

3.5.4—(1) Where leave of the court is required under the 1988 Act before the action may proceed, the pursuer shall lodge along with the initial writ or summons a motion or incidental application, as the case may be, stating the grounds upon which leave is sought.

(2) The sheriff may hear the pursuer on the motion or incidental application and may grant or refuse it or make such other order in relation to it as he considers appropriate prior to determination.

(3) Where such motion or incidental application is granted, a copy of the sheriff's interlocutor shall be served upon the defender along with the warrant of citation.

A4.xi The Copyright (Material Open to Public Inspection) (Marking of Copies of Plans and Drawings) Order 1990

(SI 1990/1427)

Made	*16th July 1990*
Laid before Parliament	*23rd July 1990*
Coming into force	*15th August 1990*

The Secretary of State, in exercise of the powers conferred upon him by section 47(4) of the Copyright, Designs and Patents Act 1988, hereby makes the following Order—

1. This Order may be cited as the Copyright (Material Open to Public Inspection) (Marking of Copies of Plans and Drawings) Order 1990 and shall come into force on 15th August 1990.

2. Subsection (2) of section 47 of the Copyright, Designs and Patents Act 1988 shall, in the case of a plan or drawing which is open to public inspection pursuant to a statutory requirement, apply only to copies of the plan or drawing marked in the following manner—

> "This copy has been made by or with the authority of [insert the name of the person required to make the plan or drawing open to public inspection] pursuant to section 47 of the Copyright, Designs and Patents Act 1988. Unless that Act provides a relevant exception to copyright, the copy must not be copied without the prior permission of the copyright owner.".

A4.xii The Copyright (Recording for Archives of Designated Class of Broadcasts and Cable Programmes) (Designated Bodies) Order 1993

(SI 1993/74)

Made	*18th January 1993*
Laid before Parliament	*21st January 1993*
Coming into force	*12th February 1993*

The Secretary of State, in exercise of powers conferred upon him by section 75 of the Copyright, Designs and Patents Act 1988 ("the Act"), and upon being satisfied that the bodies designated by this Order are not established or conducted for profit, hereby makes the following Order:

1. *This Order may be cited as the Copyright (Recording for Archives of Designated Class of Broadcasts and Cable Programmes) (Designated Bodies) Order 1993 and shall come into force on 12th February 1993.*

2. *Each of the bodies specified in the Schedule to this Order is designated as a body for which a recording of a broadcast [...] of the class designated by article 3 below, or a copy thereof, may be made for the purpose of placing the same in any archive maintained by it.*

A4 REGULATIONS MADE UNDER CDPA 1988

3. *All broadcasts other than encrypted transmissions [...] are designated as a class for the purposes of section 75 of the Act.*

4. *The Copyright (Recording for Archives of Designated Class of Broadcasts and Cable Programmes) (Designated Bodies) Order 1991 is hereby revoked.*

Note: The words "or cable programme" in art.2 and the words "and all cable programmes" in art.3 revoked by the Copyright and Related Rights Regulations 2003 (SI 2003/2498), Sch.2 with effect from October 31, 2003. For savings and transitional provisions, see Part 3 of those Regulations.

Article 2   SCHEDULE

DESIGNATED BODIES

The British Film Institute
The British Library
The British Medical Association
The British Music Information Centre
The Imperial War Museum
The Music Performance Research Centre
The National Library of Wales
The Scottish Film Council

Note: Lapsed on the repeal of the Copyright, Designs and Patents Act 1988, s.75, with effect from June 1, 2014 at 00.02 (see s.75 of the 1988 Act above, and the Copyright and Rights in Performances (Research, Education, Libraries and Archives) Regulations 2014 (SI 2014/1372), reg.8(1)).

A4.xiii The Copyright (Educational Establishments) Order 2005

(SI 2005/223)

Made	*2nd February 2005*
Laid before Parliament	*8th February 2005*
Coming into force	*1st April 2005*

The Secretary of State, in exercise of the powers conferred upon her by section 174(1)(b) of the Copyright, Designs and Patents Act 1988, hereby makes the following Order:

1. This Order may be cited as the Copyright (Educational Establishments) Order 2005 and shall come into force on 1st April 2005.

2. The descriptions of educational establishments mentioned in the Schedule to this Order are specified for the purposes of Part I of the Copyright, Designs and Patents Act 1988.

3. The Copyright (Educational Establishments) (No.2) Order 1989 is hereby revoked.

Article 2   SCHEDULE

Higher Education

1. Any university empowered by Royal Charter or Act of Parliament to award degrees and any college, or institution in the nature of a college, in such a university.

2. Any institution in England and Wales which provides a course of any description mentioned in Schedule 6 to the Education Reform Act 1988.

3. Any institution in Scotland which provides higher education within the meaning of section 38 of the Further and Higher Education (Scotland) Act 1992.

4. Any institution in Northern Ireland–
(a) which provides a course of any description mentioned in Schedule 1 to the Further Education (Northern Ireland) Order 1997; or
(b) which is a college of education within the meaning of article 2(2) of the Education and Libraries (Northern Ireland) Order 1986.

Further Education

5. Any institution in England and Wales the sole or main purpose of which is to provide further education within the meaning of section 2 of the Education Act 1996.

6. Any institution in Scotland the sole or main purpose of which is to provide further education within the meaning of either section 1(5)(b) of the Education (Scotland) Act 1980 or section 1(3) of the Further and Higher Education (Scotland) Act 1992.

7. Any institution in Northern Ireland the sole or main purpose of which is to provide further education within the meaning of article 3 of the Further Education (Northern Ireland) Order 1997.

Theological Colleges

8. Any theological college.

A4.xiv The Copyright (Regulation of Relevant Licensing Bodies) Regulations 2014

(SI 2014/898)

Made   *1st April 2014*
Coming into force   *6th April 2014*

A draft of the Regulations has been laid before and approved by each House of Parliament under paragraph 7(4) of Schedule A1 to the Copyright, Designs and Patents Act 1988.

The Secretary of State, in exercise of the powers conferred by section 116(5) of and paragraphs 1 to 7 of Schedule A1 to that Act, makes the following Regulations:

PART 1 Preliminary

Citation and commencement

1. These Regulations may be cited as the Copyright (Regulation of Relevant Licensing Bodies) Regulations 2014 and shall come into force on 6th April 2014.

Interpretation

2. In these Regulations—
"the Act" means the Copyright, Designs and Patents Act 1988;
"code reviewer" means a person who has been appointed by the Secretary of State under regulation 6;
"Comptroller" shall have the same meaning as in the Patents and Designs Act 1907;
"Extended Collective Licensing Scheme" means a collective licensing scheme under which a relevant licensing body which is authorised by the Secretary of State may grant licences in respect of—
(a) copyright works in which copyright is owned by non-member right holders; or
(b) performers' rights where the acts restricted in relation to the performance are owned by non-member right holders;
"First-tier Tribunal" means the First-tier Tribunal established by section 3(1) of the Tribunals, Courts and Enforcement Act 2007;

"licensing code ombudsman" means a person who has been appointed by the Secretary of State under regulation 7;

"micro-business" means a business with fewer than ten employees and which has a turnover or balance sheet total of less than 2 million Euros per annum;

"non-member right holder" means a right holder who is represented by the relevant licensing body under an Extended Collective Licensing Scheme but who is not a member of the relevant licensing body and whose rights are not the subject of an express contractual agreement with the relevant licensing body for the licensing of copyright works or performers' rights;

"potential licensee" means any person who has communicated with the relevant licensing body and expressed an interest in being granted a licence in respect of a copyright work or a performer's right;

"relevant licensing body" means any body that is a licensing body within the meaning of section 116(2) of the Act and which—

> (a) is authorised by way of assignment, licence or any other contractual arrangement to manage copyright or rights related to copyright on behalf of more than one right holder, for the collective benefit of those right holders, as its sole or main purpose; and

> (b) is either owned or controlled by its members or organised on a not for profit basis;

"relevant person" means a director, manager or similar officer of a relevant licensing body or, where the body's affairs are managed by its members, a member;

"right holder" means the owner of the copyright in a copyright work or of a performer's right and includes an exclusive licensee of the copyright owner;

"specified criteria" means the criteria set out in the Schedule;

"transparent" means that, in dealing with any of its members, licensees or potential licensees, the relevant licensing body provides to that member, licensee or potential licensee any information it holds which may reasonably be considered to be relevant to that particular member, licensee or potential licensee;

"working day" means any day except a Saturday or Sunday, Christmas Day, Good Friday or a day which is a bank holiday in any part of the United Kingdom under section 1 of the Banking and Financial Dealings Act 1971.

PART 2 Regulation of relevant licensing bodies

Notice of non-compliance and direction to adopt a code of practice

3.—(1) If the relevant circumstances are met, the Secretary of State may direct a relevant licensing body to adopt and publish a code of practice that complies with the specified criteria.

(2) For the purposes of paragraph (1), the relevant circumstances are—

(a) the relevant licensing body is not a micro-business;

(b) that in the opinion of the Secretary of State the relevant licensing body either—

> (i) has no code of practice; or

> (ii) has a code of practice which does not comply in material respects with the specified criteria; and

(c) where sub-paragraph (b)(ii) applies, that the Secretary of State has notified the relevant licensing body that its code of practice does not comply in material respects with the specified criteria and the relevant licensing body has not amended, within the period of 49 days from the date of the notification, its code of practice to comply in material respects with the specified criteria.

(3) In deciding whether or not any code of practice of a relevant licensing body complies in material respects with the specified criteria under paragraph (2)(b)(ii) or regulation 4, the Secretary of State may have regard to a report produced by a code reviewer.

(4) The Secretary of State may request a code reviewer to produce a report in order to assist him in making his decision under paragraph (3).

(5) A notification under paragraph (2)(c) must be given by—

(a) serving a copy on the relevant licensing body; and

(b) publishing the notification in such manner as the Secretary of State considers appropriate for the purpose of bringing the matters to which the notification relates to the attention of persons likely to be affected by them.

Effect of a direction

4.—(1) The relevant licensing body must, within 49 days of the date on which a direction under regulation 3 is made, notify to the Secretary of State a code of practice that complies with the specified criteria and that it proposes to adopt in accordance with the direction.

(2) Following receipt of a code of practice notified in accordance with paragraph (1), the Secretary of State shall inform the relevant licensing body in writing that the code of practice notified either—

(a) meets the specified criteria and is approved by the Secretary of State; or

(b) does not meet the specified criteria and that the Secretary of State intends to impose a code of practice on the relevant licensing body.

(3) Once its code of practice has been approved by the Secretary of State and the approval notified to the relevant licensing body, the body shall within 7 days of notification adopt the approved code of practice and operate its licensing activities in accordance with that code of practice.

Imposition of code of practice

5.—(1) The Secretary of State may impose a code of practice if he—

(a) is satisfied that the code of practice notified under regulation 4(1) does not meet the specified criteria or that the relevant licensing body has failed to adopt an approved code of practice in accordance regulation 4(3);

(b) gives notice to the relevant licensing body of the code of practice to be imposed upon it; and

(c) has considered any representations made by the relevant licensing body in accordance with the notice and not withdrawn.

(2) The notice must—

(a) state the reasons for the proposed refusal of approval for any code of practice notified by the relevant licensing body;

(b) contain the code of practice that the Secretary of State proposes to impose on the relevant licensing body; and

(c) state the period (not less than 14 days starting with the date of delivery of the notice) within which representations may be made in relation to the proposed imposition of the code of practice.

(3) Where the Secretary of State decides to impose the code of practice contained in the notice, the Secretary of State shall notify the relevant licensing body and give it a written statement of reasons for the decision together with the date from which the approved code of practice is to have effect as the code of practice adopted by the body (the "effective date").

(4) The relevant licensing body shall operate its licensing activities in accordance with the imposed code with effect from the effective date.

Code reviewer

6.—(1) The Secretary of State may appoint a suitably qualified person as code reviewer to review and report to the Secretary of State, when requested to do so by the Secretary of State, on the codes of practice adopted by the relevant licensing bodies, including how they relate to the specified criteria, and on compliance with the codes of practice.

(2) Before making an appointment under paragraph (1) the Secretary of State shall consult with those persons whom the Secretary of State considers to represent the interests of relevant licensing bodies, licensees, the persons on whose behalf a relevant licensing body is authorised to negotiate or grant licences and the Comptroller.

(3) The code reviewer may serve notice on any relevant licensing body requiring that relevant licensing body to provide information, documents or assistance to the code reviewer for the purposes of a review or report and may copy any information or documents provided in accordance with the notice.

(4) A relevant licensing body shall provide the code reviewer with any information, documents or assistance requested under paragraph (3) within 14 days of receipt of the request.

(5) Any reference in this regulation or in regulation 7 to the provision of information or of a document includes a reference to the provision of a legible and intelligible copy of information recorded otherwise than in legible form.

(6) The Secretary of State may pay the reasonable expenses and allowances of the code reviewer in respect of any work which the Secretary of State requests the code reviewer to carry out under these Regulations.

Licensing code ombudsman

7.—(1) The Secretary of State may appoint a suitably qualified person as licensing code ombudsman to investigate and determine disputes about a relevant licensing body's compliance with its code of practice.

(2) A relevant licensing body, licensee or a person on whose behalf a relevant licensing body is authorised to negotiate may refer a dispute about a relevant licensing body's compliance with its code of practice or other matter to the licensing code ombudsman.

(3) The licensing code ombudsman may serve notice on any relevant licensing body requiring it to provide to the licensing code ombudsman any information, documents or assistance for the purposes of investigating a dispute referred to in paragraph (1) and copy any document or information provided in accordance with the notice.

(4) A relevant licensing body shall provide the licensing code ombudsman with any information, documents or assistance requested under paragraph (3) within 14 days of receipt of the request.

(5) A relevant licensing body shall comply with a determination of the licensing code ombudsman.

(6) The Secretary of State may pay the reasonable expenses and allowances of

the licensing code ombudsman in respect of any work which the licensing code ombudsman carries out under these Regulations.

Recovery of fees by the Secretary of State

8.—(1) Subject to paragraph (2), the Secretary of State may require a relevant licensing body to pay to the Secretary of State a fee to reimburse the Secretary of State the cost of administering the operation of these Regulations.

(2) The aggregate amount of fees recovered from the relevant licensing bodies under paragraph (1) must not be more than the cost to the Secretary of State of administering the operation of these Regulations.

(3) The relevant licensing body shall pay the fee within 24 days of the date on which the relevant licensing body is notified of the fee.

PART 3 INFORMATION AND FINANCIAL PENALTIES

Secretary of State's powers to request information

9.—(1) The Secretary of State may serve notice on any relevant licensing body requiring it to supply to the Secretary of State for any purpose related to its licensing activity such information as may be specified or described in the notice, and to supply it at a time and place and in a form and manner so specified.

(2) A relevant licensing body shall supply the Secretary of State with information requested under paragraph (1) within 14 days of receipt of the request.

(3) The Secretary of State may, for a purpose described in paragraph (1), copy any document or information provided.

(4) Any reference in this regulation to the production of a document includes a reference to the production of a legible and intelligible copy of information recorded otherwise than in legible form.

Financial penalties

10.—(1) The Secretary of State may impose a financial penalty on a relevant licensing body or a relevant person if the Secretary of State is satisfied that the relevant licensing body has failed to comply with its obligations under—

  (a) regulation 4(3) (adoption of an approved code of practice), 5(4) (compliance with an imposed code of practice) or 7(5) (compliance with determination of the licensing code ombudsman); or

  (b) regulation 4(1) (notification of code of practice), 6(4) (supply of information to code reviewer), 7(4) (supply of information to licensing code ombudsman) or 9(2) (supply of information in accordance with a requirement imposed by the Secretary of State).

(2) Any financial penalty imposed under paragraph (1)(a) shall not exceed £50,000.

(3) Any financial penalty imposed under paragraphs (1)(b) or (2), may comprise—

  (a) a sum equivalent to level 5 on the standard scale; together with

  (b) a daily default fine equivalent to one tenth of level 5 on the standard scale for each day until the required action is taken, but the financial penalty shall not exceed £50,000 in total.

Imposition of a financial penalty: main procedural requirements

11.—(1) As soon as practicable after imposing a financial penalty, the Secretary of State must give notice of the financial penalty.

(2) The notice of the financial penalty must state —

    (a) that the Secretary of State has imposed a financial penalty on the relevant licensing body or a relevant person,

    (b) the amount of the financial penalty,

    (c) the acts or omissions which the Secretary of State considers constitute the contravention,

    (d) any other facts which the Secretary of State considers justify the imposition of a financial penalty; and

    (e) the period (not less than 28 days from the date of service of the notice on the relevant licensing body or relevant person) within which the financial penalty is to be paid.

(3) A notice under this regulation must be given by—

    (a) serving a copy of the notice on the relevant licensing body and any relevant person upon whom a financial penalty is imposed, and

    (b) publishing the notice in such manner as the Secretary of State considers appropriate for the purpose of bringing the matters to which the notice relates to the attention of persons likely to be affected by them.

Appeals

12.—(1) If a relevant licensing body is aggrieved by the imposition of a code of practice or by the imposition or amount of a financial penalty, the relevant licensing body may appeal to the First-tier Tribunal.

(2) If a relevant person is aggrieved by the imposition or amount of a financial penalty, the relevant person may appeal to the First-tier Tribunal.

(3) On an appeal under this regulation, the First-tier Tribunal may make such order as it considers appropriate.

(4) Where the appeal is against the imposition of a code of practice, the code shall continue in force until the First-tier Tribunal has determined the appeal.

(5) Where an appeal has been made under this regulation, the financial penalty may not be required to be paid until the appeal has been determined, withdrawn or otherwise dealt with.

13. If the time specified in these Regulations for doing any act ends on a day other than a working day, the act is done in time if it is done on the next working day.

Regulation 2   SCHEDULE

Specified Criteria

1. The specified criteria are set out in paragraphs 2– 9 of this Schedule.

Obligations to rights holders, members and licensees

2. The code of practice shall require the relevant licensing body to—

    (a) offer membership to all relevant right holders in the sector it manages;

    (b) have rules or a constitution that enables members and non-member right holders to withdraw their rights on reasonable notice;

    (c) offer fair and balanced representation of those right holders who are members of the relevant licensing body in the internal decision making process of the relevant licensing body;

    (d) provide a copy of the rules or constitution to members and to those potential members who have identified themselves and requested a copy;

    (e) act in the best interests of its members as a whole;

    (f) treat all members and non-member right holders fairly, honestly, reasonably, impartially, courteously and in accordance with its rules and membership agreement;

(g) ensure that its dealings with all members are transparent;

(h) treat its licensees and potential licensees fairly, honestly, impartially, courteously and in accordance with its rules and any licence agreement;

(i) ensure that its dealings with licensees or potential licensees are transparent;

(j) consult and negotiate fairly, reasonably and proportionately in relation to the terms and conditions of a new or significantly amended licensing scheme;

(k) provide to licensees, and to any potential licensees who have requested it, information about its licensing schemes, their terms and conditions and how it collects royalties;

(l) ensure that all licences and licensing schemes are drafted in plain English and are accompanied by suitable explanatory material.

Requirements imposed on licensees

3. The code of practice shall set out the requirements that the relevant licensing body must impose on licensees including—

(a) to respect the rights of creators and right holders including their right to receive fair payment when their works are used; and

(b) that copyright material is to be used only in accordance with the terms and conditions of a licence.

Conduct of employees, agents and representatives

4. The code of practice shall require the relevant licensing body to ensure that—

(a) its staff training procedures for employees, agents and representatives include training about conduct that complies with the obligations to members and licensees set out in this Schedule;

(b) its staff provide licensees and potential licensees with clear information, including information about cooling off periods which may apply to new licences; and

(c) its employees and agents are aware of procedures for handling complaints and resolving disputes and are able to explain those procedures to members, non-member right holders, licensees and the general public in plain English.

Information and transparency – monitoring and reporting requirements

5.

(a) inform members, licensees and potential licensees, on request, about the scope of its repertoire, any existing reciprocal representation and the territorial scope of its mandate;

(b) maintain, and make available to members on request, a clear distribution policy that includes the basis for calculating remuneration and the frequency of payments, together with clear information about deductions and what they are for;

(c) provide details of tariffs in a uniform format on its website;

(d) provide details of its code of practice and complaints procedure, accessible via a link on the website homepage;

(e) undertake that all information provided is kept up to date, is readily accessible and written in clear language that can be easily understood by licensees, potential licensees and members.

Reporting requirements

6. The code of practice shall require the relevant licensing body to publish an annual report which includes—

(a) the number of right holders represented, whether as members or through representative arrangements including, where possible and if applicable, an estimate of the number of non-member right holders represented by any Extended Collective Licensing Scheme;

(b) the distribution policy;

(c) total revenue from licences granted for its repertoire during the reporting period;

(d) total costs incurred in administering licences and licensing schemes;

(e) itemised costs incurred in administering licences and licensing schemes;

(f) allocation and distribution of payments of revenues received and extent to which these are compliant with its distribution policy;

(g) procedures for the appointment of directors of or, where appropriate, managers or similar officers in the relevant licensing body and details of any appointment during the course of the reporting period;

(h) details of remuneration of each director of or, where appropriate, managers or similar officers in the relevant licensing body during the reporting period; and

(i) a report regarding compliance with its code of practice over the past year, including data on total level of complaints and how they were dealt with.

Resolution of complaints and disputes

7. The code of practice shall provide that the relevant licensing body shall adopt and publicise procedures for dealing with complaints from members, non-member right holders, licensees and potential licensees together with arrangements for the submission of any disputes, including complaints which cannot be resolved by the complaints procedure, to the licensing code ombudsman.

8. The complaints procedure shall—

(a) define the categories of complaints and explain how each will be dealt with;

(b) ensure information on how to make complaints is readily accessible to members, licensees and potential licensees;

(c) provide reasonable assistance to a complainant when forming and lodging a complaint;

(d) specify who will handle a complaint on behalf of the relevant licensing body;

(e) indicate the timeframe for the handling of a complaint;

(f) provide that the relevant licensing body must give a written response to each complaint made in writing;

(g) provide that the relevant licensing body must give a written decision where appropriate for each complaint and give reasons for that decision;

(h) ensure that the relevant licensing body makes adequate resources available for the purpose of responding to complaints; and

(i) provide that the relevant licensing body must regularly review its complaint handling procedure and dispute resolution procedures to ensure they comply with the specified criteria.

Ombudsman Scheme

9. The code of practice shall provide that the licensing code ombudsman shall be the final arbiter on disputes between the relevant licensing body and its members or licensees in relation to those provisions of the relevant licensing body's code of practice the inclusion of which is required by these specified criteria.

A4.xv The Copyright and Rights in Performances (Extended Collective Licensing) Regulations 2014

(SI 2014/2588)

Made   *11th September 2014*

Coming into force   *1st October 2014*

A draft of the Regulations has been laid before and approved by each House of Parliament under section 116D(5) of and paragraph 1D(5) of Schedule 2A to the Copyright, Designs and Patents Act 1988.

The Secretary of State, in exercise of the powers conferred by sections 116B to 116D of and paragraphs 1B to 1D of Schedule 2A to that Act, makes the following Regulations:

Citation and commencement

1. These Regulations may be cited as the Copyright and Rights in Performances (Extended Collective Licensing) Regulations 2014 and shall come into force on 1st October 2014.

Interpretation

2. In these Regulations—

"Act" means the Copyright, Designs and Patents Act 1988;

"authorisation" means an authorisation granted by the Secretary of State to a relevant licensing body under regulation 4 or 9;

"code of practice" means the code of practice adopted and published by the relevant licensing body;

"Codes Regulations" mean the Copyright (Regulation of Relevant Licensing Bodies) Regulations 2014;

"Comptroller" means the Comptroller-General of Patents, Designs and Trade Marks;

"distribution policy" means the distribution policy adopted and published by the relevant licensing body;

"Extended Collective Licensing Scheme" means a collective licensing scheme under which a relevant licensing body may grant licences in accordance with an authorisation under regulation 4 in respect of relevant works—

(a) in which copyright is owned by non-member right holders; or

(b) in relation to which the restricted acts in relation to the performance may be permitted or prohibited by non-member right holders;

"financial year" means the financial year of the relevant licensing body;

"member" means a right holder or a body representing right holders, including other relevant licensing bodies, fulfilling the membership requirements of and admitted to membership by a relevant licensing body;

"net licence fee" means the licence fee received by a relevant licensing body under an Extended Collective Licensing Scheme in respect of a relevant work less a reasonable administration fee

"non-member right holder" means a right holder who is represented by the relevant licensing body under an Extended Collective Licensing Scheme but who is not a member of the relevant licensing body and whose rights in the relevant works are not the subject of an express contractual agreement with the relevant licensing body;

"opt out arrangements" means the steps to be followed by a right holder to limit or exclude the grant of licences under an Extended Collective Licensing Scheme;

"permitted use" means the acts—

(a) restricted by copyright, or

(b) to which sections 182, 182A, 182B, 182C, 182CA, 183 or 184 of the Act apply, which the relevant licensing body is authorised to license;

"relevant licensing body" means any body that is a licensing body within the meaning of section 116(2) of the Act and which—

(a) is authorised by way of assignment, licence or any other contractual arrangement to manage the rights of right holders in relevant works on behalf of more than one right holder, for the collective benefit of those right holders, as its sole or main purpose; and

(b) is either owned or controlled by its members or organised on a not for profit basis;

"representation" means the extent to which the relevant licensing body currently—

(a) acts on behalf of right holders in respect of relevant works of the type which will be the subject of the proposed Extended Collective Licensing Scheme; and

(b) holds right holders' rights in relevant works of the type which will be the subject of the proposed Extended Collective Licensing Scheme;

"required consent" means the informed consent of a substantial proportion of the members of the relevant licensing body who vote on the proposal;

"relevant work" has the meaning set out in regulation 3;

"restricted acts" means the acts in relation to a performance to which sections 182, 182A, 182B, 182C, 182CA, 183 or 184 of the Act apply;

"right holder" has the meaning set out in regulation 3

"specified criteria" means the criteria set out in the Schedule to the Codes Regulations.

Relevant work and right holder

3.—(1) "Relevant work" means a work which is protected by copyright or a performance in respect of which certain acts constitute restricted acts.

(2) A reference to a "relevant work" includes a reference to a work or a performance, which itself falls within the definition of "relevant work" and is embedded in or incorporated in, or constitutes an integral part of, another relevant work.

(3) "Right holder" in relation to a relevant work means—

(a) an owner of the copyright in the relevant work;

(b) a licensee under an exclusive licence in relation to the relevant work;

(c) a person with rights to permit or prohibit one or more of the restricted acts in relation to a performance recorded by the relevant work and, in the case of a performance, which is embedded in, or incorporated in or constitutes an integral part of a relevant work, a person with rights to permit or prohibit one or more of the restricted acts in relation to the performance; and

(d) a licensee under an exclusive licence in relation to those rights.

Authorisation to operate an Extended Collective Licensing Scheme

4.—(1) The Secretary of State may, if he considers it reasonable in the circumstances to do so, authorise a relevant licensing body to operate an Extended Collective Licensing Scheme after receiving an application made in accordance with regulation 5 and completion of the procedure in regulations 6 to 8.

(2) An authorisation must specify—

(a) the types of relevant work to which it applies; and

(b) the permitted use.

(3) A relevant licensing body authorised under paragraph (1) may license all rights within the scope of the Extended Collective Licensing Scheme provided that the relevant licensing body—

(a) grants scheme licences in accordance with the terms and conditions notified to the Secretary of State under regulation 5(1)(p);

(b) carries out its licensing activities in accordance with its code of practice;

(c) complies with the requirements of these Regulations; and

(d) complies with the conditions of its authorisation.

(4) The Secretary of State may only grant an authorisation to a relevant licensing body if the Secretary of State is satisfied that—

(a) at the time of the authorisation, the relevant licensing body licenses by way of collective licence relevant works of the type which are to be the subject of the proposed Extended Collective Licensing Scheme;

(b) the relevant licensing body's representation in the type of relevant works which are to be the subject of the proposed Extended Collective Licensing Scheme is significant;

(c) the code of practice of the relevant licensing body is consistent with the specified criteria including the criteria concerning the protection of non-member right holders;

(d) the opt out arrangements, including those for multiple works, are adequate to protect the interests of right holders;

(e) the arrangements for publicising the scheme, for contacting non–member right holders in order to distribute the net licence fees and for distributing any net licence fees which remain undistributed are appropriate for the proposed scheme, having regard to the interests of non-member right holders; and

(f) the relevant licensing body has obtained the required consent to the proposed Extended Collective Licensing Scheme.

(5) An authorisation is personal to the relevant licensing body and the authorisation may not be transferred to any other person or body.

(6) An authorisation continues in force until the earlier of the expiration of five years from the date of the grant of the authorisation or until revocation or cancellation in accordance with regulation 14 or 15.

Application for authorisation

5.—(1) An application for authorisation under regulation 4 must be made in writing to the Secretary of State in the form required by the Secretary of State, including in electronic form, and must contain—

(a) a summary of the application;

(b) the name of the applicant;

(c) evidence that the applicant is a relevant licensing body;

(d) an address for service on the applicant in the European Economic Area;

(e) the types of relevant work to which the Extended Collective Licensing Scheme will apply;

(f) the right holders' rights in relation to relevant works which the relevant licensing body seeks to be authorised to license;

(g) the opt out arrangements that the relevant licensing body will adopt including the steps which a non-member right holder is required to take to opt out of a proposed Extended Collective Licensing Scheme before the scheme commences and whether the consent of the Secretary of State is sought as described in regulation 16(5)(b);

(h) the number of right holders—

(i) who have notified the relevant licensing body that they wish to opt out of the proposed Extended Collective Licensing Scheme; or

(ii) whose rights, as a result of contractual arrangements with the relevant licensing body, will not fall within the Extended Collective Licensing Scheme together, in each case and to the extent that the relevant licensing body has been notified by the relevant right holder, with the number of relevant works in which those right holders have rights;

(i) evidence of the representation provided by the relevant licensing body;

(j) evidence that the relevant licensing body has obtained the required consent;

(k) the information that was provided by the relevant licensing body to the relevant members, when seeking the required consent;

(l) a copy of any collective licence, in force at the date of the application for authorisation, under which the relevant licensing body licenses relevant works of the type which will be the subject of the proposed Extended Collective Licensing Scheme;

(m) the code of practice that the relevant licensing body will operate in relation to its licensing activities if the authorisation is granted and which is consistent with the specified criteria, including the criteria concerning the protection of non-member right holders;

(n) a copy of any report relating to the code of practice adopted by the relevant licensing body which has been produced by an independent code reviewer in accordance with the terms of the self-regulatory code of practice or by a code reviewer appointed by the Secretary of State under regulation 6 of the Codes Regulations;

(o) a declaration signed on behalf of the relevant licensing body confirming that, at the time of the application, it is complying in all material respects with the terms of its code of practice;

(p) a copy of the terms and conditions of the licence which the relevant licensing body proposes to grant its licensees under the Extended Collective Licensing Scheme;

(q) a copy of the distribution policy which the relevant licensing body proposes to operate in relation to its licensing activities if the authorisation is granted;

(r) the arrangements for publicising the Extended Collective Licensing Scheme to non-member right holders and third parties before its introduction and during the life of the scheme; and

(s) the methods by which the relevant licensing body will contact non-member right holders and distribute the net licence fees to them.

(2) An application for authorisation under regulation 4 must be accompanied by an initial fee to reimburse the Secretary of State for any administrative expenses incurred in connection with the application for authorisation.

Response to an application

6.—(1) If an application, submitted in accordance with regulation 4 or 9, complies with the requirements of the relevant regulation the Secretary of State must within 14 days of its receipt inform the relevant licensing body—

(a) that the application has been received;

(b) of any additional information that the Secretary of State requires to facilitate consideration of the application; and

(c) of the date by which the application will be determined.

(2) If an application submitted in accordance with regulation 4 or 9 does not meet the requirements of the relevant regulation the Secretary of State shall within 14 days of receipt inform the relevant licensing body in writing that the application has been rejected, together with a statement of the reasons for that decision.

Authorisation procedure

7.—(1) Before granting an authorisation under regulation 4 or 9 the Secretary of State must—

(a) publish a notice setting out details of the application for authorisation in such manner as the Secretary of State considers appropriate for bringing it to the attention of persons likely to be affected by the authorisation; and

(b) consider any comments provided in accordance with the notice.

(2) The notice must state the period (which must be not less than 28 days starting with the date of publication of the notice) within which comments may be provided to the Secretary of State regarding the proposed authorisation.

Notice of decision on authorisation

8.—(1) The Secretary of State must decide whether to grant an authorisation, under regulation 4, or a renewal of an authorisation under regulation 9, and shall notify the relevant licensing body of his decision together with the reasons for the decision.

(2) If an authorisation is granted, the notification must set out the commencement date of the authorisation, whether the authorisation has been granted subject to conditions, and if so, what the conditions are.

(3) The Secretary of State may require a relevant licensing body to pay to the Secretary of State an application fee to reimburse the Secretary of State for any administrative expenses incurred in connection with the application, including those associated with a consideration of whether the requirements set out in regulation 4(4), or (as thecase may be) 9(4), are satisfied.

(4) When setting the application fee the Secretary of State must take account of any initial fee which has already been paid.

(5) The Secretary of State must notify the relevant licensing body of his decision on an application for authorisation within 90 days of the end of the period for providing comments under regulation 7, and on an application for a renewal of authorisation, within 28 days of that date.

(6) The Secretary of State must publish his decision in such manner as the Secretary of State considers appropriate for bringing it to the attention of persons likely to be affected by the authorisation.

Renewal of an authorisation

9.—(1) The Secretary of State may, if he considers it reasonable in the circumstances to do so, renew the authorisation of a relevant licensing body to operate an Extended Collective Licensing Scheme upon the application of that body, made in accordance with regulation 10, and after the completion of the procedure set out in regulations 6 to 8.

(2) A renewed authorisation must specify—

    (a) the types of relevant work to which it applies; and

    (b) the permitted use.

(3) Regulation 4(3) to (5) applies in relation to the renewal of an authorisation as it applies in relation to the original application for authorisation.

(4) The Secretary of State may renew an authorisation for a fixed period or may express the renewed authorisation to continue until the earlier of revocation or cancellation in accordance with regulations 14 or 15.

Application for the renewal of an authorisation

10.—(1) An application by a relevant licensing body for a renewal of an authorisation under regulation 9 shall be made to the Secretary of State in writing, not less than three years from the date of grant of the existing authorisation and not less than three months before the expiration of that authorisation, in the form required by the Secretary of State, including in electronic form.

(2) An application for a renewal of an authorisation under regulation 9 must contain—

    (a) a summary of the application for renewal;

    (b) confirmation that the information provided under regulation 5(b) to (h), (l), (m), (p), (q) and (s), remains as set out in the previous authorised application or details of any material changes;

(c) information demonstrating—

    (i) how the opt out arrangements have been operated during the previous period of authorisation;

    (ii) the number of right holders who, at the date of the application for renewal, have notified the relevant licensing authority that they wish to opt out of the proposed Extended Collective Licensing Scheme compared with the number of right holders who were opted out of the Extended Collective Licensing Scheme at the date of the previous application for authorisation; and

    (iii) the number of relevant works that are opted out at the date of the application for renewal compared with the number of relevant works that are opted out of the Extended Collective Licensing Scheme at the date of the previous application for authorisation and, to the extent that the relevant licensing body has been notified by the relevant right holders, the number of works in which those right holders have rights;

(d) evidence of the representation provided by the relevant licensing body at the time the application for renewal is made;

(e) evidence that the relevant licensing body has obtained the required consent;

(f) the information that was provided by the relevant licensing body to the relevant members, when seeking the required consent;

(g) a copy of any report produced within the period of the initial authorisation relating to the code of practice adopted by the relevant licensing body which has been produced by an independent code reviewer in accordance with the terms of the self-regulatory code of practice or by a code reviewer appointed by the Secretary of State in accordance with regulation 6 of the Codes Regulations;

(h) a declaration signed on behalf of the relevant licensing body confirming that, at the time of the application for renewal, it is complying in all material respects with the terms of its code of practice;

(i) a list of complaints from any non-member right holders whose works or rights have been licensed under the Extended Collective Licensing Scheme and the nature of the complaints and how they were resolved;

(j) details of the distributions which have been made to non-member right holders, any sums which have been distributed in accordance with regulation 19 and which remain undistributed;

(k) the arrangements for publicising the Extended Collective Licensing Scheme to non-member right holders and third parties during the life of the scheme together with information demonstrating how effective the publication of the Extended Collective Licensing Scheme has been; and

(l) whether the consent of the Secretary of State is sought as described in regulation 16(5)(b).

(3) An application by a relevant licensing body for a renewal of an authorisation under regulation 9 shall be accompanied by a renewal fee to reimburse the Secretary of State for any administrative expenses incurred in connection with the application for renewal.

Review of Extended Collective Licensing Scheme

11.—(1) Every three years after the date on which an authorisation was renewed, the relevant licensing body which operates an Extended Collective Licensing Scheme must provide the Secretary of State with—

(a) information demonstrating—
    (i) how the opt out arrangements have been operated during the previous period of authorisation;
    (ii) the number of right holders who, at the time of the review, have notified the relevant licensing authority that they wish to opt out of the Extended Collective Licensing Scheme compared with the number of right holders who were opted out of the Extended Collective Licensing Scheme at the date of the previous application for authorisation; and
    (iii) the number of opted out works at the time of the review compared with the number of works opted out of the Extended Collective Licensing Scheme at the date of the previous application for authorisation and, to the extent that the relevant licensing body has been notified by the relevant right holders, the number of works in which those right holders have rights;

(b) evidence of the representation provided by the relevant licensing body at the time the application for renewal is made;

(c) a copy of any report relating to the code of practice adopted by the relevant licensing body which has been produced by an independent code reviewer in accordance with the terms of the self-regulatory code of practice or by a code reviewer appointed by the Secretary of State under regulation 6 of the Codes Regulations;

(d) a declaration signed on behalf of the relevant licensing body confirming that, at the time of the review, it is complying in all material respects with the terms of its code of practice;

(e) a list of complaints from any non-member right holders whose works or rights have been licensed under the Extended Collective Licensing Scheme and the nature of the complaints and how they were resolved;

(f) details of the distributions which have been made to non-member right holders, any sums which have been distributed in accordance with regulation 19 and which remain undistributed;

(g) the arrangements for publicising the Extended Collective Licensing Scheme to non-member right holders and third parties during the life of the scheme together with information demonstrating how effective the publication of the Extended Collective Licensing Scheme has been; and

(h) confirmation that the information provided under regulation 5(b) to (h), (l), (m), (p), (q) and (s), remains as set out in the previous authorised application or details of any material changes.

(2) The Secretary of State may, in addition, require the relevant licensing body to provide to the Secretary of State, within the time period specified by the Secretary of State—

(a) evidence that the relevant licensing body has obtained the required consent to the continuation of the Extended Collective Licensing Scheme; and

(b) the information that was provided by the relevant licensing body to the relevant members, when seeking the required consent.

(3) The Secretary of State may publish information setting out details of the review and seek comments from those likely to be affected by the review.

(4) The Secretary of State may require a relevant licensing body to pay to the Secretary of State a fee to reimburse the Secretary of State for any administrative expenses incurred in connection with the review.

(5) The Secretary of State must, within three months of the date described in paragraph (1), notify the relevant licensing body of the outcome of the review of

the Extended Collective Licensing Scheme and publish the summary of findings of the review in such manner as the Secretary of State considers appropriate for bringing it to the attention of persons likely to be affected by the authorisation.

Modification of an authorisation

12.—(1) The Secretary of State may, upon the application of a relevant licensing body which operates an Extended Collective Licensing Scheme, or of the Comptroller, or following a review under regulation 11 of the scheme operated by that body, modify the conditions of an authorisation, granted under regulation 4 or 9, other than those required to be specified by regulation 4(2) or 9(2).

(2) Before making a modification under this regulation, the Secretary of State must—

(a) give notice of the proposed modification, and

(b) consider any comments provided in accordance with the notice and not withdrawn.

(3) The notice must—

(a) summarise the proposed modification;

(b) state the reasons for the proposed modification, and

(c) state the period (which must be not less than 28 days starting with the date of publication of the notice) within which representations may be made to the Secretary of State regarding the proposed modification.

(4) A notice under paragraph (2) must be given by—

(a) serving a copy of the notice on the relevant licensing body, and

(b) publishing the notice in such manner as the Secretary of State considers appropriate for the purpose of bringing the matters to which the notice relates to the attention of persons likely to be affected by them.

(5) The Secretary of State may require a relevant licensing body to pay to the Secretary of State a fee to reimburse the Secretary of State for any administrative expenses incurred in connection with the application for modification.

Notice of decision on modification

13.—(1) The Secretary of State must, within 28 days of the end of period for making representations under regulation 12, make his decision on the application for modification, publish the decision and notify the relevant licensing body in writing of the decision and of the reasons for it.

(2) If the application has been approved, the notification shall also set out whether the application has been approved subject to conditions, and if so, what the conditions are and the commencement date of the modified authorisation.

Revocation of an authorisation

14.—(1) If the Secretary of State is satisfied that the relevant licensing body has failed in respects which are relevant to the operation of the Extended Collective Licensing Scheme to operate its licensing activities in accordance with the types of relevant work or permitted use specified in the authorisation in accordance with regulations 4(2) or 9(2), the Secretary of State must revoke the authorisation.

(2) The Secretary of State may revoke the authorisation if he has reasonable grounds to believe that the relevant licensing body has failed in material respects to comply with—

(a) any other requirements of these Regulations;

(b) any conditions of its authorisation; or

(c) the specified criteria.

(3) The Secretary of State may require a relevant licensing body, whose authorisation is revoked, to pay to the Secretary of State a fee to reimburse the Secretary of State for any administrative expenses incurred in connection with administering the operation of this regulation; and a fee that falls to be paid under this paragraph is recoverable by the Secretary of State as a debt.

(4) Prior to revoking any authorisation, the Secretary of State must satisfy the requirements set out in paragraphs (5) to (7).

(5) The Secretary of State must—

(a) publish a notice in such manner as the Secretary of State considers appropriate for bringing the intention to revoke together with the reasons for taking this action to the attention of the relevant licensing body and of persons likely to be affected by the revocation; and

(b) allow the relevant licensing body and persons likely to be affected by the revocation to make comments in writing.

(6) Comments under paragraph (5)(b) must be made within 21 days from the date of the notification under paragraph (5)(a) or within such longer period as is specified in the notice.

(7) Within 42 days of the end of the period for making representations referred to in paragraph (6), the Secretary of State must provide to the relevant licensing body either the decision on revocation or the date on which the decision on revocation will be provided to the relevant licensing body.

(8) The Secretary of State's decision whether or not to revoke the authorisation must set out the reasons for the decision together, where relevant, with the date on which the authorisation shall cease.

(9) Any licences granted by the relevant licensing body under the Extended Collective Licensing Scheme shall lapse with effect from the date on which the revocation of the relevant authorisation has effect.

(10) The Secretary of State must publish his decision in such manner as the Secretary of State considers appropriate together with any conditions attached to it.

Opt out from an Extended Collective Licensing Scheme

16.—(1) A right holder may exclude or limit the grant of licences under an Extended Collective Licensing Scheme or a proposed Extended Collective Licensing Scheme in relation to their rights in a relevant work by following the opt out arrangements which are referred to in the authorisation given by the Secretary of State or in modifications to those arrangements which are made by the Secretary of State under regulation 12, including those relating to the form of opt out notice.

(2) A non-member right holder who wishes to exercise their right to opt out must provide the relevant licensing body with their name, so that the relevant licensing body may list the name under paragraph (6), and may identify the relevant works to be opted out.

(3) The opt out arrangements of each relevant licensing body shall—

(a) permit a non-member right holder to provide the relevant licensing body with an opt out notice which excludes or limits the grant of licences under an Extended Collective Licensing Scheme in relation to some or all of their relevant works;

(b) permit a non-member right holder to provide the relevant licensing body with an opt out notice which excludes or limits the grant of licences under a proposed Extended Collective Licensing Scheme in relation to some or all of their relevant works and provide that the opt out shall take effect before the commencement of the Extended Collective Licensing Scheme; and

(c) permit a member of the relevant licensing body to provide the relevant licensing body with an opt out notice which excludes or limits the grant of licences under an Extended Collective Licensing Scheme in relation to some or all of their relevant works where any agreement entered into between the member and the relevant licensing body, in relation to those relevant works, including a collective licensing agreement, enables the member to notify the relevant licensing body that it does not wish to participate in either—

(i) an Extended Collective Licensing Scheme, or

(ii) a collective licensing scheme,

operated, in either case, by the relevant licensing body.

(4) Within 14 days of receipt of a notice of opt out, the relevant licensing body shall—

(a) acknowledge receipt of the non-member right holder's request to opt out;

(b) inform the non-member right holder of the date from which the opt-out takes effect and, where a licence has been granted, of the termination date of the licence;

(c) inform any relevant licensees that the work has been opted out together with the termination date of the licence; and

(d) update the list referred to in paragraph (6).

(5) The termination date of the licence, referred to in paragraph (4)(b), shall not be later than—

(a) six months from the date of receipt by the relevant licensing body of the notice of opt out;

(b) nine months from that date, where the licensee is an educational establishment and the relevant licensing body has, in its application for authorisation or a renewal of authorisation under regulation 5 or 10, sought the consent of the Secretary of State to the later termination date for educational establishments in specified circumstances and the Secretary of State has consented to the later termination date in the notice of his decision provided under regulation 8.

(6) The relevant licensing body shall in respect of each Extended Collective Licensing Scheme maintain and make available to the public a list of—

(a) the names of those non-member right holders who have opted out;

(b) any relevant works which have been identified as opted out; and

(c) the names of any persons whose rights in relevant works are outside the scheme as a result of any contractual arrangements which those persons have entered into with the relevant licensing body.

Licensing of works or rights under an Extended Collective Licensing Scheme

17.—(1) A relevant licensing body may only grant, under an Extended Collective Licensing Scheme, a licence in respect of a relevant work owned by a non-member right holder which—

(a) permits non-exclusive use of the relevant work;

(b) has effect as if granted by the right holder in the relevant work;

(c) terminates on or before the expiration, revocation or cancellation of the authorisation of the relevant licensing body; and

(d) in a case where a non-member right holder has excluded from the

Extended Collective Licensing Scheme their rights in a relevant work, terminates on the termination date determined in accordance with regulations 16(4) and(5).

(2) The grant of a licence in accordance with these Regulations or the doing of any act permitted by a licence, which is granted in accordance with these Regulations, does not constitute an infringement of a right holder right in a relevant work for the purposes of the Act.

(3) A relevant licensing body must after the termination of a licence deliver to the relevant non- member right holders any payments due together with a written statement of account in relation to those payments, in accordance with its distribution policy.

(4) A payment referred to in paragraph (3) must be made as soon as practicable, after a termination, and no later than nine months from the end of the financial year of the relevant licensing body in which the licence fee was received.

(5) A relevant licensing body must maintain a record of the distributions of the licence fee that it has made.

Licence fee

18.—(1) The relevant licensing body may deduct a reasonable administration fee from the licence fee which it receives for the grant, under an Extended Collective Licensing Scheme, of a licence of a relevant work owned by a non-member right holder.

(2) The relevant licensing body must apply the administration fee towards the general costs of the relevant licensing body and for the benefit of both member and non-member right holders.

(3) The relevant licensing body must, as soon as practicable and no later than nine months from the end of the financial year in which a licence fee was collected, distribute the appropriate portion of the net licence fee to those non-member right holders who have been identified and located and transfer any portion of the net licence fee that remains undistributed to a designated account.

(4) A non-member right holder may, within three years from the end of the financial year in which the relevant licensing body received a licence fee under an Extended Collective Licensing Scheme, produce to the relevant licensing body evidence of either or both of—

(a) a reasonable or achieved level of licence fee, and

(b) the level of use to which the relevant work has been put during the term of the licence, and request the relevant licensing body to adjust the net licence fee which is distributed under paragraph (3) to take account of that level of licence fee or of use.

(5) A relevant licensing body shall publish information on the relevant works and other subject matter which have been licensed under the Extended Collective Licensing Scheme but for which one or more right holders have not been identified or located and shall update the information within twelve months from the end of the financial year in which the licence fee was collected.

Retention and application of undistributed licence fees

19.—(1) Subject to paragraph (2), the relevant licensing body must transfer a sum equal to the net licence fee received in respect of a non-member right holder from the designated account to the Secretary of State where—

(a) not less than three years have elapsed from the end of the financial year in which the relevant licensing body received a licence fee under an Extended Collective Licensing Scheme; and

(b) the relevant non-member right holder, who is entitled to the licence fee, has not been identified or located.

(2) Where the Secretary of State has directed the relevant licensing body to retain the licence fee in a designated account, for any period after the expiration of the initial three year period, the relevant licensing body must retain the licence fee in the designated account and then transfer the licence fee to the Secretary of State at the end of the period.

(3) The Secretary of State must retain any net licence fee, which has not been distributed by the relevant licensing body, for a period of 8 years from the date of authorisation of the Extended Collective Licensing Scheme and may then determine the use of the net licence fee, including, by applying some or all of the net licence fee to fund social, cultural and educational activities for the benefit of non-member right holders.

Secretary of State's power to request information

20.—(1) The Secretary of State may serve notice on any relevant licensing body requiring it to supply to the Secretary of State for any purpose related to an Extended Collective Licensing Scheme operated by it such information as may be specified or described in the notice, and to supply it at a time and place and in a form and manner so specified.

(2) A relevant licensing body shall supply the Secretary of State with information requested under paragraph (1) within 14 days of receipt of the request.

A4.xvi The Copyright and Rights in Performances (Licensing of Orphan Works) Regulations 2014 (SI 2014/2863)

(SI 2014/2863)

Made   *27th October 2014*
Coming into force   *29th October 2014*

A draft of the Regulations has been laid before and approved by each House of Parliament under section 116D(5) and paragraph 1D(5) of Schedule 2A to the Copyright, Designs and Patents Act 1988.

The Secretary of State, in exercise of the powers conferred by sections 116A, 116C and 116D of and paragraphs 1A, 1C and 1D of Schedule 2A to that Act, makes the following Regulations:

Citation and commencement

1. These Regulations may be cited as the Copyright and Rights in Performances (Licensing of Orphan Works) Regulations 2014 and shall come into force on 29th October 2014.

Interpretation

2. In these Regulations—
     "the Act" means the Copyright, Designs and Patents Act 1988;
     "authorising body" means the Comptroller;
     "Comptroller" means the Comptroller-General of Patents, Designs and Trade Marks;
     "diligent search" has the meaning set out in regulation 4;
     "identified right holder" is a right holder of the type referred to in regulation 12(1);
     "orphan licence" is a licence authorising the use of an orphan work;

"orphan licensee" means a person who either wishes to be granted or has been granted an orphan licence;

"orphan work" has the meaning set out in regulation 3;

"relevant work" has the meaning set out in regulation 3;

"restricted acts" means the acts in relation to a performance to which sections 182, 182A, 182B, 182C, 182CA, 183 or 184 of the Act apply;

"right holder" has the meaning set out in regulation 3.

Relevant work, right holder and orphan work

3.—(1) "Relevant work" means a work which is protected by copyright or a performance in respect of which certain acts constitute restricted acts.

(2) A reference to a "relevant work" includes a reference to a work or a performance, which itself falls within the definition of "relevant work" and is embedded in or incorporated in, or constitutes an integral part of, another relevant work.

(3) "Right holder" in relation to a relevant work means—

(a) an owner of the copyright in the relevant work;

(b) a licensee under an exclusive licence in relation to the relevant work;

(c) a person with rights to permit or prohibit one or more of the restricted acts in relation to a performance recorded by the relevant work and, in the case of a performance, which is embedded or incorporated in or constitutes an integral part of another relevant work, a person with rights to permit or prohibit one or more of the restricted acts in relation to the performance; and

(d) a licensee under an exclusive licence in relation to those rights.

(4) A relevant work is an orphan work where, after a diligent search made in accordance with regulation 4, one or more of the right holders in the relevant work have either not been identified or, if identified, have not been located.

(5) Where a relevant work has more than one right holder and, after a diligent search made in accordance with regulation 4, one or more of the right holders have either not been identified or, if identified, have not been located, then the relevant work is an orphan work to the extent that the rights of those right holders are either not identified or not located.

(6) In these Regulations, a reference to an orphan work includes a relevant work in which it is not known whether copyright or the right to permit or prohibit the restricted acts subsists, and references to a right holder who has not been identified or located are to be read as including references to a supposed right holder.

(7) A relevant work ceases to be an orphan work to the extent that a right holder is identified in accordance with regulation 12.

Diligent search

4.—(1) An orphan licensee shall, before applying for an orphan licence, carry out a diligent search or refer to an existing diligent search which is valid and, in either case, is appropriate to the orphan work which is the proposed subject matter of the orphan licence and relates to the rights in the relevant work which the orphan licensee proposes to use.

(2) A diligent search must comprise a reasonable search of the relevant sources to identify and locate the right holders of the relevant work.

(3) The sources that are relevant for the relevant work must, as a minimum, include—

(a) the relevant register maintained by the authorising body and the relevant databases maintained by the Office for Harmonization in the Internal Market; and

(b) where there is no record that the relevant work is an orphan work in the register or databases referred to in paragraph (a), any relevant sources listed for that category of work in Part 2 of Schedule ZA1 to the Act.

(4) The authorising body may issue guidance on what sources may additionally be relevant in the case of different relevant works.

(5) A diligent search is valid, for the purposes of paragraph (1), for seven years from the earlier of the date—

(a) on which an orphan licence of the orphan work was first granted by the authorising body; or

(b) that the record of a diligent search undertaken in respect of a relevant work was first made public by the Office for Harmonization in the Internal Market.

(6) An orphan licensee shall provide the authorising body with such information concerning—

(a) the diligent search; and

(b) the use that the orphan licensee proposes to make of the orphan work

as the authorising body may require in connection with the application for an orphan licence.

(7) The orphan licensee shall, when applying for an orphan licence, provide the authorising body with an application in the form required by the authorising body, including in electronic form, and the application shall—

(a) demonstrate that a diligent search has been carried out; and

(b) contain a declaration in writing by the orphan licensee stating that the information provided in the application is correct.

(8) Where an orphan licensee makes a declaration under sub-paragraph (7)(b) that the orphan licensee knows or has reason to believe is false and the orphan licensee is granted an orphan licence and carries out any of the acts restricted by copyright or the restricted acts, the orphan licensee is liable for infringement of copyright or sections 182, 182A, 182B, 182C, 182CA, 183 or 184 of the Act as appropriate.

(9) The authorising body shall take reasonable steps to ensure that the search relied upon by the orphan licensee satisfies the requirements for a diligent search.

Record and register of orphan works

5.—(1) The authorising body shall maintain and update a register which sets out the details of the orphan works in respect of which—

(a) a diligent search has been carried out and an application, for the grant of an orphan licence, has been made to and is being considered by the authorising body;

(b) orphan licences have been granted together with the permitted uses of the relevant works; and

(c) orphan licences have been refused.

(2) The authorising body shall make the register available to the public by electronic means and free of charge.

Licensing of orphan works

6.—(1) Once the authorising body has received the information set out in regulations 4(6) and (7), it may grant an orphan licence.

(2) The authorising body may only grant an orphan licence which—

(a) permits non-exclusive use of an orphan work in the United Kingdom;

(b) permits acts restricted by the copyright or sections 182, 182A, 182B,

182C, 182CA, 183 or 184 of the Act in an orphan work for a term not exceeding 7 years;

(c) prohibits the grant of sub-licences;

(d) has effect as if granted by the right holder of the relevant work;

(e) provides that the use of an orphan work does not affect the moral rights of an author under Chapter IV of Part 1 of the Act or the moral rights of a performer under Chapter 3 of Part 2 of the Act and treats those moral rights as having been asserted.

(3) Subject to the requirements set out in paragraph (2), the authorising body may grant a licence subject to conditions.

(4) An orphan licence may not be granted to a person authorised to grant licences.

(5) The authorising body may refuse to grant a licence—

(a) on the ground that, in its reasonable opinion, a proposed use or adaptation is not appropriate having regard to the circumstances of the case, including whether the proposed adaptation constitutes derogatory treatment of the work; or

(b) on any other reasonable ground.

(6) Subject to the requirements set out in paragraph (2), the authorising body may, during the term of a licence, vary the terms of an orphan licence.

Use for incidental purposes

7. Any person may, without infringing copyright or sections 182, 182A, 182B, 182C, 182CA, 183 or 184 of the Act, make reasonable use of an orphan work for purposes which are incidental to—

(a) the application for the grant of an orphan licence; and

(b) the processing of the application and the maintenance of the register referred to in regulation 5(1).

Renewal of orphan licence

8.—(1) Upon the request of the orphan licensee, submitted in the form required not less than six months before the expiration of the orphan licence, the authorising body may renew an orphan licence for a further term not exceeding 7 years.

(2) A request for a renewal of an orphan licence shall be accompanied by evidence of a diligent search carried out in accordance with regulation 4 together with the information set out in regulations 4(6) and (7).

Processing fee

9. The authorising body may charge a reasonable fee for processing an application for an orphan licence or to vary or renew an existing orphan licence.

Licence fee for an orphan licence

10.—(1) Subject to paragraph (2), on the grant of an orphan licence the authorising body—

(a) shall charge the orphan licensee a reasonable licence fee for the period of the licence calculated with regard to relevant factors which shall include the level of licence fees which are achieved under licences for a similar use of similar relevant works which are not orphan works; and

(b) may charge a reasonable additional amount in respect of the costs of the authorising body

(2) The authorising body shall—

    (a) hold all licence fees paid under this regulation in a designated account

    (b) adopt accounting procedures that ring-fence in a separate account for monies received from orphan licences; and

    (c) retain unclaimed licence fees for a period of not less than eight years from the date of the grant of the relevant orphan licence.

(3) The authorising body shall maintain and make available information that sets out, in respect of the orphan licences it grants, how the licence fee is calculated.

Reporting requirements

11.—(1) The authorising body shall publish an annual report on the operation of the orphan works scheme and the orphan licences that it has granted.

(2) The authorising body shall provide the Secretary of State with a copy of the annual report upon its publication.

Rights of identified right holder

12.—(1) This regulation applies where the right holder in an orphan work identifies themselves to the authorising body and satisfies the authorising body of their identity and of their ownership of relevant rights in the orphan work either—

    (a) in the period between the receipt by the authorising body of an application for the grant of an orphan licence and the grant by the authorising body of that licence; or

    (b) within eight years or less of the date on which the authorising body has granted an orphan licence of the orphan work.

(2) If the authorising body has verified the diligent search but has not granted an orphan licence then the work shall, to the extent of the rights of the identified right holder, cease to be an orphan work.

(3) If the authorising body has granted an orphan licence then the orphan licence shall continue for the remainder of its unexpired term or until the expiration of the notice period which is set out in the orphan licence notwithstanding the fact that the right holder is identified.

(4) The authorising body shall within two months of being satisfied that the right holder has been identified—

    (a) notify the orphan licensee that the right holder has been identified;

    (b) pay to the right holder a sum equal to the licence fee paid by the orphan licensee in respect of the orphan work.

Unclaimed licence fees of orphan works

13.—(1) Where more than 8 years have elapsed since the grant of an orphan licence and no right holder in the orphan work has identified themselves, the authorising body shall apply the licence fee, received by it in respect of that orphan licence, to pay the reasonable costs which the authorising body has incurred in connection with the orphan works scheme, including the setting up and running of the scheme.

(2) To the extent that the licence fees referred to in paragraph (1) constitute a surplus over the reasonable costs of the authorising body, the authorising body may apply the surplus to fund social, cultural and educational activities.

(3) If a right holder in an orphan work identifies themselves to the authorising body more than eight years after the grant of the orphan licence and satisfies the authorising body of their identity and of their ownership of relevant rights in the

orphan work, the authorising body may make such payment to the right holder as the body considers reasonable in all the circumstances of the case.

Appeals

14. (1) A right holder who has identified themselves to the authorising body under regulation 12, may appeal to the First-tier Tribunal on the grounds that the authorising body has either acted improperly or failed to comply with its obligations under these Regulations.

(2) An orphan licensee may appeal to the Copyright Tribunal concerning—

(a) the refusal by the authorising body to grant an orphan licence to the orphan licensee;

(b) any condition imposed by the authorising body in connection with the grant of the orphan licence; or

(c) any amount described in regulation 10(1) which the authorising body requires it to pay.

(3) On an application under paragraph (2) the Copyright Tribunal shall consider the matter and may make such order as it considers to be reasonable in the circumstances.

A5. Commencement Orders (CDPA 1988)

A5.i The Copyright, Designs and Patents Act 1988 (Commencement No. 1) Order 1989

(SI 1989/816) (c.21)

Made   *9th May 1989*

The Secretary of State, in exercise of the powers conferred upon him by section 305(3) of the Copyright, Designs and Patents Act 1988, hereby makes the following Order:

1. This Order may be cited as the Copyright, Designs and Patents Act 1988 (Commencement No. 1) Order 1989.

2. The following provisions of the Copyright, Designs and Patents Act 1988 shall come into force on 1st August 1989:

    Part I (copyright);

    Part II (rights in performances);

    Part III (design right);

    Part IV (registered designs), except—

        section 272 in so far as it relates to paragraph 21 of Schedule 3, and section 273;

    Part VI (patents), except—

        sections 293 and 294, and

        section 295 in so far as it relates to paragraphs 1 to 11 and 17 to 30 of Schedule 5;

    Part VII (miscellaneous and general), except—

        section 301,

        section 303(1) in so far as it relates to paragraphs 15, 18(2) and 21 of Schedule 7, and

        section 303(2) in so far as it relates to the references in Schedule 8 to section 32 of the Registered Designs Act 1949 and to the provisions of the Patents Act 1977, other than section 49(3) of, and paragraphs 1 and 3 of Schedule 5 to, that Act;

    Schedule 1 (copyright: transitional provisions and savings);

    Schedule 2 (rights in performance: permitted acts);

    Schedule 3 (minor and consequential amendments to the Registered Designs Act 1949), other than paragraph 21;

    Schedule 5 (patents: miscellaneous amendments), other than paragraphs 1 to 11 and 17 to 30;

    Schedule 7 (consequential amendments), other than paragraphs 15, 18(2) and 21;

    Schedule 8 (repeals), except in so far as it relates to—

        section 32 of the Registered Designs Act 1949, and

        the provisions of the Patents Act 1977, other than section 49(3) of, and paragraphs 1 and 3 of Schedule 5 to, that Act.

Note: This Order was amended by SI 1989/1303 (c.45). See A5.iv, below.

A5.ii The Copyright, Designs and Patents Act 1988 (Commencement No. 2) Order 1989

(SI 1989/955 (c.25))

Made   *9th June 1989*

The Secretary of State, in exercise of the powers conferred upon him by section 305(3) of the Copyright, Designs and Patents Act 1988 ("the Act"), hereby makes the following Order:

1. This Order may be cited as the Copyright, Designs and Patents Act 1988 (Commencement No. 2) Order 1989.

2. The provisions of the Act specified in the to this Order (which, apart from this Order, come into force on 1st August 1989) shall come into force forthwith for the purpose only of enabling the making of subordinate legislation thereunder, by the authority shown in relation to those provisions, expressed to come into force on 1st August 1989.

SCHEDULE

PROVISIONS OF THE ACT COMING INTO FORCE FORTHWITH

Provision and Authority	*Subject matter*
Regulations by the Secretary of State under sections 37 and 38 to 43	Copying by librarians and archivists of prescribed libraries and archives.
Orders by the Secretary of State under—	
section 47	Specification of material to be marked in relation to public insepection and copying of the same, and application or provisions relating to public inspection of material to material or registers maintained by international organisations.
section 52	Articles to be regarded as made by industrial process and excluded articles.
section 61	Recordings of folksongs for archival purposes for designated bodies.
section 74	Provision of subtitled copies of broadcasts and cable programmes by designated bodies.

Notes:

(1) This Order was amended by The Copyright, Designs and Patents Act 1988 (Commencement No.3) Order 1989 (SI 1989/1032 (c.27)), made on June 20, 1989, by substituting for the Schedule to this Order the Schedule in the Schedule to the amending Order. This Order is, therefore, printed with the substituted Schedule.

(2) For SI 1989/816 (c.21) see A5.i, above.

A5.iii The Copyright, Designs and Patents Act 1988 (Commencement No.3) Order 1989

(SI 1989/1032)

Made   *20th June 1989*

The Secretary of State, in exercise of the powers conferred upon him by section

305(3) of the Copyright, Designs and Patents Act 1988[1] *("the Act"), hereby makes the following Order:*

1. This Order may be cited as the Copyright, Designs and Patents Act 1988 (Commencement No. 3) Order 1989.

2. The Copyright, Designs and Patents Act 1988 (Commencement No. 2) Order 1989[2] is amended by substituting for the Schedule thereto the Schedule set out in the Schedule to this Order.

20th June 1989

SCHEDULE

Provisions of the Act Coming into Force Forthwith

Provision and Authority	Subject matter
Regulations by the Secretary of State under sections 37 and 38 to 43	Copying by librarians and archivists of prescribed libraries and archives.
Orders by the Secretary of State under—	
section 47	Specification of material to be marked in relation to public inspection and copyring of the same, and application of provisions relating to public inspection of material to material or registers maintained by international organisatgions.
section 52	Articles to be regarded as made by industrial process and excluded articles.
section 61	Recordings of folksongs for archival purposes for designated bodies.
section 74	Provision of subtitled copies of broadcasts and cable programmes by designated bodies.
section 75	Recordings for archives of designated class of broadcasts and cable programmes.
section 100 and 196	Prescribing the form of notice of seizure when infringing articles or illicit recordings are seized and detained.
Regulations by Commissioners of Customs and Excise under section 112	Prescribing the form of notices required under section 111 in respect of goods to be treated as prohibited goods.
Rules by the Lord Chancellor under sections 150, 152 and paragraph 34 of Schedule 1	Proceedings before the Copyright Tribunal.
Order in Council by Her Majesty under—	
section 159	Application of Part I of the Act to other countries.
section 168	Vesting of copyright in certain international organisations.
Order by Secretary of State under—	

---

[1] 1988 c.48.

[2] See SI 1989/955. [*Editorial Note*: see A5.ii, above.]

Provision and Authority	Subject matter
section 174	Descriptions of educational establishments for the purposes of Part I of the Act, and application of provisions relating to educational establishments to certain teachers.
Order in Council by Her Majesty under section 208	Designation of Convention countries enjoying reciprocal protection under Part II of the Act (performances).
Rules by Secretary of State under section 250	Proceedings before Comptroller under Part III of the Act (design right).
Order in Council by Her Majesty under section 256	Designation of countries enjoying reciprocal protection under Part III of the Act (design right).
section 75	Recordings for archives of designated class of broadcasts and cable programmes.
sections 100 and 196	Prescribing the form of notice of seizure when infringing articles or illicit recordings are seized and detained.
Regulations by Commissioners of Customs and Excise under section 112	Prescribing the form of notices required under section 111 in respect of goods to be treated as prohibited goods.
Rules by the Lord Chancellor under sections 150, 152 and paragraph 34 of Schedule 1	Proceedings before the Copyright Tribunal.
Order in Council by Her Majesty under—	
section 159	Application of Part I of the Act to other countries.
section 168	Vesting of copyright in certain international organisations.
Order by Secretary of State under—	
section 174	Descriptions of educational establishments for the purposes of Part I of the Act, and application of provisions relating to educational establishments to certain teachers.
Order in Council by Her Majesty under section 208	Designation of Convention countries enjoying reciprocal protection under Part II of the Act (performances).
Rules by Secretary of State under section 250	Proceedings before Comptroller under Part III of the Act (design right).
Order in Council by Her Majesty under section 256	Designation of countries enjoying reciprocal protection under Part III of the Act (design right).

A5.iv The Copyright, Designs and Patents Act 1988 (Commencement No. 4) Order 1989

(SI 1989/1303 (C.45))

Made   *27th July 1989*

The Secretary of State, in exercise of the powers conferred upon him by section 305(3) of the Copyright, Designs and Patents Act 1988, hereby makes the following Order:

1. This Order may be cited as the Copyright, Designs and Patents Act 1988 (Commencement No. 4) Order 1989.

2. Section 304(4) and (6) of the Copyright, Designs and Patents Act 1988 ("the 1988 Act") shall come into force on 28th July 1989.

3. In article 2 of the Copyright, Designs and Patents Act 1988 (Commencement No. 1) Order 1989 there shall be added to the list of the provisions of Part VII of the 1988 Act which do not come into force on 1st August 1989 a reference to section 304(4) and (6).

A5.v The Copyright, Designs and Patents Act 1988 (Commencement No. 5) Order 1990

(SI 1990/1400 (c.42))

Made   *10th July 1990*

The Secretary of State, in exercise of the powers conferred upon him by section 305(3) of the Copyright, Designs and Patents Act 1988, hereby makes the following Order:

1. This Order may be cited as the Copyright, Designs and Patents Act 1988 (Commencement No. 5) Order 1990.

2. The following provisions of the Copyright, Designs and Patents Act 1988 shall come into force on 13th August 1990—

  (a) in Part IV (registered designs)—
      section 272 in so far as it relates to paragraph 21 of Schedule 3, and section 273;

  (b) Part V (patent agents and trade mark agents) save in so far as article 3 below otherwise provides;

  (c) in Part VI (patents)—
      section 295 in so far as it relates to paragraph 27 of Schedule 5;

  (d) in Part VII (miscellaneous and general)—
      section 303(1) in so far as it relates to paragraphs 15, 18(2) and 21 of Schedule 7, and
      section 303(2) in so far as it relates to the references in Schedule 8 to—
          section 32 of the Registered Designs Act 1949, and sections 84, 85, 104, the words "within the meaning of section 104 above" in section 105, sections 114 and 115, section 123(2)(k), and the definition of "patent agent" in section 130(1), of the Patents Act 1977;

  (e) in Schedule 3 (minor and consequential amendments to the Registered Designs Act 1949) paragraph 21;

  (f) Schedule 4;

  (g) in Schedule 5 (patents: miscellaneous amendments), paragraph 27;

  (h) in Schedule 7 (consequential amendments), paragraphs 15, 18(2) and 21;

  (i) in Schedule 8 (repeals) the references to—
      section 32 of the Registered Designs Act 1949, and sections 84, 85, 104, the words "within the meaning of section 104 above" in section 105, sections 114 and 115, section 123(2)(k), and the definition of "patent agent" in section 130(1), of the Patents Act 1977.

3. For the purpose only of making rules expressed to come into force on or after 13th August 1990, any provision of Part V of the Copyright, Designs and Patents Act 1988 conferring power to make rules shall come into force forthwith.

A5.vi The Copyright, Designs and Patents Act 1988 (Commencement No. 6) Order 1990

(SI 1990/2168 (C.53))

Made   *1st November 1990*

The Secretary of State, in exercise of the powers conferred upon him by section 305(3) of the Copyright, Designs and Patents Act 1988, hereby makes the following Order—

1. This Order may be cited as the Copyright, Designs and Patents Act 1988 (Commencement No. 6) Order 1990.

2. The following provisions of the Copyright, Designs and Patents Act 1988 shall come into force on 7th January 1990—

(a) in Part VI (patents), save in so far as article 3 below otherwise provides—

section 295 in so far as it relates to paragraphs 1 to 11, 17 to 23, 25, 26, 28 and 30 of Schedule 5;

(b) in Part VII (miscellaneous and general), section 303(2) in so far as it relates to the references in Schedule 8 to—

section 14(4) and (8), paragraph (b) and the word "and" preceding it in section 28(3), section 28(5) to (9), sections 72(3) and 88, the words "88(6) and (7)" in section 130(7) of, and paragraphs 2, 7 and 8 of Schedule 5 to, the Patents Act 1977;

(c) in Schedule 5 (patents: miscellaneous amendments), save in so far as article 3 below otherwise provides—

paragraphs 1 to 11, 17 to 23, 25, 26, 28 and 30;

(d) in Schedule 8 (repeals) the references to—

section 14(4) and (8), paragraph (b) and the word "and" preceding it in section 28(3), section 28(5) to (9), sections 72(3) and 88, the words "88(6) and (7)" in section 130(7) of, and paragraphs, 2, 7 and 8 of Schedule 5 to, the Patents Act 1977.

3. For the purposes only of making rules expressed to come into force on or after 7th January 1991, any amendment to the Patents Act 1977 effected by a provision referred to in article 2(a) and (c) above which confers power to make rules or prescribe anything shall come into force forthwith.

PART B

RELATED LEGISLATION AND MATERIALS

PART B

RELATED LEGISLATION AND MATERIALS

B1. The Copyright Tribunal

B1.i The Copyright Tribunal Rules 2010

(SI 2010/791)

Made	*15th March 2010*
Laid before Parliament	*16th March 2010*
Coming into force	*6th April 2010*

ARRANGEMENT OF RULES

The Lord Chancellor in exercise of the powers conferred upon him by sections 150 and 152(2) and (3) of the Copyright, Designs and Patents Act 1988, after consultation with the Secretary of State, with the approval of the Treasury as to the fees chargeable under these Rules in respect of proceedings before the Copyright Tribunal, and after consultation with the Administrative Justice and Tribunals Council in accordance with paragraph 24(1), (3) and (4) of Schedule 7 to the Tribunals Courts and Enforcement Act 2007, makes the following Rules:

Part I

Preliminary

Citation and Commencement

1. These Rules may be cited as the Copyright Tribunal Rules 2010 and shall come into force on 6th April 2010.

Interpretation

2.—(1) In these Rules—

"the Act" means the Copyright, Designs and Patents Act 1988;

"applicant" means a person or organisation who has made a reference or application to the Tribunal in accordance with rule 7;

"application" means the application form and statement of grounds filed with the Tribunal in accordance with rule 7(1);

"application form" means the form set out in Schedule 1;

"bank holiday" has the meaning conferred by section 1 of the Banking and Financial Dealings Act 1971;

"the Chairman" means the Chairman of the Tribunal or a deputy chairman or any other member of the Tribunal appointed to act as chairman;

"costs", in relation to proceedings in Scotland, means "expenses";

"court" means —

    (a) as respects England and Wales, the High Court;

    (b) as respects Scotland, the Court of Session;

    (c) as respects Northern Ireland, the High Court of Northern Ireland;

"intervener" means a person or organisation who has applied under rule 15 to be made a party to proceedings;

"the office" means the office for the time being of the Tribunal;

"proceedings" means proceedings in respect of an application before the Tribunal;

"relevant fee" means the fee payable to the Tribunal as set out in Schedule 2;

"the Secretary" means the Secretary for the time being of the Tribunal;

"small application" has the meaning given in rule 17(6);

"standard application" has the meaning given in rule 17(6);

"statement of truth" means —

    (a) in Northern Ireland, an affidavit;

    (b) in England and Wales and Scotland a statement which meets the requirements of paragraphs (2) and (3) below;

"the Tribunal" means the Copyright Tribunal;

"the Tribunal address for service" has the meaning set out in rule 4; and

"the Tribunal Website" has the meaning set out in rule 5.

(2) A statement of truth is a statement that—

    (a) The party putting forward the document, or

    (b) in the case of a witness statement, the maker of the witness statement believes the facts stated in the document are true.

(3) A statement of truth must be signed by—

    (a) In the case of a statement of grounds, a response or a request for permission to intervene, the party or the legal representative of the party and

    (b) In the case of a witness statement, the maker of the statement.

(4) The powers conferred on the Tribunal by rules 39(3) and 42 may be exercised by either the Chairman or the Tribunal.

Overriding objective

3.—(1) The Rules set out a procedural code with the overriding objective of enabling the Tribunal to deal with cases justly.

(2) Dealing with a case justly includes, so far as practicable—

    (a) ensuring that the parties are on an equal footing;

    (b) saving expense;

    (c) dealing with the case in ways which are proportionate—

        (i) to the amount of money involved,

        (ii) to the importance of the case,

        (iii) to the complexity of the issues, and

        (iv) to the financial position of each party;

    (d) ensuring that it is dealt with expeditiously and fairly; and

    (e) allotting to it an appropriate share of the resources available to the Tribunal, while taking into account the need to allot resources to other cases.

(3) The parties are required to help the Tribunal to further the overriding objective.

Tribunal address for service

4. The address for service of documents on the Tribunal is: The Secretary of the Copyright Tribunal, 21 Bloomsbury Street, London WC1B 3HF or such other address as may be notified in the London, Edinburgh and Belfast Gazettes and on the Tribunal Website.

Tribunal Website

5. The location of the Tribunal Website is: www.ipo.gov.uk/ctribunal.htm or such other location as may be notified from time to time in such manner as the Chairman may direct.

Representation and rights of audience

6. In proceedings a party may be represented by—

    (a) a person who, for the purposes of the Legal Services Act 2007 is an authorised person in relation to an activity which constitutes the exercise of a right of audience or the conduct of litigation within the meaning of that Act;

    (b) an advocate or solicitor in Scotland or a barrister or solicitor in Northern Ireland; or

    (c) any other person allowed by the Tribunal to appear on his behalf.

PART II

COMMENCING PROCEEDINGS

Commencing proceedings

7.—(1) Proceedings are started when a person files—

    (a) an application form;

    (b) a statement of grounds; and

    (c) the relevant fee.

(2) The statement of grounds must—

(a) contain a concise statement of the facts on which the applicant relies;
(b) state the statutory provision under which the application is made;
(c) where appropriate include the terms of payment or terms of licence which the applicant believes to be unreasonable;
(d) specify the relief sought;
(e) be verified by a statement of truth.

Defective applications

8.—(1) If the Tribunal considers that an application does not comply with rule 7, or is materially incomplete, or is lacking in clarity, it may give such directions as may be necessary to ensure that those defects are remedied.

(2) The Tribunal may, if satisfied that the efficient conduct of the proceedings so requires, instruct the Secretary to defer service of the application on the respondent until after the directions referred to in paragraph (1) have been complied with.

Power to reject

9.—(1) The Tribunal may, after giving the parties an opportunity to be heard, reject an application in whole or in part at any stage in the proceedings if—
(a) it considers that the Tribunal has no jurisdiction to hear the application;
(b) it considers that the applicant
   (i) does not have a sufficient interest in the application; or
   (ii) is not an organisation that is representative of a class of persons that have a sufficient interest in the application;
(c) it considers, in accordance with relevant provision of the Act, that the application is premature;
(d) it considers that the application is an abuse of the Tribunal's process;
(e) it considers that the application discloses no reasonable grounds for bringing the application.

(2) When the Tribunal rejects an application it may make any consequential order it considers appropriate.

(3) For the purposes of paragraph (1)(c), the relevant provision means—
(a) section 118(2), where the reference is made under section 118;
(b) section 125(2), where the reference is made under section 125;
(c) paragraph 3(2) of Schedule 2A, where the reference is made under paragraph 3 of Schedule 2A and
(d) paragraph 10(2) of Schedule 2A, where the reference is made under paragraph 10 of Schedule 2A.

Amendment of application

10.—(1) The applicant may amend the application only with the permission of the Tribunal.

(2) Where the Tribunal grants permission under paragraph (1) it may do so on such terms as it thinks fit, and shall give such further or consequential directions as may be necessary.

Withdrawal of the application

11.—(1) The applicant may withdraw an application only with the permission of the Tribunal.

(2) Where the Tribunal gives permission under paragraph (1) it may—
(a) do so on such terms as it thinks fit; and
(b) instruct the Secretary to publish notice of the withdrawal on the Tribunal Website or in such other manner as the Tribunal may direct.

(3) Where an application is withdrawn any interim order of the Tribunal, other than an order made in respect of costs, shall immediately cease to have effect, unless the Tribunal directs otherwise.

PART III

RESPONSE TO THE PROCEEDINGS

Acknowledgement and notification

12.—(1) On receiving an application the Secretary must—

(a) send an acknowledgement of its receipt to the applicant; and

(b) subject to rules 8(2) and 9 send a copy of the application to the respondent marked to show the date on which that copy is sent.

The response

13.—(1) The respondent must send to the Secretary a response in the form required by this rule so that the response is received within 28 days (or such further time as the Tribunal may allow) of the date on which the Secretary sent a copy of the application to the respondent in accordance with rule 12(b).

(2) The response filed by the respondent must state—

(a) the name and address of the respondent;

(b) the name and address of the respondent's legal representatives, if any;

(c) an address for service in the European Economic Area;

and must be signed and dated by the respondent, or on the respondent's behalf by a duly authorised officer or legal representative.

(3) The response must contain—

(a) a concise statement of the facts on which the respondent relies;

(b) any relief sought by the respondent; and

(c) any directions sought pursuant to rule 20.

(4) The response must be verified by a statement of truth.

(5) Rules 8 and 10 shall apply to the response.

(6) On receiving the response, the Secretary shall send a copy to the applicant.

PART IV

INTERVENTION AND CONSOLIDATION

Publication of application

14.—(1) Subject to rules 8 and 9 the Secretary must as soon as practicable upon receipt of an application publish a notice on the Tribunal Website and in any other manner the Chairman may direct.

(2) The notice referred to in paragraph (1) must state—

(a) that an application has been received;

(b) the section of the Act under which the application is made;

(c) the name of the applicant;

(d) the particulars of the relief sought by the applicant;

(e) a summary of the principal grounds relied on; and

(f) that any person—

    (i) with substantial interest in the proceedings;

    (ii) who objects to the application on the basis that the applicant does not have a sufficient interest in the application; or

    (iii) who objects to the application on the basis that the applicant is

not representative of a class of persons that have a sufficient interest in the application,

may apply to intervene in the proceedings, in accordance with rule 15, within 28
days of publication of the notice or such other period as the Chairman may direct.

Intervention

15.—(1) Any person with substantial interest in the outcome of proceedings
may make a request to the Tribunal for permission to intervene in those
proceedings.

(2) The request must be sent to the Secretary within 28 days of the publication
of the notice in accordance with rule 14.

(3) The Secretary shall give notice of the request for permission to intervene
to the respondent and all other parties to the proceedings and invite their observations on that request within a specified period.

(4) A request for permission to intervene must state—

   (a) the title of the proceedings to which that request relates;

   (b) the name and address of the person wishing to intervene;

   (c) the name and address of their legal representative, if any;

   (d) an address for service in the European Economic Area;

   (e) the facts on which the person wishing to intervene relies and the relief
       sought.

(5) The request must be verified by a statement of truth and accompanied by
the relevant fee.

(6) The Tribunal may permit the intervention on such terms and conditions as
it thinks fit, if satisfied, having taken into account the observations of the parties,
that the intervening party has a substantial interest.

(7) On granting permission in accordance with paragraph (6), the Tribunal
shall give all such consequential directions as it considers necessary with regard,
in particular, to the service on the intervener of the documents lodged with the
Secretary, the submission by the intervener of a statement of intervention and, if
appropriate, the submission by the principal parties of a response to the statement
of intervention.

(8) The statement of intervention and any response to it shall contain—

   (a) a concise statement of the facts supporting the intervention or response;
       and

   (b) any relief sought by the intervener or the party responding to the
       intervention.

(9) The statement of intervention and any response shall be verified by a statement of truth.

(10) Rules 8 and 10 shall apply to the statement of intervention.

Consolidation

16.—(1) Where two or more applications are made relating to the same licensing scheme or proposed licensing scheme, or which involve the same or similar
issues, the Tribunal may on its own initiative, or on the request of a party, order
that the proceedings or any particular issue or matter raised in the proceedings be
consolidated or heard together.

(2) Before making an order under this rule, the Tribunal must invite the parties to the relevant proceedings to submit their observations.

PART V

ALLOCATION

Allocation

17.—(1) The Tribunal shall allocate an application to the small applications track or to the standard applications track, taking into account the factors set out in this rule;

(2) When the Tribunal makes an allocation it shall have regard to—

    (a) the financial value of the application to each of the parties;

    (b) whether the facts, legal issues, relief requested or procedures involved are simple or complex; and

    (c) the importance of the outcome of the application to other licensees or putative licensees of a licensing body.

(3) The small applications track is the normal track for an application where its financial value is less than £50,000 to each party and the facts and legal issues involved are simple.

(4) The standard track is the normal track for all other applications.

(5) When the Tribunal has allocated an application to a track the Secretary shall serve a notice of allocation on every party.

(6) Applications allocated to the small applications track are referred to as "small applications" and all other applications are referred to as "standard applications".

(7) The Rules apply to small applications with the exception of rules 22(1), (2) and (3), 23, 35 and 36.

(8) The Rules apply to standard applications with the exception of rule 21.

Change of track

18. The Tribunal may at any time on the request of a party or of its own initiative order, having considered the factors set out in rule 17(2), that—

    (a) proceedings allocated to the small applications track be transferred to the standard applications track; or

    (b) proceedings allocated to the standard applications track be transferred to the small applications track.

PART VI

CASE MANAGEMENT AND PREPARATION FOR HEARING

Case management—general

19.—(1) In determining applications the Tribunal shall actively exercise its powers set out in rules 16 (consolidation), 17 (allocation), 18 (change of track), 20 (directions), 21 (procedure for small applications) 22 (case management of standard applications) 23 (oral hearing of a standard application) 24 (evidence), 25 (expert evidence) 26 (summoning of witnesses and order to answer questions or produce documents) and 27 (failure to comply with directions) with a view to ensuring that the application is dealt with justly.

(2) The Tribunal may in particular—

    (a) encourage and facilitate the use of an alternative dispute resolution procedure if it considers it appropriate; and

    (b) dispense with the need for the parties to attend any hearing.

Directions

20.—(1) The Tribunal may at any time, on the request of a party or of its own initiative, at a case management conference, pre-hearing review, on an application for appeal or otherwise, give such directions as are provided for in paragraph (2) below or such other directions as it thinks fit to secure the just, expeditious and economical conduct of the proceedings.

(2) Where a party requests directions in accordance with paragraph (1) the request must be accompanied by the relevant fee.

(3) The Tribunal may give directions—

  (a) as to the manner in which the proceedings are to be conducted, including any time limits to be observed in the conduct of an oral hearing;

  (b) that the parties file a reply, rejoinder or other additional statements or particulars;

  (c) that part of any of the proceedings be dealt with as a preliminary issue;

  (d) that any part of the application, response or intervention be struck out;

  (e) for the dismissal of the proceedings;

  (f) to stay or, where the proceedings are in Scotland, to sist the whole or part of any proceedings or order or decision of the Tribunal either generally or until after a specified date;

  (g) for the preparation and exchange of skeleton arguments;

  (h) in relation to proceedings in England and Wales or Northern Ireland, requiring persons to attend and give evidence or to produce documents;

  (i) as to the evidence which may be required or admitted in proceedings before the Tribunal and the extent to which it shall be oral or written;

  (j) as to the submission in advance of a hearing of any witness statements or expert reports;

  (k) as to the cross-examination of witnesses;

  (l) as to the fixing of time limits with respect to any aspect of the proceedings;

  (m) as to the abridgement or extension of any time limits, whether or not expired;

  (n) for the disclosure between, or the production by, the parties of documents or classes of documents;

  (o) for the appointment and instruction of experts, whether by the Tribunal or by the parties and the manner in which expert evidence is to be given;

  (p) as to the use or further disclosure of a document which has been disclosed in the proceedings, whether or not it has been read to or by the Chairman or Tribunal or referred to at a hearing which has been held in public;

  (q) for the award of costs; and

  (r) for hearing a person who is not a party where, in any proceedings, it is proposed to make an order or give a direction in relation to that person.

(4) The Tribunal may, in particular, of its own initiative—

  (a) put questions to the parties;

  (b) invite the parties to make written or oral submissions on certain aspects of the proceedings;

  (c) ask the parties or other persons for information or particulars;

  (d) ask for documents or any papers relating to the case to be produced;

  (e) summon the parties' representatives or the parties in person to meetings.

(5) A request by a party for directions shall be made in writing as soon as practicable and shall be served by the Secretary on any other party who might be affected by such directions and determined by the Tribunal taking into account the observations of the parties.

Procedure for small applications

21.—(1) This rule contains the procedure for small applications.

(2) As soon as possible after an allocation is made in accordance with rule 17 or 18 the Tribunal shall give directions and notify the parties of the date on which the decision shall be delivered in accordance with rule 30.

(3) If any party requests a hearing or the Tribunal considers that a hearing is required, either before or after the Tribunal has given directions in accordance with paragraph (2) the Tribunal must give directions (which may include directions for a case management conference or a pre-hearing review), fix a date for the hearing and notify the parties in writing of the date, time and place of that oral hearing.

Case management of standard applications

22.—(1) This rule applies to the case management of standard applications. Paragraphs (4) and (5) of this rule apply to small applications if the Tribunal gives directions in accordance with rule 21(3).

(2) Where it appears to the Tribunal that any proceedings would be facilitated by holding a case management conference or pre-hearing review the Tribunal may, on the request of a party or of its own initiative, give directions for such a conference or review to be held.

(3) Unless the Tribunal otherwise directs, a case management conference must be held as soon as practicable after allocation in accordance with rule 17 or rule 18(a).

(4) A case management conference or pre-hearing review shall be held in private unless the Tribunal otherwise directs.

(5) The purpose of a case management conference or pre-hearing review is—

    (a) to ensure the efficient conduct of the proceedings;

    (b) to determine the points on which the parties must present further argument or which call for further evidence to be produced;

    (c) to clarify the forms of order sought by the parties, their arguments of fact and law and the points at issue between them;

    (d) to ensure that all agreements that can be reached between the parties about the matters in issue and the conduct of the proceedings are made and recorded;

    (e) to facilitate the settlement of the proceedings;

    (f) to set a timetable outlining the steps to be taken by the parties pursuant to directions in preparation for the oral hearing of the proceedings;

    (g) to set the dates within which the hearing shall take place.

Oral hearing of a standard application

23. As soon as practicable after the case management conference or pre-hearing review, the Secretary shall, after discussions with the parties, notify the parties in writing of the date, time and place for the oral hearing and of any timetable for that hearing.

Evidence

24.—(1) The Tribunal may control the evidence by giving directions as to—

    (a) the issues on which evidence is required;

    (b) the nature of the evidence required to decide those issues; and

    (c) the way in which the evidence is to be placed before the Tribunal.

(2) The Tribunal may use its power to exclude evidence that would otherwise be admissible where—

    (a) the evidence was not provided within the time allowed by a direction;

    (b) the evidence was provided in a manner that did not comply with a direction;

(c) it would be unfair to admit the evidence;

(d) the evidence is not proportionate to the issues of the case; or

(e) the evidence is not necessary for the fair disposal of the case.

(3) The Tribunal may require any witness to give evidence on oath or affirmation or, if in writing, by way of a witness statement verified by a statement of truth.

(4) The Tribunal may allow a witness to give evidence through a video link or by other means.

Expert evidence

25.—(1) Expert evidence shall be restricted to that which is proportionate to the issues of the case and necessary for the fair disposal of the case.

(2) No party may call an expert or put in expert evidence without the permission of the Tribunal.

(3) When a party applies for permission to call an expert or put in expert evidence it must identify—

(a) the field in which expert evidence shall be relied upon;

(b) the expert in that field whose evidence shall be relied upon and, if applicable, the organisation by whom the expert is employed and

(c) the principal issues which the expert will be expected to address.

(4) If the Tribunal grants permission under this rule it must be only in relation to the expert named and the field and on the issues identified in the application.

(5) The Tribunal may limit the fees and expenses of an expert that can be recovered from the parties to the litigation that did not instruct that expert.

Summoning of witnesses and orders to answer questions or produce documents

26.—(1) On the application of a party or on its own initiative, the Tribunal may—

(a) by summons require any person to attend as a witness at a hearing at the time and place specified in the summons; or

(b) order any person to answer any questions or produce any documents in that person's possession or control which relate to any issue in the proceedings.

(2) A summons under paragraph (1)(a) must—

(a) give the person required to attend not less than 14 days' notice of the hearing or such shorter period as the Tribunal may direct; and

(b) where the person is not a party, make provision for the person's necessary expenses of attendance to be paid, and state who is to pay them.

(3) No person may be compelled to give any evidence or produce any document that the person could not be compelled to give or produce on a trial of an action in a court of law in the part of the United Kingdom where the proceedings are due to be determined.

(4) This rule shall only apply to proceedings in England and Wales and Northern Ireland

Failure to comply with directions

27. If any party fails to comply with any direction given in accordance with these Rules, the Tribunal may, if it considers that the justice of the case so requires, order that such party be debarred from taking any further part in the proceedings without the permission of the Tribunal.

PART VII

The Hearing

Hearing to be in public

28. Except where the Tribunal orders otherwise, the hearing of any application must be in public.

Procedure at the hearing

29.—(1) The proceedings must be opened and directed by the Chairman who is responsible for the proper conduct of the hearing.

(2) The Tribunal shall, so far as it appears to it appropriate, seek to avoid formality in its proceedings and shall conduct the hearing in such manner as it considers most appropriate for the clarification of the issues before it and generally to the just, expeditious and economical handling of the proceedings.

(3) Unless the Tribunal otherwise directs, no witness of fact or expert may be heard unless the relevant witness statement or expert report has been submitted in advance of the hearing and in accordance with any directions of the Tribunal.

(4) The Tribunal may limit cross-examination of witnesses to any extent or in any manner it deems appropriate.

PART VIII

Delivery of the Decision

Delivery of the decision

30.—(1) The decision of the Tribunal on an application must be given in writing and must include a statement of the Tribunal's reasons.

(2) The Secretary must as soon as practicable serve on every party to the proceedings a copy of the Tribunal's decision.

(3) The Chairman must arrange for the decision of the Tribunal to be published in such manner as considered appropriate.

Orders for costs

31.—(1) The Tribunal may, at its discretion, at any stage of the proceedings make any order it thinks fit in relation to the payment of costs by one party to another in respect of the whole or part of the proceedings.

(2) Any party against whom an order for costs is made shall, if the Tribunal so directs, pay to any other party a lump sum by way of costs, or such proportion of the costs as may be just, and in the last mentioned case the Tribunal may assess the sum to be paid or may direct that it be assessed or, where appropriate, taxed by—

    (a) the Chairman;

    (b) a costs officer of the High Court;

    (c) the Master (Taxing Office) of the High Court of Northern Ireland; or

    (d) the Auditor of the Court of Session.

Effective date of order

32. Except where the operation of the order is suspended under rule 33 or 34, an order of the Tribunal shall take effect from such date, and shall remain in force for such period, as is specified in the order.

Part IX

Appeals from the Tribunal

Commencement of appeal proceedings

33.—(1) An appeal to the court under section 152 of the Act arising from a decision of the Tribunal must be brought within 28 days of the date of decision of the Tribunal or within such further period as the court may, on application to it, allow.

(2) A party appealing to the court must as soon as may be practicable serve on the Secretary a notice of such appeal accompanied by the relevant fee and shall serve a copy of the notice on every person who was a party to the proceedings giving rise to that decision.

(3) Following receipt of the notice of appeal by the Secretary the Tribunal may on its own initiative suspend the operation of any order contained in its decision.

Suspension of order

34.—(1) Unless the Tribunal orders otherwise an appeal to the Court shall not operate as a stay of any decision or order of the Tribunal.

(2) The Tribunal may endorse a consent order where all parties to an action have consented to the suspension of the operation of an order.

(3) An application to the Tribunal for an endorsement under paragraph (2) must be accompanied by the relevant fee.

(4) Where any order of the Tribunal has been suspended by the Tribunal in accordance with rule 33(3) or upon the application of a party to the proceedings in accordance with rule 34(2) the Secretary must serve notice of the suspension on all parties to the proceedings, and if particulars of the order have been advertised must cause notice of the suspension to be advertised in the same manner.

(5) Rule 30(3) applies to the publication of a decision to suspend an order.

Part X

Interim Orders and Awards

Power to make provisional awards

35. Subject to rule 36, the Tribunal shall have power to order on a provisional basis any relief which it would have power to grant in a final decision.

Awards on different issues

36.—(1) The Tribunal may make more than one award at different times on different aspects of the matters to be determined.

(2) The Tribunal may, in particular, make an award relating to—

    (a) an issue affecting the whole claim, or

    (b) a part only of the claims or cross-claims submitted to it for decision.

(3) If the Tribunal makes an award under paragraph (2) it shall specify in its award the issue, or the claim or part of a claim, which is the subject matter of that award.

Part XI

Supplementary

Enforcement—England and Wales and Northern Ireland

37. A decision made by the Tribunal may, by leave of the court, be enforced in

England and Wales or Northern Ireland in the same manner as a judgment or order of the court to the same effect.

Enforcement of Tribunal's orders in Scotland

38. Any decision of the Tribunal may be enforced in Scotland in the same way as a recorded decree arbitral.

Service of documents

39.—(1) Any notice or other document required by these Rules to be served on any person may be sent by pre-paid post to its address for service, or, where no address for service has been given, to its registered office, principal place of business or last known address, and every notice or other document required to be served on the Secretary may be sent by pre-paid post to the Secretary the Tribunal address for service during office hours.

(2) Any notice or other document required to be served on a licensing body or organisation which is not a body corporate may be sent to the secretary, manager or other similar officer.

(3) The Tribunal may direct that service of any notice or other document be dispensed with or effected otherwise than in the manner provided by these Rules.

(4) Service of any notice or document on a party's solicitor or agent shall be deemed to be service on such party, and service on a solicitor or agent acting for more than one party shall be deemed to be service on every party for whom such a solicitor or agent acts.

Time

40.—(1) Where a period expressed in days, weeks or months is to be calculated from the moment at which an event occurs or an action takes place, the day during which that event occurs or that action takes place shall not be counted as falling within the period in question.

(2) A period expressed in weeks or months shall end with the expiry of whichever day in the last week or month is the same day of the week or falls on the same date in the month, as the day during which the event or action from which the period is to be calculated occurred or took place. If, in a period expressed in months, the day on which it should expire does not occur in the last month, the period shall end with the expiry of the last day of that month.

(3) Where the time for doing any act expires on a Saturday, Sunday, Christmas Day, Good Friday or bank holiday, the act is in time if done on the next following day which is not a Saturday, a Sunday, Christmas Day, Good Friday or bank holiday in any part of the United Kingdom.

Office hours

41. The office shall be open between 10.00am and 4.00pm Monday to Friday, excluding Good Friday, Christmas Day and bank holidays in England and Wales.

Clerical mistakes and accidental slips or omissions

42. The Tribunal may at any time correct any clerical mistake or other accidental slip or omission in a decision, direction or any document produced by it, by—

(a) sending notification of the amended decision or direction, or a copy of the amended document, to each party; and

(b) making any necessary amendment to any information published in relation to the decision, direction or document.

Power of Tribunal to regulate procedure

43. Subject to the provisions of the Act and these Rules, the Tribunal shall have power to regulate its own procedure.

PART XII

TRANSITIONAL AND REVOCATION

Transitional provisions

44. Any proceedings commenced under the Act before these Rules come into force shall continue in accordance with these Rules.

Revocation

45. The Copyright Tribunal Rules 1989 are revoked.

Rule 2   SCHEDULE 1

APPLICATION FORM

APPLICATION FORM	
	Tribunal reference: Issue Date
Applicant's name and address, email address and telephone number:	
Respondent's name and address, email address and telephone number:	
Either (a) the section number of the Copyright Designs and Patents Act 1988 or Broadcasting Act 1990 or (b) name of the Regulations under which the claim is brought:	
Brief details of the facts upon which the applicant relies:	
Applicant's address for service, if different from the address above:	
Date:	

Rule 2   SCHEDULE 2

FEES

1. The relevant fee is £15 for an application for directions in accordance with rule 20, other than an application for a direction under rule 20(3)(d).

2. The relevant fee is £25 for

(a) an application for directions under rule 20(3)(d);

(b) a request for permission to intervene made under rule 15;

(c) a notice of appeal served in accordance with rule 33;

(d) an application for endorsement of a consent order made in accordance with rule 34(3);

(e) an application to the Tribunal made under rule 7 where the application is

    (i) for special leave made under section 120, 122, 127, 135F, 142 or paragraph 5 of Schedule 6 to the Act or paragraph 6(2) of Schedule 17 to the Broadcasting Act 1990;

    (ii) a reference made under section 125 or 126 of the Act;

    (iii) an appeal made under section 139 of the Act;

    (iv) made under section 135F of the Act for review of an order;

    (v) made under section 142 of the Act to settle royalty or other sums payable;

    (vi) made under section 144 of the Act to settle terms of a licence of right;

    (vii) made under paragraph 6(1) of Schedule 17 to the Broadcasting Act 1990.

3. The relevant fee is £50 for an application made under rule 7, other than an application listed in paragraph 2(e) above.

B1.ii Draft order of the Copyright Tribunal under section 190(1) of the Copyright Designs and Patents Act 1988

[order granting consent on behalf of persons entitled to the reproduction right whose identity or whereabouts cannot be ascertained]

WHEREAS the Applicants wish to make a recording from a previous recording ("the Original Recording") of [*work*] by [*author*][*insert details of any other identifying features of the Original Recording*]

UPON reading the Applicant's Notice of Application and Statement in Support of Application together with accompanying documentary evidence, and

UPON THE TRIBUNAL BEING SATISFIED THAT the identity or whereabouts of the persons entitled to the reproduction right in respect of the Original Recording [*other than A, B and C*] ("The Unidentified Persons") cannot be ascertained by reasonable enquiry and that all notices relating to the Application required by the Tribunal pursuant to section 190(3) of the Act have been duly published.

THE COPYRIGHT TRIBUNAL GIVES CONSENT TO THE MAKING OF A RECORDING FROM THE ORIGINAL RECORDING ON BEHALF THE UNIDENTIFIED PERSONS PROVIDED THAT

any such person shall be at liberty to apply to the Copyright Tribunal pursuant to section 190(6) of the Act for the Copyright Tribunal to make such Order as to any payment or other terms as it thinks fit.

B2. LICENSING SCHEMES

B2.i The Copyright (Certification of Licensing Scheme for Educational Recording of Broadcasts) (Educational Recording Agency Limited) Order 2007

(SI 2007/ 266)

Made   *1st February 2007*

The Educational Recording Agency Limited (company number 2423219), whose registered office is at New Premier House, 150 Southampton Row, London WC1B 5AL has applied to the Secretary of State to certify, for the purposes of section 35 of, and paragraph 6 of Schedule 2 to, the Copyright, Designs and Patents Act 1988 ("the Act"), a licensing scheme to be operated by it:

The Secretary of State is satisfied that the scheme enables the works to which it relates to be identified with sufficient certainty by persons likely to require licences and that it sets out clearly the charges (if any) payable and the other terms on which licences will be granted:

Accordingly, the Secretary of State, in exercise of the powers conferred upon him by section 143 of, and paragraph 16 of Schedule 2A to, the Act, hereby makes the following Order:

1. This Order may be cited as the Copyright (Certification of Licensing Scheme for Educational Recording of Broadcasts) (Educational Recording Agency Limited) Order 2007.

2. The licensing scheme set out in the Schedule to this Order is certified for the purposes of section 35 of, and paragraph 6 of Schedule 2 to, the Copyright, Designs and Patents Act 1988.

3. The certification under article 2 shall come into operation on 1st April 2007.

Article 2   SCHEDULE

THE EDUCATIONAL RECORDING AGENCY LIMITED LICENSING SCHEME

NATURE OF THE LICENCE

1. The Educational Recording Agency Limited (known as "ERA") is authorised to operate a Licensing Scheme for the purposes of both section 35 of, and paragraph 6 of Schedule 2 to the Copyright, Designs and Patents Act 1988.

2. "The Act" refers to the Copyright, Designs and Patents Act 1988 or any relevant law amending, modifying or re-enacting it from time to time.

3. Set out below are the terms of the Licensing Scheme which ERA has been authorised to operate to the extent that the same has been certified for the purposes of both section 35 of the Act and paragraph 6 of Schedule 2 to the Act ("the Licensing Scheme").

4. These terms shall form part of licences issued under the Licensing Scheme ("the Licence").

5. The Licensing Scheme and Licences issued under it shall apply only to Relevant Rights when used for non-commercial educational purposes within or on behalf of an Educational Establishment. All licensees under the Licensing Scheme shall either be or represent an Educational Establishment ("Licensee").

6. ["Educational Establishment" shall mean any school or other description of educational establishment defined by section 174 of the Act or as may be specified by order of the Secretary of State for the purposes of that section.]

ERA REPERTOIRE AND LICENSOR MEMBERS

7.—(1) The copyright works and rights in performances relevant to a Licence granted under the Licensing Scheme ("ERA Repertoire") are the works and performances in respect of which and to the extent which the Licensor Members of ERA (or persons represented by the Licensor Members) own or control Relevant Rights.

(2) "Relevant Rights" shall comprise the right:

(a) to cause or authorise the making of recordings of a broadcast and copies of such a recording and (only as a direct result of their inclusion in a broadcast) of copyright works and/or performances contained in the recorded broadcast by or on behalf of an Educational Establishment for the educational purposes of that Educational Establishment ("ERA Recordings"); and

(b) to authorise ERA Recordings to be communicated to the public by a person situated within the premises of an Educational Establishment but only to the extent that the communication cannot be received by any person situated outside the premises of that Educational Establishment.

[In addition this Licence may be relevant to terms and conditions for online services that authorise defined rights of non-commercial educational access or use to educational establishments on the condition that they hold a current licence from ERA.]

[**8.** The Licensor Members of ERA and the works and performances forming part of ERA Repertoire in respect of which the Relevant Rights are owned or controlled by such Licensors will for the purposes of Licences issued under the Licensing Scheme comprise:

AUTHORS' LICENSING AND COLLECTING SOCIETY LIMITED ("ALCS")

Those literary and dramatic works which are owned by or controlled by persons represented by ALCS and which are included in any broadcast.

[ASSOCIATION DE GESTION INTERNATIONALE COLLECTIVE DES OEUVRES AUDIOVISUELLES ("AGICOA")]

The films which are owned or controlled by persons represented by AGICOA and which are included in any broadcast from which an ERA Recording is made.

BBC WORLDWIDE LIMITED

The broadcasts of the British Broadcasting Corporation and all those copyright works owned or controlled by the British Broadcasting Corporation which are included in any broadcast.

BPI (BRITISH RECORDED MUSIC INDUSTRY) LIMITED ("BPI")

Those sound recordings which are owned or controlled by persons represented by BPI and which are included in any broadcast from which an ERA Recording is made.

[COMPACT COLLECTIONS LIMITED ("Compact") acting as agent for

(i) DISCOVERY COMMUNICATIONS EUROPE LIMITED concerning the broadcasts made on the broadcast services operated by Discovery Communications Europe Limited including Discovery Science and all those copyright works owned or controlled by Discovery Communications Europe Limited or any of its subsidiary or associated companies included in any broadcast;

(ii) NGC EUROPE LIMITED concerning the broadcasts made on the broadcast services operated by NGC Europe Limited including National Geographic Channel, National Geographic Channel HD, Wild UK, Nat Geo Wild (Europe) and Wild HD and all those copyright works owned or controlled by NGC Europe Limited or any of its subsidiary or associated companies included in any broadcast; and

(iii) AETN UK concerning the broadcasts of AETN UK or any of its subsidiary companies and all those copyright works owned or controlled by AETN UK or any of its subsidiary companies which are included in any broadcast.]

CHANNEL FOUR TELEVISION CORPORATION ("Channel 4")

The broadcasts made on Channel 4, E4 and/or Film Four and/or any other broadcast service operated by Channel 4 or any of its subsidiary companies and all those copyright works owned or controlled by Channel 4 or any of its subsidiary companies included in any broadcast.

CHANNEL 5 BROADCASTING LIMITED ("Channel 5")

The broadcasts made on Five and/or any other broadcast service operated by Channel 5 or any of its subsidiary companies and all those copyright works owned or controlled by Channel 5 or any of its subsidiary companies included in any broadcast.

DESIGN AND ARTISTS COPYRIGHT SOCIETY LIMITED ("DACS")

Those artistic works (as defined in the Act) in which the copyright is owned or controlled by the members of DACS or the members of copyright societies represented by DACS and which are included in any broadcast.

DIRECTORS UK LIMITED ("Directors UK")

The copyright works which are owned or controlled by, or in which authorship is owned or controlled by, persons represented by Directors UK and which are included in any broadcast from which an ERA Recording is made.

EQUITY

The performances by persons represented by Equity which are included in any broadcast.

[FOCAL INTERNATIONAL LIMITED (The Federation of Commercial Audio Visual Libraries) ("FOCAL")

The film and videotape clips and stills which are owned or controlled by persons represented by FOCAL or its subsidiary or associated companies and which are included in any broadcast from which an ERA Recording is made.]

THE INCORPORATED SOCIETY OF MUSICIANS ("ISM")

The literary and musical works which are owned by or controlled by persons represented by ISM and the performances by persons who are represented by ISM which are included in any broadcast.

ITV NETWORK LIMITED ("ITV Network")

The broadcasts made on the channel branded as ITV1 in England and Wales, as the STV regions (formerly known as Grampian TV and Scottish TV) in Scotland, as Ulster in Northern Ireland, and as Channel TV in the Channel Islands, on ITV 2, on ITV 3, on the ITV News Channel and/or any other broadcast service operated by ITV Network Limited or any of its associated or subsidiary companies and all those copyright works owned or controlled by ITV Network Limited or any of its subsidiary or associated companies included in any broadcast.

MECHANICAL COPYRIGHT PROTECTION SOCIETY LIMITED ("MCPS")

Those musical works and sound recordings which are owned or controlled by members of MCPS and entrusted by its members to MCPS and which are included in any broadcast from which an ERA Recording is made.

MUSICIANS' UNION ("the MU")

The performances by persons represented by the MU which are included in any broadcast.

[OPEN UNIVERSITY WORLDWIDE LIMITED

The films and other copyright works which are owned or represented by Open University Worldwide Limited or any of its subsidiary or associated companies and which are included in any broadcast made by the British Broadcasting Corporation or any other broadcast on behalf of the Open University Worldwide Limited from which an ERA Recording is made.]

THE PERFORMING RIGHT SOCIETY LIMITED ("PRS")

The musical works which are owned or controlled by the PRS or by persons represented by the PRS and which are included in any broadcast from which an ERA Recording has beenmade.

PHONOGRAPHIC PERFORMANCE LIMITED ("PPL")

Those sound recordings which are owned or represented by PPL and which are included in any broadcast from which an ERA Recording is made.

[RADIO INDEPENDENTS GROUP ("RIG")

The sound recordings and any other copyright audio works owned or controlled by members of RIG and entrusted by its members to RIG and which are included in any broadcast from which an ERA recording is made.]

SIANEL PEDWAR CYMRU ("S4C")

The broadcasts made on S4C, S4C Digital and/or S4C2 and/or any other broadcast service operated by S4C or any of its subsidiary companies and all those copyright works owned or controlled by S4C or any of its subsidiary companies included in any broadcast.

For the above purposes "broadcast" shall have the meaning provided by section 6 of the Act.

[...] If the Licensee is in any doubt as to whether a Licence covers a particular right or a particular copyright work the Licensee shall be entitled to contact ERA who shall be obliged within a reasonable time (by one of the Licensor Members) to confirm whether or not a particular right is owned or controlled by one of the Licensors.]

9. No recording or copying of a broadcast under any Licence shall be made except by or on behalf of an Educational Establishment and any such recording or copying shall be made either:

(a) on the premises of the Educational Establishment by or under the direct supervision of a teacher or employee of the Licensee; or

(b) at the residence of a teacher employed by the Licensee by that teacher; or

(c) at the premises of a third party authorised by the Licensee to make recordings or copies on behalf of the Licensee under written contractual terms and conditions which prevent the retention or use of any recordings or copies by that third party or any other third party unless ERA shall have expressly agreed that a specific third party may retain any recordings or copies for subsequent use only by authorised Licensees of ERA in accordance with the provisions of the Licensing Scheme.

Maintaining records

10. [Licensees shall be required to ensure that all ERA Recordings or copies comprising ERA Recordings made under a Licence provide for sufficient acknowledgement of the service from which the ERA Recording was acquired to be given; with each ERA Recording being marked with the name of the source, the date upon which the recording was secured by or for the Educational establishment and the title of the recording.]

To provide sufficient acknowledgement all copies shall be marked with a statement in clear and bold lettering reading:

> "This recording is to be used only for non-commercial educational purposes under the terms of the ERA Licence"

or such other wording or statement as ERA shall reasonably require from time to time.

Physical copies shall include the statement on the exterior of the copy, and /or its packaging.

When under the Licence copies are made and stored in digital form for access through a computer server, the statement shall also be included as a written opening credit or web-page which must be viewed or listened to before access to the ERA Recording is permitted.

11. Licensees may be required to record and maintain at the request of ERA details of [how ERA Recordings are acquired or accessed] and the number of copies of such recordings made under a Licence and to make available to ERA such records for inspection.

12. Licensees shall undertake that if and when any ERA Recordings are communicated to the public by a person situated within the premises of an Educational Establishment under the Licence suitable password, and other digital rights management or technological protection systems are operated and applied by the Licensee to ensure that such communication is not received or receivable by persons situated outside the premises of the licensed Educational Establishment.

13. Licensees may be required to maintain further records and answer questionnaires or surveys as ERA may reasonably require for the proper operation of the Licensing Scheme [and any agreements with third parties relevant to clause 9(c)].

14. ERA shall be entitled to inspect and Licensees shall provide for ERA to have access to all records that Licensees and licensed Educational Establishments are required to maintain under the above provisions, and further to have access to all ERA Recordings however stored under the terms of a Licence, in order to inspect the same to check compliance with the Licence.

Period of Licence and Fees

15. Licences shall be granted in consideration of payment of the agreed Licence fees and may be granted for such period or periods as may from time to time be specified by or agreed with ERA.

16. The Licence fee shall be calculated by reference to the period for which the Licence is granted and to the tariff applicable in respect of that period.

[**17.** [...]]

[**17A.** The annual tariff for students in Educational Establishments relevant to this clause 17A shall apply for each student.

For Licences taking effect on or after 1st April 2013 the annual tariff shall be:

Students in Primary schools (including Educational Establishments known as Preparatory Schools)	33p per head
Students in Secondary schools undertaking Secondary education)	59p per head
Students in Educational Establishments of Further Education (including former Sixth Form Colleges) who have not attained the age of 18 at the start of the education year	59p per head

17B. The annual tariff for students relevant to this clause 17B shall be calculated on a full-time or full-time equivalent basis by category of student in an Educational Establishment.

For Licences taking effect on or after 1st April 2013 the annual tariff shall be:

Students who have attained the age of 18 at the start of the educational year in Educational Establishments of Further Education undertaking courses of further education	£1.11p
Students in Educational Establishments of Higher Education and Students of other Educational Establishments who have attained the age of 18 at the start of the educational year when undertaking courses of Higher Education	£1.75p
Students in Educational Establishments not relevant to clause 17A or otherwise under this clause 17B but specified from time to time by the Secretary of State under s 174 of the Act.	£1.75p

Discounted rates may be negotiated at ERA's discretion to cover groups of Educational Establishments relevant to this clause.]

18. Licence fees for Licences running for a period of less than one year shall be calculated on a pro-rata basis against the applicable annual tariff.

19. Licensees shall pay agreed Licence fees together with any VAT and any other Government tax which may be applicable from time to time in addition to such Licence Fee on such a date or dates as may from time to time be required by ERA in the Licence and within 28 days of invoice.

TERMINATION

20. ERA shall be entitled to terminate Licences granted:

    (a) if Licence Fees are not paid when due; or

    (b) for any other substantial breach of the conditions of the Licence,

provided that ERA shall have given to the Licensee written notice identifying the nature of late payment or the nature of the breach.

The termination will become effective twenty eight days after receipt of the written notice unless during the relevant period of twenty eight days the Licensee makes payment of outstanding fees or remedies the breach.

21. Licences will automatically terminate:

    (a) if and when an administrator, receiver, administrative receiver or other encumbrancer takes possession of, or is appointed over, the whole or any substantial part of the assets of a Licensee;

    (b) if the Licensee enters into an arrangement or composition with or for the benefit of its creditors (including any voluntary arrangement under the Insolvency Act 1986);

(c) if a petition is presented for the purpose of considering a resolution for the making of an administration order, the winding-up or dissolution of the Licensee.

22. If punctual payment of agreed Licence Fees is not made, ERA shall be entitled to charge interest on amounts unpaid at the rate of statutory interest prescribed under section 6 of the Late Payment of Commercial Debts (Interest) Act 1998.

23. Upon expiry of a Licence without renewal or when a Licence is terminated by ERA it shall be entitled to require a Licensee to delete all ERA Recordings or copies made by the Educational Establishment to which the Licence related.

24. If a Licensee is in breach of the terms of a Licence and ERA incurs costs and expenses either in monitoring and discovering any breach of the terms of a Licence or in enforcing the conditions of any Licence, the Licensee shall be required to indemnify ERA in respect of any such costs and expenses so incurred.

25. Licensees shall be required to take all reasonable steps to ensure that rights granted by a Licence are not exceeded or abused by teachers, employees, pupils or other persons.

26. Licences issued shall be governed and interpreted in accordance with the laws of England and Wales.

Notes:

(1) Paragraph 8 was substituted by the Copyright (Certification of Licensing Scheme for Educational Recording of Broadcasts) (Educational Recording Agency Limited) (Revocation and Amendment) Order 2008 (SI 2008/211) Sch.1 para.1, with effect from April 1, 2008.

(2) The words in square brackets in para.8 substituted for the former words "ASSOCIATION DE GESTON INTERNATIONALE COLLECTIVE DES OEUVRES AUDIOVISUELLES ("AGICOA")" by the Copyright (Certification of Licensing Scheme for Educational Recording of Broadcasts) (Educational Recording Agency Limited) (Amendment) Order 2009 (SI 2009/20) art.2(2), with effect from April 1, 2009.

(3) Paragraph 6 substituted, in para.7(2) words in square brackets inserted, in para.8, entry "RADIO INDEPENDENTS GROUP ("RIG")" inserted, in para.10 first paragraph in square brackets substituted , in para.13 words in square brackets inserted, and paras 17A and 17B substituted for para.17 by the Copyright (Certification of Licensing Scheme for Educational Recording of Broadcasts) (Educational Recording Agency Limited) (Amendment) Order 2013 (SI 2013/158) art.2, with effect from April 1, 2013.

Paragraph 6 formerly read:

"6. *"Educational Establishment" shall mean any school and any other description of educational establishment as may be specified by order of the Secretary of State for the purposes of section 174 of the Act."*

In para.10, first paragraph read:

"Licensees shall be required to ensure that all ERA Recordings or copies comprising ERA Recordings made under a Licence provide for sufficient acknowledgement of the broadcast relevant to the ERA Recording to be given with each ERA Recording being marked with the name of the broadcaster, the date upon which the broadcast took place and the title of the recording."

(4) In para.8, entries "Compact Collections Limited ("Compact")" and "FOCAL INTERNATIONAL LIMITED" inserted by the Copyright (Certification of Licensing Scheme for Educational Recording of Broadcasts) (Educational Recording Agency Limited) (Amendment) Order 2011 (SI 2011/159) art.2, with effect from April 1, 2011.

(5) In para.8, entry "OPEN UNIVERSITY WORLDWIDE LIMITED" inserted, and words "However, Licences under the Licensing Scheme shall not authorise the recording of Open University programmes." revoked, by the Copyright (Certification of Licensing Scheme for Educational Recording of Broadcasts) (Educational Recording Agency Limited) (Amendment No. 2) Order 2013 (SI 2013/1924), art.2, with effect from October 1, 2013.

B2.ii The Copyright (Certification of Licensing Scheme for Educational Recording of Broadcasts) (Open University) Order 2003

(SI 2003/187)

Made   *30th January 2003*

Coming into force   *1st April 2003*

Whereas Open University Worldwide Limited (company number 01260275 previously named Open University Educational Enterprises Limited) has applied to the Secretary of State to certify for the purposes of section 35 of the Copyright, Designs and Patents Act 1988 ("the Act") a new licensing scheme to replace the licensing scheme set out in the Schedule to the Copyright (Certification of Licensing Scheme for Educational Recording of Broadcasts) (Open University Educational Enterprises Limited) Order 1993 ("the 1993 Order");

And whereas the Secretary of State is satisfied that the new scheme enables the works to which it relates to be identified with sufficient certainty by persons likely to require licences and that it sets out clearly the charges (if any) payable and the other terms on which licences will be granted;

Now, therefore, the Secretary of State in exercise of the powers conferred upon her by section 143 of the Act, hereby makes the following Order—

1. This Order may be cited as The Copyright (Certification of Licensing Scheme for Educational Recording of Broadcasts) (Open University) Order 2003 and shall come into force on 1st April 2003.

2. The licensing scheme set out in the Schedule to this Order is certified for the purposes of section 35 of the Act (recording by educational establishments of broadcasts [...]).

3. The certification under article 2 above shall for the purposes of section 35 of the Act come into operation on 1st April 2003.

4. The 1993 Order and the Copyright (Certification of Licensing Scheme for Educational Recording of Broadcasts) (Open University Educational Enterprises Limited) (Amendment) Order 1996 are hereby revoked.

5. Nothing in this Order shall affect the operation of licences granted under the 1993 scheme and in force at the coming into force of this Order.

Note: The words "and cable programmes" repealed from art.2 by the Copyright and Related Rights Regulations 2003 (SI 2003/2498), Sch.2 with effect from October 31, 2003. For savings and transitional provisions, see Part 3 of those Regulations.

Article 2   SCHEDULE

OPEN UNIVERSITY LICENSING SCHEME

Open University Worldwide Limited holds an exclusive right under copyright to licence the recording off air of all Open University television programmes in the United Kingdom by Educational Establishments and operates a licensing scheme for the off air recording of designated television programmes.

The scheme set out hereunder is operated for the purposes of section 35 of the Copyright, Designs and Patents Act 1988 ("the Act") in respect of recording of broadcasts by Educational Establishments and replaces the scheme scheduled to the Copyright (Certification of Licensing Scheme for Educational Recording of Broadcasts) (Open University Educational Enterprises Limited) Order 1993 ("the 1993 Scheme").

The charges payable under the licences are set out:

(a) in respect of Schools, in Appendix A to the licensing scheme;

(b) in respect of Educational Institutions, in Appendix B to the licensing scheme.

The Open University Licensed Off Air Recording Scheme for Educational Establishments

Licences shall be issued in accordance with the terms set out below.

DEFINITIONS

In the Scheme and the Appendices the following expressions have the meanings set opposite them:

School:	Any school as defined in section 174 of the Act.
Educational Institution:	Any educational establishment specified by order of the Secretary of State under section 174(1)(b) of the Act.
Licence Fee:	The fee payable by Schools calculated in accordance with Open University Worldwide Limited's scale of fees set out in Appendix A for the use of Designated Programmes in accordance with the terms of the Licence for a period of up to twelve months from the date of the Licence as originally granted or renewed unless or until the Licence is terminated pursuant to Clauses 2 or 6 thereof.
Programme Fee:	The fee payable by Educational Institutions calculated in accordance with Open University Worldwide Limited's scale of programme fees as set out in Appendix B for the use of a Designated Programme in accordance with the terms of the Licence for a period of up to twelve months from the date of its recording unless or until the Licence is terminated pursuant to Clauses 2 or 6 thereof.
Designated Programmes:	The television programmes broadcast by the British Broadcasting Corporation or other broadcasting organisation(s) on behalf of the Open University. The expressions "recordings of the Designated Programmes" or "recorded Designated Programmes" includes Additional Copies.
Record off air:	To record by the use of video tape, video compact disc or any available recording and/or playback device whether available now or invented in the future, a transmission by broadcast or diffusion of television programmes to be received by television or similar receiving device.
Educational Purposes:	The showing of recordings of Designated Programmes exclusively in teaching, training or study as part of a formal or informal course of instruction undertaken or carried out by the Licensee for non profit making purposes and where no charge is made on any person for the purposes of viewing the Designated Programmes, including the loan of recordings to bona fide students for such purposes.
Additional Copies:	Copies made by the Licensee of Designated Programmes recorded by it.
Business Day:	Any day except Saturday, Sunday, a Bank Holiday, Christmas Day or Good Friday.
Educational Establishment:	An educational establishment as defined in section 174 of the Act.

Grant

1. The School or the Educational Institution (hereinafter referred to as "the Licensee") shall warrant that it is a School or Educational Institution, as the case may be, and Open University Worldwide Limited shall grant to the Licensee on the terms set out below a non-exclusive Licence to Record off air Designated Programmes for Educational Purposes.

Term

2. The Licence shall continue from the date of issue for a period of twelve months and shall be automatically renewed for further periods of twelve months unless or until terminated in accordance with Clause 6, or by either side giving to the other not less than one calendar month's notice in writing, in the case of Educational Institutions, to expire on the date of the anniversary of any twelve month period.

Warranties and Obligations of Open University Worldwide Limited

3.—(1) Warranties

Open University Worldwide Limited warrants that it is duly appointed by the relevant copyright owners and/or broadcasting organisations to act as Licensor on their behalf and it has full power and authority to grant the rights set out herein.

(2) Obligations

Open University Worldwide Limited shall make available to the Licensee information about the transmission schedules of the Designated Programmes.

Obligations of the Licensee

4. The Licensee shall:

(1) ensure that all Recording off air is made by a lecturer, instructor, teacher or other suitably qualified person appointed for the purpose by the Licensee;

(2) ensure that recordings of the Designated Programmes are not edited, cut or amended in any way including by digital manipulation without prior written permission of Open University Worldwide Limited and are not shown or disclosed or passed into the possession of any third party and are not removed from the direct control of the Licensee;

(3) ensure that the recorded Designated Programmes are used for Educational Purposes only and the Licensee shall not itself or through its employees or agents, sell, lend, hire or otherwise use or dispose of recordings of Designated Programmes other than in accordance with the terms of the Licence and shall prevent any third party from duplicating, selling, lending, hiring or otherwise using or disposing of recordings of the Designated Programmes;

(4) where the Licensee is an Educational Institution, make up, retain and keep made up such detailed and accurate records as may be required by Open University Worldwide Limited of the Designated Programmes recorded and in particular shall complete the log sheets provided by or approved in writing by Open University Worldwide Limited;

(5) affix to each recording in a prominent place and shall not obscure, remove, alter or deface a label which shall include the title of the Designated Programme and the date upon which it was recorded;

(6) where the Licensee is an Educational Institution, return to Open University Worldwide Limited all duly completed log sheets on dates specified by Open University Worldwide Limited to a maximum number of three times in each twelve month licence period and on termination of the Licence;

(7) subject to paragraph (8) below, erase any and all recordings of the Designated Programmes in existence at the expiration of the licence period or upon termination of the Licence whichever shall be the sooner and shall supply to Open University Worldwide Limited a certificate of erasure within 28 days of such expiration or termination;

(8) if the licence period is automatically continued without interruption for a further period of twelve months pursuant to Clause 2 the Licensee may at its option and subject to paragraph (7) retain recordings of Designated Programmes: (a) where the Licensee is a School, for the following twelve month period and subject always to the proper Licence fee therefor being paid; (b) where the Licensee is an Educational Institution, provided such programmes remain entered into the log for the following twelve month period and subject always to the proper recording fees therefor being paid.

(9) in the event that the Licensee makes Additional Copies, report the making of such copies immediately to Open University Worldwide Limited. Upon receipt of such information from the Licensee, Open University Worldwide Limited will invoice the Licensee for the copies made and will maintain a record of the copies made.

Consideration

5. In consideration for the Licence:

(1) where the Licensee is a School,

    (a) the Licensee shall pay Open University Worldwide Limited the fees set out in Appendix A plus VAT where applicable.

    (b) Licence Fees payable under paragraph (1)(a) shall be paid within thirty days of the date of the invoice whenever sent to the Licensee by Open University Worldwide Limited;

(2) where the Licensee is an Educational Institution,

    (a) the Licensee shall pay Open University Worldwide Limited the fees set out in Appendix B plus VAT where applicable;

    (b) fees payable under paragraph (2)(a) shall be calculated by Open University Worldwide Limited annually and shall be paid within thirty days of the date of the invoice whenever sent to the Licensee by Open University Worldwide Limited;

    (c) the Licensee shall permit its records and accounts to be examined upon reasonable notice in writing from Open University Worldwide Limited by Open University Worldwide Limited's properly appointed representative at Open University Worldwide Limited's expense to verify the records and payments for which provision is made in the Licence.

Termination

6. Open University Worldwide Limited shall at its option be entitled by notice in writing to the Licensee to terminate the Licence forthwith in any of the following events that is to say if the Licensee shall:

(1) fail promptly to account and make payments hereunder or fail to perform any other obligation required of it hereunder and the Licensee shall not have cured or remedied such failure within 14 (fourteen) days of a request from Open University Worldwide Limited (time being of the essence);

(2) adopt a resolution for its winding up (otherwise than for the purpose of and followed by an amalgamation or reconstruction) or if a petition is presented for the appointment of an administrator or if a receiver or an administrative receiver is appointed in respect of, or an encumbrancer takes possession of, the whole or any part of its undertaking or assets or if the Licensee is unable to pay its debts within the meaning of section 123 of the Insolvency Act 1986;

(3) cease to carry on the business or function as a School or an Educational Institution, as the case may be.

NOTE: Discounted fees to cover groups of licensees may be negotiated at the discretion of Open University Worldwide Limited.

Alterations to Agreement

7. Any alteration or variation to the Licence shall not be valid or enforceable unless recorded in writing and signed by an authorised signatory of each party.

Assignment

8. The Licence is specific to the Licensee and the Licensee shall not assign the benefits or the obligations of the Licence.

Expenses

9. Save as otherwise expressed all expenses of and incidental to the fulfilment of the Licence shall be borne by the party incurring such expense.

Force Majeure

10. Neither party to the Licence shall be liable in any way for any delays or failure to perform its obligations thereunder resulting from any cause beyond its reasonable control.

Service of Notices

11.—(1) Notices and other communications must be sent by first class post, fax or e-mail whether or not they are required to be in writing. They must be addressed to the recipient at the postal address, fax number or e-mail address specified in the Licence unless the parties have agreed an alternative address.

(2) Notice by post will be deemed served on the third Business Day after it was posted.

(3) Notice by fax or e-mail will only be deemed served if an automatic confirmation of correct sending is received by the sender. Then, if the notice is transmitted before 4 p.m. on a Business Day, it will be deemed served on that day, otherwise it will be deemed served on the next Business Day.

Indemnity

12. The Licensee will indemnify and at all times keep Open University Worldwide Limited fully indemnified against all actions, proceedings, claims, costs and damages whatsoever made against or incurred by Open University Worldwide Limited in consequence of any breach or non-performance by the Licensee, its employees or agents of any of the covenants contained in the Licence.

Law of England

13. The law of England shall govern the Licence.

APPENDIX A

THE OPEN UNIVERSITY LICENSED OFF AIR RECORDING SCHEME SCALE OF LICENCE FEES FOR SCHOOLS

VAT is payable in addition to all fees shown

CATEGORY 1A: Primary Schools	£28 per annum
CATEGORY 1B: Secondary Schools	£78 per annum

ADDITIONAL COPIES (CAT-EGORY 1A and CATEGORY 1B)	The Licence fees shown above include the recording of any Designated Programme and up to four (4) Additional Copies thereof.
	Where the Licensee makes more than four (4) Additional Copies, the fees charged will be:
5–10 Additional Copies of any single Designated Programme	£30 for each Additional Copy
11–20 Additional Copies of any single Designated Programme	£20 for each Additional Copy
21-plus Additional Copies of any single Designated Programme	£10 for each Additional Copy

APPENDIX B

THE OPEN UNIVERSITY LICENSED OFF AIR RECORDING SCHEME

VAT is payable in addition to all fees shown

Scale of Programme Fees for Educational Institutions

Number of Recordings	Fee per Annum or Part thereof	Unit Cost per Additional Recording
Under 5	recordings will be charged at £19.36 per recording	
5	£96.80	
6–9		£19.36
10	£155.25	
11–14		£15.48
15	£212.55	
16–24		£14.20
25	£322.65	
26–49		£12.90
50	£594.75	
51–74		£11.88
75	£865.75	
76–99		£11.50
100	£1,128.50	
101–124		£11.30
125	£1,355.40	
126–149		£10.86
150	£1,552.50	
151–199		£10.38
200	£1,934.60	
201–249		£9.68
250	£2,328.70	
251–299		£9.30
300	£2,651.10	
301–399		£8.88
400	£3,290.00	
401–499		£8.22
500	£3,869.20	£7.15

1. Please note that the FEES relate to EACH EPISODE of a series. Thus a series of six programmes will attract six programme fees.

These fees apply to those programmes which are retained for use. A FREE 28 day period for PREVIEW purposes ONLY is allowed to assess suitability.

Scale of Fees for Additional Copies

ADDITIONAL COPIES	The Programme fees shown in 1. above include the recording of any Designated Programme and up to four (4) Additional Copies thereof.

Where the Licensee makes more than four (4) Additional Copies, the fees charged will be:	
5–10 Additional Copies of any single Designated Programme	£30 each
11–20 Additional Copies of any single Designated Programme	£20 each
21-plus Additional Copies of any single Designated Programme	£10 each

B3. PUBLIC LENDING RIGHT

B3.i The Public Lending Right Act 1979

(c.10)

An Act to provide public lending right for authors, and for connected purposes.
[22nd March, 1979]

Establishment of public lending right

1.—(1) In accordance with a scheme to be prepared and brought into force by the Secretary of State, there shall be conferred on authors a right, known as "public lending right", to receive from time to time out of a Central Fund payments in respect of such of their books as are lent out to the public by local library authorities in the United Kingdom.

(2) The classes, descriptions and categories of books in respect of which public lending right subsists, and the scales of payments to be made from the Central Fund in respect of it, shall be determined by or in accordance with the scheme; and in preparing the scheme the Secretary of State shall consult with representatives of authors and library authorities and of others who appear to be likely to be affected by it.

(3) [...] [T]he Schedule to this Act has effect [...].

(4) The [Board] shall be charged with the duty of establishing and maintaining in accordance with the scheme a register showing the books in respect of which public lending right subsists and the persons entitled to the right in respect of any registered book.

(5) The [Board] shall, in the case of any registered book determine in accordance with the scheme the sums (if any) due by way of public lending right; and any sum so determined to be due shall be recoverable from the [Board] as a debt due to the person for the time being entitled to that right in respect of the book.

(6) Subject to any provision made by the scheme, the duration of public lending right in respect of a book shall be from the date of the book's first publication (or, if later, the beginning of the year in which application is made for it to be registered) until 50 years have elapsed since the end of the year in which the author died.

(7) Provision shall be made by the scheme for the right—

(a) to be established by registration;

(b) to be transmissible by assignment or assignation, by testamentary disposition or by operation of law, as personal or moveable property;

(c) to be claimed by or on behalf of the person for the time being entitled;

(d) to be renounced (either in whole or in part, and either temporarily or for all time) on notice being given to the [Board] to that effect.

Notes:

(1) The original references in the Act to the Secretary of State in the Act were replaced by references to the Chancellor of the Duchy of Lancaster by art.2(1) and the Schedule to the Transfer of Functions (Arts and Libraries) Order SI 1979/907 (with effect from September 1, 1979). References to the Chancellor were replaced by references to the Secretary of State by art.2(1) and Sch.1 Pt 1 to the Transfer of Functions (Arts, Libraries and National Heritage) Order SI 1981/207 (with effect from April 1, 1981). References to the Secretary of State were replaced by references to the Lord President of the Council by art.2(1) and Sch.1 Pt 1 to the Transfer of Functions (Arts, Libraries and National Heritage) Order SI 1983/879 (with effect from July 1, 1983). References to the Lord President were replaced by references to the Chancellor of the Duchy of Lancaster by art.2(1) and Sch.1 Pt 1 to the

Transfer of Functions (Arts, Libraries and National Heritage) Order SI 1984/1814 (with effect from December 22, 1984). References to the Chancellor were replaced by references to the Lord President by art.2(1) and Sch.1 Pt 1 to the Transfer of Functions (Arts, Libraries and National Heritage) Order SI 1986/600 (with effect from April 29, 1986). Finally, references to the Lord President were replaced by references to the Secretary of State by art.3(1) and Sch.1 Pt 1 to the Transfer of Functions (National Heritage) Order SI 1992/1311 (with effect from July 3, 1992).

(2) In subs.(3) words "Secretary of State shall appoint an officer to be known as the Registrar of Public Lending Right; and the" and "with respect to the Registrar" repealed, and in subss (4), (5), (7)(d) word in square brackets substituted for word "Registrar", subject to supplementary provisions, by the Public Bodies (Abolition of the Registrar of Public Lending Right) Order 2013 (SI 2013/2352), Sch.1 para.7, with effect from October 1, 2013 (for supplementary provisions see art.8 thereof).

The Central Fund

2.—(1) The Central Fund shall be constituted by the Secretary of State and placed under the control and management of the Registrar.

(2) There shall be paid into the Fund from time to time such sums, out of money provided by Parliament, as the Secretary of State with Treasury approval determines to be required for the purpose of satisfying the liabilities of the Fund; but in respect of the liabilities of any one financial year of the Fund the total of those sums shall not exceed £2 million less the total of any sums paid in that year, out of money so provided, under paragraph 2 of the Schedule to this Act (pay, pension, etc. of [Board]).

(3) With the consent of the Treasury, the Secretary of State may from time to time by order in a statutory instrument increase the limit on the sums to be paid under subsection (2) above in respect of financial years beginning after that in which the order is made; but no such order shall be made unless a draft of it has been laid before the House of Commons and approved by a resolution of that House.

[(4) There are to be paid out of the Central Fund such sums as may in accordance with the scheme be due from time to time in respect of public lending right.]

[(5) There is to be paid into the Central Fund—

　(a) money received by the Board in respect of property disposed of in connection with its functions in relation to public lending right, and

　(b) money otherwise received by the Board in the course of its functions in relation to public lending right, or under this Act,

after deduction of any costs associated with the disposal of the property or otherwise referable to the money received.

(5A) But an amount required to be paid into the Central Fund under subsection (5) is instead to be paid into the Consolidated Fund if the Secretary of State, with the consent of the Treasury, so directs.]

(6) [...]

Notes:

(1) The limit on the sums to be paid under s.2(2) was modified by the Public Lending Right (Increase of Limit) Order 2003 (SI 2003/839), art.2 which provided:

"2. *The limit on the sums to be paid under section 2(2) of the Public Lending Right Act 1979, out of money provided by Parliament into the Central Fund to satisfy the liabilities of any one financial year of the Fund, shall be increased to—*

　(a) *£14.252 million in respect of the financial year beginning on the day this Order comes into force; and*

　(b) *£8 million in respect of financial years thereafter,*

and, in each case, that limit shall be less the total of any sums paid in that year, out of money so provided, under paragraph 2 of the Schedule to the Public Lending Right Act 1979 (pay, pension, etc. of Registrar)."

(2) The limit on the sums to be paid under s.2(2) was previously modified by the Public Lending Right (Increase of Limit) Order 1999 (SI 1999/905), art.2 which provided:

"2. *The limit on the sums to be paid under section 2(2) of the Public Lending Right Act 1979 out of money provided by Parliament into the Central Fund to satisfy the liabilities of any one financial year of the Fund shall, in respect of any financial year beginning after 31st March 1999, be increased to £5.5 million less the total of any sums paid in that year, out of money so provided, under paragraph 2 of the Schedule to that Act (pay, pension, etc. of Registrar)."*

(3) In subs.(1) word in square brackets substituted for word "Registrar", in subs.(2) words "less the total of any sums paid in that year, out of money so provided, under paragraph 2 of the Schedule to this Act (pay, pension, etc. of Registrar)" repealed, subss (4), (5), (5A) substituted, and subs.(6) repealed, subject to supplementary provisions, by the Public Bodies (Abolition of the Registrar of Public Lending Right) Order 2013 (SI 2013/2352), Sch.1 para.8, with effect from October 1, 2013 (for supplementary provisions see art.8 thereof).

The scheme and its administration

3.—(1) As soon as may be after this Act comes into force, [the Lord President of the Council] shall prepare the draft of a scheme for its purpose and lay a copy of the draft before each House of Parliament.

(2) If the draft scheme is approved by a resolution of each House, [the Lord President of the Council] shall bring the scheme into force (in the form of the draft) by means of an order in a statutory instrument, to be laid before Parliament after it is made; and the order may provide for different provisions of the scheme to come into force on different dates.

(3) The scheme shall be so framed as to make entitlement to public lending right dependent on, and its extent ascertainable by reference to, the number of occasions on which books are lent out from particular libraries, to be specified by the scheme or identified in accordance with provision made by it.

(4) For this purpose, "library" —

(a) means any one of a local library authority's collections of books held by them for the purpose of being borrowed by the public; and

(b) includes any such collection which is taken about from place to place.

(5) The scheme may provide for requiring local library authorities—

(a) to give information as and when, and in the form in which, the Registrar may call for it or the Secretary of State may direct, as to loans made by them to the public of books in respect of which public lending right subsists, or of other books; and

(b) to arrange for books to be numbered, or otherwise marked or coded, with a view to facilitating the maintenance of the register and the ascertainment and administration of public lending right.

(6) The [Board] shall [...] reimburse to local library authorities any expenditure incurred by them in giving effect to the scheme, the amount of that expenditure being ascertained in accordance with such calculations as the scheme may prescribe.

(7) Subject to the provisions of this Act (and in particular to the foregoing provisions of this section), the scheme may be varied from time to time by the Secretary of State, after such consultation as is mentioned in section 1(2) above, and the variation brought into force by an order in a statutory instrument, subject to annulment in pursuance of a resolution of either House of Parliament; and the variation may comprise such incidental and transitional provisions as the Secretary of State thinks appropriate for the purposes of continuing the scheme as varied.

(8) The Secretary of State shall in each year prepare and lay before each House of Parliament a report on the working of the scheme.

Notes:

   (1) In subss.(1), (2) words substituted for "the Secretary of State" by (SI 1983/879) and (SI 1984/1814).

   (2) In subss.(5)(a), (6) word in square brackets substituted for word "Registrar", and in subs.(6) words ", by means of payments out of the Central Fund," repealed, subject to supplementary provisions, by the Public Bodies (Abolition of the Registrar of Public Lending Right) Order 2013 (SI 2013/2352), Sch.1 para.9, with effect from October 1, 2013 (for supplementary provisions see art.8 thereof).

The register

4.—(1) The register shall be kept in such form, and contain such particulars of books and their authors, as may be prescribed.

(2) No application for an entry in the register is to be entertained in the case of any book unless it falls within a class, description or category of books prescribed as one in respect of which public lending right subsists.

(3) The scheme shall provide for the register to be conclusive both as to whether public lending right subsists in respect of a particular book and also as to the persons (if any) who are for the time being entitled to the right.

(4) Provision shall be included in the scheme for entries in the register to be made and amended, on application made in the prescribed manner and supported by prescribed particulars (verified as prescribed) so as to indicate, in the case of any book who (if any one) is for the time being entitled to public lending right in respect of it.

(5) The [Board] may direct the removal from the register of every entry relating to a book in whose case no sum has become due by way of public lending right for a period of at least 10 years, but without prejudice to a subsequent application for the entries to be restored to the register.

[(6) The Board may require the payment of fees, according to prescribed scales and rates, for supplying copies of entries in the register.

(6A) A copy of an entry in the register is, in all legal proceedings, admissible in evidence as of equal validity with the original if it is certified in writing by—

   (a) a member of the Board,

   (b) a person employed by, or contracted to provide services for, the Board with authority in that behalf (which authority it is unnecessary to prove).]

(7) It shall be an offence for any person, in connection with the entry of any matter whatsoever in the register, to make any statement which he knows to be false in a material particular or recklessly to make any statement which is false in a material particular; and a person who commits an offence under this section shall be liable on summary conviction to a fine of not more than [level 5 on the standard scale].

(8) Where an offence under subsection (7) above which has been committed by a body corporate is proved to have been committed with the consent or connivance of, or to be attributable to any neglect on the part of, a director, manager, secretary or other similar officer of the body corporate, or any person who was purporting to act in any such capacity, he (as well as the body corporate) shall be guilty of that offence and be liable to be proceeded against accordingly.

Where the affairs of a body corporate are managed by its members, this subsection applies in relation to the acts and defaults of a member in connection with his functions of management as if he were a director of the body corporate.

Notes:

   (1) In subs.(7) words substituted by virtue of (for England, Wales) the Criminal Justice

Act 1982, s.46, (for Scotland) the Criminal Procedure (Scotland) Act 1975, s.289G.

(2) In subs.(5) word in square brackets substituted for word "Registrar", and subss.(6), (6A) substituted, subject to supplementary provisions, by the Public Bodies (Abolition of the Registrar of Public Lending Right) Order 2013 (SI 2013/2352), Sch.1 para.10, with effect from October 1, 2013 (for supplementary provisions see art.8 thereof). Subs.(6) formerly read:

"(6) The Registrar may require the payment of fees, according to prescribed scales and rates, for supplying copies of entries in the register; and a copy of an entry, certified under the hand of the Registrar or an officer of his with authority in that behalf (which authority it shall be unnecessary to prove) shall in all legal proceedings be admissible in evidence as of equal validity with the original."

Citation, etc.

5.—(1) This Act may be cited as the Public Lending Right Act, 1979.

(2) In this Act any reference to "the scheme" is to the scheme prepared and brought into force by the Secretary of State in accordance with sections 1 and 3 of this Act (including the scheme as varied from time to time under section 3(7); and—

["author", in relation to a work recorded as a sound recording, includes a producer or narrator; "book" includes

["the Board" means the British Library Board established under section 1(2) of the British Library Act 1972;]

["book" includes—

(a) a work recorded as a sound recording and consisting mainly of spoken words (an "audio-book"), and

(b) a work, other than an audio-book, recorded in electronic form and consisting mainly of (or of any combination of) written or spoken words or still pictures (an "c-book");]

["lent out" —

(a) means made available to a member of the public for use away from library premises for a limited time, but

(b) does not include being communicated by means of electronic transmission to a place other than library premises,

and "loan" and "borrowed" are to be read accordingly;]

["library premises" has the meaning given in section 8(7) of the Public Libraries and Museums Act 1964;]

"local library authority" means—

(a) a library authority under the Public Libraries and Museums Act, 1964,[1]

(b) a statutory library authority within the Public Libraries (Scotland) Act, 1955,[2] and

(c) an Education and Library Board within the Education and Libraries (Northern Ireland) Order 1972[3];

"prescribed" means prescribed by the scheme;

["producer" has the meaning given in section 178 of the Copyright, Designs and Patents Act 1988;]

"the register" means the register required by section 1(4) to be established and maintained by the [Board][;]

---

[1] c. 75.
[2] c. 27.
[3] SI 1972/1263 (N.I. 12).

[...]

[" sound recording" has the meaning given in section 5A(1) of the Copyright, Designs and Patents Act 1988.]

(3) This act comes into force on a day to be appointed by an order made by the [Chancellor of the Duchy of Lancaster] in a statutory instrument to be laid before Parliament after it has been made.

(4) This Act extends to Northern Ireland.

Notes:

(1) In subs.(3) words in square brackets substituted for words "the Secretary of State" by virtue of (SI 1979/907), art.2(1), 11.

(2) In subs.(2) definition "the Board" inserted, in definition "the register" word in square brackets substituted for word "Registrar", and definition "the Registrar" repealed, , subject to supplementary provisions, by the Public Bodies (Abolition of the Registrar of Public Lending Right) Order 2013 (SI 2013/2352), Sch.1 para.11, with effect from October 1, 2013 (for supplementary provisions see art.8 thereof). Definition "the Registrar" formerly read:

"'the Registrar' means the Registrar of Public Lending Right."

(3) Definitions "author", "book", "lent out", "library premises", "producer" and "sound recording" inserted, and in definition "the Registrar", the word "and" repealed by the Digital Economy Act 2010 s.43, with effect from June 30, 2014.

Section 1(3)   SCHEDULE

[PUBLIC LENDING RIGHT: SUPPLEMENTARY PROVISION]

1.–5. [...]

[**6.** The Documentary Evidence Act 1868 shall have effect as if the Board were included in the first column of the Schedule to that Act, as if any person authorised to act on behalf of the Board were mentioned in the second column of that Schedule, and as if the regulations referred to in that Act included any documents issued by the Board, or by any such person, in relation to the Board's functions under this Act or the scheme.]

7. [...]

8. Anything authorised or required under this Act [...] or by or under the scheme, to be done by the [Board] may be done by any [person] who is authorised generally or specially in that behalf in writing by the [Board].

Note: Heading substituted for heading "The Registrar of Public Lending Right", paras 1–5, 7 repealed, and para.6 substituted, and para.8 amended, subject to supplementary provisions, by the Public Bodies (Abolition of the Registrar of Public Lending Right) Order 2013 (SI 2013/2352), Sch.1 para.12, with effect from October 1, 2013 (for supplementary provisions see art.8 thereof). Schedule (as amended by (SI 2011/1213)) formerly read:

"1. *The Registrar shall hold and vacate office as such in accordance with the terms of his appointment; but he may at any time resign his office by notice in writing addressed to the Secretary of State; and the Secretary of State may at any time remove a person from the office of Registrar on the ground of incapacity or misbehaviour.*

2.—*(1) There shall be paid to the Registrar out of money provided by Parliament such remuneration and allowances as the Secretary of State may determine with the approval of the Minister for the Civil Service.*

(2) In the case of any such holder of the office of Registrar as may be determined by the Secretary of State with that approval, there shall be paid out of money so provided such pension, allowance or gratuity to or in respect of him, or such contributions or payments towards provision of such a pension, allowance or gratuity, as may be so determined.

3. *If, when a person ceases to hold office as Registrar, it appears to the Secretary of State that there are special circumstances which make it right that he should receive compensation, there may (with the approval of the Minister for the Civil Service) be paid to him out of the Central Fund a sum by way of compensation of such amount as may be so determined.*

4. *In House of Commons Disqualification Act 1975,*[4] *in Part III of Schedule 1 (other disqualifying offices), the following shall be inserted at the appropriate place in alphabetical order—*

"Registrar of Public Lending Right":

and the like insertion shall be made in Part III of Schedule 1 to the Northern Ireland Assembly Disqualification Act 1975.[5]

5.—(1) The Registrar of Public Lending Right shall be by that name a corporation sole, with a corporate seal.

(2) He is not to be regarded as the servant or agent of the Crown.

6. The Documentary Evidence Act 1868[6] shall have effect as if the Registrar were included in the first column of the Schedule to that Act, as if the Registrar and any person authorised to act on his behalf were mentioned in the second column of that Schedule, and as if the regulations referred to in that Act included any documents issued by the Registrar or by any such person.

7.—(1) The Registrar may appoint such assistant registrars and staff as he thinks fit, subject to the approval of the Secretary of State as to their numbers; and their terms and conditions of service, and the remuneration and allowances payable to them, shall be such as the Registrar may determine.

(2) The Registrar may direct, in the case of persons appointed by him under this paragraph—

    (a) that there be paid to and in respect of them such pensions, allowances and gratuities as he may determine;

    (b) that payments be made towards the provision for them of such pensions, allowances and gratuities as he may determine; and

    (c) that schemes be provided and maintained (whether contributory or not) for the payment to and in respect of them of such pensions, allowances and gratuities as he may determine.

(3) Any money required for the payment of remuneration and allowances under this paragraph, and of pensions, allowances and gratuities, and otherwise for the purpose of sub-paragraph (2) above, shall be paid from the Central Fund.

(4) The approval of the Secretary of State and the Minister for the Civil Service shall be required for any directions or determination by the Registrar under this paragraph.

8. Anything authorised or required under this Act (except paragraph 7 of this Schedule), or by or under the scheme, to be done by the Registrar may be done by any assistant registrar or member of the Registrar's staff who is authorised generally or specially in that behalf in writing by the Registrar."

B3.ii The Public Lending Right Scheme 1982 (Commencement) Order 1982

(SI 1982/719)

Made	*17th May 1982*
Laid before Parliament	*1st June 1982*
Coming into Operation	*14th June 1982*

In exercise of the powers conferred on me by section 3 (2) of the Public Lending Right Act 1979, I hereby make the following Order:—

1. This Order may be cited as the Public Lending Right Scheme 1982 (Commencement) Order 1982 and shall come into operation on 14th June 1982.

2.—(1) The Scheme set out in the Appendix hereto, which has been approved by a resolution of each House of Parliament, shall come into force in the manner hereinafter provided.

---

[4] c. 24.
[5] c. 25.
[6] c. 37.

(2) The provisions of the Scheme specified in column 1 of the table set out below shall come into force on the dates specified in relation thereto in column 2 of that table:

(1) **Provisions of the Scheme**	(2) **Date on which provisions come into force**
Parts I, II and IV, Schedule 2 and Schedule 3 Part I	14th June 1982
Part III and Schedule 1	1st September 1982
Part V, Schedule 3 Part II and Schedule 4	1st July 1983

APPENDIX

PUBLIC LENDING RIGHT SCHEME 1982 ARRANGEMENT OF SCHEME

PART I

TITLE AND INTERPRETATION

Citation and extent

1. This Scheme may be cited as the Public Lending Right Scheme 1982, and shall extend to the whole of the United Kingdom.

General definitions

2.—(1) In this Scheme, except where the context otherwise requires, the following expressions have the meanings hereby respectively assigned to them, that is to say—

"the Act" means the Public Lending Right Act 1979;

"author", in relation to an eligible book, means a person who is, or one of a number of persons who are, treated as such by Article 4;

["EEA State" means a member State, Norway, Iceland and Lichtenstein;]

"eligible author", in relation to an eligible book, means an author of that book who is an eligible person;

"eligible book" has the meaning assigned thereto by Article 6;

"eligible person", in relation to an author, has the meaning assigned thereto by Article 5;

"financial year" means a period of twelve months ending on the 31st March;

"identifying number" means the number entered in the Register in pursuance of Article 8(1)(a)(iv);

[...]

"local library authority" has the meaning assigned thereto by section 5(2) of the Act;

["posthumously eligible book" has the meaning assigned thereto by [article 6A] ;

"posthumously eligible person" has the meaning assigned thereto by [article 5A] ;]

"the Registrar" and "the Register" have the meanings assigned thereto by section 5(2) of the Act;

"registered interest" means the interest (being the whole or a share thereof), in the Public Lending Right in respect of a particular book, shown on the Register as belonging to a particular person, and "registered owner" means the person for the time being so registered;

"the registry" means the place at which the Register is for the time being maintained in pursuance of Article 7;

"sampling year" has the meaning assigned thereto by Article 36.

(2) In this Scheme, except where the context otherwise requires, any reference to an Article or to a Part or to a Schedule shall be construed as a reference to an Article contained in, or to a Part of or a Schedule to, this Scheme, as the case may be, and any reference in any Article to a paragraph shall be construed as a reference to a paragraph in that Article.

Notes:

(1) The definition of "EEA State" was inserted by Public Lending Right Scheme 1982 (Commencement of Variations) Order (SI 2004/1258) with effect from June 1, 2004.

(2) The definition of "library" was revoked by the Public Lending Right Scheme 1982 (Commencement of Variations) Order (SI 1988/2070) with effect from December 22, 1988.

(3) The definitions of "posthumously eligible book" and "posthumously eligible person" were inserted by the Public Lending Right Scheme 1982 (Commencement of Variations) Order (SI 1988/2070) (December 22, 1988)

(4) The word "Article" in para.2(1) was substituted by the Public Lending Right Scheme 1982 (Commencement of Variations) Order (SI 1989/2188) with effect from December 21, 1989.

Delivery of documents and service of notice

3. Unless the context otherwise requires, any requirement in this Scheme for—

(a)   a document or an application to be delivered at the registry or produced to the Registrar or for notice to be given to him, shall be satisfied if the same is either—

(i)   delivered in person at the registry between the hours of 11 am and 3pm on a working day; or

(ii)   sent through the post by recorded delivery;

(b)   a local library authority or a registered owner to be notified of any matter shall be satisfied if such notification is sent through the post.

PART II

BOOKS AND AUTHORS ELIGIBLE UNDER THE SCHEME

[Authors

4.—(1) Subject to paragraph (2), a person shall be treated as an author of a book for the purpose of this Scheme if he is either –

(a)   a writer of the book, including without prejudice to the generality of that expression,

(i) a translator thereof, and

(ii) an editor or compiler thereof, who in either case has contributed more than ten per cent of the contents of the book or more than ten pages of the contents, whichever is the less [, or who is entitled to a royalty payment from the publisher in respect of the book][, and]

[(iii) in relation to an audio-book, a producer or narrator thereof; or]

(b)   an illustrator thereof, which for this purpose includes the author of a photograph [...]

[(2) Notwithstanding paragraph (1), a person shall not be treated as an author of a book unless the fact that he is an author within the meaning of paragraph (1)—

(a)   is evidenced by his being named on the title page of the book; or

[(b)   is evidenced by his entitlement to a royalty payment from the publisher in respect of the book; or

(c)   in the case of a book without a title page, is evidenced—

(i) by his being named elsewhere in the book and in the view of the Registrar his contribution to the book was such that he would have merited a mention on the title page had there been one, or

(ii) by his entitlement to a royalty payment from the publisher in respect of the book; or

[(iii) by his being named on the case with which the audio-book is sold; or
(iv) is evidenced by reference to a written contract with the publisher of the audio-book which refers expressly to his being an author within the meaning of paragraph (1).]
(d) is evidenced by a statement, signed by all the other authors of the book in respect of whom the fact that they are authors of the book is evidenced in accordance with paragraphs (a) to (c), that his contribution to the book was such that it is appropriate that he should be treated as an author of the book and the Registrar is satisfied that it is appropriate so to treat him.]]]

Notes:

(1) This paragraph was substituted by the Public Lending Right Scheme 1982 (Amendment) Order (SI 1984/1847) art.2 (December 28, 1984)
(2) The words in para.4(1)(a)(ii) inserted by the Public Lending Right Scheme 1982 (Commencement of Variations) Order (SI 1991/2618) with effect from December 18, 1991.
(3) The words in para.4(1(b) repealed by the Public Lending Right Scheme 1982 (Commencement of Variations) Order (SI 1997/1576) with effect from July 15, 1997.
(4) Paragraph 2 was substituted by the Public Lending Right Scheme 1982 (Commencement of Variations) Order (SI 1988/2070) with effect from December 22, 1988.
(5) Paragraph 4(2)(b)–(d) substituted for para.4(2)(b) by the Public Lending Right Scheme 1982 (Commencement of Variations) Order (SI 1991/2618) with effect from December 18, 1991.
(6) Paragraph (1)(a)(iii) inserted and preceding word substituted for word "; or", and para.(2)(c)(iii) and (iv) inserted, by the Public Lending Right Scheme 1982 (Commencement of Variations) Order 2014 (SI 2014/1457), App.1, para.1, with effect from July 1, 2014.

Eligible persons

5.—[(1) For the purposes of the Scheme, and in relation to each application by a person relating to an eligible book, the applicant is an eligible person if he is an author (within the meaning of Article 4) of that book who at the date of the application has his only or principal home [in an EEA State or, if he has no home, has been present in an EEA State] for not less than twelve months out of the preceding twenty-four months.]

(2) In this Article, "principal home", in the case of a person having more than one home means that one of those homes at which he has been for the longest aggregate period during the twenty-four months immediately preceding the application for registration.

Notes:

(1) Paragraph 5(1) was substituted by the Public Lending Right Scheme 1982 (Amendment) Order (SI 1984/1847) art.3 with effect from December 28, 1984.
(2) The words in brackets in para.5(1) substituted by the Public Lending Right Scheme 1982 (Commencement of Variations) Order (SI 2004/1258) with effect from June 1, 2004.

[Posthumously eligible persons

5A. For the purposes of the Scheme, and in relation to each application relating to a posthumously eligible book, an author who is dead is a posthumously eligible person if, had he been an applicant for first registration of Public Lending Right in relation to that book at the date of his death, he would have been an eligible person in accordance with article 5.]

Note: This paragraph was added by the Public Lending Right Scheme 1982 (Commencement of Variations) Order (SI 1988/2070) with effect from December 22, 1988.

Eligible books

6.—(1) For the purposes of this Scheme, an eligible book is a book (as defined in paragraph (2)) the sole author, or at least one of the authors, of which is an eligible person; and there shall be treated as a separate book—

(a)   each volume of a work published in two or more volumes, and

(b)   each new edition of a book.

[(2) In paragraph (1) "book" means a printed and bound publication (including a paper-back edition [or an audio-book or an e-book]) but does not include—

(a)   a book bearing, in lieu of the name of an author who is a natural person, the name of a body corporate or an unincorporated association;

(b)   [...]

(c)   a book which is wholly or mainly a musical score;

(d)   a book the copyright of which is vested in the Crown;

(e)   a book which has not been offered for sale to the public; [...]

(f)   a serial publication including, without prejudice to the generality of that expression, a newspaper, magazine, journal or periodical [; or]

[(g)   a book which does not have an International Standard Book Number.]]

(3) [...]

Notes:

(1) This paragraph was substituted by the Public Lending Right Scheme 1982 (Amendment) Order (SI 1984/1847) art.4(a) with effect from December 28, 1984.

(2) Paragraph 6(2)(b) was revoked by the Public Lending Right Scheme 1982 (Commencement of Variations) Order (SI 1991/2618) with effect from December 18, 1991.

(3) The word in para.6(2)(e) was repealed by the Public Lending Right Scheme 1982 (Commencement of Variations) Order (SI 1990/2360) with effect from December 27, 1990.

(4) The words in para.6(4) inserted by the Public Lending Right Scheme 1982 (Commencement of Variations) Order (SI 1990/2360) with effect from December 27, 1990.

(5) Paragraph 6(2)(g) was substituted by the Public Lending Right Scheme 1982 (Commencement of Variations) Order (SI 1999/420) with effect from July 1, 1999.

(6) Paragraph 6(3) was revoked by the Public Lending Right Scheme 1982 (Amendment) Order (SI 1984/1847) with effect from December 28, 1984.

(7) In para.(2) words in square brackets inserted by the Public Lending Right Scheme 1982 (Commencement of Variations) Order 2014 (SI 2014/1457), App.1, para.2, with effect from July 1, 2014.

[Posthumously eligible books

6A.—(1) For the purposes of the Scheme, a book is a posthumously eligible book if—

(a)   it is a book within the meaning of article 6(2),

(b)   the sole author, or at least one of the authors, of the book is a posthumously eligible person, and

(c) the book is either

(i) published within one year before or ten years after the date of that person's death and that person had made a successful application during his lifetime for registration of Public Lending Right or of an eligible author's share of the Right in respect of at least one other book, or

(ii) a book which consists of or incorporates a work of that person which had previously been the constituent of or incorporated in a book in relation to which that person had made such an application as aforesaid.]

Note: This paragraph was added by the Public Lending Right Scheme 1982 (Commencement of Variations) Order (SI 1988/2070) with effect from December 22, 1988.

PART III

REGISTRATION OF PUBLIC LENDING RIGHT

The Register

7. The Registrar shall establish and maintain a Public Lending Right Register at such place as the Secretary of State may from time to time determine, and upon each such determination notice shall be published in the London Gazette, the Edinburgh Gazette and the Belfast Gazette, of such place and the time of the commencement of registration thereat.

The content of the Register

8.—(1) The Register shall contain—

(a)   particulars of each book in respect of which Public Lending Right subsists, including—

(i)   the title of the book;

(ii)   the name or names of the persons appearing on the title page as the authors thereof;

(iii)   the true identity of an author if different from (ii) above;

(iv)   a number for that book, determined by, or in accordance with arrangements made by, the Registrar;

(b)   the name and address of each person entitled to the Right in respect of each such book and, if more than one, the share of each such person in such Right.

(2) The Registrar shall also keep at the registry an index whereby all entries in the Register can readily be traced, and for this purpose "index" includes any device or combination of devices serving the purpose of an index.

Registration

9.—[(1) Public Lending Right in respect of a book may, and may only, be registered if—

(a)   the book is an eligible book and application in that behalf is made in accordance with articles 14 and 17, or

(b)   the book is a posthumously eligible book and application in that behalf is made in accordance with articles 14A and 17B.]

(2) Subject to paragraph (3), an eligible author's share of the Public Lending Right in respect of an eligible book with two or more authors (including any who are not eligible persons) may, and may only, be registered on application in that behalf made [in accordance with articles 14 and 17].

(3) The share of the Public Lending Right in such a book as is mentioned in paragraph (2) of an author who was not an eligible person at the time when application was first made for the registration of the share of the Right of any co-author may, and may only, be registered if—

(a)   he has become and remains an eligible person, and

   (b) application in that behalf is made in accordance with Articles 14 and 17 .]

       […]

[(4) A posthumously eligible person's share of the Public Lending Right in respect of a posthumously eligible book with two or more authors (including any who are not eligible persons) may, and may only, be registered on application made in accordance with articles 14A and 17B .]

Notes:

(1) Paragraph 1 was substituted by the Public Lending Right Scheme 1982 (Commencement of Variations) Order (SI 1988/2070) with effect from December 22, 1988.

(2) The words in brackets in para.2 substituted by the Public Lending Right Scheme 1982 (Commencement of Variations) Order (SI 1988/2070) with effect from December 22, 1988.

(3) Paragraph 3(b) was substituted by the Public Lending Right Scheme 1982 (Amendment) Order (SI 1984/1847) art.5(b) with effect from December 28, 1984.

(4) Paragraph 3(c) was repealed by the Public Lending Right Scheme 1982 (Commencement of Variations) Order (SI 1988/2070) with effect from December 22, 1988.

(5) Paragraph 4 was added by the Public Lending Right Scheme 1982 (Commencement of Variations) Order (SI 1988/2070) with effect from December 22, 1988.

[Shares in Public Lending Right

9A.—(1) Subject to the following paragraphs an eligible person's registered share of Public Lending Right in respect of a book [other than an audio-book,] of which he is author shall be the whole of that Right or, where a book has two or more authors (including any who are not eligible persons), such share of the Public Lending Right as may be specified in accordance with Article 17(1)(c) in the application for first registration of the Right.

(2) A translator's share of Public Lending Right in respect of a book [other than an audio-book,] shall be thirty per cent of that Right, or if there is more than one translator (including any who are not eligible persons), an equal share of thirty per cent, but this paragraph shall not apply where a translator is an author of the book in another capacity unless he makes an application in accordance with Article 17(1)(c)(ii).

(3) An editor's or compiler's share of Public Lending Right in respect of a book [other than an audio-book,] shall be

(a)   twenty per cent of that Right, or

(b)   if he satisfies the Registrar that he has contributed more than twenty per cent of the contents of the book, the percentage equal to that percentage contribution, or

(c)   if there is more than one editor or compiler (including any who are not eligible persons), an equal share of twenty per cent or the higher percentage attributable to the editors or compilers in accordance with sub-paragraph (b).

[[(4) Each eligible person's share of Public Lending Right in respect of a book [other than an audio-book,] with two or more authors (including any who are not eligible persons but disregarding a translator, editor or compiler) shall not exceed fifty per cent. of that Right unless the Registrar is satisfied that any share exceeding fifty per cent. which is specified in accordance with article 17(1)(c) in the application for first registration of the Right or in accordance with article 17(2) in the application for first registration of an eligible author's share of the Right is reasonable in relation to that author's contribution.]]

(5) Where a book [other than an audio-book,] has two or more authors (including any who are not eligible persons) and the Registrar is satisfied that one or more of them is dead or cannot be traced at the date of application despite all reasonable steps having been taken to do so, the Public Lending Right shall be apportioned amongst all the authors (including any who are not eligible persons)

(a)   by attributing to each author the same share of Public Lending Right as has been attributed to that author in respect of any other book by the same authors or, if there is more than one such other book, the most recent book by those authors in respect of which Public Lending Right has been registered, if the Registrar is satisfied that there has been no significant change in the respective contributions of the authors;

(b)   where sub-paragraph (a) does not apply, equally, subject to

(i)   the prior application of paragraphs (2), (3) and (7), and

(ii) where the book is illustrated,

(aa) the attribution of twenty per cent of the Public Lending Right to the illustrator, or

(bb) if he satisfies the Registrar that he has contributed more than twenty per cent of the contents of the book, the attribution of the percentage equal to that percentage contribution, or

(cc) if there is more than one illustrator (including any who are not eligible persons), the attribution of an equal share of twenty per cent or the higher percentage attributable to illustrators in accordance with sub-paragraph (bb).

(6) Where paragraph 5(b)(ii) applies, an illustrator who is also an author of a book [other than an audio-book,] in another capacity shall, in addition to any share of Public Lending Right to which he is entitled under that […] paragraph, be entitled to any further share of the Right which is attributable to him as author in that other capacity.

(7) Where all the persons (including the personal representatives of a posthumously eligible person) amongst whom the Public Lending Right would otherwise be apportioned equally in accordance with paragraph (5)(b) jointly notify the Registrar in writing that they wish the Right to be apportioned in a manner other than equally, the apportionment specified by them shall apply if the Registrar is satisfied that it is reasonable in that case.

(8) Where all the authors who are party to an application under article 17(1)(c) and who are entitled under paragraphs (2), (3), and 5(b)(ii) to a share of a percentage of Public Lending Rights in respect of the relevant book specify in accordance with article 17(1)(c) that the said percentage shall be apportioned in a manner other than that provided for by those paragraphs the specified apportionment shall apply if the Registrar is satisfied that it is reasonable in that case.]]

Notes:
   (1) This paragraph was added by the Public Lending Right Scheme 1982 (Amendment) Order (SI 1984/1847) art.6 with effect from December 28, 1984.
   (2) Sub-paragraphs (4)–(6) substituted for paras 9A(4)–(8) by the Public Lending Right Scheme 1982 (Commencement of Variations) Order (SI 1988/2070) with effect from December 22, 1988.
   (3) Paragraph 9A(4) was substituted by the Public Lending Right Scheme 1982 (Commencement of Variations) Order (SI 1997/1576) with effect from July 15, 1997.
   (4) The word in brackets in para.9A(6) was repealed by the Public Lending Right Scheme 1982 (Commencement of Variations) Order (SI 1990/2360) with effect from December 27, 1990.
   (5) In paras (1), (2), (3), (4), (5) and (6), words in square brackets inserted by the Public Lending Right Scheme 1982 (Commencement of Variations) Order 2014 (SI 2014/1457), App.1 para.3, with effect from July 1, 2014.

Shares in Public Lending Right in respect of audio-books

[9B.—(1) In respect of an audio-book for which there is a writer, narrator and producer, but no editor or translator—
   (a) the writer's share shall be sixty per cent of the Public Lending Right,
   (b) the narrator's share shall be twenty per cent of that Right, and
   (c) the producer's share shall be twenty per cent of that Right.
  (2) In respect of the audio-book for which there is both an editor and a translator—
   (a) the writer's shall shall be thirty per cent of the Public Lending Right,
   (b) the narrator's share shall be twenty per cent of that Right,
   (c) the producer's share shall be twenty per cent of the Right,
   (d) the editor's share shall be twelve per cent of that Right,
   (e) the translator's share shall be eighteen percent of that Right.
  (3) In respect of an audio-book for which there is an editor, but no translator—
   (a) the writer's share shall be forty-eight per cent of that Right,
   (b) the narrator's share shall be twenty per cent of that Right,
   (c) the producer's share shall be twenty per cent of that Right, and
   (d) the editor's share shall be twelve per cent of that Right.
  (4) In respect of an audio-book for which there is a translator, but no editor—
   (a) the writer's share shall be forty-two per cent of the Public Lending Right,
   (b) the narrator's share shall be twenty per cent of that Right,
   (c) the producer's share shall be twenty per cent of that Right, and
   (d) the translator's share share be eighteen per cent of that Right.
  (5) In the case of an audio-book for which the number of writers, narrators, producers, editors or translators id greater than one (including any who are not eligible persons) the respective shares of the Public Lending Right referred to in paragraph (1) to (4) shall be divided equally.]

Note: Paragraph 9B (originally inserted by SI 2014/1457) substituted by the Public Lending Right Scheme 1982 (Commencement of Variation and Amendment) Order 2014 (SI 2014/1945), Appx, with effect from August 13, 2014.

Dealings to be effected only on the Register

10. No Public Lending Right in respect of a particular book shall subsist and no transmission of a registered interest shall be effective until such Right or such transmission has been entered in the Register by the Registrar.

Register to be conclusive

11. The Register shall be conclusive as to whether Public Lending Right subsists in respect of a particular book and also as to the persons (if any) who are for the time being entitled to the Right.

Amendment of the Register

12. The Register may be amended pursuant to an Order of a Court of competent jurisdiction or by the decision of the Registrar in any of the following cases—
(a)   in any case and at any time with the consent of the registered owner or owners of the Right in respect of a particular book;

(b)   where a Court of competent jurisdiction or the Registrar is satisfied that an entry in the Register has been obtained by fraud;

(c)   where a decision of a Court of competent jurisdiction affects any interest in an eligible book and, in consequence thereof, the Registrar is of the opinion that amendment of the Register is required;

(d)   where two or more persons are erroneously registered as being entitled to the same interest in Public Lending Right in respect of a particular book;

(e)   where an entry erroneously relates to a book which is not an eligible book;

(f)   in any other case where by reason of any error or omission in the Register, or by reason of any entry made under a mistake, it appears to the Registrar just to amend the Register.

Payments consequent upon amendment

13. The person who, as a result of an amendment of the Register pursuant to Article 12 [or 17A] becomes the registered owner of a registered interest shall be entitled to the payment of Public Lending Right in respect of that interest from the date upon which the Register was amended.

Note: The words in brackets inserted by the Public Lending Right Scheme 1982 (Amendment) Order (SI 1984/1847) art.7 with effect from December 28, 1984.

Procedure for Registration

Forms of application

14. Any application required under this Scheme [other than an application required under article 14A]—

(a)   for first registration of Public Lending Right or of an eligible author's share of the Right;

(b)   for the transfer of a registered interest, or

(c)   for renunciation of a registered interest,

shall be made in writing to the Registrar and provide the information specified in Part I, II or III of Schedule 1 (as the case may be) in such form as he may from time to time require.

Note: The words in brackets inserted by the Public Lending Right Scheme 1982 (Commencement of Variations) Order (SI 1988/2070) with effect from December 22, 1988.

[Forms of application in respect of posthumously eligible books

14A. An application under article 17B for first registration of Public Lending Right, or of a posthumously eligible person's share of the Right, in relation to a posthumously eligible book shall be made in writing to the Registrar and shall provide in such form as he may from time to time require

(a)   the information specified in paragraphs 1 to 4 of Part I of Schedule 1 other than the address specified in paragraph 4,

(b)   a statement signed by the personal representatives of the posthumously eligible person that the conditions as to eligibility specified in articles 5A and 6A are satisfied, and

(c)   in the case of a work by more than one author, a statement signed as aforesaid that the posthumously eligible person in relation to whom the application is being made was translator, editor or compiler or illustrator [or narrator or producer] of the book and that the claim to Public Lending Right in respect thereof is limited to the percentage prescribed in article 9A(2), (3)[,(5)(b)(ii) or article 9B] or that the other author, or one of the other authors, of the work is a translator and that the claim to Public Lending Right in respect thereof is limited to that share or to a share of that share to which the translator is not entitled,

and shall be accompanied, when the personal representatives have not previously made an application under article 17B in relation to that posthumously eligible person, by

(i)   the probate, letters of administration or confirmation of executors of the posthumously eligible person in relation to whom the application is being made, and

(ii)   a certificate signed by a Member of Parliament, [a member of the Scottish Parliament,] Justice of the Peace, Minister of Religion, lawyer, bank officer, school teacher, police officer, [registered medical practitioner, who need not hold a licence to practise,] or other person accepted by the Registrar as being of similar standing and stating that he had known the posthumously eligible person in relation to whom the application is being made for at least two years before the date of his death, that he was not related to him and that to the best of his knowledge the contents of the statement referred to in […] paragraph (b) are true.]

Notes:

(1) This paragraph was added by the Public Lending Right Scheme 1982 (Commencement of Variations) Order (SI 1988/2070) with effect from December 22, 1988.

(2) The words "a member of the Scottish Parliament," in para.14A(c)(ii) inserted by Scotland Act 1998 (Consequential Modifications) (No.1) Order (SI 1999/1042) Sch.1(II) para.19 with effect from May 6, 1999.

(3) The words "registered medical practitioner, who need not hold a licence to practise," in para.(c)(ii) substituted by Medical Act 1983 (Amendment) Order (SI 2002/3135) Sch.1(II) para.23 with effect from November 16, 2009 as specified on pp.14478 and 14479 of the *London Gazette* dated August 21, 2009.

(4) The word in brackets in para.14A(c)(ii) was repealed by the Public Lending Right Scheme 1982 (Commencement of Variations) Order (SI 1990/2360) with effect from December 27, 1990.

(5) In para.(c) words in square brackets inserted by the Public Lending Right Scheme 1982 (Commencement of Variations) Order 2014 (SI 2014/1457), App.1, para.5, with effect from July 1, 2014.

Recording of receipt of application

15. The Registrar shall record the date upon which each application for first registration is received by him.

Completion of registration

16.—(1) When the Registrar is satisfied as to the eligibility of a book for registration and as to the persons entitled to Public Lending Right in respect of that book and, if more than one, of their respective shares therein, the registration shall be completed and, as regards a first registration of the Right, each registration shall be effective as from the day the application was recorded by the Registrar as having been received by him.

(2) On completion of a registration the Registrar shall issue to any person so entered in the Register as having an interest in the Public Lending Right in respect of the book to which the entry relates, an acknowledgment of registration in the form of a copy of the relevant entry, indicating therein the date from which the entry takes effect.

First Registration

Application for first registration

17.—(1) An application for first registration of Public Lending Right in respect of an eligible book—

(a) shall satisfy the requirements of Article 14 and be made by delivery at the registry;

(b) shall be made by an eligible author, and

[(c) where the book has two or more authors (including any who are not eligible persons), shall specify the proposed shares of each of them and for that purpose each of those authors who is alive at the date of application shall be a party to the application, unless

(i) the Registrar is satisfied that he cannot be traced, despite all reasonable steps having been taken to do so, or

(ii) the application is made by the translator or editor or compiler [or narrator or producer] of the book and he specifies that he is making the application only in his capacity as such [or]

[(iii) any author of the book who is not a party to the application is a translator and the application specifies that it relates only to that share of Public Lending Right in the book to which the translator is not entitled. [, or]]

[(iv) the application is made by an author of the book and he specifies that he is making the application otherwise than wholly or partly in the capacity of translator, editor, or compiler [or narrator or producer] of the book, and—

(aa) there is at the date of the application an effective agreement or arrangement between each person who is an author of the book (including any author who is not an eligible person or who does not wish to register);

(bb) each such person is a party to the agreement or arrangement otherwise than wholly or partly in the capacity as translator, editor or compiler [or narrator or producer] of the book; and

(cc) the agreement or arrangement relates to the apportionment of shares of Public Lending Right in the book or, where there is any eligible person who would be entitled to a share of the Right by virtue of being a translator, editor, or compiler [or narrator or producer], to the apportionment of shares in such proportion of the Right as would remain after taking account of any such entitlement.]]

(2) An application for first registration of an eligible author's share of Public Lending Right in respect of an eligible book with two or more authors (including any who are not eligible persons)—

(a) shall satisfy the requirements of Article 14 and be made by delivery at the registry, […]

(b) shall be made by the author concerned. [, and]

[(c) shall, when made by an author otherwise than wholly or partly in the capacity as translator, editor or compiler [or narrator or producer] of the book, satisfy the requirements of paragraph (1)(c)(iv).]

(3) Anything which falls to be done by an author under this Article shall, if he is not of full age, be done by his parent or guardian and that parent or guardian shall be recorded in the Register as the person to whom are payable sums in respect of any registered interest of the author until such time as a transfer of the registration into the author's own name has been recorded in pursuance of Article 25.

Notes:

(1) Paragraph 17(1)(c) was substituted by the Public Lending Right Scheme 1982 (Amendment) Order (SI 1984/1847) art.8 with effect from December 28, 1984.

(2) Paragraph 17(1)(c)(iii) was inserted by the Public Lending Right Scheme 1982 (Commencement of Variations) Order (SI 1988/2070) with effect from December 22, 1988.

(3) The words in brackets in para.17(2)(c) added by the Public Lending Right Scheme 1982 (Commencement of Variations) Order (SI 1989/2188) with effect from December 21, 1989.

(4) Paragraph 17(2)(c) was added by the Public Lending Right Scheme 1982 (Commencement of Variations) Order (SI 1989/2188) with effect from December 21, 1989.

(5) The words in brackets in para.17(2)(a) deleted by the Public Lending Right Scheme 1982 (Commencement of Variations) Order (SI 1989/2188) with effect from December 21, 1989.

(6) In paras (1)(c), (2)(c), words in square brackets inserted by the Public Lending Right Scheme 1982 (Commencement of Variations) Order 2014 (SI 2014/1457), App.1, para.6, with effect from July 1, 2014.

[Transitional provisions for translators, editors and compilers

17A.—(1) Where an application for first registration of Public Lending Right in respect of a book was made before 28th December 1984 and a translator, editor or compiler thereof would have been party to the said application if it had been made on or after that date he may, if he is an eligible person, make an application for the registered shares of the Right to be revised.

(2) Subject to the following paragraphs, the provisions of this Scheme shall apply to an application under paragraph (1) as though it were an application for first registration of Public Lending Right.

(3) Where a successful application is made under paragraph (1)—

(a) the applicant's share of the Public Lending Right shall be that prescribed in Article 9A(2) or (3) as the case may be, and

(b) the relevant shares of his co-authors, one to another, shall remain unaltered, unless all the authors who were party to the original application before 28th December 1984 are party to the application under paragraph (1) and specify an apportionment of their shares in a different manner and the Registrar is satisfied that such apportionment is reasonable.

(4) Where a successful application is made in accordance with paragraph (1) the Registrar shall amend the Register accordingly.]

Note: This paragraph was added by the Public Lending Right Scheme 1982 (Amendment) Order (SI 1984/1847) art.9 with effect December 28, 1984.

[Application for first registration in respect of posthumously eligible books

17B.—(1) An application for first registration of Public Lending Right in respect of a posthumously eligible book and an application for first registration of a posthumously eligible person's share of Public Lending Right in respect of such a book with two or more authors (including any who are not eligible persons)—

(a) shall satisfy the requirements of article 14A and be made by delivery at the registry, and

(b) shall be made by the personal representatives of the posthumously eligible person concerned.]

Note: This paragraph was added by the Public Lending Right Scheme 1982 (Commencement of Variations) Order (SI 1988/2070) App.1 para.11 with effect from December 22, 1988.

[Evidence required in connection with the applications

18. The Registrar may require the submission of evidence to satisfy him that—

(a) a book is an eligible book,

(b) a person applying as author for the first registration of Public Lending Right, or the registration of a share of the Right, is in fact the author of that book and is an eligible person, […]

(c) […] any co-author who is not a party to an application for first registration of Public Lending Right is dead or cannot be traced despite all reasonable steps having been taken to do so, [and]

[(d) where such an application as is mentioned in article 17(1)(c)(iv) has been made in accordance with paragraph (1) or (2) of that article—

(i) there is such an agreement or arrangement as is mentioned in article 17(1)(c)(iv), and

(ii) the share of Public Lending Right of the person making the application is as specified in that agreement or arrangement.]

and may for the purpose of obtaining any such evidence require a statutory declaration to be made by any person.]

Notes:

(1) This paragraph was substituted by the Public Lending Right Scheme 1982 (Amendment) Order (SI 1984/1847) art.10 with effect from December 28, 1984.

(2) The word in brackets in para.18(b) was repealed by the Public Lending Right Scheme 1982 (Commencement of Variations) Order (SI 1989/2188) App. with effect from December 21, 1989.

(3) The word in brackets in para.18(c) was repealed and the word "and" was inserted by the Public Lending Right Scheme 1982 (Commencement of Variations) Order (SI 1989/2188) App. with effect from December 21, 1989.

(4) Paragraph 18(d) was added by the Public Lending Right Scheme 1982 (Commencement of Variations) Order (SI 1989/2188) App. with effect from December 21, 1989.

Subsequent dealings with Public Lending Right

Public Lending Right to be transmissible

19. A registered interest shall be transmissible by assignment or assignation, by testamentary disposition or by operation of law, as personal or movable property, so long, as regards a particular book, as the Right in respect of that book is capable of subsisting.

Period during which the Right may be transferred

20. The duration of Public Lending Right in respect of any book and the period during which there may be dealings therein shall be from the date of the book's first publication (or, if later, the beginning of the sampling year in which application is made for it to be registered) until [seventy] years have elapsed since the end of the sampling year in which the author died or, if the book is registered as the work of more than one author, as regards dealings in the share of the Right attributable to that author, the end of the year in which that author died.

Note: The word in brackets was substituted by the Public Lending Right Scheme 1982 (Commencement of Variations) Order (SI 1997/1576) App. para.3 with effect from July 15, 1997.

Whole interest to be assigned

21.—(1) The disposition of Public Lending Right, after the first registration thereof, shall, as respects each registered interest in any book, be for the whole of that interest.

(2) On such disposition the interest may be registered in the name of joint owners, being not more than four in number and all being of full age, but in such case the senior only shall be deemed, for the purposes of the Scheme, to be the registered owner; seniority shall be determined by the order in which names stand in the Register.

(3) Subject to Articles 29 and 30, no notice of any trusts, expressed, implied or constructive, shall be entered on the Register or be receivable by the Registrar.

Applications for transfer

22. Every application for registration of a transfer of Public Lending Right shall satisfy the requirements of Article 14 and be made by delivery at the registry.

Stamp duty

23.—(1) An application for transfer shall bear the proper Inland Revenue stamp impressed thereon to show that all duty payable (if any) in respect of the transaction has been paid.

(2) Where an application for transfer is submitted for the purpose of giving effect to a transaction under a deed or other instrument on which the Inland Revenue stamp has already been impressed, such stamped instrument shall, before completion of the registration, be produced to the Registrar to show that all duty payable (if any) in respect of the transaction has been paid.

Proof of author's existence

24. It shall be a condition of registration of every transfer that the transferee provides, and gives an undertaking to the Registrar in future to provide at such intervals and in such form as the Registrar may require, evidence that the author is still alive, or, as the case may be, evidence of the author's death.

Registration by an author on attainment of full age

25. An author whose interest is, pursuant to Article 17(3), registered in the name of his parent or guardian may, on attaining full age, make application to the Registrar in accordance with Articles 21 to 23, so far as they are applicable, for the transfer of the registration of the Right into his own name, and until such transfer has been recorded the Registrar shall be entitled to remit any sums due in respect of the Right to such parent or guardian.

Transmission on death

Registration of personal representatives

26. On production of the probate, letters of administration, or confirmation of executors of a registered owner, the personal representatives named in such probate, letters or confirmation shall, on production of the same to the Registrar, be registered as owner in place of the deceased owner with the addition of the words "executor or executrix (or administrator or administratrix) of [name] deceased".

Transfer by personal representatives

27. The personal representatives registered under the preceding Article may transfer the interest of the deceased owner, such transfer being in accordance with Articles 21 to 24 or such provisions thereof as are applicable in the circumstances of the case.

Transfer on bankruptcy, liquidation or sequestration

Registration of Official Receiver, Official Assignees or Judicial Factor

28.—(1) On the production to the Registrar of an office copy of an Order of a Court having jurisdiction in bankruptcy adjudging a registered owner bankrupt or directing the estate of a deceased registered owner to be administered [in accordance with an order under section 421 of the Insolvency Act 1986] or section 21 of the Bankruptcy Amendment Act (Northern Ireland) 1929, together with a certificate signed by the Official Receiver or Official Assignee, as the case may be, that any registered interest in the name of the bankrupt registered owner, or deceased registered owner, is part of his property divisible amongst his creditors, the Official Receiver or the Official Assignee may be registered as the registered owner in place of the bankrupt or deceased registered owner.

(2) Where there is produced to the Registrar a certified copy of an Order of a Court having competent jurisdiction in Scotland awarding sequestration of the estate of a registered owner (including a deceased registered owner) and appointing a judicial factor the Registrar shall on receipt of such a copy enter in the Register the name of the judicial factor as registered owner with the addition of the words "judicial factor in the estate of [name]".

Note: The words in brackets in para.28(1) substituted by Insolvency (Amendment of Subordinate Legislation) Order (SI 1986/2001) Sch.1 para.1 with effect from December 29, 1986.

Registration of Trustee in Bankruptcy in place of Official Receiver, Assignees in Bankruptcy or Judicial Factor

29.—(1) Where the Official Receiver or the Official Assignee has been registered as registered owner and some other person is subsequently appointed trustee, or, in Northern Ireland, a creditor's assignee is appointed, the trustee or the assignee may be registered as registered owner in place of the Official Receiver, or the Official Assignee, on production of an office copy of the certificate by the Department of Trade of his appointment as trustee, or in Northern Ireland an office copy of the certificate under section 90 of the Bankruptcy (Ireland) Amendment Act 1872 or of the certificate of the vesting of the estate and effects of the registered owner in the assignee.

(2) Where a judicial factor has been registered as an owner in terms of Article 28(2) and some other person is subsequently elected as a trustee for behoof of the creditors of the former registered owner, the Registrar, on receipt of the notification of such election and of sufficient evidence to demonstrate that that person has been so elected, shall enter in the Register the name of the trustee as registered owner with the addition of the words "trustee in the estate of [name]".

(3) If the Official Receiver or the Official Assignee has not been entered on the Register under Article 28 (1) the trustee or the assignee may be registered as registered owner on production of office copies of the Order adjudging the registered owner bankrupt and the appropriate certificate referred to in paragraph (1) with a certificate signed by the trustee or the assignee that the registered interest is part of the property of the bankrupt divisible amongst his creditors.

(4) If a judicial factor has not been entered in the Register as owner under Article 28(2) the Registrar shall, on receipt of the certified copy of an Order of a Court under Article 28(2) together with the notification and evidence referred to in paragraph (2), enter in the Register as registered owner the name of the duly elected trustee with the addition of the words "trustee in the estate of [name]".

Registration of a trust under a Scheme of Arrangement or an Arrangement under the control of the Court

30.—(1) If any registered interest is vested in a trustee under the provisions of a Scheme of Arrangement approved by a Court having jurisdiction in bankruptcy, the Official Receiver or other trustee may be registered as owner in like manner as a trustee in bankruptcy upon production of an office copy of the Scheme of Arrangement, a certificate signed by the Official Receiver, or such other trustee, that the registered interest was part of the property vested in him under the provisions of the Scheme, and in the case of a trustee other than the Official Receiver, an office copy of the certificate by the Department of Trade of his appointment as trustee.

(2) If any registered interest of an arranging debtor who is a registered owner is vested in the Official Assignee alone or jointly with other persons under section 349 of the Irish Bankrupt and Insolvent Act 1857, the Official Assignee and such other persons (if any) may be registered as owner in his place on production of an office copy of the Order of the Court approving and confirming the resolution or agreement referred to in the said section with a certificate by the Official Assignee identifying the arranging debtor named in the Order of the Court with the registered owner endorsed thereon and a certificate signed by the Official Assignee and other such person (if any) that the registered interest was part of the property vested under the resolution or agreement.

(3) If, as regards Scotland, a registered owner—

(a)   has entered into a deed of arrangement for behoof of his creditors, the Registrar shall, on receiving a certified copy of the Order of the Court approving such arrangement, enter on the Register as owner the name of the person who is under the said deed of arrangement to receive any payments due to the owner (where that person is not the registered owner at the date of approval of the arrangement);

(b)   has entered into a private trust deed or composition contract for behoof of his creditors, the trustee under such deed or contract may make an application, accompanied by such evidence as the Registrar may require, for transmission of the registered interest into his name as such trustee; and on receipt of such an application the Registrar shall make the appropriate entry in the Register.

Liquidation of a company

31. In the liquidation of a company in which an interest in Public Lending Right is vested, any resolution or order appointing a liquidator may be filed and referred to on the Register, and, when so registered, shall be deemed to be in force until it is cancelled or superseded on the Register.

Renunciation

32.—(1) On making application in that behalf which satisfies the requirements of Article 14, the registered owner of a registered interest may absolutely and unconditionally renounce that interest as provided in paragraph (2).

(2) Such renunciation may, as to extent, be in respect of either the whole or a half share of the registered interest and may be effective for all time, or in respect of such financial years as shall be specified by the registered owner.

(3) An application for renunciation shall bear the proper Inland Revenue stamp impressed thereon.

(4) The Registrar shall as at the date from which the renunciation is to have effect amend the Register—

(a)   in the case of a renunciation for all time of the whole of the registered interest by removing from the Register the entry relating to the registered owner and, if that interest represents the whole of the Public Lending Right in a book, the entry relating to that book; or

(b)   in all other cases, by noting against the relevant entry in the Register the extent of the renunciation and the period during which it is effective.

(5) Immediately upon the amendment of the Register as provided in paragraph (4), any sum due by way of Public Lending Right which, apart from the renunciation would become payable to the registered owner by 31st March in any year falling within the period to which the renunciation applies, shall cease to be so payable.

General

Neglected applications for registration

33. Where in the case of any application for first or any subsequent registration an applicant has failed to provide within three months information requested by the Registrar, notice may be given to the applicant that the application will be treated as abandoned unless the information is duly furnished within a time (not being less than one month) determined by the Registrar and specified in the notice; and if, at the expiration of that time, the information so requested is not furnished, the application may be treated as abandoned.

Removal of entries from the Register

34. Where the Registrar, pursuant to section 4(5) of the Act, directs the removal from the Register of any entry relating to a book in whose case no sum has become due by way of Public Lending Right for a period of at least ten years, any subsequent application for the entry to be restored to the Register may be made only by the person who, at the date of the removal of the entry, was the registered owner, or by his legal personal representatives.

Copies of entries in the Register

35.—(1) The Registrar shall not supply a copy of any entry in the Register otherwise than to—

(a) a registered owner, as regards any entry which relates to his registered interest; or

(b) such other person as the registered owner may direct, but if the entry in question also relates to other registered owners, only with the consent of all such owners.

(2) The Registrar may require a payment of a fee for supplying a copy of an entry in the Register, not exceeding £5 in respect of each such entry.

PART IV

ASCERTAINMENT OF THE NUMBER OF LOANS OF BOOKS

Special definitions

36. In this Part, unless the context otherwise requires—

"copy" means an individual copy of a particular book, and "copy number" means a number which distinguishes the copy to which it is applied from other copies of the same book in the same library;

"group", in relation to service points, means a group specified in Schedule 2;

["library" has the meaning assigned to it by section 3(4) of the Act;]

"loans" means loans whereby books are lent out from a service point to individual borrowers, and includes loans of books not normally held at that service point;

["mobile library service point" means a service point which is taken about from place to place;]

"month" means one of the twelve months in the calendar year;

"operative sampling point" means a sampling point at which loans are for the time being required to be recorded in pursuance of Article 40(1);

"ordinary service point" means a service point from which fewer than 500,000 loans were made during the preceding period of twelve months;

"participating period", in relation to a sampling point, means the period commencing on the date on which the local library authority having responsibility for it receives from the Registrar notice of designation pursuant to [Article 38(5)] and ending on the date specified in a notice given thereunder as the date upon which it is to cease to act as a sampling point;

"principal service point", in relation to a library authority, means any of the following—

(a) whichever of the service points for which that authority is responsible is the service point from which the greatest number of loans were made during the preceding period of twelve months;

(b) any service point for which that authority is responsible, the number of loans from which during the preceding period of twelve months was not less than three-quarters of the number of loans made from the service point referred to in [.   .] paragraph (a) during the same period;

(c) any other such service point from which 500,000 or more, loans were made during the aforesaid period;

and "principal service points" means every service point which is a principal service point in relation to any library authority;

["sampling point" means any principal service point, ordinary service point or mobile library service point [, or any number of such points in relation to any local library authority,] which has been designated, for the time being, by the Registrar under article 38;]

"sampling year" means the period of twelve months ending on 30th June;

"service point" means a place from which books comprised in a library are lent out to the public at large.

Notes:

(1) The definition of "library" was added by the Public Lending Right Scheme 1982 (Commencement of Variations) Order (SI 1988/2070) App.1 para.12(a) with effect from December 22, 1988.

(2) The definition of "mobile library service point" was added by the Public Lending Right Scheme 1982 (Commencement of Variations) Order (SI 1988/2070) App.1 para.12(b) with effect from December 22, 1988.

(3) The words in brackets in the definition of "participating period" substituted by the Public Lending Right Scheme 1982 (Commencement of Variations) Order (SI 1997/1576) App. para.4 with effect from July 15, 1997.

(4) The words in brackets in para.36(b) repealed by the Public Lending Right Scheme 1982 (Commencement of Variations) Order (SI 1990/2360) App.1 para.1 with effect from December 27, 1990.

(5) The definition of "sampling point" was substituted by the Public Lending Right Scheme 1982 (Commencement of Variations) Order (SI 1988/2070) App.1 para.12(c) with effect from December 22, 1988.

(6) The words in brackets in the definition of "sampling point" inserted by the Public Lending Right Scheme 1982 (Commencement of Variations) Order (SI 1990/2360) App.1 para.3 with effect from December 27, 1990.

Number of loans to be ascertained by means of a sample

37. The number of occasions on which a book is lent out shall be determined by means of a sample of the lendings of that book from particular service points, designated in accordance with the provisions of this Part; and for the purpose of the sample, service points shall be classified into the groups, according to local library authority areas, specified in Schedule 2.

Designation of sampling points

38.—[(1) Such local library authorities as the Registrar may require shall, not later than 30th September in each year, furnish to the Registrar lists, as at 31st March of that year, of all their principal, ordinary and mobile service points. The Registrar shall, not later than 31st December of that year, designate in accordance with paragraph (5) those service points which are to be operative sampling points or which are to be included in operative sampling points as from the beginning of the ensuing sampling year.]

[(1A) The Registrar may, at any time after he has designated a sampling point in accordance with paragraph (1), discontinue the designation of that point and designate a new sampling point, such discontinuance and new point to take effect from 1st January in the ensuing sampling year. Notice of discontinuance and designation pursuant to this paragraph shall be given in accordance with paragraph (5).]

[(2) The Registrar shall so exercise his powers under this article as to secure, subject to paragraph (4), that—

(a) at all times there shall be [not less than] 30 operative sampling points comprising—

    [(i) 5 points falling within not less than 3 local library authority areas in Group A and 5 points falling within not less than 4 local library authority areas in Group D in Schedule 2,]

    (ii) 4 points falling within [not less than 3 local library authority areas in] each of Groups B, C and E in Schedule 2,

    (iii) 3 points falling within [not less than 3 local library authority areas in] each of Groups F and G in Schedule 2, and

    (iv) 2 points falling within [not less than 2 local library authority areas in] Group H in Schedule 2;

(b) at all times the operative sampling points falling within each Group in Schedule 2 shall include, subject to paragraph (3), a principal service point and an ordinary service point;

[(c) at all times one of the 3 operative sampling points falling within Group F in Schedule 2 shall be within one of the following principal areas: Carmarthenshire, Pembrokeshire, Ceredigion, Isle of Anglesey, Gwynedd, Conwy, Denbighshire or Powys;]

(d) at all times one of the 3 operative sampling points falling within Group G in Schedule 2 shall be outside the [Cities] of Edinburgh and Glasgow;

[(e) no operative sampling point shall consist only of a mobile library service point other than an operative sampling point falling within [a principal area specified in sub-paragraph (c) above];]

(f) [during] each sampling year at least [7] operative sampling points shall be replaced by new such points; and

[(g) no operative sampling point shall remain as such for a continuous period of more than 4 years [, unless it is in Group H in Schedule 2].]]

(3) The relevant local library authority shall notify the Registrar of any change in the categorisation of a sampling point [which consists of a single principal, ordinary or mobile] service point but the Registrar shall not be required by paragraph (2)(a) to discontinue the designation of the point as a sampling point before the expiry of the sampling year in which he receives such notice or, if that year has less than six months to run, before the expiry of the next following sampling year. For the purposes of this paragraph and of paragraph (2)(a), a change in the categorisation of a sampling point shall be disregarded if it is occasioned by an increase or decrease of less than 10% in the number of loans made therefrom.

(4) The local library authority shall notify the Registrar of any decision to close [a service point which is or is included in] a sampling point and the date on which the closure takes effect but, if it is not reasonably practicable for the Registrar to satisfy the requirements of paragraph (2) before the closure takes effect, those requirements shall be treated as satisfied if satisfied as soon as is reasonably practicable thereafter.

(5) [...]

[(5) The Registrar shall give to the local library authority responsible for a sampling point—

[(a) for the purposes of designating that point under paragraphs (1) or (1A), notice in writing of such designation specifying the period ending on 31st December or 30th June, in any sampling year for which he intends the point to be an operative sampling point;]

(b) for the purpose of discontinuing that point as a sampling point, not less than six months notice in writing of such discontinuance.]

Notes:

(1) Paragraph 38(1) was substituted by the Public Lending Right Scheme 1982 (Commencement of Variations) Order (SI 1990/2360) App.1 para.4(a) with effect from December 27, 1990.

(2) Paragraph 38(1A) was added by the Public Lending Right Scheme 1982 (Commencement of Variations) Order (SI 1990/2360) App.1 para.4(b) with effect from December 27, 1990.

(3) Paragraph 38(2) was substituted by the Public Lending Right Scheme 1982 (Commencement of Variations) Order 1988/2070 App.1 para.13(b) (December 22, 1988).

(4) The words in brackets in para.38(2)(a) inserted by the Public Lending Right Scheme 1982 (Commencement of Variations) Order (SI 1990/2360) App.1 para.4(c)(i) with effect from December 27, 1990.

(5) Paragraph 28(2)(a)(i) was substituted by the Public Lending Right Scheme 1982 (Commencement of Variations) Order (SI 1990/2360) App.1 para.4(c)(ii) with effect from December 27, 1990.

(6) The words in brackets in para.38(2)(a)(ii) inserted by the Public Lending Right Scheme 1982 (Commencement of Variations) Order (SI 1990/2360) App.1 para.4(c)(iii) with effect from December 27, 1990.

(7) The words in brackets in para.(2)(a)(iii) inserted by the Public Lending Right Scheme 1982 (Commencement of Variations) Order (SI 1990/2360) App.1 para.4(c)(iv) with effect from December 27, 1990.

(8) The words in brackets in para.38(2)(a)(iv) inserted by the Public Lending Right Scheme 1982 (Commencement of Variations) Order (SI 1990/2360) App.1 para.4(c)(v) with effect from December 27, 1990.

(9) Paragraph 38(2)(c) was substituted by the Public Lending Right Scheme 1982 (Commencement of Variations) Order (SI 1996/1338) App. para.1(a) with effect from June 14, 1996.

(10) The word in brackets in para.38(2)(d) was substituted by the Public Lending Right Scheme 1982 (Commencement of Variations) Order 1996/1338 App. para.1(b) (June 14, 1996)

(11) Paragraph 38(2)(e) was substituted by the Public Lending Right Scheme 1982 (Commencement of Variations) Order 1990/2360 App.1 para.4(c)(vi) (December 27, 1990)

(12) The words in brackets in para.38(2)(e) substituted by the Public Lending Right Scheme 1982 (Commencement of Variations) Order 1996/1338 App. para.1(c) (June 14, 1996)

(13) The word in brackets in para.38(2)(f) was substituted by the Public Lending Right Scheme 1982 (Commencement of Variations) Order (SI 1990/2360) App.1 para.4(c)(vii) with effect from December 27, 1990.

(14) The figure in brackets in para.38(2)(f) was substituted by the Public Lending Right Scheme 1982 (Commencement of Variations) Order (SI 2005/1519) App. Part 1 para.1(a) with effect from July 1, 2005.

(15) Paragraph 38(2)(g) was substituted by the Public Lending Right Scheme 1982 (Commencement of Variations) Order (SI 1990/2360) App.1 para.4(c)(viii) with effect from December 27, 1990.

(16) The words in brackets in para.28(2)(g) inserted by the Public Lending Right Scheme 1982 (Commencement of Variations) Order (SI 2005/1519) App. Part 1 para.1(b) with effect from July 1, 2005.

(17) The words in brackets in para.38(3) substituted by the Public Lending Right Scheme 1982 (Commencement of Variations) Order (SI 1990/2360) App.1 para.4(d) with effect from December 27, 1990.

(18) The words in brackets in para.38(4) inserted by the Public Lending Right Scheme 1982 (Commencement of Variations) Order (SI 1990/2360) App.1 para.4(e) with effect from December 27, 1990.

(19) The existing para.38(5) was repealed and existing para.38(6) was renumbered as para.38(5) by the Public Lending Right Scheme 1982 (Commencement of Variations) Order (SI 1990/2360) App.1 para.4(f) with effect from December 27, 1990).

(20) The existing text of para.38(6) was renumbered as para.38(5) and figure substituted by the Public Lending Right Scheme 1982 (Commencement of Variations) Order (SI 1990/2360) App.1 para.4(g)(i) with effect from December 27, 1990.

(21) Paragraph 38(5)(a) was substituted by the Public Lending Right Scheme 1982 (Commencement of Variations) Order (SI 1990/2360) App.1 para.4(g)(ii) with effect from December 27, 1990.

Provision by libraries of recording facilities

39. Upon receipt of a notice under [Article 38(5)(a)] a local library authority shall—

(a) arrange for every book which may be lent out from the sampling point to which the designation refers [to be separately identified], in such form as the Registrar may require, with its identifying number and (where more than one copy may be lent out) copy number, and shall notify the Registrar at such time and in such manner as he may direct of the number of books [so identified]; and

(b) acquire, in accordance with arrangements approved by the Registrar, such equipment (including computer programs) as may be necessary to enable the authority to comply with the provision of Article 40 regarding the furnishing of information to the Registrar.

Notes:

(1) The words in brackets substituted by the Public Lending Right Scheme 1982 (Commencement of Variations) Order (SI 1996/1338) App. para.2 with effect from June 14, 1996.

(2) In para.(a) words in square brackets substituted for words "to be marked" and "so marked" respectively, by the Public Lending Right Scheme 1982 (Commencement of Variations) Order 2014 (SI 2014/1457), App.1, para.7, with effect from July 1, 2014.

Duty to record lendings

40.—(1) A local library authority which has received a notice under [Article 38(5)(a)] shall, for such period as is specified in the notice, record every occasion on which a copy of a book is lent out to the public from the sampling point to which the notice refers and shall furnish to the Registrar, in such form and at such intervals as he may direct, details of such lendings, including the identifying number and any copy number of the copy in question.

(2) For the purpose of this Article each volume of a work published in two or more volumes shall be treated as a separate book.

Note: The words in brackets in para.40(1) substituted by the Public Lending Right Scheme 1982 (Commencement of Variations) Order (SI 1996/1338) App. para.3 with effect from June 14, 1996.

Provision of book loan data

41. Each local library authority shall submit to the Registrar, in such form, at such intervals and in respect of such periods as he may direct, a return of the total number of occasions on which the books comprised in all its collections were the subject of loans.

Method of determining the number of notional loans

42.—(1) The Registrar shall, from the details of loans furnished to him by local library authorities pursuant to the provisions of this Part (upon the accuracy of which the Registrar shall be entitled to rely), calculate, in accordance with paragraph (2), the number of notional loans of each book in respect of which Public Lending Right subsists in each sampling year.

(2) The number of notional loans of each book made during a sampling year shall be the aggregate of the number of notional loans of that book made in all groups; and the number of notional loans for a group shall be determined in accordance with the following formula:—

Total notional loans in the group = $A/B \times C$

Where—

  A represents the number of loans of that book recorded during the sampling year at the operative sampling points in that group;

  B represents the total number of loans of books made to the public during the sampling year from the operative sampling points in that group; and

  C represents the aggregate of the loans of all books made to the public from all libraries (within the meaning of section 3(4) of the Act) in the area of the group during the financial year ending in the sampling year in question, or, as regards any particular library for which loan data relating to that financial year is not available to the Registrar, the most recent financial year for which he has such data.

[(3) For the purposes of paragraph (2)

  (a) Groups A, B and C in Schedule 2 shall be treated as one group; [...]

  (b) if on any occasion on which any details of lendings at a particular sampling point [which consists of a single service point are] furnished to the Registrar in accordance with article 40 [and] record loans of a copy of a book in excess of an average of one loan for each period of five days covered by the details, the loans in excess of that average shall be disregarded.

    [; and

  [(c) the Registrar may disregard any loan of a book reported from a sampling point in accordance with Article 40 where the local library authority does not specify an International Standard Book Number in respect of the book.]]]

Notes:

  (1) Paragraph 42(3) was substituted by the Public Lending Right Scheme 1982 (Commencement of Variations) Order (SI 1988/2070) App.1 para.14 with effect from December 22, 1988.

  (2) The word in brackets in para.42(3)(a) was repealed by the Public Lending Right Scheme 1982 (Commencement of Variations) Order (SI 1990/2360) App.1 para.5(a) with effect from December 27, 1990.

(3) The words in brackets in para.42(3)(b) inserted by the Public Lending Right Scheme 1982 (Commencement of Variations) Order (SI 1990/2360) App.1 para.5(b)(i) with effect from December 27, 1990.

(4) Paragraph 42(3)(c) was inserted by the Public Lending Right Scheme 1982 (Commencement of Variations) Order (SI 1990/2360) App.1 para.5(c) with effect from December 27, 1990.

(5) Paragraph 42(3)(c) was substituted by the Public Lending Right Scheme 1982 (Commencement of Variations) Order (SI 1999/420) App. para.2 with effect from July 1, 1999.

Reimbursement of local library authorities

43.—(1) The Registrar shall, subject to the provisions of this Article and Article 44, reimburse to local library authorities the net expenditure incurred by them in giving effect to this Scheme.

(2) It shall be the duty of local library authorities to keep proper accounts and records in respect of the expenditure (including overhead expenses) incurred by them in giving effect to this Scheme and the Registrar may withhold payment to a local library authority, in whole or in part, until such time as such authority has furnished to him sufficient evidence as to the amount of the expenditure so incurred.

Expense incurred in respect of sampling points

44.—(1) Without prejudice to the generality of Article 43(2) each local library authority to which a notice has been given under [Article 38(5)(a)] shall submit to the Registrar at such time and in such form as he may require estimates of the net expenditure to be incurred in giving effect to this Scheme at the sampling point or points specified in such notice.

(2) Such local library authority may from time to time during the participating period submit to the Registrar claims in respect of the expenditure incurred, or estimated to have been incurred by it, and the Registrar shall be entitled to rely upon the accuracy of such claims and to make payments on account of the expenditure incurred by that authority in giving effect to the Scheme.

(3) The total amount payable by way of reimbursement to such local library authority shall be finally determined by the Registrar after examination of such audited financial statements and such books, records, documents, and accounts relating thereto as he may require; and any balance found after such final determination to be due by or to the Registrar in account with the local library authority in question shall be paid to or recovered from such local library authority.

(4) In reckoning the net expenditure for the purposes of this Article and of Article 43, the following shall be deducted from the gross expenditure incurred by a local library authority in connection with a sampling point—

(a) any sum received in connection with the disposal (by sale, lease or otherwise) of any property or equipment purchased pursuant to [paragraph (b) of Article 39];

(b) any sum which it might reasonably be expected would have been received on such a disposal (whether or not there has been a disposal of the property or equipment in question);

(c) any insurance monies received in respect of the loss or destruction of or damage to any such property or equipment;

(d) an amount representing the appropriate proportion of the net cost (whether by way of purchase, lease, or otherwise) of any property or equipment which is used by a local library authority partly in connection with this Scheme and partly for other purposes not connected therewith:

> Provided that where deductions are made under both sub-paragraphs (a) and (b) in respect of the same property or equipment, the aggregate deductions thereunder shall not exceed whichever is the greater of the sums mentioned in those sub-paragraphs.

(5) In determining the amount finally to be paid to or recovered from a local library authority pursuant to paragraph (3), account shall be taken of any expenditure reasonably incurred by that authority in discontinuing the sampling point.

Notes:

(1) The words in brackets in para.44(1) substituted by the Public Lending Right

Scheme 1982 (Commencement of Variations) Order (SI 1997/1576) App. para.5 with effect from July 15, 1997.

(2) The words in para.44(2)(a) repealed by the Public Lending Right Scheme 1982 (Commencement of Variations) Order (SI 1990/2360) App.1 para.1 with effect from December 27, 1990.

45. [...]

Note: This paragraph was revoked by the Public Lending Right Scheme 1982 (Amendment) Order (SI 1984/1847) Sch.1 with effect from December 28, 1984.

PART V

CALCULATION AND PAYMENT OF PUBLIC LENDING RIGHT

Determination of the sum due in respect of Public Lending Right

46.—(1) For any financial year, the sum due by way of Public Lending Right in respect of a registered interest to the registered owner thereof shall be ascertained by reference to—

(a) the product of the number of notional loans attributable to that interest (calculated in accordance with paragraph (4)) and [7.67p], and

(b) the aggregate amount of that product and the like products in the case of all other registered interests which initially were registered interests of the same author [or were interests registered by the personal representatives of the same author].

(2) Subject to paragraph (3) the sum so due for the financial year shall be—

(a) except where the following sub-paragraph applies, the product mentioned in paragraph (1)(a);

(b) if the aggregate amount mentioned in paragraph (1)(b) exceeds [£6,600], the product of [**x/y and £6,600**

where—

x is the number of notional loans attributable to the interest in question, and y is the aggregate of that number and the number of notional loans attributable to all other registered interests which initially were registered interests of the same author or were interests registered by the personal representatives of the same author.]

[(3) If the aggregate of the amounts determined in accordance with paragraph (2) in respect of each registered interest of the registered owner thereof is less than [£1], the sum due in respect of the registered interest shall be nil.]

(4) For the purposes of paragraphs (1) and (2) (b), the number of notional loans attributable to any registered interest in any financial year shall be calculated by ascertaining, in accordance with Article 42(2), the number of notional loans of the book to which it relates which were made during the sampling year ending in that financial year, and shall be—

(a) if the registered interest represents the whole of the Public Lending Right in respect of that book, the total notional loans of the book in question;

(b) if the registered interest relates only to a share of the Public Lending Right in respect of that book, such proportion of the total notional loans of the book as the registered interest bears to the whole of the Public Lending Right in that book, fractions of a loan being disregarded;

(c) if the Right in respect of that registered interest has been renounced in part, such proportion of the notional loans attributable to the registered interest under sub-paragraph (a) or (b), as the case may be, which the unrenounced share bears to the whole of the registered interest, fractions of a loan being disregarded;

(d) nil, if the Right in respect of the registered interest has been wholly renounced for the financial year in question.

(5) For the purposes of paragraphs (1) and (2)(b), the references to interests which were initially registered interests of the same author include interests which, in pursuance of Article 17(3), were registered in the name of his parent or guardian.

Notes:

(1) The figure in square brackets in para.46(1)(a) was substituted by the Public Lending Right Scheme 1982 (Commencement of Variation) Order 2016 (SI 2016/15),

art.2, with effect from February 5, 2016 (figure previously "6.66p" as substituted by SI 2015/7 with effect from February 3, 2015).

(2) The words in brackets in para.46(1)(b) inserted by the Public Lending Right Scheme 1982 (Commencement of Variations) Order (SI 1989/2188) App. with effect from December 21, 1989.

(3) The figure in brackets in para.46(2)(b) was substituted by the Public Lending Right Scheme 1982 (Commencement of Variations) Order (SI 2005/1519) App. Part 2 para.2 with effect from September 1, 2006.

(4) Paragraph 46(3) was substituted by the Public Lending Right Scheme 1982 (Commencement of Variations) Order (SI 1988/2070) App.1 para.15(c) with effect from December 22, 1988.

(5) The figure in brackets in para.46(3) was substituted by the Public Lending Right Scheme 1982 (Commencement of Variations) Order (SI 2005/1519) App. Part 2 para.3 with effect from September 1, 2006.

Persons to whom the payment is due

47. The person entitled to the Public Lending Right in respect of any registered book in any financial year shall be the registered owner thereof as at 30th June of that year.

Right to be claimed

48.—(1) No payment shall be made in respect of Public Lending Right unless that Right has been claimed by or on behalf of the person for the time being entitled.

(2) A claim in respect of the Right may be made for—

(a) a specified period;

(b) an unspecified period determinable by not less than three months written notice of termination given to the Registrar by or on behalf of the person for the time being entitled to the Right.

(3) A claim shall automatically lapse in the event of any change of ownership recorded on the Register, subsequent to first registration thereof, in respect of the Right to which the claim relates.

Notification of entitlement and payment of sums due under the Scheme

49.—(1) Any sum payable by way of Public Lending Right in respect of a registered interest, for any financial year, shall (unless sooner paid) fall due for payment on the last day of that year.

(2) Any such sum may be paid by cheque or warrant sent through the post directed to the registered address of the registered owner or, in the case of joint owners, to the registered address of the senior owner (as defined in Article 21(2)), or to such person and to such address as the owner or joint owners may direct by a written payment mandate to the Registrar, delivered at the registry, in the form set out in Schedule 4 or a form to the like effect; every such cheque or warrant shall be made payable to the order of the person to whom it is sent and any one of two or more joint owners may give a good receipt for any money due to them under this Scheme.

(3) The Registrar shall at the end of each financial year, or as soon as is reasonably practicable thereafter, inform each registered owner [to whom a sum is payable by way of Public Lending Right in respect of that year], by notice posted to his registered address of—

(a) the notional number of lendings for that year of each book in respect of which he is a registered owner; and

(b) the amount of such sum.]

(4) If, after the Registrar has notified the registered owner as provided in paragraph (3), the cheque or warrant for the sum referred to therein is not presented for payment and thereby lapses—

(a) there shall be no further duty on the part of the Registrar to take steps to trace the registered owner and it shall be the responsibility of such owner to make application to the Registrar for payment; and

(b) if at the end of six years from the date upon which a payment in respect of Public Lending Right becomes due no such application has beenmade by the person entitled thereto, the entitlement to such payment shall lapse.

[(5) At the request of a registered owner to whom no notice is required to be given under paragraph (3) in respect of any financial year, the Registrar shall supply to him particulars (calculated in accordance with article 42) of the number of notional loans during the sampling year ending in that financial year of any book in respect of which he is the registered owner, provided the request is made no later than six months after the end of that financial year.]

Notes:

(1) The words in brackets in para.49(3) inserted by the Public Lending Right Scheme 1982 (Commencement of Variations) Order (SI 1990/2360) App.1 para.7(a)(i) with effect from December 27, 1990.

(2) Paragraph 49(3)(b) Substituted by the Public Lending Right Scheme 1982 (Commencement of Variations) Order (SI 1990/2360) App.1 para.7(a)(ii) with effect from December 27, 1990.

(3) Paragraph 49(5) was added by the Public Lending Right Scheme 1982 (Commencement of Variations) Order (SI 1990/2360) App.1 para.7(b) with effect from December 27, 1990.

Power to call for information

50. The Registrar may at any time require a statutory declaration or other sufficient evidence that an author or any registered owner is alive and is the person to whom money is payable under this Scheme, and may withhold payment until such declaration or evidence as he may require is produced.

Interest

51. No sum determined to be due under this Scheme shall carry interest.

52. […]

Note: This paragraph was revoked by the Public Lending Right Scheme 1982 (Amendment) Order (SI 1984/1847) Sch.1 with effect from December 28, 1984.

Article 14   SCHEDULE 1

INFORMATION TO BE PROVIDED IN CONNECTION WITH APPLICATIONS

PART I

APPLICATION FOR FIRST REGISTRATION

Each application shall provide the Registrar, in such form as he may from time to time require, with the following—

1. The title of the book to which the application relates.

[2. The name of every author (within the meaning of article 4) and the evidence on which each author relies for the purpose of being treated as an author in accordance with article 4(2).]

Note: This paragraph was substituted by the Public Lending Right Scheme 1982 (Commencement of Variations) Order (SI 1991/2618) App. para.4 with effect from December 18, 1991.

3. The true identity (if different from 2 above) of each such person, and his address.

4. The International Standard Book Number (if any) of the book.

[5. A statement signed by each applicant that in each case the conditions as to eligibility specified in Part II of the Scheme are satisfied at the date of application, accompanied, when the applicant has not previously made an application under Article 17 of this Scheme, by a certificate signed by a Member of Parliament, [a member of the Scottish Parliament,] Justice of the Peace, Minister of Religion, lawyer, bank officer, school teacher, police officer, [registered medical practitioner, who need not hold a licence to practise,] or other person accepted by the Registrar as being of similar standing and stating that he has known the appli6ant for at least two years, that he is not related to the applicant and that to the best of his knowledge the contents of the statement by the applicant are true.]

Notes:

(1) Paragraphs 5, 6 and 7 substituted for paras 5, 6, 7 and 8 by the Public Lending Right Scheme 1982 (Amendment) Order (SI 1984/1847) art.14 with effect from December 28, 1984.

(2) The words "a member of the Scottish Parliament," inserted by Scotland Act 1998 (Consequential Modifications) (No.1) Order (SI 1999/1042) Sch.1(II) para.19 with effect from May 6, 1999.

(3) The words "registered medical practitioner, who need not hold a licence to practise," substituted by Medical Act 1983 (Amendment) Order (SI 2002/3135) Sch.1(II) para.23 with effect from November 16, 2009 as specified on pp.14478 and 14479 of the *London Gazette* dated August 21, 2009.

[6. In the case of a work by more than one author—

(a) a statement signed by all the authors who are alive and can be traced at the date of application specifying—

    (i) the agreed share in the Public Lending Right of each author, and

    (ii) whether any author is translator, editor, compiler or, if any author is dead or untraced at the date of application, illustrator of the book and, if so, whether he is also an author of the book in another capacity, or

(b) a statement by the applicant that he is translator, editor or compiler of the book and that his claim to the Public Lending Right in respect thereof is limited to the percentage prescribed in Article 9A(2) or (3) as the case may be [or]

[(c) where one of the authors of the work is a translator, a statement signed by the other author or, if more than one, all the other authors who are alive and can be traced at the date of application specifying—

    (i) that another author of the book who is not a party to the application is a translator,

    (ii) that the claim to Public Lending Right in respect thereof is limited to that share to which the translator is not entitled, and

    (iii) where there is more than one author other than the translator

        (aa) the agreed share of each such author in that share of the Public Lending Right to which the translator is not entitled, and

        (bb) whether any such author is editor or compiler or, if any such author is dead or untraced at the date of application, illustrator of the book and, if so, whether he is also an author of the book in another capacity [or]]

[(d) where such an application as is mentioned in paragraph (1)(c)(iv) of article 17 is made in accordance with paragraph (1) or (2) of that article, a statement specifying the names of all the other persons whether or not party to such agreement or arrangement as is mentioned in paragraph (1)(c)(iv) of article 17, who are eligible for a share of Public Lending Right in respect of the book.]]

Notes:

(1) Paragraphs 5, 6 and 7 substituted for paras 5, 6, 7 and 8 by the Public Lending Right Scheme 1982 (Amendment) Order (SI 1984/1847) art.14 with effect from December 28, 1984.

(2) The word in brackets in para.6(b) and para.6(c) was inserted by the Public Lending Right Scheme 1982 (Commencement of Variations) Order (SI 1988/2070) App.1 para.16 with effect from December 22, 1988.

(3) The word in brackets in para.6(c)(iii)(bb) was inserted by the Public Lending Right Scheme 1982 (Commencement of Variations) Order (SI 1989/2188) App.001 with effect from December 21, 1989.

(4) Paragraph 6(d) was added by the Public Lending Right Scheme 1982 (Commencement of Variations) Order (SI 1989/2188) App. with effect from December 21, 1989.

[7. Where an editor or compiler of a book wishes to claim, or claim an equal share of, more than twenty per cent of the Public Lending Right in accordance with Article 9A(3), particulars indicating evidence of the percentage that he has, or where there are two or more editors or compilers that they have jointly, contributed to the contents of the book.]

Note: Paragraphs 5, 6 and 7 substituted for paras 5, 6, 7 and 8 by the Public Lending Right Scheme 1982 (Amendment) Order (SI 1984/1847) art.14 with effect from December 28, 1984.

[8. In the case of an author not of full age, a declaration by the applicant that he is the parent or guardian, as the case may be, of the author, and a copy of the author's birth certificate.]

Note: Paragraphs 5, 6 and 7 substituted for paras 5, 6, 7 and 8 by the Public Lending Right Scheme 1982 (Amendment) Order (SI 1984/1847) art.14 with effect from December 28, 1984.

PART II

APPLICATION FOR TRANSFER OF REGISTERED INTEREST

Each application shall provide the Registrar, in such form as he may from time to time require, with the following—

1. The title of the book.

2. The International Standard Book Number (if any) of the book.

3. The name and address of the transferor.

4. The name and address of the transferee.

5. An undertaking by the transferee to furnish to the Registrar, whenever so required, proof that the author is still alive.

PART III

APPLICATION FOR RENUNCIATION OF REGISTERED INTEREST

Each application shall provide the Registrar, in such form as he may from time to time require, with the following—

1. The name and address of the person renouncing.

2. The title of the book to which the renunciation relates.

3. The International Standard Book Number (if any) of the book.

4. The extent of the Right being renounced.

5. The period in respect of which the Right is renounced.

Articles 36–38   [SCHEDULE 2

GROUPING SERVICE POINTS]

[Service points shall be grouped according to local library authority areas as follows—

GROUP A

[Bedfordshire	Kent	Slough
Bracknell Forest	Luton	Southend
Brighton and Hove	Milton Keynes	Thurrock
Buckinghamshire	Newbury	Suffolk
Cambridgeshire	Norfolk	Surrey
East Sussex	Northamptonshire	West Sussex
Essex	Oxfordshire	Windsor and Maidenhead
Hertfordshire	Peterborough	Wokingham
Medway Council	Reading	

GROUP B

Bath and North East Somerest	Gloucestershire	Somerset
Bournemouth	Hampshire	South Gloucestershire
City of Bristol	Herefordshire	Staffordshire
City of Portsmouth	The Isle of Wight	Swindon
City of Southampton	The Isles of Scilly	Torbay
City Stoke-on-Trent	North Somerset	Warwickshire
Cornwall	Plymouth	Wiltshire
Devon	Poole	Worcestershire
Dorset	Shropshire	The Wrekin

GROUP C

Blackburn	East Riding of Yorkshire	North Lincolnshire
Blackpool	Halton	Northumberland
Cheshire	Hartlepool	North Yorkshire

City of Derby	Lancashire	Nottinghamshire
City of Kingston upon Hull	Leicestershire	Redcar and Cleveland
City of Leicester	Lincolnshire	Rutland
Cumbria	Nottingham	Stockon-on-Tees
Darlington	Middlesbrough	Warrington
Derbyshire	North East Lincolnshire	York
Durham		

GROUP D
Those within the areas of the metropolitan districts of England.
GROUP E
Those within the areas of Greater London.
GROUP F
Those in Wales.
GROUP G
Those in Scotland.
GROUP H
Those in Northern Ireland.]]

Notes:

(1) This Schedule was substituted by the Public Lending Right Scheme 1982 (Commencement of Variations) Order (SI 1988/2070) App.1 para.17 with effect from December 22, 1988.

(2) The words of this Schedule substituted by the Public Lending Right Scheme 1982 (Commencement of Variations) Order (SI 1998/1218) App. para.1 with effect from June 6, 1998.

Articles 45 and 52   SCHEDULE 3

TRANSITORY PROVISIONS

PART I

ESTABLISHMENT OF INITIAL SAMPLE

1. […]

Note: This paragraph was revoked by the Public Lending Right Scheme 1982 (Amendment) Order (SI 1984/1847) Sch.1 with effect from December 28, 1984.

2. […]

Note: This paragraph was revoked by the Public Lending Right Scheme 1982 (Amendment) Order (SI 1984/1847) Sch.1 with effect from December 28, 1984.

3. […]

Note: This paragraph was revoked by the Public Lending Right Scheme 1982 (Amendment) Order (SI 1984/1847) Sch.1 with effect from December 28, 1984.

PART II

INITIAL PAYMENT TO AUTHORS

1. […]

Note: This paragraph was revoked by the Public Lending Right Scheme 1982 (Amendment) Order (SI 1984/1847) Sch.1 with effect from December 28, 1984.

2. […]

Note: This paragraph was revoked by the Public Lending Right Scheme 1982 (Amendment) Order (SI 1984/1847) Sch.1 with effect from December 28, 1984.

Article 49   SCHEDULE 4

PAYMENT MANDATE

Article 5   [SCHEDULE 5

SPECIFIED COUNTRIES]

[...]

Note: This paragraph was revoked by the Public Lending Right Scheme 1982 (Commencement of Variations) Order (SI 2004/1258) App. para.1(c) with effect from June 1, 2004.

B4. Publication Right

See regs 1–4, 16, 17, 25–27 of the Copyright and Related Rights Regulations 1996 (SI 1996/2967) at A3.iii, above.

B5. DATABASE RIGHT

See regs 1–4, 12–30 of, Schs 1 and 2 to, the Copyright and Rights in Databases
Regulations 1997 (SI 1997/3032) at A3.iv, above.

B6. LEGAL DEPOSIT LIBRARIES ACT 2003 AND BRITISH MUSEUM REGULATIONS

B6.i The Legal Deposit Libraries Act 2003

2003 (C.28)

ARRANGEMENT OF SECTIONS

An Act to make provision in place of section 15 of the Copyright Act 1911 relating to the deposit of printed and similar publications, including on and off line publications; to make provision about the use and preservation of material deposited; and for connected purposes. [30th October 2003]

BE IT ENACTED by the Queen's most Excellent Majesty, by and with the advice and consent of the Lords Spiritual and Temporal, and Commons, in this present Parliament assembled, and by the authority of the same, as follows:—

Duty to deposit

Deposit of publications

1.—(1) A person who publishes in the United Kingdom a work to which this Act applies must at his own expense deliver a copy of it to an address specified (generally or in a particular case) by any deposit library entitled to delivery under this section.

(2) If a deposit library other than the authority controlling the Library of Trinity College, Dublin has not specified an address, the copy is to be delivered to the library.

(3) In the case of a work published in print, this Act applies to—

(a) a book (including a pamphlet, magazine or newspaper),

(b) a sheet of letterpress or music,

(c) a map, plan, chart or table, and

(d) a part of any such work;

but that is subject to any prescribed exception.

(4) In the case of a work published in a medium other than print, this Act applies to a work of a prescribed description.

(5) A prescribed description may not include works consisting only of—

(a) a sound recording or film or both, or

(b) such material and other material which is merely incidental to it.

(6) Subject to section 6(2)(h), the obligation under subsection (1) is to deliver a copy of the work in the medium in which it is published.

(7) In this section, "address" means an address in the United Kingdom or an electronic address.

New and alternative editions

2.—(1) This Act does not apply to a work which is substantially the same as one already published in the same medium in the United Kingdom.

(2) Where substantially the same work is published in the United Kingdom in more than one medium—

(a) section 1(1) applies only in relation to its publication in one of those media, and

(b) that medium is to be determined in accordance with regulations made by the Secretary of State.

(3) The Secretary of State may by regulations make provision as to circumstances in which works are or are not to be regarded for the purposes of this section as substantially the same.

Enforcement

3.—(1) This section applies where a person (in this section, "the publisher") who is required by or under this Act to deliver anything to an address specified by a deposit library, or to a deposit library, has failed to comply with that obligation.

(2) The library may, in accordance with rules of court, apply to the county court (or, in Scotland, to the sheriff) for an order requiring the publisher to comply with the obligation.

(3) If on an application under subsection (2) it appears that—

(a) the publisher is unable to comply with the obligation, or

(b) for any other reason, it is not appropriate to make an order under that subsection,

the court or sheriff may instead make an order requiring the publisher to pay to the library an amount which is not more than the cost of making good the failure to comply.

Printed publications

Printed publications: the British Library

4.—(1) The British Library Board is entitled to delivery under section 1 of a copy of every work published in print.

(2) The copy must be delivered within one month beginning with the day of publication.

(3) The copy is to be of the same quality as the best copies which, at the time of delivery, have been produced for publication in the United Kingdom.

(4) The Board must give a receipt in writing (whether sent by electronic or other means).

Printed publications: other libraries

5.—(1) Each deposit library other than the British Library Board is entitled to delivery under section 1 of a copy of any work published in print which it requests.

(2) A request under this section must be in writing (whether sent by electronic or other means).

(3) A request—
   (a) may be made before publication, and
   (b) in particular, may relate to all future numbers or parts of an encyclopae-
        dia, newspaper, magazine or other work.

(4) No request may be made after the end of 12 months beginning with the day of publication.

(5) The copy must be delivered within one month beginning with—
   (a) the day of publication, or
   (b) if later, the day on which the request is received.

(6) The copy is to be of the same quality as the largest number of copies which, at the time of delivery, have been produced for publication in the United Kingdom.

Non-print publications

Regulations: deposit of non-print publications

6.—(1) The Secretary of State may make regulations supplementing sections 1 and 2 as they apply to works published in media other than print.

(2) Regulations under this section may in particular—
   (a) make provision about the time at which or the circumstances in which
        any deposit library becomes or ceases to be entitled to delivery under
        section 1;
   (b) require the person mentioned in section 1(1) to deliver, with the copy of
        the work, a copy of any computer program and any information neces-
        sary in order to access the work, and a copy of any manual and other ma-
        terial that accompanies the work and is made available to the public;
   (c) require delivery within a time prescribed by reference to publication or
        another event;
   (d) permit or require delivery by electronic means;
   (e) where a work is produced for publication in copies of differing quality,
        specify the quality of copies to be delivered;
   (f) where a work is published or made available to the public in different
        formats, provide for the format in which any copy is to be delivered to
        be determined in accordance with requirements specified (generally or
        in a particular case) by the deposit libraries or any of them;
   (g) make provision as to the circumstances in which works published on
        line are or are not to be treated as published in the United Kingdom;
   (h) specify the medium in which a copy of a work published on line is to be
        delivered.

Restrictions on activities in relation to non-print publications

7.—(1) Subject to subsection (3), a relevant person may not do any of the activities listed in subsection (2) in relation to relevant material.

(2) The activities are—

(a) using the material (whether or not such use necessarily involves the making of a temporary copy of it);

(b) copying the material (other than by making a temporary copy where this is necessary for the purpose of using the material);

(c) in the case of relevant material comprising or containing a computer program or database, adapting it;

(d) lending the material to a third party (other than lending by a deposit library to a reader for use by the reader on library premises controlled by the library);

(e) transferring the material to a third party;

(f) disposing of the material.

(3) The Secretary of State may by regulations make provision permitting relevant persons to do any of the activities listed in subsection (2) in relation to relevant material, subject to such conditions as may be prescribed.

(4) Regulations under this section may in particular make provision about—

(a) the purposes for which relevant material may be used or copied;

(b) the time at which or the circumstances in which readers may first use relevant material;

(c) the description of readers who may use relevant material;

(d) the limitations on the number of readers who may use relevant material at any one time (whether by limiting the number of terminals in a deposit library from which readers may at any one time access an electronic publication or otherwise).

(5) In this section—

(a) "reader" means a person who, for the purposes of research or study and with the permission of a deposit library, is on library premises controlled by it;

(b) "relevant material" means—

(i) a copy delivered under section 1 of a work published in a medium other than print;

(ii) a copy delivered pursuant to regulations under section 6 of a computer program or material within section 6(2)(b);

(iii) a copy of a work to which section 10(6) applies;

(iv) a copy (at any remove) of anything within any of sub-paragraphs (i) to (iii);

(c) "relevant person" means—

(i) a deposit library or person acting on its behalf;

(ii) a reader;

(d) references to a deposit library include references to the Faculty of Advocates.

(6) A contravention of this section is actionable at the suit of a person who suffers loss as a result of the contravention, subject to the defences and other incidents applying to actions for breach of statutory duty.

Activities in relation to non-print publications: copyright etc.

8.—(1) In Chapter 3 of Part 1 of the 1988 Act (acts permitted in relation to copyright works), after section 44 insert—

Legal deposit libraries

"**44A**—(1) Copyright is not infringed by the copying of a work from the internet by a deposit library or person acting on its behalf if—

      (a) the work is of a description prescribed by regulations under section 10(5) of the 2003 Act,

      (b) its publication on the internet, or a person publishing it there, is connected with the United Kingdom in a manner so prescribed, and

      (c) the copying is done in accordance with any conditions so prescribed.

(2) Copyright is not infringed by the doing of anything in relation to relevant material permitted to be done under regulations under section 7 of the 2003 Act.

(3) The Secretary of State may by regulations make provision excluding, in relation to prescribed activities done in relation to relevant material, the application of such of the provisions of this Chapter as are prescribed.

(4) Regulations under subsection (3) may in particular make provision prescribing activities—

      (a) done for a prescribed purpose,

      (b) done by prescribed descriptions of reader,

      (c) done in relation to prescribed descriptions of relevant material,

      (d) done other than in accordance with prescribed conditions.

(5) Regulations under this section may make different provision for different purposes.

(6) Regulations under this section shall be made by statutory instrument which shall be subject to annulment in pursuance of a resolution of either House of Parliament.

(7) In this section—

      (a) "the 2003 Act" means the Legal Deposit Libraries Act 2003;

      (b) "deposit library", "reader" and "relevant material" have the same meaning as in section 7 of the 2003 Act;

      (c) "prescribed" means prescribed by regulations made by the Secretary of State."

(2) In Part III of the Copyright and Rights In Databases Regulations 1997 (SI 1997/3032) (database right), after Regulation 20 insert—

Exceptions to database right: deposit libraries

"**20A.**—(1) Database right in a database is not infringed by the copying of a work from the internet by a deposit library or person acting on its behalf if—

    (a) the work is of a description prescribed by regulations under section 10(5) of the 2003 Act,

    (b) its publication on the internet, or a person publishing it there, is connected with the United Kingdom in a manner so prescribed, and

    (c) the copying is done in accordance with any conditions so prescribed.

(2) Database right in a database is not infringed by the doing of anything in relation to relevant material permitted to be done under regulations under section 7 of the 2003 Act.

(3) Regulations under section 44A(3) of the 1988 Act exclude the application of paragraph (2) in relation to prescribed activities in relation to relevant material as (and to the extent that) they exclude the application of section 44A(2) of that Act in relation to those activities.

(4) In this Regulation—

    (a) "the 2003 Act" means the Legal Deposit Libraries Act 2003;

    (b) "deposit library" and "relevant material" have the same meaning as in section 7 of the 2003 Act."

Exemption from liability

Exemption from liability: deposit of publications etc.

9.—(1) The delivery by a person, pursuant to section 1, of a copy of a work is to be taken—

(a) not to breach any contract relating to any part of the work to which that person is a party, and

(b) not to infringe copyright, publication right or database right in relation to any part of the work or any patent.

(2) Subsection (1) applies to the delivery, pursuant to regulations under section 6, of a copy of a computer program or material within section 6(2)(b) as it applies to the delivery of a copy of a work pursuant to section 1.

Exemption from liability: activities in relation to publications

10.—(1) A deposit library, or a person acting on its behalf, is not liable in damages [...] for defamation arising out of the doing by a relevant person of an activity listed in section 7(2) in relation to a copy of a work delivered under section 1.

(2) Subsection (1) does not apply to the liability of a deposit library where—

(a) it knows, or [...] it knows of facts or circumstances from which it ought to know, that the copy contains a defamatory statement, and

(b) it has had a reasonable opportunity since obtaining that knowledge to prevent the doing of the activity in relation to the copy.

(3) Where, pursuant to section 1, a person (in this section, "the publisher") has delivered a copy of a work to an address specified by a deposit library, the publisher is not liable in damages, [...] for defamation arising out of the doing by a relevant person of an activity listed in section 7(2) in relation to the copy.

(4) Subsection (3) does not apply where—

(a) the publisher knows, or [...] the publisher knows of facts or circumstances from which it ought to know, that the copy contains a defamatory statement, and

(b) it has had a reasonable opportunity since obtaining that knowledge to inform the library of the matter, facts or circumstances known to it and has not done so.

(5) Where a work is published on the internet, subsection (6) applies to a copy of the work if—

(a) the work is of a description prescribed by regulations under this subsections,

(b) the publication of the work on the internet, or a person publishing it there, is connected with the United Kingdom in a manner so prescribed, and

(c) the copy was made by a deposit library or person acting on its behalf copying the work from the internet in accordance with any conditions so prescribed.

(6) Where this subsection applies to a copy of a work—

(a) no person other than the library is liable in damages, [...] for defamation arising out of the doing by a relevant person of an activity listed in section 7(2) in relation to the copy, and

(b) subsections (1) and (2) apply in relation to the doing of an activity in relation to the copy as they apply in relation to the doing of the activity in relation to a copy of a work delivered under section 1.

(7) In this section—

(a) "relevant person" has the same meaning as in section 7;

(b) references to activities listed in section 7(2) are references to those activities whether or not done in relation to relevant material (as defined in section 7);

(c) references to a deposit library include references to the Faculty of Advocates.

(8) The Secretary of State may by regulations provide for this section, as it applies in relation to liability in damages [...] for defamation, to apply in relation to liability (including criminal liability) of any description prescribed in the regulations, subject to such modifications as may be prescribed.

(9) Where this section applies to the doing of an activity in relation to a copy of a work it also applies to the doing of the activity in relation to a copy (at any remove) of that copy.

(10) Nothing in this section imposes liability on any person.

Note: The words omitted in s.10(1), (2)(a), (3), (4)(a), (6)(a) and (8) repealed by the Coroners and Justice Act 2009 Sch.23, with effect from January 12, 2010.

Regulations

Regulations: general

11.—(1) Any power under this Act to make regulations—

(a) includes power to make different provision for different purposes, including in particular different media, descriptions of work, deposit libraries or areas, and

(b) as well as being exercisable in relation to all cases to which it extends, may be exercised in relation to those cases subject to specified exceptions, or in relation to a particular case or class of cases.

(2) Regulations under this Act may not be made unless the Secretary of State has consulted—

(a) the deposit libraries, and

(b) the publishers appearing to the Secretary of State to be likely to be affected.

(3) Regulations under section 1(4) or 6 may not be made so as to apply to works published before the regulations are made.

(4) Regulations under section 1(4), 2 or 6 may not be made unless the Secretary of State considers that the costs likely to be incurred as a result of the regulations by persons who publish works to which the regulations relate are not disproportionate to the benefit to the public arising from the delivery of copies of such works.

(5) Regulations under section 1(4), 2, 6, 7 or 10(5) may not be made unless the Secretary of State considers that the regulations do not unreasonably prejudice the interests of persons who publish works to which the regulations relate.

(6) Any power to make regulations under this Act is exercisable by statutory instrument, and no such regulations may be made unless a draft of the instrument containing them has been laid before and approved by a resolution of each House of Parliament.

Regulations: Scotland and Wales

12.—(1) Regulations under this Act may not be made without the consent of the Scottish Ministers if they would—

(a) remove an entitlement conferred by or under this Act on [...] the National Library of Scotland, or

    (b) confer an entitlement that is not conferred on [the National Library of Scotland] on any other deposit library.

  (2) Subsection (1) does not apply where the entitlement is to delivery of copies of electronic publications and—

    (a) in the case of legal publications, the Faculty of Advocates, or

    (b) in any other case, [...] the National Library of Scotland,

is provided with a means of accessing those publications electronically.

  (3) Where subsection (1) does not apply, regulations under this Act that would affect [...] the National Library of Scotland may not be made unless the Secretary of State has consulted the Scottish Ministers.

  (4) Regulations under this Act may not be made without the consent of the National Assembly for Wales if they would—

    (a) remove an entitlement conferred by or under this Act on the authority controlling the National Library of Wales, or

    (b) confer an entitlement that is not conferred on that authority on any other deposit library;

but this does not apply where the entitlement is to delivery of copies of electronic publications and that authority is provided with a means of accessing those publications electronically.

  (5) Where subsection (4) does not apply, regulations under this Act that would affect the authority controlling the National Library of Wales may not be made unless the Secretary of State has consulted the National Assembly for Wales.

Note: In subss (1)(a), (2)(b), (3) words "the authority controlling" repealed, in subs.(1)(b) words in square brackets substituted for words "that authority", by the National Library of Scotland Act 2012, Sch.2 para.7, with effect from February 1, 2013.

Regulations: Trinity College, Dublin

  13.—(1) Regulations under this Act which confer an entitlement on the authority controlling the Library of Trinity College, Dublin may not be made unless the Secretary of State is satisfied, in relation to relevant material delivered pursuant to such an entitlement—

    (a) that as regards the restriction by section 7 (having regard to any regulations made under that section) of activities in relation to relevant material, the restriction of those activities under the laws of Ireland is not substantially less,

    (b) that as regards the protection under the laws of any part of the United Kingdom of copyright, publication right, database right and patents in relation to relevant material, the protection under the laws of Ireland of corresponding rights is not substantially less, and

    (c) that as regards the protection from liability under subsections (3) and (4) of section 10 (or those subsections as applied by regulations under that section), the protection under the laws of Ireland in relation to corresponding liability is not substantially less.

  (2) In this section "relevant material" has the same meaning as in section 7.

General

Interpretation

  14. In this Act—

    "the 1988 Act" means the Copyright, Designs and Patents Act 1988 (c. 48);

    "database right" has the meaning given by regulation 13(1) of the Copyright and Rights in Databases Regulations 1997 (SI 1997/3032);

"deposit library" means any of the British Library Board and the authorities controlling—

    (a) the National Library of Scotland,

    (b) the National Library of Wales,

    (c) the Bodleian Library, Oxford,

    (d) the University Library, Cambridge,

    (e) the Library of Trinity College, Dublin;

"electronic publication" means an on line or off line publication including any publication in electronic form (within the meaning given by section 178 of the 1988 Act);

"film" has the meaning given by section 5B of the 1988 Act;

"medium" means any medium of publication, including in particular any form of on line or off line publication;

"prescribed" means prescribed by regulations made by the Secretary of State;

"publication", in relation to a work—

    (a) means the issue of copies of the work to the public, and

    (b) includes making the work available to the public by means of an electronic retrieval system;

and related expressions are to be interpreted accordingly;

"publication right" has the meaning given by regulation 16(1) of the Copyright and Related Rights Regulations 1996 (SI 1996/2967);

"sound recording" has the meaning given by section 5A of the 1988 Act.

Consequential amendments, repeals and revocation

15.—(1) The provisions listed in the Schedule are repealed or revoked to the extent specified.

(2) Section 5 of the National Library of Scotland Act 1925 (c. 73) (transfer of privilege under section 15 of the Copyright Act 1911) is amended as follows.

(3) For subsections (1) to (3) substitute—

"(1) Copies of legal publications delivered for the Board as the authority for the Library under section 1 of the Legal Deposit Libraries Act 2003 shall be transmitted by the Board to the Faculty.

(2) The Board shall cause to be inserted in the requests made for them under section 5 of that Act such legal publications as may be named in writing to them by the Faculty."

(4) In subsections (4) and (5), for "law books" substitute "legal publications".

(5) After subsection (5) add—

"(6) In this section, "publication" includes a publication made available to the public by means of an electronic retrieval system."

Commencement and extent

16.—(1) The preceding provisions of this Act, except so far as they confer power to make regulations, come into force in accordance with provision made by the Secretary of State by order made by statutory instrument.

(2) Different provision may be made for different purposes.

(3) An order under subsection (1) may not be made unless the Secretary of State has consulted the Scottish Ministers and the National Assembly for Wales.

(4) This Act does not apply to works published before the commencement of section 1.

(5) This Act extends to Northern Ireland.

Short title

17. This Act may be cited as the Legal Deposit Libraries Act 2003.

Section 15(1)   SCHEDULE

REPEALS AND REVOCATION

Reference	Extent of repeal or revocation
Copyright Act 1911 (c. 46)	Section 15.
British Museum Act 1932 (c. 34)	The whole Act.
British Library Act 1972 (c. 54)	Section 4(1).
National Assembly for Wales (Transfer of Functions) Order 1999 (S. I. 1999/672)	In Schedule 2, the entry relating to the Copyright Act 1911.

B6.ii The British Museum (Delivery of Books) Regulation

(S.R. & O. 1915/773)

Dated   *9th August 1915*

The Board of Trade on the application of the Trustees of the British Museum, and by virtue of the powers given them by section 1 of the Copyright (British Museum) Act, 1915, hereby make the following Regulation, to come into operation as from the date hereof:

There shall be excepted from the provisions of section 15(1) of the Copyright Act, 1911, whereby the publisher of any book published in the United Kingdom is required within one month after the publication to deliver, at his own expense, a copy of the book to the Trustees of the British Museum, the following publications, *viz.*:

Trade Advertisements,	Trade Leaflets,
Trade Cards,	Trade Plans,
Trade Catalogues,	Trade Posters,
Trade Circulars,	Trade Price Lists,
Trade Coupons,	Trade Prospectuses,
Trade Designs,	Trade Show Cards,
Trade Forms,	Trade Wrappers.
Trade Labels,	

Note: References to the British Library Board are to be substituted for references to the Trustees by virtue of s.4 of the British Library Act 1972 (c.54).

B6.iii British Museum (Publications Not Required) Regulation

(S.R. & O. 1935/278)

Dated   *12th October 1932*

The Trustees of the British Museum, being empowered under the British Museum Act, 1932, by regulations to apply the said Act to publications of such classes as may be specified in such regulations being publications of the descriptions set out in the Schedule to the said Act and thereby to except certain publications from subsection (1) of section 15 of the Copyright Act, 1911, hereby make the following regulation within their said powers. The delivery by publishers of publications falling under the following categories is no longer required, unless a written demand for delivery of them or any of them is made by the Trustees:

Publications wholly or mainly in the nature of the trade advertisements. Registers of voters prepared under the Representation of the People Act, 1918, as amended by any subsequent enactment.

Specifications of inventions prepared for the purposes of the Patents and Designs Act, 1907, as amended by any subsequent enactment.

Publications wholly or mainly in the nature of time tables of passenger transport services, being publications prepared for local use.

Publications wholly or mainly in the nature of calendars.

Publications wholly or mainly in the nature of blank forms of accounts, or blank forms of receipts, or other blank forms of a similar character.

Wall sheets printed with alphabets, mottoes, religious tests or other matter for the purpose of elementary instruction.

Note: References to the British Library Board are to be substituted for references to the Trustees by virtue of s.4 of the British Library Act 1972 (c.54).

B6.iv The Legal Deposit Libraries (Non-Print Works) Regulations 2013

(SI 2013/777)

The Secretary of State makes the following Regulations in exercise of the powers conferred by sections 1(4), 2(2), 6(1), 7(3), 10(5) and 11(1) of the Legal Deposit Libraries Act 2003[1].

The Secretary of State has consulted the deposit libraries[2] and the publishers appearing to the Secretary of State to be likely to be affected by these Regulations.

The Secretary of State has consulted the Scottish Ministers and the Welsh Ministers[3].

The Secretary of State is satisfied that as regards the restriction by section 7 of the Act (having regard to these Regulations) of activities in relation to relevant material[4], the restriction of those activities under the laws of Ireland is not substantially less.

The Secretary of State is satisfied that as regards the protection under the laws of any part of the United Kingdom of copyright, publication right, database right and patents in relation to relevant material, the protection under the laws of Ireland of corresponding rights is not substantially less.

The Secretary of State is satisfied that as regards the protection from liability under subsections (3) and (4) of section 10 of the Act, the protection under the laws of Ireland in relation to corresponding liability is not substantially less.

The Secretary of State considers that the costs likely to be incurred as a result of

---

[1] Section 10(6) of the Act, to which section 10(5) of the Act refers, was amended in relation to England and Wales and Northern Ireland by Part 2 of Schedule 23 to the Coroners and Justice Act 2009 (c.25) and in relation to Scotland by paragraph 72(e) of Schedule 7 to the Criminal Justice and Licensing (Scotland) Act 2010 (2010 asp 13) to reflect changes made to common law libel offences.

[2] "Deposit library" is defined in section 14 of the Act.

[3] The requirement in section 12(5) of the Act to consult the National Assembly for Wales is to be construed as a reference to the Welsh Ministers by virtue of paragraphs 30 and 32 of Schedule 11 to the Government of Wales Act 2006 (c.32).

[4] "Relevant material" is defined in section 7(5)(b) of the Act.

these Regulations by persons who publish works to which these Regulations relate are not disproportionate to the benefit to the public arising from the delivery of copies of such works.

The Secretary of State considers that these Regulations do not unreasonably prejudice the interests of persons who publish works to which these Regulations relate.

In accordance with section 11(6) of the Act a draft of this instrument was laid before and approved by a resolution of each House of Parliament.

PART 1

INTRODUCTORY

Citation and commencement

1.—(1) These Regulations may be cited as the Legal Deposit Libraries (Non-Print Works) Regulations 2013.

(2) They come into force on the day after the day on which they are made.

Interpretation

2.—(1) In these Regulations—

"the Act" means the Legal Deposit Libraries Act 2003;

"computer terminal" means a terminal on library premises controlled by the deposit library from which a reader is permitted to view relevant material;

"database right" has the same meaning as in regulation 13 of the Copyright and Rights in Databases Regulations 1997;

"IP address" means internet protocol address;

"permanent collection" means the permanent collection held by a deposit library of non-print work delivered or copied under these Regulations;

"personal data" has the same meaning as in section 1 of the Data Protection Act 1998;

"publisher" means, in relation to a work to which the Act applies, the person to whom the obligation in section 1(1) of the Act applies in respect of that work;

"web harvester" means a computer program which is used to search the internet in order to request delivery of on line work on behalf of a deposit library;

(2) a reference to "in writing" includes text which is—

(a) transmitted by electronic means;

(b) received in legible form; and

(c) capable of being used for subsequent reference;

(3) a reference to a deposit library (whether or not to a specific deposit library) includes a person acting on behalf of the deposit library.

3. In regulations 20 and 23 to 31 references to a deposit library include reference to the Faculty of Advocates.

PART 2

EXEMPTION FOR EXISTING MICRO-BUSINESSES AND NEW BUSINESSES

The exemption

4.—(1) During the exemption period, regulations 13(1)(a), 14(2), 15, 16(3) to

16(7) and 17 do not apply in relation to a work published in a medium other than print where a person publishes the work in the course of a business, if the business is—

(a) an existing micro-business, or

(b) a new business.

(2) In relation to a work published off line that is subject to the exemption in paragraph (1)—

(a) paragraphs (1) and (2) of regulation 15 shall not require delivery of any such work;

(b) paragraph (3) of regulation 15 shall have effect as if it provided for the British Library Board (in addition to other deposit libraries) to be entitled to delivery of the work if it requests it, and paragraphs (4) to (10) of that regulation have effect accordingly.

Micro-businesses

5. A micro-business is a business that has fewer than 10 employees (see regulations 9 to 11).

Existing micro-businesses

6. An existing micro-business is a business that was a micro-business immediately before the commencement date.

New businesses

7.—(1) A new business is a business which a person, or a number of persons, ("P") begins to carry on during the period beginning with the commencement date and ending with 31 March 2014.

(2) But a business is not a new business if—

(a) P has, at any time during the period of 6 months ending immediately before the date on which P begins to carry on the business, carried on another business consisting of the activities of which the business consists (or most of them), or

(b) P carries on the business as a result of a transfer (within the meaning of paragraph (4)).

(3) Paragraph (2)(a) does not apply if the other business referred to in that paragraph was a new business (within the meaning of this regulation).

(4) P carries on a business as a result of a transfer if P begins to carry on the business on another person ceasing to carry on the activities of which it consists (or most of them) in consequence of arrangements involving P and the other person.

(5) For this purpose, P is to be taken to begin to carry on a business on another person ceasing to carry on such activities if—

(a) P begins to carry on the business otherwise than in partnership on such activities ceasing to be carried on by persons in partnership, or

(b) P is a number of persons in partnership who begin to carry on the business on such activities ceasing to be carried on—

(i) by a person, or a number of persons, otherwise than in partnership,

(ii) by persons in partnership who do not consist only of all the persons who constitute P, or

(iii) partly as mentioned in paragraph (i) and partly as mentioned in paragraph (ii).

(6) Paragraph (2)(b) does not apply if the activities referred to in paragraph (4) were, when carried on by the person who is not P referred to in that paragraph, activities of a new business (within the meaning of this regulation).

(7) P is not to be regarded as beginning to carry on a business for the purposes of paragraph (1) if—

    (a) before P begins to carry on the business, P is a party to arrangements under which P may (at any time during the period beginning with the commencement date and ending with 31 March 2014) carry on, as part of the business, activities carried on by any other person, and

    (b) the business would have been prevented by paragraph (2)(b) from being a new business if—

        (i) P had begun to carry on the activities when beginning to carry on the business, and

        (ii) the other person had at that time ceased to carry them on.

(8) "Arrangements"includes an agreement, understanding, scheme, transaction or series of transactions (whether or not legally enforceable).

The exemption period

8.—(1) The exemption period in relation to an existing micro-business starts with the commencement date and ends with 31 March 2014.

(2) The exemption period in relation to a new business starts with the date on which P begins to carry on the business and ends with 31 March 2014.

Number of employees of a business

9. For the purposes of this Part, the number of employees of a business is calculated as follows—

TH/37.5

where TH is the total number of hours per week for which all the employees of the business are contracted to work.

Employees of a business

10. For the purposes of this Part, the employees of a business are the persons who are employed for the purposes of the business.

Employees

11.—(1) In this Part, "employee" means an individual who has entered into or works under a contract of employment.

(2) In paragraph (1) "contract of employment" means a contract of service, whether express or implied, and (if it is express) whether oral or in writing.

The commencement date

12. For the purposes of this Part, "the commencement date" means the date on which these Regulations come into force.

PART 3

DEPOSIT

Non-print work to which the Act applies

13.—(1) The Act applies to the following descriptions of work published in a medium other than print—

    (a) work that is published off line, and

    (b) work that is published on line.

(2) But, the descriptions of work prescribed in paragraph (1) do not include—

    (a) work consisting only of—

    (i) a sound recording or film[5] or both, or

    (ii) such material and other material which is merely incidental to it;

  (b) work which contains personal data and which is only made available to a restricted group of persons; or

  (c) work published before these Regulations were made.

(3) The description of work that is prescribed for the purposes of section 10(5)(a) of the Act is work that is published on the internet and that does not fall within the description given in paragraph (2)(a) or (b).

New and alternative editions

14.—(1) Where substantially the same work is published in the United Kingdom in print and in one or more non-print media, the duty under section 1(1) of the Act applies only in relation to its publication in print unless the publisher and the deposit library agree that instead the duty under section 1(1) of the Act applies in relation to its publication in one of the non-print media in which the work is published.

(2) Where substantially the same work is published in the United Kingdom in two or more nonprint media (and is not published in print), the publisher and the deposit library may agree one of those non-print media as the medium in relation to which the duty under section 1(1) of the Act applies and, in the absence of agreement, the publisher may decide the non-print medium (which must be one in which the work is published) in relation to which the duty under section 1(1) of the Act applies.

Entitlement to delivery: off line work

15.—(1) The British Library Board is entitled to delivery under section 1 of the Act of a copy of every work published off line.

(2) A copy must be delivered to the British Library Board within one month beginning with the day of publication.

(3) Each deposit library other than the British Library Board is entitled to delivery under section 1 of the Act of a copy of any work published off line which it requests.

(4) The following provisions apply to a request made under paragraph (3)—

  (a) it must be in writing;

  (b) it must be made—

    (i) within 12 months beginning with the day of publication, or

    (ii) (in relation to a work published off line that is subject to the exemption in regulation 4) if later, by 30 April 2014;

  (c) it may be made before publication;

  (d) it may relate to all future numbers or parts of an encyclopaedia, newspaper, magazine or other non-print work.

(5) The copy must be delivered within one month beginning with—

  (a) the day of publication, or

  (b) if later, the day on which the request is received.

(6) The copy delivered pursuant to paragraphs (1) and (3) must be of a quality most suitable for the preservation of the work.

(7) The quality most suitable for the preservation of the work may be as agreed between the publisher and the deposit library or, in the absence of agreement, a quality which the publisher decides.

(8) Each deposit library must give a receipt in writing for the copies of work published off line that it receives.

---

[5] "Film" is defined in section 14 of the Act.

Entitlement to delivery: on line work

16.—(1) Each deposit library is entitled to delivery under section 1 of the Act of a copy of any work published on line which it requests provided that such a request is made in accordance with paragraph (2) or (3).

(2) Where there is an agreement between a publisher and a deposit library regarding the method by which a work, or works of a particular description, will be delivered—

    (a) the request for delivery of the work must be made in writing; and

    (b) the work must be delivered to the deposit library by the agreed method within one month of the request being made, and must be of a quality which is most suitable for its preservation.

(3) Where no such agreement is in place, any request for delivery of a work must be made by the deposit library by means of a web harvester from one or more IP addresses dedicated for the purpose of making requests under this paragraph to the IP address from which the work is made available to the public.

(4) A request by a deposit library under paragraph (3) made in respect of a webpage which contains a login facility will be deemed to be a request for the work or works available behind that login facility provided that the deposit library has given the publisher at least one month's notice in writing before making the request.

(5) Delivery of a work requested under paragraph (3) must be by electronic means and by automated response to the request made by the web harvester.

(6) When making a request under paragraph (3) for work or works available behind a login facility, a deposit library must use any relevant login details provided to it by the publisher.

(7) A deposit library must not use such login details for any purpose except for compliance with these Regulations.

(8) For the purposes of paragraph (2)(b), the quality most suitable for the preservation of a work shall be such as may be agreed between the publisher and the deposit library or, in the absence of agreement, shall be decided by the publisher.

Delivery of additional information

17. The publisher of a work delivered under regulation 15 or regulation 16(2) must deliver at the same time—

    (a) a copy of any computer program or any other data or information necessary to access the work; and

    (b) a copy of any manual and other material that accompanies the work and is made available to the public.

On line work: published in the United Kingdom

18.—(1) Subject to paragraph (2), a work published on line shall be treated as published in the United Kingdom if—

    (a) it is made available to the public from a website with a domain name which relates to the United Kingdom or to a place within the United Kingdom; or

    (b) it is made available to the public by a person and any of that person's activities relating to the creation or the publication of the work take place within the United Kingdom.

(2) A work published on line shall not be treated as published in the United Kingdom if access to the work is only made available to persons outside the United Kingdom.

(3) Where work is published on the internet and the publication of that work or a person publishing it there is connected with the United Kingdom in the man-

ner prescribed in paragraphs (1) and (2), that manner of connection with the United Kingdom is also prescribed for the purposes of section 10(5)(b) of the Act.

Part 4

Permitted activities

Use etc. of relevant material by deposit libraries

19. A deposit library may transfer or lend relevant material to any other deposit library.

20. A deposit library may use relevant material for the purposes of—

(a) reviewing and maintaining the relevant material, and

(b) the deposit library's own non-commercial research (whether the subject matter of the research is the permanent collection or not).

21. The National Library of Scotland may permanently transfer any relevant material that is an off line legal publication to the Faculty of Advocates.

22. The National Library of Scotland may transfer or lend any relevant material that is an on line legal publication to the Faculty of Advocates.

Reader access to relevant material

23. A deposit library must ensure that only one computer terminal is available to readers to access the same relevant material at any one time.

24. In the case of relevant material which is work published on line, at least seven days must elapse from the date of delivery of that relevant material to the deposit library before a reader may be permitted to view it.

25.—(1) A copyright owner or database right owner in relation to relevant material may make a request in writing to a deposit library to withhold access to that relevant material from readers for a specified period of time.

(2) The deposit library receiving the request must comply with that request if the following conditions are met —

(a) the period specified in the request does not exceed three years from the date on which the request is made;

(b) the deposit library is satisfied on reasonable grounds that, for the period specified in the request, viewing of the relevant material by a reader would, or would be likely to, unreasonably prejudice the interests of the person making the request.

(3) The entitlement to make a request under paragraph (1) includes an entitlement to make subsequent requests, and (subject to paragraph (4)) a deposit library must comply with a subsequent request if the conditions in paragraph (2) are met in relation to that request.

(4) If a subsequent request seeks to extend the specified period of time relating to an earlier request made under paragraph (1), that subsequent request must be made at least one month before the specified period expires.

Reader access to relevant material: visually impaired persons

26.—(1) A deposit library may make and supply for use on its premises accessible copies of relevant material for a visually impaired person if copies of the relevant material are not commercially available in a form that is accessible to the visually impaired person.

(2) Paragraph (1) does not apply in relation to relevant material that is a database in which copyright or database right subsists.

(3) A deposit library must ensure that only one reader uses an accessible copy of the same relevant material made under this regulation at any one time.

(4) An accessible copy made under paragraph (1) must be accompanied by—

(a) a statement that it is made under this regulation; and

(b) a sufficient acknowledgement.

(5) A deposit library entitled to make accessible copies under paragraph (1) may hold an intermediate copy of the relevant material which is necessarily made during the production of the accessible copies, but only—

(a) if and so long as the deposit library continues to be entitled to make accessible copies of that relevant material; and

(b) for the purposes of the production of further accessible copies.

(6) A deposit library may lend or transfer the intermediate copy to another deposit library which is entitled to make accessible copies of the relevant material under paragraph (1) provided that the intermediate copy is used only for the purposes of the production of further accessible copies.

(7) A deposit library must—

(a) keep records of accessible copies made under this regulation and of the persons to whom they are supplied;

(b) keep records of any intermediate copy lent or transferred under this regulation and of the deposit libraries to whom it is lent or transferred;

(c) allow a copyright owner or a person acting for a copyright owner, on giving reasonable notice, to inspect the records at any reasonable time.

(8) Within a reasonable time of making an accessible copy under paragraph (1) or lending or transferring an intermediate copy under paragraph (6), the deposit library must notify—

(a) each representative body; or

(b) if there is no such body, the copyright owner.

(9) A representative body is a body which—

(a) represents particular copyright owners, or owners of copyright in the type of copyright work concerned; and

(b) has given notice to the Secretary of State of the copyright owners, or the classes of copyright owner, represented by it.

(10) The requirement to notify the copyright owner under paragraph (8) does not apply—

(a) if it is not reasonably possible for the deposit library to ascertain the name and address of the copyright owner; or

(b) (where there is more than one copyright owner of the work to which the notification relates) in respect of those persons for whom it is not reasonably possible for the deposit library to ascertain their names and addresses.

(11) In this regulation—

(a) "accessible copy" and "visually impaired"have the same meaning as in section 31F of the Copyright, Designs and Patents Act 1988 ("the 1988 Act");

(b) "database"has the same meaning as in section 3A of the 1988 Act;

(c) "sufficient acknowledgement"has the same meaning as in section 178 of the 1988 Act.

27.—(1) A deposit library may, if the conditions set out in paragraph (2) are met, produce and supply to a person a copy of relevant material.

(2) Those conditions are that—

(a) in relation to relevant material in which database right does not subsist, the deposit library is satisfied that the copy is required by that person for the purposes of non-commercial research or private study, criticism or review or reporting current events, parliamentary or judicial proceedings or a Royal Commission or statutory inquiry and will not be used for any other purpose;

(b) in relation to relevant material in which database right subsists, the deposit library is satisfied that the copy is required by that person for the purposes of parliamentary or judicial proceedings or a Royal Commission or statutory inquiry and will not be used for any other purpose;

(c) that person has delivered to the deposit library a signed declaration in writing in relation to the relevant material substantially in accordance with the Form in the Schedule to these Regulations;

(d) in relation to a copy of relevant material required for the purposes of non-commercial research or private study, the deposit library is satisfied that the requirement of the person requiring the copy is not related and similar to that of another person.

(3) For the purposes of paragraph (2)(d)—

(a) requirements shall be regarded as similar if the requirements are for copies of substantially the same relevant material at substantially the same time and for substantially the same purpose; and

(b) requirements of persons shall be regarded as related if those persons receive instruction to which the relevant material is relevant at the same time and place.

(4) Unless the deposit library is aware that the signed declaration delivered under paragraph (2)(c) is false in a material particular, the deposit library may rely on it in order to determine whether a copy is required for any of the purposes specified in paragraph (2)(a) or 2(b) and may rely on it in relation to paragraph (2)(d).

28.—(1) The supply by a deposit library of a copy of relevant material under regulation 27 is subject to the following provisions of this regulation.

(2) Where the relevant material is capable of being supplied in print, a deposit library must supply a copy of the relevant material in print unless the copyright owner or database right owner (as the case may be) has given permission for a copy to be supplied in a medium other than print in which case it may be supplied in that medium.

(3) Where the relevant material is not capable of being supplied in print, a deposit library may only supply a copy of the relevant material in a medium other than print if the copyright owner or database right owner (as the case may be) has given permission for the deposit library to supply a copy in that medium.

(4) In relation to a copy of relevant material required for the purposes of non-commercial research or private study—

(a) a deposit library must not supply a person with more than one copy of the same relevant material;

(b) the copy of the relevant material supplied by a deposit library must not represent more than a reasonable proportion of the relevant material of which the element copied forms a part;

(c) if the relevant material being copied is an article in a periodical, a deposit library must not supply a person with more than one copy of that article or more than one article contained in the same edition of that periodical.

(5) The person requiring the copy of the relevant material is required to pay for that copy a sum not less than the cost (including a contribution to general expenses) attributable to its production.

Copying relevant material for the purposes of preservation

29.—(1) A deposit library may copy relevant material if the copy is made in any of the circumstances falling within paragraph (2).

(2) The circumstances are that the copy is made (whether from the relevant material itself or from a copy made by the deposit library by virtue of this regulation) in order—

(a) to preserve or replace the relevant material by placing the copy in the permanent collection in addition to or in place of the relevant material;

(b) to replace the relevant material in the permanent collection of another deposit library if that relevant material has been lost, destroyed or damaged.

(3) A copy may be made by virtue of this regulation in a different medium or format from the relevant material if the deposit library considers the change is necessary or expedient for the purpose for which the copy is made.

(4) Paragraph (1) does not apply if database right subsists in the relevant material.

Adapting relevant material for the purposes of preservation

30.—(1) A deposit library may adapt relevant material if the adaptation is made in any of the circumstances falling within paragraph (2).

(2) The circumstances are that the adaptation is made (whether from the relevant material itself or from a copy made by the deposit library by virtue of regulation 29) for the following purposes—

(a) to preserve or replace the relevant material by placing the adaptation in the permanent collection in addition to or in place of the relevant material;

(b) to replace the relevant material in the permanent collection of another deposit library if that relevant material has been lost, destroyed or damaged.

(3) An adaptation may be made by virtue of this regulation in a different medium or format from the relevant material if the deposit library considers the change is necessary or expedient for the purpose for which the adaptation is made.

(4) Paragraph (1) does not apply if database right subsists in the relevant material.

Disposing of relevant material

31.—(1) A deposit library may dispose of relevant material, or copies or adaptations of relevant material, by destroying it but must retain at least one version of any relevant material.

(2) The version or versions retained by a deposit library must be the version or versions which the deposit library considers most suitable for the preservation of the relevant material.

B7. Customs

B7.a European Materials

Regulation (EU) No 608/2013 of the European Parliament and of the Council of 12 June 2013 concerning customs enforcement of intellectual property rights and repealing Council Regulation (EC) No 1383/2003

B7.ai

THE EUROPEAN PARLIAMENT AND THE COUNCIL OF THE EUROPEAN UNION,

Having regard to the Treaty on the Functioning of the European Union, and in particular Article 207 thereof,

Having regard to the proposal from the European Commission,

After transmission of the draft legislative act to the national parliaments,

Acting in accordance with the ordinary legislative procedure[1],

Whereas:

(1) The Council requested, in its Resolution of 25 September 2008 on a comprehensive European anti-counterfeiting and anti-piracy plan, that Council Regulation (EC) No 1383/2003 of 22 July 2003 concerning customs action against goods suspected of infringing certain intellectual property rights and the measures to be taken against goods found to have infringed such rights[2], be viewed.

(2) The marketing of goods infringing intellectual property rights does considerable damage to right-holders, users or groups of producers, and to law-abiding manufacturers and traders. Such marketing could also be deceiving consumers, and could in some cases be endangering their health and safety. Such goods should, in so far as is possible, be kept off the Union market and measures should be adopted to deal with such unlawful marketing without impeding legitimate trade.

(3) The review of Regulation (EC) No 1383/2003 showed that, in the light of economic, commercial and legal developments, certain improvements to the legal framework are necessary to strengthen the enforcement of intellectual property rights by customs authorities, as well as to ensure appropriate legal certainty.

(4) The customs authorities should be competent to enforce intellectual property rights with regard to goods, which, in accordance with Union customs legislation, are liable to customs supervision or customs control, and to carry out adequate controls on such goods with a view to preventing operations in breach of intellectual property rights laws. Enforcing intellectual property rights at the border, wherever the goods are, or should have been, under customs supervision or customs control is an efficient way to quickly and effectively provide legal protection to the right-holder as well as the users and groups of producers. Where the release of goods is suspended or goods are detained by customs authorities at the border, only one legal proceeding should be required, whereas several separate proceedings should be required for the same level of enforcement for goods found on the market, which have been disaggregated and delivered to retailers. An exception should be made for goods released for free circulation under the end-use regime, as such goods remain under customs supervision, even though they have been released for free circulation. This Regulation should not apply to

---

[1] Position of the European Parliament of 3 July 2012 (not yet published in the Official Journal) and position of the Council at first reading of 16 May 2013 (not yet published in the Official Journal). Position of the European Parliament of 11 June 2013 (not yet published in the Official Journal).

[2] OJ L 196, 2.8.2003, p. 7.

goods carried by passengers in their personal luggage provided that those goods are for their own personal use and there are no indications that commercial traffic is involved.

(5) Regulation (EC) No 1383/2003 does not cover certain intellectual property rights and certain infringements are excluded from its scope. In order to strengthen the enforcement of intellectual property rights, customs intervention should be extended to other types of infringements not covered by Regulation (EC) No 1383/2003. This Regulation should therefore, in addition to the rights already covered by Regulation (EC) No 1383/2003, also include trade names in so far as they are protected as exclusive property rights under national law, topographies of semiconductor products and utility models and devices which are primarily designed, produced or adapted for the purpose of enabling or facilitating the circumvention of technological measures.

(6) Infringements resulting from so-called illegal parallel trade and overruns are excluded from the scope of Regulation (EC) No 1383/2003. Goods subject to illegal parallel trade, namely goods that have been manufactured with the consent of the right-holder but placed on the market for the first time in the European Economic Area without his consent, and overruns, namely goods that are manufactured by a person duly authorised by a right-holder to manufacture a certain quantity of goods, in excess of the quantities agreed between that person and the right-holder, are manufactured as genuine goods and it is therefore not appropriate that customs authorities focus their efforts on such goods. Illegal parallel trade and overruns should therefore also be excluded from the scope of this Regulation.

(7) Member States should, in cooperation with the Commission, provide appropriate training for customs officials, in order to ensure the correct implementation of this Regulation.

(8) This Regulation, when fully implemented, will further contribute to an internal market which ensures right-holders a more effective protection, fuels creativity and innovation and provides consumers with reliable and high-quality products, which should in turn strengthen cross-border transactions between consumers, businesses and traders.

(9) Member States face increasingly limited resources in the field of customs. Therefore, the promotion of risk management technologies and strategies to maximise resources available to customs authorities should be supported.

(10) This Regulation solely contains procedural rules for customs authorities. Accordingly, this Regulation does not set out any criteria for ascertaining the existence of an infringement of an intellectual property right.

(11) Under the 'Declaration on the TRIPS Agreement and Public Health' adopted by the Doha WTO Ministerial Conference on 14 November 2001, the Agreement on Trade-Related Aspects of Intellectual Property Rights (TRIPS Agreement) can and should be interpreted and implemented in a manner supportive of WTO Members' right to protect public health and, in particular, to promote access to medicines for all. Consequently, in line with the Union's international commitments and its development cooperation policy, with regard to medicines, the passage of which across the customs territory of the Union, with or without transhipment, warehousing, breaking bulk, or changes in the mode or means of transport, is only a portion of a complete journey beginning and terminating beyond the territory of the Union, customs authorities should, when assessing a risk of infringement of intellectual property rights, take account of any substantial likelihood of diversion of such medicines onto the market of the Union.

(12) This Regulation should not affect the provisions on the competence of courts, in particular, those of Regulation (EU) No 1215/2012 of the European

Parliament and of the Council of 12 December 2012 on jurisdiction and the recognition and enforcement of judgments in civil and commercial matters[3].

(13) Persons, users, bodies or groups of producers, who are in a position to initiate legal proceedings in their own name with respect to a possible infringement of an intellectual property right, should be entitled to submit an application.

(14) In order to ensure that intellectual property rights are enforced throughout the Union, it is appropriate to allow persons or entities seeking enforcement of Union-wide rights to apply to the customs authorities of a single Member State. Such applicants should be able to request that those authorities decide that action be taken to enforce the intellectual property right both in their own Member State and in any other Member State.

(15) In order to ensure the swift enforcement of intellectual property rights, it should be provided that, where the customs authorities suspect, on the basis of reasonable indications, that goods under their supervision infringe intellectual property rights, they may suspend the release of or detain the goods whether at their own initiative or upon application, in order to enable a person or entity entitled to submit an application to initiate proceedings for determining whether an intellectual property right has been infringed.

(16) Regulation (EC) No 1383/2003 allowed Member States to provide for a procedure allowing the destruction of certain goods without there being any obligation to initiate proceedings to establish whether an intellectual property right has been infringed. As recognised in the European Parliament Resolution of 18 December 2008 on the impact of counterfeiting on international trade[4], such procedure has proved very successful in the Member States where it has been available. Therefore, the procedure should be made compulsory with regard to all infringements of intellectual property rights and should be applied, where the declarant or the holder of the goods agrees to destruction. Furthermore, the procedure should provide that customs authorities may deem that the declarant or the holder of the goods has agreed to the destruction of the goods where he has not explicitly opposed destruction within the prescribed period.

(17) In order to reduce the administrative burden and costs to a minimum, a specific procedure should be introduced for small consignments of counterfeit and pirated goods, which should allow for such goods to be destroyed without the explicit agreement of the applicant in each case. However, a general request made by the applicant in the application should be required in order for that procedure to be applied. Furthermore, customs authorities should have the possibility to require that the applicant covers the costs incurred by the application of that procedure.

(18) For further legal certainty, it is appropriate to modify the timelines for suspending the release of or detaining goods suspected of infringing an intellectual property right and the conditions in which information about detained goods is to be passed on to persons and entities concerned by customs authorities, as provided for in Regulation (EC) No 1383/2003.

(19) Taking into account the provisional and preventive character of the measures adopted by the customs authorities when applying this Regulation and the conflicting interests of the parties affected by the measures, some aspects of the procedures should be adapted to ensure the smooth application of this Regulation, whilst respecting the rights of the concerned parties. Thus, with respect to the various notifications envisaged by this Regulation, the customs authorities should notify the relevant person, on the basis of the documents concerning the

[3] OJ L 351, 20.12.2012, p. 1.
[4] OJ C 45 E, 23.2.2010, p. 47.

customs treatment or of the situation in which the goods are placed. Furthermore, since the procedure for destruction of goods implies that both the declarant or the holder of the goods and the holder of the decision should communicate their possible objections to destruction in parallel, it should be ensured that the holder of the decision is given the possibility to react to a potential objection to destruction by the declarant or the holder of the goods. It should therefore be ensured that the declarant or the holder of the goods is notified of the suspension of the release of the goods or their detention before, or on the same day as, the holder of the decision.

(20) Customs authorities and the Commission are encouraged to cooperate with the European Observatory on Infringements of Intellectual Property Rights in the framework of their respective competences.

(21) With a view to eliminating international trade in goods infringing intellectual property rights, the TRIPS Agreement provides that WTO Members are to promote the exchange of information between customs authorities on such trade. Accordingly, it should be possible for the Commission and the customs authorities of the Member States to share information on suspected breaches of intellectual property rights with the relevant authorities of third countries, including on goods which are in transit through the territory of the Union and originate in or are destined for those third countries.

(22) In the interest of efficiency, the provisions of Council Regulation (EC) No 515/97 of 13 March 1997 on mutual assistance between the administrative authorities of the Member States and cooperation between the latter and the Commission to ensure the correct application of the law on customs or agricultural matters[5], should apply.

(23) The liability of the customs authorities should be governed by the legislation of the Member States, though the granting by the customs authorities of an application should not entitle the holder of the decision to compensation in the event that goods suspected of infringing an intellectual property right are not detected by the customs authorities and are released or no action is taken to detain them.

(24) Given that customs authorities take action upon application, it is appropriate to provide that the holder of the decision should reimburse all the costs incurred by the customs authorities in taking action to enforce his intellectual property rights. Nevertheless, this should not preclude the holder of the decision from seeking compensation from the infringer or other persons that might be considered liable under the legislation of the Member State where the goods were found. Such persons might include intermediaries, where applicable. Costs and damages incurred by persons other than customs authorities as a result of a customs action, where the release of goods is suspended or the goods are detained on the basis of a claim of a third party based on intellectual property, should be governed by the specific legislation applicable in each particular case.

(25) This Regulation introduces the possibility for customs authorities to allow goods which are to be destroyed to be moved, under customs supervision, between different places within the customs territory of the Union. Customs authorities may furthermore decide to release such goods for free circulation with a view to further recycling or disposal outside commercial channels including for awareness-raising, training and educational purposes.

(26) Customs enforcement of intellectual property rights entails the exchange of data on decisions relating to applications. Such processing of data covers also personal data and should be carried out in accordance with Union law, as set out

---

[5] OJ L 82, 22.3.1997, p. 1.

in Directive 95/46/EC of the European Parliament and of the Council of 24 October 1995 on the protection of individuals with regard to the processing of personal data and on the free movement of such data[6] and Regulation (EC) No 45/2001 of the European Parliament and of the Council of 18 December 2000 on the protection of individuals with regard to the processing of personal data by Community institutions and bodies and on the free movement of such data[7].

(27) The exchange of information relating to decisions on applications and to customs actions should be made via a central electronic database. The entity which will control and manage that database and the entities in charge of ensuring the security of the processing of the data contained in the database should be defined. Introducing any type of possible interoperability or exchange should first and foremost comply with the purpose limitation principle, namely that data should be used for the purpose for which the database has been established, and no further exchange or interconnection should be allowed other than for that purpose.

(28) In order to ensure that the definition of small consignments can be adapted if it proves to be impractical, taking into account the need to ensure the effective operation of the procedure, or where necessary to avoid any circumvention of this procedure as regards the composition of consignments, the power to adopt acts in accordance with Article 290 of the Treaty on the Functioning of the European Union should be delegated to the Commission in respect of amending the non-essential elements of the definition of small consignments, namely the specific quantities set out in that definition. It is of particular importance that the Commission carry out appropriate consultations during its preparatory work, including at expert level. The Commission, when preparing and drawing up delegated acts, should ensure a simultaneous, timely and appropriate transmission of relevant documents to the European Parliament and to the Council.

(29) In order to ensure uniform conditions for the implementation of the provisions concerning defining the elements of the practical arrangements for the exchange of data with third countries and the provisions concerning the forms for the application and for requesting the extension of the period during which customs authorities are to take action, implementing powers should be conferred on the Commission, namely to define those elements of the practical arrangements and to establish standard forms. Those powers should be exercised in accordance with Regulation (EU) No 182/2011 of the European Parliament and of the Council of 16 February 2011 laying down the rules and general principles concerning mechanisms for control by Member States of the Commission's exercise of implementing powers[8]. For establishing the standard forms, although the subject of the provisions of this Regulation to be implemented falls within the scope of the common commercial policy, given the nature and impacts of those implementing acts, the advisory procedure should be used for their adoption, because all details of what information to include in the forms follows directly from the text of this Regulation. Those implementing acts will therefore only establish the format and structure of the form and will have no further implications for the common commercial policy of the Union.

(30) Regulation (EC) No 1383/2003 should be repealed.

(31) The European Data Protection Supervisor was consulted in accordance

---

[6] OJ L 281, 23.11.1995, p. 31.
[7] OJ L 8, 12.1.2001, p. 1.
[8] OJ L 55, 28.2.2011, p. 13.

with Article 28(2) of Regulation (EC) No 45/2001 and delivered an opinion on 12 October 2011[9],

HAVE ADOPTED THIS REGULATION:

CHAPTER I

SUBJECT MATTER, SCOPE AND DEFINITIONS

Article 1

Subject Matter, Scope and Definitions

1. This Regulation sets out the conditions and procedures for action by the customs authorities where goods suspected of infringing an intellectual property right are, or should have been, subject to customs supervision or customs control within the customs territory of the Union in accordance with Council Regulation (EEC) No 2913/92 of 12 October 1992 establishing the Community Customs Code[10], particularly goods in the following situations:

   (a) when declared for release for free circulation, export or re-export;
   (b) when entering or leaving the customs territory of the Union;
   (c) when placed under a suspensive procedure or in a free zone or free warehouse.

2. In respect of the goods subject to customs supervision or customs control, and without prejudice to Articles 17 and 18, the customs authorities shall carry out adequate customs controls and shall take proportionate identification measures as provided for in Article 13(1) and Article 72 of Regulation (EEC) No 2913/92 in accordance with risk analysis criteria with a view to preventing acts in breach of intellectual property laws applicable in the territory of the Union and in order to cooperate with third countries on the enforcement of intellectual property rights.

3. This Regulation shall not apply to goods that have been released for free circulation under the end-use regime.

4. This Regulation shall not apply to goods of a non-commercial nature contained in travellers' personal luggage.

5. This Regulation shall not apply to goods that have been manufactured with the consent of the right-holder or to goods manufactured, by a person duly authorised by a right-holder to manufacture a certain quantity of goods, in excess of the quantities agreed between that person and the right-holder.

6. This Regulation shall not affect national or Union law on intellectual property or the laws of the Member States in relation to criminal procedures.

Article 2

Definitions

For the purposes of this Regulation:

   (1) 'intellectual property right' means:
       (a) a trade mark;
       (b) a design;
       (c) a copyright or any related right as provided for by national or Union law;

---

[9] OJ C 363, 13.12.2011, p. 3.
[10] OJ L 302, 19.10.1992, p. 1.

(d) a geographical indication;

(f) a supplementary protection certificate for medicinal products as provided for in Regulation (EC) No 469/2009 of the European Parliament and of the Council of 6 May 2009 concerning the supplementary protection certificate for medicinal products[11];

(g) a supplementary protection certificate for plant protection products as provided for in Regulation (EC) No 1610/96 of the European Parliament and of the Council of 23 July 1996 concerning the creation of a supplementary protection certificate for plant protection products[12];

(h) a Community plant variety right as provided for in Council Regulation (EC) No 2100/94 of 27 July 1994 on Community plant variety rights[13];

(i) a plant variety right as provided for by national law;

(j) a topography of semiconductor product as provided for by national or Union law;

(k) a utility model in so far as it is protected as an intellectual property right by national or Union law;

(l) a trade name in so far as it is protected as an exclusive intellectual property right by national or Union law;

(2) 'trade mark' means:

(a) a Community trade mark as provided for in Council Regulation (EC) No 207/2009 of 26 February 2009 on the Community trade mark[14];

(b) a trade mark registered in a Member State, or, in the case of Belgium, Luxembourg or the Netherlands, at the Benelux Office for Intellectual Property;

(c) a trade mark registered under international arrangements which has effect in a Member State or in the Union;

(3) 'design' means:

(a) a Community design as provided for in Council Regulation (EC) No 6/2002 of 12 December 2001 on Community designs[15];

(b) a design registered in a Member State, or, in the case of Belgium, Luxembourg or the Netherlands, at the Benelux Office for Intellectual Property;

(c) a design registered under international arrangements which has effect in a Member State or in the Union;

(4) 'geographical indication' means:

(a) a geographical indication or designation of origin protected for agricultural products and foodstuff as provided for in Regulation (EU) No 1151/2012 of the European Parliament and of the Council of 21 November 2012 on quality schemes for agricultural products and foodstuffs[16];

(b) a designation of origin or geographical indication for wine

[11] OJ L 152, 16.6.2009, p. 1.
[12] OJ L 198, 8.8.1996, p. 30.
[13] OJ L 227, 1.9.1994, p. 1.
[14] OJ L 78, 24.3.2009, p. 1.
[15] OJ L 3, 5.1.2002, p. 1.
[16] OJ L 343, 14.12.2012, p. 1.

as provided for in Council Regulation (EC) No 1234/2007 of 22 October 2007 establishing a common organisation of agricultural markets and on specific provisions for certain agricultural products (Single CMO Regulation)[17];

(c) a geographical designation for aromatised drinks based on wine products as provided for in Council Regulation (EEC) No 1601/91 of 10 June 1991 laying down general rules on the definition, description and presentation of aromatized wines, aromatized wine-based drinks and aromatized wine-product cocktails[18];

(d) a geographical indication of spirit drinks as provided for in Regulation (EC) No 110/2008 of the European Parliament and of the Council of 15 January 2008 on the definition, description, presentation, labelling and the protection of geographical indications of spirit drinks[19];

(e) a geographical indication for products not falling under points (a) to (d) in so far as it is established as an exclusive intellectual property right by national or Union law;

(f) a geographical indication as provided for in Agreements between the Union and third countries and as such listed in those Agreements;

(5) 'counterfeit goods' means:

(a) goods which are the subject of an act infringing a trade mark in the Member State where they are found and bear without authorisation a sign which is identical to the trade mark validly registered in respect of the same type of goods, or which cannot be distinguished in its essential aspects from such a trade mark;

(b) goods which are the subject of an act infringing a geographical indication in the Member State where they are found and, bear or are described by, a name or term protected in respect of that geographical indication;

(c) any packaging, label, sticker, brochure, operating instructions, warranty document or other similar item, even if presented separately, which is the subject of an act infringing a trade mark or a geographical indication, which includes a sign, name or term which is identical to a validly registered trade mark or protected geographical indication, or which cannot be distinguished in its essential aspects from such a trade mark or geographical indication, and which can be used for the same type of goods as that for which the trade mark or geographical indication has been registered;

(6) 'pirated goods' means: goods which are the subject of an act infringing a copyright or related right or a design in the Member State where the goods are found and which are, or contain copies, made without the consent of the holder of a copyright or related right or a design, or of a person authorised by that holder in the country of production;

(7) 'goods suspected of infringing an intellectual property right' means: goods with regard to which there are reasonable indications that, in the Member State where those goods are found, they are prima facie:

(a) goods which are the subject of an act infringing an intellectual property right in that Member State;

---

[17] OJ L 299, 16.11.2007, p. 1.
[18] OJ L 149, 14.6.1991, p. 1.
[19] OJ L 39, 13.2.2008, p. 16.

(b) devices, products or components which are primarily designed, produced or adapted for the purpose of enabling or facilitating the circumvention of any technology, device or component that, in the normal course of its operation, prevents or restricts acts in respect of works which are not authorised by the holder of any copyright or any right related to copyright and which relate to an act infringing those rights in that Member State;

(c) any mould or matrix which is specifically designed or adapted for the manufacture of goods infringing an intellectual property right, if such moulds or matrices relate to an act infringing an intellectual property right in that Member State;

(8) 'right-holder' means: the holder of an intellectual property right;

(9) 'application' means: a request made to the competent customs department for customs authorities to take action with respect to goods suspected of infringing an intellectual property right;

(10) 'national application' means: an application requesting the customs authorities of a Member State to take action in that Member State;

(11) 'Union application' means: an application submitted in one Member State and requesting the customs authorities of that Member State and of one or more other Member States to take action in their respective Member States;

(12) 'applicant' means: the person or entity in whose name an application is submitted;

(13) 'holder of the decision' means: the holder of a decision granting an application;

(14) 'holder of the goods' means: the person who is the owner of the goods suspected of infringing an intellectual property right or who has a similar right of disposal, or physical control, over such goods;

(15) 'declarant' means: the declarant as defined in point (18) of Article 4 of Regulation (EEC) No 2913/92;

(16) 'destruction' means: the physical destruction, recycling or disposal of goods outside commercial channels, in such a way as to preclude damage to the holder of the decision;

(17) 'customs territory of the Union' means: the customs territory of the Community as defined in Article 3 of Regulation (EEC) No 2913/92;

(18) 'release of the goods' means: the release of the goods as defined in point (20) of Article 4 of Regulation (EEC) No 2913/92;

(19) 'small consignment' means: a postal or express courier consignment, which:

(a) contains three units or less; or

(b) has a gross weight of less than two kilograms.

For the purpose of point (a), 'units' means goods as classified under the Combined Nomenclature in accordance with Annex I to Council Regulation (EEC) No 2658/87 of 23 July 1987 on the tariff and statistical nomenclature and on the Common Customs Tariff[20] if unpackaged, or the package of such goods intended for retail sale to the ultimate consumer. For the purpose of this definition, separate goods falling in the same Combined Nomenclature code shall be considered as different units and goods presented as sets classified in one Combined Nomenclature code shall be considered as one unit;

[20] OJ L 256, 7.9.1987, p. 1.

(20) 'perishable goods' means: goods considered by customs authorities to deteriorate by being kept for up to 20 days from the date of their suspension of release or detention;

(21) 'exclusive licence' means: a licence (whether general or limited) authorising the licensee to the exclusion of all other persons, including the person granting the licence, to use an intellectual property right in the manner authorised by the licence.

CHAPTER II

APPLICATIONS

SECTION 1

SUBMISSION OF APPLICATIONS

Article 3

Entitlement to submit an application

The following persons and entities shall, to the extent they are entitled to initiate proceedings, in order to determine whether an intellectual property right has been infringed, in the Member State or Member States where the customs authorities are requested to take action, be entitled to submit:

(1) a national or a Union application:

(a) right-holders;

(b) intellectual property collective rights management bodies as referred to in point (c) of Article 4(1) of Directive 2004/48/EC of the European Parliament and of the Council of 29 April 2004 on the enforcement of intellectual property rights[21];

(c) professional defence bodies as referred to in point (d) of Article 4(1) of Directive 2004/48/EC;

(d) groups within the meaning of point (2) of Article 3, and Article 49(1) of Regulation (EU) No 1151/2012, groups of producers within the meaning of Article 118e of Regulation (EC) No 1234/2007 or similar groups of producers provided for in Union law governing geographical indications representing producers of products with a geographical indication or representatives of such groups, in particular Regulations (EEC) No 1601/91 and (EC) No 110/2008 and operators entitled to use a geographical indication as well as inspection bodies or authorities competent for such a geographical indication;

(2) a national application:

(a) persons or entities authorised to use intellectual property rights, which have been authorised formally by the right-holder to initiate proceedings in order to determine whether the intellectual property right has been infringed;

(b) groups of producers provided for in the legislation of the Member States governing geographical indications representing producers of products with geographical indications or representatives of such groups and operators entitled to use a geographical indication, as well as inspection bodies or authorities competent for such a geographical indication;

(3) a Union application: holders of exclusive licenses covering the entire territory of two or more Member States, where those licence holders have been

---

[21] OJ L 157, 30.4.2004, p. 45.

authorised formally in those Member States by the right-holder to initiate proceedings in order to determine whether the intellectual property right has been infringed.

Article 4

Intellectual property rights covered by Union applications

A Union application may be submitted only with respect to intellectual property rights based on Union law producing effects throughout the Union.

Article 5

Submission of applications

1. Each Member State shall designate the customs department competent to receive and process applications ('competent customs department'). The Member State shall inform the Commission accordingly and the Commission shall make public a list of competent customs departments designated by the Member States.

2. Applications shall be submitted to the competent customs department. The applications shall be completed using the form referred to in Article 6 and shall contain the information required therein.

3. Where an application is submitted after notification by the customs authorities of the suspension of the release or detention of the goods in accordance with Article 18(3), that application shall comply with the following:

(a) it is submitted to the competent customs department within four working days of the notification of the suspension of the release or detention of the goods;

(b) it is a national application;

(c) it contains the information referred to in Article 6(3). The applicant may, however, omit the information referred to in point (g), (h) or (i) of that paragraph.

4. Except in the circumstances referred to in point (3) of Article 3, only one national application and one Union application may be submitted per Member State for the same intellectual property right protected in that Member State. In the circumstances referred to in point (3) of Article 3, more than one Union application shall be allowed.

5. Where a Union application is granted for a Member State already covered by another Union application granted to the same applicant and for the same intellectual property right, the customs authorities of that Member State shall take action on the basis of the Union application first granted. They shall inform the competent customs department of the Member State where any subsequent Union application was granted, which shall, amend or revoke the decision granting that subsequent Union application.

6. Where computerised systems are available for the purpose of receiving and processing applications, applications as well as attachments shall be submitted using electronic data-processing techniques. Member States and the Commission shall develop, maintain and employ such systems in accordance with the multi-annual strategic plan referred to in Article 8(2) of Decision No 70/2008/EC of the European Parliament and of the Council of 15 January 2008 on a paperless customs environment for customs and trade[22].

Article 6

Application form

1. The Commission shall establish an application form by means of imple-

---

[22] OJ L 23, 26.1.2008, p. 21.

menting acts. Those implementing acts shall be adopted in accordance with the advisory procedure referred to in Article 34(2).

2. The application form shall specify the information that has to be provided to the data subject pursuant to Regulation (EC) No 45/2001 and national laws implementing Directive 95/46/EC.

3. The Commission shall ensure that the following information is required of the applicant in the application form:

(a) details concerning the applicant;

(b) the status, within the meaning of Article 3, of the applicant;

(c) documents providing evidence to satisfy the competent customs department that the applicant is entitled to submit the application;

(d) where the applicant submits the application by means of a representative, details of the person representing him and evidence of that person's powers to act as representative, in accordance with the legislation of the Member State in which the application is submitted;

(e) the intellectual property right or rights to be enforced;

(f) in the case of a Union application, the Member States in which customs action is requested;

(g) specific and technical data on the authentic goods, including markings such as bar-coding and images where appropriate;

(h) the information needed to enable the customs authorities to readily identify the goods in question;

(i) information relevant to the customs authorities' analysis and assessment of the risk of infringement of the intellectual property right or the intellectual property rights concerned, such as the authorised distributors;

(j) whether information provided in accordance with point (g), (h) or (i) of this paragraph is to be marked for restricted handling in accordance with Article 31(5);

(k) the details of any representative designated by the applicant to take charge of legal and technical matters;

(l) an undertaking by the applicant to notify the competent customs department of any of the situations laid down in Article 15;

(m) an undertaking by the applicant to forward and update any information relevant to the customs authorities' analysis and assessment of the risk of infringement of the intellectual property right(s) concerned;

(n) an undertaking by the applicant to assume liability under the conditions laid down in Article 28;

(o) an undertaking by the applicant to bear the costs referred to in Article 29 under the conditions laid down in that Article;

(p) an agreement by the applicant that the data provided by him may be processed by the Commission and by the Member States;

(q) whether the applicant requests the use of the procedure referred to in Article 26 and, where requested by the customs authorities, agrees to cover the costs related to destruction of goods under that procedure.

SECTION 2

DECISIONS ON APPLICATIONS

Article 7

Processing of incomplete applications

1. Where, on receipt of an application, the competent customs department

considers that the application does not contain all the information required by Article 6(3), the competent customs department shall request the applicant to supply the missing information within 10 working days of notification of the request.

In such cases, the time-limit referred to in Article 9(1) shall be suspended until the relevant information is received.

2. Where the applicant does not provide the missing information within the period referred to in the first subparagraph of paragraph 1, the competent customs department shall reject the application.

Article 8
Fees

The applicant shall not be charged a fee to cover the administrative costs resulting from the processing of the application.

Article 9
Notification of decisions granting or rejecting applications

1. The competent customs department shall notify the applicant of its decision granting or rejecting the application within 30 working days of the receipt of the application. In the event of rejection, the competent customs department shall provide reasons for its decision and include information on the appeal procedure.

2. If the applicant has been notified of the suspension of the release or the detention of the goods by the customs authorities before the submission of an application, the competent customs department shall notify the applicant of its decision granting or rejecting the application within two working days of the receipt of the application.

Article 10
Decisions concerning applications

1. A decision granting a national application and any decision revoking or amending it shall take effect in the Member State in which the national application was submitted from the day following the date of adoption.

A decision extending the period during which customs authorities are to take action shall take effect in the Member State in which the national application was submitted on the day following the date of expiry of the period to be extended.

2. A decision granting a Union application and any decision revoking or amending it shall take effect as follows:

(a) in the Member State in which the application was submitted, on the day following the date of adoption;

(b) in all other Member States where action by the customs authorities is requested, on the day following the date on which the customs authorities are notified in accordance with Article 14(2), provided that the holder of the decision has fulfilled his obligations under Article 29(3) with regard to translation costs.

A decision extending the period during which customs authorities are to take action shall take effect in the Member State in which the Union application was submitted and in all other Member States where action by the customs authorities is requested the day following the date of expiry of the period to be extended.

Article 11
Period during which the customs authorities are to take action

1. When granting an application, the competent customs department shall specify the period during which the customs authorities are to take action.

That period shall begin on the day the decision granting the application takes effect, pursuant to Article 10, and shall not exceed one year from the day following the date of adoption.

2. Where an application submitted after notification by the customs authorities of the suspension of the release or detention of the goods in accordance with Article 18(3) does not contain the information referred to in point (g), (h) or (i) of Article 6(3), it shall be granted only for the suspension of the release or detention of those goods, unless that information is provided within 10 working days after the notification of the suspension of the release or detention of the goods.

3. Where an intellectual property right ceases to have effect or where the applicant ceases for other reasons to be entitled to submit an application, no action shall be taken by the customs authorities. The decision granting the application shall be revoked or amended accordingly by the competent customs department that granted the decision.

Article 12
Extension of the period during which the customs authorities are to take action

1. On expiry of the period during which the customs authorities are to take action, and subject to the prior discharge by the holder of the decision of any debt owed to the customs authorities under this Regulation, the competent customs department which adopted the initial decision may, at the request of the holder of the decision, extend that period.

2. Where the request for extension of the period during which the customs authorities are to take action is received by the competent customs department less than 30 working days before the expiry of the period to be extended, it may refuse that request.

3. The competent customs department shall notify its decision on the extension to the holder of the decision within 30 working days of the receipt of the request referred to in paragraph 1. The competent customs department shall specify the period during which the customs authorities are to take action.

4. The extended period during which the customs authorities are to take action shall run from the day following the date of expiry of the previous period and shall not exceed one year.

5. Where an intellectual property right ceases to have effect or where the applicant ceases for other reasons to be entitled to submit an application, no action shall be taken by the customs authorities. The decision granting the extension shall be revoked or amended accordingly by the competent customs department that granted the decision.

6. The holder of the decision shall not be charged a fee to cover the administrative costs resulting from the processing of the request for extension.

7. The Commission shall establish an extension request form by means of implementing acts. Those implementing acts shall be adopted in accordance with the advisory procedure referred to in Article 34(2).

Article 13
Amending the decision with regard to intellectual property rights

The competent customs department that adopted the decision granting the application may, at the request of the holder of that decision, modify the list of intellectual property rights in that decision. Where a new intellectual property right is added, the request shall contain the information referred to in points (c), (e), (g), (h) and (i) of Article 6(3).

In the case of a decision granting a Union application, any modification consisting of the addition of intellectual property rights shall be limited to intellectual property rights covered by Article 4.

Article 14

Notification obligations of the competent customs department

1. The competent customs department to which a national application has been submitted shall forward the following decisions to the customs offices of its Member State, immediately after their adoption:

(a) decisions granting the application;

(b) decisions revoking decisions granting the application;

(c) decisions amending decisions granting the application;

(d) decisions extending the period during which the customs authorities are to take action.

2. The competent customs department to which a Union application has been submitted shall forward the following decisions to the competent customs department of the Member State or Member States indicated in the Union application, immediately after their adoption:

(a) decisions granting the application;

(b) decisions revoking decisions granting the application;

(c) decisions amending decisions granting the application;

(d) decisions extending the period during which the customs authorities are to take action.

The competent customs department of the Member State or Member States indicated in the Union application shall immediately after receiving those decisions forward them to their customs offices.

3. The competent customs department of the Member State or Member States indicated in the Union application may request the competent customs department that adopted the decision granting the application to provide them with additional information deemed necessary for the implementation of that decision.

4. The competent customs department shall forward its decision suspending the actions of the customs authorities under point (b) of Article 16(1) and Article 16(2) to the customs offices of its Member State, immediately after its adoption.

Article 15

Notification obligations of the holder of the decision

The holder of the decision shall immediately notify the competent customs department that granted the application of any of the following:

(a) an intellectual property right covered by the application ceases to have effect;

(b) the holder of the decision ceases for other reasons to be entitled to submit the application;

(c) modifications to the information referred to in Article 6(3).

Article 16

Failure of the holder of the decision to fulfil his obligations

1. Where the holder of the decision uses the information provided by the customs authorities for purposes other than those provided for in Article 21, the competent customs department of the Member State where the information was provided or misused may:

(a) revoke any decision adopted by it granting a national application to that holder of the decision, and refuse to extend the period during which the customs authorities are to take action;

(b) suspend in their territory, during the period during which the customs authorities are to take action, any decision granting a Union application to that holder of the decision.

2. The competent customs department may decide to suspend the actions of the customs authorities until the expiry of the period during which those authorities are to take action, where the holder of the decision:

(a) does not fulfil the notification obligations set out in Article 15;

(b) does not fulfil the obligation on returning samples set out in Article 19(3);

(c) does not fulfil the obligations on costs and translation set out in Article 29(1) and (3);

(d) without valid reason does not initiate proceedings as provided for in Article 23(3) or Article 26(9). In the case of a Union application, the decision to suspend the actions of the customs authorities shall have effect only in the Member State where such decision is taken.

Chapter III

Action by the Customs Authorities

Section 1

Suspension of the release or detention of goods suspected of infringing an intellectual property right

Article 17

Suspension of the release or detention of the goods following the grant of an application

1. Where the customs authorities identify goods suspected of infringing an intellectual property right covered by a decision granting an application, they shall suspend the release of the goods or detain them.

2. Before suspending the release of or detaining the goods, the customs authorities may ask the holder of the decision to provide them with any relevant information with respect to the goods. The customs authorities may also provide the holder of the decision with information about the actual or estimated quantity of goods, their actual or presumed nature and images thereof, as appropriate.

3. The customs authorities shall notify the declarant or the holder of the goods of the suspension of the release of the goods or the detention of the goods within one working day of that suspension or detention.

Where the customs authorities opt to notify the holder of the goods and two or more persons are considered to be the holder of the goods, the customs authorities shall not be obliged to notify more than one of those persons.

The customs authorities shall notify the holder of the decision of the suspension of the release of the goods or the detention on the same day as, or promptly after, the declarant or the holder of the goods is notified.

The notifications shall include information on the procedure set out in Article 23.

4. The customs authorities shall inform the holder of the decision and the declarant or the holder of the goods of the actual or estimated quantity and the actual or presumed nature of the goods, including available images thereof, as appropriate, whose release has been suspended or which have been detained. The

customs authorities shall also, upon request and where available to them, inform the holder of the decision of the names and addresses of the consignee, the consignor and the declarant or the holder of the goods, of the customs procedure and of the origin, provenance and destination of the goods whose release has been suspended or which have been detained.

Article 18

Suspension of the release or detention of the goods before the grant of an application

1. Where the customs authorities identify goods suspected of infringing an intellectual property right, which are not covered by a decision granting an application, they may, except for in the case of perishable goods, suspend the release of those goods or detain them.

2. Before suspending the release of or detaining the goods suspected of infringing an intellectual property right, the customs authorities may, without disclosing any information other than the actual or estimated quantity of goods, their actual or presumed nature and images thereof, as appropriate, request any person or entity potentially entitled to submit an application concerning the alleged infringement of the intellectual property rights to provide them with any relevant information.

3. The customs authorities shall notify the declarant or the holder of the goods of the suspension of the release of the goods or their detention within one working day of that suspension or detention. Where the customs authorities opt to notify the holder of the goods and two or more persons are considered to be the holder of the goods, the customs authorities shall not be obliged to notify more than one of those persons.

The customs authorities shall notify persons or entities entitled to submit an application concerning the alleged infringement of the intellectual property rights, of the suspension of the release of the goods or their detention on the same day as, or promptly after, the declarant or the holder of the goods is notified.

The customs authorities may consult the competent public authorities in order to identify the persons or entities entitled to submit an application.

The notifications shall include information on the procedure set out in Article 23.

4. The customs authorities shall grant the release of the goods or put an end to their detention immediately after completion of all customs formalities in the following cases:

 (a) where they have not identified any person or entity entitled to submit an application concerning the alleged infringement of intellectual property rights within one working day from the suspension of the release or the detention of the goods;

 (b) where they have not received an application in accordance with Article 5(3), or where they have rejected such an application.

5. Where an application has been granted, the customs authorities shall, upon request and where available to them, inform the holder of the decision of the names and addresses of the consignee, the consignor and the declarant or the holder of the goods, of the customs procedure and of the origin, provenance and destination of the goods whose release has been suspended or which have been detained.

Article 19

Inspection and sampling of goods whose release has been suspended or which have been detained

1. The customs authorities shall give the holder of the decision and the declar-

ant or the holder of the goods the opportunity to inspect the goods whose release has been suspended or which have been detained.

2. The customs authorities may take samples that are representative of the goods. They may provide or send such samples to the holder of the decision, at the holder's request and strictly for the purposes of analysis and to facilitate the subsequent procedure in relation to counterfeit and pirated goods. Any analysis of those samples shall be carried out under the sole responsibility of the holder of the decision.

3. The holder of the decision shall, unless circumstances do not allow, return the samples referred to in paragraph 2 to the customs authorities on completion of the analysis, at the latest before the goods are released or their detention is ended.

Article 20
Conditions for storage

The conditions of storage of goods during a period of suspension of release or detention shall be determined by the customs authorities.

Article 21
Permitted use of certain information by the holder of the decision

Where the holder of the decision has received the information referred to in Article 17(4), Article 18(5), Article 19 or Article 26(8), he may disclose or use that information only for the following purposes:

(a) to initiate proceedings to determine whether an intellectual property right has been infringed and in the course of such proceedings;

(b) in connection with criminal investigations related to the infringement of an intellectual property right and undertaken by public authorities in the Member State where the goods are found;

(c) to initiate criminal proceedings and in the course of such proceedings;

(d) to seek compensation from the infringer or other persons;

(e) to agree with the declarant or the holder of the goods that the goods be destroyed in accordance with Article 23(1);

(f) to agree with the declarant or the holder of the goods of the amount of the guarantee referred to in point (a) of Article 24(2).

Article 22
Sharing of information and data between customs authorities

1. Without prejudice to applicable provisions on data protection in the Union and for the purpose of contributing to eliminating international trade in goods infringing intellectual property rights, the Commission and the customs authorities of the Member States may share certain data and information available to them with the relevant authorities in third countries according to the practical arrangements referred to in paragraph 3.

2. The data and information referred to in paragraph 1 shall be exchanged to swiftly enable effective enforcement against shipments of goods infringing an intellectual property right. Such data and information may relate to seizures, trends and general risk information, including on goods which are in transit through the territory of the Union and which have originated in or are destined for the territory of third countries concerned. Such data and information may include, where appropriate, the following:

(a) nature and quantity of goods;

(b) suspected intellectual property right infringed;

(c) origin, provenance and destination of the goods;

(d) information on movements of means of transport, in particular:

    (i) name of vessel or registration of means of transport;

    (ii) reference numbers of freight bill or other transport document;

    (iii) number of containers;

    (iv) weight of load;

    (v) description and/or coding of goods;

    (vi) reservation number;

    (vii) seal number;

    (viii) place of first loading;

    (ix) place of final unloading;

    (x) places of transhipment;

    (xi) expected date of arrival at place of final unloading;

(e) information on movements of containers, in particular:

    (i) container number;

    (ii) container loading status;

    (iii) date of movement;

    (iv) type of movement (loaded, unloaded, transhipped, entered, left, etc.);

    (v) name of vessel or registration of means of transport;

    (vi) number of voyage/journey;

    (vii) place;

    (viii) freight bill or other transport document.

3. The Commission shall adopt implementing acts defining the elements of the necessary practical arrangements concerning the exchange of data and information referred to in paragraphs 1 and 2 of this Article. Those implementing acts shall be adopted in accordance with the examination procedure referred to in Article 34(3).

Section 2

Destruction of goods, initiation of proceedings and early release of goods

Article 23

Destruction of goods and initiation of proceedings

1. Goods suspected of infringing an intellectual property right may be destroyed under customs control, without there being any need to determine whether an intellectual property right has been infringed under the law of the Member State where the goods are found, where all of the following conditions are fulfilled:

(a) the holder of the decision has confirmed in writing to the customs authorities, within 10 working days, or three working days in the case of perishable goods, of notification of the suspension of the release or the detention of the goods, that, in his conviction, an intellectual property right has been infringed;

(b) the holder of the decision has confirmed in writing to the customs authorities, within 10 working days, or three working days in the case of perishable goods, of notification of the suspension of the release or the detention of the goods, his agreement to the destruction of the goods;

(c) the declarant or the holder of the goods has confirmed in writing to the customs authorities, within 10 working days, or three working days in the case of perishable goods, of notification of the suspension of the release or the detention of the goods, his agreement to the destruction of the goods. Where the declarant or the holder of the goods has not confirmed his agreement to the destruction of the goods nor notified his opposition thereto to the customs authorities, within those deadlines, the customs authorities may deem the declarant or the holder of the goods to have confirmed his agreement to the destruction of those goods.

The customs authorities shall grant the release of the goods or put an end to their detention, immediately after completion of all customs formalities, where within the periods referred to in points (a) and (b) of the first subparagraph, they have not received both the written confirmation from the holder of the decision that, in his conviction, an intellectual property right has been infringed and his agreement to destruction, unless those authorities have been duly informed about the initiation of proceedings to determine whether an intellectual property right has been infringed.

2. The destruction of the goods shall be carried out under customs control and under the responsibility of the holder of the decision, unless otherwise specified in the national law of the Member State where the goods are destroyed. Samples may be taken by competent authorities prior to the destruction of the goods. Samples taken prior to destruction may be used for educational purposes.

3. Where the declarant or the holder of the goods has not confirmed his agreement to the destruction in writing and where the declarant or the holder of the goods has not been deemed to have confirmed his agreement to the destruction, in accordance with point (c) of the first subparagraph of paragraph 1 within the periods referred to therein, the customs authorities shall immediately notify the holder of the decision thereof. The holder of the decision shall, within 10 working days, or three working days in the case of perishable goods, of notification of the suspension of the release or the detention of the goods, initiate proceedings to determine whether an intellectual property right has been infringed.

4. Except in the case of perishable goods the customs authorities may extend the period referred to in paragraph 3 by a maximum of 10 working days upon a duly justified request by the holder of the decision in appropriate cases.

5. The customs authorities shall grant the release of the goods or put an end to their detention, immediately after completion of all customs formalities, where, within the periods referred to in paragraphs 3 and 4, they have not been duly informed, in accordance with paragraph 3, on the initiation of proceedings to determine whether an intellectual property right has been infringed.

Article 24
Early release of goods

1. Where the customs authorities have been notified of the initiation of proceedings to determine whether a design, patent, utility model, topography of semiconductor product or plant variety has been infringed, the declarant or the holder of the goods may request the customs authorities to release the goods or put an end to their detention before the completion of those proceedings.

2. The customs authorities shall release the goods or put an end to their detention only where all the following conditions are fulfilled:
  (a) the declarant or the holder of the goods has provided a guarantee that is of an amount sufficient to protect the interests of the holder of the decision;
  (b) the authority competent to determine whether an intellectual property right has been infringed has not authorised precautionary measures;
  (c) all customs formalities have been completed.

3. The provision of the guarantee referred to in point (a) of paragraph 2 shall not affect the other legal remedies available to the holder of the decision.

Article 25

Goods for destruction

1. Goods to be destroyed under Article 23 or 26 shall not be:

(a) released for free circulation, unless customs authorities, with the agreement of the holder of the decision, decide that it is necessary in the event that the goods are to be recycled or disposed of outside commercial channels, including for awareness-raising, training and educational purposes. The conditions under which the goods can be released for free circulation shall be determined by the customs authorities;

(b) brought out of the customs territory of the Union;

(c) exported;

(d) re-exported;

(e) placed under a suspensive procedure;

(f) placed in a free zone or free warehouse.

2. The customs authorities may allow the goods referred to in paragraph 1 to be moved under customs supervision between different places within the customs territory of the Union with a view to their destruction under customs control.

Article 26

Procedure for the destruction of goods in small consignments

1. This Article shall apply to goods where all of the following conditions are fulfilled:

(a) the goods are suspected of being counterfeit or pirated goods;

(b) the goods are not perishable goods;

(c) the goods are covered by a decision granting an application;

(d) the holder of the decision has requested the use of the procedure set out in this Article in the application;

(e) the goods are transported in small consignments.

2. When the procedure set out in this Article is applied, Article 17(3) and (4) and Article 19(2) and (3) shall not apply.

3. The customs authorities shall notify the declarant or the holder of the goods of the suspension of the release of the goods or their detention within one working day of the suspension of the release or of the detention of the goods. The notification of the suspension of the release or the detention of the goods shall include the following information:

(a) that the customs authorities intend to destroy the goods;

(b) the rights of the declarant or the holder of the goods under paragraphs 4, 5 and 6.

4. The declarant or the holder of the goods shall be given the opportunity to express his point of view within 10 working days of notification of the suspension of the release or the detention of the goods.

5. The goods concerned may be destroyed where, within 10 working days of notification of the suspension of the release or the detention of the goods, the declarant or the holder of the goods has confirmed to the customs authorities his agreement to the destruction of the goods.

6. Where the declarant or the holder of the goods has not confirmed his agreement to the destruction of the goods nor notified his opposition thereto to the customs authorities, within the period referred to in paragraph 5, the customs authorities may deem the declarant or the holder of the goods to have confirmed his agreement to the destruction of the goods.

7. The destruction shall be carried out under customs control. The customs authorities shall, upon request and as appropriate, provide the holder of the decision with information about the actual or estimated quantity of destroyed goods and their nature.

8. Where the declarant or the holder of the goods has not confirmed his agreement to the destruction of the goods and where the declarant or the holder of the goods has not been deemed to have confirmed such agreement, in accordance with paragraph 6, the customs authorities shall immediately notify the holder of the decision thereof and of the quantity of goods and their nature, including images thereof, where appropriate. The customs authorities shall also, upon request and where available to them, inform the holder of the decision of the names and addresses of the consignee, the consignor and the declarant or the holder of the goods, of the customs procedure and of the origin, provenance and destination of the goods whose release has been suspended or which have been detained.

9. The customs authorities shall grant the release of the goods or put an end to their detention immediately after completion of all customs formalities where they have not received information from the holder of the decision on the initiation of proceedings to determine whether an intellectual property right has been infringed within 10 working days of the notification referred to in paragraph 8.

10. The Commission shall be empowered to adopt delegated acts in accordance with Article 35 concerning the amendment of quantities in the definition of small consignments in the event that the definition is found to be impractical in the light of the need to ensure the effective operation of the procedure set out in this Article, or where necessary in order to avoid any circumvention of this procedure as regards the composition of consignments.

CHAPTER IV

LIABILITY, COSTS AND PENALTIES

Article 27

Liability of the customs authorities

Without prejudice to national law, the decision granting an application shall not entitle the holder of that decision to compensation in the event that goods suspected of infringing an intellectual property right are not detected by a customs office and are released, or no action is taken to detain them.

Article 28

Liability of the holder of the decision

Where a procedure duly initiated pursuant to this Regulation is discontinued owing to an act or omission on the part of the holder of the decision, where samples taken pursuant to Article 19(2) are either not returned or are damaged and beyond use owing to an act or omission on the part of the holder of the decision, or where the goods in question are subsequently found not to infringe an intellectual property right, the holder of the decision shall be liable towards any holder of the goods or declarant, who has suffered damage in that regard, in accordance with specific applicable legislation.

Article 29

Costs

1. Where requested by the customs authorities, the holder of the decision shall

reimburse the costs incurred by the customs authorities, or other parties acting on behalf of customs authorities, from the moment of detention or suspension of the release of the goods, including storage and handling of the goods, in accordance with Article 17(1), Article 18(1) and Article 19(2) and (3), and when using corrective measures such as destruction of goods in accordance with Articles 23 and 26. The holder of a decision to whom the suspension of release or detention of goods has been notified shall, upon request, be given information by the customs authorities on where and how those goods are being stored and on the estimated costs of storage referred to in this paragraph. The information on estimated costs may be expressed in terms of time, products, volume, weight or service depending on the circumstances of storage and the nature of the goods.

2. This Article shall be without prejudice to the right of the holder of the decision to seek compensation from the infringer or other persons in accordance with the legislation applicable.

3. The holder of a decision granting a Union application shall provide and pay for any translation required by the competent customs department or customs authorities which are to take action concerning the goods suspected of infringing an intellectual property right.

Article 30

Penalties

The Member States shall ensure that the holders of decisions comply with the obligations set out in this Regulation, including, where appropriate, by laying down provisions establishing penalties. The penalties provided for shall be effective, proportionate and dissuasive.

The Member States shall notify those provisions and any subsequent amendment affecting them to the Commission without delay.

Chapter V

Exchange of Information

Article 31

Exchange of data on decisions relating to applications and detentions between the Member States and the Commission

1. The competent customs departments shall notify without delay the Commission of the following:

(a) decisions granting applications, including the application and its attachments;

(b) decisions extending the period during which the customs authorities are to take action or decisions revoking the decision granting the application or amending it;

(c) the suspension of a decision granting the application.

2. Without prejudice to point (g) of Article 24 of Regulation (EC) No 515/97, where the release of the goods is suspended or the goods are detained, the customs authorities shall transmit to the Commission any relevant information, except personal data, including information on the quantity and type of the goods, value, intellectual property rights, customs procedures, countries of provenance, origin and destination, and transport routes and means.

3. The transmission of the information referred to in paragraphs 1 and 2 of this Article and all exchanges of data on decisions concerning applications as referred

to in Article 14 between customs authorities of the Member States shall be made via a central database of the Commission. The information and data shall be stored in that database.

4. For the purposes of ensuring processing of the information referred to in paragraphs 1 to 3 of this Article, the central database referred to in paragraph 3 shall be established in an electronic form. The central database shall contain the information, including personal data, referred to in Article 6(3), Article 14 and this Article.

5. The customs authorities of the Member States and the Commission shall have access to the information contained in the central database as appropriate for the fulfilment of their legal responsibilities in applying this Regulation. The access to information marked for restricted handling in accordance with Article 6(3) is restricted to the customs authorities of the Member States where action is requested. Upon justified request by the Commission, the customs authorities of the Member States may give access to the Commission to such information where it is strictly necessary for the application of this Regulation.

6. The customs authorities shall introduce into the central database information related to the applications submitted to the competent customs department. The customs authorities which have introduced information into the central database shall, where necessary, amend, supplement, correct or delete such information. Each customs authority that has introduced information in the central database shall be responsible for the accuracy, adequacy and relevancy of this information.

7. The Commission shall establish and maintain adequate technical and organisational arrangements for the reliable and secure operation of the central database. The customs authorities of each Member State shall establish and maintain adequate technical and organisational arrangements to ensure the confidentiality and security of processing with respect to the processing operations carried out by their customs authorities and with respect to terminals of the central database located on the territory of that Member State.

Article 32

Establishment of a central database

The Commission shall establish the central database referred to in Article 31. That database shall be operational as soon as possible and not later than 1 January 2015.

Article 33

Data protection provisions

1. The processing of personal data in the central database of the Commission shall be carried out in accordance with Regulation (EC) No 45/2001 and under the supervision of the European Data Protection Supervisor.

2. Processing of personal data by the competent authorities in the Member States shall be carried out in accordance with Directive 95/46/EC and under the supervision of the public independent authority of the Member State referred to in Article 28 of that Directive.

3. Personal data shall be collected and used solely for the purposes of this Regulation. Personal data so collected shall be accurate and shall be kept up to date.

4. Each customs authority that has introduced personal data into the central database shall be the controller with respect to the processing of this data.

5. A data subject shall have a right of access to the personal data relating to

him or her that are processed through the central database and, where appropriate, the right to the rectification, erasure or blocking of personal data in accordance with Regulation (EC) No 45/2001 or the national laws implementing Directive 95/46/EC.

6. All requests for the exercise of the right of access, rectification, erasure or blocking shall be submitted to and processed by the customs authorities. Where a data subject has submitted a request for the exercise of that right to the Commission, the Commission shall forward such request to the customs authorities concerned.

7. Personal data shall not be kept longer than six months from the date the relevant decision granting the application has been revoked or the relevant period during which the customs authorities are to take action has expired.

8. Where the holder of the decision has initiated proceedings in accordance with Article 23(3) or Article 26(9) and has notified the customs authorities of the initiation of such proceedings, personal data shall be kept for six months after proceedings have determined in a final way whether an intellectual property right has been infringed.

CHAPTER VI

COMMITTEE, DELEGATION AND FINAL PROVISIONS

Article 34

Committee procedure

1. The Commission shall be assisted by the Customs Code Committee established by Articles 247a and 248a of Regulation (EEC) No 2913/92. That committee shall be a committee within the meaning of Regulation (EU) No 182/2011.

2. Where reference is made to this paragraph, Article 4 of Regulation (EU) No 182/2011 shall apply.

3. Where reference is made to this paragraph, Article 5 of Regulation (EU) No 182/2011 shall apply.

Article 35

Exercise of the delegation

1. The power to adopt delegated acts is conferred on the Commission subject to the conditions laid down in this Article.

2. The power to adopt delegated acts referred to in Article 26(10) shall be conferred on the Commission for an indeterminate period of time from 19 July 2013.

3. The delegation of power referred to in Article 26(10) may be revoked at any time by the European Parliament or by the Council. A decision to revoke shall put an end to the delegation of the power specified in that decision. It shall take effect the day following the publication of the decision in the Official Journal of the European Union or at a later date specified therein. It shall not affect the validity of any delegated acts already in force.

4. As soon as it adopts a delegated act, the Commission shall notify it simultaneously to the European Parliament and to the Council.

5. A delegated act adopted pursuant to Article 26(10) shall enter into force only if no objection has been expressed either by the European Parliament or the Council within a period of two months of notification of that act to the European Parliament and the Council or if, before the expiry of that period the European

Parliament and the Council have both informed the Commission that they will not object. That period shall be extended by two months on the initiative of the European Parliament or of the Council.

Article 36

Mutual administrative assistance

The provisions of Regulation (EC) No 515/97 shall apply mutatis mutandis to this Regulation.

Article 37

Reporting

By 31 December 2016, the Commission shall submit to the European Parliament and to the Council a report on the implementation of this Regulation. If necessary, that report shall be accompanied by appropriate recommendations.

That report shall refer to any relevant incidents concerning medicines in transit across the customs territory of the Union that might occur under this Regulation, including an assessment of its potential impact on the Union commitments on access to medicines under the 'Declaration on the TRIPS Agreement and Public Health' adopted by the Doha WTO Ministerial Conference on 14 November 2001, and the measures taken to address any situation creating adverse effects in that regard.

Article 38

Repeal

Regulation (EC) No 1383/2003 is repealed with effect from 1 January 2014.

References to the repealed Regulation shall be construed as references to this Regulation and shall be read in accordance with the correlation table set out in the Annex.

Article 39

Transitional provisions

Applications granted in accordance with Regulation (EC) No 1383/2003 shall remain valid for the period specified in the decision granting the application during which the customs authorities are to take action and shall not be extended.

Article 40

Entry into force and application

1. This Regulation shall enter into force on the twentieth day following that of its publication in the Official Journal of the European Union.

2. It shall apply from 1 January 2014, with the exception of:

(a) Article 6, Article 12(7) and Article 22(3), which shall apply from 19 July 2013;

(b) Article 31(1) and (3) to (7) and Article 33, which shall apply from the date on which the central database referred to in Article 32 is in place. The Commission shall make that date public.

This Regulation shall be binding in its entirety and directly applicable in all Member States. Done at Strasbourg, 12 June 2013.

For the European Parliament

The President

M. SCHULZ

For the Council
The President
L. CREIGHTON

ANNEX

Correlation table

Regulation (EC) No 1383/2003	This Regulation
Article 1	Article 1
Article 2	Article 2
Article 3	Article 1
Article 4	Article 18
Article 5	Articles 3 to 9
Article 6	Articles 6 and 29
Article 7	Article 12
Article 8	Articles 10, 11, 12, 14 and 15
Article 9	Articles 17 and 19
Article 10	—
Article 11	Article 23
Article 12	Articles 16 and 21
Article 13	Article 23
Article 14	Article 24
Article 15	Article 20
Article 16	Article 25
Article 17	—
Article 18	Article 30
Article 19	Articles 27 and 28
Article 20	Articles 6, 12, 22 and 26
Article 21	Article 34
Article 22	Articles 31 and 36
Article 23	—
Article 24	Article 38
Article 25	Article 40

Note: Regulation (EU) No 608/2013 repeals and replaces Council Regulation (EC) No.1383/2003, with effect from 1 January 2014 (see Article 40 above).

B7.aii Commission Implementing Regulation (EU) No 1352/2013 of 4 December 2013 establishing the forms provided for in Regulation (EU) No 608/2013 of the European Parliament and of the Council concerning customs enforcement of intellectual property rights

THE EUROPEAN COMMISSION,

Having regard to the Treaty on the Functioning of the European Union,

Having regard to Regulation (EU) No 608/2013 of the European Parliament and of the Council of 12 June 2013 concerning customs enforcement of intellectual property rights and repealing Council Regulation (EC) No 1383/2003[1], and in particular Article 6(1) and Article 12(7) thereof,

After consulting the European Data Protection Supervisor,

---

[1] OJ L 181, 29.6.2013, p. 15.

Whereas:

(1) Regulation (EU) No 608/2013 sets out the conditions and procedures for action by the customs authorities where goods suspected of infringing an intellectual property right are, or should have been, subject to customs supervision or customs controls in accordance with Council Regulation (EEC) No 2913/922.[2]

(2) In accordance with Regulation (EU) No 608/2013 persons and entities duly entitled may submit an application to the competent customs department requesting that customs authorities take action on those goods (application) and may also request the extension of the period during which the customs authorities are to take action in accordance with a previously granted application (extension request).

(3) In order to ensure uniform conditions for the application and for the extension request, standard forms should be established.

(4) Those standard forms should replace those provided for in Commission Regulation (EC) No 1891/2004.[3]*implementing Council Regulation (EC) No 1383/2003*[4], *which is to be repealed by Regulation (EU) No 608/2013.*

(5) Regulation (EC) No 1891/2004 should therefore be repealed.

(6) Regulation (EU) No 608/2013 shall apply from 1 January 2014 and, therefore, this Regulation should also be applicable from the same date.

(7) The measures provided for in this Regulation are in accordance with the opinion of the Customs Code Committee, referred to in Article 34(1) of Regulation (EU) No 608/2013,

HAS ADOPTED THIS REGULATION:

Article 1

1. The application requesting that customs authorities take action with respect to goods suspected of infringing an intellectual property right (application) referred to in Article 6 of Regulation (EU) No 608/2013 shall be made by using the form set out in Annex I to this Regulation.

2. The request for extension of the period during which the customs authorities are to take action (extension request) referred to in Article 12 of Regulation (EU) No 608/2013 shall be made by using the form set out in Annex II to this Regulation.

3. The forms set out in Annexes I and II shall be completed in accordance with the notes on completion set out in Annex III.

Article 2

Without prejudice to Article 5(6) of Regulation (EU) No 608/2013, the forms set out in Annexes I and II to this Regulation may, where necessary, be completed legibly by hand.

Those forms shall contain no erasures, overwritten words or other alterations and shall be made up of two copies.

The handwritten forms shall be completed in ink and block capitals.

Article 3

Regulation (EC) No 1891/2004 is repealed.

---

[2] Council Regulation (EEC) No 2913/92 of 12 October 1992 establishing the Community Customs Code (OJ L 302, 19.10.1992, p. 1.).

[3] Commission Regulation (EC) No 1891/2004 of 21 October 2004 laying down provisions for the implementation of Council Regulation (EC) No 1383/2003 concerning customs action against goods suspected of infringing certain intellectual property rights and the measures to be taken against goods found to have infringed such rights (OJ L 328, 30.10.2004, p. 16.).

[4] Council Regulation (EC) No 1383/2003 of 22 July 2003 concerning customs action against goods suspected of infringing certain intellectual property rights and the measures to be taken against goods found to have infringed such rights (OJ L 196, 2.8.2003, p. 7).

Article 4

This Regulation shall enter into force on the twentieth day following that of its publication in the Official Journal of the European Union.

It shall apply from 1 January 2014.

This Regulation shall be binding in its entirety and directly applicable in all Member States.

Done at Brussels, 4 December 2013.

For the Commission
  The President
  José Manuel Barroso

ANNEX I

EUROPEAN UNION – APPLICATION FOR ACTION

<table>
<tr><td rowspan="10" style="writing-mode: vertical-lr;">COPY FOR THE COMPETENT CUSTOMS DEPARTMENT</td><td>

1   1. Applicant

Name (*):
Address (*):
Town (*):
Postal Code:
Country (*):
EORI-No:
TIN No:
National registration No:
Telephone: (+)
Mobile: (+)
Fax: (+)
Email:
Website:
</td><td>

For official use
Date of receipt

Registration number of application

INTELLECTUAL PROPERTY RIGHTS
APPLICATION FOR ACTION BY CUSTOMS AUTHORITIES
under Article 6 of Regulation (EU) No 608/2013

2 (*).   Union application   ☐
     National application   ☐
</td></tr>
</table>

3 (*). Status of applicant

☐ Right-holder   ☐ Group of producers of products with a Geographical Indication or representative of such group

☐ Person or entity authorised to use the IP right   ☐ Operator entitled to use a Geographical Indication

☐ IP collective rights management body   ☐ Inspection body or authority competent for a Geographical Indication

☐ Professional defence body   ☐ Exclusive license holder covering two or more Member States

4. Representative submitting the application in the name of the applicant:

Company:
Name (*):
Address (*):
Town (*):
Postal Code:
Country (*):
Telephone: (+)
Mobile: (+)   ☐ Evidence of the representatives power to act is enclosed
Fax: (+)

5 (*). Type of right to which the application refers

☐ National trademark (NTM)	Geographical Indication/Designation of origin:
☐ Community trademark (CTM)	☐ for agricultural products and foodstuff (CGIP)
☐ International registered trademark (ITM)	☐ for wine (CGIW)
☐ Registered national design (ND)	☐ for aromatised drinks based on wine products (CGIA)
☐ Registered Community design (CDR)	☐ for spirit drinks (CGIS)
☐ Unregistered Community design (CDU)	☐ for other products (NGI)
☐ International registered design (ICD)	☐ as listed in Agreements between the Union and third countries (CGIL)
☐ Copyright and related right (NCPR)	Plant variety right:
☐ Trade name (NTN)	☐ national (NPVR)
☐ Topography of semiconductor product (NTSP)	☐ Community (CPVR)
☐ Patent as provided for by national law (NPT)	Supplementary protection certificate:
☐ Patent as provided for by Union law (UPT)	☐ for medicinal products (SPCM)
☐ Utility model (NUM)	☐ for plant protection products (SPCP)

6 (*). Member State or, in the case of a Union application, Member States in which customs action is requested

☐ ALL MEMBER STATES   ☐ BE ☐ BG ☐ CZ ☐ DK ☐ DE ☐ EE ☐ IE ☐ EL ☐ ES ☐ FR ☐ HR ☐ IT ☐ CY ☐ LV
                   ☐ LT ☐ LU ☐ HU ☐ MT ☐ NL ☐ AT ☐ PL ☐ PT ☐ RO ☐ SI ☐ SK ☐ FI ☐ SE ☐ UK

7. Representative for legal matters	8. Representative for technical matters
Company: Name (*): Address (*): Town (*): Postal Code: Country (*): Telephone: (+) Mobile: (+) Fax: (+) Email: Website:	Company: Name (*): Address (*): Town (*): Postal Code: Country (*): Telephone: (+) Mobile: (+) Fax: (+) Email: Website:

9. In case of a Union application, the details of the designated representatives for legal and technical matters are included in annex no ....

10. Small consignment procedure

☐ I request the use of the procedure in Article 26 of Regulation (EU) No 608/2013 and, where requested by the customs authorities, agree to cover the costs related to the destruction of goods under this procedure.

(*) these are mandatory fields and shall be filled in   (+) at least one of these fields shall be filled in

11 (*). List of rights to which the application refers

No	Type of right	Registration number	Date of registration	Expiry date	List of goods to which the right refers

For further rights see annex no ...   ☐ Restricted handling

Authentic goods

12. Goods details (*)   ☐ Restricted handling
IP right no:
Goods description (*):

CN tariff number:
Customs value:
European average market value:
National market value: ☐ See enclosed annex no ...

13. Goods distinctive features (*)   ☐ Restricted handling
Position on the goods (*):
Description (*):

                                                                       ☐ See enclosed annex no ...

14. Place of production (*)   ☐ Restricted handling
Country:
Company:
Address:
Town: ☐ See enclosed annex no ...

15. Involved companies (*)   ☐ Restricted handling
Role:
Name (*):
Address:
Town: ☐ See enclosed annex no ...

16. Traders (*)   ☐ Restricted handling

                                                                       ☐ See enclosed annex no ...

17. Goods clearance details and distribution information   ☐ Restricted handling

                                                                       ☐ See enclosed annex no ...

18. Packages   ☐ Restricted handling

Kind of packages:
Number of items per package:
Description (incl. distinctive features):
                                                                       ☐ See enclosed annex no ...

19. Accompanying documents   ☐ Restricted handling
Type of document:
Description:
                                                                       ☐ See enclosed annex no ...

Infringing goods

20. Goods details ☐ Restricted handling

IP right no:

Goods description:

CN tariff number:

Minimum value:

☐ See enclosed annex no ...

21. Goods distinctive features ☐ Restricted handling

Position on the goods:

Description:

☐ See enclosed annex no ...

22. Place of production ☐ Restricted handling

Country:

Company:

Address:

Town:

☐ See enclosed annex no ...

23. Involved companies ☐ Restricted handling

Role:

Name:

Address:

Town:

☐ See enclosed annex no ...

24. Traders ☐ Restricted handling

☐ See enclosed annex no ...

25. Goods distribution information ☐ Restricted handling

☐ See enclosed annex no ...

26. Packages ☐ Restricted handling

Kind of packages:

Number of items per package:

Description (incl. distinctive features):

☐ See enclosed annex no ...

27. Accompanying documents ☐ Restricted handling

Type of document:

Description:

☐ See enclosed annex no ...

28. Additional information   ☐ Restricted handling

☐

☐ See enclosed annex no ...

29. Undertakings

By signing I undertake to:

— notify immediately the competent customs department that granted this application of any change in the information provided by me within this application or attachments in accordance with Article 15 of Regulation (EU) No 608/2013.

— forward to the competent customs department that granted this application any update on the information as referred to in point (g), (h) or (i) of Article 6(3) of Regulation (EU) No 608/2013 that are relevant to customs authorities' analysis and assessment of the risk of infringement of the intellectual property right(s) included in this application.

— assume liability under the conditions laid down in Article 28 of Regulation (EU) No 608/2013 and bear the costs as referred to in Article 29 of Regulation (EU) No 608/2013.

I agree that all the data submitted with this application may be processed by the European Commission and by the Member States.

30. Signature (*)

Date (DD/MM/YYYY)   Applicant's signature

Place   Name (Block capitals)

For official use

Decision by customs authorities (within the meaning of Section 2 of Regulation (EU) No 608/2013)

☐ The application is completely granted.

☐ The application has been partially granted (for the granted rights see attached list).

Date of adoption (DD/MM/YYYY)   Signature and stamp   Competent customs department

Expiry date of the application:

Any request for extension of the period that customs authorities are to take action should be received by the competent customs department at the latest 30 working days before the expiry date.

☐ The application has been rejected.

A reasoned decision stating the grounds for partial or complete rejection and information concerning the appeal procedure are attached.

Date (DD/MM/YYYY)   Signature and stamp   Competent customs department

Personal data protection and the central database for the processing of applications for action.

Where the European Commission processes personal data contained in this application for action Regulation (EC) No 45/2001 of the European Parliament and of the Council on the protection of individuals with regard to the processing of personal data by the Community Institutions and bodies and on the free movement of such data will apply. Where the competent customs authority of a Member State processes personal data contained in this application for action the national provisions implementing Directive 95/46/EC will apply.

The purpose of the processing of personal data of the application for action is the enforcement of intellectual property rights by customs authorities in the Union in accordance with Regulation (EU) No 608/2013 of the European Parliament and of the Council of 12 June 2013 concerning customs enforcement of intellectual property rights.

The controller with respect to the processing of the data in the central database is the national competent customs department where the application has been submitted. The list of competent customs departments is published on the website of the Commission:

http://ec.europa.eu/taxation_customs/customs/customs_controls/counterfeit_piracy/right_holders/index_en.htm.

The access to all personal data of this application is granted through UserID/Password to customs authorities in the Member States and the Commission.

Personal data forming part of the information that falls under restricted handling will only be accessible by customs authorities of the Member States as indicated in box 6 of the application through UserID/Password.

In accordance with Article 22 of Regulation (EU) No 608/2013, without prejudice to applicable provisions on data protection in the Union and for the purpose of contributing to eliminating international trade in goods infringing intellectual property rights, the Commission and the customs authorities of the Member States may share personal data and information contained in the application with the relevant authorities in third countries.

Replies to data fields marked with an * and to at least one of the fields marked "+" are obligatory to be filled in. In case of failure to fill in these obligatory data, the application shall be rejected.

The data subject has a right of access to the personal data relating to him or her that will be processed through the central database and, where appropriate, the right to rectify, erase or block personal data in accordance with Regulation (EC) No 45/2001 or the national laws implementing Directive 95/46/EC.

All requests for the exercise of the right of access, rectification, erasure or blocking shall be submitted to and processed by the competent customs department where the application was submitted.

The legal basis for processing the personal data for the enforcement of intellectual property rights is Regulation (EU) No 608/2013 of the European Parliament and of the Council of 12 June 2013 concerning customs enforcement of intellectual property rights.

Personal data shall not be stored longer than six months from the date the decision granting the application has been revoked or the relevant period during which customs authorities are to take action has expired. That period shall be specified by the competent customs department when granting the application and shall not exceed one year from the day following the date of adoption of the decision granting the application. However, where customs authorities have been notified of proceedings initiated to determine a possible infringement of goods under the application, personal data shall be kept for six months after the proceedings have been concluded.

Complaints, in case of conflict, can be addressed to the relevant national data protection authority. The contact details of the national data protection authorities are available on the web-site of the European Commission, Directorate General for Justice (http://ec.europa.eu/justice/data-protection/bodies/authorities/eu/index_en.htm#h2-1). Where the complaint concerns processing of personal data by the European Commission, it should be addressed to the European Data Protection Supervisor (http://www.edps.europa.eu/EDPSWEB/).

EUROPEAN UNION – APPLICATION FOR ACTION

COPY FOR THE APPLICANT

2	1. Applicant	For official use

1. Applicant
Name (*):
Address (*):
Town (*):
Postal Code:
Country (*):
EORI-No:
TIN No:
National registration No:
Telephone: (+)
Mobile: (+)
Fax: (+)
Email:
Website:

For official use
Date of receipt

Registration number of application

INTELLECTUAL PROPERTY RIGHTS

APPLICATION FOR ACTION BY CUSTOMS AUTHORITIES

under Article 6 of Regulation (EU) No 608/2013

2 (*). Union application ☐
National application ☐

3 (*). Status of applicant
☐ Right-holder
☐ Group of producers of products with a Geographical Indication or representative of such group
☐ Person or entity authorised to use the IP right
☐ Operator entitled to use a Geographical Indication
☐ IP collective rights management body
☐ Inspection body or authority competent for a Geographical Indication
☐ Professional defence body
☐ Exclusive license holder covering two or more Member States

4. Representative submitting the application in the name of the applicant:
Company:
Name (*):
Address (*):
Town (*):
Postal Code:
Country (*):
Telephone: (+)
Mobile: (+)
Fax: (+)

☐ Evidence of the representatives power to act is enclosed

5 (*). Type of right to which the application refers

☐ National trademark (NTM)
☐ Community trademark (CTM)
☐ International registered trademark (ITM)
☐ Registered national design (ND)
☐ Registered Community design (CDR)
☐ Unregistered Community design (CDU)
☐ International registered design (ICD)
☐ Copyright and related right (NCPR)
☐ Trade name (NTN)
☐ Topography of semiconductor product (NTSP)
☐ Patent as provided for by national law (NPT)
☐ Patent as provided for by Union law (UPT)
☐ Utility model (NUM)

Geographical Indication/Designation of origin:
☐ for agricultural products and foodstuff (CGIP)
☐ for wine (CGIW)
☐ for aromatised drinks based on wine products (CGIA)
☐ for spirit drinks (CGIS)
☐ for other products (NGI)
☐ as listed in Agreements between the Union and third countries (CGIL)
Plant variety right:
☐ national (NPVR)
☐ Community (CPVR)
Supplementary protection certificate:
☐ for medicinal products (SPCM)
☐ for plant protection products (SPCP)

6 (*). Member State or, in the case of a Union application, Member States in which customs action is requested

☐ ALL MEMBER STATES
☐ BE ☐ BG ☐ CZ ☐ DK ☐ DE ☐ EE ☐ IE ☐ EL ☐ ES ☐ FR ☐ HR ☐ IT ☐ CY ☐ LV
☐ LT ☐ LU ☐ HU ☐ MT ☐ NL ☐ AT ☐ PL ☐ PT ☐ RO ☐ SI ☐ SK ☐ FI ☐ SE ☐ UK

7. Representative for legal matters
Company:
Name (*):
Address (*):
Town (*):
Postal Code:
Country (*):
Telephone: (+)
Mobile: (+)
Fax: (+)
Email:
Website:

8. Representative for technical matters
Company:
Name (*):
Address (*):
Town (*):
Postal Code:
Country (*):
Telephone: (+)
Mobile: (+)
Fax: (+)
Email:
Website:

9. In case of a Union application, the details of the designated representatives for legal and technical matters are included in annex no ....

10. Small consignment procedure
☐ I request the use of the procedure in Article 26 of Regulation (EU) No 608/2013 and, where requested by the customs authorities, agree to cover the costs related to the destruction of goods under this procedure.

(*) these are mandatory fields and shall be filled in   (+) at least one of these fields shall be filled in

No	Type of right	Registration number	Date of registration	Expiry date	List of goods to which the right refers

11 (*). List of rights to which the application refers

For further rights see annex no ...   ☐ Restricted handling

Authentic goods

12. Goods details (*)   ☐ Restricted handling
IP right no:
Goods description (*):

CN tariff number:
Customs value:
European average market value:
National market value: ☐ See enclosed annex no ...

13. Goods distinctive features (*)   ☐ Restricted handling
Position on the goods (*):
Description (*):

          ☐ See enclosed annex no ...

14. Place of production (*)   ☐ Restricted handling
Country:
Company:
Address:
Town: ☐ See enclosed annex no ...

15. Involved companies (*)   ☐ Restricted handling
Role:
Name (*):
Address:
Town: ☐ See enclosed annex no ...

16. Traders (*)   ☐ Restricted handling

          ☐ See enclosed annex no ...

17. Goods clearance details and distribution information   ☐ Restricted handling

          ☐ See enclosed annex no ...

18. Packages   ☐ Restricted handling

Kind of packages:
Number of items per package:
Description (incl. distinctive features):   ☐ See enclosed annex no ...

19. Accompanying documents   ☐ Restricted handling
Type of document:
Description: ☐ See enclosed annex no ...

Infringing goods	
20. Goods details IP right no: Goods description: CN tariff number: Minimum value:	☐ Restricted handling ☐ See enclosed annex no ...
21. Goods distinctive features Position on the goods: Description:	☐ Restricted handling ☐ See enclosed annex no ...
22. Place of production Country: Company: Address: Town:	☐ Restricted handling ☐ See enclosed annex no ...
23. Involved companies Role: Name: Address: Town:	☐ Restricted handling ☐ See enclosed annex no ...
24. Traders	☐ Restricted handling ☐ See enclosed annex no ...
25. Goods distribution information	☐ Restricted handling ☐ See enclosed annex no ...
26. Packages Kind of packages: Number of items per package: Description (incl. distinctive features):	☐ Restricted handling ☐ See enclosed annex no ...
27. Accompanying documents Type of document: Description:	☐ Restricted handling ☐ See enclosed annex no ...

28. Additional information	☐ Restricted handling
☐	
	☐ See enclosed annex no ...

29. Undertakings

By signing I undertake to:

— notify immediately the competent customs department that granted this application of any change in the information provided by me within this application or attachments in accordance with Article 15 of Regulation (EU) No 608/2013.

— forward to the competent customs department that granted this application any update on the information as referred to in point (g), (h) or (i) of Article 6(3) of Regulation (EU) No 608/2013 that are relevant to customs authorities' analysis and assessment of the risk of infringement of the intellectual property right(s) included in this application.

— assume liability under the conditions laid down in Article 28 of Regulation (EU) No 608/2013 and bear the costs as referred to in Article 29 of Regulation (EU) No 608/2013.

I agree that all the data submitted with this application may be processed by the European Commission and by the Member States.

30. Signature (*)

Date (DD/MM/YYYY)	Applicant's signature
Place	Name (Block capitals)

For official use

Decision by customs authorities (within the meaning of Section 2 of Regulation (EU) No 608/2013)

☐ The application is completely granted.

☐ The application has been partially granted (for the granted rights see attached list).

Date of adoption (DD/MM/YYYY)	Signature and stamp	Competent customs department

Expiry date of the application:

Any request for extension of the period that customs authorities are to take action should be received by the competent customs department at the latest 30 working days before the expiry date.

☐ The application has been rejected.

A reasoned decision stating the grounds for partial or complete rejection and information concerning the appeal procedure are attached.

Date (DD/MM/YYYY)	Signature and stamp	Competent customs department

> **Personal data protection and the central database for the processing of applications for action.**

Where the European Commission processes personal data contained in this application for action Regulation (EC) No 45/2001 of the European Parliament and of the Council on the protection of individuals with regard to the processing of personal data by the Community Institutions and bodies and on the free movement of such data will apply. Where the competent customs authority of a Member State processes personal data contained in this application for action the national provisions implementing Directive 95/46/EC will apply.

The purpose of the processing of personal data of the application for action is the enforcement of intellectual property rights by customs authorities in the Union in accordance with Regulation (EU) No 608/2013 of the European Parliament and of the Council of 12 June 2013 concerning customs enforcement of intellectual property rights.

The controller with respect to the processing of the data in the central database is the national competent customs department where the application has been submitted. The list of competent customs departments is published on the website of the Commission:

http://ec.europa.eu/taxation_customs/customs/customs_controls/counterfeit_piracy/right_holders/index_en.htm.

The access to all personal data of this application is granted through UserID/Password to customs authorities in the Member States and the Commission.

Personal data forming part of the information that falls under restricted handling will only be accessible by customs authorities of the Member States as indicated in box 6 of the application through UserID/Password.

In accordance with Article 22 of Regulation (EU) No 608/2013, without prejudice to applicable provisions on data protection in the Union and for the purpose of contributing to eliminating international trade in goods infringing intellectual property rights, the Commission and the customs authorities of the Member States may share personal data and information contained in the application with the relevant authorities in third countries.

Replies to data fields marked with an * and to at least one of the fields marked "+" are obligatory to be filled in. In case of failure to fill in these obligatory data, the application shall be rejected.

The data subject has a right of access to the personal data relating to him or her that will be processed through the central database and, where appropriate, the right to rectify, erase or block personal data in accordance with Regulation (EC) No 45/2001 or the national laws implementing Directive 95/46/EC.

All requests for the exercise of the right of access, rectification, erasure or blocking shall be submitted to and processed by the competent customs department where the application was submitted.

The legal basis for processing the personal data for the enforcement of intellectual property rights is Regulation (EU) No 608/2013 of the European Parliament and of the Council of 12 June 2013 concerning customs enforcement of intellectual property rights.

Personal data shall not be stored longer than six months from the date the decision granting the application has been revoked or the relevant period during which customs authorities are to take action has expired. That period shall be specified by the competent customs department when granting the application and shall not exceed one year from the day following the date of adoption of the decision granting the application. However, where customs authorities have been notified of proceedings initiated to determine a possible infringement of goods under the application, personal data shall be kept for six months after the proceedings have been concluded.

Complaints, in case of conflict, can be addressed to the relevant national data protection authority. The contact details of the national data protection authorities are available on the web-site of the European Commission, Directorate General for Justice (http://ec.europa.eu/justice/data-protection/bodies/authorities/eu/index_en.htm#h2-1). Where the complaint concerns processing of personal data by the European Commission, it should be addressed to the European Data Protection Supervisor (http://www.edps.europa.eu/EDPSWEB/).

ANNEX II

EUROPEAN UNION – REQUEST FOR EXTENSION

1	**1. Holder of the decision**

<table>
<tr><td rowspan="6" style="writing-mode:vertical-lr">COPY FOR THE COMPETENT CUSTOMS DEPARTMENT</td><td>

1. Holder of the decision

Name (*):

Address (*):

Town (*):

Postal Code:

Country (*):

Telephone: (+)

Mobile: (+)

Fax: (+)

Email:
</td><td>

For official use

Date of receipt

INTELLECTUAL PROPERTY RIGHTS

REQUEST FOR EXTENSION OF THE PERIOD FOR ACTION

under Article 12 of Regulation (EU) No 608/2013
</td></tr>
</table>

2 (*). I request the extension of the period during which the customs authorities are to take action in respect of the following application

Registration number of application: /

☐ I confirm, that there are no changes in the information concerning the application for action and its annexes.

☐ I provide the following information concerning the application for action.

See enclosed annex no ...

1 Any request for extension of the period that customs authorities are to take action should be received by the competent customs department at the latest 30 working days before the expiry date.

---

3. Signature (*)

Date (DD/MM/YYYY)   Signature of the holder of the decision

Place   Name (Block capitals)

For official use

Decision by customs authorities (within the meaning of Section 2 of Regulation (EU) No 608/2013)

☐ The request for extension is completely granted.

☐ The request for extension has been partially granted (for the granted rights see attached list).

Date (DD/MM/YYYY)   Signature and stamp   Competent customs department

Expiry date of the application:

☐ The request for extension has been rejected.

A reasoned decision stating the grounds for partial or complete rejection and information concerning the appeal procedure are attached.

Date (DD/MM/YYYY)   Signature and stamp   Competent customs department

(*) these are mandatory fields and shall be filled in   (+) at least one of these fields shall be filled in

Personal data protection and the central database for the processing of applications for action.

Where the European Commission processes personal data contained in this extension request Regulation (EC) No 45/2001 of the European Parliament and of the Council on the protection of individuals with regard to the processing of personal data by the Community institutions and bodies and on the free movement of such data will apply. Where the competent customs authority of a Member State processes personal data contained in this extension request the national provisions implementing Directive 95/46/EC will apply.

The purpose of the processing of personal data of the application for action is the enforcement of intellectual property rights by customs authorities in the Union in accordance with Regulation (EU) No 608/2013 of the European Parliament and of the Council of 12 June 2013 concerning customs enforcement of intellectual property rights.

The controller with respect to the processing of the data in the central database is the national competent customs department where the application has been submitted. The list of competent customs departments is published on the website of the Commission: http://ec.europa.eu/taxation_customs/customs/customs_controls/counterfeit_piracy/right_holders/index_en.htm.

The access to all personal data of the application is granted through UserID/Password to customs authorities in the Member States and the Commission.

Personal data forming part of the information that falls under restricted handling will only be accessible by customs authorities of the Member States as indicated in box 6 of the application through UserID/Password. In accordance with Article 22 of Regulation (EU) No 608/2013, without prejudice to applicable provisions on data protection in the Union and for the purpose of contributing to eliminating international trade in goods infringing intellectual property rights, the Commission and the customs authorities of the Member States may share personal data and information contained in the application with the relevant authorities in third countries. Replies to data fields marked with an * are obligatory to be filled in. In case of failure to fill in these obligatory data, the extension request shall be rejected.

The data subject has a right of access to the personal data relating to him or her that will be processed through the central database and, where appropriate, the right to rectify, erase or block personal data in accordance with Regulation (EC) No 45/2001 or the national laws implementing Directive 95/46/EC.

All requests for the exercise of the right of access, rectification, erasure or blocking shall be submitted to and processed by the competent customs department where the application was submitted.

The legal basis for processing the personal data for the enforcement of intellectual property rights is Regulation (EU) No 608/2013 of the European Parliament and of the Council of 12 June 2013 concerning customs enforcement of intellectual property rights.

Personal data shall not be stored longer than six months from the date the decision granting the application has been revoked or the relevant period during which customs authorities are to take action has expired. That period shall be specified by the competent customs department when granting the extension request and shall not exceed one year from the day following the date of adoption of the decision granting the extension request. However, where customs authorities have been notified of proceedings initiated to determine a possible infringement of goods under the application, personal data shall be kept for six months after the proceedings have been concluded.

Complaints, in case of conflict, can be addressed to the relevant national data protection authority. The contact details of the national data protection authorities are available on the web-site of the European Commission, Directorate General for Justice (http://ec.europa.eu/justice/data-protection/bodies/authorities/eu/index_en.htm#h2-1). Where the complaint concerns processing of personal data by the European Commission, it should be addressed to the European Data Protection Supervisor (http://www.edps.europa.eu/EDPSWEB/).

EUROPEAN UNION – REQUEST FOR EXTENSION

2	**1. Holder of the decision** Name (*): Address (*): Town (*): Postal Code: Country (*): Telephone: (+) Mobile: (+) Fax: (+) Email:	**For official use** Date of receipt INTELLECTUAL PROPERTY RIGHTS REQUEST FOR EXTENSION OF THE PERIOD FOR ACTION under Article 12 of Regulation (EU) No 608/2013

COPY FOR THE APPLICANT

2 (*). I request the extension of the period during which the customs authorities are to take action in respect of the following application

Registration number of application: /

☐ I confirm, that there are no changes in the information concerning the application for action and its annexes.

☐ I provide the following information concerning the application for action.

See enclosed annex no …

Any request for extension of the period that customs authorities are to take action should be received by the competent customs department at the latest 30 working days before the expiry date.

3. Signature (*)

Date (DD/MM/YYYY)   Signature of the holder of the decision

Place   Name (Block capitals)

For official use

Decision by customs authorities (within the meaning of Section 2 of Regulation (EU) No 608/2013)

☐ The request for extension is completely granted.

☐ The request for extension has been partially granted (for the granted rights see attached list).

Date (DD/MM/YYYY)   Signature and stamp   Competent customs department

Expiry date of the application:

☐ The request for extension has been rejected.

A reasoned decision stating the grounds for partial or complete rejection and information concerning the appeal procedure are attached.

Date (DD/MM/YYYY)   Signature and stamp   Competent customs department

(*) these are mandatory fields and shall be filled in   (+) at least one of these fields shall be filled in

---

Personal data protection and the central database for the processing of applications for action.

Where the European Commission processes personal data contained in this extension request Regulation (EC) No 45/2001 of the European Parliament and of the Council on the protection of individuals with regard to the processing of personal data by the Community institutions and bodies and on the free movement of such data will apply. Where the competent customs authority of a Member State processes personal data contained in this extension request the national provisions implementing Directive 95/46/EC will apply.

The purpose of the processing of personal data of the application for action is the enforcement of intellectual property rights by customs authorities in the Union in accordance with Regulation (EU) No 608/2013 of the European Parliament and of the Council of 12 June 2013 concerning customs enforcement of intellectual property rights.

The controller with respect to the processing of the data in the central database is the national competent customs department where the application has been submitted. The list of competent customs departments is published on the website of the Commission: http://ec.europa.eu/taxation_customs/customs/customs_controls/counterfeit_piracy/right_holders/index_en.htm.

The access to all personal data of the application is granted through UserID/Password to customs authorities in the Member States and the Commission.

Personal data forming part of the information that falls under restricted handling will only be accessible by customs authorities of the Member States as indicated in box 6 of the application through UserID/Password. In accordance with Article 22 of Regulation (EU) No 608/2013, without prejudice to applicable provisions on data protection in the Union and for the purpose of contributing to eliminating international trade in goods infringing intellectual property rights, the Commission and the customs authorities of the Member States may share personal data and information contained in the application with the relevant authorities in third countries. Replies to data fields marked with an * are obligatory to be filled in. In case of failure to fill in these obligatory data, the extension request shall be rejected.

The data subject has a right of access to the personal data relating to him or her that will be processed through the central database and, where appropriate, the right to rectify, erase or block personal data in accordance with Regulation (EC) No 45/2001 or the national laws implementing Directive 95/46/EC.

All requests for the exercise of the right of access, rectification, erasure or blocking shall be submitted to and processed by the competent customs department where the application was submitted.

The legal basis for processing the personal data for the enforcement of intellectual property rights is Regulation (EU) No 608/2013 of the European Parliament and of the Council of 12 June 2013 concerning customs enforcement of intellectual property rights.

Personal data shall not be stored longer than six months from the date the decision granting the application has been revoked or the relevant period during which customs authorities are to take action has expired. That period shall be specified by the competent customs department when granting the extension request and shall not exceed one year from the day following the date of adoption of the decision granting the extension request. However, where customs authorities have been notified of proceedings initiated to determine a possible infringement of goods under the application, personal data shall be kept for six months after the proceedings have been concluded.

Complaints, in case of conflict, can be addressed to the relevant national data protection authority. The contact details of the national data protection authorities are available on the web-site of the European Commission, Directorate General for Justice (http://ec.europa.eu/justice/data-protection/bodies/authorities/eu/index_en.htm#h2-1). Where the complaint concerns processing of personal data by the European Commission, it should be addressed to the European Data Protection Supervisor (http://www.edps.europa.eu/EDPSWEB/).

ANNEX III

NOTES ON COMPLETION

I. *SPECIFICATIONS OF THE BOXES OF THE APPLICATION FOR ACTION FORM SET OUT IN ANNEX I TO BE FILLED IN BY THE APPLICANT*

Fields in the form marked with an asterisk (*) are mandatory fields and shall be filled in.

Where in a box one or more fields are marked with a plus sign (+) at least one of those fields shall be filled in.

No data shall be entered in the boxes marked "for official use".

Box 1: Applicant

Details concerning the applicant shall be entered in this box. It shall contain information on the name and complete address of the applicant and his telephone, mobile telephone or fax number. The applicant may, where appropriate, enter his Taxpayer Identification Number, any other national registration number and his

Economic Operator Registration and Identification Number (EORI-No), which is a number, unique throughout the Union, assigned by a customs authority in a Member State to economic operators involved in customs activities. The applicant may also enter, where appropriate, his e-mail address and his website address.

Box 2: Union/National application

The appropriate box shall be ticked to indicate whether the application is a National or a Union application, as referred to in points (10) and (11) of Article 2 of Regulation (EU) No 608/2013.

Box 3: Status of the applicant

The appropriate box shall be ticked to indicate the status of the applicant within the meaning of Article 3 of Regulation (EU) No 608/2013. The application shall include documents providing evidence to satisfy the competent customs department that the applicant is entitled to submit an application.

Box 4: Representative submitting the application in the name of the applicant

Where the application is submitted by the applicant by means of a representative, details concerning that representative shall be entered in this box. The application shall include evidence of his powers to act as a representative in accordance with the legislation of the Member State in which the application is submitted and the corresponding box shall be ticked.

Box 5: Type of right to which the application refers

The type(s) of the intellectual property rights (IPR) to be enforced shall be indicated by ticking the appropriate box.

Box 6: Member State or, in the case of a Union application, Member States in which customs action is requested

The Member State or, in the case of a Union application, Member States in which customs action is requested shall be indicated by ticking the appropriate box.

Box 7: Representative for legal matters

The details of the representative designated by the applicant to take charge of legal matters shall be indicated in this box.

Box 8: Representative for technical matters

In case the representative for technical matters is different from the representative indicated in box 7, the details of the representative for technical matters shall be indicated in this box.

Box 9: Details of the designated representatives for legal and technical matters in case of a Union application

In case of a Union application, the details of the representative or representatives designated by the applicant to take charge of technical and legal matters in the Member States indicated in box 6 shall be provided in a separate annex which shall contain the elements of information requested in boxes 7 and 8. In case a representative has been designated for more than one Member State, it shall be clearly indicated for which Member States he has been designated.

Box 10: Small consignment procedure

Where the applicant wishes to request the use of the procedure for destruction of goods in small consignments set out in Article 26 of Regulation (EU) No 608/2013, this box shall be ticked.

Box 11: List of rights to which the application refers

Information on the right or rights to be enforced shall be entered in this box.

In the column "No", sequential numbers shall be entered for each of the intellectual property rights to which the application refers.

In the column "Type of right", the type of IPR shall be indicated by using the appropriate abbreviations which appear in box 5 in brackets.

In the column "list of goods to which the right refers", the type of goods which are covered by the relevant IPR and with regard to which the applicant wishes to request customs enforcement shall be entered.

Sub-box "Restricted handling" in boxes 12-28

Where the applicant wishes to request that information provided by him in boxes 12-28 be the subject of restricted handling within the meaning of Article 31(5) of Regulation (EU) No 608/2013, this sub-box shall be ticked.

Page 2: Information on authentic goods in boxes 12-19

The applicant shall enter in boxes 12-19, as appropriate, specific and technical data on the authentic goods, information needed to enable the customs authorities to readily identify goods suspected of infringing IPR and information relevant to the customs authorities' analysis and assessment of the risk of infringement of the IPR(s) concerned.

Box 12: Goods details

Box 12 shall contain a description of the authentic goods, including get-up and graphic symbols, their Combined Nomenclature code and their value in the EU internal market. The applicant, where appropriate, shall provide images of those goods. The information shall be arranged per different type of goods or different assortment of goods.

Box 13: Goods distinctive features

Box 13 shall contain information on the typical features of the authentic goods, such as markings, labels, security threads, holograms, buttons, hangtags and barcoding, indicating the exact position of the features on the goods and their appearance.

Box 14: Place of production

Box 14 shall contain information on the place of production of the authentic goods.

Box 15: Involved companies

Box 15 shall contain information on authorised importers, suppliers, manufacturers, carriers, consignees or exporters. The information shall be arranged per different type of goods.

Box 16: Traders

Box 16 shall contain information on persons or entities authorised to trade in products involving the use of the IPR(s) for which enforcement is sought. The information shall refer to name, address and registration numbers, such as EORI number, of those persons or entities. Likewise, the information shall comprise information on how licensees may demonstrate their authorisation to use the IPR(s) in question.

Box 17: Goods clearance details and distribution information

Box 17 shall contain information on channels of distribution of the authentic goods, such as information related to central warehouses, dispatch departments, means of transport, transport routes and delivery, and on customs procedures and offices where the clearance of the authentic goods is carried out.

Box 18: Packages

This box shall contain information on the packaging of the authentic goods, such as information on the following:

(a) the kind of packages, indicated by using the relevant codes as given in Annex 38 to Commission Regulation (EEC) No 2454/93[5];

(b) typical features of the packages (for instance, markings, labels, security threads, holograms, buttons, hangtags and bar-coding), including the exact position of the features in the package;

(c) special package designs (colour, shape);

(d) where appropriate, images of those goods.

Box 19: Accompanying documents

Box 19 shall contain information on documents accompanying the authentic goods, such as brochures, operating instructions, warranty documents or other similar items.

Page 3: Information on infringing goods in boxes 20-27

The applicant shall enter in boxes 20-27, as appropriate, information relevant to the customs authorities' analysis and assessment of the risk of infringement of the IPR(s) concerned.

Box 20: Goods details

Box 20 shall contain a description of goods suspected of infringing an intellectual property right (infringing goods), including get-up and graphic symbols. The applicant, where appropriate, shall provide images of those goods. The information shall be arranged per different type of goods or different assortment of goods.

Box 21: Goods distinctive features

Box 21 shall contain information on the typical features of the suspected infringing goods, such as markings, labels, security threads, holograms, buttons, hangtags and bar-coding, indicating the exact position of the features on the goods and their appearance.

Box 22: Place of production

Box 22 shall contain information on the known or suspected place of origin, provenance and delivery of the infringing goods.

Box 23: Involved companies

Box 23 shall contain information on importers, suppliers, manufacturers, carriers, consignees or exporters who are suspected of being involved in infringements of the relevant intellectual property rights.

Box 24: Traders

Box 24 shall contain information on persons or entities not authorised to trade

---

[5] Commission Regulation (EEC) No 2454/93 of 2 July 1993 laying down provisions for the implementation of Council Regulation (EEC) No 2913/92 establishing the Community Customs Code (OJ L 253, 11.10.1993, p. 1).

in products involving the use of the IPR(s) for which enforcement is sought and who have been trading the products in the Union in the past.

Box 25: Goods distribution information

Box 25 shall contain information on channels of distribution of the infringing goods, such as information related to warehouses, dispatch departments, means of transport, transport routes and places of delivery, and on customs procedures and offices where the clearance of the infringing goods is carried out.

Box 26: Packages

This box shall contain information on the packaging of the suspected infringing goods, such as information on the following:

(a) the kind of packages, indicated by using the relevant codes as given in Annex 38 to Regulation (EEC) No 2454/93;

(b) typical features of the packages (for instance, markings, labels, holograms, buttons, hangtags and bar-coding), including the exact position of the features in the package;

(c) special package designs (colour, shape);

(d) where appropriate, images of those goods.

Box 27: Accompanying documents

Box 27 shall contain information on documents accompanying the suspected infringing goods, such as brochures, operating instructions, warranty documents or other similar items.

Box 28: Additional information

The applicant may provide in box 28 any additional information relevant to the customs authorities' analysis and assessment of the risk of infringement of the IPR(s) concerned such as specific information concerning planned deliveries of suspected infringing goods, including specific and detailed information on means of transport, containers and persons involved.

Box 29: Undertakings

Do not amend the wording, or enter data in this box.

Box 30: Signature

In box 30, the applicant or the representative of the applicant indicated in box 4 shall enter the place and date of completion of the application and shall sign. The signatory's name shall be given in block capitals.

II. *SPECIFICATIONS OF THE BOXES OF THE REQUEST FOR EXTENSION FORM SET OUT IN ANNEX II TO BE FILLED IN BY THE HOLDER OF THE DECISION*

Fields in the form marked with an asterisk (*) are mandatory fields and shall be filled in.

In boxes where fields are marked with a plus (+) at least one of these fields shall be filled in.

Do not enter data in the boxes marked "for official use".

Box 1: Details concerning the holder of the decision

Details concerning the holder of the decision shall be entered in this box.

Box 2: Extension request

The application registration number including the first two digits representing the iso/alpha-2 code of the Member State that granted the application shall be entered in this box. The holder of the decision shall indicate whether he is requesting modifications to the information contained in the application by ticking the appropriate box.

Box 3: Signature

In box 3, the holder of the decision or the representative of the holder of the decision shall enter the place and date of completion of the request and shall sign. The signatory's name shall be given in block capitals.

B7.B UK MATERIALS

B7.bi The Copyright (Customs) Regulations 1989

(SI 1989/1178)

Made	*10th July 1989*
Laid before Parliament	*11th July 1989*
Coming into force	*1st August 1989*

The Commissioners of Customs and Excise, in exercise of the powers conferred on them by section 112(1), (2) and (3) of the Copyright, Designs and Patents Act 1988[1] and of all other powers enabling them in that behalf, hereby make the following Regulations:

1. These Regulations may be cited as the Copyright (Customs) Regulations 1989 and shall come into force on 1st August 1989.

2.—(1) Notice given under section 111(1) of the Copyright, Designs and Patents Act 1988 shall be in the form set out in Schedule 1 or a form to the like effect approved by the Commissioners; and a separate notice shall be given in respect of each work.

(2) Notice given under section 111(3) of that Act shall be in the form set out in Schedule 2 or a form to the like effect approved by the Commissioners; and a separate notice given shall be given in respect of each work and in respect of each expected importation into the United Kingdom.

(3) In regulations 3 to 9 "notice" means a notice given under either of those subsections.

3. The notice shall contain full particulars of the matters specified therein and shall contain a declaration by the signatory that the information given by him in the notice is true.

4. A fee of £30 (plus value added tax) in respect of the notice shall be paid to the Commissioners at the time it is given.

5. The person giving the notice shall furnish to the Commissioners a copy of the work specified in the notice at the time the notice is given and at that time or at the time the goods to which the notice relates are imported shall furnish to them such evidence as they may reasonably require to establish—

(a) his ownership of the copyright in such work;

(b) that goods detained are infringing copies; or

(c) that a person who has signed the notice as agent is duly authorised.

6. The person giving the notice shall give security or further security within such time and in such manner, whether by bond or by deposit of a sum of money, as the Commissioners may require, in respect of any liability or expense which they may incur in consequence of the notice by reason of the detention of any article or anything done to an article detained.

---

[1] 1988 c.48.

7. In every case, whether any security or further security is given or not, the person who has given the notice shall keep the Commissioners indemnified against all such liability and expense as is mentioned in regulation 6.

8. The person giving the notice shall notify the Commissioners in writing of any change in the ownership of the copyright in the work specified in the notice or other change affecting the notice within fourteen days of such change.

9. The notice shall be deemed to have been withdrawn—

    (a) as from the expiry of fourteen days from any change in ownership of the copyright specified in the notice, whether notified to the Commissioners in accordance with regulation 8 or not; or

    (b) if the person giving the notice has failed to comply with the requirement of these Regulations.

10. The Copyright (Customs) Regulations 1957[2] and the Copyright (Customs) (Amendment) Regulations 1982[3] are revoked.

Regulation 2(1)   SCHEDULE 1

Notice under the Copyright, Designs & Patents Act 1988 Requesting Infringing Copies of a Literary, Dramatic or Musical Work to be treated as Prohibited Goods.

Please read these notes before completing this notice.

1. This notice may only be given by the owner of the copyright in a published literary, dramatic or musical work or a person acting on his behalf. A separate notice must be given for each work.

2. The period specified in part 1 shall not exceed 5 years and shall not extend beyond the period for which copyright is to subsist.

3. A fee of £30(plus VAT) is payable. Please enclose a cheque for the required amount made payable to "Commissioners of Customs and Excise".

4. A copy of the work specified in part 2 should be enclosed.

5. The person who has given the notice shall keep the Commissioners of Customs and Excise indemnified against any liability or expense which they may incur as a result of detaining any article or anything done to an article detained because of this notice. You may need to provide the Commissioners with security to cover this indemnity. You will be informed when this is required.

6. Part 3 is not obligatory, but please give as many details as possible.

Part 1.

I, ... give notice that

                Full name of signatory in BLOCK LETTERS

. . . .

                Name and address of Owner of Copyright

. . . .

. . . .

is the owner of the copyright in the work specified below which subsists under the Copyright, Designs and Patents Act 1988 and I request that any infringing copies of the said work be treated as prohibited goods for a period starting

on .... and ending on ....

Part 2.

Particulars of Work

Title: . . . .

. . . .

---

[2] SI 1957/875.
[3] SI 1982/766.

Full name of author/authors: . . . .

. . . .

Date copyright expires: . . . .

Part 3.

Details of expected importation

   a) Date of importation . . . .

   b) Place of customs declaration . . . .

   c) Place of unloading . . . .

   d) Country of origin . . . .

   e) Country from which goods consigned . . . .

   f) Bill of loading/airway bill/consignment reference number . . . .

   g) Name of ship/aircraft flight number/vehicle registration number . . . .

   h) Name and address of importer/consignee . . . .

      . . . .

   i) Tariff classification and commodity code . . . .

Part 4.

Declaration

I declare that the information given by me in this notice is true.

Signature . . . . Date . . . .

   (*Owner of copyright/Authorised agent)

Delete as necessary

Part 5.

Please send the completed notice, enclosing fee and a copy of the work, to:—

HM Customs and Excise

CDB3(B)

Dorset House

Stamford Street

LONDON SE1 9PS

Regulation 2(2)   SCHEDULE 2

NOTICE UNDER THE COPYRIGHT, DESIGNS & PATENTS ACT 1988 REQUESTING INFRINGING COPIES
OF A SOUND RECORDING OR FILM TO BE TREATED AS PROHIBITED GOODS.

Please read these notes before completing this notice.

1. This notice may only be given by the owner of the copyright in a sound recording or film or a person acting on his behalf. A separate notice must be given in respect of each work and each expected importation of infringing copies of the work.

2. A fee of £30(plus VAT) is payable. Please enclose a cheque for the required amount made payable to "Commissioners of Customs and Excise".

3. A copy of the work specified in part 2 should be enclosed.

4. The person who has given the notice shall keep the Commissioners of Customs and Excise indemnified against any liability or expense which they may incur as a result of detaining any article or any thing done to an article detained because of this notice.

You may need to provide the Commissioners with security to cover this indemnity.
You will be informed when this is required.

5. Part 4 is not obligatory, but please give as many details as possible.

Part 1.

I, ...

give notice that

Full name of signatory in BLOCK LETTERS

. . . .

Name and address of Owner of Copyright

. . . .

. . . .

is the owner of the copyright in the work specified below which subsists under the Copyright, Designs and Patents Act 1988 and that infringing copies of the work are expected to be imported into the United Kingdom and I request that these copies be treated as prohibited goods.

Part 2.
Particulars of Work
Title: . . . .
. . . .
Label, marking or statement borne by work: . . . .
. . . .
Date copyright expires: . . . .
Part 3.
Expected arrival in United Kingdom
Date . . . .
Place . . . .
Part 4.
Details of expected importation
         Place of customs declaration . . . .
         Place of unloading . . . .
         Country of origin . . . .
         Country from which goods consigned . . . .
         Bill of lading/airway bill/consignment reference number . . . .
         Name of ship/aircraft flight number/vehicle registration number . . . .
         Name and address of importer/consignee . . . .
         . . . .
         Tariff classification and commodity code . . . .
Part 5.
Declaration
I declare that the information given by me in this notice is true.
Signature . . . . Date . . . .
    (*Owner of copyright/Authorised agent)
*Delete as necessary
Part 6.
Please send the completed notice, enclosing fee and a copy of the work, to:—
HM Customs and Excise
CDB3(B)
Dorset House
Stamford Street
LONDON SE1 9PS

B7.bii The Goods Infringing Intellectual Property Rights (Customs) Regulations 2004

(SI 2004/ 1473)

Made   *4th June 2004*
Laid before Parliament   *7th June 2004*
Coming into force   *1st July 2004*

The Commissioners of Customs and Excise, in exercise of the powers conferred on them by section 2(2) of the European Communities Act 1972, being a Department designated for the purposes of that subsection in relation to counterfeit and pirated goods, goods infringing a patent, goods infringing a supplementary protection certificate, goods infringing Community plant variety rights and goods infringing plant breeders' rights, designations of origin, geographical indications and geographical designations, hereby make the following Regulations:

1. These Regulations may be cited as the Goods Infringing Intellectual Property Rights (Customs) Regulations 2004 and shall come into force on 1st July 2004.

Interpretation

2.—(1) In these Regulations—

"the 1979 Act" means the Customs and Excise Management Act 1979;

"application" means an application under Article 5 of the Council Regulation;

"the Commissioners" means the Commissioners of Customs and Excise;

[...;]

"the Council Regulation" means Council Regulation (EC) No 1383/2003 concerning customs action against goods suspected of infringing certain intellectual property rights and the measures to be taken against goods found to have infringed such rights;

"the customs and excise Acts" has the meaning given in section 1(1) of the 1979 Act;

"database rights" has the meaning given in regulation 13 of the Copyright and Rights in Databases Regulations 1997;

"decision" means a decision granting an application in accordance with Article 8 of the Council Regulation;

"declarant" has the meaning given in Article 4(18) of Council Regulation (EEC) No 2913/1992 establishing the Community Customs Code;

[...;]

"goods infringing an intellectual property right" has the meaning given in Article 2(1) of the Council Regulation and related expressions shall be construed accordingly;

[...;]

"publication rights" has the meaning given in regulation 16 of the Copyright and Related Rights Regulations 1996;

[...;]

"right-holder" has the meaning given in Article 2(2) of the Council Regulation;

[...;]

"working days" has the meaning given in Article 3(1) of Council Regulation (EEC, Euratom) No 1182/1971 determining the rules applicable to periods, dates and time limits.

(2) For the purposes of these Regulations, any reference in the Council Regulation to "copyright or related right" is to be construed as a reference to "copyright, rights in performances, publication rights or database rights".

(3) These Regulations shall apply to goods which fall to be treated by virtue of [Article 2] of the Council Regulation as being goods infringing an intellectual property right; but these Regulations shall not apply to any goods in relation to which the Council Regulation does not apply by virtue of [Article 3] thereof.

Note: In reg.2(1) the definitions of "Community design", "Community plant variety right", "design right", "designation of origin", "European patent (UK)", "geographical designation", "geographical indication", "patent", "plant breeders' right", "registered design" and "supplementary protection certificate" (in italics) omitted and in reg. 2(3) the words in square brackets substituted for the former words "Article 2(3)" and "Article 3(1)" by the Goods Infringing Intellectual Property Rights (Customs) (Amendment) (No.2) Regulations 2010 (SI 2010/992), regs 3 and 4, with effect from April 16, 2010.

Infringing goods liable to forfeiture

3. [...]

Note: Regulation 3 was omitted by the Goods Infringing Intellectual Property Rights (Customs) (Amendment) Regulations 2010 (SI 2010/324) reg.2(1), with effect from March 10, 2010.

Application for action

4. [...]

Notes:

(1) Regulation 4(2) was omitted by the Goods Infringing Intellectual Property Rights (Customs) (Amendment) Regulations 2010 (SI 2010/324) reg.2(1), with effect from March 10, 2010.

(2) The remainder of reg.4 was omitted by the Goods Infringing Intellectual Property Rights (Customs) (Amendment) (No.2) Regulations 2010 (SI 2010/992) reg.5, with effect from April 16, 2010.

Decision to cease to have effect

5. A decision shall have no further effect where—

(a) any change, following the making of the application, which takes place in the ownership or authorised use of the intellectual property right specified in the application, is not communicated in writing to the Commissioners; or

(b) the intellectual property right specified in the application expires.

Samples of goods

6. [...]

Note: Regulation 6 was omitted by the Goods Infringing Intellectual Property Rights (Customs) (Amendment) (No.2) Regulations 2010 (SI 2010/992) reg.5, with effect from April 16, 2010.

Simplified procedure

7.—[(1) The Commissioners may treat as abandoned for destruction goods which have been suspended from release or detained by virtue of [Article 9 of the Council Regulation] where the right-holder has informed the Commissioners in writing within the specified period that those goods infringe an intellectual property right and either of the following conditions applies—

(a) the right-holder has provided the Commissioners with the written agreement of the declarant, the holder or the owner of the goods ("the interested parties") that the goods may [be] destroyed; or

(b) none of the interested parties has specifically opposed the destruction of the goods within the specified period.

(2) The Commissioners may not treat the goods as abandoned for destruction where one interested party has given its written agreement as mentioned in regulation 7(1)(a), but either or both of the other interested parties has specifically opposed destruction within the specified period.

(3) The Commissioners may, at their discretion, accept the written agreement mentioned in regulation 7(1)(a) directly from the interested party.

(4) Where goods are treated as abandoned for destruction by virtue of paragraph (1)—

(a) the right-holder must bear the expense and the responsibility for the destruction of the goods, unless otherwise specified by the Commissioners; and

(b) the Commissioners must retain a sample of the goods in such conditions that it can be used if required as evidence in legal proceedings.

(5) The specified period means ten working days from receipt of the notification to the right-holder provided for in [Article 9 of the Council Regulation], or three working days in the case of perishable goods. The Commissioners may, at their discretion, extend this period by a further ten working days.

(6) A reference in this regulation to the Commissioners is to be construed as a reference to the Secretary of State.]

Notes:
  (1) Regulation 7 was substituted by the Goods Infringing Intellectual Property Rights (Customs) (Amendment) Regulations 2010 (SI 2010/324) reg.2(2), with effect from March 10, 2010.
  (2) The words in the first set of square brackets in reg.7(1) in the square brackets in reg.7(5) substituted for the former by "regulation 4(1)(c)" and the word "by" in reg. 7(1)(a) was inserted by the Goods Infringing Intellectual Property Rights (Customs) (Amendment) (No. 2) Regulations 2010 (SI 2010/992) regs 6, 7, with effect from April 16, 2010.

Detention and seizure of goods infringing specified intellectual property rights

8. [...]

Note: Regulation 8 was omitted by the Goods Infringing Intellectual Property Rights (Customs) (Amendment) Regulations 2010 (SI 2010/324) reg.2(1), with effect from March 10, 2010.]

Initiation of proceedings

9. [...]

Note: Regulation 9 was omitted by the Goods Infringing Intellectual Property Rights (Customs) (Amendment) Regulations 2010 (SI 2010/324) reg.2(1), with effect from March 10, 2010.

Relationship with other powers

10. Nothing in these Regulagtions shall be taken to affect—
  (a) any power of the Commissioners conferred otherwise than by any provision of these Regulations to suspend the release of, or detain, any goods; or
  (b) the power of any court to grant any relief, including any power to make an order by way of interim relief.

Misuse of information by a right-holder

11.—(1) Where the Commissioners have reasonable grounds for believing that there has been a misuse of information by a right-holder the Commissioners may suspend the decision in force at the time of the misuse of information, in relation to a relevant intellectual property right, for the remainder of its period of validity.

(2) Where the Commissioners have reasonable grounds for believing that there has been a further misuse of information within three years of a previous misuse of information by that right-holder the Commissioners may—
  (a) suspend the decision in force at the time of the further misuse of information, in relation to a relevant intellectual property right, for the remainder of its period of validity; and
  (b) for a period of up to one year from its expiry, refuse to renew the decision in force at the time of the further misuse of information, or to accept a new application, in relation to a relevant intellectual property right.

(3) In this regulation—
  (a) "misuse of information" means the use of information supplied to a right-holder pursuant to the first sub-paragraph of Article 9(3) of the Council Regulation other than for the purposes specified in Articles 10, 11 and 13(1) of the Council Regulation, or pursuant to an enactment or order of a court, and related expressions shall be construed accordingly;
  (b) "relevant intellectual property right" means any intellectual property

right in relation to a suspected infringement of which information was supplied to a right-holder pursuant to the first sub-paragraph of Article 9(3) of the Council Regulation, and in relation to which the Commissioners have reasonable grounds for believing that there has been a misuse of that information.

Amendment of the Copyright, Designs and Patents Act 1988

12. For subsection (3B) of section 111 of the Copyright, Designs and Patents Act 1988 there shall be substituted—

> "(3B) This section does not apply to goods placed in, or expected to be placed in, one of the situations referred to in Article 1(1), in respect of which an application may be made under Article 5(1), of Council Regulation (EC) No 1383/2003 concerning customs action against goods suspected of infringing certain intellectual property rights and the measures to be taken against goods found to have infringed such rights.".

Amendment of the Trade Marks Act 1994

13. For subsection (3) of section 89 of the Trade Marks Act 1994 there shall be substituted—

> "(3) This section does not apply to goods placed in, or expected to be placed in, one of the situations referred to in Article 1(1), in respect of which an application may be made under Article 5(1), of Council Regulation (EC) No 1383/2003 concerning customs action against goods suspected of infringing certain intellectual property rights and the measures to be taken against goods found to have infringed such rights.".

Revocations

14. The Regulations listed in the Schedule are hereby revoked.

Regulation 14   SCHEDULE

REVOCATIONS

Regulations revoked	*References*
The Trade Marks (EC Measures Relating to Counterfeit Goods) Regulations 1995.	SI 1995/1444
The Goods Infringing Intellectual Property Rights (Customs) Regulations 1999.	SI 1999/1601
The Goods Infringing Intellectual Property Rights (Consequential Provisions) Regulations 1999.	SI 1999/1618
The Goods Infringing Intellectual Property Rights (Customs) Regulations 2003.	SI 2003/2316

B7.biii Customs Notice No.34

Published 6 December 2013

Contents

1. Foreword
  2. Introduction
  3. European Union Legislation
  4. Application procedures
  5. Role of IP Authorisation Unit (IPAU)

6. Action taken by Border Force when suspect goods are detected at the border
7. Additional information
8. United Kingdom legislation facilitating action against grey market goods
9. Your rights and obligations
10. Do you have any comments or suggestions?
11. Putting things right
12. How we use your information

Foreword

This notice cancels and replaces Notice 34 (November 2012).

1. Introduction

1.1 What this Notice is about?

This notice explains how we operate the EU procedures on customs enforcement of intellectual property (IP) rights at the external border including:

- trade marks
- design rights
- copyright or any related rights
- geographical indications
- patents
- supplementary protection certificate for medical products or for plant protection products
- plant variety rights
- topography of a semi conductor

A full description of the rights can be found in Article 2 of Regulation 608/2013.

Note the regulation also includes utility model and trade name in the list of IP rights however the UK does not feature a utility model as an IP right and trade name is not recognised as an exclusive IP right. For this reason no customs intervention is possible for these rights at the UK external border.

The notice also explains the UK legislation on:

- customs action in relation to goods infringing trade marks and copyright (Grey Market goods)

1.2 What's changed

This Notice has been amended as a result of significant changes in legislation and procedure. This was caused by the entry into force of Regulation (EU) No 608/2013 and the consequential repeal of Council Regulation 1383/2003.

1.3 The law

The procedures in this notice are based on the following:

- Regulation (EU) No 608/2013
- Commission Regulation (awaiting details)
- Trade Marks Act 1994
- Trade Marks (Customs) Regulations 1994
- Copyright, Designs and Patents Act 1988
- Copyright (Customs) Regulations 1989

This notice is not the law, it is our view on what the law says and nothing in this notice takes the place of or amends the law.

1.4 Responsibilities

HM Revenue and Customs (HMRC) is the UK customs authority responsible for national policy governing IP rights enforcement at the UK external border.

Border Force (BF) is a law enforcement command within the Home Office responsible for carrying out the frontier interventions that implement this policy, under the terms of a

Partnership Agreement between the Commissioners of HMRC and the Home Office. References in this notice to 'us', 'we' etc refer to either HMRC or BF as appropriate.

The Customs enforcement action described in this notice is possible only where IP right protection has been granted by an appropriate organisation or, in the case of any copyright, related right or unregistered design where it arises by operation of law. The official government body within the UK for approving, registering and providing advice on IP is the Intellectual Property Office (IPO). The IPO website describes their work and provides advice.

IP rights covering the EU can be registered via the Office for Harmonisation in the Internal Market (OHIM). The OHIM website describes their work and provides advice.

2. European Union legislation

2.1 Regulation (EU) 608/2013

Regulation (EU) No 608/2013 of the European Parliament and of the Council (from this point simply referred to as the Regulation) establishes mandatory rules and other procedures which customs authorities use to facilitate the enforcement of certain IP rights at the external frontier of the EU. The Regulation is procedural in nature and does not introduce, amend or in any way affect national or EU law on IP or law relating to criminal procedures.

Significant elements of the Regulation include:

- the scope of customs intervention
- goods excluded from the scope of the Regulation
- list of IP rights included and their definitions
- application for action process
- simplified destruction procedure for infringing goods
- obligations of the IP rights applicant including sanctions where appropriate
- procedure for the notification of detention to both sides involved plus a clear time line of events
- use of information by the right holder
- procedure for the destruction of counterfeit or pirated goods in small consignments without reference to the right holder
- establishment and use of a central database
- legal authority for an implementing act to designate new forms for application for action, request for extension and so on

2.2 Definitions

For the purpose of this Notice, the following definitions apply:

2.2.1 Counterfeit goods

Goods, including any packaging, label, sticker, brochure, operating instructions, warranty document or similar item (even if presented separately) which are subject of an act infringing:

- a trade mark in the Member State where they are found and bear without authorisation a sign which is identical to the trade mark validly registered in respect of the same type of goods, or which cannot be distinguished in its essential aspects from such a trade mark
- a geographical indication in the Member State where they are found and, bear or are described by, a name or term protected in respect of that geographical indication

2.2.2 Pirated goods

Goods which are the subject of an act infringing a copyright or related right or a design in the Member State where the goods are found and which are, or contain copies, made without the consent of the holder of a copyright or related right or a design, or of a person authorised by that holder in the country of production.

2.2.3 Right-holder

The holder of an IP right.

2.2.4 The declarant or the holder of the goods

The 'declarant' is the person making a summary declaration or a re-export notification to Customs or making a Customs declaration in his own name or the person in whose name such a declaration is made.

The 'holder' means the person who is the owner of the goods or who has a similar right of disposal over them or who has physical control over them.

2.2.5 Perishable goods

Goods considered by customs authorities to deteriorate by being kept for up to 20 working days from the date of their suspension of release or detention.

2.2.6 Destruction

The physical destruction, recycling, or disposal of goods outside of commercial channels in such a way as to preclude damage to the right holder.

2.2.7 Small consignment

A postal or express courier shipment which:
  - (a) contains 3 units or less
  - (b) has a gross weight of less than 2 kilograms

2.2.8 Grey Market goods

  - goods manufactured with the consent of the right-holder but marketed without consent
  - goods manufactured by a person duly authorised by a right holder to manufacture a certain quantity of goods but which have been produced in excess of that agreed amount

2.2.9 Entry into the EU

  - placing of goods under Customs supervision
  - declaration of goods for free circulation within the EU
  - placing of goods under a suspensive procedure
  - placing of imported goods in a free zone or free warehouse

2.2.10 Working day

All days other than public holidays, Sundays and Saturdays. The day upon which an event takes place shall not be considered as falling within the period in question.

The period for responding to a detention begins the first working day after detention was notified and ends with the expiry of the last hour of the last day of the period.

2.2.11 Initiation of proceedings

For the purposes of proceedings required by articles 26 and 29 of the Regulation the 'initiating process' is complied with when the claim form is issued by the Court. This is regardless of whether or not it contains (or is accompanied by) the particulars of claim at that time. To ensure the continuation of a detention the claimant must serve the claim on the defendant no later than the date allowed under the Civil Procedure Rules.

2.2.12 Suspect goods

Goods where there are reasonable indications that they are the subject of an act infringing an intellectual property right in the Member State in which they are found.

2.3 Exclusions

2.3.1 Regulation 608/2013 does not apply to:

  - grey market goods (but see Section 7 regarding possible action under UK national law)
  - goods of a non commercial nature contained in travellers' personal luggage
  - goods in free circulation in the EU moving between Member States

3. Application procedures

3.1 I hold an intellectual property (IP) right; how do I apply for protection?

If you:
  - want Customs action at the UK border only you should complete a National IP Rights Application for Action (AFA)

- hold an EU IP Right and you want Customs action in two or more Member States, you should complete an EU AFA
- you must use the appropriate form as set out in Commission Regulation (Regulation Number not known - will be added later)

3.2 Who can submit an AFA?

A full description of the persons and entities entitled to submit either a national or Union AFA can be found in Article 3 of the Regulation and includes:

- right holders
- IP collective rights management bodies
- professional defence bodies
- in respect of geographical indicators; groups of producers or similar groups, inspection bodies or similar competent authorities
- persons or entities duly authorised by the right holder to initiate proceedings in order to determine whether an IP right has been infringed
- holders of exclusive licences duly authorised by the right holder to initiate proceedings in order to determine whether an IP right has been infringed

3.3 What information will the applicant be asked to provide?

As set out in Article 6 of the Regulation you must provide:

- name, address and contact details along with your status within the meaning of Article 3 of the Regulation
- IP right or rights to be protected
- documentary evidence that you hold the relevant rights or are authorised to act on behalf of the owner
- for a Union AFA you must also list the Member States in which you require action to be taken, as well as the contact details of the right-holder for each Member State concerned
- a sufficiently detailed description of the goods to enable us to recognise them
- specific technical data on the authentic goods, for example markings, bar codes, and images as appropriate
- the name and contact details of your appointed legal and technical experts
- agreement that data provided may be processed by the Commission and other Member States
- whether you wish to request the use of the "small consignment" procedure and agree to cover the costs of goods destroyed under that procedure

The applicant will also be required to provide undertakings as follows:

- to notify the IP Authorisation Unit (IPAU) where an IP right ceases to have effect
- forward and update information that will enable customs authorities to analyse and assess the risk of an IP infringement
- to assume liability towards the holder of the goods where, following detention:
  (a) action is discontinued due to an act or omission on the part of the applicant
  (b) samples are either not returned or are damaged and beyond use due to an act or omission on the part of the applicant
  (c) the goods in question are found not to infringe an IP right
- to reimburse, where requested, the costs incurred by customs authorities or other persons acting on their behalf, from the moment of detention. This includes costs associated with the storage and handling of the goods and, if appropriate, their destruction

3.4 Additional information

Wherever applicable and if known you should also include within the application:

- any specific information concerning the type or pattern of fraud
- the port or country from which the goods are consigned and their intended port of arrival in the EU/UK
- details identifying the consignment or packages; for example descriptions, marks and numbers, the container number, waybill or manifest details

- the expected date of arrival or departure of the goods
- the means of transport and the identity of the carrier, logistics operator and/or customs broker/agent involved
- the identity (including address and postcode) of the importer or exporter. If known please also supply their Economic Operator Registration and Identification number
- the country or countries of production and the routes used by traffickers
- the technical differences, if known, between the authentic and suspected infringing goods
- the pre-tax value of the original goods on the legitimate market in the country in which the application for action is lodged

You should also provide details on the form, no matter how trivial, of any other intelligence you may have about the trade in infringing goods in order to help us intercept such goods. Any information that you wish to make available after the acceptance of the application for action can be sent by post or email to the address in section 3.6.

3.5 When should I send my application?

Wherever possible you should send us your completed AFA 30 working days before you expect the infringing goods to be imported or exported, or you want the monitoring period to commence.

If you have not submitted an AFA, we may notify you of any suspected infringing goods we discover during the course of our checks and invite you to submit an application (ex officio action). We are only authorised to detain these goods for 4 working days following the notification of detention to allow you to submit an application, we cannot extend this period.

3.6 Where should I send the completed application?

You should send the completed AFA to:

HM Revenue and Customs
CITEX Authorisations and Returns
Intellectual Property Authorisation Unit
Fitz Roy House
Castle Meadow Road
Nottingham
NG2 1BD

Telephone: 03000 564 280 or 03000 564 097
Fax: 03000 564 569
Email: approvals.ip@hmrc.gsi.gov.uk

You may also contact this office for advice on completing an IP application.

3.7 Administrative fees, validity periods and renewals

You will not be charged a fee for new applications, or requests for extensions, submitted under the Regulation. However we reserve the right to pass on to you any costs we incur in from the moment of detention including handling, storage and for destroying the suspect goods.

The validity period of an AFA shall not exceed one year but may be extended upon request. To ensure continuity of coverage the renewal should be received at least 30 working days before expiry of the application and in any event must be received before the expiry date or a new AFA may be required. The request shall be forwarded to the authorising customs office using the model form as set out in the Commission Regulation.

Please note that an AFA granted prior to 1 January 2014 under Council Regulation 1383/2003 cannot be renewed beyond its expiry date by a simple extension request. From 1 January a new AFA must be submitted under the provisions of the 2013 Regulation. Thereafter the AFA may be renewed on request.

Should an IP right cease to have effect you must inform the appropriate customs authority so the AFA can be amended or revoked. Similarly where an applicant ceases for any reason to be entitled to submit an AFA they must inform the appropriate customs authority; the AFA will be revoked.

Where an AFA is submitted in response to an ex-officio detention which does not contain all of the mandatory information regarding technical data etc it shall be granted only for the detention period of the goods in question.

A comprehensive manual covering completion of the AFA as well as copies of the various forms can be found on the European Commission's website.

3.8 Liability for costs

When you submit an application the right-holder is required to complete an undertaking to pay all costs and liabilities incurred under the Regulation. These may include:

- storage and other handling charges for correctly detained and abandoned goods
- costs incurred in the destruction of the goods, including those destroyed under the small consignment procedure

Additionally Article 28 establishes a civil liability in respect of legal costs and compensation for any loss suffered by the owner of the goods if you or the court confirm that the goods are not infringing or the action is discontinued owing to an act or omission on you part.

3.9 Disclosure of information

The Regulation establishes a gateway that allows us to disclose to a third party information that would otherwise be confidential. This information is disclosed on the understanding that it may only be used for the following purposes:

- to initiate proceedings to determine whether an IP right has been infringed and in the course of those proceedings
- in connection with criminal investigations related to the infringement of an IP right undertaken by a public body in the Member State in which the goods are found (for example Trading Standards)
- for criminal proceedings
- to seek compensation from the infringer or other persons
- to agree with the declarant or holder that goods may be abandoned for destruction
- to agree with the declarant or holder an appropriate level of security allowing early release of goods suspected of infringing a design, patent, semi-conductor topography, or plant variety (see section 6.1)

Misuse of information provided under the terms of the Regulation may result in the revocation or suspension of the application in force or a refusal to extend the period of validity of the AFA.

4. Role of IP Authorisation Unit (IPAU)

The IPAU will accept and process applications for action and extensions and can provide help and guidance on all aspects of the application process.

The IPAU should also be the first point of contact for information and intelligence on expected arrivals of suspect goods. Consider using either the Red Alert or New Trends form provided by the Commission.

They are not able to comment or give advice on goods detained by BF at the frontier, enquiries concerning such matters should be addressed to the BF case officer.

Matters of customs IP policy should be referred to the Policy Unit at ron.johnson@hmrc.gsi.gov.uk.

General customs enquires should be referred to the helpline on Telephone: 0300 200 3700.

4.1 Processing of an application for action

Step	Procedure
1	We will consider your AFA and advise you as soon as possible whether we can accept it. For minor changes or clarifications the applicant may be contacted by phone or e-mail

2   Where we reject an AFA we will tell you why and give you the opportunity to amend the AFA or ask us to reconsider our decision

3   When your AFA is accepted we will confirm this in writing by means of a formal decision. We have 30 working days from the receipt of a perfect AFA to complete this action

4   For an AFA lodged in response to an ex-officio detention the frontier officer concerned will be notified if the AFA has been accepted. The goods will then be dealt with accordingly. You will be notified of the decision within two working-days of the receipt of the AFA

5   Once an AFA has been agreed the details will be loaded onto the EU database called COPIS. This will make the details available to BF officers and, in the case of a Union AFA, to the customs authorities in the Member States for which action is requested

6   We will not issue a reminder advising of the imminent expiry of an AFA. We accept no responsibility for loss of coverage as a result of a right holder failing to renew an AFA in good time

5. Action taken by Border Force when suspect goods are detected at the border

When we intercept goods that we have reason to believe are infringing and are covered by a valid application or notice, we will deal with them in accordance with the relevant EU or UK legislation.

5.1 An application for action is in place

When suspect goods are detected at the border BF will:

(a) detain the goods

(b) notify the declarant or holder of the goods of their detention within one working day of the decision to detain and give them 10 working days in which to either consent or object to their abandonment for destruction

(c) notify the right holder of the detention on the same working day or promptly after. Invite them to confirm whether or not the believe the goods to be infringing and if so whether they agree to their destruction, they will be given 10 working days to respond

(d) provide in the notification the consignment details allowed under Article 17.4 of the Regulation and the consequences of failing to respond within 10 working days

(e) give all parties the opportunity to inspect the goods; in the case of goods suspected of being counterfeit or pirated, the right holder may request a sample for further analysis

(f) detain the goods pending a response from all parties or the expiry of both of the respective detention periods

Goods can be considered as abandoned for destruction under the following conditions:

- the right holder confirms in writing that, in their opinion, the goods infringe an IP right covered by the AFA and consents to destruction plus
- the declarant or holder of the goods confirms in writing that they agree to their destruction

BF may deem that consent has been given where:

- the right holder confirms in writing that, in their opinion, the goods infringe an IP right covered by the AFA and consents to destruction plus
- the declarant or holder of the goods has not confirmed his agreement to destruction nor notified his opposition to it; for example by failing to respond within the period set out

Destruction is carried out under customs control and under the responsibility of the right holder. Samples may be taken and retained.

The prescribed detention period is 10 working days from the notification of detention. In the case of perishable goods this is reduced to 3 working days.

If the declarant or holder of the goods objects to their destruction BF will notify the right holder accordingly. If the right holder has not provided satisfactory evidence to BF that they have initiated proceedings to determine whether their IP right has been infringed before the end of the detention period, including any extension, the goods must be released from detention; subject to the completion of all other customs formalities.

Except in the case of perishable goods BF may, at the request of the right holder and where they agree it is justified, extend the detention period by a maximum of a further 10 working days. The total period cannot exceed 20 working days.

5.2 When no application for action is in place (ex-officio detention)

Except where they are perishable when goods suspected of infringing an IP right are detected by BF but no valid AFA is in place they:

(a) may, prior to detention seek to identify the relevant right holder. BF can give basic information to a likely right holder but cannot disclose anything that may identify an individual or company

(b) must release the goods if no right holder has been identified within 1 day of the detection; subject to the completion of all other customs formalities

(c) will detain the goods if an entitled right holder is identified and he expresses an intention to lodge an AFA covering any IP right he believes is infringed by the consignment

(d) will notify the declarant or holder of the goods of their detention within one working day of the decision to detain, give them 10 working days in which to either consent or object to their abandonment for destruction and informing them of the consequences of failing to respond

(e) notify the right holder of the detention on the same working day or promptly after and:

- invite them to submit a national AFA to the IPAU covering the goods and the right in question
- to confirm whether or not the believe the goods to be infringing and if so whether they agree to their destruction
- given 10 working days to respond but must send an acceptable national AFA to the IPAU before the end of 4 working days
- informed of the consequences of failing to respond within the deadlines set out

(f) will not disclose names and addresses of any party involved to the right holder until a valid AFA has been received by the IPAU

(g) must release the goods, subject to the completion of all other customs formalities, if after four working days of the detention the right holder has not lodged an acceptable AFA with the IPAU

(h) will on request disclose all available information as set out in Article 18.5 to the right holder if an AFA is accepted. The case proceeds as from 5.1 (e)

5.3 Procedure for the destruction of goods in small consignments

The Regulation establishes an option procedure whereby goods in small consignments may be abandoned for destruction at the right holder's expense without any reference to the right holder or the need for the right holder to commence legal proceedings.

5.3.1 Eligibility for use of the small consignment procedure

Before the small consignment procedure can be used all of the following conditions must be fulfilled:

- the goods are suspected of being counterfeit or pirated
- the goods are not perishable
- there is an extant AFA already in place covering the goods in question
- the right holder has requested the use of the procedure when they submitted their AFA
- the goods are transported as a small consignment (see 2.2.7)

5.3.2 Initial detention and offer to the declarant or holder of the goods

When suspect goods eligible for the small consignment procedure are detected at the border BF will:

(a) detain the goods notify and the declarant or holder of the goods that they intend to destroy the goods unless they oppose the destruction. The right holder is not notified of the detention at this stage

(b) give the declarant or holder 10 working days from the notification of detention to express their points of view and informing them of the consequences of failing to respond before the deadline expires

(c) if consent to destroy the goods is given they will be considered as abandoned and destroyed

(d) if the declarant or holder of the goods has neither confirmed his agreement to destruction nor notified his opposition at the close of the 10 day detention period, for example by failing to respond to the request; BF may deem that consent to destroy the goods has been given

(e) destruction is carried out under customs control and under the responsibility of the right holder. At the request of the right holder BF may provide information about the quantity and nature of the goods destroyed but are unable to provide any other details concerning the goods

5.3.3 *Procedure if the declarant or holder objects to destruction*

If the declarant or holder has notified his opposition to destruction or, in the absence of an objection, BF have chosen not to deem that consent has been given; the right holder must be given the opportunity of initiating proceedings to protect his IP right.

(a) BF will detain the goods for 10 working days, notify the right holder and invite him to initiate proceedings to determine whether an IP right has been infringed. There is no facility to further extend this period

(b) BF will disclose full consignment details to the right holder as set out in Article 26.8 of the Regulation and inform them of the consequences of failing to respond within the deadline set

(c) if upon expiry of the deadline BF has not received confirmation from the right holder that he has initiated proceedings then the goods must be released; subject to the completion of all other customs formalities

5.4 Information for the right holder following detention

When suspect goods are detained by BF they will write to you giving details of the consignment and explaining your options under the Regulation. It is important that you act and respond with alacrity and ensure that any time limits notified to you are strictly observed.

On receipt of the detention notice from BF consider the status of the goods and your options.

You only have 10 working days from notification of the detention (3 working days in the case of perishable goods) to complete all of the following:

- decide whether you believe the goods infringe any of your IP rights and if so what course of action you wish to take
- if infringing notify BF of that fact and whether you agree to their destruction
- should you believe the goods do infringe your IP rights but you do not consent to their destruction you must either initiate court proceedings or the goods will be released
- if BF notify you that the declarant or holder of the goods has objected to their destruction you must initiate court proceedings and inform BF accordingly or the goods must be released

Contact the BF if you require further consignment information, wish to exercise your right to inspect the goods or to receive a sample.

Should the goods not infringe your IP rights, or you do not intend to take any action, inform the BF without delay so that early release can be arranged.

If you believe that the goods do infringe you IP rights, write to the BF confirming this, identifying the specific right concerned and whether or not you wish the goods to be destroyed . You also have the option of contacting the declarant or holder of the goods to seek their consent to destroy the goods.

Should the declarant or holder of the goods object to their destruction, or where BF has not exercised their right to deem consent to destruction has been given, BF will inform you. In such a case the goods will be released from detention unless you initiate court proceedings to determine whether your IP right has been infringed and notify BF of this fact before expiry of the detention period.

As an alternative to the procedure leading to voluntary abandonment of the goods for destruction you may wish instead to immediately initiate court proceedings. If this is the case write to BF withholding consent for destruction and confirm that proceedings are to be undertaken. Before expiry of the detention period you must show that proceedings have been commenced by providing, for example:

- a court issued claim form (England and Wales) or a writ (Northern Ireland) or signeted summons (Scotland)
- proof that the proceedings cover the goods in question

Release is automatic unless abandonment is agreed by both parties, is deemed by BF or you have given notice of proceedings before the expiry of the detention period, including any extension.

Except in the case of perishable goods or where the goods were originally dealt with under the small consignment procedure you may seek an extension of the detention period by writing to the case officer and setting out your reasons. You must do this before the expiry of the 10th working day.

Should BF notify you of ex-officio detection or detention you should decide whether you hold the right in question and if so whether you wish to take action.

If you do not intend to lodge an AFA, you believe the goods do not infringe, or you are not the right holder; inform BF immediately so that the goods can be released.

If you intend to lodge an AFA inform BF who will take steps to detain (or continue to detain) the goods. You must then complete a national AFA and lodge it with the IPAU.

You have only 4 working days to lodge an acceptable AFA or the goods must be released; there is no facility to extend this lodgement period.

In signing the AFA you have given an undertaking to assume certain liabilities and bear the costs arising out of the detention and disposal of the goods. Your attention is drawn to Article 16 of the Regulation concerning the failure to fulfil certain obligations including the misuse of information provided by customs. Failure to abide by the conditions set out may lead to the revocation or suspension of your AFA.

If you have opted in to the small consignment procedure and BF detect a consignment that fulfils the conditions set out in the Regulation they will follow the procedure as set out in section 5.3. If the declarant or holder consents to the destruction of the goods, or BF deem that consent has been given, the goods will be destroyed at your expense.

You may request information about the actual or estimated quantity of the destroyed goods and their nature but we are unable to provide the names and addresses of any third party. Should the declarant or holder not agree to the destruction of the goods BF will detain them for 10 working days and disclose the information set out in Article 26.8 of the Regulation to allow you to initiate proceedings if you so desire. There is no facility to extend this period further.

5.5 Information for the declarant or holder of the goods following detention

When suspect goods are detained BF are required to inform the declarant or the holder of the goods; there is no requirement to inform all interested parties.

BF will write to one or more of the interested parties giving details of the consignment and your options under the Regulation and the date by which you must reply. It is important that the recipient acts and responds with alacrity, ensuring any time limits notified are strictly observed.

On receipt of the detention notice from BF consider whether you believe the goods infringe an IP right and your options. If you do not have title to the goods immediately bring the situation to the attention of the owner.

You only have 10 working days from notification of the detention (3 working days in the case of perishable goods) to complete all of the following:

- decide if you believe the goods infringe an IP right and the course of action you will to take
- if applicable notify BF that you agree to abandon the goods for destruction
- if you do not believe that an IP right has been infringed and you do not agree to their destruction; immediately inform BF that you withhold consent for their disposal

Contact BF if you require further consignment information or wish to exercise your right to inspect the goods.

If you do not believe that the goods infringe an IP right and thus intend to object to their destruction you must respond to the case officer setting out your objection before the expiry of the detention period.

You may contact the right holder, or the right holder may contact you to discuss options.

The right holder may seek an extension to the detention period to complete their investigations but there is no facility for you to seek an extension. It is important therefore that you respond to the case officer within the 10 working day period allocated to you.

BF may deem that consent to destroy the goods has been given and arrange for their disposal without further reference to you if you:

- do not respond to BF or object to their disposal before the expiry of the detention period
- the right holder asserts that the goods infringe their IP right and give consent for their destruction

Costs for the storage and destruction for detained goods are the responsibility of the right holder although they may exercise their right to initiate civil proceedings against you to recover their costs.

As part of the AFA process the right holder must provide an undertaking accepting liability towards the holder of the goods or declarant should the detention be discontinued or where the goods are found not to infringe an IP right. Should you wish to take advantage of this option you must contact the right holder or their representative.

If the right holder has opted in to the small consignment procedure and BF detect a consignment that fulfils the conditions set out in the Regulation they will follow the procedure as set out in Section 5.3 and detain the goods for 10 working days.

You will be given the option of abandoning the goods for destruction under customs control and at the expense of the right holder.

No information about the consignment that could identify you or any other third party is provided to the right holder unless you object to the destruction of the goods.

It is important to you respond to BF before expiry of the 10 day detention period or they may deem that you have agreed to the destruction of the goods.

If you inform BF that you object to the destruction of the goods they will disclose the consignment details to the right holder and detain the consignment for a further 10 working days.

This is to give the right holder the opportunity to decide whether an IP right has been infringed and to initiate court proceedings, should they so desire.

6. Additional information

6.1 Early release of goods

Where a right holder has initiated proceedings to determine whether a design right, patent, topography semiconductor product or plant variety right has been infringed the declarant or holder of the goods may request their release from detention before the completion of the proceedings.

Release will only be allowed where:

- a sufficient level of security has beenagreed with the right holder
- no precautionary measures have been imposed by the court or other competent body
- all customs formalities have been complied with

The declarant or holder should reach an agreement with the right holder on the level and nature of the security and inform BF accordingly. Neither BF nor HMRC will hold the security.

6.2 Storage and destruction of goods

The conditions of storage of the goods shall be determined by BF.

Goods to be destroyed shall not be:

- released for free circulation however BF, with the agreement of the right holder, may allow goods to be recycled or disposed of outside of commercial channels including for the purposes of publicity, training or education. The conditions under which goods can be released for free circulation shall be determined by the customs authorities

- brought out of the customs territory of the Union
- exported
- re-exported
- placed under a suspensive procedure
- placed in a free zone or free warehouse

Goods may be moved under customs supervision between different places within the customs territory to facilitate their destruction under customs control.

6.3 Liability of the customs authority

Article 27 of the Regulation specifies that the granting of an AFA shall not entitle the right holder concerned to compensation in the event that goods suspected of infringing an IP right are not detected and are released or no action is taken to detain them.

7. United Kingdom legislation facilitating action against grey market goods

7.1 Law

The EU Regulation does not apply to grey market goods however Section 89 of the Trade Marks Act 1994 (TMA) allows the proprietor or the licensee of a registered trade mark to give notice in writing that goods expected to arrive in the UK will infringe their trade mark and should therefore be treated as prohibited.

Section 111 of the Copyright, Designs and Patents Act 1988 (CDPA) allows the owner of a copyright to give notice in writing that infringing copies of certain types of works expected to arrive in the UK on a specified date, are to be treated as prohibited.

These sections apply only to infringing goods arriving in the UK from outside the European Economic Area, or from within that area but not having been entered for free circulation. Goods that are prohibited are liable to forfeiture and may be seized under UK customs law.

7.2 Exclusions

TMA Section 89 and CDPA Section 111 do not apply to:

- goods for which action may be undertaken using Regulation (EU) No 608/2013
- infringing goods intended for the private and domestic use of the importer
- goods already in free circulation within the European Economic Area
- goods which have already arrived in the UK, irrespective of their customs status

7.3 Application and enforcement procedures

The procedures are set out in the Schedules to the Trade Marks (Customs) Regulations 1994 (SI 1994 No 2625) and the Copyright (Customs) Regulation 1989 (SI 1989 No 1178). You are required, on request, to provide as much specific information about the expected shipment as possible, otherwise we may be unable to target it successfully.

Send your application and fee to:

> HM Revenue and Customs
> CITEX Authorisations and Returns
> Intellectual Property Authorisation Unit
> Fitz Roy House
> Castle Meadow Road
> Nottingham
> NG2 1BD

Telephone: 03000 564 280 or 03000 564 479
Fax: 03000 564 569
Email: approvals.ip@hmrc.gsi.gov.uk

Having accepted an application under these arrangements we will seek to target and intercept infringing consignments arriving in the UK. Any detention or seizure of goods at the frontier will be carried out under the Customs and Excise Management Act 1979.

7.4 Fees

You are required to pay an administration fee of £30 (plus VAT) in respect of each notice you lodge under Section 89 or Section 111. You should make payment at the time the notice is given and make cheques payable to 'HM Revenue and Customs'.

7.5 Indemnity

Both Acts specify that the person giving the notice shall keep us indemnified against any liability and expense incurred as a result of activities carried out in relation to the goods that are specified in the notice.

7.6 Security

We can, under the Acts, at any time require a security by cash deposit or guarantee in respect of the notice and the goods to which it relates. We will notify you if and when we require security.

7.7 Action following detection of goods included in a notice

When we intercept goods covered by a notice lodged under either TMA s89 or CDPA s111 we will inform the applicant and upon confirmation that the goods are infringing we will seize them under the Customs and Excise Management Act 1979 as being liable to forfeiture. The goods will be destroyed under customs supervision unless the owner of the goods objects to this course of action by lodging a 'Notice of Claim'.

7.8 Liability

We do not accept liability for any infringing goods covered by applications or notices under either EU or UK legislation which we do not detect and are released or no action is taken to detain them.

Your rights and obligations

Your Charter explains what you can expect from us and what we expect from you. For more information go to Your Charter.

Do you have any comments or suggestions?

If you have any comments or suggestions to make about this notice, please write to:

> HM Revenue and Customs
> Intellectual Property Policy Team
> 10th Floor North Central
> Alexander House
> 21 Victoria Avenue
> Southend on Sea
> SS99 1AA

Please note this address is not for general enquiries.

For your general enquiries please phone our helpline on Telephone: 0300 200 3700.

Putting things right

If you are unhappy with our service, please contact the person or office you have been dealing with. They will try to put things right. If you are still unhappy, they will tell you how to complain.

If you want to know more about making a complaint go to www.hmrc.gov.uk and under quick links, select Complaints and appeals.

How we use your information

HMRC is a Data Controller under the Data Protection Act 1998. We hold information for the purposes specified in our notification to the Information Commissioner, including the assessment and collection of tax and duties, the payment of benefits and the prevention and detection of crime, and may use this information for any of them.

We may get information about you from others, or we may give information to them. If we do, it will only be as the law permits to:

- check the accuracy of information
- prevent or detect crime
- protect public funds

We may check information we receive about you with what is already in ourrecords. This can include information provided by you, as well as by others, such as other government departments or agencies and overseas tax and customs authorities. We will not give information to anyone outside HMRC unless the law permits us to do so. For more information go to www.hmrc.gov.uk and look for Data Protection Act within the Search facility.

B RELATED LEGISLATION AND MATERIALS

B8. Designs

B8.i Registered Designs Act 1949

(12, 13 & 14 Geo. 6, c.88)

Arrangement of Sections

Registrable designs and proceedings for registration

Effect of registration, &c.

International Arrangements

Property in and dealing with registered designs and applications

B RELATED LEGISLATION AND MATERIALS

Supplemental

An Act to consolidate certain enactments relating to registered designs.

[16th December 1949]

Note: This Act is printed as amended by the Registered Designs Regulations 2001 (SI 2001/3949). For the Isle of Man, the Act has been amended in substantially the same way by the Registered Designs (Isle of Man) Order 2001 (SI 2001/3678).

Registrable designs and proceedings for registration

Registration of designs.

[1.—(1) A design may, subject to the following provisions of this Act, be registered under this Act on the making of an application for registration.

(2) In this Act "design" means the appearance of the whole or a part of a product resulting from the features of, in particular, the lines, contours, colours, shape, texture or materials of the product or its ornamentation.

(3) In this Act—

     "complex product" means a product which is composed of at least two replaceable component parts permitting disassembly and reassembly of the product; and

     "product" means any industrial or handicraft item other than a computer program; and, in particular, includes packaging, get-up, graphic symbols, typographic type-faces and parts intended to be assembled into a complex product.]

Note: This section was substituted by the Registered Designs Regulations 2001 (SI 2001/3949), reg.2 with effect from December 9, 2001.

Substantive grounds for refusal of registration.

1A. [...]

Notes:

     (1) Section 1A was omitted by the Regulatory Reform (Registered Designs) Order 2006 (SI 2006/1974), art.3, with effect from October 1, 2006.

     (2) This section was originally inserted by the Registered Designs Regulations 2001 (SI 2001/3949), reg.2 with effect from December 9, 2001. The words in square

brackets in subs.(2)(b) inserted by the Registered Designs Regulations 2003 (SI 2003/550), reg.2 with effect from April 1, 2003, subject to transitional provisions contained in those Regulations:

Substantive grounds for refusal of registration.

"**1A.**—(1) *The following shall be refused registration under this Act—*

    (a) *anything which does not fulfil the requirements of section 1(2) of this Act;*

    (b) *designs which do not fulfil the requirements of sections 1B to 1D of this Act;*

    (c) *designs to which a ground of refusal mentioned in Schedule A1 to this Act applies.*

(2) *A design ("the later design") shall be refused registration under this Act if it is not new or does not have individual character when compared with a design which—*

    (a) *has been made available to the public on or after the relevant date; but*

    (b) *is protected as from a date prior to the relevant date by virtue of registration under this Act [or the Community Design Regulation] or an application for such registration.*

(3) *In subsection (2) above "the relevant date" means the date on which the application for the registration of the later design was made or is treated by virtue of section 3B(2), (3) or (5) or 14(2) of this Act as having been made."*

Requirement of novelty and individual character.

[**1B.**—(1) A design shall be protected by a right in a registered design to the extent that the design is new and has individual character.

(2) For the purposes of subsection (1) above, a design is new if no identical design or no design whose features differ only in immaterial details has been made available to the public before the relevant date.

(3) For the purposes of subsection (1) above, a design has individual character if the overall impression it produces on the informed user differs from the overall impression produced on such a user by any design which has been made available to the public before the relevant date.

(4) In determining the extent to which a design has individual character, the degree of freedom of the author in creating the design shall be taken into consideration.

(5) For the purposes of this section, a design has been made available to the public before the relevant date if—

    (a) it has been published (whether following registration or otherwise), exhibited, used in trade or otherwise disclosed before that date; and

    (b) the disclosure does not fall within subsection (6) below.

(6) A disclosure falls within this subsection if—

    (a) it could not reasonably have become known before the relevant date in the normal course of business to persons carrying on business in the European Economic Area and specialising in the sector concerned;

    (b) it was made to a person other than the designer, or any successor in title of his, under conditions of confidentiality (whether express or implied);

    (c) it was made by the designer, or any successor in title of his, during the period of 12 months immediately preceding the relevant date;

    (d) it was made by a person other than the designer, or any successor in title of his, during the period of 12 months immediately preceding the relevant date in consequence of information provided or other action taken by the designer or any successor in title of his; or

    (e) it was made during the period of 12 months immediately preceding the relevant date as a consequence of an abuse in relation to the designer or any successor in title of his.

(7) In subsections (2), (3), (5) and (6) above "the relevant date" means the date on which the application for the registration of the design was made or is treated by virtue of section 3B(2), (3) or (5) or 14(2) of this Act as having been made.

(8) For the purposes of this section, a design applied to or incorporated in a product which constitutes a component part of a complex product shall only be considered to be new and to have individual character—

   (a) if the component part, once it has been incorporated into the complex product, remains visible during normal use of the complex product; and

   (b) to the extent that those visible features of the component part are in themselves new and have individual character.

(9) In subsection (8) above "normal use" means use by the end user; but does not include any maintenance, servicing or repair work in relation to the product.]

Note: This section was inserted by the Registered Designs Regulations 2001 (SI 2001/3949), reg.2 with effect from December 9, 2001.

Designs dictated by their technical function.

[1C.—(1) A right in a registered design shall not subsist in features of appearance of a product which are solely dictated by the product's technical function.

(2) A right in a registered design shall not subsist in features of appearance of a product which must necessarily be reproduced in their exact form and dimensions so as to permit the product in which the design is incorporated or to which it is applied to be mechanically connected to, or placed in, around or against, another product so that either product may perform its function.

(3) Subsection (2) above does not prevent a right in a registered design subsisting in a design serving the purpose of allowing multiple assembly or connection of mutually interchangeable products within a modular system.]

Note: This section was inserted by the Registered Designs Regulations 2001 (SI 2001/3949), reg.2 with effect from December 9, 2001.

Designs contrary to public policy or morality.

[1D. A right in a registered design shall not subsist in a design which is contrary to public policy or to accepted principles of morality.]

Note: This section was inserted by the Registered Designs Regulations 2001 (SI 2001/3949), reg.2 with effect from December 9, 2001.

Proprietorship of designs

2.—(1) The author of a design shall be treated for the purposes of this Act as the original proprietor of the design, subject to the following provisions.

(1A) [...]

(1B) Where [...] a design is created by an employee in the course of his employment, his employer shall be treated as the original proprietor of the design.

(2) Where a design [...] becomes vested, whether by assignment, transmission or operation of law, in any person other than the original proprietor, either alone or jointly with the original proprietor, that other person, or as the case may be the original proprietor and that other person, shall be treated for the purposes of this Act as the proprietor of the design [...].

(3) In this Act the "author" of a design means the person who creates it.

(4) In the case of a design generated by computer in circumstances such that there is no human author, the person by whom the arrangements necessary for the creation of the design are made shall be taken to be the author.

Notes:

    (1) In subs.(2), the words ", or the right to apply any design to any article," and "or as the proprietor of the design in relation to that article" repealed by the Registered Designs Regulations 2001 (SI 2001/3949), reg.9, Sch.2 with effect from December 9, 2001.

    (2) Subsection (1A) repealed and in subs.(1B) words omitted repealed, subject to transitional provisions, by the Intellectual Property Act 2014, s.6(1), with effect from October 1, 2014 (for transitional provisions see (SI 2014/2330), art.4). Subsections (1A) and (1B) formerly read:

"(1) Where a design is created in pursuance of a commission for money or money's worth, the person commissioning the design shall be treated as the original proprietor of the design.

(1B) Where, in a case not falling within subsection (1A), a design is created by an employee in the course of his employment, his employer shall be treated as the original proprietor of the design."

Applications for registration.

[**3.**—(1) An application for the registration of a design [or designs] [...] shall be filed at the Patent Office in the prescribed manner.

(2) [...]

(3) An application for the registration of a design [or designs] in which national unregistered design right subsists shall be made by the person claiming to be the design right owner.

(4) [...]

(5) An application for the registration of a design which, owing to any default or neglect on the part of the applicant, has not been completed so as to enable registration to be effected within such time as may be prescribed shall be deemed to be abandoned.]

Notes:

    (1) This section was substituted by the Registered Designs Regulations 2001 (SI 2001/3949), reg.4 with effect from December 9, 2001. The section formerly provided:

Applications for registration.

*"**3.**—(1) An application for the registration of a design shall registration be made in the prescribed form and shall be filed at the Patent Office in the prescribed manner.*

    (2) An application for the registration of a design in which design right subsists shall not be entertained unless made by the person claiming to be the design right owner.

    (3) For the purpose of deciding whether a design is new, the registrar may make such searches, if any, as he thinks fit.

    (4) The registrar may, in such cases as may be prescribed, direct that for the purpose of deciding whether a design is new an application shall be treated as made on a date earlier or later than that on which it was in fact made.

    (5) The registrar may refuse any application for the registration of a design or may register the design in pursuance of the application subject to such modifications, if any, as he thinks fit; and a design when registered shall be registered as of the date on which the application was made or is treated as having been made.

    (6) An application which, owing to any default or neglect on the part of the applicant, has not been completed so as to enable registration to be effected within such time as may be prescribed shall be deemed to be abandoned.

(7) *An appeal lies from any decision of the registrar under this section.*"

(2) The words in square brackets in s.3(1) to (3) inserted and s.3(4) was omitted by the Regulatory Reform (Registered Designs) Order 2006 (SI 2006/1974), art.4 and art.11, with effect from October 1, 2006.

(3) Section 3(4) has been omitted. It previously read:

"(4) *For the purpose of deciding whether, and to what extent, a design is new or has individual character, the registrar may make such searches (if any) as he thinks fit.*"

(4) In subs.(1) words "shall be made in the prescribed form and" repealed and subs.(2) repealed, subject to transitional provisions, by the Intellectual Property Act 2014, ss.6(2), 12(2), with effect from October 1, 2014 (for transitional provisions see (SI 2014/2330), art.4). Subsection (2) formerly read:

"(2) *An application for the registration of a design [or designs] shall be made by the person claiming to be the proprietor of the design [or designs].*"

Determination of applications for registration.

[3A.—(1) Subject as follows, the registrar shall not refuse [to register a design included in an application under this Act].

(2) If it appears to the registrar that an application for the registration of a design [or designs] has not been made in accordance with any rules made under this Act, he may refuse [to register any design included in it].

(3) If it appears to the registrar that [the applicant is not under section 3(2) or (3) or 14 entitled to apply for the registration of a design included in the application, he shall refuse to register that design.]

[(4) If it appears to the registrar that the application for registration includes—

    (a) something which does not fulfil the requirements of section 1(2) of this Act;

    (b) a design that does not fulfil the requirements of section 1C or 1D of this Act; or

    (c) a design to which a ground of refusal mentioned in Schedule A1 to this Act applies, he shall refuse to register that thing or that design.]].

Notes:

(1) This section was inserted by the Registered Designs Regulations 2001 (SI 2001/3949), reg.4 with effect from December 9, 2001.

(2) The words in square brackets in s.3A(1) to (3) inserted and s.3A(4) was substituted by the Regulatory Reform (Registered Designs) Order 2006 (SI 2006/1974), art.5 and art.12, with effect from October 1, 2006. Read literally, the effect of art.12(3)(a) of SI 2006/1974 is to substitute the words "or designs" in s.3A(2) for the words "a design". It seems clear that this is an error and art.12(3)(a) should have provided for the *addition* of the words "or designs" after "a design". In this supplement the text of s.3A(2) has been amended so as to give effect to this clear intention.

Modification of applications for registration.

[3B.—(1) The registrar may, at any time before an application for the registration of a design [or designs] is determined, permit the applicant to make such modifications of the application as the registrar thinks fit.

(2) Where an application for the registration of a design [or designs] has been modified before it has been determined in such a way that [any design included in the application] has been altered significantly, the registrar may, for the purpose of deciding whether and to what extent the design is new or has individual character, direct that the application [so far as relating to that design] shall be treated as having been made on the date on which it was so modified.

(3) Where—

(a) an application for the registration of [more than one design] has been modified before it has been determined to exclude one or more designs from the application; and

(b) a subsequent application for the registration of a design so excluded has, within such period (if any) as has been prescribed for such applications, been made by the person who made the earlier application or his successor in title,

the registrar may, for the purpose of deciding whether and to what extent the design is new or has individual character, direct that the subsequent application shall be treated as having been made on the date on which the earlier application was, or is treated as having been, made.

(4) Where [...] the registration of a design has been refused on any ground mentioned in [section 3A(4)(b) or (c)] of this Act, the application [for the design-]may be modified by the applicant if it appears to the registrar that—

(a) the identity of the design is retained; and

(b) the modifications have been made in accordance with any rules made under this Act.

(5) An application modified under subsection (4) above shall be treated as the original application and, in particular, as made on the date on which the original application was made or is treated as having been made.

(6) Any modification under this section may, in particular, be effected by making a partial disclaimer in relation to the application.]

Notes:

(1) This section was inserted by the Registered Designs Regulations 2001 (SI 2001/3949), reg.4 with effect from December 9, 2001.

(2) The words in square brackets in s.3B(1) to (4) substituted or inserted by the Regulatory Reform (Registered Designs) Order 2006 (SI 2006/1974), art.6 and art.13, with effect from October 1, 2006.

Date of registration of designs.

[3C.—(1) Subject as follows, a design, when registered, shall be registered as of the date on which the application was made or is treated as having been made.

(2) Subsection (1) above shall not apply to an application which is treated as having been made on a particular date by section 14(2) of this Act or by virtue of the operation of section 3B(3) or (5) of this Act by reference to section 14(2) of this Act.

(3) A design, when registered, shall be registered as of—

(a) in the case of an application which is treated as having been made on a particular date by section 14(2) of this Act, the date on which the application was made;

(b) in the case of an application which is treated as having been made on a particular date by virtue of the operation of section 3B(3) of this Act by reference to section 14(2) of this Act, the date on which the earlier application was made;

(c) in the case of an application which is treated as having been made on a particular date by virtue of the operation of section 3B(5) of this Act by reference to section 14(2) of this Act, the date on which the original application was made.]

Note: This section was inserted by the Registered Designs Regulations 2001 (SI 2001/3949), reg.4 with effect from December 9, 2001.

Appeals in relation to applications for registration.

[3D. An appeal lies from any decision of the registrar under section 3A or 3B of this Act.]

Note: This section was inserted by the Registered Designs Regulations 2001 (SI 2001/3949), reg.4 with effect from December 9, 2001.

Registration of same design in respect of other articles, etc.

4. [...]

Note: This section was repealed by the Registered Designs Regulations 2001 (SI 2001/3949), reg.9, Sch.2 with effect from December 9, 2001. The section formerly provided:

Registration of same design in respect of other articles, etc.

"**4.**—(1) *Where the registered proprietor of a design registered in respect of any article makes an application—*

    (a) *for registration in respect of one or more other articles, of the registered design, or*

    (b) *for registration in respect of the same or one or more other articles, of a design consisting of the registered design with modifications or variations not sufficient to alter the character or substantially to affect the identity thereof,*

the application shall not be refused and the registration made on that application shall not be invalidated by reason only of the previous, registration or publication of the registered design:

Provided that the period of copyright in a design registered by virtue of this section shall not extend beyond the expiration of the original and any extended period of copyright in the original registered design.

(2) *Where any person makes an application for the registration of a design in respect of any article and either—*

    (a) *that design has been previously registered by another person in respect of some other article; or*

    (b) *the design to which the application relates consists of a design previously registered by another person in respect of the same or some other article with modifications or variations not sufficient to alter the character or substantially to affect the identity thereof,*

then, if at any time while the application is pending the applicant becomes the registered proprietor of the design previously registered, the foregoing provisions of this section shall apply as if at the time of making the application the applicant had been the registered proprietor of that design."

Provisions for secrecy of certain designs.

5.—(1) Where, either before or after the commencement of this Act, an application for the registration of a design has been made, and it appears to the registrar that the design is one of a class notified to him by the Secretary of State as relevant for defence purposes, he may give directions for prohibiting or restricting the publication of information with respect to the design, or the communication of such information to any person or class of persons specified in the directions.

(2) The Secretary of State shall by rules make provision for securing that where such directions are given—

    (a) the representation or specimen of the design, [....]

    (b) [...]

shall not be open to public inspection at the Patent Office during the continuance in force of the directions.

(3) Where the registrar gives any such directions as aforesaid, he shall give notice of the application and of the directions to the Secretary of State, and thereupon the following provisions shall have effect, that is to say:

(a) the Secretary of State shall, upon receipt of such notice, consider whether the publication of the design would be prejudicial to the defence of the realm and unless a notice under paragraph (c) of this subsection has previously been given by that authority to the registrar, shall reconsider that question before the expiration of nine months from the date of filing of the application for registration of the design and at least once in every subsequent year;

(b) for the purpose aforesaid, the Secretary of State may, at any time after the design has been registered or, with the consent of the applicant, at any time before the design has been registered, inspect the representation or specimen of the design [...] filed in pursuance of the application;

(c) if upon consideration of the design at any time it appears to the Secretary of State that the publication of the design would not, or would no longer, be prejudicial to the defence of the realm, he shall give notice to the registrar to that effect;

(d) on the receipt of any such notice the registrar shall revoke the directions and may, subject to such conditions, if any, as he thinks fit, extend the time for doing anything required or authorised to be done by or under this Act in connection with the application or registration, whether or not that time has previously expired.

(4) No person resident in the United Kingdom shall, except under the authority of a written permit granted by or on behalf of the registrar, make or cause to be made any application outside the United Kingdom for the registration of a design of any class prescribed for the purposes of this section unless—

(a) an application for registration of the same design has been made in the United Kingdom not less than six weeks before the application outside the United Kingdom; and

(b) either no directions have been given under subsection (1) of this section in relation to the application in the United Kingdom or all such directions have been revoked:

Provided that this subsection shall not apply in relation to a design for which an application for protection has first been filed in a country outside the United Kingdom by a person resident outside the United Kingdom.

(5) [...].

Note: Subsection (2)(b) (previously reading "any evidence filed in support of the applicant's contention that the appearance of an article is material (for the purposes of section 1(3) of this Act)"), the word "and" immediately before it and the words ", or any such evidence as is mentioned in subsection (2)(b) above" in subs.(3)(b) repealed by the Registered Designs Regulations 2001 (SI 2001/3949), reg.9, Sch.2 with effect from December 9, 2001.

Provisions as to confidential disclosure, etc.

6. [...]

Note: This section was repealed by the Registered Designs Regulations 2001 (SI 2001/3949), reg.9, Sch.2 with effect from December 9, 2001. The section formerly provided:

Provisions as to confidential disclosure, etc.

"6.—(1) *An application for the registration of a design shall not be refused, and the registration of a design shall not be invalidated, by reason only of—*

(a) *the disclosure of the design by the proprietor to any other person in such circumstances as would make it contrary to good faith for that other person to use or publish the design;*

(b) *the disclosure of the design in breach of good faith by any person other than the proprietor of the design; or*

(c) *in the case of a new or original textile design intended for registration, the acceptance of a first and confidential order for goods bearing the design.*

(2) *An application for the registration of a design shall not be refused and the registration of a design shall not be invalidated by reason only—*

(a) *that a representation of the design, or any article to which the design has been applied, has been displayed, with the consent of the proprietor of the design, at an exhibition certified by the Secretary of State for the purposes of this subsection;*

(b) *that after any such display as aforesaid, and during the period of the exhibition, a representation of the design or any such article as aforesaid has been displayed by any person without the consent of the proprietor; or*

(c) *that a representation of the design has been published in consequence of any such display as is mentioned in paragraph (a) of this subsection,*

if the application for registration of the design is made not later than six months after the opening of the exhibition.

(3) *An application for the registration of a design shall not be refused, and the registration of a design shall not be invalidated, by reason only of the communication of the design by the proprietor thereof to a government department or to any person authorised by a government department to consider the merits of the design, or of anything done in consequence of such a communication.*

(4) *Where an application is made by or with the consent of the owner of copyright in an artistic work for the registration of a corresponding design, the design shall not be treated for the purposes of this Act as being other than new by reason only of any use previously made of the artistic work, subject to subsection (5).*

(5) *Subsection (4) does not apply if the previous use consisted of or included the sale, letting for hire or oer or exposure for sale or hire of articles to which had been applied industrially—*

(a) *the design in question, or*

(b) *a design differing from it only in immaterial details or in features which are variants commonly used in the trade,*

and that previous use was made by or with the consent of the copyright owner.

(6) *The Secretary of State may make provision by rules as to the circumstances in which a design is to be regarded for the purposes of this section as "applied industrially" to articles, or any description of articles."*

Effect of registration, &c.

Right given by registration.

[7.—(1) The registration of a design under this Act gives the registered proprietor the exclusive right to use the design and any design which does not produce on the informed user a different overall impression.

(2) For the purposes of subsection (1) above and section 7A of this Act any reference to the use of a design includes a reference to—

(a) the making, offering, putting on the market, importing, exporting or using of a product in which the design is incorporated or to which it is applied; or

(b) stocking such a product for those purposes.

(3) In determining for the purposes of subsection (1) above whether a design produces a different overall impression on the informed user, the degree of freedom of the author in creating his design shall be taken into consideration.

(4) The right conferred by subsection (1) above is subject to any limitation attaching to the registration in question (including, in particular, any partial disclaimer or any declaration by the registrar or a court of partial invalidity).]

Note: This section was substituted by the Registered Designs Regulations 2001 (SI 2001/3949), reg.5 with effect from December 9, 2001. The section formerly provided:

Right given by registration.

"**7.**—(1) *The registration of a design under this Act gives the registered proprietor the exclusive right—*

      (a) *to make or import—*

            (i) *for sale or hire, or*

            (ii) *for use for the purposes of a trade or business, or*

      (b) *to sell, hire or offer or expose for sale or hire,*

an article in respect of which the design is registered and to which that design or a design not substantially different from it has been applied.

(2) *The right in the registered design is infringed by a person who without the licence of the registered proprietor does anything which by virtue of subsection (1) is the exclusive right of the proprietor.*

(3) *The right in the registered design is also infringed by a person who, without the licence of the registered proprietor makes anything or enabling any such article to be made, in the United Kingdom or elsewhere, as mentioned in subsection (1).*

(4) *The right in the registered design is also infringed by a person who without the licence of the registered proprietor—*

      (a) *does anything in relation to a kit that would be an infringement if done in relation to the assembled article (see subsection (1)), or*

      (b) *makes anything for enabling a kit to be made or assembled, in the United Kingdom or elsewhere, if the assembled article would be such an article as is mentioned in subsection (1);*

and for this purpose a "kit" means a complete or substantially complete set of components intended to be assembled into an article.

(5) *No proceedings shall be taken in respect of an infringement committed before the date on which the certificate of registration of the design under this Act is granted.*

(6) *The right in a registered design is not infringed by the reproduction of a feature of the design which, by virtue of section 1(1)(b), is left out of account in determining whether the design is registrable.*

Infringements of rights in registered designs.

[7A.—(1) Subject as follows, the right in a registered design is infringed by a person who, without the consent of the registered proprietor, does anything which by virtue of section 7 of this Act is the exclusive right of the registered proprietor.

(2) The right in a registered design is not infringed by—

      (a) an act which is done privately and for purposes which are not commercial;

      (b) an act which is done for experimental purposes;

      (c) an act of reproduction for teaching purposes or for the purpose of making citations provided that the conditions mentioned in subsection (3) below are satisfied;

      (d) the use of equipment on ships or aircraft which are registered in another country but which are temporarily in the United Kingdom;

      (e) the importation into the United Kingdom of spare parts or accessories for the purpose of repairing such ships or aircraft; or

      (f) the carrying out of repairs on such ships or aircraft,

(3) The conditions mentioned in this subsection are—

      (a) the act of reproduction is compatible with fair trade practice and does not unduly prejudice the normal exploitation of the design; and

      (b) mention is made of the source.

(4) The right in a registered design is not infringed by an act which relates to a

product in which any design protected by the registration is incorporated or to which it is applied if the product has been put on the market in the European Economic Area by the registered proprietor or with his consent.

(5) The right in a registered design of a component part which may be used for the purpose of the repair of a complex product so as to restore its original appearance is not infringed by the use for that purpose of any design protected by the registration.

(6) No proceedings shall be taken in respect of an infringement of the right in a registered design committed before the date on which the certificate of registration of the design under this Act is granted.]

Note: This section was inserted by the Registered Designs Regulations 2001 (SI 2001/3949), reg.5 with effect from December 9, 2001.

Right of prior use

[7B.—(1) A person who, before the application date, used a registered design in good faith or made serious and effective preparations to do so may continue to use the design for the purposes for which, before that date, the person had used it or made the preparations to use it.

(2) In subsection (1), the "application date", in relation to a registered design, means—

    (a) the date on which an application for the registration was made under section 3, or

    (b) where an application for the registration was treated as having been made by virtue of section 14(2), the date on which it was treated as having been so made.

(3) Subsection (1) does not apply if the design which the person used, or made preparations to use, was copied from the design which was subsequently registered.

(4) The right conferred on a person by subsection (1) does not include a right to licence another person to use the design.

(5) Nor may the person on whom the right under subsection (1) is conferred assign the right, or transmit it on death (or in the case of a body corporate on its dissolution), unless—

    (a) the design was used, or the preparations for its use were made, in the course of a business, and

    (b) the right is assigned or transmitted with the part of the business in which the design was used or the preparations for its use were made.]

Note: Section 7B inserted, subject to transitional provisions, by the Intellectual Property Act 2014, s.7(1), with effect from October 1, 2014 (for transitional provisions see (SI 2014/2330), art.4).

Duration of right in registered design.

8.—(1) The right in a registered design subsists in the first instance for a period of five years from the date of the registration of the design.

(2) The period for which the right subsists may be extended for a second, third, fourth and fifth period of five years, by applying to the registrar for an extension and paying the prescribed renewal fee.

(3) If the first, second, third or fourth period expires without such application and payment being made, the right shall cease to have effect; and the registrar shall, in accordance with rules made by the Secretary of State, notify the proprietor of that fact.

(4) If during the period of six months immediately following the end of that period an application for extension is made and the prescribed renewal fee and any prescribed additional fee is paid, the right shall be treated as if it had never expired, with the result that—

 (a) anything done under or in relation to the right during that further period shall be treated as valid,

 (b) an act which would have constituted an infringement of the right if it had not expired shall be treated as an infringement, and

 (c) an act which would have constituted use of the design for the services of the Crown if the right had not expired shall be treated as such use.

[…]

Notes:

 (1) Subsection (6) was amended by the Merchant Shipping Act 1995 Sch.13 para.26.

 (2) Transitional provisions relating to subs.(2) are contained in the Registered Designs Regulations 2001 (SI 2001/3949), reg.13(8) which provide:

 "(8) In section 8(2) of the Act of 1949 as it has effect in relation to pre-1989 registrations (period of copyright)—

 (a) *after the words 'second period', where they appear for the second time, there shall be inserted 'and for a fourth period of five years from the expiration of the third period and for a fifth period of five years from the expiration of the fourth period';*

 (b) *after the words 'second or third' there shall be inserted 'or fourth or fifth'; and*

 (c) *after the words 'second period', where they appear for the third time, there shall be inserted 'or the third period or the fourth period'."*

 (3) Subsections (5) and (6) repealed by the Registered Designs Regulations 2001 (SI 2001/3949), reg.9, Sch.2 with effect from December 9, 2001. They formerly provided:

 "(5) Where it is shown that a registered design—

 (a) *was at the time it was registered a corresponding design in relation to an artistic work in which copyright subsists, and*

 (b) *by reason of a previous use of that work would not have been registrable but for section 6(4) of this Act (registration despite certain prior applications of design),*

 the right in the registered design expires when the copyright in that work expires, if that is earlier than the time at which it would otherwise expire, and it may not thereafter be renewed.

 (6) The above provisions have effect subject to the proviso to section 4(1) (registration of same design in respect of other articles, &c.) [and, in the case of the right of the Secretary of State in any design forming part of the British mercantile marine uniform registered under this Act, to that right's subsisting so long as the design remains on the register.]"

Restoration of lapsed right in design.

8A.—(1) Where the right in a registered design has expired by reason of a failure to extend, in accordance with section 8(2) or (4), the period for which the right subsists, an application for the restoration of the right in the design may be made to the registrar within the prescribed period.

(2) The application may be made by the person who was the registered proprietor of the design or by any other person who would have been entitled to the right in the design if it had not expired; and where the design was held by two or more persons jointly, the application may, with the leave of the registrar, be made by one or more of them without joining the others.

(3) Notice of the application shall be published by the registrar in the prescribed manner.

(4) If the registrar is satisfied that the [failure of the proprietor] to see that the period for which the right subsisted was extended in accordance with section 8(2) or (4) [was unintentional], he shall, on payment of any unpaid renewal fee and any prescribed additional fee, order the restoration of the right in the design.

(5) The order may be made subject to such conditions as the registrar thinks fit, and if the proprietor of the design does not comply with any condition the registrar may revoke the order and give such consequential directions as he thinks fit.

(6) Rules altering the period prescribed for the purposes of subsection (1) may contain such transitional provisions and savings as appear to the Secretary of State to be necessary or expedient.

Note: The words in square brackets in s.8A(4) inserted by the Regulatory Reform (Registered Designs) Order 2006 (SI 2006/1974), art.17, with effect from October 1, 2006.

Effect of order for restoration of right.

8B.—(1) The effect of an order under section 8A for the restoration of the right in a registered design is as follows.

(2) Anything done under or in relation to the right during the period between expiry and restoration shall be treated as valid.

(3) Anything done during that period which would have constituted an infringement if the right had not expired shall be treated as an infringement—

(a) if done at a time when it was possible for an application for extension to be made under section 8(4); or

(b) if it was a continuation or repetition of an earlier infringing act.

(4) If after it was no longer possible for such an application for extension to be made, and before publication of notice of the application for restoration, a person—

(a) began in good faith to do an act which would have constituted an infringement of the right in the design if it had not expired, or

(b) made in good faith effective and serious preperations to do such an act,

he has the right to continue to do the act or, as the case may be, to do the act, notwithstanding the restoration of the right in the design; but this does not extend to granting a licence to another person to do the act.

(5) If the act was done, or the preparations were made, in the course of a business, the person entitled to the right conferred by subsection (4) may—

(a) authorise the doing of that act by any partners of his for the time being in that business, and

(b) assign that right, or transmit it on death (or in the case of a body corporate on its dissolution), to any person who acquires that part of the business in the course of which the act was done or the preparations were made.

(6) Where [a product] is disposed of to another in exercise of the rights conferred by subsection (4) or subsection (5), that other and any person claiming through him may deal with [the product] in the same way as if it had been disposed of by the registered proprietor of the design.

(7) The above provisions apply in relation to the use of a registered design for the services of the Crown as they apply in relation to infringement of the right in the design.

Note: The words in square brackets in subs.(6) substituted for the former words "an article" and "the article" by the Registered Designs Regulations 2001 (SI 2001/3949), reg.9, Sch.1 para.2 with effect from December 9, 2001.

Exemption of innocent infringer from liability for damages.

9. [...]

Notes:

(1) Section 9 was repealed by the Intellectual Property (Enforcement, etc.) Regulations 2006 (SI 2006/1028) Sch.4, with effect from April 29, 2006.

(2) In the original version, below, the words in square brackets in subs.(1) substituted for the former words "an article" and "the article" by the Registered Designs Regulations 2001 (SI 2001/3949), reg.9, Sch.1 para.3 with effect from December 9, 2001:

Exemption of innocent infringer from liability for damages.

"**9.**—(1) *In proceedings for the infringement of the right in a registered design damages shall not be awarded against a defendant who proves that at the date of the infringement he was not aware, and had no reasonable ground for supposing, that the design was registered; and a person shall not be deemed to have been aware or to have had reasonable grounds for supposing as aforesaid by reason only of the marking of [a product] with the word "registered" or any abbreviation thereof, or any word or words expressing or implying that the design applied to [, or incorporated in, the product] has been registered, unless the number of the design accompanied the word or words or the abbreviation in question.*

(2) *Nothing in this section shall affect the power of the court to grant an injunction in any proceedings for infringement of the right in a registered design.*"

Compulsory licence in respect of registered design.

10. [...]

Note: This section was repealed by the Registered Designs Regulations 2001 (SI 2001/3949), reg.6, reg.9, Sch.2 with effect from December 9, 2001. The section formerly provided:

Compulsory licence in respect of registered design.

"**10.**—(1) *At any time after a design has been registered any person interested may apply to the registrar for the grant of a compulsory licence in respect of the design on the ground that the design is not applied in the United Kingdom by any industrial process or means to the article in respect of which it is registered to such an extent as is reasonable in the circumstances of the case; and the registrar may make such order on the application as he thinks fit.*

(2) *An order for the grant of a licence shall, without prejudice to any other method of enforcement, have effect as if it were a deed executed by the registered proprietor and all other necessary parties, granting a licence in accordance with the order.*

(3) *No order shall be made under this section which would be at variance with any treaty, convention, arrangement or engagement applying to the United Kingdom and any convention country.*

(4) *An appeal shall lie from any order of the registrar under this section.*"

Cancellation of registration.

[**11.** The registrar may, upon a request made in the prescribed manner by the registered proprietor, cancel the registration of a design.]

Note: This section was substituted by the Registered Designs Regulations 2001 (SI 2001/3949), reg.7 with effect from December 9, 2001. The section formerly provided:

Cancellation of registration.

"**11.**—(1) *The registrar may, upon a request made in the prescribed manner by the registered proprietor, cancel the registration of a design.*

(2) *At any time after a design has been registered any person interested may apply to the registrar for the cancellation of the registration of the design on the ground*

that the design was not, at the date of the registration thereof, new ..., or on any other ground on which the registrar could have refused to register the design; and the registrar may make such order on the application as he thinks fit.

(3) *At any time after a design has been registered, any person interested may apply to the registrar for the cancellation of the registration on the ground that—*

   (a) *the design was at the time it was registered a corresponding design in relation to an artistic work in which copyright subsisted, and*

   (b) *the right in the registered design has expired in accordance with section 8(4) of this Act (expiry of right in registered design on expiry of copyright in artistic work);*

and the registrar may make such order on the application as he thinks fit.

(4) *A cancellation under this section takes effect—*

   (a) *in the case of cancellation under subsection (1), from the date of the registrars decision,*

   (b) *in the case of cancellation under subsection (2), from the date of registration,*

   (c) *in the case of cancellation under subsection (3), from the date on which the right in the registered design expired, or, in any case, from such other date as the registrar may direct.*

(5) *An appeal lies from any order of the registrar under this section."*

Grounds for invalidity of registration.

[**11ZA.**—(1) The registration of a design may be declared invalid

   [(a) on the ground that it does not fulfil the requirements of section 1(2)of this Act;

   (b) on the ground that it does not fulfil the requirements of sections 1B to 1D of this Act; or

   (c) where any ground of refusal mentioned in Schedule A1 to this Act applies.]

[(1A) The registration of a design ("the later design") may be declared invalid if it is not new or does not have individual character when compared to a design which—

   (a) has been made available to the public on or after the relevant date; but

   [(b) is protected as from a date prior to the relevant date—

      (i) by virtue of registration under this Act or the Community Design Regulation or an application for such registration, or

      (ii) by virtue of an international registration (within the meaning of Articles 106a to 106f of that Regulation) designating the Community.]

(1B) In subsection (1A) "the relevant date" means the date on which the application for the registration of the later design was made or is treated by virtue of section 3B(2), (3) or (5) or 14(2) of this Act as having been made.]

(2) The registration of a design may be declared invalid on the ground of the registered proprietor not being the proprietor of the design and the proprietor of the design objecting.

(3) The registration of a design involving the use of an earlier distinctive sign may be declared invalid on the ground of an objection by the holder of rights to the sign which include the right to prohibit in the United Kingdom such use of the sign.

(4) The registration of a design constituting an unauthorised use of a work protected by the law of copyright in the United Kingdom may be declared invalid on the ground of an objection by the owner of the copyright.

(5) In this section and sections 11ZB, 11ZC and 11ZE of this Act (other than section 11ZE(1)) references to the registration of a design include references to

the former registration of a design; and these sections shall apply, with necessary modifications, in relation to such former registrations.]

Notes:

(1) This section was inserted by the Registered Designs Regulations 2001 (SI 2001/ 3949), reg.7 with effect from December 9, 2001.

(2) The words in square brackets in s.11ZA(1) and s.11ZA(1A) and (1B) inserted by the Regulatory Reform (Registered Designs) Order 2006 (SI 2006/1974), art.7, with effect from October 1, 2006; subs.(1A)(b) was substituted by the Designs (International Registrations Designating the European Community) Regulations 2007 (SI 2007/3378), reg.2, with effect from January 1, 2008.

Applications for declaration of invalidity.

[**11ZB.**—(1) Any person interested may make an application to the registrar for a declaration of invalidity [under section 11ZA(1)(a) or (b)] of this Act.

(2) Any person concerned by the use in question may make an application to the registrar for a declaration of invalidity [under section 11ZA(1)(c)] of this Act.

(3) The relevant person may make an application to the registrar for a declaration of invalidity [under section 11ZA(1A)] of this Act.

(4) In subsection (3) above "the relevant person" means, in relation to an earlier design protected by virtue of registration under this Act or an application for such registration, the registered proprietor of the design or (as the case may be) the applicant.

(5) The person able to make an objection under subsection (2), (3) or (4) of section 11ZA of this Act may make an application to the registrar for a declaration of invalidity [under] that subsection.

(6) An application may be made under this section in relation to a design at any time after the design has been registered.]

Notes:

(1) This section was inserted by the Registered Designs Regulations 2001 (SI 2001/ 3949), reg.7 with effect from December 9, 2001. The words in square brackets in subs.(4) inserted by the Registered Designs Regulations 2003 (SI 2003/550), reg.2 with effect from April 1, 2003

(2) The words in square brackets in s.11ZB(1), (2), (3) and (5) substituted by the Regulatory Reform (Registered Designs) Order 2006 (SI 2006/1974), art.8, with effect from October 1, 2006.

Determination of applications for declaration of invalidity.

[**11ZC.**—(1) This section applies where an application has been made to the registrar for a declaration of invalidity in relation to a registration.

(2) If it appears to the registrar that the application has not been made in accordance with any rules made under this Act, he may refuse the application.

(3) If it appears to the registrar that the application has not been made in accordance with section 11ZB of this Act, he shall refuse the application.

(4) Subject to subsections (2) and (3) above, the registrar shall make a declaration of invalidity if it appears to him that the ground of invalidity specified in the application has been established in relation to the registration.

(5) Otherwise the registrar shall refuse the application.

(6) A declaration of invalidity may be a declaration of partial invalidity.]

Note: This section was inserted by the Registered Designs Regulations 2001 (SI 2001/ 3949), reg.7 with effect from December 9, 2001.

Modification of registration.

[**11ZD.**—(1) Subsections (2) and (3) below apply where the registrar intends to declare the registration of a design invalid [under section 11ZA(1)(b) or (c), (1A), (3) or (4)] of this Act.

(2) The registrar shall inform the registered proprietor of that fact.

(3) The registered proprietor may make an application to the registrar for the registrar to make such modifications to the registration of the design as the registered proprietor specifies in his application.

(4) Such modifications may, in particular, include the inclusion on the register of a partial disclaimer by the registered proprietor.

(5) If it appears to the registrar that the application has not been made in accordance with any rules made under this Act, the registrar may refuse the application.

(6) If it appears to the registrar that the identity of the design is not retained or the modified registration would be invalid by virtue of section 11ZA of this Act, the registrar shall refuse the application.

(7) Otherwise the registrar shall make the specified modifications.

(8) A modification of a registration made under this section shall have effect, and be treated always to have had effect, from the grant of registration.]

Notes:
  (1) This section was inserted by the Registered Designs Regulations 2001 (SI 2001/ 3949), reg.7 with effect from December 9, 2001.
  (2) The words in square brackets in s.11ZD(1) substituted by the Regulatory Reform (Registered Designs) Order 2006 (SI 2006/1974), art.9, with effect from October 1, 2006.

Effect of cancellation or invalidation of registration.

[**11ZE.**—(1) A cancellation of registration under section 11 of this Act takes effect from the date of the registrar's decision or from such other date as the registrar may direct.

(2) Where the registrar declares the registration of a design invalid to any extent, the registration shall to that extent be treated as having been invalid from the date of registration or from such other date as the registrar may direct.]

Note: This section was inserted by the Registered Designs Regulations 2001 (SI 2001/ 3949), reg.7 with effect from December 9, 2001.

Appeals in relation to cancellation or invalidation.

[**11ZF.** An appeal lies from any decision of the registrar under section 11 to 11ZE of this Act.]

Note: This section was inserted by the Registered Designs Regulations 2001 (SI 2001/ 3949), reg.7 with effect from December 9, 2001.

Powers exercisable for protection of the public interest.

11A.—(1) Where a report of the [Competition and Markets Authority] has been laid before Parliament containing conclusions to the effect—
  (a) [...]
  (b) [...]
  (c) on a competition reference, that a person was engaged in an anti-competitive practice which operated or may be expected to operate against the public interest, or
  (d) on a reference under section 11 of the Competition Act 1980 (reference of public bodies and certain other persons), that a person is pursuing a course of conduct which operates against the public interest,

the appropriate Minister or Ministers may apply to the registrar to take action under this section.

(2) Before making an application the appropriate Minister or Ministers shall publish, in such manner as he or they think appropriate, a notice describing the nature of the proposed application and shall consider any representations which may be made within 30 days of such publication by persons whose interests appear to him or them to be affected.

(3) If on an application under this section it appears to the registrar that the matters specified in the Commission's report as being those which in the [Competition and Markets Authority's report as being those which in the opinion of the Competition and Markets Authority] operate, or operated or may be expected to operate, against the public interest include—

    (a) conditions in licences granted in respect of a registered design by its proprietor restricting the use of the design by the licensee or the right of the proprietor to grant other licences,

    (b) [...]

he may by order cancel or modify any such condition.

    (4) [...]

    (5) [...]

    (6) An appeal lies from any order of the registrar under this section.

    (7) In this section "the appropriate Minister or Ministers" means the Minister or Ministers to whom the report of the [Competition and Markets Authority] was made.

Notes:

    (1) The words in square brackets in subs.(1) and (7) substituted for the former words "Monopolies and Mergers Commission" by the Competition Act 1998 (Competition Commission) Transitional, Consequential and Supplemental Provisions Order 1999 (SI 1999/506), art.9 with effect from April 1, 1999.

    (2) Subsection (1)(a) and (b) repealed by the Enterprise Act 2002 (c.40), Sch.25, para.1, Sch.26 with effect from June 20, 2003, subject to transitional provisions in relation to subs.(1)(b) contained in the Enterprise Act 2002 (Commencement No.3, Transitional and Transitory Provisions and Savings) Order 2003 (SI 2003/1397), art.3(1). The former subs.(1)(a) and (b) provided:

        "(b) *on a monopoly reference, that a monopoly situation exists and facts found by the Commission operate or may be expected to operate against the public interest,*

        (c) *on a merger reference, that a merger situation qualifying for investigation has been created and the creation of the situation, or particular elements in or consequences of it specied in the report, operate or may be expected to operate against the public interest,".*

    (3) The words "or may, instead or in addition, make an entry in the register to the effect that licences in respect of the design are to be available as of right" in subs.(3) and subss.(4) and (5) repealed by the Registered Designs Regulations 2001 (SI 2001/3949), reg.6, reg.9, Sch.2, with effect from December 9, 2001. The former subss.(4) and (5) provided:

        "(4) *The terms of a licence available by virtue of this section shall, in default of agreement, be settled by the registrar on an application by the person requiring the licence; and terms so settled shall authorise the licensee to do everything which would be an infringement of the right in the registered design in the absence of a licence.*

        (5) *Where the terms of a licence are settled by the registrar, the licence has effect from the date on which the application to him was made.".*

    (4) In subss (1), (7) words in square brackets substituted for words "[Competition Commission]" and in subs.(3) words in square brackets substituted for words "Commission's report as being those which in the Commission's opinion", by the

Enterprise and Regulatory Reform Act 2013 (Competition) (Consequential, Transitional and Saving Provisions) Order 2014 (SI 2014/892), Sch.1 para.20, with effect from April 1, 2014.

Powers exercisable following merger and market investigations.

[**11AB.**—(1) Subsection (2) below applies where—
(a) section 41(2), 55(2), 66(6), 75(2), 83(2), 138(2), 147(2)[, 147A(2)] or 160(2) of, or paragraph 5(2) or 10(2) of Schedule 7 to, the Enterprise Act 2002 (powers to take remedial action following merger or market investigations) applies;
(b) the [Competition and Markets Authority] or (as the case may be) the Secretary of State considers that it would be appropriate to make an application under this section for the purpose of remedying, mitigating or preventing a matter which cannot be dealt with under the enactment concerned; and
(c) the matter concerned involves conditions in licences granted in respect of a registered design by its proprietor restricting the use of the design by the licensee or the right of the proprietor to grant other licences.

(2) The [Competition and Markets Authority] or (as the case may be) the Secretary of State may apply to the registrar to take action under this section.

(3) Before making an application the [Competition and Markets Authority] or (as the case may be) the Secretary of State shall publish, in such manner as it or he thinks appropriate, a notice describing the nature of the proposed application and shall consider any representations which may be made within 30 days of such publication by persons whose interests appear to it or him to be affected.

(4) The registrar may, if it appears to him on an application under this section that the application is made in accordance with this section, by order cancel or modify any condition concerned of the kind mentioned in subsection (1)(c) above.

(5) An appeal lies from any order of the registrar under this section.

[(6) References in this section to the Competition and Markets Authority are references to a CMA group except where—
(a) section 75(2) of the Enterprise Act 2002 applies; or
(b) any other enactment mentioned in subsection (1)(a) above applies and the functions of the Competition and Markets Authority under that enactment are being performed by the CMA Board by virtue of section 34C(3) or 133A(2) of the Enterprise Act 2002.]

(7) References in section 35, 36, 47, 63, 134[, 141 or 141A] of the Enterprise Act 2002 (questions to be decided by the [Competition and Markets Authority] in its reports) to taking action under section 41(2), 55, 66, 138[, 147 or 147A] shall include references to taking action under subsection (2) above.

(8) An order made by virtue of this section in consequence of action under subsection (2) above where an enactment mentioned in subsection (1)(a) above applies shall be treated, for the purposes of sections 91(3), 92(1)(a), 162(1) and 166(3) of the Enterprise Act 2002 (duties to register and keep under review enforcement orders etc.), as if it were made under the relevant power in Part 3 or (as the case may be) 4 of that Act to make an enforcement order (within the meaning of the Part concerned).]

[(9) In subsection (6) "CMA Board" and "CMA group" have the same meaning as in Schedule 4 to the Enterprise and Regulatory Reform Act 2013.]

Notes:
(1) This section was inserted by the Enterprise Act 2002 (c.40), Sch.25, para.1(3) with effect from June 20, 2003 (Enterprise Act 2002 (Commencement No.3, Transitional and Transitory Provisions and Savings) Order 2003 (SI 2003/1397)).

(2) In subss.(1)(b), (2), (3), (7) words in square brackets substituted for words "Competition Commission", in subs.(1)(a) reference inserted, subs.(6) substituted, in subs.(7) references in square brackets substituted for references ", 141 or 141A" and ", 147 or 147A" respectively, and subs.(9) inserted, by the Enterprise and Regulatory Reform Act 2013 (Competition) (Consequential, Transitional and Saving Provisions) Order 2014 (SI 2014/892), Sch.1 para.21, with effect from April 1, 2014. Subs.(6) formerly read:

"(6) References in this section to the Competition Commission shall, in cases where section 75(2) of the Enterprise Act 2002 applies, be read as references to the Office of Fair Trading."

Undertaking to take licence of right in infringement proceedings.

11B. [...]

Note: This section was repealed by the Registered Designs Regulations 2001 (SI 2001/ 3949), reg.9, Sch.2 with effect from December 9, 2001. The provision formerly read:

Undertaking to take licence of right in infringement proceedings.

"**11B.**—(1) *If in proceedings for infringement of the right in a registered design in respect of which a licence is available as of right under section 11A of this Act the defendant undertakes to take a licence on such terms as may be agreed or, in default of agreement, settled by the registrar under that section—*

(a) *no injunction shall be granted against him, and*

(b) *the amount recoverable against him by way of damages or on account of profits shall not exceed double the amount which would have been payable by him as licensee if such a licence on those terms had been granted before the earliest infringement.*

(2) *An undertaking may be given at any time before final order in the proceedings, without any admission of liability.*

(3) *Nothing in this section affects the remedies available in respect of an infringement committed before licences of right were available.*"

Use for services of the Crown.

12. The provisions of the First Schedule to this Act shall have effect with respect to the use of registered designs for the services of the Crown and the rights of third parties in respect of such use.

International Arrangements

Orders in Council as to convention countries.

13.—(1) His Majesty may, with a view to the fulfilment of a treaty, convention, arrangement or engagement, by Order in Council declare that any country specified in the Order is a convention country for the purposes of this Act:

Provided that a declaration may be made as aforesaid for the purposes either of all or of some only of the provisions of this Act, and a country in the case of which a declaration made for the purposes of some only of the provisions of this Act is in force shall be deemed to be a convention country for the purposes of those provisions only.

(2) His Majesty may by Order in Council direct that any of the Channel Islands, any colony, ... shall be deemed to be a convention country for the purposes of all or any of the provisions of this Act; and an Order made under this subsection may direct that any such provisions shall have effect, in relation to the territory in question, subject to such conditions or limitations, if any, as may be specified in the Order.

(3) For the purposes of subsection (1) of this section, every colony, protector-ate, territory subject to the authority or under the suzerainty of another country, and territory administered by another country ... under the trusteeship system of the United Nations, shall be deemed to be a country in the case of which a decla-ration may be made under that subsection.

Registration of design where application for protection in convention country has been made.

14.—(1) An application for registration of a design [or designs] in respect of which protection has been applied for in a convention country may be made in accordance with the provisions of this Act by the person by whom the application for protection was made or his personal representative or assignee:

Provided that no application shall be made by virtue of this section after the expiration of six months from the date of the application for protection in a convention country or, where more than one such application for protection has been made, from the date of the first application.

(2) Where an application for registration of a design [or designs] is made by virtue of this section, the application shall be treated, for the purpose of determin-ing whether [(and to what extent)] that or any other design is new [or has individ-ual character], as made on the date of the application for protection in the conven-tion country or, if more than one such application was made, on the date of the first such application.

(3) Subsection (2) shall not be construed as excluding the power to give direc-tions under [section 3B(2) or (3)] of this Act in relation to an application made by virtue of this section.

(4) Where a person has applied for protection for a design by an application which—

    (a) in accordance with the terms of a treaty subsisting between two or more convention countries, is equivalent to an application duly made in any one of those convention countries; or

    (b) in accordance with the law of any convention country, is equivalent to an application duly made in that convention country,

he shall be deemed for the purposes of this section to have applied in that conven-tion country.

Notes:

    (1) The words "or designs" in square brackets in s.14(1) and (2) inserted by the Regulatory Reform (Registered Designs) Order 2006 (SI 2006/1974), art.14, with effect from October 1, 2006.

    (2) The words in square brackets in subs.(2) inserted and the words in square brackets in subs.(3) substituted for the former words "section 3(4)" by the Registered Designs Regulations 2001 (SI 2001/3949), reg.9, Sch.1 para.4 with effect from December 9, 2001.

Extension of time for applications under s.14 in certain cases.

15.—(1) If the Secretary of State is satisfied that provision substantially equiv-alent to the provision to be made by or under this section has been or will be made under the law of any convention country, he may make rules empowering the registrar to extend the time for making application under subsection (1) of section 14 of this Act for registration of a design in respect of which protection has been applied for in that country in any case where the period specified in the proviso to that subsection expires during a period prescribed by the rules.

(2) Rules made under this section—

(a) may, where any agreement or arrangement has been made between His Majesty's Government in the United Kingdom and the government of the convention country for the supply or mutual exchange of information or [products], provide, either generally or in any class of case specified in the rules, that an extension of time shall not be granted under this section unless the design has been communicated in accordance with the agreement or arrangement;

(b) may, either generally or in any class of case specified in the rules, fix the maximum extension which may be granted under this section;

(c) may prescribe or allow any special procedure in connection with applications made by virtue of this section;

(d) may empower the registrar to extend, in relation to an application made by virtue of this section, the time limited by or under the foregoing provisions of this Act for doing any act, subject to such conditions, if any, as may be imposed by or under the rules;

(e) may provide for securing that the rights conferred by registration on an application made by virtue of this section shall be subject to such restrictions or conditions as may be specified by or under the rules and in particular to restrictions and conditions for the protection of persons (including persons acting on behalf of His Majesty) who, otherwise than as the result of a communication made in accordance with such an agreement or arrangement as is mentioned in paragraph (a) of this subsection, and before the date of the application in question or such later date as may be allowed by the rules, may have imported or made [products] to which the design is applied [or in which it is incorporated] or may have made any application for registration of the design.

Note: The word in square brackets in subs.(2)(a) and in the first set of square brackets in subs.(2)(e) substituted for the former word "articles" and the words in the second set of square brackets in subs.(2)(e) inserted by the Registered Designs Regulations 2001 (SI 2001/3949), reg.9, Sch.1 para.5 with effect from December 9, 2001.

Protection of designs communicated under international agreements.

16. [...]

Note: This section was repealed by the Registered Designs Regulations 2001 (SI 2001/3949), reg.9, Sch.2 with effect from December 9, 2001. The provision formerly read:

Protection of designs communicated under international agreements.

"16.—(1) *Subject to the provisions of this section, the Secretary of State may make rules for securing that, where a design has been communicated in accordance with an agreement or arrangement made between His Majesty's Government in the United Kingdom and the government of any other country for the supply or mutual exchange of information or articles,—*

(a) *an application for the registration of the design made by the person from whom the design was communicated or his personal representative or assignee shall not be prejudiced, and the registration of the design in pursuance of such an application shall not be invalidated, by reason only that the design has been communicated as aforesaid or that in consequence thereof—*

(i) *the design has been published or applied, or*

(ii) *an application for registration of the design has been made by any other person, or the design has been registered on such an application;*

(b) *any application for the registration of a design made in consequence of such a communication as aforesaid may be refused and any registration of a design made on such an application may be cancelled.*

(2) Rules made under subsection (1) of this section may provide that the publication or application of a design, or the making of any application for registration thereof shall, in such circumstances and subject to such conditions or exceptions as may be prescribed by the rules, be presumed to have been in consequence of such a communication as is mentioned in that subsection.

(3) The powers of the Secretary of State under this section, so far as they are exercisable for the benefit of persons from whom designs have been communicated to His Majesty's Government in the United Kingdom by the government of any other country, shall only be exercised if and to the extent that the Secretary of State is satisfied that substantially equivalent provision has been or will be made under the law of that country for the benefit of persons from whom designs have been communicated by His Majesty's Government in the United Kingdom to the government of that country.

(4) References in the last foregoing subsection to the communication of a design to or by His Majesty's Government or the government of any other country shall be construed as including references to the communication of the design by or to any person authorised in that behalf by the government in question."

Property in and dealing with registered designs and applications

The nature of registered designs.

[**15A.** A registered design or an application for a registered design is personal property (in Scotland, incorporeal moveable property).]

Note: Section 15A was added by Intellectual Property (Enforcement, etc.) Regulations 2006/1028 Sch.1 para.2 with effect from April 29, 2006.

Accession to the Hague Agreement

[**15ZA**—(1) The Secretary of State may by order make provision for giving effect in the United Kingdom to the provisions of the Geneva Act of the Hague Agreement Concerning the International Registration of Industrial Designs adopted by the Diplomatic Conference on 2 July 1999.

(2) An order under this section may, in particular, make provision about—

(a) the making of applications for international registrations at the Patent Office;

(b) the procedures to be followed where an international registration designates the United Kingdom;

(c) the effect of an international registration which designates the United Kingdom;

(d) the communication of information to the International Bureau;

(e) the payment of fees.

(3) An order under this section may—

(a) amend this Act;

(b) apply specified provisions of this Act with such modifications as may be specified.

(4) An expression used in subsection (2) and in the Agreement referred to in subsection (1) has the same meaning in that subsection as it has in the Agreement.]

Assignment, &c of registered designs and applications for registered designs.

[**15B.**—(1) A registered design or an application for a registered design is transmissible by assignment, testamentary disposition or operation of law in the same way as other personal or moveable property, subject to the following provisions of this section.

(2) Any transmission of a registered design or an application for a registered design is subject to any rights vested in any other person of which notice is entered in the register of designs, or in the case of applications, notice is given to the registrar.

(3) An assignment of, or an assent relating to, a registered design or application for a registered design is not effective unless it is in writing signed by or on behalf of the assignor or, as the case may be, a personal representative.

(4) Except in Scotland, the requirement in subsection (3) may be satisfied in a case where the assignor or personal representative is a body corporate by the affixing of its seal.

(5) Subsections (3) and (4) apply to assignment by way of security as in relation to any other assignment.

(6) A registered design or application for a registered design may be the subject of a charge (in Scotland, security) in the same way as other personal or moveable property.

(7) The proprietor of a registered design may grant a licence to use that registered design.

(8) Any equities (in Scotland, rights) in respect of a registered design or an application for a registered design may be enforced in like manner as in respect of any other personal or moveable property.]

Note: Section 15B was added by Intellectual Property (Enforcement, etc.) Regulations 2006/1028 Sch.1 para.2 with effect from April 29, 2006.

Exclusive licences.

[**15C.**—(1) In this Act an "exclusive licence" means a licence in writing signed by or on behalf of the proprietor of the registered design authorising the licensee to the exclusion of all other persons, including the person granting the licence, to exercise a right which would otherwise be exercisable exclusively by the proprietor of the registered design.

(2) The licensee under an exclusive licence has the same rights against any successor in title who is bound by the licence as he has against the person granting the licence.]

Note: Section.15C was added by the Intellectual Property (Enforcement, etc.) Regulations 2006 (SI 2006/1028), Sch.1 para.2, with effect from April 29, 2006.

Register of designs, etc.

Register of designs.

17.—(1) The registrar shall maintain the register of designs, in which shall be entered—

    (a) the names and addresses of proprietors of registered designs;

    (b) notices of assignments and of transmissions of registered designs; and

    (c) such other matters as may be prescribed or as the registrar may think fit.

(2) No notice of any trust, whether express, implied or constructive, shall be entered in the register of designs, and the registrar shall not be affected by any such notice.

(3) The register need not be kept in documentary form.

(4) Subject to the provisions of this Act and to rules made by the Secretary of State under it, the public shall have a right to inspect the register at the Patent Office at all convenient times.

(5) Any person who applies for a certified copy of an entry in the register or a certified extract from the register shall be entitled to obtain such a copy or extract on payment of a fee prescribed in relation to certified copies and extracts; and rules made by the Secretary of State under this Act may provide that any person who applies for an uncertified copy or extract shall be entitled to such a copy or extract on payment of a fee prescribed in relation to uncertified copies and extracts.

(6) Applications under subsection (5) above or rules made by virtue of that subsection shall be made in such manner as may be prescribed.

(7) In relation to any portion of the register kept otherwise than in documentary form—

> (a) the right of inspection conferred by subsection (4) above is a right to inspect the material on the register; and
>
> (b) the right to a copy or extract conferred by subsection (5) above or rules is a right to a copy or extract in a form in which it can be taken away and in which it is visible and legible.

(8) [...]The register shall be prima facie evidence of anything required or authorised to be entered in it and in Scotland shall be sufficient evidence of any such thing.

(9) A certificate purporting to be signed by the registrar and certifying that any entry which he is authorised by or under this Act to make has or has not been made, or that any other thing which he is so authorised to do has or has not been done, shall be prima facie evidence, and in Scotland shall be sufficient evidence, of the matters so certified.

(10) Each of the following—

> (a) a copy of an entry in the register or an extract from the register which is supplied under subsection (5) above;
>
> (b) a copy or any representation, specimen or document kept in the Patent Office or an extract from any such document,

which purports to be a certified copy or certified extract shall [...] be admitted in evidence without further proof and without production of any original; and in Scotland such evidence shall be sufficient evidence.

[...]

(12) In this section "certified copy" and "certified extract" means a copy and extract certified by the registrar and sealed with the seal of the Patent Office.

Notes:

> (1) Subsection (11) was repealed by the Youth Justice and Criminal Evidence Act 1999 (c.23), s.67 and Sch.6 with effect from April 14, 2000 (Youth Justice and Criminal Evidence Act 1999 (Commencement No. 2) Order 2000 (SI 2000/1034)). Subsection (11) formerly provided:
>
> > "(11) *In the application of this section to England and Wales nothing in it shall be taken as detracting from section 69 or 70 of the Police and Criminal Evidence Act 1984 or any provision made by virtue of either of them.*"
>
> (2) Subsections (8) and (10) were amended by the Criminal Justice Act 2003 (c.44), Sch.37, Pt 6 with effect from April 4, 2005.

Certificate of registration.

18.—(1) The registrar shall grant a certificate of registration in the prescribed form to the registered proprietor of a design when the design is registered.

(2) The registrar may, in a case where he is satisfied that the certificate of registration has been lost or destroyed, or in any other case in which he thinks it expedient, furnish one or more copies of the certificate.

Registration of assignments, etc.

19.—(1) Where any person becomes entitled by assignment, transmission or operation of law to a registered design or to a share in a registered design, or becomes entitled as mortgagee, licensee or otherwise to any other interest in a registered design, he shall apply to the registrar in the prescribed manner for the registration of his title as proprietor or co-proprietor or, as the case may be, of notice of his interest, in the register of designs.

(2) Without prejudice to the provisions of the foregoing subsection, an application for the registration of the title of any person becoming entitled by assignment to a registered design or a share in a registered design, or becoming entitled by virtue of a mortgage, licence or other instrument to any other interest in a registered design, may be made in the prescribed manner by the assignor, mortgagor, licensor or other party to that instrument, as the case may be.

(3) Where application is made under this section for the registration of the title of any person, the registrar shall, upon proof of title to his satisfaction—

    (a) where that person is entitled to a registered design or a share in a registered design, register him in the register of designs as proprietor or co-proprietor of the design, and enter in that register particulars of the instrument or event by which he derives title; or

    (b) where that person is entitled to any other interest in the registered design, enter in that register notice of his interest, with particulars of the instrument (if any) creating it.

(3A) [...]

(3B) Where [national unregistered design right] subsists in a registered design and the proprietor of the registered design is also the design right owner, an assignment of the [national unregistered design right] shall be taken to be also an assignment of the right in the registered design, unless a contrary intention appears.

(4) [...]

(5) Except for the purposes of an application to rectify the register under the following provisions of this Act, a document in respect of which no entry has been made in the register of designs under subsection (3) of this section shall not be admitted in any court as evidence of the title of any person to a registered design or share of or interest in a registered design unless the court otherwise directs.

Notes:

    (1) The words in square brackets in subs.(3B) substituted for the former words "design right" by the Registered Designs Regulations 2001 (SI 2001/3949), reg.9, Sch.1, para.6 with effect from December 9, 2001.

    (2) Section 19(4) was repealed by the Intellectual Property (Enforcement, etc.) Regulations 2006 (SI 2006/1028), Sch.4, with effect from April 29, 2006. The subsection previously read:

        "(4) *Subject to any rights vested in any other person of which notice is entered in the register of designs, the person or persons registered as proprietor of a registered design shall have power to assign, grant licences under, or otherwise deal with the design, and to give effectual receipts for any consideration for any such assignment, licence or dealing.*

      Provided that any equities in respect of the design may be enforced in like manner as in respect of any other personal property."

    (3) Subsection (3A) repealed by the Intellectual Property Act 2014, s.9(1), with effect from October 1, 2014 (see (SI 2014/2330)). Subsection (3A) (as amended by (SI 2001/3949)) formerly read:

"(3A) Where [national unregistered design right] subsists in a registered design, the reg-

istrar shall not register an interest under subsection (3) unless he is satis- fied that the person entitled to that interest is also entitled to a corresponding interest in the- [national unregistered design right]."

Rectification of register.

20.—(1) The court may, on the application of [the relevant person], order the register of designs to be rectified by the making of any entry therein or the variation or deletion of any entry therein.

(1A) In subsection (1) above "the relevant person" means—

- (a) in the case of an application invoking any ground referred to in [section 11ZA(1)(c)] of this Act, any person concerned by the use in question;
- (b) in the case of an application invoking the ground mentioned in [section 11ZA(1A)] of this Act, the appropriate person;
- (c) in the case of an application invoking any ground mentioned in section 11ZA(2), (3) or (4) of this Act, the person able to make the objection;
- (d) in any other case, any person aggrieved.

(1B) In subsection (1A) above "the appropriate person" means, in relation to an earlier design protected by virtue of registration under this Act [or the Community Design Regulation] or an application for such registration, the registered proprietor of the design [, the holder of the registered Community design] or (as the case may be) the applicant.]

(2) In proceedings under this section the court may determine any question which it may be necessary or expedient to decide in connection with the rectification of the register.

(3) Notice of any application to the court under this section shall be given in the prescribed manner to the registrar, who shall be entitled to appear and be heard on the application, and shall appear if so directed by the court.

(4) Any order made by the court under this section shall direct that notice of the order shall be served on the registrar in the prescribed manner; and the registrar shall, on receipt of the notice, rectify the register accordingly.

(5) A rectification of the register under this section has effect as follows—

- (a) an entry made has effect from the date on which it should have been made,
- (b) an entry varied has effect as if it had originally been made in its varied form, and
- (c) an entry deleted shall be deemed never to have had effect,

unless, in any case, the court directs otherwise.

[(6) Orders which may be made by the court under this section include, in particular, declarations of partial invalidity.]

Notes:

- (1) The words in square brackets in subs.(1) substituted for the former words "any person aggrieved" and subss.(1A), (1B) and (6) inserted by the Registered Designs Regulations 2001 (SI 2001/3949), reg.8 with effect from December 9, 2001.
- (2) The words in internal square brackets in subs.(1B) inserted by the Registered Designs Regulations 2003 (SI 2003/550), reg.2 with effect from April 1, 2003.
- (3) The words in square brackets in s.20(1A) substituted by the Regulatory Reform (Registered Designs) Order 2006 (SI 2006/1974), art.10, with effect from October 1, 2006.

Power to correct clerical errors.

21.—(1) The registrar may, in accordance with the provisions of this section, correct any error in an application for the registration or in the representation of a design, or any error in the register of designs.

(2) A correction may be made in pursuance of this section either upon a request in writing made by any person interested and accompanied by the prescribed fee, or without such a request.

(3) Where the registrar proposes to make any such correction as aforesaid otherwise than in pursuance of a request made under this section, he shall give notice of the proposal to the registered proprietor or the applicant for registration of the design, as the case may be, and to any other person who appears to him to be concerned, and shall give them an opportunity to be heard before making the correction.

Inspection of registered designs.

22.—(1) Where a design has been registered under this Act, there shall be open to inspection at the Patent Office on and after the day on which the certificate of registration is [granted]—

    (a) the representation or specimen of the design, [*and*

  (aa) *every document kept at the Patent Office in connection with that design.]*

    (b) [...]

This subsection has effect subject to [subsection (4)] [*subsections (4) to (7)*] and to any rules made under section 5(2) of this Act.

  (2) [...]

  (3) [...]

[(4) Where registration of a design has been refused pursuant to an application under this Act, or an application under this Act has been abandoned in relation to any design—

    (a) the application, so far as relating to that design, and

    (b) any representation, specimen or other document which has been filed and relates to that design, shall not at any time be open to inspection at the Patent Office or be published by the registrar.]"

[(5) *For the purposes of subsection (1), a document is not to be regarded as open for inspection unless (in addition to being open for inspection in hard copy) it is made available by electronic transmission in such a way that members of the public may access it at a place and time individually chosen by them.*]

[(6) *The Secretary of State may by rules specify cases or circumstances in which a document kept at the Patent Office in connection with a registered design may not be inspected.*

  (7) *Rules made under subsection (6) may confer a discretion on the registrar.*]

Notes:

  (1) Subsection (1)(b) was repealed by the Registered Designs Regulations 2001 (SI 2001/3949), reg.9, Sch.2, with effect from December 9, 2001. It formerly provided:

    "(b) *any evidence filed in support of the applicant's contention that the appearance of an article is material (for the purposes of section 1(3) of this Act).*"

  (2) Subsections (2) and (3) repealed by the Regulatory Reform (Registered Designs) Order 2006 (SI 2006/1974), art.16, with effect from October 1, 2006. The subsections formerly read:

    "(2) *[Where—*

    (a) *a design has been registered;*

    (b) *a product to which the design was intended to be applied or in which it was intended to be incorporated was specified, in accordance with rules made under section 36 of this Act, in the application for the registration of the design; and*

    (c) *the product so specified falls within any class prescribed for the purposes of this subsection, no] representation, specimen or evidence filed in pursuance of the application shall, until the expiration of such period after the day on which the certificate of registration is issued as may be prescribed in relation to [products] of that class, be open to inspection at the Patent Office except by the registered proprietor, a person authorised in writing by the registered proprietor, or a person authorised by the registrar or by the court:*

Provided that where the registrar proposes to refuse an application for the registration of any other design on the ground that [, by reference to the firstmentioned design, it is not new or does not have individual character], the applicant shall be entitled to inspect the representation or specimen of the firstmentioned design filed in pursuance of the application for registration of that design.

(3) In the case of a [registered design and a specified product which falls within any class] prescribed for the purposes of the last foregoing subsection, the representation, specimen or evidence shall not, during the period prescribed as aforesaid, be inspected by any person by virtue of this section except in the presence of the registrar or of an officer acting under him; and except in the case of an inspection authorised by the proviso to that subsection, the person making the inspection shall not be entitled to take a copy of the representation, specimen or evidence or any part thereof."

(3) Subsection (4) and the words in square brackets in subsection (1) substituted by the Regulatory Reform (Registered Designs) Order 2006 (SI 2006/1974) arts 15 and 16, with effect from October 1, 2006.

(4) Subsection (1)(aa) in italics prospectively inserted, in the last sentence of subs.(1), words "subsections (4) to (7)" in italics prospectively substituted for words "subsection (4)", and subs.(5), (6), (7) prospectively inserted, by the Intellectual Property Act 2014, s.9(2)–(5), with effect from a date to be appointed.

Information as to existence of right in registered design.

23. On the request of a person furnishing such information as may enable the registrar to identify the design, and on payment of the prescribed fee, the registrar shall inform him—

(a) whether the design is registered [...], and

(b) whether any extension of the period of the right in the registered design has been granted,

and shall state the date of registration and the name and address of the registered proprietor.

Note: In subs.(a), the words "and, if so, in respect of what articles" repealed by the Registered Designs Regulations 2001 (SI 2001/3949), reg.9, Sch.2, with effect from December 9, 2001.

Evidence of entries, documents, etc.

24. [...]

Note: Section 24 was repealed by the Repealed by Patents, Designs and Marks Act 1986 (c.39), s.3(1), Sch.3 Pt I. The original provision was as follows:

Evidence of entries, documents, etc.

"**24.**—(1) *A certificate purporting to be signed by the registrar and certifying that any entry which he is authorised by or under this Act to make has or has not been made, or that any other thing which he is so authorised to do has or has not been done shall be prima facie evidence of the matters so certified.*

(2) A copy of any entry in the register of designs or of any representation, specimen or document kept in the Patent Office or an extract from the register or any such document, purporting to be certified by the registrar and to be sealed with the seal of the Patent Office, shall be admitted in evidence without further proof and without production of the original."

Legal proceedings and Appeals

Action for infringement.

[24A.—(1) An infringement of the right in a registered design is actionable by the registered proprietor.

(2) In an action for infringement all such relief by way of damages, injunctions, accounts or otherwise is available to him as is available in respect of the infringement of any other property right.

(3) This section has effect subject to section 24B of this Act (exemption of innocent infringer from liability).]

Note: Section 24A was added by the Intellectual Property (Enforcement, etc.) Regulations 2006 (SI 2006/1028) Sch.1 para.3 with effect from April 29, 2006.

Exemption of innocent infringer from liability.

[24B.—(1) In proceedings for the infringement of the right in a registered design damages shall not be awarded [...] against a defendant who proves that at the date of the infringement he was not aware, and had no reasonable ground for supposing, that the design was registered.

(2) For the purposes of subsection (1), a person shall not be deemed to have been aware or to have had reasonable grounds for supposing that the design was registered by reason only of the marking of a product with—

(a) the word "registered" or any abbreviation thereof, or
(b) any word or words expressing or implying that the design applied to, or incorporated in, the product has been registered,

unless the number of the design accompanied the word or words or the abbreviation in question.

(3) Nothing in this section shall affect the power of the court to grant an injunction in any proceedings for infringement of the right in a registered design.]

Notes:

(1) Section 24B was added by the Intellectual Property (Enforcement, etc.) Regulations 2006 (SI 2006/1028) Sch.1 para.3 with effect from April 29, 2006.
(2) In subs.(1) words ", and no order shall be made for an account of profits," repealed by the Intellectual Property Act 2014, s.10(1), with effect from October 1, 2014 (see (SI 2014/2330)).

Order for delivery up.

[24C.—(1) Where a person—

(a) has in his possession, custody or control for commercial purposes an infringing article, or
(b) has in his possession, custody or control anything specifically designed or adapted for making articles to a particular design which is a registered design, knowing or having reason to believe that it has been or is to be used to make an infringing article,

the registered proprietor in question may apply to the court for an order that the infringing article or other thing be delivered up to him or to such other person as the court may direct.

(2) An application shall not be made after the end of the period specified in the following provisions of this section; and no order shall be made unless the court also makes, or it appears to the court that there are grounds for making, an order under section 24D of this Act (order as to disposal of infringing article, &c.).

(3) An application for an order under this section may not be made after the end of the period of six years from the date on which the article or thing in question was made, subject to subsection (4).

(4) If during the whole or any part of that period the registered proprietor—

(a) is under a disability, or

(b) is prevented by fraud or concealment from discovering the facts entitling him to apply for an order,

an application may be made at any time before the end of the period of six years from the date on which he ceased to be under a disability or, as the case may be, could with reasonable diligence have discovered those facts.

(5) In subsection (4) "disability"—

(a) in England and Wales, has the same meaning as in the Limitation Act 1980;

(b) in Scotland, means legal disability within the meaning of the Prescription and Limitation (Scotland) Act 1973;

(c) in Northern Ireland, has the same meaning as in the Statute of Limitations (Northern Ireland) 1958.

(6) A person to whom an infringing article or other thing is delivered up in pursuance of an order under this section shall, if an order under section 24D of this Act is not made, retain it pending the making of an order, or the decision not to make an order, under that section.

(7) The reference in subsection (1) to an act being done in relation to an article for "commercial purposes" are to its being done with a view to the article in question being sold or hired in the course of a business.

(8) Nothing in this section affects any other power of the court.]

Note: Section 24C was added by the Intellectual Property (Enforcement, etc.) Regulations 2006 (SI 2006/1028) Sch.1 para.3 with effect from April 29, 2006.

Order as to disposal of infringing articles, &c.

[**24D.**—(1) An application may be made to the court for an order that an infringing article or other thing delivered up in pursuance of an order under section 24C of this Act shall be—

(a) forfeited to the registered proprietor, or

(b) destroyed or otherwise dealt with as the court may think fit,

or for a decision that no such order should be made.

(2) In considering what order (if any) should be made, the court shall consider whether other remedies available in an action for infringement of the right in a registered design would be adequate to compensate the registered proprietor and to protect his interests.

(3) Where there is more than one person interested in an article or other thing, the court shall make such order as it thinks just and may (in particular) direct that the thing be sold, or otherwise dealt with, and the proceeds divided.

(4) If the court decides that no order should be made under this section, the person in whose possession, custody or control the article or other thing was before being delivered up is entitled to its return.

(5) References in this section to a person having an interest in an article or other thing include any person in whose favour an order could be made in respect of it—

(a) under this section;

(b) under section 19 of Trade Marks Act 1994 (including that section as applied by regulation 4 of the Community Trade Mark Regulations 2006 (SI 2006/1027));

(c) under section 114, 204 or 231 of the Copyright, Designs and Patents Act 1988; or

(d) under regulation 1C of the Community Design Regulations 2005 (SI 2005/2339).]

Note: Section 24D was added by the Intellectual Property (Enforcement, etc.) Regulations 2006 (SI 2006/1028) Sch.1 para.3 with effect from April 29, 2006.

Jurisdiction of county court and sheriff court.

[**24E.**—(1) In Northern Ireland a county court may entertain proceedings under the following provisions of this Act—

section 24C (order for delivery up of infringing article, &c.),

section 24D (order as to disposal of infringing article, &c.), or

section 24F(8) (application by exclusive licensee having concurrent rights),

where the value of the infringing articles and other things in question does not exceed the county court limit for actions in tort.

(2) In Scotland proceedings for an order under any of those provisions may be brought in the sheriff court.

(3) Nothing in this section shall be construed as affecting the jurisdiction of the Court of Session or the High Court in Northern Ireland.]

Note: Section 24E was added by the Intellectual Property (Enforcement, etc.) Regulations 2006 (SI 2006/1028) Sch.1 para.3 with effect from April 29, 2006.

Rights and remedies of exclusive licensee.

[**24F.**—(1) In relation to a registered design, an exclusive licensee has, except against the registered proprietor, the same rights and remedies in respect of matters occurring after the grant of the licence as if the licence had been an assignment.

(2) His rights and remedies are concurrent with those of the registered proprietor; and references to the registered proprietor in the provisions of this Act relating to infringement shall be construed accordingly.

(3) In an action brought by an exclusive licensee by virtue of this section a defendant may avail himself of any defence which would have been available to him if the action had been brought by the registered proprietor.

(4) Where an action for infringement of the right in a registered design brought by the registered proprietor or an exclusive licensee relates (wholly or partly) to an infringement in respect of which they have concurrent rights of action, the proprietor or, as the case may be, the exclusive licensee may not, without the leave of the court, proceed with the action unless the other is either joined as a claimant or added as a defendant.

(5) A registered proprietor or exclusive licensee who is added as a defendant in pursuance of subsection (4) is not liable for any costs in the action unless he takes part in the proceedings.

(6) Subsections (4) and (5) do not affect the granting of interlocutory relief on the application of the registered proprietor or an exclusive licensee.

(7) Where an action for infringement of the right in a registered design is brought which relates (wholly or partly) to an infringement in respect of which the registered proprietor and an exclusive licensee have concurrent rights of action—

(a) the court shall, in assessing damages, take into account—

(i) the terms of the licence, and

(ii) any pecuniary remedy already awarded or available to either of them in respect of the infringement;

(b) no account of profits shall be directed if an award of damages has been made, or an account of profits has been directed, in favour of the other of them in respect of the infringement; and

(c) the court shall if an account of profits is directed apportion the profits between them as the court considers just, subject to any agreement between them;

and these provisions apply whether or not the proprietor and the exclusive licensee are both parties to the action.

(8) The registered proprietor shall notify any exclusive licensee having concurrent rights before applying for an order under section 24C of this Act (order for delivery up of infringing article, &c); and the court may on the application of the licensee make such order under that section as it thinks fit having regard to the terms of the licence.]

Note: Section 24F was added by the Intellectual Property (Enforcement, etc.) Regulations 2006 (SI 2006/1028) Sch.1 para.3 with effect from April 29, 2006.

Meaning of "infringing article".

[**24G.**—(1) In this Act "infringing article", in relation to a design, shall be construed in accordance with this section.

(2) An article is an infringing article if its making to that design was an infringement of the right in a registered design.

(3) An article is also an infringing article if—

(a) it has been or is proposed to be imported into the United Kingdom, and

(b) its making to that design in the United Kingdom would have been an infringement of the right in a registered design or a breach of an exclusive licensing agreement relating to that registered design.

(4) Where it is shown that an article is made to a design which is or has been a registered design, it shall be presumed until the contrary is proved that the article was made at a time when the right in the registered design subsisted.

(5) Nothing in subsection (3) shall be construed as applying to an article which may be lawfully imported into the United Kingdom by virtue of an enforceable [EU] right within the meaning of section 2(1) of the European Communities Act 1972.]

Notes:

(1) Section 24G was added by the Intellectual Property (Enforcement, etc.) Regulations 2006 (SI 2006/1028), Sch.1 para.3, with effect from April 29, 2006.

(2) In subs.(5) the expression "EU" was substituted for the word "Community" by the Treaty of Lisbon (Changes in Terminology) Order 2011 (SI 2011/1043) art.6(1)(f) with effect from April 22, 2011.

Certificate of contested validity of registration.

25.—(1) If in any proceedings before the court the validity of the registration of a design is contested, and it is found by the court that the design is [, to any extent,] validly registered, the court may certify that the validly of the registration of the design was contested in those proceedings.

(2) Where any such certificate has been granted, then if in any subsequent proceedings before the court for infringement of the right in the registered design or for [invalidation] of the registration of the design, a final order or judgment is made or given in favour of the registered proprietor, he shall, unless the court otherwise directs, be entitled to his costs as between solicitor and client:

Provided that this subsection shall not apply to the costs of any appeal in any such proceedings as aforesaid.

Note: In subs.(1), the words in square brackets inserted and in subs.(2) the word in square brackets was substituted for the former word "substitution" by the Registered Designs Regulations 2001 (SI 2001/3949), reg.9, Sch.1, para.8, with effect from December 9, 2001.

Remedy for groundless threats of infringement proceedings.

26.—(1) Where any person (whether entitled to or interested in a registered design or an application for registration of a design or not) by circulars, advertisements or otherwise threatens any other person with proceedings for infringement of the right in a registered design, any person aggrieved thereby may bring an action against him for any such relief as is mentioned in the next following subsection.

(2) Unless in any action brought by virtue of this section the defendant proves that the acts in respect of which proceedings were threatened constitute or, if done, would constitute, an infringement of the right in a registered design the registration of which is not shown by the [claimant] to be invalid, the [claimant] shall be entitled to the following relief, that is to say:

    (a) a declaration to the effect that the threats are unjustifiable;

    (b) an injunction against the continuance of the threats; and

    (c) such damages, if any, as he has sustained thereby.

(2A) Proceedings may not be brought under this section in respect of a threat to bring proceedings for an infringement alleged to consist of the making or importing of anything.

(3) For the avoidance of doubt it is hereby declared that a mere notification that a design is registered does not constitute a threat of proceedings within the meaning of this section.

Note: Subsection (2) was amended by the Intellectual Property (Enforcement, etc.) Regulations 2006 (SI 2006/1028), Sch.1 para.4, with effect from April 29, 2006.

The court.

27.—(1) In this Act "the court" means—

    (a) in England and Wales, the High [Court] [(subject to section 27A(6))] having jurisdiction by virtue of an order under section 287 of the Copyright, Designs and Patents Act 1988,

    (b) in Scotland, the Court of Session, and

    (c) in Northern Ireland, the High Court.

(2) Provision may be made by rules of court with respect to proceedings in the High Court in England and Wales for references and applications under this Act to be dealt with by such judge of that court as the [Lord Chief Justice of England and Wales may, after consulting the Lord Chancellor, select] for the purpose.

[(3) The Lord Chief Justice may nominate a judicial office holder (as defined in section 109(4) of the Constitutional Reform Act 2005) to exercise his functions under subsection (2).]

Notes:

    (1) Subsection (2) was amended and subs.(3) was inserted by the Constitutional Reform Act 2005 (c.4), Sch.4 para.36, with effect from April 3, 2006.

    (2) In subs.(1)(a) first word substituted for words "Court or any patents county court", subject to transitional provisions and savings, by the Crime and Courts Act 2013, Sch.9 para.21, with effect from October 1, 2013 (see SI 2013/1725) (for transitional provisions and savings see s.15, Sch.8 of the Act).

(3) In subs.(1)(a) second words inserted by the Intellectual Property Act 2014, s.10(3), with effect from April 6, 2015 (see (SI 2015/165)).

Appeals from decisions of registrar

[27A.—(1) An appeal against a decision of the registrar under this Act may be made to—
  (a) a person appointed by the Lord Chancellor (an "appointed person"), or
  (b) the court.
(2) On an appeal under this section to an appointed person, the appointed person may refer the appeal to the court if—
  (a) it appears to the appointed person that a point of general legal importance is involved,
  (b) the registrar requests that the appeal be so referred, or
  (c) such a request is made by any party to the proceedings before the registrar in which the decision appealed against was made.
(3) Before referring an appeal to the court under subsection (2), the appointed person must give the appellant and any other party to the appeal an opportunity to make representations as to whether it should be so referred.
(4) Where, on an appeal under this section to an appointed person, the appointed person does not refer the appeal to the court—
  (a) the appointed person must hear and determine the appeal, and
  (b) the appointed person's decision is final.
(5) Sections 30 and 31 (costs, evidence) apply to proceedings before an appointed person as they apply to proceedings before the registrar.
(6) In the application of this section to England and Wales, "the court" means the High Court.

Note: Sections 27A and 27B inserted by the Intellectual Property Act 2014, s.10(2), with effect for certain purposes from July 15, 2014 (see SI 2014/1715), and with effect for remaining purposes from April 6, 2015 (see SI 2015/165).

Persons appointed to hear and determine appeals

[27B.—(1) A person is not eligible for appointment under section 27A(1)(a) unless the person—
  (a) satisfies the judicial-appointment eligibility condition on a 5-year basis,
  (b) is an advocate or solicitor in Scotland of at least 5 years' standing,
  (c) is a member of the Bar of Northern Ireland or solicitor of the Court of Judicature of Northern Ireland of at least 5 years' standing, or
  (d) has held judicial office.
(2) An appointed person must hold and vacate office in accordance with his terms of appointment, subject to subsections (3) to (5).
(3) An appointed person is to be paid such remuneration (whether by way of salary or fees) and such allowances as the Secretary of State may with the approval of the Treasury decide.
(4) An appointed person may resign office by notice in writing to the Lord Chancellor.
(5) The Lord Chancellor may by notice in writing remove an appointed person ("A") from office if—
  (a) A has become bankrupt or made an arrangement with A's creditors or, in Scotland, A's estate has been sequestrated or A has executed a trust deed for A's creditors or entered into a composition contract,
  (b) A is incapacitated by physical or mental illness, or

(c) A is, in the opinion of the Lord Chancellor, otherwise unable or unfit to perform A's duties as an appointed person.

(6) Before exercising a power under section 27A or this section, the Lord Chancellor must consult the Secretary of State.

(7) The Lord Chancellor may remove a person from office under subsection (5) only with the concurrence of the appropriate senior judge.

(8) The appropriate senior judge is the Lord Chief Justice of England and Wales, unless—

(a) the person to be removed exercises functions wholly or mainly in Scotland, in which case it is the Lord President of the Court of Session, or

(b) the person to be removed exercises functions wholly or mainly in Northern Ireland, in which case it is the Lord Chief Justice of Northern Ireland.]

Note: Sections 27A and 28B inserted by the Intellectual Property Act 2014, s.10(2), with effect for certain purposes from July 15, 2014 (see SI 2014/1715), and with effect for remaining purposes from April 6, 2015 (see SI 2015/165).

The Appeal Tribunal

28. [...]

Note: Section 28 repealed by the Intellectual Property Act 2014, s.10(4), with effect from April 6, 2015 (see SI 2015/165). Section 28 (as amended by the Administration of Justice Act 1970, the Constitutional Reform Act 2005, (SI 2006/1028)) formerly read:

The Appeal Tribunal.

"*[28.—(1) Any appeal from the registrar under this Act shall lie to the Appeal Tribunal.*

(2) The Appeal Tribunal shall consist of

(a) one or more judges of the High Court nominated [by the Lord Chief Justice of England and Wales after consulting the Lord Chancellor], and

(b) one judge of the Court of Session nominated by the Lord President of that Court.

(2A) At any time when it consists of two or more judges, the jurisdiction of the Appeal Tribunal—

(a) where in the case of any particular appeal the senior of those judges so directs, shall be exercised in relation to that appeal by both of the judges, or (if there are more than two) by two of them, sitting together, and

(b) in relation to any appeal in respect of which no such direction is given, may be exercised by any one of the judges;

and, in the exercise of that jurisdiction, different appeals may be heard at the same time by different judges.

(3) The expenses of the Appeal Tribunal shall be defrayed and the fees to be taken therein may be fixed as if the Tribunal were a court of the High Court.

(4) The Appeal Tribunal may examine witnesses on oath and administer oaths for that purpose.

(5) Upon any appeal under this Act the Appeal Tribunal may by order award to any party such costs [. . .] as the Tribunal may consider reasonable and direct how and by what parties the costs [. . .] are to be paid; and any such order may be enforced

(a) in England and Wales or Northern Ireland, in the same way as an order of the High Court;

(b) in Scotland, in the same way as a decree for expenses granted by the Court of Session.

(6) [...]

(7) Upon any appeal under this Act the Appeal Tribunal may exercise any power which could have been exercised by the registrar in the proceeding from which the appeal is brought.

(8) Subject to the foregoing provisions of this section the Appeal Tribunal may make rules for regulating all matters relating to proceedings before it under this Act, including right of audience.

(8A) At any time when the Appeal Tribunal consists of two or more judges, the power to make rules under subsection (8) of this section shall be exercisable by the senior of those judges:

Provided that another of those judges may exercise that power if it appears to him that it is necessary for rules to be made and that the judge (or, if more than one, each of the judges) senior to him is for the time being prevented by illness, absence or otherwise from making them.

(9) An appeal to the Appeal Tribunal under this Act shall not be deemed to be a proceeding in the High Court.

(10) In this section "the High Court" means the High Court in England and Wales; and for the purposes of this section the seniority of judges shall be reckoned by reference to the dates on which they were appointed judges of that court or the Court of Session.

[(11) The Lord Chief Justice may nominate a judicial office holder (as defined in section 109(4) of the Constitutional Reform Act 2005) to exercise his functions under subsection (2)(a).]] "

Opinions on designs

[28A.—(1) The Secretary of State may by regulations make provision about the making of requests to the registrar for an opinion on specified matters relating to—

    (a) designs registered under this Act;

    (b) designs of such other description as may be specified.

(2) The regulations must require the registrar to give an opinion in response to a request made under the regulations, except—

    (a) in specified cases or circumstances, or

    (b) where for any reason the registrar considers it inappropriate in all the circumstances to do so.

(3) The regulations may provide that a request made under the regulations must be accompanied by—

    (a) a fee of a specified amount;

    (b) specified information.

(4) The regulations must provide that an opinion given by the registrar under the regulations is not binding for any purposes.

(5) The regulations must provide that neither the registrar nor any examiner or other officer of the Patent Office is to incur any liability by reason of or in connection with—

    (a) any opinion given under the regulations, or

    (b) any examination or investigation undertaken for the purpose of giving such an opinion.

(6) An opinion given by the registrar under the regulations is not to be treated as a decision of the registrar for the purposes of section 27A.

(7) But the regulations must provide for an appeal relating to an opinion given

under the regulations to be made to a person appointed under section 27A; and the regulations may make further provision in relation to such appeals.

(8) The regulations may confer discretion on the registrar.

(9) Regulations under this section—

(a) may make different provision for different purposes;

(b) may include consequential, incidental, supplementary, transitional, transitory or saving provision.

(10) In this section, *"specified"* means specified in regulations under this section.]

Note: Section 28A inserted by the Intellectual Property Act 2014, s.11(1), with effect from October 1, 2014 (see SI 2014/2330).

Powers and duties of Registrar

Exercise of discretionary powers of registrar.

29. Without prejudice to any provisions of this Act requiring the registrar to hear any party to proceedings thereunder, or to give to any such party an opportunity to be heard, [rules made by the Secretary of State under this Act shall require the registrar to give] to any applicant for registration of a design an opportunity to be heard before exercising adversely to the applicant any discretion vested in the registrar by or under this Act.

Note: The words in square brackets substituted by the Copyright, Designs and Patents Act 1988 (c.48), s.272, Sch.3 para.18.

Costs and security for costs.

30.—(1) Rules made by the Secretary of State under this Act may make provision empowering the registrar, in any proceedings before him under this Act—

(a) to award any party such costs as he may consider reasonable, and

(b) to direct how and by what parties they are to be paid.

(2) Any such order of the registrar may be enforced—

(a) in England and Wales or Northern Ireland, in the same way as an order of the High Court,

(b) in Scotland, in the same way as a decree for expenses granted by the Court of Session.

(3) Rules made by the Secretary of State under this Act may make provision empowering the registrar to require a person, in such cases as may be prescribed, to give security for the costs of—

(a) an application for [invalidation] of the registration of a design,

(b) [...]

(c) an appeal from any decision of the registrar under this Act,

and enabling the application or appeal to be treated as abandoned in default of such security being given.

Note: In subs.(3)(a), the word in square brackets was substituted for the former word "substitution" and subs.(3)(b) was repealed by the Registered Designs Regulations 2001 (SI 2001/3949), reg.9, Sch.1 para.9, Sch.2, with effect from December 9, 2001.

Evidence before registrar.

31. Rules made by the Secretary of State under this Act may make provision—

(a) as to the giving of evidence in proceedings before the registrar under this Act by affidavit or statutory declaration;

(b) conferring on the registrar the powers of an official referee of the [Senior Courts] [or of the Court of Judicature] as regards the examination of witnesses on oath and the discovery and production of documents; and

(c) applying in relation to the attendance of witnesses in proceedings before the registrar the rules applicable to the attendance of witnesses in proceedings before such a referee.

Note: In subs.(b), the words in square brackets substituted by the Constitutional Reform Act 2005 (c.4) Sch.11 with effect from October 1, 2009.

Power to require use of forms

[**31A.**—(1) The registrar may require the use of such forms as the registrar may direct for—

(a) an application for the registration of a design;

(b) representations or specimens of designs or other documents which may be filed at the Patent Office.

(2) The forms, and any directions by the registrar about their use, are to be published in the prescribed manner.]

Note: Section 31A inserted by the Intellectual Property Act 2014, s.12(1), with effect from October 1, 2014 (see SI 2014/2330).

Power of registrar to refuse to deal with certain agents.

32. [...]

Note: Section 32 was repealed by the Copyright, Designs and Patents Act 1988 (c.48), ss.272, 303(2), Sch.3 para.21, Sch.8. The original provision was as follows:

Power of registrar to refuse to deal with certain agents.

"**32.**—(1) *Rules made by the Board of Trade under this Act may authorise the registrar to refuse to recognise as agent in may authorise the registrar to refuse to recognise as agent in—*

(a) *any individual whose name has been erased from, and not restored to, the register of patent agents kept in pursuance of rules made under the Patents Act, 1949;*

(b) *any individual who is for the time being suspended in accordance with those rules from acting as a patent agent;*

(c) *any person who has been convicted of an offence under section eighty-eight of the Patents Act, 1949;*

(d) *any person who is found by the Board of Trade (after being given an opportunity to be heard) to have been convicted of any offence or to have been guilty of any such misconduct as, in the case of an individual registered in the register of patent agents aforesaid, would render him liable to have his name erased therefrom;*

(e) *any person, not being registered as a patent agent, who in the opinion of the registrar is engaged wholly or mainly in acting as agent in applying for patents in the United Kingdom or elsewhere in the name or for the benefit of a person by whom he is employed;*

(f) *any company or firm, if any person whom the registrar could refuse to recognise as agent in respect of any business under this Act is acting as a director or manager of the company or is a partner in the firm.*

(2) *The registrar shall refuse to recognise as agent in respect of any business under this Act any person who neither resides nor has a place of business in the United Kingdom or the Isle of Man.*"

Offences

Offences under s.5.

33.—(1) If any person fails to comply with any direction under section five of this Act or makes or causes to be made an application for the registration of a design in contravention of that section, he shall be guilty of an offence and liable—

(a) on conviction on indictment to imprisonment for a term not exceeding two years or a fine, or both;

(b) on summary conviction to imprisonment for a term not exceeding six months or a fine not exceeding the statutory maximum, or both.

(2) [...]

Note: Subsection (2) was repealed by the Copyright, Designs and Patents Act 1988 (c.48), ss.272, 303(2), Sch.3 para.22(3), (4), Sch.8. The original subsection was as follows:

"(2) *Where an offence under section five of this Act is committed by a body corporate, every person who at the time of the commission of the offence is a director, general manager, secretary or other similar officer of the body corporate, or is purporting to act in any such capacity, shall be deemed to be guilty of that offence unless he proves that the offence was committed without his consent or connivance and that he exercised all such diligence to prevent the commission of the offence as he ought to have exercised having regard to the. nature of his functions in that capacity and to all the circumstances."*

Falsification of register, etc.

34. If any person makes or causes to be made a false entry in the register of designs, or a writing falsely purporting to be a copy of an entry in that register, or produces or tenders or causes to be produced or tendered in evidence any such writing, knowing the entry or writing to be false, he [shall be guilty of an offence and liable—

(a) on conviction on indictment to imprisonment for a term not exceeding two years or a fine, or both;

(b) on summary conviction to imprisonment for a term not exceeding six months or a fine not exceeding the statutory maximum, or both.]

Note: The words in the square brackets in s.34 substituted by the Copyright, Designs and Patents Act 1988 (c.48), Sch.3 para.23(1)(2).

Fine or falsely representing a design as registered.

35.—(1) If any person falsely represents that a design applied to any article [, or incorporated in, any product] sold by him is registered [...], he shall be liable on summary conviction to a fine not exceeding level 3 on the standard scale; and for the purposes of this provision a person who sells [a product] having stamped, engraved or impressed thereon or otherwise applied thereto the word "registered", or any other word expressing or implying the design applied to [, or incorporated in, the product] is registered, shall be deemed to represent that the design applied to [, or incorporated in, the product] is registered [...].

(2) If any person, after the right in a registered design has expired, marks [any product] to which the design has been applied [or in which it has been incorporated] with the word "registered", or any word or words implying that there is a subsisting right in the design under this Act, or causes any [such product] to be so marked, he shall be liable on summary conviction to a fine not exceeding level 1 on the standard scale.

[(3) For the purposes of this section, the use in the United Kingdom in relation to a design—

(a) of the word "registered", or

(b) of any other word or symbol importing a reference (express or implied) to registration, shall be deemed to be a representation as to registration under this Act unless it is shown that the reference is to registration elsewhere than in the United Kingdom and that the design is in fact so registered.]

Notes:

(1) In subs.(1), the words in the first set of square brackets inserted; the words "in respect of that article" repealed; the words in the second set of square brackets substituted for the former words "an article"; the words in the third set of square brackets substituted for the former words "the article"; the words in the fourth set of square brackets substituted for the former words "the article"; and the words "in respect of the article" repealed by the Registered Designs Regulations 2001 (SI 2001/3949), reg.9, Sch.1, para.10, Sch.2, with effect from December 9, 2001.

(2) In subs.(2), the words in the first set of square brackets substituted for the former words "any article"; the words in the second set of square brackets inserted and the words in the third set of square brackets substituted for the former words "such article" by the Registered Designs Regulations 2001 (SI 2001/3949), reg.9, Sch.1, para.10, with effect from December 9, 2001.

(3) Subsection (3) was inserted by the Community Design Regulations 2005 (SI 2005/2339), reg.6, with effect from October 1, 2005.

Offence of unauthorised copying etc. of design in course of business

[35ZA.—*(1) A person commits an offence if—*

(a) in the course of a business, the person intentionally copies a registered design so as to make a product—

(i) exactly to that design, or

(ii) with features that differ only in immaterial details from that design, and

(b) the person does so—

(i) knowing, or having reason to believe, that the design is a registered design, and

(ii) without the consent of the registered proprietor of the design.

(2) Subsection (3) applies in relation to a product where a registered design has been intentionally copied so as to make the product—

(a) exactly to the design, or

(b) with features that differ only in immaterial details from the design.

(3) A person commits an offence if—

(a) in the course of a business, the person offers, puts on the market, imports, exports or uses the product, or stocks it for one or more of those purposes,

(b) the person does so without the consent of the registered proprietor of the design, and

(c) the person does so knowing, or having reason to believe, that—

(i) a design has been intentionally copied without the consent of the registered proprietor so as to make the product exactly to the design or with features that differ only in immaterial details from the design, and

(ii) the design is a registered design.

(4) It is a defence for a person charged with an offence under this section to show that the person reasonably believed that the registration of the design was invalid.

(5) It is also a defence for a person charged with an offence under this section to show that the person—

    (a) did not infringe the right in the design, or

    (b) reasonably believed that the person did not do so.

(6) The reference in subsection (3) to using a product in the course of a business does not include a reference to using it for a purpose which is merely incidental to the carrying on of the business.

(7) In this section "registered design" includes a registered Community design; and a reference to the registered proprietor is, in the case of a registered Community design, to be read as a reference to the holder.

(8) A person guilty of an offence under this section is liable—

    (a) on conviction on indictment, to imprisonment for a term not exceeding ten years or to a fine or to both;

    (b) on summary conviction in England and Wales or Northern Ireland, to imprisonment for a term not exceeding six months or to a fine not exceeding the statutory maximum or to both;

    (c) on summary conviction in Scotland, to imprisonment for a term not exceeding 12 months or to a fine not exceeding the statutory maximum or to both.]

Note: Sections 35ZA to 35ZD inserted by the Intellectual Property Act 2014, s.13, with effect from October 1, 2014 (see SI 2014/2330).

Section 35ZA: enforcement

[35ZB.—(1A) For the investigatory powers available to a local weights and measures authority or the Department of Enterprise, Trade and Investment in Northern Ireland for the purposes of the enforcement of section 35ZA, see Schedule 5 to the Consumer Rights Act 2015.

(2) Any enactment which authorises the disclosure of information for the purpose of facilitating the enforcement of the Trade Descriptions Act 1968 applies—

    (a) as if section 35ZA were a provision of that Act, and

    (b) as if the functions of any person in relation to the enforcement of that section were functions under that Act.

(3) Nothing in this section is to be construed as authorising a local weights and measures authority to bring proceedings in Scotland.]

Notes:

    (1) Sections 35ZA to 35ZD inserted by the Intellectual Property Act 2014, s.13, with effect from October 1, 2014 (see SI 2014/2330).

    (2) Subsection (1) repealed, and new subs.(1A) inserted, by the Consumer Rights Act 2015, Sch.6, para.1, with effect from October 1, 2015 (SI 2015/1630). Subs.(1A) formerly read:

(1) The following provisions of the Trade Descriptions Act 1968 (which provide for the enforcement of that Act by local weights and measures authorities or the relevant Northern Ireland Department) apply as if section 35ZA were a provision of that Act—

    (a) section 27 (power to make test purchases);

    (b) section 28 (power to enter premises and inspect and seize goods and documents);

    (c) section 29 (obstruction of authorised officers);

    (d) section 33 (compensation for loss etc. of seized goods).

Section 35ZA: forfeiture in England and Wales or Northern Ireland

[35ZC.—(1) In England and Wales or Northern Ireland, a person who, in connection with the investigation or prosecution of an offence under section 35ZA, has come into the possession of relevant products or articles may apply under this section for an order for the forfeiture of the products or articles.

(2) "Relevant product" means a product which is made exactly to a registered design, or with features that differ only in immaterial details from a registered design, by copying that design intentionally.

(3) "Relevant article" means an article which is specifically designed or adapted for making copies of a registered design intentionally.

(4) An application under this section may be made—

    (a) where proceedings have been brought in any court for an offence under section 35ZA relating to some or all of the products or articles, to that court;

    (b) where no application for the forfeiture of the products or articles has been made under paragraph (a), by way of complaint to a magistrates' court.

(5) On an application under this section, the court may make an order for the forfeiture of products or articles only if it is satisfied that an offence under section 35ZA has been committed in relation to the products or articles.

(6) A court may infer for the purposes of this section that such an offence has been committed in relation to any products or articles if it is satisfied that such an offence has been committed in relation to products or articles which are representations of them (whether by reason of being of the same design or part of the same consignment or batch or otherwise).

(7) Any person aggrieved by an order made under this section by a magistrates' court, or by a decision of such a court not to make such an order, may appeal against that order or decision—

    (a) in England and Wales, to the Crown Court;

    (b) in Northern Ireland, to the county court.

(8) An order so made may contain such provision as appears to the court to be appropriate for delaying the coming into force of the order pending the making and determination of any appeal (including any application under section 111 of the Magistrates' Courts Act 1980 or Article 146 of the Magistrates' Courts (Northern Ireland) Order 1981).

(9) Subject to subsection (10), any products or articles forfeited under this section are to be destroyed in accordance with such directions as the court may give.

(10) On making an order under this section, the court may, if it considers it appropriate to do so, direct that the products or articles to which the order relates shall (instead of being destroyed) be released to such person and on such conditions as the court may specify.]

Note: Sections 35ZA to 35ZD inserted by the Intellectual Property Act 2014, s.13, with effect from October 1, 2014 (see SI 2014/2330).

Section 35ZA: forfeiture in Scotland

[**35ZD.**—(1) In Scotland, the court may make an order for the forfeiture of any relevant products or articles (as defined by section 35ZC).

(2) An order under this section may be made—

    (a) on an application by the procurator fiscal made in the manner specified in section 134 of the Criminal Procedure (Scotland) Act 1995, or

    (b) where a person is convicted of an offence under section 35ZA, in addition to any other penalty which the court may impose.

(3) On an application under subsection (2)(a), the court may make an order for

the forfeiture of relevant products or articles only if it is satisfied that an offence under section 35ZA has been committed in relation to the relevant products or articles.

(4) The court may infer for the purposes of this section that such an offence has been committed in relation to any relevant products or articles which are representative of them (whether by reason of being of the same design or part of the same consignment or batch or otherwise).

(5) The procurator fiscal making the application under subsection (2)(a) must serve on any person appearing to the procurator fiscal to be the owner of, or otherwise have an interest in, the products or articles to which an application under this section relates is entitled to appear at the hearing of the application to show cause why the products or articles should not be forfeited.

(6) Service under subsection (5) must be carried out, and such service may be proved, in the manner specified for citation of an accused in summary proceedings under the Criminal Procedure (Scotland) Act 1995.

(7) Any person upon whom notice is served under subsection (5) and any other person claiming to be the owner of, or otherwise have an interest in, products or articles to which an application under this section relates is entitled to appear at the hearing of the application to show cause why the products or articles should not be forfeited.

(8) The court must not make an order following an application under subsection (2)(a)—

    (a) if any person on whom notice is served under subsection (5) does not appear, unless service of the notice on that person is proved, or

    (b) if no notice under subsection (5) has been served, unless the court is satisfied that in the circumstances it was reasonable not to serve such notice.

(9) Where an order for the forfeiture of any products or articles is made following an application under subsection (2)(a), any person who appeared, or was entitled to appear, to show cause why goods, material or articles should not be forfeited may, within 21 days of making the order, appeal to the High Court of Justiciary by bill of suspension.

(10) Section 182(5)(a) to (e) of the Criminal Procedure (Scotland) Act 1995 applies to an appeal under subsection (9) as it applies to a stated case under Part 2 of that Act.

(11) An order following an application under subsection (2)(a) does not take effect—

    (a) until the end of the period of 21 days beginning with the day after the day on which the order is made, or

    (b) if an appeal is made under subsection (9) within that period, until the appeal is dismissed or abandoned.

(12) An order under subsection (2)(b) does not take effect—

    (a) until the end of the period within which an appeal against the order could be brought under the Criminal Procedure (Scotland) Act 1995, or

    (b) if an appeal is made within that period, until the appeal is determined or abandoned.

(13) Subject to subsection (14), products or articles forfeited under this section must be destroyed in accordance with such directions as the court may give.

(14) On making an order under this section, the court may, if it considers it appropriate to do so, direct that the products or articles to which the order relates shall (instead of being destroyed) be released, to such person and on such conditions as the court may specify.

(15) In this section, "the court" means—

(a) in relation to an order made on an application under subsection (2)(a), the sheriff;

(b) in relation to an order made under subsection (2)(b), the court which imposed the penalty.]

Note: Sections 35ZA to 35ZD inserted by the Intellectual Property Act 2014, s.13, with effect from October 1, 2014 (see (SI 2014/2330)).

Offence by body corporate: liability of officers.

[**35A.**—(1) Where an offence under this Act committed by a body corporate is proved to have been committed with the consent or connivance of a director, manager, secretary or other similar officer of the body, or a person purporting to act in any such capacity, he as well as the body corporate is guilty of the offence and liable to be proceeded against and punished accordingly.

(2) In relation to a body corporate whose affairs are managed by its members "director" means a member of the body corporate.]

[(3) Proceedings for an offence under this Act alleged to have been committed by a partnership are to be brought against the partnership in the name of the firm and not in that of the partners; but without prejudice to any liability of the partners under subsection (6) or (7).

(4) The following provisions apply for the purposes of such proceedings as in relation to a body corporate—

(a) any rules of court relating to the service of documents;

(b) in England and Wales, Schedule 3 to the Magistrates' Courts Act 1980;

(c) in Northern Ireland, Schedule 4 to the Magistrates' Courts (Northern Ireland) Order 1981.

(5) A fine imposed on a partnership (other than a Scottish partnership) on its conviction in such proceedings must be paid out of the partnership assets.

(6) Where a partnership (other than a Scottish partnership) is guilty of an offence under this Act, every partner, other than a partner who is proved to have been ignorant of or to have attempted to prevent the commission of the offence, is also guilty of the offence and liable to be proceeded against and punished accordingly.

(7) Where an offence under this Act committed by a Scottish partnership is proved to have been committed with the consent or connivance of a partner in the partnership, or a person purporting to act in that capacity, he as well as the partnership is guilty of the offence and liable to be proceeded against and punished accordingly.]

Notes:

(1) Section 35A inserted by the Copyright, Designs and Patents Act 1988 (c.48) Sch.3 para.25(1), (2).

(2) Subsections (3)-(7) inserted by the Intellectual Property Act 2014, s.14 with effect from October 1, 2014 (see SI 2014/2330).

Rules, etc.

General power of Secretary of State to make rules, etc.

36.—(1) Subject to the provisions of this Act, the Secretary of State may make such rules as he thinks expedient for regulating the business of the Patent Office in relation to designs and for regulating all matters by this Act placed under the direction or control of the registrar or the Secretary of State.

(1A) Rules may, in particular, make provision—

(a) prescribing the form of applications for registration of designs and of any representations or specimens of designs or other documents which may be filed at the Patent Office, and requiring copies to be furnished of any such representations, specimens or documents;

[(ab) requiring applications for registration of designs to specify—

    (i) the products to which the designs are intended to be applied or in which they are intended to be incorporated;

    (ii) the classification of the designs by reference to such test as may be prescribed;]

(b) regulating the procedure to be followed in connection with any application or request to the registrar or in connection with any proceeding before him, and authorising the rectification of irregularities of procedure;

(c) providing for the appointment of advisers to assist the registrar in proceedings before him;

(d) regulating the keeping of the register of designs;

(e) authorising the publication and sale of copies of representations of designs and other documents in the Patent Office;

(f) prescribing anything authorised or required by this Act to be prescribed by rules.

(1B) The remuneration of an adviser appointed to assist the registrar shall be determined by the Secretary of State with the consent of the Treasury and shall be defrayed out of money provided by Parliament.

(2) Rules made under this section may provide for the establishment of branch offices for designs and may authorise any document or thing required by or under this Act to be filed or done at the Patent Office to be filed or done at the branch office at Manchester or any other branch office established in pursuance of the rules.

Note: Subsection (1A)(ab) was inserted by the Registered Designs Regulations 2001 (SI 2001/3949), reg.9, Sch.1 para.11, with effect from December 9, 2001.

Provisions as to rules and Orders.

37.—(1) [...]

(2) Any rules made by the Secretary of State in pursuance of [section 15 [*or 22(6)*] of this Act], and any order made, direction given, or other action taken under the rules by the registrar, may be made, given or taken so as to have effect as respects things done or omitted to be done on or after such date, whether before or after the coming into operation of the rules or of this Act, as may be specified in the rules.

(3) Any power to make rules conferred by this Act on the Secretary of State [. . .][and the power to make an order under section 15ZA] [and the power to make regulations under section 28A] shall be exercisable by statutory instrument [. . .].

(4) Any statutory instrument containing rules made by the Secretary of State under this Act [or regulations under section 28A] shall be subject to annulment in pursuance of a resolution of either House of Parliament.

[(4A) Subsection (4) does not apply to the first regulations to be made under section 28A, but the Secretary of State may not make those regulations unless a draft of the statutory instrument containing them has been laid before, and approved by a resolution of, each House of Parliament.]

[(4B) The Secretary of State may not make an order under section 15ZA unless a draft of the statutory instrument containing the order has been laid before, and approved by a resolution of, each House of Parliament.]

(5) Any Order in Council made under this Act may be revoked or varied by a subsequent Order in Council.

Notes:

(1) Subsection (1) was repealed by the Copyright, Designs and Patents Act 1988 (c.48) Sch.3 para.27(2), Sch.8. The subsection originally read:

"(1) *Any rules made by the Board of Trade under this Act shall be advertised twice in the Journal.*"

(2) In subs.(2) the words in square brackets substituted for the former words "section 15 or section 16 of this Act" by the Registered Designs Regulations 2001 (SI 2001/3949), reg.9, Sch.1 para.12, Sch.2, with effect from December 9, 2001.

(3) Subsection (3) was amended by the Tribunals, Courts and Enforcement Act 2007, s.146, Sch.23, Pt.6.

(4) In subss.(3) and (4) words in square brackets inserted and subss.(4A) and (4B) inserted by the Intellectual Property Act 2014, s.8(2), 11(3), with effect from October 1, 2014 (see (SI 2014/2330)).

(5) In subs.(3) words repealed by the Intellectual Property Act 2014, s.10(5), with effect from April 6, 2015 (see (SI 2015/165)). Subsection (3) formerly read:

"*(3) Any power to make rules conferred by this Act on the Secretary of State or on the Appeal Tribunal shall be exercisable by statutory instrument; and the Statutory Instruments Act 1946 shall apply to a statutory instrument containing rules made by the Appeal Tribunal in like manner as if the rules had been made by a Minister of the Crown.*"

(6) In subs.(2) reference "or 22(6)" inserted after reference "section 15" by the Intellectual Property Act 2014, s.9(6), with effect from a day to be appointed.

Use of electronic communications.

[37A.—(1) The registrar may give directions as to the form and manner in which documents to be delivered to the registrar—

(a) in electronic form; or

(b) using electronic communications, are to be delivered to him.

(2) A direction under subsection (1) may provide that in order for a document to be delivered in compliance with the direction it shall be accompanied by one or more additional documents specified in the direction.

(3) Subject to subsections (11) and (12), if a document to which a direction under subsection (1) or (2) applies is delivered to the registrar in a form or manner which does not comply with the direction the registrar may treat the document as not having been delivered.

(4) Subsection (5) applies in relation to a case where—

(a) a document is delivered using electronic communications, and

(b) there is a requirement for a fee to accompany the document.

(5) The registrar may give directions specifying—

(a) how the fee shall be paid; and

(b) when the fee shall be deemed to have been paid.

(6) The registrar may give directions specifying that a person who delivers a document to the registrar in electronic form or using electronic communications cannot treat the document as having been delivered unless its delivery has been acknowledged.

(7) The registrar may give directions specifying how a time of delivery is to be accorded to a document delivered to him in electronic form or using electronic communications.

(8) A direction under this section may be given—

(a) generally;

(b) in relation to a description of cases specified in the direction;

(c) in relation to a particular person or persons.

(9) A direction under this section may be varied or revoked by a subsequent direction under this section.

(10) The delivery using electronic communications to any person by the registrar of any document is deemed to be effected, unless the registrar has otherwise specified, by transmitting an electronic communication containing the document to an address provided or made available to the registrar by that person as an address of his for the receipt of electronic communications; and unless the contrary is proved such delivery is deemed to be effected immediately upon the transmission of the communication.

(11) A requirement of this Act that something must be done in the prescribed manner is satisfied in the case of something that is done—

(a) using a document in electronic form, or

(b) using electronic communications, only if the directions under this section that apply to the manner in which it is done are complied with

(12) In the case of an application made as mentioned insubsection (11)(a) or (b) above, a reference in this Act to the application not having been made in accordance with rules under this Act includes a reference to its not having been made in accordance with any applicable directions under this section.

(13) This section applies—

(a) to delivery at the Patent Office as it applies to delivery to the registrar; and

(b) to delivery by the Patent Office as it applies to delivery by the registrar.]

Note: Section 37A was inserted by the Registered Designs Act 1949 and Patents Act 1977 (Electronic Communications) Order 2006 (SI 2006/1229), art.2, with effect from October 1, 2006.

Proceedings of Board of Trade.

38. [...]

Note: Section 38 was repealed by the Copyright, Designs and Patents Act 1988 (c.48), Sch.3 para.28, Sch.8. The original wording of the provision was as follows:

Proceedings of Board of Trade.

"38.—(1) *Anything required or authorised by this Act to be done by, to or before the-Board of Trade may be done by, to or before the President of the Board of Trade, any secretary, under-secretary or assistant secretary of the Board, or any person authorised in that behalf by the President.*

(2) *All documents purporting to be orders made by the Board of Trade and to be sealed with the seal of the Board,. or to be signed by a secretary, under-secretary or assistant secretary of the Board, or by any person authorised in that behalf by the President of the Board, shall be received in evidence and shall be deemed to be such orders without further proof, unless the contrary is shown.*

(3) *A certificate, signed by the President of the Board of Trade, that any order made or act done is the order or act of the Board, shall be conclusive evidence of the fact so certified."*

Supplemental

Hours of business and excluded days.

39.—(1) [The registrar may give directions specifying] the hour at which the Patent Office shall be deemed to be closed on any day for purposes of the transaction by the public of business under this Act or of any class of such business, [and specifying] days as excluded days for any such purposes.

(2) Any business done under this Act on any day after the hour specified as aforesaid in relation to business of that class, or on a day which is an excluded day in relation to business of that class, shall be deemed to have been done on the next following day not being an excluded day; and where the time for doing anything under this Act expires on an excluded day, that time shall be extended to the next following day not being an excluded day.

Notes:
(1) The words in square brackets in subs.(1) substituted by the Copyright, Designs and Patents Act 1988 (c.48), Sch.3 para.29.
(2) In subs.(1) words in square brackets substituted by the Intellectual Property Act 2014, s.12(4), with effect from October 1, 2014 (see (SI 2014/2330)). Subsection (1) formerly read:
"(1) Rules made by [the Secretary of State] under this Act may specify the hour at which the Patent Office shall be deemed to be closed on any day for purposes of the transaction by the public of business under this Act or of any class of such business, and may specify days as excluded days for any such purposes."

Fees.

40. There shall be paid in respect of the registration of designs and applications therefor, and in respect of other matters relating to designs arising under this Act, such fees as may be prescribed by rules made by [the Secretary of State] with the consent of the Treasury.

Note: The words in square brackets in substituted by the Copyright, Designs and Patents Act 1988 (c.48), Sch.3 para.30.

Service of notices, etc., by post.

41. Any notice required or authorised to be given by or under this Act, and any application or other document so authorised or required to be made or filed, may be given, made or filed by post.

Annual report of registrar.

42. The Comptroller-General of Patents, Designs and Trade Marks shall, in his annual report with respect to the execution of [the Patents Act 1977], include a report with respect to the execution of this Act as if it formed a part of or was included in that Act.

Note: The words in square brackets substituted by the Patents Act 1977 (c. 37), Sch.5 para.3.

Savings.

43.—(1) [...]
(2) Nothing in this Act shall affect the right of the Crown or of any person deriving title directly or indirectly from the Crown to sell or use [products] forfeited under the laws relating to customs or excise.

Notes:
(1) Subsection (1) was repealed by the Registered Designs Regulations 2001 (SI 2001/ 3949) Sch.2 para.1 with effect from December 9, 2001. The original wording was as follows:
"(1) Nothing in this Act shall be construed as authorising or requiring the registrar to register a design the use of which would, in his opinion, be contrary to law or morality."

(2) In subs.(2) the words in square brackets substituted for the former words "section 15 or section 16 of this Act" by the Registered Designs Regulations 2001 (SI 2001/3949), reg.9, Sch.1 para.12, Sch.2, with effect from December 9, 2001.

Interpretation.

44.—(1) In this Act, except where the context otherwise requires, the following expressions have the meanings hereby respectively assigned by them, that is to say—

[…]

[…]

"assignee" includes the personal representative of a deceased assignee, and references to the assignee of any person include references to the assignee of the personal representative or assignee of that person;

"author", in relation to a design, has the meaning given by section 2(3) and (4);

[…]

["Community Design Regulation" means Council Regulation (EC) 6/2002 of 12th December 2001 on Community Designs;]

["complex product" has the meaning assigned to it by section 1(3) of this Act;]

[…]

"the court" shall be construed in accordance with section 27 of this Act;

"design" has the meaning assigned to it by [section 1(2)] of this Act;

"electronic communication" has the same meaning as in the Electronic Communications Act 2000;

"employee", "employment" and "employer" refer to employment under a contract of service or of apprenticeship;

[…]

["national unregistered design right" means design right within the meaning of Part III of the Copyright, Designs and Patents Act 1988;]

"prescribed" means prescribed by rules made by the Secretary of State under this Act;

["product" has the meaning assigned to it by section 1(3) of this Act;]

"proprietor" has the meaning assigned to it by section two of this Act;

["registered Community design" means a design that complies with the conditions contained in, and is registered in the manner provided for in, the Community Design Regulation;]

"registered proprietor" means the person or persons for the time being entered in the register of designs as proprietor of the design;

"registrar" means the Comptroller-General of Patents Designs and Trade-Marks;

[…]

(2) [...]

(3) [...]

(4) For the purposes of subsection (1) of [section 14 of this Act], the expression "personal representative," in relation to a deceased person, includes the legal representative of the deceased appointed in any country outside the United Kingdom.

Notes:

(1) In subs.(1), the definitions of "article", "artistic work", "corresponding design" and "set of articles" repealed and the definitions of "complex product", "national

unregistered design right" and "product" inserted; the words in square brackets in the definition of "design" substituted for the former words "section 1(1)" and in subs.(4), the words in square brackets substituted for the former words "section 14 and of section 16 of this Act" by the Registered Designs Regulations 2001 (SI 2001/3949), reg.9, Sch.1, para.12, Sch.2, with effect from December 9, 2001. The former definitions provided:

> *""article" means any article of manufacture and includes any part of an article if that part is made and sold separately;*
>
> *"artistic work" has the same meaning as in Part I of the Copyright, Designs and Patents Act 1988;*
>
> *"corresponding design", in relation to an artistic work, means a design which if applied to an article would produce something which would be treated for the purposes of Part I of the Copyright, Designs and Patents Act 1988 as a copy of that work;*
>
> *"set of articles" means a number of articles of the same general character ordinarily on sale or intended to be used together, to each of which the same design, or the same design with modifications or variations not sufficient to alter the character or substantially to affect the identity thereof, is applied."*

(2) In subs.(1) the definitions of "Community Design Regulation" and "registered Community design" inserted by the Registered Designs Regulations 2003 (SI 2003/550), reg.2 with effect from April 1, 2003.

(3) The definition of "electronic communication", also in subs.(1) was inserted by the Registered Designs Act 1949 and Patents Act 1977 (Electronic Communications) Order 2006 (SI 2006/1229), art.3, with effect from October 1, 2006; the definition of "Appeal Tribunal" was repealed by the Intellectual Property Act 2014, s.10(6) with effect from April 6, 2015.

(4) Subsections (2) and (3) repealed by the Registered Designs Regulations 2001 (SI 2001/3949) Sch.2 para.1 with effect from December 9, 2001. The subsections previously read:

> *"(2) Any reference in this Act to an article in respect of which a design is registered shall, in the case of a design registered in respect of a set of articles, be construed as a reference to any article of that set.*
>
> *(3) Any question arising under this Act whether a number of articles constitute a set of articles shall be determined by the registrar; and notwithstanding anything in this Act any determination of the registrar under this subsection shall be final."*

(5) Definition *"Appeal Tribunal"* repealed by the Intellectual Property Act 2014, s.10(6), with effect from April 6, 2015 (see (SI 2015/165)). Definition formerly read:

> *" Appeal Tribunal" means the Appeal Tribunal constituted and acting in accordance with section 28 of this Act as amended by the Administration of Justice Act 1969;".*

Application to Scotland.

[**45.**—(1) In the application of this Act to Scotland—

> "account of profits" means accounting and payment of profits;
>
> "accounts" means count, reckoning and payment;
>
> "arbitrator" means arbiter;
>
> "assignment" means assignation;
>
> "claimant" means pursuer;
>
> "costs" means expenses;
>
> "defendant" means defender;
>
> "delivery up" means delivery;
>
> "injunction" means interdict;
>
> "interlocutory relief" means interim remedy.

(2) References to the Crown shall be construed as including references to the Crown in right of the Scottish Administration.]

Note: Section 45 was substituted by the Intellectual Property (Enforcement, etc.) Regulations 2006 (SI 2006/1028), Sch.1 para.5, with effect from April 29, 2006.

Application to Northern Ireland.

46. In the application of this Act to Northern Ireland—

(1) [...]

(2) [...]

(3) References to enactments include enactments comprised in Northern Ireland legislation:

(3A) References to the Crown include the Crown in right of Her Majesty's Government in Northern Ireland:

(4) References to a government department shall be construed as including references to a Northern Ireland department, and in relation to a Northern Ireland department references to the Treasury shall be construed as references to the Department of Finance and Personnel.

[(4A) Any reference to a claimant includes a reference to a plaintiff.]

(5) [...]

Notes:

(1) Section 46(4A) was inserted by the Intellectual Property (Enforcement, etc.) Regulations 2006 (SI 2006/1028), Sch.1 para.6, with effect from April 29, 2006.

(2) Subsections (1) and (2) repealed by the Copyright, Designs and Patents Act 1988 (c.48), Sch.3 para.33(2), Sch.8. The original wording was as follows:

"(1) *The provisions of this Act conferring a special jurisdiction on the court, as defined by this Act, shall not, except so far as the jurisdiction extends, affect the jurisdiction of any court in Northern Ireland in any proceedings relating to designs; and with reference to any such proceedings the term " the Court" means the High Court in Northern Ireland:*

(2) *If any rectification of a register under this Act is required in pursuance of any proceeding in a court, a copy of the order, decree, or other authority for the rectification shall be served on the registrar, and he shall rectify the register accordingly:".*

(3) Subsection (5) was Northern Ireland Act 1962 (c.30), Sch.4 Pt. IV. The original wording was as follows:

"(5) *The expression "summary conviction" shall be construed as meaning conviction subject to, and in accordance with, the Petty Sessions (Ireland) Act, 1851, and any Act (including any Act of the Parliament of Northern Ireland) amending that Act.".*

Application to Isle of Man.

[**47.** This Act extends to the Isle of Man, subject to any modifications contained in an Order made by Her Majesty in Council, and accordingly, subject to any such Order, references in this Act to the United Kingdom shall be construed as including the Isle of Man.]

Note: Section 47 was substituted by the Copyright, Designs and Patents Act 1988 (c.48), Sch.3 para.34. The section originally read:

Application to Isle of Man.

"**47.** *This Act shall extend to the Isle of Man subject to the following modifications:—*

(1) *Nothing in this Act shall affect the jurisdiction of the courts in the Isle of Man in proceedings for infringement or in any action or proceeding respecting a design competent to those courts ;*

(2) *The punishment for a misdemeanour under this Act in the Isle of Man shall be imprisonment for any term not exceeding two years, with or without hard labour,*

and with or without a fine not exceeding one hundred pounds, at the discretion of the court;

(3) *Any offence under this Act committed in the Isle of Man which would in England be punishable on summary conviction may be prosecuted, and any fine in respect thereof recovered, at the instance of any person aggrieved, in the manner in which offences punishable on summary conviction may for the time being be prosecuted.*"

Territorial waters and the continental shelf.

[47A.—(1) For the purposes of this Act the territorial waters of the United Kingdom shall be treated as part of the United Kingdom.

(2) This Act applies to things done in the United Kingdom sector of the continental shelf on a structure or vessel which is present there for purposes directly connected with the exploration of the sea bed or subsoil or the exploitation of their natural resources as it applies to things done in the United Kingdom.

(3) The United Kingdom sector of the continental shelf means the areas designated by order under section 1(7) of the Continental Shelf Act 1964.]

Note: Section 47A was inserted by the Copyright, Designs and Patents Act 1988 (c.48), Sch.3 para.35.

Repeals, savings, and transitional provisions.

48.—(1) [...]

(2) Subject to the provisions of this section, any Order in Council, rule, order, requirement, certificate, notice, decision, direction, authorisation, consent, application, request or thing made, issued given or done under any enactment repealed by this Act shall, if in force at the commencement of this Act, and so far as it could have been made, issued, given or done under this Act, continue in force and have effect as if made, issued, given or done under the corresponding enactment of this Act.

(3) Any register kept under the Patents and Designs Act 1907 shall be deemed to form part of the corresponding register under this Act.

(4) Any design registered before the commencement of this Act shall be deemed to be registered under this Act in respect of articles of the class in which it is registered.

(5) [...]

(6) Any document referring to any enactment repealed by this Act shall be construed as referring to the corresponding enactment of this Act.

(7) Nothing in the foregoing provisions of this section shall be taken as prejudicing the operation of section 38 of the Interpretation Act 1889 (which relates to the effect of repeals).

Notes:

(1) Subsection (5) was repealed by the Registered Designs Regulations 2001 (SI 2001/ 3949), reg.9, Sch.2, with effect from December 9, 2001. Subsection (5) originally read:

"(5) *Where, in relation to any design the time for giving notice to the registrar under section fifty-nine of the Patents and Designs Act, 1907, expired before the commencement of this Act and the notice was not given, subsection (2) of section six of this Act shall not apply in relation to that design or any registration of that design.*"

(2) Subsection (1) was repealed by the Copyright, Designs and Patents Act 1988 (c.48), Sch.3 para.36, Sch.8. Subsection (1) originally read:

"(1) *Subject to the provisions of this section the enactments specified in the Second Schedule to this Act are hereby repealed to the extent specified in the third column of that Schedule.*"

Short title and commencement.

49.—(1) This Act may be cited as the Registered Designs Act 1949.

(2) This Act shall come into operation on the first day of January, nineteen hundred and fifty, immediately after the coming into operation of the Patents and Designs Act 1949.

[SCHEDULE A1

GROUNDS FOR REFUSAL OF REGISTRATION IN RELATION TO EMBLEMS ETC.

Grounds for refusal in relation to certain emblems etc.

1.—(1) A design shall be refused registration under this Act if it involves the use of—

(a) the Royal arms, or any of the principal armorial bearings of the Royal arms, or any insignia or device so nearly resembling the Royal arms or any such armorial bearing as to be likely to be mistaken for them or it;

(b) a representation of the Royal crown or any of the Royal flags;

(c) a representation of Her Majesty or any member of the Royal family, or any colourable imitation thereof; or

(d) words, letters or devices likely to lead persons to think that the applicant either has or recently has had Royal patronage or authorisation;

unless it appears to the registrar that consent for such use has been given by or on behalf of Her Majesty or (as the case may be) the relevant member of the Royal family.

(2) A design shall be refused registration under this Act if it involves the use of—

(a) the national flag of the United Kingdom (commonly known as the Union Jack); or

(b) the flag of England, Wales, Scotland, Northern Ireland or the Isle of Man,

and it appears to the registrar that the use would be misleading or grossly offensive.

(3) A design shall be refused registration under this Act if it involves the use of—

(a) arms to which a person is entitled by virtue of a grant of arms by the Crown; or

(b) insignia so nearly resembling such arms as to be likely to be mistaken for them;

unless it appears to the registrar that consent for such use has been given by or on behalf of the person concerned and the use is not in any way contrary to the law of arms.

(4) A design shall be refused registration under this Act if it involves the use of a controlled representation within the meaning of the Olympic Symbol etc. (Protection) Act 1995 unless it appears to the registrar that—

(a) the application is made by the person for the time being appointed under section 1(2) of the Olympic Symbol etc. (Protection) Act 1995 (power of Secretary of State to appoint a person as the proprietor of the Olympics association right); or

(b) consent for such use has been given by or on behalf of the person mentioned in paragraph (a) above.

Grounds for refusal in relation to emblems etc. of Paris Convention countries

2.—(1) A design shall be refused registration under this Act if it involves the use of the flag of a Paris Convention country unless—

(a) the authorisation of the competent authorities of that country has been given for the registration; or

(b) it appears to the registrar that the use of the flag in the manner proposed is permitted without such authorisation.

(2) A design shall be refused registration under this Act if it involves the use of the armorial bearings or any other state emblem of a Paris Convention country which is protected under the Paris Convention unless the authorisation of the competent authorities of that country has been given for the registration.

(3) A design shall be refused registration under this Act if—

(a) the design involves the use of an official sign or hallmark adopted by a Paris Convention country and indicating control and warranty;

(b) the sign or hallmark is protected under the Paris Convention; and

(c) the design could be applied to or incorporated in goods of the same, or a similar, kind as those in relation to which the sign or hallmark indicates control and warranty;

unless the authorisation of the competent authorities of that country has been given for the registration.

(4) The provisions of this paragraph as to national flags and other state emblems, and official signs or hallmarks, apply equally to anything which from a heraldic point of view imitates any such flag or other emblem, or sign or hallmark.

(5) Nothing in this paragraph prevents the registration of a design on the application of a national of a country who is authorised to make use of a state emblem, or official sign or hallmark, of that country, notwithstanding that it is similar to that of another country.

Grounds for refusal in relation to emblems etc. of certain international organisations
3.—(1) This paragraph applies to—
    (a) the armorial bearings, flags or other emblems; and
    (b) the abbreviations and names,
of international intergovernmental organisations of which one or more Paris Convention countries are members.

(2) A design shall be refused registration under this Act if it involves the use of any such emblem, abbreviation or name which is protected under the Paris Convention unless—
    (a) the authorisation of the international organisation concerned has been given for the registration; or
    (b) it appears to the registrar that the use of the emblem, abbreviation or name in the manner proposed—
        (i) is not such as to suggest to the public that a connection exists between the organisation and the design; or
        (ii) is not likely to mislead the public as to the existence of a connection between the user and the organisation.

(3) The provisions of this paragraph as to emblems of an international organisation apply equally to anything which from a heraldic point of view imitates any such emblem.

(4) Nothing in this paragraph affects the rights of a person whose *bona fide* use of the design in question began before 4th January 1962 (when the relevant provisions of the Paris Convention entered into force in relation to the United Kingdom).

Paragraphs 2 and 3: supplementary
4.—(1) For the purposes of paragraph 2 above state emblems of a Paris Convention country (other than the national flag), and official signs or hallmarks, shall be regarded as protected under the Paris Convention only if, or to the extent that—
    (a) the country in question has notified the United Kingdom in accordance with Article 6ter(3) of the Convention that it desires to protect that emblem, sign or hallmark;
    (b) the notification remains in force; and
    (c) the United Kingdom has not objected to it in accordance with Article 6ter(4) or any such objection has been withdrawn.

(2) For the purposes of paragraph 3 above the emblems, abbreviations and names of an international organisation shall be regarded as protected under the Paris Convention only if, or to the extent that—
    (a) the organisation in question has notified the United Kingdom in accordance with Article 6ter(3) of the Convention that it desires to protect that emblem, abbreviation or name;
    (b) the notification remains in force; and
    (c) the United Kingdom has not objected to it in accordance with Article 6ter(4) or any such objection has been withdrawn.

(3) Notification under Article 6ter(3) of the Paris Convention shall have effect only in relation to applications for the registration of designs made more than two months after the receipt of the notification.

Interpretation
5. In this Schedule—
    "a Paris Convention country" means a country, other than the United Kingdom, which is a party to the Paris Convention; and
    "the Paris Convention" means the Paris Convention for the Protection of Industrial Property of 20th March 1883.]

Note: Schedule A1 was inserted by the Registered Designs Regulations 2001 (SI 2001/3949), reg.3, with effect from December 9, 2001.

Section 12   SCHEDULE 1

Provisions as to the Use of Registered Designs for the Services of the Crown and as to the Rights of Third Parties in Respect of Such Use

Use of registered designs for services of the Crown

1.—(1) Notwithstanding anything in this Act, any Government department, and any person authorised in writing by a Government department, may use any registered design for the services of the Crown in accordance with the following provisions of this paragraph.

(2) If and so far as the design has before the date of registration thereof been duly recorded by or applied by or on behalf of a Government department otherwise than in consequence of the communication of the design directly or indirectly by the registered proprietor or any person from whom he derives title, any use of the design by virtue of this paragraph may be made free of any royalty or other payment to the registered proprietor.

(3) If and so far as the design has not been so recorded or applied as aforesaid, any use of the design made by virtue of this paragraph at any time after the date of registration thereof, or in consequence of any such communication as aforesaid, shall be made upon such terms as may be agreed upon, either before or after the use, between the Government department and the registered proprietor with the approval of the Treasury, or as may in default of agreement be determined by the court on a reference under paragraph 3 of this Schedule.

(4) The authority of a Government department in respect of a design may be given under this paragraph either before or after the design is registered and either before or after the acts in respect of which the authority is given are done, and may be given to any person whether or not he is authorised directly or indirectly by the registered proprietor to use the design.

(5) Where any use of a design is made by or with the authority of a Government department under this paragraph, then, unless it appears to the department that it would be contrary to the public interest so to do, the department shall notify the registered proprietor as soon as practicable after the use is begun and furnish him with such information as to the extent of the use as he may from time to time require.

(6) For the purposes of this and the next following paragraph "the services of the Crown" shall be deemed to include—

    (a) the supply to the government of any country outside the United Kingdom, in pursuance of an agreement or arrangement between Her Majesty's Government in the United Kingdom and the government of that country, of [products] required—

        (i) for the defence of that country; or

        (ii) for the defence of any other country whose government is party to any agreement or arrangement with Her Majesty's said Government in respect of defence matters;

    (b) the supply to the United Nations, or the government of any country belonging to that organisation, in pursuance of an agreement or arrangement between Her Majesty's Government and that organisation or government, of [products] required for any armed forces operating in pursuance of a resolution of that organisation or any organ of that organisation;

and the power of a Government department or a person authorised by a Government department under this paragraph to use a design shall include power to sell to any such government or to the said organisation any [products] the supply of which is authorised by this sub-paragraph, and to sell to any person any [products] made in the exercise of the powers conferred by this paragraph which are no longer required for the purpose for which they were made.

(7) The purchaser of any [products] sold in the exercise of powers conferred by this paragraph, and any person claiming through him, shall have power to deal with them in the same manner as if the rights in the registered design were held on behalf of His Majesty.

Note: In sub-paras.(6) and (7), the words in square brackets substituted for the former words "products" by the Registered Design Regulations 2001 (SI 2001/3949), reg.9, Sch.1 para.15 with effect from December 9, 2001. This paragraph was modified by the Visiting Forces and International Headquarters (Application of Law) Order 1999 (SI 1999/1736), art.4, Sch.4 para.1 with effect from June 23, 1999.

Rights of third parties in respect of Crown use

2.—(1) In relation to any use of a registered design, or a design in respect of which an application for registration is pending, made for the services of the Crown—

(a) by a Government department or a person authorised by a Government department under the last foregoing paragraph; or

(b) by the registered proprietor or applicant for registration to the order of a Government department,

the provisions of any licence, assignment or agreement made, whether before or after the commencement of this Act, between the registered proprietor or applicant for registration or any person who derives title from him or from whom he derives title and any person other than a Government department shall be of no effect so far as those provisions restrict or regulate the use of the design, or any model, document or information relating thereto, or provide for the making of payments in respect of any such use, or calculated by reference thereto; and the reproduction or publication of any model or document in connection with the said use shall not be deemed to be an infringement of any copyright or [national unregistered design right] subsisting in the model or document.

(2) Where an exclusive licence granted otherwise than for royalties or other benefits determined by reference to the use of the designs is in force under the registered design then—

(a) in relation to any use of the design which, but for the provisions of this and the last foregoing paragraph, would constitute an infringement of the rights of the licensee, sub-paragraph (3) of the last foregoing paragraph shall have effect as if for the reference to the registered proprietor there were substituted a reference to the licensee; and

(b) in relation to any use of the design by the licensee by virtue of an authority given under the last foregoing paragraph, that paragraph shall have effect as if the said sub-paragraph (3) were omitted.

(3) Subject to the provisions of the last foregoing sub-paragraph, where the registered design or the right to apply for or obtain registration of the design has been assigned to the registered proprietor in consideration of royalties or other benefits determined by reference to the use of the design, then—

(a) in relation to any use of the design by virtue of paragraph 1 of this Schedule, sub-paragraph (3) of that paragraph shall have effect as if the reference to the registered proprietor included a reference to the assignor, and any sum payable by virtue of that sub-paragraph shall be divided between the registered proprietor and the assignor in such proportion as may be agreed upon between them or as may in default or agreement be determined by the court on a reference under the next following paragraph; and

(b) in relation to any use of the design made for the services of the Crown by the registered proprietor to the order of a Government department, sub- paragraph (3) of paragraph 1 of this Schedule shall have effect as if that use were made by virtue of an authority given under that paragraph.

(4) Where, under sub-paragraph (3) of paragraph 1 of this Schedule, payments are required to be made by a Government department to a registered proprietor in respect of any use of a design, any person being the holder of an exclusive licence under the registered design (not being such a licence as is mentioned in sub-paragraph (2) of this paragraph) authorising him to make that use of the design shall be entitled to recover from the registered proprietor such part (if any) of those payments as may be agreed upon between that person and the registered proprietor, or as may in default of agreement be determined by the court under the next following paragraph to be just having regard to any expenditure incurred by that person—

(a) in developing the said design; or

(b) in making payments to the registered proprietor, other than royalties or other payments determined by reference to the use of the design, in consideration of the licence;

and if, at any time before the amount of any such payment has been agreed upon between the Government department and the registered proprietor, that person gives notice in writing of his interest to the department, any agreement as to the amount of that payment shall be of no effect unless it is made with his consent.

(5) In this paragraph "exclusive licence" means a licence from a registered proprietor which confers on the licensee, or on the licensee and persons authorised by him, to the exclusion of all other persons (including the registered proprietor), any right in respect of the registered design.

Note: In sub-para.(1), the words in square brackets substituted for the former words "design right" by the Registered Design Regulations 2001 (SI 2001/3949), reg.9, Sch.1 para.15 with effect from December 9, 2001. This paragraph was modified by the Visiting Forces and International Headquarters (Application of Law) Order 1999 (SI 1999/1736), art.4, Sch.4 para.1 with effect from June 23, 1999.

Compensation for loss of profit

2A.—(1) Where Crown use is made of a registered design, the government department concerned shall pay—

(a) to the registered proprietor, or

(b) if there is an exclusive licence in force in respect of the design, to the exclusive licensee,

compensation for any loss resulting from his not being awarded a contract to supply the [products] to which the design is applied [or in which it is incorporated].

(2) Compensation is payable only to the extent that such a contract could have been fulfilled from his existing manufacturing capacity; but is payable notwithstanding the existence of circumstances rendering him ineligible for the award of such a contract.

(3) In determining the loss, regard shall be had to the profit which would have been made on such a contract and to the extent to which any manufacturing capacity was under-used.

(4) No compensation is payable in respect of any failure to secure contracts for the supply of [products] to which the design is applied [or in which it is incorporated] otherwise than for the services of the Crown.

(5) The amount payable under this paragraph shall, if not agreed between the registered proprietor or licensee and the government department concerned with the approval of the Treasury, be determined by the court on a reference under paragraph 3; and it is in addition to any amount payable under paragraph 1 or 2 of this schedule.

(6) In this paragraph—

"Crown use", in relation to a design, means the doing of anything by virtue of paragraph 1 which would otherwise be an infringement of the right in the design; and

"the government department concerned", in relation to such use, means the government department by whom or on whose authority the act was done.

Note: In sub-paras.(1) and (4), the word in the first set of square brackets substituted for the former word "articles" and the words in the second set of square brackets inserted by the Registered Design Regulations 2001 (SI 2001/3949), reg.9, Sch.1, para.15 with effect from December 9, 2001. This paragraph was modified by the Visiting Forces and International Headquarters (Application of Law) Order 1999 (SI 1999/1736), art.4, Sch.4, para.1 with effect from June 23, 1999.

Reference of disputes as to Crown use

3.—(1) Any dispute as to—

(a) the exercise by a Government department, or a person authorised by a Government department, of the powers conferred by paragraph 1 of this Schedule,

(b) terms for the use of a design for the services of the Crown under that paragraph,

(c) the right of any person to receive any part of a payment made under paragraph 1(3), or

    (d) the right of any person to receive a payment under paragraph 2A,

may be referred to the court by either party to the dispute.

    (2) In any proceedings under this paragraph to which a Government department are a party, the department may—

        (a) if the registered proprietor is a party to the proceedings [and the department are a relevant person within the meaning of section 20 of this Act], apply for [invalidation] of the registration of the design upon any ground upon which the registration of a design may be [declared invalid] on an application to the court under section twenty of this Act;

        (b) in any case [and provided that the department would be the relevant person within the meaning of section 20 of this Act if they had made an application on the grounds for invalidity being raised], put in issue the validity of the registration of the design without applying for its [invalidation].

    (3) If in such proceedings as aforesaid any question arises whether a design has been recorded or applied as mentioned in paragraph 1 of this Schedule, and the disclosure of any document recording the design, or of any evidence of the application thereof, would in the opinion of the department be prejudicial to the public interest, the disclosure may be made confidentially to counsel for the other party or to an independent expert mutually agreed upon.

    (4) In determining under this paragraph any dispute between a Government department and any person as to terms for the use of a design for the services of the Crown, the court shall have regard to any benefit or compensation which that person or any person from whom he derives title may have received or may be entitled to receive, directly or indirectly from any Government department in respect of the design in question.

    (5) In any proceedings under this paragraph the court may at any time order the whole proceedings or any question or issue of fact arising therein to be referred to a special or official referee or an arbitrator on such terms as the court may direct; and references to the court in the foregoing provisions of this paragraph shall be construed accordingly.

    Note: In sub-para.2(1)(a), the words in the first set of square brackets inserted; the word in the second set of square brackets was substituted for the former word "cancellation"; the word in the third set of square brackets was substituted for the former word "cancelled" and in subs.(2)(b) the words in the first set of square brackets inserted; the word in the second set of square brackets was substituted for the former word "cancellation" by the Registered Design Regulations 2001 (SI 2001/3949), reg.9, Sch.1, para.15 with effect from December 9, 2001. This paragraph was modified by the Visiting Forces and International Headquarters (Application of Law) Order 1999 (SI 1999/1736), art.4, Sch.4 para.1 with effect from June 23, 1999.

Special provisions as to Crown use during emergency

    4.—(1) During any period of emergency within the meaning of this paragraph, the powers exercisable in relation to a design by a Government department, or a person authorised by a Government department under paragraph 1 of this Schedule shall include power to use the design for any purpose which appears to the department necessary or expedient—

        (a) for the efficient prosecution of any war in which His Majesty may be engaged;

        (b) for the maintenance of supplies and services essential to the life of the community;

        (c) for securing a sufficiency of supplies and services essential to the well-being of the community;

        (d) for promoting the productivity of industry, commerce and agriculture;

        (e) for fostering and directing exports and reducing imports, or imports of any classes, from all or any countries and for redressing the balance of trade;

        (f) generally for ensuring that the whole resources of the community are available for use, and are used, in a manner best calculated to serve the interests of the community; or

        (g) for assisting the relief of suffering and the restoration and distribution of essential supplies and services in any part of His Majesty's dominions or any foreign countries that are in grave distress as the result of war;

and any reference in this Schedule to the services of the Crown and shall be construed as including a reference to the purposes aforesaid.

(2) In this paragraph the expression "period of emergency" means a period beginning on such date as may be declared by Order in Council to be the commencement, and ending on such date as may be so declared to be the termination, of a period of emergency for the purposes of this paragraph.

(3) No Order in Council under this paragraph shall be submitted to Her Majesty unless a draft of it has been laid before and approved by a resolution of each House of Parliament.

SCHEDULE 2

[...]

Note: Repealed by the Copyright, Designs and Patents Act 1988 (c.48) Sch.3 para.38, Sch.8. Schedule 2 in its original form is not printed here.

B8.ii The Copyright (Industrial Process and Excluded Articles) (No. 2) Order 1989

(SI 1989/1070)

Made	*26th June 1989*
Laid before Parliament	*4th July 1989*
Coming into force	*1st August 1989*

The Secretary of State, in exercise of the powers conferred upon him by section 52(4) of the Copyright, Designs and Patents Act 1988 ("the Act"), hereby makes the following Order:—

1. This Order may be cited as the Copyright (Industrial Process and Excluded Articles) (No. 2) Order 1989 and shall come into force on 1st August 1989.

2. An article is to be regarded for the purposes of section 52 of the Act (limitation of copyright protection for design derived from artistic work) as made by an industrial process if—

(a) it is one of more than fifty articles which—

(i) all fall to be treated for the purposes of Part I of the Act as copies of a particular artistic work, but

(ii) do not all together constitute a single set of articles as defined in section 44(1) of the Registered Designs Act 1949; or

(b) it consists of goods manufactured in lengths or pieces, not being hand-made goods.

3.—(1) There are excluded from the operation of section 52 of the Act—

(a) works of sculpture, other than casts or models used or intended to be used as models or patterns to be multiplied by any industrial process;

(b) wall plaques, medals and medallions; and

(c) printed matter primarily of a literary or artistic character, including book jackets, calendars, certificates, coupons, dress-making patterns, greetings cards, labels, leaflets, maps, plans, playing cards, postcards, stamps, trade advertisements, trade forms and cards, transfers and similar articles.

(2) Nothing in article 2 of this Order shall be taken to limit the meaning of "industrial process" in paragraph (1)(a) of this article.

4. The Copyright (Industrial Designs) Rules 1957[i] and the Copyright (Industrial Process and Excluded Articles) Order 1989[ii] are hereby revoked.

B8.iii The Design Right (Proceedings before Comptroller) Rules 1989

(SI 1989/1130)

Made	*4th July 1989*
Laid before Parliament	*10th July 1989*
Coming into force	*1st August 1989*

The Secretary of State, in exercise of the powers conferred upon him by section 250 of the Copyright, Designs and Patents Act 1988, with the consent of the Treasury pursuant to subsection (3) of that section as to the fees prescribed under these Rules, and after consultation with the Council on Tribunals in accordance with section 10(1) of the Tribunal and Inquiries Act 1971, hereby makes the following Rules:

Citation and commencement

1. These Rules may be cited as the Design Right (Proceedings before Comptroller) Rules 1989 and shall come into force on 1st August 1989.

Interpretation

2.—(1) In these Rules, unless the context otherwise requires—
"the Act" means the Copyright, Designs and Patents Act 1988;
"applicant" means a person who has referred a dispute or made an application to the Comptroller;
"application" means an application to the Comptroller to settle or vary the terms of a licence of right or to adjust the terms of a licence;
"dispute" means a dispute as to any of the matters referred to in rule 3(1); and
"proceedings" means proceedings before the Comptroller in respect of a dispute or application.

(2) A rule or schedule referred to by number means the rule or schedule so numbered in these Rules; and a requirement under these Rules to use a form set out in Schedule 1 is satisfied by the use either of a replica of that form or of a form which contains the information required by the form set out in the said Schedule and which is acceptable to the Comptroller.

Proceedings in respect of a dispute

3.—(1) Proceedings under section 246 of the Act in respect of a dispute as to—
(a) the subsistence of design right,
(b) the term of design right, or
(c) the identity of the person in whom design right first vested,
shall be commenced by the service by the applicant on the Comptroller of a notice in Form 1 in Schedule 1. There shall be served with that notice a statement in duplicate setting out the name and address of the other party to the dispute (hereinafter in this rule referred to as the respondent), the issues in dispute, the applicant's case and the documents relevant to his case.

(2) Within 14 days of the receipt of the notice the Comptroller shall send a

---

[i] *Editorial Note:* SI 1957/867 (*Copinger*, 12th edn para. 1742).
[ii] *Editorial Note:* SI 1989/1010: made but not laid before Parliament.

copy of the notice, together with a copy of the applicant's statement, to the respondent.

(3) Within 28 days of the receipt by him of the documents referred to in paragraph (2) above, the respondent shall serve on the Comptroller a counter-statement and shall at the same time serve a copy of it on the applicant. Such counter-statement shall set out full particulars of the grounds on which he contests the applicant's case, any issues on which he and the applicant are in agreement and the documents relevant to his case.

(4) Within 21 days of the service on him of the counter-statement, the applicant may serve a further statement on the Comptroller setting out the grounds on which he contests the respondent's case, and shall at the same time serve a copy of it on the respondent.

(5) No amended statement or further statement shall be served by either party except by leave or direction of the Comptroller.

4.—(1) The Comptroller shall give such directions as to the further conduct of proceedings as he considers appropriate [including directing the party or parties to attend a case management conference or a pre-hearing review or both.]

(2) If a party fails to comply with any direction given under this rule, the Comptroller may in awarding costs take account of such default.

Note: The words in square brackets inserted by the Design Right (Proceedings before Comptroller) (Amendment) Rules 1999 (SI 1999/3195), r.3 with effect from December 22, 1999.

5.—(1) Unless the Comptroller otherwise directs, all evidence in the proceedings shall be by statutory declaration [, witness statement] or affidavit.

(2) Where the Comptroller thinks fit in any particular case to take oral evidence in lieu of or in addition to evidence by statutory declaration [, witness statement] or affidavit he may so direct and, unless he directs otherwise, shall allow any witness to be cross-examined on his evidence.

(3) A party to the proceedings who desires to make oral representations shall so notify the Comptroller and the Comptroller shall, unless he and the parties agree to a shorter period, give at least 14 days' notice of the time and place of the hearing to the parties.

(4) If a party intends to refer at a hearing to any document not already referred to in the proceedings, he shall, unless the Comptroller and the other party agree to a shorter period, give 14 days' notice of his intention, together with particulars of every document to which he intends to refer, to the Comptroller and the other party.

(5) At any stage of the proceedings the Comptroller may direct that such documents, information or evidence as he may require shall be filed within such time as he may specify.

(6) The hearing of any proceedings, or part of proceedings, under this rule shall be in public, unless the Comptroller, after consultation with the parties, otherwise directs.

[(7) The Comptroller may give a direction as he thinks fit in any particular case that evidence shall be given by affidavit or statutory declaration instead of or in addition to a witness statement.

(8) Where in proceedings before the Comptroller, a party adduces evidence of a statement made by a person otherwise than while giving oral evidence in the proceedings and does not call that person as a witness, the Comptroller may, if he thinks fit, permit any other party to the proceedings to call that person as a witness and cross-examine him on the statement as if he had been called by the first-mentioned party and as if the statement were his evidence in chief.]

Note: The words in square brackets in sub-rules (1) and (2) and sub-rules (7) and (8) inserted by the Design Right (Proceedings before Comptroller) (Amendment) Rules 1999 (SI 1999/3195), r.4 with effect from December 22, 1999.

6.—(1) Any party to the proceedings may appear in person or be represented by counsel or a solicitor (of any part of the United Kingdom) or, subject to paragraph (4) below, a patent [attorney] or any other person whom he desires to represent him.

(2) Anything required or authorised by these Rules to be done by or in relation to any person may be done by or in relation to his agent.

(3) Where after a person has become a party to the proceedings he appoints an agent for the first time or appoints an agent in substitution for another, the newly appointed agent shall give written notice of his appointment to the Comptroller and to every other party to the proceedings.

(4) The Comptroller may refuse to recognise as such an agent in respect of any proceedings before him—

> (a) a person who has been convicted of an offence under section 88 of the Patents Act 1949 or section 114 of the Patents Act 1977 [or section 276 of the Act];
>
> (b) [a person] whose name has been erased from and not restored to, or who is suspended from, the register of patent [attorneys] (kept [in accordance with] [section 275 of the Act]) on the ground of misconduct;
>
> (c) a person who is found by the Secretary of State to have been guilty of such conduct as would, in the case of [a person] registered in the register of patent [attorneys], render [the person] liable to have [the person's] name erased from the register on the ground of misconduct;
>
> (d) a partnership or body corporate of which one of the partners or directors is a person whom the Comptroller could refuse to recognise under sub-paragraphs (a), (b) or (c) above.

Note: The words in square brackets in r. 6(1), (4)(b) and (4)(c) substituted by the Legal Services Act 2007 (Consequential Amendments) Order 2009 (SI 2009/3348) art. 8, with effect from January 1, 2010.

7.—(1) A person who claims to have a substantial interest in a dispute in respect of which proceedings have been commenced may apply to the Comptroller to be made a party to the dispute in Form 2 in Schedule 1, supported by a statement of his interest. He shall serve a copy of his application, together with his statement, on every party to the proceedings.

(2) The Comptroller shall, upon being satisfied of the substantial interest of that person in the dispute, grant the application and shall give such directions or further directions under rule 4(1) as may be necessary to enable that person to participate in the proceedings as a party to the dispute.

8. A party (including a person made a party to the proceedings under rule 7) may at any time before the Comptroller's decision withdraw from the proceedings by serving a notice to that effect on the Comptroller and every other party to the proceedings, but such withdrawal shall be without prejudice to the Comptroller's power to make an order as to the payment of costs incurred up to the time of service of the notice.

9. After hearing the party or parties desiring to be heard, or if none of the parties so desires, then without a hearing, the Comptroller shall decide the dispute and notify his decision to the parties, giving written reasons for his decision if so required by any party.

Proceedings in respect of application to settle terms of licence of right or adjust terms of licence

10.—(1) Proceedings in respect of an application to the Comptroller—

(a) under section 247 of the Act, to settle the terms of a licence available as of right by virtue of section 237 or under an order under section 238 of the Act, or

(b) under paragraph 19(2) of Schedule 1 to the Act, to settle the terms of a licence available as of right in respect of a design recorded or embodied in a design document or model before 1st August 1989, or

(c) brought by virtue of paragraph 19(5) of Schedule 1 to the Act, to adjust the terms of a licence granted before 1st August 1989 in respect of a design referred to in sub-paragraph (b) above,

shall be commenced by the service by the applicant on the Comptroller of a notice in Form 3 in Schedule 1.

(2) There shall be served with the notice a statement in duplicate setting out—

(a) in the case of an application referred to in paragraph (1)(a) or (b) above, the terms of the licence which the applicant requires the Comptroller to settle and, unless the application is one to which rule 13 relates, the name and address of the owner of the design right or, as the case may be, the copyright owner of the design;

(b) in the case of an application referred to in paragraph (1)(c) above, the date and terms of the licence and the grounds on which the applicant requires the Comptroller to adjust those terms and the name and address of the grantor of the licence.

(3) Within 14 days of the receipt of the notice the Comptroller shall send a copy of it, together with a copy of the applicant's statement, to the person (hereinafter in this rule referred to as the respondent) shown in the application as the design right owner, copyright owner or grantor of the licence, as appropriate.

(4) Within 6 weeks of the receipt by him of the notice sent under paragraph (3) above the respondent shall, if he does not agree to the terms of the licence required by the applicant to be settled or, as the case may be, adjusted, serve a notice of objection on the Comptroller with a statement setting out the grounds of his objection and at the same time shall serve a copy of the same on the applicant.

(5) Within 4 weeks of the receipt of the notice of objection the applicant may serve on the Comptroller a counter-statement and at the same time serve a copy of it on the respondent.

(6) No amended statement or further statement shall be served by either party except by leave or direction of the Comptroller.

11. Rules 4, 5, 6 and 8 shall apply in respect of proceedings under r.10 as they apply in respect of proceedings under r.3.

12. After hearing the party or parties desiring to be heard, or if none of the parties so desires, then without a hearing, the Comptroller shall decide the application and notify his decision to the parties, giving written reasons for his decision if so required by any party.

Settlement of terms where design right owner unknown

13.—(1) Where a person making an application under rule 10(1)(a) or (b) is unable (after making such inquiries as he considers reasonable) to discover the identity of the design right owner or, as the case may be, the copyright owner, he shall serve with his notice under that rule a statement to that effect, setting out particulars of the inquiries made by him as to the identity of the owner of the right and the results of those inquiries.

(2) The Comptroller may require the applicant to make such further inquiries into the identity of the owner of the right as he thinks fit and, may for that purpose, require him to publish in such a manner as the Comptroller considers appropriate particulars of the application.

(3) The Comptroller shall, upon being satisfied from the applicant's statement or the further inquiries made under paragraph (2) above that the identity of the owner of the right cannot be discovered, consider the application and settle the terms of the licence.

Proceedings in respect of application by design right owner to vary terms of licence

14.—(1) Where the Comptroller has, in settling the terms of the licence under rule 13, ordered that the licence shall be free of any obligation as to royalties or other payments, the design right owner or copyright owner (as the case may be) may serve on the Comptroller a notice in Form 4 in Schedule 1 applying for the terms of the licence to be varied from the date of his application. There shall be served with the notice a statement in duplicate setting out the particulars of the grounds for variation and the terms required to be varied.

(2) Within 14 days of the receipt of the notice the Comptroller shall send a copy of the notice, together with the design right or copyright owner's statement, to the applicant under rule 10 (hereinafter in this rule referred to as the licensee).

(3) The licensee shall, if he does not agree to the terms as required to be varied by the design right or copyright owner, within 6 weeks of the receipt of the notice serve notice of objection on the Comptroller with a statement setting out the grounds of his objection and at the same time shall serve a copy of the same on the design right or copyright owner, as the case may be.

(4) Within 4 weeks of the receipt of the notice of objection the design right or copyright owner may serve on the Comptroller a counter-statement, and at the same time shall serve a copy of it on the licensee.

(5) No amended statement or further statement shall be served by either party except by leave or direction of the Comptroller.

15. Rules 4, 5, 6 and 8 shall apply in respect of proceedings under rule 14 as they apply in respect of proceedings under rule 3.

16. After hearing the party or parties desiring to be heard, or if none of the parties so desires, then without a hearing, the Comptroller shall decide the application and notify his decision to the parties, giving written reasons for his decision if so required by any party.

General

17. Any document filed in any proceedings may, if the Comptroller thinks fit, be amended, and any irregularity in procedure may be rectified by the Comptroller on such terms as he may direct.

18.—(1) Any statutory declaration or affidavit filed in any proceedings shall be made and subscribed as follows—

    (a) in the United Kingdom, before any justice of the peace or any commissioner or other officer authorised by law in any part of the United Kingdom to administer an oath for the purpose of any legal proceedings;

    (b) in any other part of Her Majesty's dominions or in the Republic of Ireland, before any court, judge, justice of the peace or any officer authorised by law to administer an oath there for the purpose of any legal proceedings; and

(c) elsewhere, before a British Minister, or person exercising the functions of a British Minister, or a Consul, Vice-Consul or other person exercising the functions of a British Consul or before a notary public, judge or magistrate.

(2) Any document purporting to have fixed, impressed or subscribed thereto or thereon the seal or signature of any person authorised by paragraph (1) above to take a declaration may be admitted by the Comptroller without proof of the genuineness of the seal or signature or of the official character of the person or his authority to take the declaration.

(3) In England and Wales, the Comptroller shall, in relation to the giving of evidence (including evidence on oath), the attendance of witnesses and the discovery and production of documents, have all the powers of a judge of the High Court, other than the power to punish summarily for contempt of court.

(4) In Scotland, the Comptroller shall, in relation to the giving of evidence (including evidence on oath), have all the powers which a Lord Ordinary of the Court of Session has in an action before him, other than the power to punish summarily for contempt of court, and, in relation to the attendance of witnesses and the recovery and production of documents, have all the powers of the Court of Session.

[18A. Any witness statement filed under these Rules shall—

(a) be a written statement signed and dated by a person which contains the evidence which the person signing it would be allowed to give orally; and

(b) include a statement by the intended witness that he believes the facts in it are true.]

Note: This rule was inserted by the Design Right (Proceedings before Comptroller) (Amendment) Rules 1999 (SI 1999/3195) r.5 with effect from December 22, 1999.

19. The Comptroller may appoint an adviser to assist him in any proceedings and shall settle the question or instructions to be submitted or given to such an adviser.

20.—[(1) The times or periods prescribed by these Rules for doing any act or taking any proceedings thereunder may be extended or shortened by the Comptroller if he thinks fit, upon such notice and upon such terms as he may direct, and an extension may be granted although the time for doing such act or taking such proceedings has already expired.]

(2) Where the last day for the doing of any act falls on a day on which the Patent Office is closed and by reason thereof the act cannot be done on that day, it may be done on the next day on which the Office is open.

Note: Sub-rule (1) was substituted by the Design Right (Proceedings before Comptroller) (Amendment) Rules 1999 (SI 1999/3195), r.6 with effect from December 22, 1999. It formerly provided:

"(1) *The times or periods prescribed by these Rules for doing any act or taking any proceedings thereunder may be extended by the Comptroller if he thinks fit, upon such notice and upon such terms as he may direct, and such extension may be granted although the time for doing such act or taking such proceedings has already expired.*"

21. For the purposes of these Rules the Patent Office shall be open Monday to Friday—

(a) between [9.00 a.m.] and midnight, for the filing of applications, forms and other documents, and

(b) between [9.00 a.m.] and [5.00 p.m.] for all other purposes,
excluding Good Friday, Christmas Day [Tuesday 4th January 2000] and any day specified or proclaimed to be a bank holiday under section 1 of the Banking and Financial Dealings Act 1971.

Note: The times in square brackets in sub-rule (a) and in the first set of square brackets in sub-rule (b) substituted for the former times "10.00 a.m.", the time in second set of square brackets in sub-rule (b) was substituted for the former time "4.00 p.m." and the words in square brackets after "Christmas Day" inserted by the Design Right (Proceedings before Comptroller) (Amendment) Rules 1999 (SI 1999/3195), r.7 with effect from December 22, 1999.

22.—(1) The Comptroller may, in respect of any proceedings, by order award such costs or, in Scotland, such expenses as he considers reasonable and direct how, to what party and from what parties they are to be paid.

(2) Where any applicant or a person making an application under rule 7 neither resides nor carries on business in the United Kingdom or another member State of the European Economic Community the Comptroller may require him to give security for the costs or expenses of the proceedings and in default of such security being given may treat the reference or application as abandoned.

23.—(1) Every person concerned in any proceedings to which these Rules relate shall furnish to the Comptroller an address for service [...], and that address may be treated for all purposes connected with such proceedings as the address of the person concerned.

[(1A) The address for service shall be an address in the United Kingdom, unless in a particular case the comptroller otherwise directs.]

Where any document or part of a document which is in a language other than English is served on the Comptroller or any party to proceedings or filed with the Comptroller in pursuance of these Rules, it shall be accompanied by a translation into English of the document or part, verified to the satisfaction of the Comptroller as corresponding to the original text.

Note: Rule 23(1) was repealed in part and r.23(1A) was inserted by the Patents, Trade Marks and Designs (Address For Service and Time Limits, etc) Rules 2006 (SI 2006/760), r.3, with effect from April 6, 2006.

24. The fees specified in Schedule 2 shall be payable in respect of the matters there mentioned.

Note: These Rules are printed as amended, the amendments being indicated by square brackets. In Rule 6(4) parts (a) and (b) were amended by the Design Right (Proceedings Before Comptroller) (Amendment) Rules 1990 (SI 1990/1453). Schedule 2 is printed as substituted by the Design Right (Proceedings Before Comptroller) (Amendment) Rules 1992 (SI 1992/615); this substitution replaced the version of Schedule 2 previously substituted by the Design Right (Proceedings Before Comptroller) (Amendment) (No. 2) Rules 1990 (SI 1990/1699).

Rules 3(1), 7(1), 10(1) and 14(1)   SCHEDULE 1

FORMS

DESIGN RIGHT FORM 1

SCHEDULE 1   Rules 3(1), 7(1), 10(1) and 14(1)

FORMS

The
Patent
Office

Design Right Form 1

**Reference of dispute
to Comptroller**

For Official Use

Copyright, Designs
& Patents Act 1988

Notes

Please type or write in dark ink using
BLOCK LETTERS. For details of
prescribed fees please contact the
Patent Office.

Rule 3 of the Design Right
(Proceedings before Comptroller)
Rules 1989 is the main rule governing
the completion and filing of this form.

This form must be filed together with a
statement in duplicate setting out the
matters referred to in Rule 3(1).

1. Your reference

2. Please give full name and address of person making the reference.
Name

Address

                              Postcode

ADP number (if known)

3. Please give an address for service in the United Kingdom to which all
correspondence will be sent.
Name

Address

                              Postcode

ADP number (if known)

❶ Identification may be made by
providing drawings, photographs or
other identifying material.

4. Please identify the design which is the subject of the proceedings.

Please mark correct box (es)

5. The dispute to be settled is in respect of :-

the subsistence of the design right ☐

the term of the design right ☐

the identity of the person in whom design right first vested ☐

6. Please give the name and address of the other party to the dispute.
Name

Address

                              Postcode

ADP number (if known)

Please sign here ➤ Signed _____ Date _____
                                                              day   month   year

Reminder
Have you attached   the statement of case in duplicate? ☐

                                  the prescribed fee? ☐

dti
the department for Enterprise

Issued   1989

The
**Patent
Office**

Design Right Form 2

**Application to be
made a party to
proceedings.**

For Official Use

Copyright, Designs
& Patents Act 1988

Notes

Please type or write in dark ink using
BLOCK LETTERS. For details of
prescribed fees please contact the
Patent Office.

Rule 7 of the Design Right
(Proceedings before Comptroller)
Rules 1989 is the main rule governing
the completion and filing of this form.

A statement to show your substantial
interest in the dispute in respect of
which proceedings have been
commenced must accompany this
form. You must also serve a copy of
the form and statement on every party
to the proceedings.

1. Your reference

2. Please give full name and address of person applying to be made a
party to dispute.
Name

Address

                            Postcode

ADP number (if known)

3. Please give an address for service in the United Kingdom to which all
correspondence will be sent.
Name

Address

                            Postcode

ADP number (if known)

4. Please identify the proceedings relating to the dispute in which you
claim to have a substantial interest.

Please sign here ➤   Signed _____ Date _____

                                            day   month   year

Reminder
Have you attached   a statement of your interest? ☐

                                      the prescribed fee? ☐

dti
the department for Enterprise

Issued   1989

DESIGN RIGHT FORM 3

The
Patent Office

Copyright, Designs
& Patents Act 1988

Design Right Form 3

Application to settle terms of Licence of Right or to adjust terms of Licence granted before 1st August 1989

For Official Use

Notes

Please type or write in dark ink using BLOCK LETTERS. For details of prescribed fees please contact the Patent Office.

Rules 10 and 13 of the Design Right (Proceedings before Comptroller) Rules 1989 are the main rules governing the completion and filing of this form.

This form must be filed, by the person requiring the settlement or adjustment of the licence, together with a statement in duplicate setting out the terms required. Where the applicant has been unable to discover the identity of the design right or copyright owner a statement must also be filed setting out the particulars of and result of the inquiries made to try to identify the owner.

❶ Identification may be made by providing drawings, photographs or other identifying material.

❺ If part 6(a) of this form applies, give the name and address of the design right or copyright owner (if known). If part 6(b) applies give the name and address of the grantor of the licence in question.

Please mark correct box

1. Your reference

2. Please give full name and address of applicant.
Name

Address

Postcode
ADP number (if known)

3. Please give an address for service in the United Kingdom to which all correspondence will be sent.
Name

Address

Postcode
ADP number (if known)

4. Please identify the design which is the subject of these proceedings.

5. Please give the name and address of the respondent (see note 5).
Name

Address

Postcode
ADP number (if known)

6. Application is made to the Comptroller:
(a) to settle the terms of a licence for the design which is available as of right by virtue of:

Section 237 ☐

an order under Section 238 ☐

paragraph 19(2) of Schedule 1 ☐

(b) to adjust terms of a licence under paragraph 19(5) of Schedule 1 ☐

Please sign here ➤

Signed _____ Date _____
day month year

Important note
This form is **not** for use by the design right or copyright owner.

dti
the department for Enterprise

Reminder
Have you attached

the prescribed fee? ☐

the statement in duplicate of the terms required ? ☐

a statement of inquiries made to identify the design right or copyright owner (if inquiries unsuccessful)? ☐

Issued 1989

DESIGN RIGHT FORM 4

The Patent Office

Copyright, Designs
& Patents Act 1988

Design Right Form 4

**Application by
Design Right or
Copyright owner to
vary terms of
licence of right.**

For Official Use

Notes

Please type or write in dark ink using BLOCK LETTERS. For details of prescribed fees please contact the Patent Office.

Rule 14 of the Design Right (Proceedings before Comptroller) Rules 1989 is the main rule governing the completion and filing of this form.

This form must be filed together with a statement in duplicate setting out the particulars of the grounds for variation and the terms required to be varied.

1. Your reference

2. Please give full name and address of applicant.
Name

Address

Postcode

ADP number (if known)

3. Please give an address for service in the United Kingdom to which all correspondence will be sent.
Name

Address

Postcode

ADP number (if known)

4. Please identify the licence which is the subject of the application.

5. Please give the name and address of the licence holder.
Name

Address

Postcode

ADP number (if known)

Please sign here ➤

Signed _____ Date _____
day month year

Reminder

Have you attached

a statement in duplicate of the grounds for variation and the terms required? ☐

the prescribed fee? ☐

dti
the department for Enterprise

Issued 1989

Rule 24

[SCHEDULE 2

FEES

1. On reference of dispute (Form 1) under rule 3(1)	£65
2. On application (Form 2) under rule 7(1)	£40
3. On application (Form 3) under rule 10(1)	£65
4. On application (Form 4) under rule 14(1)	£65]

B8.iv The Registered Designs Regulations 2001

(SI 2001/3949)

Made   *8th December 2001*

Coming into force   *9th December 2001*

Whereas a draft of the following Regulations has been approved by resolution of each House of Parliament:

Now, therefore, the Secretary of State, being designated for the purposes of section 2(2) of the European Communities Act 1972] in relation to measures relating to the legal protection of designs, in exercise of the powers conferred on her by the said section 2(2) hereby makes the following Regulations:

Citation, commencement and extent

1.—(1) These Regulations may be cited as the Registered Designs Regulations 2001 and shall come into force on the day after the day on which they are made.

(2) Subject to paragraph (3), these Regulations extend to England and Wales, Scotland and Northern Ireland.

(3) The amendments made by these Regulations to the Chartered Associations (Protection of Names and Uniforms) Act 1926 do not extend to Northern Ireland.

[...]

Note: Regulations 2–9 are not reprinted in this Work.

Transitional provisions: pending applications

10.—(1) This Regulation applies to applications for registration under the Registered Designs Act 1949 which have been made but not finally determined before the coming into force of these Regulations ("pending applications").

(2) The Act of 1949 as it has effect immediately before the coming into force of these Regulations shall continue to apply in relation to pending applications so far as it relates to the determination of such applications.

(3) Accordingly the amendments and repeals made by these Regulations shall not apply in relation to the determination of such applications.

Transitional provisions: transitional registrations

11.—(1) This Regulation applies to any registration under the Registered Designs Act 1949 which results from the determination of a pending application (within the meaning of Regulation 10).

(2) The Act of 1949 as it has effect immediately before the coming into force of these Regulations shall continue to apply in relation to registrations to which this Regulation applies ("transitional registrations") so far as the Act relates to the cancellation or invalidation of such registrations (other than cancellation by virtue of section 11(3) of that Act).

(3) Accordingly the amendments and repeals made by these Regulations shall, so far as they relate to the cancellation or invalidation of registrations, not apply in relation to transitional registrations.

(4) The amendments and repeals made by these Regulations shall otherwise (and subject to paragraphs (5) to (9) and Regulation 14) apply in relation to transitional registrations.

(5) In the application by virtue of paragraph (4) of the amendments made by Regulation 5, the fact that transitional registrations are in respect of any articles, or sets of articles, shall be disregarded.

(6) The amendments made by Regulation 4 shall not operate so as to determine the dates of registration of designs to which transitional registrations apply; and these dates shall be determined by reference to the Act of 1949 as it has effect immediately before the coming into force of these Regulations.

(7) Where—

(a) any such date of registration for the purposes of calculating the period for which the right in a registered design subsists, or any extension of that period, under section 8 of the Act of 1949 is determined by virtue of section 14(2) of that Act; and

(b) that date is earlier than the date which would otherwise have been the date of registration for those purposes;

the difference between the two dates shall be added to the first period of five years for which the right in the registered design is to subsist.

(8) Any reference in section 8 of the Act of 1949 to a period of five years shall, in the case of any such period which is extended by virtue of paragraph (7), be treated as a reference to the extended period.

(9) The repeal by these Regulations of the proviso in section 4(1) of the Act of 1949 and of the reference to it in section 8 of that Act shall not apply to the right in a design to which a transitional registration applies.

Transitional provisions: post-1989 registrations

12.—(1) This Regulation applies to—

(a) any registration under the Registered Designs Act 1949 which—

(i) has resulted from an application made on or after 1st August 1989 and before the coming into force of these Regulations; and

(ii) has given rise to a right in a registered design which is in force at the coming into force of these Regulations;

(b) any registration under the Act of 1949 which—

(i) has resulted from an application made on or after 1st August 1989 and before the coming into force of these Regulations; and

(ii) has given rise to a right in a registered design which is not in force at the coming into force of these Regulations but which is capable of being treated as never having ceased to be in force by virtue of section 8(4) of the Act of 1949 or of being restored by virtue of sections 8A and 8B of that Act; and

(c) any registration which subsequently ceases to fall within sub-paragraph (b) because the right in the registered design has been treated or restored as mentioned in paragraph (ii) of that sub-paragraph.

(2) The Act of 1949 as it has effect immediately before the coming into force of these Regulations shall continue to apply in relation to registrations to which this Regulation applies ("post-1989 registrations") so far as the Act relates to the cancellation or invalidation of such registrations (other than cancellation by virtue of section 11(3) of that Act and by reference to an expiry of copyright occurring on or after the coming into force of these Regulations).

(3) Accordingly the amendments and repeals made by these Regulations shall, so far as they relate to the cancellation or invalidation of registrations, not apply in relation to post-1989 registrations.

(4) The amendments and repeals made by these Regulations shall otherwise apply (subject to paragraphs (5) to (9) andRegulation 14) in relation to post-1989 registrations.

(5) In the application by virtue of paragraph (4) of the amendments made by Regulation 5, the fact that post-1989 registrations are in respect of any articles, or sets of articles, shall be disregarded.

(6) The amendments made by Regulation 4 shall not operate so as to alter the dates of registration of designs to which post-1989 registrations apply.

(7) Where—

(a) any such date of registration for the purposes of calculating the period for which the right in a registered design subsists, or any extension of that period, under section 8 of the Act of 1949 was determined by virtue of section 14(2) of that Act; and

(b) that date is earlier than the date which would otherwise have been the date of registration for those purposes;

the difference between the two dates shall be added to any period of five years which is current on the coming into force of these Regulations or, if no such period is current but a subsequent extension or restoration is effected under section 8, or sections 8A and 8B, of the Act of 1949, to the period resulting from that extension or restoration.

(8) Any reference in section 8 of the Act of 1949 to a period of five years shall, in the case of any such period which is extended by virtue of paragraph (7), be treated as a reference to the extended period.

(9) The repeal by these Regulations of the proviso in section 4(1) of the Act of 1949 and the reference to it in section 8 of that Act shall not apply to the right in a design to which a post-1989 registration applies.

Transitional provisions: pre-1989 registrations

13.—(1) This Regulation applies to—

(a) any registration under the Registered Designs Act 1949 which—

   (i) has resulted from an application made before 1st August 1989; and

   (ii) has given rise to a copyright in a registered design which is in force at the coming into force of these Regulations;

(b) any registration under the Act of 1949 which—

   (i) has resulted from an application made before 1st August 1989; and

   (ii) has given rise to a copyright in a registered design which is not in force at the coming into force of these Regulations but which would be capable of coming back into force by virtue of an extension of the period of copyright under section 8(2) of the Act of 1949 if that provision were amended as set out in paragraph (8); and

(c) any registration which subsequently ceases to fall within sub-paragraph (b) because the copyright in the registered design has come back into force by virtue of an extension of the period of copyright under section 8(2) of the Act of 1949 as amended by paragraph (8).

(2) Subject as follows, the amendments and repeals made by these Regulations shall not apply to any provision of the Act of 1949 which only has effect in relation to applications for registration made before 1st August 1989 or any registrations resulting from such applications.

(3) Any such provision and any other provision of the Act of 1949 as it has effect immediately before the coming into force of these Regulations in relation to registrations which fall within paragraph (1) ("pre-1989 registrations") shall continue to apply so far as it relates to the cancellation or invalidation of pre-1989 registrations (other than cancellation by virtue of section 11(3) of that Act and by reference to an expiry of copyright occurring on or after the coming into force of these Regulations).

(4) Accordingly the amendments and repeals made by these Regulations shall, so far as they relate to the cancellation or invalidation of registrations, not apply in relation to pre-1989 registrations.

(5) The amendments and repeals made by these Regulations shall otherwise apply (subject to paragraphs (2) and (9) to (12) and Regulation 14) in relation to pre-1989 registrations.

(6) Amendments and repeals corresponding to the amendments and repeals made by these Regulations (other than those relating to the cancellation or invalidation of registrations) shall be treated as having effect, with necessary modifications and subject to Regulation 14, in relation to any provision of the Act of 1949 which only has effect in relation to applications for registration made before 1st August 1989 or any registrations resulting from such applications.

(7) In the application by virtue of paragraph (6) of amendments corresponding to those made by Regulation 5, the fact that pre-1989 registrations are in respect of any articles, or sets of articles, shall be disregarded.

(8) In section 8(2) of the Act of 1949 as it has effect in relation to pre-1989 registrations (period of copyright)—

(a) after the words "second period", where they appear for the second time, there shall be inserted "and for a fourth period of five years from the expiration of the third period and for a fifth period of five years from the expiration of the fourth period";

(b) after the words "second or third" there shall be inserted "or fourth or fifth"; and

(c) after the words "second period", where they appear for the third time, there shall be inserted "or the third period or the fourth period".

(9) The amendments made by Regulation 4 shall not operate so as to alter the dates of registration of designs to which pre-1989 registrations apply.

(10) Where—

(a) the date of registration for the purposes of calculating the period of copyright, or any extension of that period, under section 8(2) of the Act of 1949 as it has effect in relation to pre-1989 registrations was determined by virtue of section 14(2) of that Act; and

(b) that date is earlier than the date which would otherwise have been the date of registration for those purposes;

the difference between the two dates shall be added to any period of five years which is current on the coming into force of these Regulations or, if no such period is current but a subsequent extension is effected under section 8 of the Act of 1949 as amended by paragraph (8), to the period resulting from that extension.

(11) Any reference in section 8(2) of the Act of 1949 as amended by paragraph (8) to a period of five years shall, in the case of any such period which is extended by virtue of paragraph (10), be treated as a reference to the extended period.

(12) The repeal by these Regulations of the proviso in section 4(1) of the Act of 1949 shall not apply to the right in a design to which a pre-1989 registration applies.

Other transitional provisions

14.—(1) Any licence which—

(a) permits anything which would otherwise be an infringement under the Registered Designs Act 1949 of the right in a registered design or the copyright in a registered design; and

(b) was granted by the registered proprietor of the design, or under section 10 or 11A of the Act of 1949, before the coming into force of these Regulations,

shall continue in force, with necessary modifications, on or after the making of these Regulations.

(2) In determining the effect of any such licence on or after the coming into force of these Regulations, regard shall be had to the purpose for which the licence was granted; and, in particular, a licence granted for the full term or

extent of the right in a registered design or the copyright in a registered design shall be treated as applying, subject to its other terms and conditions, to the full term or extent of that right as extended by virtue of these Regulations.

(3) The right in a registered design conferred by virtue of these Regulations in relation to registrations to which Regulation 11, 12 or 13 applies shall not enable the registered proprietor to prevent any person from continuing to carry out acts begun by him before the coming into force of these Regulations and which, at that time, the registered proprietor or, in the case of registrations to which Regulation 11 applies, a registered proprietor would have been unable to prevent.

(4) The right in a registered design conferred by virtue of these Regulations in relation to registrations to which Regulation 12 or 13 applies shall, in particular, not apply in relation to infringements committed in relation to those registrations before the coming into force of these Regulations.

(5) The repeals by these Regulations in section 5 of the Registered Designs Act 1949 shall not apply in relation to any evidence filed in support of an application made before the coming into force of these Regulations.

(6) The amendments and repeals made by these Regulations in section 22 of the Act of 1949 (other than the amendment to the proviso in subsection (2) of that section) shall not apply in relation to any registration which has resulted from an application made before the coming into force of these Regulations.

(7) The amendment to the proviso in section 22(2) of the Act of 1949 shall not apply where—

(a) the registration of the first-mentioned design resulted from an application made before the coming into force of these Regulations; and

(b) the application for the registration of the other design was also made before the coming into force of these Regulations.

(8) The amendments and repeals made by these Regulations in section 35 of the Act of 1949 shall not apply in relation to any offences committed before the coming into force of these Regulations.

(9) The repeal by these Regulations of provisions in section 44 of the Act of 1949 which relate to the meaning of a set of articles shall not apply so far as those provisions are required for the purposes of paragraph 6(2)(a) of Schedule 1 to the Copyright, Designs and Patents Act 1988.

(10) Any amendment or repeal by these Regulations of a provision in section 44 of the Act of 1949 or in any enactment other than the Act of 1949 shall not apply so far as that provision is required for the purposes of any other transitional provision made by these Regulations.

(11) The Act of 1949 as it has effect immediately before the coming into force of these Regulations shall continue to apply in relation to former registrations, whose registration resulted from an application made before the coming into force of these Regulations, so far as the Act relates to the cancellation or invalidation of such registrations.

(12) Paragraph (13) applies in relation to any registration to which Regulation 11, 12 or 13 applies which is in respect of any features of shape, configuration, pattern or ornament which do not fall within the new definition of "design" inserted into section 1 of the Act of 1949 by Regulation 2 of these Regulations.

(13) The Act of 1949 shall, so far as it applies in relation to any such registration, apply as if the features concerned were included within the new definition of "design" in that Act.

[...]

Note: Schedules 1 and 2 are not reprinted in this Work.

Note: For the equivalent SI in relation to the Isle of Man, see the Registered Designs (Isle of Man) Order 2001 (SI 2001/3678).

B8.v The Registered Designs Regulations 2003

(SI 2003/ 550)

Made	*6th March 2003*
Laid before Parliament	*7th March 2003*
Coming into force	*1st April 2003*

The Secretary of State, being designated for the purposes of section 2(2) of the European Communities Act 1972 in relation to measures relating to the legal protection of designs, in exercise of powers conferred on her by the said section 2(2) hereby makes the following Regulations:

Citation, commencement and extent

1.—(1) These Regulations may be cited as the Registered Designs Regulations 2003 and shall come into force on 1st April 2003.

(2) These Regulations extend to England and Wales, Scotland and Northern Ireland.

Amendment to the Registered Designs Act 1949

2. [Amendments have been taken into the Act]

Transitional provisions: pending applications

3.—(1) This Regulation applies to applications for registration under the Act that have been made after the coming into force of the Registered Designs Regulations 2001 ("2001 Regulations") and before the coming into force of these Regulations but that have not been finally determined before the coming into force of these Regulations ("pending applications").

(2) The Act as it has effect immediately before the coming into force of these Regulations shall continue to apply in relation to pending applications.

(3) Accordingly the amendments made by these Regulations shall not apply in relation to such applications.

Transitional provisions: transitional registrations

4.—(1) This Regulation applies to any registration under the Act that results from the determination of a pending application (within the meaning of Regulation 3).

(2) The Act as it has effect immediately before the coming into force of these Regulations shall continue to apply in relation to registrations to which this Regulation applies ("transitional registrations").

(3) Accordingly the amendments made by these Regulations shall not apply in relation to transitional registrations.

Transitional provisions: resulting registrations

5.—(1) This Regulation applies to any registration made under the Act before the coming into force of these Regulations that results from the determination of an application made under the Act after the coming into force of the 2001 Regulations.

(2) The Act as it has effect immediately before the coming into force of these Regulations shall continue to apply in relation to registrations to which this Regulation applies ("resulting registrations").

(3) Accordingly the amendments made by these Regulations shall not apply in relation to resulting registrations.

B8.vi The Designs (Convention Countries) Order 2007

(SI 2007/ 277)

Made   *7th February 2007*
Coming into force   *6th April 2007*

At the Court at Buckingham Palace, the 7th day of February 2007

Present,

The Queen's Most Excellent Majesty in Council

Her Majesty, by and with the advice of Her Privy Counsel, in exercise of the powers conferred upon Her by sections 13(1) and 37(5) of the Registered Designs Act 1949 makes the following Order:

1.—(1) This Order may be cited as the Designs (Convention Countries) Order 2007 and shall come into force on 6th April 2007.

(2) The Designs (Convention Countries) Order 2006 is revoked.

2. The countries specified in the Schedule are declared to be convention countries for the purposes of all the provisions of the Registered Designs Act 1949.

Christine Cook
Deputy Clerk of the Privy Council

Article 2   SCHEDULE

CONVENTION COUNTRIES

Albania
Algeria
Andorra
Angola
Antigua and Barbuda
Argentina
Armenia
Australia
Austria
Azerbaijan
Bahamas
Bahrain
Bangladesh
Barbados
Belarus
Belgium
Belize
Benin
Bhutan
Bolivia
Bosnia and Herzegovina
Botswana
Brazil
Brunei Darussalam
Bulgaria
Burkina Faso
Burundi
Cambodia
Cameroon
Canada
[Cape Verde]

Central African Republic
Chad
Chile
China
Columbia
Comoros
Congo
Congo, Democratic Republic of the
Costa Rica
Cote d'Ivoire
Croatia
Cuba
Cyprus
Czech Republic
Denmark
Djibouti
Dominica
Dominican Republic
Ecuador
Egypt
El Salvador
Equatorial Guinea
Estonia
Faeroe Islands
Fiji
Finland
France (including overseas Departments and Territories)
Gabon
Gambia
Georgia
Germany
Ghana
Greece
Grenada
Guatemala
Guinea
Guinea-Bissau
Guyana
Haiti
Holy See
Honduras
Hong Kong
Hungary
Iceland
India
Indonesia
Iran, Islamic Republic of
Iraq
Ireland
Israel
Italy
Jamaica
Japan
Jordan
Kazakhstan
Kenya
Korea, Democratic People's Republic of
Korea, Republic of
Kuwait
Kyrgyzstan

Lao People's Democratic Republic
Latvia
Lebanon
Lesotho
Liberia
Libyan Arab Jamahiriya
Liechtenstein
Lithuania
Luxembourg
Macao
Macedonia, Former Yugoslav Republic of
Madagascar
Malawi
Malaysia
Maldives
Mali
Malta
Mauritania
Mauritius
Mexico
Moldova, Republic of
Monaco
Mongolia
Montenegro
Morocco
Mozambique
Myanmar
Namibia
Nepal
Netherlands
Netherlands Antilles and Aruba
New Zealand (including the Cook Islands, Niue and Tokelau)
Nicaragua
Niger
Nigeria
Norway
Oman
Pakistan
Panama
Papua New Guinea
Paraguay
Peru
Philippines
Poland
Portugal
Qatar
Romania
Russian Federation
Rwanda
Saint Kitts and Nevis
Saint Lucia
Saint Vincent and the Grenadines
[Samoa]
San Marino
Sao Tome and Principe
Saudi Arabia
Senegal
Serbia
Seychelles
Sierra Leone

Singapore
Slovakia
Slovenia
Solomon Islands
South Africa
Spain
Sri Lanka
Sudan
Suriname
Swaziland
Sweden
Switzerland
Syrian Arab Republic
Taiwan
Tajikistan
Tanzania, United Republic of
Thailand
Togo
Tonga
Trinidad and Tobago
Tunisia
Turkey
Turkmenistan
Uganda
Ukraine
United Arab Emirates
United States of America (including Puerto Rico and all territories and possessions)
Uruguay
Uzbekistan
[Vanuatu]
Venezuela
Viet Nam
Yemen
Zambia
Zimbabwe

Notes:

(1) "Cape Verde" was added to the list of countries in this Schedule by the Designs (Convention Countries) (Amendment) Order 2009 (SI 2009/2747) art.2, with effect from November 12, 2009.

(2) "Samoa" and "Vanuatu" were added to the list of countries in this Schedule by the Designs (Convention Countries) (Amendment) Order 2013 (SI 2013/539), art.2(2)(a), (b) with effect from April 16, 2013.

B8.vii Directive 98/71/EC of the European Parliament and of the Council of 13 October 1998 on the legal protection of designs

See below, **H.5.**

B8.viii Council Regulation 6/2002 of 12 December 2001 on Community designs[i]

THE COUNCIL OF THE EUROPEAN UNION,

Having regard to the Treaty establishing the European Community, and in particular Article 308 thereof,

---

[i] *Editorial note*: The footnote numbering in the original Regulation is reproduced below.

Having regard to the proposal from the Commission[1],

Having regard to the opinion of the European Parliament[2],

Having regard to the opinion of the Economic and Social Committee[3],

Whereas:

(1) A unified system for obtaining a Community design to which uniform protection is given with uniform effect throughout the entire territory of the Community would further the objectives of the Community as laid down in the Treaty.

(2) Only the Benelux countries have introduced a uniform design protection law. In all the other Member States the protection of designs is a matter for the relevant national law and is confined to the territory of the Member State concerned. Identical designs may be therefore protected differently in different Member States and for the benefit of different owners. This inevitably leads to conflicts in the course of trade between Member States.

(3) The substantial differences between Member States' design laws prevent and distort Community-wide competition. In comparison with domestic trade in, and competition between, products incorporating a design, trade and competition within the Community are prevented and distorted by the large number of applications, offices, procedures, laws, nationally circumscribed exclusive rights and the combined administrative expense with correspondingly high costs and fees for the applicant. Directive 98/71/EC of the European Parliament and of the Council of 13 October 1998 on the legal protection of designs[4] contributes to remedying this situation.

(4) The effect of design protection being limited to the territory of the individual Member States whether or not their laws are approximated, leads to a possible division of the internal market with respect to products incorporating a design which is the subject of national rights held by different individuals, and hence constitutes an obstacle to the free movement of goods.

(5) This calls for the creation of a Community design which is directly applicable in each Member State, because only in this way will it be possible to obtain, through one application made to the Office for Harmonisation in the Internal Market (Trade Marks and Design) in accordance with a single procedure under one law, one design right for one area encompassing all Member States.

(6) Since the objectives of the proposed action, namely, the protection of one design right for one area encompassing all the Member States, cannot be sufficiently achieved by the Member States by reason of the scale and the effects of the creation of a Community design and a Community design authority and can therefore, be better achieved at Community level, the Community may adopt measures, in accordance with the principle of subsidiarity as set out in Article 5 of the Treaty. In accordance with the principle of proportionality, as set out in that Article, this Regulation does not go beyond what is necessary in order to achieve those objectives.

(7) Enhanced protection for industrial design not only promotes the contribution of individual designers to the sum of Community excellence in the field, but also encourages innovation and development of new products and investment in their production.

(8) Consequently a more accessible design-protection system adapted to the needs of the internal market is essential for Community industries.

(9) The substantive provisions of this Regulation on design law should be aligned with the respective provisions in Directive 98/71/EC.

---

[1] OJ C 29, 31.1.1994, p. 20 and OJ C 248, 29.8.2000, p. 3.

[2] OJ C 67, 1.3.2001, p. 318.

[3] OJ C 110, 2.5.1995 and OJ C 75, 15.3.2000, p. 35.

[4] OJ L 289, 28.10.1998, p. 28.

(10) Technological innovation should not be hampered by granting design protection to features dictated solely by a technical function. It is understood that this does not entail that a design must have an aesthetic quality. Likewise, the interoperability of products of different makes should not be hindered by extending protection to the design of mechanical fittings. Consequently, those features of a design which are excluded from protection for those reasons should not be taken into consideration for the purpose of assessing whether other features of the design fulfil the requirements for protection.

(11) The mechanical fittings of modular products may nevertheless constitute an important element of the innovative characteristics of modular products and present a major marketing asset, and therefore should be eligible for protection.

(12) Protection should not be extended to those component parts which are not visible during normal use of a product, nor to those features of such part which are not visible when the part is mounted, or which would not, in themselves, fulfil the requirements as to novelty and individual character. Therefore, those features of design which are excluded from protection for these reasons should not be taken into consideration for the purpose of assessing whether other features of the design fulfil the requirements for protection.

(13) Full-scale approximation of the laws of the Member States on the use of protected designs for the purpose of permitting the repair of a complex product so as to restore its original appearance, where the design is applied to or incorporated in a product which constitutes a component part of a complex product upon whose appearance the protected design is dependent, could not be achieved through Directive 98/71/EC. Within the framework of the conciliation procedure on the said Directive, the Commission undertook to review the consequences of the provisions of that Directive three years after the deadline for transposition of the Directive in particular for the industrial sectors which are most affected. Under these circumstances, it is appropriate not to confer any protection as a Community design for a design which is applied to or incorporated in a product which constitutes a component part of a complex product upon whose appearance the design is dependent and which is used for the purpose of the repair of a complex product so as to restore its original appearance, until the Council has decided its policy on this issue on the basis of a Commission proposal.

(14) The assessment as to whether a design has individual character should be based on whether the overall impression produced on an informed user viewing the design clearly differs from that produced on him by the existing design corpus, taking into consideration the nature of the product to which the design is applied or in which it is incorporated, and in particular the industrial sector to which it belongs and the degree of freedom of the designer in developing the design.

(15) A Community design should, as far as possible, serve the needs of all sectors of industry in the Community.

(16) Some of those sectors produce large numbers of designs for products frequently having a short market life where protection without the burden of registration formalities is an advantage and the duration of protection is of lesser significance. On the other hand, there are sectors of industry which value the advantages of registration for the greater legal certainty it provides and which require the possibility of a longer term of protection corresponding to the foreseeable market life of their products.

(17) This calls for two forms of protection, one being a short-term unregistered design and the other being a longer term registered design.

(18) A registered Community design requires the creation and maintenance of a register in which will be registered all those applications which comply with formal conditions and which have been accorded a date of filing. This registra-

tion system should in principle not be based upon substantive examination as to compliance with requirements for protection prior to registration, thereby keeping to a minimum the registration and other procedural burdens on applicants.

(19) A Community design should not be upheld unless the design is new and unless it also possesses an individual character in comparison with other designs.

(20) It is also necessary to allow the designer or his successor in title to test the products embodying the design in the market place before deciding whether the protection resulting from a registered Community design is desirable. To this end it is necessary to provide that disclosures of the design by the designer or his successor in title, or abusive disclosures during a period of 12 months prior to the date of the filing of the application for a registered Community design should not be prejudicial in assessing the novelty or the individual character of the design in question.

(21) The exclusive nature of the right conferred by the registered Community design is consistent with its greater legal certainty. It is appropriate that the unregistered Community design should, however, constitute a right only to prevent copying. Protection could not therefore extend to design products which are the result of a design arrived at independently by a second designer. This right should also extend to trade in products embodying infringing designs.

(22) The enforcement of these rights is to be left to national laws. It is necessary therefore to provide for some basic uniform sanctions in all Member States. These should make it possible, irrespective of the jurisdiction under which enforcement is sought, to stop the infringing acts.

(23) Any third person who can establish that he has in good faith commenced use even for commercial purposes within the Community, or has made serious and effective preparations to that end, of a design included within the scope of protection of a registered Community design, which has not been copied from the latter, may be entitled to a limited exploitation of that design.

(24) It is a fundamental objective of this Regulation that the procedure for obtaining a registered Community design should present the minimum cost and difficulty to applicants, so as to make it readily available to small and medium-sized enterprises as well as to individual designers.

(25) Those sectors of industry producing large numbers of possibly short-lived designs over short periods of time of which only some may be eventually commercialised will find advantage in the unregistered Community design. Furthermore, there is also a need for these sectors to have easier recourse to the registered Community design. Therefore, the option of combining a number of designs in one multiple application would satisfy that need. However, the designs contained in a multiple application may be dealt with independently of each other for the purposes of enforcement of rights, licensing, rights in rem, levy of execution, insolvency proceedings, surrender, renewal, assignment, deferred publication or declaration of invalidity.

(26) The normal publication following registration of a Community design could in some cases destroy or jeopardise the success of a commercial operation involving the design. The facility of a deferment of publication for a reasonable period affords a solution in such cases.

(27) A procedure for hearing actions concerning validity of a registered Community design in a single place would bring savings in costs and time compared with procedures involving different national courts.

(28) It is therefore necessary to provide safeguards including a right of appeal to a Board of Appeal, and ultimately to the Court of Justice. Such a procedure would assist the development of uniform interpretation of the requirements governing the validity of Community designs.

(29) It is essential that the rights conferred by a Community design can be enforced in an efficient manner throughout the territory of the Community.

(30) The litigation system should avoid as far as possible "forum shopping". It is therefore necessary to establish clear rules of international jurisdiction.

(31) This Regulation does not preclude the application to designs protected by Community designs of the industrial property laws or other relevant laws of the Member States, such as those relating to design protection acquired by registration or those relating to unregistered designs, trade marks, patents and utility models, unfair competition or civil liability.

(32) In the absence of the complete harmonisation of copyright law, it is important to establish the principle of cumulation of protection under the Community design and under copyright law, whilst leaving Member States free to establish the extent of copyright protection and the conditions under which such protection is conferred.

(33) The measures necessary for the implementation of this Regulation should be adopted in accordance with Council Decision 1999/468/EC of 28 June 1999 laying down the procedures for the exercise of implementing powers conferred on the Commission[5],

HAS ADOPTED THIS REGULATION:

TITLE I

GENERAL PROVISIONS

Article 1

Community design

1. A design which complies with the conditions contained in this Regulation is hereinafter referred to as a "Community design".

2. A design shall be protected:

(a) by an "unregistered Community design", if made available to the public in the manner provided for in this Regulation;

(b) by a "registered Community design", if registered in the manner provided for in this Regulation.

3. A Community design shall have a unitary character. It shall have equal effect throughout the Community. It shall not be registered, transferred or surrendered or be the subject of a decision declaring it invalid, nor shall its use be prohibited, save in respect of the whole Community. This principle and its implications shall apply unless otherwise provided in this Regulation.

Article 2

Office

The Office for Harmonisation in the Internal Market (Trade Marks and Designs), hereinafter referred to as "the Office", instituted by Council Regulation (EC) No 40/94 of 20 December 1993 on the Community trade mark[6], hereinafter referred to as the "Regulation on the Community trade mark", shall carry out the tasks entrusted to it by this Regulation.

---

[5] OJ L 184, 17.7.1999, p. 23.
[6] OJ L 11, 14.1.1994, p. 1. Regulation as last amended by Regulation (EC) No 3288/94 (OJ L 349, 31.12.1994, p. 83).

TITLE II

THE LAW RELATING TO DESIGNS

SECTION 1

REQUIREMENTS FOR PROTECTION

Article 3

Definitions

Definitions

(a) "design" means the appearance of the whole or a part of a product resulting from the features of, in particular, the lines, contours, colours, shape, texture and/or materials of the product itself and/or its ornamentation;

(b) "product" means any industrial or handicraft item, including inter alia parts intended to be assembled into a complex product, packaging, get-up, graphic symbols and typographic typefaces, but excluding computer programs;

(c) "complex product" means a product which is composed of multiple components which can be replaced permitting disassembly and re-assembly of the product.

Article 4

Requirements for protection

1. A design shall be protected by a Community design to the extent that it is new and has individual character.

2. A design applied to or incorporated in a product which constitutes a component part of a complex product shall only be considered to be new and to have individual character:

(a) if the component part, once it has been incorporated into the complex product, remains visible during normal use of the latter; and

(b) to the extent that those visible features of the component part fulfil in themselves the requirements as to novelty and individual character.

3. "Normal use" within the meaning of paragraph (2)(a) shall mean use by the end user, excluding maintenance, servicing or repair work.

Article 5

Novelty

1. A design shall be considered to be new if no identical design has been made available to the public:

(a) in the case of an unregistered Community design, before the date on which the design for which protection is claimed has first been made available to the public;

(b) in the case of a registered Community design, before the date of filing of the application for registration of the design for which protection is claimed, or, if priority is claimed, the date of priority.

2. Designs shall be deemed to be identical if their features differ only in immaterial details.

Article 6

Individual character

1. A design shall be considered to have individual character if the overall

impression it produces on the informed user differs from the overall impression produced on such a user by any design which has been made available to the public:

(a) in the case of an unregistered Community design, before the date on which the design for which protection is claimed has first been made available to the public;

(b) in the case of a registered Community design, before the date of filing the application for registration or, if a priority is claimed, the date of priority.

2. In assessing individual character, the degree of freedom of the designer in developing the design shall be taken into consideration.

Article 7
Disclosure

1. For the purpose of applying Articles 5 and 6, a design shall be deemed to have been made available to the public if it has been published following registration or otherwise, or exhibited, used in trade or otherwise disclosed, before the date referred to in Articles 5(1)(a) and 6(1)(a) or in Articles 5(1)(b) and 6(1)(b), as the case may be, except where these events could not reasonably have become known in the normal course of business to the circles specialised in the sector concerned, operating within the Community. The design shall not, however, be deemed to have been made available to the public for the sole reason that it has been disclosed to a third person under explicit or implicit conditions of confidentiality.

2. A disclosure shall not be taken into consideration for the purpose of applying Articles 5 and 6 and if a design for which protection is claimed under a registered Community design has been made available to the public:

(a) by the designer, his successor in title, or a third person as a result of information provided or action taken by the designer or his successor in title; and

(b) during the 12-month period preceding the date of filing of the application or, if a priority is claimed, the date of priority.

3. Paragraph 2 shall also apply if the design has been made available to the public as a consequence of an abuse in relation to the designer or his successor in title.

Article 8
Designs dictated by their technical function and designs of interconnections

1. A Community design shall not subsist in features of appearance of a product which are solely dictated by its technical function.

2. A Community design shall not subsist in features of appearance of a product which must necessarily be reproduced in their exact form and dimensions in order to permit the product in which the design is incorporated or to which it is applied to be mechanically connected to or placed in, around or against another product so that either product may perform its function.

3. Notwithstanding paragraph 2, a Community design shall under the conditions set out in Articles 5 and 6 subsist in a design serving the purpose of allowing the multiple assembly or connection of mutually interchangeable products within a modular system.

Article 9
Designs contrary to public policy or morality

A Community design shall not subsist in a design which is contrary to public policy or to accepted principles of morality.

SECTION 2

SCOPE AND TERM OF PROTECTION

Article 10

Scope of protection

1. The scope of the protection conferred by a Community design shall include any design which does not produce on the informed user a different overall impression.

2. In assessing the scope of protection, the degree of freedom of the designer in developing his design shall be taken into consideration.

Article 11

Commencement and term of protection of the unregistered Community design

1. A design which meets the requirements under Section 1 shall be protected by an unregistered Community design for a period of three years as from the date on which the design was first made available to the public within the Community.

2. For the purpose of paragraph 1, a design shall be deemed to have been made available to the public within the Community if it has been published, exhibited, used in trade or otherwise disclosed in such a way that, in the normal course of business, these events could reasonably have become known to the circles specialised in the sector concerned, operating within the Community. The design shall not, however, be deemed to have been made available to the public for the sole reason that it has been disclosed to a third person under explicit or implicit conditions of confidentiality.

Article 12

Commencement and term of protection of the registered Community design

Upon registration by the Office, a design which meets the requirements under Section 1 shall be protected by a registered Community design for a period of five years as from the date of the filing of the application. The right holder may have the term of protection renewed for one or more periods of five years each, up to a total term of 25 years from the date of filing.

Article 13

Renewal

1. Registration of the registered Community design shall be renewed at the request of the right holder or of any person expressly authorised by him, provided that the renewal fee has been paid.

2. The Office shall inform the right holder of the registered Community design and any person having a right entered in the register of Community designs, referred to in Article 72, hereafter referred to as the "register" in respect of the registered Community design, of the expiry of the registration in good time before the said expiry. Failure to give such information shall not involve the responsibility of the Office.

3. The request for renewal shall be submitted and the renewal fee paid within a period of six months ending on the last day of the month in which protection ends. Failing this, the request may be submitted and the fee paid within a further period of six months from the day referred to in the first sentence, provided that an additional fee is paid within this further period.

4. Renewal shall take effect from the day following the date on which the existing registration expires. The renewal shall be entered in the register.

SECTION 3

RIGHT TO THE COMMUNITY DESIGN

Article 14
Right to the Community design

1. The right to the Community design shall vest in the designer or his successor in title.

2. If two or more persons have jointly developed a design, the right to the Community design shall vest in them jointly.

3. However, where a design is developed by an employee in the execution of his duties or following the instructions given by his employer, the right to the Community design shall vest in the employer, unless otherwise agreed or specified under national law.

Article 15
Claims relating to the entitlement to a Community design

1. If an unregistered Community design is disclosed or claimed by, or a registered Community design has been applied for or registered in the name of, a person who is not entitled to it under Article 14, the person entitled to it under that provision may, without prejudice to any other remedy which may be open to him, claim to become recognised as the legitimate holder of the Community design.

2. Where a person is jointly entitled to a Community design, that person may, in accordance with paragraph 1, claim to become recognised as joint holder.

3. Legal proceedings under paragraphs 1 or 2 shall be barred three years after the date of publication of a registered Community design or the date of disclosure of an unregistered Community design. This provision shall not apply if the person who is not entitled to the Community design was acting in bad faith at the time when such design was applied for or disclosed or was assigned to him.

4. In the case of a registered Community design, the following shall be entered in the register:

(a) the mention that legal proceedings under paragraph 1 have been instituted;
(b) the final decision or any other termination of the proceedings;
(c) any change in the ownership of the registered Community design resulting from the final decision.

Article 16
Effects of a judgement on entitlement to a registered Community design

1. Where there is a complete change of ownership of a registered Community design as a result of legal proceedings under Article 15(1), licences and other rights shall lapse upon the entering in the register of the person entitled.

2. If, before the institution of the legal proceedings under Article 15(1) has been registered, the holder of the registered Community design or a licensee has exploited the design within the Community or made serious and effective preparations to do so, he may continue such exploitation provided that he requests within the period prescribed by the implementing regulation a non-exclusive licence from the new holder whose name is entered in the register. The licence shall be granted for a reasonable period and upon reasonable terms.

3. Paragraph 2 shall not apply if the holder of the registered Community design or the licensee was acting in bad faith at the time when he began to exploit the design or to make preparations to do so.

Article 17

Presumption in favour of the registered holder of the design

The person in whose name the registered Community design is registered or, prior to registration, the person in whose name the application is filed, shall be deemed to be the person entitled in any proceedings before the Office as well as in any other proceedings.

Article 18

Right of the designer to be cited

The designer shall have the right, in the same way as the applicant for or the holder of a registered Community design, to be cited as such before the Office and in the register. If the design is the result of teamwork, the citation of the team may replace the citation of the individual designers.

SECTION 4

EFFECTS OF THE COMMUNITY DESIGN

Article 19

Rights conferred by the Community design

1. A registered Community design shall confer on its holder the exclusive right to use it and to prevent any third party not having his consent from using it. The aforementioned use shall cover, in particular, the making, offering, putting on the market, importing, exporting or using of a product in which the design is incorporated or to which it is applied, or stocking such a product for those purposes.

2. An unregistered Community design shall, however, confer on its holder the right to prevent the acts referred to in paragraph 1 only if the contested use results from copying the protected design.

The contested use shall not be deemed to result from copying the protected design if it results from an independent work of creation by a designer who may be reasonably thought not to be familiar with the design made available to the public by the holder.

3. Paragraph 2 shall also apply to a registered Community design subject to deferment of publication as long as the relevant entries in the register and the file have not been made available to the public in accordance with Article 50(4).

Article 20

Limitation of the rights conferred by a Community design

1. The rights conferred by a Community design shall not be exercised in respect of:
(a) acts done privately and for non-commercial purposes;
(b) acts done for experimental purposes;
(c) acts of reproduction for the purpose of making citations or of teaching, provided that such acts are compatible with fair trade practice and do not unduly prejudice the normal exploitation of the design, and that mention is made of the source.

2. In addition, the rights conferred by a Community design shall not be exercised in respect of:

(a) the equipment on ships and aircraft registered in a third country when these temporarily enter the territory of the Community;

(b) the importation in the Community of spare parts and accessories for the purpose of repairing such craft;

(c) the execution of repairs on such craft.

Article 21

Exhaustion of rights

The rights conferred by a Community design shall not extend to acts relating to a product in which a design included within the scope of protection of the Community design is incorporated or to which it is applied, when the product has been put on the market in the Community by the holder of the Community design or with his consent.

Article 22

Rights of prior use in respect of a registered Community design

1. A right of prior use shall exist for any third person who can establish that before the date of filing of the application, or, if a priority is claimed, before the date of priority, he has in good faith commenced use within the Community, or has made serious and effective preparations to that end, of a design included within the scope of protection of a registered Community design, which has not been copied from the latter.

2. The right of prior use shall entitle the third person to exploit the design for the purposes for which its use had been effected, or for which serious and effective preparations had been made, before the filing or priority date of the registered Community design.

3. The right of prior use shall not extend to granting a licence to another person to exploit the design.

4. The right of prior use cannot be transferred except, where the third person is a business, along with that part of the business in the course of which the act was done or the preparations were made.

Article 23

Government use

Any provision in the law of a Member State allowing use of national designs by or for the government may be applied to Community designs, but only to the extent that the use is necessary for essential defence or security needs.

SECTION 5

INVALIDITY

Article 24

Declaration of invalidity

1. A registered Community design shall be declared invalid on application to the Office in accordance with the procedure in Titles VI and VII or by a Community design court on the basis of a counterclaim in infringement proceedings.

2. A Community design may be declared invalid even after the Community design has lapsed or has been surrendered.

3. An unregistered Community design shall be declared invalid by a Community design court on application to such a court or on the basis of a counterclaim in infringement proceedings.

Article 25

Grounds for invalidity

1. A Community design may be declared invalid only in the following cases:
(a) if the design does not correspond to the definition under Article 3(a);
(b) if it does not fulfil the requirements of Articles 4 to 9;
(c) if, by virtue of a court decision, the right holder is not entitled to the Community design under Article 14;
(d) if the Community design is in conflict with a prior design which has been made available to the public after the date of filing of the application or, if priority is claimed, the date of priority of the Community design, and which is protected from a date prior to the said date
   [(i) by a registered Community design or an application for such a design, or
   (ii) by a registered design right of a Member State, or by an application for such a right, or
   (iii) by a design right registered under the Geneva Act of the Hague Agreement concerning the international registration of industrial designs, adopted in Geneva on 2 July 1999, hereinafter referred to as "the Geneva Act", which was approved by Council Decision 954/2006 and which has effect in the Community, or by an application for such a right;]
(e) if a distinctive sign is used in a subsequent design, and Community law or the law of the Member State governing that sign confers on the right holder of the sign the right to prohibit such use;
(f) if the design constitutes an unauthorised use of a work protected under the copyright law of a Member State;
(g) if the design constitutes an improper use of any of the items listed in Article 6ter of the "Paris Convention" for the Protection of Industrial Property hereafter referred to as the "Paris Convention", or of badges, emblems and escutcheons other than those covered by the said Article 6ter and which are of particular public interest in a Member State.

2. The ground provided for in paragraph (1)(c) may be invoked solely by the person who is entitled to the Community design under Article 14.

3. The grounds provided for in paragraph (1)(d), (e) and (f) may be invoked solely by the applicant for or holder of the earlier right.

4. The ground provided for in paragraph (1)(g) may be invoked solely by the person or entity concerned by the use.

5. Paragraphs 3 and 4 shall be without prejudice to the freedom of Member States to provide that the grounds provided for in paragraphs 1(d) and (g) may also be invoked by the appropriate authority of the Member State in question on its own initiative.

6. A registered Community design which has been declared invalid pursuant to paragraph (1)(b), (e), (f) or (g) may be maintained in an amended form, if in that form it complies with the requirements for protection and the identity of the design is retained. "Maintenance" in an amended form may include registration accompanied by a partial disclaimer by the holder of the registered Community design or entry in the register of a court decision or a decision by the Office declaring the partial invalidity of the registered Community design.

Note: The words in square brackets in art.25(1)(d) amended by Council Regulation (EC) No 1891/2006 of December 18, 2006 (OJ L 386/14).

Article 26

Consequences of invalidity

1. A Community design shall be deemed not to have had, as from the outset, the effects specified in this Regulation, to the extent that it has been declared invalid.

2. Subject to the national provisions relating either to claims for compensation for damage caused by negligence or lack of good faith on the part of the holder of the Community design, or to unjust enrichment, the retroactive effect of invalidity of the Community design shall not affect:

  (a) any decision on infringement which has acquired the authority of a final decision and been enforced prior to the invalidity decision;

  (b) any contract concluded prior to the invalidity decision, in so far as it has been performed before the decision; however, repayment, to an extent justified by the circumstances, of sums paid under the relevant contract may be claimed on grounds of equity.

TITLE III

COMMUNITY DESIGNS AS OBJECTS OF PROPERTY

Article 27

Dealing with Community designs as national design rights

1. Unless Articles 28, 29, 30, 31 and 32 provide otherwise, a Community design as an object of property shall be dealt with in its entirety, and for the whole area of the Community, as a national design right of the Member State in which:

  (a) the holder has his seat or his domicile on the relevant date; or

  (b) where point (a) does not apply, the holder has an establishment on the relevant date.

2. In the case of a registered Community design, paragraph 1 shall apply according to the entries in the register.

3. In the case of joint holders, if two or more of them fulfil the condition under paragraph 1, the Member State referred to in that paragraph shall be determined:

  (a) in the case of an unregistered Community design, by reference to the relevant joint holder designated by them by common agreement;

  (b) in the case of a registered Community design, by reference to the first of the relevant joint holders in the order in which they are mentioned in the register.

4. Where paragraphs 1, 2 and 3 do not apply, the Member State referred to in paragraph 1 shall be the Member State in which the seat of the Office is situated.

Article 28

Transfer of the registered Community design

The transfer of a registered Community design shall be subject to the following provisions:

  (a) at the request of one of the parties, a transfer shall be entered in the register and published;

(b) until such time as the transfer has been entered in the register, the successor in title may not invoke the rights arising from the registration of the Community design;

(c) where there are time limits to be observed in dealings with the Office, the successor in title may make the corresponding statements to the Office once the request for registration of the transfer has been received by the Office;

(d) all documents which by virtue of Article 66 require notification to the holder of the registered Community design shall be addressed by the Office to the person registered as holder or his representative, if one has been appointed.

Article 29

Rights in rem on a registered Community design

1. A registered Community design may be given as security or be the subject of rights in rem.

2. On request of one of the parties, the rights mentioned in paragraph 1 shall be entered in the register and published.

Article 30

Levy of execution

1. A registered Community design may be levied in execution.

2. As regards the procedure for levy of execution in respect of a registered Community design, the courts and authorities of the Member State determined in accordance with Article 27 shall have exclusive jurisdiction.

3. On request of one of the parties, levy of execution shall be entered in the register and published.

Article 31

Insolvency proceedings

1. The only insolvency proceedings in which a Community design may be involved shall be those opened in the Member State within the territory of which the centre of a debtor's main interests is situated.

2. In the case of joint proprietorship of a Community design, paragraph 1 shall apply to the share of the joint proprietor.

3. Where a Community design is involved in insolvency proceedings, on request of the competent national authority an entry to this effect shall be made in the register and published in the Community Designs Bulletin referred to in Article 73(1).

Article 32

Licensing

1. A Community design may be licensed for the whole or part of the Community. A licence may be exclusive or non-exclusive.

2. Without prejudice to any legal proceedings based on the law of contract, the holder may invoke the rights conferred by the Community design against a licensee who contravenes any provision in his licensing contract with regard to its duration, the form in which the design may be used, the range of products for which the licence is granted and the quality of products manufactured by the licensee.

3. Without prejudice to the provisions of the licensing contract, the licensee may bring proceedings for infringement of a Community design only if the right

holder consents thereto. However, the holder of an exclusive licence may bring such proceedings if the right holder in the Community design, having been given notice to do so, does not himself bring infringement proceedings within an appropriate period.

4. A licensee shall, for the purpose of obtaining compensation for damage suffered by him, be entitled to intervene in an infringement action brought by the right holder in a Community design.

5. In the case of a registered Community design, the grant or transfer of a licence in respect of such right shall, at the request of one of the parties, be entered in the register and published.

Article 33
Effects vis-à-vis third parties

1. The effects vis-à-vis third parties of the legal acts referred to in Articles 28, 29, 30 and 32 shall be governed by the law of the Member State determined in accordance with Article 27.

2. However, as regards registered Community designs, legal acts referred to in Articles 28, 29 and 32 shall only have effect vis-à-vis third parties in all the Member States after entry in the register. Nevertheless, such an act, before it is so entered, shall have effect vis-à-vis third parties who have acquired rights in the registered Community design after the date of that act but who knew of the act at the date on which the rights were acquired.

3. Paragraph 2 shall not apply to a person who acquires the registered Community design or a right concerning the registered Community design by way of transfer of the whole of the undertaking or by any other universal succession.

4. Until such time as common rules for the Member States in the field of insolvency enter into force, the effects vis-à-vis third parties of insolvency proceedings shall be governed by the law of the Member State in which such proceedings are first brought under the national law or the regulations applicable in this field.

Article 34
The application for a registered Community design as an object of property

1. An application for a registered Community design as an object of property shall be dealt with in its entirety, and for the whole area of the Community, as a national design right of the Member State determined in accordance with Article 27.

2. Articles 28, 29, 30, 31, 32 and 33 shall apply mutatis mutandis to applications for registered Community designs. Where the effect of one of these provisions is conditional upon an entry in the register, that formality shall be performed upon registration of the resulting registered Community design.

TITLE IV

APPLICATION FOR A REGISTERED COMMUNITY DESIGN

SECTION 1

FILING OF APPLICATIONS AND THE CONDITIONS WHICH GOVERN THEM

Article 35
Filing and forwarding of applications

1. An application for a registered Community design shall be filed, at the option of the applicant:

(a) at the Office; or

(b) at the central industrial property office of a Member State; or

(c) in the Benelux countries, at the Benelux Design Office.

2. Where the application is filed at the central industrial property office of a Member State or at the Benelux Design Office, that office shall take all steps to forward the application to the Office within two weeks after filing. It may charge the applicant a fee which shall not exceed the administrative costs of receiving and forwarding the application.

3. As soon as the Office has received an application which has been forwarded by a central industrial property office of a Member State or by the Benelux Design Office, it shall inform the applicant accordingly, indicating the date of its receipt at the Office.

4. No less than 10 years after the entry into force of this Regulation, the Commission shall draw up a report on the operation of the system of filing applications for registered Community designs, accompanied by any proposals for revision that it may deem appropriate.

Article 36

Conditions with which applications must comply

1. An application for a registered Community design shall contain:

(a) a request for registration;

(b) information identifying the applicant;

(c) a representation of the design suitable for reproduction. However, if the object of the application is a two-dimensional design and the application contains a request for deferment of publication in accordance with Article 50, the representation of the design may be replaced by a specimen.

2. The application shall further contain an indication of the products in which the design is intended to be incorporated or to which it is intended to be applied.

3. In addition, the application may contain:

(a) a description explaining the representation or the specimen;

(b) a request for deferment of publication of the registration in accordance with Article 50;

(c) information identifying the representative if the applicant has appointed one;

(d) the classification of the products in which the design is intended to be incorporated or to which it is intended to be applied according to class;

(e) the citation of the designer or of the team of designers or a statement under the applicant's responsibility that the designer or the team of designers has waived the right to be cited.

4. The application shall be subject to the payment of the registration fee and the publication fee. Where a request for deferment under paragraph 3(b) is filed, the publication fee shall be replaced by the fee for deferment of publication.

5. The application shall comply with the conditions laid down in the implementing regulation.

6. The information contained in the elements mentioned in paragraph 2 and in paragraph 3(a) and (d) shall not affect the scope of protection of the design as such.

Article 38

Date of filing

1. The date of filing of an application for a registered Community design shall

be the date on which documents containing the information specified in Article 36(1) are filed with the Office by the applicant, or, if the application has been filed with the central industrial property office of a Member State or with the Benelux Design Office, with that office.

2. By derogation from paragraph 1, the date of filing of an application filed with the central industrial property office of a Member State or with the Benelux Design Office and reaching the Office more than two months after the date on which documents containing the information specified in Article 36(1) have been filed shall be the date of receipt of such documents by the Office.

Article 39

Equivalence of Community filing with national filing

An application for a registered Community design which has been accorded a date of filing shall, in the Member States, be equivalent to a regular national filing, including where appropriate the priority claimed for the said application.

Article 40

Classification

For the purpose of this Regulation, use shall be made of the Annex to the Agreement establishing an International Classification for Industrial Designs, signed at Locarno on 8 October 1968 .

SECTION 2

PRIORITY

Article 41

Right of priority

1. A person who has duly filed an application for a design right or for a utility model in or for any State party to the Paris Convention for the Protection of Industrial Property, or to the Agreement establishing the World Trade Organisation, or his successors in title, shall enjoy, for the purpose of filing an application for a registered Community design in respect of the same design or utility model, a right of priority of six months from the date of filing of the first application.

2. Every filing that is equivalent to a regular national filing under the national law of the State where it was made or under bilateral or multilateral agreements shall be recognised as giving rise to a right of priority.

3. "Regular national filing" means any filing that is sufficient to establish the date on which the application was filed, whatever may be the outcome of the application.

4. A subsequent application for a design which was the subject of a previous first application, and which is filed in or in respect of the same State, shall be considered as the first application for the purpose of determining priority, provided that, at the date of the filing of the subsequent application, the previous application has been withdrawn, abandoned or refused without being open to public inspection and without leaving any rights outstanding, and has not served as a basis for claiming priority. The previous application may not thereafter serve as a basis for claiming a right of priority.

5. If the first filing has been made in a State which is not a party to the Paris Convention, or to the Agreement establishing the World Trade Organisation, paragraphs 1 to 4 shall apply only in so far as that State, according to published findings, grants, on the basis of a filing made at the Office and subject to condi-

tions equivalent to those laid down in this Regulation, a right of priority having equivalent effect.

Article 42

Claiming priority

An applicant for a registered Community design desiring to take advantage of the priority of a previous application shall file a declaration of priority and a copy of the previous application. If the language of the latter is not one of the languages of the Office, the Office may require a translation of the previous application in one of those languages.

Article 43

Effect of priority right

The effect of the right of priority shall be that the date of priority shall count as the date of the filing of the application for a registered Community design for the purpose of Articles 5, 6, 7, 22, 25(1)(d) and 50(1).

Article 44

Exhibition priority

1. If an applicant for a registered Community design has disclosed products in which the design is incorporated, or to which it is applied, at an official or officially recognised international exhibition falling within the terms of the Convention on International Exhibitions signed in Paris on 22 November 1928 and last revised on 30 November 1972, he may, if he files the application within a period of six months from the date of the first disclosure of such products, claim a right of priority from that date within the meaning of Article 43.

2. An applicant who wishes to claim priority pursuant to paragraph 1, under the conditions laid down in the implementing regulation, must file evidence that he has disclosed at an exhibition the products in or to which the design is incorporated or applied.

3. An exhibition priority granted in a Member State or in a third country does not extend the period of priority laid down in Article 41.

TITLE V

REGISTRATION PROCEDURE

Article 45

Examination as to formal requirements for filing

1. The Office shall examine whether the application complies with the requirements laid down in Article 36(1) for the accordance of a date of filing.

2. The Office shall examine whether:

(a) the application complies with the other requirements laid down in Article 36(2), (3), (4) and (5) and, in the case of a multiple application, Article 37(1) and (2);

(b) the application meets the formal requirements laid down in the implementing regulation for the implementation of Articles 36 and 37;

(c) the requirements of Article 77(2) are satisfied;

(d) the requirements concerning the claim to priority are satisfied, if a priority is claimed.

3. The conditions for the examination as to the formal requirements for filing shall be laid down in the implementing regulation.

Article 46

Remediable deficiencies

1. Where, in carrying out the examination under Article 45, the Office notes that there are deficiencies which may be corrected, the Office shall request the applicant to remedy them within the prescribed period.

2. If the deficiencies concern the requirements referred to in Article 36(1) and the applicant complies with the Office's request within the prescribed period, the Office shall accord as the date of filing the date on which the deficiencies are remedied. If the deficiencies are not remedied within the prescribed period, the application shall not be dealt with as an application for a registered Community design.

3. If the deficiencies concern the requirements, including the payment of fees, as referred to in Article 45(2)(a), (b) and (c) and the applicant complies with the Office's request within the prescribed period, the Office shall accord as the date of filing the date on which the application was originally filed. If the deficiencies or the default in payment are not remedied within the prescribed period, the Office shall refuse the application.

4. If the deficiencies concern the requirements referred to in Article 45(2)(d), failure to remedy them within the prescribed period shall result in the loss of the right of priority for the application.

Article 47

Grounds for non-registrability

1. If the Office, in carrying out the examination pursuant to Article 45, notices that the design for which protection is sought:
  (a) does not correspond to the definition under Article 3(a); or
  (b) is contrary to public policy or to accepted principles of morality, it shall refuse the application.

2. The application shall not be refused before the applicant has been allowed the opportunity of withdrawing or amending the application or of submitting his observations.

Article 48

Registration

If the requirements that an application for a registered Community design must satisfy have been fulfilled and to the extent that the application has not been refused by virtue of Article 47, the Office shall register the application in the Community design Register as a registered Community design. The registration shall bear the date of filing of the application referred to in Article 38.

Article 49

Publication

Upon registration, the Office shall publish the registered Community design in the Community Designs Bulletin as mentioned in Article 73(1). The contents of the publication shall be set out in the implementing regulation.

Article 50

Deferment of publication

1. The applicant for a registered Community design may request, when filing

the application, that the publication of the registered Community design be deferred for a period of 30 months from the date of filing the application or, if a priority is claimed, from the date of priority.

2. Upon such request, where the conditions set out in Article 48 are satisfied, the registered Community design shall be registered, but neither the representation of the design nor any file relating to the application shall, subject to Article 74(2), be open to public inspection.

3. The Office shall publish in the Community Designs Bulletin a mention of the deferment of the publication of the registered Community design. The mention shall be accompanied by information identifying the right holder in the registered Community design, the date of filing the application and any other particulars prescribed by the implementing regulation.

4. At the expiry of the period of deferment, or at any earlier date on request by the right holder, the Office shall open to public inspection all the entries in the register and the file relating to the application and shall publish the registered Community design in the Community Designs Bulletin, provided that, within the time limit laid down in the implementing regulation:

(a) the publication fee and, in the event of a multiple application, the additional publication fee are paid;

(b) where use has been made of the option pursuant to Article 36(1)(c), the right holder has filed with the Office a representation of the design.

If the right holder fails to comply with these requirements, the registered Community design shall be deemed from the outset not to have had the effects specified in this Regulation.

5. In the case of multiple applications, paragraph 4 need only be applied to some of the designs included therein.

6. The institution of legal proceedings on the basis of a registered Community design during the period of deferment of publication shall be subject to the condition that the information contained in the register and in the file relating to the application has been communicated to the person against whom the action is brought.

TITLE VI

SURRENDER AND INVALIDITY OF THE REGISTERED COMMUNITY DESIGN

Article 51

Surrender

1. The surrender of a registered Community design shall be declared to the Office in writing by the right holder. It shall not have effect until it has been entered in the register.

2. If a Community design which is subject to deferment of publication is surrendered it shall be deemed from the outset not to have had the effects specified in this Regulation.

3. A registered Community design may be partially surrendered provided that its amended form complies with the requirements for protection and the identity of the design is retained.

4. Surrender shall be registered only with the agreement of the proprietor of a right entered in the register. If a licence has been registered, surrender shall be entered in the register only if the right holder in the registered Community design proves that he has informed the licensee of his intention to surrender. This entry shall be made on expiry of the period prescribed by the implementing regulation.

5. If an action pursuant to Article 14 relating to the entitlement to a registered Community design has been brought before a Community design court, the Office shall not enter the surrender in the register without the agreement of the claimant.

Article 52

Application for a declaration of invalidity

1. Subject to Article 25(2), (3), (4) and (5), any natural or legal person, as well as a public authority empowered to do so, may submit to the Office an application for a declaration of invalidity of a registered Community design.

2. The application shall be filed in a written reasoned statement. It shall not be deemed to have been filed until the fee for an application for a declaration of invalidity has been paid.

3. An application for a declaration of invalidity shall not be admissible if an application relating to the same subject matter and cause of action, and involving the same parties, has been adjudicated on by a Community design court and has acquired the authority of a final decision.

Article 53

Examination of the application

1. If the Office finds that the application for a declaration of invalidity is admissible, the Office shall examine whether the grounds for invalidity referred to in Article 25 prejudice the maintenance of the registered Community design.

2. In the examination of the application, which shall be conducted in accordance with the implementing regulation, the Office shall invite the parties, as often as necessary, to file observations, within a period to be fixed by the Office, on communications from the other parties or issued by itself.

3. The decision declaring the registered Community design invalid shall be entered in the register upon becoming final.

Article 54

Participation in the proceedings of the alleged infringer

1. In the event of an application for a declaration of invalidity of a registered Community design being filed, and as long as no final decision has been taken by the Office, any third party who proves that proceedings for infringement of the same design have been instituted against him may be joined as a party in the invalidity proceedings on request submitted within three months of the date on which the infringement proceedings were instituted.

The same shall apply in respect of any third party who proves both that the right holder of the Community design has requested that he cease an alleged infringement of the design and that he has instituted proceedings for a court ruling that he is not infringing the Community design.

2. The request to be joined as a party shall be filed in a written reasoned statement. It shall not be deemed to have been filed until the invalidity fee, referred to in Article 52(2), has been paid. Thereafter the request shall, subject to any exceptions laid down in the implementing regulation, be treated as an application for a declaration of invalidity.

TITLE VII

APPEALS

Article 55

Decisions subject to appeal

1. An appeal shall lie from decisions of the examiners, the Administration of Trade Marks and Designs and Legal Division and Invalidity Divisions. It shall have suspensive effect.

2. A decision which does not terminate proceedings as regards one of the parties can only be appealed together with the final decision, unless the decision allows separate appeal.

Article 56

Persons entitled to appeal and to be parties to appeal proceedings

Any party to proceedings adversely affected by a decision may appeal. Any other parties to the proceedings shall be parties to the appeal proceedings as of right.

Article 57

Time limit and form of appeal

Notice of appeal must be filed in writing at the Office within two months after the date of notification of the decision appealed from. The notice shall be deemed to have been filed only when the fee for appeal has been paid. Within four months after the date of notification of the decision, a written statement setting out the grounds of appeal must be filed.

Article 58

Interlocutory revision

1. If the department whose decision is contested considers the appeal to be admissible and well founded, it shall rectify its decision. This shall not apply where the appellant is opposed by another party to the proceedings.

2. If the decision is not rectified within one month after receipt of the statement of grounds, the appeal shall be remitted to the Board of Appeal without delay and without comment as to its merits.

Article 59

Examination of appeals

1. If the appeal is admissible, the Board of Appeal shall examine whether the appeal is to be allowed.

2. In the examination of the appeal, the Board of Appeal shall invite the parties, as often as necessary, to file observations, within a period to be fixed by the Board of Appeal, on communications from the other parties or issued by itself.

Article 60

Decisions in respect of appeals

1. Following the examination as to the merits of the appeal, the Board of Appeal shall decide on the appeal. The Board of Appeal may either exercise any power within the competence of the department which was responsible for the

decision appealed against or remit the case to that department for further prosecution.

2. If the Board of Appeal remits the case for further prosecution to the department whose decision was appealed, that department shall be bound by the ratio decidendi of the Board of Appeal, in so far as the facts are the same.

3. The decisions of the Boards of Appeal shall take effect only from the date of expiry of the period referred to in Article 61(5) or, if an action has been brought before the Court of Justice within that period, from the date of rejection of such action.

Article 61

Actions before the Court of Justice

1. Actions may be brought before the Court of Justice against decisions of the Boards of Appeal on appeals.

2. The action may be brought on grounds of lack of competence, infringement of an essential procedural requirement, infringement of the Treaty, of this Regulation or of any rule of law relating to their application or misuse of power.

3. The Court of Justice has jurisdiction to annul or to alter the contested decision.

4. The action shall be open to any party to proceedings before the Board of Appeal adversely affected by its decision.

5. The action shall be brought before the Court of Justice within two months of the date of notification of the decision of the Board of Appeal.

6. The Office shall be required to take the necessary measures to comply with the judgment of the Court of Justice.

TITLE VIII

PROCEDURE BEFORE THE OFFICE

SECTION 1

GENERAL PROVISIONS

Article 62

Statement of reasons on which decisions are based

Decisions of the Office shall state the reasons on which they are based. They shall be based only on reasons or evidence on which the parties concerned have had an opportunity to present their comments.

Article 63

Examination of the facts by the Office of its own motion

1. In proceedings before it the Office shall examine the facts of its own motion. However, in proceedings relating to a declaration of invalidity, the Office shall be restricted in this examination to the facts, evidence and arguments provided by the parties and the relief sought.

2. The Office may disregard facts or evidence which are not submitted in due time by the parties concerned.

Article 64

Oral proceedings

1. If the Office considers that oral proceedings would be expedient, they shall

be held either at the instance of the Office or at the request of any party to the proceedings.

2. Oral proceedings, including delivery of the decision, shall be public, unless the department before which the proceedings are taking place decides otherwise in cases where admission of the public could have serious and unjustified disadvantages, in particular for a party to the proceedings.

Article 65

Taking of evidence

1. In any proceedings before the Office the means of giving or obtaining evidence shall include the following:

(a) hearing the parties;
(b) requests for information;
(c) the production of documents and items of evidence;
(d) hearing witnesses;
(e) opinions by experts;
(f) statements in writing, sworn or affirmed or having a similar effect under the law of the State in which the statement is drawn up.

2. The relevant department of the Office may commission one of its members to examine the evidence adduced.

3. If the Office considers it necessary for a party, witness or expert to give evidence orally, it shall issue a summons to the person concerned to appear before it.

4. The parties shall be informed of the hearing of a witness or expert before the Office. They shall have the right to be present and to put questions to the witness or expert.

Article 66

Notification

The Office shall, as a matter of course, notify those concerned of decisions and summonses and of any notice or other communication from which a time limit is reckoned, or of which those concerned must be notified under other provisions of this Regulation or of the implementing regulation, or of which notification has been ordered by the President of the Office.

Article 67

Restitutio in integrum

1. The applicant for or holder of a registered Community design or any other party to proceedings before the Office who, in spite of all due care required by the circumstances having been taken, was unable to observe a time limit vis-à-vis the Office shall, upon application, have his rights re-established if the non-observance in question has the direct consequence, by virtue of the provisions of this Regulation, of causing the loss of any rights or means of redress.

2. The application must be filed in writing within two months of the removal of the cause of non-compliance with the time limit. The omitted act must be completed within this period. The application shall only be admissible within the year immediately following the expiry of the unobserved time limit. In the case of non-submission of the request for renewal of registration or of non-payment of a renewal fee, the further period of six months provided for in the second sentence of Article 13(3) shall be deducted from the period of one year.

3. The application must state the grounds on which it is based and must set out

the facts on which it relies. It shall not be deemed to be filed until the fee for the re-establishment of rights has been paid.

4. The department competent to decide on the omitted act shall decide upon the application.

5. The provisions of this Article shall not be applicable to the time limits referred to in paragraph 2 and Article 41(1).

6. Where the applicant for or holder of a registered Community design has his rights re-established, he may not invoke his rights vis-à-vis a third party who, in good faith, in the course of the period between the loss of rights in the application for or registration of the registered Community design and publication of the mention of re-establishment of those rights, has put on the market products in which a design included within the scope of protection of the registered Community design is incorporated or to which it is applied.

7. A third party who may avail himself of the provisions of paragraph 6 may bring third party proceedings against the decision re-establishing the rights of the applicant for or holder of the registered Community design within a period of two months as from the date of publication of the mention of re-establishment of those rights.

8. Nothing in this Article shall limit the right of a Member State to grant restitutio in integrum in respect of time limits provided for in this Regulation and to be complied with vis-à-vis the authorities of such State.

Article 68

Reference to general principles

In the absence of procedural provisions in this Regulation, the implementing regulation, the fees regulation or the rules of procedure of the Boards of Appeal, the Office shall take into account the principles of procedural law generally recognised in the Member States.

Article 69

Termination of financial obligations

1. Rights of the Office to the payment of fees shall be barred four years from the end of the calendar year in which the fee fell due.

2. Rights against the Office for the refunding of fees or sums of money paid in excess of a fee shall be barred after four years from the end of the calendar year in which the right arose.

3. The periods laid down in paragraphs 1 and 2 shall be interrupted, in the case covered by paragraph 1, by a request for payment of the fee and, in the case covered by paragraph 2, by a reasoned claim in writing. On interruption it shall begin again immediately and shall end at the latest six years after the end of the year in which it originally began, unless in the meantime judicial proceedings to enforce the right have begun. In this case the period shall end at the earliest one year after the judgment has acquired the authority of a final decision.

SECTION 2

COSTS

Article 70

Apportionment of costs

1. The losing party in proceedings for a declaration of invalidity of a registered Community design or appeal proceedings shall bear the fees incurred by the

other party as well as all costs incurred by him essential to the proceedings, including travel and subsistence and the remuneration of an agent, adviser or advocate, within the limits of scales set for each category of costs under the conditions laid down in the implementing regulation.

2. However, where each party succeeds on some and fails on other heads, or if reasons of equity so dictate, the Invalidity Division or Board of Appeal shall decide a different apportionment of costs.

3. A party who terminates the proceedings by surrendering the registered Community design or by not renewing its registration or by withdrawing the application for a declaration of invalidity or the appeal, shall bear the fees and the costs incurred by the other party as stipulated in paragraphs 1 and 2.

4. Where a case does not proceed to judgment, the costs shall be at the discretion of the Invalidity Division or Board of Appeal.

5. Where the parties conclude before the Invalidity Division or Board of Appeal a settlement of costs differing from that provided for in paragraphs 1, 2, 3 and 4, the body concerned shall take note of that agreement.

6. On request, the registry of the Invalidity Division or Board of Appeal shall fix the amount of the costs to be paid pursuant to the preceding paragraphs. The amount so determined may be reviewed by a decision of the Invalidity Division or Board of Appeal on a request filed within the period prescribed by the implementing regulation.

Article 71

Enforcement of decisions fixing the amount of costs

1. Any final decision of the Office fixing the amount of costs shall be enforceable.

2. Enforcement shall be governed by the rules of civil procedure in force in the State in the territory of which it is carried out. The order for its enforcement shall be appended to the decision, without any other formality than verification of the authenticity of the decision, by the national authority which the government of each Member State shall designate for this purpose and shall make known to the Office and to the Court of Justice.

3. When these formalities have been completed on application by the party concerned, the latter may proceed to enforcement in accordance with the national law, by bringing the matter directly before the competent authority.

4. Enforcement may be suspended only by a decision of the Court of Justice. However, the courts of the Member State concerned shall have jurisdiction over complaints that enforcement is being carried out in an irregular manner.

SECTION 3

INFORMING THE PUBLIC AND THE OFFICIAL AUTHORITIES OF THE MEMBER STATES

Article 72

Register of Community designs

The Office shall keep a register to be known as the register of Community designs, which shall contain those particulars of which the registration is provided for by this Regulation or by the implementing regulation. The register shall be open to public inspection, except to the extent that Article 50(2) provides otherwise.

Article 73

Periodical publications

1. This Office shall periodically publish a Community Designs Bulletin

containing entries open to public inspection in the register as well as other particulars the publication of which is prescribed by this Regulation or by the implementing regulation.

2. Notices and information of a general character issued by the President of the Office, as well as any other information relevant to this Regulation or its implementation, shall be published in the Official Journal of the Office.

Article 74

Inspection of files

1. The files relating to applications for registered Community designs which have not yet been published or the files relating to registered Community designs which are subject to deferment of publication in accordance with Article 50 or which, being subject to such deferment, have been surrendered before or on the expiry of that period, shall not be made available for inspection without the consent of the applicant for or the right holder in the registered Community design.

2. Any person who can establish a legitimate interest may inspect a file without the consent of the applicant for or holder of the registered Community design prior to the publication or after the surrender of the latter in the case provided for in paragraph 1.

This shall in particular apply if the interested person proves that the applicant for or the holder of the registered Community design has taken steps with a view to invoking against him the right under the registered Community design.

3. Subsequent to the publication of the registered Community design, the file may be inspected on request.

4. However, where a file is inspected pursuant to paragraph 2 or 3, certain documents in the file may be withheld from inspection in accordance with the provisions of the implementing regulation.

Article 75

Administrative cooperation

Unless otherwise provided in this Regulation or in national laws, the Office and the courts or authorities of the Member States shall on request give assistance to each other by communicating information or opening files for inspection.

Where the Office opens files to inspection by courts, public prosecutors' offices or central industrial property offices, the inspection shall not be subject to the restrictions laid down in Article 74.

Article 76

Exchange of publications

1. The Office and the central industrial property offices of the Member States shall despatch to each other on request and for their own use one or more copies of their respective publications free of charge.

2. The Office may conclude agreements relating to the exchange or supply of publications.

SECTION 4

REPRESENTATION

Article 77

General principles of representation

1. Subject to paragraph 2, no person shall be compelled to be represented before the Office.

2. Without prejudice to the second subparagraph of paragraph 3, natural or legal persons not having either their domicile or their principal place of business or a real and effective industrial or commercial establishment in the Community must be represented before the Office in accordance with Article 78(1) in all proceedings before the Office established by this Regulation, other than in filing an application for a registered Community design; the implementing regulation may permit other exceptions.

3. Natural or legal persons having their domicile or principal place of business or a real and effective industrial or commercial establishment in the Community may be represented before the Office by one of their employees, who must file with it a signed authorisation for inclusion in the files, the details of which are set out in the implementing regulation.

An employee of a legal person to which this paragraph applies may also represent other legal persons which have economic connections with the first legal person, even if those other legal persons have neither their domicile nor their principal place of business nor a real and effective industrial or commercial establishment within the Community.

Article 78

Professional representation

1. Representation of natural or legal persons in proceedings before the Office under this Regulation may only be undertaken by:

(a) any legal practitioner qualified in one of the Member States and having his place of business within the Community, to the extent that he is entitled, within the said State, to act as a representative in industrial property matters; or

(b) any professional representatives whose name has been entered on the list of professional representatives referred to in Article 89(1)(b) of the Regulation on the Community trade mark; or

(c) persons whose names are entered on the special list of professional representatives for design matters referred to in paragraph 4.

2. The persons referred to in paragraph 1(c) shall only be entitled to represent third persons in proceedings on design matters before the Office.

3. The implementing regulation shall provide whether and under what conditions representatives must file with the Office a signed authorisation for insertion on the files.

4. Any natural person may be entered on the special list of professional representatives in design matters, if he fulfils the following conditions:

(a) he must be a national of one of the Member States;

(b) he must have his place of business or employment in the Community;

(c) he must be entitled to represent natural or legal persons in design matters before the central industrial property office of a Member State or before the Benelux Design Office. Where, in that State, the entitlement to represent in design matters is not conditional upon the requirement of special professional qualifications, persons applying to be entered on the list must have habitually acted in design matters before the central industrial property office of the said State for at least five years. However, persons whose professional qualification to represent natural or legal persons in design matters before the central industrial property office of one of the Member States is officially recognised in accordance with the regulations laid by such State shall not be subject to the condition of having exercised the profession.

5. Entry on the list referred to in paragraph 4 shall be effected upon request,

accompanied by a certificate furnished by the central industrial property office of the Member State concerned, which must indicate that the conditions laid down in the said paragraph are fulfilled.

6. The President of the Office may grant exemption from:

(a) the requirement of paragraph 4(a) in special circumstances;

(b) the requirement of paragraph 4(c), second sentence, if the applicant furnishes proof that he has acquired the requisite qualification in another way.

7. The conditions under which a person may be removed from the list shall be laid down in the implementing regulation.

TITLE IX

JURISDICTION AND PROCEDURE IN LEGAL ACTIONS RELATING TO COMMUNITY DESIGNS

SECTION 1

JURISDICTION AND ENFORCEMENT

Article 79

Application of the Convention on Jurisdiction and Enforcement

1. Unless otherwise specified in this Regulation, the Convention on Jurisdiction and the Enforcement of Judgements in Civil and Commercial Matters, signed in Brussels on 27 September 1968[7], hereinafter referred to as the "Convention on Jurisdiction and Enforcement", shall apply to proceedings relating to Community designs and applications for registered Community designs, as well as to proceedings relating to actions on the basis of Community designs and national designs enjoying simultaneous protection.

2. The provisions of the Convention on Jurisdiction and Enforcement which are rendered applicable by the paragraph 1 shall have effect in respect of any Member State solely in the text which is in force in respect of that State at any given time.

3. In the event of proceedings in respect of the actions and claims referred to in Article 85:

(a) Articles 2, 4, 5(1), (3), (4) and (5), 16(4) and 24 of the Convention on Jurisdiction and Enforcement shall not apply;

(b) Articles 17 and 18 of that Convention shall apply subject to the limitations in Article 82(4) of this Regulation;

(c) the provisions of Title II of that Convention which are applicable to persons domiciled in a Member State shall also be applicable to persons who do not have a domicile in any Member State but have an establishment therein.

4. The provisions of the Convention on Jurisdiction and Enforcement shall not have effect in respect of any Member State for which that Convention has not yet entered into force. Until such entry into force, proceedings referred to in paragraph 1 shall be governed in such a Member State by any bilateral or multilateral convention governing its relationship with another Member State concerned, or, if no such convention exists, by its domestic law on jurisdiction, recognition and enforcement of decisions.

---

[7] OJ L 299, 31.12.1972, p. 32. Convention as amended by the Conventions on the Accession to that Convention of the States acceding to the European Communities.

Section 2

Disputes concerning the infringement and validity of Community designs

Article 80
Community design courts

1. The Member States shall designate in their territories as limited a number as possible of national courts and tribunals of first and second instance (Community design courts) which shall perform the functions assigned to them by this Regulation.

2. Each Member State shall communicate to the Commission not later than 6 March 2005 a list of Community design courts, indicating their names and their territorial jurisdiction.

3. Any change made after communication of the list referred to in paragraph 2 in the number, names or territorial jurisdiction of the Community design courts shall be notified without delay by the Member State concerned to the Commission.

4. The information referred to in paragraphs 2 and 3 shall be notified by the Commission to the Member States and published in the Official Journal of the European Communities.

5. As long as a Member State has not communicated the list as stipulated in paragraph 2, jurisdiction for any proceedings resulting from an action covered by Article 81 for which the courts of that State have jurisdiction pursuant to Article 82 shall lie with that court of the State in question which would have jurisdiction ratione loci and ratione materiae in the case of proceedings relating to a national design right of that State.

Article 81
Jurisdiction over infringement and validity

The Community design courts shall have exclusive jurisdiction:

(a) for infringement actions and—if they are permitted under national law—actions in respect of threatened infringement of Community designs;

(b) for actions for declaration of non-infringement of Community designs, if they are permitted under national law;

(c) for actions for a declaration of invalidity of an unregistered Community design;

(d) for counterclaims for a declaration of invalidity of a Community design raised in connection with actions under (a).

Article 82
International jurisdiction

1. Subject to the provisions of this Regulation and to any provisions of the Convention on Jurisdiction and Enforcement applicable by virtue of Article 79, proceedings in respect of the actions and claims referred to in Article 81 shall be brought in the courts of the Member State in which the defendant is domiciled or, if he is not domiciled in any of the Member States, in any Member State in which he has an establishment.

2. If the defendant is neither domiciled nor has an establishment in any of the Member States, such proceedings shall be brought in the courts of the Member State in which the plaintiff is domiciled or, if he is not domiciled in any of the Member States, in any Member State in which he has an establishment.

3. If neither the defendant nor the plaintiff is so domiciled or has such an

establishment, such proceedings shall be brought in the courts of the Member State where the Office has its seat.

4. Notwithstanding paragraphs 1, 2 and 3:

(a) Article 17 of the Convention on Jurisdiction and Enforcement shall apply if the parties agree that a different Community design court shall have jurisdiction;

(b) Article 18 of that Convention shall apply if the defendant enters an appearance before a different Community design court.

5. Proceedings in respect of the actions and claims referred to in Article 81(a) and (d) may also be brought in the courts of the Member State in which the act of infringement has been committed or threatened.

Article 83

Extent of jurisdiction on infringement

1. A Community design court whose jurisdiction is based on Article 82(1), (2) (3) or (4) shall have jurisdiction in respect of acts of infringement committed or threatened within the territory of any of the Member States.

2. A Community design court whose jurisdiction is based on Article 82(5) shall have jurisdiction only in respect of acts of infringement committed or threatened within the territory of the Member State in which that court is situated.

Article 84

Action or counterclaim for a declaration of invalidity of a Community design

1. An action or a counterclaim for a declaration of invalidity of a Community design may only be based on the grounds for invalidity mentioned in Article 25.

2. In the cases referred to in Article 25(2), (3), (4) and (5) the action or the counterclaim may be brought solely by the person entitled under those provisions.

3. If the counterclaim is brought in a legal action to which the right holder of the Community design is not already a party, he shall be informed thereof and may be joined as a party to the action in accordance with the conditions set out in the law of the Member State where the court is situated.

4. The validity of a Community design may not be put in issue in an action for a declaration of non-infringement.

Article 85

Presumption of validity—defence as to the merits

1. In proceedings in respect of an infringement action or an action for threatened infringement of a registered Community design, the Community design court shall treat the Community design as valid. Validity may be challenged only with a counterclaim for a declaration of invalidity. However, a plea relating to the invalidity of a Community design, submitted otherwise than by way of counterclaim, shall be admissible in so far as the defendant claims that the Community design could be declared invalid on account of an earlier national design right, within the meaning of Article 25(1)(d), belonging to him.

2. In proceedings in respect of an infringement action or an action for threatened infringement of an unregistered Community design, the Community design court shall treat the Community design as valid if the right holder produces proof that the conditions laid down in Article 11 have been met and indicates what constitutes the individual character of his Community design. However, the defendant may contest its validity by way of a plea or with a counterclaim for a declaration of invalidity.

Article 86

Judgements of invalidity

1. Where in a proceeding before a Community design court the Community design has been put in issue by way of a counterclaim for a declaration of invalidity:

(a) if any of the grounds mentioned in Article 25 are found to prejudice the maintenance of the Community design, the court shall declare the Community design invalid;

(b) if none of the grounds mentioned in Article 25 is found to prejudice the maintenance of the Community design, the court shall reject the counterclaim.

2. The Community design court with which a counterclaim for a declaration of invalidity of a registered Community design has been filed shall inform the Office of the date on which the counterclaim was filed. The latter shall record this fact in the register.

3. The Community design court hearing a counterclaim for a declaration of invalidity of a registered Community design may, on application by the right holder of the registered Community design and after hearing the other parties, stay the proceedings and request the defendant to submit an application for a declaration of invalidity to the Office within a time limit which the court shall determine. If the application is not made within the time limit, the proceedings shall continue; the counterclaim shall be deemed withdrawn. Article 91(3) shall apply.

4. Where a Community design court has given a judgment which has become final on a counterclaim for a declaration of invalidity of a registered Community design, a copy of the judgment shall be sent to the Office. Any party may request information about such transmission. The Office shall mention the judgment in the register in accordance with the provisions of the implementing regulation.

5. No counterclaim for a declaration of invalidity of a registered Community design may be made if an application relating to the same subject matter and cause of action, and involving the same parties, has already been determined by the Office in a decision which has become final.

Article 87

Effects of the judgement on invalidity

When it has become final, a judgment of a Community design court declaring a Community design invalid shall have in all the Member States the effects specified in Article 26.

Article 88

Applicable law

1. The Community design courts shall apply the provisions of this Regulation.

2. On all matters not covered by this Regulation, a Community design court shall apply its national law, including its private international law.

3. Unless otherwise provided in this Regulation, a Community design court shall apply the rules of procedure governing the same type of action relating to a national design right in the Member State where it is situated.

Article 89

Sanctions in actions for infringement

1. Where in an action for infringement or for threatened infringement a Com-

munity design court finds that the defendant has infringed or threatened to infringe a Community design, it shall, unless there are special reasons for not doing so, order the following measures:

(a) an order prohibiting the defendant from proceeding with the acts which have infringed or would infringe the Community design;

(b) an order to seize the infringing products;

(c) an order to seize materials and implements predominantly used in order to manufacture the infringing goods, if their owner knew the effect for which such use was intended or if such effect would have been obvious in the circumstances;

(d) any order imposing other sanctions appropriate under the circumstances which are provided by the law of the Member State in which the acts of infringement or threatened infringement are committed, including its private international law.

2. The Community design court shall take such measures in accordance with its national law as are aimed at ensuring that the orders referred to in paragraph 1 are complied with.

Article 90

Provisional measures, including protective measures

1. Application may be made to the courts of a Member State, including Community design courts, for such provisional measures, including protective measures, in respect of a Community design as may be available under the law of that State in respect of national design rights even if, under this Regulation, a Community design court of another Member State has jurisdiction as to the substance of the matter.

2. In proceedings relating to provisional measures, including protective measures, a plea otherwise than by way of counterclaim relating to the invalidity of a Community design submitted by the defendant shall be admissible. Article 85(2) shall, however, apply mutatis mutandis.

3. A Community design court whose jurisdiction is based on Article 82(1), (2), (3) or (4) shall have jurisdiction to grant provisional measures, including protective measures, which, subject to any necessary procedure for recognition and enforcement pursuant to Title III of the Convention on Jurisdiction and Enforcement, are applicable in the territory of any Member State. No other court shall have such jurisdiction.

Article 91

Specific rules on related actions

1. A Community design court hearing an action referred to in Article 81, other than an action for a declaration of non-infringement, shall, unless there are special grounds for continuing the hearing, of its own motion after hearing the parties, or at the request of one of the parties and after hearing the other parties, stay the proceedings where the validity of the Community design is already in issue before another Community design court on account of a counterclaim or, in the case of a registered Community design, where an application for a declaration of invalidity has already been filed at the Office.

2. The Office, when hearing an application for a declaration of invalidity of a registered Community design, shall, unless there are special grounds for continuing the hearing, of its own motion after hearing the parties, or at the request of one of the parties and after hearing the other parties, stay the proceedings where the validity of the registered Community design is already in issue on account of

a counterclaim before a Community design court. However, if one of the parties to the proceedings before the Community design court so requests, the court may, after hearing the other parties to these proceedings, stay the proceedings. The Office shall in this instance continue the proceedings pending before it.

3. Where the Community design court stays the proceedings it may order provisional measures, including protective measures, for the duration of the stay.

Article 92

Jurisdiction of Community design courts of second instance—further appeal

1. An appeal to the Community design courts of second instance shall lie from judgments of the Community design courts of first instance in respect of proceedings arising from the actions and claims referred to in Article 81.

2. The conditions under which an appeal may be lodged with a Community design court of second instance shall be determined by the national law of the Member State in which that court is located.

3. The national rules concerning further appeal shall be applicable in respect of judgments of Community design courts of second instance.

SECTION 3

OTHER DISPUTES CONCERNING COMMUNITY DESIGNS

Article 93

Supplementary provisions on the jurisdiction of national courts other than Community design courts

1. Within the Member State whose courts have jurisdiction under Article 79(1) or (4), those courts shall have jurisdiction for actions relating to Community designs other than those referred to in Article 81 which would have jurisdiction ratione loci and ratione materiae in the case of actions relating to a national design right in that State.

2. Actions relating to a Community design, other than those referred to in Article 81, for which no court has jurisdiction pursuant to Article 79(1) and (4) and paragraph 1 of this Article may be heard before the courts of the Member State in which the Office has its seat.

Article 94

Obligation of the national court

A national court which is dealing with an action relating to a Community design other than the actions referred to in Article 81 shall treat the design as valid. Articles 85(2) and 90(2) shall, however, apply mutatis mutandis.

TITLE X

EFFECTS ON THE LAWS OF THE MEMBER STATES

Article 95

Parallel actions on the basis of Community designs and national design rights

1. Where actions for infringement or for threatened infringement involving

the same cause of action and between the same parties are brought before the courts of different Member States, one seized on the basis of a Community design and the other seized on the basis of a national design right providing simultaneous protection, the court other than the court first seized shall of its own motion decline jurisdiction in favour of that court. The court which would be required to decline jurisdiction may stay its proceedings if the jurisdiction of the other court is contested.

2. The Community design court hearing an action for infringement or threatened infringement on the basis of a Community design shall reject the action if a final judgment on the merits has been given on the same cause of action and between the same parties on the basis of a design right providing simultaneous protection.

3. The court hearing an action for infringement or for threatened infringement on the basis of a national design right shall reject the action if a final judgment on the merits has been given on the same cause of action and between the same parties on the basis of a Community design providing simultaneous protection.

4. Paragraphs 1, 2 and 3 shall not apply in respect of provisional measures, including protective measures.

Article 96

Relationship to other forms of protection under national law

1. The provisions of this Regulation shall be without prejudice to any provisions of Community law or of the law of the Member States concerned relating to unregistered designs, trade marks or other distinctive signs, patents and utility models, typefaces, civil liability and unfair competition.

2. A design protected by a Community design shall also be eligible for protection under the law of copyright of Member States as from the date on which the design was created or fixed in any form. The extent to which, and the conditions under which, such a protection is conferred, including the level of originality required, shall be determined by each Member State.

TITLE XI

SUPPLEMENTARY PROVISIONS CONCERNING THE OFFICE

SECTION 1

GENERAL PROVISIONS

Article 97

General provision

Unless otherwise provided in this Title, Title XII of the Regulation on the Community trade mark shall apply to the Office with regard to its tasks under this Regulation.

Article 98

Language of proceedings

1. The application for a registered Community design shall be filed in one of the official languages of the Community.

2. The applicant must indicate a second language which shall be a language of the Office the use of which he accepts as a possible language of proceedings before the Office.

If the application was filed in a language which is not one of the languages of the Office, the Office shall arrange to have the application translated into the language indicated by the applicant.

3. Where the applicant for a registered Community design is the sole party to proceedings before the Office, the language of proceedings shall be the language used for filing the application. If the application was made in a language other than the languages of the Office, the Office may send written communications to the applicant in the second language indicated by the applicant in his application.

4. In the case of invalidity proceedings, the language of proceedings shall be the language used for filing the application for a registered Community design if this is one of the languages of the Office. If the application was made in a language other than the languages of the Office, the language of proceedings shall be the second language indicated in the application.

The application for a declaration of invalidity shall be filed in the language of proceedings.

Where the language of proceedings is not the language used for filing the application for a registered Community design, the right holder of the Community design may file observations in the language of filing. The Office shall arrange to have those observations translated into the language of proceedings.

The implementing regulation may provide that the translation expenses to be borne by the Office may not, subject to a derogation granted by the Office where justified by the complexity of the case, exceed an amount to be fixed for each category of proceedings on the basis of the average size of statements of case received by the Office. Expenditure in excess of this amount may be allocated to the losing party in accordance with Article 70.

5. Parties to invalidity proceedings may agree that a different official language of the Community is to be the language of the proceedings.

Article 99

Publication and register

1. All information the publication of which is prescribed by this Regulation or the implementing regulation shall be published in all the official languages of the Community.

2. All entries in the Register of Community designs shall be made in all the official languages of the Community.

3. In cases of doubt, the text in the language of the Office in which the application for a registered Community design was filed shall be authentic. If the application was filed in an official language of the Community other than one of the languages of the Office, the text in the second language indicated by the applicant shall be authentic.

Article 100

Supplementary powers of the President

In addition to the functions and powers conferred on the President of the Office by Article 119 of the Regulation on the Community trade mark, the President may place before the Commission any proposal to amend this Regulation, the implementing regulation, the fees regulation and any other rule to the extent that they apply to registered Community designs, after consulting the Administrative Board and, in the case of the fees regulation, the Budget Committee.

Article 101

Supplementary powers of the Administrative Board

In addition to the powers conferred on it by Article 121 et seq of the Regulation on the Community trade mark or by other provisions of this Regulation, the Administrative Board;

(a) shall set the date for the first filing of applications for registered Community designs pursuant to Article 111(2);

(b) shall be consulted before adoption of the guidelines for examination as to formal requirements, examination as to grounds for refusal of registration and invalidity proceedings in the Office and in the other cases provided for in this Regulation.

SECTION 2

PROCEDURES

Article 102

Competence

For taking decisions in connection with the procedures laid down in this Regulation the following shall be competent:

(a) examiners;

(b) the Administration of Trade Marks and Designs and Legal Division;

(c) Invalidity Divisions;

(d) Boards of Appeal.

Article 103

Examiners

An examiner shall be responsible for taking decisions on behalf of the Office in relation to an application for a registered Community design.

Article 104

The Administration of Trade Marks and Designs and Legal Division

1. The Administration of Trade Marks and Legal Division provided for by Article 128 of the Regulation on the Community trade mark shall become the Administration of Trade Marks and Designs and Legal Division.

2. In addition to the powers conferred upon it by the Regulation on the Community trade mark, it shall be responsible for taking those decisions required by this Regulation which do not fall within the competence of an examiner or an Invalidity Division. It shall in particular be responsible for decisions in respect of entries in the register.

Article 105

Invalidity Divisions

1. An Invalidity Division shall be responsible for taking decisions in relation to applications for declarations of invalidity of registered Community designs.

2. An Invalidity Division shall consist of three members. At least one of the members must be legally qualified.

Article 106

Boards of Appeal

In addition to the powers conferred upon it by Article 131 of the Regulation on the Community trade mark, the Boards of Appeal instituted by that Regulation shall be responsible for deciding on appeals from decisions of the examiners, the

Invalidity Divisions and from the decisions of the Administration of Trade Marks and Designs and Legal Division as regards their decisions concerning Community designs.

TITLE XIA

INTERNATIONAL REGISTRATION OF DESIGNS

SECTION 1

GENERAL PROVISIONS

Article 106a

Application of provisions

1. Unless otherwise specified in this title, this Regulation and any Regulations implementing this Regulation adopted pursuant to Article 109 shall apply, mutatis mutandis, to registrations of industrial designs in the international register maintained by the International Bureau of the World Intellectual Property Organisation (hereinafter referred to as "international registration" and "the International Bureau") designating the Community, under the Geneva Act.

2. Any recording of an international registration designating the Community in the International Register shall have the same effect as if it had been made in the register of Community designs of the Office, and any publication of an international registration designating the Community in the Bulletin of the International Bureau shall have the same effect as if it had been published in the Community Designs Bulletin.

SECTION 2

INTERNATIONAL REGISTRATIONS DESIGNATING THE COMMUNITY

Article 106b

Procedure for filing the international application

International applications pursuant to Article 4(1) of the Geneva Act shall be filed directly at the International Bureau.

Article 106c

Designation fees

The prescribed designation fees referred to in Article 7(1) of the Geneva Act are replaced by an individual designation fee.

Article 106d

Effects of international registration designating the European Community

1. An international registration designating the Community shall, from the date of its registration referred to in Article 10(2) of the Geneva Act, have the same effect as an application for a registered Community design.

2. If no refusal has been notified or if any such refusal has been withdrawn, the international registration of a design designating the Community shall, from the date referred to in paragraph 1, have the same effect as the registration of a design as a registered Community design.

3. The Office shall provide information on international registrations referred

to in paragraph 2, in accordance with the conditions laid down in the Implementing Regulation.

Article 106e
Refusal

1. The Office shall communicate to the International Bureau a notification of refusal not later than six months from the date of publication of the international registration, if in carrying out an examination of an international registration, the Office notices that the design for which protection is sought does not correspond to the definition under Article 3(a), or is contrary to public policy or to accepted principles of morality.

The notification shall state the grounds on which the refusal is based.

2. The effects of an international registration in the Community shall not be refused before the holder has been allowed the opportunity of renouncing the international registration in respect of the Community or of submitting observations.

3. The conditions for the examination as to the grounds for refusal shall be laid down in the Implementing Regulation.

Article 106f
Invalidation of the effects of an international registration

1. The effects of an international registration in the Community may be declared invalid partly or in whole in accordance with the procedure in Titles VI and VII or by a Community design court on the basis of a counterclaim in infringement proceedings.

2. Where the Office is aware of the invalidation, it shall notify it to the International Bureau.

Note: Title XIa, and arts 106(a)–106(f) inserted by the Council Regulation (EC) No 1891/2006 of December 18, 2006 (OJ L 386/14).

TITLE XII

FINAL PROVISIONS

Article 107
Implementing regulation

1. The rules implementing this Regulation shall be adopted in an implementing regulation.

2. In addition to the fees already provided for in this Regulation, fees shall be charged, in accordance with the detailed rules of application laid down in the implementing regulation and in a fees regulation, in the cases listed below:

(a) late payment of the registration fee;
(b) late payment of the publication fee;
(c) late payment of the fee for deferment of publication;
(d) late payment of additional fees for multiple applications;
(e) issue of a copy of the certificate of registration;
(f) registration of the transfer of a registered Community design;
(g) registration of a licence or another right in respect of a registered Community design;
(h) cancellation of the registration of a licence or another right;

(i) issue of an extract from the register;

(j) inspection of the files;

(k) issue of copies of file documents;

(l) communication of information in a file;

(m) review of the determination of the procedural costs to be refunded;

(n) issue of certified copies of the application.

3. The implementing regulation and the fees regulation shall be adopted and amended in accordance with the procedure laid down in Article 109(2).

Article 108

Rules of procedure of the Boards of Appeal

The rules of procedure of the Boards of Appeal shall apply to appeals heard by those Boards under this Regulation, without prejudice to any necessary adjustment or additional provision, adopted in accordance with the procedure laid down in Article 109(2).

Article 109

Committee

1. The Commission shall be assisted by a Committee.

2. Where reference is made to this paragraph, Articles 5 and 7 of Decision 1999/468/EC shall apply. The period laid down in Article 5(6) of Decision 1999/468/EC shall be set at three months.

3. The Committee shall adopt its rules of procedure

Article 110

Transitional provision

1. Until such time as amendments to this Regulation enter into force on a proposal from the Commission on this subject, protection as a Community design shall not exist for a design which constitutes a component part of a complex product used within the meaning of Article 19(1) for the purpose of the repair of that complex product so as to restore its original appearance.

2. The proposal from the Commission referred to in paragraph 1 shall be submitted together with, and take into consideration, any changes which the Commission shall propose on the same subject pursuant to Article 18 of Directive 98/71/EC.

Article 111

Entry into force

1. This Regulation shall enter into force on the 60th day following its publication in the Official Journal of the European Communities.

2. Applications for registered Community designs may be filed at the Office from the date fixed by the Administrative Board on the recommendation of the President of the Office.

3. Applications for registered Community designs filed within three months before the date referred to in paragraph 2 shall be deemed to have been filed on that date.

This Regulation shall be binding in its entirety and directly applicable in all Member States.

Done at Brussels, 12 December 2001.

B8.ix The Community Designs (Designation of Community Design Courts) Regulations 2005

(SI 2005/ 696)

Made	*10th March 2005*
Laid before Parliament	*16th March 2005*
Coming into force	*6th April 2005*

The Secretary of State, being a Minister designated for the purposes of section 2(2) of the European Communities Act 1972 in relation to measures relating to the legal protection of designs, in exercise of powers conferred on her by that section makes the following Regulations:

1. These Regulations may be cited as the Community Designs (Designation of Community Design Courts) Regulations 2005 and shall come into force on 6th April 2005.

2.—(1) For the purposes of Article 80 of the Council Regulation (EC) No. 6/2002 of 12th December 2001 on Community designs, the following courts are designated as Community design courts–
    (a) in England and Wales–
        (i) the High Court; and
        (ii) any county court designated as a patents county court under section 287(1) of the Copyright, Designs and Patents Act 1988;
    (b) in Scotland, the Court of Session; and
    (c) in Northern Ireland, the High Court.
(2) For the purpose of hearing appeals from judgments of the courts designated by paragraph (1), the following courts are designated as Community design courts–
    (a) in England and Wales, the Court of Appeal;
    (b) in Scotland, the Court of Session;
    (c) in Northern Ireland, the Court of Appeal.

B8.x The Community Design Regulations 2005

(SI 2005/ 2339)

Made	*15th August 2005*
Laid before Parliament	*23rd August 2005*
Coming into force	*1st October 2005*

The Secretary of State, being a Minister designated for the purposes of section 2(2) of the European Communities Act 1972 in relation to measures relating to the legal protection of designs, in exercise of the powers conferred on him by that section makes the following Regulations:

Introductory and interpretation

1.—(1) These Regulations may be cited as the Community Design Regulations 2005 and shall come into force on 1st October 2005.
(2) In these Regulations—
    "the Community Design Regulation" means Council Regulation (EC) 6/2002 of 12th December 2001 on Community Designs;
    ["Community design court" means a court designated as such by the Community Designs (Designation of Community Design Courts) Regulations 2005;]

"Community design", "registered Community design" and "unregistered Community design" have the same meanings as in the Community Design Regulation[; and "international registration" has the same meaning as in Articles 106a to 106f of the Community Design Regulation] [; and.

" international registration" has the same meaning as in Articles 106a to 106f of the Community Design Regulation]

[(3) In addition, references to a Community design and a registered Community design include a reference to a design protected by virtue of an international registration designating the Community.]

Note: In reg.1(2) the definition of "Community design court" was inserted by the Intellectual Property (Enforcement, etc.) Regulations 2006 (SI 2006/1028), Sch.3 para.8, with effect from April 29, 2006. In reg.1(2) the definition of "international registration" was inserted by the Designs (International Registrations Designating the European Community) Regulations 2007 (SI 2007/3378) reg.3, with effect from January 1, 2008. Regulation 1(3) was inserted by the Designs (International Regulations Designating the European Community) Regulations 2007 (SI 2007/3378) reg.3(1)(a), with effect from January 1, 2008.

Infringement proceedings

[1A.—(1) This regulation and regulations 1B to 1D are without prejudice to the duties of the Community design court under the provisions of Article 89(1)(a) to (c) of the Community Design Regulation.

(2) [Subject to paragraphs (3) to (5), in an action] for infringement of a Community design all such relief by way of damages, injunctions, accounts or otherwise is available to the holder of the Community design as is available in respect of the infringement of any other property right.]

[(3) In an action for the infringement of the right in a registered Community design damages shall not be awarded against a person who proves that at the date of the infringement they were not aware, and had no reasonable ground for supposing, that the design was registered.

(4) For the purpose of paragraph (3), a person shall not be deemed to have been aware or to have had reasonable grounds for supposing that the design was registered by reason only of the marking of a product with—

(a) the word "registered" or any abbreviation of that word, or

(b) any word or words expressing or implying that the design applied to, or incorporated in, the product has been registered,

unless the number of the design accompanied the word or words or the abbreviation in question.

(5) In an action for the infringement of an unregistered Community design, damages shall not be awarded against a person who proves that at the date of the infringement that they were not aware, and had no reason to believe, that the design to which the action relates was protected as an unregistered Community design.]

Notes:

(1) Regulation 1A was inserted by the Intellectual Property (Enforcement, etc.) Regulations 2006 (SI 2006/1028), Sch.3 para.9, with effect from April 29, 2006.

(2) Words in square brackets substituted for words "In an action", and subss (3) (5) inserted, by Community Design (Amendment) Regulations 2014 (SI 2014/2400), reg.3, with effect from October 1, 2014.

Order for delivery up

[1B.—(1) Where a person—

    (a) has in his possession, custody or control for commercial purposes an infringing article, or

    (b) has in his possession, custody or control anything specifically designed or adapted for making articles to a particular design which is a Community design, knowing or having reason to believe that it has been or is to be used to make an infringing article,

the holder of the Community design in question may apply to the Community design court for an order that the infringing article or other thing be delivered up to him or to such other person as the court may direct.

(2) An application shall not be made after the end of the period specified in the following provisions of this regulation; and no order shall be made unless the court also makes, or it appears to the court that there are grounds for making, an order under regulation 1C (order as to disposal of infringing articles, &c.).

(3) An application for an order under this regulation may not be made after the end of the period of six years from the date on which the article or thing in question was made, subject to paragraph (4).

(4) If during the whole or any part of that period the holder of the Community design—

    (a) is under a disability, or

    (b) is prevented by fraud or concealment from discovering the facts entitling him to apply for an order,

an application may be made at any time before the end of the period of six years from the date on which he ceased to be under a disability or, as the case may be, could with reasonable diligence have discovered those facts.

(5) In paragraph (4) "disability"—

    (a) in England and Wales, has the same meaning as in the Limitation Act 1980;

    (b) in Scotland, means legal disability within the meaning of the Prescription and Limitation (Scotland) Act 1973;

    (c) in Northern Ireland, has the same meaning as in the Statute of Limitations (Northern Ireland) 1958.

(6) A person to whom an infringing article or other thing is delivered up in pursuance of an order under this regulation shall, if an order under regulation 1C is not made, retain it pending the making of an order, or the decision not to make an order, under that regulation.

(7) The reference in paragraph (1) to an act being done in relation to an article for "commercial purposes" are to its being done with a view to the article in question being sold or hired in the course of a business.

(8) Nothing in this regulation affects any other power of the court.]

Note: Regulation 1B was inserted by the Intellectual Property (Enforcement, etc.) Regulations 2006 (SI 2006/1028), Sch.3 para.9, with effect from April 29, 2006.

Order as to disposal of infringing articles, &c

[1C.—(1) An application may be made to the Community design court for an order that an infringing article or other thing delivered up in pursuance of an order under regulation 1B shall be—

    (a) forfeited to the holder of the Community design, or

    (b) destroyed or otherwise dealt with as the court may think fit,

or for a decision that no such order should be made.

(2) In considering what order (if any) should be made, the court shall consider whether other remedies available in an action for infringement of the right in a Community design would be adequate to compensate the holder and to protect his interests.

(3) Where there is more than one person interested in an article or other thing, the court shall make such order as it thinks just and may (in particular) direct that the thing be sold, or otherwise dealt with, and the proceeds divided.

(4) If the court decides that no order should be made under this regulation, the person in whose possession, custody or control the article or other thing was before being delivered up is entitled to its return.

(5) References in this regulation to a person having an interest in an article or other thing include any person in whose favour an order could be made in respect of it—

    (a) under this regulation;

    (b) under section 24D of the Registered Designs Act 1949;

    (c) under section 114, 204 or 231 of the Copyright, Designs and Patents Act 1988; or

    (d) under section 19 of the Trade Marks Act 1994 (including that section as applied by regulation 4 of the Community Trade Mark Regulations 2006 (SI 2006/1027)).]

Note: Regulation 1C was inserted by the Intellectual Property (Enforcement, etc.) Regulations 2006 (SI 2006/1028), Sch.3 para.9, with effect from April 29, 2006.

Meaning of "infringing article"

[**1D.**—(1) In these Regulations "infringing article", in relation to a design, shall be construed in accordance with this regulation.

(2) An article is an infringing article if its making to that design was an infringement of a [EU] design.

(3) An article is also an infringing article if—

    (a) it has been or is proposed to be imported into the United Kingdom, and

    (b) its making to that design in the United Kingdom would have been an infringement of a [EU] design or a breach of an exclusive licensing agreement relating to that [EU] design.

(4) Where it is shown that an article is made to a design which is or has been a [EU] design, it shall be presumed until the contrary is proved that the article was made at a time when the right in the [EU] design subsisted.

(5) Nothing in paragraph (3) shall be construed as applying to an article which may be lawfully imported into the United Kingdom by virtue of an enforceable [EU] right within the meaning of section 2(1) of the European Communities Act 1972.]

Notes:

    (1) Regulation 1D was inserted by the Intellectual Property (Enforcement, etc.) Regulations 2006 (SI 2006/1028), Sch.3 para.9, with effect from April 29, 2006.

    (2) In reg.1D(5) the expression "EU" was substituted for the word "Community" by the Treaty of Lisbon (Changes in Terminology) Order 2011 (SI 2011/1043) art.6(1)(f) with effect from April 22, 2011.

Remedy for groundless threats of infringement proceedings

2.—(1) Where any person (whether entitled to or interested in a Community design or not) by circulars, advertisements or otherwise threatens any other person with proceedings for infringement of a Community design, any person aggrieved thereby may bring an action against him for any such relief as is mentioned in paragraph (2).

(2) Subject to paragraphs (3) and (4), the claimant shall be entitled to the following relief—

(a) a declaration to the effect that the threats are unjustifiable;

(b) an injunction against the continuance of the threats; and

(c) such damages, if any, as he has sustained by reason of the threats.

(3) If the defendant proves that the acts in respect of which proceedings were threatened constitute or, if done, would constitute an infringement of a registered Community design the claimant shall be entitled to the relief claimed only if he shows that the registration is invalid.

(4) If the defendant proves that the acts in respect of which proceedings were threatened constitute or, if done, would constitute an infringement of an unregistered Community design the claimant shall not be entitled to the relief claimed.

(5) Proceedings may not be brought under this regulation in respect of a threat to bring proceedings for an infringement alleged to consist of the making or importing of anything.

(6) Mere notification that a design is—

(a) a registered Community design; or

(b) protected as an unregistered Community design,

does not constitute a threat of proceedings for the purpose of this regulation.

[(6A) In relation to a design protected by virtue of an international registration designating the Community, the reference in paragraph (3) to a registration being invalid includes a reference to the effects of the international registration being declared invalid in accordance with Article 106f of the Community Design Regulation.]

(7) [...]

Notes:

(1) Regulation 2(7) was revoked by the Intellectual Property (Enforcement, etc.) Regulations 2006 (SI 2006/1028) Sch.4, with effect from April 29, 2006.

(2) Regulation 2(6A) was inserted by the Designs (International Registrations Designating the European Community) Regulations 2007 (SI 2007/3378) reg.3, with effect from January 1, 2008.

Falsely representing a design as a registered Community design

3.—(1) It is an offence for a person falsely to represent that a design applied to, or incorporated in, any product sold by him is a registered Community design.

(2) It is an offence for a person, after a registered Community design has expired, to represent (expressly or by implication) that a design applied to, or incorporated in, any product sold is still registered in the manner provided for in the Community Design Regulation.

(3) A person guilty of an offence under paragraph (1) is liable on summary conviction to a fine not exceeding level 3 on the standard scale.

(4) A person guilty of an offence under paragraph (2) is liable on summary conviction to a fine not exceeding level 1 on the standard scale.

Privilege for communications with those on the special list of professional design representatives

4.—(1) This regulation applies to communications as to any matter relating to the protection of any design.

(2) Any such communication—

(a) between a person and his professional designs representative, or

(b) for the purposes of obtaining, or in response to a request for, information which a person is seeking for the purpose of instructing his professional designs representative, is privileged from, or in Scotland protected against, disclosure in legal proceedings in the same way as a communication between a person and his solicitor or, as the case may be, a communication for the purpose of obtaining, or in response to a request for, information which a person is seeking for the purpose of instructing his solicitor.

(3) In paragraph (2) "professional designs representative" means a person who is on the special list of professional representatives for design matters referred to in Article 78 of the Community Design Regulation.

Use of Community design for services of the Crown

5. The provisions of the Schedule to these Regulations shall have effect with respect to the use of registered Community designs and unregistered Community designs for the services of the Crown and the rights of third parties in respect of such use.

Application to Scotland and Northern Ireland

[**5A.**—(1) In the application of these Regulations to Scotland—

"accounts" means count, reckoning and payment;

"claimant" means pursuer;

"defendant" means defender;

"delivery up" means delivery;

"injunction" means interdict.

(2) In the application of these Regulations to Northern Ireland, "claimant" includes plaintiff.]

Note: Regulation 5A was inserted by the Intellectual Property (Enforcement, etc.) Regulations 2006 (SI 2006/1028), Sch.3 para.10, with effect from April 29, 2006.

Amendment of section 35 of the Registered Designs Act 1949

6. In section 35 of the Registered Designs Act 1949 (fine for falsely representing a design as registered), after subsection (2) there shall be inserted—

"(3) For the purposes of this section, the use in the United Kingdom in relation to a design—

(a) of the word "registered", or

(b) of any other word or symbol importing a reference (express or implied) to registration,

shall be deemed to be a representation as to registration under this Act unless it is shown that the reference is to registration elsewhere than in the United Kingdom and that the design is in fact so registered.".

Regulation 5   SCHEDULE

USE OF COMMUNITY DESIGNS FOR SERVICES OF THE CROWN

Use of Community design for services of the Crown

1.—(1) A government department, or a person authorised in writing by a government department, may without the consent of the holder of a Community design—

(a)   do anything for the purpose of supplying products for the services of the Crown, or

(b)   dispose of products no longer required for the services of the Crown;

and nothing done by virtue of this paragraph infringes the Community design.

(2) References in this Schedule to "the services of the Crown" are limited to those which are necessary for essential defence or security needs.

(3) In this Schedule—

"Crown use", in relation to a Community design, means the doing of anything by virtue of this paragraph which would otherwise be an infringement of the Community design; and

"the government department concerned", in relation to such use, means the government department by whom or on whose authority the act was done.

(4) The authority of a government department in respect of Crown use of a Community design may be given to a person either before or after the use and whether or not he is authorised, directly or indirectly, by the holder of the Community design to do anything in relation to the design.

(5) A person acquiring anything sold in the exercise of powers conferred by this paragraph, and any person claiming under him, may deal with it in the same manner as if the Crown was the holder of the Community design.

Settlement of terms for Crown use

2.—(1) Where Crown use is made of a Community design, the government department concerned shall—

(a)   notify the holder of the Community design as soon as practicable, and

(b)   give him such information as to the extent of the use as he may from time to time require,

unless it appears to the department that it would be contrary to the public interest to do so or the identity of the holder of the Community design cannot be ascertained on reasonable inquiry.

(2) Crown use of a Community design shall be on such terms as, either before or after the use, are agreed between the government department concerned and the holder of the Community design with the approval of the Treasury or, in default of agreement, are determined by the court.

(3) In the application of sub-paragraph (2) to Northern Ireland the reference to the Treasury shall, where the government department referred to in that sub-paragraph is a Northern Ireland department, be construed as a reference to the Department of Finance and Personnel.

(4) In the application of sub-paragraph (2) to Scotland, where the government department referred to in that sub-paragraph is any part of the Scottish Administration, the words "with the approval of the Treasury" are omitted.

(5) Where the identity of the holder of the Community design cannot be ascertained on reasonable inquiry, the government department concerned may apply to the court who may order that no royalty or other sum shall be payable in respect of Crown use of the Community design until the holder agrees terms with the department or refers the matter to the court for determination.

Rights of third parties in case of Crown use

3.—(1) The provisions of any licence, assignment or agreement made between the holder of the Community design (or anyone deriving title from him or from whom he derives title) and any person other than a government department are of no effect in relation to Crown use of a Community design, or any act incidental to Crown use, so far as they—

(a)   restrict or regulate anything done in relation to the Community design, or the use of any model, document or other information relating to it, or

(b)   provide for the making of payments in respect of, or calculated by reference to such use;

and the copying or issuing to the public of copies of any such model or document in connection with the thing done, or any such use, shall be deemed not to be an infringement of any copyright in the model or document.

(2) Sub-paragraph (1) shall not be construed as authorising the disclosure of any such model, document or information in contravention of the licence, assignment or agreement.

(3) Where an exclusive licence is in force in respect of the Community design—

(a)   if the licence was granted for royalties—

(i)   any agreement between the holder of the Community design and a government department under paragraph 2 (settlement of terms for Crown use) requires the consent of the licensee, and

(ii)   the licensee is entitled to recover from the holder of the Community design such part of the payment for Crown use as may be agreed between them or, in default of agreement, determined by the court;

(b)   if the licence was granted otherwise than for royalties—

(i)   paragraph 2 applies in relation to anything done which but for paragraph 1 (Crown use) and sub-paragraph (1) would be an infringement of the rights of the licensee with the substitution for references to the holder of the Community design of references to the licensee, and

(ii)   paragraph 2 does not apply in relation to anything done by the licensee by virtue of an authority given under paragraph 1.

(4) Where the Community design has been assigned to the holder of the Community design in consideration of royalties—

(a)   paragraph 2 applies in relation to Crown use of the Community design as if the references to the holder of the Community design included the assignor, and any payment for Crown use shall be divided between them in such proportion as may be agreed or, in default of agreement, determined by the court; and

(b)   paragraph 2 applies in relation to any act incidental to Crown use as it applies in relation to Crown use of the Community design.

(5) Where any model, document or other information relating to a Community design is used in connection with Crown use of the design, or any act incidental to Crown use, paragraph 2 applies to the use of the model, document or other information with the substitution for the references to the holder of the Community design of references to the person entitled to the benefit of any provision of an agreement rendered inoperative by sub-paragraph (1).

(6) In this paragraph—

"act incidental to Crown use" means anything done for the services of the Crown to the order of a government department by the holder of the Community design in respect of a design;

"payment for Crown use" means such amount as is payable by the government department concerned by virtue of paragraph 2; and

"royalties" includes any benefit determined by reference to the use of the Community design.

Crown use: compensation for loss of profit

4.—(1) Where Crown use is made of a Community design, the government department concerned shall pay—

(a)   to the holder of the Community design, or

(b)   if there is an exclusive licence in force in respect of the Community design, to the exclusive licensee,

compensation for any loss resulting from his not being awarded a contract to supply the products to which the Community design is applied or in which it is incorporated.

(2) Compensation is payable only to the extent that such a contract could have been fulfilled from his existing manufacturing capacity; but is payable notwithstanding the existence of circumstances rendering him ineligible for the award of such a contract.

(3) In determining the loss, regard shall be had to the profit which would have been made on such a contract and to the extent to which any manufacturing capacity was under-used.

(4) No compensation is payable in respect of any failure to secure contracts for the supply of products to which the Community design is applied or in which it is incorporated otherwise than for the services of the Crown.

(5) The amount payable shall, if not agreed between the holder of the Community design or licensee and the government department concerned with the approval of the Treasury, be determined by the court on a reference under paragraph 5; and it is in addition to any amount payable under paragraph 2 or 3.

(6) In the application of this paragraph to Northern Ireland, the reference in sub-paragraph (5) to the Treasury shall, where the government department concerned is a

Northern Ireland department, be construed as a reference to the Department of Finance and Personnel.

(7) In the application of this paragraph to Scotland, where the government department referred to in sub-paragraph (5) is any part of the Scottish Administration, the words "with the approval of the Treasury" in that sub-paragraph are omitted.

Reference of disputes relating to Crown use

5.—(1) A dispute as to any matter which falls to be determined by the court in default of agreement under—

(a)   paragraph 2 (settlement of terms for Crown use),

(b)   paragraph 3 (rights of third parties in case of Crown use), or

(c)   paragraph 4 (Crown use: compensation for loss of profit),

may be referred to the court by any party to the dispute.

(2) In determining a dispute between a government department and any person as to the terms for Crown use of a Community design the court shall have regard to—

(a)   any sums which that person or a person from whom he derives title has received or is entitled to receive, directly or indirectly, from any government department in respect of the Community design; and

(b)   whether that person or a person from whom he derives title has in the court's opinion without reasonable cause failed to comply with a request of the department for the use of the Community design on reasonable terms.

(3) One of two or more joint holders of the Community design may, without the concurrence of the others, refer a dispute to the court under this paragraph, but shall not do so unless the others are made parties; and none of those others is liable for any costs unless he takes part in the proceedings.

(4) Where the consent of an exclusive licensee is required by paragraph 3(3)(a)(i) to the settlement by agreement of the terms for Crown use of a Community design, a determination by the court of the amount of any payment to be made for such use is of no effect unless the licensee has beennotified of the reference and given an opportunity to be heard.

(5) On the reference of a dispute as to the amount recoverable as mentioned in paragraph 3(3)(a)(ii) (right of exclusive licensee to recover part of amount payable to holder of Community design) the court shall determine what is just having regard to any expenditure incurred by the licensee—

(a)   in developing the design, or

(b)   in making payments to the holder of the Community design in consideration of the licence (other than royalties or other payments determined by reference to the use of the design).

(6) In this Schedule "the court" means—

(a) in England and Wales, the High Court or any patents county court having jurisdiction by virtue of an order under section 287 of the Copyright, Designs and Patents Act 1988,

(b) in Scotland, the Court of Session, and

(c) in Northern Ireland, the High Court.

B9. Semiconductor Topographies

B9.i The Design Right (Semiconductor Topographies) Regulations 1989

(SI 1989/1100)

Made	*29th June 1989*
Coming into force	*1st August 1989*

Whereas a draft of the following Regulations has been approved by resolution of each House of Parliament:

Now, therefore, the Secretary of State, being designated[1] for the purposes of section 2(2) of the European Communities Act 1972[2] in relation to the conferment and protection of exclusive rights in the topographies of semiconductor products, in exercise of the powers conferred on him by the said section 2(2) hereby makes the following Regulations:

Citation and commencement

1. These Regulations may be cited as the Design Right (Semiconductor Topographies) Regulations 1989 and shall come into force on 1st August 1989.

Interpretation

2.—(1) In these Regulations—

"the Act" means the Copyright, Designs and Patents Act 1988;

"semiconductor product" means an article the purpose, or one of the purposes, of which is the performance of an electronic function and which consists of two or more layers, at least one of which is composed of semiconducting material and in or upon one or more of which is fixed a pattern appertaining to that or another function; and

"semiconductor topography" means a design within the meaning of section 213(2) of the Act which is a design of either of the following:

(a) the pattern fixed, or intended to be fixed, in or upon—

(i) a layer of a semiconductor product, or

(ii) a layer of material in the course of and for the purpose of the manufacture of a semiconductor product, or

(b) the arrangement of the patterns fixed, or intended to be fixed, in or upon the layers of a semiconductor product in relation to one another.

(2) Except where the context otherwise requires, these Regulations shall be construed as one with Part III of the Act (design right).

Application of Copyright, Designs and Patents Act 1988, Part III

3. In its application to a design which is a semiconductor topography, Part III of the Act shall have effect subject to regulations 4 to 9 below.

Qualification

4.—(1) Section 213(5) of the Act has effect subject to paragraphs (2) to (4) below.

[(2) Part III of the Act has effect as if for section 217(3) there was substituted the following—

---

[1] SI 1987/448.
[2] c. 68.

"(3) In this section "qualifying country" means—
    (a) the United Kingdom,
    (b) another member State,
    (c) the Isle of Man, Gibraltar, the Channel Islands or any colony,
    (d) a country listed in the Schedule to the Design Right (Semiconductor Topographies) Regulations 1989."]

(3) Where a semiconductor topography is created in pursuance of a commission or in the course of employment and the designer of the topography is, by virtue of section 215 of the Act (as substituted by regulation 5 below), the first owner of design right in that topography, section 219 of the Act does not apply and section 218(2) to (4) of the Act shall apply to the topography as if it had not been created in pursuance of a commission or in the course of employment.

(4) Section 220 of the Act has effect subject to regulation 7 below and as if for subsection (1) there was substituted the following:

"**220.**—(1) A design which does not qualify for design right protection under section 218 or 219 (as modified by regulation 4(3) of the Design Right (Semiconductor Topographies) Regulations 1989) or under the said regulation 4(3) qualifies for design right protection if the first marketing of articles made to the design—
    (a) is by a qualifying person who is exclusively authorised to put such articles on the market in every member State of the European Economic Community, and
    (b) takes place within the territory of any member State.";
and subsection (4) of section 220 accordingly has effect as if the words "in the United Kingdom" omitted.

Note: Regulation 4(2) was substituted by the Design Right (Semiconductor Topographies) (Amendment) Regulations 2006 (SI 2006/1833), reg.3 with effect from August 1, 2006.

Ownership of design right

5. Part III of the Act has effect as if for section 215 of the Act there was substituted the following:

"**215.**—(1) The designer is the first owner of any design right in a design which is not created in pursuance of a commission or in the course of employment.

(2) Where a design is created in pursuance of a commission, the person commissioning the design is the first owner of any design right in it subject to any agreement in writing to the contrary.

(3) Where, in a case not falling within subsection (2) a design is created by an employee in the course of his employment, his employer is the first owner of any design right in the design subject to any agreement in writing to the contrary.

(4) If a design qualifies for design right protection by virtue of section 220 (as modified by regulation 4(4) of the Design Right (Semiconductor Topographies) Regulations 1989), the above rules do not apply and, subject to regulation 7 of the said Regulations, the person by whom the articles in question are marketed is the first owner of the design right.".

Duration of design right

6.—(1) Part III of the Act has effect as if for section 216 of the Act there was substituted the following:

"**216.** The design right in a semiconductor topography expires—
    (a) ten years from the end of the calendar year in which the topography or articles made to the topography were first made available for sale or hire anywhere in the world by or with the licence of the design right owner, or
    (b) if neither the topography nor articles made to the topography are so made available within a period of fifteen years commencing with the earlier of

the time when the topography was first recorded in a design document or the time when an article was first made to the topography, at the end of that period.".

(2) Subsection (2) of section 263 of the Act has effect as if the words "or a semiconductor topography" were inserted after the words "in relation to an article".

(3) The substitute provision set out in paragraph (1) above has effect subject to regulation 7 below.

Confidential information

7. In determining, for the purposes of section 215(4), 216 or 220 of the Act (as modified by these Regulations), whether there has been any marketing, or anything has been made available for sale or hire, no account shall be taken of any sale or hire, or any offer or exposure for sale or hire, which is subject to an obligation of confidence in respect of information about the semiconductor topography in question unless either—

(a) the article or semiconductor topography sold or hired or offered or ex- posed for sale or hire has beensold or hired on a previous occasion (whether or not subject to an obligation of confidence), or

(b) the obligation is imposed at the behest of the Crown, or of the govern- ment of any country outside the United Kingdom, for the protection of security in connection with the production of arms, munitions or war material.

Infringement

8.—(1) Section 226 of the Act has effect as if for subsection (1) there was substituted the following:

"**226.**—(1) Subject to subsection (1A), the owner of design right in a design has the exclusive right to reproduce the design—

(a) by making articles to that design, or

(b) by making a design document recording the design for the purpose of en- abling such articles to be made.

(1A) Subsection (1) does not apply to—

(a) the reproduction of a design privately for non-commercial aims; or

(b) the reproduction of a design for the purpose of analysing or evaluating the design or analysing, evaluating or teaching the concepts, processes, systems or techniques embodied in it.".

(2) Section 227 of the Act does not apply if the article in question has previously been sold or hired within—

(a) the United Kingdom by or with the licence of the owner of design right in the semiconductor topography in question, or

(b) the territory of any other member State of the European Economic Com- munity or the territory of Gibraltar by or with the consent of the person for the time being entitled to import it into or sell or hire it within that territory.

(3) Section 228(6) of the Act does not apply.

(4) It is not an infringement of design right in a semiconductor topography to—

(a) create another original semiconductor topography as a result of an analy- sis or evaluation of the first topography or of the concepts, processes, systems or techniques embodied in it, or

(b) reproduce that other topography.

(5) Anything which would be an infringement of the design right in a semiconduc- tor topography if done in relation to the topography as a whole is an infringement of the design right in the topography if done in relation to a substantial part of the topography.

Licences of right

9. Section 237 of the Act does not apply.

Revocation and transitional provisions

10.—(1) The Semiconductor Products (Protection of Topography) Regulations 1987 are hereby revoked.

(2) Sub-paragraph (1) of paragraph 19 of Schedule 1 to the Act shall not apply in respect of a semiconductor topography created between 7th November 1987 and 31st July 1989.

(3) In its application to copyright in a semiconductor topography created before 7th November 1987, sub-paragraph (2) of the said paragraph 19 shall have effect as if the reference to sections 237 to 239 were a reference to sections 238 and 239; and subparagraph (3) of that paragraph accordingly shall not apply to such copyright.

[SCHEDULE 1

QUALIFYING COUNTRIES

Albania
Angola
Antigua and Barbuda
Argentina
Armenia
Australia
Bahrain, Kingdom of
Bangladesh
Barbados
Belize
Benin
Bolivia
Botswana
Brazil
Brunei Darussalam
Bulgaria
Burkina Faso
Burundi
Cambodia
Cameroon
Canada
Central African Republic
Chad
Chile
China
Colombia
Congo
Costa Rica
Côte d'Ivoire
Croatia
Cuba
Democratic Republic of the Congo
Djibouti
Dominica
Dominican Republic
Ecuador
Egypt
El Salvador

Fiji
Former Yugoslav Republic of Macedonia
French overseas territories
Gabon
The Gambia
Georgia
Ghana
Grenada
Guatemala
Guinea
Guinea Bissau
Guyana
Haiti
Honduras
Hong Kong
Iceland
India
Indonesia
Israel
Jamaica
Japan
Jordan
Kenya
Korea, Republic of
Kuwait
Kyrgyz Republic
Lesotho
Liechtenstein
Macao, China
Madagascar
Malawi
Malaysia
Maldives
Mali
Mauritania
Mauritius
Mexico
Moldova
Mongolia
Morocco
Mozambique
Myanmar
Namibia
Nepal
Netherlands Antilles
New Zealand
Nicaragua
Niger
Nigeria
Norway
Oman
Pakistan
Panama
Papua New Guinea
Paraguay
Peru
Philippines
Qatar
Romania
Rwanda

Saint Kitts and Nevis
Saint Lucia
Saint Vincent & the Grenadines
Saudi Arabia
Senegal
Sierra Leone
Singapore
Solomon Islands
South Africa
Sri Lanka
Suriname
Swaziland
Switzerland
Chinese Taipei
Tanzania
Thailand
Togo
[Tonga]
Trinidad and Tobago
Tunisia
Turkey
Uganda
[Ukraine]
United Arab Emirates
United States of America
Uruguay
Venezuela
[Vietnam]
Zambia
Zimbabwe]

Notes:

(1) Schedule 1 was substituted by the Design Right (Semiconductor Topographies) (Amendment) Regulations 2006 (SI 2006/1833), reg.4 with effect from August 1, 2006; and amended by the Design Right (Semiconductor Topographies) (Amendment) (No.2) Regulations 2008 (SI 2008/1434), reg.3, with effect from July 1, 2008.

(2) "Tonga", "Ukraine" and "Vietnam" inserted by the Design Right (Semiconductor Topographies) (Amendment) (No.2) Regulations 2008 (SI 2008/1434) reg.3 with effect from July 1, 2008.

B10. E-Commerce

B10.i The Electronic Commerce (EC Directive) Regulations 2002

(SI 2002/2013)

Made	*30th July 2002*
Laid before Parliament	*31st July 2002*
Coming into force	*1st August 1989*
Regulation 16	*23rd October 2002*
Remainder	*21st August 2002*

The Secretary of State, being a Minister designated for the purposes of section 2(2) of the European Communities Act 1972 in relation to information society services, in exercise of the powers conferred on her by that section, hereby makes the following Regulations:—

Citation and commencement

1.—(1) These Regulations may be cited as the Electronic Commerce (EC Directive) Regulations 2002 and except for regulation 16 shall come into force on 21st August 2002.

(2) Regulation 16 shall come into force on 23rd October 2002.

Interpretation

2.—(1) In these Regulations and in the Schedule—

"commercial communication" means a communication, in any form, designed to promote, directly or indirectly, the goods, services or image of any person pursuing a commercial, industrial or craft activity or exercising a regulated profession, other than a communication—

(a) consisting only of information allowing direct access to the activity of that person including a geographic address, a domain name or an electronic mail address; or

(b) relating to the goods, services or image of that person provided that the communication has been prepared independently of the person making it (and for this purpose, a communication prepared without financial consideration is to be taken to have been prepared independently unless the contrary is shown);

"the Commission" means the Commission of the European Communities;

"consumer" means any natural person who is acting for purposes other than those of his trade, business or profession;

"coordinated field" means requirements applicable to information society service providers or information society services, regardless of whether they are of a general nature or specifically designed for them, and covers requirements with which the service provider has to comply in respect of—

(a) the taking up of the activity of an information society service, such as requirements concerning qualifications, authorisation or notification, and

(b) the pursuit of the activity of an information society service, such as requirements concerning the behaviour of the service provider, requirements regarding the quality or content of the service including those applicable to advertising and contracts, or requirements concerning the liability of the service provider, but does not cover requirements such as those applicable to goods as such, to the delivery of goods or to services not provided by electronic means;

"the Directive" means Directive 2000/31/EC of the European Parliament and of the Council of 8 June 2000 on certain legal aspects of information society services, in particular electronic commerce, in the Internal Market (Directive on electronic commerce);

"EEA Agreement" means the Agreement on the European Economic Area signed at Oporto on 2 May 1992 as adjusted by the Protocol signed at Brussels on 17 March 1993;

["EEA Enactment" has the meaning given by Schedule 1 to the Interpretation Act 1978;]

"enactment" includes an enactment comprised in Northern Ireland legislation and comprised in, or an instrument made under, an Act of the Scottish Parliament;

"enforcement action" means any form of enforcement action including, in particular—

    (a) in relation to any legal requirement imposed by or under any enactment, any action taken with a view to or in connection with imposing any sanction (whether criminal or otherwise) for failure to observe or comply with it; and

    (b) in relation to a permission or authorisation, anything done with a view to removing or restricting that permission or authorisation;

"enforcement authority" does not include courts but, subject to that, means any person who is authorised, whether by or under an enactment or otherwise, to take enforcement action;

"established service provider" means a service provider who is a national of a member State or a company or firm as mentioned in [Article 54] of the Treaty and who effectively pursues an economic activity by virtue of which he is a service provider using a fixed establishment in a member State for an indefinite period, but the presence and use of the technical means and technologies required to provide the information society service do not, in themselves, constitute an establishment of the provider; in cases where it cannot be determined from which of a number of places of establishment a given service is provided, that service is to be regarded as provided from the place of establishment where the provider has the centre of his activities relating to that service; references to a service provider being established or to the establishment of a service provider shall be construed accordingly;

"information society services" (which is summarised in recital 17 of the Directive as covering "any service normally provided for remuneration, at a distance, by means of electronic equipment for the processing (including digital compression) and storage of data, and at the individual request of a recipient of a service") has the meaning set out in Article 2(a) of the Directive, (which refers to Article 1(2) of Directive 98/34/EC of the European Parliament and of the Council of 22 June 1998 laying down a procedure for the provision of information in the field of technical standards and regulations, as amended by Directive 98/48/EC of 20 July 1998);

"member State" includes a State which is a contracting party to the EEA Agreement;

"recipient of the service" means any person who, for professional ends or otherwise, uses an information society service, in particular for the purposes of seeking information or making it accessible;

"regulated profession" means any profession within the meaning of either Article 1(d) of Council Directive 89/48/EEC of 21 December 1988 on a general system for the recognition of higher-education diplomas awarded on completion of professional education and training of at least three years' duration or of Article 1(f) of Council Directive 92/51/EEC of 18 June 1992 on a second general system for the recognition of professional education and training to supplement Directive 89/48/EEC;

"service provider" means any person providing an information society service;

"the Treaty" means [the Treaty on the Functioning of the European Union].

(2) In regulation 4 and 5, "requirement" means any legal requirement under the law of the United Kingdom, or any part of it, imposed by or under any enactment or otherwise.

(3) Terms used in the Directive other than those in paragraph (1) above shall have the same meaning as in the Directive.

Notes:

(1) Definition *"EEA Agreement"* substituted by the Broadcasting and Communications (Amendment) Regulations 2013 (SI 2013/2217), reg.8, with effect from October 1, 2013. Definition formerly read:

"EEA Agreement" means the Agreement on the European Economic Area signed at Oporto on 2 May 1992 as adjusted by the Protocol signed at Brussels on 17 March 1993;"

(2) In definition "the Treaty" words substituted for words "the treaty establishing the European Community", and in definition "established service provider" words in square brackets substituted for words "Article 48", subject to savings, by the Treaty of Lisbon (Changes in Terminology or Numbering) Order 2012 (SI 2012/1809), Sch.1 para.1, with effect from August 1, 2012 (for savings see (SI 2012/1809), art.2(2)).

Exclusions

3.—(1) Nothing in these Regulations shall apply in respect of—

(a) the field of taxation;

(b) questions relating to information society services covered by the Data Protection Directive and the Telecommunications Data Protection Directive and Directive 2002/58/EC of the European Parliament and of the Council of 12th July 2002 concerning the processing of personal data and the protection of privacy in the electronic communications sector (Directive on privacy and electronic communications);

(c) questions relating to agreements or practices governed by cartel law; and

(d) the following activities of information society services—

(i) the activities of a public notary or equivalent professions to the extent that they involve a direct and specific connection with the exercise of public authority,

(ii) the representation of a client and defence of his interests before the courts, and

(iii) betting, gaming or lotteries which involve wagering a stake with monetary value.

(2) These Regulations shall not apply in relation to any Act passed on or after the date these Regulations are made or in exercise of a power to legislate after that date.

(3) In this regulation—

"cartel law" means so much of the law relating to agreements between undertakings, decisions by associations of undertakings or concerted practices as relates to agreements to divide the market or fix prices;

"Data Protection Directive" means Directive 95/46/EC of the European Parliament and of the Council of 24 October 1995 on the protection of individuals with regard to the processing of personal data and on the free movement of such data; and

"Telecommunications Data Protection Directive" means Directive 97/66/EC of the European Parliament and of the Council of 15 December 1997 concerning the processing of personal data and the protection of privacy in the telecommunications sector.

Note: Regulations 4–16 are not reprinted in this Work.

Mere conduit

17.—(1) Where an information society service is provided which consists of the transmission in a communication network of information provided by a recipient of the service or the provision of access to a communication network, the service provider (if he otherwise would) shall not be liable for damages or for any other pecuniary remedy or for any criminal sanction as a result of that transmission where the service provider—

(a) did not initiate the transmission;

(b) did not select the receiver of the transmission; and

(c) did not select or modify the information contained in the transmission.

(2) The acts of transmission and of provision of access referred to in paragraph (1) include the automatic, intermediate and transient storage of the information transmitted where:

(a) this takes place for the sole purpose of carrying out the transmission in the communication network, and

(b) the information is not stored for any period longer than is reasonably necessary for the transmission.

Caching

18. Where an information society service is provided which consists of the transmission in a communication network of information provided by a recipient of the service, the service provider (if he otherwise would) shall not be liable for damages or for any other pecuniary remedy or for any criminal sanction as a result of that transmission where—

(a) the information is the subject of automatic, intermediate and temporary storage where that storage is for the sole purpose of making more efficient onward transmission of the information to other recipients of the service upon their request, and

(b) the service provider—

(i) does not modify the information;

(ii) complies with conditions on access to the information;

(iii) complies with any rules regarding the updating of the information, specified in a manner widely recognised and used by industry;

(iv) does not interfere with the lawful use of technology, widely recognised and used by industry, to obtain data on the use of the information; and

(v) acts expeditiously to remove or to disable access to the information he has stored upon obtaining actual knowledge of the fact that the information at the initial source of the transmission has been removed from the network, or access to it has been disabled, or that a court or an administrative authority has ordered such removal or disablement.

Hosting

19. Where an information society service is provided which consists of the storage of information provided by a recipient of the service, the service provider (if he otherwise would) shall not be liable for damages or for any other pecuniary remedy or for any criminal sanction as a result of that storage where—

(a) the service provider—
  (i) does not have actual knowledge of unlawful activity or information and, where a claim for damages is made, is not aware of facts or circumstances from which it would have been apparent to the service provider that the activity or information was unlawful; or
  (ii) upon obtaining such knowledge or awareness, acts expeditiously to remove or to disable access to the information, and
(b) the recipient of the service was not acting under the authority or the control of the service provider.

Protection of rights

20.—(1) Nothing in regulations 17, 18 and 19 shall—

(a) prevent a person agreeing different contractual terms; or
(b) affect the rights of any party to apply to a court for relief to prevent or stop infringement of any rights.

(2) Any power of an administrative authority to prevent or stop infringement of any rights shall continue to apply notwithstanding regulations 17, 18 and 19.

Defence in Criminal Proceedings: burden of proof

21.—(1) This regulation applies where a service provider charged with an offence in criminal proceedings arising out of any transmission, provision of access or storage falling within regulation 17, 18 or 19 relies on a defence under any of regulations 17, 18 and 19.

(2) Where evidence is adduced which is sufficient to raise an issue with respect to that defence, the court or jury shall assume that the defence is satisfied unless the prosecution proves beyond reasonable doubt that it is not.

Notice for the purposes of actual knowledge

22. In determining whether a service provider has actual knowledge for the purposes of regulations 18(b)(v) and 19(a)(i), a court shall take into account all matters which appear to it in the particular circumstances to be relevant and, among other things, shall have regard to—

(a) whether a service provider has received a notice through a means of contact made available in accordance with regulation 6(1)(c), and
(b) the extent to which any notice includes—
  (i) the full name and address of the sender of the notice;
  (ii) details of the location of the information in question; and
  (iii) details of the unlawful nature of the activity or information in question.

B11. ENFORCEMENT

B11.i The Intellectual Property (Enforcement, etc.) Regulations 2006

(SI 2006/ 1028)

Made	*5th April 2006*
Laid before Parliament	*6th April 2006*
Coming into force	*29th April 2006*

The Secretary of State has been designated for the purposes of section 2(2) of the European Communities Act 1972 in relation to intellectual property (including both registered and unregistered rights).

He makes the following Regulations under the powers conferred by that section:

Citation and commencement

1. These Regulations may be cited as the Intellectual Property (Enforcement, etc.) Regulations 2006 and shall come into force on 29th April 2006.

Amendments of legislation

2.—(1) Schedule 1 (amendments to the Registered Designs Act 1949) shall have effect.

(2) Schedule 2 (amendments to other primary legislation) shall have effect.

(3) Schedule 3 (amendments to secondary legislation) shall have effect.

(4) The enactments set out in Schedule 4 (repeals) shall be repealed or revoked to the extent specified.

Assessment of damages

3.—(1) Where in an action for infringement of an intellectual property right the defendant knew, or had reasonable grounds to know, that he engaged in infringing activity, the damages awarded to the claimant shall be appropriate to the actual prejudice he suffered as a result of the infringement.

(2) When awarding such damages—

    (a) all appropriate aspects shall be taken into account, including in particular—

        (i) the negative economic consequences, including any lost profits, which the claimant has suffered, and any unfair profits made by the defendant; and

        (ii) elements other than economic factors, including the moral prejudice caused to the claimant by the infringement; or

    (b) where appropriate, they may be awarded on the basis of the royalties or fees which would have been due had the defendant obtained a licence.

(3) This regulation does not affect the operation of any enactment or rule of law relating to remedies for the infringement of intellectual property rights except to the extent that it is inconsistent with the provisions of this regulation.

(4) In the application of this regulation to—

    (a) Scotland, "claimant" includes pursuer; "defendant" includes defender; and "enactment" includes an enactment comprised in, or an instrument made under, an Act of the Scottish Parliament; and

    (b) Northern Ireland, "claimant" includes plaintiff.

Order in Scotland for disclosure of information

4.—(1) This regulation applies to proceedings in Scotland concerning an infringement of an intellectual property right.

(2) The pursuer may apply to the court for an order that information regarding the origin and distribution networks of goods or services which infringe an intellectual property right shall be disclosed to him by the relevant person.

(3) The court may only order the information to be disclosed where it considers it just and proportionate having regard to the rights and privileges of the relevant person and others; such an order may be subject to such conditions as the court thinks fit.

(4) The relevant person is—

(a) the alleged infringer,

(b) any person who—

    (i) was found in possession of the infringing goods on a commercial scale,

    (ii) was found to be using the infringing services on a commercial scale, or

    (iii) was found to be providing services on a commercial scale, which are used in activities which infringe an intellectual property right, or

(c) any person who has been identified by a person specified in sub-paragraph (b) as being involved in—

    (i) the production, manufacture or distribution of the infringing goods, or

    (ii) the provision of the infringing services.

(5) For the purposes of paragraph (3), the court may order the disclosure of any of the following types of information—

(a) the names and addresses of—

    (i) each producer, manufacturer, distributor or supplier of the infringing goods or services;

    (ii) any person who previously possessed the infringing goods; and

    (iii) the intended wholesaler and retailer of the infringing goods or services; and

(b) information relating to—

    (i) the quantities of infringing goods or the amount of infringing services provided, produced, manufactured, delivered, received or ordered; and

    (ii) the price paid for the infringing goods or infringing services in question.

(6) Nothing in this regulation affects—

(a) any right of the pursuer to receive information under any other enactment (including an enactment comprised in, or an instrument made under, an Act of the Scottish Parliament) or rule of law; and

(b) any other power of the court.

(7) For the purposes of this regulation and regulation 5, "court" means the Court of Session or the sheriff.

Order in Scotland for publication of judgments

5. In Scotland, where the court finds that an intellectual property right has been infringed, the court may, at the request of the pursuer, order appropriate measures for the dissemination and publication of the judgment to be taken at the defender's expense.

Schedules 1–4

[Not reproduced.]

B11.ii The Communications Act 2003

(c.21)

*An Act to confer functions on the Office of Communications; to make provision
about the regulation of the provision of electronic communications networks
and services and of the use of the electro-magnetic spectrum; to make
provision about the regulation of broadcasting and of the provision of
television and radio services; to make provision about mergers involving
newspaper and other media enterprises and, in that connection, to amend the
Enterprise Act 2002; and for connected purposes.*

[17th July 2003]

*BE IT ENACTED by the Queen's most Excellent Majesty, by and with the advice
and consent of the Lords Spiritual and Temporal, and Commons, in this
present Parliament assembled, and by the authority of the same, as follows:—*

Preliminary

Meaning of electronic communications networks and services

32.—(1) In this Act "electronic communications network" means—
(a) a transmission system for the conveyance, by the use of electrical,
    magnetic or electro-magnetic energy, of signals of any description; and
(b) such of the following as are used, by the person providing the system
    and in association with it, for the conveyance of the signals—
    (i) apparatus comprised in the system;
    (ii) apparatus used for the switching or routing of the signals; [...]
    (iii) software and stored data[; and
    (iv) (except for the purposes of sections 125 to 127) other resources,
        including network elements which are not active.]

(2) In this Act "electronic communications service" means a service consisting in, or having as its principal feature, the conveyance by means of an electronic
communications network of signals, except in so far as it is a content service.

[(3) In this Act "associated facility" means a facility, element or service which
is available for use, or has the potential to be used, in association with the use of
an electronic communications network or electronic communications service
(whether or not one provided by the person making the facility, element or service available) for the purpose of—
(a) making the provision of that network or service possible;
(b) making possible the provision of other services provided by means of
    that network or service; or
(c) supporting the provision of such other services.]

(4) In this Act—
(a) references to the provision of an electronic communications network
    include references to its establishment, maintenance or operation;
(b) references, where one or more persons are employed or engaged to
    provide the network or service under the direction or control of another
    person, to the person by whom an electronic communications network
    or electronic communications service is provided are confined to refer-
    ences to that other person; and
(c) references, where one or more persons are employed or engaged to make
    facilities available under the direction or control of another person, to
    the person by whom any associated facilities are made available are
    confined to references to that other person.

(5) Paragraphs (a) and (b) of subsection (4) apply in relation to references in subsection (1) to the provision of a transmission system as they apply in relation to references in this Act to the provision of an electronic communications network.

(6) The reference in subsection (1) to a transmission system includes a reference to a transmission system consisting of no more than a transmitter used for the conveyance of signals.

(7) In subsection (2) "a content service" means so much of any service as consists in one or both of the following—

    (a) the provision of material with a view to its being comprised in signals conveyed by means of an electronic communications network;

    (b) the exercise of editorial control over the contents of signals conveyed by means of a such a network.

(8) In this section references to the conveyance of signals include references to the transmission or routing of signals or of parts of signals and to the broadcasting of signals for general reception.

(9) For the purposes of this section the cases in which software and stored data are to be taken as being used for a particular purpose include cases in which they—

    (a) have been installed or stored in order to be used for that purpose; and

    (b) are available to be so used.

(10) In this section "signal" includes—

    (a) anything comprising speech, music, sounds, visual images or communications or data of any description; and

    (b) signals serving for the impartation of anything between persons, between a person and a thing or between things, or for the actuation or control of apparatus.

Note: In subs.(1)(b)(ii) word "and" repealed, subs.(1)(b)(iv) inserted, and subs.(3) substituted, subject to savings and transitional provisions, by the Electronic Communications and Wireless Telegraphy Regulations 2011 (SI 2011/1210), Sch.1 para.9(a)(i), with effect from May 26, 2011 (for savings and transitional provisions, see (SI 2011/1210), Sch.3 para.2). Subsection (3) formerly read:

"(3) In this Act "associated facility" means a facility which—

    (a) is available for use in association with the use of an electronic communications network or electronic communications service (whether or not one provided by the person making the facility available); and

    (b) is so available for the purpose of—

        (i) making the provision of that network or service possible;

        (ii) making possible the provision of other services provided by means of that network or service; or

        (iii) supporting the provision of such other services."

Online infringement of copyright: obligations of internet service providers

Obligation to notify subscribers of copyright infringement reports

124A.—(1) This section applies if it appears to a copyright owner that—

    (a) a subscriber to an internet access service has infringed the owner's copyright by means of the service; or

    (b) a subscriber to an internet access service has allowed another person to use the service, and that other person has infringed the owner's copyright by means of the service.

(2) The owner may make a copyright infringement report to the internet service provider who provided the internet access service if a code in force under section 124C or 124D (an "initial obligations code") allows the owner to do so.

(3) A "copyright infringement report" is a report that—

(a) states that there appears to have been an infringement of the owner's copyright;

(b) includes a description of the apparent infringement;

(c) includes evidence of the apparent infringement that shows the subscriber's IP address and the time at which the evidence was gathered;

(d) is sent to the internet service provider within the period of 1 month beginning with the day on which the evidence was gathered; and

(e) complies with any other requirement of the initial obligations code.

(4) An internet service provider who receives a copyright infringement report must notify the subscriber of the report if the initial obligations code requires the provider to do so.

(5) A notification under subsection (4) must be sent to the subscriber within the period of 1 month beginning with the day on which the provider receives the report.

(6) A notification under subsection (4) must include—

(a) a statement that the notification is sent under this section in response to a copyright infringement report;

(b) the name of the copyright owner who made the report;

(c) a description of the apparent infringement;

(d) evidence of the apparent infringement that shows the subscriber's IP address and the time at which the evidence was gathered;

(e) information about subscriber appeals and the grounds on which they may be made;

(f) information about copyright and its purpose;

(g) advice, or information enabling the subscriber to obtain advice, about how to obtain lawful access to copyright works;

(h) advice, or information enabling the subscriber to obtain advice, about steps that a subscriber can take to protect an internet access service from unauthorised use; and

(i) anything else that the initial obligations code requires the notification to include.

(7) For the purposes of subsection (6)(h) the internet service provider must take into account the suitability of different protection for subscribers in different circumstances.

(8) The things that may be required under subsection (6)(i), whether in general or in a particular case, include in particular—

(a) a statement that information about the apparent infringement may be kept by the internet service provider;

(b) a statement that the copyright owner may require the provider to disclose which copyright infringement reports made by the owner to the provider relate to the subscriber;

(c) a statement that, following such a disclosure, the copyright owner may apply to a court to learn the subscriber's identity and may bring proceedings against the subscriber for copyright infringement; and

(d) where the requirement for the provider to send the notification arises partly because of a report that has already been the subject of a notification under subsection (4), a statement that the number of copyright infringement reports relating to the subscriber may be taken into account for the purposes of any technical measures.

(9) In this section "notify", in relation to a subscriber, means send a notification to the electronic or postal address held by the internet service provider for the subscriber (and sections 394 to 396 do not apply).

Note: Section 124A was inserted by the Digital Economy Act 2010 s.3 with effect from June 8, 2010 (see s.47(1) of the Act).

Obligation to provide copyright infringement lists to copyright owners

124B.—(1) An internet service provider must provide a copyright owner with a copyright infringement list for a period if—
 (a) the owner requests the list for that period; and
 (b) an initial obligations code requires the internet service provider to provide it.
 (2) A "copyright infringement list" is a list that—
 (a) sets out, in relation to each relevant subscriber, which of the copyright infringement reports made by the owner to the provider relate to the subscriber, but
 (b) does not enable any subscriber to be identified.
 (3) A subscriber is a "relevant subscriber" in relation to a copyright owner and an internet service provider if copyright infringement reports made by the owner to the provider in relation to the subscriber have reached the threshold set in the initial obligations code.

Note: Section 124B was inserted by the Digital Economy Act 2010 s.4 with effect from June 8, 2010 (see s.47(1) of the Act).

Approval of code about the initial obligations

124C.—(1) The obligations of internet service providers under sections 124A and 124B are the "initial obligations".
 (2) If it appears to OFCOM—
 (a) that a code has been made by any person for the purpose of regulating the initial obligations; and
 (b) that it would be appropriate for them to approve the code for that purpose,
they may by order approve it, with effect from the date given in the order.
 (3) The provision that may be contained in a code and approved under this section includes provision that—
 (a) specifies conditions that must be met for rights and obligations under the copyright infringement provisions or the code to apply in a particular case;
 (b) requires copyright owners or internet service providers to provide any information or assistance that is reasonably required to determine whether a condition under paragraph (a) is met.
 (4) The provision mentioned in subsection (3)(a) may, in particular, specify that a right or obligation does not apply in relation to a copyright owner unless the owner has made arrangements with an internet service provider regarding—
 (a) the number of copyright infringement reports that the owner may make to the provider within a particular period; and
 (b) payment in advance of a contribution towards meeting costs incurred by the provider.
 (5) The provision mentioned in subsection (3)(a) may also, in particular, provide that—
 (a) except as provided by the code, rights and obligations do not apply in re-

lation to an internet service provider unless the number of copyright infringement reports the provider receives within a particular period reaches a threshold set in the code; and

(b) if the threshold is reached, rights or obligations apply with effect from the date when it is reached or from a later time.

(6) OFCOM must not approve a code under this section unless satisfied that it meets the criteria set out in section 124E.

(7) Not more than one approved code may have effect at a time.

(8) OFCOM must keep an approved code under review.

(9) OFCOM may by order, at any time, for the purpose mentioned in subsection (2)—

(a) approve modifications that have been made to an approved code; or

(b) withdraw their approval from an approved code,

with effect from the date given in the order, and must do so if the code ceases to meet the criteria set out in section 124E.

(10) The consent of the Secretary of State is required for the approval of a code or the modification of an approved code.

(11) An order made by OFCOM under this section approving a code or modification must set out the code or modification.

(12) Section 403 applies to the power of OFCOM to make an order under this section.

(13) A statutory instrument containing an order made by OFCOM under this section is subject to annulment in pursuance of a resolution of either House of Parliament.

Note: Section 124C was inserted by the Digital Economy Act 2010 s.5 with effect from April 8, 2010 (see s.47(2) of the Act).

Initial obligations code by OFCOM in the absence of an approved code

124D.—(1) For any period when sections 124A and 124B are in force but for which there is no approved initial obligations code under OFCOM must by order make a code for the purpose of regulating the initial obligations.

(2) OFCOM may but need not make a code under subsection (1) for a time before the end of—

(a) the period of six months beginning with the day on which sections 124A and 124B come into force, or

(b) such longer period as the Secretary of State may specify by notice to OFCOM.

(3) The Secretary of State may give a notice under subsection (2)(b) only if it appears to the Secretary of State that it is not practicable for OFCOM to make a code with effect from the end of the period mentioned in subsection (2)(a) or any longer period for the time being specified under subsection (2)(b).

(4) A code under this section may do any of the things mentioned in section 124C(3) to (5).

(5) A code under this section may also—

(a) confer jurisdiction with respect to any matter (other than jurisdiction to determine appeals by subscribers) on OFCOM themselves;

(b) provide for OFCOM, in exercising such jurisdiction, to make awards of compensation, to direct the reimbursement of costs, or to do both;

(c) provide for OFCOM to enforce, or to participate in the enforcement of, any awards or directions made under the code;

(d) make other provision for the enforcement of such awards and directions;

(e) establish a body corporate, with the capacity to make its own rules and establish its own procedures, for the purpose of determining subscriber appeals;

(f) provide for a person with the function of determining subscriber appeals to enforce, or to participate in the enforcement of, any awards or directions made by the person;

(g) make other provision for the enforcement of such awards and directions; and

(h) make other provision for the purpose of regulating the initial obligations.

(6) OFCOM must not make a code under this section unless they are satisfied that it meets the criteria set out in section 124E.

(7) OFCOM must—

(a) keep a code under this section under review; and

(b) by order make any amendment of it that is necessary to ensure that while it is in force it continues to meet the criteria set out in section 124E.

(8) The consent of the Secretary of State is required for the making or amendment by OFCOM of a code under this section.

(9) Section 403 applies to the power of OFCOM to make an order under this section.

(10) A statutory instrument containing an order made by OFCOM under this section is subject to annulment in pursuance of a resolution of either House of Parliament.

Note: Section 124D was inserted by the Digital Economy Act 2010 s.6 with effect from April 8, 2010 (see s.47(1) of the Act).

Contents of initial obligations code

124E.—(1) The criteria referred to in sections 124C(6) and 124D(6) are—

(a) that the code makes the required provision about copyright infringement reports (see subsection (2));

(b) that it makes the required provision about the notification of subscribers (see subsections (3) and (4));

(c) that it sets the threshold applying for the purposes of determining who is a relevant subscriber within the meaning of section 124B(3) (see subsections (5) and (6));

(d) that it makes provision about how internet service providers are to keep information about subscribers;

(e) that it limits the time for which they may keep that information;

(f) that it makes any provision about contributions towards meeting costs that is required to be included by an order under section 124M;

(g) that the requirements concerning administration and enforcement are met in relation to the code (see subsections (7) and (8));

(h) that the requirements concerning subscriber appeals are met in relation to the code (see section 124K);

(i) that the provisions of the code are objectively justifiable in relation to the matters to which it relates;

(j) that those provisions are not such as to discriminate unduly against particular persons or against a particular description of persons;

(k) that those provisions are proportionate to what they are intended to achieve; and

(l) that, in relation to what those provisions are intended to achieve, they are transparent.

(2) The required provision about copyright infringement reports is provision that specifies—

    (a) requirements as to the means of obtaining evidence of infringement of copyright for inclusion in a report;

    (b) the standard of evidence that must be included; and

    (c) the required form of the report.

(3) The required provision about the notification of subscribers is provision that specifies, in relation to a subscriber in relation to whom an internet service provider receives one or more copyright infringement reports—

    (a) requirements as to the means by which the provider identifies the subscriber;

    (b) which of the reports the provider must notify the subscriber of; and

    (c) requirements as to the form, contents and means of the notification in each case.

(4) The provision mentioned in subsection (3) must not permit any copyright infringement report received by an internet service provider more than 12 months before the date of a notification of a subscriber to be taken into account for the purposes of the notification.

(5) The threshold applying in accordance with subsection (1)(c) may, subject to subsection (6), be set by reference to any matter, including in particular one or more of—

    (a) the number of copyright infringement reports;

    (b) the time within which the reports are made; and

    (c) the time of the apparent infringements to which they relate.

(6) The threshold applying in accordance with subsection (1)(c) must operate in such a way that a copyright infringement report received by an internet service provider more than 12 months before a particular date does not affect whether the threshold is met on that date; and a copyright infringement list provided under section 124B must not take into account any such report.

(7) The requirements concerning administration and enforcement are—

    (a) that OFCOM have, under the code, the functions of administering and enforcing it, including the function of resolving owner-provider disputes;

    (b) that there are adequate arrangements under the code for OFCOM to obtain any information or assistance from internet service providers or copyright owners that OFCOM reasonably require for the purposes of administering and enforcing the code; and

    (c) that there are adequate arrangements under the code for the costs incurred by OFCOM in administering and enforcing the code to be met by internet service providers and copyright owners.

(8) The provision mentioned in subsection (7) may include, in particular—

    (a) provision for the payment, to a person specified in the code, of a penalty not exceeding the maximum penalty for the time being specified in section 124L(2);

    (b) provision requiring a copyright owner to indemnify an internet service provider for any loss or damage resulting from the owner's failure to comply with the code or the copyright infringement provisions.

(9) In this section "owner-provider dispute" means a dispute that—

    (a) is between persons who are copyright owners or internet service providers; and

    (b) relates to an act or omission in relation to an initial obligation or an initial obligations code.

Note: Section 124E was inserted by the Digital Economy Act 2010 s.7 with effect from April 8, 2010 (see s.47(1) of the Act).

Progress reports

124F.—(1) OFCOM must prepare the following reports for the Secretary of State about the infringement of copyright by subscribers to internet access services.

(2) OFCOM must prepare a full report for—

(a) the period of 12 months beginning with the first day on which there is an initial obligations code in force; and

(b) each successive period of 12 months.

(3) OFCOM must prepare an interim report for—

(a) the period of 3 months beginning with the first day on which there is an initial obligations code in force; and

(b) each successive period of 3 months, other than one ending at the same time as a period of 12 months under subsection (2).

But this is subject to any direction by the Secretary of State under subsection (4).

(4) The Secretary of State may direct that subsection (3) no longer applies, with effect from the date given in the direction.

(5) A full report under this section must include—

(a) an assessment of the current level of subscribers' use of internet access services to infringe copyright;

(b) a description of the steps taken by copyright owners to enable subscribers to obtain lawful access to copyright works;

(c) a description of the steps taken by copyright owners to inform, and change the attitude of, members of the public in relation to the infringement of copyright;

(d) an assessment of the extent of the steps mentioned in paragraphs (b) and (c);

(e) an assessment of the extent to which copyright owners have made copyright infringement reports;

(f) an assessment of the extent to which they have brought legal proceedings against subscribers in relation to whom such reports have been made;

(g) an assessment of the extent to which any such proceedings have been against subscribers in relation to whom a substantial number of reports have been made; and

(h) anything else that the Secretary of State directs OFCOM to include in the report.

(6) An interim report under this section must include—

(a) the assessments mentioned in subsection (5)(a), (e) and (f); and

(b) anything else that the Secretary of State directs OFCOM to include in the report.

(7) OFCOM must send a report prepared under this section to the Secretary of State as soon as practicable after the end of the period for which it is prepared.

(8) OFCOM must publish every full report under this section—

(a) as soon as practicable after they send it to the Secretary of State, and

(b) in such manner as they consider appropriate for bringing it to the attention of persons who, in their opinion, are likely to have an interest in it.

(9) OFCOM may exclude information from a report when it is published under subsection (8) if they consider that it is information that they could refuse to disclose in response to a request under the Freedom of Information Act 2000.

Note: Section 124F was inserted by the Digital Economy Act 2010 s.8 with effect from June 8, 2010 (see s.47(1) of the Act).

Obligations to limit internet access: assessment and preparation

124G.—(1) The Secretary of State may direct OFCOM to—

(a) assess whether one or more technical obligations should be imposed on internet service providers;

(b) take steps to prepare for the obligations;

(c) provide a report on the assessment or steps to the Secretary of State.

(2) A "technical obligation", in relation to an internet service provider, is an obligation for the provider to take a technical measure against some or all relevant subscribers to its service for the purpose of preventing or reducing infringement of copyright by means of the internet.

(3) A "technical measure" is a measure that—

(a) limits the speed or other capacity of the service provided to a subscriber;

(b) prevents a subscriber from using the service to gain access to particular material, or limits such use;

(c) suspends the service provided to a subscriber; or

(d) limits the service provided to a subscriber in another way.

(4) A subscriber to an internet access service is "relevant" if the subscriber is a relevant subscriber, within the meaning of section 124B(3), in relation to the provider of the service and one or more copyright owners.

(5) The assessment and steps that the Secretary of State may direct OFCOM to carry out or take under subsection (1) include, in particular—

(a) consultation of copyright owners, internet service providers, subscribers or any other person;

(b) an assessment of the likely efficacy of a technical measure in relation to a particular type of internet access service; and

(c) steps to prepare a proposed technical obligations code.

(6) Internet service providers and copyright owners must give OFCOM any assistance that OFCOM reasonably require for the purposes of complying with any direction under this section.

(7) The Secretary of State must lay before Parliament any direction under this section.

(8) OFCOM must publish every report under this section—

(a) as soon as practicable after they send it to the Secretary of State, and

(b) in such manner as they consider appropriate for bringing it to the attention of persons who, in their opinion, are likely to have an interest in it.

(9) OFCOM may exclude information from a report when it is published under subsection (8) if they consider that it is information that they could refuse to disclose in response to a request under the Freedom of Information Act 2000.

Note: Section 124G was inserted by the Digital Economy Act 2010 s.9 with effect from June 8, 2010 (see s.47(1) of the Act).

Obligations to limit internet access

124H.—(1) The Secretary of State may by order impose a technical obligation on internet service providers if—

(a) OFCOM have assessed whether one or more technical obligations should be imposed on internet service providers; and

(b) taking into account that assessment, reports prepared by OFCOM under section 124F, and any other matter that appears to the Secretary of State to be relevant, the Secretary of State considers it appropriate to make the order.

(2) No order may be made under this section within the period of 12 months beginning with the first day on which there is an initial obligations code in force.

(3) An order under this section must specify the date from which the technical obligation is to have effect, or provide for it to be specified.

(4) The order may also specify—

(a) the criteria for taking the technical measure concerned against a subscriber;

(b) the steps to be taken as part of the measure and when they are to be taken.

(5) No order is to be made under this section unless—

(a) the Secretary of State has complied with subsections (6) to (10), and

(b) a draft of the order has been laid before Parliament and approved by a resolution of each House.

(6) If the Secretary of State proposes to make an order under this section, the Secretary of State must lay before Parliament a document that—

(a) explains the proposal, and

(b) sets it out in the form of a draft order.

(7) During the period of 60 days beginning with the day on which the document was laid under subsection (6) ("the 60-day period"), the Secretary of State may not lay before Parliament a draft order to give effect to the proposal (with or without modifications).

(8) In preparing a draft order under this section to give effect to the proposal, the Secretary of State must have regard to any of the following that are made with regard to the draft order during the 60-day period—

(a) any representations, and

(b) any recommendations of a committee of either House of Parliament charged with reporting on the draft order.

(9) When laying before Parliament a draft order to give effect to the proposal (with or without modifications), the Secretary of State must also lay a document that explains any changes made to the proposal contained in the document laid before Parliament under subsection (6).

(10) In calculating the 60-day period, no account is to be taken of any time during which Parliament is dissolved or prorogued or during which either House is adjourned for more than 4 days.

Note: Section 124H was inserted by the Digital Economy Act 2010 s.10 with effect from June 8, 2010 (see s.47(1) of the Act).

Code by OFCOM about obligations to limit internet access

124I.—(1) For any period during which there are one or more technical obligations in force under section 124H, OFCOM must by order make a technical obligations code for the purpose of regulating those obligations.

(2) The code may be made separately from, or in combination with, any initial obligations code under section 124D.

(3) A code under this section may—

(a) do any of the things mentioned in section 124C(3) to (5) or section 124D(5)(a) to (g); and

(b) make other provision for the purpose of regulating the technical obligations.

(4) OFCOM must not make a code under this section unless they are satisfied that it meets the criteria set out in section 124J.

(5) OFCOM must—

(a) keep a code under this section under review; and

(b) by order make any amendment of it that is necessary to ensure that while it is in force it continues to meet the criteria set out in section 124J.

B RELATED LEGISLATION AND MATERIALS

(6) The consent of the Secretary of State is required for the making or amendment by OFCOM of a code under this section.

(7) Section 403 applies to the power of OFCOM to make an order under this section.

(8) A statutory instrument containing an order made by OFCOM under this section is subject to annulment in pursuance of a resolution of either House of Parliament.

Note: Section 124I was inserted by the Digital Economy Act 2010 s.11 with effect from June 8, 2010 (see s.47(1) of the Act).

Contents of code about obligations to limit internet access

124J.—(1) The criteria referred to in section 124I(4) are—

(a) that the requirements concerning enforcement and related matters are met in relation to the code (see subsections (2) and (3));

(b) that the requirements concerning subscriber appeals are met in relation to the code (see section 124K);

(c) that it makes any provision about contributions towards meeting costs that is required to be included by an order under section 124M;

(d) that it makes any other provision that the Secretary of State requires it to make;

(e) that the provisions of the code are objectively justifiable in relation to the matters to which it relates;

(f) that those provisions are not such as to discriminate unduly against particular persons or against a particular description of persons;

(g) that those provisions are proportionate to what they are intended to achieve; and

(h) that, in relation to what those provisions are intended to achieve, they are transparent.

(2) The requirements concerning enforcement and related matters are—

(a) that OFCOM have, under the code, the functions of administering and enforcing it, including the function of resolving owner-provider disputes;

(b) that there are adequate arrangements under the code for OFCOM to obtain any information or assistance from internet service providers or copyright owners that OFCOM reasonably require for the purposes of administering and enforcing the code; and

(c) that there are adequate arrangements under the code for the costs incurred by OFCOM in administering and enforcing the code to be met by internet service providers and copyright owners.

(3) The provision made concerning enforcement and related matters may also (unless the Secretary of State requires otherwise) include, in particular—

(a) provision for the payment, to a person specified in the code, of a penalty not exceeding the maximum penalty for the time being specified in section 124L(2);

(b) provision requiring a copyright owner to indemnify an internet service provider for any loss or damage resulting from the owner's infringement or error in relation to the code or the copyright infringement provisions.

(4) In this section "owner-provider dispute" means a dispute that—

(a) is between persons who are copyright owners or internet service providers; and

(b) relates to an act or omission in relation to a technical obligation or a technical obligations code.

Note: Section 124J was inserted by the Digital Economy Act 2010 s.12 with effect from June 8, 2010 (see s.47(1) of the Act).

Subscriber appeals

124K.—(1) The requirements concerning subscriber appeals are—

   (a) for the purposes of section 124E(1)(h), the requirements of subsections (2) to (8); and

   (b) for the purposes of section 124J(1)(b), the requirements of subsections (2) to (11).

(2) The requirements of this subsection are—

   (a) that the code confers on subscribers the right to bring a subscriber appeal and, in the case of a technical obligations code, a further right of appeal to the First-tier Tribunal;

   (b) that there is a person who, under the code, has the function of determining subscriber appeals;

   (c) that that person is for practical purposes independent (so far as determining subscriber appeals is concerned) of internet service providers, copyright owners and OFCOM; and

   (d) that there are adequate arrangements under the code for the costs incurred by that person in determining subscriber appeals to be met by internet service providers, copyright owners and the subscriber concerned.

(3) The code must provide for the grounds of appeal (so far as an appeal relates to, or to anything done by reference to, a copyright infringement report) to include the following—

   (a) that the apparent infringement to which the report relates was not an infringement of copyright;

   (b) that the report does not relate to the subscriber's IP address at the time of the apparent infringement.

(4) The code must provide for the grounds of appeal to include contravention by the copyright owner or internet service provider of the code or of an obligation regulated by the code.

(5) The code must provide that an appeal on any grounds must be determined in favour of the subscriber unless the copyright owner or internet service provider shows that, as respects any copyright infringement report to which the appeal relates or by reference to which anything to which the appeal relates was done (or, if there is more than one such report, as respects each of them)—

   (a) the apparent infringement was an infringement of copyright, and

   (b) the report relates to the subscriber's IP address at the time of that infringement.

(6) The code must provide that, where a ground mentioned in subsection (3) is relied on, the appeal must be determined in favour of the subscriber if the subscriber shows that—

   (a) the act constituting the apparent infringement to which the report relates was not done by the subscriber, and

   (b) the subscriber took reasonable steps to prevent other persons infringing copyright by means of the internet access service.

(7) The powers of the person determining subscriber appeals must include power—

   (a) to secure so far as practicable that a subscriber is not prejudiced for the purposes of the copyright infringement provisions by an act or omission in respect of which an appeal is determined in favour of the subscriber;

(b) to make an award of compensation to be paid by a copyright owner or internet service provider to a subscriber affected by such an act or omission; and

(c) where the appeal is determined in favour of the subscriber, to direct the copyright owner or internet service provider to reimburse the reasonable costs of the subscriber.

(8) The code must provide that the power to direct the reimbursement of costs under subsection (7)(c) is to be exercised to award reasonable costs to a subscriber whose appeal is successful, unless the person deciding the appeal is satisfied that it would be unjust to give such a direction having regard to all the circumstances including the conduct of the parties before and during the proceedings.

(9) In the case of a technical obligations code, the powers of the person determining subscriber appeals must include power—

(a) on an appeal in relation to a technical measure or proposed technical measure—

(i) to confirm the measure;

(ii) to require the measure not to be taken or to be withdrawn;

(iii) to substitute any other technical measure that the internet service provider has power to take;

(b) to exercise the power mentioned in paragraph (a)(ii) or (iii) where an appeal is not upheld but the person determining it is satisfied that there are exceptional circumstances that justify the exercise of the power;

(c) to take any steps that OFCOM could take in relation to the act or omission giving rise to the technical measure; and

(d) to remit the decision whether to confirm the technical measure, or any matter relating to that decision, to OFCOM.

(10) In the case of a technical obligations code, the code must make provision—

(a) enabling a determination of a subscriber appeal to be appealed to the First-tier Tribunal, including on grounds that it was based on an error of fact, wrong in law or unreasonable;

(b) giving the First-tier Tribunal, in relation to an appeal to it, the powers mentioned in subsections (7) and (9); and

(c) in relation to recovery of costs awarded by the Tribunal.

(11) In the case of a technical obligations code, the code must include provision to secure that a technical measure is not taken against a subscriber until—

(a) the period for bringing a subscriber appeal, or any further appeal to the First-tier Tribunal, in relation to the proposed measure has ended (or the subscriber has waived the right to appeal); and

(b) any such subscriber appeal or further appeal has been determined, abandoned or otherwise disposed of.

Note: Section 124K was inserted by the Digital Economy Act 2010 s.13 with effect from June 8, 2010 (see s.47(1) of the Act).

Enforcement of obligations

124L.—(1) Sections 94 to 96 apply in relation to a contravention of an initial obligation or a technical obligation, or a contravention of an obligation under section 124G(6), as they apply in relation to a contravention of a condition set out under section 45.

(2) The amount of the penalty imposed under section 96 as applied by this section is to be such amount not exceeding £250,000 as OFCOM determine to be—

(a) appropriate; and

(b) proportionate to the contravention in respect of which it is imposed.

(3) In making that determination OFCOM must have regard to—

(a) any representations made to them by the internet service provider or copyright owner on whom the penalty is imposed;

(b) any steps taken by the provider or owner towards complying with the obligations contraventions of which have been notified to the provider or owner under section 94 (as applied); and

(c) any steps taken by the provider or owner for remedying the consequences of those contraventions.

(4) The Secretary of State may by order amend this section so as to substitute a different maximum penalty for the maximum penalty for the time being specified in subsection (2).

(5) No order is to be made containing provision authorised by subsection (4) unless a draft of the order has been laid before Parliament and approved by a resolution of each House.

Note: Section 124L was inserted by the Digital Economy Act 2010 s.14 with effect from June 8, 2010 (see s.47(1) of the Act).

Sharing of costs

124M.—(1) The Secretary of State may by order specify provision that must be included in an initial obligations code or a technical obligations code about payment of contributions towards costs incurred under the copyright infringement provisions.

(2) Any provision specified under subsection (1) must relate to payment of contributions by one or more of the following only—

(a) copyright owners;

(b) internet service providers;

(c) in relation to a subscriber appeal or a further appeal by a subscriber to the First-tier Tribunal, the subscriber.

(3) Provision specified under subsection (1) may relate to, in particular—

(a) payment by a copyright owner of a contribution towards the costs that an internet service provider incurs;

(b) payment by a copyright owner or internet service provider of a contribution towards the costs that OFCOM incur.

(4) Provision specified under subsection (1) may include, in particular—

(a) provision about costs incurred before the provision is included in an initial obligations code or a technical obligations code;

(b) provision for payment in advance of expected costs (and for reimbursement of overpayments where the costs incurred are less than expected);

(c) provision about how costs, expected costs or contributions must be calculated;

(d) other provision about when and how contributions must be paid.

(5) No order is to be made under this section unless a draft of the order has been laid before Parliament and approved by a resolution of each House.

Note: Section 124M was inserted by the Digital Economy Act 2010 s.15 with effect from April 8, 2010 (see s.47(2) of the Act).

Interpretation

124N. In sections 124A to 124M and this section—

"apparent infringement", in relation to a copyright infringement report, means the infringement of copyright that the report states appears to have taken place;

"copyright infringement list" has the meaning given in section 124B(2);

"copyright infringement provisions" means sections 124A to 124M and this section;

"copyright infringement report" has the meaning given in section 124A(3);

"copyright owner" means —

> (a) a copyright owner within the meaning of Part 1 of the Copyright, Designs and Patents Act 1988 (see section 173 of that Act); or

> (b) someone authorised by that person to act on the person's behalf;

"copyright work" has the same meaning as in Part 1 of the Copyright, Designs and Patents Act 1988 (see section 1(2) of that Act);

"initial obligations" has the meaning given in section 124C(1);

"initial obligations code" has the meaning given in section 124A(2);

"internet access service" means an electronic communications service that—

> (a) is provided to a subscriber;

> (b) consists entirely or mainly of the provision of access to the internet; and

> (c) includes the allocation of an IP address or IP addresses to the subscriber to enable that access;

"internet service provider" means a person who provides an internet access service;

"IP address" means an internet protocol address;

"subscriber", in relation to an internet access service, means a person who—

> (a) receives the service under an agreement between the person and the provider of the service; and

> (b) does not receive it as a communications provider;

"subscriber appeal" means —

> (a) in relation to an initial obligations code, an appeal by a subscriber on grounds specified in the code in relation to—

>> (i) the making of a copyright infringement report;

>> (ii) notification under section 124A(4);

>> (iii) the inclusion or proposed inclusion of an entry in a copyright infringement list; or

>> (iv) any other act or omission in relation to an initial obligation or an initial obligations code;

> (b) in relation to a technical obligations code, an appeal by a subscriber on grounds specified in the code in relation to—

>> (i) the proposed taking of a technical measure; or

>> (ii) any other act or omission in relation to a technical obligation or a technical obligations code;

"technical measure" has the meaning given in section 124G(3);

"technical obligation" has the meaning given in section 124G(2);

"technical obligations code" means a code in force under section 124I.

Note: Section 124N was inserted by the Digital Economy Act 2010 s.16(1) with effect from April 8, 2010 (see s.47(2) of the Act).

B11.iii Civil Procedure Rules 45.30 to 45.32

VII. SCALE COSTS FOR CLAIMS IN THE INTELLECTUAL PROPERTY ENTERPRISE COURT

Scope and interpretation

45.30.—(1) Subject to paragraph (2), this Section applies to proceedings in [the Intellectual Property Enterprise Court].

(2) This Section does not apply where—

(a) the court considers that a party has behaved in a manner which amounts to an abuse of the court's process; or

(b) the claim concerns the infringement or revocation of a patent or registered design [or registered trade mark] the validity of which has been certified by a court [or by the Comptroller-General of Patents, Designs and Trade Marks] in earlier proceedings.

(3) The court will make a summary assessment of the costs of the party in whose favour any order for costs is made. Rules 44.2(8), 44.7(b) and Part 47 do not apply to this Section.

(4) "Scale costs" means the costs set out in Table A and Table B of the Practice Direction supplementing this Part.

Notes:

(1) In subs.(1) words in square brackets substituted by the Civil Procedure (Amendment No.7) Rules 2013/1974, r.20(f)(i) with effect from October 1, 2013.

(2) In subs.2(b) first words in square brackets inserted by Civil Procedure (Amendment) Rules 2014/407, r.19 with effect from April 6, 2014. In subs.2(b) words in second square brackets inserted by the Civil Procedure (Amendment No.7) Rules 2013/1974, r.20(f)(ii) with effect from (October 1, 2013.

Amount of scale costs

45.31—(1) Subject to rule 45.32, the court will not order a party to pay total costs of more than—

(a) £50,000 on the final determination of a claim in relation to liability; and

(b) £25,000 on an inquiry as to damages or account of profits.

(2) The amounts in paragraph (1) apply after the court has applied the provision on set off in accordance with rule 44.12(a).

(3) The maximum amount of scale costs that the court will award for each stage of the claim is set out in Practice Direction 45.

(4) The amount of the scale costs awarded by the court in accordance with paragraph (3) will depend on the nature and complexity of the claim.

[(4A Subject to assessment where appropriate, the following may be recovered in addition to the amount of the scale costs set out in Practice Direction 45 – Fixed Costs—

(a) court fees;

(b) costs relating to the enforcement of any court order; and

(c) wasted costs.]

(5) Where appropriate, [VAT] may be recovered in addition to the amount of the scale costs and any reference in this Section to scale costs is a reference to those costs net of any such VAT.

Note: Subsection (4A) added and in subs.(5) words in square brackets substituted by the Civil Procedure (Amendment No.7) Rules 2013/1974, r.20(g)(i) with effect from October 1, 2013.

Summary assessment of the costs of an application where a party has behaved unreasonably

45.32 Costs awarded to a party under rule 63.26(2) are in addition to the total costs that may be awarded to that party under rule 45.31.]

Note: Section IV (rr.45.30 to 32) substituted for existing Section VII (rr.45.41 to 43), subject to transitional provisions, by the Civil Procedure (Amendment) Rules 2013 (SI 2013/262), Sch.1 para.1, with effect from April 1, 2013 (for transitional provisions see (SI 2013/262), r.22(8)).

B11.iv Civil Procedure Rules 63.13 and 63.17–26

II. REGISTERED TRADE MARKS AND OTHER INTELLECTUAL PROPERTY RIGHTS

Allocation

63.13. Claims relating to matters arising out of the 1994 Act and other intellectual property rights set out in [Practice Direction 63] must be started in—
    (a) the Chancery Division;
    (b) [the Intellectual Property Enterprise Court]; or
    (c) save as set out in [Practice Direction 63], a [County Court hearing centre] where there is also a Chancery District Registry.

Notes:
    (1) In first sentence and para.(c) first words in brackets substituted by the Civil Procedure (Amendment No.2) Rules (SI 2009/3390) r.38(a) with effect from April 6, 2010.
    (2) In para.(b) words in square brackets substituted for words "a patents county court", subject to saving, by the Civil Procedure (Amendment No.7) Rules 2013 (SI 2013/ 1974) r.26(g), with effect from October 1, 2013 (for saving see r.30).
    (3) In para.(c) second words in square brackets substituted for words "county court" by the Civil Procedure (Amendment) Rules 2014 (SI 2014/407), r.27(a), with effect from April 22, 2014 (being the date on which the Crime and Courts Act 2013, s.17(1) and (2) came into force for all purposes).

V. [INTELLECTUAL PROPERTY ENTERPRISE COURT]

Scope of this Section

[63.17. This Part, as modified by this Section, applies to claims started in or transferred to [the Intellectual Property Enterprise Court].]

Note:
    (1) In heading, words in square brackets substituted for words "a patents county court", subject to saving, by Civil Procedure (Amendment No.7) Rules 2013 (SI 2013/1974), r.26(h), with effect from October 1, 2013 (for saving see r.30).
    (2) This rule was added by the Civil Procedure (Amendment No.2) Rules (SI 2010/ 1953) Sch.2 para.1 with effect from October 1, 2010.
    (3) Words in square brackets substituted for words "a patents county court", subject to saving, by Civil Procedure (Amendment No.7) Rules 2013 (SI 2013/1974), r.26(I), with effect from October 1, 2013 (for saving see r.30).

[63.17A—(1) In proceedings in the Intellectual Property Enterprise Court in which a claim is made for damages or an account of profits, the amount or value of that claim shall not exceed £500,000.
    (2) In determining the amount or value of a claim for the purpose of paragraph (1), a claim for—

(a) interest, other than interest payable under an agreement; or

(b) costs,

shall be disregarded.

(3) Paragraph (1) shall not apply if the parties agree that the Intellectual Property Enterprise Court shall have jurisdiction to award damages or profits in excess of £500,000.]

Note: Rule 17A inserted, subject to saving, by Civil Procedure (Amendment No.7) Rules 2013 (SI 2013/1974), r.26(j), with effect from October 1, 2013 (for saving see r.30).

Transfer of proceedings

[**63.18.**—(1) Rule 30.5 applies save for the modifications—

(a) a judge sitting in the County Court or the general Chancery Division may order proceedings to be transferred to the Intellectual Property Enterprise Court; and

(b) an application for the transfer of proceedings from the County Court or the general Chancery Division to the Intellectual Property Enterprise Court may be made to a judge sitting in the County Court or the general Chancery Division respectively.

(2) When considering whether to transfer proceedings to or from the Intellectual Property Enterprise Court, the court will have regard to the provisions of Practice Direction 30.]

Note: Rule 63.18 substituted by Civil Procedure (Amendment No.7) Rules 2013 (SI 2013/1974), s.26(k), with effect from October 1, 2013 (for saving see r.30). Rule 63.18 (as inserted by SI 2010/1953) formerly read:

"63.18 When considering whether to transfer proceedings to or from a patents county court, the court will have regard to the provisions of Practice Direction 30."

[Enterprise judges and [District Judges]]

[**63.19.**—(1) Subject to paragraph (2), proceedings in [the Intellectual Property Enterprise Court will be dealt with by an enterprise judge.]

[(1A) For the purposes of the Practice Direction 52A – Appeals: General Provisions, a decision of the enterprise judge shall be treated as a decision by a circuit judge hearing a specialist claim in the County Court.]

[(2) Unless the court otherwise orders, the following matters will be dealt with by a district judge—

(a) allocation of claims to the small claims track or multi-track in accordance with rule 63.27(3);

(b) claims allocated to the small claims track; and

(c) all proceedings for the enforcement of any financial element of an Intellectual Property Enterprise Court judgment.

(3) For the purposes of the Practice Direction 52A – Appeals: General Provisions, a decision of a district judge shall be treated as a decision by a district judge hearing a specialist claim in the County Court. An appeal from such a decision shall be heard by an enterprise judge.]

Note:

(1) This rule was added by the Civil Procedure (Amendment No.2) Rules (SI 2010/1953) Sch.2 para.1 with effect from October 1, 2010.

(2) Heading substituted for words "Patents judge", in para.(1) words in square brackets substituted for words "a patents county court will be dealt with by the patents judge of that court", and paras (1A), (2), (3) inserted by Civil Procedure (Amendment No.7) Rules 2013 (SI 2013/1974), s.26(l), with effect from October 1, 2013 (for saving see r.30).

(3) In heading words substituted by the Civil Procedure (Amendment) Rules 2014 (SI 2014/407), r.4(a), with effect from April 22, 2014 (being the date on which the Crime and Courts Act 2013, s.17(1) and (2) came into force for all purposes).

Statements of case

[**63.20.**—(1) Part 16 applies with the modification that a statement of case must set out concisely all the facts and arguments upon which the party serving it relies.

(2) The particulars of claim must state whether the claimant has complied with paragraph 7.1(1) and Annex A (paragraph 2) of the Practice Direction (Pre-Action Conduct).]

Note: This rule was added by the Civil Procedure (Amendment No.2) Rules (SI 2010/1953) Sch.2 para.1 with effect from October 1, 2010.

Statement of truth

[**63.21.** Part 22 applies with the modification that the statement of truth verifying a statement of case must be signed by a person with knowledge of the facts alleged, or if no one person has knowledge of all the facts, by persons who between them have knowledge of all the facts alleged.]

Note: This rule was added by the Civil Procedure (Amendment No.2) Rules (SI 2010/1953) Sch.2 para.1 with effect from October 1, 2010.

Defence and reply

[**63.22.**—(1) Rule 63.7 does not apply and Part 15 applies with the following modifications.

(2) Where the particulars of claim contain a confirmation in accordance with rule 63.20(2), the period for filing a defence [where the defendant files an acknowledgment of service under Part 10] is 42 days after service of the particulars of claim unless rule 15.4(2) provides for a longer period to do so.

(3) Where the particulars of claim do not contain a confirmation in accordance with rule 63.20(2), the period for filing a defence [where the defendant files an acknowledgment of service under Part 10] is 70 days after service of the particulars of claim.

(4) Where the claimant files a reply to a defence it must be filed and served on all other parties within 28 days of service of the defence.

(5) Where the defendant files a reply to a defence to a counterclaim it must be filed and served on all other parties within 14 days of service of the defence to the counterclaim.

(6) The periods in this rule may only be extended by order of the court and for good reason.]

Notes:
(1) This rule was added by the Civil Procedure (Amendment No.2) Rules (SI 2010/1953) Sch.2 para.1 with effect from October 1, 2010.
(2) In paras (2), (3) words in square brackets inserted by the Civil Procedure (Amendment No.7) Rules 2013 (SI 2013/197), s.26(m), with effect from October 1, 2013 (for saving see r.30).

Case management

[**63.23.**—(1) At the first case management conference after those defendants who intend to file and serve a defence have done so, the court will identify the issues and decide whether to make an order in accordance with paragraph 29.1 of Practice Direction 63.

(2) Save in exceptional circumstances the court will not [permit] by a party to submit material in addition to that ordered under paragraph (1).

(3) The court may determine the claim on the papers where all parties consent.]

Notes:

    (1) This rule was added by the Civil Procedure (Amendment No.2) Rules (SI 2010/1953), Sch.2 para.1 with effect from October 1, 2010.

    (2) In para.(2) words in square brackets substituted for words "consider an application by" by the Civil Procedure (Amendment No.7) Rules 2013 (SI 2013/1974), s.26(n), with effect from October 1, 2013 (for saving see r.30).

Disclosure and inspection

[63.24.—(1) Rule 63.9 does not apply.

(2) Part 31 applies save that the provisions on standard disclosure do not apply.]

Note: This rule was added by the Civil Procedure (Amendment No.2) Rules (SI 2010/1953) Sch.2 para.1 with effect from October 1, 2010.

Applications

[63.25.—(1) Part 23 applies with the modifications set out in this rule.

(2) Except at the case management conference provided for in rule 63.23(1), a respondent to an application must file and serve on all relevant parties a response within 5 days of the service of the application notice.

(3) The court will deal with an application without a hearing unless the court considers it necessary to hold a hearing.

(4) An application to transfer the claim to the [Patents Court or general Chancery Division] or to stay proceedings must be made before or at the case management conference provided for in rule 63.23(1).

(5) The court will consider an application to transfer the claim later in the proceedings only where there are exceptional circumstances.]

Notes:

    (1) This rule was added by the Civil Procedure (Amendment No.2) Rules (SI 2010/1953) Sch.2 para.1 with effect from October 1, 2010.

    (2) In para.(4) words in square brackets substituted for words "High Court or" by the Civil Procedure (Amendment No.7) Rules 2013 (SI 2013/1974), s.26(o), with effect from October 1, 2013 (for saving see r.30).

Costs

[63.26.—(1) Subject to paragraph (2), the court will reserve the costs of an application to the conclusion of the trial when they will be subject to summary assessment.

(2) Where a party has behaved unreasonably the court [may] make an order for costs at the conclusion of the hearing.

(3) Where the court makes a summary assessment of costs, it will do so in accordance with [Section IV] of Part 45.]

Notes:

    (1) This rule was added by the Civil Procedure (Amendment No.2) Rules (SI 2010/1953) Sch.2 para.1 with effect from October 1, 2010.

    (2) In paras (2), (3) words in square brackets substituted for words "will" and "Section VII" respectively by the Civil Procedure (Amendment No.7) Rules 2013 (SI 2013/1974), s.26(o), with effect from October 1, 2013 (for saving see r.30).

Allocation to the small claims track

[63.27—(1) A claim started in or transferred to [the Intellectual Property Enterprise Court] will be allocated to the small claims track if—

    (a) rule 63.13, but not rule 63.2, applies to the claim;

    (b) the value of the claim is not more than [£10,000];

    (c) it is stated in the particulars of claim that the claimant wishes the claim to be allocated to the small claims track; and

    (d) no objection to the claim being allocated to the small claims track is raised by the defendant in the defence.

  [(2) [...]

  (3) If either—

    (a) the requirements of rule 63.27(1)(a), (b) and (c) are satisfied, but in the defence the defendant objects to the claim being allocated to the small claims track; or

    (b) the requirements of rule 63.27(1)(a) and (b) are satisfied, but not (c), and in the defence the defendant requests that the claim be allocated to the small claims track, the court will allocate the claim to the small claims track or the multi-track in accordance with Part 26 (case management – preliminary stage). [For that purpose the court will send the parties a directions questionnaire and require them to file completed directions questionnaires and to serve them on all other parties within 14 days.]

  (4) Part 27 (small claims track) shall apply to claims allocated to the small claims track in [the Intellectual Property Enterprise Court] with the modification to rule 27.2(1)(a) that Part 25 (interim remedies) shall not apply to such claims at all. [Section IV] of Part 45 (scale costs for claims in [the Intellectual Property Enterprise Court]) shall not apply to claims allocated to the small claims track in [the Intellectual Property Enterprise Court].]

Notes:

    (1) In para.(1)(b) figure in square brackets substituted for figure "£5,000", subject to savings and transitional provisions, by the Civil Procedure (Amendment) Rules 2013 (SI 2013/262), r.19, with effect from April 1, 2013 (for savings and transitional provisions, see SI 2013/262 r.22(3)).

    (2) Para.(2) revoked, in para.(3) words in square brackets inserted, and in paras (1), (4) words in square brackets substituted for words "a patents county court" and in para.(4) words "Section IV" substituted for words "Section VII" by the Civil Procedure (Amendment No.7) Rules 2013 (SI 2013/1974), s.26(q), with effect from October 1, 2013 (for saving see r.30).

Extent to which rules in this Part apply to small claims

[63.28—(1) To the extent provided by this rule, this Part shall apply to a claim allocated to, or requested to be allocated to, the small claims track in [the Intellectual Property Enterprise Court].

  (2) Rules 63.1, 63.13, 63.18, 63.20, 63.21, 63.22, 63.25, 63.26(1) and (2), and 63.27 shall apply to the claim.

  (3) No other rules in this Part shall apply.]

Note: In para.(1) words in square brackets substituted for words "a patents county court" by the Civil Procedure (Amendment) Rules 2013 (SI 2013/262), r.26(r) with effect from April 1, 2013 (for savings and transitional provisions, see SI 2013/262 r.22(3)).

B11.v Practice Direction 45 — Fixed Costs

SECTION IV SCALE COSTS FOR PROCEEDINGS IN THE INTELLECTUAL PROPERTY ENTERPRISE COURT

3.1 Tables A and B set out the maximum amount of scale costs which the court will award for each stage of a claim in the Intellectual Property Enterprise Court.

3.2 Table A sets out the scale costs for each stage of a claim up to determination of liability.

3.3 Table B sets out the scale costs for each stage of an inquiry as to damages or account of profits.

TABLE A

Stage of a claim	Maximum amount of costs
Particulars of claim	£7,000
Defence and counterclaim	£7,000
Reply and defence to counterclaim	£7,000
Attendance at a case management conference	£3,000
Making or responding to an application	£3,000
Providing or inspecting disclosure or product/process description	£6,000
Performing or inspecting experiments	£3,000
Preparing witness statements	£6,000
Preparing experts' report	£8,000
Preparing for and attending trial and judgment	£16,000
Preparing for determination on the papers	£5,500

TABLE B

Stage of a claim	Maximum amount of costs
Points of claim	£3,000
Points of defence	£3,000
Attendance at a case management conference	£3,000
Making or responding to an application	£3,000
Providing or inspecting disclosure	£3,000
Preparing witness statements	£6,000
Preparing experts' report	£6,000
Preparing for and attending trial and judgment	£8,000
Preparing for determination on the papers	£3,000

B11.vi Practice Direction 63—Intellectual Property Claims

SECTION II. PROVISIONS ABOUT REGISTERED TRADE MARKS AND OTHER INTELLECTUAL PROPERTY RIGHTS

Allocation (rule 63.13)

16.1 The other intellectual property rights referred to in rule 63.13 are—

(1) copyright;

(2) rights in performances;

(3) rights conferred under Part VII of the 1988 Act ;
(4) design right;
(5) Community design right;
(6) association rights;
(7) moral rights;
(8) database rights
(9) unauthorised decryption rights;
(10) hallmarks;
(11) claims in respect of technical trade secrets;
(12) passing off;
(13) protected designations of origin, protected geographical indications and traditional speciality guarantees;
(14) registered trade marks; and
(15) Community trade marks.

16.2 There are Chancery district registries at Birmingham, Bristol, Caernarfon, Cardiff, Leeds, Liverpool, Manchester, Mold, Newcastle upon Tyne and Preston.
16.3 The County Court hearing centres at Caernarfon, Mold and Preston do not have jurisdiction in relation to registered trade marks and Community trade marks.

Starting the claim

17.1 Except for claims started in the Intellectual Property Enterprise Court, a claim form to which Section II of Part 63 applies must be marked in the top right hand corner 'Intellectual Property' below the title of the court in which it is issued.
17.2 In the case of claims concerning registered trade marks and Community trade marks, the claim form must state the registration number of any trade mark to which the claim relates.

Claim for additional damages under section 97(2), section 191J(2) or section 229(3) of the 1988 Act

22.1 Where a claimant seeks to recover additional damages under section 97(2), section 191J(2) or section 229(3) of the 1988 Act, the particulars of claim must include—
(1) a statement to that effect; and
(2) the grounds for claiming them.

Application for delivery up or forfeiture under the 1988 Act

23.1 An applicant who applies under section 99, 114, 195, 204, 230 or 231 of the 1988 Act for delivery up or forfeiture must serve—
(1) the claim form; or
(2) application notice, where appropriate,
on all identifiable persons who have an interest in the goods, material or articles within the meaning of section 114, 204 or 231 of the 1988 Act.

SECTION IV. PROVISIONS ABOUT FINAL ORDERS

Costs

26.1 Where the court makes an order for delivery up or destruction of infringing goods, or articles designed or adapted to make such goods, the person against whom the order is made must pay the costs of complying with that order unless the court orders otherwise.
26.2 Where the court finds that an intellectual property right has been infringed,

the court may, at the request of the applicant, order appropriate measures for the dissemination and publication of the judgment to be taken at the expense of the infringer.

SECTION V. PROVISIONS ABOUT PROCEEDINGS IN THE INTELLECTUAL PROPERTY ENTERPRISE COURT

Scope of Section V

27.1 Except as provided for in paragraph 27.2 this Practice Direction, as modified by this Section, applies to claims in the Intellectual Property Enterprise Court.

27.2 Paragraph 5.2, paragraphs 5.10 to 9.1 and paragraph 9.2(3) do not apply to a claim in the Intellectual Property Enterprise Court.

Claims for infringement or challenge to validity

28.1 Paragraph 4.2(2) is modified so that the grounds for invalidity must be included in the statement of case and not in a separate document.

Case management (rule 63.23)

29.1 At the case management conference referred to in rule 63.23 the court may order any of the following—

(1) specific disclosure;

(2) a product or process description (or a supplementary product or process description where one has already been provided);

(3) experiments;

(4) witness statements;

(5) experts' reports;

(6) cross examination at trial;

(7) written submissions or skeleton arguments

29.2 The court will make an order under paragraph 29.1 only —

(1) in relation to specific and identified issues; and

(2) if the court is satisfied that the benefit of the further material in terms of its value in resolving those issues appears likely to justify the cost of producing and dealing with it.

Applications (rule 63.25)

30.1 Where the court considers that a hearing is necessary under rule 63.25(3) the court will conduct a hearing by telephone or video conference in accordance with paragraphs 6.2 to 7 of Practice Direction 23A unless it considers that a hearing in person would be more cost effective for the parties or is otherwise necessary in the interests of justice.

Determination of the claim

31.1 Where possible, the court will determine the claim solely on the basis of the parties' statements of case and oral submissions.

31.2 The court will set the timetable for the trial and will, so far as appropriate, allocate equal time to the parties. Cross-examination will be strictly controlled by the court. The court will endeavour to ensure that the trial lasts no more than 2 days.

B12. PUBLIC SECTOR INFORMATION

B12.i Directive 2003/98/EC of the European Parliament and of the Council of 17 November 2003 on the re-use of public sector information

See below, **H10**.

B12.ii The Re-use of Public Sector Information Regulations 2015

(SI 2015/ 1415)

Made	*24th June 2015*
Laid before Parliament	*25th June 2015*
Coming into force	*18th July 2015*

The Secretary of State is designated for the purposes of section 2(2) of the European Communities Act 1972 in relation to the re-use of public sector information. The Secretary of State makes the following Regulations in exercise of the powers conferred by that section.

Citation and commencement

1. These Regulations may be cited as the Re-use of Public Sector Information Regulations 2015 and come into force on 18th July 2015.

Interpretation

2. In these Regulations–
"the 1998 Act" means the Data Protection Act 1998;
"the 2000 Act" means the Freedom of Information Act 2000;
"the 2002 Act" means the Freedom of Information (Scotland) Act 2002;
"the 2004 Regulations" means the Environmental Information Regulations 2004;
"the 2004 Scottish Regulations" means the Environmental Information (Scotland) Regulations 2004;
"the 2009 Regulations" means the INSPIRE (Scotland) Regulations 2009;
"applicant" means a person who makes a request for re-use of a document to a public sector body;
"document" means any information recorded in any form, including any part of such information, whether in writing or stored in electronic form or as a sound, visual or audio-visual recording, other than a computer program;
"formal open standard" means a standard which has been laid down in written form, detailing specifications for the requirements of how to ensure software interoperability;
"government department" includes a Northern Ireland department and any other body or authority exercising statutory functions on behalf of the Crown;
"information access legislation" means the 1998 Act, the 2000 Act, the 2002 Act, the 2004 Regulations, the 2004 Scottish Regulations, the 2009 Regulations and the 2009 Scottish Regulations;

"machine-readable format" means a file format structured so that software applications can easily identify, recognise and extract specific data, including individual statements of fact, and their internal structure;

"open format" means a file format that is platform-independent and made available to the public without any restriction that impedes the re-use of documents;

"public sector body" has the meaning ascribed to it by regulation 3;

"relevant intellectual property rights" means any of the following rights–

    (a) copyright (within the meaning of section 1 of the Copyright, Designs and Patents Act 1988);

    (b) database right (within the meaning of regulation 13 of the Copyright and Rights in Database Regulations 1997);

    (c) publication right (within the meaning of regulation 16 of the Copyright and Related Rights Regulations 1996);

    (d) rights in performances (meaning the rights conferred by Part 2 of the Copyright, Designs and Patents Act 1988);

"re-use" and cognate expressions have the meaning ascribed to them in regulation 4;

"university" means any public sector body that provides post-secondary school higher education leading to academic degrees;

"working day" means any day other than a Saturday or a Sunday, Christmas Day, Good Friday or any day which is a bank holiday under the Banking and Financial Dealings Act 1971 in any part of the United Kingdom.

"writing" includes text which is–

    (a) transmitted by electronic means;

    (b) received in legible form; and

    (c) capable of being used for subsequent reference.

Public Sector Body

3.—(1) For the purposes of these Regulations each of the following is a public sector body–

(a) a Minister of the Crown;

(b) a government department;

(c) the Corporate Officer of the House of Commons;

(d) the Corporate Officer of the House of Lords;

(e) the Northern Ireland Assembly Commission;

(f) Scottish Ministers;

(g) the Scottish Parliament;

(h) the Scottish Parliamentary Corporate Body;

(i) the National Assembly for Wales Commission;

(j) Welsh Ministers;

(k) a local authority;

(l) a fire and rescue authority constituted by a scheme under section 2 of the Fire and Rescue Services Act 2004 or a scheme to which section 4 of that Act applies;

(m) the Northern Ireland Fire and Rescue Service Board;

(n) a police and crime commissioner elected under section 1 of the Police Reform and Social Responsibility Act 2011;

(o) a chief constable of a police force appointed under section 2 of that Act;

(p) The Mayor's Office for Policing and Crime established under section 3 of that Act;

(q) the Commissioner of Police of the Metropolis appointed under section 4 of that Act;

(r) the Scottish Police Authority established under section 1 of the Police and Fire Reform (Scotland) Act 2012;

(s) the Police Service of Scotland established under section 6 of that Act;

(t) the Northern Ireland Policing Board;

(u) an authority established under section 10 of the Local Government Act 1985;

(v) a joint authority established by Part IV of that Act;

(w) any body established pursuant to an order under section 67 of that Act;

(x) the Broads Authority;

(y) any joint board the constituent members of which consist of any of the bodies specified in paragraphs (k) and (l), (n) to (s) and (u) to (x);

(z) a National Park authority established by an Order under section 63 of the Environment Act 1995;

(aa) a corporation established or a group of individuals appointed to act together for the specific purposes of meeting needs in the general interest, not having an industrial or commercial character, and–

(i) financed wholly or mainly by another public sector body, or

(ii) subject to management supervision by another public sector body, or

(iii) more than half of the board of directors or members of which, or in the case of a group of individuals, more than half of those individuals, are appointed by another public sector body;

(bb) an association of or formed by one or more public sector bodies.

(cc) a community justice authority established under section 3 of the Management of Offenders etc. (Scotland) Act 2005.

(2) In the application of these Regulations to England, "local authority" means–

(a) a county council, a district council, a London borough council, a parish council or the Council of the Isles of Scilly;

(b) the Common Council of the City of London in its capacity as local authority or police authority;

(c) the Greater London Authority or a functional body within the meaning of the Greater London Authority Act 1999.

(3) In the application of these Regulations to Wales, "local authority" means a county borough council or community council.

(4) In the application of these Regulations to Scotland, "local authority" means a council constituted under section 2 of the Local Government etc. (Scotland) Act 1994 and also includes a joint board or joint committee within the meaning of that section.

(5) In the application of these Regulations to Northern Ireland, "local authority" means a district council within the meaning of the Local Government Act (Northern Ireland) 1972.

Re-use of documents

4.—(1) Subject to paragraph (2), re-use means the use by a person of a document held by a public sector body for a purpose other than the initial purpose within that public sector body's public task for which the document was produced.

(2) Re-use shall not include–

(a) the transfer for use of a document within a public sector body for the purpose of carrying out its own public task; or

(b) the transfer for use of a document from one public sector body to another for the purpose of either public sector body carrying out its public task.

Exclusions

5.—(1) These Regulations do not apply to a document where–
- (a) the activity of supplying the document is one which falls outside the public task of the public sector body, provided that the scope of the public task of that body is transparent and subject to review; or
- (b) a third party owns relevant intellectual property rights in the document.

(2) These Regulations do not apply to a document unless it–
- (a) has been identified by the public sector body as being available for re-use;
- (b) has been provided to the applicant; or
- (c) is accessible by means other than by making a request for it within the meaning of the 1998 Act, the 2000 Act (or where appropriate the 2002 Act) or the 2004 Regulations (or where appropriate the 2004 Scottish Regulations).

(3) These Regulations do not apply to documents held by–
- (a) public service broadcasters and their subsidiaries, and other bodies and their subsidiaries for the purposes of the provision of programme services or the conduct of any activities which a public service broadcaster is required or empowered to provide or to engage in by or under any enactment or other public instrument;
- (b) educational and research establishments including organisations established for the transfer of research results, schools and universities (except university libraries); or
- (c) cultural establishments, other than libraries, museums and archives.

(4) For the purposes of paragraph (3), "public service broadcaster" has the same meaning given by section 264(12) of the Communications Act 2003, "subsidiary" has the meaning given by section 1159 of the Companies Act 2006 and "programme services" has the meaning given by section 405(1) of the Communications Act 2003.

(5) These Regulations do not apply in any situation in which a person is under a legal obligation to prove an interest in order to gain access to documents.

(6) These Regulations do not apply to parts of documents containing only logos, crests or insignia.

(7) These Regulations do not apply to—
- (a) a document where access is excluded or restricted under information access legislation including on the grounds of protection of personal data, protection of national security, defence or public security, statistical confidentiality or commercial confidentiality (including business, professional or company secrets); or
- (b) any part of a document which—
  - (i) is accessible under information access legislation; and
  - (ii) contains personal data the re-use of which would be incompatible with the law concerning the protection of individuals with regard to the processing of personal data.

Request for re-use

6. A person who wishes to make a request for re-use must ensure that the request—

(a) is in writing;

(b) states the name of the applicant and an address for correspondence;

(c) specifies the document requested; and

(d) states the purpose for which the document is to be re-used.

Permitting re-use

7.—(1) Subject to paragraph (2), a public sector body must permit re-use where it receives a request made in accordance with regulation 6.

(2) A public sector body which is a library (including a university library), museum or archive holding intellectual property rights in a document may permit re-use of that document.

(3) Where a public sector body permits re-use, it must do so in accordance with regulations 11 to 16.

Responding to a request for re-use

8.—(1) A public sector body must respond to a request for re-use promptly and in any event before the end of the twentieth working day beginning with the day after receipt.

(2) Where documents requested for re-use are extensive in quantity or the request raises complex issues the public sector body may extend the period for responding by such time as is reasonable in the circumstances.

(3) Where paragraph (2) applies, the public sector body must, before the end of the twentieth working day beginning with the day after receipt, notify the applicant in writing—

(a) that no decision on re-use has yet been reached; and

(b) of an estimated date by which it expects to respond to the request for re-use.

(4) In this regulation, responding to a request for re-use means—

(a) refusing the request for re-use;

(b) making the requested document available to the applicant for re-use; or

(c) where conditions are to be imposed on re-use under regulation 12, finalising the offer to the applicant of the conditions on which re-use will be permitted.

Notification of refusal

9.—(1) Subject to paragraph (2), where a public sector body refuses a request for re-use, it must notify the applicant in writing of the reasons for refusal.

(2) Where a public sector body refuses a request for re-use because these Regulations do not apply to the document by virtue of regulation 5(3) it shall not be obliged to comply with regulation 8(1) or paragraph (1) of this regulation.

(3) A notification under paragraph (1) must contain a reference to the means of redress available to the applicant.

(4) Subject to paragraphs (5) and (6), where a request for re-use is refused because these Regulations do not apply to the document by virtue of regulation 5(1)(b), the notification under paragraph (1) must identify, where known, the name of the person—

(a) who owns the relevant intellectual property rights; or

(b) from whom the public sector body obtained the document.

(5) The obligation in paragraph (4) does not apply where complying with it would contravene the 1998 Act.

(6) Paragraph (4) does not apply where the public sector body providing the

notification under paragraph (1) is a library (including a university library), museum or archive.

Processing requests for re-use

10. Where possible and appropriate, a public sector body must ensure that the procedure for processing a request for re-use in accordance with these Regulations is capable of being carried out by electronic means.

Format of documents

11.—(1) A public sector body must make a document available to an applicant under regulation 8(4)(b) or (c)—
    (a) in the format and language in which it is held on the date of the request for re-use; and
    (b) where possible and appropriate, in open format and machine-readable format together with its metadata.

(2) The format and the metadata referred to in paragraph (1)(b) should, insofar as possible, comply with formal open standards.

(3) Where possible and appropriate, a public sector body must make a document available for re-use by electronic means.

(4) Nothing in these Regulations obliges a public sector body to do any of the following—
    (a) create or adapt a document or provide an extract from it in order to comply with a request for re-use where to do so would involve disproportionate effort;
    (b) continue to produce or store a certain type of document for the purposes of re-use by another person.

Conditions

12.—(1) A public sector body may impose conditions on re-use, where appropriate through a licence.

(2) Where conditions are imposed they must not unnecessarily restrict–
    (a) the way in which a document can be re-used; or
    (b) competition.

Non-discrimination

13.—(1) A condition imposed under regulation 12 must not discriminate between applicants who make a request for re-use for comparable purposes.

(2) If a public sector body which holds a document wishes to re-use the document for activities which fall outside the scope of its public task, the same conditions must apply to that re-use as would apply to re-use by any other applicant for comparable purposes.

Prohibition of exclusive arrangements

14.—(1) Subject to paragraphs (2) and (6), a public sector body may not enter into an exclusive arrangement with any person.

(2) A public sector body may, where necessary for the provision of a service in the public interest, enter into an exclusive arrangement.

(3) The validity of the reason for granting an exclusive arrangement under paragraph (2) must be reviewed at least once every three years.

(4) Any exclusive arrangement permitted under paragraph (2) and entered into on or after 31st December 2003 must be published by the public sector body.

(5) Paragraphs (2) to (4) do not apply to the digitisation of cultural resources.

(6) A public sector body may enter into an exclusive arrangement in relation to the digitisation of cultural resources.

(7) The period of exclusivity of an arrangement under paragraph (6) should not normally exceed 10 years.

(8) Where the period of exclusivity referred to in paragraph (7) exceeds 10 years, the duration of the period of exclusivity must be reviewed during the 11th year and, if applicable, every 7 years thereafter.

(9) Any exclusive arrangement permitted under paragraph (6) must be published by the public sector body.

(10) As part of any exclusive arrangement permitted under paragraph (6), the public sector body concerned must be provided free of charge with a copy of the digitised cultural resources.

(11) The copy must be available for re-use at the end of the period of exclusivity.

(12) Any exclusive arrangement existing on 17th July 2013 and to which neither paragraph (2) nor paragraph (6) applies must be terminated at the earlier of—

(a) the date on which it comes to an end in accordance with its terms; or

(b) 18th July 2043.

(13) In this regulation, "exclusive arrangement" means a contract or other arrangement granting an exclusive right to re-use a document.

Charging

15.—(1) A public sector body may charge for permitting re-use.

(2) Subject to paragraph (3), any charge for re-use must be limited to the marginal costs incurred in respect of the reproduction, provision and dissemination of documents.

(3) Paragraph (2) shall not apply to the following–

(a) a public sector body that is required to generate revenue to cover a substantial part of its costs relating to the performance of its public task;

(b) documents for which the public sector body making the charge is required to generate sufficient revenue to cover a substantial part of the costs relating to their collection, production, reproduction or dissemination; or

(c) libraries (including university libraries), museums and archives.

(4) The requirement referred to in paragraph (3)(b) means a requirement defined—

(a) by law or by other binding rules; or

(b) in the absence of such rules, in accordance with common administrative practice.

(5) In any case where paragraph (3)(a) or (b) applies, the public sector body must calculate the total charge in relation to a document in accordance with paragraph (6).

(6) The total charge shall not exceed the sum of—

(a) direct costs;

(b) a reasonable apportionment of indirect and overhead costs attributable to chargeable activity; and

(c) a reasonable return on investment.

(7) In any case where paragraph (3)(c) applies, the total income of the public sector body from supplying and permitting re-use of documents over the appropriate accounting period must not exceed the aggregate of the amounts calculated in accordance with paragraph (8) for each document.

(8) For each document, the amount is the sum of—

   (a) direct costs;

   (b) a reasonable apportionment of indirect and overhead costs attributable to chargeable activity; and

   (c) a reasonable return on investment.

(9) Any charges for re-use must, so far as is reasonably practicable, be calculated in accordance with the accounting principles applicable to the public sector body from time to time.

(10) A public sector body must not charge an applicant for—

   (a) direct costs; or

   (b) indirect and overhead costs,

if the same applicant has been charged in respect of those same costs by that public sector body for access to the same document under information access legislation.

(11) In this regulation—

   "apportionment", in relation to indirect and overhead costs, means the allocation of such costs to each activity of the body in connection with which the costs are incurred;

   "chargeable activity", in relation to a document and a public sector body, means—

      (a) in the case of a body referred to in paragraph (3)(a) or (b), the body's collection, production, reproduction and dissemination of the document; and

      (b) in the case of a body referred to in paragraph 3(c), the body's collection, production, reproduction, dissemination, preservation and rights clearance of the document;

   "direct costs"", in relation to a document and a public sector body, means costs which are incurred by the body only as a consequence of it undertaking chargeable activity;

   "indirect and overhead costs"", in relation to a document and a public sector body, means costs which are not direct costs and which are incurred by the body in connection with—

      (a) chargeable activity; and

      (b) any other of the body's activities.

Information to be published by a public sector body

16.—(1) Where a public sector body charges for re-use it shall, so far as is reasonably practicable, determine standard charges.

(2) Where a public sector body establishes standard charges it shall, so far as is reasonably practicable, establish—

   (a) any applicable conditions for re-use;

   (b) the actual amount of any charges; and

   (c) the basis on which such charges have been calculated.

(3) Where paragraph (2) applies, the public sector body must ensure that the information specified in that paragraph is made available to the public.

(4) Where a standard charge for re-use has not been established, a public sector body—

   (a) must indicate at the outset which factors have been taken into account in the calculation of a charge for re-use; and

   (b) if requested to do so by an applicant, must specify in writing the way in which any such charge has been calculated in relation to a specific request for re-use.

(5) Where regulation 15(3)(b) applies, a public sector body must, so far as is reasonably practicable, predetermine the requirement by which it must generate the revenue specified in that regulation.

(6) A public sector body must, where possible and appropriate, make the information referred to in paragraphs (2) and (5) available by electronic means.

(7) A public sector body must ensure that the following information is made available to the public—

(a) a list of its main documents available for re-use with relevant metadata; and

(b) details of the means of redress available under these Regulations.

(8) In relation to paragraph (7)(a) a public sector body must ensure that—

(a) where possible and appropriate, the list of its main documents is available in machine- readable format;

(b) where possible and appropriate, potential applicants are able to search the list of documents and relevant metadata by electronic means; and

(c) where possible, a public sector body must facilitate the cross-linguistic search for documents.

Internal complaints procedure

17.—(1) A public sector body must establish an internal complaints procedure for determining complaints relating to its compliance with these Regulations.

(2) A person who believes that a public sector body has failed to comply with any requirement of these Regulations may complain in writing to the public sector body in accordance with its internal complaints procedure.

(3) A public sector body must determine any complaint made under paragraph (2) within a reasonable time and thereafter notify the person of its determination without delay.

(4) Notification under paragraph (3) must be in writing and give reasons for the determination.

Enforcement and appeals provisions: general

18.—(1) Except where regulation 19 applies, the relevant enforcement and appeals provisions of the 2000 Act apply for the purposes of these Regulations as they apply for the purposes of the 2000 Act, but with the modifications in paragraph (3) of this regulation.

(2) In this regulation, "the relevant enforcement and appeals provisions of the 2000 Act" means the following sections of the 2000 Act—

(a) section 50 (application for decision by Commissioner);

(b) section 51 (information notices);

(c) section 52 (enforcement notices);

(d) section 54 (failure to comply with notice);

(e) section 56 (no action against public authority);

(f) section 57 (appeal against notices served under Part IV);

(g) section 58 (determination of appeals).

(3) The relevant enforcement and appeals provisions of the 2000 Act apply as mentioned in paragraph (1) as if—

(a) for any reference to "public authority", "an authority" or "the authority", there were substituted a reference to "public sector body", "a body" or "the body" respectively;

(b) in section 50—

(i) in subsection (1)—

          (aa) for "information" there were substituted "re-use";

          (bb) for "Part I" there were substituted "the Re-use of Public Sector Information Regulations 2015";

     (ii) in subsection (2)(a), the words "in conformity with the code of practice under section 45" were omitted;

   (iii) paragraph (a) of subsection (4) and the "or" at the end of that paragraph were omitted;

   (iv) in subsection (4)(b), for the words "sections 11 and 17" there were substituted "the Re-use of Public Sector Information Regulations 2015";

    (v) subsection (7) were omitted;

  (c) in section 51—

     (i) in subsection (1)—

          (aa) in paragraph (b)(i), for "Part I, or" there were substituted "the Re-use of Public Sector Information Regulations 2015,";

          (bb) paragraph (b)(ii) were omitted;

          (cc) in the closing words, for the words from "application" to the end there were substituted "application, or to compliance with those Regulations, as is so specified";

     (ii) in subsection (2)(b)(i), for the words "either of the purposes" there were substituted "the purpose";

  (d) in section 52—

     (i) in subsections (1) and (2), for "Part I" there were substituted "the Re-use of Public Sector Information Regulations 2005";

     (ii) subsection (5) were omitted;

  (e) in section 56(1), for "by or under this Act" there were substituted "by the Re-use of Public Sector Information Regulations 2015";

  (f) in section 57, subsection (3) were omitted.

Enforcement and appeals provisions: regulation 15(5) charging exceptions

19.—(1) This regulation applies where (and only to the extent that) a complaint under regulation 17 alleges that a public sector body has either—

  (a) failed to comply with regulation 15(5); or

  (b) applied regulation 15(5) in a case where regulation 15(3)(a) or (b) does not apply.

(2) The relevant enforcement and appeals provisions of the 2000 Act apply for the purposes of this Regulation as they apply for the purposes of the 2000 Act, but with the modifications in paragraph (4) of this regulation.

(3) In this regulation, "the relevant enforcement and appeals provisions of the 2000 Act" means the following sections of the 2000 Act—

  (a) section 50 (application for decision by Commissioner);

  (b) section 56 (no action against public authority);

  (c) section 57 (appeal against notices served under Part IV);

  (d) section 58 (determination of appeals).

(4) The relevant enforcement and appeals provisions of the 2000 Act apply as mentioned in paragraph (2) as if—

  (a) for any reference to "public authority", "an authority" or "the authority", there were substituted a reference to "public sector body", "a body" or "the body" respectively;

  (b) for any reference to "decision" or "decision notice" (including in the heading of section 50 but excluding any reference in text treated as inserted by this regulation), there were substituted a reference to "recommendation" or "recommendation notice", as the case may be;

(c) in section 50—

    (i) in subsection (1)—

        (aa) for "information" there were substituted "re-use";

        (bb) for "Part I" there were substituted "the Re-use of Public Sector Information Regulations 2015";

    (ii) in subsection (2)(a), the words "in conformity with the code of practice under section 45" were omitted;

    (iii) for subsections (4) to (7), there were substituted the following —

"(4) Where a recommendation notice has been served, the public sector body shall—

(a) decide what action, if any, it will take as a result of the recommendation and the date by which any such action will be taken; and

(b) notify the Commissioner and the complainant of its decision and the reasons for it.

(5) Action referred to in subsection (4) may include (but is not limited to)—

(a) reaffirming, varying or substituting any response by the public sector body to the complainant's request for re-use; or

(b) taking no further steps.

(6) The public sector body must comply with subsection (4) promptly and in any event not later than the twentieth working day following the date of receipt by the public sector body of the recommendation.

(7) In this section "working day" means any day other than a Saturday, a Sunday, Christmas Day, Good Friday or a day which is a bank holiday under the Banking and Financial Dealings Act 1971in any part of the United Kingdom.";

(d) in section 56(1)—

    (i) for "by or under this Act" there were substituted "by the Re-use of Public Sector Information Regulations 2015";

    (ii) subsection (2) were omitted;

(e) in section 57—

    (i) in the heading, after "served" there were inserted "and decisions notified";

    (ii) subsection (1) were omitted;

    (iii) in subsection (2), for "information notice or an enforcement notice" there were substituted "recommendation notice";

    (iv) for subsection (3), there were substituted the following —

"(3) Where a public sector body has provided notification of its decision under section 50(4), the complainant may appeal to the First-tier Tribunal against the decision.

(4) Where a public sector body has failed to provide a notification or its reasons under section 50(4) within the period referred to in section 50(6), the complainant may, without further delay, appeal to the First-tier Tribunal in respect of any matter complained of under section 50(1).";

(f) in section 58—

    (i) in subsection (1), for "57" there were substituted "57(2)";

    (ii) for subsection (2) there were substituted—

"(2) If on an appeal under section 57(3) the Tribunal considers that the decision is not in accordance with the law, the Tribunal shall allow the appeal; and in any other case the Tribunal shall dismiss the appeal.

(3) If on an appeal under section 57(4) the Tribunal considers that the request

for re-use made by the complainant to the public sector body was not dealt with in accordance with regulation 15(5) of the Re-use of Public Sector Information Regulations 2015 or that the body applied that regulation in a case where regulation 15(3) (a) or (b) did not apply, the Tribunal shall allow the appeal; and in any other case the Tribunal shall dismiss the appeal.

(4) On an appeal, the Tribunal may review any finding of fact on which the notice in question was based.".

Information sharing

20.—(1) The Information Commissioner must notify the Scottish Information Commissioner on receipt of an appeal brought under regulations 18 or 19 that relates to a Scottish Public Authority designated as such by or under the 2002 Act, and must provide an opportunity for the Scottish Information Commissioner to provide information relating to the appeal.

(2) The Information Commissioner may disclose to the Scottish Information Commissioner any information obtained under or for the purposes of these Regulations which is considered to be necessary in order to carry out any of the functions conferred by or under them.

(3) The Scottish Information Commissioner may disclose to the Information Commissioner any information obtained under or for the purposes of the 2002 Act, the 2004 Regulations or these Regulations which is considered to be necessary in order to carry out any of the functions conferred by or under these Regulations.

Amendments to the Freedom of Information Act 2000

21.—(1) The 2000 Act is amended as follows.

(2) In section 11A (release of datasets for re-use), after subsection (1) insert—

"(1A) But if the whole of the relevant copyright work is a document to which the Re-use of Public Sector Information Regulations 2015 apply, this section does not apply to the relevant copyright work.

(1B) If part of the relevant copyright work is a document to which those Regulations apply—

   (a) this section does not apply to that part, but

   (b) this section does apply to the part to which the Regulations do not apply (and references in the following provisions of this section to the relevant copyright work are to be read as references to that part).".

(3) In section 19 (publication schemes)—

   (a) in subsection (2A)(c), before "where" insert "subject to subsections (2AA) and (2AB).";

   (b) (b) after subsection (2A), insert—

"(2AA) If the whole of the relevant copyright work is a document to which the Re-use of Public Sector Information Regulations 2015 apply, subsections (2A)(c) and (2B) to (2F) do not apply to the relevant copyright work.

(2AB) If part of the relevant copyright work is a document to which those Regulations apply—

   (a) subsections (2A)(c) and (2B) to (2F) do not apply to that part, but

   (b) those provisions do apply to the part to which the Regulations do not apply (and references in the following provisions of this section to the relevant copyright work are to be read as references to that part).".

Revocation, transitional and saving provisions

22.—(1) In this regulation—

"the 2005 Regulations" means the Re-use of Public Sector Information Regulations 2005;

"the coming into force date" means the day on which these Regulations come into force.

(2) Subject to paragraphs (3) to (7), the 2005 Regulations are revoked.

(3) Subject to paragraphs (4) to (7) the 2005 Regulations shall continue to have effect in respect of any request for re-use received prior to the coming into force date and in respect of which a decision was not made by a public sector body prior to that date.

(4) During the period of three months beginning with the coming into force date, the 2005 Regulations shall continue to have effect in respect of any complaint or request for a review which was made prior to that date and which was—

(a) a complaint referred to the Office of Public Sector Information under regulation 18(1) of those Regulations;

(b) a complaint referred to the Advisory Panel on Public Sector Information under regulation 18(3) of those Regulations; or

(c) a request for a review referred to the Advisory Panel on Public Sector Information under regulation 20(1) of those Regulations.

(5) Paragraphs (5) and (6) apply to a matter relating to the 2005 Regulations which was the subject of a complaint or request for a review under those Regulations made prior to the coming into force date and in respect of which a recommendation has not been made under those Regulations.

(6) Subject to paragraph (6), after the end of the period referred to in paragraph (3), a matter to which this paragraph applies shall be dealt with in accordance with regulation 18 or 19 of these Regulations (as the case may be) as if it were a matter relating to these Regulations.

(7) Sections 52, 54, 56, 57 and 58 of the 2000 Act do not apply to a matter to which this paragraph applies.

(8) Despite the amendments made by regulation 21, sections 11A and 19 of the 2000 Act shall continue to have effect for all purposes on and after the coming into force date, as they had effect immediately before that date, in respect of any—

(a) information falling within section 11A(1) of that Act which was requested before the coming into force date; or

(b) publication scheme published before the coming into force date.

PART C

ORDERS IN COUNCIL

PART C

ORDERS IN COUNCIL

C1. THE COPYRIGHT (INTERNATIONAL ORGANISATIONS) ORDER 1989

(SI 1989/989)

Made	*13th June 1989*
Laid before Parliament	*21st June 1989*
Coming into force	*1st August 1989*

At the Court at Buckingham Palace, the 13th day of June 1989

Present,

The Queen's Most Excellent Majesty in Council

Her Majesty, by virtue of the authority conferred upon Her by section 168(2) of the Copyright, Designs and Patents Act 1988, is pleased, by and with the advice of Her Privy Council, to order, and it is hereby ordered, as follows:

1. This Order may be cited as the Copyright (International Organisations) Order 1989 and shall come into force on 1st August 1989.

2. It is hereby declared to be expedient that section 168 of the Copyright, Designs and Patents Act 1988 (copyright vesting in certain international organisations) should apply to the United Nations, the Specialised Agencies of the United Nations and the Organisation of American States.

C2. THE DESIGN RIGHT (RECIPROCAL PROTECTION) (NO.2) ORDER 1989

(SI 1989/1294)

Made	*28th July 1989*
Laid before Parliament	*31st July 1989*
Coming into force	*1st August 1989*

At the Court at Windsor Castle, the 28th day of July 1989

Present,

The Queen's Most Excellent Majesty in Council

Whereas, it appears to Her Majesty that the laws of the countries mentioned in article 2 of this Order provide adequate protection for British designs:

Now, therefore, Her Majesty, by virtue of the authority conferred upon Her by section 256(1) of the Copyright, Designs and Patents Act 1988, is pleased, by and with the advice of Her Privy Council, to order, and it is hereby ordered, as follows:

1. This Order may be cited as the Design Right (Reciprocal Protection) (No. 2) Order 1989 and shall come into force on 1st August 1989.

2. The following countries are hereby designated as enjoying reciprocal protection under Part III of the Copyright, Designs and Patents Act 1988 (design right)—

> Anguilla
> Bermuda
> British Indian Ocean Territory
> British Virgin Islands
> Cayman Islands
> Channel Islands
> Falkland Islands
> Gibraltar
> Hong Kong
> Isle of Man
> Montserrat
> New Zealand
> Pitcairn, Henderson, Ducie and Oeno Islands
> [St Helena, Ascension and Tristan da Cunha]
> South Georgia and the South Sandwich Islands
> Turks and Caicos Islands.

Note: Words in square brackets substituted for words "St Helena and Dependencies" by the Overseas Territories (Change of Name) (No. 10) Order 2011 (SI 2011/2983) art.2(2) with effect from January 14, 2012.

3. The Design Right (Reciprocal Protection) Order 1989[1] is hereby revoked.

---

[1] SI 1989/990.

C3. THE COPYRIGHT (STATUS OF FORMER DEPENDENT TERRITORIES) ORDER 1990

(SI 1990/1512)

Made	*24th July 1990*
Laid before Parliament	*1st August 1990*
Coming into force	*22nd August 1990*

At the Court at Buckingham Palace, the 24th day of July 1990

Present,

The Queen's Most Excellent Majesty in Council

Her Majesty, by virtue of the authority conferred on Her by paragraph 37(1) and (2)(b) of Schedule 1 to the Copyright, Designs and Patents Act 1988 ("the Act"), is pleased, by and with the advice of Her Privy Council, to order, and it is hereby ordered, as follows—

1. This Order may be cited as the Copyright (Status of Former Dependent Territories) Order 1990 and shall come into force on 22nd August 1990).

2. It is hereby declared for the purposes of paragraph 37(1) of Schedule 1 to the Act (copyright status of former dependent territories) that immediately before the commencement of Part I of the Act on 1st August 1989 each of the countries specified in Schedule 1 to this Order was a country to which the Copyright Act 1956 extended or was treated as such a country by virtue of paragraph 39(2) of Schedule 7 to that Act (countries to which the Copyright Act 1911 extended or was treated as extending).

3. It is hereby declared that each of the countries specified in Schedule 2 to this Order shall cease to be treated as a country to which Part I of the Act extends for the purposes of sections 154 to 156 of the Act (qualification for copyright protection) by reason of the fact that the provisions of the Copyright Act 1956 or, as the case may be, the Copyright Act 1911, which extended there as part of the law of that country have been repealed or amended.

Article 2	SCHEDULE 1

Countries to which the Copyright Act 1956 extended or was treated as extending immediately before 1st August 1989:

> Antigua
> Botswana
> Dominica
> Gambia
> Grenada
> Guyana
> Jamaica
> Kiribati
> Lesotho
> St. Christopher-Nevis
> St. Lucia
> Seychelles
> Solomon Islands
> Swaziland
> Tuvalu
> Uganda

Article 3	SCHEDULE 2

Countries ceasing to be treated as countries to which Part I of the Copyright, Designs and Patents Act 1988 extends:

Botswana
Seychelles
Solomon Islands
Uganda

C4. THE COPYRIGHT AND PERFORMANCES (APPLICATION TO OTHER COUNTRIES) ORDER 2013

(SI 2013/536)

Made	*13th March 2013*
Laid before Parliament	*15th March 2013*
Coming into force	*6th April 2013*

At the Court at Buckingham Palace, the 13th day of March 2013

Present,

The Queen's Most Excellent Majesty in Council

Her Majesty is satisfied, to the extent this Order relates to a country which is neither a Convention country nor another member State of the European Union, that provision has been or will be made under the law of that country, giving adequate protection to the owners of copyright in respect of works under Part I of the Copyright, Designs and Patents Act 1988 and to the owners of rights in respect of British performances.

Accordingly, Her Majesty, by and with the advice of Her Privy Council, in exercise of the powers conferred upon Her by sections 159 and 208 of the Copyright, Designs and Patents Act 1988 and by section 2(2) of the European Communities Act 1972, makes the following Order:

Introductory

1.—(1) This Order may be cited as the Copyright and Performances (Application to Other Countries) Order 2013 and shall come into force on 6th April 2013.

(2) In this Order—

"Act" means the Copyright, Designs and Patents Act 1988;

"Berne Convention" means the Convention for the Protection of Literary and Artistic Works adopted in Berne in 1886 and its revisions; "first published" has the meaning ascribed to it by section 155(3) of the Act;

"Part I" means Part I of the Act (copyright);

"Part II" means Part II of the Act (rights in performances);

"relevant country" means, in relation to the works referred to in article 2(1), each country listed in the first column of the Table and in relation to the works referred to in article 2(2) to (4), each country listed in the first column of the Table corresponding to an entry in the second to fourth columns of the Table;

"relevant declaration under the Rome Convention" means a declaration under Article 16(1)(a)(i) of the Rome Convention (which allows for reservations) by a country party to the Rome Convention that it will not apply the provisions of Article 12 (which provides for payment of a single equitable remuneration for secondary uses of phonograms);

"relevant declaration under the WPPT" means a declaration under Article 15(3) of the WPPT by a country party to the WPPT that it will apply the provisions of Article 15(1) of the WPPT (which confers on performers and producers of phonograms a right to remuneration for broadcasting and communication to the public) only in respect of certain uses, or that it will limit their application in some other way, or that it will not apply these provisions at all;

"Rome Convention" means the International Convention for the Protection

of Performers, Producers of Phonograms and Broadcasting Organisations done at Rome on 6th October 1961;

"Table" means the table set out in the Schedule;

"WPPT" means the World Intellectual Property Organisation Performances
and Phonograms Treaty adopted in Geneva on 20th December 1996;
and

"WTO TRIPS" means the Agreement establishing the World Trade Organisation (including the Agreement on Trade-Related Aspects of
Intellectual Property Rights) signed in Marrakesh on 15th April 1994.

(3) The Copyright and Performances (Application to Other Countries) Order
2012 and the Copyright and Performances (Application to Other Countries)
(Amendment) Order 2012 are revoked.

Application of Part I

2.—(1) All the provisions of Part I relating to literary, dramatic, musical and
Copyright and Performances (Application to Other Countries) 541 artistic works,
films and typographical arrangement of published editions apply in relation to a
relevant country in the manner set out in paragraph (5), subject to article 3.

(2) Where an entry in the second column of the Table shows a plus sign (+),
all the provisions of Part I apply to sound recordings in relation to a relevant
country in the manner set out in paragraph (5).

(3) Where there is an entry in the third column of the Table, all the provisions
of Part I apply to wireless broadcasts in relation to a relevant country in the manner set out in paragraph (5), subject to article 5.

(4) Where there is an entry in the fourth column of the Table, all the provisions of Part I apply to broadcasts other than wireless broadcasts in relation to a
relevant country in the manner set out in paragraph (5).

(5) The provisions of Part I apply in relation to—

(a) a person who is a citizen or subject of, or is domiciled or resident in, a
relevant country as they apply to a person who is a British citizen or is
domiciled or resident in the United Kingdom,

(b) a body incorporated under the law of a relevant country as they apply in
relation to a body incorporated under the law of a part of the United
Kingdom,

(c) the works referred to in paragraphs (1) and (2) first published in a relevant country as they apply in relation to such works first published in the
United Kingdom, and

(d) broadcasts referred to in paragraphs (3) and (4) made from a relevant
country as they apply in relation to broadcasts made from the United
Kingdom.

Exception relating to literary, dramatic, musical or artistic works

3. Where a literary, dramatic, musical or artistic work was first published before
1st June 1957 it shall not qualify for copyright protection under section 154 of
the Act (qualification by reference to author).

Exceptions and modifications relating to sound recordings

4.—(1) Where the entry for a country in the second column of the Table does
not include a plus (+) or minus (-) sign, the country is neither a party to the Rome
Convention nor the WPPT but is a party to the Berne Convention or the WTO
TRIPS or both, and accordingly the provisions of Part I, in so far as they relate to
sound recordings, apply in relation to that country, except for the following—

    (a) section 18A (infringement by rental or lending of work to the public) in so far as it applies to lending;

    (b) section 19 (infringement by playing of work in public);

    (c) section 20 (infringement by communication to the public);

    (d) section 26 (secondary infringement: provision of apparatus for infringing performance, etc); and

    (e) section 107(2A) and (3) (criminal liability for communicating to the public or playing a sound recording).

(2) Where the entry for a country in the second column of the Table includes a minus sign (-), the country is not a party to the Rome Convention but is a party to the WPPT, and accordingly the provisions of Part I, in so far as they relate to sound recordings, apply in relation to that country with the following modifications—

    (a) section 18A (infringement by rental or lending of work to the public), except in so far as it applies to lending;

    (b) section 20 (infringement by communication to the public), except that references to communication to the public do not include the broadcasting of a sound recording; and

    (c) section 107(2A) (criminal liability for communicating to the public), except that it does not apply in relation to the broadcasting of a sound recording.

Exceptions relating to wireless broadcasts

5.—(1) Where the entry for a country in the third column of the Table includes a minus sign (-), the country is not a party to the Rome Convention but is a party to the WTO TRIPS, and accordingly the following provisions of Part I, in so far as they relate to wireless broadcasts, do not apply in relation to that country—

    (a) section 18A (infringement by rental or lending of work to the public);

    (b) section 19 (infringement by showing or playing of work in public), but only in so far as it relates to broadcasts other than television broadcasts;

    (c) section 20 (infringement by communication to the public), except in relation to broadcasting by wireless telegraphy;

    (d) section 26 (secondary infringement: provision of apparatus for infringing performance, etc), but only in so far as it relates to broadcasts other than television broadcasts;

    (e) section 107(2A) (criminal liability for communicating to the public), except in relation to broadcasting by wireless telegraphy.

(2) The provisions of Part I do not apply in relation to a wireless broadcast made from a place in a country, referred to in paragraph (1), before the relevant date.

(3) The relevant date in relation to a country—

    (a) where its entry in the third column of the Table includes an "(X)", is 1st June 1957;

    (b) where its entry in the third column of the Table includes a "(Y)", is 1st January 1996; or

    (c) where there is a date next to its entry in the third column of the Table, is that date.

Application of Part II

6.—(1) Where the entry for a country in the fifth column of the Table is the word "designated", the country—

   (a) is a party to the Rome Convention and has not made a relevant declaration under the Rome Convention, or

   (b) has made or will make provision giving adequate protection for British performances under its law,

and accordingly that country is designated as enjoying reciprocal protection under Part II.

(2) Where the entry for a country in the fifth column of the Table is the word "deemed", the country is not a party to the Rome Convention but is a party to the WPPT, and accordingly that country shall be treated as if it were designated as enjoying reciprocal protection under Part II, except as provided in paragraph (6) and article 7(1).

(3) Where the entry for a country is a minus sign (-) in the fifth column of the Table, the country is neither a party to the Rome Convention nor the WPPT but is a party to the WTO TRIPS, and accordingly that country shall be treated as if it were designated as enjoying reciprocal protection under Part II, except as provided in paragraph (6) and article 7(1) and (2).

(4) Where the entry for a country includes an asterisk (*) in the fifth column of the Table, the country is a party to the Rome Convention but has made a relevant declaration under the Rome Convention, and accordingly that country shall be treated as if it were designated as enjoying reciprocal protection under Part II, except as provided in article 7(3).

(5) Where the entry for a country includes a hash sign (#) in the fifth column of the Table, the country is a party to the WPPT but has made a relevant declaration under the WPPT, and accordingly that country shall be treated as if it were designated as enjoying reciprocal protection under Part II, except as provided in paragraph (6) and article 7(1) and (4).

(6) In relation to the provisions of Part II—

   (a) as applied by paragraphs (2) and (3), and

   (b) to the extent applied by paragraph (5),

the definition of "recording", in section 180(2) (rights conferred on performers and persons having recording rights), shall be construed as applying only to sound recordings (and not to films).

Exceptions to application of Part II

7.—(1) In relation to article 6(2), (3) and (5), the following provisions of Part II shall not apply—

   (a) section 182C (consent required for rental or lending of copies to public), in so far as it relates to lending;

   (b) section 183 (infringement of performer's rights by use of recording made without consent);

   (c) sections 185 to 188 (rights of person having recording rights);

   (d) section 198(2) (criminal liability for playing or communicating to the public).

(2) In relation to article 6(3), the following provisions of Part II shall not apply—

   (a) section 182CA (consent required for making available to the public);

   (b) section 182D (right to equitable remuneration for exploitation of sound recording);

   (c) section 198(1A) (criminal liability for making available to the public).

(3) In relation to article 6(4), to the extent that the relevant declaration under the Rome Convention is in force in the law of the country in relation to British performances, the provisions of Part II shall not apply to grant the protection

provided under Article 12 of the Rome Convention, unless the recording has been first published in a country which is party to the Rome Convention and which has not made a relevant declaration under that Convention.

(4) In relation to article 6(5), where a country is a party to the WPPT and has made a relevant declaration under the WPPT, the provisions of Part II shall not apply to protect the right provided for in Article 15(1) of the WPPT to the extent the declaration is in force in the law of that country in relation to British performances.

Savings

8.—(1) For the purposes of this article an act is an "excluded act" where—
- (a) a person (A) has incurred any expenditure or liability in connection with the act; and
- (b) he—
  - (i) began in good faith to do the act, or
  - (ii) made in good faith effective and serious preparations to do the act,

at a time when the act neither infringed nor was restricted by the relevant rights in the work or performance.

(2) Where another person (B) acquires those relevant rights on or after the coming into force of this Order, A has the right—
- (a) to continue to do the excluded act, or
- (b) to do the excluded act,

notwithstanding that the excluded act infringes or is restricted by those relevant rights under this Order.

(3) Where B, or his exclusive licensee, pays reasonable compensation to A paragraph (2) no longer applies.

(4) Where—
- (a) B offers to pay compensation to A under paragraph (3); but
- (b) A and B cannot agree on what compensation is reasonable, either person may refer the matter to arbitration.

(5) In this article "relevant rights" means copyright, the rights conferred by Chapter 4 of Part I (moral rights) and the rights conferred by Part II.

Articles 2 to 6 SCHEDULE

APPLICATION OF PARTS I AND II

Country	Article 2(2) (sound record-ings)	Article 2(3) (wireless broadcasts)	Article 2(4) (other broadcasts)	Article 6 (performances)
Albania	Applies (+)	Applies (1st September 2000)		Designated
Algeria	Applies (+)	Applies (22nd April 2007)		Designated
Andorra	Applies (+)	Applies (25th May 2004)		Designated
Angola	Applies	Applies (−) (23rd November 1996)		(−)
Antigua and Barbuda	Applies	Applies (−) (Y)		(−)

Country	Article 2(2) (sound recordings)	Article 2(3) (wireless broadcasts)	Article 2(4) (other broadcasts)	Article 6 (performances)
Argentina	Applies (+)	Applies (2nd March 1992)		Designated
Armenia	Applies (+)	Applies (31st January 2003)		Designated
Australia (including Norfolk Island)	Applies (+)	Applies (30th September 1992)		Designated(*)(#)
Austria	Applies (+)	Applies (X)	Applies	
Azerbaijan	Applies (+)	Applies (5th October 2005)		Designated
Bahamas	Applies			
Bahrain	Applies (+)	Applies (Y)		Designated
Bangladesh	Applies (+)	Applies (−) (Y)		(−)
Barbados	Applies (+)	Applies (18th September 1983)		Designated
Belarus	Applies (+)	Applies (27th May 2003)		Designated
Belgium	Applies (+)	Applies (X)	Applies	
Belize	Applies	Applies (−) (Y)		(−)
Benin	Applies(−)	Applies (+) (22nd February 1996)		Deemed
Bermuda	Applies	Applies (6th August 1962)	Applies	Designated
Bhutan	Applies			
Bolivia	Applies (+)	Applies (24th November 1993)		Designated
Bosnia and Herzegovina	Applies(+)	Applies (19th May 2009)		Designated
Botswana	Applies (−)	Applies (−) (Y)		Deemed
Brazil	Applies (+)	Applies (29th September 1965)		Designated
Brunei Darussalam	Applies	Applies (−) (Y)		(−)
Bulgaria	Applies (+)	Applies (X)	Applies	
Burkina Faso	Applies (+)	Applies (14th January 1988)		Designated
Burundi	Applies	Applies (−) (Y)		(−)
Cambodia	Applies	Applies (−) (13th October 2004)		(−)
Cameroon	Applies	Applies (−) (Y)		(−)
Canada	Applies (+)	Applies (Y)		Designated
Cape Verde	Applies (+)	Applies (3rd July 1997)		Designated

Country	Article 2(2) (sound record-ings)	Article 2(3) (wireless broadcasts)	Article 2(4) (other broadcasts)	Article 6 (performances)
Central African Republic	Applies	Applies (−) (Y)		(−)
Chad	Applies	Applies (−) (19th October 1996)		(−)
Chile	Applies (+)	Applies (5th September 1974)		Designated(#)
China	Applies(−)	Applies (−) (11th December 2001)		Deemed(#)
Colombia	Applies (+)	Applies (17th September 1976)		Designated
Comoros	Applies			
Congo	Applies (+)	Applies (18th May 1964)		Designated(*)
Costa Rica	Applies (+)	Applies (9th September 1971)		Designated(#)
Cote d'Ivoire	Applies	Applies (−) (Y)		(−)
Croatia	Applies (+)	Applies (20th April 2000)		Designated
Cuba	Applies	Applies (−) (Y)		(−)
Cyprus	Applies (+)	Applies (X)	Applies	
Czech Republic	Applies (+)	Applies (X)	Applies	
Democratic Republic of the Congo	Applies	Applies (−) (1st January 1997)		(−)
Denmark	Applies (+)	Applies (X)	Applies	
Djibouti	Applies	Applies (−) (Y)		(−)
Dominica	Applies (+)	Applies (Y)		Designated
Dominican Re-public	Applies (+)	Applies (27th January 1987)		Designated
Ecuador	Applies (+)	Applies (18th May 1964)		Designated
Egypt	Applies	Applies (−) (Y)		(−)
El Salvador	Applies (+)	Applies (29th June 1979)		Designated
Equatorial Guinea	Applies			
Estonia	Applies (+)	Applies (X)	Applies	
Faeroe Islands	Applies	Applies (1st February 1962)		Designated
Fiji	Applies (+)	Applies (11th April 1972)		Designated(*)
Finland	Applies (+)	Applies (X)	Applies	

Country	Article 2(2) (sound record-ings)	Article 2(3) (wireless broadcasts)	Article 2(4) (other broadcasts)	Article 6 (performances)
France (includ-ing Overseas Departments and Territories)	Applies (+)	Applies (X)	Applies	
Gabon	Applies (−)	Applies (−) (Y)		Deemed
Gambia	Applies	Applies (−) (23rd October 1996)		(−)
Georgia	Applies (+)	Applies (14th August 2004)		Designated
Germany	Applies (+)	Applies (X)	Applies	
Ghana	Applies (+)	Applies (−) (Y)		Deemed
Gibraltar	Applies (+)	Applies (X)	Applies	Designated
Greece	Applies (+)	Applies (X)	Applies	
Greenland	Applies	Applies (1st February 1962)		Designated
Grenada	Applies	Applies (−) (22nd February 1996)		(−)
Guatemala	Applies (+)	Applies (14th January 1977)		Designated
[Guernsey, the Bailiwick of	Applies (+)	Applies (X)		Applies Designated]
Guinea	Applies (−)	Applies (−) (Y)		Deemed
Guinea-Bissau	Applies	Applies (−) (Y)		(−)
Guyana	Applies	Applies (−) (Y)		(−)
Haiti	Applies	Applies (−) (30th January 1996)		(−)
Holy See	Applies			
Honduras	Applies (+)	Applies (16th February 1990)		Designated
Hong Kong	Applies (+)	Applies (X)		(−)
Hungary	Applies (+)	Applies (X)	Applies	
Iceland	Applies (+)	Applies (X)	Applies	Designated(*)
India	Applies (+)	Applies (−) (Y)		(−)
Indonesia	Applies (+)	Applies (X)	Applies	Deemed
Ireland	Applies (+)	Applies (X)	Applies	
Isle of Man	Applies (+)	Applies (X)	Applies	Designated
Israel	Applies (+)	Applies (Y)		Designated
Italy	Applies (+)	Applies (X)	Applies	
Jamaica	Applies (+)	Applies (27th January 1994)		Designated
Japan	Applies (+)	Applies (26th October 1989)		Designated
Jersey, the Bal-liwick of	Applies (+)	Applies (X)	Applies	

Country	Article 2(2) (sound recordings)	Article 2(3) (wireless broadcasts)	Article 2(4) (other broadcasts)	Article 6 (performances)
Jordan	Applies (−)	Applies (−) (11th April 2000)		Deemed
Kazakhstan	Applies (−)			Deemed
Kenya	Applies	Applies (−) (Y)		(−)
Korea, Democratic People's Republic of	Applies			
Korea, Republic of	Applies(+)	Applies (18th March 2009)		Designated(#)
Kuwait	Applies	Applies (−) (Y)		(−)
Kyrgyzstan	Applies (+)	Applies (20th December 1998)		Designated
Lao People's Democratic Republic	Applies	Applies (−) 3rd February 2013		(−)
Latvia	Applies (+)	Applies (X)	Applies	
Lebanon	Applies (+)	Applies (12th August 1997)		Designated
Lesotho	Applies (+)	Applies (26th January 1990)		Designated
Liberia	Applies(+)	Applies (16th December 2005)		Designated
Libyan Arab Jamahiriya	Applies			
Liechtenstein	Applies (+)	Applies (X)	Applies	Designated
Lithuania	Applies (+)	Applies (X)	Applies	
Luxembourg	Applies (+)	Applies (X)	Applies	
Macao	Applies	Applies (−) (Y)		(−)
Macedonia, The Former Yugoslav Republic of	Applies (+)	Applies (2nd March 1998)		Designated(*)(#)
Madagascar	Applies	Applies (−) (Y)		(−)
Malawi	Applies (+)	Applies (22nd June 1989)		Deemed (−)
Malaysia	Applies (+)	Applies (X)		Deemed
Maldives	Applies	Applies (−) (Y)		(−)
Mali	Applies (−)	Applies (−) (Y)		Deemed
Malta	Applies (+)	Applies (X)	Applies	
Mauritania	Applies	Applies (−) (Y)		(−)
Mauritius	Applies	Applies (−) (Y)		(−)

Country	Article 2(2) (sound recordings)	Article 2(3) (wireless broadcasts)	Article 2(4) (other broadcasts)	Article 6 (performances)
Mexico	Applies (+)	Applies (18th May 1964)		Designated
Micronesia, Federated States of	Applies			
Moldova, Republic of	Applies (+)	Applies (5th December 1995)		Designated
Monaco	Applies (+)	Applies (6th December 1985)	Designated(*)	
Mongolia	Applies (−)	Applies (−) (29th January 1997)		Deemed
Montenegro	Applies (+)	Applies (10th June 2003)		Designated
Morocco	Applies (−)	Applies (−) (Y)		Deemed
Mozambique	Applies	Applies (−) (Y)		(−)
Myanmar	Applies	Applies (−) (Y)		(−)
Namibia	Applies	Applies (−) (Y)		(−)
Nepal	Applies	Applies (−) (23rd April 2004)		(−)
Netherlands	Applies (+)	Applies (X)	Applies	
Netherlands Antilles, Curacao, Sint Maarten and Aruba	Applies	Applies (−) (Y)		Deemed
New Zealand	Applies (+)	Applies (−) (Y)		(−)
Nicaragua	Applies (+)	Applies (Y)		Designated
Niger	Applies (+)	Applies (18th May 1964)		Designated(*)
Nigeria	Applies (+)	Applies (29th October 1993)		Designated
Norway	Applies (+)	Applies (X)	Applies	Designated
Oman	Applies	Applies (−) (9th November 2000)		Deemed
Pakistan	Applies (+)	Applies (−) (Y)		(−)
Panama	Applies (+)	Applies (2nd September 1983)		Designated
Papua New Guinea	Applies	Applies (−) (9th June 1996)		Deemed (−)
Paraguay	Applies (+)	Applies (26th February 1970)		Designated
Peru	Applies (+)	Applies (7th August 1985)		Designated

Country	Article 2(2) (sound record-ings)	Article 2(3) (wireless broadcasts)	Article 2(4) (other broadcasts)	Article 6 (performances)
Philippines	Applies (+)	Applies (25th September 1984)		Designated
Poland	Applies (+)	Applies (X)	Applies	
Portugal	Applies (+)	Applies (X)	Applies	
Qatar	Applies	Applies (−) (13th January 1996)		Deemed
Romania	Applies (+)	Applies (X)	Applies	
Russian Federation	Applies (+)	Applies (26th May 2003)		Designated
Rwanda	Applies	Applies (−) (22nd May 1996)		(−)
Saint Kitts and Nevis	Applies	Applies (−) (21st February 1996)		(−)
Saint Lucia	Applies (+)	Applies (Y)		Designated
Saint Vincent and the Grenadines	Applies (−)	Applies (−) (Y)		Deemed
Samoa	Applies	Applies (−) 10th May 2012		(−)
Saudi Arabia	Applies	Applies (−) (11th December 2005)		(−)
Senegal	Applies (−)	Applies (+)(Y)		Deemed
Serbia	Applies (+)	Applics (10th June 2003)		Designated
Sierra Leone	Applies	Applies (−) (Y)		(−)
Singapore	Applies (−)	Applies (X)	Applies	Deemed(#)
Slovak Republic	Applies (+)	Applies (X)	Applies	
Slovenia	Applies (+)	Applies (X)	Applies	
Solomon Islands	Applies	Applies (−) (26th July 1996)		Deemed (−)
South Africa	Applies	Applies (−) (Y)		(−)
Spain	Applies (+)	Applies (X)	Applies	
Sri Lanka	Applies	Applies (−) (Y)		(−)
Sudan	Applies			
Suriname	Applies	Applies (−) (Y)		(−)
Swaziland	Applies	Applies (−) (Y)		(−)
Sweden	Applies (+)	Applies (X)	Applies	
Switzerland	Applies (+)	Applies (X)	Applies	Designated
Syrian Arab Republic	Applies (+)	Applies (13th May 2006)		Designated

Country	Article 2(2) (sound recordings)	Article 2(3) (wireless broadcasts)	Article 2(4) (other broadcasts)	Article 6 (performances)
Taiwan	Applies (+)	Applies (−) (1st January 2002)		(−)
Tajikistan	Applies(+)	Applies (19th May 2008)		Designated
Tanzania, United Republic of	Applies	Applies (+)(Y)		(−)
Thailand	Applies (+)	Applies (−) (Y)		(−)
Togo	Applies (+)	Applies (Y)		Designated
Tonga	Applies	Applies (−) (27th July 2007)		(−)
Trinidad and Tobago	Applies (−)	Applies (−) (Y)		Deemed
Tunisia	Applies	Applies (−) (Y)		(−)
Turkey	Applies (+)	Applies (Y)		Designated
Uganda	Applies	Applies (−) (Y)		(−)
Ukraine	Applies (+)	Applies (12th June 2002)		Designated
United Arab Emirates	Applies (+)	Applies (10th April 1996)		Designated
United States of America (including Puerto Rico and all territories and possessions)	Applies (−)	Applies (−) (Y)		Deemed(#)
Uruguay	Applies (+)	Applies (4th July 1977)		Designated
Uzbekistan	Applies			
Vanuatu	Applies	Applies (−) (24th August 2012)		(−)
Venezuela	Applies (+)	Applies (Y)		Designated
Vietnam	Applies (+)	Applies (1st March 2007)		Designated(*)
Yemen	Applies			
Zambia	Applies	Applies (−) (Y)		(−)
Zimbabwe	Applies	Applies (−) (Y)		(−)

Note: Entry relating to Guernsey inserted by the Copyright and Performances (Application to Other Countries) (Amendment) Order 2015 (SI 2015/216), art.2, with effect from April 6, 2015.

PART D

TABLES OF PARLIAMENTARY DEBATES

PART D

TABLES OF PARLIAMENTARY DEBATES

D1. THE COPYRIGHT, DESIGNS AND PATENTS ACT 1988

The following is a table of the main debates on particular sections of the Bill. References to "H.C., SCD", "H.C., SCE" and "H.C., SCF" are to the debates in the House of Commons of Standing Committee D in 1996, Standing Committee E in 1988 and Standing Committee F in 1990 respectively. References to "H.C., SC4" are to the debates in the House of Commons of the Fourth Standing Committee on Delegated Legislation in 1997.

Section 1(1)	H.L. Vol. 490, cols. 822, 823; H.L. Vol. 493, cols. 1054, 1055 (on removal of distinction between Parts I and II in 1956 Act).
Section 1(1)(a)	H.L. Vol 490, cols. 813–822; H.L. Vol. 493, cols. 1072–1074 (photograph).
Section 1(1)(b), (c)	H.L. Vol. 493, cols. 1055–1058.
Section 1(1)(c)	H.L. Vol. 490, col. 823.
Section 1(3)	H.C., SCE col. 21.
Section 2	H.L. Vol. 490, cols. 827, 828; H.L. Vol. 494, cols. 607, 610.
Section 3(1)	"Literary work": H.L. Vol. 490, cols. 828–832; H.C., SCE cols. 21–25, 36–39. "Table or compilation": H.L. Vol. 490, cols. 832, 834; H.C., SCE cols. 21–25. "Musical work": H.L. Vol. 490, cols. 828, 832; H.C., SCE cols. 36–39. "Dramatic work": H.L. Vol. 490, cols. 830, 836, 837; H.C., SCE cols. 33–38.
Section 3(2)	H.L. Vol. 490, cols. 828, 834–836; H.L. Vol. 493, cols. 1058, 1059; H.C., SCE cols. 33–39; H.L. Vol. 501, cols. 197–200.
Section 3(3)	H.L. Vol. 490, col. 835; Vol. 493, cols. 1058–1059; H.C., SCE cols. 34–39; Vol. 495, cols. 610–611.
Section 3A	H.L. Vol. 584, col. 793; H.C. Vol. 5.
Section 4(1)(a)	H.L. Vol. 490, cols. 838–841 ("Irrespective of artistic quality") H.L. Vol. 490, cols. 843–847; Vol. 493, cols. 1067–1069 ("Typeface"). H.L. Vol. 490, col. 849; Vol. 493, cols. 1066, 1067 ("Collage").
Section 4(1)(b)	H.L. Vol. 490, cols. 841–843.
Section 4(1)(c)	H.L. Vol. 490, cols. 846–848.
Section 4(2)	H.L. Vol. 493, cols. 1069–1071 ("Building"). H.L. Vol. 490, cols. 852–854; Vol. 493, cols. 1071, 1072 ("Graphic work"). H.L. Vol. 490, cols. 849–852; Vol. 493, cols. 1063–1066, 1072–1074; Vol 495, cols, 611–615 ("Photograph").

Section 5(1)	H.L. Vol. 490, cols. 854, 856, 858–859; H.C., SCE Cols. 40–43 ("Sound recording"). H.L. Vol. 490, cols. 856–859; Vol. 493, col. 1072; H.C., SCE cols. 40–43 ("Film").
Section 5(2)	H.L. Vol. 493, cols. 1072–1074.
Section 6(1)	H.L. Vol. 490, cols. 859–863; Vol. 493, cols. 1074, 1075; H.C., SCE cols. 44–48; H.L. Vol. 501, cols. 201–203.
Section 6(2)	H.L. Vol. 501, cols. 201–203.
Section 6(3)	H.L. Vol. 490, cols. 863–866; Vol. 493, cols. 1075–1076; Vol. 495, col. 615; H.C., SCE cols. 44–49; H.L. Vol. 501, cols. 201–203.
Section 6(6)	H.C., SCE cols. 49–51.
Section 6A(2)(b)	H.C. Vol. 284, col. 1379.
Section 7	H.C. Vol. 138, cols. 112–115; H.L. Vol. 501, cols. 203–206.
Section 7(1), (2)	H.L. Vol. 490, cols. 866–870; Vol. 495, cols. 615–617; H.C., SCE cols. 51–53.
Section 8(1)	H.L. Vol. 490, cols. 870–874.
Section 9(1)	H.L. Vol. 490, cols. 879–886 (photograph).
Section 9(2)(a)	H.L. Vol. 490, cols. 886–891; H.L. Vol. 493, cols. 1076–1081; H.C., SCE cols. 57–65.
Section 9(2)(d)	H.L. Vol. 490, cols. 891–893.
Sections 9(4), (5)	H.L. Vol. 490, cols. 893, 894; H.L. Vol. 493, cols. 1081–1084.
Section 10	H.C., SCE cols. 65–70.
Section 10(1)	H.L. Vol. 490, cols. 903, 904; H.L. Vol. 493, cols. 1084, 1085.
Section 11	(Commissioned works) H.L. Vol. 490, cols. 916–917; H.L. Vol. 493, cols. 1095–1098.
Section 11(2)	H.L. Vol. 490, cols. 895–902, 904–911, 911–915 (photographs); H.C., SCE cols. 70–90; H.C. Vol. 138, cols. 115–127; H.L. Vol. 493, cols. 1085–1095.
Section 12(1)	H.L. Vol. 490, cols. 1149–1154, 1160; H.C., SCE cols. 107–115. (Photographs): H.L. Vol. 490, cols. 1154–1158;
Section 12(2)	H.L. Vol. 490, cols. 1153, 1154, 1158–1160; H.L. Vol. 493, cols. 1081–1084, 1098, 1099; H.C., SCE cols. 115–120.
Section 12(3)	H.C., SCE cols. 120–121; H.L. Vol. 501, cols. 206–208.
Section 13(1)	H.L. Vol. 490, cols. 1160–1162; H.L. Vol. 493, cols. 1099–1103.
Section 14(1), (2)	H.L. Vol. 490, cols. 1162, 1163.
Section 15	H.L. Vol. 490, cols. 1163–1165.
Section 16	H.L. Vol. 490, cols. 1165–1167 (knowledge).
Section 16(2)	H.L. Vol. 490, cols. 824–827 (authorise).

Section 16(3)	H.L. Vol. 493, cols. 1105, 1106.
Section 16(3)(a)	H.L. Vol. 490, cols. 1167–1174.
Section 16(3)(b)	H.L. Vol. 490, cols. 1184, 1185.
Section 17(1)	H.L. Vol. 490, col. 1191 (parody).
Section 17(2)	H.L. Vol. 490, cols. 1177–1184, 1190; H.L. Vol. 493, cols. 1103–1105; H.C., SCE cols. 121–128; 130–136; H.L. Vol. 501, cols. 208–214 (storing by electronic means and transient copying).
Section 17(2)	H.L. Vol. 490, cols. 1186–1189 (photograph).
Section 17(4)	H.L. Vol. 490, cols. 1189, 1190, H.L. Vol. 493, cols. 1106–1109.
Section 17(5)	H.L. Vol. 490, cols. 1191, 1192.
Section 17(6)	[see *supra*, section 17(2)].
Section 18	H.L. Vol. 501, cols. 214–224; H.C. Vol. 140, cols. 270, 271.
Section 18(2)	H.L. Vol. 490, cols. 1192–1205; H.L. Vol. 493, cols. 1109–1120; H.L. Vol. 495, cols. 619–623, 650; H.C., SCE cols. 139–149, 259–345 (rental); H.C. Vol. 138, cols. 128, 146–173; H.L. Vol. 501, cols. 217–224.
Section 18A	H.L. Vol. 576, col. 37.
Section 19(1)	H.C., SCE cols. 150–162 ("in public").
Section 19(2)	H.L. Vol. 490, cols. 1205, 1206.
Section 21	H.C., SCE cols. 162–164 (sampling).
Section 21(3)(a)(iii)	H.L. Vol. 490, cols. 1206, 1208.
Section 22	H.L. Vol. 490, cols. 1208, 1209 ("export").
Sections 22, 23, 24	H.L. Vol. 490, cols. 1212–1214; H.L. Vol. 493, cols. 1129–1132 ("reason to believe", etc.).
Section 23(a)	H.L. Vol. 490, cols. 1214–1216; H.L. Vol. 493, cols. 1132–1133.
Section 24(1)	H.L. Vol. 490, cols. 1216, 1217. ("Specifically designed or adapted":) H.L. Vol. 490, cols. 1216, 1217; H.L. Vol. 493, cols. 1133–1135.
Section 24(1)(c)	H.L. Vol. 493, cols. 1135–1137.
Section 24(2)	H.L. Vol. 490, cols. 1209–1211; H.C., SCE cols. 165, 166; H.C. Vol. 138, col. 129.
Section 25	H.L. Vol. 490, cols. 1218–1221.
Section 25(1)	H.L. Vol. 490, col. 1218; H.L. Vol. 493, cols. 1140–1144; H.L. Vol. 495, col. 625 (grounds for belief).
Section 26	H.L. Vol. 490, cols. 1221, 1222.
Section 26(2)(b)	H.L. Vol. 493, cols. 1144, 1145.
Section 27(3)(b)	H.L. Vol. 490, cols. 1222, 1223; H.C., SCE cols. 169–174.

Section 27(5)	H.L. Vol. 490, cols. 1223–1227; H.L. Vol. 493, cols. 1145, 1146; H.C., SCE cols. 169–174.
Section 27(6)	H.L. Vol. 495, cols. 626, 627; H.C., SCE cols. 174–177; H.L. Vol. 501, cols. 225–227.
Section 28	H.L. Vol. 491, cols. 72–75; H.L. Vol. 501, cols. 227–232.
Section 28(1)	H.L. Vol. 493, cols. 1146–1152; H.L. Vol. 495, cols. 673, 674; H.C., SCE cols. 177–180; H.L. Vol. 501, cols. 227–232.
Section 29	H.L. Vol. 491, cols. 85–111; H.L. Vol. 493, cols. 1153–1162; H.L. Vol. 495, cols. 627, 628; H.C, SCE cols. 180–204; H.C. Vol. 138, cols. 129–136.
Section 29(3)	H.C., SCE cols. 197–199; H.C. Vol. 138, cols. 137–139; H.L. Vol. 501, cols. 232–236.
Section 30(2)	H.L. Vol. 491, cols. 111–115;. H.C., SCE cols. 205–217; H.C. Vol. 138, cols. 139–140; H.L. Vol. 501, cols. 236, 237.
Section 30(3)	H.L. Vol. 491, cols. 115, 116.
Section 31(1)	H.L. Vol. 491, cols. 120–124.
Section 31(3)	H.C., SCE cols. 217–220; H.L. Vol. 501, cols. 237, 238.
Section 32(2)	H.L. Vol. 491, cols. 124–127; H.L. Vol. 493, cols. 1164–1166.
Section 32(4)	H.C., SCE cols. 220, 221; H.L. Vol. 501, cols. 238, 239.
Section 32(5)	H.C. Vol. 138, cols. 140, 141.
Section 33	H.L. Vol. 491, cols. 128–136; H.C., SCE cols. 221, 222; H.L. Vol. 501, cols. 239, 240.
Section 33(2)	H.L. Vol. 491, cols. 135–136.
Section 33(4)	H.L. Vol. 493, col. 1166.
Section 34(1), (2)	H.L. Vol. 493, cols. 1166–1168.
Section 34(2)	H.C., SCE cols. 222, 223.
Section 34	H.L. Vol. 491, cols. 148–151.
Section 35	H.C., SCE cols. 224, 225.
Section 36(2)	H.L. Vol. 491, cols. 151–159; H.L. Vol. 493, cols. 1169–1172.
Section 36(4)	H.L. Vol. 491, cols. 159–166.
Section 36A	H.L. Vol. 576, col. 38.
Section 37(2)	H.L. Vol. 493, cols. 1171–1173.
Section 38	H.L. Vol. 491, cols. 167–177; H.L. Vol. 495, cols. 635–637.
Section 39	H.L. Vol. 491, cols. 177–180; H.L. Vol. 495, cols. 637–640; H.C., SCE cols. 226–229.
Section 40	H.L. Vol. 491, cols. 180, H.C., SCE cols. 229–231.
Section 42	H.C., SCE cols. 231, 232; H.L. Vol. 501, cols. 240, 241.

Section 43	H.C., SCE cols. 232, 233.
Section 45	H.L. Vol. 491, cols. 181–183.
Section 45(2)	H.L. Vol. 493, cols. 1173–1176.
Section 46(4)	H.L. Vol. 493, cols. 1176, 1177; H.L. Vol. 495, cols. 640, 641.
Section 47	H.C., SCE col. 234; H.L. Vol. 501, cols. 241, 242.
Section 48(2)	H.L. Vol. 493, cols. 1177, 1178; H.L. Vol. 495, cols. 641–643.
Section 50	H.L. Vol. 495, col. 643; H.C. Vol. 138, col. 142; H.L. Vol. 501, cols. 242–245.
Section 50D	H.L. Vol. 584, col. 793; H.L., SC4, col. 6.
Section 51	H.L. Vol. 490, cols. 1174–1176, 1184, 1185; H.L. Vol. 491, cols. 183–188; H.L. Vol. 493, cols. 1178–1180; H.L. Vol. 495, cols. 618, 619, 643–646; H.C., SCE cols. 237–249.
Section 52	H.L. Vol. 491, cols. 188, 189.
Section 52(6)	H.C., SCE cols. 249, 250; H.L. Vol. 501, cols. 245, 246.
Section 53	H.C., SCE col. 251.
Section 54	H.L. Vol. 493, cols. 1180, 1181; H.L. Vol. 495, col. 646.
Section 55	H.L. Vol. 493, cols. 1181, 1182.
Section 56	H.L. Vol. 495, cols. 647–648; H.C., SCE cols. 251, 256; H.L. Vol. 501, cols. 208–214; 249.
Section 57	H.L. Vol. 493, col. 1182; H.C., SCE cols. 256, 257; H.L. Vol. 501, cols. 206–208.
Section 58	H.L. Vol. 491, cols. 116–120; H.L. Vol. 493, cols. 1060–1063; H.L. Vol. 495, cols. 648, 649; H.C., SCE cols. 25–33; H.C., SCE cols. 484, 485; H.L. Vol. 501, cols. 197–200.
Section 59	H.L. Vol. 491, cols. 189, 190; H.C., SCE cols. 257–259; H.C. Vol. 138, cols. 142–143; H.L. Vol. 501, cols. 197–200.
Section 60	H.L. Vol. 491, cols. 105–111; H.L. Vol. 495, cols. 628–630; H.C. Vol. 138, cols. 143–145; H.L. Vol. 501, cols. 251–252. (See also s.29).
Section 61	H.C. Vol. 138, cols. 104–112; H.L. Vol. 501, cols. 252–254.
Section 62	H.L. Vol. 491, col. 190; H.L. Vol. 493, cols. 1182–1184; H.C. Vol. 138, cols. 145, 146.
Section 63	H.L. Vol. 493, cols. 1184–1186; H.L. Vol. 495, cols. 626, 627; H.C. Vol. 138, col. 141.
Section 64	H.L. Vol. 491, cols. 190–192; H.L. Vol. 493, cols. 1186, 1187.

Section 66	H.L. Vol. 495, cols. 650, 651; H.C., SCE cols. 259–345; H.C. Vol. 138, cols. 146–173; H.L. Vol. 501, cols. 214–224.
Section 66(6)	H.L. Vol. 495, col. 650.
Section 67	H.L. Vol. 493, cols. 1188, 1189; H.C., SCE cols. 345, 346.
Section 68	H.L. Vol. 495, cols. 654, 655; H.C., SCE cols. 346–348; H.L. Vol. 501, cols. 242–245.
Section 69	H.L. Vol. 495, cols. 655, 656.
Section 69(2), (3)	H.C., SCD cols. 763–765; H.L. Vol. 574, cols. 1013, 1137–1140.
Section 70	H.C., SCE cols. 348, 349, 470–482; H.C. Vol. 138, cols. 72–78; H.L. Vol. 501, cols. 255–270.
Section 72	H.L. Vol. 491, cols. 340–343; H.L. Vol. 493, cols. 1190–1192; H.C., SCE cols. 349–353.
Section 72(2)(b)	H.L. Vol. 493, col. 1192.
Section 73	H.L. Vol. 491, cols. 343–345; H.C., SCE cols. 353, 354.
Section 73, 73A	H.C. Vol. 280, cols. 593–594; H.L. Vol. 574, cols. 1057–1070, 1096.
Section 74	H.L. Vol. 491, cols. 345, 346; H.C., SCE cols. 354, 355; H.L. Vol. 501, cols. 271, 272; H.L. Vol. 140, cols. 271–272.
Section 75	H.C., SCE cols. 355, 356.
Section 76	H.L. Vol. 491, cols. 127, 128.
Section 77	H.L. Vol. 491, cols. 346–361; H.C., SCE cols. 357–367.
Section 77(4)(c), (5)	H.L. Vol. 493, cols. 1298–1300.
Section 77(8)	H.L. Vol. 493, col. 1300; H.L. Vol. 501, cols. 272, 273.
Section 78	H.L. Vol. 491, cols. 361–366; H.L. Vol. 493, cols. 1300–1303; H.C., SCE cols. 367, 368; H.C. Vol. 138, cols. 174, 175.
Section 79	H.L. Vol. 491, cols. 366, 367, 375–388; H.L. Vol. 493, cols. 1326–1329; H.L. Vol. 495, cols. 657–661; H.C., SCE cols. 368–386; H.C. Vol. 138, cols. 175–182.
Section 79(2)	H.L. Vol. 493, col. 1305.
Section 79(3)	H.L. Vol. 491, cols. 375–384; H.L. Vol. 493, cols. 1305–1314.
Section 79(4)	H.L. Vol. 491, cols. 385, 386; H.L. Vol. 501, col. 273.
Section 79(4), (5)	H.L. Vol. 495, cols. 657–660.
Section 79(4)(e)	H.L. Vol. 501, col. 273.
Section 79(4)(h)	H.L. Vol. 501, cols. 206–208.
Section 80	H.L. Vol. 491, cols. 387–391; H.C., SCE cols. 386–389; H.C. Vol. 138, cols. 182–184.

Section 80(2)(b)	H.L. Vol. 493, cols. 1329–1331; H.L. Vol. 495, cols. 661, 662.
Section 80(7)	H.L. Vol. 491, cols. 389–391.
Section 81	H.L. Vol. 491, cols. 391–394; H.C., SCE col. 389.
Section 81(6)	H.L. Vol. 493, cols. 1329–1331; H.L. Vol. 495, col. 664, H.L. Vol. 501, cols. 242–245.
Section 82	H.L. Vol. 493, cols. 1332, 1333; H.L. Vol. 495, cols. 662, 663.
Section 85	H.L. Vol. 495, cols. 607–610.
Section 87	H.L. Vol. 491, cols. 394–398; H.L. Vol. 493, cols. 1334–1342; H.C., SCE cols. 390, 391.
Section 88	H.L. Vol. 495, cols. 666, 667.
Section 90(2)	H.L. Vol. 491, cols. 398–401; H.L. Vol. 493, cols. 1342, 1343; H.L. Vol. 495, cols. 667, 668; H.C., SCE col. 392; H.L. Vol. 501, col. 275.
Section 93A, 93B	H.L. Vol. 576, col. 51.
Section 95	H.L. Vol. 491, cols. 401–404; H.L. Vol. 493, cols. 1343–1345; H.L. Vol. 495, col. 666.
Section 95(4)	H.L. Vol. 501, cols. 276, 277.
Section 96	H.L. Vol. 491, cols. 404–406; H.C., SCE cols. 395, 396.
Section 97	H.L. Vol. 491, cols. 407, 408.
Section 97(1)	H.L. Vol. 491, cols. 406–407; H.L. Vol. 493, cols. 1345–1347.
Section 97(2)	H.C., SCE cols. 396–399.
Section 98	H.L. Vol. 501, cols. 277–283.
Section 98(1)	H.C., SCE cols. 486–488.
Section 99	H.L. Vol. 491, cols. 408–410; H.L. Vol. 493, cols. 1347–1350; H.C., SCE cols. 399–403; H.L. Vol. 501, cols. 246–249.
Section 100	H.L. Vol. 491, cols. 410–414; H.L. Vol. 493, cols. 1359–1363; H.L. Vol. 495, col. 669; H.C., SCE cols. 403–407; H.L. Vol. 501, cols. 246–249.
Section 101	H.C., SCE cols. 407–411.
Section 102	H.L. Vol. 491, cols. 414, 415; H.L. Vol. 501, cols. 284, 285.
Section 103	H.L. Vol. 491, cols. 415–417; H.L. Vol. 493, cols. 1363–1365.
Section 103(2)	H.L. Vol. 491, cols. 417, 418.
Section 104	H.L. Vol. 491, cols. 418–420; H.L. Vol. 493, cols. 1365–1368; H.L. Vol. 495, cols. 670, 671.
Section 104–106	H.C., SCE cols. 490–500.
Section 105	H.C. Vol. 138, cols. 186–189; H.L. Vol. 501, cols. 286, 287.
Section 107(1)(c)	H.L. Vol. 491, cols. 420, 421.

Section 107(5)	H.L. Vol. 491, cols. 421–423.
Section 107(6)	H.L. Vol. 491, cols. 423, 424.
Section 108	H.L. Vol. 491, cols. 424, 425; H.L. Vol. 501, cols. 246–249.
Section 110	H.L. Vol. 491, col. 425; H.L. Vol. 493, cols. 1369, 1370.
Section 111	H.L. Vol. 491, cols. 425, 426; H.L. Vol. 493, cols. 1370–1373; H.L. Vol. 495, cols. 671–673; H.C., SCE cols. 411–415.
Section 113	H.C., SCE col. 416.
Section 114	H.L. Vol. 501, cols. 246–248; H.C. Vol. 140, cols. 272, 273.
Section 116	H.L. Vol. 491, cols. 486–489; H.L. Vol. 493, cols. 1373, 1374; H.L. Vol. 495, cols. 673–675; H.C., SCE cols. 417–426.
Section 117	H.L. Vol. 491, col. 489; H.C., SCE cols. 426–428; H.C. Vol. 140, cols. 273, 274.
Section 118	H.L. Vol. 491, cols. 489–492; H.L. Vol. 495, cols. 675, 676; H.C. Vol. 138, cols. 190, 191.
Section 119	H.L. Vol. 491, col. 492.
Section 120	H.L. Vol. 491, col. 493.
Section 121	H.L. Vol. 491, cols. 494, 495; H.L. Vol. 493, col. 1375.
Section 122	H.L. Vol. 491, cols. 496, 497.
Section 123(3)	H.L. Vol. 491, cols. 497, 498; H.L. Vol. 501, cols. 291–294.
Section 124	H.L. Vol. 491, cols. 499, 500.
Section 125	H.L. Vol. 493, cols. 1376–1378.
Section 126	H.C., SCE cols. 428–431; H.L. Vol. 501, cols. 298–302.
Section 127	H.L. Vol. 501, cols. 294–298.
Section 128	H.L. Vol. 493, col. 1378.
Section 129	H.L. Vol. 491, cols. 504–512; H.L. Vol. 493, cols. 1378, 1379; H.C., SCE cols. 431–435; H.L. Vol. 501, col. 304.
Section 130	H.L. Vol. 491, cols. 520–522.
Section 131	H.L. Vol. 491, cols. 522–524.
Section 134	H.L. Vol. 491, cols. 524–527.
Section 134(1), (3A)	H.C. Vol. 280, cols. 593–594; H.L. Vol. 574, cols. 1067–1070, 1096.
Section 135	H.L. Vol. 491, cols. 527, 528.
Section 135A–G	H.C., SCE cols. 444–456; H.C. Vol. 164, col. 49; H.C., SCE cols. 1454–1464; Vol. 172, cols. 345, 346; H.L. Vol. 521, cols. 1657–1695; Vol. 522, cols. 839–848, 1188; H.C. Vol. 178, col. 612.

Section 135H	H.C., SCD, cols. 756–761; H.C. Vol. 280, cols. 591–593; H.L. Vol. 574, cols. 1097–1100.
Section 136	H.L. Vol. 491, cols. 528–531; H.L. Vol. 493, col. 1379.
Section 138	H.C., SCE cols. 435, 436.
Section 139	H.L. Vol. 501, cols. 305, 306.
Section 140	H.L. Vol. 491, cols. 531–533.
Section 141	H.L. Vol. 491, cols. 533, 534; H.L. Vol. 493, cols. 1379–1381.
Section 143	H.L. Vol. 491, cols. 534, 535.
Section 143(1)(b)	H.C., SCE cols. 436, 437.
Section 143(2)(a)	H.L. Vol. 501, cols. 306, 307.
Section 144	H.C., SCE cols. 136–139; H.C., SCE cols. 485–488.
Section 144(3)	H.C. Vol. 138, col. 194.
Section 144A	H.L. Vol. 576, col. 37; H.L. Vol. 284, col. 1385.
Section 145	H.L. Vol. 491, cols. 536, 537; H.L. Vol. 493, cols. 1383–1384.
Section 145(2)	H.C., SCE cols. 437–441.
Section 146	H.L. Vol. 491, cols. 537, 538.
Section 149, 150, 152	H.L. Vol. 501, cols. 308–310.
Section 148(2)	H.L. Vol. 493, col. 1385.
Section 149(a)	H.C. Vol. 280, cols. 593–594; H.L. Vol. 574, cols. 1067–1070, 1096.
Section 150	H.C., SCE col. 441.
Section 151(1)	H.C. Vol. 138, cols. 195–197.
Section 151A	H.C. Vol. 280, cols. 591–593; H.L. Vol. 574, cols. 1097–1100.
Section 152	H.L. Vol. 491, cols. 538–542; H.C., SCE cols. 441, 442.
Section 153(3)	H.L. Vol. 491, col. 542.
Section 154(1)	H.L. Vol. 491, cols. 543, 544.
Section 155	H.L. Vol. 491, cols. 544–547; H.C., SCE cols. 444–456.
Section 157	H.C. Vol. 138, cols. 198, 199.
Section 157(5)	H.C., SCE cols. 456–458.
Section 160(1)	H.L. Vol. 495, col. 677.
Section 161, 162	H.L. Vol. 491, cols. 549–553; H.L. Vol. 493, cols. 1387–1398; H.C., SCE cols. 458–461; H.L. Vol. 501, cols. 312, 313.
Section 163	H.L. Vol. 491, cols. 553–562; H.L. Vol. 493, cols. 1389–1396; H.L. Vol. 495, cols. 677, 678, H.L. Vol. 501, cols. 193–197.
Section 163, 165	H.C., SCE cols. 91–107.
Section 164	H.C. Vol. 138, col. 94; H.L. Vol. 501, cols. 193–197.

D Tables of Parliamentary Debates

Section 165	H.L. Vol. 501, cols. 193–197.
Section 168	H.L. Vol. 491, cols. 562, 563; H.L. Vol. 493, col. 1396.
Section 169	H.C., SCE cols. 461–463.
Section 171(1)(e)	H.L. Vol. 491, cols. 563–566.
Section 171(3)	H.L. Vol. 490, cols. 1174–1176 (spare parts exception). H.L. Vol. 491, cols. 75–78; H.L. Vol. 493, cols. 1162–1164; H.L. Vol. 495, cols. 630–635 (public interest defence).
Section 172(2)	H.L. Vol. 491, cols. 568–570.
Section 172(3)	H.L. Vol. 491, cols. 567, 568; H.L. Vol. 501, cols. 315, 316.
Section 174	H.L. Vol. 493, cols. 1396, 1397.
Section 175	H.L. Vol. 491, cols. 570, 571; H.L. Vol. 493, cols. 1397, 1398; H.C. Vol. 138, cols. 199, 200.
Section 176	H.L. Vol. 493, col. 1399.
Section 178	H.L. Vol. 491, cols. 571, 572; H.C., SCE col. 464; H.L. Vol. 501, cols. 208–214 ("electronic"); H.C., SCE col. 465 ("writing"); H.L. Vol. 501, col. 316 ("computer generated", "judicial proceedings").
Section 180	H.C., SCE cols. 503, 504.
Section 182(1)	H.L. Vol. 491, cols. 869–882; H.L. Vol. 493, cols. 1402–1404.
Section 183	H.L. Vol. 491, cols. 882–885; H.L. Vol. 495, cols. 679–680.
Section 184(1)	H.L. Vol. 493, col. 1405.
Section 184(2)	H.L. Vol. 491, cols. 885, 886.
Section 185	H.L. Vol. 491, cols. 886, 887.
Section 187	H.L. Vol. 491, cols. 887–889; H.L. Vol. 495, cols. 680, 681; H.C., SCE cols. 504, 505.
Section 189	H.L. Vol. 501, cols. 318, 319.
Section 190	H.C., SCE cols. 510–514; H.L. Vol. 501, cols. 320–322.
Section 191	H.L. Vol. 491, cols. 890, 891.
Section 191G	H.L. Vol. 576, cols. 37, 39.
Section 192	H.L. Vol. 493, cols. 1406, 1407; H.C., SCE col. 506.
Section 193	H.L. Vol. 491, cols. 891, 892.
Section 195	H.L. Vol. 491, cols. 892–895.
Section 197	H.L. Vol. 491, cols. 900, 901; H.L. Vol. 501, cols. 324, 325.
Section 198	H.C., SCE cols. 506, 507.
Section 198(1)	H.L. Vol. 491, cols. 895, 896.
Section 198(3)	H.L. Vol. 491, cols. 896, 897.
Section 199	H.L. Vol. 491, col. 897.

Section 201(1)	H.L. Vol. 491, cols. 897, 898.
Section 205B(1)(CC)	H.C. Vol. 280, cols. 593–594; H.L. Vol. 574, cols. 1067–1070, 1096.
Section 206	H.L. Vol. 491, col. 898.
Section 208	H.L. Vol. 493, cols. 1408, 1409.
Section 209, 210	H.L. Vol. 491, cols. 899, 900.
Section 210	H.L. Vol. 501, cols. 312–313.
Section 211	H.L. Vol. 495, col. 697.
Section 213	H.L. Vol. 491, cols. 1088–1115; H.L. Vol. 494, cols. 104–111; H.L. Vol. 495, cols. 697–700; H.C., SCE cols. 519–577; H.C. Vol. 138, cols. 36–63; H.L. Vol. 501, cols. 328–332.
Section 213(4)	H.L. Vol. 494, cols. 111, 112; H.C. Vol. 138, cols. 63–72.
Section 215(2)	H.L. Vol. 491, cols. 1115–1118; H.L. Vol. 494, cols. 112–116; H.C., SCE cols. 577–582.
Section 216	H.L. Vol. 491, cols. 1118–1126; H.L. Vol. 494, cols. 116–121; H.L. Vol. 495, cols. 700–702; H.C., SCE cols. 582–590.
Section 217	H.L. Vol. 491, cols. 1127–1129; H.L. Vol. 494, cols. 121, 122.
Section 220(4)	H.L. Vol. 494, cols. 122, 123.
Section 223	H.L. Vol. 491, cols. 1129, 1130.
Section 226	H.L. Vol. 491, cols. 1131–1134; H.L. Vol. 494, cols. 123–127; H.L. Vol. 495, cols. 702–704; H.C. SCE col. 591, 592.
Section 228	H.L. Vol. 494, cols. 127–130.
Section 236	H.L. Vol. 491, cols. 1135–1137.
Section 237	H.L. Vol. 491, cols. 1138–1141; H.L. Vol. 494, cols. 133–135; H.C., SCE cols. 593–560.
Section 238	H.L. Vol. 491, cols. 1153–1154.
Section 239	H.L. Vol. 491, cols. 1154–1157; H.L. Vol. 494, cols. 135, 136.
Sections 240, 243	H.L. Vol. 491, cols. 1157–1161; H.L. Vol. 494, cols. 136–140; H.L. Vol. 495, cols. 706–710; H.C., SCE cols. 600–609; H.C. Vol. 138, cols. 85–93.
Section 240(3)(a)	H.C. Vol. 138, col. 87.
Section 243	H.C. Vol. 138, cols. 86–93; H.L. Vol. 501, cols. 335, 336.
Section 246	H.L. Vol. 494, cols. 140, 141; H.C., SCE cols. 609–611.
Section 247	H.C., SCE cols. 611, 612.
Section 248	H.C., SCE cols. 612–614.
Section 250	H.C., SCE col. 614; H.L. Vol. 501, cols. 337, 338.

Section 252	H.L. Vol. 495, col. 710.
Section 253	H.L. Vol. 501, col. 338.
Section 253(3)	H.L. Vol. 491, col. 1162; H.L. Vol. 494, cols. 142, 143.
Section 255	H.C., SCE cols. 615, 616.
Section 256	H.C., SCE cols. 616, 617.
Section 257	H.C., SCE cols. 617, 618.
Section 287	H.L. Vol. 491, cols. 1192–1194; H.L. Vol. 495, cols 719–722.
Section 288	H.L. Vol. 495, cols. 722–724.
Section 289	H.L. Vol. 495, cols. 724–276.
Section 290	H.L. Vol. 495, cols. 726–727.
Section 291	H.L. Vol. 495, cols. 727–728.
Section 293	H.L. Vol. 495, cols. 728–729.
Section 296	H.L. Vol. 501, cols. 350, 351.
Section 296B	H.L. Vol. 584, col. 793; SC4, col. 6.
Section 297A, 298(2)(a)	H.C., SCD, cols. 756–761; H.C. Vol. 280, cols. 587–588; H.L. Vol. 574, cols. 1100, 1105.
Sections 297A, 299(2), (5)	H.L. Vol. 521, col. 1695; Vol. 522, col. 1188; H.C. Vol. 178, cols. 612–614.
Sections 298, 299	H.L. Vol. 501, cols. 351–353.
Schedule 1	H.L. Vol. 491, cols. 573–589.
Schedule 1, para. 8(2)	H.L. Vol. 501, col. 357.
Schedule 1, para. 10	H.L. Vol. 501, cols. 357, 358.
Schedule 1, para. 14(6)	H.C., SCE col. 466.
Schedule 1, para. 31(2)	H.L. Vol. 493, cols. 1401, 1402.
Schedule 2	H.L. Vol. 501, cols. 318, 319.
Schedule 2, para. 3(1)	H.L. Vol. 491, cols. 902, 903.
Schedule 2, para. 16	H.L. Vol. 491, col. 904.
Schedule 2, para. 17(2), (3)	H.C. SCD, cols. 763–765; H.L. Vol. 574, cols. 1013, 1137–1140.
Schedule 2, paras. 19, 19A	H.C. Vol. 280, cols. 593–594; H.L. Vol. 574, cols. 1067–1070, 1096.

D2. The Broadcasting Act 1990

Section 176, Schedule 17   H.C. Vol. 164, col. 49; H.C., SCF cols. 1345–1362, 1364–1384, 1466, 1499–1501; Vol. 172, cols. 346–348; H.L. Vol. 521, cols. 1700–1710; Vol. 522, cols. 850–853; H.C. Vol. 178, cols. 592–594.

D3. THE COPYRIGHT (COMPUTER PROGRAMS) REGULATIONS 1992

See in general: H.L. Vol. 541, cols. 514–516.

D4. THE DURATION OF COPYRIGHT AND RIGHTS IN PERFORMANCES REGULATIONS 1995

See in general:	H.L. Vol. 567, cols. 1468–1480; H.C. Vol. 268, cols. 1254–1273.
Regulation 18	H.L. Vol. 567, col. 1470.
Regulation 19	H.L. Vol. 567, cols. 1470, 1478.
Regulation 23	H.L. Vol. 567, cols. 1471, 1476; H.C. Vol. 268, cols. 1263, 1268, 1271.
Regulation 24	H.L. Vol. 567, col. 1476; H.C. Vol. 268, col. 1269.

D TABLES OF PARLIAMENTARY DEBATES

D5. THE COPYRIGHT AND RELATED RIGHTS REGULATIONS 1996

See in general:	H.L. Vol. 576, cols. 34–52; H.C. Vol. 284, cols. 1375–1388.
Regulation 27	H.L. Vol. 576, col. 45.
Regulation 33	H.L. Vol. 576, cols. 39, 45; H.C. Vol. 291, col. 585W.

D6. The Broadcasting Act 1996

Section 137   H.C. Vol. 280, col. 291; H.L. Vol. 574, col. 1096.

D7. THE COPYRIGHT AND RIGHTS IN DATABASES REGULATIONS 1997

See in general:	H.C., SC4 (3 December 1997); H.C. Vol. 302, col. 1149; H.L. Vol. 584, cols. 792–800.
Regulation 12	H.C., SC4, cols. 9, 18.
Regulation 13	H.C., SC4, col. 9.
Regulation 21	H.C., SC4, col. 9.
Regulation 28	H.C., SC4, col. 19.
Regulation 30	H.C., SC4, col. 18.

D8. THE COMMUNICATIONS ACT 2003

s.124A	H.L. Vol. 716 (12 Jan 2010) cols. 440–443; H.C. Vol. 508 (7 Apr 2010) cols. 1107–1131
s.124A(1)	H.L. Vol. 716 (12 Jan 2010) cols. 443–463; Vol. 717 (1 Mar 2010) cols. 1287–1289
s.124A(3)	H.L. Vol. 716 (12 Jan 2010) cols. 463–474; Vol. 717 (1 Mar 2010) cols. 1289–1292
s.124A(5)	H.L. Vol. 717 (1 Mar 2010) col. 1292
s.124A(6)	H.L. Vol. 716 (18 Jan 2010) cols. 791–804; Vol. 717 (1 Mar 2010) cols. 1292–1294
s.124A(7)	H.L. Vol. 717 (1 Mar 2010) col. 1294
s.124A(8)	H.L. Vol. 716 (18 Jan 2010) cols. 804–806; Vol. 717 (1 Mar 2010) cols. 1294–1295
s.124A(9)	H.L. Vol. 716 (18 Jan 2010) cols. 804–814; Vol. 718 (15 Mar 2010) cols. 458–467
ss.124A–124M	H.L. Vol. 715 (2 Dec 2009) cols. 771, 782, 785
s.124B(1)	H.L. Vol. 716 (18 Jan 2010) cols. 819–823
s.124B(2)	H.L. Vol. 716 (18 Jan 2010) cols. 823–827
s.124B(3)	H.L. Vol. 716 (18 Jan 2010) cols. 827–828; Vol. 717 (1 Mar 2010) cols. 1295–1297
ss.124B–124N	H.C. Vol. 508 (6 Apr 2010) cols. 883–885
s.124C	H.C. Vol. 508 (7 Apr 2010) cols. 1131 1134
s.124C(2)	H.L. Vol. 716 (18 Jan 2010) cols. 828–829
s.124C(3)	H.L. Vol. 716 (18 Jan 2010) cols. 829–837; Vol. 717 (1 Mar 2010) cols. 1300–1305
s.124C(4)	II.L. Vol. 716 (18 Jan 2010) cols. 837–839
s.124C(5)	H.L. Vol. 716 (18 Jan 2010) cols. 839–843; Vol. 717 (1 Mar 2010) cols. 1305–1306
s.124C(5)(b)	H.L. Vol. 715 (2 Dec 2009) cols. 753–754
s.124C(6)	H.L. Vol. 716 (18 Jan 2010) cols. 843–844; Vol. 717 (1 Mar 2010) cols. 1306–1307
s.124C(7)	H.L. Vol. 716 (18 Jan 2010) cols. 844–846
s.124C(9)	H.L. Vol. 716 (18 Jan 2010) col. 846
s.124C(10)	H.L. Vol. 716 (18 Jan 2010) cols. 846–847
s.124C(11)	H.L. Vol. 716 (18 Jan 2010) col. 847
s.124C(12)	H.L. Vol. 716 (18 Jan 2010) col. 847
s.124C(13)	H.L. Vol. 716 (18 Jan 2010) col. 847
s.124D	H.C. Vol. 508 (7 Apr 2010) col. 1134
s.124D(1)	H.L. Vol. 716 (18 Jan 2010) cols. 847–848
s.124D(2)	H.L. Vol. 716 (18 Jan 2010) cols. 847–851; Vol. 717 (1 Mar 2010) cols. 1307–1308
s.124D(3)	H.L. Vol. 716 (18 Jan 2010) cols. 849–851
s.124D(5)	H.L. Vol. 716 (18 Jan 2010) cols. 851–854; Vol. 717 (1 Mar 2010) cols. 1308–1309
s.124E	H.C. Vol. 508 (7 Apr 2010) cols. 1135–1139; Vol. 718 (8 Apr 2010) cols. 1718–1723

s.124E(1)	H.L. Vol. 716 (18 Jan 2010) cols. 854–862; Vol. 717 (1 Mar 2010) cols. 1309–1313, (3 Mar 2010) cols. 1453–1472
s.124E(2)	H.L. Vol. 716 (18 Jan 2010) cols. 862–866; Vol. 717 (3 Mar 2010) cols. 1472
s.124E(3)	H.L. Vol. 716 (18 Jan 2010) cols. 867–868
s.124E(4)	H.L. Vol. 717 (3 Mar 2010) cols. 1472–1473
s.124E(5)	H.L. Vol. 717 (3 Mar 2010) cols. 1472–1473
s.124E(6)	H.L. Vol. 717 (3 Mar 2010) cols. 1472–1473
s.124E(7)	H.L. Vol. 716 (20 Jan 2010) cols. 1009–1032; Vol. 717 (3 Mar 2010) cols. 1472–1473; Vol. 718 (15 Mar 2010) cols. 467–468
s.124E(8)	H.L. Vol. 716 (20 Jan 2010) cols. 1032–1038; Vol. 718 (15 Mar 2010) cols. 468
s.124E(9)	H.L. Vol. 717 (3 Mar 2010) cols. 1472–1473
s.124F	H.L. Vol. 716 (20 Jan 2010) cols. 1065–1066; H.C. Vol. 508 (7 Apr 2010) col. 1139
s.124F(3)	H.L. Vol. 717 (3 Mar 2010) cols. 1473–1474
s.124F(4)	H.L. Vol. 717 (3 Mar 2010) cols. 1473–1474
s.124F(5)	H.L. Vol. 716 (20 Jan 2010) cols. 1044–1054; Vol. 717 (3 Mar 2010) cols. 1474–1477
s.124F(8)	H.L. Vol. 717 (3 Mar 2010) col. 1477
s.124F(9)	H.L. Vol. 717 (3 Mar 2010) col. 1477
s.124G	H.L. Vol. 715 (2 Dec 2009) col. 787; Vol. 716 (20 Jan 2010) cols. 1075–1076; H.C. Vol. 508 (6 Apr 2010) col. 921; (7 Apr 2010) col. 1139
s.124G(1)	H.L. Vol. 716 (20 Jan 2010) cols. 1066–1075
s.124G(2)	H.L. Vol. 716 (20 Jan 2010) cols. 1076–1079; Vol. 717 (3 Mar 2010) col. 1478
s.124G(3)	H.L. Vol. 716 (20 Jan 2010) cols. 1079–1089
s.124G(4)	H.L. Vol. 716 (20 Jan 2010) cols. 1089–1090; Vol. 718 (15 Mar 2010) col. 468
s.124G(5)	H.L. Vol. 716 (26 Jan 2010) cols. 1301–1316
s.124G(6)	H.L. Vol. 716 (26 Jan 2010) cols. 1316–1319; Vol. 717 (3 Mar 2010) cols. 1478–1479
s.124G(8)	H.L. Vol. 717 (3 Mar 2010) col. 1479
s.124G(9)	H.L. Vol. 717 (3 Mar 2010) col. 1479
s.124H	H.L. Vol. 715 (2 Dec 2009) col. 791; Vol. 716 (26 Jan 2010) cols. 1322–1325; H.C. Vol. 508 (6 Apr 2010) cols. 849, 858; (7 Apr 2010) col. 1139; H.L. Vol 718 (8 Apr 2010) cols. 1723–1727
s.124H(1)	H.L. Vol. 716 (26 Jan 2010) cols. 1320–1322; Vol. 717 (3 Mar 2010) cols. 1479–1486
s.124H(5)	H.L. Vol. 716 (26 Jan 2010) col. 1323
ss.124H–124N	H.C. Vol. 508 (6 Apr 2010) col. 924
s.124I	H.L. Vol. 715 (2 Dec 2009) col. 787; H.C. Vol. 508 (7 Apr 2010) col. 1139

s.124I(3)	H.L. Vol. 717 (3 Mar 2010) cols. 1486; Vol. 718 (15 Mar 2010) col. 469
s.124J	H.L. Vol. 715 (2 Dec 2009) col. 787; H.C. Vol. 508 (7 Apr 2010) col. 1139
s.124J(1)	H.L. Vol. 716 (26 Jan 2010) cols. 1326–1332; Vol. 717 (3 Mar 2010) cols. 1486–1488
s.124J(2)	H.L. Vol. 716 (26 Jan 2010) cols. 1332–1337; Vol. 717 (3 Mar 2010) col. 1488; Vol. 718 (15 Mar 2010) col. 469
s.124J(3)	H.L. Vol. 716 (26 Jan 2010) cols. 1337–1338; Vol. 717 (3 Mar 2010) col. 1488
s.124J(4)	H.L. Vol. 717 (3 Mar 2010) col. 1488
s.124K	H.L. Vol. 717 (3 Mar 2010) cols. 1488–1493; H.C. Vol. 508 (7 Apr 2010) col. 1139
s.124K(5)	H.L. Vol. 718 (15 Mar 2010) col. 469
s.124K(11)	H.L. Vol. 718 (15 Mar 2010) col. 469
s.124L	H.L. Vol 718 (8 Apr 2010) cols. 1727–1728; H.C. Vol. 508 (7 Apr 2010) col. 1139
s.124L(2)	H.L. Vol. 716 (26 Jan 2010) cols. 1338–1341
s.124L(3)	H.L. Vol. 717 (3 Mar 2010) col. 1493
s.124M(1)	H.L. Vol. 716 (26 Jan 2010) cols. 1341–1343
s.124M(2)	H.L. Vol. 716 (26 Jan 2010) col. 1344; Vol. 717 (3 Mar 2010) col. 1494; Vol. 718 (15 Mar 2010) cols. 469–471
s.124M(3)	H.L. Vol. 717 (3 Mar 2010) cols. 1494–1497
s.124M(5)	H.L. Vol. 716 (26 Jan 2010) col. 1344
s.124N	H.L. Vol. 716 (26 Jan 2010) cols. 1344–1346; Vol. 717 (3 Mar 2010) cols. 1497 ("subscriber appeal"); Vol. 718 (15 Mar 2010) col. 471 ("subscriber appeal"); II.C. Vol. 508 (6 Apr 2010) col. 857

D9. THE DIGITAL ECONOMY ACT 2010

D10. THE INTELLECTUAL PROPERTY ACT 2014

Hansard

Debates on the Intellectual Property Bill in the House of Lords can be found here:

> http://www.publications.parliament.uk/pa/ld201314/ldhansrd/text/
> 130723-0001.htm#13072350000686; and
>
> http://www.publications.parliament.uk/pa/ld201314/ldhansrd/text/
> 130730-0001.htm#13073026000417.

PART E

REPEALED STATUTES

PART E

REPEALED STATUTES

E1. THE COPYRIGHT ACT 1956[i]

(4 & 5 ELIZ. 2, C.74)

ARRANGEMENT OF SECTIONS

---

[i] *Editorial Note*: This Act (and the Copyright (Computer Software) Amendment Act 1985) repealed by the CDPA 1988, above as from August 1, 1989. Comparative Tables showing the correspondence of this Act to the 1988 Act, and of the 1988 to this Act are printed at E2, below.

An Act to make new provision in respect of copyright and related matters, in substitution for the provisions of the Copyright Act, 1911, and other enactments relating thereto; to amend the Registered Designs Act, 1949, with respect to designs related to artistic works in which copyright subsists, and to amend the Dramatic and Musical Performers' Protection Act, 1925; and for purposes connected with the matters aforesaid.

[5th November, 1956]

PART I

COPYRIGHT IN ORIGINAL WORKS

Nature of copyright under this Act

1.—(1) In this Act "copyright" in relation to a work (except where the context otherwise requires) means the exclusive right, by virtue and subject to the provisions of this Act, to do, and to authorise other persons to do, certain acts in relation to that work in the United Kingdom or in any other country to which the relevant provision of this Act extends.

The said acts, in relation to a work of any description, are those acts which, in the relevant provision of this Act, are designated as the acts restricted by the copyright in a work of that description.

(2) In accordance with the preceding subsection, but subject to the following provisions of this Act, the copyright in a work is infringed by any person who, not being the owner of the copyright, and without the licence of the owner thereof, does, or authorises another person to do, any of the said acts in relation to the work in the United Kingdom or in any other country to which the relevant provision of this Act extends.

(3) In the preceding subsections references to the relevant provision of this Act, in relation to a work of any description, are references to the provision of this Act whereby it is provided that (subject to compliance with the conditions specified therein) copyright shall subsist in works of that description.

(4) The preceding provisions of this section shall apply, in relation to any subject-matter (other than a work) of a description to which any provision of Part II of the Act relates, as they apply in relation to a work.

(5) For the purposes of any provision of this Act which specifies the conditions under which copyright may subsist in any description of work or other subject-matter, "qualified person"—

[ii] *Editorial Note*: By virtue of the Sound Broadcasting Act 1972 (c.31) s.1 repealed and replaced by the Independent Broadcasting Authority Act 1973 (c.19) ss.1, 38 and 39, repealed and replaced by the Broadcasting Act 1981 (c.68) s.65 and Sch.8, references to "Independent Broadcasting Authority" inter alia in the 1956 Act are to be substituted for "Independent Television Authority". This Act is therefore printed with the necessary substituted references. The Broadcasting Act 1981 was repealed by s.203(3) of and Sch.21 to the Broadcasting Act 1990 (c.42) as provided by the Broadcasting Act 1990 (Commencement No.1 and Transitional Provisions) Order 1990 (SI 1990/2347) (c.61). See s.127 of the 1990 Act and SI 1990/2347 (c.61) as to the dissolution of the IBA.

   (a) in the case of an individual, means a person who is a British subject or British protected person or a citizen of the Republic of Ireland or (not being a British subject or British protected person or a citizen of the Republic of Ireland) is domiciled or resident in the United Kingdom or in another country to which that provision extends, and

   (b) in the case of a body corporate, means a body incorporated under the laws of any part of the United Kingdom or of another country to which that provision extends.

In this subsection "British protected person" has the same meaning as in [the British Nationality Act, 1981.]

Note: This section was amended by the British Nationality (Modification of Enactments) Order 1982 (SI 1982/1832) and is printed as amended. As to "British subject" see British Nationality Act 1981 (c.61) s. 51(1) and *Milltronics Ltd v Hycontrol Ltd* [1990] F.S.R. 273.

Copyright in literary, dramatic and musical works

2.—(1) Copyright shall subsist, subject to the provisions of this Act, in every original literary, dramatic or musical work which is unpublished, and of which the author was a qualified person at the time when the work was made, or, if the making of the work extended over a period, was a qualified person for a substantial part of that period.

(2) Where an original literary, dramatic or musical work has been published, then, subject to the provisions of this Act, copyright shall subsist in the work (or, if copyright in the work subsisted immediately before its first publication, shall continue to subsist) if, but only if,—

   (a) the first publication of the work took place in the United Kingdom, or in another country to which this section extends, or

   (b) the author of the work was a qualified person at the time when the work was first published, or

   (c) the author had died before that time, but was a qualified person immediately before his death.

(3) Subject to the last preceding subsection, copyright subsisting in a work by virtue of this section shall continue to subsist until the end of the period of fifty years from the end of the calendar year in which the author died, and shall then expire:

Provided that if before the death of the author none of the following acts had been done, that is to say,—

   (a) the publication of the work,

   (b) the performance of the work in public,

   (c) the offer for sale to the public of records of the work,

   (d) the broadcasting of the work,

   [(e) the inclusion of the work in a cable programme.]

the copyright shall continue to subsist until the end of the period of fifty years from the end of the calendar year which includes the earliest occasion on which one of those acts is done.

(4) In the last preceding subsection references to the doing of any act in relation to a work include references to the doing of that act in relation to an adaptation of the work.

(5) The acts restricted by the copyright in a literary, dramatic or musical work are—

   (a) reproducing the work in any material form;

   (b) publishing the work;

(c) performing the work in public;

(d) broadcasting the work;

[(e) including the work in a cable programme;]

(f) making any adaptation of the work;

(g) doing, in relation to an adaptation of the work, any of the acts specified in relation to the work in paragraphs (a) to (e) of this subsection.

(6) In this Act "adaptation"—

(a) in relation to a literary or dramatic work, means any of the following, that is to say,—

(i) in the case of a non-dramatic work, a version of the work (whether in its original language or a different language) in which it is converted into a dramatic work;

(ii) in the case of a dramatic work, a version of the work (whether in its original language or a different language) in which it is converted into a non-dramatic work;

(iii) a translation of the work;

(iv) a version of the work in which the story or action is conveyed wholly or mainly by means of pictures in a form suitable for reproduction in a book, or in a newspaper, magazine or similar periodical; and

(b) in relation to a musical work, means an arrangement or transcription of the work,

so however that the mention of any matter in this definition shall not affect the generality of paragraph (a) of the last preceding subsection.

Note: This section was amended by the Cable and Broadcasting Act 1984 (c.46) and is printed as amended.

Copyright in artistic works

3.—(1) In this Act "artistic work" means a work of any of the following descriptions, that is to say,—

(a) the following, irrespective of artistic quality, namely paintings, sculptures, drawings, engravings and photographs;

(b) works of architecture, being either buildings or models for buildings;

(c) works of artistic craftsmanship, not falling within either of the preceding paragraphs.

(2) Copyright shall subsist, subject to the provisions of this Act, in every original artistic work which is unpublished, and of which the author was a qualified person at the time when the work was made, or, if the making of the work extended over a period, was a qualified person for a substantial part of that period.

(3) Where an original artistic work has been published, then, subject to the provisions of this Act, copyright shall subsist in the work (or, if copyright in the work subsisted immediately before its first publication, shall continue to subsist) if, but only if,—

(a) the first publication of the work took place in the United Kingdom, or in another country to which this section extends, or

(b) the author of the work was a qualified person at the time when the work was first published, or

(c) the author had died before that time, but was a qualified person immediately before his death.

(4) Subject to the last preceding subsection, copyright subsisting in a work by virtue of this section shall continue to subsist until the end of the period of fifty years from the end of the calendar year in which the author died, and shall then expire:

Provided that—

    (a) in the case of an engraving, if before the death of the author the engraving had not been published, the copyright shall continue to subsist until the end of the period of fifty years from the end of the calendar year in which it is first published;

    (b) the copyright in a photograph shall continue to subsist until the end of the period of fifty years from the end of the calendar year in which the photograph is first published, and shall then expire.

(5) The Acts restricted by the copyright in an artistic work are—

    (a) reproducing the work in any material form;

    (b) publishing the work;

    (c) including the work in a television broadcast;

    [(d) including the work in a cable programme.]

Note: This section was amended by the Cable and Broadcasting Act 1984 (c.46) and is printed as amended.

Ownership of copyright in literary, dramatic, musical and artistic works

4.—(1) Subject to the provisions of this section, the author of a work shall be entitled to any copyright subsisting in the work by virtue of this Part of this Act.

(2) Where a literary, dramatic or artistic work is made by the author in the course of his employment by the proprietor of a newspaper, magazine or similar periodical under a contract of service or apprenticeship, and is so made for the purpose of publication in a newspaper, magazine or similar periodical, the said proprietor shall be entitled to the copyright in the work in so far as the copyright relates to publication of the work in any newspaper, magazine or similar periodical, or to reproduction of the work for the purpose of its being so published; but in all other respects the author shall be entitled to any copyright subsisting in the work by virtue of this Part of this Act.

(3) Subject to the last preceding subsection, where a person commissions the taking of a photograph, or the painting or drawing of a portrait, or the making of an engraving, and pays or agrees to pay for it in money or money's worth, and the work is made in pursuance of that commission, the person who so commissioned the work shall be entitled to any copyright subsisting therein by virtue of this Part of this Act.

(4) Where, in a case not falling within either of the two last preceding subsections, a work is made in the course of the author's employment by another person under a contract of service or apprenticeship, that other person shall be entitled to any copyright subsisting in the work by virtue of this Part of this Act.

(5) Each of the three last preceding subsections shall have effect subject, in any particular case, to any agreement excluding the operation thereof in that case.

(6) The preceding provisions of this section shall all have effect subject to the provisions of Part VI of this Act.

Infringements by importation, sale and other dealings

5.—(1) Without prejudice to the general provisions of section one of this Act as to infringements of copyright, the provisions of this section shall have effect in relation to copyright subsisting by virtue of this Part of this Act.

(2) The copyright in a literary, dramatic, musical or artistic work is infringed by any person who, without the licence of the owner of the copyright, imports an article (otherwise than for his private and domestic use) into the United Kingdom, or into any other country to which this section extends, if to his knowledge the making of that article constituted an infringement of that copyright, or would

have constituted such an infringement if the article had been made in the place into which it is so imported.

(3) The copyright in a literary, dramatic, musical or artistic work is infringed by any person who, in the United Kingdom, or in any other country to which this section extends, and without the licence of the owner of the copyright,—

(a) sells, lets for hire, or by way of trade offers or exposes for sale or hire any article, or

(b) by way of trade exhibits any article in public,

if to his knowledge the making of the article constituted an infringement of that copyright, or (in the case of an imported article) would have constituted an infringement of that copyright if the article had been made in the place into which it was imported.

(4) The last preceding subsection shall apply in relation to the distribution of any articles either—

(a) for purposes of trade, or

(b) for other purposes, but to such an extent as to affect prejudicially the owner of the copyright in question,

as it applies in relation to the sale of an article.

(5) The copyright in a literary, dramatic or musical work is also infringed by any person who permits a place of public entertainment to be used for a performance in public of the work, where the performance constitutes an infringement of the copyright in the work:

Provided that this subsection shall not apply in a case where the person permitting the place to be so used—

(a) was not aware, and had no reasonable grounds for suspecting, that the performance would be an infringement of the copyright, or

(b) gave the permission gratuitously, or for a consideration which was only nominal or (if more than nominal) did not exceed a reasonable estimate of the expenses to be incurred by him in consequence of the use of the place for the performance.

(6) In this section "place of public entertainment" includes any premises which are occupied mainly for other purposes, but are from time to time made available for hire to such persons as may desire to hire them for purposes of public entertainment.

General exceptions from protection of literary, dramatic and musical works

6.—(1) No fair dealing with a literary, dramatic or musical work for purposes of research or private study shall constitute an infringement of the copyright in the work.

(2) No fair dealing with a literary, dramatic or musical work shall constitute an infringement of the copyright in the work if it is for purposes of criticism or review, whether of that work or of another work, and is accompanied by a sufficient acknowledgement.

(3) No fair dealing with a literary, dramatic or musical work shall constitute an infringement of the copyright in the work if it is for the purpose of reporting current events—

(a) in a newspaper, magazine or similar periodical, or

(b) by means of broadcasting, or in a cinematograph film,

and, in a case falling within paragraph (a) of this subsection, is accompanied by a sufficient acknowledgement.

(4) The copyright in a literary, dramatic or musical work is not infringed by reproducing it for the purposes of a judicial proceeding, or for the purposes of a report of a judicial proceeding.

(5) The reading or recitation in public by one person of any reasonable extract from a published literary or dramatic work, if accompanied by a sufficient acknowledgement, shall not constitute an infringement of the copyright in the work:

Provided that this subsection shall not apply to anything done for the purposes of broadcasting.

(6) The copyright in a published literary or dramatic work is not infringed by the inclusion of a short passage therefrom in a collection intended for the use of schools, if—

(a) the collection is described in its title, and in any advertisements thereof issued by or on behalf of the publisher, as being so intended, and

(b) the work in question was not published for the use of schools, and

(c) the collection consists mainly of material in which no copyright subsists, and

(d) the inclusion of the passage is accompanied by a sufficient acknowledgment:

Provided that this subsection shall not apply in relation to the copyright in a work if, in addition to the passage in question, two or more other excerpts from works by the author thereof (being works in which copyright subsists at the time when the collection is published) are contained in that collection, or are contained in that collection taken together with every similar collection (if any) published by the same publisher within the period of five years immediately preceding the publication of that collection.

(7) Where by virtue of an assignment or licence a person is authorised to broadcast a literary, dramatic or musical work from a place in the United Kingdom, or in another country to which section two of this Act extends, but (apart from this subsection) would not be entitled to make reproductions of it in the form of a record or of a cinematograph film, the copyright in the work is not infringed by his making such a reproduction of the work solely for the purpose of broadcasting the work:

Provided that this subsection shall not apply if—

(a) the reproduction is used for making any further reproduction therefrom, or for any other purpose except that of broadcasting in accordance with the assignment or licence, or

(b) the reproduction is not destroyed before the end of the period of twenty-eight days beginning with the day on which it is first used for broadcasting the work in pursuance of the assignment or licence, or such extended period (if any) as may be agreed between the person who made the reproduction and the person who (in relation to the making of reproductions of the description in question) is the owner of the copyright.

(8) The preceding provisions of this section shall apply to the doing of any act in relation to an adaptation of a work as they apply in relation to the doing of that act in relation to the work itself.

(9) The provisions of this section shall apply where a work, or adaptation of a work, is [included in a cable programme] as they apply where a work or adaptation is broadcast.

(10) In this Act "sufficient acknowledgment" means an acknowledgment identifying the work in question by its title or other description and, unless the work is anonymous or the author has previously agreed or required that no acknowledgment of his name should be made, also identifying the author.

Note: This section was amended by the Cable and Broadcasting Act 1984 (c.46) and is printed as amended.

Special exceptions as respects libraries and archives

7.—(1) The copyright in an article contained in a periodical publication is not infringed by the making or supplying of a copy of the article, if the copy is made or supplied by or on behalf of the librarian of a library of a class prescribed by regulations made under this subsection by the Board of Trade, and the conditions prescribed by those regulations are complied with.

(2) In making any regulations for the purposes of the preceding subsection the Board of Trade shall make such provision as the Board may consider appropriate for securing—

(a) that the libraries to which the regulations apply are not established or conducted for profit;

(b) that the copies in question are supplied only to persons satisfying the librarian, or a person acting on his behalf, that they require them for purposes of research or private study and will not use them for any other purpose;

(c) that no person is furnished under the regulations with two or more copies of the same article;

(d) that no copy extends to more than one article contained in any one publication; and

(e) that persons to whom copies are supplied under the regulations are required to pay for them a sum not less than the cost (including a contribution to the general expenses of the library) attributable to their production,

and may impose such other requirements (if any) as may appear to the Board to be expedient.

(3) The copyright in a published literary, dramatic or musical work, other than an article contained in a periodical publication, is not infringed by the making or supplying of a copy of part of the work, if the copy is made or supplied by or on behalf of the librarian of a library of a class prescribed by regulations made under this subsection by the Board of Trade, and the conditions prescribed by those regulations are complied with:

Provided that this subsection shall not apply if, at the time when the copy is made, the librarian knows the name and address of a person entitled to authorise the making of the copy, or could by reasonable inquiry ascertain the name and address of such a person.

(4) The provisions of subsection (2) of this section shall apply for the purposes of the last preceding subsection:

Provided that paragraph (d) of the said subsection (2) shall not apply for those purposes, but any regulations made under the last preceding subsection shall include such provision as the Board of Trade may consider appropriate for securing that no copy to which the regulations apply extends to more than a reasonable proportion of the work in question.

(5) The copyright in a published literary, dramatic or musical work is not infringed by the making or supplying of a copy of the work, or of part of it, by or on behalf of the librarian of a library of a class prescribed by regulations made under this subsection by the Board of Trade, if—

(a) the copy is supplied to the librarian of any library of a class so prescribed;

(b) at the time when the copy is made, the librarian by or on whose behalf it is supplied does not know the name and address of any person entitled to authorise the making of the copy, and could not by reasonable inquiry ascertain the name and address of such a person; and

(c) any other conditions prescribed by the regulations are complied with:

Provided that the condition specified in paragraph (b) of this subsection shall not apply in the case of an article contained in a periodical publication.

(6) Where, at a time more than fifty years from the end of the calendar year in which the author of a literary, dramatic or musical work died, and more than one hundred years after the time, or the end of the period, at or during which the work was made,—

(a) copyright subsists in the work, but

(b) the work has not been published, and

(c) the manuscript or a copy of the work is kept in a library, museum or other institution where (subject to any provisions regulating the institution in question) it is open to public inspection,

the copyright in the work is not infringed by a person who reproduces the work for purposes of research or private study, or with a view to publication.

(7) Where a published literary, dramatic or musical work (in this subsection referred to as "the new work") incorporates the whole or part of a work (in this subsection referred to as "the old work") in the case of which the circumstances specified in the last preceding subsection existed immediately before the new work was published, and—

(a) before the new work was published, such notice of the intended publication as may be prescribed by regulations made under this subsection by the Board of Trade had been given, and

(b) immediately before the new work was published, the identity of the owner of the copyright in the old work was not known to the publisher of the new work,

then for the purposes of this Act—

(i) that publication of the new work, and

(ii) any subsequent publication of the new work, either in the same or in an altered form,

shall, in so far as it constitutes a publication of the old work, not be treated as an infringement of the copyright in the old work or as an unauthorised publication of the old work:

Provided that this subsection shall not apply to a subsequent publication incorporating a part of the old work which was not included in the new work as originally published, unless (apart from this subsection) the circumstances specified in the last preceding subsection, and in paragraphs (a) and (b) of this subsection, existed immediately before that subsequent publication.

(8) In so far as the publication of a work, or of part of a work, is, by virtue of the last preceding subsection, not to be treated as an infringement of the copyright in the work, a person who subsequently broadcasts the work, or that part thereof, as the case may be, or [includes it in a cable programme,] or performs it in public, or makes a record of it, does not thereby infringe the copyright in the work.

(9) In relation to an article or other work which is accompanied by one or more artistic works provided for explaining or illustrating it (in this subsection referred to as "illustrations"), the preceding provisions of this section shall apply as if—

(a) wherever they provide that the copyright in the article or work is not infringed, the reference to that copyright included a reference to any copyright in any of the illustrations;

(b) in subsections (1) and (2), references to a copy of the article included references to a copy of the article together with a copy of the illustrations or any of them;

(c) in subsections (3) to (5), reference to a copy of the work included references to a copy of the work together with a copy of the illustrations or any of them, and references to a copy of part of the work included references to a copy of that part of the work together with a copy of any of the illustrations which were provided for explaining or illustrating that part; and

(d) in subsections (6) and (7), references to the doing of any act in relation to the work included references to the doing of that act in relation to the work together with any of the illustrations.

(10) In this section "article" includes an item of any description.

Note: This section was amended by the Cable and Broadcasting Act 1984 (c.46) and is printed as amended.

Special exception in respect of records of musical works

8.—(1) The copyright in a musical work is not infringed by a person (in this section referred to as "the manufacturer") who makes a record of the work or of an adaptation thereof in the United Kingdom, if—

(a) records of the work, or, as the case may be, of a similar adaptation of the work, have previously been made in, or imported into, the United Kingdom for the purposes of retail sale, and were so made or imported by, or with the licence of, the owner of the copyright in the work;

(b) before making the record, the manufacturer gave to the owner of the copyright the prescribed notice of his intention to make it;

(c) the manufacturer intends to sell the record by retail, or to supply it for the purpose of its being sold by retail by another person, or intends to use it for making other records which are to be so sold or supplied; and

(d) in the case of a record which is sold by retail, the manufacturer pays to the owner of the copyright, in the prescribed manner and at the prescribed time, a royalty of an amount ascertained in accordance with the following provisions of this section.

(2) Subject to the following provisions of this section, the royalty mentioned in paragraph (d) of the preceding subsection shall be of an amount equal to six and one-quarter per cent of the ordinary retail selling price of the record, calculated in the prescribed manner:

Provided that, if the amount so calculated includes a fraction of a farthing, that fraction shall be reckoned as one farthing, and if, apart from this proviso, the amount of the royalty would be less than three-farthings, the amount thereof shall be three-farthings.

(3) If, at any time after the end of the period of one year beginning with the coming into operation of this section, it appears to the Board of Trade that the ordinary rate of royalty, or the minimum amount thereof, in accordance with the provisions of the last preceding subsection, or in accordance with those provisions as last varied by an order under this subsection, has ceased to be equitable, either generally or in relation to any class of records, the Board may hold a public inquiry in the prescribed manner; and if, in consequence of such an inquiry, the Board are satisfied of the need to do so, the Board may make an order prescribing such different rate or amount, either generally or in relation to any one or more classes of records, as the Board may consider just:

Provided that—

(a) no order shall be made under this subsection unless a draft of the order has been laid before Parliament and approved by a resolution of each House of Parliament; and

(b) where an order comprising a class of records (that is to say, either a general order or an order relating specifically to that class, or to that class together with one or more other classes of records) has been made under this sub-section, no further order comprising that class of records shall be made thereunder less than five years after the date on which the previous order comprising that class (or, if more than one, the last previous order comprising that class) was made thereunder.

(4) In the case of a record which comprises (with or without other material, and either in their original form or in the form of adaptations) two or more musical works in which copyright subsists—

    (a) the minimum royalty shall be three-farthings in respect of each of those works, or, if a higher or lower amount is prescribed by an order under the last preceding subsection as the minimum royalty, shall be that amount in respect of each of those works; and

    (b) if the owners of the copyright in the works are different persons, the royalty shall be apportioned among them in such manner as they may agree or as in default of agreement, may be determined by arbitration.

(5) Where a record comprises (with or without other material) a performance of a musical work, or of an adaptation of a musical work, in which words are sung, or are spoken incidentally to or in association with the music, and either no copyright subsists in that work or, if such copyright subsists, the conditions specified in subsection (1) of this section are fulfilled in relation to that copyright, then if—

    (a) the words consist or form part of a literary or dramatic work in which copyright subsists, and

    (b) such previous records as are referred to in paragraph (a) of subsection (1) of this section were made or imported by, or with the licence of, the owner of the copyright in that literary or dramatic work, and

    (c) the conditions specified in paragraphs (b) and (d) of subsection (1) of this section are fulfilled in relation to the owner of that copyright,

the making of the record shall not constitute an infringement of the copyright in the literary or dramatic work:

Provided that this subsection shall not be construed as requiring more than one royalty to be paid in respect of a record; and if copyright subsists both in the musical work and in the literary or dramatic work, and their owners are different persons, the royalty shall be apportioned among them (or among them and any other person entitled to a share thereof in accordance with the last preceding subsection) as they may agree or as, in default of agreement, may be determined by arbitration.

(6) For the purposes of this section an adaptation of a work shall be taken to be similar to an adaptation thereof contained in previous records if the two adaptations do not substantially differ in their treatment of the work, either in respect of style or (apart from any difference in numbers) in respect of the performers required for performing them.

(7) Where, for the purposes of paragraph (a) of subsection (1) of this section, the manufacturer requires to know whether such previous records as are mentioned in that paragraph were made or imported as therein mentioned, the manufacturer may make the prescribed inquiries; and if the owner of the copyright fails to reply to those inquiries within the prescribed period, the previous records shall be taken to have been made or imported, as the case may be, with the licence of the owner of the copyright.

(8) The preceding provisions of this section shall apply in relation to records of part of a work or adaptation as they apply in relation to records of the whole of it:

Provided that subsection (1) of this section—

    (a) shall not apply to a record of the whole of a work or adaptation unless the previous records referred to in paragraph (a) of that subsection were records of the whole of the work or of a similar adaptation, and

    (b) shall not apply to a record of part of a work or adaptation unless those previous records were records of, or comprising, that part of the work or of a similar adaptation.

(9) In relation to musical works published before the first day of July, nineteen hundred and twelve, the preceding provisions of this section shall apply as if paragraph (a) of subsection (1), paragraph (b) of subsection (5), subsections (6) and (7), and the proviso to the last preceding subsection, were omitted:

Provided that this subsection shall not extend the operation of subsection (5) of this section to a record in respect of which the condition specified in paragraph (b) of that subsection is not fulfilled, unless the words comprised in the record (as well as the musical work) were published before the first day of July, nineteen hundred and twelve, and were so published as words to be sung to, or spoken incidentally to or in association with, the music.

(10) Nothing in this section shall be construed as authorising the importation of records which could not lawfully be imported apart from this section; and accordingly, for the purposes of any provision of this Act relating to imported articles, where the question arises whether the making of a record made outside the United Kingdom would have constituted an infringement of copyright if the record had been made in the United Kingdom, that question shall be determined as if subsection (1) of this section had not been enacted.

(11) In this section "prescribed" means prescribed by regulations made under this section by the Board of Trade; and any such regulations made for the purposes of paragraph (d) of subsection (1) of this section may provide that the taking of such steps as may be specified in the regulations (being such steps as the Board consider most convenient for ensuring the receipt of the royalties by the owner of the copyright) shall be treated as constituting payment of the royalties in accordance with that paragraph.

General exceptions from protection of artistic works

9.—(1) No fair dealing with an artistic work for purposes of research or private study shall constitute an infringement of the copyright in the work.

(2) No fair dealing with an artistic work shall constitute an infringement of the copyright in the work if it is for purposes of criticism or review, whether of that work or of another work, and is accompanied by a sufficient acknowledgment.

(3) The copyright in a work to which this subsection applies which is permanently situated in a public place, or in premises open to the public, is not infringed by the making of a painting, drawing, engraving or photograph of the work, or the inclusion of the work in a cinematograph film or in a television broadcast.

This subsection applies to sculptures, and to such works of artistic craftsmanship as are mentioned in paragraph (c) of subsection (1) of section three of this Act.

(4) The copyright in a work of architecture is not infringed by the making of a painting, drawing, engraving or photograph of the work, or the inclusion of the work in a cinematograph film or in a television broadcast.

(5) Without prejudice to the two last preceding subsections, the copyright in an artistic work is not infringed by the inclusion of the work in a cinematograph film or in a television broadcast, if its inclusion therein is only by way of background or is otherwise only incidental to the principal matters represented in the film or broadcast.

E REPEALED STATUTES

(6) The copyright in an artistic work is not infringed by the publication of a painting, drawing, engraving, photograph or cinematograph film, if by virtue of any of the three last preceding subsections the making of that painting, drawing, engraving, photograph or film did not constitute an infringement of the copyright.

(7) The copyright in an artistic work is not infringed by reproducing it for the purposes of judicial proceeding or for the purposes of a report of a judicial proceeding.

(8) The making of an object of any description which is in three dimensions shall not be taken to infringe the copyright in an artistic work in two dimensions, if the object would not appear, to persons who are not experts in relation to objects of that description, to be a reproduction of the artistic work.

(9) The copyright in an artistic work is not infringed by the making of a subsequent artistic work by the same author, notwithstanding that part of the earlier work—

(a) is reproduced in the subsequent work, and

(b) is so reproduced by the use of a mould, cast, sketch, plan, model or study made for the purposes of the earlier work,

if in making the subsequent work the author does not repeat or imitate the main design of the earlier work.

(10) Where copyright subsists in a building as a work of architecture, the copyright is not infringed by any reconstruction of that building; and where a building has been constructed in accordance with architectural drawings or plans in which copyright subsists, and has been so constructed by, or with the licence of, the owner of that copyright, any subsequent reconstruction of the building by reference to those drawings or plans shall not constitute an infringement of that copyright.

(11) The provisions of this section shall apply in relation to a [cable programme] as they apply in relation to a television broadcast.

Note: This section was amended by the Cable and Broadcasting Act 1984 (c.46) and is printed as amended.

Special exception in respect of industrial designs

10.—[(1) *Where copyright subsists in an artistic work, and a corresponding design is registered under the Registered Designs Act, 1949 (in this section referred to as "the Act of 1949"), it shall not be an infringement of the copyright in the work—*

(a) *to do anything, during the subsistence of the copyright in the registered design under the Act of 1949, which is within the scope of the copyright in the design, or*

(b) *to do anything, after the copyright in the registered design has come to an end, which, if it had been done while the copyright in the design subsisted, would have been within the scope of that copyright as extended to all associated designs and articles:*

Provided that this subsection shall have effect subject to the provisions of the First Schedule to this Act in cases falling within that Schedule.

(2) *Where copyright subsists in an artistic work, and—*

(a) *a corresponding design is applied industrially by or with the licence of the owner of the copyright in the work, and*

(b) *articles to which the design has been so applied are sold, let for hire, or offered for sale or hire, and*

(c) *at the time when those articles are sold, let for hire, or offered for sale or hire, they are not articles in respect of which the design has been registered under the Act of 1949, the following provisions of this section shall apply.*

(3) *Subject to the next following subsection,—*

(a) *during the relevant period of fifteen years, it shall not be an infringement of the copyright in the work to do anything which, at the time when it is done, would have been within the scope of the copyright in the design if the design had, immediately before that time, been registered in respect of all relevant articles; and*

(b) *after the end of the relevant period of fifteen years, it shall not be an infringement of the copyright in the work to do anything which, at the time when it is done, would, if the design had been registered immediately before that time, have been within the scope of the copyright in the design as extended to all associated designs and articles.*

In this subsection "the relevant period of fifteen years" means the period of fifteen years beginning with the date on which articles, such as are mentioned in paragraph (b) of the last preceding subsection, were first sold, let for hire, or offered for sale or hire in the circumstances mentioned in paragraph (c) of that subsection; and "all relevant articles", in relation to any time within that period, means all articles falling within the said paragraph (b) which had before that time been sold, let for hire, or offered for sale or hire in those circumstances.]

[(2) Where copyright subsists in an artistic work, and—

(a) a corresponding design is applied industrially by or with the licence of the owner of the copyright in the work, and

(b) articles to which the design has been so applied are sold, let for hire, or offered for sale or hire whether in the United Kingdom or elsewhere, and[iii]

the following provisions of this section shall apply.

(3) Subject to the next following subsection, after the end of the relevant period of fifteen years it shall not be an infringement of the copyright in the work to do anything which at the time when it was done would, if a corresponding design had been registered under the Registered Designs Act 1949 (in this section referred to as "the Act of 1949") immediately before that time, have been within the scope of the copyright in the design as extended to all associated designs and articles.

In this subsection "the relevant period of fifteen years" means the period of fifteen years beginning with the date on which articles, such as are mentioned in paragraph (b) of the last preceding subsection, were first sold, let for hire or offered for sale or hire, whether in the United Kingdom or elsewhere.]

(4) For the purposes of subsection (2) and (3) of this section, no account shall be taken of any articles in respect of which, at the time when they were sold, let for hire, or offered for sale or hire, the design in question was excluded from registration under the Act of 1949 by rules made under subsection (4) of section one of that Act (which relates to the exclusion of designs for articles which are primarily literary or artistic in character); and for the purposes of any proceedings under this Act a design shall be conclusively presumed to have been so excluded if—

(a) before the commencement of those proceedings, an application for the registration of the design under the Act of 1949 in respect of those articles had been refused;

(b) the reason or one of the reasons stated for the refusal was that the design was excluded from such registration by rules made under the said subsection (4); and

---

[iii] *Editorial Note:* Sic. Although it deleted sub-para.(c), the 1968 Act did not delete the word "and" between sub-para.(c) and sub-para.(b).

(c) no appeal against that refusal had been allowed before the date of the commencement of the proceedings or was pending on that date.

(5) The power of the Board of Trade to make rules under section thirty-six of the Act of 1949 shall include power to make rules for the purposes of this section for determining the circumstances in which a design is to be taken to be applied industrially.

(6) In this section, references to the scope of the copyright in a registered design are references to the aggregate of the things, which, by virtue of section seven of the Act of 1949, the registered proprietor of the design has the exclusive right to do, and references to the scope of the copyright in a registered design as extended to all associated designs and articles are references to the aggregate of the things which, by virtue of that section, the registered proprietor would have had the exclusive right to do if—

    (a) when that design was registered, there had at the same time been registered every possible design consisting of that design with modifications or variations not sufficient to alter the character or substantially to affect the identity thereof, and the said proprietor had been registered as the proprietor of every such design, and

    (b) the design in question, and every other design such as is mentioned in the preceding paragraph, had been registered in respect of all the articles to which it was capable of being applied.

(7) In this section "corresponding design", in relation to an artistic work, means a design which, when applied to an article, results in a reproduction of that work.

Note: This section and the First Schedule were amended by the Design Copyright Act 1968 (c.68). The amendment to this section consisted of deleting subs.(1), amending subs.(2) and substituting a new subs.(3). The original subss.(1), (2) and (3) are printed in italics. The word "and" at the end of subs.(2)(b) was not deleted by the 1968 Act.

Provisions as to anonymous and pseudonymous works, and works of joint authorship

11.—(1) The preceding provisions of this Part of this Act shall have effect subject to the modifications specified in the Second Schedule to this Act in the case of works published anonymously or pseudonymously.

(2) The provisions of the Third Schedule to this Act shall have effect with respect to works of joint authorship.

(3) In this Act "work of joint authorship" means a work produced by the collaboration of two or more authors in which the contribution of each author is not separate from the contribution of the other author or authors.

Part II

Copyright in Sound Recordings, Cinematograph Films, Broadcasts, etc.

Copyright in sound recordings

12.—(1) Copyright shall subsist, subject to the provisions of this Act, in every sound recording of which the maker was a qualified person at the time when the recording was made.

(2) Without prejudice to the preceding subsection, copyright shall subsist, subject to the provisions of this Act, in every sound recording which has been published, if the first publication of the recording took place in the United Kingdom or in another country to which this section extends.

(3) Copyright subsisting in a sound recording by virtue of this section shall continue to subsist until the end of the period of fifty years from the end of the calendar year in which the recording is first published, and shall then expire.

(4) Subject to the provisions of this Act, the maker of a sound recording shall be entitled to any copyright subsisting in the recording by virtue of this section:

Provided that where a person commissions the making of a sound recording, and pays or agrees to pay for it in money or money's worth, and the recording is made in pursuance of that commission, that person, in the absence of any agreement to the contrary, shall, subject to the provisions of Part VI of this Act, be entitled to any copyright subsisting in the recording by virtue of this section.

(5) The acts restricted by the copyright in a sound recording are the following, whether a record embodying the recording is utilised directly or indirectly in doing them, that is to say,—

(a) making a record embodying the recording;

(b) causing the recording to be heard in public;

(c) broadcasting the recording [or including it in a cable programme].

(6) The copyright in a sound recording is not infringed by a person who does any of those Acts in the United Kingdom in relation to a sound recording, or part of a sound recording, if—

(a) records, embodying that recording, or that part of the recording, as the case may be, have previously been issued to the public in the United Kingdom, and

(b) at the time when those records were so issued, neither the records nor the containers in which they were so issued bore a label or other mark indicating the year in which the recording was first published:

Provided that this subsection shall not apply if it is shown that the records in question were not issued by or with the licence of the owner of the copyright, or that the owner of the copyright had taken all reasonable steps for securing that records embodying the recording or part thereof would not be issued to the public in the United Kingdom without such a label or mark either on the records themselves or on their containers.

(7) Where a sound recording is caused to be heard in public—

(a) at any premises where persons reside or sleep, as part of the amenities provided exclusively or mainly for residents or inmates therein, or

(b) as part of the activities of, or for the benefit of, a club, society or other organisation which is not established or conducted for profit and whose main objects are charitable or are otherwise concerned with the advancement of religion, education or social welfare,

the Act of causing it to be so heard shall not constitute an infringement of the copyright in the recording:

Provided that this subsection shall not apply—

(i) in the case of such premises as are mentioned in paragraph (a) of this subsection, if a special charge is made for admission to the part of the premises where the recording is to be heard; or

(ii) in the case of such an organisation as is mentioned in paragraph (b) of this subsection, if a charge is made for admission to the place where the recording is to be heard, and any of the proceeds of the charge are applied otherwise than for the purposes of the organisation.

(8) For the purposes of this Act a sound recording shall be taken to be made at the time when the first record embodying the recording is produced, and the maker of a sound recording is the person who owns that record at the time when the recording is made.

(9) In this Act "sound recording" means the aggregate of the sounds embodied in, and capable of being reproduced by means of, a record of any description, other than a sound-track associated with a cinematograph film; and "publication", in relation to a sound recording, means the issue to the public of records embodying the recording or any part thereof.

Note: This section was amended by the Cable and Broadcasting Act 1984 (c.46) and is printed as amended.

Copyright in cinematograph films

13.—(1) Copyright shall subsist, subject to the provisions of this Act, in every cinematograph film of which the maker was a qualified person for the whole or a substantial part of the period during which the film was made.

(2) Without prejudice to the preceding subsection, copyright shall subsist, subject to the provisions of this Act, in every cinematograph film which has been published, if the first publication of the film took place in the United Kingdom or in another country to which this section extends.

(3) Copyright subsisting in a cinematograph film by virtue of this section—

[(a) in the case of any film which was registered under a former enactment relating to the registration of films, shall continue until the end of the period of fifty years from the end of the calendar year in which it was so registered;]

(b) in the case [of any other film], shall continue until the film is published, and thereafter until the end of the period of fifty years from the end of the calendar year which includes the date of its first publication, or, if copyright in the film subsists by virtue only of the last preceding subsection, shall continue as from the date of first publication until the end of the period of fifty years from the end of the calendar year which includes that date,

and then shall expire:

[In this subsection "former enactment relating to the registration of films" means Part II of the Films Act 1960 or Part III of the Cinematograph Films Act 1938.]

(4) Subject to the provisions of Part VI of this Act, the maker of a cinematograph film shall be entitled to any copyright subsisting in the film by virtue of this section.

(5) The Acts restricted by the copyright in a cinematograph film are—

(a) making a copy of the film;

(b) causing the film, in so far as it consists of visual images, to be seen in public, or, in so far as it consists of sounds, to be heard in public;

(c) broadcasting the film;

[(d) including the film in a cable programme.]

(6) The copyright in a cinematograph film is not infringed by making a copy of it for the purposes of a judicial proceeding, or by causing it to be seen or heard in public for the purposes of such a proceeding.

(7) Where by virtue of this section copyright has subsisted in a cinematograph film, a person who, after that copyright has expired, causes the film to be seen, or to be seen and heard, in public does not thereby infringe any copyright subsisting by virtue of Part I of this Act in any literary, dramatic, musical or artistic work.

(8) In the case of [any film consisting wholly or mainly of photographs which, at the time when they were taken, were means of communicating news,] the copyright in the film is not infringed by causing it to be seen or heard in public after the end of the period of fifty years from the end of the calendar year in which the principal events depicted in the film occurred.

(9) For the purposes of this Act a cinematograph film shall be taken to include the sounds embodied in any sound-track associated with the film, and references to a copy of a cinematograph film shall be construed accordingly:

Provided that where those sounds are also embodied in a record, other than such a sound-track or a record derived (directly or indirectly) from such a sound-track, the copyright in the film is not infringed by any use made of that record.

(10) In this Act—

"cinematograph film" means any sequence of visual images recorded on material of any description (whether translucent or not) so as to be capable, by the use of that material,—

(a) of being shown as a moving picture, or

(b) of being recorded on other material (whether translucent or not), by the use of which it can be so shown;

"the maker", in relation to a cinematograph film, means the person by whom the arrangements necessary for the making of the film are undertaken;

"publication", in relation to a cinematograph film, means the sale, letting on hire, or offer for sale or hire, of copies of the film to the public;

"copy", in relation to a cinematograph film, means any print, negative, tape or other article on which the film or part of it is recorded,

and references in this Act to a sound-track associated with a cinematograph film are references to any record of sounds which is incorporated in any print, negative, tape or other article on which the film or part of it, in so far as it consists of visual images, is recorded, or which is issued by the maker of the film for use in conjunction with such an article.

Note: This section, as amended by the Films Act 1960 (8 & 9 Eliz. 2. c.57), was further amended by the Films Act 1985 (c.21), which repealed the Films Act 1960. A new subs.(5)(d) was substituted by the Cable and Broadcasting Act 1984 (c.46). The section is printed as amended by the 1984 and 1985 Acts.

Copyright in television broadcasts and sound broadcasts

14.—(1) Copyright shall subsist, subject to the provisions of this Act,—

(a) in every television broadcast made by the British Broadcasting Corporation (in this Act referred to as "the Corporation") or by the Independent [Broadcasting] Authority (in this Act referred to as "the Authority") from a place in the United Kingdom or in any other country to which this section extends, and

(b) in every sound broadcast made by the Corporation or the Authority from such a place.

(2) Subject to the provisions of this Act, the Corporation or the Authority, as the case may be, shall be entitled to any copyright subsisting in a television broadcast or sound broadcast made by them; and any such copyright shall continue to subsist until the end of the period of fifty years from the end of the calendar year in which the broadcast is made, and shall then expire.

(3) In so far as a television broadcast or sound broadcast is a repetition (whether the first or any subsequent repetition) of a television broadcast or sound broadcast previously made as mentioned in subsection (1) of this section (whether by the Corporation or by the Authority), and is made by broadcasting material recorded on film, records or otherwise,—

(a) copyright shall not subsist therein by virtue of this section if it is made after the end of the period of fifty years from the end of the calendar year in which the previous broadcast was made; and

   (b) if it is made before the end of that period, any copyright subsisting therein by virtue of this section shall expire at the end of that period.

(4) The Acts restricted by the copyright in a television broadcast or sound broadcast are—

   (a) in the case of a television broadcast in so far as it consists of visual images, making, otherwise than for private purposes, a cinematograph film of it or a copy of such a film;

   (b) in the case of a sound broadcast, or of a television broadcast in so far as it consists of sounds, making, otherwise than for private purposes, a sound recording of it or a record embodying such a recording;

   (c) in the case either of a television broadcast, causing it, in so far as it consists of visual images, to be seen in public, or, in so far as it consists of sounds, to be heard in public, if it is seen or heard by a paying audience;

   (d) in the case either of a television broadcast or of a sound broadcast, re-broadcasting it [or including it in a cable programme].

(5) The restrictions imposed by virtue of the last preceding subsection in relation to a television broadcast or sound broadcast made by the Corporation or by the Authority shall apply whether the act in question is done by the reception of the broadcast or by making use of any record, print, negative, tape or other article on which the broadcast has been recorded.

(6) In relation to copyright in television broadcasts, in so far as they consist of visual images, the restrictions imposed by virtue of subsection (4) of this section shall apply to any sequence of images sufficient to be seen as a moving picture; and accordingly, for the purpose of establishing an infringement of such copyright, it shall not be necessary to prove that the act in question extended to more than such a sequence of images.

(7) For the purposes of subsection (4) of this section a cinematograph film or a copy thereof, or a sound recording or a record embodying a recording, shall be taken to be made otherwise than for private purposes if it is made for the purposes of the doing by any person of any of the following acts, that is to say,—

   (a) the sale or letting for hire of any copy of the film, or, as the case may be, of any record embodying the recording;

   (b) broadcasting the film or recording [or including it in a cable programme];

   (c) causing the film or recording to be seen or heard in public.

(8) for the purposes of paragraph (c) of subsection (4) of this section, a television broadcast shall be taken to be seen or heard by a paying audience if it is seen or heard by persons who either—

   (a) have been admitted for payment to the place where the broadcast is to be seen or heard, or have been admitted for payment to a place of which that place forms part, or

   (b) have been admitted to the place where the broadcast is to be seen or heard in circumstances where goods or services are supplied there at prices which exceed the prices usually charged at that place and are partly attributable to the facilities afforded for seeing or hearing the broadcast:

Provided that for the purposes of paragraph (a) of this subsection no account shall be taken—

   (i) of persons admitted to the place in question as residents or inmates therein, or

   (ii) of persons admitted to that place as members of a club or society, where the payment is only for membership of the club or society and the provision of facilities for seeing or hearing television broadcasts is only incidental to the main purposes of the club or society.

[(8A) The copyright in a television broadcast or sound broadcast is not infringed by any person who, by the reception and immediate re-transmission of the broadcast, includes a programme in a cable programme service—

(a) if the programme is so included in pursuance of a requirement imposed under subsection (1) of section 13 of the Cable and Broadcasting Act 1984; or

(b) where the broadcast is made otherwise than in a DBS service (as defined in subsection (6) of that section) or an additional teletext service (as so defined), if and to the extent that it is made for reception in the area in which the cable programme service is provided.]

(9) The copyright in a television broadcast or sound broadcast is not infringed by anything done in relation to the broadcast for the purposes of a judicial proceeding.

(10) In this Act "television broadcast" means visual images broadcast by way of television, together with any sounds broadcast for reception along with those images, and "sound broadcast" means sound broadcast otherwise than as part of a television broadcast; and for the purposes of this Act a television broadcast or sound broadcast shall be taken to be made by the body by whom, at the time when, and from the place from which,

[(a) the visual images or sounds in question, or both, as the case may be, are broadcast; or

(b) in the case of a television broadcast or sound broadcast made by the technique known as direct broadcasting by satellite, the visual images or sounds in question, or both, as the case may be, are transmitted to the satellite transponder.]

(11) The foregoing provisions of this section shall have effect as if references in those provisions and in section 12(9) of this Act to sounds included references to signals serving for the impartation of matter otherwise than in the form of sounds or visual images.]

Note: This section was amended by the Cable and Broadcasting Act 1984 (c.46) and is printed as amended.

Copyright in cable programmes

[14A.—(1) Copyright shall subsist, subject to the provisions of this Act, in every cable programme which is included in a cable programme service provided by a qualified person in the United Kingdom or in any other country to which this section extends.

(2) Copyright shall not subsist in a cable programme by virtue of this section if the programme is included in the cable programme service by the reception and immediate re-transmission of a television broadcast or a sound broadcast.

(3) Subject to the provisions of this Act, a person providing a cable programme service shall be entitled to any copyright subsisting in a cable programme included in that service and any such copyright shall continue to subsist until the end of the period of fifty years from the end of the calendar year in which the cable programme is so included, and shall then expire.

(4) In so far as a cable programme is a repetition (whether the first or any subsequent repetition) of a cable programme previously included as mentioned in subsection (1) of this section—

(a) copyright shall not subsist therein by virtue of this section if it is so included after the end of the period of fifty years from the end of the calendar year in which it was previously so included; and

(b) if it is so included before the end of that period any copyright subsisting therein by virtue of this section shall expire at the end of that period.

(5) The Acts restricted by the copyright in a cable programme are—

(a) in so far as it consists of visual images, making, otherwise than for private purposes, a cinematograph film of it or a copy of such a film;

(b) in so far as it consists of sounds, making, otherwise than for private purposes, a sound recording of it or a record embodying such a recording;

(c) causing it, in so far as it consists of visual images, to be seen in public, or, in so far as it consists of sounds, to be heard in public, if it is seen or heard by a paying audience;

(d) broadcasting it or including it in a cable programme service.

(6) The restrictions imposed by virtue of the last preceding subsection in relation to a cable programme shall apply whether the act in question is done by the reception of the programme or by making use of any record, print, negative, tape or other article on which the programme has been recorded.

(7) In relation to copyright in cable programmes, in so far as they consist of visual images, the restrictions imposed by virtue of subsection (5) of this section shall apply to any sequence of images sufficient to be seen as a moving picture; and accordingly, for the purpose of establishing an infringement of such copyright, it shall not be necessary to prove that the act in question extended to more than such a sequence of images.

(8) For the purposes of subsection (5) of this section a cinematograph film or a copy thereof, or a sound recording or a record embodying a recording, shall be taken to be made otherwise than for private purposes if it is made for the purposes of the doing by any person of any of the following acts, that is to say—

(a) the sale or letting for hire of any copy of the film, or, as the case may be, of any record embodying the recording;

(b) broadcasting the film or recording or including it in a cable programme service;

(c) causing the film or recording to be seen or heard in public.

(9) For the purposes of paragraph (c) of subsection (5) of this section, a cable programme shall be taken to be seen or heard by a paying audience if it is seen or heard by persons who either—

(a) have been admitted for payment to the place where the programme is to be seen or heard, or have been admitted for payment to a place of which that place forms part, or

(b) have been admitted to the place where the programme is to be seen or heard in circumstances where goods or services are supplied there at prices which exceed the prices usually charged at that place and are partly attributable to the facilities afforded for seeing or hearing the programme:

Provided that for the purposes of paragraph (a) of this subsection no account shall be taken—

(i) of persons admitted to the place in question as residents or inmates therein, or

(ii) of persons admitted to that place as members of a club or society, where payment is only for membership of the club or society and the provision of facilities for seeing or hearing cable programmes is only incidental to the main purposes of the club or society.

(10) The copyright in a cable programme is not infringed by anything done in relation to the programme for the purposes of a judicial proceeding.

(11) In this Act—

"cable programme" means a programme which is included, after the commencement of section 22 of the Cable and Broadcasting Act 1984, in a cable programme service;

"cable programme service" means a cable programme service within the meaning of the said Act of 1984 or a service provided outside the United Kingdom which would be such a service if subsection (7) of section 2 of that Act and references in subsection (1) of that section to the United Kingdom were omitted;

"programme", in relation to a cable programme service, includes any item included in that service.

(12) The foregoing provisions of this section shall have effect as if references in those provisions and in section 12(9) of this Act to sounds included references to signals serving for the impartation of matter otherwise than in the form of sounds or visual images.]

Note: Section 14A was added by the Cable and Broadcasting Act 1984 (c.46). The 1984 Act was repealed by s.203(3) of and Sch.21 to the Broadcasting Act 1990 (c.42) as provided by the Broadcasting Act 1990 (Commencement No.1 and Transitional Provisions) Order 1990 (SI 1990/2347 (c.61)) A2.ii, above.

Copyright in published editions of works

15.—(1) Copyright shall subsist, subject to the provisions of this Act, in every published edition of any one or more literary, dramatic or musical works in the case of which either—

(a) the first publication of the edition took place in the United Kingdom, or in another country to which this section extends, or

(b) the publisher of the edition was a qualified person at the date of the first publication thereof:

Provided that this subsection does not apply to an edition which reproduces the typographical arrangement of a previous edition of the same work or works.

(2) Subject to the provisions of this Act, the publisher of an edition shall be entitled to any copyright subsisting in the edition by virtue of this section; and any such copyright shall continue to subsist until the end of the period of twenty-five years from the end of the calendar year in which the edition was first published, and shall then expire.

(3) The act restricted by the copyright subsisting by virtue of this section in a published edition is the making, by any photographic or similar process, of a reproduction of the typographical arrangement of the edition.

(4) The copyright under this section in a published edition is not infringed by the making by or on behalf of a librarian of a reproduction of the typographical arrangement of the edition, if he is the librarian of a library of a class prescribed by regulations made under this subsection by the Board of Trade, and the conditions prescribed by those regulations are complied with.

Supplementary provisions for purposes of Part II

16.—(1) The provisions of this section shall have effect with respect to copyright subsisting by virtue of this Part of this Act in sound recordings, cinematograph films, television broadcasts, [sound broadcasts and cable programmes,] and in published editions of literary, dramatic and musical works; and in those provisions references to the relevant provision of this Part of this Act, in relation to copyright in a subject-matter of any of those descriptions, are references to the provision of this Part of this Act whereby it is provided that (subject to compliance with the conditions specified therein) copyright shall subsist in that description of subject-matter.

(2) Any copyright subsisting by virtue of this Part of this Act is infringed by any person who, without the licence of the owner of the copyright, imports an article (otherwise than for his private and domestic use) into the United Kingdom, or into any other country to which the relevant provision of this Part of this Act extends, if to his knowledge the making of that article constituted an infringement of that copyright, or would have constituted such an infringement if the article had been made in the place into which it is so imported.

(3) Any such copyright is also infringed by any person who, in the United Kingdom, or in any other country to which the relevant provision of this Part of this Act extends, and without the licence of the owner of the copyright,—

    (a) sells, lets for hire, or by way of trade offers or exposes for sale or hire any article, or

    (b) by way of trade exhibits any article in public,

if to his knowledge the making of the article constituted an infringement of that copyright, or (in the case of an imported article) would have constituted an infringement of that copyright if the article had been made in the place into which it was imported.

(4) The last preceding subsection shall apply in relation to the distribution of any articles either—

    (a) for purposes of trade, or

    (b) for other purposes, but to such an extent as to affect prejudicially the owner of the copyright in question.

as it applies in relation to the sale of an article.

(5) The three last preceding subsections shall have effect without prejudice to the general provisions of section one of this Act as to infringements of copyright.

(6) Where by virtue of this Part of this Act copyright subsists in a sound recording, cinematograph film, broadcast, [cable programme] or other subject-matter, nothing in this Part of this Act shall be construed as affecting the operation of Part I of this Act in relation to any literary, dramatic, musical or artistic work from which that subject-matter is wholly or partly derived; and copyright subsisting by virtue of this Part of this Act shall be additional to, and independent of, any copyright subsisting by virtue of Part I of this Act:

Provided that this subsection shall have effect subject to the provisions of subsection (7) of section thirteen of this Act.

(7) The subsistence of copyright under any of the preceding sections of this Part of this Act shall not affect the operation of any other of those sections under which copyright can subsist.

Note: This section was amended by the Cable and Broadcasting Act 1984 (c.46) and is printed as amended.

Part III

Remedies for Infringements of Copyright

Action by owner of copyright for infringement

17.—(1) Subject to the provisions of this Act, infringements of copyright shall be actionable at the suit of the owner of the copyright; and in any action for such an infringement all such relief, by way of damages, injunction, accounts or otherwise, shall be available to the plaintiff as is available in any corresponding proceedings in respect of infringements of other proprietary rights.

(2) Where in an action for infringement of copyright it is proved or admitted—

(a) that an infringement was committed, but

(b) that at the time of the infringement the defendant was not aware, and had no reasonable grounds for suspecting, that copyright subsisted in the work or other subject-matter to which the action relates,

the plaintiff shall not be entitled under this section to any damages against the defendant in respect of the infringement, but shall be entitled to an account of profits in respect of the infringement whether any other relief is granted under this section or not.

(3) Where in an action under this section an infringement of copyright is proved or admitted, and the court, having regard (in addition to all other material considerations) to—

(a) the flagrancy of the infringement, and

(b) any benefit shown to have accrued to the defendant by reason of the infringement,

is satisfied that effective relief would not otherwise be available to the plaintiff, the court, in assessing damages for the infringement, shall have power to award such additional damages by virtue of this subsection as the court may consider appropriate in the circumstances.

(4) In an action for infringement of copyright in respect of the construction of a building, no injunction or other order shall be made—

(a) after the construction of the building has been begun, so as to prevent it from being completed, or

(b) so as to require the building in so far as it has been constructed, to be demolished.

(5) In this Part of this Act "action" includes a counterclaim, and references to the plaintiff and to the defendant in an action shall be construed accordingly.

(6) In the application of this Part of this Act to Scotland, "injunction" means an interdict and "interlocutory injunction" means an interim interdict, "accounts" means count, reckoning and payment, "an account of profits" means an accounting and payment of profits, "plaintiff" means pursuer, "defendant" means defender and "costs" means expenses.

Rights of owner of copyright in respect of infringing copies, etc.

18.—(1) Subject to the provisions of this Act, the owner of any copyright shall be entitled to all such rights and remedies, in respect of the conversion or detention by any person of any infringing copy, or of any plate used or intended to be used for making infringing copies, as he would be entitled to if he were the owner of every such copy or plate and had been the owner thereof since the time when it was made:

Provided that if, by virtue of subsection (2) of section three of the Limitation Act, 1939 (which relates to successive conversions or detentions), or of any corresponding provision which may be enacted by the Parliament of Northern Ireland, the title of the owner of the copyright to such a copy or plate would (if he had then been the owner of the copy or plate) have been extinguished at the end of the period mentioned in that subsection or corresponding provision, he shall not be entitled to any rights or remedies under this subsection in respect of anything done in relation to that copy or plate after the end of that period.

(2) A plaintiff shall not be entitled by virtue of this section to any damages or to any other pecuniary remedy (except costs) if it is proved or admitted that, at the time of the conversion or detention in question,—

(a) the defendant was not aware, and had no reasonable grounds for suspecting, that copyright subsisted in the work or other subject-matter to which the action relates, or

(b) where the articles converted or detained were infringing copies, the defendant believed, and had reasonable grounds for believing, that they were not infringing copies, or

(c) where the article converted or detained was a plate used or intended to be used for making any articles, the defendant believed, and had reasonable grounds for believing, that the articles so made or intended to be made were not, or (as the case may be) would not be, infringing copies.

(3) In this Part of this Act "infringing copy" —

(a) in relation to a literary, dramatic, musical or artistic work, or to such a published edition as is mentioned in section fifteen of this Act, means a reproduction otherwise than in the form of a cinematograph film,

(b) in relation to a sound recording, means a record embodying that recording,

(c) in relation to a cinematograph film, means a copy of the film, and

(d) in relation to a television broadcast or [a sound broadcast or a cable programme], means a copy of a cinematograph film of it or a record embodying a sound recording of it,

being (in any such case) an article the making of which constituted an infringement of the copyright in the work, edition, recording, film, [broadcast or programme,] or, in the case of an imported article, would have constituted an infringement of that copyright if the article had been made in the place into which it was imported: and "plate" includes any stereotype, stone, block, mould, matrix, transfer, negative or other appliance.

(4) In the application of this section to Scotland, for any reference to the conversion or detention by any person of an infringing copy there shall be substituted a reference to an intromission by any person with an infringing copy, and for any reference to articles converted or detained there shall be substituted a reference to articles intromitted with.

Notes:

(1) This section was amended by the Cable and Broadcasting Act 1984 (c.46) and is printed as amended.

(2) The Limitation Act 1939 was repealed by the Limitation Act 1980 (c.58) s.40(3) and Sch.4.

Proceedings in case of copyright subject to exclusive licence

19.—(1) The provisions of this section shall have effect as to proceedings in the case of any copyright in respect of which an exclusive licence has been granted and is in force at the time of the events to which the proceedings relate.

(2) Subject to the following provisions of this section—

(a) the exclusive licensee shall (except against the owner of the copyright) have the same rights of action, and be entitled to the same remedies, under section seventeen of this Act as if the licence had been an assignment, and those rights and remedies shall be concurrent with the rights and remedies of the owner of the copyright under that section;

(b) the exclusive licensee shall (except against the owner of the copyright) have the same rights of action, and be entitled to the same remedies, by virtue of the last preceding section as if the licence had been an assignment; and

(c) the owner of the copyright shall not have any rights of action, or be entitled to any remedies, by virtue of the last preceding section which he would not have had or been entitled to if the licence had been an assignment.

(3) Where an action is brought either by the owner of the copyright or by the exclusive licensee, and the action, in so far as it is brought under section seventeen of this Act, relates (wholly or partly) to an infringement in respect of which they have concurrent rights of action under that section, the owner or licensee, as the case may be, shall not be entitled, except with the leave of the court, to proceed with the action, in so far as it is brought under that section and relates to that infringement, unless the other party is either joined as a plaintiff in the action or added as a defendant:

Provided that this subsection shall not affect the granting of an interlocutory injunction on the application of either of them.

(4) In any action brought by the exclusive licensee by virtue of this section, any defence which would have been available to a defendant in the action, if this section had not been enacted and the action had been brought by the owner of the copyright, shall be available to that defendant as against the exclusive licensee.

(5) Where an action is brought in the circumstances mentioned in subsection (3) of this section, and the owner of the copyright and the exclusive licensee are not both plaintiffs in the action, the court, in assessing damages in respect of any such infringement as is mentioned in that subsection,—

(a) if the plaintiff is the exclusive licensee, shall take into account any liabilities (in respect of royalties or otherwise) to which the licence is subject, and

(b) whether the plaintiff is the owner of the copyright or the exclusive licensee, shall take into account any pecuniary remedy already awarded to the other party under section seventeen of this Act in respect of that infringement, or, as the case may require, any right of action exercisable by the other party under that section in respect thereof.

(6) Where an action, in so far as it is brought under section seventeen of this Act, relates (wholly or partly) to an infringement in respect of which the owner of the copyright and the exclusive licensee have concurrent rights of action under that section, and in that action (whether they are both parties to it or not) an account of profits is directed to be taken in respect of that infringement, then, subject to any agreement of which the court is aware, whereby the application of those profits is determined as between the owner of the copyright and the exclusive licensee, the court shall apportion the profits between them as the court may consider just, and shall give such directions as the court may consider appropriate for giving effect to that apportionment.

(7) In an action brought either by the owner of the copyright or by the exclusive licensee,—

(a) no judgment or order for the payment of damages in respect of an infringement of copyright shall be given or made under section seventeen of this Act, if a final judgment or order has been given or made awarding an account of profits to the other party under that section in respect of the same infringement; and

(b) no judgment or order for an account of profits in respect of an infringement of copyright shall be given or made under that section, if a final judgment or order has been given or made awarding either damages or an account of profits to the other party under that section in respect of the same infringement.

(8) Where, in an action brought in the circumstances mentioned in subsection (3) of this section, whether by the owner of the copyright or by the exclusive licensee, the other party is not joined as a plaintiff (either at the commencement of the action or subsequently), but is added as a defendant, he shall not be liable for any costs in the action unless he enters an appearance and takes part in the proceedings.

(9) In this section "exclusive licence" means a licence in writing, signed by or on behalf of an owner or prospective owner of copyright, authorising the licensee, to the exclusion of all other persons, including the grantor of the licence, to exercise a right which by virtue of this Act would (apart from the licence) be exercisable exclusively by the owner of the copyright, and "exclusive licensee" shall be construed accordingly; "the other party", in relation to the owner of the copyright, means the exclusive licensee, and, in relation to the exclusive licensee, means the owner of the copyright; and "if the licence had been an assignment" means if, instead of the licence, there had been granted (subject to terms and conditions corresponding as nearly as may be with those subject to which the licence was granted) an assignment of the copyright in respect of its application to the doing, at the places and times authorised by the licence, of the acts so authorised.

Proof of facts in copyright actions

20.—(1) In any action brought by virtue of this Part of this Act—
  (a) copyright shall be presumed to subsist in the work or other subject-matter to which the action relates, if the defendant does not put in issue the question whether copyright subsists therein, and
  (b) where the subsistence of the copyright is proved or admitted, or is presumed in pursuance of the preceding paragraph, the plaintiff shall be presumed to be the owner of the copyright, if he claims to be the owner of the copyright and the defendant does not put in issue the question of his ownership thereof.

(2) Subject to the preceding subsection, where, in the case of a literary, dramatic, musical or artistic work, a name purporting to be that of the author appeared on copies of the work as published, or, in the case of an artistic work, appeared on the work when it was made, the person whose name so appeared (if it was his true name or a name by which he was commonly known) shall, in any action brought by virtue of this Part of this Act, be presumed, unless the contrary is proved,—
  (a) to be the author of the work, and
  (b) to have made the work in circumstances not falling within subsection (2), subsection (3) or subsection (4) of section four of this Act.

(3) In the case of a work alleged to be a work of joint authorship, the last preceding subsection shall apply in relation to each person alleged to be one of the authors of the work, as if references in that subsection to the author were references to one of the authors.

(4) Where, in an action brought by virtue of this Part of this Act, with respect to a literary, dramatic, musical or artistic work, subsection (2) of this section does not apply, but it is established—
  (a) that the work was first published in the United Kingdom, or in another country to which section two, or, as the case may be, section three, of this Act extends, and was so published within the period of fifty years ending with the beginning of the calendar year in which the action was brought, and
  (b) that a name purporting to be that of the publisher appeared on copies of the work as first published,
then, unless the contrary is shown, copyright shall be presumed to subsist in the work and the person whose name so appeared shall be presumed to have been the owner of that copyright at the time of the publication.

For the purposes of this subsection a fact shall be taken to be established if it is proved or admitted, or if it is presumed in pursuance of the following provisions of this section.

(5) Where in an action brought by virtue of this Part of this Act with respect to a literary, dramatic, musical or artistic work it is proved or admitted that the author of the work is dead,—

    (a) the work shall be presumed to be an original work unless the contrary is proved, and

    (b) if it is alleged by the plaintiff that a publication specified in the allegation was the first publication of the work, and that it took place in a country and on a date so specified, that publication shall be presumed, unless the contrary is proved, to have been the first publication of the work, and to have taken place in that country and on that date.

(6) Paragraphs (a) and (b) of the last preceding subsection shall apply where a work has been published, and—

    (a) the publication was anonymous, or was under a name alleged by the plaintiff to have been a pseudonym, and

    (b) it is not shown that the work has ever been published under the true name of the author, or under a name by which he was commonly known, or that it is possible for a person without previous knowledge of the facts to ascertain the identity of the author by reasonable inquiry.

as those paragraphs apply in a case where it is proved that the author is dead.

(7) In any action brought by virtue of this Part of this Act with respect to copyright in a sound recording, if records embodying that recording or part thereof have been issued to the public, and at the time when those records were so issued they bore a label or other mark comprising any one or more of the following statements, that is to say,—

    (a) that a person named on the label or mark was the maker of the sound recording;

    (b) that the recording was first published in a year specified on the label or mark;

    (c) that the recording was first published in a country specified on the label or mark;

that label or mark shall be sufficient evidence of the facts so stated except in so far as the contrary is proved.

Penalties and summary proceedings in respect of dealings which infringe copyright

21.—(1) Any person who, at a time when copyright subsists in a work,—

    (a) makes for sale or hire, or

    (b) sells or lets for hire, or by way of trade offers or exposes for sale or hire, or

    (c) by way of trade exhibits in public, or

    (d) imports into the United Kingdom, otherwise than for his private and domestic use,

any article which he knows to be an infringing copy of the work, shall be guilty of an offence under this subsection.

(2) Any person who, at a time when copyright subsists in a work, distributes, either—

    (a) for purposes of trade, or

    (b) for other purposes, but to such an extent as to affect prejudicially the owner of the copyright,

articles which he knows to be infringing copies of the work, shall be guilty of an offence under this subsection.

(3) Any person who, at a time when copyright subsists in a work, makes or

has in his possession a plate, knowing that it is to be used for making infringing copies of the work, shall be guilty of an offence under this subsection.

(4) The preceding subsections shall apply in relation to copyright subsisting in any subject-matter by virtue of Part II of this Act, as they apply in relation to copyright subsisting by virtue of Part I of this Act.

[(4A) Any person who, at a time when copyright subsists in a sound recording or in a cinematograph film, by way of trade has in his possession any article which he knows to be an infringing copy of the sound recording or cinematograph film, as the case may be, shall be guilty of an offence under this subsection.]

(5) Any person who causes a literary, dramatic or musical work to be performed in public, knowing that copyright subsists in the work and that the performance constitutes an infringement of the copyright, shall be guilty of an offence under this subsection.

(6) The preceding provisions of this section apply only in respect of acts done in the United Kingdom.

(7) A person guilty of an offence under subsection (1) [or subsection (2) of this section, other than an offence for which a penalty is provided by subsection (7A) or (7B) of this section,] shall on summary conviction—

(a) if it is his first conviction of an offence under this section, be liable to a fine not exceeding forty shillings for each article to which the offence relates;

(b) in any other case, be liable to such a fine, or to imprisonment for a term not exceeding two months:

Provided that a fine imposed by virtue of this subsection shall not exceed fifty pounds in respect of articles comprised in the same transaction.

[(7A) A person guilty of an offence under subsection (1)(b) or (c) or (4A) of this section relating to an infringing copy of a sound recording or cinematograph film shall be liable on summary conviction to a fine not exceeding level 5 on the standard scale or imprisonment for a term not exceeding two months or to both.

(7B) A person guilty of an offence under subsection (1)(a) or (d) or (2) of this section relating to an infringing copy of a sound recording or cinematograph film shall be liable—

(a) on summary conviction, to a fine not exceeding the statutory maximum;

(b) on conviction on indictment, to a fine or to imprisonment for a term not exceeding two years or to both.

(7C) In subsection (7A) of this section "the standard scale" has the meaning given by section 75 of the Criminal Justice Act 1982 and for the purposes of that subsection—

(a) section 37 of that Act; and

(b) an order under section 143 of the Magistrates' Courts Act 1980 which alters the sums specified in subsection (2) of the said section 37,

shall extend to Northern Ireland and the said section 75 shall have effect as if after the words "England and Wales" there were inserted the words "or Northern Ireland".

(7D) In subsection (7B) of this section "statutory maximum" has the meaning given by section 74 of the Criminal Justice Act 1982 and for the purposes of that subsection—

(a) section 32 of the Magistrates' Courts Act 1980; and

(b) an order made under section 143 of that Act which alters the sum specified in the definition of "the prescribed sum" in subsection (9) of the said section 32,

shall extend to Northern Ireland and subsection (1) of the said section 74 shall have effect as if after the words "England and Wales" there were inserted the words "or Northern Ireland".]

(8) A person guilty of an offence under subsection (3) or subsection (5) of this section shall on summary conviction—

(a) if it is his first conviction of an offence under this section, be liable to a fine not exceeding fifty pounds;

(b) in any other case, be liable to such a fine, or to imprisonment for a term not exceeding two months.

(9) The court before which a person is charged with an offence under this section may, whether he is convicted of the offence or not, order that any article in his possession which appears to the court to be an infringing copy, or to be a plate used or intended to be used for making infringing copies, shall be destroyed or delivered up to the owner of the copyright in question or otherwise dealt with as the court may think fit.

(10) An appeal shall lie to a court of quarter sessions from any order made under the last preceding subsection by a court of summary jurisdiction; and where such an order is made by the sheriff there shall be a like right of appeal against the order as if it were a conviction.

Note: This section was amended by the Copyright Act 1956 (Amendment) Act 1982 (c.35) and again by the Copyright (Amendment) Act 1983 (c.42) and is printed as amended by such Acts.

Search warrants

[**21A.**—(1) Where, on information on oath given by a constable, a justice of the peace is satisfied that there are reasonable grounds for believing—

(a) that an offence under subsection (1)(a) or (d) or (2) of section 21 of this Act relating to an infringing copy of a sound recording or a cinematograph film has been or is about to be committed in any premises, and

(b) that evidence that the offence has been or is about to be committed is in those premises,

he may issue a warrant authorising a constable to enter and search the premises, using such reasonable force as is necessary.

(2) A warrant under this section may authorise persons to accompany any constable who is executing it and must be executed within twenty-eight days from the date of its issue.

(3) In executing a warrant issued under this section a constable may seize any article if he reasonably believes that it is evidence that an offence under subsection (1), (2) or (4A) of section 21 of this Act relating to an infringing copy of a sound recording or a cinematograph film has been or is about to be committed.

(4) In this section "premises" includes land, buildings, moveable structures, vehicles, vessels, aircraft and hovercraft.

(5) This section shall have effect in Northern Ireland as if in subsection (1)—

(a) for the reference to an information there were substituted a reference to a complaint, and

(b) for the reference to a justice of the peace there were substituted a reference to a resident magistrate.

(6) This section shall not extend to Scotland.

Persons accompanying constable under search warrant or order of court in Scotland

21B.—(1) Where in Scotland an application is made for a warrant or order of court to authorise a constable to enter and search any premises where there are reasonable grounds for believing that an offence under subsection (1)(a) or (d) or (2) of section 21 of this Act relating to an infringing copy of a sound recording or a cinematograph film has been or is about to be committed, the court may in any such warrant or order of court authorise any person named in the warrant or order to accompany any constable who is executing the warrant or order.

(2) In this section "premises" includes land, buildings, moveable structures, vehicles, vessels, aircraft and hovercraft.

(3) This section applies to Scotland only.]

Note: Sections 21A and 21B added by the Copyright (Amendment) Act 1983 (c.42).

Provision for restricting importation of printed copies

22.—(1) The owner of the copyright in any published literary, dramatic or musical work may give notice in writing to the Commissioners of Customs and Excise (in this section referred to as "the Commissioners")—

(a) that he is the owner of the copyright in the work, and

(b) that he requests the Commissioners, during a period specified in the notice, to treat as prohibited goods copies of the work to which this section applies:

Provided that the period specified in a notice under this subsection shall not exceed five years and shall not extend beyond the end of the period for which the copyright is to subsist.

(2) This section applies, in the case of a work, to any printed copy made outside the United Kingdom which, if it had been made in the United Kingdom, would be an infringing copy of the work.

(3) Where a notice has been given under this section in respect of a work, and has not been withdrawn, the importation into the United Kingdom, at a time before the end of the period specified in the notice, of any copy of the work to which this section applies shall, subject to the following provisions of this section, be prohibited:

Provided that this subsection shall not apply to the importation of any article by a person for his private and domestic use.

(4) The Commissioners may make regulations prescribing the form in which notices are to be given under this section, and requiring a person giving such a notice, either at the time of giving the notice or at the time when the goods in question are imported, or at both those times, to furnish the Commissioners with such evidence, and to comply with such other conditions (if any), as may be specified in the regulations; and any such regulations may include such incidental and supplementary provisions as the Commissioners consider expedient for the purposes of this section.

(5) Without prejudice to the generality of the last preceding subsection, regulations made under that subsection may include provision for requiring a person who has given a notice under subsection (1) of this section, or a notice purporting to be a notice under that subsection,—

(a) to pay such fees in respect of the notice as may be prescribed by the regulations;

(b) to give to the Commissioners such security as may be so prescribed, in respect of any liability or expense which they may incur in consequence of the detention, at any time within the period specified in the notice, of any copy of the work to which the notice relates, or in consequence of anything done in relation to a copy so detained;

(c) whether any such security is given or not, to keep the Commissioners indemnified against any such liability, or expense as is mentioned in the last preceding paragraph.

(6) For the purpose of section 17 of the Customs and Excise Management Act

1979 (which relates to the disposal of duties), any fees paid in pursuance of regulations made under this section shall be treated as money collected on account of [duties (whether of customs or excise) charged on imported goods.]

(7) Notwithstanding anything in [the Customs and Excise Management Act 1979] a person shall not be liable to any penalty under that Act (other than forfeiture of the goods) by reason that any goods are treated as prohibited goods by virtue of this section.

Note: Subsections (6) and (7) amended by the Customs and Excise Management Act 1979 (c.2) s.177(1) and Sch.4 and are printed as amended.

PART IV

PERFORMING RIGHT TRIBUNAL

Establishment of tribunal

23.—(1) There shall be established a tribunal, to be called the Performing Right Tribunal (in this Act referred to as "the tribunal"), for the purpose of exercising the jurisdiction conferred by the provisions of this Part of this Act.

(2) The tribunal shall consist of a chairman appointed by the Lord Chancellor, who shall be a barrister, advocate or solicitor of not less than seven years' standing or a person who has held judicial office, and of not less than two nor more than four other members appointed by the Board of Trade.

[(3) *A person shall be disqualified for being appointed, or being, a member of the tribunal so long as he is a member of the Commons House of Parliament, or of the Senate or House of Commons of Northern Ireland.*]

(4) The provisions of the Fourth Schedule to this Act shall have effect with respect to the tribunal.

(5) There shall be paid to the members of the tribunal such remuneration (whether by way of salaries or fees), and such allowances, as the Board of Trade, with the approval of the Treasury, may determine in the case of those members respectively.

(6) The Board of Trade may appoint such officers and servants of the tribunal as the Board, with the approval of the Treasury as to numbers and remuneration, may determine.

(7) The remuneration and allowances of members of the tribunal, the remuneration of any officers and servants appointed under the last preceding subsection, and such other expenses of the tribunal as the Board of Trade with the approval of the Treasury may determine shall be paid out of moneys provided by Parliament.

Note: Subsection (3) was repealed by the House of Commons Disqualification Act 1957 (5 & 6 Eliz. 2, c.20) which was itself repealed by the House of Commons Disqualification Act 1975 (c.24) and the Northern Ireland Assembly Disqualification Act 1975 (c.25), which provide instead that a person is disqualified for membership of the House of Commons and the Northern Ireland Assembly, who for the time being is a member of the Performing Right Tribunal.

General provisions as to jurisdiction of tribunal

24.—(1) Subject to the provisions of this Part of this Act, the function of the tribunal shall be to determine disputes arising between licensing bodies and persons requiring licences, or organisations claiming to be representative of such persons, either—

    (a) on the reference of a licence scheme to the tribunal, or

    (b) on the application of a person requiring a licence either in accordance with a licence scheme or in a case not covered by a licence scheme.

  (2) In this Part of this Act "licence" means a licence granted by or on behalf of the owner, or prospective owner, of the copyright in a literary, dramatic or musical work, or in a sound recording or a television broadcast, being—

    (a) in the case of a literary, dramatic or musical work, a licence to perform in public, or to broadcast, the work or an adaptation thereof, or to [include the work or an adaptation thereof in a cable programme];

    (b) in the case of a sound recording, a licence to cause it to be heard in public, [to broadcast it or to include it in a cable programme];

    (c) in the case of a television broadcast, a licence to cause it, in so far it consists of visual images, to be seen in public and, in so far as it consists of sounds, to be heard in public.

  (3) In this Part of this Act "licensing body" —

    (a) in relation to such licences as are mentioned in paragraph (a) of the last preceding subsection, means a society or other organisation which has as its main object, or one of its main objects, the negotiation or granting of such licences, either as owner or prospective owner of copyright or as agent for the owners or prospective owners thereof;

    (b) in relation to such licences as are mentioned in paragraph (b) of the last preceding subsection, means any owner or prospective owner of copyright in sound recordings, or any person or body of persons acting as agent for any owners or prospective owners of copyright in sound recordings in relation to the negotiation or granting of such licences; and

    (c) in relation to such licences as are mentioned in paragraph (c) of the last preceding subsection, means the Corporation or the Authority or any organisation appointed by them, or either of them, in accordance with the provisions of the Fifth Schedule to this Act:

Provided that paragraph (a) of this subsection shall not apply to an organisation by reason that its objects include the negotiation or granting of individual licences, each relating to a single work or the works of a single author, if they do not include the negotiation or granting of general licences, each extending to the works of several authors.

  (4) In this Part of this Act "licence scheme", in relation to licences of any description, means a scheme made by one or more licensing bodies, setting out the classes of cases in which they, or the persons on whose behalf they act, are willing to grant licences of that description, and the charges (if any), and terms and conditions, subject to which licences would be granted in those classes of cases; and in this subsection "scheme" includes anything in the nature of a scheme, whether described therein as a scheme or as a tariff or by any other name.

  (5) References in this Part of this Act to terms and conditions are references to any terms and conditions other than those relating to the amount of a charge for a licence; and references to giving an opportunity to a person of presenting his case are references to giving him an opportunity, at his option, of submitting representations in writing, or of being heard, or of submitting representations in writing and being heard.

Note: This section was amended by the Cable and Broadcasting Act 1984 (c.46) and is printed as amended.

Reference of licence schemes to tribunal

  25.—(1) Where, at any time while a licence scheme is in operation, a dispute arises with respect to the scheme between the licensing body operating the scheme and—

(a) an organisation claiming to be representative of persons requiring licences in cases of a class to which the scheme applies, or

(b) any person claiming that he requires a licence in a case of a class to which the scheme applies,

the organisation or person in question may refer the scheme to the tribunal in so far as it relates to cases of that class.

(2) The parties to a reference under this section shall be—

(a) the organisation or person at whose instance the reference is made;

(b) the licensing body operating the scheme to which the reference relates; and

(c) such other organisations or persons (if any) as apply to the tribunal to be made parties to the reference and, in accordance with the next following subsection, are made parties thereto.

(3) Where an organisation (whether claiming to be representative of persons requiring licences or not) or a person (whether requiring a licence or not) applies to the tribunal to be made a party to a reference, and the tribunal is satisfied that the organisation or person has a substantial interest in the matter in dispute, the tribunal may, if it thinks fit, make that organisation or person a party to the reference.

(4) The tribunal shall not entertain a reference under this section by an organisation unless the tribunal is satisfied that the organisation is reasonably representative of the class of persons which it claims to represent.

(5) Subject to the last preceding subsection, the tribunal, on any reference under this section, shall consider the matter in dispute, and, after giving to the parties to the reference an opportunity of presenting their cases respectively, shall make such order, either confirming or varying the scheme, in so far as it relates to cases of the class to which the reference relates, as the tribunal may determine to be reasonable in the circumstances.

(6) An order of the tribunal under this section may, notwithstanding anything contained in the licence scheme to which it relates, be made so as to be in force either indefinitely or for such period as the tribunal may determine.

(7) Where a licence scheme has been referred to the tribunal under this section, then, notwithstanding anything contained in the scheme,—

(a) the scheme shall remain in operation until the tribunal has made an order in pursuance of the reference, and

(b) after such an order has been made, the scheme shall remain in operation, in so far as it relates to the class of cases in respect of which the order was made, so long as the order remains in force:

Provided that this subsection shall not apply in relation to a reference as respects any period after the reference has been withdrawn, or has been discharged by virtue of subsection (4) of this section.

Further reference of scheme to tribunal

26.—(1) Where the tribunal has made an order under the last preceding section with respect to a licence scheme, then, subject to the next following subsection, at any time while the order remains in force,—

(a) the licensing body operating the scheme, or

(b) any organisation claiming to be representative of persons requiring licences in cases of the class to which the order applies, or

(c) any person claiming that he requires a licence in a case of that class,

may refer the scheme again to the tribunal in so far as it relates to cases of that class.

(2) A licence scheme shall not, except with the special leave of the tribunal, be referred again to the tribunal under the preceding subsection at a time earlier than—

(a) the end of the period of twelve months beginning with the date on which the order in question was made, in the case of an order made so as to be in force indefinitely or for a period exceeding fifteen months, or

(b) the beginning of the period of three months ending with the date of expiry of the order, in the case of an order made so as to be in force for fifteen months or less.

(3) The parties to a reference under this section shall be—

(a) the licensing body, organisation or person at whose instance the reference is made;

(b) the licensing body operating the scheme to which the reference relates, if the reference is not made at their instance; and

(c) such other organisations or persons (if any) as apply to the tribunal to be made parties to the reference and, in accordance with the provisions applicable in that behalf by virtue of subsection (5) of this section, are made parties thereto.

(4) Subject to the next following subsection, the tribunal, on any reference under this section, shall consider the matter in dispute, and after giving to the parties to the reference an opportunity of presenting their cases respectively, shall make such order in relation to the scheme as previously confirmed or varied, in so far as it relates to cases of the class in question, either by way of confirming, varying or further varying the scheme, as the tribunal may determine to be reasonable in the circumstances.

(5) Subsections (3), (4), (6) and (7) of the last preceding section shall apply for the purposes of this section.

(6) The preceding provisions of this section shall have effect in relation to orders made under this section as they have effect in relation to orders made under the last preceding section.

(7) Nothing in this section shall be construed as preventing a licence scheme, in respect of which an order has been made under the last preceding section, from being again referred to the tribunal under that section, either—

(a) at any time, in so far as the scheme relates to cases of a class to which the order does not apply, or

(b) after the expiration of the order, in so far as the scheme relates to cases of the class to which the order applied while it was in force.

Applications to tribunal

27.—(1) For the purposes of this Part of this Act a case shall be taken to be covered by a licence scheme if, in accordance with a licence scheme for the time being in operation, licences would be granted in cases of the class to which that case belongs:

Provided that where, in accordance with the provisions of a licence scheme,—

(a) the licences which would be so granted would be subject to terms and conditions whereby particular matters would be excepted from the licences, and

(b) the case in question relates to one or more matters falling within such an exception,

that case shall be taken not to be covered by the scheme.

(2) Any person who claims, in a case covered by a licence scheme, that the licensing body operating the scheme have refused or failed to grant him a licence

in accordance with the provisions of the scheme, or to procure the grant to him of such a licence, may apply to the tribunal under this section.

(3) Any person who claims that he requires a licence in a case not covered by a licence scheme, and either—

(a) that a licensing body have refused or failed to grant the licence, or to procure the grant thereof, and that in the circumstances it is unreasonable that the licence should not be granted, or

(b) that any charges, terms or conditions subject to which a licensing body propose that the licence should be granted are unreasonable,

may apply to the tribunal under this section.

(4) Where an organisation (whether claiming to be representative of persons requiring licences or not) or a person (whether requiring a licence or not) applies to the tribunal to be made a party to an application under the preceding provisions of this section, and the tribunal is satisfied that the organisation or person has a substantial interest in the matter in dispute, the tribunal may, if it thinks fit, make that organisation or person a party to the application.

(5) On any application under subsection (2) or subsection (3) of this section the tribunal shall give to the applicant and to the licensing body in question and to every other party (if any) to the application an opportunity of presenting their cases respectively; and if the tribunal is satisfied that the claim of the applicant is well founded, the tribunal shall make an order declaring that, in respect of the matters specified in the order, the applicant is entitled to a licence on such terms and conditions, and subject to the payment of such charges (if any) as—

(a) in the case of an application under subsection (2) of this section, the tribunal may determine to be applicable in accordance with the licence scheme, or

(b) in the case of an application under subsection (3) of this section, the tribunal may determine to be reasonable in the circumstances.

(6) Any reference in this section to a failure to grant or procure the grant of a licence shall be construed as a reference to a failure to grant it, or to procure the grant thereof, within a reasonable time after being requested to do so.

Applications for review by tribunal of orders

[27A.—(1) Where the tribunal has made an order under subsection (5) of the last preceding section, then subject to the next following subsection, at any time while the order remains in force,—

(a) the licensing body in question, or

(b) the original applicant

may apply to the tribunal to review its original order.

(2) An application shall not be made pursuant to subsection (1) of this section, except with the special leave of the tribunal, at a time earlier than—

(a) the end of a period of twelve months beginning with the date on which the original order was made, in the case of an order made so as to be in force indefinitely or for a period exceeding fifteen months, or

(b) the beginning of the period of three months ending with the date of expiry of the order in the case of an order made so as to be in force for fifteen months or less.

(3) the parties to an application under this section shall be—

(a) the parties to the original application proceedings; and

(b) any organisation or person who is made party thereto pursuant to subsection (5) of this section.

(4) The tribunal, on any application under this section, after giving all the par-

ties an opportunity of presenting their cases shall make such order in relation to the application either by way of confirming or varying the order in question as—

(a) in the case of an order made pursuant to an application under subsection (2) of the last preceding section, the tribunal may determine to be applicable in accordance with the licence scheme, or

(b) in the case of an order made pursuant to an application under subsection (3) of the last preceding section, the tribunal may determine to be reasonable in the circumstances.

(5) Subsection (4) of section 27 (applications by organisations and person to be made party to proceedings) shall apply in relation to proceedings under this section as it applies in relation to proceedings under that section.

(6) The preceding provisions of this section shall have effect in relation to orders made under this section as they have in relation to orders made under the last preceding section.]

Note: This section was inserted by the Copyright (Amendment) Act, 1971 (c.4).

Exercise of jurisdiction of tribunal in relation to inclusion of broadcasts in cable programmes

[27B.—(1) On a reference to the tribunal under this Part of this Act relating to licences to broadcast works or sound recordings for reception in any area, the tribunal shall exercise its powers under this Part of this Act so as to secure that the charges payable for the licences adequately reflect the extent to which the works or recordings will be included, in pursuance of requirements imposed under section 13(1) of the Cable and Broadcasting Act 1984, in cable programme services provided in areas parts of which fall outside that area.

(2) The preceding subsection shall have effect, with the necessary notifications, in relation to applications under this Part of this Act as it has effect in relation to references thereunder.]

Note: This section was inserted by the Cable and Broadcasting Act 1984 (c.46). See the Note to s.14A, above.

Exercise of jurisdiction of tribunal in relation to diffusion of foreign broadcasts

28.—(1) Where, on a reference to the tribunal under this Part of this Act relating to licences to [include works or sound recordings in a cable programme service provided] in the United Kingdom, the tribunal is satisfied—

(a) that the licences are required wholly or partly for the purpose of [including in such a service] programmes broadcast, from a place outside the United Kingdom, by an organisation other than the Corporation and the Authority, and

(b) that, under the arrangements in accordance with which the programmes are broadcast by that organisation, charges are payable by or on behalf of the organisation to another body, as being the body entitled under the relevant copyright law to authorise the broadcasting of those works [or recordings] from that place, the tribunal shall, subject to the next following subsection, exercise its powers under this Part of this Act as the tribunal may consider appropriate for securing that the persons requiring the licences are exempted from the payment of any charges for them in so far as the licences are required for the purpose of [including those programmes in a cable programme service].

(2) If on such a reference as is mentioned in the last preceding subsection the

tribunal is satisfied as to the matters mentioned in paragraphs (a) and (b) of that subsection, but it is shown to the satisfaction of the tribunal that the charges payable by or on behalf of the organisation, as mentioned in paragraph (b) of that subsection,—

(a) make no allowance for the fact that, in consequence of the broadcasting of the works [or recordings] in question by that organisation, the persons requiring the licences may be enabled to [include those works or recordings in cable programme services provided] in the United Kingdom, or

(b) do not adequately reflect the extent to which it is likely that those persons will [so include those works or recordings] in consequence of their being so broadcast,

the last preceding subsection shall not apply, but the tribunal shall exercise its powers under this Part of this Act so as to secure that the charges payable for the licences, in so far as the licences are required for the purpose mentioned in the last preceding subsection, are on a scale not exceeding that appearing to the tribunal to be requisite for making good the deficiency (as mentioned in paragraph (a) or paragraph (b) of this subsection, as the case may be) in the charges payable by or on behalf of the organisation broadcasting the works [or recordings].

(3) The preceding provisions of this section shall have effect, with the necessary modifications, in relation to applications under this Part of this Act as they have effect in relation to references thereunder.

(4) In this section "the relevant copyright law", in relation to works [or sound recordings] broadcast from a place outside the United Kingdom, means so much of the laws of the country in which that place is situated as confers rights similar to copyright under this Act or as otherwise relates to such rights; and any reference to works includes a reference to adaptations thereof.

Note: This section was amended by the Cable and Broadcasting Act 1984 (c.46) and is printed as amended.

Effect of orders of tribunal, and supplementary provisions relating thereto

29.—(1) Where an order made on a reference under this Part of this Act with respect to a licence scheme is for the time being in force, any person who, in a case covered by the scheme as confirmed or varied by the order, does anything which—

(a) apart from this subsection would be an infringement of copyright, but

(b) would not be such an infringement if he were the holder of a licence granted in accordance with the scheme, as confirmed or varied by the order, in so far as the scheme relates to cases comprised in the order,

shall, if he has complied with the requirements specified in the next following subsection, be in the like position, in any proceedings for infringement of that copyright, as if he had at the material time been the holder of such a licence.

(2) The said requirements are—

(a) that, at all material times, the said person has complied with the terms and conditions which, in accordance with the licence scheme as confirmed or varied by the order, would be applicable to a licence covering the case in question, and

(b) if, in accordance with the scheme as so confirmed or varied, any charges are payable in respect of such a licence, that at the material time he had paid those charges to the licensing body operating the scheme, or, if at that time the amount payable could not be ascertained, he had given an undertaking to the licensing body to pay the charges when ascertained.

(3) Where the tribunal has made an order under section twenty-seven [or sec-

tion twenty-seven A] of this Act declaring that a person is entitled to a licence in respect of any matters specified in the order, then if—

(a) that person has complied with the terms and conditions specified in the order, and

(b) in a case where the order requires the payment of charges, he has paid those charges to the licensing body in accordance with the order, or, if the order so provides, has given to the licensing body an undertaking to pay the charges when ascertained,

he shall be in the like position, in any proceedings for infringement of copyright relating to any of those matters, as if he had at all material times been the holder of a licence granted by the owner of the copyright in question on the terms and conditions specified in the order.

(4) In the exercise of its jurisdiction in respect of licences relating to television broadcasts, the tribunal shall have regard (among other matters) to any conditions imposed by the promoters of any entertainment or other event which is to be comprised in the broadcasts; and, in particular, the tribunal shall not hold a refusal or failure to grant a licence to be unreasonable if it could not have been granted consistently with those conditions:

Provided that nothing in this subsection shall require the tribunal to have regard to any such conditions in so far as they purport to regulate the charges to be imposed in respect of the grant of licences, or in so far as they relate to payments to be made to the promoters of any event in consideration of the grant of facilities for broadcasting.

(5) Where, on a reference to the tribunal under this Part of this Act,—

(a) the reference relates to licences in respect of copyright in sound recordings or in television broadcasts, and

(b) the tribunal is satisfied that any of the licences in question are required for the purposes of organisations such as are mentioned in paragraph (b) of subsection (7) of section twelve of this Act,

the tribunal may, if it thinks fit, exercise its powers under this Part of this Act so as to reduce, in the case of those organisations, to such extent as the tribunal thinks fit, the charges which it determines generally to be reasonable in relation to cases of the class to which the reference relates, or, if it thinks fit, so as to exempt those organisations from the payment of any such charges.

(6) The last preceding subsection shall have effect, with the necessary modifications, in relation to applications under this Part of this Act as it has effect in relation to references thereunder.

(7) In relation to copyright in a literary, dramatic or musical work, any reference in this section to proceedings for infringement of copyright includes a reference to proceedings brought by virtue of subsection (5) of section twenty-one of this Act.

Note: The words in square brackets in subs.(3) inserted by the Copyright (Amendment) Act 1971 (c.4).

Reference of questions of law to the court

30.—(1) Any question of law arising in the course of proceedings before the tribunal may, at the request of any party to the proceedings, be referred by the tribunal to the court for decision, whether before or after the tribunal has given its decision in the proceedings.

Provided that a question shall not be referred to the court by virtue of this subsection in pursuance of a request made after the date on which the tribunal gave its decision, unless the request is made before the end of such period as may be prescribed by rules made under the Fourth Schedule to this Act.

(2) If the tribunal, after giving its decision in any proceedings, refuses any such request to refer a question to the court, the party by whom the request was made may, within such period as may be prescribed by rules of court, apply to the court for an order directing the tribunal to refer the question to the court.

(3) On any reference to the court under this section with respect to any proceedings before the tribunal, and on any application under the last preceding subsection with respect to any such proceedings, every party to the proceedings before the tribunal shall be entitled to appear and to be heard.

(4) Where, after the tribunal has given its decision in any proceedings, the tribunal refers to the court under this section a question of law which arose in the course of the proceedings, and the court decides that the question was erroneously determined by the tribunal,—

    (a) the tribunal, if it considers it requisite to do so for the purpose of giving effect to the decision of the court, shall give to the parties to the proceedings a further opportunity of presenting their cases respectively;

    (b) in any event, the tribunal shall reconsider the matter in dispute in conformity with the decision of the court;

    (c) if on such reconsideration it appears to the tribunal to be appropriate to do so, the tribunal shall make such order revoking or modifying any order previously made by it in the proceedings, or, in the case of proceedings under section twenty-seven of this Act where the tribunal refused to make an order, shall make such order under that section, as on such reconsideration that tribunal determines to be appropriate.

(5) Any reference of a question by the tribunal to the court under this section shall be by way of stating a case for the opinion of the court; and the decision of the court on any such reference shall be final.

(6) In this section "the court"—

    (a) in relation to any proceedings of the tribunal in England or Wales, or in Northern Ireland, means the High Court; and

    (b) in relation to any proceedings of the tribunal in Scotland, means the Court of Session.

Note: By virtue of s.7 of and Sch.1 to the Northern Ireland Act, 1962 (10 & 11 Eliz. 2, c.30), s.30 of the Copyright Act 1956, in its application to proceedings in Northern Ireland, was to have effect with the omission, from subs.(2), of the words "within such period as may be prescribed by rules of court." This section and Schedule repealed by the Judicature (Northern Ireland) Act 1978 (c.23).

See as to the meaning of "High Court" the Interpretation Act 1978 (c.30) s.5 and Sch.1.

PART V

EXTENSION OR RESTRICTION OF OPERATION OF ACT

Extension of Act to Isle of Man, Channel Islands, colonies and dependencies

31.—(1) Her Majesty may by Order in Council direct that any of the provisions of this Act specified in the Order (including any enactments for the time being in force amending or substituted for those provisions) shall extend, subject to such exceptions and modifications (if any) as may be specified in the Order, to—

    (a) the Isle of Man;

    (b) any of the Channel Islands;

    (c) any colony;

    (d) any country outside Her Majesty's dominions in which for the time being Her Majesty has jurisdiction;

(e) any country consisting partly of one or more colonies and partly of one or more such countries as are mentioned in the last preceding paragraph.

(2) The powers conferred by the preceding subsection shall be exercisable in relation to any Order in Council made under the following provisions of this Part of this Act, as those powers are exercisable by virtue of that subsection in relation to the provisions of this Act.

(3) The legislature of any country to which any provisions of this Act have been extended may modify or add to those provisions, in their operation as part of the law of that country, in such manner as that legislature may consider necessary to adapt the provisions to the circumstances of that country:

Provided that no such modifications or additions, except in so far as they relate to procedure and remedies, shall be made so as to apply to any work or other subject-matter in which copyright can subsist unless—

(a) in the case of a literary, dramatic, musical or artistic work, the author of the work, or, in the case of a sound recording or a cinematograph film, the maker of the recording or film, was domiciled or resident in that country at the time when, or during the period while, the work, recording or film was made, or

(b) in the case of a published edition of a literary, dramatic or musical work, the publisher of the edition was domiciled or resident in that country at the date of its first publication, or

(c) in the case of a literary, dramatic, musical or artistic work, or of a sound recording or a cinematograph film or a published edition, it was first published in that country, or

(d) in the case of a television broadcast or sound broadcast, it was made from a place in that country, [or

(e) in the case of a cable programme, it was sent from a place in that country.]

(4) For the purposes of any proceedings under this Act in the United Kingdom, where the proceedings relate to an act done in a country to which any provisions of this Act extend subject to exceptions, modifications or additions,—

(a) the procedure applicable to the proceedings, including the time within which they may be brought, and the remedies available therein, shall be in accordance with this Act in its operation as part of the law of the United Kingdom; but

(b) if the act in question does not constitute an infringement of copyright under this Act in its operation as part of the law of the country where the act was done, it shall (notwithstanding anything in this Act) be treated as not constituting an infringement of copyright under this Act in its operation as part of the law of the United Kingdom.

Note: This section was amended by the Cable and Broadcasting Act 1984 (c.46) and is printed as amended.

Application of Act to countries to which it does not extend

32.—(1) Her Majesty may by Order in Council make provision for applying any of the provisions of this Act specified in the Order, in the case of a country to which those provisions do not extend, in any one or more of the following ways, that is to say, so as to secure that those provisions—

(a) apply in relation to literary, dramatic, musical or artistic works, sound recordings, cinematograph films or editions first published in that country as they apply in relation to literary, dramatic, musical or artistic works, sound recordings, cinematograph films or editions first published in the United Kingdom;

(b) apply in relation to persons who, at a material time, are citizens or subjects of that country as they apply in relation to persons who, at such a time, are British subjects;

(c) apply in relation to persons who, at a material time, are domiciled or resident in that country as they apply in relation to persons who, at such a time, are domiciled or resident in the United Kingdom;

(d) apply in relation to bodies incorporated under the laws of that country as they apply in relation to bodies incorporated under the laws of any part of the United Kingdom;

(e) apply in relation to television broadcasts and sound broadcasts made from places in that country, by one or more organisations constituted in, or under the laws of, that country, as they apply in relation to television broadcasts and sound broadcasts made from places in the United Kingdom by the Corporation or the Authority;

[(f) apply in relation to cable programmes sent from places in that country as they apply in relation to cable programmes sent from places in the United Kingdom.]

(2) An Order in Council under this section—

(a) may apply the provisions in question as mentioned in the preceding subsection, but subject to exceptions or modifications specified in the Order;

(b) may direct that the provisions in question shall so apply either generally or in relation to such classes of works, or other classes of cases, as may be specified in the Order.

(3) Her Majesty shall not make an Order in Council under this section applying any of the provisions of this Act in the case of a country, other than a country which is a party to a Convention relating to copyright to which the United Kingdom is also a party, unless Her Majesty is satisfied that, in respect of the class of works or other subject-matter to which those provisions relate, provision has been or will be made under the laws of that country whereby adequate protection will be given to owners of copyright under this Act.

Note: This section was amended by the Cable and Broadcasting Act 1984 (c.46) and is printed as amended.

Provisions as to international organisations

33.—(1) Where it appears to Her Majesty that one or more sovereign Powers, or the government or governments thereof, are members of an organisation, and that is expedient that the provisions of this section should apply to that organisation, Her Majesty may by Order in Council declare that the organisation is one to which this section applies.

(2) Where an original literary, dramatic, musical or artistic work is made by or under the direction or control of an organisation to which this section applies in such circumstances that—

(a) copyright would not subsist in the work apart from this subsection, but

(b) if the author of the work had been a British subject at the time when it was made, copyright would have subsisted in the work immediately after it was made and would thereupon have vested in the organisation,

copyright shall subsist in the work as if the author had been a British subject when it was made, that copyright shall continue to subsist so long as the work remains unpublished, and the organisation shall, subject to the provisions of this Act, be entitled to that copyright.

(3) Where an original literary, dramatic, musical or artistic work is first published by or under the direction or control of an organisation to which this

section applies, in such circumstances that, apart from this subsection, copyright does not subsist in the work immediately after the first publication thereof, and either—

(a) the work is so published in pursuance of an agreement with the author which does not reserve to the author the copyright (if any) in the work, or

(b) the work was made in such circumstances that, if it had been first published in the United Kingdom, the organisation would have been entitled to the copyright in the work,

copyright shall subsist in the work (or, if copyright in the work subsisted immediately before its first publication, shall continue to subsist) as if it had been first published in the United Kingdom, that copyright shall subsist until the end of the period of fifty years from the end of the calendar year in which the work was first published, and the organisation shall, subject to the provisions of Part VI of this Act, be entitled to that copyright.

(4) The provisions of Part I of this Act, with the exception of provisions thereof relating to the subsistence, duration or ownership of copyright, shall apply in relation to copyright subsisting by virtue of this section as they apply in relation to copyright subsisting by virtue of the said Part I.

(5) An organisation to which this section applies which otherwise has not, or at some material time otherwise had not, the legal capacities of a body corporate shall have, and shall be deemed at all material times to have had, the legal capacities of a body corporate for the purpose of holding, dealing with and enforcing copyright and in connection with all legal proceedings relating to copyright.

Extended application of provisions relating to broadcasts

34. Her Majesty may by Order in Council provide that, subject to such exceptions and modifications (if any) as may be specified in the Order, such provisions of this Act relating to television broadcasts or to sound broadcasts as may be so specified shall apply in relation to the operation of wireless telegraphy apparatus by way of the emission (as opposed to reception) of electro-magnetic energy—

(a) by such persons or classes of persons, other than the Corporation and the Authority, as may be specified in the Order, and

(b) for such purposes (whether involving broadcasting or not) as may be so specified,

as they apply in relation to television broadcasts, or, as the case may be, to sound broadcasts, made by the Corporation and the Authority.

Denial of copyright to citizens of countries not giving adequate protection to British works

35.—(1) If it appears to Her Majesty that the laws of a country fail to give adequate protection to British works to which this section applies, or fail to give such protection in the case of one or more classes of such works (whether the lack of protection relates to the nature of the work or the country of its author or both), Her Majesty may make an Order in Council designating that country and making such provision in relation thereto as is mentioned in the following provisions of this section.

(2) An Order in Council under this section shall provide that, either generally or in such classes of cases as are specified in the Order, copyright under this Act shall not subsist in works to which this section applies which were first published after a date specified in the Order, if at the time of their first publication the authors thereof were—

(a) citizens or subjects of the country designated by the Order, not being at that time persons domiciled or resident in the United Kingdom or in another country to which the relevant provision of this Act extends, or

(b) bodies incorporated under the laws of the country designated by the Order.

(3) In making an Order in Council under this section Her Majesty shall have regard to the nature and extent of the lack of protection for British works in consequence of which the Order is made.

(4) This section applies to the following works, that is to say, literary, dramatic musical and artistic works, sound recordings and cinematograph films.

(5) In this section—

"British work" means a work of which the author, at the time when the work was made, was a qualified person for the purposes of the relevant provision of this Act;

"author", in relation to a sound recording or a cinematograph film, means the maker of the recording or film;

"the relevant provision of this Act", in relation to literary, dramatic and musical works means section two, in relation to artistic works means section three, in relation to sound recordings means section twelve, and in relation to cinematograph films means section thirteen, of this Act.

PART VI

MISCELLANEOUS AND SUPPLEMENTARY PROVISIONS

Assignments and licences in respect of copyright

36.—(1) Subject to the provisions of this section, copyright shall be transmissible by assignment, by testamentary disposition, or by operation of law, as personal or moveable property.

(2) An assignment of copyright may be limited in any of the following ways, or in any combination of two or more of those ways, that is to say,—

(a) so as to apply to one or more, but not all, of the classes of acts which by virtue of this Act the owner of the copyright has the exclusive right to do (including any one or more classes of acts not separately designated in this Act as being restricted by the copyright, but falling within any of the classes of acts so designated);

(b) so as to apply to any one or more, but not all, of the countries in relation to which the owner of the copyright has by virtue of this Act that exclusive right;

(c) so as to apply to part, but not the whole, of the period for which the copyright is to subsist;

and references in this Act to a partial assignment are references to an assignment so limited.

(3) No assignment of copyright (whether total or partial) shall have effect unless it is in writing signed by or on behalf of the assignor.

(4) A licence granted in respect of any copyright by the person who, in relation to the matters to which the licence relates, is the owner of the copyright shall be binding upon every successor in title to his interest in the copyright, except a purchaser in good faith for valuable consideration and without notice (actual or constructive) of the licence or a person deriving title from such a purchaser; and references in this Act, in relation to any copyright, to the doing of anything with,

or (as the case may be) without, the licence of the owner of the copyright shall be construed accordingly.

Prospective ownership of copyright

37.—(1) Where by an agreement made in relation to any future copyright, and signed by or on behalf of the prospective owner of the copyright, the prospective owner purports to assign the future copyright (wholly or partially) to another person (in this subsection referred to as "the assignee"), then if, on the coming into existence of the copyright, the assignee or a person claiming under him would, apart from this subsection, be entitled as against all other persons to require the copyright to be vested in him (wholly or partially, as the case may be), the copyright shall, on its coming into existence, vest in the assignee or his successor in title accordingly by virtue of this subsection and without further assurance.

(2) Where, at the time when any copyright comes into existence, the person who, if he were then living, would be entitled to the copyright is dead, the copyright shall devolve as if it had subsisted immediately before his death and he had then been the owner of the copyright.

(3) Subsection (4) of the last preceding section shall apply in relation to a licence granted by a prospective owner of any copyright as it applies in relation to a licence granted by the owner of a subsisting copyright, as if any reference in that subsection to the owner's interest in the copyright included a reference to his prospective interest therein.

(4) The provisions of the Fifth Schedule to this Act shall have effect with respect to assignments and licences in respect of copyright (including future copyright) in television broadcasts.

(5) In this Act "future copyright" means copyright which will or may come into existence in respect of any future work or class of works or other subject-matter, or on the coming into operation of any provisions of this Act, or in any other future event, and "prospective owner" shall be construed accordingly and, in relation to any such copyright, includes a person prospectively entitled thereto by virtue of such an agreement as is mentioned in subsection (1) of this section.

Copyright to pass under will with unpublished work

38. Where under a bequest (whether specific or general) a person is entitled, beneficially or otherwise, to the manuscript of a literary, dramatic or musical work, or to an artistic work, and the work was not published before the death of the testator, the bequest shall, unless a contrary intention is indicated in the testator's will or a codicil thereto, be construed as including the copyright in the work in so far as the testator was the owner of the copyright immediately before his death.

Provisions as to Crown and Government departments

39.—(1) In the case of every original literary, dramatic, musical or artistic work made by or under the direction or control of Her Majesty or a Government department,—

(a) if apart from this section copyright would not subsist in the work, copyright shall subsist therein by virtue of this subsection, and

(b) in any case, Her Majesty shall, subject to the provisions of this Part of this Act, be entitled to the copyright in the work.

(2) Her Majesty shall, subject to the provisions of this Part of this Act, be entitled—

(a) to the copyright in every original literary, dramatic or musical work first published in the United Kingdom, or in another country to which section two of this Act extends, if first published by or under the direction or control of Her Majesty or a Government department;

(b) to the copyright in every original artistic work first published in the United Kingdom, or in another country to which section three of this Act extends, if first published by or under such direction or control.

(3) Copyright in a literary, dramatic or musical work, to which Her Majesty is entitled in accordance with either of the preceding subsections,—

(a) where the work is unpublished, shall continue to subsist so long as the work remains unpublished, and

(b) where the work is published, shall subsist (or, if copyright in the work subsisted immediately before its first publication, shall continue to subsist) until the end of the period of fifty years from the end of the calendar year in which the work was first published, and shall then expire.

(4) Copyright in an artistic work to which Her Majesty is entitled in accordance with the preceding provisions of this section shall continue to subsist until the end of the period of fifty years from the end of the calendar year in which the work was made, and shall then expire:

Provided that where the work in question is an engraving or a photograph, the copyright shall continue to subsist until the end of the period of fifty years from the end of the calendar year in which the engraving or photograph is first published.

(5) In the case of every sound recording or cinematograph film made by or under the direction or control of Her Majesty or a Government department,—

(a) if apart from this section copyright would not subsist in the recording or film, copyright shall subsist therein by virtue of this subsection, and

(b) in any case, Her Majesty shall, subject to the provisions of this Part of this Act, be entitled to the copyright in the recording or film, and it shall subsist for the same period as if it were copyright subsisting by virtue of, and owned in accordance with, section twelve or, as the case may be, section thirteen of this Act.

(6) The preceding provisions of this section shall have effect subject to any agreement made by or on behalf of Her Majesty or a Government department with the author of the work, or the maker of the sound recording or cinematograph film, as the case may be, whereby it is agreed that the copyright in the work, recording or film shall vest in the author or maker, or in another person designated in the agreement in that behalf.

(7) In relation to copyright subsisting by virtue of this section—

(a) in the case of a literary, dramatic, musical or artistic work, the provisions of Part I of this Act, with the exception of provisions thereof relating to the subsistence, duration or ownership of copyright, and

(b) in the case of a sound recording or cinematograph film, the provisions of Part II of this Act, with the exception of provisions thereof relating to the subsistence or ownership of copyright,

shall apply as those provisions apply in relation to copyright subsisting by virtue of Part I or, as the case may be, Part II of this Act.

(8) For the avoidance of doubt, it is hereby declared that the provisions of section three of the Crown Proceedings Act, 1947 (which relates to infringements of industrial property by servants or agents of the Crown) apply to copyright under this Act.

(9) In this section "Government department" means any department of Her

Majesty's Government in the United Kingdom or of the Government of Northern Ireland, or any department or agency of the Government of any other country to which this section extends.

Broadcasts of sound recordings and cinematograph films, and diffusion of broadcast programmes

40.—(1) Where a sound broadcast or television broadcast is made by the Corporation or the Authority, and a person, by the reception of that broadcast, causes a sound recording to be heard in public, he does not thereby infringe the copyright (if any) in that recording under section twelve of this Act.

(2) Where a television broadcast or sound broadcast is made by the Corporation or the Authority, and the broadcast is an authorised broadcast, any person who, by the reception of the broadcast, causes a cinematograph film to be seen or heard in public shall be in the like position, in any proceedings for infringement of the copyright (if any) in the film under section thirteen of this Act, as if he had been the holder of a licence granted by the owner of that copyright to cause the film to be seen or heard in public by the reception of the broadcast.

[(3) Where a television broadcast or sound broadcast is made by the Corporation or the Authority and the broadcast is an authorised broadcast, then, subject to subsection (3A) below, any person who, by the reception and immediate retransmission of the broadcast, includes a programme in a cable programme service, being a programme comprising a literary, dramatic or musical work, or an adaptation of such a work, or an artistic work, or a sound recording or cinematograph film, shall be in the like position, in any proceedings for infringement of the copyright (if any) in the work, recording or film, as if he had been the holder of a licence granted by the owner of that copyright to include the work, adaptation, recording or film in any programme so included in that service.

(3A) Subsection (3) above applies only—
- (a) if the programme is included in the service in pursuance of a requirement imposed under section 13(1) of the Cable and Broadcasting Act 1984; or
- (b) if and to the extent that the broadcast is made for reception in the area in which the service is provided.]

(4) If, in the circumstances mentioned in either of the two last preceding subsections, the person causing the cinematograph film to be seen or heard, or [including the programme in a cable programme service,] as the case may be, infringed the copyright in question, by reason that the broadcast was not an authorised broadcast,—
- (a) no proceedings shall be brought against that person under this Act in respect of his infringement of that copyright, but
- (b) it shall be taken into account in assessing damages in any proceedings against the Corporation or the Authority, as the case may be, in respect of that copyright, in so far as that copyright was infringed by them in making the broadcast.

(5) For the purposes of this section, a broadcast shall be taken, in relation to a work [or sound recording] or cinematograph film, to be an authorised broadcast if, but only if, it is made by, or with the licence of, the owner of the copyright in the work [or recording] or film.

Note: This section was amended by the Cable and Broadcasting Act 1984 (c.46) and is printed as amended. See Note to s.14A above.

Inclusion of sound recordings and cinematograph films in cable programmes

[**40A.**—(1) Where a cable programme is sent and a person, by the reception of that programme, causes a sound recording to be heard in public, he does not thereby infringe the copyright (if any) in that recording under section 12 of this Act.

(2) Where a cable programme is sent and the programme is an authorised programme, any person who, by the reception of the programme, causes a cinematograph film to be seen or heard in public shall be in the like position, in any proceedings for infringement of copyright (if any) in the film under section 13 of this Act, as if he had been the holder of a licence granted by the owner of that copyright to cause the film to be seen or heard in public by the reception of the programme.

(3) If, in the circumstances mentioned in the last preceding subsection, a person causing a cinematograph film to be seen or heard infringes the copyright in the film by reason that the cable programme was not an authorised programme—

(a) no proceedings shall be brought against that person under this Act in respect of his infringement of that copyright, but

(b) it shall be taken into account in assessing damages in any proceedings against the person sending the programme, in so far as that copyright was infringed by him in sending the programme.

(4) For the purposes of this section, a cable programme shall be taken, in relation to a cinematograph film, to be an authorised programme if, but only if, it is sent by, or with the licence of, the owner of the copyright in the film.]

Note: This section was inserted by the Cable and Broadcasting Act 1984 (c 46).

Use of copyright material for education

41.—(1) Where copyright subsists in a literary, dramatic, musical or artistic work, the copyright shall not be taken to be infringed by reason only that the work is reproduced, or an adaptation of the work is made or reproduced,—

(a) in the course of instruction, whether at a school or elsewhere, where the reproduction or adaptation is made by a teacher or pupil otherwise than by the use of a duplicating process, or

(b) as part of the questions to be answered in an examination, or in an answer to such a question.

(2) Nothing in the preceding subsection shall apply to the publication of a work or of an adaptation of a work; and, for the purposes of section five of this Act, the fact that to a person's knowledge the making of an article would have constituted an infringement of copyright but for the preceding subsection shall have the like effect as if, to his knowledge, the making of it had constituted such an infringement.

(3) For the avoidance of doubt it is hereby declared that, where a literary, dramatic or musical work—

(a) is performed in class, or otherwise in the presence of an audience, and

(b) is so performed in the course of the activities of a school, by a person who is a teacher in, or a pupil in attendance at, the school,

the performance shall not be taken for the purposes of this Act to be a performance in public if the audience is limited to persons who are teachers in, or pupils in attendance at, the school, or are otherwise directly connected with the activities of the school.

(4) For the purposes of the last preceding subsection a person shall not be taken to be directly connected with the activities of a school by reason only that he is a parent or guardian of a pupil in attendance at the school.

(5) The two last preceding subsections shall apply in relation to sound record-

ings, cinematograph films [television broadcasts and cable programmes] as they apply in relation to literary, dramatic and musical works, as if any reference to performance were a reference to the act of causing the sounds or visual images in question to be heard or seen.

(6) Nothing in this section shall be construed—

(a) as extending the operation of any provision of this Act as to the acts restricted by copyright of any description, or

(b) as derogating from the operation of any exemption conferred by any provision of this Act other than this section.

(7) In this section "school"—

(a) in relation to England and Wales, has the same meaning as in the Education Act, 1944;

(b) in relation to Scotland, has the same meaning as in the Education (Scotland) Act, 1946, except that it includes an approved school within the meaning of the Children and Young Persons (Scotland) Act, 1937; and

(c) in relation to Northern Ireland, has the same meaning as in the Education Act (Northern Ireland), 1947;

and "duplicating process" means any process involving the use of an appliance for producing multiple copies.

Notes:

(1) This section was amended by the Cable and Broadcasting Act 1984 (c.46) and is printed as amended.

(2) The definition of "approved school" in ss.83 and 110 of the Children and Young Persons (Scotland) Act 1937 (1 Edw. 8 and 1 Geo. 6, c.37) was repealed as to Scotland by the Social Work (Scotland) Act 1968 (c.49). The Education (Scotland) Act 1946 (9 & 10 Geo. 6, c.72) was repealed by the Education (Scotland) Act 1962 (10 & 11 Eliz. 2, c.47). The Education Act (Northern Ireland) 1947 (c.3) was repealed by the Education and Libraries (Northern Ireland) Order 1972 (2010/1263) (N.I. 12), which was itself repealed by the Education and Libraries (Northern Ireland) Order 1986 (1986/594) (N.I. 3).

Special provisions as to public records

42.—(1) Where any work in which copyright subsists, or a reproduction of any such work, is comprised in—

(a) any records belonging to Her Majesty which are under the charge and superintendence of the Master of the Rolls by virtue of an Order in Council under section two of the Public Record Office Act, 1838, and are open to public inspection in accordance with rules made under that Act, or

(b) any public records to which the Public Records Act (Northern Ireland), 1923, applies; being records which are open to public inspection in accordance with Rules made under that Act,

the copyright in the work is not infringed by the making, or the supplying to any person, of any reproduction of the work by or under the direction of any officer appointed under the said Act of 1838 or the said Act of 1923, as the case may be.

(2) In the preceding subsection "records"—

(a) in paragraph (a) of that subsection has the same meaning as in the Public Record Office Act, 1838;

(b) in paragraph (b) of that subsection has the same meaning as in the Public Records Act (Northern Ireland), 1923.

(3) Any reference in this section to the Public Records Act (Northern Ireland), 1923, shall be construed as including a reference to that Act as for the time being

amended or re-enacted (with or without modifications) by any enactment of the Parliament of Northern Ireland.

Note: The Public Record Office Act 1838, was repealed by s.13 of and Sch.4 to the Public Records Act 1958 (6 & 7 Eliz. 2, c.51) and by virtue of s.11 of and Sch.3 to that Act, as respects any reproduction made after the commencement of that Act, the reference in s.42(1)(a) of the Copyright Act 1956, to records of the description there mentioned is to be taken as a reference to public records which are open to public inspection in pursuance of the provisions of the 1958 Act. See as to the Public Records Act (Northern Ireland) 1923, the Administration of Justice Act 1969 (c.58) s.27 and the Statute Law (Repeals) Act 1978 (c.45) s.1 and Schs 1 and 2.

False attribution of authorship

43.—(1) The restrictions imposed by this section shall have effect in relation to literary, dramatic, musical or artistic works; and any reference in this section to a work shall be construed as a reference to such a work.

(2) A person (in this subsection referred to as "the offender") contravenes those restrictions as respects another person if, without the licence of that other person, he does any of the following acts in the United Kingdom, that is to say, he—

(a) inserts or affixes that other person's name in or on a work of which that person is not the author, or in or on a reproduction of such a work, in such a way as to imply that the other person is the author of the work, or

(b) publishes, or sells or lets for hire, or by way of trade offers or exposes for sale or hire, or by way of trade exhibits in public, a work in or on which the other person's name has been so inserted or affixed, if to the offender's knowledge that person is not the author of the work, or

(c) does any of the acts mentioned in the last preceding paragraph in relation to, or distributes, reproductions of a work, being reproductions in or on which the other person's name has been so inserted or affixed, if to the offender's knowledge that person is not the author of the work, or

(d) performs in public, [broadcasts or includes in a cable programme] a work of which the other person is not the author, as being a work of which he is the author, if to the offender's knowledge that person is not the author of the work.

(3) The last preceding subsection shall apply where, contrary to the fact, a work is represented as being an adaptation of the work of another person as it applies where a work is so represented as being the work of another person.

(4) In the case of an artistic work which has been altered after the author parted with the possession of it, the said restrictions are contravened, in relation to the author, by a person who in the United Kingdom, without the licence of the author,—

(a) publishes, sells or lets for hire, or by way of trade offers or exposes for sale or hire the work as so altered, as being the unaltered work of the author, or

(b) publishes, sells or lets for hire, or by way of trade offers or exposes for sale or hire a reproduction of the work as so altered, as being a reproduction of the unaltered work of the author,

if to his knowledge it is not the unaltered work, or, as the case may be, a reproduction of the unaltered work, of the author.

(5) The three last preceding subsections shall apply with respect to anything done in relation to another person after that person's death, as if any reference to that person's licence were a reference to a licence given by him or by his personal representatives:

Provided that nothing in those subsections shall apply to anything done in relation to a person more than twenty years after that person's death.

(6) In the case of an artistic work in which copyright subsists, the said restrictions are also contravened, in relation to the author of the work, by a person who in the United Kingdom—

(a) publishes or sells or lets for hire, or by way of trade offers or exposes for sale or hire, or by way of trade exhibits in public, a reproduction of the work, as being a reproduction made by the author of the work, or

(b) distributes reproductions of the work as being reproductions made by the author of the work,

if (in any such case) the reproduction or reproductions was or were to his knowledge not made by the author.

(7) The preceding provisions of this section shall apply (with the necessary modifications) with respect to acts done in relation to two or more persons in connection with the same work.

(8) The restrictions imposed by this section shall not be enforceable by any criminal proceedings; but any contravention of those restrictions, in relation to a person, shall be actionable at his suit, or, if he is dead, at the suit of his personal representatives, as a breach of statutory duty.

(9) Any damages recovered under this section by personal representatives, in respect of a contravention committed in relation to a person after his death, shall devolve as part of his estate, as if the right of action had subsisted and had been vested in him immediately before his death.

(10) Nothing in this section shall derogate from any right of action or other remedy (whether civil or criminal) in proceedings instituted otherwise than by virtue of this section:

Provided that this subsection shall not be construed as requiring any damages recovered by virtue of this section to be disregarded in assessing damages in any proceedings instituted otherwise than by virtue of this section and arising out of the same transaction.

(11) In this section "name" includes initials or a monogram.

Note: This section was amended by the Cable and Broadcasting Act 1984 (c.46) and is printed as amended.

Amendments of Registered Designs Act, 1949

44.—(1) In section six of the Registered Designs Act, 1949, (under which the disclosure of a design in certain circumstances is not to be a reason for refusing registration), the following subsections shall be inserted after subsection (3):

"(4) Where copyright under the Copyright Act, 1956, subsists in an artistic work, and an application is made by, or with the consent of, the owner of that copyright for the registration of a corresponding design, that design shall not be treated for the purposes of this Act as being other than new or original by reason only of any use previously made of the artistic work, unless—

(a) the previous use consisted of or included the sale, letting for hire, or offer for sale or hire of articles to which the design in question (or a design differing from it only as mentioned in subsection (2) of section one of this Act) had been applied industrially, other than articles of a description specified in rules made under subsection (4) of section one of this Act, and

(b) that previous use was made by, or with the consent of, the owner of the copyright in the artistic work.

(5) Any rules made by virtue of subsection (5) of section ten of the Copyright Act, 1956 (which relates to rules for determining the circumstances in which a design

is to be taken to be applied industrially) shall apply for the purposes of the last foregoing subsection."

(2) The following subsection shall be added at the end of section eight of the said Act of 1949 (which relates to the period of copyright in registered designs):

"(3) Where in the case of a registered design it is shown—

    (a) that the design, at the time when it was registered, was a corresponding design in relation to an artistic work in which copyright subsisted under the Copyright Act, 1956;

    (b) that, by reason of a previous use of that artistic work, the design would not have been registrable under this Act but for subsection (4) of section six of this Act; and

    (c) that the copyright in that work under the Copyright Act, 1956, expired before the date of expiry of the copyright in the design,

the copyright in the design shall, notwithstanding anything in this section, be deemed to have expired at the same time as the copyright in the artistic work, and shall not be renewable after that time."

(3) In section eleven of the said Act of 1949 (which relates to cancellation of the registration of designs), the following subsection shall be inserted after subsection (2):

"(2A) At any time after a design has been registered, any person interested may apply to the registrar for the cancellation of the registration of the design on the grounds—

    (a) that the design, at the time when it was registered, was a corresponding design in relation to an artistic work in which copyright subsisted under the Copyright Act, 1956;

    (b) that, by reason of a previous use of that artistic work, the design would not have been registrable under this Act but for subsection (4) of section six of this Act; and

    (c) that the copyright in that work under the Copyright Act, 1956, has expired;

and the registrar may make such order on the application as he thinks fit."

(4) In subsection (3) of the said section eleven, for the words "the last foregoing subsection" there shall be substituted the words "either of the two last foregoing subsections."

(5) In subsection (1) of section forty-four of the said Act of 1949 (which relates to the interpretation of that Act)—

    (a) after the definition of "article" there shall be inserted the words "'artistic work' has the same meaning as in the Copyright Act, 1956"; and

    (b) after the definition of "copyright" there shall be inserted the words "'corresponding design' has the same meaning as in section ten of the Copyright Act, 1956".

Amendment of Dramatic and Musical Performers' Protection Act, 1925

[45. *In the Dramatic and Musical Performers' Protection Act, 1925,—*

    (a) *after section one there shall be inserted the two sections set out in Part I of the Sixth Schedule to this Act; and*

    (b) *after section three there shall be inserted the two sections set out in Part II of that Schedule;*

and the provisions of that Act specified in Part III of that Schedule shall have effect subject to the amendments set out in relation thereto in the second column of the said Part III (being minor amendments of that Act and amendments consequential upon the insertion therein of the sections referred to in paragraphs (a) and (b) of this section).]

Note: This provision and the Sixth Schedule repealed by the Dramatic and Musical Performers' Protection Act 1958 (6 & 7 Eliz. 2, c.44), which also repealed the Dramatic and Musical Performers' Protection Act 1925 (15 & 16 Geo. 5, c.46).

Savings

46.—(1) Any rights conferred on universities and colleges by the Copyright Act, 1775, which continued to subsist in accordance with section thirty-three of the Copyright Act, 1911, notwithstanding the repeal of the said Act of 1775, shall continue to subsist in accordance with the said Act of 1775, notwithstanding any repeal effected by this Act:

Provided that no proceedings shall be brought under the Copyright Act, 1775, but the provisions of Part III of this Act shall apply for the enforcement of those rights as if they were copyright subsisting by virtue of this Act.

(2) Nothing in this Act shall affect any right or privilege of the Crown subsisting otherwise than by virtue of an enactment; and nothing in this Act shall affect any right or privilege of the Crown or of any other person under any enactment (including any enactment of the Parliament of Northern Ireland), except in so far as that enactment is expressly repealed, amended or modified by this Act.

(3) Nothing in this Act shall affect the right of the Crown or of any person deriving title from the Crown to sell, use or otherwise deal with articles forfeited under the laws relating to customs or excise, including any articles so forfeited by virtue of this Act or of any enactment repealed by this Act.

(4) Nothing in this Act shall affect the operation of any rule of equity relating to breaches of trust or confidence.

(5) Subject to the preceding provisions of this section, no copyright, or right in the nature of copyright, shall subsist otherwise than by virtue of this Act or of some other enactment in that behalf.

General provisions as to Orders in Council, regulations, rules and orders, and as to Board of Trade

47.—(1) Any power to make regulations, rules or orders under this Act shall be exercisable by statutory instrument.

(2) Any statutory instrument containing—

(a) any Order in Council or regulations made under this Act, or

(b) any rules made by the Lord Chancellor under the Fourth Schedule to this Act,

shall be subject to annulment in pursuance of a resolution of either House of Parliament.

(3) Any Order in Council, or other order, made under any of the preceding provisions of this Act may be varied or revoked by a subsequent Order in Council or order made thereunder.

(4) Where a power to make regulations or rules is conferred by any provision of this Act, regulations or rules under that power may be made either as respects all, or as respects any one or more, of the matters to which the provision relates; and different provision may be made by any such regulations or rules as respects different classes of cases to which the regulations or rules apply.

[(5) *Anything required or authorised by or under this Act to be done by, to or before the Board of Trade may be done by, to or before the President of the Board of Trade, any Minister of State with duties concerning the affairs of the Board, any secretary, under-secretary or assistant secretary of the Board, or any person authorised in that behalf by the President.*]

(6) In this section "order" does not include an order of a court or of the tribunal.

Note: Subsection (5) was repealed by s.18 of and Sch.4 to the Industrial Expansion Act 1968, (c.32) s.14 of which provides that anything authorised or required by or under that

Act or any other enactments (including an enactment of the Parliament of Northern Ireland), whether passed before or after that Act, to be done by, to or before the Board of Trade may be done by, to or before the President of the Board or any person acting with his authority. See as to concurrent exercise of functions by the Secretary of State, The Secretary of State for Trade and Industry Order 1970 (SI 1970/1537), as amended.

Interpretation

48.—(1) In this Act, except in so far as the context otherwise requires, the following expressions have the meanings hereby assigned to them respectively, that is to say:

"adaptation", in relation to a literary, dramatic or musical work, has the meaning assigned to it by section two of this Act;

"artistic work" has the meaning assigned to it by section three of this Act;

"assignment", in relation to Scotland, means an assignation;

"building" includes any structure;

["cable programme", "cable programme service" and "programme" have the meanings assigned to them by section 14A of this Act;]

"cinematograph film" has the meaning assigned to it by section thirteen of this Act;

"construction" includes erection, and references to reconstruction shall be construed accordingly;

"the Corporation" and "the Authority" have the meanings assigned to them by section fourteen of this Act;

"country" includes any territory;

"dramatic work" includes a choreographic work or entertainment in dumb show if reduced to writing in the form in which the work or entertainment is to be presented, but does not include a cinematograph film, as distinct from a scenario or script for a cinematograph film;

"drawing" includes any diagram, map, chart or plan;

"engraving" includes any etching, lithograph, woodcut, print or similar work, not being a photograph;

"future copyright" and "prospective owner" have the meanings assigned to them by section thirty-seven of this Act;

"judicial proceeding" means a proceeding before any court, tribunal or person having by law power to hear, receive and examine evidence on oath;

"literary work" includes any written table or compilation;

"manuscript", in relation to a work, means the original document embodying the work, whether written by hand or not;

"performance" includes delivery, in relation to lectures, addresses, speeches and sermons, and in general, subject to the provisions of subsection (5) of this section, includes any mode of visual or acoustic presentation, including any such presentation by the operation of wireless telegraphy apparatus, or by the exhibition of a cinematograph film, or by the use of a record, or by any other means, and references to performing a work or an adaptation of a work shall be construed accordingly;

"photograph" means any product of photography or of any process akin to photography, other than a part of a cinematograph film, and "author", in relation to a photograph, means the person who, at the time when the photograph is taken, is the owner of the material on which it is taken;

"qualified person" has the meaning assigned to it by section one of this Act;

"record" means any disc, tape, perforated roll or other device in which sounds are embodied so as to be capable (with or without the aid of some other instrument) of being automatically reproduced therefrom, and references to a record of a work or other subject-matter are references to a record (as herein defined) by means of which it can be performed;

"reproduction", in the case of a literary, dramatic or musical work, includes a reproduction in the form of a record or of a cinematograph film, and, in the case of an artistic work, includes a version produced by converting the work into a three-dimensional form, or, if it is in three dimensions, by converting it into a two-dimensional form, and references to reproducing a work shall be construed accordingly;

"sculpture" includes any cast or model made for purposes of sculpture;

"sound recording" has the meaning assigned to it by section twelve of this Act;

"sufficient acknowledgment" has the meaning assigned to it by section six of this Act;

"television broadcast" and "sound broadcast" have the meanings assigned to them by section fourteen of this Act;

"wireless telegraphy apparatus" has the same meaning as in the Wireless Telegraphy Act, 1949;

"work of joint authorship" has the meaning assigned to it by section eleven of this Act;

"writing" includes any form of notation, whether by hand or by printing, typewriting or any similar process.

(2) References in this Act to broadcasting are references to broadcasting by wireless telegraphy (within the meaning of the Wireless Telegraphy Act, 1949), whether by way of sound broadcasting or of television.

[(3) References in this Act to the inclusion of a programme in a cable programme service are references to its inclusion in such a service by the person providing that service.

(3A) For the purposes of this Act no account shall be taken of a cable programme service if, and to the extent that, it is provided for—

(a) a person providing another such service;

(b) the Corporation; or

(c) the Authority;

and for the purposes of this subsection a cable programme service provided for the Welsh Fourth Channel Authority, the subsidiary mentioned in section 12(2) of the Broadcasting Act 1981 or a programme contractor within the meaning of that Act shall be treated as provided for the Authority.

(3B) For the purposes of this Act no account shall be taken of a cable programme service which is only incidental to a business of keeping or letting premises where persons reside or sleep, and is operated as part of the amenities provided exclusively or mainly for residents or inmates therein.]

(4) References in this Act to the doing of any act by the reception of a television broadcast or sound broadcast made by the Corporation or the Authority are references to the doing of that act by means of receiving the broadcast either—

(a) from the transmission whereby the broadcast is made by the Corporation or the Authority, as the case may be, or

(b) from a transmission made by the Corporation or the Authority, as the case may be, otherwise than by way of broadcasting, but simultaneously with the transmission mentioned in the preceding paragraph,

whether (in either case) the reception of the broadcast is directly from the transmission in question or from a re-transmission thereof made by any person from any place, whether in the United Kingdom or elsewhere; and in this subsection "re-transmission" means any re-transmission, whether over paths provided by a material substance or not, including any re-transmission made by making use of any record, print, negative, tape or other article on which the broadcast in question has been recorded.

(5) For the purposes of this Act, broadcasting, or [including a work or other subject matter in a cable programme] shall not be taken to constitute performance, or to constitute causing visual images or sounds to be seen or heard; and where visual images or sounds are displayed or emitted by any receiving apparatus, to which they are conveyed by the transmission of electromagnetic signals (whether over paths provided by a material substance or not),—

    (a) the operation of any apparatus whereby the signals are transmitted directly or indirectly, to the receiving apparatus shall not be taken to constitute performance or to constitute causing the visual images or sounds to be seen or heard; but

    (b) in so far as the display or emission of the images or sounds constitutes a performance, or causes them to be seen or heard, the performance, or the causing of the images or sounds to be seen or heard, as the case may be, shall be taken to be effected by the operation of the receiving apparatus.

(6) Without prejudice to the last preceding subsection, where a work or an adaptation of a work is performed, or visual images or sounds are caused to be seen or heard, by the operation of any apparatus to which this subsection applies, being apparatus provided by or with the consent of the occupier of the premises where the apparatus is situated, the occupier of those premises shall, for the purposes of this Act, be taken to be the person giving the performance, or causing the images or sounds to be seen or heard, whether he is the person operating the apparatus or not.

This subsection applies to any such receiving apparatus as is mentioned in the last preceding subsection, and to any apparatus for reproducing sounds by the use of a record.

(7) Except in so far as the context otherwise requires, any reference in this Act to an enactment shall be construed as a reference to that enactment as amended or extended by or under any other enactment.

Note: This section was amended by the Cable and Broadcasting Act 1984 (c.46) and is printed as amended.

Supplementary provisions as to interpretation

49.—(1) Except in so far as the context requires, any reference in this Act to the doing of an act in relation to a work or other subject-matter shall be taken to include a reference to the doing of that act in relation to a substantial part thereof, and any reference to a reproduction, adaptation or copy of a work, or a record embodying a sound recording, shall be taken to include a reference to a reproduction, adaptation or copy of a substantial part of the work, or a record embodying a substantial part of the sound recording, as the case may be:

Provided that, for the purposes of the following provisions of this Act, namely subsections (1) and (2) of section two, subsections (2) and (3) of section three, subsections (2) and (3) of section thirty-three, section thirty-eight, and subsections (2) to (4) of section thirty-nine, this subsection shall not affect the construction of any reference to the publication, or absence of publication, of a work.

(2) With regard to publication, the provisions of this subsection shall have effect for the purposes of this Act, that is to say,—

    (a) the performance, or the issue of records, of a literary, dramatic or musical work, the exhibition of an artistic work, the construction of a work of architecture, and the issue of photographs or engravings of a work of architecture or of a sculpture, do not constitute publication of the work;

(b) except in so far as it may constitute an infringement of copyright, or a contravention of any restriction imposed by section forty-three of this Act, a publication which is merely colourable, and not intended to satisfy the reasonable requirements of the public, shall be disregarded;

(c) subject to the preceding paragraphs, a literary, dramatic or musical work, or an edition of such a work, or an artistic work, shall be taken to have been published if, but only if, reproductions of the work or edition have been issued to the public;

(d) a publication in the United Kingdom, or in any other country, shall not be treated as being other than the first publication by reason only of an earlier publication elsewhere, if the two publications took place within a period of not more than thirty days;

and in determining, for the purposes of paragraph (c) of this subsection, whether reproductions of a work or edition have been issued to the public, the preceding subsection shall not apply.

(3) In determining for the purposes of any provision of this Act—

(a) whether a work or other subject-matter has been published, or

(b) whether a publication of a work or other subject-matter was the first publication thereof, or

(c) whether a work or other subject-matter was published or otherwise dealt with in the lifetime of a person,

no account shall be taken of any unauthorised publication or of the doing of any other unauthorised act; and (subject to subsection (7) of section seven of this Act) a publication or other act shall for the purposes of this subsection be taken to have been unauthorised—

(i) if copyright subsisted in the work or other subject-matter and the act in question was done otherwise than by, or with the licence of, the owner of the copyright, or

(ii) if copyright did not subsist in the work or other subject-matter, and the act in question was done otherwise than by, or with the licence of, the author (or, in the case of a sound recording or a cinematograph film, or an edition of a literary, dramatic or musical work, the maker or publisher, as the case may be) or persons lawfully claiming under him:

Provided that nothing in this subsection shall affect any provisions of this Act as to the acts restricted by any copyright or as to acts constituting infringements of copyrights, or any provisions of section forty-three of this Act.

(4) References in this Act to the time at which, or the period during which, a literary, dramatic or musical work was made are references to the time or period at or during which it was first reduced to writing or some other material form.

(5) In the case of any copyright to which (whether in consequence of a partial assignment or otherwise) different persons are entitled in respect of the application of the copyright—

(a) to the doing of different acts or classes of acts, or

(b) to the doing of one or more acts or classes of acts in different countries or at different times,

the owner of the copyright, for any purpose of this Act, shall be taken to be the person who is entitled to the copyright in respect of its application to the doing of the particular act or class of acts, or, as the case may be, to the doing thereof in the particular country or at the particular time, which is relevant to the purpose in question; and, in relation to any future copyright to which different persons are prospectively entitled, references in this Act to the prospective owner of the copyright shall be construed accordingly.

(6) Without prejudice to the generality of the last preceding subsection, where under any provision of this Act a question arises whether an article of any description has been imported or sold, or otherwise dealt with, without the licence of the owner of any copyright, the owner of the copyright, for the purpose of determining that question, shall be taken to be the person entitled to the copyright in respect of its application to the making of articles of that description in the country into which the article was imported, or, as the case may be, in which it was sold or otherwise dealt with.

(7) Where the doing of anything is authorised by the grantee of a licence, or a person deriving title from the grantee, and it is within the terms (including any implied terms) of the licence for him to authorise it, it shall for the purposes of this Act be taken to be done with the licence of the grantor and of every other person (if any) upon whom the licence is binding.

(8) References in this Act to deriving title are references to deriving title either directly or indirectly.

(9) Where, in the case of copyright of any description,—

    (a) provisions contained in this Act specify certain acts as being restricted by the copyright, or as constituting infringements thereof, and

    (b) other provisions of this Act specify certain acts as not constituting infringements of the copyright,

the omission or exclusion of any matter from the latter provisions shall not be taken to extend the operation of the former provisions.

(10) Any reference in this Act to countries to which a provision of this Act extends includes a country to which that provision extends subject to exceptions, modifications or additions.

Transitional provisions, and repeals

50.—(1) The transitional provisions contained in the Seventh Schedule to this Act shall have effect for the purposes of this Act; and the provisions of the Eighth Schedule to this Act shall have effect in accordance with those transitional provisions.

[(2) *Subject to the said transitional provisions, the enactments specified in the Ninth Schedule to this Act are hereby repealed to the extent specified in the third column of that Schedule.*]

Note: Subsection (2) of this section and Sch.9 repealed by the Statute Law (Repeals) Act 1974 (c.22).

Short title, commencement and extent

51.—(1) This Act may be cited as the Copyright Act, 1956.

(2) This Act shall come into operation on such day as the Board of Trade may by order appoint; and different days may be appointed for the purposes of different provisions of this Act, and, for the purposes of any provision of this Act whereby enactments are repealed, different days may be appointed for the operation of the repeal in relation to different enactments, including different enactments contained in the same Act.

(3) It is hereby declared that this Act extends to Northern Ireland.

SCHEDULES

Section 10   FIRST SCHEDULE

FALSE REGISTRATION OF INDUSTRIAL DESIGNS

1. The provisions of this Schedule shall have effect where—
(a) copyright subsists in an artistic work, and proceedings are brought under this Act relating to that work;
(b) a corresponding design has been registered under the Act of 1949, and the copyright in the design subsisting by virtue of that registration has not expired by effluxion of time before the commencement of those proceedings; and
(c) it is proved or admitted in the proceedings that the person registered as the proprietor of the design was not the proprietor thereof for the purposes of the Act of 1949, and was so registered without the knowledge of the owner of the copyright in the artistic work.

2. For the purposes of those proceedings (but subject to the next following paragraph) the registration shall be treated as never having been effected, and accordingly, in relation to that registration, [*subsection (1) of section ten of this Act shall not apply, and*] nothing in section seven of the Act of 1949 shall be construed as affording any defence in those proceedings.

3. Notwithstanding anything in the last preceding paragraph, if in the proceedings it is proved or admitted that any act to which the proceedings relate—
(a) was done in pursuance of an assignment or licence made or granted by the person registered as proprietor of the design, and
(b) was so done in good faith in reliance upon the registration, and without notice of any proceedings for the cancellation of the registration or for rectifying the entry in the register of designs relating thereto,
[*subsection (1) of section ten of this Act shall apply in relation to that act for the purposes of the first-mentioned proceedings*] [this shall be a good defence to such proceedings.]

4. In this Schedule "the Act of 1949" means the Registered Designs Act, 1949, and "corresponding design" has the meaning assigned to it by subsection (7) of section ten of this Act.

Note: Paragraphs 2 and 3 amended by the Design Copyright Act 1968 (c.68) by deleting the words in italics and by substituting new words at the end of para.3 as shown in square brackets.

Section 11   SECOND SCHEDULE

DURATION OF COPYRIGHT IN ANONYMOUS AND PSEUDONYMOUS WORKS

1. Where the first publication of a literary, dramatic, or musical work, or of an artistic work other than a photograph, is anonymous or pseudonymous, then subject to the following provisions of this Schedule—
(a) subsection (3) of section two of this Act, or, as the case may be, subsection (4) of section three of this Act, shall not apply, and
(b) any copyright subsisting in the work by virtue of either of those sections shall continue to subsist until the end of the period of fifty years from the end of the calendar year in which the work was first published, and shall then expire.

2. The preceding paragraph shall not apply in the case of a work if, at any time before the end of the period mentioned in that paragraph, it is possible for a person without previous knowledge of the facts to ascertain the identity of the author by reasonable inquiry.

3. For the purposes of this Act a publication of a work under two or more names shall not be taken to be pseudonymous unless all those names are pseudonyms.

Section 12   THIRD SCHEDULE

WORKS OF JOINT AUTHORSHIP

1. In relation to a work of joint authorship, the references to the author in subsections (1) and (2) of section two of this Act, in subsections (2) and (3) of section three of this Act, and in paragraph 2 of the Second Schedule to this Act, shall be construed as references to any one or more of the authors.

2. In relation to a work of joint authorship, other than a work to which the next following paragraph applies, references to the author in subsection (3) of section two, in subsection (4) of section three, and in subsection (6) of section seven, of this Act, shall be construed as references to the author who died last.

3.—(1) This paragraph applies to any work of joint authorship which was first published under two or more names, of which one or more (but not all) were pseudonyms.

(2) This paragraph also applies to any work of joint authorship which was first published under two or more names all of which were pseudonyms, if, at any time within the period of fifty years from the end of the calendar year in which the work was first published, it is possible for a person without previous knowledge of the facts to ascertain the identity of any one or more (but not all) of the authors by reasonable inquiry.

(3) In relation to a work to which this paragraph applies, references to the author in subsection (3) of section two of this Act, and in subsection (4) of section three of this Act, shall be construed as references to the author whose identity was disclosed, or, if the identity of two or more of the authors was disclosed, as references to that one of those authors who died last.

(4) For the purposes of this paragraph the identity of an author shall be taken to have been disclosed if either—

(a) in his case, the name under which the work was published was not a pseudonym, or

(b) it is possible to ascertain his identity as mentioned in subparagraph (2) of this paragraph.

4.—(1) In relation to a work of joint authorship of which one or more of the authors are persons to whom this paragraph applies, subsection (1) of section four of this Act shall have effect as if the author or authors, other than persons to whom this paragraph applies, had been the sole author, or (as the case may be) sole joint authors of the work.

(2) This paragraph applies, in the case of a work, to any person such that, if he had been the sole author of the work, copyright would not have subsisted in the work, by virtue of Part I of this Act.

5. In the proviso to subsection (6) of section six of this Act, the reference to other excerpts from works by the author of the passage in question—

(a) shall be taken to include a reference to excerpts from works by the author of that passage in collaboration with any other person, or

(b) if the passage in question is from a work of joint authorship, shall be taken to include a reference to excerpts from works by any one or more of the authors of that passage, or by any one or more of those authors in collaboration with any other person.

Subject to the preceding provisions of this Schedule, any reference in this Act to the author of a work shall (unless it is otherwise expressly provided) be construed, in relation to a work of joint authorship, as a reference to all the authors of the work.

Sections 23, 30, 47   FOURTH SCHEDULE

Provisions as to Performing Right Tribunal

1.—(1) Subject to the provisions of this paragraph, the members of the tribunal shall hold office for such period as may be determined at the time of their respective appointments: and a person who ceases to hold office as a member of the tribunal shall be eligible for re-appointment.

(2) Any member of the tribunal may at any time by notice in writing to the Board of Trade, or, in the case of the chairman of the tribunal, to the Lord Chancellor, resign his appointment.

(3) The Board of Trade, or, in the case of the chairman of the tribunal, the Lord Chancellor, may declare the office of any member of the tribunal vacant on the ground of his unfitness to continue in office or incapacity to perform the duties thereof.

2. If any member of the tribunal is, by reason of illness, absence or other reasonable

cause, for the time being unable to perform the duties of his office, either generally or in relation to any particular proceedings, the Board of Trade, or, in the case of the chairman of the tribunal, the Lord Chancellor, may appoint some other duly qualified person to discharge the duties of that member for any period, not exceeding six months at one time, or, as the case may be, in relation to those proceedings; and a person so appointed shall, during that period or in relation to those proceedings, have the same powers as the person in whose place he is appointed.

3. If at any time there are more than two members of the tribunal, in addition to the chairman, then, for the purposes of any proceedings, the tribunal may consist of the chairman together with any two or more of those members.

4. If the members of the tribunal dealing with any reference or application are unable to agree as to the order to be made by the tribunal, a decision shall be taken by the votes of the majority; and, in the event of an equality of votes, the chairman shall be entitled to a second or casting vote.

5. The tribunal may order that the costs or expenses of any proceedings before it incurred by any party shall be paid by any other party, and may tax or settle the amount of any costs or expenses to be paid under any such order or direct in what manner they are to be taxed.

6.—(1) The Lord Chancellor may make rules as to the procedure in connection with the making of references and applications to the tribunal, and for regulating proceedings before the tribunal and, subject to the approval of the Treasury, as to the fees chargeable in respect of those proceedings.

(2) Any such rules may apply in relation to the tribunal—

- (a) as respects proceedings in England and Wales, any of the provisions of the Arbitration Act, 1950, and
- (b) as respects proceedings in Northern Ireland, any of the provisions of the Arbitration Act (Northern Ireland), 1937.

(3) Any such rules may include provision—

- (a) for prescribing the period within which, after the tribunal has given its decision in any proceedings, a request may be made to the tribunal to refer a question of law to the court;
- (b) for requiring notice of any intended application to the court under subsection (2) of section thirty of this Act to be given to the tribunal and to the other parties to the proceedings, and for limiting the time within which any such notice is to be given;
- (c) for suspending, or authorising or requiring the tribunal to suspend, the operation of orders of the tribunal, in cases where, after giving its decision, the tribunal refers a question of law to the court;
- (d) for modifying, in relation to orders of the tribunal whose operation is suspended, the operation of any provisions of Part IV of this Act as to the effect of orders made thereunder;
- (e) for the publication of notices, or the taking of any other steps, for securing that persons affected by the suspension of an order of the tribunal will be informed of its suspension;
- (f) for regulating or prescribing any other matters incidental to or consequential upon any request, application, order or decision under section thirty of this Act.

(4) Provision shall be made by rules of court for limiting the time for instituting proceedings under subsection (2) of section thirty of this Act, and for authorising or requiring the court, where it makes an order directing the tribunal to refer a question of law to the court, to provide in the order for suspending the operation of any order made by the tribunal in the proceedings in which the question of law arose.

(5) In this paragraph "the court" has the same meaning as in section thirty of this Act.

7. As respects proceedings in Scotland, the tribunal shall have the like powers for securing the attendance of witnesses and the production of documents, and with regard to the examination of witnesses on oath, as if the tribunal were an arbiter under a submission.

8. Without prejudice to any method available by law for the proof of orders of the tribunal, a document purporting to be a copy of any such order, and to be certified by the chairman of the tribunal to be a true copy thereof, shall, in any legal proceedings, be sufficient evidence of the order unless the contrary is proved.

Sections 24, 37 FIFTH SCHEDULE

APPOINTMENT OF TELEVISION COPYRIGHT ORGANISATIONS BY BRITISH BROADCASTING CORPORA-
TION AND INDEPENDENT [BROADCASTING] AUTHORITY

1. In this Schedule—
  (a) references to a right to which this Schedule applies are references to the copyright (including any future copyright) in any television broadcast, in so far as the copyright relates, or when it comes into existence will relate, to the acts specified in paragraph (c) of subsection (4) of section fourteen of this Act;
  (b) references to the purposes of this Schedule are references to the purposes of negotiating or granting licences in respect of rights to which this Schedule applies.

2. The Corporation and the Authority may jointly appoint an organisation for the purposes of this Schedule; and if they do so, no other organisation shall be appointed by them or either of them for those purposes until the appointment of that organisation has been duly terminated.

3. Subject to the last preceding paragraph, the Corporation or the Authority, or each of them, may appoint an organisation for the purposes of this Schedule; and if an organisation is so appointed by the Corporation or by the Authority, no other organisation shall be appointed for the purposes of this Schedule by the Corporation or the Authority, as the case may be, until the appointment of that organisation has been duly terminated.

4. A right to which this Schedule applies shall not be assignable by the Corporation or by the Authority except to an organisation duly appointed for the purposes of this Schedule; and where such a right has been assigned to such an organisation, it shall not be assignable by the organisation except to the Corporation or the Authority, as the case may be, or to another organisation subsequently appointed for the purposes of this Schedule.

5.—(1) Neither the Corporation nor the Authority shall authorise any organisation or person, other than any person in their employment under a contract of service, to negotiate or act for them with respect to the granting of licences in respect of rights to which this Schedule applies, except an organisation duly appointed for the purposes of this Schedule.

(2) An organisation appointed for the purposes of this Schedule shall not authorise any other organisation or person, other than any person in their employment under a contract of service, to negotiate or act for them, or for the Corporation or the Authority, with respect to the granting of licences in respect of rights to which this Schedule applies.

6. The appointment, or the termination of the appointment, of an organisation for the purposes of this Schedule shall not have effect unless, not less than fourteen days before the appointment or termination is to take effect, a notice is published in the London Gazette, the Edinburgh Gazette and the Belfast Gazette, specifying the name and address of the organisation, and the date on which the appointment or termination is to take effect, and stating whether the appointment, or termination of appointment, is made by the Corporation or the Authority or by both of them.

7. Where notice of the appointment of an organisation for the purposes of this Schedule has been given under the last preceding paragraph, the organisation shall be taken for the purposes of this Act to be authorised to act in accordance with the appointment until their appointment is duly terminated in pursuance of a notice published in accordance with that paragraph.

Section 45 [SIXTH SCHEDULE

AMENDMENT OF DRAMATIC AND MUSICAL PERFORMERS' PROTECTION ACT, 1925

PART I

NEW SECTIONS 1A AND 1B

Penalties for making, etc., cinematograph films without consent of performers

1A. Subject to the provisions of this Act, if any person knowingly—
  (a) *makes a cinematograph film, directly or indirectly, from or by means of the performance of any dramatic or musical work without the consent in writing of the performers, or*

(b) *sells or lets for hire, or distributes for the purposes of trade, or by way of trade exposes or offers for sale or hire, a cinematograph film made in contravention of this Act, or*

(c) *uses for the purposes of exhibition to the public a cinematograph film made in contravention of this Act,*

he shall be guilty of an offence under this Act, and shall be liable on summary conviction to a fine not exceeding fifty pounds:

Provided that, where a person is charged with an offence under paragraph (a) of this section, it shall be a defence to prove that the cinematograph film was made for his private and domestic use only.

Penalties for broadcasting without consent of performers

1B. *Subject to the provisions of this Act, any person who, otherwise than by the use of a record or a cinematograph film, knowingly broadcasts a performance of any dramatic or musical work, or any part of such a performance, without the consent in writing of the performers shall be guilty of an offence under this Act, and shall be liable on summary conviction to a fine not exceeding fifty pounds.*

PART II

NEW SECTIONS 3A AND 3B

Special defences

3A. *Notwithstanding anything in the preceding provisions of this Act, it shall be a defence to any proceedings under this Act to prove—*

(a) *that the record, cinematograph film or broadcast to which the proceedings relate was made only for the purpose of reporting current events, or*

(b) *that the inclusion of the performance in question in the record, cinematograph film or broadcast to which the proceedings relate was only by way of background or was otherwise only incidental to the principal matters comprised or represented in the record, film or broadcast.*

Consent on behalf of performers

3B. *Where in any proceedings under this Act it is proved—*

(a) *that the record, cinematograph film or broadcast to which the proceedings relate was made with the consent in writing of a person who, at the time of giving the consent, represented that he was authorised by the performers to give it on their behalf, and*

(b) *that the person making the record, film or broadcast had no reasonable grounds for believing that the person giving the consent was not so authorised,*

the provisions of this Act shall apply as if it had been proved that the performers had themselves consented in writing to the making of the record, film or broadcast.

PART III

MINOR AND CONSEQUENTIAL AMENDMENTS

Provision amended	Amendment
Section one ...	At the beginning of the section there shall be inserted the words
	"Subject to the provisions of this Act"; and at the end of the section, for the words "not made for purposes of trade" there shall be substituted the words "made for his private and domestic use only."
Section three ...	For the words "records or" there shall be substituted the words "records, cinematograph films."
Section four ...	At the end of the definition of the expression "record" there shall be inserted the words "including the soundtrack of a cinematograph film"; and at the end of the section there shall be inserted the following definitions:

Provision amended	*Amendment*

"The expression 'cinematograph film' means any print, negative, tape or other article on which a performance of a dramatic or musical work or part thereof is recorded for the purposes of visual reproduction, and any reference to the making of a cinematograph film is a reference to the carrying out of any process whereby such a performance or part thereof is so recorded;

The expression 'broadcast' means broadcast by wireless telegraphy (within the meaning of the Wireless Telegraphy Act, 1949) whether by way of sound broadcasting or of television."]

Note: The provisions of this Schedule and s.45 repealed by the Dramatic and Musical Performers' Protection Act, 1958 (6 & 7 Eliz. 2, c.44), which also repealed the Dramatic and Musical Performers' Protection Act, 1925 (15 & 16 Geo. 5, c.46).

Section 50 SEVENTH SCHEDULE

Transitional Provisions

PART I

Provisions Relating to Part I of Act

Conditions for subsistence of copyright

1. In the application of sections two and three to works first published before the commencement of those sections, subsection (2) of section two, and subsection (3) of section three, shall apply as if paragraphs (b) and (c) of those subsections were omitted.

Duration of copyright

2. In relation to any photograph taken before the commencement of section three, subsection (4) of that section shall not apply, but, subject to subsection (3) of that section, copyright subsisting in the photograph by virtue of that section shall continue to subsist until the end of the period of fifty years from the end of the calendar year in which the photograph was taken, and shall then expire.

Ownership of copyright

3.—(1) Subsections (2) to (4) of section four shall not apply—
  (a) to any work as mentioned in subsection (2) or subsection (4) of that section, if the work was so made before the commencement of that section, or
  (b) to any work made as mentioned in subsection (3) of that section, if the work was or is so made in pursuance of a contract made before the commencement of that section.

(2) In relation to any work to which the preceding sub-paragraph applies, subsection (1) of section four shall have effect subject to the proviso set out in paragraph 1 of the Eighth Schedule to this Act (being the proviso to subsection (1) of section five of the Act of 1911).

Infringements of copyright

4. For the purposes of section five, the fact that, to a person's knowledge, the making of an article constituted an infringement of copyright under the Act of 1911, or would have constituted such an infringement if the article had been made in the place into which it is imported, shall have the like effect as if, to that person's knowledge, the making of the article had constituted an infringement of copyright under this Act.

5. Subsection (7) of section six does not apply to assignments made or licences granted before the commencement of that section.

6.—(1) References in section eight to records previously made by, or with the licence of, the owner of the copyright in a work include references to records previously made by, or with the consent of, the owner of the copyright in that work under the Act of 1911.

(2) The repeal by this Act of any provisions of section nineteen of the Act of 1911, or of the provisions of the Copyright Order Confirmation (Mechanical Instruments: Royalties) Act, 1928, shall not affect the operation of those provisions, or of any regulations or order made thereunder, in relation to a record made before the repeal.

7.—(1) In relation to a painting, drawing, engraving, photograph or cinematograph film made before the commencement of section nine, subsection (6) of that section shall apply if, by virtue of subsection (3) or subsection (4) of that section, the making of the painting, drawing, engraving, photograph or film would not have constituted an infringement of copyright under this Act if this Act had been in operation at the time when it was made.

(2) In subsection (10) of section nine, the reference to construction by, or with the licence of, the owner of the copyright in any architectural drawings or plans includes a reference to construction by, or with the licence of, the person who, at the time of the construction, was the owner of the copyright in the drawings or plans under the Act of 1911, or under any enactment repealed by that Act.

8.—(1) Section ten and the First Schedule to this Act do not apply to artistic works made before the commencement of that section.

(2) Copyright shall not subsist by virtue of this Act in any artistic work made before the commencement of section ten which, at the time when the work was made, constituted a design capable of registration under the Registered Designs Act, 1949, or under the enactments repealed by that Act, and was used, or intended to be used, as a model or pattern to be multiplied by any industrial process.

(3) The provisions set out in paragraph 2 of the Eighth Schedule to this Act (being the relevant provisions of the Copyright (Industrial Designs) Rules, 1949) shall apply for the purposes of the last preceding sub-paragraph.

9.—(1) Where, before the repeal by this Act of section three of the Act of 1911, a person has, in the case of a work, given the notice requisite under the proviso set out in paragraph 3 of the Eighth Schedule to this Act (being the proviso to the said section three), then, as respects reproductions by that person of that work after the repeal of that section by this Act, that proviso shall have effect as if it had been re-enacted in this Act as a proviso to subsection (2) of section one:

Provided that the said proviso shall so have effect subject to the provisions set out in paragraphs 4 and 5 of the Eighth Schedule to this Act (being so much of subsection (1) of sections sixteen and seventeen respectively of the Act of 1911 as is applicable to the said proviso), as if those provisions had also been re-enacted in this Act.

(2) For the purposes of the operation of the said proviso in accordance with the preceding sub-paragraph, any regulations made by the Board of Trade thereunder before the repeal of section three of the Act of 1911 shall have effect as if they had been made under this Act, and the power of the Board of Trade to make further regulations thereunder shall apply as if the proviso had been re-enacted as mentioned in the preceding sub-paragraph.

Works of joint authorship

10.—(1) Notwithstanding anything in section eleven, or in the Third Schedule to this Act, copyright shall not subsist by virtue of Part I of this Act in any work of joint authorship first published before the commencement of section eleven, if the period of copyright had expired before the commencement of that section.

(2) In this paragraph "the period of copyright" means whichever is the longer of the following periods, that is to say,—

(a) the life of the author who died first and a term of fifty years after his death, and

(b) the life of the author who died last.

PART II

PROVISIONS RELATING TO PART II OF ACT

Sound recordings

11. In the case of a sound recording made before the commencement of section twelve,

subsection (3) of that section shall apply with the substitution, for the period mentioned in that subsection, of the period of fifty years from the end of the calendar year in which the recording was made.

12. Subsection (6) of section twelve shall not apply to a sound recording made before the commencement of that section.

13. Notwithstanding anything in section twelve, copyright shall not subsist by virtue of that section in a sound recording made before the first day of July, nineteen hundred and twelve, unless, immediately before the commencement of that section, a corresponding copyright subsisted, in relation to that recording, by virtue of subsection (8) of section nineteen of the Act of 1911 (which relates to records made before the commencement of that Act).

Cinematograph films

14. Section thirteen shall not apply to cinematograph films made before the commencement of that section.

15. Where a cinematograph film made before the commencement of section thirteen was an original dramatic work within the definition of "dramatic work" set out in paragraph 9 of the Eighth Schedule to this Act (being the definition thereof in the Act of 1911), the provisions of this Act, including the provisions of this Schedule other than this paragraph, shall have effect in relation to the film as if it had been an original dramatic work within the meaning of this Act; and the person who was the author of the work for the purposes of the Act of 1911 shall be taken to be the author thereof for the purposes of the said provisions as applied by this paragraph.

16. The provisions of this Act shall have effect in relation to photographs forming part of a cinematograph film made before the commencement of section thirteen as those provisions have effect in relation to photographs not forming part of a cinematograph film.

Television broadcasts and sound broadcasts

17. Copyright shall not subsist by virtue of section fourteen in any television broadcast or sound broadcast made before the commencement of that section.

18. For the purposes of subsection (3) of section fourteen, a previous television broadcast or sound broadcast shall be disregarded if it was made before the commencement of that section.

Supplementary

19. For the purposes of subsections (2) to (4) of section sixteen, the fact that, to a person's knowledge, the making of an article constituted an infringement of copyright under the Act of 1911, or would have constituted such an infringement if the article had been made in the place into which it is imported, shall have the like effect as if, to that person's knowledge, the making of the article had constituted an infringement of copyright under this Act.

PART III

Provisions Relating to Part III of Act

20. Nothing in section seventeen shall apply to any infringement of copyright under the Act of 1911, or shall affect any proceedings under that Act, whether begun before or after the commencement of that section.

21. Section eighteen shall not apply with respect to any article made, or, as the case may be, imported, before the commencement of that section; but, notwithstanding the repeal by this Act of section seven of the Act of 1911 (which contains provisions corresponding to subsection (1) of section eighteen), proceedings may (subject to the provisions of that Act) be brought or continued by virtue of the said section seven in respect of any article made or imported before the repeal, although the proceedings relate to the conversion or detention thereof after the repeal took effect.

22. Section nineteen shall not apply to any licence granted before the commencement of that section, and shall not affect any proceedings under the Act of 1911, whether begun before or after the commencement of that section.

23. For the purposes of section twenty-one the definition of "infringing copy" in section eighteen shall apply as if any reference to copyright in that definition included a reference to copyright under the Act of 1911.

24. Where before the commencement of section twenty-two a notice had been given in respect of a work under section fourteen of the Act of 1911 (which contains provisions corresponding to section twenty-two), and that notice had not been withdrawn and had not otherwise ceased to have effect before the commencement of section twenty-two, the notice shall have effect after the commencement of that section as if it had been duly given thereunder.

Provided that a notice shall not continue to have effect by virtue of this paragraph after the end of the period of six months beginning with the commencement of section twenty-two.

PART IV

PROVISIONS RELATING TO PART IV OF ACT

25. The provisions of Part IV of this Act shall apply in relation to licence schemes made before the commencement of that Part as they apply in relation to licence schemes made thereafter, as if references in Part IV of this Act to copyright included references to copyright under the Act of 1911.

26. In section twenty-seven, references to a refusal or failure to grant or procure the grant of a licence, or to a proposal that a licence should be granted, do not include a refusal or failure which occurred, or a proposal made, before the commencement of that section.

PART V

PROVISIONS RELATING TO PART V OF ACT

27. In section thirty-three, subsection (2) shall not apply to works made before the commencement of that section, and subsection (3) shall not apply to works first published before the commencement of that section.

PART VI

PROVISIONS RELATING TO PART VI OF ACT

Assignments, licences and bequests

28.—(1) Where by virtue of any provision of this Act copyright subsists in a work, any document or event which—

  (a) was made or occurred before the commencement of that provision, and

  (b) had any operation affecting the title to copyright in the work under the Act of 1911, or would have had such an operation if the Act of 1911 had continued in force,

shall have the corresponding operation in relation to the copyright in the work under this Act:

Provided that, if the operation of any such document was or would have been limited to a period specified in the document, it shall not have any operation in relation to the copyright under this Act, except in so far as that period extends beyond the commencement of the provision of this Act by virtue of which copyright subsists in the work.

(2) For the purposes of the operation of a document in accordance with the preceding sub-paragraph,—

  (a) expressions used in the document shall be construed in accordance with their effect immediately before the commencement of the provision in question, notwithstanding that a different meaning is assigned to them for the purposes of this Act; and

  (b) subsection (1) of section thirty-seven shall not apply.

(3) Without prejudice to the generality of sub-paragraph (1) of this paragraph, the proviso set out in paragraph 6 of the Eighth Schedule to this Act (being the proviso to subsection (2) of section five of the Act of 1911) shall apply to assignments and licences having effect in relation to copyright under this Act in accordance with that sub-paragraph, as if that proviso had been re-enacted in this Act.

(4) In relation to copyright under this Act in a sound recording or in a cinematograph film, the preceding provisions of this paragraph shall apply subject to the following modifications that is to say,—

(a) in the case of a sound recording, references to the copyright under the Act of 1911 shall be construed as references to the copyright under that Act in records embodying the recording, and

(b) in the case of a cinematograph film, references to the copyright under the Act of 1911 shall be construed as references to any copyright under that Act in the film (in so far as it constituted a dramatic work for the purposes of the Act of 1911) or in photographs forming part of the film.

(5) In this paragraph "operation affecting the title", in relation to copyright under the Act of 1911, means any operation affecting the ownership of that copyright, or creating, transferring or terminating an interest, right or licence in respect of that copyright.

29. Section thirty-eight shall not apply to a bequest contained in the will, or a codicil to the will, of a testator who died before the commencement of that section.

(2) In the case of an author who died before the commencement of section thirty-eight, the provisions set out in paragraph 7 of the Eighth Schedule to this Act (being subsection (2) of section seventeen of the Act of 1911) shall have effect as if it had been re-enacted in this Act.

Crown and Government departments

30. Subsection (4) of section thirty-nine shall apply in relation to photographs taken before the commencement of that section as if the proviso to that subsection were omitted.

31.—(1) In the application of subsection (5) of section thirty-nine to a sound recording made before the commencement of that section, paragraph (b) of that subsection shall apply as if for the period mentioned in that paragraph there were substituted the period of fifty years from the end of the calendar year in which the recording was made.

(2) With respect to cinematograph films made before the commencement of section thirty-nine—

(a) subsection (5) of that section shall not apply, but

(b) in the case of a cinematograph film made as mentioned in that subsection, but before the commencement of section thirty-nine, if it was an original dramatic work as mentioned in paragraph 15 of this Schedule, the provisions of subsections (1) to (3) of section thirty-nine shall apply in accordance with that paragraph, and

(c) in relation to photographs forming part of such a cinematograph film the provisions of subsections (1), (2) and (4) of section thirty-nine (as modified by the last preceding paragraph) shall apply as they apply in relation to photographs not forming part of a cinematograph film.

False attribution of authorship

32.—(1) Paragraphs (b) and (c) of subsection (2) of section forty-three shall apply to any such act as is therein mentioned, if done after the commencement of that section, notwithstanding that the name in question was inserted or affixed before the commencement of that section.

(2) Subject to the preceding sub-paragraph, no act done before the commencement of section forty-three shall be actionable by virtue of that section.

(3) In this paragraph "name" has the same meaning as in section forty-three.

Other provisions

33.—(1) In the application of subsection (2) of section forty-nine to a publication effected before the commencement of that section, the reference in paragraph (d) to thirty days shall be treated as a reference to fourteen days.

(2) For the purposes of the application of subsection (3) of section forty-nine to an act done before the commencement of a provision of this Act to which that subsection applies, references to copyright include references to copyright under the Act of 1911, and, in relation to copyright under that Act, references to the licence of the owner are references to the consent or acquiescence of the owner.

PART VII

WORKS MADE BEFORE 1ST JULY, 1912

34.—(1) This part of this Schedule applies to works made before the first day of July, nineteen hundred and twelve.

(2) In this Part of this Schedule "right conferred by the Act of 1911", in relation to a work, means such a substituted right as, by virtue of section twenty-four of the Act of 1911, was conferred in place of a right subsisting immediately before the commencement of that Act.

35. Notwithstanding anything in Part I of this Schedule, neither subsection (1) nor subsection (2) of section two, nor subsection (2) or subsection (3) of section three, shall apply to a work to which this Part of this Schedule applies, unless a right conferred by the Act of 1911 subsisted in the work immediately before the commencement of section two or section three as the case may be.

36.—(1) Where, in the case of a dramatic or musical work to which this Part of this Schedule applies, the right conferred by the Act of 1911 did not include the sole right to perform the work in public, then, in so far as copyright subsists in the work by virtue of this Act, the acts restricted by the copyright shall be treated as not including those specified in sub-paragraph (3) of this paragraph.

(2) Where, in the case of a dramatic or musical work to which this Part of this Schedule applies, the right conferred by the Act of 1911 consisted only of the sole right to perform the work in public, then, in so far as copyright subsists in the work by virtue of this Act, the acts restricted by the copyright shall be treated as consisting only of those specified in sub-paragraph (3) of this paragraph.

(3) The said acts are—

  (a) performing the work or an adaptation thereof in public;

  (b) broadcasting the work or an adaptation thereof;

  [(c) including the work or an adaptation thereof in a cable programme.]

37. Where a work to which this Part of this Schedule applies consists of an essay, article or portion forming part of and first published in a review, magazine or other periodical or work of a like nature, and immediately before the commencement of section two a right of publishing the work in a separate form subsisted by virtue of the provision set out in paragraph 8 of the Eighth Schedule to this Act (being the note appended to the First Schedule to the Act of 1911), that provision shall have effect, in relation to that work, as if it had been re-enacted in this Act with the substitution, for the word "right" where it first occurs, of the word "copyright".

38.—(1) Without prejudice to the generality of sub-paragraph (1) of paragraph 28 of this Schedule, the provisions of this paragraph shall have effect where—

  (a) the author of a work to which this Part of this Schedule applies had, before the commencement of the Act of 1911, made such an assignment or grant as is mentioned in paragraph (a) of the proviso to subsection (1) of section twenty-four of that Act (which relates to transactions whereby the author had assigned, or granted an interest in, the copyright or performing right in a work for the full term of that right under the law in force before the Act of 1911), and

  (b) copyright subsists in the work by virtue of any provision of this Act.

(2) If, before the commencement of that provision of this Act, any event occurred, or notice was given, which in accordance with paragraph (a) of the said proviso had any operation affecting the ownership of the right conferred by the Act of 1911 in relation to the work, or creating, transferring or terminating an interest, right or licence in respect of that right, that event or notice shall have the corresponding operation in relation to the copyright in the work under this Act.

(3) Any right which, at a time after the commencement of that provision of this Act, would, by virtue of paragraph (a) of the said proviso, have been exercisable in relation to the work, or to the right conferred by the Act of 1911, if this Act had not been passed, shall be exercisable in relation to the work or to the copyright therein under this Act, as the case may be.

(4) If, in accordance with paragraph (a) of the said proviso, the right conferred by the Act of 1911 would have reverted to the author or his personal representatives on the date referred to in that paragraph, and the said date falls after the commencement of the provision of this Act whereby copyright subsists in the work, then on that date—

(a) the copyright in the work under this Act shall revert to the author or his personal representatives, as the case may be, and

(b) any interest of any other person in that copyright which subsists on that date by virtue of any document made before the commencement of the Act of 1911 shall thereupon determine.

PART VIII

General and Supplementary Provisions

39.—(1) The provisions of this paragraph shall have effect for the construction of any reference in any provision of this Act—

(a) to countries to which that provision extends, or

(b) to qualified persons.

(2) Where, at any time after the commencement of any provisions of this Act, a provision which contains such a reference—

(a) has not yet been extended by virtue of section thirty-one to a country to which the Act of 1911 extended (or which, by virtue of that Act, was to be treated as a country to which it extended), and

(b) has not been applied in the case of that country by virtue of section thirty-two, then, with respect to any time before the provision is so extended or applied, the reference shall be construed as if the provision did extend to that country.

(3) For the purpose of determining whether copyright subsists in any work or other subject-matter at a time when a provision containing such a reference has been extended to a country other than the United Kingdom, the reference shall be construed, in relation to past events, as if that provision had always been in operation and had always extended to that country.

(4) In relation to photographs taken before the commencement of section three, and to sound recordings made before the commencement of section twelve, the definition of "qualified person" in subsection (5) of section one shall apply as if, in paragraph (b) of that subsection, for the words "body incorporated under the laws of" there were substituted the words "body corporate which has established a place of business in".

[**40.**—(1) *The provisions of the two next following sub-paragraphs shall apply where—*

(a) *immediately before the date on which any provisions of the Act of 1911 (in this paragraph referred to as "the repealed provisions") are repealed in the law of the United Kingdom by this Act, the repealed provisions have effect as applied by an Order in Council made in respect of a foreign country under section twenty-nine of the Act of 1911; and*

(b) *no Order in Council under section thirty-two of this Act, applying any provisions of this Act in the case of that country, is made so as to come into force on or before that date.*

(2) *The repealed provisions, as applied by the Order in Council under section twenty-nine of the Act of 1911 (or by that Order as varied by any subsequent Order thereunder), shall continue to have effect, notwithstanding the repeal, until the occurrence of whichever of the following events first occurs, that is to say—*

(a) *the revocation of the Order in Council under section twenty-nine of the Act of 1911;*

(b) *the coming into operation of an Order in Council under section thirty-two of this Act applying any of the provisions of this Act in the case of the foreign country in question;*

(c) *the expiration of the period of two years beginning with the date mentioned in the preceding sub-paragraph.*

(3) *For the purposes of continuing, varying or terminating the operation of the repealed provisions in accordance with the last preceding sub-paragraph, and for the purposes of any proceedings arising out of the operation of those provisions in accordance with that sub-paragraph, all the provisions of the Act of 1911 (including the power to revoke or vary Orders in Council under section twenty-nine of that Act) shall be treated as continuing in force as if none of those provisions had been repealed by this Act.*

(4) *In relation to a country in respect of which an Order in Council has been made under subsection (3) of section twenty-six of the Act of 1911 (which relates to countries*

therein referred to as self-governing dominions to which that Act does not extend), the preceding provisions of this paragraph shall apply as they apply in relation to a foreign country, with the substitution, for references to section twenty-nine of the Act of 1911, of references to the said subsection (3).]

41. In so far as the Act of 1911 or any Order in Council made thereunder forms part of the law of any country other than the United Kingdom, at a time after that Act has been wholly or partly repealed in the law of the United Kingdom, it shall, so long as it forms part of the law of that country, be construed and have effect as if that Act had not been so repealed.

42. The mention of any particular matter in the preceding provisions of this Schedule with regard to the repeal of any of the provisions of the Act of 1911 shall not affect the general application to this Act of section thirty-eight of the Interpretation Act, 1889[iv] (which relates to the effect of repeals), either in relation to the Act of 1911 or to any other enactment repealed by this Act.

43. For the purposes of the application, by virtue of any of the preceding paragraphs of this Schedule, of any of the provisions set out in the Eighth Schedule to this Act,—

(a) the expressions of which definitions are set out in paragraph 9 of that Schedule (being the definitions of those expressions in the Act of 1911) shall, notwithstanding anything in this Act, be construed in accordance with those definitions; and

(b) where, for those purposes, any of those provisions is to be treated as if re-enacted in this Act, it shall be treated as if it had been so re-enacted with the substitution, for the words "this Act", wherever the reference is to the passing or the commencement of the Act of 1911, of the words "the Copyright Act, 1911".

44. Without prejudice to the operation of any of the preceding provisions of this Schedule—

(a) any enactment or other document referring to an enactment repealed by this Act shall be construed as referring (or as including a reference) to the corresponding enactment of this Act;

(b) any enactment or other document referring to copyright, or to works in which copyright subsists, if apart from this Act it would be construed as referring to copyright under the Act of 1911, or to works in which copyright subsists under that Act, shall be construed as referring (or as including a reference) to copyright under this Act, or, as the case may be, to works or any other subject-matter in which copyright subsists under this Act;

(c) any reference to an enactment or other document to the grant of an interest in copyright by licence shall be construed, in relation to copyright under this Act, as a reference to the grant of a licence in respect of that copyright.

45.—(1) Except in so far as it is otherwise expressly provided in this Schedule, the provisions of this Act apply in relation to things existing at the commencement of those provisions as they apply in relation to things coming into existence thereafter.

(2) For the purposes of any reference in this Schedule to works, sound recordings or cinematograph films made before the commencement of a provision of this Act, a work, recording or film, the making of which extended over a period, shall not be taken to have been so made unless the making of it was completed before the commencement of that provision.

46.—(1) Any reference in this Schedule to a numbered section shall, unless the reference is to a section of a specified Act, be construed as a reference to the section bearing that number in this Act.

(2) Any reference in this Schedule to the commencement of a provision of this Act is a reference to the date on which that provision comes into operation as part of the law of the United Kingdom.

47.—(1) In this Schedule "photograph" has the meaning assigned to it in the definition set out in paragraph 9 of the Eighth Schedule to this Act, and not the meaning assigned to it by section forty-eight.

[iv] *Editorial Note:* The Interpretation Act 1889 (52 & 53 Vict., c.63) was repealed almost entirely by the Interpretation Act 1978 (c.30); see ss.16, 17, 22, 26 of Sch.2, Pt. I to the latter Act.

(2) In this Schedule "the Act of 1911" means the Copyright Act, 1911.

Notes:

(1) Paragraph 36(3) was amended by the Cable and Broadcasting Act 1984 (c.46) and is printed as amended.
(2) Paragraph 40 was repealed by the Statute Law (Repeals) Act 1986 (c.12).

Section 50   EIGHTH SCHEDULE

PROVISIONS OF COPYRIGHT ACT, 1911, AND RULES, REFERRED TO IN SEVENTH SCHEDULE

1. *Proviso to s.5(1) of the (referred to in paragraph 3 of Seventh Schedule):*Provided that—

(a) where, in the case of an engraving, photograph, or portrait, the plate or other original was ordered by some other person and was made for valuable consideration in pursuance of that order, then, in the absence of any agreement to the contrary, the person by whom such plate or other original was ordered shall be the first owner of the copyright; and

(b) where the author was in the employment of some other person under a contract of service or apprenticeship and the work was made in the course of his employment by that person, the person by whom the author was employed shall, in the absence of any agreement to the contrary, be the first owner of the copyright, but where the work is an article or other contribution to a newspaper, magazine, or similar periodical, there shall, in the absence of any agreement to the contrary, be deemed to be reserved to the author a right to restrain the publication of the work, otherwise than as part of a newspaper, magazine, or similar periodical.

2. *Rule 2 of the Copyright (Industrial Design) Rules, 1949 (referred to in paragraph 8 of Seventh Schedule):*

A design shall be deemed to be used as a model or pattern to be multiplied by any industrial process—

(a) when the design is reproduced or is intended to be reproduced on more than fifty single articles, unless all the articles in which the design is reproduced or is intended to be reproduced together form only a single set of articles as defined in subsection (1) of section 44 of the Registered Designs Act, 1949, or

(b) when the design is to be applied to—
(i) printed paper hangings,
(ii) carpets, floor cloths or oil cloths, manufactured or sold in lengths or pieces,
(iii) textile piece goods, or textile goods manufactured or sold in lengths or pieces, or
(iv) lace, not made by hand.

3. *Proviso to s.3 of the Copyright Act, 1911 (referred to in paragraph 9 of Seventh Schedule):*

Provided that at any time after the expiration of twenty-five years, or in the case of a work in which copyright subsists at the passing of this Act thirty years, from the death of the author of a published work, copyright in the work shall not be deemed to be infringed by the reproduction of the work for sale if the person reproducing the work proves that he has given the prescribed notice in writing of his intention to reproduce the work, and that he has paid in the prescribed manner to, or for the benefit of, the owner of the copyright royalties in respect of all copies of the work sold by him calculated at the rate of ten per cent on the price at which he publishes the work; and, for the purposes of this proviso, the Board of Trade may make regulations prescribing the mode in which notices are to be given, and the particulars to be given in such notices, and the mode, time, and frequency of the payment of royalties, including (if they think fit) regulations requiring payment in advance or otherwise securing the payment of royalties.

4. *S.16(1) of the Copyright Act, 1911 (referred to in paragraph 9 of Seventh Schedule):*

In the case of a work of joint authorship ... references in this Act to the period after the expiration of any specified number of years from the death of the author shall be construed as references to the period after the expiration of the like number of years from the death of the author who dies first or after the death of the author who dies last, whichever period may be the shorter ...

5. *S.17(1) of Copyright Act, 1911 (referred to in paragraph 9 of Seventh Schedule):*

In the case of a literary, dramatic or musical work, or an engraving, in which copyright subsists at the date of the death of the author or, in the case of a work of joint authorship, at or immediately before the date of the death of the author who dies last, but which has not been published, nor, in the case of a dramatic or musical work, been performed in public, nor, in the case of a lecture, been delivered in public, before that date, ... the proviso to section three of this Act shall ... apply as if the author had died at the date of such publication or performance or delivery in public as aforesaid.

6. *Proviso to s.5(2) of the Copyright Act, 1911 (referred to in paragraph 28 of Seventh Schedule):*

Provided that, where the author of a work is the first owner of the copyright therein, no assignment of the copyright, and no grant of any interest therein, made by him (otherwise than by will) after the passing of this Act, shall be operative to vest in the assignee or grantee any rights with respect to the copyright in the work beyond the expiration of twenty-five years from the death of the author, and the reversionary interest in the copyright expectant on the termination of that period shall, on the death of the author, notwithstanding any agreement to the contrary, devolve on his legal personal representatives as part of his estate, and any agreement entered into by him as to the disposition of such reversionary interest shall be null and void, but nothing in this proviso shall be construed as applying to the assignment of the copyright in a collective work or a licence to publish a work or part of a work as part of a collective work.

7. *S.17(2) of the Copyright Act, 1911 (referred to in paragraph 29 of Seventh Schedule):*

The ownership of an author's manuscript after his death, where such ownership has been acquired under a testamentary disposition made by the author and the manuscript is of a work which has not been published nor performed in public nor delivered in public, shall be prima facie proof of the copyright being with the owner of the manuscript.

8. *Note to First Schedule to the Copyright Act, 1911 (referred to in paragraph 37 of Seventh Schedule):*

In the case of an essay, article, or portion forming part of and first published in a review, magazine, or other periodical or work of a like nature, the right shall be subject to any right of publishing the essay, article, or portion in a separate form to which the author is entitled at the commencement of this Act, or would, if this Act had not been passed, have become entitled under section eighteen of the Copyright Act, 1842.

9. *Definitions in s.35(1) of the Copyright Act, 1911 (referred to in paragraphs 15, 43 and 47 of Seventh Schedule):*

"literary work" includes maps, charts, plans, tables, and compilations;

"dramatic work" includes any piece for recitation, choreographic work or entertainment in dumb show the scenic arrangement or acting form of which is fixed in writing or otherwise, and any cinematograph production where the arrangement or acting form or the combination of incidents represented give the work an original character;

"performance" means any acoustic representation of a work and any visual representation of any dramatic action in a work, including such a representation made by means of any mechanical instrument;

"photograph" includes photo-lithograph and any work produced by any process analogous to photography;

"collective work" means—

(a) any encyclopedia, dictionary, year book, or similar work;

(b) a newspaper, review, magazine, or similar periodical; and

(c) any work written in distinct parts by different authors, or in which works or parts of works of different authors are incorporated;

"delivery" in relation to a lecture, includes delivery by means of any mechanical instrument;

"lecture" includes address, speech and sermon.

Note—In this Schedule "this Act" means the Copyright Act, 1911.

Section 50   [NINTH SCHEDULE

ENACTMENTS REPEALED

Session and Chapter	Short Title	Extent of Repeal
25 & 26 Vict. c.68.	*The Fine Arts Copyright Act, 1862.*	*The whole Act.*
2 Edw. 7, c.15.	*The Musical (Summary Proceedings) Copyright Act, 1902.*	*The whole Act.*
6 Edw. 7, c.36.	*The Musical Copyright Act, 1906.*	*The whole Act.*
1 & 2 Geo. 5, c.46.	*The Copyright Act, 1911.*	*The whole Act, except sections fifteen, thirty-four and thirty-seven thereof.*
18 & 19 Geo. 5, c.1ii.	*The Copyright Order Confirmation (Mechanical Instruments: Royalties) Act, 1928.*	*The whole Act.*
11 & Geo. 6, c.7.	*The Ceylon Independence Act, 1947.*	*Paragraph 10 of the Second Schedule.*

TABLE OF STATUTES REFERRED TO IN THIS ACT

Short Title	Session and Chapter
Copyright Act, 1775	*15 Geo. 3, c.53.*
Public Record Office Act, 1838	*1 & 2 Vict. c.94.*
Interpretation Act, 1889	*52 & 53 Vict. c.63.*
Copyright Act, 1911	*1 & 2 Geo. 5, c.46.*
Dramatic and Musical Performers' Protection Act, 1925	*15 & 16 Geo. 5, c.46.*
Children and Young Persons (Scotland) Act, 1937	*1 Edw. 8 & 1 Geo. 6, c.37.*
Cinematograph Films Act, 1938	*1 & 2 Geo. 6, c.17.*
Limitation Act, 1939	*2 & 3 Geo. 6, c.21.*
Education Act, 1944	*7 & 8 Geo. 6, c.31.*
Education (Scotland) Act, 1946	*9 & 10 Geo. 6, c.72.*
Crown Proceedings Act, 1947	*10 & 11 Geo. 6, c.44.*
British Nationality Act, 1948	*11 & 12 Geo. 6, c.56.*
Wireless Telegraphy Act, 1949	*12, 13 & 14 Geo. 6, c.54.*
Registered Designs Act, 1949	*12, 13 & 14 Geo. 6, c.88.*
Arbitration Act, 1950	*14 Geo. 6, c.27.*
Customs and Excise Act, 1952	*15 & 16 Geo. 6, & 1 Eliz. 2, c.44.*]

Note: Subsection (2) of s.50 and Sch.9 repealed by the Statute Law (Repeals) Act 1974 (c.22).

E REPEALED STATUTES

E2. COMPARATIVE TABLES I AND II

COMPARATIVE TABLE—I

Copyright Act 1956 compared with Copyright, Designs and Patents Act 1988

1956	1988	1956	1988
s. 1 (1)	ss. 2 (1), 157 (1)	s. 9 (1)	s. 29
(2), (3), (4)	16 (1), (2)	(2)	30 (1), (3)
(5)	153, 154	(3), (4)	62
2 (1), (2)	1, 153, 154, 155	(5), (6)	31
(3), (4)	s. 12	(7)	s. 45
(5) (a)	17	(8)	—
(b)	18	(9)	64
(c)	19	(10)	65
(d), (e)	20	(11)	—
(f), (g)	21	10	ss. 51–53
(6)	21	11 (1)	—
3 (1)	4 (1), (2)	(2)	—
(2), (3)	ss. 1, 153, 154, 155	(3)	s. 10 (1), (2)
(4)	s. 12	s. 12 (1), (2)	ss. 1, 153, 154, 155
(5) (a)	17	(3)	s. 13
(b)	18	(4)	11
(c), (d)	20	(5) (a)	17
4	11	(b)	19
5 (1)	—	(c)	20
(2)	22	(6)	—
(3), (4)	23	(7)	67
(5), (6)	25	(8)	9 (1)–(3)
6 (1)	29	(9)	5 (1)
(2)	30 (1), (3)	13 (1), (2)	ss. 1, 153, 154, 155
(3)	30 (2), (3)	(3)	s. 13
(4)	45	(4)	11
(5)	59	(5) (a)	17
(6)	33	(b)	19
(7)	68	(c), (d)	20
(8)	76	(6)	45
(9)	—	(7), (8), (9)	—
(10)	178	(10)	ss. 5 (1), 9 (1)–(3)
7 (1)–(5), (9)	ss. 37–42	(11)	—
(6)–(8), (9)	s. 43	14 (1)	1, 9 (1)–(3), 153, 156
8	—		

1956	1988	1956	1988
s. 14 (2), (3)	ss. 11, 14	s. 19 (4)	s. 101
(4) (a), (b)	s. 17	(5), (6), (7)	102 (4)
(c)	19	(8)	(2)
(d)	20	(9)	ss. 92, 176 (1)
(5)	—	20 (1)	—
(6)	17 (4)	(2), (3)	s. 104 (1), (2),
(7)	—		(3)
(8)	72	(4)	(4)
(8A)	73	(5), (6)	s. 105
(9)	45	(7)	105 (1)
(10)	6 (3), (4)	21 (1), (2), (4),	107 (1)
(11)	—	(4A)	
14A (1), (2),	ss. 1, 153, 154, 156	(3), (4)	s. 107 (2)
(4)		(5)	(3)
(3), (4)	9 (1)–(3), 11, 14	(6)	—
(5) (a),	s. 17	(7), (7A),	107 (4), (5)
(b)		(7B), (7C),	
(c)	19	(7D), (8)	
(d)	20	(9)	ss. 108, 114
(6)	—	(10)	s. 108
(7)	17 (4)	21 (A)	s. 109
(8)	—	(B)	109
(9)	72	22	ss. 111, 112
(10)	45	ss. 23, 24	145–152
(11)	7	25–27A	116–128
(12)	—	27B, 28	129–135
15 (1)	ss. 1, 8 (1), (2)	s. 29	123, 128
(1) (a)	ss. 153, 155	s. 30	s. 152
(b)	153, 154	31	157 (2)–(5)
(2)	9 (1)–(3), 11,	32	159
	15	33	168
(3)	s. 17	34	156
(4)	ss. 37–42	35	160
16 (1)	—	36	ss. 90, 176 (1)
(2)	s. 22	37	91, 176 (1)
(3), (4)	23	38	s. 93
(5), (6), (7)	—	39	163
17 (1)	96	40 (1), (2)	—
(2)	97 (1)	(3), (3A),	73
(3)	(2)	(4), (5)	
(4), (5)	—	40A	—
(6)	177	41 (1), (5)	ss. 32, 76,
18 (1)	99		174 (5)
(2)	—	(2)	36, 76
(3)	27	(3), (4), (5)	34, 174 (5)
(4)	177	(6)	—
19 (1)	—	(7)	s. 174
(2)	101	42	49
(3)	102 (1), (3)	43	84

1956	1988	1956	1988
s. 44	ss. 265–273, Sched. 3	para. 2 3	para. 12 11
45	ss. 180–212	paras. 4–7	paras. 14–16
46	s. 171	para. 9	—
47	Individual sections	11 19	para. 12 —
48	s. 178	paras. 20–24	paras. 31–33
(1)	Individual sections	25, 26	para. 34
(2)	s. 6 (1)	para. 27	44
(3), (3A),		para. 28 (1), (2),	25 (1), (2)
(3B)	7	(4), (5)	
(4)	—	(3), (4)	
(5)	19 (4)	(5) and	
(6)	26	Sched. 8	
(7)	—	paras. 6,	
49 (1)	16 (3)	9	27
(2), (3)	175	29	30
(2) (d)	155 (3)	paras. 30, 31	paras. 40–42
(4)	3 (2), (3)	para. 32	22–24
(5), (6)	173	paras. 34–36	para. 17
(7)–(10)	—	para. 37	18
50 (1)	170	38	28
(2)	303	paras. 39, 40	—
51 (1)	306	para. 41	36
(2)	305	paras. 42, 43	—
s. 15 (3)	ss. 157 (1), 304	para. 44	4
Sched. 1	51–53	45 (1)	3
Scheds. 2, 3	9 (4), (5), 10 (3), 12, 153, 154	(2)	1 (3)
Sched. 4	145–152	paras. 46, 47 Sched. 8	paras. 1, 2 —
Sched. 5	—	para. 2	Sched. 1, paras. 5–9, 35
Sched. 6	180–212	paras. 6, 9	para. 27
Sched. 7	Sched. 1	Sched. 9	Sched. 8
paras. 1, 8, 10, 12, 13, 14–16, 17–18, 33 and Sched. 8, para. 2	paras. 5–9, 35		

Comparative Table—II

Copyright, Designs and Patents Act 1988 compared with Copyright Act 1956

1988	1956	1988	1956
s. 1	ss. 2 (1), (2), 3	s. 16 (3)	s. 49 (1)
	(2), (3), 12	(4)	—
	(1), (2), 13	17	ss. 2 (5) (a), 3 (5)
	(1), (2), 14		(a), 12 (5)
	(1), 14A (1),		(a), 13 (5)
	(2), (4), 15 (1)		(a), 14 (4)
2 (1)	s. 1 (1)		(a), (b), (6),
(2)	—		14A (5) (a),
3 (1)	48 (1)		(b), (7), 15 (3)
(2), (3)	49 (4)	(3)	s. 48 (1)
4 (1), (2)	ss. 3 (1), 48 (1)	18	ss. 2 (5) (b), 3 (5)
5 (1)	12 (9), 13 (10)		(b)
(2)	—	19	2 (5) (c), 12
6 (1)	s. 48 (2)		(5) (b), 13
(2)	—		(5), (6), 14
(3), (4)	14 (10)		(4) (c), 14A
(5), (6)	—		(5) (c)
7	ss. 14A, (11), 48	(2)	s. 48 (1)
	(3),(3A),(3B)	(4)	48 (5)
8 (1), (2)	s. 15 (1)	20	ss. 2 (5) (d), (e),
9 (1)–(3)	ss. 12 (8), 13 (10),		3 (5) (c),
	14 (1), 14A		(d), 12 (5)
	(3), 15 (2),		(c), 13 (5)
	48 (1)		(c), (d), 14
(4), (5)	Scheds. 2, 3		(4) (d), 14A
10 (1), (2)	s. 11 (3)		(5) (d)
(3)	Sched. 3	21	s. 2 (5) (f), (g),
11	ss. 4, 12 (4), 13		(6)
	(4), 14 (2),	22	ss. 5 (2), 16 (2)
	14A (3), 15	23	5 (3), (4), 16
	(2)		(3), (4)
12	2 (3), (4),	24	—
	3 (4),	25	s. 5 (5), (6)
	Scheds. 2, 3	26	48 (6)
13	ss. 12 (3), 13 (3)	27	18 (3)
14	14 (2), (3),	28	—
	14A (3), (4)	29	ss. 6 (1), 9 (1)
15	s. 15 (2)	30 (1), (3)	6 (2), 9 (2)
16 (1), (2)	1 (2), (3), (4)	(2), (3)	s. 6 (3)

1988	1956	1988	1956
s. 31	ss. 9 (5), (6)	s. 92	s. 19 (9)
32	41 (1), (5)	93	38
33	6 (6)	ss. 94, 95	—
34	41 (3), (4), (5)	s. 96	17 (1)
35	—	97 (1)	(2)
36	41 (2)	(2)	(3)
ss. 37–42	ss. 7 (1)–(5), (9),	98	—
	15 (4)	99	18 (1)
s. 43	s. 7 (6)–(8), (9)	100	—
44	—	101	19 (2), (4)
45	ss. 6 (4), 9 (7), 13	102 (1), (3)	(3)
	(6), 14 (9),	(2)	(8)
	14A (10)	(4)	(5), (6), (7)
46	—	(5)	—
47	—	103	
48	—	(1), (2),	
49	42	(3)	20 (2), (3)
50	—	s. 104 (4)	20 (4)
ss. 51–53	s. 10, Sched. 1	(5)	(5), (6)
54, 55	—	105 (1)	(7)
s. 56	—	(2)–(5)	—
57	—	106	—
58	—	107 (1)	21 (1), (2),
59	6 (5)		(4), (4A)
60	—	(2)	(3), (4)
61	—	(3)	(5)
62	9 (3), (4)	(4), (5)	(7), (7A),
63	—		(7B), (7C),
64	9 (9)		(7D), (8)
65	9 (10)		
66	—	(6)	—
67	12 (7)	108	21 (9), (10)
68	6 (7)	109	ss. 21 (A), 21 (B)
69	—	110	—
70	—	ss. 111, 112	s. 22
71	—	s. 113	—
72	ss. 14 (8), 14A (9)	114	21 (9)
73	14 (8A), 40	115	—
	(3), (3A),	ss. 116–128	ss. 25–27A, 29
	(4), (5)	129–135	27 (B), 28
74	—	135A–135G	—
75	—	136–144	—
76	6 (8), 41 (1),	145–152	ss. 23, 24, 30,
	(2)		Sched. 4
ss. 77–83	—	153, 154	ss. 1 (5), 2 (1), 3
s. 84	s. 43		(2), 12 (1),
ss. 85–89	—		13 (1), 14A
s. 90	36		(1), 15 (1)
91	37		(b), Sched. 3

1988	1956	1988	1956
ss. 153, 155	ss. 2 (2), 3 (3), 12 (2), 13 (2), 15 (1) (a)	para. 3	para. 45 (1)
		4	44
s. 155 (3)	s. 49 (2) (d)	paras. 5–9	paras. 1, 8, 10, 12, 13, 14, 16,
ss. 153, 156	ss. 14 (1), 14A (1), 34		17, 18, 33
s. 157 (1)	1 (1), 51 (3)		para. 2, Sched. 8
157 (2)–(5)	s. 31	para. 10	—
158	—	11	para. 3
159	32	12	paras. 2, 11
160	35	13	—
ss. 161, 162	39	paras. 14–16	4–7
s. 163	39	para. 17	34–36
ss. 164–167	—	18	37
ss. 168	s. 33	paras. 19, 20, 21	—
169	—	paras. 22–24	32
170	s. 50 (1)	para. 25(1), (2)	28(1), (2), (4), (5)
s. 171	46		
172	—	26	—
173	49 (5), (6)	27	paras. 28 (3), (4),
174	41 (7)		(5), paras. 6, 9,
(5)	(1), (3), (4)		Sched. 8
175	49 (2), (3)	28	para. 38
176 (1)	ss. 19 (9), 36 (3), 37 (1)	29	—
		30	39
(2)	—	paras. 31–33	paras. 20–24
177	17 (6), 18 (4), 48 (1)	para. 34	25, 26
		35	paras. 1, 8, 10,
178	s. 48 and individual sections		12, 13, 14–16, 17–18, 33, para. 2,
179	—		Sched. 8
ss. 180–212	s. 45, Sched. 6	36	para. 41
213–264	—	37	—
265–273	s. 44	paras. 38, 39	—
274–286	—	40–42	paras. 30, 31
287–292	—	43	—
293–295	—	44	para. 27
296–297	—	45	—
297A–299	—	46	—
s. 300	—	Sched. 2	—
301	—	Sched. 3	s. 44
302	—	Sched. 4	—
303	50 (2)	Sched. 5	—
304	51 (3)	Sched. 6	—
305	(2)	Sched. 7	—
306	(1)	Sched. 8	Sched. 9
Sched. 1	Sched. 7		
paras. 1, 2	paras. 45 (2), 46, 47		

E3. COPYRIGHT ACT 1911

Copyright Act 1911

(1 & 2 GEO. 5, C.46)

An Act to amend and consolidate the Law relating to Copyright.

[16th December, 1911]

PART I

IMPERIAL COPYRIGHT

Rights

Copyright

1.—(1) Subject to the provisions of this Act,[i] copyright shall subsist throughout the parts of His Majesty's dominions to which this Act extends for the term hereinafter mentioned in every original literary dramatic musical and artistic work, if—

(a) in the case of a published work, the work was first published within such parts of His Majesty's dominions as aforesaid; and

(b) in the case of an unpublished work, the author was at the date of the making of the work a British subject or resident within such parts of His Majesty's dominions as aforesaid;

but in no other works, except so far as the protection conferred by this Act is extended by Orders in Council thereunder relating to self-governing dominions to which this Act does not extend and to foreign countries.

(2) For the purposes of this Act, "copyright" means the sole right to produce or reproduce the work or any substantial part thereof in any material form whatsoever, to perform, or in the case of a lecture to deliver, the work or any substantial part thereof in public; if the work is unpublished, to publish the work or any substantial part thereof; and shall include the sole right,—

(a) to produce, reproduce, perform, or publish any translation of the work;

(b) in the case of a dramatic work, to convert it into a novel or other non-dramatic work;

(c) in the case of a novel or other non-dramatic work, or of an artistic work, to convert it into a dramatic work, by way of performance in public or otherwise;

(d) in the case of a literary, dramatic, or musical work, to make any record, perforated roll, cinematograph film, or other contrivance by means of which the work which the work may be mechanically performed or delivered,

and to authorise any such acts as aforesaid.

(3) For the purposes of this Act, publication, in relation to any work, means the issue of copies of the work to the public, and does not include the performance in public of a dramatic or musical work, the delivery in public of a lecture, the exhibition in public of an artistic work, or the construction of an architectural

---

[i] *Editorial Note*: This Act was repealed by the Copyright Act 1956, above, as from June 1, 1957 with the exception of ss.15, 34, 37. Sections 34 and 37(2) repealed by the Statute Law (Repeals) Act 1986 (c.12). Comparative Tables showing the correspondence of this Act to the 1956 Act, and of the 1956 Act to this Act, are printed at E4, below.

work of art, but, for the purposes of this provision, the issue of photographs and engravings of works of sculpture and architectural works of art shall not be deemed to be publication of such works.

Infringement of copyright

2.—(1) Copyright in a work shall be deemed to be infringed by any person who, without the consent of the owner of the copyright, does anything the sole right to do which is by this Act conferred on the owner of the copyright: Provided that the following acts shall not constitute an infringement of copyright:

    (i) Any fair dealing with any work for the purposes of private study, research, criticism, review, or newspaper summary:

    (ii) Where the author of an artistic work is not the owner of the copyright therein, the use by the author of any mould, cast, sketch, plan, model, or study made by him for the purpose of the work, provided that he does not thereby repeat or imitate the main design of that work:

    (iii) The making or publishing of paintings, drawings, engravings, or photographs of a work of sculpture or artistic craftsmanship, if permanently situate in a public place or building, or the making or publishing of paintings, drawings, engravings, or photographs (which are not in the nature of architectural drawings or plans) of any architectural work of art:

    (iv) The publication in a collection, mainly composed of non-copyright matter, bona fide intended for the use of schools, and so described in the title and in any advertisements issued by the publisher, of short passages from published literary works not themselves published for the use of schools in which copyright subsists: provided that not more than two of such passages from works by the same author are published by the same publisher within five years, and that the source from which such passages are taken is acknowledged:

    (v) The publication in a newspaper of a report of a lecture delivered in public, unless the report is prohibited by conspicuous written or printed notice affixed before and maintained during the lecture at or about the main entrance of the building in which the lecture is given, and, except whilst the building is being used for public worship, in a position near the lecturer; but nothing in this paragraph shall affect the provisions in paragraph (i) as to newspaper summaries:

    (vi) The reading or recitation in public by one person of any reasonable extract from any published work.

(2) Copyright in a work shall also be deemed to be infringed by any person who—

    (a) sells or lets for hire, or by way of trade exposes or offers for sale or hire; or

    (b) distributes either for the purposes of trade or to such an extent as to affect prejudicially the owner of the copyright; or

    (c) by way of trade exhibits in public; or

    (d) imports for sale or hire into any party of His Majesty's dominions to which this Act extends.

any work which to his knowledge infringes copyright or would infringe copyright if it had been made within the part of His Majesty's dominions in or into which the sale or hiring, exposure, offering for sale or hire, distribution, exhibition, or importation took place.

(3) Copyright in a work shall also be deemed to be infringed by any person who for his private profit permits a theatre or other place of entertainment to be used for the performance in public of the work without the consent of the owner of the copyright, unless he was not aware, and had no reasonable ground for suspecting, that the performance would be an infringement of copyright.

Term of copyright

3. The term for which copyright shall subsist shall, except as otherwise expressly provided by this Act, be the life of the author and a period of fifty years after his death:

Provided that at any time after the expiration of twenty-five years, or in the case of a work in which copyright subsists at the passing of this act thirty years, from the death of the author of a published work, copyright in the work shall not be deemed to be infringed by the reproduction of the work for sale if the person reproducing the work proves that he has given the prescribed notice in writing of his intention to reproduce the work, and that he has paid in the prescribed manner to, or for the benefit of, the owner of the copyright royalties in respect of all copies of the work sold by him calculated at the rate of ten per cent. on the price at which he publishes the work; and, for the purposes of this proviso, the Board of Trade may make regulations prescribing the mode in which notices are to be given, and the particulars to be given such notices, and the mode, time, and frequency of the payment of royalties, including (if they think fit) regulations requiring payment in advance or otherwise securing the payment of royalties.

Compulsory licences

4. If at any time after the death of the author of a literary, dramatic, or musical work which has been published or performed in public a complaint is made to the Judicial Committee of the Privy Council that the owner of the copyright in the work has refused to republish or to allow the republication of the work or has refused to allow the performance in public of the work, and that by reason of such refusal the work is withheld from the public, the owner of the copyright may be ordered to grant a licence to reproduce the work or perform the work in public, as the case may be, on such terms and subject to such conditions as the Judicial Committee may think fit.

Ownership of copyright, etc.

5.—(1) Subject to the provisions of this Act, the author of a work shall be the first owner of the copyright therein:

Provided that—

(a) where, in the case of an engraving, photograph, or portrait, the plate or other original was ordered by some other person and was made for valuable consideration in pursuance of that order, then, in the absence of any agreement to the contrary, the person by whom such plate or other original was ordered shall be the first owner of the copyright; and

(b) where the author was in the employment of some other person under a contract of service or apprenticeship and the work was made in the course of his employment by that person, the person by whom the author was employed shall, in the absence of any agreement to the contrary, be the first owner of the copyright, but where the work is an article or other contribution to a newspaper, magazine, or similar periodical, there shall, in the absence of any agreement to the contrary, be deemed to be reserved to the author a right to restrain the publication of the work, otherwise than as part of a newspaper, magazine, or similar periodical.

(2) The owner of the copyright in any work may assign the right, either wholly or partially, and either generally or subject to limitations to the United Kingdom or any self-governing dominion or other part of His Majesty's dominions to which this Act extends, and either for the whole term of the copyright or for any part thereof, and may grant any interest in the right by licence, but no such assignment or grant shall be valid unless it is in writing signed by the owner of the right in respect of which the assignment or grant is made, or by his duly authorised agent:

Provided that, where the author of a work is the first owner of the copyright therein, no assignment of the copyright, and no grant of any interest therein, made by him (otherwise than by will) after the passing of this Act, shall be operative to vest in the assignee or grantee any rights with respect to the copyright in the work beyond the expiration of twenty-five years from the death of the author, and the reversionary interest in the copyright expectant on the termination of that period shall, on the death of the author, notwithstanding any agreement to the contrary, devolve on his legal personal representatives as part of his estate, and any agreement entered into by him as to the disposition of such reversionary interest shall be null and void, but nothing in this proviso shall be construed as applying to the assignment of the copyright in a collective work or a licence to publish a work or part of a work as part of a collective work.

(3) Where, under any partial assignment of copyright, the assignee becomes entitled to any right comprised in copyright, the assignee as respects the right so assigned, and the assignor as respects the rights not assigned, shall be treated for the purposes of this Act as the owner of the copyright, and the provisions of this Act shall have effect accordingly.

Civil Remedies

Civil remedies for infringement of copyright

6.—(1) Where copyright in any work has been infringed, the owner of the copyright shall, except as otherwise provided by this Act, be entitled to all such remedies by way of injunction or interdict, damages, accounts, and otherwise, as are or may be conferred by law for the infringement of a right.

(2) The costs of all parties in any proceedings in respect of the infringement of copyright shall be in the absolute discretion of the court.

(3) In any action for infringement of copyright in any work, the work shall be presumed to be a work in which copyright subsists and the plaintiff shall be presumed to be the owner of the copyright, unless the defendant puts in issue the existence of the copyright, or, as the case may be, the title of the plaintiff, and where any such question is in issue, then—

(a) if a name purporting to be that of the author of the work is printed or otherwise indicated thereon in the usual manner, the person whose name is so printed or indicated shall, unless the contrary is proved, be presumed to be the author of the work;

(b) if no name is so printed or indicated, or if the name so printed or indicated is not the author's true name or the name by which he is commonly known, and a name purporting to be that of the publisher or proprietor of the work is printed or otherwise indicated thereon in the usual manner the person whose name is so printed or indicated shall, unless the contrary is proved, be presumed to be the owner of the copyright in the work for the purposes of proceedings in respect of the infringement of copyright therein.

Rights of owner against persons possessing or dealing with infringing copies, etc.

7. All infringing copies of any work in which copyright subsists, or of any substantial part thereof, and all plates used or intended to be used for the production of such infringing copies, shall be deemed to be the property of the owner of the copyright, who accordingly may take proceedings for the recovery of the possession thereof or in respect of the conversion thereof.

Exemption of innocent infringer from liability pay damages, etc.

8. Where proceedings are taken in respect of the infringement of the copyright in any work and the defendant in his defence alleges that he was not aware of the existence of the copyright in the work, the plaintiff shall not be entitled to any remedy other than an injunction or interdict in respect of the infringement if the defendant proves that at the date of the infringement he was not aware and had no reasonable ground for suspecting that copyright subsisted in the work.

Restriction on remedies in the case of architecture

9.—(1) Where the construction of a building or other structure which infringes or which, if completed, would infringe the copyright in some other work has been commenced, the owner of the copyright shall not be entitled to obtain an injunction or interdict to restrain the construction of such building or structure or to order its demolition.

(2) Such of the other provisions of this Act as provide that an infringing copy of a work shall be deemed to be the property of the owner of the copyright, or as impose summary penalties, shall not apply in any case to which this section applies.

Limitation of actions

10. An action in respect of infringement of copyright shall not be commenced after the expiration of three years next after the infringement.

Summary Remedies

Penalties for dealing with infringing copies, etc.

11.—(1) If any person knowingly—
- (a) makes for sale or hire any infringing copy of a work in which copyright subsists; or
- (b) sells or lets for hire, or by way of trade exposes or offers for sale or hire any infringing copy of any such work; or
- (c) distributes infringing copies of any such work either for the purposes of trade or to such an extent as to affect prejudicially the owner of the copyright; or
- (d) by way of trade exhibits in public any infringing copy of any such work; or
- (e) imports for sale or hire into the United Kingdom any infringing copy of any such work:

he shall be guilty of an offence under this Act and be liable on summary conviction to a fine not exceeding forty shillings for every copy dealt with in contravention of this section, but not exceeding fifty pounds in respect of the same transaction; or, in the case of a second or subsequent offence, either to such fine or to imprisonment with or without hard labour for a term not exceeding two months.

(2) If any person knowingly makes or has in his possession any plate for the purpose of making infringing copies of any work in which copyright subsists, or knowingly and for his private profit causes any such work to be performed in public without the consent of the owner of the copyright, he shall be guilty of an offence under this Act, and be liable on summary conviction to a fine not exceeding fifty pounds, or, in the case of a second or subsequent offence, either to such fine or to imprisonment with or without hard labour for a term not exceeding two months.

(3) The court before which any such proceedings are taken may, whether the alleged offender is convicted or not, order that all copies of the work or all plates in the possession of the alleged offender, which appear to it to be infringing copies or plates for the purpose of making infringing copies, be destroyed or delivered up to the owner of the copyright or otherwise dealt with as the court may think fit.

(4) Nothing in this section shall, as respects musical works, affect the provisions of the Musical (Summary Proceedings) Copyright Act, 1902, or the Musical Copyright Act, 1906.

Appeals to quarter sessions

12. Any person aggrieved by a summary conviction of an offence under the foregoing provisions of this Act may in England and Ireland appeal to a court of quarter sessions and in Scotland under and in terms of the Summary Jurisdiction (Scotland) Acts.

Extent of provisions as to summary remedies

13. The provisions of this Act with respect to summary remedies shall extend only to the United Kingdom.

Importation of Copies

Importation of copies

14.—(1) Copies made out of the United Kingdom of any work in which copyright subsists which if made in the United Kingdom would infringe copyright, and as to which the owner of the copyright gives notice in writing by himself or his agent to the Commissioners of Customs and Excise, that he is desirous that such copies should not be imported into the United Kingdom, shall not be so imported, and shall, subject to the provisions of this section, be deemed to be included in the table of prohibitions and restrictions contained in section forty-two of the Customs Consolidation Act, 1876, and that section shall apply accordingly.

(2) Before detaining any such copies or taking any further proceedings with a view to the forfeiture thereof under the law relating to the Customs, the Commissioners of Customs and Excise may require the regulations under this section, whether as to information, conditions, or other matters, to be complied with, and may satisfy themselves in accordance with those regulations that the copies are such as are prohibited by this section to be imported.

(3) The Commissioners of Customs and Excise may make regulations, either general or special, respecting the detention and forfeiture of copies the importation of which is prohibited by this section, and the conditions, if any, to be fulfilled before such detention and forfeiture, and may, by such regulations, determine the information, notices, and security to be given, and the evidence requisite for any of the purposes of this section, and the mode of verification of such evidence.

(4) The regulations may apply to copies of all works the importation of copies of which is prohibited by this section, or different regulations may be made respecting different classes of such works.

(5) The regulations may provide for the informant reimbursing the Commissioners of Customs and excise all expenses and damages incurred in respect of any detention made on his information, and of any proceedings consequent on such detention and may provide for notices under any enactment repealed by this Act being treated as notices given under this section.

(6) The foregoing provisions of this section shall have effect as if they were part of the Customs Consolidation Act, 1876: Provided that, notwithstanding anything in that Act, the Isle of Man shall not be treated as part of the United Kingdom for the purposes of this section.

(7) This section shall, with the necessary modifications, apply to the importation into a British possession to which this Act extends of copies of works made out of that possession.

Note: In subs.(1) the words "and shall, subject to the provisions of this section" onwards repealed by the Customs and Excise Act 1952 (15 & 16 Geo. 6 and 1 Eliz. 2, c.44) s.320, Sch.12 Pt I.

Delivery of Books to Libraries

Delivery of copies to British Museum and other libraries

15.—(1) The publisher of every book published in the United Kingdom shall, within one month after the publication, deliver, at his own expense, a copy of the book to the [British Library Board] who shall give a written receipt for it.

(2) He shall also, if written demand is made before the expiration of twelve months after publication, deliver within one month after receipt of that written demand or, if the demand was made before publication, within one month after publication, to some depôt in London named in the demand a copy of the book for, or in accordance with the directions of, the authority having the control of each of the following libraries, namely: the Bodleian Library, Oxford, the University Library, Cambridge, the [National Library of Scotland] and the Library of Trinity College, Dublin, and subject to the provisions of this section the National Library of Wales. In the case of an encyclopaedia, newspaper, review, magazine, or work published in a series of numbers or parts, the written demand may include all numbers or parts of the work which may be subsequently published.

(3) The copy delivered to the [British Library Board] shall be a copy of the whole book with all maps and illustrations belonging thereto, finished and coloured in the same manner as the best copies of the book are published, and shall be bound, sewed, or stitched together, and on the best paper on which the book is printed.

(4) The copy delivered for the other authorities mentioned in this section shall be on the paper on which the largest number of copies of the book is printed for sale, and shall be in the like condition as the books prepared for sale.

(5) The books of which copies are to be delivered to the National Library of Wales shall not include books of such classes as may be specified in regulations to be made by the [Lord President of the Council].

(6) If a publisher fails to comply with this section, he shall be liable on summary conviction to a fine not exceeding five pounds and the value of the book, and the fine shall be paid to the [British Library Board] or authority to whom the book ought to have been delivered.

(7) For the purposes of this section, the expression "book" includes every part or division of a book, pamphlet, sheet of letterpress, sheet of music, map, plan, chart or table separately published, but shall not include any second or subsequent edition of a book unless such edition contains additions or alterations either in the letterpress or in the maps, prints, or other engravings belonging thereto.

Notes:

(1) This section was repealed by the Legal Deposit Libraries Act 2003 (c.28) s.15, Sch. with effect from February 1, 2004 (Legal Deposit Libraries Act 2003 (Commencement) Order 2004 (SI 2004/130)).

(2) This section was not repealed by the 1956 Act, nor by the 1988 Act, but was amended by the British Library Act 1972 (c.54), s.4 to substitute references to the British Library Board for the trustees of the British Museum.

(3) A proviso added to subs.(1) by the Copyright (British Museum) Act 1915 (5 & 6 Geo. 5, c.38), was repealed by the British Museum Act 1932 (22 & 23 Geo. 5, c.34) s.2(2).

(4) The National Library of Scotland was substituted in subs.(2) for the Library of the Faculty of Advocates at Edinburgh by the National Library of Scotland Act 1925 (15 & 16 Geo. 5, c.73) s.5.

(5) The Lord President of the Council was substituted for the Board of Trade by the Transfer of Functions (Arts, Libraries and National Heritage) Order 1986 (SI 1986/600).

Special Provisions as to certain Works

Works of joint authors

16.—(1) In the case of a work of joint authorship, copyright shall subsist during the life of the author who first dies and for a term of fifty years after his death, or during the life of the author who dies last, whichever period is the longer, and references in this Act to the period after the expiration of any specified number of years from the death of the author shall be construed as references to the period after the expiration of the like number of years from the death of the author who dies first or after the death of the author who dies last, whichever period may be the shorter, and in the provisions of this Act with respect to the grant of compulsory licences a reference to the date of the death of the author who dies last shall be substituted for the reference to the date of the death of the author.

(2) Where, in the case of a work of joint authorship, some one or more of the joint authors do not satisfy the conditions conferring copyright laid down by this Act, the work shall be treated for the purposes of this Act as if the other author or authors had been the sole author or authors thereof:

Provided that the term of the copyright shall be the same as it would have been if all the authors had satisfied such conditions as aforesaid.

(3) For the purposes of this Act, "a work of a joint authorship" means a work produced by the collaboration of two or more authors in which the contribution of one author is not distinct from the contribution of the other author or authors.

(4) Where a married woman and her husband are joint authors of a work the interest of such married woman therein shall be her separate property.

Note: In subs.(4) the word "separate" was repealed by the Law Reform (Married Woman and Tortfeasors) Act 1935 (25 & 26 Geo. 5, c.30) s.5, Sch.2.

Posthumous works

17.—(1) In the case of a literary dramatic or musical work, or an engraving, in which copyright subsists at the date of the death of the author or, in the case of a work of joint authorship, at or immediately before the date of the death of the author who dies last, but which has not been published, nor, in the case of a dramatic or musical work, been performed in public, nor, in the case of a lecture, been delivered in public, before that date, copyright shall subsist till publication, or performance or delivery in public, whichever may first happen, and for a term of fifty years thereafter, and the proviso to section three of this Act shall, in the case of such a work, apply as if the author had died at the date of such publication or performance or delivery in public as aforesaid.

(2) The ownership of an author's manuscript after his death, where such ownership has been acquired under a testamentary disposition made by the author and the manuscript is of a work which has not been published nor performed in public nor delivered in public, shall be prima facie proof of the copyright being with the owner of the manuscript.

Provisions as to Government publications

18. Without prejudice to any rights or privileges of the Crown, where any work has, whether before or after the commencement of this Act, been prepared or published by or under the direction or control of His Majesty or any Government department, the copyright in the work shall, subject to any agreement with the author, belong to His Majesty, and in such case shall continue for a period of fifty years from the date of the first publication of the work.

Provisions as to mechanical instruments

19.—(1) Copyright shall subsist in records, perforated rolls, and other contrivances by means of which sounds may be mechanically reproduced, in like manner as if such contrivances were musical works, but the term of copyright shall be fifty years from the making of the original plate from which the contrivance was directly or indirectly derived, and the person who was the owner of such original plate at the time when such plate was made shall be deemed to be the author of the work, and, where such owner is a body corporate, the body corporate shall be deemed for the purposes of this Act to reside within the parts of His Majesty's dominions to which this Act extends if it has established a place of business within such parts.

(2) It shall not be deemed to be an infringement of copyright in any musical work for any person to make within the parts of His Majesty's dominions to which this Act extends records, perforated rolls, or other contrivances by means of which the work may be mechanically performed, if such person proves—

(a) that such contrivances have previously been made by, or with the consent or acquiescence of, the owner of the copyright in the work; and

(b) that he has given the prescribed notice of his intention to make the contrivances, and has paid in the prescribed manner to, or for the benefit of, the owner of the copyright in the work royalties in respect of all such contrivances sold by him, calculated at the rate hereinafter mentioned:

Provided that—

(i) nothing in this provision shall authorise any alterations in, or omissions from, the work reproduced, unless contrivances reproducing the work subject to similar alterations and omissions have been previously made by, or with the consent or acquiescence of, the owner of the copyright, or unless such alterations or omissions are reasonably necessary for the adaptation of the work to the contrivances in question; and

(ii) for the purposes of this provision, a musical work shall be deemed to include any words so closely associated therewith as to form part of the same work, but shall not be deemed to include a contrivance by means of which sounds may be mechanically reproduced.

(3) The rate at which such royalties as aforesaid are to be calculated shall—

(a) in the case of contrivances sold within two years after the commencement of this Act by the person making the same, be two and one-half per cent.; and

(b) in the case of contrivances sold as aforesaid after the expiration of that period, five per cent.

on the ordinary retail selling price of the contrivance calculated in the prescribed manner, so however that the royalty payable in respect of a contrivance shall, in no case, be less than a halfpenny for each separate musical work in which copyright subsists reproduced thereon, and, where the royalty calculated as aforesaid includes a fraction of a farthing, such fraction shall be reckoned as a farthing:

Provided that, if, at any time after the expiration of seven years from the commencement of this Act, it appears to the Board of Trade that such rate as aforesaid is no longer equitable, the Board of Trade may, after holding a public inquiry, make an order either decreasing or increasing that rate to such extent as under the circumstances may seem just, but any order so made shall be provisional only and shall not have any effect unless and until confirmed by Parliament; but, where an order revising the rate has been so made and confirmed, no further revision shall be made before the expiration of fourteen years from the date of the last revision.

(4) If any such contrivance is made reproducing two or more different works in which copyright subsists and the owners of the copyright therein are different persons, the sums payable by way of royalties under this section shall be apportioned amongst the several owners of the copyright in such proportions as, failing agreement, may be determined by arbitration.

(5) When any such contrivances by means of which a musical work may be mechanically performed have been made, then, for the purposes of this section, the owner of the copyright in the work shall, in relation to any person who makes the prescribed inquiries, be deemed to have given his consent to the making of such contrivances if he fails to reply to such inquiries within the prescribed time.

(6) For the purposes of this section, the Board of Trade may make regulations prescribing anything which under this section is to be prescribed, and prescribing the mode in which notices are to be given and the particulars to be given in such notices, and the mode, time, and frequency of the payment of royalties, and any such regulations may, if the Board think fit, include regulations requiring payment in advance or otherwise securing the payment of royalties.

(7) In the case of musical works published before the commencement of this Act, the foregoing provisions shall have effect, subject to the following modifications and additions:

(a) The conditions as to the previous making by, or with the consent or acquiescence of, the owner of the copyright in the work, and the restrictions as to alterations in or omissions from the work, shall not apply:

(b) The rate of two and one-half per cent. shall be substituted for the rate of five per cent. as the rate at which royalties are to be calculated, but no royalties shall be payable in respect of contrivances sold before the first day of July, nineteen hundred and thirteen, if contrivances reproducing the same work had been lawfully made, or placed on sale, within the parts of His Majesty's dominions to which this Act extends before the first day of July, nineteen hundred and ten:

(c) Notwithstanding any assignment made before the passing of this Act of the copyright in a musical work, any rights conferred by this Act in respect of the making, or authorising the making, of contrivances by means of which the work may be mechanically performed shall belong to the author or his legal personal representatives and not to the assignee, and the royalties aforesaid shall be payable to, and for the benefit of, the author of the work or his legal personal representatives:

(d) The saving contained in this Act of the rights and interests arising from, or in connexion with, action taken before the commencement of this Act shall not be construed as authorising any person who has made contrivances by means of which the work may be mechanically performed to sell any such contrivances, whether made before or after the passing of this Act, except on the terms and subject to the conditions laid down in this section:

(e) Where the work is a work on which copyright is conferred by an Order in Council relating to a foreign country, the copyright so conferred shall not, except to such extent as may be provided by the Order, include any rights with respect to the making of records, perforated rolls, or other contrivances by means of which the work may be mechanically performed.

(8) Notwithstanding anything in this Act, where a record, perforated roll, or other contrivance by means of which sounds may be mechanically reproduced has been made before the commencement of this Act, copyright shall, as from the commencement of this Act, subsist therein in like manner and for the like term as if this Act had been in force at the date of the making of the original plate from which the contrivance was directly or indirectly derived:

Provided that—

(i) the person who, at the commencement of this Act, is the owner of such original plate shall be the first owner of such copyright; and

(ii) nothing in this provision shall be construed as conferring copyright in any such contrivance if the making thereof would have infringed copyright in some other such contrivance, if this provision had been in force at the time of the making of the first-mentioned contrivance.

Provision as to political speeches

20. Notwithstanding anything in this Act, it shall not be an infringement of copyright in an address of a political nature delivered at a public meeting to publish a report thereof in a newspaper.

Provisions as to photographs

21. The term for which copyright shall subsist in photographs shall be fifty years from the making of the original negative from which the photograph was directly or indirectly derived, and the person who was the owner of such negative at the time when such negative was made shall be deemed to be the author of the work, and, where such owner is a body corporate, the body corporate shall be deemed for the purposes of this Act to reside within the parts of His Majesty's dominions to which this Act extends if it has established a place of business within such parts.

Provisions as to designs registrable under 7 Edw. 7, c.29

22.—(1) This Act shall not apply to designs capable of being registered under the Patents and Designs Act, 1907, except designs which, though capable of being so registered, are not used or intended to be used as models or patterns to be multiplied by any industrial process.

(2) General rules under section eighty-six of the Patents and Designs Act, 1907, may be made for determining the conditions under which a design shall be deemed to be used for such purposes as aforesaid.

Works of foreign authors first published in parts of His Majesty's dominions to which Act extends

23. If it appears to His Majesty that a foreign country does not give, or has not undertaken to give, adequate protection to the works of British authors, it shall be lawful for His Majesty by Order in Council to direct that such of the provisions of this Act as confer copyright on works first published within the parts of His Majesty's dominions to which this Act extends, shall not apply to works published after the date specified in the Order, the authors whereof are subjects or citizens of such foreign country, and are not resident in His Majesty's dominions, and thereupon those provisions shall not apply to such works.

Existing works

24.—(1) Where any person is immediately before the commencement of this Act entitled to any such right in any work as is specified in the first column of the First Schedule to this Act, or to any interest in such a right, he shall, as from that date, be entitled to the substituted right set forth in the second column of that schedule, or to the same interest in such a substituted right, and to no other right or interest, and such substituted right shall subsist for the term for which it would have subsisted if this Act had been in force at the date when the work was made and the work had been one entitled to copyright thereunder:

Provided that—

  (a) if the author of any work in which any such right as is specified in the first column of the First Schedule to this Act subsists at the commencement of this Act has, before that date, assigned the right or granted any interest therein for the whole term of the right, then at the date when, but for the passing of this Act, the right would have expired the substituted right conferred by this section shall, in the absence of express agreement, pass to the author of the work, and any interest therein created before the commencement of this Act and then subsisting shall determine; but the person who immediately before the date at which the right would so have expired was the owner of the right or interest shall be entitled at his option either—

    (i) on giving such notice as hereinafter mentioned, to an assignment of the right or the grant of a similar interest therein for the remainder of the term of the right for such consideration as, failing agreement, may be determined by arbitration; or

    (ii) without any such assignment or grant, to continue to reproduce or perform the work in like manner as theretofore subject to the payment, if demanded by the author within three years after the date at which the right would have so expired, of such royalties to the author as, failing agreement, may be determined by arbitration, or, where the work is incorporated in a collective work and the owner of the right or interest is the proprietor of that collective work, without any such payment;

    The notice above referred to must be given not more than one year nor less than six months before the date at which the right would have so expired, and must be sent by registered post to the author, or, if he cannot with reasonable diligence be found, advertised in the *London Gazette* and in two London newspapers:

(b) where any person has, before the twenty-sixth day of July nineteen hundred and ten, taken any action whereby he has incurred any expenditure or liability in connexion with the reproduction or performance of any work in a manner which at the time was lawful, or for the purpose of or with a view to the reproduction or performance of a work at a time when such reproduction or performance would, but for the passing of this Act, have been lawful, nothing in this section shall diminish or prejudice any rights or interest arising from or in connexion with such action which are subsisting and valuable at the said date, unless the person who by virtue of this section becomes entitled to restrain such reproduction or performance agrees to pay such compensation as, failing agreement, may be determined by arbitration.

(2) For the purposes of this section, the expression "author" includes the legal personal representatives of a deceased author.

(3) Subject to the provisions of section nineteen subsections (7) and (8) and of section thirty-three of this Act, copyright shall not subsist in any work made before the commencement of this Act, otherwise than under, and in accordance with, the provisions of this section.

Application to British Possessions

Application of Act to British dominions

25.—(1) This Act, except such of the provisions thereof as are expressly restricted to the United Kingdom, shall extend throughout His Majesty's dominions: Provided that it shall not extend to a self-governing dominion, unless declared by the Legislature of that dominion to be in force therein either without any modifications or additions, or with such modifications and additions relating exclusively to procedure and remedies, or necessary to adapt this Act to the circumstances of the dominion, as may be enacted by such Legislature.

(2) If the Secretary of State certifies by notice published in the *London Gazette* that any self-governing dominion has passed legislation under which works, the authors whereof were at the date of the making of the works British subjects resident elsewhere than in the dominion or (not being British subjects) were resident in the parts of His Majesty's dominions to which this Act extends, enjoy within the dominion rights substantially identical with those conferred by this Act, then, whilst such legislation continues in force, the dominion shall, for the purposes of the rights conferred by this Act, be treated as if it were a dominion to which this Act extends; and it shall be lawful for the Secretary of State to give such a certificate as aforesaid, notwithstanding that the remedies for enforcing the rights, or the restrictions on the importation of copies of works, manufactured in a foreign country, under the law of the dominion, differ from those under this Act.

Legislative powers of self-governing dominions

26.—(1) The Legislature of any self-governing dominion may, at any time, repeal all or any of the enactments relating to copyright passed by Parliament (including this Act) so far as they are operative within that dominion: Provided that no such repeal shall prejudicially affect any legal rights existing at the time of the repeal, and that, on this Act or any part thereof being so repealed by the Legislature of a self-governing dominion, that dominion shall cease to be a dominion to which this Act extends.

(2) In any self-governing dominion to which this Act does not extend, the enactments repealed by this Act shall, so far as they are operative in that dominion, continue in force until repealed by the Legislature of that dominion.

(3) Where His Majesty in Council is satisfied that the law of a self-governing dominion to which this Act does not extend provides adequate protection within the dominion for the works (whether published or unpublished) of authors who at the time of the making of the work were British subjects resident elsewhere than in that dominion, His Majesty in Council may, for the purpose of giving reciprocal protection, direct that this Act, except such parts (if any) thereof as may be specified in the Order, and subject to any conditions contained therein, shall, within the parts of His Majesty's dominions to which this Act extends, apply to works the authors whereof were, at the time of the making of the work, resident within the first-mentioned dominion, and to works first published in that dominion; but, save as provided by such an Order, works the authors whereof were resident in a dominion to which this Act does not extend shall not, whether they are British subjects or not, be entitled to any protection under this Act except such protection as is by this Act conferred on works first published within the parts of His Majesty's dominions to which this Act extends:

Provided that no such Order shall confer any rights within a self-governing dominion, but the Governor in Council of any self-governing dominion to which this Act extends, may, by Order, confer within that dominion the like rights as His Majesty in Council is, under the foregoing provisions of this subsection, authorised to confer within other parts of His Majesty's dominions.

For the purposes of this subsection, the expression "a dominion to which this Act extends" includes a dominion which is for the purposes of this Act to be treated as if it were a dominion to which this Act extends.

Power of Legislatures of British possessions to pass supplemental legislation

27. The Legislature of any British possession to which this Act extends may modify or add to any of the provisions of this Act in its application to the possession, but, except so far as such modifications and additions relate to procedure and remedies, they shall apply only to works the authors whereof were, at the time of the making of the work, resident in the possession, and to works first published in the possession.

Application to protectorates

28. His Majesty may, by Order in Council, extend this Act to any territories under his protection and to Cyprus, and, on the making of any such Order, this Act shall, subject to the provisions of the Order, have effect as if the territories to which it applies or Cyprus were part of His Majesty's dominions to which this Act extends.

PART II.—INTERNATIONAL COPYRIGHT

Power to extend Act to foreign works

29.—(1) His Majesty may, by Order in Council, direct that this Act (except such parts, if any, thereof as may be specified in the Order) shall apply—
  (a) to works first published in a foreign country to which the Order relates, in like manner as if they were first published within the parts of His Majesty's dominions to which this Act extends;
  (b) to literary, dramatic, musical, and artistic works, or any class thereof, the authors whereof were at the time of the making of the work subjects or

citizens of a foreign country to which the Order relates, in like manner as if the authors were British subjects;

(c) in respect of residence in a foreign country to which the Order relates, in like manner as if such residence were residence in the parts of His Majesty's dominions to which this Act extends;

and thereupon, subject to the provisions of this Part of this Act and of the Order, this Act shall apply accordingly:

Provided that—

(i) before making an Order in Council under this section in respect of any foreign country (other than a country with which His Majesty has entered into a convention relating to copyright), His Majesty shall be satisfied that that foreign country has made, or has undertaken to make, such provisions, if any, as it appears to His Majesty expedient to require for the protection of works entitled to copyright under the provisions of Part I of this Act;

(ii) the Order in Council may provide that the term of copyright within such parts of His Majesty's dominions as aforesaid shall not exceed that conferred by the law of the country to which the Order relates;

(iii) the provisions of this Act as to the delivery of copies of books shall not apply to works first published in such country, except so far as is provided by the Order;

(iv) the Order in Council may provide that the enjoyment of the rights conferred by this Act shall be subject to the accomplishment of such conditions and formalities (if any) as may be prescribed by the Order.

(v) in applying the provision of this Act as to ownership of copyright, the Order in Council may make such modifications as appear necessary having regard to the law of the foreign country;

(vi) in applying the provisions of this Act as to existing works, the Order in Council may make such modifications as appear necessary, and may provide that nothing in those provisions as so applied shall be construed as reviving any right of preventing the production or importation of any translation in any case where the right has ceased by virtue of section five of the International Copyright Act, 1886.

(2) An Order in Council under this section may extend to all the several countries named or described therein.

Application of Part II to British possessions

30.—(1) An Order in Council under this Part of this Act shall apply to all His Majesty's dominions to which this Act extends except self-governing dominions and any other possession specified in the Order with respect to which it appears to His Majesty expedient that the Order should not apply.

(2) The Governor in Council of any self-governing dominion to which this Act extends may, as respects that dominion, make the like orders as under this Part of this Act His Majesty in Council is authorised to make with respect to His Majesty's dominions other than self-governing dominions, and the provisions of this Part of this Act shall with the necessary modifications, apply accordingly.

(3) Where it appears to His Majesty expedient to except from the provisions of any Order any part of his dominions not being a self-governing dominion, it shall be lawful for his Majesty by the same or any other Order in Council to declare that such Order and this Part of this Act shall not, and the same shall not,

apply to such part, except so far as is necessary for preventing any prejudice to any rights acquired previously to the date of such Order.

Part III.—Supplemental Provisions

Abrogation of common law rights

31. No person shall be entitled to copyright or any similar right in any literary, dramatic, musical, or artistic work, whether published or unpublished, otherwise than under and in accordance with the provisions of this Act, or of any other statutory enactment for the time being in force, but nothing in this section shall be construed as abrogating any right or jurisdiction to restrain a breach of trust or confidence.

Provisions as to Orders in Council

32.—(1) His Majesty in Council may make Orders for altering, revoking, or varying any Order in Council made under this Act, or under any enactments repealed by this Act, but any Order made under this section shall not affect prejudicially any rights or interests acquired or accrued at the date when the Order comes into operation, and shall provide for the protection of such rights and interests.

(2) Every Order in Council made under this Act shall be published in the *London Gazette* and shall be laid before both Houses of Parliament as soon as may be after it is made, and shall have effect as if enacted in this Act.

Saving of university copyright

33. Nothing in this Act shall deprive any of the universities and colleges mentioned in the Copyright Act, 1775, of any copyright they already possess under the Act, but the remedies and penalties for infringement of any such copyright shall be under this Act and not under that Act.

Saving of compensation to certain libraries

34. There shall continue to be charged on, and paid out of, the Consolidated Fund of the United Kingdom such annual compensation as was immediately before the commencement of this Act payable in pursuance of any Act as compensation to a library for the loss of the right to receive gratuitous copies of books:

Provided that this compensation shall not be paid to a library in any year, unless the Treasury are satisfied that the compensation for the previous year has been applied in the purchase of books for the use of and to be preserved in the library.

Note: This section was not repealed by the 1956 Act, but was repealed by the Statute Law (Repeals) Act 1986 (c.12).

Interpretation

35.—(1) In this Act, unless the context otherwise requires—
"Literary work" includes maps, charts, plans, tables, and compilations;
"Dramatic work" includes any piece for recitation, choreographic work or entertainment in dumb show, the scenic arrangement or acting form of which is fixed in writing or otherwise, any cinematograph production where the arrangement or acting form or the combination of incidents represented give the work an original character;

"Artistic work" includes works of painting, drawing, sculpture and artistic craftsmanship, and architectural works of art and engravings and photographs;

"Work of sculpture" includes casts and models;

"Architectural work of art" means any building or structure having an artistic character or design, in respect of such character or design, or any model for such building or structure, provided that the protection afforded by this Act shall be confined to the artistic character and design, and shall not extend to processes or methods of construction;

"Engravings" include etchings, lithographs, wood-cuts, prints, and other similar works, not being photographs;

"Photograph" includes photo-lithograph and any work produced by any process analogous to photography;

"Cinematograph" includes any work produced by any process analogous to cinematography;

"Collective work" means—

(a) an encyclopaedia, dictionary, year book, or similar work;

(b) a newspaper, review, magazine, or similar periodical; and

(c) any work written in distinct parts by different authors, or in which works or parts of works of different authors are incorporated;

"Infringing", when applied a copy of a work in which copyright subsists, means any copy, including any colourable imitation, made, or imported in contravention of the provisions of this Act;

"Performance" means any acoustic representation of a work and any visual representation of any dramatic action in a work, including such a representation made by means of any mechanical instrument:

"Delivery", in relation to a lecture, includes delivery by means of any mechanical instrument:

"Plate" includes any stereotype or other plate, stone, block, mould, matrix, transfer, or negative used or intended to be used for printing or reproducing copies of any work, and any matrix or other appliance by which records, perforated rolls or other contrivances for the acoustic representation of the work are or are intended to be made;

"Lecture" includes address, speech, and sermon;

"Self-governing domination" means the Dominion of Canada, the Commonwealth of Australia, the Dominion of New Zealand, the Union of South Africa, and Newfoundland.

(2) For the purposes of this Act (other than those relating to infringements of copyright), a work shall not be deemed to be published or performed in public, and a lecture shall not be deemed to be delivered in public, if published, performed in public, or delivered in public, without the consent or acquiescence of the author, his executors administrators or assigns.

(3) For the purposes of this Act, a work shall be deemed to be first published within the parts of His Majesty's dominions to which this Act extends, notwithstanding that it has been published simultaneously in some other place, unless the publication in such parts of His Majesty's dominions as aforesaid is colourable only and is not intended to satisfy the reasonable requirements of the public, and a work shall be deemed to be published simultaneously in two places if the time between the publication in one such place and the publication in the other place does not exceed fourteen days, or such longer period as may, for the time being, be fixed by Order in Council.

(4) Where, in the case of an unpublished work, the making of a work has

extended over a considerable period, the conditions of this Act conferring copyright shall be deemed to have been compiled with, if the author was, during any substantial part of that period, a British subject or a resident within the parts of His Majesty's dominions to which this Act extends.

(5) For the purposes of the provisions of this Act as to residence, an author of a work shall be deemed to be a resident in the parts of His Majesty's dominions to which this Act extends if he is domiciled within any such part.

Repeal

36. Subject to the provisions of this Act, the enactments mentioned in the Second Schedule to this Act are hereby repealed to the extent specified in the third column of that schedule:

Provided that this repeal shall not take effect in any part of His Majesty's dominions until this Act comes into operation in that part.

Short title and commencement

37.—(1) This Act may be cited as the Copyright Act, 1911.

(2) This Act shall come into operation—

    (a) in the United Kingdom, on the first day of July nineteen hundred and twelve or such earlier date as may be fixed by Order in Council;

    (b) in a self-governing dominion to which this Act extends, at such date as may be fixed by the Legislature of that dominion;

    (c) in the Channel Islands, at such date as may be fixed by the States of those islands respectively;

    (d) in any other British possession to which this Act extends, on the proclamation thereof within the possession by the Governor.

Note: This section was not repealed by the 1956 Act, but subs.(2) thereof was repealed by the Statute Law (Repeals) Act 1986 (c.12).

SCHEDULES

Section 24

FIRST SCHEDULE

EXISTING RIGHTS

Existing Right	Substituted Right
(a) In the case of Works other than Dramatic and Musical Works.	
Copyright	Copyright as defined by this Act.
(b) In the case of Musical and Dramatic Works.	
Both copyright and performing right	Copyright as defined by this Act.
Copyright, but not performing right	Copyright as defined by this Act, except the sole right to perform the work or any substantial part thereof in public.
Performing right, but not copyright	The sole right to perform the work in public, but none of the other rights comprised in copyright as defined by this Act.

For the purposes of this Schedule, the following expressions, where used in the first column thereof, have the following meanings:

"Copyright", in the case of a work which according to the law in force immediately before the commencement of this Act has not been published before that date and statutory copyright wherein depends on publication, includes the right at common law (if any) to restrain publication or other dealing with the work;

* In the case of an essay, article, or portion forming part of and first published in a review, magazine, or other periodical or work of a like nature, the right shall be subject to any right of publishing the essay, article, or portion in a separate form to which the author is entitled at the commencement of this Act, or would, if this Act had not been passed, have become entitled under section eighteen of the Copyright Act, 1842.

"Performing right", in the case of a work which has not been performed in public before the commencement of this Act, includes the right at common law (if any) to restrain the performance thereof in public.

Section 36

SECOND SCHEDULE

ENACTMENTS REPEALED

Session and Chapter	Short Title	Extent of Repeal
8 Geo. 2, c.13.	The Engraving Copyright Act, 1734.	The whole Act.
7 Geo. 3, c.38	The Engraving Copyright Act, 1767.	The whole Act.
15 Geo. 3, c.53.	The Copyright Act, 1775.	The whole Act.
17 Geo. 3, c.57.	The Prints Copyright Act, 1777.	The whole Act.
54 Geo. 3, c.56.	The Sculpture Copyright Act, 1814.	The whole Act.
3 & 4 Will. 4, c.15.	The Dramatic Copyright Act, 1833.	The whole Act.
5 & 6 Will. 4, c.65.	The Lectures Copyright Act, 1835.	The whole Act.
6 &7 Will. 4, c.59.	The Prints and Engravings Copyright (Ireland) Act, 1836.	The whole Act.
6 & 7 Will. 4, c.110.	The Copyright Act, 1836.	The whole Act.
5 & 6 Vict. c.45.	The Copyright Act, 1842.	The whole Act.
7 & 8 Vict. c.12.	The International Copyright Act, 1844.	The whole Act.
10 & 11 Vict. c.95.	The Colonial Copyright Act, 1847.	The whole Act.
15 & 16 Vict. c.12.	The International Copyright Act, 1852.	The whole Act.
25 & 26 Vict. c.68.	The Fine Arts Copyright Act, 1862.	Sections one to six. In section eight the words "and pursuant to any Act for the protection of copyright engravings," and "and in any such Act as aforesaid." Sections nine to twelve.
38 & 39 Vict. c.12.	The International Copyright Act, 1875.	The whole Act.
39 & 40 Vict. c.36.	The Customs Consolidation Act, 1876.	Section forty-two, from "Books wherein" to "such copyright will expire." Sections forty-four, forty-five, and one hundred and fifty-two.
45 & 46 Vict. c.40.	The Copyright (Musical Compositions) Act, 1882.	The whole Act.
49 & 50 Vict. c.33.	The International Copyright Act, 1886.	The whole Act.

Session and Chapter	Short Title	Extent of Repeal
51 & 52 Vict. c.17.	The Copyright (Musical Compositions) Act, 1888.	The whole Act.
52 & 53 Vict. c.42.	The Revenue Act, 1889.	Section one, form "Books first published" to "as provided in that section."
6 Edw. 7, c.36.	The Musical Copyright Act, 1906.	In section three the words "and which has been registered in accordance" with the provisions of the "Copyright Act, 1842, or" of the International "Copyright Act, 1844," which registration may "be effected notwithstanding anything in the International Copyright"Act, 1886."

E4. COMPARATIVE TABLES III AND IV

COMPARATIVE TABLE—III

Copyright Act 1911 compared with Copyright Act 1956

1911	1956	1911	1956	1911	1956
s. 1 (1) (a)	ss. 2 (2), 3	s. 5 (1) (b)	s. 4 (2), (5)	s. 19 (6)	s. 8 (11)
	(3)	(2)	36 (1), (2),	(7)	(9)
(b)	1 (5), 2		(3)	(8)	omitted
	(1), 3 (2)	proviso	omitted	20	omitted
(2)	1 (1), 2	(3)	49 (5)	21	3 (4)
	(5), 3 (5)	6 (1)	17 (1)	22	ss. 10, 44
	46 (1),	(2)	omitted	23	s. 35
	48 (1),	(3)	20 (1)	24	omitted
	49 (1),	(a)	20 (2)	25	ss. 1 (1), 31
(a) (b) (c)	s. 2 (6)	(b)	20 (4)	26	omitted
(d)	ss. 2 (5), 3	7	18 (1)	27	s. 31 (3)
	(5), 48 (1)	8	ss. 17 (2) 18	28	(1)
(3)	s. 49 (2)		(2)	29	32
2 (1)	1 (2)	9 (1)	s. 17 (4)	30	omitted
(i)	6 (1), (2),	(2)	omitted	31	46 (4), (5)
	(3)	10	omitted	32	47
	9 (1), (2)	11	21	33	46 (1)
(ii)	9 (9)	12	21 (10)	34	not repealed
(iii)	9 (3),	13	21 (6)	35 (1)	ss. 3 (1), 13
	(4), (6)	14	22		(10)
(iv)	6 (6)	15	not repealed		18 (3), 48
(v) (vi)	omitted	16	11, Sch. 3		(1)
(2) (a)	5 (3)	(4)	16 (3)		s. 49 (2), (3)
(b)	(4)	17 (1)	ss. 2 (3), 3		
(c)	(3)		(4)	(2)	49 (3)
(d)	(2)	(2)	s. 38	(3)	(2)
(3)	(5)	18	39	(4)	(9)
3	ss. 2 (3), 3	19 (1)	12 (1)	(5)	1 (5) (a)
	(4)	(2)	8 (1), (5),		
proviso	omitted		(6), (8)	36	omitted
4	omitted	(3)	(2)	37	not repealed
5 (1)	s. 4 (1)	(3)	(3)	Sch. 1	omitted
(a)	(3), (5)	proviso		Sch. 2	omitted
		(4)	(4)		
		(5)	(7)		

COMPARATIVE TABLE—IV

Copyright Act 1956 compared with Copyright Act 1911

1956	1911	1956	1911	1956	1911
s.1 (1)	s.1 (2)	s.9 (1), (2)	s.2 (1) (i)	s.31 (2)	—
(2)	2 (1)	(3), (4)	(iii)	32 (3)	s.27
(3), (4)	—	(5)	—	ss.33, 34	29
(5)	1 (1) (b)	(6)	2 (1) (iii)	s.35	—
2 (1)	(b)	(7), (8)	—	36	23
(2)	(a)	(9)	2 (1) (ii)	37	5 (2)
(3)	ss.3, 17	(10), (11)	—	38	—
(4)	—	10	—	39	17 (2)
(5)	s.1 (2)	11 (1)	—	ss.40–45	18
(6)	(2)	(2), (3)	16	s.46 (1)	—
3 (1)	35 (1)	12	19 (1)	(2)	33
(2)	1 (1) (b)	ss.13–16	—	(3)	18
(3)	(a)	s.17 (1)	6 (1)	(4)	—
(4)	ss.3, 17, 21	(2)	(8)	(5), (6)	31
(5)	s.1 (2)	(3)	—	47	32
4 (1)	5 (1)	(4)	9 (1)	48 (1)	35 (1)
(2)	(b)	18 (1)	7	(2)–(7)	—
(3)	(a)	(2) (a)	8 (1)	49 (1)	1 (2)
(4)	(b)	(b), (c)	—	(2)	ss.1 (3), 35, (3)
(5)	5 (1)	(3)	35 (1)	(3)	s.35 (2)
(6)	—	19	—	(4)	(4)
5	2 (2), (3)	20 (1), (2)	6 (3)	(5)	5 (3)
6 (1)		(3)	—	(6)–(10)	(3)
(3)	(1) (i)	(4)	6 (3)	50	24
(4)	—	(5), (6)	—	51	—
(5)	2 (1) (ii)	21	ss.11, 12	Schs 1, 2	—
(6)	(iv)	22	s.14	Schs 3	16
(7)–(10)	—	ss.23–30	—	Schs 4–9	—
7	—	s.31 (1)	28		
8	19 (2)–(7)				

E5. PRE-1911 ACT STATUTES

E5.i Statute of Anne 1709

ANNO OCTAVO ANNÆ REGINÆ.

An Act for the Encouragement of Learning, by Vesting the Copies of Printed Books in the Authors or Purchasers of such Copies, during the Times therein mentioned.

Whereas Printers, Booksellers, and other Persons, have of late frequently taken the Liberty of Printing, Reprinting, and Publishing, or causing to be Printed, Reprinted, and Published Books, and other Writings, without the Consent of the Authors or Proprietors of such Books and Writings, to their very great Detriment, and too often to the Ruin of them and their Families: For Preventing therefore such Practices for the future, and for the Encouragement of Learned Men to Compose and Write useful Books; May it please Your Majesty, that it may be Enacted, and be it Enacted by the Queens most Excellent Majesty, by and with the Advice and Consent of the Lords Spiritual and Temporal, and Commons in this present Parliament Assembled, and by the Authority of the same, That from and after the Tenth Day of April, One thousand seven hundred and ten, the Author of any Book or Books already Printed, who hath not Transferred to any other the Copy or Copies of such Book or Books, Share or Shares thereof, or the Bookseller or Booksellers, Printer or Printers, or other Person or Persons, who hath or have Purchased or Acquired the Copy or Copies of any Book or Books, in order to Print or Reprint the same, shall have the sole Right and Liberty of Printing such Book and Books for the Term of One and twenty Years, to Commence from the said Tenth Day of April, and no longer; and that the Author of any Book or Books already Composed and not Printed and Published, or that shall hereafter be Composed, and his Assignee, or Assigns, shall have the sole Liberty of Printing and Reprinting such Book and Books for the Term of four-teen Years, to Commence from the Day of the First Publishing the same, and no longer; And that if any other Bookseller, Printer, or other Person whatsoever, from and after the Tenth Day of April, One thousand seven hundred and ten, within the times Granted and Limited by this Act, as aforesaid, shall Print, Reprint, or Import, or cause to be Printed, Reprinted, or Imported any such Book or Books, without the Consent of the Proprietor or Proprietors thereof first had and obtained in Writing, Signed in the Presence of Two or more Credible Witnesses; or knowing the same to be so Printed or Reprinted, without the Consent of the Proprietors, shall Sell, Publish, or Expose to Sale, or cause to be Sold, Published, or Exposed to Sale, any such Book or Books, without such Consent first had and obtained, as aforesaid, Then such Offender or Offenders shall Forfeit such Book or Books, and all and every Sheet or Sheets, being part of such Book or Books, to the Proprietor or Proprietors of the Copy thereof, who shall forthwith Damask and make Waste-Paper of them: And further, That every such Offender or Offenders, shall Forfeit One Peny for every sheet which shall be found in his, her, or their Custody, either Printed or Printing, Published or Exposed to Sale, contrary to the true intent and meaning of this Act, the one Moiety thereof to the Queens most Excellent Majesty, Her Heirs and Successors, and the other Moiety thereof to any Person or Persons that shall Sue for the same, to be Recovered in any of Her Majesties Courts of Record at Westminster, by Action of Debt, Bill, Plaint, or Information, in which no Wager of Law, Essoign, Privilege, or Protection, or more than one Imparlance, shall be allowed.

And whereas many Persons may through Ignorance Offend against this Act, unless some Provision be made whereby the Property in every such Book, as is intended by this Act to be Secured to the proprietor or Proprietors thereof, may be ascertained, as likewise the Consent of such Proprietor or Proprietors for the Printing or Reprinting of such Book or Books may from time to time be known; Be it therefore further Enacted by the Authority aforesaid, That nothing in this Act contained shall be construed to extend to subject any Bookseller, Printer, or other Person whatsoever, to the Forfeitures or Penalties therein mentioned, for or by reason of the Printing or Reprinting of any Book or Books without such Consent, as aforesaid, unless the Title to the Copy of such Book or Books hereafter Published shall, before such Publication be Entred, in the Register-Book of the Company of Stationers, in such manner as hath been usual, which Register-Book shall at all times be kept at the Hall of the said Company, and unless such Consent of the Proprietor or Proprietors be in like manner Entred, as aforesaid, for every of which several Entries, Six Pence shall be Paid, and no more; which said Register-Book may, at all Seasonable and Convenient times, be Resorted to, and Inspected by any Bookseller, Printer, or other Person, for the Purposes before mentioned, without any Fee or Reward; and the Clerk of the said Company of Stationers, shall, when and as often as thereunto required, give a Certificate under his Hand of such Entry or Entries, and for every such Certificate, may take a Fee not exceeding Six Pence.

Provided nevertheless, That if the Clerk of the said Company of Stationers, for the time being shall Refuse or Neglect to Register, or make such Entry or Entries, or to give such Certificate, being thereunto Required by the Author or Proprietor of such Copy or Copies, in the Presence of Two or more Credible Witnesses, That then such Person and Persons so refusing, Notice being first duly given of such Refusal, by an Advertisement in the Gazette, shall have the like Benefit, as if such Entry or Entries, Certificate or Certificates had been duly made and given; and that the Clerks so refusing, shall, for any such Offence, Forfeit to the Proprietor of such Copy or Copies the Sum of Twenty Pounds, to be Recovered in any of Her Majesties Courts of Record at Westminster, by Action of Debt, Bill, Plaint, or Information, in which no Wager of Law, Essoign, Privilege or Protection, or more than one Imparlance shall be allowed.

Provided nevertheless, and it is hereby further Enacted by the Authority aforesaid, That if any Bookseller or Booksellers, Printer or Printers, shall, after the said Five and twentieth Day of March, One thousand seven hundred and ten, set a Price upon, or Sell or Expose to Sale, any Book or Books at such a Price or Rate as shall be Conceived by any Person or Persons to be High and Unreasonable; It shall and may be Lawful for any Person or Persons to make Complaint thereof to the Lord Archbishop of Canterbury for the time being; the Lord Chancellor, or Lord Keeper of the Great Seal of Great Britain for the time being; the Lord Bishop of London for the time being; the Lord Chief Justice of the Court of Queens Bench, the Lord Chief Justice of the Court of Common Pleas, the Lord Chief Baron of the Court of Exchequer, for the time being; the Vice-Chancellors of the Two Universities for the time being, in that part of Great Britain called England; the Lord President of the Sessions for the time being; the Lord Justice General for the time being; the Lord Chief Baron of the Exchequer for the time being; the Rector of the College of Edinburgh for the time being, in that part of Great Britain called Scotland; who, or any one of them, shall and have hereby full Power and Authority from time to time, to Send for, Summon, or Call before him or them such Bookseller or Booksellers, Printer or Printers, and to Examine and Enquire of the reason of the Dearness and Inhauncement of the Price or Value of such Book or Books by him or them so Sold or Exposed to Sale; and if upon such Enquiry and Examination it shall be found, that the Price of such Book or Books is Inhaunced, or any wise too High or Unreasonable, Then and in such case, the said Archbishop of Canterbury, Lord Chancellor or Lord Keeper, Bishop of London, two Chief Justices, Chief Baron, Vice Chancellors of the Universities, in that part of Great Britain called England, and the said Lord President of the Sessions, Lord Justice General, Lord Chief Baron, and Rector of the College of Edinburgh, in that part of Great Britain called Scotland, or any one or more of them, so Enquiring and Examining, have hereby full Power and Authority to Reform and Redress the same, and to Limit and Settle the Price of every such Printed Book and Books, from time to time, according to the best of their Judgements, and as to them shall seem Just and Reasonable; and in case of Alteration of the Rate or Price from what was Set or Demanded by such Bookseller or Booksellers, Printer or Printers, to Award and Order such Bookseller and Booksellers, Printer and Printers, to Pay all the Costs and Charges that the Person or Persons so Complaining shall be put unto, by reason of such Complaint, and of the causing such Rate or Price to be so Limited and Settled; all which shall be done by the said Archbishop of Canterbury, Lord Chancellor, or Lord Keeper, Bishop of London, two Chief Justices, Chief Baron, Vice Chancellors of the Two Universities, in that part of Great Britain called England, and the said Lord President of the Sessions, Lord Justice General, Lord Chief Baron, and Rector of the College of Edinburgh, in that part of Great Britain called Scotland, or any one of them, by Writing under their Hands and Seals, and thereof Publick Notice shall be forthwith given by the said Bookseller or Booksellers, Printer or Printers, by an Advertisement in the Gazette; and if any Bookseller or Booksellers, Printer or Printers, shall, after such Settlement made of the said Rate and Price, Sell, or expose to Sale any Book or Books, at a higher or greater Price than what shall have been so Limited and Settled, as aforesaid, then and in every such case such Bookseller and Booksellers, Printer and Printers, shall Forfeit the Sum of Five Pounds for every such Book so by him, her, or them Sold or Exposed to Sale; One Moiety thereof to the Queens most Excellent Majesty, Her Heirs and Successors, and the other Moiety to any Person or Persons that shall Sue for the same, to be Recovered, with Costs of Suit, in any of Her Majesties Courts of Record at Westminster, by Action of Debt, Bill, Plaint or Information, in which no Wager of Law, Essoign, Privilege or Protection, or more than one Imparlance, shall be allowed.

Provided always, and it is hereby Enacted, That Nine Copies of each Book or Books, upon the best Paper, that from and after the said Tenth Day of April, One thousand seven hundred and ten, shall be Printed and Published, as aforesaid, or Reprinted and Published with Additions, shall, by the Printer and Printers thereof, be Delivered to the Warehouse-Keeper of the said Company of Stationers for the time being, at the Hall of the said Company, before such Publication made, for the Use of the Royal Library, the Libraries of the Universities of Oxford and Cambridge, the Libraries of the Four Universities in Scotland, the Library of Sion College in London, and the Library commonly called the Library belonging to the Faculty of Advocates at Edinburgh respectively; which said Warehouse-Keeper, is hereby required, within Ten Days after Demand by the Keepers of the respective Libraries, or any Person or Persons by them or any of them Authorised to Demand the said Copy, to Deliver the same, for the Use of the aforesaid Libraries; and if any Proprietor, Bookseller or Printer, or the said Warehouse-Keeper of the said Company of Stationers, shall not observe the Direction of this Act therein, That then he and they, so making Default in not Delivering the said Printed Copies, as aforesaid, shall Forfeit, besides the value of the said Printed Copies, the sum of Five Pounds for every Copy not so Delivered, as also the value of the said Printed Copy not so Delivered, the same to be Recovered by the Queens Majesty, Her Heirs and Successors, and by the Chancellor, Masters, and Scholars of any of the said Universities, and by the President and Fellows of Sion College, and the said Faculty of Advocates at Edinburgh, with their full Costs respectively.

Provided always, and be it further Enacted, That if any Person or Persons incur the Penalties contained in this Act, in that part of Great Britain called Scotland, they shall be recoverable by any Action before the Court of Session there.

Provided, That nothing in this Act contained do extend, or shall be construed to extend, to Prohibit the Importation, Vending, or Selling of any Books in Greek, Latin, or any other Foreign Language Printed beyond the Seas; Any thing in this Act contained to the contrary notwithstanding.

And be it further Enacted by the Authority aforesaid, That if any Action or Suit shall be Commenced or Brought against any Person or Persons whatsoever, for doing or causing to be done any thing in pursuance of this Act, the Defendants in such Action may Plead the General Issue, and give the Special Matter in Evidence; and if upon such Action a Verdict be given for the Defendant, or the Plaintiff become Nonsuited, or Discontinue his Action, then the Defendant shall have and recover his full Costs, for which he shall have the same Remedy as a Defendant in any case by Law hath.

Provided, That nothing in this Act contained shall extend, or be construed to extend, either to Prejudice or Confirm any Right that the said Universities, or any of them, or any Person or Persons have, or claim to have, to the Printing or Reprinting any Book or Copy already Printed, or hereafter to be Printed.

Provided nevertheless, That all Actions, Suits, Bills, Indictments, or Informations for any Offence that shall be Committed against this Act, shall be Brought, Sued, and Commenced within Three Months next after such Offence Committed, or else the same shall be Void and of none Effect.

Provided always, That after the Expiration of the said Term of Fourteen Years, the sole Right of Printing or Disposing of Copies shall return to the Authors thereof, if they are then Living, for another Term of Fourteen Years.

FINIS

E5.ii The Engraving Copyright Act 1734 section 1

(8 GEO. II C.13)

An Act for the Encouragement of the Art of designing, engraving, and etching historical and other Prints, by vesting the Properties thereof in the Inventors and Engravers during the Time therein mentioned.

1. That from and after the twenty-fourth day of June which shall be in the year of our Lord one thousand seven hundred and thirty-five, every person who shall invent and design, engrave, etch, or work, in mezzotinto or chiaro-oscuro, or from his own works and invention shall cause to be designed and engraved, etched, or worked, in mezzotinto or chiaro-oscuro, any historical or other print or prints, shall have the sole right and liberty of printing and reprinting the same for the term of fourteen years, to commence from the day of the first publishing thereof, which shall be truly engraved with the name of the proprietor on each plate, and printed on every such print or prints; and that if any print-seller or other person whatsoever, from and after the said twenty-fourth day of June one thousand seven hundred and thirty-five, within the time limited by this Act, shall engrave, etch, or work as aforesaid, or in any other manner copy and sell, or cause to be engraved, etched, or copied and sold, in the whole or in part, by varying, adding to, or diminishing from the main design, or shall print, reprint, or import for sale, or cause to be printed, reprinted, or imported for sale, any such print or prints, or any parts thereof, without the consent of the proprietor or proprietors thereof first had and obtained in writing signed by him or them respectively in the presence of two or more credible witnesses, or, knowing the same to be so printed or reprinted without the consent of the proprietor or proprietors shall publish, sell, or expose for sale, or otherwise or in any other manner disposed of, or cause to be published, sold, or exposed to sale, or otherwise or in any other manner disposed of, any such print or prints, without such consent first had and obtained as aforesaid, then such offender or offenders shall forfeit the plate or plates on which such print or prints are or shall be copied, and all and every sheet or sheets (being part of or whereon such print or prints are or shall be so copied or printed), to the proprietor or proprietors of such original print or prints, who shall forthwith destroy and damask the same.

E5.iii The Engraving Copyright Act 1766 sections 1, 2, 3

(7 GEO. III C.38)

An Act to amend and render more effectual an Act made in the Eighth Year of the Reign of King George the Second, for Encouragement of the Arts of designing, engraving, and etching historical and other Prints; and for vesting in, and securing to, Jane Hogarth, Widown, the Property in certain Prints.

1. That from and after the first day of January, one thousand seven hundred and sixty-seven, all and every person and persons who shall invent or design, engrave, etch, or work in mezzotinto or chiaro-oscuro, or, from his own work, design, or invention, shall cause or procure to be designed, engraved, etched, or worked in mezzotinto or chiaro-oscuro, any historical print or prints, or any print or prints of any portrait, conversation, landscape, or architecture, map, chart, or plan, or any other print or prints whatsoever, shall have, and are hereby declared to have, the benefit and protection of the said Act and this Act, under the restrictions and limitations hereinafter mentioned.

2. And be it further enacted by the authority aforesaid, That from and after the said first day of January one thousand seven hundred and sixty-seven, all and every person and persons who shall engrave, etch, or work in mezzotinto or chiaro-oscuro, or cause to be engraved, etched or worked, any print, taken from any picture, drawing, model, or sculpture, either ancient or modern, shall have, and are hereby declared to have, the benefit and protection of [the Engraving Copyright Act 1734] and this Act, for the term hereinafter mentioned, in like manner as if such print had been graved or drawn from the original design of such graver, etcher, or draftsman; and if any person shall engrave, print and publish, or import for sale, any copy of any such print, contrary to the true intent and meaning of this and the said former Act, every such person shall be liable to the penalties contained in the said Act, to be recovered as therein and hereinafter is mentioned.

6. And be it further enacted by the authority aforesaid, That the sole right and liberty of printing and reprinting intended to be secured and protected by the said former Act and this Act, shall be extended, continued, and be vested in the respective proprietors, for the space of twenty-eight years, to commence from the day of the first publishing of any of the works respectively hereinbefore and in the said former act mentioned.

E5.iv The Prints Copyright Act 1777 section 1

(17 GEO. III C.57)

An Act for more effectually securing the Property of Prints to Inventors and Engravers, by enabling them to sue for and recover Penalties in certain Cases.

1. That from and after the twenty-forth day of June, one thousand seven hundred and seventy-seven, if any engraver, etcher, print-seller, or other person shall, within the time limited by [the Engraving Act 1734 and the Engraving Act 1766], or either of them, engrave, etch, or work, or cause or procure to be engraved, etched, or worked, in mezzotinto or chiaro-oscuro, or otherwise, or in any other manner copy, in the whole or in part, by varying, adding to, or diminishing from the main design, or shall print, reprint, or import for sale, or cause or procure to be printed, reprinted, or imported for sale, or shall publish, sell, or otherwise dispose of, any copy or copies of any historical print or prints, or any print or prints of any portrait, conversation, landscape, or architecture, map, chart, or plan, or any other print or prints whatsoever, which hath or have been, or shall be engraved, etched, drawn, or designed, in any part of Great Britain, without the express consent of the proprietor or proprietors thereof first had and obtained in writing, signed by him, her, or them respectively, with his, her, or their own hand or hands, in the presence of and attested by two or more credible witnesses, then every such proprietor or proprietors shall and may, by and in a special action upon the case, to be brought against the person or persons so offending, recover such damages as a jury on the trial of such action or on the execution of a writ of inquiry thereon, shall give or assess, together with double costs of suit.

E5.v The Sculpture Copyright Act 1814 sections 1, 2, 6

(54 Geo. III. c.56)

An Act to amend and render more effectual an Act of His present Majesty, for encouraging the Art of making new Models and Casts of Busts, and other Things therein mentioned; and for giving further Encouragement to such Arts.

1. That from and after the passing of this Act, every person or persons who shall make or cause to be made any new and original sculpture or model, or copy or cast, of the human figure, or human figures, or of any bust or busts, or of any part or parts of the human figure, clothed in drapery or otherwise, or of any animal or animals, or of any part or parts of any animal combined with the human figure or otherwise, or of any subject being matter of invention in sculpture, or of any alto or bassorclievo representing any of the matters or things hereinbefore mentioned, or any cast from nature of the human figure, or of any part or parts of the human figure, or of any cast from nature of any animal, or of any part or parts of any animal, or of any such subject containing or representing any of the matters and things hereinbefore mentioned, whether separate or combined, shall have the sole right and property of all and in every such new and original sculpture, model, copy, and cast of the human figure or human figures, and of all and in every such busts or busts, and of all and in every such part or parts of the human figure, clothed in drapery or otherwise, and of all and in every such new and original sculpture, model, copy, and cast, representing any animal or animals, and of all and in every such work representing any part or parts of any animal combined with the human figure or otherwise, and of all and in every such new and original sculpture, model, copy, and cast of any subject, being matter of invention in sculpture and of all and in every such new and original sculpture, model, copy, and cast in alto or basso relievo, representing any of the matters or things hereinbefore mentioned, and of every such cast from nature, for the term of fourteen years from first putting forth or publishing the same: Provided, in all and in every case, the proprietor or proprietors do cause his, her, or their name or names, with the date, to be put on all and every such new and original sculpture, model, copy, or cast, and on every such cast from nature, before the same shall be put forth or published.

2. And be it further enacted, That the sole right and property of all works, which have been put forth or published under the protection of the said recited Act, shall be extended, continued to and vested in the respective proprietors thereof for the term of fourteen years, to commence from the date when such last mentioned works respectively were put forth or published.

6. Provided always, and be it further enacted, That from and immediately after the expiration of the said term of fourteen years, the sole right of making and disposing of such new and original sculpture or model, or copy, or cast of any of the matters or things hereinbefore mentioned, shall return to the person or persons who originally made or caused to be made the same, if he or they shall be then living, for the further term of fourteen years, excepting in the case or cases where such person or persons shall by sale or otherwise have divested himself, herself, or themselves, of such right of making or disposing of any new and original sculpture, model, or copy, or cast of any of the matters or things hereinbefore mentioned, previous to the passing of this Act.

E5.vi The Dramatic Copyright Act 1833 section 1

(3 WILL. IV. c.15)

An Act to amend the Laws relating to dramatic literary Property.

1. That from and after the passing of this Act the author of any tragedy, comedy, play, opera, farce, or any other dramatic piece or entertainment, composed, and not printed and published by the author thereof, or his assignee, or which hereafter shall be composed, and not printed or published by the author thereof or his assignee, or the assignee of such author, shall have as his own property the sole liberty of representing, or causing to be represented, at any place or places of dramatic entertainment whatsoever, in any part of the United Kingdom of Great Britain and Ireland, in the Isles of Man, Jersey, and Guernsey, or in any part of the British dominions, any such production as aforesaid, not printed and published by the author thereof or his assignee, and shall be deemed and taken to be the proprietor thereof; and that the author of any such production, printed and published within ten years before the passing of this Act by the author thereof of his assignee, or which shall hereafter be so printed and published, or the assignee of such author, shall from the time of passing this Act, or from the time of such publication respectively, until the end of twenty-eight years from the day of such first publication of the same, and also, if the author or authors, or the survivor of the authors, shall be living at the end of that period, during the residue of his natural life, have as his own property the sole liberty of representing, or causing to be represented, the same at any such place of dramatic entertainment as aforesaid, and shall be deemed and taken to be the proprietor thereof.

E5.vii The Lectures Copyright Act 1835 sections 1, 5

(5 & 6 WILL. IV. c.65.)

An Act for preventing the Publication of Lectures without Consent

1. That from and after the first day of September one thousand eight hundred and thirty-five the author of any lecture or lectures, or the person to whom he hath sold or otherwise conveyed the copy thereof, in order to deliver the same in any school, seminary, institution, or other place, or for any other purpose, shall have the sole right and liberty of printing and publishing such lecture or lectures; and that if any person shall, by taking down the same in short-hand or otherwise in writing, or in any other way, obtain or make a copy of such lecture or lectures, and shall print or lithograph or otherwise copy and publish the same, or cause the same to be printed, lithographed, or otherwise copied and published, without leave of the author thereof, or of the person to whom the author thereof hath sold or otherwise conveyed the same, and every person who, knowing the same to have been printed or copied and published without such consent, shall sell, publish, or expose to sale, or cause to be sold, published, or exposed to sale, any such lecture or lectures, shall forfeit such printed or otherwise copied lecture or lectures, or parts thereof, together with one penny for every sheet thereof which shall be found in his custody, either printed, lithographed, or copied, or printing, lithographing, or copying, published or exposed to sale, contrary to the true intent and meaning of this Act, the one moiety thereof to His Majesty, his heirs or successors, and the other moiety thereof to any person who shall sue for the same, to be recovered in any of His Majesty's Courts of Record in Westminster, by action of debt, bill, plaint, or information, in which no wager of law, essoign, privilege, or protection, or more than one imparlance shall be allowed.

5. Provided further, That nothing in this Act shall extend to any lecture or lectures, or the printing, copying, or publishing any lecture or lectures, or parts thereof, of the delivering of which notice in writing shall not have been given to two justices living within five miles from the place where such lecture or lectures shall be delivered two days at the least before delivering the same, or to any lecture or lectures delivered in any university or public school or college, or on any public foundation, or by any individual in virtue of or according to any gift, endowment, or foundation; and that the law relating thereto shall remain the same as if this Act had not been passed.

E5.viii The Copyright Act 1842 sections 2, 3, 18, 20, 22

(5 & 6 VICT. C.45)

An Act to amend the Law of Copyright

2. And be it enacted, That in the construction of this Act the word "book" shall be construed to mean and include every volume, part or division of a volume, pamphlet, sheet of letter-press, sheet of music, map, chart, or plan separately published: that the words "dramatic piece" shall be construed to mean and include every tragedy, comedy, play, opera, farce, or other scenic, musical, or dramatic entertainment; that the word "copyright" shall be construed to mean the sole and exclusive liberty of printing or otherwise multiplying copies of any subject to which the said word is herein applied; that the words "personal representative" shall be construed to mean and include every executor, administrator, and next of kin entitled to administration; that the word "assigns" shall be construed to mean and include every person in whom the interest of an author in copyright shall be vested, whether derived from such author before or after the publication of any book, and whether acquired by sale, gift, bequest, or by operation of law, or otherwise; that the words "British Dominions" shall be construed to mean and include all parts of the United Kingdom of Great Britain and Ireland, the Islands of Jersey and Guernsey, all parts of the East and West Indies, and all the colonies, settlements, and possessions of the Crown which now are or hereafter may be acquired; and that whenever in this Act, in describing any person, matter, or thing the word importing the singular number or the masculine gender only is used, the same shall be understood to include and to be applied to several persons as well as one person, and females as well as males, and several matters or things as well as one matter or thing, respectively, unless there shall be something in the subject or context repugnant to such construction.

3. And be it enacted, That the copyright in every book which shall after the passing of this Act be published in the lifetime of its author shall endure for the natural life of such author, and for the further term of seven years, commencing at the time of his death, and shall be the property of such author and his assigns: Provided always, that if the said term of seven years shall expire before the end of forty-two years from the first publication of such book, the copyright shall in that case endure for such period of forty-two years; and that the copyright in every book which shall be published after the death of its author shall endure for the term of forty-two years from the first publication thereof, and shall be the property of the proprietor of the author's manuscript from which such book shall be first published, and his assigns.

18. And be it enacted, That when any publisher or other person shall, before or at the time of the passing of this Act, have projected, conducted, and carried on, or shall hereafter project, conduct, and carry on, or be the proprietor of any encyclopaedia, review, magazine, periodical work, or work published in a series of books or parts, or any book whatsoever, and shall have employed or shall employ any persons to compose the same, or any volumes, parts, essays, articles, or portions thereof, for publication in or as part of the same, and such work, volumes, parts, essays, articles, or portions shall have been or shall hereafter be composed under such employment, on the terms that the copyright therein shall belong to such proprietor, projector, publisher or conductor, and paid for by such proprietor, projector, publisher, or conductor, the copyright in every such encyclopaedia, review, magazine periodical work, and work published in a series of books or parts, and in every volume, part, essay, article, and portion so composed and paid for, shall be the property of such proprietor, projector, publisher, or other conductor, who shall enjoy the same rights as if he were the actual author thereof, and shall have such term of copyright therein as is given to the authors of books by this Act; except only that in the case of essays, articles, or portions forming part of and first published in reviews, magazines, or other periodical works of a like nature, after the term of twenty-eight years from the first publication thereof respectively the right of publishing the same in a separate form shall revert to the author for the remainder of the term given by this Act: Provided always, that during the term of twenty-eight years the said proprietor, projector, publisher, or conductor shall not publish any such essay, article, or portion separately or singly, without the consent previously obtained, of the author thereof, or his assigns: Provided, also, that nothing herein contained shall alter or affect the right of any person who shall have been or who shall be employed as aforesaid to publish any such his composition in a separate form who by any contract, express or implied, may have reserved or may hereafter reserve to himself such right; but every author reserving, retaining, or having such right shall be entitled to the copyright in such composition when published in a separate form, according to this Act, without prejudice to the right of such proprietor, projector, publisher, or conductor as aforesaid.

20. And whereas an Act was passed in the third year of the reign of His late Majesty, to amend the law relating to dramatic literary property, and it is expedient to extend the term of the sole liberty of representing dramatic pieces given by that Act to the full time by this Act provided for the continuance of copyright: And whereas it is expedient to extend to musical compositions the benefits of that Act, and also of this Act, be it therefore enacted, That the provisions of the said Act of His late Majesty, and of this Act, shall apply to musical compositions, and that the sole liberty of representing or performing, or causing or permitting to be represented or performed, any dramatic piece or musical composition, shall endure and be the property of the author thereof, and his assigns, for the term in this Act provided for the duration of copyright in books: and the provisions hereinbefore enacted in respect of the property of such copyright, and of registering the same, shall apply to the liberty of representing or performing any dramatic piece of musical composition, as if the same were herein expressly re-enacted and applied thereto, save and except that the first public representation or performance of any dramatice piece or musical composition shall be deemed equivalent, in the construction of this Act, to the first publication of any book: Provided always, that in case of any dramatic piece, or musical composition in manuscript, it shall be sufficient for the person having the sole liberty of representing or performing, or causing to be represented or performed, the same to register only the title thereof, the name and place of abode of the author or composer thereof, the name and place of abode of the proprietor thereof, and the time and place of its first representation or performance.

22. And be it enacted, That no assignment of the copyright of any book consisting of or containing a dramatic piece or musical composition shall be holden to convey to the assignee the right of representing or performing such dramatic piece or musical composition, unless an entry in the said registry book shall be made of such assignment, wherein shall be expressed the intention of the parties that such right should pass by such assignment.

E5.ix The International Copyright Act 1852 section 14

(15 & 16 VICT. C.12.)

An Act to explain the Acts relating to Copyright in engravings

14. It is hereby declared, That the provisions of the [Engraving Copyright] Acts are intended to include prints taken by lithography, or any other mechanical process by which prints or impressions of drawings or designs are capable of being multiplied indefinitely, and the said Acts shall be construed accordingly.

E5.x Fine Arts Copyright Act 1862, sections 1, 3

(25 & 26 VICT.C.68)

An Act for amending the Law relating to Copyright in Works of the Fine Arts, and for repressing the Commission of Fraud in the Production and Sale of such Works.

1. The author, being a British subject or resident within the dominions of the Crown, of every original painting, drawing, and photograph which shall be or shall have been made either in the British dominions or elsewhere, and which shall not have been sold or disposed of before the commencement of this Act, and his assigns shall have the sole and exclusive right of copying, engraving, reproducing, and multiplying such painting or drawing, and the design thereof, or such photograph, and the negative thereof, by any means and of any size, for the term of the natural life of such author and seven years after his death; provided that when any painting or drawing, or the negative of any photograph, shall for the first time after the passing of this Act be sold or disposed of, or shall be made or executed for or on behalf of any other person for a good or a valuable consideration, the person so selling or disposing of or making or executing the same shall not retain the copyright thereof, unless it be expressly reserved to him by agreement in writing signed, at or before the time of such sale or disposition, by the vendee or assignee of such painting or drawing, or of such negative of a photograph, or by the person for or on whose behalf the same shall be so made or executed, but the copyright shall belong to the vendee or assignee of such painting or drawing, or of such negative of a photograph, or to the person for or on whose behalf the same shall have been made or executed; nor shall the vendee or assignee thereof be entitled to any such copyright, unless, at or before the time of such sale or disposition, an agreement in writing, signed by the person so selling or disposing of the same, or by his agent duly authorized, shall have been made to that effect.

3. All copyright under this Act shall be deemed personal or moveable estate, and shall be assignable at law, and every assignment thereof, and every licence to use or copy by any means or process the design or work which shall be the subject of such copyright, shall be made by some note or memorandum in writing, to be signed by the proprietor of the copyright, or by his agent appointed for that purpose in writing.

E6. Performers' Protection Acts

E6.i Dramatic and Musical Performers' Protection Act 1958

(6 & 7 Eliz. 2, c.44)

An Act to consolidate the Dramatic and Musical Performers' Protection Act 1925, and the provisions of the Copyright Act, 1956, amending it.[i]

[23rd July 1958]

Penalization of making, etc., records without consent of performers

1. Subject to the provisions of this Act, if a person knowingly—

    (a) makes a record, directly or indirectly from or by means of the performance of a dramatic or musical work without the consent in writing of the performers, or

    (b) sells or lets for hire, or distributes for the purposes of trade, or by way of trade exposes or offers for sale or hire, a record made in contravention of this Act, or

    (c) uses for the purposes of a public performance a record so made,

he shall be guilty of an offence under this Act, and shall be liable, on summary conviction, to a fine not exceeding forty shillings for each record in respect of which an offence is proved, but not exceeding fifty pounds in respect of any one transaction:

Provided that, where a person is charged with an offence under paragraph (a) of this section, it shall be a defence to prove that the record was made for his private and domestic use only.

Penalization of making, etc., cinematograph films without consent of performers

2. Subject to the provisions of this Act, if a person knowingly—

    (a) makes a cinematograph film, directly or indirectly, from or by means of the performance of a dramatic or musical work without consent in writing of the performers, or

    (b) sells or lets for hire, or distributes for the purposes of trade, or by way of trade exposes or offers for sale or hire, a cinematograph film made in contravention of this Act, or

    (c) uses for the purposes of exhibition to the public a cinematograph film so made:

he shall be guilty of an offence under this Act and shall be liable, on summary conviction, to a fine not exceeding fifty pounds:

Provided that, where a person is charged with an offence under paragraph (a) of this section, it shall be a defence to prove that the cinematograph film was made for his private and domestic use only.

Penalization of broadcasting without consent of performers

3. Subject to the provisions of this Act, a person who, otherwise than by the use of a record or cinematograph film, knowingly broadcasts a performance of a dramatic or musical work, or any part of such a performance, without the consent in writing of the performers, shall be guilty of an offence under this Act, and shall be liable, on summary conviction, to a fine not exceeding fifty pounds.

---

[i] *Editorial Note*: This Act, and the Performers' Protection Act 1963 and the Performers' Protection Act 1972 repealed by the 1988 Act, above, as from August 1, 1989.

Penalization of making or having plates, etc., for making records in contravention of Act

4. If a person makes, or has in his possession, a plate or similar contrivance for the purpose of making records in contravention of this Act, he shall be guilty of an offence under this Act, and shall be liable, on summary conviction, to a fine not exceeding fifty pounds for each plate or similar contrivance in respect of which an offence is proved.

Power of court to order destruction of records, etc., contravening Act

5. The court before which any proceedings are taken under this Act may, on conviction of the offender, order that all records, cinematograph films, plates or similar contrivances in the possession of the offender which appear to the court to have been made in contravention of this Act, or to be adapted for the making of records in contravention of this Act, and in respect of which the offender has been convicted, be destroyed, or otherwise dealt with as the court may think fit.

Additional Offence

(1) A person who, otherwise than by the use of a record or cinematograph film or the reception [and re-transmission] of a broadcast, knowingly [includes a performance to which the Principal Act applies, or any part of such performance, in a cable programme without the consent in writing of the performers,] shall be guilty of an offence and shall be liable, on summary conviction, to a fine not exceeding fifty pounds.[ii]

Special defences

6. Notwithstanding anything in the preceding provisions of this Act, it shall be a defence to any proceedings under this Act to prove—

    (a) that the record, cinematograph film [*, broadcast or [cable programme]*][iii] to which the proceedings relate was made [*or included*][iv] only for the purpose of reporting current events, or

    (b) that the inclusion of the performance in question in the record, cinematograph film[*, broadcast or [cable programme]*][v] to which the proceedings relate was only by way of background or was otherwise only incidental to the principal matters comprised or represented in the record, film[*, broadcast or [cable programme]*][vi].

Consent on behalf of performers

7. Where in any proceedings under this Act it is proved—

    (a) that the record, cinematograph film[*, broadcast or [cable programme]*][vii] to which the proceedings relate was made [*or included*][viii] with the consent in writing of a person who, at the time of giving the consent,

---

[ii] *Editorial Note*: This Act (the Dramatic and Musical Performers' Protection Act 1958) is the "Principal Act" referred to in the italicised passage of text. Subsection 3(3) of the Performers' Protection Act 1963, below, provides that the 1958 Act shall have effect as if this passage (subs.3(1) of the 1963 Act) was inserted at this point. It is printed as amended by the Cable and Broadcasting 1984 (c.46)

[iii] *Editorial Note*: See subs.3(3) of the Performers' Protection Act 1963, below.

[iv] *Editorial Note*: See subs.3(3) of the Performers' Protection Act 1963, below.

[v] *Editorial Note*: See subs.3(3) of the Performers' Protection Act 1963, below.

[vi] *Editorial Note*: See subs.3(3) of the Performers' Protection Act 1963, below.

[vii] *Editorial Note*: See subs.3(3) of the Performers' Protection Act 1963, below.

[viii] *Editorial Note*: See subs.3(3) of the Performers' Protection Act 1963, below.

represented that he was authorised by the performers to give it on their behalf, and

(b) that the person making [*or including*][ix] the record, film[*, broadcast or [cable programme]*][x] had no reasonable grounds for believing that the person giving the consent was not so authorised,

the provisions of this Act shall apply as if it had been proved that the performers had themselves consented in writing to the making [*or including*][xi] of the record, film or broadcast.

Interpretation

8.—(1) In this Act, unless the context otherwise requires, the following expressions have the meanings hereby respectively assigned to them, that is to say,—

"broadcast" means broadcast by wireless telegraphy (within the meaning of the Wireless Telegraphy Act, 1949), whether by way of sound broadcasting or of television;

["cable programme" means a programme included in a cable programme service, and references to the inclusion of a cable programme shall be construed accordingly;

"cable programme service" means a cable programme service within the meaning of the Cable and Broadcasting Act 1984 or a service provided outside the United Kingdom which would be such a service if subsection (7) of section 2 of that Act and references in subsection (1) of that section to the United Kingdom were omitted];

"cinematograph film" means any print, negative, tape or other article on which a performance of a dramatic or musical work or part thereof is recorded for the purposes of visual reproduction;

"performance of a dramatic or musical work" includes any performance, mechanical or otherwise, of any such work, being a performance rendered or intended to be rendered audible by mechanical or electrical means;

"performers", in the case of a mechanical performance, means the persons whose performance is mechanically reproduced;

["programme", in relation to a cable programme service, include any item included in that service;]

"record" means any record or similar contrivance for reproducing sound, including the sound-track of a cinematograph film.

(2) Any reference in this Act to the making of a cinematograph film is a reference to the carrying out of any process whereby a performance of a dramatic or musical work or part thereof is recorded for the purposes of visual reproduction.

(3) Section 48(3) of the Copyright Act 1956 (which explains the meaning of references in that Act to the inclusion of a programme in a cable programme service) shall apply for the purposes of this Act as it applies for the purposes of that Act.]

Short title, extent, repeal and commencement

9.—(1) This Act may be cited as the Dramatic and Musical Performers' Protection Act, 1958.

(2) It is hereby declared that this Act extends to Northern Ireland.

[ix] *Editorial Note*: See subs.3(3) of the Performers' Protection Act 1963, below.
[x] *Editorial Note*: See subs.3(3) of the Performers' Protection Act 1963, below.
[xi] *Editorial Note*: See subs.3(3) of the Performers' Protection Act 1963, below.

[(3) The Dramatic and Musical Performers' Protection Act, 1925, and section forty-five of, and the Sixth Schedule to, the Copyright Act, 1956, are hereby repealed.]

(4) This Act shall come into operation at the expiration of a period of one month beginning with the date of its passing.

Notes:

(1) The 1958 Act was amended by the Cable and Broadcasting Act 1984 (c.46). It is printed as amended. The 1958 Act should be read in conjunction with the Performers' Protection Act 1963, below.

(2) Subsection (3) of s.9 was repealed by the Statute Law (Repeals) Act 1974 (c.22).

E6.ii The Performers' Protection Act 1963

(c.53)

An Act to amend the law relating to the protection of performers so as to enable effect to be given to a Convention entered into Rome on 26th October 1961.

[31st July 1963]

Performances to which principal Act applies

1.—(1) The principal Act[i] shall have effect as if for references therein to the performance of a dramatic or musical work there were substituted references to the performance of any actors, singers, musicians, dancers or other persons who act, sing, deliver, declaim, play in or otherwise perform literary, dramatic, musical or artistic works, and the definition contained in section 8(1) of that Act of the expression "performance of a dramatic or musical work" (by which that expression is made to include a performance rendered or intended or to be rendered audible by mechanical or electrical means) shall be construed accordingly.

(2) For the avoidance of doubt it is hereby declared that the principal Act applies as respects anything done in relation to a performance notwithstanding that the performance took place out of the United Kingdom, but this shall not cause anything done out of the United Kingdom to be treated as an offence.

Sales, etc., of records made abroad

2. For the purposes of paragraphs (b) and (c) of section 1 of the principal Act (by which sales of, and other dealings with, records made in contravention of the Act are rendered punishable), a record made in a country outside the United Kingdom directly or indirectly from or by means of a performance to which the principal Act applies shall, where the civil or criminal law of that country contains a provision for the protection of performers under which the consent of any person to the making of the record was required, be deemed to have been made in contravention of the principal Act if, whether knowingly or not, it was made without the consent so required and without the consent in writing of the performers.

Relaying of performers

3.—(1) A person who, otherwise than by the use of a record or cinematograph film or the reception [and immediate re-transmission] of a broadcast, knowingly [includes a performance to which the principal Act applies, or any part of such

---

[i] *Editorial Note*: The Preamble to the 1963 Act defines the Dramatic and Musical Performers' Protection Act 1958 (6 & 7 Eliz. 2, c.44), for the purposes of the 1963 Act, as "the principal Act".

performance, in a cable programme without the consent in writing of the performers,] shall be guilty of an offence, and shall be liable, on summary conviction, to a fine not exceeding fifty pounds.

[…]

(3) Section 6 of the principal Act (which provides for special defences) shall have effect as if the preceding subsections were inserted immediately before that section, and that section and section 7 of the principal Act (which provides for the giving of consent on behalf of performers) shall have effect as if for the words "or broadcast" in each place where they occur there were substituted the words "broadcast or transmission".

Giving of consent without authority

4.—(1) Where—

(a) a record, cinematograph film, [or broadcast is made or a cable programme is included] with the consent in writing of a person who, at the time of giving the consent, represented that he was authorised by the performers to give it on their behalf when to his knowledge he was not so authorised, and

(b) if proceedings were brought against the person to whom the consent was given, the consent would by virtue of section 7 of the principal Act afford a defence to those proceedings,

the person giving the consent shall be guilty of an offence, and shall be liable, on summary conviction, to a fine not exceeding fifty pounds.

(2) The said section 7 shall not apply to proceedings under this section.

Citation, construction, commencement and extent

5.—(1) This Act may be cited as the Performers' Protection Act, 1963, and the principal Act and this Act may be cited together as the Performers' Protection Acts, 1958 and 1963.

(2) This Act shall be construed as one with the principal Act.

(3) This Act shall come into operation at the expiration of the period of one month beginning with the date of its passing, and shall apply only in relation to performances taking place after its commencement.

(4) It is hereby declared that this Act extends to Northern Ireland.

Notes:

(1) The 1963 Act was amended by the Cable and Broadcasting Act 1984 (c.46) and is printed as amended. See also s.3 of the Performers' Protection Act 1972, below, which inserted, after s.4 of the 1963 Act, a new s.4A (which is not re-printed here).

(2) The 1984 Act also amended ss.6 and 7 of the Dramatic and Musical Performers' Protection Act 1958 (E6.i, above): see s.3 of the 1963 Act below. The amendments were as follows. In s.6, for the word "transmission," in each place where it occurs, the words "cable programme" substituted and after the word "made" the words "or included" inserted. In s.7, for the word "transmission", in each place where it occurs, the words "cable programme" substituted, after the word "made" the words "or included" inserted and after the word "making," in both places where it occurs, the words "or including" inserted.

E6.iii The Performers' Protection Act 1972

(c.32)

An Act to amend the Performers' Protection Acts 1958 and 1963.

[29th June, 1972]

Increase of fines under Performers' Protection Acts, 1958 and 1963

1. The enactments specified in column 1 of the Schedule to this Act (being enactments creating the offences under the Performers' Protection Acts 1958 and 1963 broadly described in column 2 of that Schedule) shall each have effect as if the maximum fine which may be imposed on summary conviction of any offence specified in that enactment were a fine not exceeding the amount specified in column 4 of that Schedule instead of a fine not exceeding the amount specified in column 3 of that Schedule.

Amendment of section 1 of Dramatic and Musical Performers' Protection Act, 1958

2. Section 1 of the Dramatic and Musical Performers' Protection Act 1958 (by which the making of records without the consent of the performers and sales of, and other dealings with, such records are rendered punishable) shall have effect as if after the word "transaction" there were inserted the words "or, on conviction on indictment, to imprisonment for a term not exceeding two years, or to a fine, or to both".

Amendment of Performers' Protection Act, 1963

3. In the Performers' Protection Act, 1963, there shall be inserted after section 4 the following section:

Offences by bodies corporate

"**4A.** Where an offence under the principal Act or this Act committed by a body corporate is proved to have been committed with the consent or connivance of, or to be attributable to any neglect on the part of, any director, manager, secretary or other similar officer of the body corporate or any person who was purporting to act in any such capacity, he, as well as the body corporate, shall be guilty of that offence and shall be liable to be proceeded against and punished accordingly."

Citation, construction, commencement and extent

4.—(1) This Act may be cited as the Performers' Protection Act, 1972, and the Performers' Protection Acts, 1958 and 1963 and this Act may be cited together as the Performers' Protection Acts, 1958 to 1972.

(2) This Act shall come into operation at the expiration of the period of one month beginning with the date of its passing, but nothing in this Act shall affect the punishment for an offence committed before the commencement of this Act.

(3) It is hereby declared that this Act extends to Northern Ireland.

Section I   SCHEDULE

INCREASE OF FINES

(1) Enactment	(2) Description of Offence	(3) Old Maximum Fine	(4) New Maximum Fine
The Dramatic and Musical Performers' Protection Act 1958—			
Section 1	Making, etc., records without consent of performers.	£2 for each record in respect of which an offence is proved subject ot a limit of £50 in respect of any one trnsaction.	£20 for each record in respect of which an offence is proved subject to a limit of £400 in respect of any one transaction.
Section 2	Making, etc., cinematograph films without consent of performers.	£50	£400
Section 3	Broadcasting without consent of performers.	£50	£400
Section 4	Making or having plates, etc., for making records in contravention of Act.	£50	£400
The Performers' Protection Act 1963—			
Section 3(1)	Relaying performances without consent of performers.	£50	£400
Section 4(1)	Giving consent without authority.	£50	£400

E7. THE COPYRIGHT (COMPUTER SOFTWARE) AMENDMENT ACT 1985

(c.41)

An Act to amend the Copyright Act 1956 in its application to computer programs and computer storage.

[16th July 1985]

Be it Enacted by the Queen's most Excellent Majesty by and with the advice and consent of the Lords Spiritual and Temporal, and Commons, in this present Parliament assembled, and by the authority of the same, as follows—

Copyright in computer programs

1.—(1) The Copyright Act 1956 shall apply in relation to a computer program (including one made before the commencement of this Act) as it applies in relation to a literary work and shall so apply whether or not copyright would subsist in that program apart from this Act.

(2) For the purposes of the application of the said Act of 1956 in relation to a computer program, a version of the program in which it is converted into or out of a computer language or code, or into a different computer language or code, is an adaptation of the program.

Computer storage

2. References in the Copyright Act 1956 to the induction of any work to a material form, or to the reproduction of any work in a material form, shall include references to the storage of that work in a computer.

Offences and search warrants

3. Where an infringing copy of a computer program consists of a disc, tape or chip or of any other device which embodies signals serving for the impartation of the program or part of it, sections 21 to 21B of the Copyright Act 1956 (offences and search warrants) shall apply in relation to that copy as they apply in relation to an infringing copy of a sound recording or cinematograph film.

Short title, interpretation, commencement and extent

4.—(1) This Act may be cited as the Copyright (Computer Software) Amendment Act 1985.

(2) This Act shall be construed as one with the Copyright Act 1956 and Part V of that Act (extension and restriction of operation of Act) shall apply in relation to the provisions of this Act as it applies in relation to the provisions of that Act.

(3) This Act shall come into force at the end of the period of two months beginning with the day on which it is passed.

(4) Nothing in this Act shall affect—

    (a) the determination of any question as to whether anything done before the commencement of this Act was an infringement of copyright or an offence under section 21 of the said Act of 1956; or

    (b) the penalty which may be imposed for any offence under that section committed before the commencement of this Act.

(5) This Act extends to Northern Ireland.

PART F

COPYRIGHT CONVENTIONS AND AGREEMENTS

PART F

COPYRIGHT CONVENTIONS AND AGREEMENTS

F1. BERNE COPYRIGHT CONVENTION

PARIS ACT 1971[i]

The International Convention for the Protection of Literary and Artistic Works signed at Berne on 9th September, 1886, completed at Paris on 4th May 1896, revised at Berlin in 1908, at Rome in 1928, at Brussels in 1948 and Stockholm in 1967, was further revised in Paris in 1971 and amended in 1979.

The 1979 amendments occur in Articles 22 and 23 which are printed as amended.

Article 1

The countries to which this Convention applies constitute a Union for the protection of the rights of authors in their literary and artistic works.

Article 2

(1) The expression "literary and artistic works" shall include every production in the literary, scientific and artistic domain, whatever may be the mode or form of its expression, such as books, pamphlets and other writings; lectures, addresses, sermons and other works of the same nature; dramatic or dramatico-musical works; choreographic works and entertainments in dumb show; musical compositions with or without words; cinematographic works to which are assimilated works expressed by a process analogous to cinematography; works of drawing, painting, architecture, sculpture, engraving and lithography; photographic works to which are assimilated works expressed by a process analogous to photography; works of applied art; illustrations, maps, plans, sketches and three-dimensional works relative to geography, topography, architecture or science.

(2) It shall, however, be a matter for legislation in the countries of the Union to prescribe that works in general or any specified categories of works shall not be protected unless they have been fixed in some material form.

(3) Translations, adaptations, arrangements of music and other alterations of a literary or artistic work shall be protected as original works without prejudice to the copyright in the original work.

(4) It shall be a matter for legislation in the countries of the Union to determine the protection to be granted to official texts of a legislative administrative and legal nature, and to official translations of such texts.

(5) Collections of literary or artistic works such as encyclopaedias and anthologies which, by reason of the selection and arrangement of their contents, constitute intellectual creations shall be protected as such, without prejudice to the copyright in each of the works forming part of such collections.

(6) The works mentioned in this Article shall enjoy protection in all countries of the Union. This protection shall operate for the benefit of the author and his successors in title.

(7) Subject to the provisions of Article 7(4) of this Convention, it shall be a matter for legislation in the countries of the Union to determine the extent of the application of their laws to works of applied art and industrial designs and models, as well as the conditions under which such works, designs and models shall be protected. Works protected in the country of origin solely as designs and models

---

[i] *Editorial Note*: Cmnd. 5002.

shall be entitled in another country of the Union only to such special protection as is granted in that country to designs and models; however, if no such special protection is granted in that country, such works shall be protected as artistic works.

(8) The protection of this Convention shall not apply to news of the day or to miscellaneous facts having the character of mere items of press information.

Article 2bis

(1) It shall be a matter for legislation in the countries of the Union to exclude, wholly or in part, from the protection provided by the preceding Article political speeches and speeches delivered in the course of legal proceedings.

(2) It shall also be a matter for legislation in the countries of the Union to determine the conditions under which lectures, addresses and other works of the same nature which are delivered in public may be reproduced by the press, broadcast, communicated to the public by wire and made the subject of public communication as envisaged in Article 11bis (1) of this Convention, when such use is justified by the informatory purpose.

(3) Nevertheless, the author shall enjoy the exclusive right of making a collection of his works mentioned in the preceding paragraphs.

Article 3

The protection of this Convention shall apply to:
- (a) authors who are nationals of one of the countries of the Union, for their works, whether published or not;
- (b) authors who are not nationals of one of the countries of the Union, for their works first published in one of those countries, or simultaneously in a country outside the Union and in a country of the Union.

(2) Authors who are not nationals of one of the countries of the Union but who have their habitual residence in one of them shall, for the purposes of this Convention, be assimilated to nationals of that country.

(3) The expression "published works" means works published with the consent of their authors, whatever may be the means of manufacture of the copies, provided that the availability of such copies has been such as to satisfy the reasonable requirements of the public, having regard to the nature of the work. The performance of a dramatic, dramatico-musical, cinematographic or musical work, the public recitation of a literary work, the communication by wire or the broadcasting of literary or artistic works, the exhibition of a work of art and the construction of a work of architecture shall not constitute publication.

(4) A work shall be considered as having been published simultaneously in several countries if it has been published in two or more countries within thirty days of its first publication.

Article 4

The protection of this Convention shall apply, even if the conditions of Article 3 are not fulfilled, to:
- (a) authors of cinematographic works the maker of which has his headquarters or habitual residence in one of the countries of the Union;
- (b) authors of works of architecture erected in a country of the Union or of other artistic works incorporated in a building or other structure located in a country of the Union.

Article 5

(1) Authors shall enjoy, in respect of works for which they are protected under

this Convention, in countries of the Union other than the country of origin, the rights which their respective laws do now or may hereafter grant to their nationals, as well as the rights specially granted by this Convention.

(2) The enjoyment and the exercise of these rights shall not be subject to any formality; such enjoyment and such exercise shall be independent of the existence of protection in the country of origin of the work. Consequently, apart from the provisions of this Convention the extent of protection, as well as the means of redress afforded to the author to protect his rights, shall be governed exclusively by the laws of the country where protection is claimed.

(3) Protection in the country of origin is governed by domestic law. However, when the author is not a national of the country of origin of the work for which he is protected under this Convention, he shall enjoy in that country the same rights as national authors.

(4) The country of origin shall be considered to be:

(a) in the case of works first published in a country of the Union, that country; in the case of works published simultaneously in several countries of the Union which grant different terms of protection, the country whose legislation grants the shortest term of protection;

(b) in the case of works published simultaneously in a country outside the Union and in a country of the Union, the latter country;

(c) in the case of unpublished works or of works first published in a country outside the Union, without simultaneous publication in a country of the Union, the country of the Union of which the author is a national, provided that:

(i) when these are cinematographic works the maker of which has his headquarters or his habitual residence in a country of the Union, the country of origin shall be that country, and

(ii) when these are works of architecture erected in a country of the Union or other artistic works incorporated in a building or other structure located in a country of the Union, the country of origin shall be that country.

Article 6

(1) Where any country outside the Union fails to protect in an adequate manner the works of authors who are nationals of one of the countries of the Union, the latter country may restrict the protection given to the works of authors who are, at the date of the first publication thereof, nationals of the other country and are not habitually resident in one of the countries of the Union. If the country of first publication avails itself of this right, the other countries of the Union shall not be required to grant to works thus subjected to special treatment a wider protection than that granted to them in the country of first publication.

(2) No restrictions introduced by virtue of the preceding paragraph shall effect the rights which an author may have acquired in respect of a work published in a country of the Union before such restrictions were put into force.

(3) The countries of the Union which restrict the grant of copyright in accordance with this Article shall give notice thereof to the Director General of the World Intellectual Property Organization (hereinafter designated as "the Director General") by a written declaration specifying the countries in regard to which protection is restricted, and the restrictions to which rights of authors who are nationals of those countries are subjected. The Director General shall immediately communicate this declaration to all the countries the Union.

Article 6bis

(1) Independently of the author's economic rights, and even after the transfer

of the said rights, the author shall have the right to claim authorship of the work and to object to any distortion, mutilation or other modification of, or other derogatory action in relation to, the said work, which would be prejudicial to his honour or reputation.

(2) The rights granted to the author in accordance with the preceding paragraph shall, after his death, be maintained, at least until the expiry of the economic rights, and shall be exercisable by the persons or institutions authorised by the legislation of the country where protection is claimed. However, those countries whose legislation, at the moment of their ratification of or accession to this Act, does not provide for the protection after the death of the author of all the rights set out in the preceding paragraph may provide that some of these rights may, after his death, cease to be maintained.

(3) The means of redress for safeguarding the rights granted by this Article shall be governed by the legislation of the country where protection is claimed.

Article 7

(1) The term of protection granted by this Convention shall be the life of the author and fifty years after his death.

(2) However, in the case of cinematographic works, the countries of the Union may provide that the term of protection shall expire fifty years after the work has been made available to the public with the consent of the author, or, failing such an event within fifty years from the making of such a work, fifty years after the making.

(3) In the case of anonymous or pseudonymous works, the term of protection granted by this Convention shall expire fifty years after the work has been lawfully made available to the public. However, when the pseudonym adopted by the author leaves no doubt as to his identity, the term of protection shall be that provided in paragraph (1). If the author of an anonymous or pseudonymous work discloses his identity during the above-mentioned period, the term of protection applicable shall be that provided in paragraph (1). The countries of the Union shall not be required to protect anonymous or pseudonymous works in respect of which it is reasonable to presume that their author has been dead for fifty years.

(4) It shall be a matter for legislation in the countries of the Union to determine the term of protection of photographic works and that of works of applied art in so far as they are protected as artistic works; however, this term shall last at least until the end of a period of twenty-five years from the making of such a work.

(5) The term of protection subsequent to the death of the author and the terms provided by paragraphs (2), (3) and (4) shall run from the date of death or of the event referred to in those paragraphs, but such terms shall always be deemed to begin on the first of January of the year following the death or such event.

(6) The countries of the Union may grant a term of protection in excess of those provided by the preceding paragraphs.

(7) Those countries of the Union bound by the Rome Act of this Convention which grant, in their national legislation in force at the time of signature of the present Act, shorter terms of protection than those provided for in the preceding paragraphs shall have the right to maintain such terms when ratifying or acceding to the present Act.

(8) In any case, the term shall be governed by the legislation of the country where protection is claimed; however, unless the legislation of that country otherwise provides, the term shall not exceed the term fixed in the country of origin of the work.

Article 7bis

The provisions of the preceding Article shall also apply in the case of a work of joint authorship, provided that the terms measured from the death of the author shall be calculated from the death of the last surviving author.

Article 8

Authors of literary and artistic works protected by this Convention shall enjoy the exclusive right of making and of authorising the translation of their works throughout the term of protection of their rights in the original works.

Article 9

(1) Authors of literary and artistic works protected by this Convention shall have the exclusive right of authorising the reproduction of these works, in any manner or form.

(2) It shall be a matter for legislation in the countries of the Union to permit the reproduction of such works in certain special cases, provided that such reproduction does not conflict with a normal exploitation of the work and does not unreasonably prejudice the legitimate interests of the author.

(3) Any sound or visual recording shall be considered as a reproduction for the purposes of this Convention.

Article 10

(1) It shall be permissible to make quotations from a work which has already been lawfully made available to the public, provided that their making is compatible with fair practice, and their extent does not exceed that justified by the purpose, including quotations from newspaper articles and periodicals in the form of press summaries.

(2) It shall be a matter for legislation in the countries of the Union, and for special agreements existing or to be concluded between them, to permit the utilisation, to the extent justified by the purpose, of literary or artistic works by way of illustration in publications, broadcasts or sound or visual recordings for teaching, provided such utilisation is compatible with fair practice.

(3) Where use is made of works in accordance with the preceding paragraphs of this Article, mention shall be made of the source, and of the name of the author if it appears thereon.

Article 10bis

(1) It shall be a matter for legislation in the countries of the Union to permit the reproduction by the press, the broadcasting or the communication to the public by wire of articles published in newspapers or periodicals on current economic, political or religious topics, and of broadcast works of the same character, in cases in which the reproduction, broadcasting or such communication thereof is not expressly reserved. Nevertheless, the source must always be clearly indicated; the legal consequence of a breach of this obligation shall be determined by the legislation of the country where protection is claimed.

(2) It shall also be a matter for legislation in the countries of the Union to determine the conditions under which, for the purpose of reporting current events by means of photography, cinematography, broadcasting or communications to the public by wire, literary or artistic works seen or heard in the course of the event may, to the extent justified by the informatory purpose, be reproduced and made available to the public.

Article 11

(1) Authors of dramatic, dramatico-musical and musical works shall enjoy the exclusive rights of authorising:

   (i) the public performance of their works, including such public performance by any means or process;

(ii) any communication to the public of the performance of their works.

(2) Authors of dramatic or dramatico-musical works shall enjoy, during the full term of their rights in the original works, the same rights with respect to translations thereof.

Article 11bis

(1) Authors of literary and artistic works shall enjoy the exclusive right of authorising:

- (i) the broadcasting of their works or the communication thereof to the public by any other means of wireless diffusion of signs, sounds or images;
- (ii) any communication to the public by wire or by rebroadcasting of the broadcast of the work, when this communication is made by an organization other than the original one;
- (iii) the public communication by loudspeaker or any other analogous instrument transmitting, by signs, sounds or images, the broadcast of the work.

(2) It shall be a matter for legislation in the countries of the Union to determine the conditions under which the rights mentioned in the preceding paragraph may be exercised, but these conditions shall apply only in the countries where they have been prescribed. They shall not in any circumstances be prejudicial to the moral rights of the author, nor to his right to obtain equitable remuneration which, in the absence of agreement, shall be fixed by competent authority.

(3) In the absence of any contrary stipulation, permission granted in accordance with paragraph (1) of this Article shall not imply permission to record, by means of instruments recording sounds or images, the work broadcast. It shall, however, be a matter for legislation in the countries of the Union to determine the regulations for ephemeral recordings made by a broadcasting organization by means of its own facilities and used for its own broadcasts. The preservation of these recordings in official archives may, on the ground of their exceptional documentary character, be authorised by such legislation.

Article 11ter

(1) Authors of literary works shall enjoy the exclusive right of authorising:

- (i) the public recitation of their works, including such public recitation by any means or process;
- (ii) any communication to the public of the recitation of their works.

(2) Authors of literary works shall enjoy, during the full term of their rights in the original works, the same rights with respect to translations thereof.

Article 12

Authors of literary or artistic works shall enjoy the exclusive right of authorising adaptations, arrangements and other alterations of their works.

Article 13

(1) Each country of the Union may impose for itself reservations and conditions on the exclusive right granted to the author of a musical work and to the author of any words, the recording of which together with the musical work has already been authorised by the latter, to authorise the sound recording of that musical work, together with such words, if any; but all such reservations and conditions shall apply only in the countries which have imposed them and shall not, in any circumstances, be prejudicial to the rights of these authors to obtain equitable remuneration which, in the absence of agreement, shall be fixed by competent authority.

(2) Recordings of musical works made in a country of the Union in accor-

dance with Article 13(3) of the Conventions signed at Rome on June 2, 1928, and at Brussels on June 26, 1948, may be reproduced in that country without the permission of the author of the musical work until a date two years after that country becomes bound by this Act.

(3) Recordings made in accordance with paragraphs (1) and (2) of this Article and imported without permission from the parties concerned into a country where they are treated as infringing recordings shall be liable to seizure.

Article 14

(1) Authors of literary or artistic works shall have the exclusive right of authorising:

(i) the cinematographic adaptation and reproduction of these works, and the distribution of the works thus adapted or reproduced;

(ii) the public performance and communication to the public by wire of the works thus adapted or reproduced.

(2) The adaptation into any other artistic form of a cinematographic production derived from literary or artistic works shall, without prejudice to the authorization of the author of the cinematographic production, remain subject to the authorization of the authors of the original works.

(3) The provision of Article 13(1) shall not apply.

Article 14bis

(1) Without prejudice to the copyright in any work which may have been adapted or reproduced, a cinematographic work shall be protected as an original work. The owner of copyright in a cinematographic work shall enjoy the same rights as the author of an original work, including the rights referred to in the preceding Article.

(2)(a) Ownership of copyright in a cinematographic work shall be a matter for legislation in the country where protection is claimed.

(b) However, in the countries of the Union which, by legislation, include among the owners of copyright in a cinematographic work authors who have brought contributions to the making of the work, such authors, if they have undertaken to bring such contributions, may not, in the absence of any contrary or special stipulation, object to the reproduction, distribution, public performance, communication to the public by wire, broadcasting or any other communication to the public, or to the subtitling or dubbing of texts, of the work.

(c) The question whether or not the form of the undertaking referred to above should, for the application of the preceding subparagraph (b), be in a written agreement or a written act of the same effect shall be a matter for the legislation of the country where the maker of the cinematographic work has his headquarters or habitual residence. However, it shall be a matter for the legislation of the country of the Union where protection is claimed to provide that the said undertaking shall be in a written agreement or a written act of the same effect. The countries whose legislation so provides shall notify the Director General by means of a written declaration, which will be immediately communicated by him to all the other countries of the Union.

(d) By "contrary or special stipulation" is meant any restrictive condition which is relevant to the aforesaid undertaking

(3) Unless the national legislation provides to the contrary, the provisions of paragraph (2)(b) above shall not be applicable to authors of scenarios, dialogues and musical works created for the making of the cinematographic work, or to the

principal director thereof. However, those countries of the Union whose legislation does not contain rules providing for the application of the said paragraph (2)(b) to such director shall notify the Director General by means of a written declaration, which will be immediately communicated by him to all other countries of the Union.

Article 14ter

(1) The author, or after his death the persons or institutions authorized by national legislation, shall, with respect to original works of art and original manuscripts of writers and composers, enjoy the inalienable right to an interest in any sale of the work subsequent to the first transfer by the author of the work.

(2) The protection provided by the preceding paragraph may be claimed in a country of the Union only if the legislation in the country to which the author belongs so permits, and to the extent permitted by the country where this protection is claimed.

(3) The procedure for collection and the amounts shall be matters for determination by national legislation.

Article 15

(1) In order that the author of a literary or artistic work protected by this Convention shall, in the absence of proof to the contrary, be regarded as such, and consequently be entitled to institute infringement proceedings in the countries of the Union, it shall be sufficient for his name to appear on the work in the usual manner. This paragraph shall be applicable even if this name is a pseudonym, where the pseudonym adopted by the author leaves no doubt as to his identity.

(2) The person or body corporate whose name appears on a cinematographic work in the usual manner shall, in the absence of proof to the contrary, be presumed to be the maker of the said work.

(3) In the case of anonymous and pseudonymous works, other than those referred to in paragraph (1) above, the publisher whose name appears on the work shall, in the absence of proof to the contrary, be deemed to represent the author, and in this capacity he shall be entitled to protect and enforce the author's rights. The provisions of this paragraph shall cease to apply when the author reveals his identity and establishes his claim to authorship of the work.

(4)(a)In the case of unpublished works where the identity of the author is unknown, but where there is every ground to presume that he is a national of a country of the Union, it shall be a matter for legislation in that country to designate the competent authority which shall represent the author and shall be entitled to protect and enforce his rights in the countries of the Union.

(b) Countries of the Union which make such designation under the terms of this provision shall notify the Director General by means of a written declaration giving full information concerning the authority thus designated. The Director General shall at once communicate this declaration to all other countries of the Union.

Article 16

(1) Infringing copies of a work shall be liable to seizure in any country of the Union where the work enjoys legal protection.

(2) The provisions of the preceding paragraph shall also apply to reproductions coming from a country where the work is not protected, or has ceased to be protected.

(3) The seizure shall take place in accordance with the legislation of each country.

Article 17

The provisions of this Convention cannot in any way affect the right of the Government of each country of the Union to permit, to control, or to prohibit, by legislation or regulation, the circulation, presentation, or exhibition of any work or production in regard to which the competent authority may find it necessary to exercise that right.

Article 18

(1) This Convention shall apply to all works which, at the moment of its coming into force, have not yet fallen into the public domain in the country of origin through the expiry of the term of protection.

(2) If, however, through the expiry of the term of protection which was previously granted, a work has fallen into the public domain of the country where protection is claimed, that work shall not be protected anew.

(3) The application of this principle shall be subject to any provisions contained in special conventions to that effect existing or to be concluded between countries of the Union. In the absence of such provisions, the respective countries shall determine, each in so far as it is concerned, the conditions of application of this principle.

(4) The preceding provisions shall also apply in the case of new accessions to the Union and to cases in which protection is extended by the application of Article 7 or by the abandonment of reservations.

Article 19

The provisions of this Convention shall not preclude the making of a claim to the benefit of any greater protection which may be granted by legislation in a country of the Union.

Article 20

The Governments of the countries of the Union reserve the right to enter into special agreements among themselves, in so far as such agreements grant to authors more extensive rights than those granted by the Convention, or contain other provisions not contrary to this Convention. The provisions of existing agreements which satisfy these conditions shall remain applicable.

Article 21

(1) Special provisions regarding developing countries are included in the Appendix.

(2) Subject to the provisions of Article 28(1)(b), the Appendix forms an integral part of this Act.

Article 22

(1)(a)The Union shall have an Assembly consisting of those countries of the Union which are bound by Articles 22 to 26.
  (b) The Government of each country shall be represented by one delegate, who may be assisted by alternative delegates, advisors and experts.
  (c) The expenses of each delegation shall be borne by the Government which has appointed it.

(2)(a)The Assembly shall:
   (i) deal with all matters concerning the maintenance and development of the Union and the implementation of this Convention;
   (ii) give directions concerning the preparation for conferences of revision to the International Bureau of Intellectual Property (hereinafter designated as "the International Bureau") referred to in the Convention Establishing

the World Intellectual Property Organization (hereinafter designated as "the Organization"), due account being taken of any comments made by those countries of the Union which are not bound by Articles 22 to 26;

(iii) review and approve the reports and activities of the Director General of the Organization concerning the Union, and give all necessary instructions concerning matters within the competence of the Union;

(iv) elect the members of the Executive Committee of the Assembly;

(v) review and approve the reports and activities of its Executive Committee, and give instructions to such Committee;

(vi) determine the programme and adopt the triennial budget of the Union and approve its final accounts;

(vii) adopt the financial regulations of the Union;

(viii) establish such committees of experts and working groups as may be necessary for the work of the Union;

(ix) determine which countries not members of the Union and which intergovernmental and international non-governmental organizations shall be admitted to its meetings as observers;

(x) adopt amendments to Articles 22 to 26;

(xi) take any other appropriate action designed to further the objectives of the Union;

(xii) exercise such other functions as are appropriate under this Convention;

(xiii) subject to its acceptance, exercise such rights as are given to it in the Convention establishing the Organization.

(b) With respect to matters which are of interest also to other Unions administered by the Organization, the Assembly shall make its decisions after having heard the advice of the Co-ordination Committee of the Organization.

(3)(a) Each country member of the Assembly shall have one vote.

(b) One-half of the countries members of the Assembly shall constitute a quorum.

(c) Notwithstanding the provisions of subparagraph (b), if, in any session, the number of countries represented is less than one-half but equal to or more than one-third of the countries members of the Assembly, the Assembly may make decisions but, with the exception of decisions concerning its own procedure, all such decisions shall take effect only if the following conditions are fulfilled. The International Bureau shall communicate the said decisions to the countries members of the Assembly which were not represented and shall invite them to express in writing their vote or abstention within a period of three months from the date of the communication. If, at the expiration of this period, the number of countries having thus expressed their vote or abstention attains the number of countries which was lacking for attaining the quorum in the session itself, such decisions shall take effect provided that at the same time the required majority still obtains.

(d) Subject to the provisions of Article 26(2), the decisions of the Assembly shall require two-thirds of the votes cast.

(e) Abstentions shall not be considered as votes.

(f) A delegate may represent, and vote in the name of, one country only.

(g) Countries of the Union not members of the Assembly shall be admitted to its meetings as observers.

(4)(a) The Assembly shall meet once in every second calendar year in ordinary session upon convocation by the Director General and, in the absence of exceptional circumstances, during the same period and at the same place as the General Assembly of the Organization.

(b) The Assembly shall meet in extraordinary session upon convocation by the Director General, at the request of the Executive Committee or at the request of one-fourth of the countries members of the Assembly.

(5) The Assembly shall adopt its own rules of procedure.

Article 23

(1) The Assembly shall have an Executive Committee.

(2)(a)The Executive Committee shall consist of countries elected by the Assembly from among countries members of the Assembly. Furthermore, the country on whose territory the Organisation has its headquarters shall, subject to the provisions of Article 25(7)(b), have an *ex officio* seat on the Committee.

(b) The Government of each country member of the Executive Committee shall be represented by one delegate, who may be assisted by alternate delegates, advisors and experts.

(c) The expenses of each delegation shall be borne by the Government which has appointed it.

(3) The number of countries members of the Executive Committee shall correspond to one-fourth of the number of countries members of the Assembly. In establishing the number of seats to be filled, remainders after division by four shall be disregarded.

(4) In electing the members of the Executive Committee, the Assembly shall have due regard to an equitable geographical distribution and to the need for countries party to the Special Agreements which might be established in relation with the Union to be among the countries constituting the Executive Committee.

(5)(a)Each member of the Executive Committee shall serve from the close of the session of the Assembly which elected it to close of the next ordinary session of the Assembly.

(b) Members of the Executive Committee may be re-elected, but not more than two-thirds of them.

(c) The Assembly shall establish the details of the rules governing the election and possible re-election of the members of the Executive Committee.

(6)(a)The Executive Committee shall:

  (i) prepare the draft agenda of the Assembly;

  (ii) submit proposals to the Assembly respecting the draft programme and triennial budget of the Union prepared by the Director General;

  (iii) *[deleted]*

  (iv) submit, with appropriate comments, to the Assembly the periodical reports of the Director General and the yearly audit reports on the accounts;

  (v) in accordance with the decisions of the Assembly and having regard to circumstances arising between two ordinary sessions of the Assembly, take all necessary measures to ensure the execution of the programme of the Union by the Director General;

  (vi) perform such other functions as are allocated to it under this Convention.

(b) With respect to matters which are of interest also to other Unions administered by the Organization, the Executive Committee shall make its decisions after having heard the advice of the Co-ordination Committee of the Organization.

(7)(a)The Executive Committee shall meet once a year in ordinary session upon convocation by the Director General, preferably during the same period and at the same place as the Co-ordination Committee of the Organization.

(b) The Executive Committee shall meet in extraordinary session upon convocation by the Director General, either on his own initiative, or at the request of its Chairman or one-fourth of its members.

(8)(a)Each country member of the Executive Committee shall have one vote.

(b) One-half of the members of the Executive Committee shall constitute a quorum.

(c) Decisions shall be made by a simple majority of the votes cast.

(d) Abstentions shall not be considered as votes.

(e) A delegate may represent, and vote in the name of, one country only.

(9) Countries of the Union not members of the Executive Committee shall be admitted to its meetings as observers.

(10) The Executive Committee shall adopt its own rules of procedure.

Article 24

(1)(a)The administrative tasks with respect to the Union shall be performed by the International Bureau, which is a continuation of the Bureau of the Union united with the Bureau of the Union established by the International Convention for the Protection of Industrial Property.

(b) In particular, the International Bureau shall provide the secretariat of the various organs of the Union.

(c) The Director General of the Organization shall be the chief executive of the Union and he shall represent the Union.

(2) The International Bureau shall assemble and publish information concerning the protection of copyright. Each country of the Union shall promptly communicate to the International Bureau all new laws and official texts concerning the protection of copyright.

(3) The International Bureau shall publish a monthly periodical.

(4) The International Bureau shall, on request, furnish information to any country of the Union on matters concerning the protection of copyright.

(5) The International Bureau shall conduct studies, and shall provide services, designed to facilitate the protection of copyright.

(6) The Director General and any staff member designated by him shall participate, without the right to vote, in all meetings of the Assembly, the Executive Committee and any other committee of experts or working group. The Director General, or a staff member designated by him, shall be *ex officio* secretary of these bodies.

(7)(a)The International Bureau shall, in accordance with the directions of the Assembly and in cooperation with the Executive Committee, make the preparations for the conferences of revision of the provisions of the Convention other than Articles 22 to 26.

(b) The International Bureau may consult with inter-governmental and international non-governmental organizations concerning preparations for conferences of revision.

(c) The Director General and persons designated by him shall take part, without the right to vote, in the discussions at these conferences.

(8) The International Bureau shall carry out any other tasks assigned to it.

Article 25

(1)(a)The Union shall have a budget.

(b) The budget of the Union shall include the income and expense proper to the Union, its contribution to the budget of expenses common to the Unions, and, where applicable, the sum made available to the budget of the Conference of the Organization.

(c) Expenses not attributable exclusively to the Union but also to one or more other Unions administered by the Organization shall be considered as expenses common to the Unions. The share of the Union in such common expenses shall be in proportion to the interest the Union has in them.

(2) The budget of the Union shall be established with due regard to the requirements of co-ordination with the budgets of the other Unions administered by the Organisation.

(3) The budget of the Union shall be financed from the following sources:

(i) contributions of the countries of the Union;

(ii) fees and charges due for services performed by the International Bureau in relation to the Union;

(iii) sale of, or royalties on, the publications of the International Bureau concerning the Union;

(iv) gifts, bequests, and subventions;

(v) rent, interests, and other miscellaneous income.

(4)(a) For the purpose of establishing its contribution towards the budget, each country of the Union shall belong to a class, and shall pay its annual contributions on the basis of a number of units fixed as follows:

Class	I	....	25
Class	II	....	20
Class	III	....	15
Class	IV	....	10
Class	V	....	5
Class	VI	....	3
Class	VII	....	1

(b) Unless it has already done so, each country shall indicate, concurrently with depositing its instrument of ratification or accession, the class to which it wishes to belong. Any country may change class. If it chooses a lower class, the country must announce it to the Assembly at one of its ordinary sessions. Any such change shall take effect at the beginning of the calendar year following the session.

(c) The annual contribution of each country shall be an amount in the same proportion to the total sum to be contributed to the annual budget of the Union by all countries as the number of units is to the total of the units of all contributing countries.

(d) Contributions shall become due on the first of January of each year.

(e) A country which is in arrears in the payment of its contributions shall have no vote in any of the organs of the Union of which it is a member if the amount of its arrears equals or exceeds the amount of the contributions due from it for the preceding two full years. However, any organ of the Union may allow such a country to continue to exercise its vote in that organ if, and as long as, it is satisfied that the delay in payment is due to exceptional and unavoidable circumstances.

(f) If the budget is not adopted before the beginning of a new financial period, it shall be at the same level as the budget of the previous year, in accordance with the financial regulations.

(5) The amount of the fees and charges due for services rendered by the International Bureau in relation to the Union shall be established, and shall be reported to the Assembly and the Executive Committee, by the Director General.

(6)(a) The Union shall have a working capital fund which shall be constituted by a single payment made by each country of the Union. If the fund becomes insufficient, an increase shall be decided by the Assembly.

(b) The amount of the initial payment of each country to the said fund or of its participation in the increase thereof shall be a proportion of the contribution of that country for the year in which the fund is established or the increase decided.

(c) The proportion and the terms of payment shall be fixed by the Assembly on the proposal of the Director General and after it has heard the advice of the Co-ordination Committee of the Organization.

(7)(a)In the headquarters agreement concluded with the country on the territory of which the Organization has its headquarters, it shall be provided that, whenever the working capital fund is insufficient, such country shall grant advances. The amount of these advances and the conditions on which they are granted shall be the subject of separate agreements, in each case, between such country and the Organization. As long as it remains under the obligation to grant advances, such country shall have an *ex officio* seat on the Executive Committee.

(b) The country referred to in sub-paragraph (a) and the Organization shall each have the right to denounce the obligation to grant advances, by written notification. Denunciation shall take effect three years after the end of the year in which it has been notified.

(8) The auditing of the accounts shall be effected by one or more of the countries of the Union or by external auditors, as provided in the financial regulations. They shall be designated, with their agreement, by the Assembly.

Article 26

(1) Proposals for the amendment of Articles 22, 23, 24, 25 and the present Article, may be initiated by any country member of the Assembly, by the Executive Committee, or by the Director General. Such proposals shall be communicated by the Director General to the members countries of the Assembly at least six months in advance of their consideration by the Assembly.

(2) Amendment to the Articles referred to in paragraph (1) shall be adopted by the Assembly. Adoption shall require three-fourths of the votes cast, provided that any amendments of Article 22, and of the present paragraph, shall require four-fifths of the votes cast.

(3) Any amendment to the Articles referred to in paragraph (1) shall enter into force one month after written notifications of acceptance, effected in accordance with their respective constitutional processes, have been received by the Director General from three-fourths of the countries members of the Assembly at the time it adopted the amendment. Any amendment to the said Articles thus accepted shall bind all the countries which are members of the Assembly at the time the amendment enters into force, or which become members thereof at a subsequent date, provided that any amendment increasing the financial obligations of countries of the Union shall bind only those countries which have notified their acceptance of such amendment.

Article 27

(1) This Convention shall be submitted to revision with a view to the introduction of amendments designed to improve the system of the Union.

(2) For this purpose, conferences shall be held successively in one of the countries of the Union among the delegates of the said countries.

(3) Subject to the provisions of Article 26 which apply to the amendment of Articles 22 to 26, any revision of this Act, including the Appendix, shall require the unanimity of the votes cast.

Article 28

(1)(a)Any country of the Union which has signed this Act may ratify it, and if it has not signed it, may accede to it. Instruments of ratification or accession shall be deposited with the Director General.

(b) Any country of the Union may declare in its instrument of ratification or accession that its ratification or accession shall not apply to Articles 1 to 21 and the Appendix, provided that, if such country has previously made a declaration under Article VI(1) of the Appendix, then it may declare in the said instrument only that its ratification or accession shall not apply to Articles 1 to 20.

(c) Any country of the Union, which in accordance with sub-paragraph (b), has excluded provisions therein referred to from the effects of its ratification or accession may at any later time declare that it extends the effects of its ratification or accession to those provisions. Such declaration shall be deposited with the Director General.

(2)(a) Articles 1 to 21 and the Appendix shall enter into force three months after both of the following two conditions are fulfilled:

(i) at least five countries of the Union have ratified or acceded to this Act without making a declaration under paragraph (1)(b),

(ii) France, Spain, the United Kingdom of Great Britain and Northern Ireland, and the United States of America, have become bound by the Universal Copyright Convention as revised at Paris on July 24, 1971.

(b) The entry into force referred to in sub-paragraph (a) shall apply to those countries of the Union which, at least three months before the said entry into force, have deposited instruments of ratification or accession not containing a declaration under paragraph (1)(b).

(c) With respect to any country of the Union not covered by sub-paragraph (b) and which ratifies or accedes to this Act without making a declaration under paragraph (1)(b), Articles 1 to 21 and the Appendix shall enter into force three months after the date on which the Director General has notified the deposit of the relevant instrument of ratification or accession, unless a subsequent date has been indicated in the instrument deposited. In the latter case, Articles 1 to 21 and the Appendix shall enter into force with respect to that country on the date thus indicated.

(d) The provisions of subparagraphs (a) to (c) do not affect the application of Article VI of the Appendix.

(3) With respect to any country of the Union which ratifies or accedes to this Act with or without a declaration made under paragraph (1)(b), Articles 22 to 38 shall enter into force three months after the date on which the Director General has notified the deposit of the relevant instrument of ratification or accession, unless a subsequent date has been indicated in the instrument deposited. In the latter case, Articles 22 to 38 shall enter into force with respect to that country on the date thus indicated.

Article 29

(1) Any country outside the Union may accede to this Act and thereby become party to this Convention and a member of the Union. Instruments of accession shall be deposited with the Director General.

(2)(a) Subject to subparagraph (b), this Convention shall enter into force with respect to any country outside the Union three months after the date on which the Director General has notified the deposit of its instrument of accession, unless a subsequent date has been indicated in the instrument deposited. In the latter case, this Convention shall enter into force with respect to that country on the date thus indicated.

(b) If the entry into force according to subparagraph (a) precedes the entry into force of Articles 1 to 21 and the Appendix according to Article 28(2)(a), the said country shall, in the meantime, be bound, instead by Articles 1 to 21 and the Appendix, by Articles 1 to 20 of the Brussels Act of this Convention.

Article 29bis

Ratification of or accession to this Act by any country not bound by Articles 22 to 38 of the Stockholm Act of this Convention shall, for the sole purposes of Article 14(2) of the Convention establishing the Organization, amount to ratification of or accession to the said Stockholm Act with the limitation set forth in Article 28(1)(b)(i) thereof.

Article 30

(1) Subject to the exceptions permitted by paragraph (2) of this Article, by Article 28(1)(b), by Article 33(2), and by the Appendix, ratification or accession shall automatically entail acceptance of all the provisions and admission to all the advantages of this Convention.

(2)(a) Any country of the Union ratifying or acceding to this Act may, subject to Article V (2) of the Appendix, retain the benefit of the reservations it has previously formulated on condition that it makes a declaration to that effect at the time of the deposit of its instrument of ratification or accession.

(b) Any country outside the Union may declare, in acceding to this Convention and subject to Article V(2) of the Appendix, that it intends to substitute, temporarily at least, for Article 8 of this Act concerning the right of translation, the provisions of Article 5 of the Union Convention of 1886, as completed at Paris in 1896, on the clear understanding that the said provisions are applicable only to translations into a language in general use in the said country. Subject to Article I(6)(b) of the Appendix, any country has the right to apply, in relation to the right of translation of works whose country of origin is a country availing itself of such a reservation, a protection which is equivalent to the protection granted by the latter country.

(c) Any country may withdraw such reservations at any time by notification addressed to the Director General.

Article 31

(1) Any country may declare in its instrument of ratification or accession, or may inform the Director General by written notification at any time thereafter, that this Convention shall be applicable to all or part of those territories, designated in the declaration or notification, for the external relations of which it is responsible.

(2) Any country which has made such a declaration or given such a notification may, at any time, notify the Director General that this Convention shall cease to be applicable to all or part of such territories.

(3)(a) Any declaration made under paragraph (1) shall take effect on the same date as the ratification or accession in which it was included, and any notification given under that paragraph shall take effect three months after its notification by the Director General.

(b) Any notification given under paragraph (2) shall take effect twelve months after its receipt by the Director General.

(4) This Article shall in no way be understood as implying the recognition of tacit acceptance by a country of the Union of the factual situation concerning a territory to which this Convention is made applicable by another country of the Union by virtue of a declaration under paragraph (1).

Article 32

(1) This Act shall, as regards relations between the countries of the Union, and to the extent that it applies, replace the Berne Convention of September 9, 1886, and the subsequent Acts of revision. The Acts previously in force shall continue to be applicable, in their entirety or to the extent that this Act does not replace them by virtue of the preceding sentence, in relations with countries of the Union which do not ratify or accede to this Act.

(2) Countries outside the Union which become party to this Act shall, subject to paragraph (3), apply it with respect to any country of the Union not bound by this Act or which, although bound by this Act, has made a declaration pursuant to Article 28(1)(b). Such countries recognize that the said country of the Union, in its relations with them:

(i) may apply the provisions of the most recent Act by which it is bound, and

(ii) subject to Article 1(6) of the Appendix, has the right to adapt the protection to the level provided for by this Act.

(3) Any country which has availed itself of any of the faculties provided for in the Appendix may apply the provisions of the Appendix relating to the faculty or faculties of which it has availed itself in its relations with any other country of the Union which is not bound by this Act, provided that the latter country has accepted the application of the said provisions.

Article 33

(1) Any dispute between two or more countries of the Union concerning the interpretation or application of this Convention, not settled by negotiation, may, by any one of the countries concerned, be brought before the International Court of Justice by application in conformity with the Statute of the Court, unless the countries concerned agree on some other method of settlement. The country bringing the dispute before the Court shall inform the International Bureau; the International Bureau shall bring the matter to the attention of the other countries of the Union.

(2) Each country may, at the time it signs this Act or deposits its instrument of ratification or accession, declare that it does not consider itself bound by the provisions of paragraph (1). With regard to any dispute between such country and any other country of the Union, the provisions of paragraph (1) shall not apply.

(3) Any country having made a declaration in accordance with the provisions of paragraph (2) may, at any time, withdraw its declaration by notification addressed to the Director General.

Article 34

(1) Subject to Article 29*bis*, no country may ratify or accede to earlier Acts of this Convention once Articles 1 to 21 and the Appendix have entered into force.

(2) Once Articles 1 to 21 and the Appendix have entered into force, no country may make a declaration under Article 5 of the Protocol Regarding Developing Countries attached to the Stockholm Act.

Article 35

(1) This Convention shall remain in force without limitation as to time.

(2) Any country may denounce this Act by notification addressed to the Director General. Such denunciation shall constitute also denunciation of all earlier Acts and shall affect only the country making it, the Convention remaining in full force and effect as regards the other countries of the Union.

(3) Denunciation shall take effect one year after the day on which the Director General has received the notification.

(4) The right of denunciation provided by this Article shall not be exercised by any country before the expiration of five years from the date upon which it becomes a member of the Union.

Article 36

(1) Any country party to this Convention undertakes to adopt, in accordance with its constitution, the measures necessary to ensure the application of this Convention.

(2) It is understood that, at the time a country becomes bound by this Convention, it will be in a position under its domestic law to give effect to the provisions of this Convention.

Article 37

(1)(a) This Act shall be signed in a single copy in the French and English languages and, subject to paragraph (2), shall be deposited with the Director General.

(b) Official texts shall be established by the Director General, after consultation with the interested Governments, in the Arabic, German, Italian, Portuguese and Spanish languages, and such other languages as the Assembly may designate.

(c) In the case of differences of opinion on the interpretation of the various texts, the French text shall prevail.

(2) This Act shall remain open for signature until January 31, 1972. Until that date, the copy referred to in paragraph (1)(a) shall be deposited with the Government of the French Republic.

(3) The Director General shall certify and transmit two copies of the signed text of this Act to the Governments of all countries of the Union and, on request, to the Government of any other country.

(4) The Director General shall register this Act with the Secretariat of the United Nations.

(5) The Director General shall notify the Governments of all countries of the Union of signatures, deposits of instruments of ratification or accession and any declarations included in such instruments or made pursuant to Articles 28(1)(c), 30(2)(a) and (b), and 33(2), entry into force of any provisions of this Act, notifications of denunciation and notifications pursuant to Articles 30(2)(c), 31(1) and (2), 33(3), and 38(1), as well as the Appendix.

Article 38

(1) Countries of the Union, which have not ratified or acceded to this Act and which are not bound by Articles 22 to 26 of the Stockholm Act of this Convention may, until April 16, 1975, exercise, if they so desire, the rights provided under the said Articles as if they were bound by them. Any country desiring to exercise such rights shall give written notification to this effect to the Director General; this notification shall be effective on the date of its receipt. Such countries shall be deemed to be members of the Assembly until the said date.

(2) As long as all the countries of the Union have not become Members of the Organization, the International Bureau of the Organization shall also function as the Bureau of the Union, and the Director General as Director of the said Bureau.

(3) Once all the countries of the Union have become Members of the Organization, the rights, obligations, and property, of the Bureau of the Union shall devolve on the International Bureau of the Organization.

APPENDIX

ARTICLE I

(1) Any country regarded as a developing country in conformity with the established

practice of the General Assembly of the United Nations which ratifies or accedes to this Act of which this Appendix forms an integral part, and which, having regard to its economic situation and its social or cultural needs, does not consider itself immediately in a position to make provision for the protection of all the rights as provided for in this Act, may, by a notification deposited with the Director General at the time of depositing its instrument of ratification or accession or, subject to Article V(1)(c), at any time thereafter, declare that it will avail itself of the faculty provided for in Article II, or of the faculty provided for in Article III, or of both of those faculties. It may, instead of availing itself of the faculty provided for in Article II, make a declaration according to Article V(1)(a).

(2)(a) Any declaration under paragraph (1) notified before the expiration of the period of ten years from the entry into force of Articles 1 to 21 and this Appendix according to Article 28(2) shall be effective until the expiration of the said period. Any such declaration may be renewed in whole or in part for periods of ten years each by a notification deposited with the Director General not more than fifteen months and not less than three months before the expiration of the ten-year period then running.

(b) Any declaration under paragraph (1) notified after the expiration of the period of ten years from the entry into force of Articles 1 to 21 and this Appendix according to Article 28(2) shall be effective until the expiration of the ten-year period then running. Any such declaration may be renewed as provided for in the second sentence of subparagraph (a).

(3) Any country of the Union which has ceased to be regarded as a developing country as referred to in paragraph (1) shall no longer be entitled to renew its declaration as provided in paragraph (2), and, whether or not it formally withdraws its declaration, such country shall be precluded from availing itself of the faculties referred to in paragraph (1) from the expiration of the ten-year period then running or from the expiration of a period of three years after it has ceased to be regarded as a developing country, whichever period expires later.

(4) Where, at the time when the declaration made under paragraph (1) or (2) ceases to be effective, there are copies in stock which were made under a licence granted by virtue of this Appendix, such copies may continue to be distributed until their stock is exhausted.

(5) Any country which is bound by the provisions of this Act and which has deposited a declaration or a notification in accordance with Article 31(1) with respect to the application of this Act to a particular territory, the situation of which can be regarded as analogous to that of the countries referred to in paragraph (1), may, in respect of such territory, make the declaration referred to in paragraph (1) and the notification of renewal referred to in paragraph (2). As long as such declaration or notification remains in effect, the provisions of this Appendix shall be applicable to the territory in respect of which it was made.

(6)(a) The fact that a country avails itself of any of the faculties referred to in paragraph (1) does not permit another country to give less protection to works of which the country of origin is the former country than it is obliged to grant under Articles 1 to 20.

(b) The right to apply reciprocal treatment provided for in Article 30(2)(b), second sentence, shall not, until the date on which the period applicable under Article I(3) expires, be exercised in respect of works the country of origin of which is a country which has made a declaration according to Article V(1)(a).

ARTICLE II

(1) Any country which has declared that it will avail itself of the faculty provided for in this Article shall be entitled, so far as works published in printed or analogous forms of reproduction are concerned, to substitute for the exclusive right of translation provided for in Article 8 a system of non-exclusive and non-transferable licenses, granted by the competent authority under the following conditions and subject to Article IV.

(2)(a) Subject to paragraph (3), if, after the expiration of a period of three years, or of any longer period determined by the national legislation of the said country, commencing on the date of the first publication of the work, a translation of such work has not been published in a language in general use in that country by the owner of the right of translation, or with his authorization, any national of such country may obtain a licence to make a translation of the work in the said language and publish the translation in printed or analogous forms of reproduction.

(b) A licence under the conditions provided for in this Article may also be granted if all the editions of the translation published in the language concerned are out of print.

(3)(a) In the case of translations into a language which is not in general use in one or more developed countries which are members of the Union, a period of one year shall be substituted for the period of three years referred to in paragraph (2)(a).

(b) Any country referred to in paragraph (1) may, with the unanimous agreement of the developed countries which are members of the Union and in which the same language is in general use, substitute, in the case of translations into that language, for the period of three years referred to in paragraph (2)(a) a shorter period as determined by such agreement but not less than one year. However, the provisions of the foregoing sentences shall not apply where the language in question is English, French or Spanish. The Director General shall be notified of any such agreement by the Governments which have concluded it.

(4)(a) No licence obtainable after three years shall be granted under this Article until a further period of six months has elapsed, and no licence obtainable after one year shall be granted under this Article until a further period of nine months has elapsed

(i) from the date on which the applicant complies with the requirements mentioned in Article IV(1), or

(ii) where the identity or the address of the owner of the right of translation is unknown, from the date on which the applicant sends, as provided for in Article IV(2), copies of his application submitted to the authority competent to grant the licence.

(b) If, during the said period of six or nine months, a translation in the language in respect of which the application was made is published by the owner of the right of translation or with his authorization, no licence under this Article shall be granted.

(5) Any licence under this Article shall be granted only for the purpose of teaching, scholarship or research.

(6) If a translation of a work is published by the owner of the right of translation or with his authorization at a price reasonably related to that normally charged in the country for comparable works, any licence granted under this Article shall terminate if such translation is in the same language and with substantially the same content as the translation published under the licence. Any copies already made before the licence terminates may continue to be distributed until their stock is exhausted.

(7) For works which are composed mainly of illustrations, a licence to make and publish a translation of the text and to reproduce and publish the illustrations may be granted only if the conditions of Article III are also fulfilled.

(8) No licence shall be granted under this Article when the author has withdrawn from circulation all copies of his work.

(9)(a) A licence to make a translation of a work which has been published in printed or analogous forms of reproduction may also be granted to any broadcasting organization having its headquarters in a country referred to in paragraph (1), upon an application made to the competent authority of that country by the said organization, provided that all of the following conditions are met:

(i) the translation is made from a copy made and acquired in accordance with the laws of the said country;

(ii) the translation is only for use in broadcasts intended exclusively for teaching or for the dissemination of the results of a specialized technical or scientific research to experts in a particular profession;

(iii) the translation is used exclusively for the purposes referred to in condition (ii) through broadcasts made lawfully and intended for recipients on the territory of the said country, including broadcasts made through the medium of sound or visual recordings lawfully and exclusively made for the purpose of such broadcasts;

(iv) all uses made of the translation are without any commercial purpose.

(b) Sound or visual recordings of a translation which was made by a broadcasting organization under a licence granted by virtue of this paragraph may, for the purposes and subject to the conditions referred to in subparagraph (a) and with the agreement of that organization, also be used by any other broadcasting organization having its headquarters in the country whose competent authority granted the licence in question.

(c) Provided that all of the criteria and conditions set out in subparagraph (a) are met, a licence may also be granted to a broadcasting organization to translate any text incorporated in an audio-visual fixation where such fixation was itself prepared and published for the sole purpose of being used in connection with systematic instructional activities.

(d) Subject to subparagraphs (a) to (c), the provisions of the preceding paragraphs shall apply to the grant and exercise of any licence granted under this paragraph.

ARTICLE III

(1) Any country which has declared that it will avail itself of the faculty provided for in this Article shall be entitled to substitute for the exclusive right of reproduction provided for in Article 9 a system of non-exclusive and non-transferable licences, granted by the competent authority under the following conditions and subject to Article IV.

(2)(a) If, in relation to a work to which this Article applies by virtue of paragraph (7), after the expiration of

  (i) the relevant period specified in paragraph (3), commencing on the date of first publication of a particular edition of the work, or

  (ii) any longer period determined by national legislation of the country referred to in paragraph (1), commencing on the same date,

    copies of such edition have not been distributed in that country to the general public or in connection with systematic instructional activities, by the owner of the right of reproduction or with his authorization, at a price reasonably related to that normally charged in the country for comparable works, any national of such country may obtain a licence to reproduce and publish such edition at that or a lower price for use in connection with systematic instructional activities.

(b) A licence to reproduce and publish an edition which has been distributed as described in subparagraph (a) may also be granted under the conditions provided for in this Article if, after the expiration of the applicable period, no authorised copies of that edition have been on sale for a period of six months in the country concerned to the general public or in connection with systematic instructional activities at a price reasonably related to that normally charged in the country for comparable works.

(3) The period referred to in paragraph (2)(a)(i) shall be five years, except that

  (i) for works of the natural and physical sciences, including mathematics, and of technology, the period shall be three years;

  (ii) for works of fiction, poetry, drama and music, and for art books, the period shall be seven years.

(4)(a) No licence obtainable after three years shall be granted under this Article until a period of six months has elapsed

  (i) from the date on which the applicant complies with the requirements mentioned in Article IV(1), or

  (ii) where the identity or the address of the owner of the right of reproduction is unknown, from the date on which the applicant sends, as provided for in Article IV(2), copies of his application submitted to the authority competent to grant the licence.

(b) Where licences are obtainable after other periods and Article IV(2) is applicable, no licence shall be granted until a period of three months has elapsed from the date of the dispatch of the copies of the application.

(c) If, during the period of six or three months referred to in subparagraphs (a) and (b), a distribution as described in paragraph (2)(a) has taken place, no licence shall be granted under this Article.

(d) No licence shall be granted if the author has withdrawn from circulation all copies of the edition for the reproduction and publication of which the licence has been applied for.

(5) A licence to reproduce and publish a translation of a work shall not be granted under this Article in the following cases:

  (i) where the translation was not published by the owner of the right of translation or with his authorization, or

(ii) where the translation is not in a language in general use in the country in which the licence is applied for.

(6) If copies of an edition of a work are distributed in the country referred to in paragraph (1) to the general public or in connection with systematic instructional activities, by the owner of the right of reproduction or with his authorization, at a price reasonably related to that normally charged in the country for comparable works, any licence granted under this Article shall terminate if such edition is in the same language and with substantially the same content as the edition which was published under the said licence. Any copies already made before the licence terminates may continue to be distributed until their stock is exhausted.

(7)(a) Subject to subparagraph (b), the works to which this Article applies shall be limited to works published in printed or analogous forms of reproduction.

(b) This Article shall also apply to the reproduction in audio-visual form of lawfully made audio-visual fixations including any protected works incorporated therein and to the translation of any incorporated text into a language in general use in the country in which the licence is applied for, always provided that the audio-visual fixations in question were prepared and published for the sole purpose of being used in connection with systematic instructional activities.

Article IV

(1) A licence under Article II or Article III may be granted only if the applicant, in accordance with the procedure of the country concerned, establishes either that he has requested, and has been denied, authorization by the owner of the right to make and publish the translation or to reproduce and publish the edition, as the case may be, or that, after due diligence on his part, he was unable to find the owner of the right. At the same time as making the request, the application shall inform any national or international information centre referred to in paragraph (2).

(2) If the owner of the right cannot be found, the applicant for a licence shall send, by registered airmail, copies of his application, submitted to the authority competent to grant the licence, to the publisher whose name appears on the work and to any national or international information centre which may have been designated, in a notification to that effect deposited with the Director General, by the Government of the country in which the publisher is believed to have his principal place of business.

(3) The name of the author shall be indicated on all copies of the translation or reproduction published under a licence granted under Article II or Article III. The title of the work shall appear on all such copies. In the case of a translation, the original title of the work shall appear in any case on all the said copies.

(4)(a) No licence granted under Article II or Article III shall extend to the export of copies, and any such licence shall be valid only for publication of the translation or of the reproduction, as the case may be, in the territory of the country in which it has been applied for.

(b) For the purposes of subparagraph (a), the notion of export shall include the sending of copies from any territory to the country which, in respect of that territory, has made a declaration under Article I(5).

(c) Where a governmental or other public entity of a country which has granted a licence to make a translation under Article II into a language other than English, French or Spanish sends copies of a translation published under such licence to another country, such sending of copies shall not, for the purposes of subparagraph (a), be considered to constitute export if all of the following conditions are met:

(i) the recipients are individuals who are nationals of the country whose competent authority has granted the licence, or organizations grouping such individuals;

(ii) the copies are to be used only for the purpose of teaching, scholarship or research;

(iii) the sending of the copies and their subsequent distribution to recipients is without any commercial purpose; and

(iv) the country to which the copies have been sent has agreed with the country whose competent authority has granted the licence to allow the receipt, or distribution, or both, and the Director General has been notified of the agreement by the Government of the country in which the licence has been granted.

(5) All copies published under a licence granted by virtue of Article II or Article III

shall bear a notice in the appropriate language stating that the copies are available for distribution only in the country or territory to which the said licence applies.

(6)(a) Due provision shall be made at the national level to ensure

(i) that the licence provides, in favour of the owner of the right of translation or of reproduction, as the case may be, for just compensation that is consistent with standards of royalties normally operating on licences freely negotiated between persons in the two countries concerned, and

(ii) payment and transmittal of the compensation: should national currency regulations intervene, the competent authority shall make all efforts, by the use of international machinery, to ensure transmittal in internationally convertible currency or its equivalent.

(b) Due provision shall be made by national legislation to ensure a correct translation of the work, or an accurate reproduction of the particular edition, as the case may be.

ARTICLE V

(1)(a) Any country entitled to make a declaration that it will avail itself of the faculty provided for in Article II may, instead, at the time of ratifying or acceding to this Act:

(i) if it is a country to which Article 30(2)(a) applies, make a declaration under that provision as far as the right of translation is concerned;

(ii) if it is a country to which Article 30(2)(a) does not apply, and even if it is not a country outside the Union, make a declaration as provided for in Article 30(2)(b), first sentence.

(b) In the case of a country which ceases to be regarded as a developing country as referred to in Article I(1), a declaration made according to this paragraph shall be effective until the date on which the period applicable under Article I(3) expires.

(c) Any country which has made a declaration according to this paragraph may not subsequently avail itself of the faculty provided for in Article II even if it withdraws the said declaration.

(2) Subject to paragraph (3), any country which has availed itself of the faculty provided for in Article II may not subsequently make a declaration according to paragraph (1).

(3) Any country which has ceased to be regarded as a developing country as referred to in Article I(1) may, not later than two years prior to the expiration of the period applicable under Article I(3), make a declaration to the effect provided for in Article 30(2)(b), first sentence, notwithstanding the fact that it is not a country outside the Union. Such declaration shall take effect at the date on which the period applicable under Article I(3) expires.

ARTICLE VI

(1) Any country of the Union may declare, as from the date of this Act, and at any time before becoming bound by Articles 1 to 21 and this Appendix:

(i) if it is a country which, were it bound by Articles 1 to 21 and this Appendix, would be entitled to avail itself of the faculties referred to in Article I(1), that it will apply the provisions of Article II or of Article III or of both to works whose country of origin is a country which, pursuant to (ii) below, admits the application of those Articles to such works, or which is bound by Articles 1 to 21 and this Appendix; such declaration may, instead of referring to Article II, refer to Article V;

(ii) that it admits the application of this Appendix to works of which it is the country of origin by countries which have made a declaration under (i) above or a notification under Article I.

(2) Any declaration made under paragraph (1) shall be in writing and shall be deposited with the Director General. The declaration shall become effective from the date of its deposit.

DECLARATION BY THE UNITED KINGDOM UNDER ARTICLE VI(1)(ii) OF THE APPENDIX

In a communication deposited with the Director General of the World Intellectual Property Organisation on 27 September, 1971, the Government of the United Kingdom declared that the United Kingdom admits the application of the Appendix to works of which it is the country of origin by countries which have made a declaration under Article VI(1)(i) of the Appendix or a notification under Article I of the Appendix.

F2. UNIVERSAL COPYRIGHT CONVENTION

PARIS ACT 1971

The Universal Copyright Convention signed at Geneva on September 6, 1952[i] was revised in Paris in 1971.[ii]

Editorial Note: Because there are differences in the texts both texts are printed so that a comparison may be made. The omissions from the 1952 text and the changes in the 1971 text are printed in italics.

Geneva	*Paris*
Article I	*Article I*
Each Contracting State undertakes to provide for the adequate and effective protection of the rights of authors and other copyright proprietors in literary, scientific and artistic works, including writings, musical, dramatic and cinematographic works, and paintings, engravings and sculpture.	Each Contracting State undertakes to provide for the adequate and effective protection of the rights of authors and other copyright proprietors in literary, scientific and artistic works, including writings, musical, dramatic and cinematographic works, and paintings, engravings and sculpture.
Have, by common agreement, accepted the terms of the following declaration:	Have, by common agreement, accepted the terms of the following declaration:
(a) Works which, according to the Berne Convention, have as their country of origin a country which has withdrawn from the International Union created by the said Convention, after January 1, 1951, shall not be protected by the Universal Copyright Convention in the countries of the Berne Union;	(a) *Except as provided by paragraph (b)*, works which, according to the Berne Convention, have as their country of origin a country which has withdrawn from the *Berne Union* after 1 January 1951, shall not be protected by the Universal Copyright Convention in the countries of the Berne Union;

---

[i] *Editorial Note*: Cmnd. 8912.
[ii] *Editorial Note*: Cmnd. 4905.

(b) *Where a Contracting State is regarded as a developing country in conformity with the established practice of the General Assembly of the United Nations, and has deposited with the Director-General of the United Nations Educational, Scientific and Cultural Organization, at the time of its withdrawal from the Berne Union, a notification to the effect that it regards itself as a developing country, the provisions of paragraph (a) shall not be applicable as long as such State may avail itself of the exceptions provided for by this Convention in accordance with Article V^{bis};*

(b) The Universal Copyright Convention shall not be applicable to the relationships among countries of the Berne Union in so far as it relates to the protection of works having as their country of origin, within the meaning of the Berne Convention, a country of the International Union created by the said Convention.

(c) *The Universal Copyright Convention shall not be applicable to the relationships among countries of the Berne Union in so far as it relates to the protection of works having as their country of origin, within the meaning of the Berne Convention, a country of the Berne Union.*

Resolution Concerning Article XI

The Intergovernmental Copyright Conference,
Having considered the problems relating to the Intergovernmental Committee provided for in Article XI of the Universal Copyright Convention, resolves:
1. The first members of the Committee shall be representatives of the following twelve States, each of those States designating one representative and an alternate: Argentina, Brazil, France, Germany, India, Italy, Japan, Mexico, Spain, Switzerland, United Kingdom and United States of America.
2. The Committee shall be constituted as soon as the Convention comes into force in accordance with Article XI of this Convention.

Resolution Concerning Article XI

The Conference for Revision of the Universal Copyright Convention,
Having considered the problems relating to the Intergovernmental Committee provided for in Article XI of this Convention, to which this resolution is annexed,
Resolves that:
1. At its inception, the Committee shall include representatives of the twelve States members of the Intergovernmental Committee established under Article XI of the 1952 Convention and the resolution annexed to it, and in addition, representatives of the following States: Algeria, Australia, Japan, Mexico, Senegal and Yugoslavia.

2. Any States that are not party to the 1952 Convention and have not acceded to this Convention before the first ordinary session of the Committee following the entry into force of this Convention shall be replaced by other States to be selected by the Committee at its first ordinary session in conformity with the provisions of Article XI (2) and (3).

3. As soon as this Convention comes into force the Committee as provided for in paragraph 1 shall be deemed to be constituted in accordance with Article XI of this Convention.

4. A session of the Committee shall take place within one year after the coming into force of this Convention; thereafter the Committee shall meet in ordinary session at intervals of not more than two years.

3. The Committee shall elect its Chairman and one Vice-Chairman. It shall establish its rules of procedure having regard to the following principles:

(a) the normal duration of the term of office of the representatives shall be six years; with one-third retiring every two years;

5. The Committee shall elect its Chairman and *two* Vice-Chairmen. It shall establish its rules of procedure having regard to the following principles:

(a) The normal duration of the term of office of the *members represented on the Committee* shall be six years with one-third retiring every two years, *it being however understood that, of the original terms of office, one-third shall expire at the end of the Committee's second ordinary session which will follow the entry into force of this Convention, a further third at the end of its third ordinary session, and the remaining third at the end of its fourth ordinary session.*

(b) before the expiration of the term of office of any members, the Committee shall decide which States shall cease to be represented on it and which States shall be called upon to designate representatives; the representatives of those States which have not ratified, accepted or acceded shall be the first to retire;

(c) the different parts of the world shall be fairly represented;

and expresses the wish that the United Nations Educational, Scientific and Cultural Organisation provide its Secretariat.

(b) *The rules governing the procedure whereby the Committee shall fill vacancies, the order in which terms of membership expire, eligibility for re-election, and election procedures, shall be based upon a balancing of the needs for continuity of membership and rotation of representation, as well as the considerations set out in Article XI (3).*

Expresses the wish that the United Nations Educational, Scientific and Cultural Organisation provide its Secretariat.

***

Protocol 1 annexed to the Universal Copyright Convention as Revised at Paris on 24 July 1971 concerning the Application of that Convention to works of Stateless Persons and Refugees

The States parties hereto, being also parties to the Universal Copyright Convention (hereinafter referred to as the "Convention") have accepted the following provisions:

1. Stateless persons and refugees who have their habitual residence in a State party to this Protocol shall, for the purposes of the Convention, be assimilated to the nationals of that State.

Protocol 1 annexed to the Universal Copyright Convention as Revised at Paris on 24 July 1971 concerning the Application of that Convention to works of Stateless Persons and Refugees

The States party hereto, being also party to the Universal Copyright Convention *as revised at Paris on 24 July 1971* (hereinafter *called* "the *1971* Convention"),

Have accepted the following provisions:

1. Stateless persons and refugees who have their habitual residence in a State party to this Protocol shall, for the purposes of the 1971 Convention, be assimilated to the nationals of that State.

2. (a) This Protocol shall be signed and shall be subject to ratification or acceptance, or may be acceded to, as if the provisions of Article VIII of the Convention applied hereto.

(b) This Protocol shall enter into force in respect of each State on the date of deposit of the instrument of ratification, acceptance or accession of the State concerned or on the date of entry into force of the Convention with respect to such State, whichever is the later.

2. (a) This Protocol shall be signed and be subject to ratification or acceptance, or may be acceded to, as if the provisions of Article VIII of the *1971* Convention applied hereto.

(b) This Protocol shall enter into force in respect of each State, on the date of deposit of the instrument of ratification, acceptance or accession of the State concerned or on the date of entry into force of the *1971* Convention with respect to such State, whichever is the later.

(c) On the entry into force of this Protocol in respect of a State not party to Protocol 1 annexed to the 1952 Convention, the latter Protocol shall be deemed to enter into force in respect of such State.

Protocol 2 annexed to the Universal Copyright Convention, concerning the application of that Convention to the works of certain International Organisations

The State parties hereto, being also parties to the Universal Copyright Convention (hereinafter referred to as the "Convention"),
Have accepted the following provisions:

1. (a) The protection provided for in Article II (1) of the Convention shall apply to works published for the first time by the United Nations, by the Specialised Agencies in relationship therewith, or by the Organisation of American States;

(b) Similarly, Article II (2) of the Convention shall apply to the said organisation or agencies.

Protocol 2 annexed to the Universal Copyright Convention as revised at Paris on 24 July 1971 concerning the application of that Convention to the works of certain International Organizations

The State party hereto, being also party to the Universal Copyright Convention *as revised at Paris on 24 July 1971* (hereinafter *called* "the *1971* Convention"),
Have accepted the following provisions:

1. (a) The protection provided for in Article II (1) of the *1971* Convention shall apply to works published for the first time by the United Nations, by the Specialized Agencies in relationship therewith, or by the Organisation of American States;

(b) Similarly, Article II (2) of the *1971* Convention shall apply to the said organization or agencies.

2.
(a) This Protocol shall be signed and shall be subject to ratification or acceptance, or may be acceded to, as if the provisions of Article VIII of the 1971 Convention applied hereto.

(b) This Protocol shall enter into force for each State on the date of deposit of the instrument of ratification, acceptance or accession of the State concerned or on the date of entry into force of the Convention with respect to such State, whichever is the later.

2.
(a) This Protocol shall be signed and shall be subject to ratification or acceptance, or may be acceded to, as if the provisions of Article VIII of the *1971* Convention applied hereto.

(b) This Protocol shall enter into force for each State on the date of deposit of the instrument of ratification, acceptance or accession of the State concerned or on the date of entry into force of the *1971* Convention with respect to such State, whichever is the later.

Protocol 3 annexed to the Universal Copyright Convention concerning the effective date of Instruments of Ratification or Acceptance of or Accession to that Convention

States parties hereto,
Recognising that the application of the
Universal Copyright Convention (hereinafter referred to as the "Convention") to States participating in all the international copyright systems already in force will contribute greatly to the value of the Convention.
Have agreed as follows:

1. Any State party hereto may, on depositing its instrument of ratification or acceptance of or accession to the Convention, notify the Director-General of the United Nations Educational, Scientific and Cultural Organisation (hereinafter referred to as "Director-General") that that instrument shall not take effect for the purposes of Article IX of the Convention until any other State named in such notification shall have deposited its instrument.

2. The notification referred to in paragraph 1 above shall accompany the instrument to which it relates.

3. The Director-General shall inform all States signatory or which have then acceded to the Convention of any notifications received in accordance with this Protocol.

4. This Protocol shall bear the same date and shall remain open for signature for the same period as the Convention.

5. It shall be subject to ratification or acceptance by the signatory States. Any State which has not signed this Protocol may accede thereto.

6.—Ratification or acceptance or accession shall be effected by the deposit of an instrument to that effect with the Director-General.

This Protocol shall enter into force on the date of deposit of not less than four instruments of ratification or acceptance or accession. The Director-General shall inform all interested States of this date. Instruments deposited after such date shall take effect on the date of their deposit.

Geneva	Paris
Article I	*Article I*

Each Contracting State undertakes to provide for the adequate and effective protection of the rights of authors and other copyright proprietors in literary, scientific and artistic works, including writings, musical, dramatic and cinematographic works, and paintings, engravings and sculpture.

Each Contracting State undertakes to provide for the adequate and effective protection of the rights of authors and other copyright proprietors in literary, scientific and artistic works, including writings, musical, dramatic and cinematographic works, and paintings, engravings and sculpture.

Article II

1. Published works of nationals of any Contracting State and works first published in that State shall enjoy in each other Contracting State the same protection as that other State accords to works of its nationals first published in its own territory.

Article II

1. Published works of nationals of any Contracting State and works first published in that State shall enjoy in each other Contracting State the same protection as that other State accords to works of its nationals first published in its own territory, *as well as the protection specially granted by this Convention.*

2. Unpublished works of nationals of each Contracting State shall enjoy in each other Contracting State the same protecton as that other State accords to unpublished works of its own nationals.

3. For the purpose of this Convention any Contracting State may, by domestic legislation, assimilate to its own nationals any person domiciled in that State.

Article III

1. Any Contracting State which, under its domestic law, requires as a condition of copyright, compliance with formalities such as deposit, registration, notice, notarial certificates, payment of fees or manufacture or publication in that Contracting State, shall regard these requirements as satisfied with respect to all works protected in accordance with this Convention and first published outside its territory and the author of which is not one of its nationals, if from the time of the first publication all the copies of the work published with the authority of the author or other copyright proprietor bear the symbol © accompanied by the name of the copyright proprietor and the year of first publication placed in such manner and location as to give reasonable notice of claim of copyright.

2. The provisions of paragraph 1 *of this Article* shall not preclude any Contracting State from requiring formalities or other conditions for the acquisition and enjoyment of copyright in respect of works first published in its territory or works of its nationals wherever published.

2. Unpublished works of nationals of each Contracting State shall enjoy in each other Contracting State the same protection as that other State accords to unpublished works of its own nationals, *as well as the protection specially granted by this Convention.*

3. For the purpose of this Convention any Contracting State may, by domestic legislation, assimilate to its own nationals any person domiciled in that State.

Article III

1. Any Contracting State which, under its domestic law, requires as a condition of copyright, compliance with formalities such as deposit, registration, notice, notarial certificates, payment of fees or manufacture or publication in that Contracting State, shall regard these requirements as satisfied with respect to all works protected in accordance with this Convention and first published outside its territory and the author of which is not one of its nationals, if from the time of the first publication all the copies of the work published with the authority of the author or other copyright proprietor bear the symbol © accompanied by the name of the copyright proprietor and the year of first publication placed in such manner and location as to give reasonable notice of claim of copyright.

2. The provisions of paragraph 1 shall not preclude any Contracting State from requiring formalities or other conditions for the acquisition and enjoyment of copyright in respect of works first published in its territory or works of its nationals wherever published.

3. The provisions of paragraph 1 *of this Article* shall not preclude any Contracting State from providing that a person seeking judicial relief must, in bringing the action, comply with procedural requirements, such as that the complainant must appear through domestic counsel or that the complainant must deposit with the court or an administrative office, or both, a copy of the work involved in the litigation; provided that failure to comply with such requirements shall not affect the validity of the copyright, nor shall any such requirement be imposed upon a national of another Contracting State if such requirement is not imposed on nationals of the State in which protection is claimed.

4. In each Contracting State there shall be legal means of protecting without formalities the unpublished works of nationals of other Contracting States.

5. If a Contracting State grants protection for more than one term of copyright and the first term is for a period longer than one of the minimum periods prescribed in Article IV, such State shall not be required to comply with the provisions of paragraph 1 of this Article III in respect of the second or any subsequent term of copyright.

Article IV

1. The duration of protection of a work shall be governed, in accordance with the provisions of Article II and this Article, by the law of the Contracting State in which protection is claimed.

3. The provisions of paragraph 1 shall not preclude any Contracting State from providing that a person seeking judicial relief must, in bringing the action, comply with procedural requirements, such as that the complainant must appear through domestic counsel or that the complainant must deposit with the court or an administrative office, or both, a copy of the work involved in the litigation; provided that failure to comply with such requirements shall not affect the validity of the copyright, nor shall any such requirement be imposed upon a national of another Contracting State if such requirement is not imposed on nationals of the State in which protection is claimed.

4. In each Contracting State there shall be legal means of protecting without formalities the unpublished works of nationals of other Contracting States.

5. If a Contracting State grants protection for more than one term of copyright and the first term is for a period longer than one of the minimum periods prescribed in Article IV, such State shall not be required to comply with the provisions of paragraph 1 of this Article in respect of the second or any subsequent term of copyright.

Article IV

1. The duration of protection of a work shall be governed, in accordance with the provisions of Article II and this Article, by the law of the Contracting State in which protection is claimed.

2. The term of protection for works protected under this Convention shall not be less than the life of the author and 25 years after his death. However, any Contracting State which, on the effective date of this Convention in that State has limited this term for certain classes of works to a period computed from the first publication of the work, shall be entitled to maintain these exceptions and to extend them to other classes of works. For all these classes the term of protection shall not be less than twenty-five years from the date of first publication.

Any Contracting State which, upon the effective date of this Convention in that State, does not compute the term of protection upon the basis of the life of the author, shall be entitled to compute the term of protection from the date of the first publication of the work or from its registration prior to publication, as the case may be, provided the term of protection shall not be less than twenty-five years from the date of first publication or from its registration prior to publication, as the case may be.

If the legislation of a Contracting State grants two or more successive terms of protection, the duration of the first term shall not be less than one of the minimum periods specified above.

2. (a) The term of protection for works protected under this Convention shall not be less than the life of the author and twenty-five years after his death. However, any Contracting State which, on the effective date of this Convention in that State, has limited this term for certain classes of works to a period computed from the first publication of the work, shall be entitled to maintain these exceptions and to extend them to other classes of works. For all these classes the term of protection shall not be less than twenty-five years from the date of first publication.

(b) Any Contracting State which, upon the effective date of this Convention in that State, does not compute the term of protection upon the basis of the life of the author, shall be entitled to compute the term of protection from the date of the first publication of the work or from its registration prior to publication, as the case may be, provided the term of protection shall not be less than twenty-five years from the date of first publication or from its registration prior to publication, as the case may be.

(c) If the legislation of a Contracting State grants two or more successive terms of protection, the duration of the first term shall not be less than one of the minimum periods specified *in subparagraphs* (a) *and* (b).

3. The provisions of paragraph 2 *of this Article* shall not apply to photographic works or to works of applied art; provided however, that the term of protection in those Contracting States which protect photographic works, or works of applied art in so far as they are protected as artistic works, shall not be less than ten years for each of said classes of works.

4. No Contracting State shall be obliged to grant protection to a work for a period longer than that fixed for the classes of works to which the work in question belongs, in the case of unpublished works by the law of the Contracting State of which the author is a national, and in the case of published works by the law of the Contracting State in which the work has been first published.

For the purposes of the application of the preceding provision, if the law of any Contracting State grants two or more successive terms of protection, the period of protection of that State shall be considered to be the aggregate of those terms. However, if a specified work is not protected by such State during the second or any subsequent term for any reason, the other Contracting State shall not be obliged to protect it during the second or any subsequent term.

3. The provisions of paragraph 2 shall not apply to photographic works or to works of applied art; provided, however, that the term of protection in those Contracting States which protect photographic works, or works of applied art in so far as they are protected as artistic works, shall not be less than ten years for each of said classes of works.

4.   (a)   No Contracting State shall be obliged to grant protection to a work for a period longer than that fixed for the classes of works to which the work in question belongs, in the case of unpublished works by the law of the Contracting State of which the author is a national, and in the case of published works by the law of the Contracting State in which the work has been first published.

     (b)   For the purposes of the application of *subparagraph* (a), if the law of any Contracting State grants two or more successive terms of protection, the period of protection of that State shall be considered to be the aggregate of those terms. However, if a specified work is not protected by such State during the second or any subsequent term for any reason, the other Contracting States shall not be obliged to protect it during the second or any subsequent term.

5. For the purposes of the application of paragraph 4 *of this Article*, the work of a national of a Contracting State, first published in a non-Contracting State, shall be treated as though first published in the Contracting State of which the author is a national.

6. For the purposes of the application of paragraph 4 *of this Article*, in case of simultaneous publication in two or more Contracting States, the work shall be treated as though first published in the State which affords the shortest term; any work published in two or more Contracting States within thirty days of its first publication shall be considered as having been published simultaneously in said Contracting States.

Article V

1. Copyright shall include the exclusive right of the author to make, publish, and authorise the making and publication of translations of works protected under this Convention.

5. For the purposes of the application of paragraph 4, the work of a national of a Contracting State, first published in a non-Contracting State, shall be treated as though first published in the Contracting State of which the author is a national.

6. For the purposes of the application of paragraph 4, in case of simultaneous publication in two or more Contracting States, the work shall be treated as though first published in the State which affords the shortest term; any work published in two or more Contracting States within thirty days of its first publication shall be considered as having been published simultaneously in said Contracting States.

Article IVbis

1. The rights referred to in Article I shall include the basic rights ensuring the author's economic interests, including the exclusive right to authorize reproduction by any means, public performance and broadcasting. The provisions of this Article shall extend to works protected under this Convention either in their original form or in any form recognizably derived from the original.

2. However, any Contracting State may, by its domestic legislation, make exceptions that do not conflict with the spirit and provisions of this Convention, to the rights mentioned in paragraph 1 of this Article. Any State whose legislation so provides, shall nevertheless accord a reasonable degree of effective protection to each of the rights to which exception has been made.

Article V

1. *The rights referred to in Article I* shall include the exclusive right of the author to make, publish and authorize the making and publication of translations of works protected under this Convention.

2. However, any Contracting State may, by its domestic legislation, restrict the right of translation of writings, but only subject to the following provisions:

If, after the expiration of a period of seven years from the date of the first publication of a writing, a translation of such writing has not been published in the national language or languages, as the case may be, of the Contracting State, by the owner of the right of translation or with his authorisation, any national of such Contracting State may obtain a non-exclusive licence from the competent authority thereof to translate the work and publish the work so translated *in any of the national languages in which it has not been published; provided that* such national, in accordance with the procedure of the State concerned, establishes either that he has requested, and been denied, authorisation by the proprietor of the right to make and publish the translation, or that, after due diligence on his part, he was unable to find the owner of the right. A licence may also be granted on the same conditions if all previous editions of a translation in such language are out of print.

2. However, any Contracting State may, by its domestic legislation restrict the right of translation of writings, but only subject to the following provisions:

(a) If, after the expiration of a period of seven years from the date of the first publication of a writing, a translation of such writing has not been published *in a language in general use in the Contracting State*, by the owner of the right of translation or with his authorization, any national of such Contracting State may obtain a non-exclusive licence from the competent authority thereof to translate the work into that language and publish the work so translated.

(b) Such national shall in accordance with the procedure of the State concerned, establish either that he has requested, and been denied, authorization by the proprietor of the right to make and publish the translation, or that, after due diligence on his part, he was unable to find the owner of the right. A licence may also be granted on the same conditions if all previous editions of a translation in *a language in general use in the Contracting State* are out of print.

If the owner of the right of translation cannot be found, then the applicant for a licence shall send copies of his application to the publisher whose name appears on the work and, if the nationality of the owner of the right of translation is known, to the diplomatic or consular representative of the State of which such owner is a national, or to the organisation which may have been designated by the government of that State. The licence shall not be granted before the expiration of a period of two months from the date of the despatch of the copies of the application.

Due provision shall be made by domestic legislation to assure to the owner of the right of translation a compensation which is just and conforms to international standards to assure payment and transmittal of such compensation, and to assure a correct translation of the work.

(c) If the owner of the right of translation cannot be found, then the applicant for a licence shall send copies of his application to the publisher whose name appears on the work and, if the nationality of the owner of the right of translation is known, to the diplomatic or consular representative of the State of which such owner is a national, or to the organization which may have been designated by the government of that State. The licence shall not be granted before the expiration of a period of two months from the date of the dispatch of the copies of the application.

(d) Due provision shall be made by domestic legislation *to ensure* to the owner of the right of translation a compensation which is just and conforms to international standards, *to ensure* payment and transmittal of such compensation, and *to ensure* a correct translation of the work.

The original title and the name of the author of the work shall be printed on all copies of the published translation. The licence shall be valid only for publication of the translation in the territory of the Contracting State where it has been applied for. Copies so published may be imported and sold in another Contracting State if one of the national languages of such other State is the same language as that into which the work has been so translated, and if the domestic law in such other State makes provision for such licences and does not prohibit such importation and sale. Where the foregoing conditions do not exist, the importation and sale of such copies in a Contracting State shall be governed by its domestic law and its agreements. The licence shall not be transferred by the licensee. The licence shall not be granted when the author has withdrawn from circulation all copies of the work.

(e) The original title and the name of the author of the work shall be printed on all copies of the published translation. The licence shall be valid only for publication of the translation in the territory of the Contracting State where it has been applied for. Copies so published may be imported and sold in another Contracting State if *a language in general use in such other State* is the same language as that into which the work has been so translated, and if the domestic law in such other State makes provision for such licences and does not prohibit such importation and sale. Where the foregoing conditions do not exist, the importation and sale of such copies in a Contracting State shall be governed by its domestic law and its agreements. The licence shall not be transferred by the licensee.

(f) The licence shall not be granted when the author has withdrawn from circulation all copies of the work.

*Article V*bis

1. Any Contracting State regarded as a developing country in conformity with the established practice of the General Assembly of the United Nations may, by a notification deposited with the Director-General of the United Nations Educational, Scientific and Cultural Organization (hereinafter called "the Director-General") at the time of its ratification, acceptance or accession or thereafter, avail itself of any or all of the exceptions provided for in Articles Vter and Vquater.

2. Any such notification shall be effective for ten years from the date of coming into force of this Convention, or for such part of that ten-year period as remains at the date of deposit of the notification, and may be renewed in whole or in part for further periods of ten years each if, not more than fifteen or less than three months before the expiration of the relevant ten-year period, the Contracting State deposits a further notification with the Director-General. Initial notifications may also be made during these further periods of ten years in accordance with the provisions of this Article.

3. Notwithstanding the provisions of paragraph 2, a Contracting State that has ceased to be regarded as a developing country as referred to in paragraph 1 shall no longer be entitled to renew its notification made under the provisions of paragraph 1 or 2, and whether or not it formally withdraws the notification such State shall be precluded from availing itself of the exceptions provided for in Articles V ter and V quater at the end of the current ten-year period, or at the end of three years after it has ceased to be regarded as a developing country, whichever period expires later.

4. Any copies of a work already made under the exceptions provided for in Articles Vter and Vquater may continue to be distributed after the expiration of the period for which notifications under this Article were effective until their stock is exhausted.

5. Any Contracting State that has deposited a notification in accordance with Article XIII with respect to the application of this Convention to a particular country or territory, the situation of which can be regarded as analogous to that of the States referred to in paragraph 1 of this Article, may also deposit notifications and renew them in accordance with the provisions of this Article with respect to any such country or territory. During the effective period of such notifications, the provisions of Articles Vter and Vquater may be applied with respect to such country or territory. The sending of copies from the country or territory to the Contracting State shall be considered as export within the meaning of Articles Vter and Vquater

Article Vter

1.   (a)   *Any Contracting State to which Article Vbis (1) applies may substitute for the period of seven years provided for in Article V (2) a period of three years or any longer period prescribed by its legislation. However, in the case of a translation into a language not in general use in one or more developed countries that are party to this Convention or only the 1952 Convention, the period shall be one year instead of three.*

(b)   *A Contracting State to which Article V^{bis} (1) applies may, with the unanimous agreement of the developed countries party to this Convention or only the 1952 Convention and in which the same language is in general use, substitute, in the case of translation into that language, for the period of three years provided for in sub-paragraph (a) another period as determined by such agreement but not shorter than one year. However, this sub-paragraph shall not apply where the language in question is English, French or Spanish. Notification of any such agreement shall be made to the Director-General.*

(c)   The licence may only be granted if the applicant, in accordance with the procedure of the State concerned, establishes either that he has requested, and been denied, authorization by the owner of the right of translation, or that, after due diligence on his part, he was unable to find the owner of the right. At the same time as he makes his request he shall inform either the International Copyright Information Centre established by the United Nations Educational, Scientific and Cultural Organization or any national or regional information centre which may have been designated in a notification to that effect deposited with the Director-General by the government of the State in which the publisher is believed to have his principal place of business.

(d)   If the owner of the right of translation cannot be found, the applicant for a licence shall send, by registered airmail, copies of his application to the publisher whose name appears on the work and to any national or regional information centre as mentioned in subparagraph (c). If no such centre is notified he shall also send a copy to the International Copyright Information Centre established by the United Nations Educational, Scientific and Cultural Organization.

2.   (a)   *Licences obtainable after three years shall not be granted under this Article until a further period of six months has elapsed and licences obtainable after one year until a further period of nine months has elapsed. The further period shall begin either from the date of the request for permission to translate mentioned in paragraph 1 (c) or, if the identity or address of the owner of the right of translation is not known, from the date of dispatch of the copies of the application for a licence mentioned in paragraph 1 (d).*

      (b)   *Licences shall not be granted if a translation has been published by the owner of the right of translation or with his authorization during the said period of six or nine months.*

3. *Any licence under this Article shall be granted only for the purpose of teaching, scholarship or research.*

4.   (a)   *Any licence granted under this Article shall not extend to the export of copies and shall be valid only for publication in the territory of the Contracting State where it has been applied for.*

(b)   *Any copy published in accordance with a licence granted under this Article shall bear a notice in the appropriate language stating that the copy is available for distribution only in the Contracting State granting the licence. If the writing bears the notice specified in Article III (1) the copies shall bear the same notice.*

(c)   *The prohibition of export provided for subparagraph (a) shall not apply where a governmental or other public entity of a State which has granted a licence under this Article to translate a work into a language other than English, French or Spanish sends copies of a translation prepared under such licence to another country if:*

(i) the recipients are individuals who are nationals of the Contracting State granting the licence, or organizations grouping such individuals;

(ii) the copies are to be used only for the purpose of teaching, scholarship or research;

(iii) the sending of the copies and their subsequent distribution to recipients is without the object of commercial purpose; and

(iv) the country to which the copies have been sent has agreed with the Contracting State to allow the receipt, distribution or both and the Director-General has been notified of such agreement by any one of the governments which have concluded it.

5. Due provision shall be made at the national level to ensure:

(a) that the licence provides for just compensation that is consistent with standards of royalties normally operating in the case of licences freely negotiated between persons in the two countries concerned; and

(b) payment and transmittal of the compensation; however, should national currency regulations intervene, the competent authority shall make all efforts, by the use of international machinery, to ensure transmittal in internationally convertible currency or its equivalent.

6. *Any licence granted by a Contracting State under this Article shall terminate if a translation of the work in the same language with substantially the same content as the edition in respect of which the licence was granted is published in the said State by the owner of the right of translation or with his authorization, at a price reasonably related to that normally charged in the same State for comparable works. Any copies already made before the licence is terminated may continue to be distributed until their stock is exhausted.*

7. *For works which are composed mainly of illustrations a licence to translate the text and to reproduce the illustrations may be granted only if the conditions of Article V^{quater} are also fulfilled.*

8. *A licence to translate a work*
(a) *protected under this Convention, published in printed or analogous forms of reproduction, may also be granted to a broadcasting organization having its headquarters in a Contracting State to which Article V^{bis} (1) applies, upon an application made in that State by the said organization under the following conditions:*

(i) *the translation is made from a copy made and acquired in accordance with the laws of the Contracting State;*

(ii) *the translation is for use only in broadcasts intended exclusively for teaching or for the dissemination of the results of specialized technical or scientific research to experts in a particular profession;*

(iii)   the translation is used exclusively for the purposes set out in condition (ii), through broadcasts lawfully made which are intended for recipients on the territory of the Contracting State, including broadcasts made through the medium of sound or visual recordings lawfully and exclusively made for the purpose of such broadcasts;

(iv)   sound or visual recordings of the translation may be exchanged only between broadcasting organizations having their headquarters in the Contracting State granting the licence; and

(v)   all uses made of the translation are without any commercial purpose.

(b)   Provided all of the criteria and conditions set out in subparagraph (a) are met, a licence may also be granted to a broadcasting organisation to translate any text incorporated in an audiovisual fixation which was itself prepared and published for the sole purpose of being used in connection with systematic instructional activities.

(c)   Subject to sub-paragraphs (a) and (b), the other provisions of this Article shall apply to the grant and exercise of the licence.

9. Subject to the provisions of this Article, any licence granted under this Article shall be governed by the provisions of Article V, and shall continue to be governed by the provisions of Article V and of this Article, even after the seven-year period provided for in Article V (2) has expired. However, after the said period has expired, the licensee shall be free to request that the said licence be replaced by a new licence governed exclusively by the provisions of Article V.

*Article V*quater

*1. Any Contracting State to which Article V*bis *(1) applies may adopt the following provisions:*

(a) *If, after the expiration of (i) the relevant period specified in sub-paragraph (c) commencing from the date of first publication of a particular edition of a literary, scientific or artistic work referred to in paragraph 3, or (ii) any longer period determined by national legislation of the State, copies of such edition have not been distributed in that State to the general public or in connexion with systematic instructional activities at a price reasonably related to that normally charged in the State for comparable works, by the owner of the right of reproduction or with his authorisation, any national of such State may obtain a non-exclusive licence from the competent authority to publish such edition at that or a lower price for use in connexion with systematic instructional activities. The licence may only be granted if such national, in accordance with the procedure of the State concerned, establishes either that he has requested, and been denied, authorization by the proprietor of the right to publish such work, or that, after due diligence on his part, he was unable to find the owner of the right. At the same time as he makes his request he shall inform either the International Copyright Information Centre established by the United Nations Educational, Scientific and Cultural Organization or any national or regional information centre referred to in subparagraph (d).*

(b)   *A licence may also be granted on the same conditions if, for a period of six months, no authorized copies of the edition in question have been on sale in the State concerned to the general public or in connexion with systematic instructional activities at a price reasonably related to that normally charged in the State for comparable works.*

(c)   *The period referred to in subparagraph (a) shall be five years except that:*

    (i)   *for works of the natural and physical sciences, including mathematics, and of technology, the period shall be three years;*

    (ii)   *for works of fiction, poetry, drama and music, and for art books, the period shall be seven years.*

(d)   *If the owner of the right of reproduction cannot be found, the applicant for a licence shall send, by registered air mail, copies of his application to the publisher whose name appears on the work and to any national or regional information centre identified as such in a notification deposited with the Director-General by the State in which the publisher is believed to have his principal place of business. In the absence of any such notification, he shall also send a copy to the International Copyright Information Centre established by the United Nations Educational, Scientific and Cultural Organization. The licence shall not be granted before the expiration of a period of three months from the date of dispatch of the copies of the application.*

(e)   *Licences obtainable after three years shall not be granted under this Article:*

(i) *until a period of six months has elapsed from the date of the request for permission referred to in sub-paragraph (a) or, if the identity or address of the owner of the right of reproduction is unknown, from the date of the dispatch of the copies of the application for a licence referred to in sub-paragraph (d);*

(ii) *if any such distribution of copies of the edition as is mentioned in sub-paragraph (a) has taken place during that period.*

(f) *The name of the author and the title of the particular edition of the work shall be printed on all copies of the published reproduction. The licence shall not extend to the export of copies and shall be valid only for publication in the territory of the Contracting State where it has been applied for. The licence shall not be transferable by the licensee.*

(g) *Due provision shall be made by domestic legislation to ensure an accurate reproduction of the particular edition in question.*

(h) *A licence to reproduce and publish a translation of a work shall not be granted under this Article in the following cases:*

(i) *where the translation was not published by the owner of the right of translation or with his authorization;*

(ii) *where the translation is not in a language in general use in the State with power to grant the licence.*

2. The exceptions provided for in paragraph 1 are subject to the following additional provisions:

    (a)   *Any copy published in accordance with a licence granted under this Article shall bear a notice in the appropriate language stating that the copy is available for distribution only in the Contracting State to which the said licence applies. If the edition bears the notice specified in Article III (1), the copies shall bear the same notice.*

    (b)   *Due provision shall be made at the national level to ensure:*

        (i)   *that the licence provides for just compensation that is consistent with standards of royalties normally operating in the case of licences freely negotiated between persons in the two countries concerned; and*

        (ii)   *payment and transmittal of the compensation; however, should national currency regulations intervene, the competent authority shall make all efforts, by the use of international machinery, to ensure transmittal in internationally convertible currency or its equivalent.*

(c) Whenever copies of an edition of a work are distributed in the Contracting State to the general public or in connexion with systematic instructional activities by the owner of the right of reproduction or with his authorization, at a price reasonably related to that normally charged in the State for comparable works, any licence granted under this Article shall terminate if such edition is in the same language and is substantially the same in content as the edition published under the licence. Any copies already made before the licence is terminated may continue to be distributed until their stock is exhausted.

(d) No licence shall be granted when the author has withdrawn from circulation all copies of the edition in question.

3. Subject to sub-paragraph (b),

(a) the literary, scientific or artistic works to which this Article applies shall be limited to works published in printed or analogous forms of reproduction.

(b) The provisions of this Article shall also apply to reproduction in audio-visual form of lawfully made audio-visual fixations including any protected works incorporated therein and to the translation of any incorporated text into a language in general use in the State with power to grant the licence; always provided that the audio-visual fixations in question were prepared and published for the sole purpose of being used in connexion with systematic instructional activities.

Article VI

Article VI

"Publication," as used in this Convention, means the reproduction in tangible form and the general distribution to the public of copies of a work from which it can be read or otherwise visually perceived.

Article VII

This Convention shall not apply to works or rights in works which, at the effective date of the Convention in a Contracting State where protection is claimed, are permanently in the public domain in the said Contracting State.

Article VIII

1. This Convention, which shall bear the date of September 6, 1952, shall be deposited with the Director-General *of the United Nations Educational, Scientific and Cultural Organisation* and shall remain open for signatures by all States for a period of 120 days after that date. It shall be subject to ratification or acceptance by the signatory States.

2. Any State which has not signed this Convention may accede thereto.

3. Ratification, acceptance or accession shall be effected by the deposit of an instrument to that effect with the Director-General *of the United Nations Educational, Scientific and Cultural Organisation.*

Article IX

1. This Convention shall come into force three months after the deposit of twelve instruments of ratification, acceptance or accession, *among which there shall be those of four States which are not members of the International Union for the Protection of Literary and Artistic Works.*

2. Subsequently, this Convention shall come into force in respect of each State three months after that State has deposited its instrument of ratification, acceptance or accession.

"Publication," as used in this Convention, means the reproduction in tangible form and the general distribution to the public of copies of a work from which it can be read or otherwise visually perceived.

Article VII

This Convention shall not apply to works or rights in works which, at the effective date of the Convention in a Contracting State where protection is claimed, are permanently in the public domain in the said Contracting State.

Article VIII

1. This Convention, which shall bear the date of *24 July 1971*, shall be deposited with the Director-General and shall remain open for signature by all States *party to the 1952 Convention* for a period of 120 days after *the date of this Convention*. It shall be subject to ratification or acceptance by the signatory States.

2. Any State which has not signed this Convention may accede thereto.

3. Ratification, acceptance or accession shall be effected by the deposit of an instrument to that effect with the Director-General.

Article IX

1. This Convention shall come into force three months after the deposit of twelve instruments of ratification, acceptance or accession.

2. Subsequently, this Convention shall come into force in respect of each State three months after that State has deposited its instrument of ratification, acceptance or accession.

3. Accession to this Convention by a State not party to the 1952 Convention shall also constitute accession to that Convention; however, if its instrument of accession is deposited before this Convention comes into force, such State may make its accession to the 1952 Convention conditional upon the coming into force of this Convention. After the coming into force of this Convention, no State may accede solely to the 1952 Convention.

4. Relations between States party to this Convention and States that are party only to the 1952 Convention, shall be governed by the 1952 Convention. However, any State party only to the 1952 Convention may, by a notification deposited with the Director-General declare that it will admit the application of the 1971 Convention to works of its nationals or works first published in its territory by all States party to this Convention.

Article X

1. Each State party to this Convention undertakes to adopt, in accordance with its Constitution, such measures as are necessary to ensure the application of this Convention.

2. It is understood, *however*, that at the time an instrument of ratification, acceptance or accession is deposited on behalf of any State, such State must be in a position under its domestic law to give effect to the terms of this Convention.

Article X

1. Each Contracting State undertakes to adopt, in accordance with its Constitution, such measures as are necessary to ensure the application of this Convention.

2. It is understood that at the *date this Convention comes into force in respect of any State, that* State must be in a position under its domestic law to give effect to the terms of this Convention.

Article XI

1. An Intergovernmental Committee is hereby established with the following duties:

(a)   to study the problems concerning the application and operation of this Convention;

(b)   to make preparation for periodic revision of this Convention;

Article XI

1. An Intergovernmental Committee is hereby established with the following duties:

(a)   to study the problems concerning the application and operation of *the Universal Copyright Convention*;

(b)   to make preparation for periodic revisions of this Convention;

(c)   to study any other problems concerning the international protection of copyright, in co-operation with the various interested international organisations, such as the United Nations Educational, Scientific and Cultural Organisation, the International Union for the Protection of Literary and Artistic Works, and the Organisation of American States;

(d)   to inform the Contracting States as to its activities.

2. The Committee shall consist of the representatives of twelve Contracting States to be selected with due consideration to fair geographical representation and in conformity with the Resolution relating to this article, annexed to this Convention.

The Director-General of the United Nations Educational, Scientific and Cultural Organisation, the Director of the Bureau of the International Union for the Protection of Literary and Artistic Works and the Secretary-General of the Organisation of American States, or their representatives, may attend meetings of the Committee in an advisory capacity.

Article XII

The Intergovernmental Committee shall convene a conference for revision *of this Convention* whenever it deems necessary, or at the request of at least ten Contracting States, or a majority of Contracting States if there are less than twenty Contracting States.

Article XIII

(c)   to study any other problems concerning the international protection of copyright, in co-operation with the various interested international organizations, such as the United Nations Educational, Scientific and Cultural Organization, the International Union for the Protection of Literary and Artistic Works, and the Organization of American States;

(d)   to inform *States party to the Universal Copyright Convention* as to its activities.

2. The Committee shall consist of the representatives of *eighteen States party to this Convention or only to the 1952 Convention.*
3. The Committee shall be selected with due consideration to a fair balance of national interests on the basis of geographical location, population, languages and stages of development.
4. The Director-General of the United Nations Educational, Scientific and Cultural Organization, the *Director-General of the World Intellectual Property Organization,* and the Secretary-General of the Organization of American States, or their representatives, may attend meetings of the Committee in an advisory capacity.

Article XII

The Intergovernmental Committee shall convene a conference for revision *whenever it deems necessary, or at the request of at least ten States party to this Convention.*

Article XIII

Any Contracting State may, at the time of deposit of its instrument of ratification, acceptance or accession, or at any time thereafter, declare by notification addressed to the Director-General *of the United Nations Educational, Scientific and Cultural Organisation* that this Convention shall apply to all or any of the countries or territories for the international relations of which it is responsible and this Convention shall thereupon apply to the countries or territories named in such notification after the expiration of the term of three months provided for in Article IX. In the absence of such notification, this Convention shall not apply to any such country or territory.

1. Any Contracting State may, at the time of deposit of its instrument of ratification, acceptance or accession, or at any time thereafter, declare by notification addressed to the Director-General that this Convention shall apply to all or any of the countries or territories for the international relations of which it is responsible and this Convention shall thereupon apply to the countries or territories named in such notification after the expiration of the term of three months provided for in Article IX. In the absence of such notification, this Convention shall not apply to any such country or territory.

2. However, nothing in this Article should be understood as implying the recognition or tacit acceptance by a Contracting State of the factual situation concerning a country or territory to which this Convention is made applicable by another Contracting State in accordance with the provisions of this Article.

Article XIV

1. Any Contracting State may denounce this Convention in its own name or on behalf of all or any of the countries or territories as to which a notification has been given under Article XIII. The denunciation shall be made by notification addressed to the Director-General *of the United Nations Educational, Scientific and Cultural Organisation.*

2. Such denunciation shall operate only in respect of the State or of the country or territory on whose behalf it was made and shall not take effect until twelve months after the date of receipt of the notification.

Article XV

1. Any Contracting State may denounce this Convention in its own name or on behalf of all or any of the countries or territories *with respect to* which a notification has been given under Article XIII. The denunciation shall be made by notification addressed to the Director-General. *Such denunciation shall also constitute denunciation of the 1952 Convention.*

2. Such denunciation shall operate only in respect of the State or of the country or territory on whose behalf it was made and shall not take effect until twelve months after the date of receipt of the notification.

Article XV

A dispute between two or more Contracting States concerning the interpretation or application of this Convention, not settled by negotiation, shall unless the States concerned agree on some other method of settlement be brought before the International Court of Justice for determination by it.

Article XVI

1. This Convention shall be established in English, French and Spanish. The three texts shall be signed and shall be equally authoritative.

2. Official texts of this Convention shall be established in German, Italian and Portuguese.

Any Contracting State or group of Contracting States shall be entitled to have established by the Director-General *of the United Nations Educational, Scientific and Cultural Organisation* other texts in the language of its choice by arrangement with the Director-General.

All such texts shall be annexed to the signed texts of this Convention.

Article XVII

1. This Convention shall not in any way affect the provisions of the Berne Convention for the Protection of Literary and Artistic Works or membership in the Union created by that Convention.

2. In application of the foregoing paragraph, a Declaration has been annexed to the present Article. This Declaration is an integral part of this Convention for the States bound by the Berne Convention on January 1, 1951, or which have or may become bound to it at a later date. The signature of this Convention by such States shall also constitute signature of the said Declaration, and ratification, acceptance or accession by such States shall include the Declaration as well as the Convention.

A dispute between two or more Contracting States concerning the interpretation or application of this Convention, not settled by negotiation, shall, unless the States concerned agree on some other method of settlement, be brought before the International Court of Justice for determination by it.

Article XVI

1. This Convention shall be established in English, French and Spanish. The three texts shall be signed and shall be equally authoritative.

2. Official texts of this Convention shall be established *by the Director-General, after consultation with the governments concerned, in Arabic, German, Italian and Portuguese.*

3. Any Contracting State or group of Contracting States shall be entitled to have established by the Director-General other texts in the language of its choice by arrangement with the Director-General.

4. All such texts shall be annexed to the signed texts of this Convention.

Article XVII

1. This Convention shall not in any way affect the provisions of the Berne Convention for the Protection of Literary and Artistic Works or membership in the Union created by that Convention.

2. In application of the foregoing paragraph, a Declaration has been annexed to the present Article. This Declaration is an integral part of this Convention for the States bound by the Berne Convention on 1 January 1951, or which have or may become bound to it at a later date. The signature of this Convention by such States shall also constitute signature of the said Declaration, and ratification, acceptance or accession by such States shall include the Declaration, as well as *this* Convention.

Article XVIII

This Convention shall not abrogate multilateral or bilateral copyright conventions or arrangements that are or may be in effect exclusively between two or more American Republics. In the event of any difference either between the provisions of such existing convention or arrangements and the provisions of this Convention, or between the provisions of this Convention and those of any new convention or arrangement which may be formulated between two or more American Republics after this Convention comes into force, the convention or arrangement most recently formulated shall prevail between the parties thereto. Rights in works acquired in any Contracting State under existing conventions or arrangements before the date this Convention comes into force in such State shall not be affected.

Article XIX

This Convention shall not abrogate multilateral or bilateral conventions or arrangements in effect between two or more Contracting States. In the event of any difference between the provisions of such existing conventions or ar rangements and the provisions of this Convention, the provisions of this Convention shall prevail. Rights in works acquired in any Contracting State under existing conventions or arrangements before the date on which this Convention comes into force in such State shall not be affected. Nothing in this Article shall affect the provisions of Articles XVII and XVIII *of this Convention*

Article XX

Reservations to this Convention shall not be permitted.

Article XXI

Article XVIII

This Convention shall not abrogate multilateral or bilateral copyright conventions or arrangements that are or may be in effect exclusively between two or more American Republics. In the event of any difference either between the provisions of such existing conventions or arrangements and the provisions of this Convention, or between the provisions of this Convention and those of any new convention or arrangement which may be formulated between two or more American Republics after this Convention comes into force, the convention or arrangement most recently formulated shall prevail between the parties thereto. Rights in works acquired in any Contracting State under existing conventions or arrangements before the date this Convention comes into force in such State shall not be affected.

Article XIX

This Convention shall not abrogate multilateral or bilateral conventions or arrangements in effect between two or more Contracting States. In the event of any difference between the provisions of such existing conventions or arrangements and the provisions of this Convention, the provisions of this Convention, shall prevail. Rights in works acquired in any Contracting State under existing conventions or arrangements before the date on which this Convention comes into force in such State shall not be affected. Nothing in this Article shall affect the provisions of Articles XVII and XVIII.

Article XX

Reservations to this Convention shall not be permitted.

Article XXI

The Director-General *of the United Nations Educational, Scientific and Cultural Organisation* shall send duly certified copies of this Convention to the States interested, *to the Swiss Federal Council* and to the Secretary-General of the United Nations for registration by him.

He shall also inform all interested States of the ratifications, acceptances and accessions which have been deposited, the date on which this Convention comes into force, the notifications under Article XIII *of* this Convention, and denunciations under Article XIV.

Appendix Declaration Relating to Article XVII

The States which are members of the International Union for the Protection of Literary and Artistic Works, and which are signatories to the Universal Copyright Convention.

Desiring to reinforce their mutual relations on the basis of the said Union and to avoid any conflict which might result from the co-existence of the Convention of Berne and the Universal Convention,

Have, by common agreement, accepted the terms of the following declaration:

(a) Works which, according to the Berne Convention, have as their country of origin a country which has withdrawn from the International Union created by the said Convention, after January 1, 1951, shall not be protected by the Universal Copyright Convention in the countries of the Berne Union;

1. The Director-General shall send duly certified copies of this Convention to the States interested and to the Secretary-General of the United Nations for registration by him.

2. He shall also inform all interested States of the ratifications, acceptances and accessions which have been deposited, the date on which this Convention comes into force, the notifications under this Convention and denunciations under Article XIV.

Appendix Declaration Relating to Article XVII

The States which are members of the International Union for the Protection of Literary and Artistic Works, (*hereinafter call "the Berne Union"*) and which are signatories to this Convention.

Desiring to reinforce their mutual relations on the basis of the said Union and to avoid any conflict which might result from the co-existence of the Berne Convention and the Universal Copyright Convention,

Recognizing the temporary need of some States to adjust their level of copyright protection in accordance with their stage of cultural, social and economic development,

Have, by common agreement, accepted the terms of the following declaration:

(a) *Except as provided by paragraph (b)*, works which, according to the Berne Convention, have as their country of origin a country which has withdrawn from the *Berne Union* after 1 January 1951, shall not be protected by the Universal Copyright Convention in the countries of the Berne Union;

(b)   The Universal Copyright Convention shall not be applicable to the relationships among countries of the Berne Union in so far as it relates to the protection of works having as their country of origin, within the meaning of the Berne Convention, a country of the International Union created by the said Convention.

Resolution Concerning Article XI

The Intergovernmental Copyright Conference,

Having considered the problems relating to the Intergovernmental Committee provided for in Article XI of the Universal Copyright Convention, resolves:

1. The first members of the Committee shall be representatives of the following twelve States, each of those States designating one representative and an alternate: Argentina, Brazil, France, Germany, India, Italy, Japan, Mexico, Spain, Switzerland, United Kingdom and United States of America.

2. The Committee shall be constituted as soon as the Convention comes into force in accordance with Article XI of this Convention.

(b)   *Where a Contracting State is regarded as a developing country in conformity with the established practice of the General Assembly of the United Nations, and has deposited with the Director-General of the United Nations Educational, Scientific and Cultural Organization, at the time of its withdrawal from the Berne Union, a notification to the effect that it regards itself as a developing country, the provisions of paragraph (a) shall not be applicable as long as such State may avail itself of the exceptions provided for by this Convention in accordance with Article V^bis;*

(c)   The Universal Copyright Convention shall not be applicable to the relationships among countries of the Berne Union in so far as it relates to the protection of works having as their country of origin, within the meaning of the Berne Convention, a country of the *Berne Union.*

Resolution Concerning Article XI

The Conference for Revision of the Universal Copyright Convention,

Having considered the problems relating to the Intergovernmental Committee provided for in Article XI of this Convention, to which this resolution is annexed,

Resolves that:

1. At its inception, the Committee shall include representatives of the twelve States members of the Intergovernmental Committee established under Article XI of the 1952 Convention and the resolution annexed to it, and in addition, representatives of the following States: Algeria, Australia, Japan, Mexico, Senegal and Yugoslavia.

2. Any States that are not party to the 1952 Convention and have not acceded to this Convention before the first ordinary session of the Committee following the entry into force of this Convention shall be replaced by other States to be selected by the Committee at its first ordinary session in conformity with the provisions of Article XI (2) and (3).

3. As soon as this Convention comes into force the Committee as provided for in paragraph 1 shall be deemed to be constituted in accordance with Article XI of this Convention.

4. A session of the Committee shall take place within one year after the coming into force of this Convention; thereafter the Committee shall meet in ordinary session at intervals of not more than two years.

3. The Committee shall elect its Chairman and one Vice-Chairman. It shall establish its rules of procedure having regard to the following principles:

(a)   the normal duration of the term of office of the representatives shall be six years; with one-third retiring every two years;

5. The Committee shall elect its Chairman and *two* Vice-Chairmen. It shall establish its rules of procedure having regard to the following principles:

(a)   The normal duration of the term of office of the *members represented on the Committee* shall be six years with one-third retiring every two years, *it being however understood that, of the original terms of office, one-third shall expire at the end of the Committee's second ordinary session which will follow the entry into force of this Convention, a further third at the end of its third ordinary session, and the remaining third at the end of its fourth ordinary session.*

(b)   before the expiration of the term of office of any members, the Committee shall decide which States shall cease to be represented on it and which States shall be called upon to designate representatives; the representatives of those States which have not ratified, accepted or acceded shall be the first to retire;

(c)   the different parts of the world shall be fairly represented;

(b)   *The rules governing the procedure whereby the Committee shall fill vacancies, the order in which terms of membership expire, eligibility for re-election, and election procedures, shall be based upon a balancing of the needs for continuity of membership and rotation of representation, as well as the considerations set out in Article XI (3).*

and expresses the wish that the United Nations Educational, Scientific and Cultural Organisation provide its Secretariat.

Expresses the wish that the United Nations Educational, Scientific and Cultural Organisation provide its Secretariat.

***

Protocol 1 annexed to the Universal Copyright Convention as Revised at Paris on 24 July 1971 concerning the Application of that Convention to works of Stateless Persons and Refugees

The States parties hereto, being also parties to the Universal Copyright Convention (hereinafter referred to as the "Convention") have accepted the following provisions:

1. Stateless persons and refugees who have their habitual residence in a State party to this Protocol shall, for the purposes of the Convention, be assimilated to the nationals of that State.

Protocol 1 annexed to the Universal Copyright Convention as Revised at Paris on 24 July 1971 concerning the Application of that Convention to works of Stateless Persons and Refugees

The States party hereto, being also party to the Universal Copyright Convention *as revised at Paris on 24 July 1971* (hereinafter *called* "the *1971* Convention"),

Have accepted the following provisions:

1. Stateless persons and refugees who have their habitual residence in a State party to this Protocol shall, for the purposes of the 1971 Convention, be assimilated to the nationals of that State.

2.
(a) This Protocol shall be signed and shall be subject to ratification or acceptance, or may be acceded to, as if the provisions of Article VIII of the Convention applied hereto.

(b) This Protocol shall enter into force in respect of each State on the date of deposit of the instrument of ratification, acceptance or accession of the State concerned or on the date of entry into force of the Convention with respect to such State, whichever is the later.

2.
(a) This Protocol shall be signed and be subject to ratification or acceptance, or may be acceded to, as if the provisions of Article VIII of the *1971* Convention applied hereto.

(b) This Protocol shall enter into force in respect of each State, on the date of deposit of the instrument of ratification, acceptance or accession of the State concerned or on the date of entry into force of the *1971* Convention with respect to such State, whichever is the later.

(c) On the entry into force of this Protocol in respect of a State not party to Protocol 1 annexed to the 1952 Convention, the latter Protocol shall be deemed to enter into force in respect of such State.

Protocol 2 annexed to the Universal Copyright Convention, concerning the application of that Convention to the works of certain International Organisations

The State parties hereto, being also parties to the Universal Copyright Convention (hereinafter referred to as the "Convention"),
Have accepted the following provisions:

1.
(a) The protection provided for in Article II (1) of the Convention shall apply to works published for the first time by the United Nations, by the Specialised Agencies in relationship therewith, or by the Organisation of American States;

(b) Similarly, Article II (2) of the Convention shall apply to the said organisation or agencies.

Protocol 2 annexed to the Universal Copyright Convention as revised at Paris on 24 July 1971 concerning the application of that Convention to the works of certain International Organizations

The State party hereto, being also party to the Universal Copyright Convention *as revised at Paris on 24 July 1971* (hereinafter *called* "the *1971* Convention"),
Have accepted the following provisions:

1.
(a) The protection provided for in Article II (1) of the *1971* Convention shall apply to works published for the first time by the United Nations, by the Specialized Agencies in relationship therewith, or by the Organisation of American States;

(b) Similarly, Article II (2) of the *1971* Convention shall apply to the said organization or agencies.

2. (a) This Protocol shall be signed and shall be subject to ratification or acceptance, or may be acceded to, as if the provisions of Article VIII of the 1971 Convention applied hereto.

(b) This Protocol shall enter into force for each State on the date of deposit of the instrument of ratification, acceptance or accession of the State concerned or on the date of entry into force of the Convention with respect to such State, whichever is the later.

Protocol 3 annexed to the Universal Copyright Convention concerning the effective date of Instruments of Ratification or Acceptance of or Accession to that Convention

States parties hereto,
Recognising that the application of the
Universal Copyright Convention (hereinafter referred to as the "Convention") to States participating in all the international copyright systems already in force will contribute greatly to the value of the Convention.
Have agreed as follows:
1. Any State party hereto may, on depositing its instrument of ratification or acceptance of or accession to the Convention, notify the Director-General of the United Nations Educational, Scientific and Cultural Organisation (hereinafter referred to as "Director-General") that that instrument shall not take effect for the purposes of Article IX of the Convention until any other State named in such notification shall have deposited its instrument.
2. The notification referred to in paragraph 1 above shall accompany the instrument to which it relates.

2. (a) This Protocol shall be signed and shall be subject to ratification or acceptance, or may be acceded to, as if the provisions of Article VIII of the *1971* Convention applied hereto.

(b) This Protocol shall enter into force for each State on the date of deposit of the instrument of ratification, acceptance or accession of the State concerned or on the date of entry into force of the *1971* Convention with respect to such State, whichever is the later.

3. The Director-General shall inform all States signatory or which have then acceded to the Convention of any notifications received in accordance with this Protocol.

4. This Protocol shall bear the same date and shall remain open for signature for the same period as the Convention.

5. It shall be subject to ratification or acceptance by the signatory States. Any State which has not signed this Protocol may accede thereto.

6.—Ratification or acceptance or accession shall be effected by the deposit of an instrument to that effect with the Director-General.

This Protocol shall enter into force on the date of deposit of not less than four instruments of ratification or acceptance or accession. The Director-General shall inform all interested States of this date. Instruments deposited after such date shall take effect on the date of their deposit.

EUROPEAN AGREEMENT ON THE PROTECTION OF TELEVISION BROADCASTS

Strasbourg, June 22, 1960

The Governments signatory hereto, being Members of the Council of Europe,

Considering that the object of the Council is to achieve a greater unity between its Members;

Considering that exchanges of television programmes between the countries of Europe are calculated to further the achievement of that object;

Considering that these exchanges are hampered by the fact that the majority of television organisations are at present powerless to restrain the re-broadcasting fixation or public performance of their broadcasts, whereas the organisers of musical or dramatic performances or the like, and the promoters of sports meetings, make their consent to broadcasting to other countries conditional upon an undertaking that the relays will not be used for purposes other than private viewing;

Considering that the international protection of television broadcasts will in no way affect any rights of third parties in these broadcasts;

Considering that the problem is one of some urgency, in view of the installations and links now being brought into service throughout Europe, which are such as to make it easy from the technical point of view for European television organisations to exchange their programmes;

Considering that, pending the conclusion of a potentially universal Convention on "neighbouring rights" at present in contemplation, it is fitting to conclude a regional Agreement restricted in scope to television broadcasts and of limited duration.

HAVE AGREED AS FOLLOWS:

Article 1

Broadcasting organisations constituted in the territory and under the laws of a Party to this Agreement or transmitting from such territory shall enjoy, in respect of all their television broadcasts:

1. in the territory of all Parties to this Agreement, the right to authorise or prohibit:

  (a) the re-broadcasting of such broadcasts;

  (b) the diffusion of such broadcasts to the public by wire;

  (c) the communication of such broadcasts to the public by means of any instrument for the transmission of signs, sounds or images;

  (d) any fixation of such broadcasts or still photographs thereof, and any reproduction of such a fixation; and

  (e) re-broadcasting, wire diffusion or public performance with the aid of the fixations or reproductions referred to in sub-paragraph (d) of this paragraph, except where the organisation in which the right vests has authorised the sale of the said fixations or reproductions to the public;

2. in the territory of any other Party to this Agreement, the same protection as that other Party may extend to organisations constituted in its territory and under its laws or transmitting from its territory, where such protection is greater than that provided for in paragraph 1 above.

Article 2

Subject to paragraph 2 of Article 1, and Articles 13 and 14, the protection provided for in paragraph 1 of Article 1 shall last not less than a period of twenty years from the end of the year in which the broadcast took place.[1]

Article 3

1. Parties to this Agreement, by making a declaration as provided in Article 10, and in respect of their own territory, may:

(a) withhold the protection provided for in sub-paragraph 1(b) of Article 1 as regards broadcasting organisations constituted in their territory or transmitting from such territory, and restrict the exercise of such protection, as regards broadcasts by broadcasting organisations constituted in the territory of another Party to this Agreement or transmitting from such territory, to a percentage of the transmissions by such organisations, which shall not be less than 50% of the average weekly duration of the broadcasts of each of these organisations;

(b) withhold the protection provided for in sub-paragraph 1(c) of Article 1, where the communication is not a paying audience within the meaning of their domestic law;

(c) withhold the protection provided for in sub-paragraph 1(d) of Article 1, where the fixation or reproduction of the fixation is made for private use, or solely for educational purposes;

(d) withhold the protection provided for in sub-paragraph 1(d) and (e) of Article 1, in respect of still photographs or reproductions of such photographs;

(e) without prejudice to sub-paragraph 1(a) of this article, withhold all protection provided for in this Agreement from television broadcasts by broadcasting organisations constituted in their territory and under their laws or transmitting from such territory, where such broadcasts enjoy protection under their domestic law;

(f) restrict the operation of this Agreement to broadcasting organisations constituted in the territory and under the laws of a Party to this Agreement and also transmitting from the territory of such party.

2. It shall be open to the aforesaid Parties, in respect of their own territory, to provide exceptions to the protection of television broadcasts:

(a) for the purpose of reporting current events, in respect of the re-broadcasting, fixation or reproduction of the fixation, wire diffusion or public performance of short extracts from a broadcast which itself constitutes the whole or part of the event in question;

(b) in respect of the making of ephemeral fixations of television broadcasts by a broadcasting organisation by means of its own facilities and for its own broadcasts.

3. The aforesaid Parties may, in respect of their own territory, provide for a body with jurisdiction over cases where the right of diffusion to the public by wire referred to in sub-paragraph 1(b) of Article 1, or the right of communication to the public referred to in sub-paragraph 1(c) of Article 1, has been unreasonably refused or granted on unreasonable terms by the broadcasting organisation in which the said right vests.

Article 4

1. Fixations of a broadcast in which protection under this Agreement subsists, or still photographs thereof, as well as reproductions of such photographs, made in a territory to which this Agreement does not apply and imported into the territory of a Party to this Agreement where they would be unlawful without the consent of the broadcasting organisation in which the right vests, shall be liable to seizure in the latter territory.

2. The provisions of the last preceding paragraph shall apply to the importation into the territory of a Party to this Agreement of still photographs of a broadcast in which protection under this Agreement subsists and of reproductions of such

photographs, where such photographs or reproductions are made in the territory of another Party to this Agreement by virtue of sub-paragraph 1(d) of Article 3.

3. Seizure shall be effected in accordance with the domestic law of each Party to this Agreement.

4. No Party to this Agreement shall be required to provide protection in respect of still photographs, or the reproduction of such photographs, of broadcasts made by a broadcasting organisation constituted in the territory and under the laws of another Party to this Agreement or transmitting from such territory, if the said other Party has availed itself of the reservation provided for in sub-paragraph 1(d) of Article 3.

Article 5

The protection afforded by this Agreement shall apply both in relation to the visual element and in relation to the sound element of a television broadcast. It shall not affect the sound element when broadcast separately.

Article 6

1. The protection provided for in Article 1 shall not affect any rights in respect of a television broadcast that may accrue to third parties, such as authors, performers, film makers, manufacturers of phonographic records or organisers of entertainments.

2. It shall likewise be without prejudice to any protection of television broadcasts that may be accorded apart from this Agreement.

Article 7

1. This Agreement shall be open to signature by the Members of the Council of Europe, who may become Parties to it either by

(a) signature without reservation in respect of ratification; or

(b) signature with reservation in respect of ratification, followed by the deposit of an instrument of ratification.

2. Instruments of ratification shall be deposited with the Secretary-General of the Council of Europe.

Article 8

1. This Agreement shall enter into force one month after the date on which three Members of the Council of Europe shall, in accordance with Article 7 thereof, have signed it without reservation in respect of ratification or shall have ratified it.

2. In the case of any Member of the Council of Europe who shall subsequently sign the Agreement without reservation in respect of ratification or who shall ratify it, the Agreement shall enter into force one month after the date of such signature or deposit of the instrument of ratification.

Article 9

1. After this Agreement has come into force, any European Government which is not a Member of the Council of Europe or any non-European Government having political ties with a Member of the Council of Europe may accede to it, subject to the prior approval of the Committee of Ministers of the Council of Europe.

2. Such accession shall be effected by the deposit of an instrument of accession with the Secretary-General of the Council of Europe and shall take effect one month after the date of deposit.

Article 10

Signature, ratification or accession shall imply full acceptance of all the provisions of this Agreement; provided always that any country may declare,[i] at the time of signature or of deposit of its instrument of ratification or accession, that it intends to avail itself of one or more of the options in paragraph 1 of Article 3 above.

Article 11

The Secretary-General of the Council of Europe shall notify Members of the Council, the Governments of any counties which may have acceded to this Agreement and the Director of the Bureau of the International Union for the Protection of Literary and Artistic Works:

(a) of any signature, together with any reservations as to ratification, of the deposit of instruments of ratification and of the date of entry into force of this Agreement;

(b) of the deposit of any instruments of accession in accordance with Article 9;

(c) of any declaration or notification received in accordance with Articles 12, 13 or 14;

(d) of any decision of the Committee of Ministers taken in pursuance of paragraph 2 of Article 12.

Article 12

1. This Agreement shall apply to the metropolitan territories of the Parties.

2. Any Party may, at the time of signature, of the deposit of its instrument of ratification or accession, or at any later date, declare by notice addressed to the Secretary-General of the Council of Europe that this Agreement shall extend to any or all of the territories for whose international relations it is responsible.

3. Any Government which has made a declaration under paragraph 2 of this Article extending this Agreement to any territory for whose international relations it is responsible may denounce the Agreement separately in respect of that territory in accordance with Article 14 thereof.

Article 13

1. This Agreement shall remain in force indefinitely.

2. Nevertheless, as from 1st January 1990, no State may remain or become a Party to this Agreement unless it is also a Party to the International Convention for the Protection of Performers, Producers of Phonograms and Broadcasting Organisations signed in Rome on 26th October 1961.

---

[i] *Editorial Note*: The instrument of ratification deposited with the Secretary-General of the Council of Europe by the Permanent Representative of the United Kingdom contains the following reservations: "(1) The Government of the United Kingdom of Great Britain and Northern Ireland withold the protection provided for in sub-paragraph (b) of paragraph 1 of Article 1 of the said Agreement; (2) The Government of the United Kingdom of Great Britain and Northern Ireland withhold the protection provided for in sub-paragraph (c) of paragraph 1 of Article 1 of the said Agreement, where the communication is not to a paying audience within the meaning of the domestic law of the United Kingdom of Great Britain and Northern Ireland; (3) The Government of the United Kingdom of Great Britain and Northern Ireland withhold the protection provided for in sub-paragraph (d) of paragraph 1 of Article 1 of the said Agreement, where the fixation or reproduction of the fixation is made for private use or solely for educational purposes; (4) The Government of the United Kingdom of Great Britain and Northern Ireland withhold the protection provided for in sub-paragraphs (d) and (e) of paragraph 1 of Article 1 of the said Agreement, in respect of still photographs or reproductions of such photographs; (5) The Government of the United Kingdom of Great Britain and Northern Ireland restrict the operation of the said Agreement to broadcasting organisations constituted in the territory and under the laws of a Party to the said Agreement and also transmitting from the territory of such Party."

Article 14

Any Contracting Party may denounce this Agreement by giving one year's notice to that effect to the Secretary-General of the Council of Europe.

In witness whereof, the undersigned,[ii] being duly authorised thereto, have signed this Agreement.

Done at Strasbourg, this 22nd day of June, 1960, in English and French, both texts being equally authoritative, in a single copy, which shall remain in the archives of the Council of Europe and of which the Secretary-General shall send certified copies to each of the signatory and acceding Governments and to the Director of the Bureau of the International Union for the Protection of Literary and Artistic Works.

Notes:

(1) Text amended according to the provisions of Protocol (ETS No. 54), which entered into force on March 24, 1965.

(2) Text amended according to the provisions of Protocol (ETS No. 54), which entered into force on March 24, 1965. This Protocol provides in art.2, para.4, that "Any State which in accordance with Article 10 of the Agreement has, before the entry into force of this Protocol, availed itself of the option in sub-paragraph 1.a of Article 3 of the Agreement may, notwithstanding anything in paragraph 1 of the present article, maintain the application of such option".

(3) Text amended according to the provisions of Protocol (ETS No. 54), which entered into force on March 24, 1965, of Additional Protocol to the Protocol (ETS No. 81), which entered into force on December 31, 1965 and of Additional Protocol to the Protocol (ETS No. 113), which entered into force on January 1, 1985.

F3.i Protocol to the European Agreement on the Protection of Television Broadcasts[i]

Strasbourg, January 22, 1965

The member States of the Council of Europe, signatory hereto.

Considering the desirability of amending the European Agreement on the Protection of Television Broadcasts, signed at Strasbourg on 22nd June 1960,[ii] hereinafter referred to as "the Agreement";

Considering that the International Convention for the Protection of Performers, Producers of Phonograms and Broadcasting Organisations, signed in Rome on 26th October 1961, entered into force on 18th May 1964,[iii]

HAVE AGREED AS FOLLOWS:

Article 1

1. Paragraph 1 of Article 2 of the Agreement shall be amended as follows:

"Subject to paragraph 2 of Article 1, and Articles 13 and 14, the protection provided for in paragraph 1 of Article 1 shall last not less than a period of twenty years form the end of the year in which the broadcast took place."

2. Paragraph 2 of Article 2 of the Agreement shall be deleted.

Article 2

1. Subparagraph 1(a) of Article 3 of the Agreement shall be amended as follows:

[ii] *Editorial Note*: At the time of signature by the United Kingdom, the following declaration was made: "Her Majesty's Government understand the word 'signature' in the first line of Article 10 to refer only to signature without reservation as to ratification."

[i] *Editorial Note*: Cmnd.2744. Signed without reservation in respect of ratification by the United Kingdom on February 23, 1965, and entered into force on March 24, 1965.

[ii] *Editorial Note*: F3, above.

[iii] *Editorial Note*: F5, below.

"(a) withhold the protection provided for in sub-paragraph 1(b) of Article 1 as regards broadcasting organisations constituted in their territory or transmitting from such territory, and restrict the exercise of such protection, as regards broadcasts by broadcasting organisations constituted in the territory of another Party to this Agreement or transmitting from such territory, to a percentage of the transmissions by such organisations, which shall not be less than 500f the average weekly duration of the broadcasts of each of these organisations."

2. Sub-paragraph 1(e) of Article 3 of the Agreement shall be amended as follows:

"(e) without prejudice to sub-paragraph 1(a) of this Article, withhold all protection provided for in this Agreement from television broadcasts by broadcasting organisations constituted by their territory and under their laws or transmitting from such territory, where such broadcasts enjoy protection under their domestic law."

3. Paragraph 3 of Article 3 of the Agreement shall be amended as follows:

"3. The aforesaid Parties may, in respect of their own territory, provide for a body with jurisdiction over cases where the right of diffusion to the public by wire referred to in sub-paragraph 1(b) of Article 1, or the right of communication to the public referred to in sub-paragraph 1(c) of Article 1, has been unreasonably refused or granted on unreasonable terms by the broadcasting organisation in which the said right vests."

4. Any State which in accordance with Article 10 of the Agreement has, before the entry into force of this Protocol, availed itself of the option in sub-paragraph 1(a) of Article 3 of the Agreement may, notwithstanding anything in paragraph 1 of the present Article, maintain the application of such option.

Article 3

Article 13 of the Agreement shall be deleted and replaced by the following:

"1. This Agreement shall remain in force indefinitely.

2. Nevertheless, as from 1st January 1975, no State may remain or become a Party to this Agreement unless it is also a Party to the International Convention for the Protection of Performers, Producers of Phonograms and Broadcasting Organisations signed in Rome on 26th October 1961."

Article 4

1. The Governments signatory to the Agreement and the Governments having acceded thereto may become Parties to this Protocol by the procedure laid down in Article 7 or Article 9 of the Agreement, according to whether they are Member States of the Council of Europe or not.

2. This Protocol shall enter into force one month after the date on which all the Parties to the Agreement have signed this Protocol without reservation in respect of ratification, or deposited their instrument of ratification or accession in accordance with the provisions of the preceding paragraph.

3. As from the date on which this Protocol enters into force, no State may become a Party to the Agreement without becoming also a Party to this Protocol.

Article 5

The Secretary-General of the Council of Europe shall notify member States of the Council, other States Parties to the Agreement, and the Director of the Bureau of the International Union for the Protection of Literary and Artistic Works of any signature of this Protocol, together with any reservations as to ratification, and of the deposit of any instrument of ratification of the Protocol or of accession to it, and of the date referred to in paragraph 2 of Article 4 of this Protocol.

In witness whereof the undersigned, being duly authorised thereto have signed this Protocol.

Done at Strasbourg, this 22nd day of January 1965 in English and in French, both texts being equally authoritative, in a single copy which shall remain deposited in the archives of the Council of Europe. The Secretary-General of the Council of Europe shall transmit certified copies of each of the signatory and acceding states.

F3.ii Additional Protocol to the Protocol to the European Agreement on the Protection of Television Broadcasts[i]

Strasbourg, January 14, 1974

The member States of the Council of Europe, signatory hereto,

Considering the desirability of extending the duration of the European Agreement on the Protection of Television Broadcasts and the Protocol to this Agreement for the benefit of States which are not yet Parties to the International Convention for the Protection of Performers, Producers of Phonograms and Broadcasting Organisations, signed in Rome on 26 October 1961,

HAVE AGREED AS FOLLOWS:

Article 1

Paragraph 2 of Article 3 of the Protocol to the Agreement is substituted by the following:

"2. Nevertheless, as from 1 January 1985, no State may remain or become a Party to this Agreement unless it is also a Party to the International Convention for the Protection of Performers, Producers of Phonograms and Broadcasting Organisations, signed in Rome on 26 October 1961."

Article 2

1. The States signatory to the Agreement and the Protocol thereto may become Parties to this Additional Protocol in accordance with the procedure laid down in Article 7 of the Agreement.

2. The States having acceded to the Agreement and to the Protocol may become Parties to this Additional Protocol by the deposit of an instrument of accession with the Secretary General of the Council of Europe.

Article 3

1. This Additional Protocol shall enter into force one month after the date on which all the Parties to the Agreement and the Protocol have signed this Additional Protocol without reservation in respect of ratification, or have deposited their instrument of ratification or accession in conformity with the provisions of Article 2.

2. After the date of entry into force of this Additional Protocol, no State may become a Party to the Agreement and the Protocol without becoming also a Party to this Additional Protocol.

Article 4

The Secretary General of the Council of Europe shall notify member States of

---

[i] *Editorial Note*: Cmnd.5954. Signed by the United Kingdom without reservation in respect of ratification on March 15, 1974, and entered into force on December 31, 1974.

the Council, other Contracting Parties to the Agreement and the Director General of the World Intellectual Property Organisation of any signature of this Additional Protocol, together with any reservations as to ratification, and of the deposit of any instrument of ratification of the Additional Protocol or of accession to it, and of the date referred to in paragraph 1 of Article 3 of this Additional Protocol.

In witness whereof the undersigned, being duly authorised thereto, have signed this Additional Protocol.

Done at Strasbourg, this 14th day of January 1974, in the English and French languages, both texts equally authoritative, in a single copy which shall remain deposited in the archives of the Council of Europe. The Secretary General of the Council of Europe shall transmit certified copies to each of the signatory and acceding States.

F3.iii Additional Protocol to the Protocol to the European Agreement on the Protection of Television Broadcasts[i]

Strasbourg, March 21, 1983

The members States of the Council of Europe, signatory hereto,

Having regard to the European Agreement on the protection of television broadcasts of 22 June 1960, hereinafter called "the Agreement", as modified by the Protocol of 22 January 1965 and the Additional Protocol of 14 January 1974;

Having regard to the fact that the date given in Article 13, paragraph 2, of the Agreement was extended by the said Additional Protocol of 14 January 1974;

Considering the desirability of further extending this date for the benefit of States which are not yet Parties to the International Convention for the Protection of Performers, Producers of Phonograms and Broadcasting Organisations, signed in Rome on 26 October 1961,

HAVE AGREED AS FOLLOWS:

Article 1

Paragraph 2 of Article 13 of the Agreement, as last modified by Article 1 of the Additional Protocol of 14 January 1974, is replaced by the following text:

"2. Nevertheless, as from 1 January 1990, no State may remain or become a Party to this Agreement unless it is also a Party to the International Convention for the Protection of Performers, Producers of Phonograms and Broadcasting Organisations signed in Rome on 26 October 1961."

Article 2

1. This Additional Protocol shall be open for signature by member States of the Council of Europe which have signed or acceded to the Agreement, which may become Parties to this Additional Protocol by:

(a) signature without reservation as to ratification, acceptance or approval, or

(b) signature subject to ratification, acceptance or approval, followed by ratification, acceptance or approval.

2. Any State not a member of the Council which has acceded to the Agreement may also accede to this Additional Protocol.

3. Instruments of ratification, acceptance, approval or accession shall be deposited with the Secretary General of the Council of Europe.

---

[i] *Editorial Note*: Cmnd.9459. Signed by the United Kingdom on July 4, 1983 and entered into force on January 1, 1985.

Article 3

This Additional Protocol shall enter into force on the first day of the month following the date on which all the Parties to the Agreement have become Parties to this Additional Protocol in accordance with provisions of Article 2.

Article 4

From the date of entry into force of this Additional Protocol, no State may become a Party to the Agreement without at the same time becoming a Party to this Additional Protocol.

Article 5

The Secretary General of the Council of Europe shall notify the member States of the Council of Europe, any State which has acceded to the Agreement and the Director General of the World Intellectual Property Organisation of:

(a) any signature of this Additional Protocol;
(b) the deposit of any instrument of ratification, acceptance, approval or accession;
(c) the date of entry into force of this Additional Protocol, in accordance with Article 3.

In witness whereof the undersigned, being duly authorised thereto, have signed this Additional Protocol.

Done at Strasbourg, this 21st day of March 1983, in English and French, both texts being equally authoritative, in a single copy which shall be deposited in the archives of the Council of Europe. The Secretary General of the Council of Europe shall transmit certified copies to each member State of the Council of Europe, to any State invited to accede to the Agreement and to the Director General of the World Intellectual Property Organisation.

F3.iv Additional Protocol to the Protocol to the European Agreement on the Protection of Television Broadcasts

Strasbourg, April 20, 1989

The member States of the Council of Europe, signatories hereto,

Having regard to the European Agreement on the Protection of Television Broadcasts of 22 June 1960, hereinafter called "the Agreement", as modified by the Protocol of 22 January 1965 and the Additional Protocols of 14 January 1974 and of 21 March 1983;

Having regard to the fact that the date given in Article 13, paragraph 2, of the Agreement was extended by the said Additional Protocols of 14 January 1974 and of 21 March 1983;

Considering the desirability of further extending this date for the benefit of States which are not yet Parties to the International Convention for the Protection of Performers, Producers of Phonograms and Broadcasting Organisations, signed in Rome on 26 October 1961,

HAVE AGREED AS FOLLOWS:

Article 1

Paragraph 2 of Article 3 of the Protocol to the Agreement and, consequently, paragraph 2 of Article 13 of the Agreement are replaced by the following text:

> "2. Nevertheless, as from 1 January 1995, no State may remain or become a Party to this Agreement unless it is also a Party to the International Convention for the Protection of Performers, Producers of Phonograms and Broadcasting Organisations, signed in Rome on 26 October 1961."

Article 2

1. This Additional Protocol shall be open for signature by the member States of the Council of Europe which have signed or acceded to the Agreement, which may become Parties to this Additional Protocol by:

(a) signature without reservation as to ratification, acceptance or approval, or

(b) signature subject to ratification, acceptance or approval, followed by ratification, acceptance or approval.

2. No member State of the Council of Europe shall sign without reservation as to ratification, acceptance or approval, or deposit an instrument of ratification, acceptance or approval, unless it is already or becomes simultaneously a Party to the Agreement.

3. Any State, not a member of the Council of Europe, which has acceded to the Agreement may also accede to this Additional Protocol.

4. Instruments of ratification, acceptance, approval or accession shall be deposited with the Secretary General of the Council of Europe.

Article 3

This Additional Protocol shall enter into force on the first day of the month following the date on which all the Parties to the Agreement have expressed their consent to be bound by this Additional Protocol in accordance with the provisions of Article 2.

Article 4

From the date of entry into force of this Additional Protocol, no State may become a Party to the Agreement without at the same time becoming a Party to this Additional Protocol.

Article 5

The Secretary General of the Council of Europe shall notify the member States of the Council of Europe, any State having acceded to the Agreement and the Director General of the World Intellectual Property Organisation of:

(a) any signature of this Additional Protocol;

(b) the deposit of any instrument of ratification, acceptance, approval or accession;

(c) the date of entry into force of this Additional Protocol in accordance with Article 3.

In witness whereof the undersigned, being duly authorised thereto, have signed this Additional Protocol.

Done at Strasbourg, the 20th April 1989 in English and in French, both texts being equally authentic, in a single copy which shall be deposited in the archives of the Council of Europe. The Secretary General of the Council of Europe shall transmit certified copies to each member State of the Council of Europe, to any State invited to accede to the Agreement and to the Director General of the World Intellectual Property Organisation.

Signed by the United Kingdom on December 18, 1989 without reservation as to ratification.

F4. European Agreement Concerning Programme Exchanges by Means of Television Films[i]

Paris, December 15, 1958

The Governments signatory hereto, being Members of the Council of Europe.

Considering that the aim of the Council of Europe is to achieve a greater unity between its Members;

Considering that it is important in the interests of European cultural and economic unity that programmes may be exchanged by means of television films between the member countries of the Council of Europe as freely as possible;

Considering that national legislations allow different conclusions as regards the legal nature of television films and as regards the rights which they grant in respect of such films;

Considering that it is necessary to resolve the difficulties arising from this situation;

Having regard to Article 20 of the Berne Convention for the Protection of Literary and Artistic Works, by the terms of which the Governments of the countries of the Union reserve to themselves the right to enter into special arrangements which do not embody stipulations contrary to that Convention.

Have agreed as follows:

Article 1

In the absence of any contrary or special stipulation within the meaning of Article 4 of the present Agreement, a broadcasting organisation under the jurisdiction of a country which is a Party to this Agreement has the right to authorise in the other countries which are Parties thereto the exploitation for television of television films of which it is the maker.

Article 2

1. All visual or sound and visual recordings intended for television shall be deemed to be television films within the meaning of the present Agreement.

2. A broadcasting organisation shall be deemed to be the maker if it has taken the initiative in, and responsibility for, the making of a television film.

Article 3

1. If the television film has been made by a maker other than the one defined in Article 2, paragraph 2, the latter is entitled, in the absence of contrary or special stipulations within the meaning of Article 4, to transfer to a broadcasting organisation the right provided in Article 1.

2. The provision contained in the preceding paragraph applies only if the maker and the broadcasting organisation are under the jurisdiction of countries which are Parties to the present Agreement.

Article 4

By "contrary of special stipulation" is meant any restrictive condition agreed between the maker and persons who contribute to the making of the television film.

Article 5

This Agreement shall not affect the following rights, which shall be entirely reserved:

---

[i] *Editorial Note*: Cmnd.1509. Signed by the United Kingdom without reservation in respect of ratification on December 15, 1958, and entered into force on July 1, 1961.

(a) any moral right recognised in relation to films;

(b) the copyright in literary, dramatic or artistic works from which the television film is derived;

(c) the copyright in a musical work, with or without words, accompanying a television film;

(d) the copyright in films other than television films;

(e) the copyright in the exploitation of television films otherwise than on television.

Article 6

1. This Agreement shall be open to signature by the Member of the Council of Europe, who may accede to it either by:

(a) signature without reservation in respect of ratification; or

(b) signature with reservation in respect of ratification, followed by the deposit of an instrument of ratification.

2. Instruments of ratification shall be deposited with the Secretary-General of the Council of Europe.

Article 7

1. This Agreement shall enter into force thirty days after the date on which three Members of the Council shall, in accordance with Article 6 thereof, have signed it without reservation in respect of ratification or shall have ratified it.

2. In the case of any Member of the Council who shall subsequently sign the Agreement without reservation in respect of ratification or who shall ratify it, the Agreement shall enter into force thirty days after the date of such signature or deposit of the instrument of ratification.

Article 8

1. After this Agreement has come into force, any country which is not a Member of the Council of Europe may accede to it, subject to the prior approval of the Committee of Ministers of the Council of Europe.

2. Such accession shall be effected by the deposit of an instrument of accession with the Secretary-General of the Council of Europe, and shall take effect thirty days after the date of deposit.

Article 9

Signature without reservation in respect of ratification, acceptance or accession shall imply full acceptance of all the provisions of this Agreement.

Article 10

The Secretary-General of the Council of Europe shall notify Members of the Council, the Governments of any countries which may have acceded to this Agreement and the Director of the Bureau of the International Union for the protection of literary and artistic works:

(a) of the date of entry into force of this Agreement and the names of any Members of the Council which have become Parties thereto;

(b) of the deposit of any instruments of accession in accordance with Article 8 of the present Agreement;

(c) of any declaration or notification received in accordance with Articles 11 and 12 thereof.

Article 11

1. This Agreement shall apply to the metropolitan territories of the Contracting Parties.

2. Any Contracting Party may, at the time of signature, ratification or accession, or at any later date, declare by notice addressed to the Secretary-General of the Council of Europe that this Agreement shall apply to any territory or territories mentioned in the said declaration and for whose international relations it is responsible.

3. Any declaration made in accordance with the preceding paragraph may, in respect of any territory mentioned in such a declaration, be withdrawn under the conditions laid down in Article 12 of this Agreement.

Article 12

1. This Agreement shall remain in force for an unlimited period.

2. Any Contracting Party may denounce this Agreement at one year's notice by notification to this effect to the Secretary-General of the Council of Europe.

In witness whereof, the undersigned, being duly authorised thereto, have signed this Agreement.

Done at Paris, this 15th day of December 1958, in English and French, both texts being equally authoritative, in a single copy, which shall remain in the archives of the Council of Europe and of which the Secretary-General shall send certified copies to each of the signatory and acceding Governments and to the Director of the International Bureau for the Protection of Literary and Artistic Works.

F5. INTERNATIONAL CONVENTION FOR THE PROTECTION OF PERFORMERS, PRODUCERS OF PHONOGRAMS AND BROADCASTING ORGANISATIONS[i]

Rome, October 26, 1961

The Contracting States, moved by the desire to protect the right of performers, producers of phonograms, and broadcasting organisations,

HAVE AGREED AS FOLLOWS:

Article 1

Protection granted under this Convention shall leave intact and shall in no way affect the protection of copyright in literary and artistic works. Consequently, no provision of this Convention may be interpreted as prejudicing such protection.

Article 2

1. For the purposes of this Convention, national treatment shall mean the treatment accorded by the domestic law of the Contracting State in which protection is claimed:

   (a) to performers who are its nationals, as regards performances taking place, broadcast, or first fixed, on its territory;

   (b) to producers of phonograms who are its nationals, as regards phonograms first fixed or first published on its territory;

   (c) to broadcasting organisations which have their headquarters on its territory, as regards broadcasts transmitted from transmitters situated on its territory.

2. National treatment shall be subject to the protection specifically guaranteed, and the limitations specifically provided for, in this Convention.

Article 3

For the purposes of this Convention:

(a) "Performers" means actors, singers, musicians, dancers, and other persons who act, sing, deliver, declaim, play in, or otherwise perform literary or artistic works;

(b) "Phonogram" means any exclusively aural fixation of sounds of a performance or of other sounds;

(c) "Producer of phonograms" means the person who, or the legal entity which, first fixes the sounds of a performance or other sounds;

(d) "Publication" means the offering of copies of a phonogram to the public in reasonable quantity;

(e) "Reproduction" means the making of a copy or copies of a fixation;

(f) "Broadcasting" means the transmission by wireless means for public reception of sounds or of images and sounds;

(g) "Rebroadcasting" means the simultaneous broadcasting by one broadcasting organisation of the broadcast of another broadcasting organisation.

Article 4

Each Contracting State shall grant national treatment to performers if any of the following conditions is met:

(a) the performance takes place in another Contracting State;

---

[i] *Editorial Note*: Cmnd.2425. Ratified by the United Kingdom on October 30, 1963, and entered into force on May 18, 1964.

(b) the performance is incorporated in a phonogram which is protected under Article 5 of this Convention;

(c) the performance, not being fixed on a phonogram; is carried by a broadcast which is protected by Article 6 of this Convention.

Article 5

1. Each Contracting State shall grant national treatment to producers of phonograms if any of the following conditions is met:

(a) the producer of the phonogram is a national of another Contracting State (criterion of nationality);

(b) the first fixation of the sound was made in another Contracting State (criterion of fixation);

(c) the phonogram was first published in another Contracting State (criterion of publication).

2. If a phonogram was first published in a non-contracting State but if it was also published, within thirty days of its first publication, in a Contracting State (simultaneous publication), it shall be considered as first published in the Contracting State.

3. By means of a notification deposited with the Secretary-General of the United Nations, any Contracting State may declare that it will not apply the criterion of publication or, alternatively, the criterion of fixation. Such notification may be deposited at the time of ratification, acceptance or accession, or at any time thereafter; in the last case, it shall become effective six months after it has been deposited.

Article 6

1. Each Contracting State shall grant national treatment to broadcasting organisations if either of the following conditions is met:

(a) the headquarters of the broadcasting organisation is situated in another Contracting State;

(b) the broadcast was transmitted from a transmitter situated in another Contracting State.

2. By means of a notification deposited with the Secretary-General of the United Nations, any Contracting State may declare that it will protect broadcasts only if the headquarters of the broadcasting organization is situated in another Contracting State and the broadcast was transmitted from a transmitter situated in the same Contracting State. Such notification may be deposited at the time of ratification, acceptance or accession, or at any time thereafter; in the last case, it shall become effective six months after it has been deposited.

Article 7

1. The protection provided for performers by this Convention shall include the possibility of preventing:

(a) the broadcasting and the communication to the public, without their consent, of their performance, except where the performance used in the broadcasting or the public communication is itself already a broadcast performance or is made from a fixation;

(b) the fixation, without their consent, of their unfixed performance;

(c) the reproduction, without their consent, of a fixation of their performance,

   (i) if the original fixation itself was made without their consent;

   (ii) if the reproduction is made for purposes different from those for which the performers gave their consent;

   (iii) if the original fixation was made in accordance with the provisions of

Article 15, and the reproduction is made for purposes different from those referred to in those provisions.

2.

(1) If broadcasting was consented to by the performers, it shall be a matter for the domestic law of the Contracting State where protection is claimed to regulate the protection against rebroadcasting, fixation for broadcasting purposes, and the reproduction of such fixation for broadcasting purposes.

(2) The terms and conditions governing the use by broadcasting organisations of fixations made for broadcasting purposes shall be determined in accordance with the domestic law of the Contracting State where protection is claimed.

(3) However, the domestic law referred to in sub-paragraphs (1) and (2) of this paragraph shall not operate to deprive performers of the ability to control, by contract, their relations with broadcasting organisations.

Article 8

Any Contracting State may, by its domestic laws and regulations, specify the manner in which performers will be represented in connexion with the exercise of their rights if several of them participate in the same performance.

Article 9

Any Contracting State may, by its domestic laws and regulations, extend the protection provided for in this Convention to artistes who do not perform literary or artistic works.

Article 10

Producers of phonograms shall enjoy the right to authorise or prohibit the direct or indirect reproduction of their phonograms.

Article 11

If, as a condition of protecting the rights of producers of phonograms, or of performers, or both, in relation to phonograms, a Contracting State, under its domestic law, requires compliance with formalities, these shall be considered as fulfilled if all the copies in commerce of the published phonogram or their containers bear a notice consisting of the symbol P, accompanied by the year date of the first publication, placed in such a manner as to give reasonable notice of claim of protection; and if the copies or their containers do not identify the producer or the licensee of the producer (by carrying his name, trade mark or other appropriate designation), the notice shall also include the name of the owner of the rights of the producer; and furthermore, if the copies or their containers do not identify the principal performers, the notice shall also include the name of the person who, in the country in which the fixation was effected, owns the rights of such performers.

Article 12

If a phonogram published for commercial purposes, or a reproduction of such phonogram, is used directly for broadcasting or for any communication to the public, a single equitable remuneration shall be paid by the user to the performers, or to the producers of the phonograms, or to both. Domestic law may, in the absence of agreement between these parties, lay down the conditions as to the sharing of this remuneration.

Article 13

Broadcasting organisations shall enjoy the right to authorise or prohibit:

(a) the rebroadcasting of their broadcasts;

(b) the fixation of their broadcasts;
(c) the reproduction:
  (i) of fixations, made without their consent, of their broadcasts;
  (ii) of fixations, made in accordance with the provisions of Article 15, of their broadcasts, if the reproduction is made for purposes different from those referred to in those provisions;
(d) the communication to the public of their television broadcasts if such communication is made in places accessible to the public against payment of an entrance fee; it shall be a matter for the domestic law of the State where protection of this right is claimed to determine the conditions under which it may be exercised.

Article 14

The term of protection to be granted under this Convention shall last at least until the end of a period of twenty years computed from the end of the year in which:
(a) the fixation was made—for phonograms and for performances incorporated therein;
(b) the performance took place—for performances not incorporated in phonograms;
(c) the broadcast took place—for broadcasts.

Article 15

1. Any Contracting State may, in its domestic laws and regulations, provide for exceptions to the protection guaranteed by this Convention as regards:
(a) private use;
(b) use of short excerpts in connexion with the reporting of current events;
(c) ephemeral fixation by a broadcasting organisation by means of its own facilities and for its own broadcasts;
(d) use solely for the purposes of teaching or scientific research.

2. Irrespective of paragraph 1 of this Article, any Contracting State may, in its domestic laws and regulations, provide for the same kinds of limitations with regard to the protection of performers, producers of phonograms and broadcasting organisations, as it provides for, in its domestic laws and regulations, in connexion with the protection of copyright in literary and artistic works. However, compulsory licences may be provided for only to the extent to which they are compatible with this Convention.

Article 16

1. Any State, upon becoming party to this Convention, shall be bound by all the obligations and shall enjoy all the benefits thereof. However a State may at any time, in a notification deposited with the Secretary-General of the United Nations, declare that:
(a) as regards Article 12:
  (i) it will not apply the provisions of that Article;
  (ii) it will not apply the provisions of that Article in respect of certain uses;
  (iii) as regards phonograms the producer of which is not a national of another Contracting State, it will not apply that Article;
  (iv) as regards phonograms the producer of which is a national of another Contracting State, it will limit the protection provided for by that Article to the extent to which, and to the term for which, the latter State grants protection to phonograms first fixed by a national of the State making the declaration; however, the fact that the Contracting State of which the pro-

ducer is a national does not grant the protection to the same beneficiary or beneficiaries as the State making the declaration shall not be considered as a difference in the extent of the protection;

(b) as regards Article 13, it will not apply item (d) of that Article; if a Contracting State makes such a declaration, the other Contracting States shall not be obliged to grant the right referred to in Article 13, item (d), to broadcasting organisations whose headquarters are in that State.

2. If the notification referred to in paragraph 1 of this Article is made after the date of the deposit of the instrument of ratification, acceptance or accession, the declaration will become effective six months after it has been deposited.

Article 17

Any State which, on October 26, 1961, grants protection to producers of phonograms solely on the basis of the criterion of fixation may, by a notification deposited with the Secretary-General of the United Nations at the time of ratification, acceptance or accession, declare that it will apply, for the purposes of Article 5, the criterion of fixation alone and, for the purposes of paragraph 1(a)(iii) and (iv) of Article 16, the criterion of fixation instead of the criterion of nationality.

Article 18

Any State which has deposited a notification under paragraph 3 of Article 5, paragraph 2 of Article 6, paragraph 1 of Article 16 or 17, may, by a further notification deposited with the Secretary-General of the United Nations, reduce its scope or withdraw it.

Article 19

Notwithstanding anything in this Convention, once a performer has consented to the incorporation of his performance in a visual or audio-visual fixation, Article 7 shall have no further application.

Article 20

1. This Convention shall not prejudice rights as acquired in any Contracting State before the date of coming into force of this Convention for that State.

2. No Contracting State shall be bound to apply the provisions of this Convention to performances or broadcasts which took place, or to phonograms which were fixed, before the date of coming into force of this Convention for that State.

Article 21

The protection provided for in this Convention shall not prejudice any protection otherwise secured to performers, producers of phonograms and broadcasting organisations.

Article 22

Contracting States reserve the right to enter into special agreements among themselves in so far as such agreements grant to performers, producers of phonograms or broadcasting organisations more extensive rights than those granted by this Convention or contain other provisions not contrary to this Convention.

Article 23

This Convention shall be deposited with the Secretary-General of the United Nations. It shall be open until June 30, 1962 for signature by any State invited to the Diplomatic Conference on the International Protection of Performers, Producers of Phonograms and Broadcasting Organisations which is a party to the

Universal Copyright Convention or a member of the International Union for the Protection of Literary and Artistic Works.

Article 24

1. This Convention shall be subject to ratification or acceptance by the signatory States.

2. This Convention shall be open for accession by any State invited to the Conference referred to in Article 23, and by any State Member of the United Nations, provided that in either case such State is a party to the Universal Copyright Convention or a member of the International Union for the Protection of Literary and Artistic Works.

3. Ratification, acceptance or accession shall be effected by the deposit of an instrument to that effect with the Secretary-General of the United Nations.

Article 25

1. This Convention shall come into force three months after the date of deposit of the sixth instrument of ratification, acceptance or accession.

2. Subsequently, this Convention shall come into force in respect of each State three months after the date of deposit of its instrument of ratification, acceptance or accession.

Article 26

1. Each Contracting State undertakes to adopt, in accordance with its Constitution, the measures necessary to ensure the application of this Convention.

2. At the time of deposit of its instrument of ratification, acceptance or accession, each State must be in a position under its domestic law to give effect to the terms of this Convention.

Article 27

1. Any State may, at the time of ratification, acceptance or accession, or at any time thereafter, declare by notification addressed to the Secretary-General of the United Nations that this Convention shall extend to all or any of the territories for whose international relations it is responsible, provided that the Universal Copyright Convention or the International Convention for the Protection of Literary and Artistic Works applies to the territory or territories concerned. This notification shall take effect three months after the date of its receipt.

2. The notification referred to in paragraph 3 of Article 5, paragraph 2 of Article 6, paragraph 2 of Article 16 and Articles 17 and 18, may be extended to cover all or any of the territories referred to in paragraph 1 of this Article.

Article 28

1. Any Contracting State may denounce this Convention, on its own behalf, or on behalf of all or any of the territories referred to in Article 27.

2. The denunciation shall be effected by a notification addressed to the Secretary-General of the United Nations and shall take effect twelve months after the date of receipt of the notification.

3. The right of denunciation shall not be exercised by a Contracting State before the expiry of a period of five years from the date on which the Convention came into force with respect to that State.

4. A Contracting State shall cease to be a party to this Convention from that time when it is neither a party to the Universal Copyright Convention nor a member of the International Union for the Protection of Literary and Artistic Works.

5. This Convention shall cease to apply to any territory referred to in Article 27 from that time when neither the Universal Copyright Convention nor the International Convention for the Protection of Literary and Artistic Works applies to that territory.

Article 29

1. After this Convention has been in force for five years, any Contracting State may, by notification addressed to the Secretary-General of the United Nations, request that a conference be convened for the purpose of revising the Convention. The Secretary-General shall notify all Contracting States of this request. If, within a period of six months following the date of notification by the Secretary-General of the United Nations, not less than one half of the Contracting States notify him of their concurrence with the request, the Secretary-General shall inform the Director-General of the International Labour Office, the Director-General of the United Nations Educational, Scientific and Cultural Organization and the Director of the Bureau of the International Union for the Protection of Literary and Artistic Works, who shall convene a revision conference in co-operation with the Intergovernmental Committee provided for in Article 32.

2. The adoption of any revision of this Convention shall require an affirmative vote by two-thirds of the States attending the revision conference, provided that this majority includes two-thirds of the States which, at the time of the revision conference, are parties to the Convention.

3. In the event of adoption of a Convention revising this Convention in whole or in part, and unless the revising Convention provides otherwise:
  (a) this Convention shall cease to be open to ratification, acceptance or accession as from the date of entry into force of the revising Convention;
  (b) this Convention shall remain in force as regards relations between or with Contracting States which have not become parties to the revising Convention.

Article 30

Any dispute which may arise between two or more Contracting States concerning the interpretation or application of this Convention and which is not settled by negotiation shall, at the request of any one of the parties to the dispute, be referred to the International Court of Justice for decision, unless they agree to another mode of settlement.

Article 31

Without prejudice to the provisions of paragraph 3 of Article 5, paragraph 2 of Article 6, paragraph 1 of Article 16 and Article 17, no reservation may be made to this Convention.

Article 32

1. An Intergovernmental Committee is hereby established with the following duties:
  (a) to study questions concerning the application and operation of this Convention; and
  (b) to collect proposals and to prepare documentation for possible revision of this Convention.

2. The Committee shall consist of representatives of the Contracting States, chosen with due regard to equitable geographical distribution. The number of members shall be six if there are twelve Contracting States or less, nine if there are thirteen to eighteen Contracting States and twelve if there are more than eighteen Contracting States.

3. The Committee shall be constituted twelve months after the Convention comes into force by an election organised among the Contracting States, each of which shall have one vote, by the Director-General of the International Labour Office, the Director-General of the United Nations Educational, Scientific and Cultural Organization and the Director of the Bureau of the International Union for the Protection of Literary and Artistic Works, in accordance with rules previously approved by a majority of all Contracting States.

4. The Committee shall elect its Chairman and officers. It shall establish its own rules of procedure. These rules shall in particular provide for the future operation of the Committee and for a method of selecting its members for the future in such a way as to ensure rotation among the various Contracting States.

5. Officials of the International Labour Office, the United Nations Educational, Scientific and Cultural Organization and the Bureau of the International Union for the Protection of Literary and Artistic Works, designated by the Directors-General and the Director thereof, shall constitute the Secretariat of the Committee.

6. Meetings of the Committee, which shall be convened whenever a majority of its members deems it necessary, shall be held successively at the headquarters of the International Labour Office, the United Nations Educational, Scientific and Cultural Organization and the Bureau of the International Union for the Protection of Literary and Artistic Works.

7. Expenses of members of the Committee shall be borne by their respective Governments.

Article 33

1. The present Convention is drawn up in English, French and Spanish, the three texts being equally authentic.

2. In addition, official texts of the present Convention shall be drawn up in German, Italian and Portuguese.

Article 34

1. The Secretary-General of the United Nations shall notify the States invited to the Conference referred to in Article 23 and every State Member of the United Nations, as well as the Director-General of the International Labour Office, the Director-General of the United Nations Educational, Scientific and Cultural Organization and the Director of the Bureau of the International Union for the Protection of Literary and Artistic Works:

(a) of the deposit of each instrument of ratification, acceptance or accession;

(b) of the date of entry into force of the Convention;

(c) of all notifications, declarations[ii] or communications provided for in this Convention;

[ii] *Editorial Note*: The United Kingdom ratification was accompanied by the following declaration: "(1) in respect of Article 5(1)(b) and in accordance with Article 5(3) of the Convention, the United Kingdom will not apply, in respect of phonograms, the criterion of fixation; (2) in respect of Article 6(1) and in accordance with Article 6(2) of the Convention, the United Kingdom will protect broadcasts only if the headquarters of the broadcasting organisation is situated in another Contracting State and the broadcast was transmitted from a transmitter situated in the same Contracting State; (3) in respect of Article 12 and in accordance with Article 16(1) of the Convention, (a) the United Kingdom will not apply the provisions of Article 12 in respect of the following uses: (i) the causing of a phonogram to be heard in public at any premises where persons reside or sleep, as part of the amenities provided exclusively or mainly for residents or inmates therein except where a special charge is made for admission to the part of the premises where the phonogram is to be heard, (ii) the causing of a phonogram to be heard in public as part of the activities of, or for the benefit of, a club, society or other organisation which is not established or conducted for profit and whose main objects are charitable or are otherwise concerned with the advancement of religion, education or social welfare, except where a charge is made for admission to the place where the phonogram is to be heard, and any of the proceeds of the charge are

(d) if any of the situations referred to in paragraphs 4 and 5 of Article 28 arise.

2. The Secretary-General of the United Nations shall also notify the Director-General of the International Labour Office, the Director-General of the United Nations Educational, Scientific and Cultural Organization and the Director of the Bureau of the International Union for the Protection of Literary and Artistic Works of the requests communicated to him in accordance with Article 29, as well as of any communication received from the Contracting States concerning the revision of the Convention.

IN FAITH WHEREOF the undersigned, being duly authorised thereto, have signed this Convention.

DONE at Rome, this twenty-sixth day of October 1961, in a single copy in the English, French and Spanish languages. Certified true copies shall be delivered by the Secretary-General of the United Nations to all the States invited to the Conference referred to in Article 23 and to every State Member of the United Nations, as well as to the Director-General of the International Labour Office, the Director-General of the United Nations Educational, Scientific and Cultural Organization and the Director of the Bureau of the International Union for the Protection of Literary and Artistic Works.

---

applied otherwise than for the purpose of the organisation; (b) as regards phonograms the producer of which is not a national of another Contracting State or as regards phonograms the producer of which is a national of a Contracting State which has made a declaration under Article 16(1)(a)(i) stating that it will not apply the provisions of Article 12, the United Kingdom will not grant the protection provided for by Article 12, unless, in either event, the phonogram has been published in a Contracting State which has made no such declaration."

F6. European Agreement for the Prevention of Broadcasts Transmitted from Stations Outside National Territories

Paris, 1965

The member States of the Council of Europe signatory hereto,

Considering that the aim of the Council of Europe is to achieve a greater unity between its Members;

Considering that the Radio Regulations annexed to the International Telecommunication Convention prohibit the establishment and use of broadcasting stations on board ships, aircraft or any other floating or airborne objects outside national territories;

Considering also the desirability of providing for the possibility of preventing the establishment and use of broadcasting stations on objects affixed to or supported by the bed of the sea outside national territories;

Considering the desirability of European collaboration in this matter,

Have agreed as follows:

Article 1

This Agreement is concerned with broadcasting stations which are installed or maintained on board ships, aircraft, or any other floating or airborne objects and which, outside national territories, transmit broadcasts intended for reception or capable of being received, wholly or in part, within the territory of any Contracting Party, or which cause harmful interference to any radio-communication service operating under the authority of a Contracting Party in accordance with the Radio Regulations.

Article 2

1. Each Contracting Party undertakes to take appropriate steps to make punishable as offences, in accordance with its domestic law, the establishment or operation of broadcasting stations referred to in Article 1, as well as acts of collaboration knowingly performed.

2. The following shall, in relation to broadcasting stations referred to in Article 1, be acts of collaboration:

  (a) the provision, maintenance or repairing of equipment;
  (b) the provision of supplies;
  (c) the provision of transport for, or the transporting of, persons, equipment or supplies;
  (d) the ordering of production of material of any kind, including advertisements, to be broadcast;
  (e) the provision of services concerning advertising for the benefit of the stations.

Article 3

Each Contracting Party shall, in accordance with its domestic law, apply the provisions of this Agreement in regard to:

  (a) its nationals who have committed any act referred to in Article 2 on its territory, ships, or aircraft, or outside national territories on any ships, aircraft or any other floating or airborne object;
  (b) non-nationals who, on its territory, ships or aircraft, or on board any floating or airborne object under its jurisdiction have committed any act referred to in Article 2.

Article 4

Nothing in this Agreement shall be deemed to prevent a Contracting Party:

(a) from also treating as punishable offences acts other than those referred to in Article 2 and also applying the provisions concerned to persons other than those referred to in Article 3;

(b) from also applying the provisions of this Agreement to broadcasting stations installed or maintained on objects affixed to or supported by the bed of the sea.

Article 5

The Contracting Parties may elect not to apply the provisions of this Agreement in respect of the services of performers which have been provided elsewhere than on the stations referred to in Article 1.

Article 6

The provisions of Article 2 shall not apply to any acts performed for the purpose of giving assistance to a ship or aircraft or any other floating or airborne object in distress or of protecting human life.

Article 7

No reservation may be made to the provisions of this Agreement.

Article 8

1. This Agreement shall be open to signature by the member States of the Council of Europe, which may become Parties to it either by:

(a) signature without reservation in respect of ratification or acceptance, or

(b) signature with reservation in respect of ratification or acceptance followed by ratification or acceptance.

2. Instruments of ratification or acceptance shall be deposited with the Secretary-General of the Council of Europe.

Article 9

1. This Agreement shall enter into force one month after the date on which three member States of the Council shall, in accordance with the provisions of Article 8, have signed the Agreement without reservation in respect of ratification or acceptance, or shall have deposited their instrument of ratification or acceptance.

2. As regards any member State which shall subsequently sign the Agreement without reservation in respect of ratification or acceptance or which shall ratify or accept it, the Agreement shall enter into force one month after the date of such signature or the date of deposit of the instrument of ratification or acceptance.

Article 10

1. After this Agreement has entered into force, any Member or Associate Member of the International Telecommunication Union which is not a Member of the Council of Europe may accede to it subject to the prior agreement of the Committee of Ministers.

2. Such accession shall be effected by depositing with the Secretary-General of the Council of Europe an instrument of accession which shall take effect one month after the date of its deposit.

Article 11

1. Any Contracting Party may, at the time of signature or when depositing its

instrument of ratification, acceptance or accession, specify the territory or territories to which this Agreement shall apply.

2. Any Contracting Party may, when depositing its instrument of ratification, acceptance or accession or at any later date, by declaration addressed to the Secretary-General of the Council of Europe, extend this Agreement to any other territory or territories specified in the declaration and for whose international relations it is responsible or on whose behalf it is authorised to give undertakings.

3. Any declaration made in pursuance of the preceding paragraph may, in respect of any territory mentioned in such declaration, be withdrawn according to the procedure laid down in Article 12 of this Agreement.

Article 12

1. This Agreement shall remain in force indefinitely.

2. Any Contracting Party may, in so far as it is concerned, denounce this Agreement by means of a notification addressed to the Secretary-General of the Council of Europe.

3. Such denunciation shall take effect six months after the date of receipt by the Secretary-General of such notification.

Article 13

The Secretary-General of the Council of Europe shall notify the member States of the Council and the Government of any State which has acceded to this Agreement, of:

(a) any signature without reservation in respect of ratification or acceptance;

(b) any signature with reservation in respect of ratification or acceptance;

(c) any deposit of an instrument of ratification, acceptance or accession;

(d) any date of entry into force of this Agreement in accordance with Articles 9 and 10 thereof;

(e) any declaration received in pursuance of paragraphs 2 and 3 of Article 11;

(f) any notification received in pursuance of the provisions of Article 12 and that date on which denunciation takes effect.

IN WITNESS WHEREOF the undersigned, being duly authorised thereto, have signed this Agreement.

DONE at Strasbourg, this 22nd day of January 1965 in English and French, both texts being equally authoritative, in a single copy which shall remain deposited in the archives of the Council of Europe. The Secretary General of the Council of Europe shall transmit certified copies to each of the signatory and acceding States.

F7. Convention Establishing the World Intellectual Property Organization[i]

Stockholm, July 14, 1967 [as amended on September 28, 1979]

The Contracting Parties

Desiring to contribute to better understanding and co-operation among States for their mutual benefit on the basis of respect for their sovereignty and equality,

Desiring, in order to encourage creative activity, to promote the protection of intellectual property throughout the world,

Desiring to modernize and render more efficient the administration of the Unions established in the fields of the protection of industrial property and the protection of literary and artistic works, while fully respecting the independence of each of the Unions,

Agree as follows:

Article 1

Establishment of the Organization

The World Intellectual Property Organization is hereby established.

Article 2

Definitions

For the purposes of this Convention:

(i) "Organization" shall mean the World Intellectual Property Organization (WIPO);

(ii) "International Bureau" shall mean the International Bureau of Intellectual Property;

(iii) "Paris Convention" shall mean the Convention for the Protection of Industrial Property signed on March 20, 1883, including any of its revisions;

(iv) "Berne Convention" shall mean the Convention for the Protection of Literary and Artistic Works signed on September 9, 1886, including any of its reservations;

(v) "Paris Union" shall mean the International Union established by the Paris Convention;

(vi) "Berne Union" shall mean the International Union established by the Berne Convention;

(vii) "Unions" shall mean the Paris Union, the Special Unions and Agreements established in relation with that Union, the Berne Union, and any other international agreement designed to promote the protection of intellectual property whose administration is assumed by the Organization according to Article 4(iii);

(viii) "intellectual property" shall include the rights relating to:

— literary, artistic and scientific works,

— performances of performing artists, phonograms, and broadcasts,

— inventions in all fields of human endeavour,

— scientific discoveries,

— industrial designs,

---

[i] *Editorial Note*: Cmnd.4408. Ratified by the United Kingdom on February 26, and entered into force on April 26, 1970.

— trademarks, service marks, and commercial names and designations,

—protection against unfair competition,

and all other rights resulting from intellectual activity in the industrial, scientific, literary or artistic fields.

Article 3

Objectives of the Organization

The objectives of the Organization are:

(i) to promote the protection of intellectual property throughout the world through co-operation among States and, where appropriate, in collaboration with any other international organization,

(ii) to ensure administrative co-operation among the Unions.

Article 4

Functions

In order to attain the objectives described in Article 3, the Organization, through its appropriate organs, and subject to the competence of each of the Unions:

(i) shall promote the development of measures designed to facilitate the efficient protection of intellectual property throughout the world and to harmonize national legislations in this field;

(ii) shall perform the administrative tasks of the Paris Union, the Special Unions established in relation with that Union, and the Berne Union;

(iii) may agree to assume, or participate in, the administration of any other international agreement designed to promote the protection of intellectual property;

(iv) shall encourage the conclusion of international agreements designed to promote the protection of intellectual property;

(v) shall offer its co-operation to States requesting legal-technical assistance in the field of intellectual property;

(iv) shall assemble and disseminate information concerning the protection of intellectual property, carry out and promote studies in this field, and publish the results of such studies;

(vii) shall maintain services facilitating the international protection of intellectual property and, where appropriate, provide for registration in this field and the publication of the data concerning the registrations;

(viii) shall take all other appropriate action.

Article 5

Membership

(1) Membership in the Organization shall be open to any State which is a member of any of the Unions as defined in Article 2 (vii).

(2) Membership in the Organization shall be equally open to any State not a member of any of the Unions, provided that:

(i) it is a member of the United Nations, any of the Specialized Agencies brought into relationship with the United Nations, or the International Atomic Energy Agency, or is a party to the Statute of the International Court of Justice, or

(ii) it is invited by the General Assembly to become a party to this Convention.

Article 6

General Assembly

(1)(a) There shall be a General Assembly consisting of the States party to this Convention which are members of any of the Unions.

(b) The Government of each State shall be represented by one delegate, who may be assisted by alternate delegates, advisors, and experts.

(c) The expenses of each delegation shall be borne by the Government which has appointed it.

(2) The General Assembly shall:

(i) appoint the Director-General upon nomination by the Co-ordination Committee;

(ii) review and approve reports of the Director-General concerning the Organization and give him all necessary instructions;

(iii) review and approve the reports and activities of the Co-ordination Committee and give instructions to such Committee;

(iv) adopt the triennial budget of expenses common to the Unions;

(v) approve the measures proposed by the Director-General concerning the administration of the international agreements referred to in Article 4(iii);

(vi) adopt the financial regulations of the Organization;

(vii) determine the working languages of the Secretariat, taking into consideration the practice of the United Nations;

(viii) invite States referred to under Article 5(2)(ii) to become party to this Convention;

(ix) determine which States not Members of the Organization and which intergovernmental and international non-governmental organizations shall be admitted to its meetings as observers;

(x) exercise such other functions as are appropriate under this Convention.

(3)(a) Each State, whether member of one or more Unions, shall have one vote in the General Assembly.

(b) One-half of the States members of the General Assembly shall constitute a quorum.

(c) Notwithstanding the provisions of sub-paragraph (b), if, in any session, the number of States represented is less than one-half but equal to or more than one-third of the States members of the General Assembly, the General Assembly may make decisions but, with the exception of decisions concerning its own procedure, all such decisions shall take effect only if the following conditions are fulfilled. The International Bureau shall communicate the said decisions to the States members of the General Assembly which were not represented and shall invite them to express in writing their vote or abstention within a period of three months from the date of the communication. If, at the expiration of this period, the number of States having thus expressed their vote or abstention attains the number of States which was lacking for attaining the quorum in the session itself, such decisions shall take effect provided that at the same time the required majority still obtains.

(d) Subject to the provisions of sub-paragraphs (e) and (f), the General Assembly shall make its decisions by a majority of two-thirds of the votes cast.

(e) The approval of measures concerning the administration of international agreements referred to in Article 4(iii) shall require a majority of three-fourths of the votes cast.

(f) The approval of an agreement with the United Nations under Articles 57 and 63 of the Charter of the United Nations shall require a majority of nine-tenths of the votes cast.[ii]

(g) For the appointment of the Director-General (paragraph (2)(i)), the approval of measures proposed by the Director-General concerning the administration of international agreements (paragraph (2)(v)), and the transfer of headquarters (Article 10), the required majority must be attained not only in the General Assembly but also in the Assembly of the Paris Union and the Assembly of the Berne Union.

(h) Abstentions shall not be considered as votes.

(i) A delegate may represent, and vote in the name of, one State only.

(4)(a) The General Assembly shall meet once in every third calendar year in ordinary session, upon convocation by the Director-General.

(b) The General Assembly shall meet in extraordinary session upon convocation by the Director-General either at the request of the Co-ordination Committee or at the request of one-fourth of the States members of the General Assembly.

(c) Meetings shall be held at the headquarters of the Organization.

(5) States party to this Convention which are not members of any of the Unions shall be admitted to the meetings of the General Assembly as observers.

(6) The General Assembly shall adopt its own rules of procedure.

Article 7

Conference

(1)(a) There shall be a Conference consisting of the States party to this Convention whether or not they are members of any of the Unions.

(b) The Government of each State shall be represented by one delegate, who may be assisted by alternate delegates, advisors, and experts.

(c) The expenses of each delegation shall be borne by the Government which has appointed it.

(2) The Conference shall:

(i) discuss matters of general interest in the field of intellectual property and may adopt recommendations relating to such matters, having regard for the competence and autonomy of the Unions;

(ii) adopt the triennial budget of the Conference;

(iii) within the limits of the budget of the Conference, establish the triennial programme of legal-technical assistance;

(iv) adopt amendments to this Convention as provided in Article 17;

(v) determine which States not Members of the Organization and which intergovernmental and international non-governmental organizations shall be admitted to its meetings as observers;

(vi) exercise such other functions as are appropriate under this Convention.

(3)(a) Each Member State shall have one vote in the Conference.

(b) One-third of the Member States shall constitute a quorum.

(c) Subject to the provisions of Article 17, the Conference shall make its decisions by a majority of two-thirds of the votes cast.

(d) The amounts of the contributions of States party to this Convention not members of any of the Unions shall be fixed by a vote in which only the delegates of such States shall have the right to vote.

[ii] *Editorial Note*: See the 1974 Agreement between the United Nations and the World Intellectual Property Organiztion and the 1975 Protocol thereto " *Copyright*," January and February 1975.

   (e) Abstentions shall not be considered as votes.

   (f) A delegate may represent, and vote in the name of, one State only.

(4)(a)The Conference shall meet in ordinary session, upon convocation by the Director-General, during the same period and at the same place as the General Assembly.

  (b) The Conference shall meet in extraordinary session, upon convocation by the Director-General, at the request of the majority of the Member States.

  (5) The Conference shall adopt its own rules procedure.

Article 8
Co-ordination Committee

(1)(a)There shall be a Co-ordination Committee consisting of the States party to this Convention which are members of the Executive Committee of the Paris Union, or the Executive Committee of the Berne Union, or both. However, if either of these Executive Committees is composed of more than one-fourth of the number of the countries members of the Assembly which elected it, then such Executive Committee shall designate from among its members the States which will be members of the Co-ordination Committee, in such a way that their number shall not exceed the one-fourth referred to above, it being understood that the country on the territory of which the Organization has its head-quarters shall not be included in the computation of the said one-fourth.

  (b) The Government of each State member of the Co-ordination Committee shall be represented by one delegate, who may be assisted by alternate delegates, advisors, and experts.

  (c) Whenever the Co-ordination Committee considers either matters of direct interest to the programme or budget of the Conference and its agenda, or proposals for the amendment of this Convention which would affect the rights or obligations of States party to this Convention not members of any of the Unions, one-fourth of such States shall participate in the meetings of the Co-ordination Committee with the same rights as members of that Committee. The Conference shall, at each of its ordinary sessions, designate these States.

  (d) The expenses of each delegation shall be borne by the Government which has appointed it.

  (2) If the other Unions administered by the Organization wish to be represented as such in the Co-ordination Committee, their representatives must be appointed from among the States members of the Co-ordination Committee.

  (3) The Co-ordination Committee shall:

   (i) give advice to the organs of the Unions, the General Assembly, the Conference, and the Director-General, on all administrative, financial and other matters of common interest either to two or more of the Unions, or to one or more of the Unions and the Organization, and in particular on the budget of expenses common to the Unions;

  (ii) prepare the draft agenda of the General Assembly;

  (iii) prepare the draft agenda and the draft programme and budget of the Conference;

  (iv) on the basis of the triennial budget of expenses common to the Unions and the triennial budget of the Conference, as well as on the basis of the triennial programme of legal-technical assistance, establish the corresponding annual budgets and programmes;

  (v) when the term of office of the Director-General is about to expire, or when there is a vacancy in the post of the Director-General, nominate a candidate for appointment to such position by the General Assembly; if the General Assembly does not appoint its nominee, the Co-ordination Committee shall nominate another candidate; this procedure shall be repeated until the latest nominee is appointed by the General Assembly;

(vi) if the post of the Director-General becomes vacant between two sessions of the General Assembly, appoint an Acting Director-General for the term preceding the assuming of office by the new Director-General;

(vii) perform such other functions as are allocated to it under this Convention.

(4)(a) The Co-ordination Committee shall meet once every year in ordinary session, upon convocation by the Director-General. It shall normally meet at the headquarters of the Organization.

(b) The Co-ordination Committee shall meet in extraordinary session, upon convocation by the Director-General, either on his own initiative, or at the request of its Chairman or one-fourth of its members.

(5)(a) Each State, whether a member of one or both of the Executive Committees referred to in paragraph (1)(a), shall have one vote in the Co-ordination Committee.

(b) One-half of the members of the Co-ordination Committee shall constitute a quorum.

(c) A delegate may represent, and vote in the name, of one State only.

(6)(a) The Co-ordination Committee shall express its opinions and make its decisions by a simple majority of the votes cast. Abstentions shall not be considered as votes.

(b) Even if a simple majority is obtained, any member of the Co-ordination Committee may, immediately after the vote, request that the votes be the subject of a special recount in the following manner: two separate lists shall be prepared, one containing the names of the States members of the Executive Committee of the Paris Union and the other the names of the States members of the Executive Committee of the Berne Union; the vote of each State shall be inscribed opposite its name in each list in which it appears. Should this special recount indicate that a simple majority has not been obtained in each of those lists, the proposal shall not be considered as carried.

(7) Any State Member of the Organization which is not a member of the Co-ordination Committee may be represented at the meetings of the Committee by observers having the right to take part in the debates but without the right to vote.

(8) The Co-ordination Committee shall establish its own rules of procedure.

Article 9

International Bureau

(1) The International Bureau shall be the Secretariat of the Organization.

(2) The International Bureau shall be directed by the Director-General, assisted by two or more Deputy Directors-General.

(3) The Director-General shall be appointed for a fixed term, which shall be not less than six years. He shall be eligible for reappointment for fixed terms. The periods of the initial appointment and possible subsequent appointments, as well as all other conditions of the appointment, shall be fixed by the General Assembly.

(4)(a) The Director-General shall be the chief executive of the Organization.

(b) He shall represent the Organization.

(c) He shall report to, and conform to the instructions of, the General Assembly as to the internal and external affairs of the Organization.

(5) The Director-General shall prepare the draft programmes and budgets and periodical reports on activities. He shall transmit them to the Governments of the interested States and to the competent organs of the Unions and the Organization.

(6) The Director-General and any staff member designated by him shall participate, without the right to vote, in all meetings of the General Assembly, the Conference, the Co-ordination Committee, and any other committee or working group. The Director-General or a staff member designated by him shall be *ex officio* secretary of these bodies.

(7) The Director-General shall appoint the staff necessary for the efficient performance of the tasks of the International Bureau. He shall appoint the Deputy Directors-General after approval by the Co-ordination Committee. The conditions of employment shall be fixed by the staff regulations to be approved by the Co-ordination Committee on the proposal of the Director-General. The paramount consideration in the employment of the staff and in the determination of the conditions of service shall be the necessity of securing the highest standards of efficiency, competence, and integrity. Due regard shall be paid to the importance of recruiting the staff on as wide a geographical basis as possible.

(8) The nature of the responsibilities of the Director-General and of the staff shall be exclusively international. In the discharge of their duties they shall not seek or receive instructions from any Government or from any authority external to the Organization. They shall refrain from any action which might prejudice their position as international officials. Each Member State undertakes to respect the exclusively international charActer of the responsibilities of the Director-General and the staff, and not to seek to influence them in the discharge of their duties.

Article 10

Headquarters

(1) The headquarters of the Organization shall be at Geneva.

(2) Its transfer may be decided as provided for in Article 6(3)(d) and (g).

Article 11

Finances

(1) The Organization shall have two separate budgets: the budget of expenses common to the Unions, and the budget of the Conference.

(2)(a)The budget of expenses common to the Unions shall include provision for expenses of interest to several Unions.

(b) This budget shall be financed from the following sources:

(i) contributions of the Unions, provided that the amount of the contribution of each Union shall be fixed by the Assembly of that Union, having regard to the interest the Union has in the common expenses;

(ii) charges due for services performed by the International Bureau not in direct relation with any of the Unions or not received for services rendered by the International Bureau in the field of legal-technical assistance;

(iii) sale of, or royalties on, the publications of the International Bureau not directly concerning any of the Unions;

(iv) gifts, bequests, and subventions, given to the Organization, except those referred to in paragraph (3)(b)(iv);

(v) rents, interests, and other miscellaneous income, of the Organization.

(3)(a)The budget of the Conference shall include provision for the expenses of holding sessions of the Conference and for the cost of the legal-technical assistance programme.

(b) This budget shall be financed from the following sources:

 (i) contributions of States party to this Convention not members of any of the Unions;

 (ii) any sums made available to this budget by the Unions, provided that the amount of the sum made available by each Union shall be fixed by the Assembly of that Union and that each Union shall be free to abstain from contributing to the said budget;

 (iii) sums received for services rendered by the International Bureau in the field of legal-technical assistance;

 (iv) gifts, bequests and subventions, given to the Organization for the purposes referred to in sub-paragraph (a).

(4)(a)For the purpose of establishing its contribution towards the budget of the Conference, each State party to this Convention not a member of any of the Unions shall belong to a class, and shall pay its annual contributions on the basis of a number of units fixed as follows:

Class A 10

Class B 3

Class C 1

(b) Each such State shall, concurrently with taking action as provided in Article 14(1), indicate the class to which it wishes to belong. Any such State may change class. If it chooses a lower class, the State must announce it to the Conference at one of its ordinary sessions. Any such change shall take effect at the beginning of the calendar year following the session.

(c) The annual contribution of each such State shall be an amount in the same proportion to the total sum to be contributed to the budget of the Conference by all such States as the number of its units is to the total of the units of all the said States.

(d) Contributions shall become due on the first of January of each year.

(e) If the budget is not adopted before the beginning of a new financial period, the budget shall be at the same level as the budget of the previous year, in accordance with the financial regulations.

(5) Any State party to this Convention not member of any of the Unions which is in arrears in the payment of its financial contributions under the present Article, and any State party to this Convention member of any of the Unions which is in arrears in the payment of its contributions to any of the Unions, shall have no vote in any of the bodies of the Organization of which it is a member, if the amount of its arrears equals or exceeds the amount of the contributions due from it for the preceding two full years. However, any of these bodies may allow such a State to continue to exercise its vote in that body if, and as long as, it is satisfied that the delay in payment arises from exceptional and unavoidable circumstances.

(6) The amount of the fees and charges due for services rendered by the International Bureau in the field of legal-technical assistance shall be established, and shall be reported to the Co-ordination Committee, by the Director-General.

(7) The Organization, with the approval of the Co-ordination Committee, may receive gifts, bequests, and subventions, directly from Governments, public or private institutions, associations or private persons.

(8)(a)The Organizations shall have a working capital fund which shall be constituted by a single payment made by the Unions and by each State party to this Convention not member of any Union. If the fund becomes insufficient, it shall be increased.

(b) The amount of the single payment of each Union and its possible participation in any increase shall be decided by its Assembly.

(c) The amount of the single payment of each State party to this Convention not member of any Union and its part in any increase shall be a proportion of the contribution of that State for the year in which the fund is established or the increase decided. The proportion and the terms of payment shall be fixed by the Conference on the proposal of the Directors-General and after it has heard the advice of the Co-ordination Committee.

(9)(a) In the headquarters agreement concluded with the State on the territory of which the Organization has its headquarters, it shall be provided that, whenever the working capital fund is insufficient, such State shall grant advances. The amount of these advances and the conditions on which they are granted shall be the subject of separate agreements, in each case, between such State and the Organization. As long as it remains under the obligation to grant advances, such State shall have an *ex officio* seat on the Co-ordination Committee.

(b) The State referred to in sub-paragraph (a) and the Organization shall each have the right to denounce the obligation to grant advances, by written notification. Denunciation shall take effect three years after the end of the year in which it has been notified.

(10) The auditing of the accounts shall be effected by one or more Member States, or by external auditors, as provided in the financial regulations. They shall be designated, with their agreement, by the General Assembly.

Article 12

Legal Capacity; Privileges and Immunities

(1) The Organization shall enjoy on the territory of each Member State, in conformity with the laws of that State, such legal capacity as may be necessary for the fulfillment of the Organization's objectives and for the exercise of its functions.

(2) The Organization shall conclude a headquarters agreement with the Swiss Confederation and with any other State in which the head-quarters may subsequently be located.

(3) The Organization may conclude bilateral or multilateral agreements with the other Member States with a view to the enjoyment by the Organization, its officials, and representatives of all Member States, of such privileges and immunities as may be necessary for the fulfillment of its objectives and for the exercise of its functions.

(4) The Director-General may negotiate and, after approval by the Co-ordination Committee, shall conclude and sign on behalf of the Organization the agreements referred to in paragraphs (2) and (3).

Article 13

Relations with other Organizations

(1) The Organization shall, where appropriate, establish working relations and co-operate with other intergovernmental organizations. Any general agreement to such effect entered into with such organizations shall be concluded by the Director-General after approval by the Co-ordination Committee.

(2) The Organization may, on matters within its competence, make suitable arrangements for consultation and co-operation with international non-governmental organizations and, with the consent of the Governments concerned, with national organizations, governmental or non-governmental. Such arrangements shall be made by the Director-General after approval by the Co-ordination Committee.

Article 14
Becoming Party to the Convention

(1) States referred to in Article 5 may become party to this Convention and Member of the Organization by:

  (i) signature without reservation as to ratification, or

  (ii) signature subject to ratification followed by the deposit of an instrument of ratification, or

  (iii) deposit of an instrument of accession.

(2) Notwithstanding any other provision of this Convention, a State party to the Paris Convention, the Berne Convention, or both Conventions, may become party to this Convention only if it concurrently ratifies or accedes to, or only after it has ratified or acceded to:

either the Stockholm Act of the Paris Convention in its entirety or with only the limitations set forth in Article 20(1)(b)(i) thereof, or the Stockholm Act of the Berne Convention in its entirety or with only the limitation set forth in Article 28(1)(b)(i) thereof.

(3) Instruments of ratification or accession shall be deposited with the Director-General.

Article 15
Entry into Force of the Convention

(1) This Convention shall enter into force three months after ten States members of the Paris Union and seven States members of the Berne Union have taken action as provided in Article 14(1), it being understood that, if a State is a member of both Unions, it will be counted in both groups. On that date, this Convention shall enter into force also in respect of States which, not being members of either of the two Unions, have taken action as provided in Article 14(1) three months or more prior to that date.

(2) In respect to any other State, this Convention shall enter into force three months after the date on which such State takes action as provided in Article 14(1).

Article 16
Reservations

No reservations to this Convention are permitted.

Article 17
Amendments

(1) Proposals for the amendment of this Convention may be initiated by any Member State, by the Co-ordination Committee, or by the Director-General. Such proposals shall be communicated by the Director-General to the Member States at least six months in advance of their consideration by the Conference.

(2) Amendments shall be adopted by the Conference. Whenever amendments would affect the rights and obligations of States party to this Convention not members of any of the Unions, such States shall also vote. On all other amendments proposed, only States party to this Convention members of any Union shall vote. Amendments shall be adopted by a simple majority of the votes cast, provided that the Conference shall vote only on such proposals for amendments as have previously been adopted by the Assembly of the Paris Union and the Assembly of the Berne Union according to the rules applicable in each of them regarding the adoption of amendments to the administrative provisions of their respective Conventions.

(3) Any amendment shall enter into force one month after written notifications of acceptance, effected in accordance with their respective constitutional processes, have been received by the Director-General from three-fourths of the States members of the Organization, entitled to vote on the proposal for amendment pursuant to paragraph (2), at the time the Conference adopted the amendment. Any amendments thus accepted shall bind all the States which are Members of the Organization at the time the amendment enters into force or which become Members at a subsequent date, provided that any amendment increasing the financial obligations of Member States shall bind only those States which have notified their acceptance of such amendment.

Article 18

Denunciation

(1) Any Member State may denounce this Convention by notification addressed to the Director-General.

(2) Denunciation shall take effect six months after the day on which the Director-General has received the notification.

Article 19

Notifications

The Director-General shall notify the Governments of all Member States of:
 (i) the date of entry into force of the Convention,
 (ii) signatures and deposits of instruments of ratification or accession,
 (iii) acceptances of an amendment to this Convention, and the date upon which the amendment enters into force,
 (iv) denunciations of this Convention.

Article 20

Final Provisions

(1)(a) This Convention shall be signed in a single copy in English, French, Russian and Spanish, all texts being equally authentic, and shall be deposited with the Government of Sweden.

 (b) This Convention shall remain open for signature at Stockholm until January 13, 1968.

(2) Official texts shall be established by the Director-General, after consultation with the interested Governments, in German, Italian and Portuguese, and such other languages as the Conference may designate.

(3) The Director-General shall transmit two duly certified copies of this Convention and of each amendment adopted by the Conference to the Governments of the States members of the Paris or Berne Unions, to the Government of any other State when it accedes to this Convention, and, on request, to the Government of any other State. The copies of the signed text of the Convention transmitted to the Governments shall be certified by the Government of Sweden.

(4) The Director-General shall register this Convention with the Secretariat of the United Nations.

Article 21

Transitional Provisions

(1) Until the first Director-General assumes office, references in this Convention to the International Bureau or to the Director-General shall be deemed to be

references to the United International Bureaux for the Protection of Industrial, Literary and Artistic Property (also called the United International Bureaux for the Protection of Intellectual Property (BIRPI)), or its Director, respectively.

(2)(a) States which are members of any of the Unions but which have not become party to this Convention may, for five years from the date of entry into force of this Convention, exercise, if they so desire, the same rights as if they had become party to this Convention. Any State desiring to exercise such rights shall give written notification to this effect to the Director-General; this notification shall be effective on the date of its receipt. Such States shall be deemed to be members of the General Assembly and the Conference until the expiration of the said period.

(b) Upon expiration of this five-year period, such States shall have no right to vote in the General Assembly, the Conference, and the Co-ordination Committee.

(c) Upon becoming party to this Convention, such States shall regain such right to vote.

(3)(a) As long as there are States members of the Paris or Berne Unions which have not become party to this Convention, the International Bureau and the Director-General shall also function as the United International Bureaux for the Protection of Industrial, Literary and Artistic Property, and its Director, respectively.

(b) The staff in the employment of the said Bureaux on the date of entry into force of this Convention shall, during the transitional period referred to in sub-paragraph (a), be considered as also employed by the International Bureau.

(4)(a) Once all the States members of the Paris Union have become Members of the Organization, the rights, obligations, and property, of the Bureau of that Union shall devolve on the International Bureau of the Organization.

(b) Once all the States members of the Berne Union have become Members of the Organization, the rights, obligations, and property, of the Bureau of that Union shall devolve on the International Bureau of the Organization.[iii]

[iii] *Editorial Note*: See the 1974 Agreement between the United Nations and the World Intellectual Property Organiztion and the 1975 Protocol thereto " *Copyright*," January and February 1975.

F8. CONVENTION FOR THE PROTECTION OF PRODUCERS OF PHONOGRAMS AGAINST UNAUTHORISED DUPLICATION OF THEIR PHONOGRAMS[i]

Geneva, October 29, 1971

THE CONTRACTING STATES,

concerned at the widespread and increasing unauthorized duplication of phonograms and the damage this is occasioning to the interests of authors, performers and producers of phonograms;

convinced that the protection of producers of phonograms against such acts will also benefit the performers whose performances, and the authors whose works, are recorded on the said phonograms;

recognizing the value of the work undertaken in this field by the United Nations Educational, Scientific and Cultural Organization and the World Intellectual Property Organization;

anxious not to impair in any way international agreements already in force and in particular in no way to prejudice wider acceptance of the Rome Convention of October 26, 1961, which affords protection to performers and to broadcasting organizations as well as to producers of phonograms;

HAVE AGREED AS FOLLOWS:

Article 1

For the purposes of this Convention:

(a) "phonogram" means any exclusively aural fixation of sounds of a performance or of other sounds;

(b) "producer of phonograms" means the person who, or the legal entity which, first fixes the sounds of a performance or other sounds;

(c) "duplicate" means an article which contains sounds taken directly or indirectly from a phonogram and which embodies all or a substantial part of the sounds fixed in that phonogram;

(d) "distribution to the public" means any act by which duplicates of a phonogram are offered, directly or indirectly, to the general public or any section thereof.

Article 2

Each Contracting State shall protect producers of phonograms who are nationals of other Contracting States against the making of duplicates without the consent of the producer and against the importation of such duplicates, provided that any such making or importation is for the purpose of distribution to the public, and against the distribution of such duplicates to the public.

Article 3

The means by which this Convention is implemented shall be a matter for the domestic law of each Contracting State and shall include one or more of the following: protection by means of the grant of a copyright or other specific right; protection by means of the law relating to unfair competition; protection by means of penal sanctions.

Article 4

The duration of the protection given shall be a matter for the domestic law of

---

[i] *Editorial Note*: Cmnd.5275. Ratified by the United Kingdom on December 5, 1972, and entered into force on April 18, 1973.

each Contracting State. However, if the domestic law prescribes a specific duration for the protection, that duration shall not be less than twenty years from the end either of the year in which the sounds embodied in the phonogram were first fixed or of the year in which the phonogram was first published.

Article 5

If, as a condition of protecting the producers of phonograms, a Contracting State, under its domestic law, requires compliance with formalities, these shall be considered as fulfilled if all the authorized duplicates of the phonogram distributed to the public or their containers bear a notice consisting of the symbol P, accompanied by the year date of the first publication, placed in such manner as to give reasonable notice of claim of protection; and, if the duplicates or their containers do not identify the producer, his successor in title or the exclusive licensee (by carrying his name, trademark or other appropriate designation), the notice shall also include the name of the producer, his successor in title or the exclusive licensee.

Article 6

Any contracting State which affords protection by means of copyright or other specific right, or protection by means of penal sanctions, may in its domestic law provide, with regard to the protection of producers of phonograms, the same kinds of limitations as are permitted with respect to the protection of authors of literary and artistic works. However, no compulsory licences may be permitted unless all of the following conditions are met:

(a) the duplication is for use solely for the purpose of teaching or scientific research;

(b) the licence shall be valid for duplication only within the territory of the Contracting State whose competent authority has granted the licence and shall not extend to the export of duplicates;

(c) the duplication made under the licence gives rise to an equitable remuneration fixed by the said authority taking into account, *inter alia*, the number of duplicates which will be made.

Article 7

(1) This Convention shall in no way be interpreted to limit or prejudice the protection otherwise secured to authors, to performers, to producers of phonograms or to broadcasting organizations under any domestic law or international agreement.

(2) It shall be a matter for the domestic law of each Contracting State to determine the extent, if any, to which performers whose performances are fixed in a phonogram are entitled to enjoy protection and the conditions for enjoying any such protection.

(3) No Contracting State shall be required to apply the provisions of this Convention to any phonogram fixed before this Convention entered into force with respect to that State.

(4) Any Contracting State which, on October 29, 1971, affords protection to producers of phonograms solely on the basis of the place of first fixation may, by a notification deposited with the Director General of the World Intellectual Property Organization, declare that it will apply this criterion instead of the criterion of the nationality of the producer.

Article 8

(1) The International Bureau of the World Intellectual Property Organization

shall assemble and publish information concerning the protection of phonograms. Each Contracting State shall promptly communicate to the International Bureau all new laws and official texts on this subject.

(2) The International Bureau shall, on request, furnish information to any Contracting State on matters concerning this Convention, and shall conduct studies and provide services designed to facilitate the protection provided for therein.

(3) The International Bureau shall exercise the functions enumerated in paragraphs (1) and (2) above in co-operation, for matters within their respective competence, with the United Nations Educational, Scientific and Cultural Organization and the International Labour Organization.

Article 9

(1) This Convention shall be deposited with the Secretary-General of the United Nations. It shall be open until April 30, 1972, for signature by any State that is a member of the United Nations, any of the Specialized Agencies brought into relationship with the United Nations, or the International Atomic Energy Agency, or is a party to the Statute of the International Court of Justice.

(2) This Convention shall be subject to ratification or acceptance by the signatory States. It shall be open for accession by any State referred to in paragraph (1) of this Article.

(3) Instruments of ratification, acceptance or accession shall be deposited with the Secretary-General of the United Nations.

(4) It is understood that, at the time a State becomes bound by this Convention, it will be in a position in accordance with its domestic law to give effect to the provisions of the Convention.

Article 10

No reservations to this Convention are permitted.

Article 11

(1) This Convention shall enter into force three months after deposit of the fifth instrument of ratification, acceptance or accession.

(2) For each State ratifying, accepting or acceding to this Convention after the deposit of the fifth instrument of ratification, acceptance or accession, the Convention shall enter into force three months after the date on which the Director-General of the World Intellectual Property Organization informs the States, in accordance with Article 13, paragraph (4), of the deposit of its instrument.

(3) Any State may, at the time of ratification, acceptance or accession or at any later date, declare by notification addressed to the Secretary-General of the United Nations that this Convention shall apply to all or any of the territories for whose international affairs it is responsible. This notification will take effect three months after the date on which it is received.

(4) However, the preceding paragraph may in no way be understood as implying the recognition or tacit acceptance by a Contracting State of the factual situation concerning a territory to which this Convention is made applicable by another Contracting State by virtue of the said paragraph.

Article 12

(1) Any Contracting State may denounce this Convention, on its own behalf or on behalf of any of the territories referred to in Article 11, paragraph (3), by written notification addressed to the Secretary-General of the United Nations.

(2) Denunciation shall take effect twelve months after the date on which the Secretary-General of the United Nations has received the notification.

Article 13

(1) This Convention shall be signed in a single copy in English, French, Russian and Spanish, the four texts being equally authentic.

(2) Official texts shall be established by the Director-General of the World Intellectual Property Organization, after consultation with the interested Governments, in the Arabic, Dutch, German, Italian and Portuguese languages.

(3) The Secretary-General of the United Nations shall notify the Director-General of the World Intellectual Property Organization, the Director-General of the United Nations Educational, Scientific and Cultural Organization and the Director-General of the International Labour Office of:

(a) signature to this Convention;

(b) the deposit of instruments of ratification, acceptance or accession;

(c) the date of entry into force of this Convention;

(d) any declaration notified pursuant to Article 11, paragraph (3);

(e) the receipt of notifications of denunciation.

(4) The Director General of the World Intellectual Property Organization shall inform the States referred to in Article 9, paragraph (1), of the notifications received pursuant to the preceding paragraph and of any declarations made under Article 7, paragraph (4). He shall also notify the Director-General of the United Nations Educational, Scientific and Cultural Organization and the Director-General of the International Labour Office of such declarations.

(5) The Secretary-General of the United Nations shall transmit two certified copies of this Convention to the States referred to in Article 9, paragraph (1).

F9. Vienna Agreement for the Protection of Type Faces and their International Deposit

Done at Vienna on June 12, 1973

Table of contents[i]

Introductory Provisions

---

[i] *Editorial Note*: This Table of Contents is added for the convenience of the readers. It does not appear in the signed text of the Agreement.

CHAPTER V

Revision and Amendment

Article 31:   Revision of the Agreement.

Article 32:   Amendment of Certain Provisions of the Agreement.

CHAPTER VI

Final Provisions

Article 33:   Becoming Party to the Agreement.

Article 34:   Declaration Concerning National Protection.

Article 35:   Entry Into Force of the Agreement.

Article 36:   Reservations.

Article 37:   Loss of Status of Party to the Agreement.

Article 38:   Denunciation of the Agreement.

Article 39:   Signature and Languages of the Agreement.

Article 40:   Depositary Functions.

Article 41:   Notifications.

THE CONTRACTING STATES,

Desiring, in order to encourage the creation of type faces, to provide an effective protection thereof,

Conscious of the role which type faces play in the dissemination of culture and of the special requirements which their protection must fulfil,

HAVE AGREED AS FOLLOWS:

Introductory Provisions

Article 1

Establishment of a Union

The States party to this Agreement constitute a Union for the protection of type faces.

Article 2

Definitions

For the purposes of this Agreement and the Regulations,

(i) "type faces" means sets of designs of:

(a) letters and alphabets as such with their accessories such as accents and punctuation marks,

(b) numerals and other figurative signs such as conventional signs, symbols and scientific signs,

(c) ornaments such as borders, fleurons and vignettes,

which are intended to provide means for composing texts by any graphic technique. The term "type faces" does not include type faces of a form dictated by purely technical requirements;

(ii) "International Register" means the International Register of Type Faces;

(iii) "international deposit" means the deposit effected for the purposes of recording in the International Register;

(iv) "applicant" means the natural person who, or the legal entity which, effects an international deposit;

(v) "owner of the international deposit" means the natural person or the legal entity in whose name the international deposit is recorded in the International Register;

(vi) "Contracting States" means the States party to this Agreement;

(vii) "Union" means the Union established by this Agreement;

(viii) "Assembly" means the Assembly of the Union;

(ix) "Paris Convention" means the Convention for the Protection of Industrial Property signed on March 20, 1883, including any of its revisions;

(x) "Organization" means the World Intellectual Property Organization;

(xi) "International Bureau" means the International Bureau of the Organization and, as long as it subsists, the United International Bureaux for the Protection of Intellectual Property (BIRPI);

(xii) "Director General" means the Director General of the Organization;

(xiii) "Regulations" means the Regulations under this Agreement.

CHAPTER I

NATIONAL PROTECTION

Article 3

Principle and Kinds of Protection

The Contracting States undertake, in accordance with the provisions of this Agreement, to ensure the protection of type faces, by establishing a special national deposit, or by adapting the deposit provided for in their national industrial design laws, or by their national copyright provisions. These kinds of protection may be cumulative.

Article 4

Natural Persons and Legal Entities Protected

(1) In Contracting States which declare under Article 34 that they intend to ensure protection by establishing a special national deposit or by adapting their national industrial design laws, the protection of this Agreement shall apply to natural persons who, or legal entities which, are residents or nationals of a Contracting State.

(2)(a) In Contracting States which declare under Article 34 that they intend to ensure protection by their national copyright provisions, the protection of this Agreement shall apply to:

(i) creators of type faces who are nationals of one of the Contracting States;

(ii) creators of type faces who are not nationals of one of the Contracting States but whose type faces are published for the first time in one of such States.

(b) Any Contracting State referred to in subparagraph (a) may assimilate creators of type faces who have their habitual residence or domicile in a Contracting State to creators of type faces who are nationals of that State.

(3) For the purposes of the Agreement, any association of natural persons or legal entities which, under the national law of the State according to which it is constituted, may acquire rights and assume obligations, notwithstanding the fact that it is not a legal entity, shall be assimilated to a legal entity. However, any Contracting State may protect, in lieu of the said association, the natural persons or legal entities constituting it.

Article 5

National Treatment

(1) Each Contracting State shall be obliged to grant to all natural persons and

legal entities entitled to claim the benefits of this Agreement the protection afforded to its nationals according to the kind of protection which such Contracting State declares under Article 34.

(2) If a Contracting State referred to in Article 4(2) requires, under its domestic law, compliance with formalities as a condition of protecting type faces, these should be considered as fulfilled, with respect to type faces whose creators are referred to in Article 4(2), if all the copies of the type faces published with the authority of the creator or other owner entitled to protection are accompanied by or, as the case may be, bear a notice consisting of the symbol © accompanied by the name of the owner entitled to protection and the year date of the first such publication placed in such a manner as to give reasonable notice of claim of protection.

Article 6

Concepts of Residence and Nationality

(1)(a) Any natural person shall be regarded as a resident of a Contracting State for the purposes of Articles 4(1) and 13 if:
  (i) according to the national law of that State he is a resident of that State, or
  (ii) he has a real and effective industrial or commercial establishment in that State.
  (b) Any natural person shall be regarded as a national of a Contracting State for the purposes of Articles 4(1) and 13 if, according to the national law of that State, he is a national of that State.
(2)(a) Any legal entity shall be regarded as a resident of a Contracting State for the purposes of Articles 4(1) and 13 if it has a real and effective industrial or commercial establishment in that State.
  (b) Any legal entity shall be regarded as a national of a Contracting State for the purposes of Articles 4(1) and 13 if it is constituted according to the national law of that State.

(3) Where any natural person or legal entity invoking the benefits of this Agreement is a resident of one State and a national of another State, and where only one of those States is a Contracting State, the Contracting States alone shall be considered for the purposes of this Agreement and the Regulations.

Article 7

Conditions of Protection

(1) The protection of type faces shall be subject to the condition that they be novel, or to the condition that they be original, or to both conditions.

(2) The novelty and the originality of type faces shall be determined in relation to their style or overall appearance, having regard, if necessary, to the criteria recognized by the competent professional circles.

Article 8

Content of Protection

(1) Protection of type faces shall confer upon the owner thereof the right to prohibit:
  (i) the making, without his consent, of any reproduction, whether identical or slightly modified, intended to provide means for composing texts by any graphic technique, irrespective of the technical means or material used;
  (ii) the commercial distribution or importation of such reproductions without his consent.
(2)(a) Subject to subparagraph (b), the right defined in paragraph (1) applies irre-

spective of whether or not the protected type faces have been known to the maker of the reproduction.

(b) Contracting States in which originality is a condition of protection are not required to apply subparagraph (a).

(3) The right provided for in paragraph (1) shall also cover any reproduction of type faces obtained by the distortion, by any purely technical means, of the protected type faces, where the essential features thereof remain recognizable.

(4) The making of elements of type faces, by a person acquiring type faces, during the ordinary course of the composition of texts, shall not be considered a reproduction within the meaning of paragraph (1)(i).

(5) Contracting States may take legislative measures to avoid abuses which might result from the exercise of the exclusive right provided under this Agreement in cases where, apart from the protected type faces in question, no other type faces are available in order to achieve a particular purpose in the public interest. The legislative measures shall not, however, prejudice the right of the owner to just remuneration for the use of his type faces. Nor shall the protection of type faces under any circumstances be subject to any forfeiture either by reason of failure to work or by reason of the importation of reproductions of the protected type faces.

Article 9

Term of Protection

(1) The term of protection may not be less than fifteen years.

(2) The term of protection may be divided into several periods, each extension being granted only at the request of the owner of the protected type faces.

Article 10

Cumulative Protection

The provisions of this Agreement shall not preclude the making of a claim to the benefit of any more extensive protection granted by national laws and shall in no way affect the protection granted by other international conventions.

Article 11

Right of Priority

For the purposes of the right of priority, if applicable, national deposits of type faces shall be considered deposits of industrial designs.

Chapter II

International Deposit

Article 12

International Deposit and Recording

(1) Subject to the provisions of paragraph (2), the international deposit shall be effected direct with the International Bureau, which shall record it in the International Register in accordance with this Agreement and the Regulations.

(2)(a) The national law of any Contracting State may provide that international deposits by natural persons or legal entities residing in the respective State may be effected through the intermediary of the competent Office of State.

(b) Where an international deposit is effected, as provided for in subparagraph (a), through the intermediary of a competent Office of a Contracting State, that Office shall indicate the date on which it received the international deposit and shall transmit the said deposit in good time to the International Bureau in the manner provided for in the Regulations.

Article 13

Right to Effect International Deposits and to Own Such Deposits

(1) Any natural person who, or legal entity which, is a resident or a national of a Contracting State may effect and be the owner of international deposits.

(2)(a) Any association of natural persons or legal entities which, under the national law of the State according to which it is constituted, may acquire rights and assume obligations, notwithstanding the fact that it is not a legal entity, shall have the right to effect international deposits and to own such deposits if it is a resident or national of a Contracting State.

(b) Subparagraph (a) shall be without prejudice to the application of the national law of any Contracting State. However, no such State shall refuse or cancel the effects provided for in Article 18 with respect to an association of the kind referred to in subparagraph (a) on the ground that it is not a legal entity if, within two months from the date of an invitation addressed to it by the competent Office of that State, the said association files with that Office a list of the names and addresses of all the natural persons or legal entities constituting it, together with a declaration that is members are engaged in a joint enterprise. In such a case, the said State may consider the natural persons or legal entities constituting the said association to be the owners of the international deposit, in lieu of the association itself, provided that the said persons or entities fulfil the conditions set forth in paragraph (1).

Article 14

Contents and Form of the International Deposit

(1) The international deposit shall contain:
   (i) a signed instrument of international deposit declaring that the deposit is effected under this Agreement, and indicating the identity, residence, nationality and address of the applicant as well as the name of the creator of the type faces for which protection is sought or that the creator has renounced being mentioned as such;
   (ii) a representation of the type faces;
   (iii) payment of the prescribed fees.

(2) The instrument of international deposit may contain:
   (i) a declaration claiming the priority of one or moire earlier deposits effected in or for one or more States party to the Paris Convention;
   (ii) an indication of the denomination given to the type faces by the applicant;
   (iii) the appointment of a representative;
   (iv) such additional indications as are provided for in the Regulations.

(3) The instrument of international deposit shall be in one of the languages prescribed by the Regulations.

Article 15

Recording or Declining of the International Deposit

(1) Subject to paragraph (2), the International Bureau shall promptly record

the international deposit in the International Register. The date of the international deposit shall be the date on which it was received by the International Bureau or, if the international deposit has been effected, as provided for in Article 12(2), through the intermediary of the competent Office of a Contracting State, the date on which that Office received the deposit, provided that the deposit reaches the International Bureau before the expiration of a period of one month following that date.

(2)(a) Where the International Bureau finds any of the following defects, it shall invite the applicant, unless it is clearly impossible to reach him, to correct the defect within three months from the date on which it sent the invitation:

  (i) the instrument of international deposit does not contain an indication that it is effected under this Agreement;

  (ii) the instrument of international deposit does not contain such indications concerning the residence and nationality of the applicant as to permit the conclusion that he has the right to effect international deposits;

  (iii) the instrument of international deposit does not contain such indications concerning the applicant as are necessary to permit him to be identified and reached by mail;

  (iv) the instrument of international deposit does not contain an indication of the name of the creator of the type faces or of the fact that the creator has renounced being mentioned as such;

  (v) the instrument of international deposit is not signed;

  (vi) the instrument of international deposit is not in one of the languages prescribed by the Regulations;

  (vii) the international deposit does not contain a representation of the type faces;

  (viii) the prescribed fees have not been paid.

 (b) If the defect or defects are corrected in the time, the International Bureau shall record the international deposit in the International Register, and the date of the international deposit shall be the date on which the International Bureau receives the correction of the said defect or defects.

 (c) If the defect or defects are not corrected in due time, the International Bureau shall decline the international deposit, inform the applicant accordingly, and reimburse to him part of the fees paid, as provided in the Regulations. If the international deposit is effected through the intermediary of the competent Office of a Contracting State, as provided for in Article 12(2), the International Bureau shall also inform that Office of the declining.

Article 16
Avoiding Certain Effects of Declining

(1) Where the International Bureau has declined the international deposit, the applicant may, within two months from the date of the notification of the declining, effect, in respect of the type faces that were the subject of the international deposit, a national deposit with the competent Office of any Contracting State which ensures the protection of type faces by establishing a special national deposit or by adapting the deposit provided for in its national industrial design law.

(2) If the competent Office or any other competent authority of that Contracting State finds that the International Bureau has declined the international deposit in error, and provided the national deposit complies with all the requirements of the national law of the said State, the said national deposit shall be treated as if it had been effected on the date which would have been the date of the international deposit had that international deposit not been declined.

Article 17

Publication and Notification of the International Deposit

International deposits recorded in the International Register shall be published by the International Bureau and notified by the latter to the competent Offices of the Contracting States.

Article 18

Effect of the International Deposit

(1) In Contracting States which declare in accordance with Article 34 that they intend to ensure the protection of type faces by establishing a special national deposit or by adapting the deposit provided for in their national industrial design laws, the international deposit recorded in the International Register shall have the same effect as a national deposit effected on the same date.

(2) The Contracting States referred to in paragraph (1) may not require that the applicant comply with any additional formality, with the exception of such formalities as may be prescribed by their national laws for the exercise of the rights. However, Contracting States which undertake an ex officio novelty examination or make provision for opposition proceedings may prescribe the formalities required by such examination or such proceedings and charge the fees, with the exception of the publication fee, provided for in their national laws for such examination, the grant of protection and the renewal thereof.

Article 19

Right of Priority

(1) For the purposes of the right of priority, if applicable, the international deposit of type faces shall be considered an industrial design deposit within the meaning of Article 4A of the Paris Convention.

(2) The international deposit shall be a regular filing within the meaning of Article 4A of the Paris Convention if it is not declined pursuant to Article 15(2)(c) of this Agreement, and shall be considered to have been effected on the date accorded to it under Article 15(1) or (2)(b) of this Agreement.

Article 20

Change in the Ownership of the International Deposit

(1) Any change in the ownership of the international deposit shall, on request, be recorded in the International Register by the International Bureau.

(2) The change in the ownership of the international deposit shall not be recorded in the International Register if, according to the indications furnished by the person requesting the recording of the change, the new owner of the international deposit does not have the right to effect international deposits.

(3) The change in the ownership of the international deposit may relate to one or more of the Contracting States referred to in Article 18(1). In such a case, renewal of the international deposit must subsequently be applied for separately by each of the owners of the international deposit as far as he is concerned.

(4) The request for the recording of a change in the ownership of the international deposit shall be presented in the form, and accompanied by the fee, prescribed in the Regulations.

(5) The International Bureau shall record the change in the ownership of the international deposit in the International Register, shall publish it, and shall notify it to the competent Offices of the Contracting States.

(6) The recording of the change in the ownership of the international deposit

in the International Register shall have the same effect as if the request for such recording had been filed direct with the competent Office of each of the Contracting States referred to in Article 18(1) which are concerned by the said change in ownership.

Article 21
Withdrawal and Renunciation of the International Deposit

(1) The applicant may withdraw his international deposit by a declaration addressed to the International Bureau.

(2) The owner of the international deposit may at any time renounce his international deposit by a declaration addressed to the International Bureau.

(3) Withdrawal and renunciation may relate to a part or the whole of the type faces which are the subject of the international deposit, or to their denomination, and to one or more of the Contracting States referred to in Article 18(1).

(4) The International Bureau shall record the renunciation in the International Register, shall publish it, and shall notify it to the competent Offices of the Contracting States.

(5) Renunciation recorded in the International Register shall have the same effect as if it had been communicated direct to the competent Office of each of the Contracting States referred to in Article 18(1).

Article 22
Other Amendments to the International Deposit

(1) The owner of the international deposit may at any time amend the indications appearing in the instrument of international deposit.

(2) Type faces which are the subject of an international deposit may not be amended.

(3) Amendments shall be subject to the payment of the fees prescribed in the Regulations.

(4) The International Bureau shall record amendments in the International Register, shall publish them, and shall notify them to the competent Offices of the Contracting States.

(5) Amendments recorded in the International Register shall have the same effect as if they had been communicated direct to the competent Office of each of the Contracting States referred to in Article 18(1).

Article 23
Term and Renewal of the International Deposit

(1) The international deposit shall have effect for an initial term of ten years from the date of such deposit.

(2) The effect of the international deposit may be extended for terms of five years on the basis of demands for renewal submitted by the owner of the international deposit.

(3) Each new term shall commence on the day following that on which the previous term expires.

(4) The demand for renewal shall be presented in the form, and accompanied by the fees, prescribed by the Regulations.

(5) The International Bureau shall record the renewal in the International Register, shall publish it, and shall notify it to the competent Offices of the Contracting States.

(6) Renewal of the international deposit shall replace such renewals as may be

provided for in the national laws. However, the international deposit may not, in any Contracting State referred to in Article 18(1), have effect after the maximum term of protection provided for in the national law of that State has expired.

Article 24
Regional Treaties

(1) Two or more Contracting States may notify the Director-General that a common Office shall be substituted for the national Office of each of them, and that their territories, as a whole, shall be deemed a single State for the purposes of international deposit.

(2) Such notification shall take effect three months after the date on which the Director General receives it.

Article 25
Representation Before the International Bureau

(1) Applicants and owners of international deposits may be represented before the International Bureau by any person empowered by them to that effect (hereinafter referred to as "the duly appointed representative").

(2) Any invitation, notification or other communication addressed by the International Bureau to the duly appointed representative shall have the same effect as if it had been addressed to the applicant or the owner of the international deposit. Any deposit, request, demand, declaration or other document whose signature by the applicant or the owner of the international deposit is required in proceedings before the International Bureau, except the document appointing the representative or revoking his appointment, may be signed by his duly appointed representative, and any communication from the duly appointed representative to the International Bureau shall have the same effect as if it had been effected by the applicant or the owner of the international deposit.

(3)(a) Where there are several applicants, they shall appoint a common representative. In the absence of such appointment, the applicant first named in the instrument of international deposit shall be considered the duly appointed representative of all the applicants.

(b) Where there are several owners of an international deposit, they shall appoint a common representative. In the absence of such appointment, the natural person or legal entity first named among the said owners in the International Register shall be considered the duly appointed common representative of all the owners of the international deposit.

(c) Subparagraph (b) shall not apply to the extent that the owners own the international deposit in respect of different Contracting States.

CHAPTER III
ADMINISTRATIVE PROVISIONS

Article 26
Assembly

(1)(a) The Assembly shall consist of the Contracting States.

(b) The Government of each Contracting State shall be represented by one delegate, who may be assisted by alternate delegates, advisors, and experts.

(2)(a) The Assembly shall:

(i) deal with all matters concerning the maintenance and development of the Union and the implementation of this Agreement;

    (ii) exercise such rights and perform such tasks as are specially conferred upon it or assigned to it under this Agreement;

    (iii) give directions to the Director General concerning the preparation for revision conferences;

    (iv) review and approve the reports and activities of the Director General concerning the Union, and given him all necessary instructions concerning matters within the competence of the Union;

    (v) determine the program, adopt the triennial budget of the Union, and approve its final accounts;

    (vi) adopt the financial regulations of the Union;

    (vii) establish such committees and working groups as it deems appropriate to facilitate the work of the Union and of its organs;

    (viii) determine which States other than Contracting States and which intergovernmental and international non-governmental organizations shall be admitted to its meetings as observers;

    (ix) take any other appropriate action designed to further the objectives of the Union and perform such other functions as are appropriate under this Agreement.

  (b) With respect to matters which are of interest also to other Unions administered by the Organization, the Assembly shall make its decisions after having heard the advice of the Coordination Committee of the Organization.

  (3) A delegate may represent, and vote in the name of, one Contracting State only.

  (4) Each Contracting State shall have one vote.

(5)(a) One-half of the Contracting States shall constitute a quorum.

  (b) In the absence of the quorum, the Assembly may make decisions but, with the exception of decisions concerning its own procedure, all such decisions shall take effect only if the quorum and the required majority are attained through voting by correspondence as provided in the Regulations.

(6)(a) Subject to the provisions of Articles 29(3) and 32(2)(b), the decisions of the Assembly shall require a majority of the votes cast.

  (b) Abstentions shall not be considered as votes.

(7)(a) The Assembly shall meet once in every third calendar year in ordinary session upon convocation by the Director General, preferably during the same period and at the same place as the General Assembly of the Organization.

  (b) The Assembly shall meet in extraordinary session upon convocation by the Director General, either on his own initiative or at the request of one-fourth of the Contracting States.

  (8) The Assembly shall adopt its own rules of procedure.

Article 27

International Bureau

  (1) The International Bureau shall:

    (i) perform the administrative tasks concerning the Union; in particular, it shall perform such tasks as are specifically assigned to it under this Agreement or by the Assembly;

    (ii) provide the secretariat of revision conferences, of the Assembly, of committees and working groups established by the Assembly, and of any other meeting convened by the Director General and dealing with matters of concern to the Union.

  (2) The Director General shall be the chief executive of the Union and shall represent the Union.

(3) The Director General shall convene any committee and working group established by the Assembly and all other meetings dealing with matters of concern to the Union.

(4)(a)The Director General and any staff member designated by him shall participate, without the right to vote, in all meetings of the Assembly, the committees and working groups established by the Assembly, and any other meeting convened by the Director General and dealing with matters of concern to the Union.

  (b) The Director General, or a staff member designated by him, shall be ex officio secretary of the Assembly, and of the committees, working groups and other meetings referred to in subparagraph (a).

(5)(a)The Director General shall, in accordance with the directions of the Assembly, make the preparations for revision conferences.

  (b) The Director General may consult with intergovernmental and international non-governmental organizations concerning the preparations for revision conferences.

  (c) The Director General and persons designated by him shall take part, without the right to vote, in the discussions at revision conferences.

  (d) The Director General, or a staff member designated by him, shall be ex officio secretary of any revision conference.

Article 28

Finances

(1)(a)The Union shall have a budget.

  (b) The budget of the Union shall include the income and expenses proper to the Union, its contribution to the budget of expenses common to the Unions administered by the Organization and any sum made available to the budget of the Conference of the Organization.

  (c) Expenses not attributable exclusively to the Union but also to one or more other Unions administered by the Organization shall be regarded as expenses common to the Unions. The share of the Union in such common expenses shall be in proportion to the interest the Union has in them.

(2) The budget of the Union shall be established with due regard to the requirements of coordination with the budgets of the other Unions administered by the Organization.

(3)(a)The budget of the Union shall be financed from the following sources:

    (i) fees and other charges due for services rendered by the International Bureau in relation to the Union;

    (ii) sale of, or royalties on, the publications of the International Bureau concerning the Union;

    (iii) gifts, bequests, and subventions;

    (iv) rents, interests, and other miscellaneous income;

    (v) the contributions of Contracting States, in so far as income deriving from the sources mentioned under (i) to (iv) is not sufficient to cover the expenses of the Union.

  (b) The amounts of fees and charges due to the International Bureau under subparagraph (a)(i) and the prices of its publications shall be so fixed that they should, under normal circumstances, be sufficient to cover the expenses of the International Bureau connected with the administration of this Agreement.

  (c) If the income exceeds the expenses, the difference shall be credited to a reserve fund.

(d) If the budget is not adopted before the beginning of a new financial period, it shall be at the same level as the budget of the previous year, as provided in the financial regulations.

(4)(a)For the purpose of establishing its contribution as provided in paragraph (3)(a)(v), each Contracting State shall belong to a class, and shall pay it contribution on the basis of a number of units fixed as follows:

Class I	25
Class II	20
Class III	15
Class IV	10
Class V	5
Class VI	3
Class VII	1

(b) Unless it has already done so, each Contracting State shall indicate, concurrently with depositing its instrument of ratification or accession, the class to which it wishes to belong. Any country may change class. If it chooses a lower class, it must announce such change to the Assembly at one of its ordinary sessions. Any such change shall take effect at the beginning of the calendar year following the said session.

(c) The contribution of each Contracting State shall be an amount in the same proportion to the total sum to be contributed as the number of its units is to the total of the units of all the Contracting States.

(d) Contributions shall be payable on the first of January of the year for which they are due.

(5)(a)The Union shall have a working capital fund which shall be constituted by a single payment made by each Contracting State. If the fund becomes insufficient, the Assembly shall arrange to increase it. If part of the fund is no longer needed, it shall be reimbursed.

(b) The amount of the initial payment of each Contracting State to the said fund or of its participation in the increase thereof shall be a proportion of the contribution which that State may be required to pay under paragraph (3)(a)(v) for the year in which the fund is established or the decision to increase it is made.

(c) The proportion and the terms of payment shall be fixed by the Assembly on the proposal of the Director General and after it has heard the advice of the Coordination Committee of the Organization.

(d) Any reimbursement under subparagraph (a) shall be proportionate to the amounts paid by each Contracting State, taking into account the dates at which they were paid.

(e) If a working capital fund of sufficient amount can be constituted by borrowing from the reserve fund, the Assembly may suspend the application of subparagraphs (a) to (d).

(6)(a)In the headquarters agreement concluded with the State on the territory of which the Organization has its headquarters, it shall be provided that, whenever the working capital fund is insufficient, such State shall grant advances. The amount of those advances and the conditions on which they are granted shall be the subject of separate agreements, in each case, between such State and Organization. As long as it remains under the obligation to grant advances, such State shall have an ex officio seat in the Assembly if it is not a Contracting State.

(b) The State referred to in subparagraph (a) and the Organization shall each have the right to denounce the obligation to grant advances, by written notification. Denunciation shall take effect three years after the end of the year in which it has been notified.

(7) The auditing of the accounts shall be effected by one or more of the Contracting States or by external auditors, as provided in the financial regulations. They shall be designated, with their agreement, by the Assembly.

Article 29

Regulations

(1) The Regulations provide rules:

(i) concerning matters in respect of which this Agreement expressly refers to the Regulations or expressly provides that they are or shall be prescribed;

(ii) concerning any administrative requirements, matters or procedures;

(iii) concerning any details useful in the implementation of this Agreement.

(2) The Regulations adopted at the same time as this Agreement are annexed to this Agreement.

(3) The Assembly may amend the Regulations, and such amendments shall require two-thirds of the votes cast.

(4) In the case of conflict between the provisions of this Agreement and those of the Regulations, the provisions of this Agreement shall prevail.

Chapter IV

Disputes

Article 30

Disputes

(1) Any dispute between two or more Contracting States concerning the interpretation or application of this Agreement or the Regulations, not settled by negotiation, may, by any of the Contracting States concerned, be brought before the International Court of Justice by application in conformity with the Statute of the Court, unless the Contracting States concerned agree on some other method of settlement. The Contracting State bringing the dispute before the Court shall inform the International Bureau; the International Bureau shall bring the matter to the attention of the other Contracting States.

(2) Each Contracting State may, at the time it signs this Agreement or deposits its instrument of ratification or accession, declare that it does not consider itself bound by the provisions of paragraph (1). With regard to any dispute between any Contracting State having made such a declaration and any other Contracting State, the provisions of paragraph (1) shall not apply.

(3) Any Contracting State having made a declaration in accordance with the provisions of paragraph (2) may, at any time, withdraw its declaration by notification addressed to the Director General.

Chapter V

Revision and Amendment

Article 31

Revision of the Agreement

(1) This Agreement may be revised from time to time by a conference of the Contracting States.

(2) The convocation of any revision conference shall be decided by the Assembly.

(3) Articles 26, 27, 28 and 32 may be amended either by a revision conference or according to the provisions of Article 32.

Article 32

Amendment of Certain Provisions of the Agreement

(1)(a) Proposals for the amendment of Articles 26, 27, 28 and the present Article, may be initiated by any Contracting State or by the Director General.

(b) Such proposals shall be communicated by the Director General to the Contracting States at least six months in advance of their consideration by the Assembly.

(2)(a) Amendments to the Articles referred to in paragraph (1) shall be adopted by the Assembly.

(b) Adoption shall require three-fourths of the votes cast, provided that adoption of any amendment to Article 26 and to the present subparagraph shall require four-fifths of the votes cast.

(3)(a) Any amendment to the Articles referred to in paragraph (1) shall enter into force one month after written notifications of acceptance, effected in accordance with their respective constitutional processes, have been received by the Director General from three-fourths of the Contracting States members of the Assembly at the time the Assembly adopted the amendment.

(b) Any amendment to the said Articles thus accepted shall bind all the Contracting States which were Contracting States at the time the amendment was adopted by the Assembly, provided that any amendment increasing the financial obligations of the said Contracting States shall bind only those States which have notified their acceptance of such amendment.

(c) Any amendment which has been accepted and which has entered into force in accordance with the provisions of subparagraph (a) shall bind all States which become Contracting States after the date on which the amendment was adopted by the Assembly.

CHAPTER VI

FINAL PROVISIONS

Article 33

Becoming Party to the Agreement

(1)(a) Subject to subparagraph (b), any State member of either the International Union for the Protection of Industrial Property or the International Union for the Protection of Literary and Artistic Works, or party to the Universal Copyright Convention or to the latter Convention as revised, may become party to this Agreement by:

(i) signature followed by the deposit of an instrument of ratification, or

(ii) deposit of an instrument of accession.

(b) States which intend to ensure the protection of type faces by establishing a special national deposit or by adapting the deposit provided for in their national industrial design laws may only become party to this Agreement if they are members of the International Union for the Protection of Industrial Property. States which intend to ensure the protection of type faces by their national copyright provisions may only become party to this Agreement if they are either members of the International Union for the Protection of Literary and Artistic Works or party to the Universal Copyright Convention or to the latter Convention as revised.

(2) Instruments of ratification or accession shall be deposited with the Director General.

(3) The provisions of Article 24 of the Stockholm Act of the Paris Convention for the Protection of Industrial Property shall apply to this Agreement.

(4) Paragraph (3) shall in no way be understood as implying the recognition or tacit acceptance by a Contracting State of the factual situation concerning a territory to which this Agreement is made applicable by another Contracting State by virtue of the said paragraph.

Article 34
Declarations Concerning National Protection

(1) At the time of depositing its instrument of ratification or accession, each State shall, by a notification addressed to the Director General, declare whether it intends to ensure the protection of type faces by establishing a special national deposit, or by adapting the deposit provided for in its national industrial design laws, or by its national copyright provisions or by more than one of these kinds of protection. Any such State which intends to ensure protection by its national copyright provisions shall declare at the same time whether it intends to assimilate creators of type faces who have their habitual residence or domicile in a Contracting State to creators of type faces who are nationals of that State.

(2) Any subsequent modification of the declarations made in accordance with paragraph (1) shall be indicated by a further notification addressed to the Director General.

Article 35
Entry Into Force of the Agreement

(1) This Agreement shall enter into force three months after five States have deposited their instruments of ratification or accession.

(2) Any State which is not among those referred to in paragraph (1) shall become bound by this Agreement three months after the date on which it has deposited its instrument of ratification or accession, unless a later date has been indicated in the instrument of ratification or accession. In the latter case, this Agreement shall enter into force with respect to that State on the date thus indicated.

(3) The provisions of Chapter II of this Agreement shall become applicable, however, only on the date on which at least three of the States for which this Agreement has entered into force under paragraph (1) afford protection to type faces by establishing a special national deposit or by adapting the deposit provided for in their national industrial design laws. For the purpose of this paragraph, the States party to the same regional treaty which gave notification under Article 24 shall count as one State only.

Article 36
Reservations

No reservations to this Agreement other than the reservation under Article 30(2) are permitted.

Article 37
Loss of Status of Party to the Agreement

Any Contracting State shall cease to be party to this Agreement when it no longer meets the conditions set forth in Article 33(1)(b).

Article 38

Denunciation of the Agreement

(1) Any Contracting State may denounce this Agreement by notification addressed to the Director General.

(2) Denunciation shall take effect one year after the day on which the Director General has received the notification.

(3) The right of denunciation provided for in paragraph (1) shall not be exercised by any Contracting State before the expiration of five years from the date on which it becomes party to this Agreement.

(4)(a) The effects of this Agreement on type faces enjoying the benefits of Articles 12 to 25 on the day preceding the day on which the denunciation by any Contracting State takes effect shall subsist in that State until the expiration of the term of protection which, subject to Article 23(6), was running on that date according to Article 23.

(b) The same shall apply to Contracting States other than the denouncing State in respect of international deposits owned by resident or national of the denouncing State.

Article 39

Signature and Language of the Agreement

(1)(a) This Agreement shall be signed in a single original in the English and French languages, both texts being equally authentic.

(b) Official texts shall be established by the Director General, after consultation with the interested Governments, in the German, Italian, Japanese, Portuguese, Russian and Spanish languages, and such other languages as the Assembly may designate.

(2) This Agreement shall remain open for signature at Vienna until December 31, 1973.

Article 40

Depository Functions

(1) The original of this Agreement, when no longer open for signature, shall be deposited with the Director General.

(2) The Director General shall transmit two copies, certified by him, of this Agreement and the Regulations annexed thereto the Governments of all the States referred to in Article 33(1)(a) and, on request, to the Government of any other State.

(3) The Director General shall register this Agreement with the Secretariat of the United Nations.

(4) The Director General shall transmit two copies, certified by him, of any amendment to this Agreement and to the regulations to the Governments of the Contracting States and, on request, to the Government of any other State.

Article 41

Notifications

The Director General shall notify the Governments of States referred to in Article 33(1)(a) of:

(i) signatures under Article 39;

(ii) deposits of instruments of ratification or accession under Article 33(2);

(iii) the date of entry into force of this Agreement under Article 35(1) and the date from which Chapter II is applicable in accordance with Article 35(3);

   (iv) declarations concerning national protection notified under Article 34;

   (v) notifications concerning regional treaties under Article 24;

   (vi) declarations made under Article 30(2);

 (vii) withdrawals of any declarations, notified under Article 30(3);

(viii) declarations and notifications made in accordance with Article 33(3);

  (ix) acceptances of amendments to this Agreement under Article 32(3);

   (x) the dates on which such amendments enter into force;

  (xi) denunciations received under Article 38.

Protocol to the Vienna Agreement for the Protection of Type Faces and their International Deposit Concerning the Term of Protection

The States party to the Vienna Agreement for the Protection of Type Faces and their International Deposit (hereinafter referred to as "the Agreement"), and party to this Protocol.

  Have agreed to the following provisions:

  1. The term of protection shall be a minimum of twenty five years instead of the minimum of fifteen years referred to in Article 9(1) of the Agreement.

(2)(a) This Protocol shall be open for signature by the States which have signed the Agreement.

  (b) This Protocol may be ratified by the States which have signed the Protocol and ratified the Agreement.

  (c) This Protocol shall be open to accession by States which have not signed the Protocol but have ratified or aceded to the Agreement.

  (d) This Protocol shall enter into force three months after three States have deposited their instruments of ratification of or accession to this Protocol, but not before the Agreement itself enters into force.

  (e) This Protocol may be revised by conferences of the States party to the Protocol which shall be convened by the Director General at the request of at least one-half of those States. The expenses attributable to any conference for the revision of this Protocol which is not held during the same period and at the same place as a conference for the revision of the Agreement shall be borne by the States party to this Protocol.

  (f) the provisions of Article 30, 33, 35(2), 36, 37, 38, 39, 40 and 41 (i), (ii), (iii), (vi), (vii), (viii) and (xi) of the Agreement shall apply *mutatis mutandis*.

F10. CONVENTION RELATING TO THE DISTRIBUTION OF PROGRAMME-CARRYING SIGNALS TRANSMITTED BY SATELLITE[i]

Brussels, May 21, 1974

THE CONTRACTING STATES,

Aware that the use of satellites for the distribution of programme-carrying signals is rapidly growing both in volume and geographical coverage;

Concerned that there is no world-wide system to prevent distributors from distributing programme-carrying signals transmitted by satellite which were not intended for those distributors, and that this lack is likely to hamper the use of satellite communications;

Recognizing, in this respect, the importance of the interests of authors, performers, producers of phonograms and broadcasting organizations;

Convinced that an international system should be established under which measures would be provided to prevent distributors from distributing programme-carrying signals transmitted by satellite which were not intended for those distributors;

Conscious of the need not to impair in any way international agreements already in force, including the International Telecommunication Convention and the Radio Regulations annexed to that Convention, and in particular in no way to prejudice wider acceptance of the Rome Convention of October 26, 1961, which affords protection to performers, producers of phonograms and broadcasting organizations,

HAVE AGREED AS FOLLOWS:

Article 1

For the purposes of this Convention:

  (i) "signal" is an electronically-generated carrier capable of transmitting programmes;

 (ii) "programme" is a body of live or recorded material consisting of images, sounds or both, embodied in signals emitted for the purpose of ultimate distribution;

(iii) "satellite" is any device in extraterrestrial space capable of transmitting signals;

 (iv) "emitted signal" or "signal emitted" is any programme-carrying signal that goes to or passes through a satellite;

  (v) "derived signal" is a signal obtained by modifying the technical characteristics of the emitted signal, whether or not there have been one or more intervening fixations;

 (vi) "originating organization" is the person or legal entity that decides what programme the emitted signals will carry;

(vii) "distributor" is the person or legal entity that decides that the transmission of the derived signals to the general public or any section thereof should take place;

(viii) "distribution" is the operation by which a distributor transmits derived signals to the general public or any section thereof.

Article 2

(1) Each Contracting State undertakes to take adequate measures to prevent

---

[i] *Editorial Note*: The United Kingdom is not a signatory. This Convention has entered into force.

the distribution on or from its territory of any programme-carrying signal by any distributor for whom the signal emitted to or passing through the satellite is not intended. This obligation shall apply where the originating organization is a national of another Contracting State and where the signal distributed is a derived signal.

(2) In any Contracting State in which the application of the measures referred to in paragraph (1) is limited in time, the duration thereof shall be fixed by its domestic law. The Secretary-General of the United Nations shall be notified in writing of such duration at the time of ratification, acceptance or accession, or if the domestic law comes into force or is changed thereafter, within six months of the coming into force of that law or of its modification.

(3) The obligation provided for in paragraph (1) shall not apply to the distribution of derived signals taken from signals which have already been distributed by a distributor for whom the emitted signals were intended.

Article 3

This Convention shall not apply where the signals emitted by or on behalf of the originating organization are intended for direct reception from the satellite by the general public.

Article 4

No Contracting State shall be required to apply the measures referred to in Article 2(1) where the signal distributed on its territory by a distributor for whom the emitted signal is not intended

  (i) carries short excerpts of the programme carried by the emitted signal, consisting of reports of current events, but only to the extent justified by the informatory purpose of such excerpts, or

  (ii) carries, as quotations, short excerpts of the programme carried by the emitted signal, provided that such quotations are compatible with fair practice and are justified by the informatory purpose of such quotations, or

  (iii) carries, where the said territory is that of a Contracting State regarded as a developing country in conformity with the established practice of the General Assembly of the United Nations, a programme carried by the emitted signal, provided that the distribution is solely for the purpose of teaching, including teaching in the framework of adult education, or scientific research.

Article 5

No Contracting State shall be required to apply this Convention with respect to any signal emitted before this Convention entered into force for that State.

Article 6

This Convention shall in no way be interpreted to limit or prejudice the protection secured to authors, performers, producers of phonograms, or broadcasting organizations, under any domestic law or international agreement.

Article 7

This Convention shall in no way be interpreted as limiting the right of any Contracting State to apply its domestic law in order to prevent abuses of monopoly.

Article 8

(1) Subject to paragraphs (2) and (3), no reservation to this Convention shall be permitted.

(2) Any Contracting State whose domestic law, on May 21, 1974, so provides may, by a written notification deposited with the Secretary-General of the United Nations, declare that, for its purposes, the words "where the originating organization is a national of another Contracting State" appearing in Article 2(1) shall be considered as if they were replaced by the words "where the signal is emitted from the territory of another Contracting State."

(3)(a)any Contracting State which, on May 21, 1974, limits or denies protection with respect to the distribution of programme-carrying signals by means of wires, cable or other similar communications channels to subscribing members of the public may, by a written notification deposited with the Secretary-General of the United Nations, declare that, to the extent that and as long as its domestic law limits or denies protection, it will not apply this Convention to such distributions.

(b) Any State that has deposited a notification in accordance with subparagraph (a) shall notify the Secretary-General of the United Nations in writing, within six months of their coming into force, of any changes in its domestic law whereby the reservation under that subparagraph becomes inapplicable or more limited in scope.

Article 9

(1) This Convention shall be deposited with the Secretary-General of the United Nations. It shall be open until March 31, 1975, for signature by any State that is a member of the United Nations, any of the Specialized Agencies brought into relationship with the United Nations, or the International Atomic Energy Agency, or is a party to the Statute of the International Court of Justice.

(2) This Convention shall be subject to ratification or acceptance by the signatory States. It shall be open for accession by any State referred to in paragraph (1).

(3) Instruments of ratification, acceptance or accession shall be deposited with the Secretary-General of the United Nations.

(4) It is understood that, at the time a State becomes bound by this Convention, it will be in a position in accordance with its domestic law to give effect to the provisions of the Convention.

Article 10

(1) This Convention shall enter into force three months after the deposit of the fifth instrument of ratification, acceptance or accession.

(2) For each State ratifying, accepting or acceding to this Convention after the deposit of the fifth instrument of ratification, acceptance or accession, this Convention shall enter into force three months after the deposit of its instrument.

Article 11

(1) Any Contracting State may denounce this Convention by written notification deposited with the Secretary-General of the United Nations.

(2) Denunciation shall take effect twelve months after the date on which the notification referred to in paragraph (1) is received.

Article 12

(1) This Convention shall be signed in a single copy in English, French, Russian and Spanish, the four texts being equally authentic.

(2) Official texts shall be established by the Director-General of the United Nations Educational, Scientific and Cultural Organization and the Director General of the World Intellectual Property Organization, after consultation with the

interested Governments, in the Arabic, Dutch, German, Italian and Portuguese languages.

(3) The Secretary-General of the United Nations shall notify the States referred to in Article 9(1), as well as the Director-General of the United Nations Educational, Scientific and Cultural Organization, the Director General of the World Intellectual Property Organization, the Director-General of the International Labour Office and the Secretary-General of the International Telecommunication Union, of

  (i) signatures to this Convention;

  (ii) the deposit of instruments of ratification, acceptance or accession;

  (iii) the date of entry into force of this Convention under Article 10(1);

  (iv) the deposit of any notification relating to Article 2(2) or Article 8(2) or (3), together with its text;

  (v) the receipt of notifications of denunciation.

(4) The Secretary-General of the United Nations shall transmit two certified copies of this Convention to all States referred to in Article 9(1).

F11. Agreement on Trade-Related Aspects of Intellectual Property Rights[i]

Table of Contents

Members,

Desiring to reduce distortions and impediments to international trade, and taking into account the need to promote effective and adequate protection of intellectual property rights, and to ensure that measures and procedures to enforce intellectual property rights do not themselves become barriers to legitimate trade;

Recognizing, to this end, the need for new rules and disciplines concerning:

(a) the applicability of the basic principle of the GATT 1994 and of relevant international intellectual property agreements or conventions;

(b) the provision of adequate standards and principles concerning the availability, scope and use of trade-related intellectual property rights;

(c) the provisions of effective and appropriate means for the enforcement of

---

[i] *Editorial Note*: Annex 1C to the Agreement Establishing the World Trade Organization, done at Marrakesh, April 15, 1994. The footnote numbering in the original Agreement is reproduced below.

trade-related intellectual property rights, taking into account differences in national legal systems;

(d) the provision of effective and expeditious procedures for the multilateral prevention and settlement of disputes between governments; and

(e) transitional arrangements aiming at the fullest participation in the results of the negotiations;

Recognizing the need for a multilateral framework of principles, rules and disciplines dealing with international trade in counterfeit goods;

Recognizing that intellectual property rights are private rights;

Recognizing the underlying public policy objectives of national systems for the protection of intellectual property, including developmental and technological objectives;

Recognizing also the special needs of the least-developed country Members in respect of maximum flexibility in the domestic implementation of laws and regulations in order to enable them to create a sound and viable technological base;

Emphasizing the importance of reducing tensions by reaching strengthened commitments to resolve disputes on trade-related intellectual property issues through multilateral procedures;

Desiring to establish a mutually supportive relationship between the WTO and the World Intellectual Property Organization (referred to in this Agreement as "WIPO") as well as other relevant international organisations;

Hereby agree as follows:

PART I

GENERAL PROVISIONS AND BASIC PRINCIPLES

Article 1
Nature and Scope of Obligations

1. Members shall give effect to the provisions of this Agreement. Members may, but shall not be obliged to, implement in their law more extensive protection than is required by this Agreement, provided that such protection does not contravene the provisions of this Agreement. Members shall be free to determine the appropriate method of implementing the provisions of this Agreement within their own legal system and practice.

2. For the purposes of this Agreement, the term "intellectual property" refers to all categories of intellectual property that are the subject of Sections 1 through 7 of Part II.

3. Members shall accord the treatment provided for in this Agreement to the nationals of other Members.[1] In respect of the relevant intellectual property right, the nationals of other Members shall be understood as those natural or legal persons that would meet the criteria for eligibility for protection provided for in the Paris Convention (1967), the Berne Convention (1971), the Rome Convention and the Treaty on Intellectual Property in Respect of Integrated Circuits, were all Members of the WTO members of those conventions.[2] Any Member availing itself of the possibilities provided in paragraph 3 of Article 5 or

---

[1] When "nationals" are referred to in this Agreement, they shall be deemed, in the case of a separate customs territory Member of the WTO, to mean persons, natural or legal, who are domiciled or who have a real and effective industrial or commercial establishment in that customs territory.

[2] In this Agreement, "Paris Convention" refers to the Paris Convention for the Protection of Industrial Property: "Paris Convention (1967)" refers to the Stockholm Act of this Convention of

paragraph 2 of Article 6 of the Rome Convention shall make a notification as foreseen in those provisions to the Council for Trade-Related Aspects of Intellectual Property Rights (the "Council for Trips").

Article 2

Intellectual Property Conventions

1. In respect of Parts II, III and IV of this Agreement, Members shall comply with Articles 1 through 12, and Article 19, of the Paris Convention (1967).

2. Nothing in Parts I to IV of this Agreement shall derogate from existing obligations that Members may have to each other under the Paris Convention, the Berne Convention, the Rome Convention and the Treaty on Intellectual Property in Respect of Integrated Circuits.

Article 3

National Treatment

1. Each Member shall accord to the nationals of other Members treatment no less favourable than that it accords to its own nationals with regard to the protection[3] of intellectual property, subject to the exceptions already provided in, respectively, the Paris Convention (1967), the Berne Convention (1971), the Rome Convention or the Treaty on Intellectual Property in Respect of Integrated Circuits. In respect of performers, producers of phonograms and broadcasting organizations, this obligation only applies in respect of the rights provided under this Agreement. Any Member availing itself of the possibilities provided in Article 6 of the Berne Convention (1971) or paragraph 1(b) of Article 16 of the Rome Convention shall make a notification as foreseen in those provisions to the Council for TRIPS.

2. Members may avail themselves of the exceptions permitted under paragraph 1 in relation to judicial and administrative procedures, including the designation of an address for service or the appointment of an agent within the jurisdiction of a Member, only where such exceptions are necessary to secure compliance with laws and regulations which are not inconsistent with the provisions of this Agreement and where such practices are not applied in a manner which would constitute a disguised restriction on trade.

Article 4

Most-Favoured-Nation Treatment

With regard to the protection of intellectual property, any advantage, favour, privilege or immunity granted by a Member to the nationals of any other country shall be accorded immediately and unconditionally to the nationals of all other Members. Exempted from this obligation are any advantage, favour, privilege or immunity accorded by a Member:

(a) deriving from international agreements on judicial assistance or law

---

14 July 1967. "Berne Convention" refers to the Berne Convention for the Protection of Literary and Artistic Works: "Berne Convention (1971)" refers to the Paris Act of this Convention of 24 July 1971. "Rome Convention" refers to the International Convention for the Protection of Performers, Producers of Phonograms and Broadcasting Organisations, adopted at Rome on 26 October 1961. "Treaty on Intellectual Property in Respect of Integrated Circuits" (IPIC Treaty) refers to the Treaty on Intellectual Property in Respect of Integrated Circuits, adopted at Washington on 26 May 1989. "WTO Agreement" refers to the Agreement Establishing the WTO.

[3] For the purposes of Articles 3 and 4, "protection" shall include matters affecting the availability, acquisition, scope, maintenance and enforcement of intellectual property rights as well as those matters affecting the use of intellectual property rights specifically addressed in this Agreement.

enforcement of a general nature and not particularly confined to the protection of intellectual property;

(b) granted in accordance with the provisions of the Berne Convention (1971) or the Rome Convention authorizing that the treatment accorded be a function not of national treatment but of the treatment accorded in another country;

(c) in respect of the rights of performers, producers of phonograms and broadcasting organizations not provided under this Agreement;

(d) deriving from international agreements related to the protection of intellectual property which entered into force prior to the entry into force of the WTO Agreement, provided that such agreements are notified to the Council for TRIPS and do not constitute an arbitrary or unjustifiable discrimination against nationals of other Members.

Article 5

Multilateral Agreements on Acquisition or Maintenance of Protection

The obligations under Articles 3 and 4 above do not apply to procedures provided in multilateral agreements concluded under the auspices of WIPO relating to the acquisition or maintenance of intellectual property rights.

Article 6

Exhaustion

For the purposes of dispute settlement under this Agreement, subject to the provisions of Articles 3 and 4 nothing in this Agreement shall be used to address the issue of the exhaustion of intellectual property rights.

Article 7

Objectives

The protection and enforcement of intellectual property rights should contribute to the promotion of technological innovation and to the transfer and dissemination of technology, to the mutual advantage of producers and users of technological knowledge and in a manner conducive to social and economic welfare, and to a balance of rights and obligations.

Article 8

Principles

1. Members may, in formulating or amending their laws and regulations, adopt measures necessary to protect public health and nutrition, and to promote the public interest in sectors of vital importance to their socio-economic and technological development, provided that such measures are consistent with the provisions of this Agreement.

2. Appropriate measures, provided that they are consistent with the provisions of this Agreement, may be needed to prevent the abuse of intellectual property rights by right holders or the resort to practices which unreasonably restrain trade or adversely affect the international transfer of technology.

PART II

STANDARDS CONCERNING THE AVAILABILITY, SCOPE AND USE OF
INTELLECTUAL PROPERTY RIGHTS

Section 1 —Copyright and Related Rights

Article 9

Relation to the Berne Convention

1. Members shall comply with Articles 1 through 21 and the Berne Convention (1971) and the Appendix thereto. However, Members shall not have rights or obligations under this Agreement in respect of the rights conferred under Article 6*bis* of that Convention or of the rights derived therefrom.

2. Copyright protection shall extend to expressions and not to ideas, procedures, methods of operation or mathematical concepts as such.

Article 10

Computer Programs and Compilations of Data

1. Computer programs, whether in source or object code, shall be protected as literary works under the Berne Convention (1971).

2. Compilations of data or other material, whether in machine readable or other form, which by reason of the selection or arrangement of their contents constitute intellectual creations shall be protected as such. Such protection, which shall not extend to the data or material itself, shall be without prejudice to any copyright subsisting in the data or material itself.

Article 11

Rental Rights

In respect of at least computer programs and cinematographic works, a Member shall provide authors and their successors in title the right to authorize or to prohibit the commercial rental to the public of originals or copies of their copyright works. A Member shall be excepted from this obligation in respect of cinematographic works unless such rental has led to widespread copying of such works which is materially impairing the exclusive right of reproduction conferred in that Member on authors and their successors in title. In respect of computer programs, this obligation does not apply to rentals where the program itself is not the essential object of the rental.

Article 12

Term of Protection

Whenever the term of protection of a work, other than a photographic work or a work of applied art, is calculated on a basis other than the life of a natural person, such term shall be no less than 50 years from the end of the calendar year of authorized publication or, failing such authorised publication within 50 years from the making of the work, 50 years from the end of the calendar year of making.

Article 13

Limitations and Exceptions

Members shall confine limitations or exceptions to exclusive rights to certain special cases which do not conflict with a normal exploitation of the work and do not unreasonably prejudice the legitimate interests of the right holder.

Article 14

Protection of Performers, Producers of Phonograms (Sound Recordings) and Broadcasting Organizations

1. In respect of a fixation of their performance on a phonogram, performers shall have the possibility of preventing the following acts when undertaken without their authorization: the fixation of their unfixed performance and the reproduction of such fixation. Performers shall also have the possibility of preventing the following acts when undertaken without their authorization: the broadcasting by wireless means and the communication to the public of their live performance.

2. Producers of phonograms shall enjoy the right to authorize or prohibit the direct or indirect reproduction of their phonograms.

3. Broadcasting organizations shall have the right to prohibit the following acts when undertaken without their authorization: the fixation, the reproduction of fixations, and the rebroadcasting by wireless means of broadcasts, as well as the communication to the public of television broadcasts of the same. Where Members do not grant such rights to broadcasting organizations, they shall provide owners of copyright in the subject matter of broadcasts with the possibility of preventing the above acts, subject to the provisions of the Berne Convention (1971).

4. The provisions of Article 11 in respect of computer programs shall apply *mutatis mutandis* to producers of phonograms and any other right holders in phonograms as determined in a Member's law. If on 15 April 1994 a Member has in force a system of equitable remuneration of right holders in respect of the rental of phonograms, it may maintain such system provided that the commercial rental of phonograms is not giving rise to the material impairment of the exclusive rights of reproduction of right holders.

5. The term of the protection available under this Agreement to performers and producers of phonograms shall last at least until the end of a period of 50 years computed from the end of the calendar year in which the fixation was made or the performance took place. The term of protection granted pursuant to paragraph 3 shall last for a least 20 years from the end of the calendar year in which the broadcast took place.

6. Any Member may, in relation to the rights conferred under paragraphs 1, 2 and 3, provide for conditions, limitations, exceptions and reservations to the extent permitted by the Rome Convention. However, the provisions of Article 18 of the Berne Convention (1971) shall also apply, *mutatis mutandis*, to the rights of performers and producers of phonograms in phonograms.

Section 2 —Trademarks

Article 15

Protectable Subject-Matter

1. Any sign, or any combination of signs, capable of distinguishing the goods or services of one undertaking from those of other undertakings, shall be capable of constituting a trademark. Such signs, in particular words including personal names, letters, numerals, figurative elements and combinations of colours as well as any combination of such signs, shall be eligible for registration as trademarks. Where signs are not inherently capable of distinguishing the relevant goods or

services, Members may make registrability depend on distinctiveness acquired through use. Members may require, as a condition of registration, that signs be visually perceptible.

2. Paragraph 1 shall not be understood to prevent a Member from denying registration of a trademark on other grounds, provided that they do not derogate from the provisions of the Paris Convention (1967).

3. Members may make registrability depend on use. However, actual use of a trademark shall not be a condition for filing an application for registration. An application shall not be refused solely on the ground that intended use has not taken place before the expiry of a period of three years from the date of application.

4. The nature of the goods or services to which a trademark is to be applied shall in no case form an obstacle to registration of the trademark.

5. Members shall publish each trademark either before it is registered or promptly after it is registered and shall afford a reasonable opportunity for petitions to cancel the registration. In addition, Members may afford an opportunity for the registration of a trademark to be opposed.

Article 16

Rights Conferred

1. The owner of a registered trademark shall have the exclusive right to prevent all third parties not having the owners' consent from using in the course of trade identical or similar signs for goods or services which are identical or similar to those in respect of which the trademark is registered where such use would result in a likelihood of confusion. In case of the use of an identical sign for identical goods or services, a likelihood of confusion shall be presumed. The rights described above shall not prejudice any existing prior rights, nor shall they affect the possibility of Members making rights available on the basis of use.

2. Article 6bis of the Paris Convention (1967) shall apply, *mutatis mutandis*, to services. In determining whether a trademark is well-known, Members shall take account of the knowledge of the trademark in the relevant sector of the public, including knowledge in the Member concerned which has been obtained as a result of the promotion of the trademark.

3. Article 6bis of the Paris Convention (1967) shall apply, *mutatis mutandis*, to goods or services which are not similar to those in respect of which a trademark is registered, provided that use of that trademark in relation to those goods or services would indicate a connection between those goods or services and the owner of the registered trademark and provided that the interests of the owner of the registered trademark are likely to be damaged by such use.

Article 17

Exceptions

Members may provide limited exceptions to the rights conferred by a trademark, such as fair use of descriptive terms, provided that such exceptions take account of the legitimate interests of the owner of the trademark and of third parties.

Article 18

Term of Protection

Initial registration, and each renewal of registration, of a trademark shall be for a term of no less than seven years. The registration of a trademark shall be renewable indefinitely.

Article 19

Requirement of Use

1. If use is required to maintain a registration, the registration may be cancelled only after an uninterrupted period of at least three years of non-use, unless valid reasons based on the existence of obstacles to such use are shown by the trademark owner. Circumstances arising independently of the will of the owner of the trademark which constitute an obstacle to the use of the trademark, such as import restrictions on or other government requirements for goods or services protected by the trademark, shall be recognized as valid reasons for non-use.

2. When subject to the control of its owner, use of a trademark by another person shall be recognized as use of the trademark for the purpose of maintaining the registration.

Article 20

Other Requirements

The use of a trademark in the course of trade shall not be unjustifiably encumbered by special requirements, such as use with another trademark, use in a special form or use in a manner detrimental to its capability to distinguish the goods or services of one undertaking form those of other undertakings, This will not preclude a requirement prescribing the use of the trademark identifying the undertaking producing the goods or services along with, but without linking it to, the trademark distinguishing the specific goods or services in question of that undertaking.

Article 21

Licensing and Assignment

Members may determine conditions on the licensing and assignment of trademarks, it being understood that the compulsory licensing of trademarks shall not be permitted and that the owner of a registered trademark shall have the right to assign his trademark with or without the transfer of the business to which the trademark belongs.

Section 3 —Geographical Indications

Article 22

Protection of Geographical Indications

1. Geographical indications are, for the purposes of this Agreement, indications which identify a good as originating in the territory of a Member, or a region or locality in that territory, where a given quality, reputation or other characteristic of the good is essentially attributable to its geographical origin.

2. In respect of geographical indications, Members shall provide the legal means for interested parties to prevent:

(a) the use of any means in the designation or presentation of a good that indicates or suggests that the good in question originates in a geographical area other than the true place of origin in a manner which misleads the public as to the geographical origin of the good;

(b) any use which constitutes an act of unfair competition within the meaning of Article 10*bis* of the Paris Convention (1967).

3. A Member shall, *ex officio* if its legislation so permits or at the request of an interested party, refuse or invalidate the registration of a trademark which contains or consists of a geographical indication with respect to goods not

originating in the territory indicated, if use of the indication in the trademark for such goods in that Member is of such a nature as to mislead the public as to the true place of origin.

4. The protection under paragraphs 1, 2 and 3 shall be applicable against a geographical indication which, although literally true as to the territory, region or locality in which the goods originate, falsely represents to the public that the goods originate in another territory.

Article 23

Additional Protection for Geographical Indications for Wines and Spirits

1. Each Member shall provide the legal means for interested parties to prevent use of a geographical indication identifying wines for wines not originating in the place indicated by the geographical indication in question or identifying spirits for spirits not originating in the place indicated by the geographical indication in question, even where the true origin of the goods is indicated or the geographical indication is used in translation or accompanied by expressions such as "kind", "type", "style", "imitation" or the like.[4]

2. The registration of a trademark for wines which contains or consists of a geographical indication identifying wines or for spirits which contains or consists of a geographical indication identifying spirits shall be refused or invalidated, *ex officio* if a Member's legislation so permits or at the request of an interested party, with respect to such wines or spirits not having this origin.

3. In the case of homonymous geographical indications for wines, protection shall be accorded to each indication, subject to the provisions of paragraph 4 of Article 22. Each Member shall determine the practical conditions under which the homonymous indications in question will be differentiated from each other, taking into account the need to ensure equitable treatment of the producers concerned and that consumers are not misled.

4. In order to facilitate the protection of geographical indications for wines, negotiations shall be undertaken in the Council for TRIPS concerning the establishment of a multilateral system of notification and registration of geographical indications for wines eligible for protection in those Members participating in the system.

Article 24

International Negotiations; Exceptions

1. Members agree to enter into negotiations aimed at increasing the protection of individual geographical indications under Article 23. The provisions of paragraphs 4 through 8 below shall not be used by a Member to refuse to conduct negotiations or to conclude bilateral or multilateral agreements. In the context of such negotiations, Members shall be willing to consider the continued applicability of these provisions to individual geographical indications whose use was the subject of such negotiations.

2. The Council for TRIPS shall keep under review the application of the provisions of this Section; the first such review shall take place within two years of the entry into force of the WTO Agreement. Any matter affecting the compliance with the obligations under these provisions may be drawn to the attention of the Council, which, at the request of a Member, shall consult with any Member or Members in respect of such matter in respect of which it has not been possible to

---

[4] Notwithstanding the first sentence of Article 42, Members may, with respect to these obligations, instead provide for enforcement by administrative action.

find a satisfactory solution through bilateral or plurilateral consultations between the Members concerned. The Council shall take such action as may be agreed to facilitate the operation and further the objectives of this Section.

3. In implementing this Section, a Member shall not diminish the protection of geographical indications that existed in that Member immediately prior to the date of entry into force of the WTO Agreement.

4. Nothing in this Section shall require a Member to prevent continued and similar use of a particular geographical indication of another Member identifying wines or spirits in connection with goods or services by any of its nationals or domiciliaries who have used that geographical indication in a continuous manner with regard to the same or related goods or services in the territory of that Member either (*a*) for at least 10 years preceding 15 April 1994 or (*b*) in good faith preceding that date.

5. Where a trademark has been applied for or registered in good faith, or where rights to a trademark have been acquired through use in good faith either:

(a) before the date of application of these provisions in that Member as defined in Part VI; or

(b) before the geographical indication is protected in its country of origin;

measures adopted to implement this Section shall not prejudice eligibility for or the validity of the registration of a trademark, or the right to use a trademark, on the basis that such a trademark is identical with, or similar to, a geographical indication.

6. Nothing in this Section shall require a Member to apply its provisions in respect of a geographical indication of any other Member with respect to goods or services for which the relevant indication is identical with the term customary in common language as the common name for such goods or services in the territory of that Member. Nothing in this Section shall require a Member to apply its provisions in respect of a geographical indication of any other Member with respect to products of the vine for which the relevant indication is identical with the customary name of a grape variety existing in the territory of that Member as of the date of entry into force of the WTO Agreement.

7. A Member may provide that any request made under this Section in connection with the use or registration of a trademark must be presented within five years after the adverse use of the protected indication has become generally known in that Member or after the date of registration of the trademark in that Member provided that the trademark has been published by that date, if such date is earlier than the date on which the adverse use became generally known in that Member, provided that the geographical indication is not used or registered in bad faith.

8. The provisions of this Section shall in no way prejudice the right of any person to use, in the course of trade, that person's name or the name of that person's predecessor in business, except where such name is used in such a manner as to mislead the public.

9. There shall be no obligation under this Agreement to protect geographical indications which are not or cease to be protected in their country of origin, or which have fallen into disuse in that country.

Section 4 —Industrial Designs

Article 25

Requirements for Protection

1. Members shall provide for the protection of independently created industrial designs that are new or original. Members may provide that designs are not new

or original if they do not significantly differ from known designs or combinations of known design features. Members may provide that such protection shall not extend to designs dictated essentially by technical or functional considerations.

2. Each Member shall ensure that requirements for securing protection for textile designs, in particular in regard to any cost, examination or publication, do not unreasonably impair the opportunity to seek and obtain such protection. Members shall be free to meet this obligation through industrial design law or through copyright law.

Article 26

Protection

1. The owner of a protected industrial design shall have the right to prevent third parties not having the owner's consent from making, selling or importing articles bearing or embodying a design which is a copy, or substantially a copy, of the protected design, when such acts are undertaken for commercial purposes.

2. Members may provide limited exceptions to the protection of industrial designs, provided that such exceptions do not unreasonably conflict with the normal exploitation of protected industrial designs and do not unreasonably prejudice the legitimate interests of the owner of the protected design, taking account of the legitimate interests of third parties.

3. The duration of protection available shall amount to at least 10 years.

Section 5 —Patents

Article 27

Patentable Subject-Matter

1. Subject to the provisions of paragraphs 2 and 3, patents shall be available for any inventions, whether products or processes, in all fields of technology, provided that they are new, involve an inventive step and are capable of industrial application.[5] Subject to paragraph 4 of Article 65, paragraph 8 of Article 70 and paragraph 3 of this Article, patents shall be available and patent rights enjoyable without discrimination as to the place of invention, the field of technology and whether products are imported or locally produced.

2. Members may exclude from patentability inventions, the prevention within their territory of the commercial exploitation of which is necessary to protect *ordre public* or morality, including to protect human, animal or plant life or health or to avoid serious prejudice to the environment, provided that such exclusion is not made merely because the exploitation is prohibited by their law.

3. Members may also exclude from patentability:

(a) diagnostic, therapeutic and surgical methods for the treatment of humans or animals;

(b) plants and animals other than micro-organisms, and essentially biological processes for the production of plants or animals other than non-biological and microbiological processes. However, Members shall provide for the protection of plant varieties either by patents or by an effective *sui generis* system or by any combination thereof. The provisions of this subparagraph shall be reviewed four years after the date of entry into force of the WTO Agreement.

---

[5] For the purposes of this Article, the terms "inventive step" and "capable of industrial application" may be deemed by a Member to be synonymous with the terms "non-obvious" and "useful" respectively.

Article 28

Rights Conferred

1. A patent shall confer on its owner the following exclusive rights:

(a) where the subject matter of a patent is a product, to prevent third parties not having the owner's consent from the acts of: making, using, offering for sale, selling, or importing[6] for these purposes that product;

(b) where the subject matter of a patent is a process, to prevent third parties not having the owner's consent from the act of using the process, and from the acts of: using, offering for sale, selling, or importing for these purposes at least the product obtained directly by that process.

2. Patent owners shall also have the right to assign, or transfer by succession, the patent and to conclude licensing contracts.

Article 29

Conditions on Patent Applicants

1. Members shall require that an applicant for a patent shall disclose the invention in a manner sufficiently clear and complete for the invention to be carried out by a person skilled in the art and may require the applicant to indicate the best mode for carrying out the invention known to the inventor at the filing date or, where priority is claimed, at the priority date of the application.

2. Members may require an applicant for a patent to provide information concerning the applicant's corresponding foreign applications and grants.

Article 30

Exceptions to Rights Conferred

Members may provide limited exceptions to the exclusive rights conferred by a patent, provided that such exceptions do not unreasonably conflict with a normal exploitation of the patent and do not unreasonably prejudice the legitimate interests of the patent owner, taking account of the legitimate interests of third parties.

Article 31

Other Use Without Authorization of the Right Holder

Where the law of a Member allows for other use[7] of the subject matter of a patent without the authorization of the right holder, including use by the government or third parties authorized by the government, the following provisions shall be respected:

(a) authorization of such use shall be considered on its individual merits;

(b) such use may only be permitted if, prior to such use, the proposed user has made efforts to obtain authorization from the right holder on reasonable commercial terms and conditions and that such efforts have not been successful within a reasonable period of time. This requirement may be waived by a Member in the case of a national emergency or other circumstances of extreme urgency or in cases of public non-commercial use. In situations of national emergency or other circumstances of extreme urgency, the right holder shall, nevertheless, be notified as soon as reasonably practicable. In

---

[6] This right, like all other rights conferred under this Agreement in respect of the use, sale, importation or other distribution of goods, is subject to the provisions of Article 6.

[7] "Other use" refers to use other than that allowed under Article 30.

the case of public non-commercial use, where the government or contractor, without making a patent search, knows or has demonstrable grounds to know that a valid patent is or will be used by or for the government, the right holder shall be informed promptly;

(c) the scope and duration of such use shall be limited to the purpose for which it was authorized, and in the case of semi-conductor technology shall only be for public non-commercial use or to remedy a practice determined after judicial or administrative process to be anti-competitive.

(d) such use shall be non-exclusive;

(e) such use shall be non-assignable, except with that part of the enterprise or goodwill which enjoys such use;

(f) any such use shall be authorized predominantly for the supply of the domestic market of the Member authorizing such use;

(g) authorization for such use shall be liable, subject to adequate protection of the legitimate interests of the persons so authorized, to be terminated if and when the circumstances which led to it cease to exist and are unlikely to recur. The competent authority shall have the authority to review, upon motivated request, the continued existence of these circumstances;

(h) the right holder shall be paid adequate remuneration in the circumstances of each case, taking into account the economic value of the authorization;

(i) the legal validity of any decision relating to the authorization of such use shall be subject to judicial review or other independent review by a distinct higher authority in that Member;

(j) any decision relating to the remuneration provided in respect of such use shall be subject to judicial review or other independent review by a distinct higher authority in that Member;

(k) Members are not obliged to apply the conditions set forth in sub-paragraphs (b) and (f) where such use is permitted to remedy a practice determined after judicial or administrative process to be anti-competitive. The need to correct anti-competitive practices may be taken into account in determining the amount of remuneration in such cases. Competent authorities shall have the authority to refuse termination of authorization if and when the conditions which led to such authorization are likely to recur;

(l) where such use is authorized to permit the exploitation of a patent ("the second patent") which cannot be exploited without infringing another patent ("the first patent"), the following additional conditions shall apply:

   (i) the invention claimed in the second patent shall involve an important technical advance of considerable economic significance in relation to the invention claimed in the first patent;

   (ii) the owner of the first patent shall be entitled to a cross-licence on reasonable terms to use the invention claimed in the second patent; and

   (iii) the use authorized in respect of the first patent shall be non-assignable except with the assignment of the second patent.

Article 32

Revocation/Forfeiture

An opportunity for judicial review of any decision to revoke or forfeit a patent shall be available.

Article 33
Term of Protection

The term of protection available shall not end before the expiration of a period of twenty years counted from the filing date.[8]

Article 34
Process Patents: Burden of Proof

1. For the purposes of civil proceedings in respect of the infringement of the rights of the owner referred to in paragraph 1(b) of Article 28, if the subject matter of a patent is a process for obtaining a product, the judicial authorities shall have the authority to order the defendant to prove that the process to obtain an identical product is different from the patented process. Therefore, Members shall provide, in at least one of the following circumstances, that any identical product when produced without the consent of the patent owner shall, in the absence of proof to the contrary, be deemed to have been obtained by the patented process:

(a) if the product obtained by the patented process is new;

(b) if there is a substantial likelihood that the identical product was made by the process and the owner of the patent has been unable through reasonable efforts to determine the process actually used.

2. Any Member shall be free to provide that the burden of proof indicated in paragraph 1 shall be on the alleged infringer only if the condition referred to in subparagraph (a) is fulfilled or only if the condition referred to in subparagraph (b) is fulfilled.

3. In the adduction of proof to the contrary, the legitimate interests of defendants in protecting their manufacturing and business secrets shall be taken into account.

Section 6 —Layout-Designs (Topographies) of Integrated Circuits

Article 35
Relation to the IPIC Treaty

Members agree to provide protection to the layout-designs (topographies) of integrated circuits (referred to in this Agreement as "layout-designs") in accordance with Articles 2 through 7 (other than paragraph 3 of Article 6), Article 12 and paragraph 3 of Article 16 of the Treaty on Intellectual Property in Respect of Integrated Circuits and, in addition, to comply with the following provisions.

Article 36
Scope of the Protection

Subject to the provisions of paragraph 1 of Article 37 below, Members shall consider unlawful the following acts if performed without the authorization of the right holder[9]: importing, selling, or otherwise distributing for commercial purposes a protected layout-design, an integrated circuit in which a protected layout-design is incorporated, or an article incorporating such an integrated circuit only in so far as it continues to contain an unlawfully reproduced layout-design.

---

[8] It is understood that those Members which do not have a system of original grant may provide that the term of protection shall be computed from the filing date in the system of original grant.

[9] The term "right holder" in this Section shall be understood as having the same meaning as the term "holder of the right" in the IPIC Treaty.

Article 37

Acts Not Requiring the Authorization of the Right Holder

1. Notwithstanding Article 36, no Member shall consider unlawful the performance of any of the acts referred to in that Article in respect of an integrated circuit incorporating an unlawfully reproduced layout-design or any article incorporating such an integrated circuit where the person performing or ordering such acts did not know and had no reasonable ground to know, when acquiring the integrated circuit or article incorporating such an integrated circuit, that it incorporated an unlawfully reproduced layout-design. Members shall provide that, after the time that such person has received sufficient notice that the layout-design was unlawfully reproduced, that person may perform any of the acts with respect to the stock on hand or ordered before such time, but shall be liable to pay to the right holder a sum equivalent to a reasonable royalty such as would be payable under a freely negotiated licence in respect of such a layout-design.

2. The conditions set out in subparagraphs (a) through (k) of Article 31 shall apply *mutatis mutandis* in the event of any non-voluntary licensing of a layout-design or of its use by or for the government without the authorization of the right holder.

Article 38

Term of Protection

1. In Members requiring registration as a condition of protection, the term of protection of layout-design shall not end before the expiration of a period of 10 years counted from the date of filing an application for registration or from the first commercial exploitation wherever in the world it occurs.

2. In Members not requiring registration as a condition for protection, layout-designs shall be protected for a term of no less than 10 years from the date of the first commercial exploitation wherever in the world it occurs.

3. Notwithstanding paragraphs 1 and 2, a Member may provide that protection shall lapse 15 years after the creation of the layout-design.

Section 7 —Protection of Undisclosed Information

Article 39

1. In the course of ensuring effective protection against unfair competition as provided in Article 10*bis* of the Paris Convention (1967), Members shall protect undisclosed information in accordance with paragraph 2 and data submitted to governments or governmental agencies in accordance with paragraph 3.

2. Natural and legal persons shall have the possibility of preventing information lawfully within their control from being disclosed to, acquired by, or used by others without their consent in a manner contrary to honest commercial practices[10] so long as such information:

(a) is secret in the sense that it is not, as a body or in the precise configuration and assembly of its components, generally known among or readily accessible to persons within the circles that normally deal with the kind of information in question:

(b) has commercial value because it is secret; and

(c) has been subject to reasonable steps under the circumstances, by the person lawfully in control of the information, to keep it secret.

---

[10] For the purpose of this provision, "a manner contrary to honest commercial practices" shall mean at least practices such as breach of contract, breach of confidence and inducement to breach, and includes the acquisition of undisclosed information by third parties who knew, or were grossly negligent in failing to know, that such practices were involved in the acquisition.

3. Members, when requiring, as a condition of approving the marketing of pharmaceutical or of agricultural chemical products which utilize new chemical entities, the submission of undisclosed test or other data, the origination of which involves a considerable effort, shall protect such data against unfair commercial use. In addition, Members shall protect such data against disclosure, except where necessary to protect the public, or unless steps are taken to ensure that the data are protected against unfair commercial use.

Section 8 —Control of Anti-Competitive Practices in Contractual Licences

Article 40

1. Members agree that some licensing practices or conditions pertaining to intellectual property rights which restrain competition may have adverse effects on trade and may impede the transfer and dissemination of technology.

2. Nothing in this Agreement shall prevent Members from specifying in their legislation licensing practices or conditions that may in particular cases constitute an abuse of intellectual property rights having an adverse effect on competition in the relevant market. As provided above, a Member may adopt, consistently with the other provisions of this Agreement, appropriate measures to prevent or control such practices, which may include for example exclusive grantback conditions, conditions preventing challenges to validity and coercive package licensing, in the light of the relevant laws and regulations of that Member.

3. Each Member shall enter, upon request, into consultations with any other Member which has cause to believe that an intellectual property right owner that is a national or domiciliary of the Member to which the request for consultations has been addressed is undertaking practices in violation of the requesting Member's laws and regulations on the subject-matter of this Section, and which wishes to secure compliance with such legislation, without prejudice to any action under the law and to the full freedom of an ultimate decision of either Member. The Member addressed shall accord full and sympathetic consideration to, and shall afford adequate opportunity for, consultations with the requesting Member, and shall cooperate through supply of publicly available non-confidential information of relevance to the matter in question and of other information available to the Member, subject to domestic law and to the conclusion of mutually satisfactory agreements concerning the safeguarding of its confidentiality by the requesting Member.

4. A Member whose nationals or domiciliaries are subject to proceedings in another Member concerning alleged violation of that other Member's laws and regulations on the subject matter of this Section shall, upon request, be granted an opportunity for consultations by the other Member under the same conditions as those foreseen in paragraph 3.

PART III

ENFORCEMENT OF INTELLECTUAL PROPERTY RIGHTS

Section 1 —General Obligations

Article 41

1. Members shall ensure that enforcement procedures as specified in this Part are available under their law so as to permit effective action against any act of infringement of intellectual property rights covered by this Agreement, including expeditious remedies to prevent infringements and remedies which constitute a deterrent to further infringements. These procedures shall be applied in such a

manner as to avoid the creation of barriers to legitimate trade and to provide for safeguards against their abuse.

2. Procedures concerning the enforcement of intellectual property rights shall be fair and equitable. They shall not be unnecessarily complicated or costly, or entail unreasonable time-limits or unwarranted delays.

3. Decisions on the merits of a case shall preferably be in writing and reasoned. They shall be made available at least to the parties to the proceeding without undue delay. Decisions on the merits of a case shall be based only on evidence in respect of which parties were offered the opportunity to be heard.

4. Parties to a proceeding shall have an opportunity for review by a judicial authority of final administrative decisions and, subject to jurisdictional provisions in a Member's law concerning the importance of a case, of at least the legal aspects of initial judicial decisions on the merits of a case. However, there shall be no obligation to provide an opportunity for review of acquittals in criminal cases.

5. It is understood that this Part does not create any obligation to put in place a judicial system for the enforcement of intellectual property rights distinct from that for the enforcement of law in general, nor does it affect the capacity of Members to enforce their law in general. Nothing in this Part creates any obligation with respect to the distribution of resources as between enforcement of intellectual property rights and the enforcement of law in general.

Section 2 —Civil and Administrative Procedures and Remedies

Article 42

Fair and Equitable Procedures

Members shall make available to right holders[11] civil judicial procedures concerning the enforcement of any intellectual property right covered by this Agreement. Defendants shall have the right to written notice which is timely and contains sufficient detail, including the basis of the claims. Parties shall be allowed to be represented by independent legal counsel, and procedures shall not impose overly burdensome requirements concerning mandatory personal appearances. All parties to such procedures shall be duly entitled to substantiate their claims and to present all relevant evidence. The procedure shall provide a means to identify and protect confidential information, unless this would be contrary to existing constitutional requirements.

Article 43

Evidence

1. The judicial authorities shall have the authority, where a party has presented reasonably available evidence sufficient to support its claims and has specified evidence relevant to substantiation of its claims which lies in the control of the opposing party, to order that this evidence be produced by the opposing party, subject in appropriate cases to conditions which ensure the protection of confidential information.

2. In cases in which a party to a proceeding voluntarily and without good reason refuses access to, or otherwise does not provide necessary information within a reasonable period, or significantly impedes a procedure relating to an enforcement action, a Member may accord judicial authorities the authority to make pre-

---

[11] For the purpose of this Part, the term "right holder" includes federations and associations having legal standing to assert such rights.

liminary and final determinations, affirmative or negative, on the basis of the information presented to them, including the complaint or the allegation presented by the party adversely affected by the denial of access to information, subject to providing the parties an opportunity to be heard on the allegations or evidence.

Article 44

Injunctions

1. The judicial authorities shall have the authority to order a party to desist from an infringement, *inter alia* to prevent the entry into the channels of commerce in their jurisdiction of imported goods that involve the infringement of an intellectual property right, immediately after customs clearance of such goods. Members are not obliged to accord such authority in respect of protected subject matter acquired or ordered by a person prior to knowing or having reasonable grounds to know that dealing in such subject matter would entail the infringement of an intellectual property right.

2. Notwithstanding the other provisions of this Part and provided that the provisions of Part II specifically addressing use by governments, or by third parties authorized by a government, without the authorization of the right holder are complied with, Members may limit the remedies available against such use to payment of remuneration in accordance with subparagraph (h) of Article 31. In other cases, the remedies under this Part shall apply or, where these remedies are inconsistent with a Member's law, declaratory judgments and adequate compensation shall be available.

Article 45

Damages

1. The judicial authorities shall have the authority to order the infringer to pay the right holder damages adequate to compensate for the injury the right holder has suffered because of an infringement of that person's intellectual property right by an infringer who knowingly, or with reasonable grounds to know, engaged in infringing activity.

2. The judicial authorities shall also have the authority to order the infringer to pay the right holder expenses, which may include appropriate attorney's fees. In appropriate cases, Members may authorize the judicial authorities to order recovery of profits and/or payment of pre-established damages even where the infringer did not knowingly, or with reasonable grounds to know, engage in infringing activity.

Article 46

Other Remedies

In order to create an effective deterrent to infringement, the judicial authorities shall have the authority to order that goods that they have found to be infringing be, without compensation of any sort, disposed of outside the channels of commerce in such a manner as to avoid any harm caused to the right holder, or, unless this would be contrary to existing constitutional requirements, destroyed. The judicial authorities shall also have the authority to order that materials and implements the predominant use of which has been in the creation of the infringing goods be, without compensation of any sort, disposed of outside the channels of commerce in such a manner as to minimize the risks of further infringements. In considering such requests, the need for proportionality between the seriousness of the infringement and the remedies ordered as well as the interests of third parties shall be taken into account. In regard to counterfeit trademark goods, the simple removal of the trademark unlawfully affixed shall not be sufficient, other than in exceptional cases, to permit release of the goods into the channels of commerce.

Article 47

Right of Information

Members may provide that the judicial authorities shall have the authority, unless this would be out of proportion to the seriousness of the infringement, to order the infringer to inform the right holder of the identity of third persons involved in the production and distribution of the infringing goods or services and of their channels of distribution.

Article 48

Indemnification of the Defendant

1. The judicial authorities shall have the authority to order a party at whose request measures were taken and who has abused enforcement procedures to provide to a party wrongfully enjoined or restrained adequate compensation for the injury suffered because of such abuse. The judicial authorities shall also have the authority to order the applicant to pay the defendant expenses, which may include appropriate attorney's fees.

2. In respect of the administration of any law pertaining to the protection or enforcement of intellectual property rights, Members shall only exempt both public authorities and officials from liability to appropriate remedial measures where actions are taken or intended in good faith in the course of the administration of that law.

Article 49

Administrative Procedures

To the extent that any civil remedy can be ordered as a result of administrative procedures on the merits of a case, such procedures shall conform to principles equivalent in substance to those set forth in this Section.

Section 3 —Provisional Measures

Article 50

1. The judicial authorities shall have the authority to order prompt and effective provisional measures:

  (a) to prevent an infringement of any intellectual property right from occurring, and in particular to prevent the entry into the channels of commerce in their jurisdiction of goods, including imported goods immediately after customs clearance;

  (b) to preserve relevant evidence in regard to the alleged infringement.

2. The judicial authorities shall have the authority to adopt provisional measures *inaudita altera parte* where appropriate, in particular where any delay is likely to cause irreparable harm to the right holder, or where there is a demonstrable risk of evidence being destroyed.

3. The judicial authorities shall have the authority to require the applicant to provide any reasonably available evidence in order to satisfy themselves with a sufficient degree of certainty that the applicant is the right holder and that the applicant's right is being infringed or that such infringement is imminent, and to order the applicant to provide a security or equivalent assurance sufficient to protect the defendant and to prevent abuse.

4. Where provisional measures have been adopted *inaudita altera parte*, the parties affected shall be given notice, without delay after the execution of the measures at the latest. A review, including a right to be heard, shall take place upon request of the defendant with a view to deciding, within a reasonable period after the notification of the measures, whether these measures shall be modified, revoked or confirmed.

5. The applicant may be required to supply other information necessary for the identification of the goods concerned by the authority that will execute the provisional measures.

6. Without prejudice to paragraph 4, provisional measures taken on the basis of paragraphs 1 and 2 shall, upon request by the defendant, be revoked or otherwise cease to have effect, if proceedings leading to a decision on the merits of the case are not initiated within a reasonable period, to be determined by the judicial authority ordering the measures where a Member's law so permits or, in the absence of such a determination, not to exceed 20 working days or 31 calendar days, whichever is the longer.

7. Where the provisional measures are revoked or where they lapse due to any act or omission by the applicant, or where it is subsequently found that there has been no infringement or threat of infringement of an intellectual property right, the judicial authorities shall have the authority to order the applicant, upon request of the defendant, to provide the defendant appropriate compensation for any injury caused by these measures.

8. To the extent that any provisional measure can be ordered as a result of administrative procedures, such procedures shall conform to principles equivalent in substance to those set forth in this Section.

Section 4 —Special Requirements Related to Border Measures[12]

Article 51

Suspension of Release by Customs Authorities

Members shall, in conformity with the provisions set out below, adopt procedures[13] to enable a right holder, who has valid grounds for suspecting that the importation of counterfeit trademark or pirated copyright goods[14] may take place, to lodge an application in writing with competent authorities, administrative or judicial, for the suspension by the customs authorities of the release into free circulation of such goods. Members may enable such an application to be made in respect of goods which involve other infringements of intellectual property rights, provided that the requirements of this Section are met. Members may also provide for corresponding procedures concerning the suspension by the customs authorities of the release of infringing goods destined for exportation from their territories.

---

[12] Where a Member has dismantled substantially all controls over movement of goods across its border with another Member with which it forms part of a customs union, it shall not be required to apply the provisions of this Section at that border.

[13] It is understood that there shall be no obligation to apply such procedures to imports of goods put on the market in another country by or with the consent of the right holder, or to goods in transit.

[14] For the purposes of this Agreement: (a) "counterfeit trademark goods" shall mean any goods, including packaging, bearing without authorization a trademark which is identical to the trademark validly registered in respect of such goods, or which cannot be distinguished in its essential aspects from such a trademark, and which thereby infringes the rights of the owner of the trademark in question under the law of the country of importation; (b) "pirated copyright goods" shall mean any goods which are copies made without the consent of the right holder or person duly authorized by the right holder in the country of production and which are made directly or indirectly from an article where the making of that copy would have constituted an infringement of a copyright or a related right under the law of the country of importation.

Article 52

Application

Any right holder initiating the procedures under Article 51 above shall be required to provide adequate evidence to satisfy the competent authorities that, under the laws of the country of importation, there is *prima facie* an infringement of the right holder's intellectual property right and to supply a sufficiently detailed description of the goods to make them readily recognizable by the customs authorities. The competent authorities shall inform the applicant within a reasonable period whether they have accepted the application and, where determined by the competent authorities, the period for which the customs authorities will take action.

Article 53

Security or Equivalent Assurance

1. The competent authorities shall have the authority to require an applicant to provide a security or equivalent assurance sufficient to protect the defendant and the competent authorities and to prevent abuse. Such security or equivalent assurance shall not unreasonably deter recourse to these procedures.

2. Where pursuant to an application under this Section the release of goods involving industrial designs, patents, layout-designs or undisclosed information into free circulation has been suspended by customs authorities on the basis of a decision other than by a judicial or other independent authority, and the period provided for in Article 55 has expired without the granting of provisional relief by the duly empowered authority, and provided that all other conditions for importation have been complied with, the owner, importer, or consignee of such goods shall be entitled to their release on the posting of a security in an amount sufficient to protect the right holder for any infringement. Payment of such security shall not prejudice any other remedy available to the right holder, it being understood that the security shall be released if the right holder fails to pursue the right of action within a reasonable period of time.

Article 54

Notice of Suspension

The importer and the applicant shall be promptly notified of the suspension of the release of goods according to Article 51.

Article 55

Duration of Suspension

If, within a period not exceeding 10 working days after the applicant has been served notice of the suspension, the customs authorities have not been informed that proceedings leading to a decision on the merits of the case have been initiated by a party other than the defendant, or that the duly empowered authority has taken provisional measures prolonging the suspension of the release of the goods, the goods shall be released, provided that all other conditions for importation or exportation have been complied with; in appropriate cases, this time-limit may be extended by another 10 working days. If proceedings leading to a decision on the merits of the case have been initiated, a review, including a right to be heard, shall take place upon request of the defendant with a view to deciding, within a reasonable period, whether these measures shall be modified, revoked or confirmed. Notwithstanding the above, where the suspension of the release of goods is carried out or continued in accordance with a provisional judicial measure, the provisions of paragraph 6 of Article 50 shall apply.

Article 56

Indemnification of the Importer and of the Owner of the Goods

Relevant authorities shall have the authority to order the applicant to pay the importer, the consignee and the owner of the goods appropriate compensation for any injury caused to them through the wrongful detention of goods or through the detention of goods released pursuant to Article 55.

Article 57

Right of Inspection and Information

Without prejudice to the protection of confidential information, Members shall provide the competent authorities the authority to give the right holder sufficient opportunity to have any goods detained by the customs authorities inspected in order to substantiate the right holder's claims. The competent authorities shall also have authority to give the importer an equivalent opportunity to have any such product inspected. Where a positive determination has been made on the merits of a case, Members may provide the competent authorities the authority to inform the right holder of the names and addresses of the consignor, the importer and the consignee and of the quantity of the goods in question.

Article 58

Ex Officio Action

Where Members require competent authorities to act upon their own initiative and to suspend the release of goods in respect of which they have acquired *prima facie* evidence that an intellectual property right is being infringed:

(a) the competent authorities may at any time seek from the right holder any information that may assist them to exercise these powers:

(b) the importer and the right holder shall be promptly notified of the suspension. Where the importer has lodged an appeal against the suspension with the competent authorities, the suspension shall be subject to the conditions, *mutatis mutandis*, set out at Article 55;

(c) Members shall only exempt both public authorities and officials from liability to appropriate remedial measures where actions are taken or intended in good faith.

Article 59

Remedies

Without prejudice to other rights of action open to the right holder and subject to the right of the defendant to seek review by a judicial authority, competent authorities shall have the authority to order the destruction or disposal of infringing goods in accordance with the principles set out in Article 46. In regard to counterfeit trademark goods, the authorities shall not allow the re-exportation of the infringing goods in an unaltered state or subject them to a different customs procedure, other than in exceptional circumstances.

Article 60

De Minimis Imports

Members may exclude from the application of the above provisions small quantities of goods of a non-commercial nature contained in travellers' personal luggage or sent in small consignments.

Section 5 —Criminal Procedures

Article 61

Members shall provide for criminal procedures and penalties to be applied at least in cases of wilful trademark counterfeiting or copyright piracy on a commercial scale. Remedies available shall include imprisonment and/or monetary fines sufficient to provide a deterrent, consistently with the level of penalties applied for crimes of a corresponding gravity. In appropriate cases, remedies available shall also include the seizure, forfeiture and destruction of the infringing goods and of any materials and implements the predominant use of which has been in the commission of the offence. Members may provide for criminal procedures and penalties to be applied in other cases of infringement of intellectual property rights, in particular where they are committed wilfully and on a commercial scale.

PART IV

ACQUISITION AND MAINTENANCE OF INTELLECTUAL PROPERTY RIGHTS AND RELATED INTER-PARTES PROCEDURES

Article 62

1. Members may require, as a condition of the acquisition or maintenance of the intellectual property rights provided for under Sections 2 through 6 of Part II, compliance with reasonable procedures and formalities. Such procedures and formalities shall be consistent with the provisions of this Agreement.

2. Where the acquisition of an intellectual property right is subject to the right being granted or registered, Members shall ensure that the procedures for grant or registration, subject to compliance with the substantive conditions for acquisition of the right, permit the granting or registration of the right within a reasonable period of time so as to avoid unwarranted curtailment of the period of protection.

3. Article 4 of the Paris Convention (1967) shall apply *mutatis mutandis* to service marks.

4. Procedures concerning the acquisition or maintenance of intellectual property rights and, where a Member's law provides for such procedures, administrative revocation and *inter partes* procedures such as opposition, revocation and cancellation, shall be governed by the general principles set out in paragraphs 2 and 3 of Article 41.

5. Final administrative decisions in any of the procedures referred to under paragraph 4 shall be subject to review by a judicial or quasi-judicial authority. However, there shall be no obligation to provide an opportunity for such review of decisions in cases of unsuccessful opposition or administrative revocation, provided that the grounds for such procedures can be the subject of invalidation procedures.

PART V

DISPUTE PREVENTION AND SETTLEMENT

Article 63

Transparency

1. Laws and regulations, and final judicial decisions and administrative rulings of general application, made effective by a Member pertaining to the subject matter of this Agreement (the availability, scope, acquisition, enforcement and prevention of the abuse of intellectual property rights) shall be published, or where such publication is not practicable made publicly available, in a national language, in such a manner as to enable governments and right holders to become acquainted with them. Agreements concerning the subject matter of this Agree-

ment which are in force between the government or a governmental agency of a Member and the government or a governmental agency of another Member shall also be published.

2. Members shall notify the laws and regulations referred to in paragraph 1 to the Council for TRIPS in order to assist that Council in its review of the operation of this Agreement. The Council shall attempt to minimize the burden on Members in carrying out this obligation and may decide to waive the obligation to notify such laws and regulations directly to the Council if consultations with WIPO on the establishment of a common register containing these laws and regulations are successful. The Council shall also consider in this connection any action required regarding notifications pursuant to the obligations under this Agreement stemming from the provisions of Article 6*ter* of the Paris Convention (1967).

3. Each Member shall be prepared to supply, in response to a written request from another Member, information of the sort referred to in paragraph 1. A Member, having reason to believe that a specific judicial decision or administrative ruling or bilateral agreement in the area of intellectual property rights affects its rights under this Agreement, may also request in writing to be given access to or be informed in sufficient detail of such specific judicial decisions or administrative rulings or bilateral agreements.

4. Nothing in paragraphs 1, 2 and 3 shall require Members to disclose confidential information which would impede law enforcement or otherwise be contrary to the public interest or would prejudice the legitimate commercial interests of particular enterprises, public or private.

Article 64

Dispute Settlement

1. The provisions of Articles XXII and XXIII of GATT 1994 as elaborated and applied by the Dispute Settlement Understanding shall apply to consultations and the settlement of disputes under this Agreement except as otherwise specifically provided herein.

2. Sub-paragraphs 1(b) and 1(c) of Article XXIII of GATT 1994 shall not apply to the settlement of disputes under this Agreement for a period of five years from the entry into force of the WTO Agreement.

3. During the time period referred to in paragraph 2, the Council for TRIPS shall examine the scope and modalities for complaints of the type provided for under subparagraphs 1(b) and 1(c) of Article XXIII of GATT 1994 made pursuant to this Agreement, and submit its recommendations to the Ministerial Conference for approval. Any decision of the Ministerial Conference to approve such recommendations or to extend the period in paragraph 2 shall be made only by consensus, and approved recommendations shall be effective for all Members without further formal acceptance process.

PART VI

TRANSITIONAL ARRANGEMENTS

Article 65

Transitional Arrangements

1. Subject to the provisions of paragraphs 2, 3 and 4, no Member shall be obliged to apply the provisions of this Agreement before the expiry of a general period of one year following the date of entry into force of the WTO Agreement.

2. Any developing country Member is entitled to delay for a further period of four years the date of application, as defined in paragraph 1, of the provisions of this Agreement other than Articles 3, 4, and 5.

3. Any other Member which is in the process of transformation from a centrally-planned into a market, free-enterprise economy and which is undertaking structural reform of its intellectual property system and facing special problems in the preparation and implementation of intellectual property laws and regulations, may also benefit from a period of delay as foreseen in paragraph 2.

4. To the extent that a developing country Member is obliged by this Agreement to extend product patent protection to areas of technology not so protectable in its territory on the general date of application of this Agreement for that Member, as defined in paragraph 2, it may delay the application of the provisions on product patents of Section 5 of Part II to such areas of technology for an additional period of five years.

5. A Member availing itself of a transitional period under paragraphs 1, 2, 3 or 4 shall ensure that any changes in its laws, regulations and practice made during that period do not result in a lesser degree of consistency with the provisions of this Agreement.

Article 66

Least-Developed Country Members

1. In view of their special needs and requirements of least-developed country Members, their economic, financial and administrative constraints, and their need for flexibility to create a viable technological base, such Members shall not be required to apply the provisions of this Agreement, other than Articles 3, 4 and 5, for a period of 10 years from the date of application as defined under paragraph 1 of Article 65. The Council for TRIPS shall, upon duly motivated request by a least-developed country Member, accord extensions of this period.

2. Developed country Members shall provide incentives to enterprises and institutions in their territories for the purpose of promoting and encouraging technology transfer to least-developed country Members in order to enable them to create a sound and viable technological base.

Article 67

Technical Cooperation

In order to facilitate the implementation of this Agreement, developed country Members shall provide, on request and on mutually agreed terms and conditions, technical and financial cooperation in favour of developing and least-developed country Members. Such cooperation shall include assistance in the preparation of laws and regulations on the protection and enforcement of intellectual property rights as well as on the prevention of their abuse, and shall include support regarding the establishment or reinforcement of domestic offices and agencies relevant to these matters, including the training of personnel.

PART VII

INSTITUTIONAL ARRANGEMENTS; FINAL PROVISIONS

Article 68

Council for Trade-Related Aspects of Intellectual Property Rights

The Council for TRIPS shall monitor the operation of this Agreement and, in particular, Members' compliance with their obligations hereunder, and shall afford Members the opportunity of consulting on matters relating to the trade-related aspects of intellectual property rights. It shall carry out such other responsibilities as assigned to it by the Members, and it shall, in particular, provide any assistance requested by them in the context of dispute settlement procedures. In carrying out its functions, the Council for TRIPS may consult with and seek information from any source it deems appropriate. In consultation with WIPO, the Council shall seek to establish, within one year of its first meeting, appropriate arrangements for cooperation with bodies of that Organization.

Article 69

International Cooperation

Members agree to cooperate with each other with a view to eliminating international trade in goods infringing intellectual property rights. For this purpose, they shall establish and notify contact points in their administrations and be ready to exchange information on trade in infringing goods. They shall, in particular, promote the exchange of information and cooperation between customs authorities with regard to trade in counterfeit trademark goods and pirated copyright goods.

Article 70

Protection of Existing Subject-Matter

1. This Agreement does not give rise to obligations in respect of acts which occurred before the date of application of the Agreement for the Member in question.

2. Except as otherwise provided for in this Agreement, this Agreement gives rise to obligations in respect of all subject matter existing at the date of application of this Agreement for the Member in question, and which is protected in that Member on the said date, or which meets or comes subsequently to meet the criteria for protection under the terms of this Agreement. In respect of this paragraph and paragraphs 3 and 4, copyright obligations with respect to existing works shall be solely determined under Article 18 of the Berne Convention (1971), and obligations with respect to the rights of producers of phonograms and performers in existing phonograms shall be determined solely under Article 18 of the Berne Convention (1971) as made applicable under paragraph 6 of Article 14 of this Agreement.

3. There shall be no obligation to restore protection to subject matter which on the date of application of this Agreement for the Member in question has fallen into the public domain.

4. In respect of any acts in respect of specific objects embodying protected subject matter which become infringing under the terms of legislation in conformity with this Agreement, and which were commenced, or in respect of which a significant investment was made, before the date of acceptance of the WTO Agreement by that Member, any Member may provide for a limitation of the remedies available to the right holder as to the continued performance of such acts after the date of application of this Agreement for that Member. In such cases the Member shall, however, at least provide for the payment of equitable remuneration.

5. A Member is not obliged to apply the provisions of Article 11 and of paragraph 4 of Article 14 with respect to originals or copies purchased prior to the date of application of this Agreement for that Member.

6. Members shall not be required to apply Article 31, or the requirement in

paragraph 1 of Article 27 that patent rights shall be enjoyable without discrimination as to the field of technology, to use without the authorization of the right holder where authorization for such use was granted by the government before the date this Agreement became known.

7. In the case of intellectual property rights for which protection is conditional upon registration, applications for protection which are pending on the date of application of this Agreement for the Member in question shall be permitted to be amended to claim any enhanced protection provided under the provisions of this Agreement. Such amendments shall not include new matter.

8. Where a Member does not make available as of the date of entry into force of the WTO Agreement patent protection for pharmaceutical and agricultural chemical products commensurate with its obligations under Article 27, that Member shall:

(a) notwithstanding the provisions of Part VI, provide as from the date of entry into force of the WTO Agreement a means by which applications for patents for such inventions can be filed;

(b) apply to these applications, as of the date of application of this Agreement, the criteria for patentability as laid down in this Agreement as if those criteria were being applied on the date of filing in that Member or, where priority is available and claimed, the priority date of the application; and

(c) provide patent protection in accordance with this Agreement as from the grant of the patent and for the remainder of the patent term, counted from the filing date in accordance with Article 33 of this Agreement, for those of these applications that meet the criteria for protection referred to in subparagraph (b) above.

9. Where a product is the subject of a patent application in a Member in accordance with paragraph 8(a), exclusive marketing rights shall be granted, notwithstanding the provisions of Part VI, for a period of five years after obtaining market approval in that Member or until a product patent is granted or rejected in that Member, whichever period is shorter, provided that, subsequent to the entry into force of the WTO Agreement, a patent application has been filed and a patent granted for that product in another Member and marketing approval obtained in such other Member.

Article 71

Review and Amendment

1. The Council for TRIPS shall review the implementation of this Agreement after the expiration of the transitional period referred to in paragraph 2 of Article 65. The Council shall, having regard to the experience gained in its implementation, review it two years after that date, and at identical intervals thereafter. The Council may also undertake reviews in the light of any relevant new developments which might warrant modification or amendment of this Agreement.

2. Amendments merely serving the purpose of adjusting to higher levels of protection of intellectual property rights achieve, and in force, in other multilateral agreements and accepted under those agreements by all Members of the WTO may be referred to the Ministerial Conference for action in accordance with paragraph 6 of Article X of the WTO Agreement on the basis of a consensus proposal from the Council for TRIPS.

Article 72

Reservations

Reservations may not be entered in respect of any of the provisions of this Agreement without the consent of the other Members.

Article 73
Security Exceptions

Nothing in this Agreement shall be construed:

(a) to require any Member to furnish any information the disclosure of which it considers contrary to its essential security interests; or

(b) to prevent a Member from taking any action which it considers necessary for the protection of its essential security interests:

    (i) relating to fissionable materials or the materials from which they are derived;

    (ii) relating to the traffic in arms, ammunition and implements of war and to such traffic in other goods and materials as is carried on directly or indirectly for the purpose of supplying a military establishment;

    (iii) taken in time of war or other emergency in international relations; or

(c) to prevent a Member from taking any action in pursuance of its obligations under the United Nations Charter for the maintenance of international peace and security.

F12. EUROPEAN CONVENTION RELATING TO QUESTIONS ON COPYRIGHT LAW AND NEIGHBOURING RIGHTS IN THE FRAMEWORK OF TRANSFRONTIER BROADCASTING BY SATELLITE

Strasbourg, 11.V.1994

PREAMBLE

The member States of the Council of Europe and the other States Party to the European Cultural Convention, signatory hereto,

Considering that the aim of the Council of Europe is to achieve a greater unity between its members for the purpose of safeguarding and realising the ideals and principles which are their common heritage and facilitating their economic and social progress;

Recalling their commitment to freedom of expression and information and the free flow of information and ideas as expressed, in particular, in the Declaration of 29 April 1982 of the Committee of Ministers of the Council of Europe on the freedom of expression and information;

Bearing in mind the concerns which inspired the adoption, by the Committee of Ministers, of Recommendation No. R (86) 2 on principles relating to copyright law questions in the field of television by satellite and cable, notably the need to safeguard the rights and interests of authors and other contributors when protected works and other contributions are broadcast by satellite;

Having regard to technical developments, in particular in the field of broadcasting by satellite, which have resulted in the blurring of the technical differences between direct broadcasting satellites and fixed service satellites, making it necessary to consider further legal aspects of broadcasting by satellite from the viewpoint of copyright law and neighbouring rights;

Bearing in mind, at the same time, the need not to hamper these new technical developments as well as the interest of the general public in having access to the media;

Concerned to promote the broadest possible harmonisation of the law of the member States, and the other States Party to the European Cultural Convention, on copyright and neighbouring rights with regard to new technical developments in the field of broadcasting by satellite,

HAVE AGREED AS FOLLOWS

For the purposes of copyright and neighbouring rights:

CHAPTER I

THE NOTION AND ACT OF BROADCASTING

Article 1

The notion of broadcasting

1. The transmission of works and other contributions by direct broadcasting satellite is broadcasting.

2. The transmission of works and other contributions by fixed service satellite under conditions which, as far as individual direct reception by the general public is concerned, are comparable to those prevailing in the case of direct broadcasting satellites, shall be treated as broadcasting.

3. The transmission of programme-carrying signals is encrypted form is considered to be broadcasting, in cases where the means for decoding the

broadcast are made available to the general public by the broadcasting organisation, or with its consent.

Article 2
The act of broadcasting

An act of broadcasting by satellite shall be considered to comprise both the up-link to the satellite and the down-link to the earth.

Chapter II

The Applicable Law

Article 3
The applicable law

1. A transmission of works and other contributions covered by Article 1 occurs in the State Party in the territory of which the transmission originates and, therefore, shall be governed exclusively by the law of that State.

2. The State Party in the territory of which the transmission originates means the State Party in which the programme-carrying signals transmitted by satellite are introduced, under the control and responsibility of the broadcasting organisation, into an uninterrupted chain of communication via the up-link and down to the earth.

3. When the transmission originates in a State which is not a party to this Convention, the law of which does not provide the level of protection of right holders foreseen in Articles 4 and 5 of this Convention, and when the programme-carrying signals are transmitted by satellite from an up-link station situated in a State Party to this Convention, the transmission shall be deemed to originate in the State Party concerned. Such shall also be deemed to be the case when a broadcasting organisation established in a State Party to this Convention is responsible for the transmission.

Article 4
Copyright

1. Authors of works mentioned in Article 2 of the Berne Convention for the Protection of Literary and Artistic Works shall, as far as transfrontier broadcasting by satellite is concerned, be protected in conformity with the provisions of that Convention (Paris Act, 1971). In particular, rights for transfrontier broadcasting by satellite concerning such works shall be acquired contractually.

2. Subject to the provisions of paragraph 3 and where the relevant applicable law according to Article 3 of this Convention has already provided so on the date of opening for signature of this Convention, a collective agreement concluded with a broadcasting organisation for a given category of works may be extended to right-holders of the same category who are not represented, on the following conditions:

— a non-represented right-holder, at any time, shall have the possibility of excluding, in his respect, the effect of an extended collective agreement and of exercising his rights on an individual basis. He may do so himself or through a collective organisation entitled to manage his rights;

— the transmission by satellite shall simulcast a terrestrial broadcast by the same broadcasting organisation.

3. The preceding paragraph shall not apply to cinematographic works, including works created by a process analogous to cinematography.

4. Where a State Party's legislation provides for the extension of a collective agreement in accordance with the provisions of paragraph 2, that State Party shall determine the broadcasting organisations entitled to avail themselves of such legislation.

Article 5
Neighbouring rights

1. As far as transfrontier broadcasting by satellite is concerned, performers, producers of phonograms and broadcasting organisations from States Parties to this Convention shall be protected, as a minimum, in accordance with the provisions of the Rome Convention for the Protection of Performers, Producers of Phonograms and Broadcasting Organisations (1961).

2. However, for the purposes of the present Convention, the rights of performers regarding the fixation and the reproduction of their performance shall be exclusive rights to authorise or prohibit. The same applies to the rights of performers concerning the broadcasting and the communication to the public of their performance, except where the performance is itself already a broadcast performance or made from a fixation.

3. A State Party shall not avail itself of the faculty provided for under Article 19 of the Rome Convention for the Protection of Performers, Producers of Phonograms and Broadcasting Organisations (1961).

4. Without prejudice to the provisions of the preceding paragraph, a State Party may provide that the signing of a contract concluded between a performer and a film producer concerning the production of a film has the effect of authorising the acts mentioned in the preceding paragraph provided that such contract provides for an equitable remuneration which cannot be waived by the performer.

5. For the purposes of this Convention, when phonograms published for commercial purposes, or reproductions thereof, are used for transfrontier broadcasting by satellite, States Parties shall provide a right under their national legislation in order to ensure that a single equitable remuneration is paid by the broadcasting organisation concerned and that this remuneration is shared between the relevant performers and producers of such phonograms.

Chapter III

Field of Application

Article 6
Retransmission

The simultaneous, complete and unchanged retransmission by terrestrial means of broadcasts by satellite are not, as such, covered by this Convention.

Article 7
Multilateral consultations

1. The Parties shall, within two years from the entry into force of this Convention and every two years thereafter, and, in any event, whenever a Party so requests, hold multilateral consultations within the Council of Europe to examine the application of this Convention and the advisability of revising it or extending any of its provisions. These consultations shall take place at meetings convened by the Secretary General of the Council of Europe.

2. Each Party shall have the right to appoint a representative to participate in these consultations. Any State referred to in Article 10 of this Convention, which is not a party to the Convention, and the European Community, shall have the right to be represented by an observer in these consultations.

3. After each consultation, the Parties shall forward to the Committee of Ministers of the Council of Europe a report on the consultation and on the functioning of the Convention, including, if they consider it necessary, proposals for the amendment of the Convention.

CHAPTER V

AMENDMENTS

Article 8

Amendments

1. Any proposal for the amendment of this Convention made in accordance with the provisions of Article 7, paragraph 3, of this Convention, shall be subject to the approval of the Committee of Ministers of the Council of Europe. After its approval, the text shall be forwarded to the Parties for acceptance.

2. Any amendment shall enter into force on the thirtieth day after all the Parties have informed the Secretary General of their acceptance thereof.

CHAPTER VI

OTHER INTERNATIONAL AGREEMENTS OR ARRANGEMENTS

Article 9

Other international agreements or arrangements

1. In their mutual relations, Parties which are members of the European Community shall apply Community rules and shall not therefore apply the rules arising from this Convention, except in so far as there is no Community rule governing the particular subject concerned.

2. Parties reserve the right to enter into international agreements among themselves in so far as such agreements grant to authors, performers, producers of phonograms or broadcasting organisations at least as extensive protection of their rights as that granted by this Convention or contain other provisions supplementing this Convention or facilitating the application of its provisions. The provisions of existing agreements which satisfy these conditions shall remain applicable.

3. Parties which avail themselves of the faculty provided for in the preceding paragraph shall notify the Secretary General of the Council of Europe who shall transmit this notification to the other Parties to this Convention.

CHAPTER VIII

FINAL CLAUSES

Article 10

Signature and entry into force

1. This Convention shall be open for signature by the member States of the

Council of Europe and the other States party to the European Cultural Convention, and by the European Community, which may express their consent to be bound by:

(a) signature without reservation as to ratification, acceptance or approval; or
(b) signature subject to ratification, acceptance or approval, followed by ratification, acceptance or approval.

2. Instruments of ratification, acceptance or approval shall be deposited with the Secretary General of the Council of Europe.

3. The Convention shall enter into force on the first day of the month following the expiration of a period of three months after the date on which seven States, of which at least five member States of the Council of Europe, have expressed their consent to be bound by the Convention in accordance with the provisions of this article.

4. In order to avoid any delay in the implementation of this Convention, a State may, at the time of signature or at any later date prior to the entry into force of the Convention in respect of that State, declare that it shall apply the Convention provisionally.

5. In respect of any signatory State, or the European Community, which subsequently expresses its consent to be bound by it, this Convention shall enter into force on the first day of the month following the expiration of a period of three months after the date of signature or of the deposit of the instrument of ratification, acceptance or approval.

Article 11

Accession by other States

1. After the entry into force of this Convention, the Committee of Ministers of the Council of Europe, after consulting the Contracting States, may invite any State which is not referred to in Article 10, paragraph 1, to accede to the Convention by a decision taken by the majority provided for in Article 20.d of the Statute of the Council of Europe and by the unanimous vote of the representatives of the Contracting States entitled to sit on the Committee of Ministers.

2. In respect of any acceding State, the Convention shall enter into force on the first day of the month following the expiration of a period of three months after the date of the deposit of the instrument of accession with the Secretary General of the Council of Europe.

Article 12

Territorial application

1. Any State may, at the time of signature or when depositing its instrument of ratification, acceptance, approval or accession, specify the territory or territories to which this Convention shall apply.

2. Any State may, at any later date, by declaration addressed to the Secretary General of the Council of Europe, extend the application of this Convention to any other territory specified in the declaration. In respect of such territory the Convention shall enter into force on the first day of the month following the expiration of a period of three months after the date of receipt of such declaration by the Secretary General.

3. Any declaration made under the two preceding paragraphs may, in respect of any territory mentioned in such declaration, be withdrawn by a notification addressed to the Secretary General. Such withdrawal shall become effective on the first day of the month following the expiration of a period of six months after the date of receipt of the notification by the Secretary General.

Article 13

Transitional arrangements

A State shall, at the time of signature or when depositing its instrument of ratification, acceptance, approval or accession, specify what rules shall apply to existing contracts. These rules should provide in particular that:

(a) agreements concerning the exploitation of works and other protected subject matter which are in force on 1 January 1995 shall be subject to the provisions of Article 3 as from 1 January 2000, if they expire after that date;

(b) where an international co-production agreement concluded before 1 January 1995 between a co-producer from a State Party and one or more co-producers from other States Parties or a third State expressly provides for a system of division of exploitation rights between the co-producers by geographical areas for all means of communication to the public, without distinguishing the arrangement applicable to communication to the public by satellite from the provisions applicable to the other means of communication, and where communication to the public by satellite of the co-production could prejudice the exclusivity, in particular the language exclusivity of one of the co-producers or his assignees in a given territory, the authorisation by one of the co-producers or his assignees for a communication to the public by satellite shall require the prior consent of the holder of that exclusivity, whether co-producer or assignee.

Article 14

Reservations

No reservation may be made in respect of the provisions of this Convention.

Article 15

Notification of legislation

A State, the legislation of which provides for the extension of collective agreements, as foreseen in Article 4 of this Convention, shall, at the time of signature, ratification, acceptance or approval in accordance with Article 10, paragraph 1.a or b, notify to the Secretary General of the Council of Europe the text of the said legislation, together with a list of broadcasters entitled to avail themselves of such extended collective agreements. Thereafter, the State concerned shall notify the Secretary General of the Council of Europe of any subsequent modification of the said legislation and of the list of broadcasters entitled to avail themselves of it.

Article 16

Denunciation

1. Any Party may, at any time, denounce this Convention by means of a notification addressed to the Secretary General of the Council of Europe.

2. Such denunciation shall become effective on the first day of the month following the expiration of a period of six months after the date of receipt of the notification by the Secretary General.

Article 17

Notifications

The Secretary General of the Council of Europe shall notify the member States of the Council of Europe, the other States Party to the European Cultural Convention, the European Community and any other State which has acceded or has been invited to accede to this Convention of:

 (a) any signature in accordance with Article 10;
 (b) the deposit of any instrument of ratification, acceptance, approval or accession in accordance with Articles 10 or 11;
 (c) any date of entry into force of this Convention in accordance with Articles 10 or 11;
 (d) any notification made in accordance with Articles 10, paragraph 4 and 15;
 (e) any other act, declaration, notification or communication relating to this Convention.

In witness whereof the undersigned, being duly authorised thereto, have signed this Convention.

Done at Strasbourg, this 11th day of May 1994, in English and French, both texts being equally authentic, in a single copy which shall be deposited in the archives of the Council of Europe. The Secretary General of the Council of Europe shall transmit certified copies to each member State of the Council of Europe, to the other states party to the European Cultural Convention, to the European Community and to any State invited to accede to this Convention.

F13. WIPO COPYRIGHT TREATY

Geneva, December 2 to 20, 1996

CONTENTS.

PREAMBLE

THE CONTRACTING PARTIES,

Desiring to develop and maintain the protection of the rights of authors in their literary and artistic works in a manner as effective and uniform as possible,

Recognizing the need to introduce new international rules and clarify the interpretation of certain existing rules in order to provide adequate solutions to the questions raised by new economic, social, cultural and technological developments,

Recognizing the profound impact of the development and convergence of information and communication technologies on the creation and use of literary and artistic works,

Emphasizing the outstanding significance of copyright protection as an incentive for literary and artistic creation,

Recognizing the need to maintain a balance between the rights of authors and the larger public interest, particularly education, research and access to information, as reflected in the Berne Convention,

Have agreed as follows:

F COPYRIGHT CONVENTIONS AND AGREEMENTS

Article 1

Relation to the Berne Convention

(1) This Treaty is a special agreement within the meaning of Article 20 of the Berne Convention for the Protection of Literary and Artistic Works, as regards Contracting Parties that are countries of the Union established by that Convention. This Treaty shall not have any connection with treaties other than the Berne Convention, nor shall it prejudice any rights and obligations under any other treaties.

(2) Nothing in this Treaty shall derogate from existing obligations that Contracting Parties have to each other under the Berne Convention for the Protection of Literary and Artistic Works.

(3) Hereinafter, "Berne Convention" shall refer to the Paris Act of July 24, 1971 of the Berne Convention for the Protection of Literary and Artistic Works.

(4) Contracting Parties shall comply with Articles 1 to 21 and the Appendix of the Berne Convention.

Article 2

Scope of Copyright Protection

Copyright protection extends to expressions and not to ideas, procedures, methods of operation or mathematical concepts as such.

Article 3

Application of Articles 2 to 6 of the Berne Convention

Contracting Parties shall apply *mutatis mutandis* the provisions of Articles 2 to 6 of the Berne Convention in respect of the protection provided for in this Treaty.

Article 4

Computer Programs

Computer programs are protected as literary works within the meaning of Article 2 of the Berne Convention. Such protection applies to computer programs, whatever may be the mode or form of their expression.

Article 5

Compilations of Data (Databases)

Compilations of data or other material, in any form, which by reason of the selection or arrangement of their contents constitute intellectual creations, are protected as such. This protection does not extend to the data or the material itself and is without prejudice to any copyright subsisting in the data or material contained in the compilation.

Article 6

Right of Distribution

(1) Authors of literary and artistic works shall enjoy the exclusive right of authorizing the making available to the public of the original and copies of their works through sale or other transfer of ownership.

(2) Nothing in this Treaty shall affect the freedom of Contracting Parties to determine the conditions, if any, under which the exhaustion of the right in paragraph (1) applies after the first sale or other transfer of ownership of the original or a copy of the work with the authorization of the author.

Article 7
Right of Rental

(1) Authors of
(i) computer programs;
(ii) cinematographic works; and
(iii) works embodied in phonograms, as determined in the national law of Contracting Parties,

shall enjoy the exclusive right of authorizing commercial rental to the public of the originals or copies of their works.

(2) Paragraph (1) shall not apply
(i) in the case of computer programs, where the program itself is not the essential object of the rental; and
(ii) in the case of cinematographic works, unless such commercial rental has led to widespread copying of such works materially impairing the exclusive right of reproduction.

(3) Notwithstanding the provisions of paragraph (1), a Contracting Party that, on April 15, 1994, had and continues to have in force a system of equitable remuneration of authors for the rental of copies of their works embodied in phonograms may maintain that system provided that the commercial rental of works embodied in phonograms is not giving rise to the material impairment of the exclusive right of reproduction of authors.

Article 8
Right of Communication to the Public

Without prejudice to the provisions of Articles 11(1)(ii), 11*bis*(1)(i) and (ii), 11*ter*(1)(ii), 14(1)(ii) and 14*bis*(1) of the Berne Convention, authors of literary and artistic works shall enjoy the exclusive right of authorizing any communication to the public of their works, by wire or wireless means, including the making available to the public of their works in such a way that members of the public may access these works from a place and at a time individually chosen by them.

Article 9
Duration of the Protection of Photographic Works

In respect of photographic works, the Contracting Parties shall not apply the provisions of Article 7(4) of the Berne Convention.

Article 10
Limitations and Exceptions

(1) Contracting Parties may, in their national legislation, provide for limitations of or exceptions to the rights granted to authors of literary and artistic works under this Treaty in certain special cases that do not conflict with a normal exploitation of the work and do not unreasonably prejudice the legitimate interests of the author.

(2) Contracting Parties shall, when applying the Berne Convention, confine any limitations of or exceptions to rights provided for therein to certain special cases that do not conflict with a normal exploitation of the work and do not unreasonably prejudice the legitimate interests of the author.

Article 11
Obligations concerning Technological Measures

Contracting Parties shall provide adequate legal protection and effective legal remedies against the circumvention of effective technological measures that are used by authors in connection with the exercise of their rights under this Treaty or the Berne Convention and that restrict acts, in respect of their works, which are not authorized by the authors concerned or permitted by law.

Article 12

Obligations concerning Rights Management Information

(1) Contracting Parties shall provide adequate and effective legal remedies against any person knowingly performing any of the following acts knowing, or with respect to civil remedies having reasonable grounds to know, that it will induce, enable, facilitate or conceal an infringement of any right covered by this Treaty or the Berne Convention:

  (i) to remove or alter any electronic rights management information without authority;

  (ii) to distribute, import for distribution, broadcast or communicate to the public, without authority, works or copies of works knowing that electronic rights management information has been removed or altered without authority.

(2) As used in this Article, "rights management information" means information which identifies the work, the author of the work, the owner of any right in the work, or information about the terms and conditions of use of the work, and any numbers or codes that represent such information, when any of these items of information is attached to a copy of a work or appears in connection with the communication of a work to the public.

Article 13

Application in Time

Contracting Parties shall apply the provisions of Article 18 of the Berne Convention to all protection provided for in this Treaty.

Article 14

Provisions on Enforcement of Rights

(1) Contracting Parties undertake to adopt, in accordance with their legal systems, the measures necessary to ensure the application of this Treaty.

(2) Contracting Parties shall ensure that enforcement procedures are available under their law so as to permit effective action against any act of infringement of rights covered by this Treaty, including expeditious remedies to prevent infringements and remedies which constitute a deterrent to further infringements.

Article 15

Assembly

(1)(a) The Contracting Parties shall have an Assembly.

  (b) Each Contracting Party shall be represented by one delegate who may be assisted by alternate delegates, advisors and experts.

  (c) The expenses of each delegation shall be borne by the Contracting Party that has appointed the delegation. The Assembly may ask the World Intellectual Property Organization (hereinafter referred to as "WIPO") to grant financial assistance to facilitate the participation of delegations of Contracting Parties that are regarded as developing countries in conformity with the established practice of the General Assembly of the United Nations or that are countries in transition to a market economy.

(2)(a) The Assembly shall deal with matters concerning the maintenance and development of this Treaty and the application and operation of this Treaty.

(b) The Assembly shall perform the function allocated to it under Article 17(2) in respect of the admission of certain intergovernmental organizations to become party to this Treaty.

(c) (c) The Assembly shall decide the convocation of any diplomatic conference for the revision of this Treaty and give the necessary instructions to the Director General of WIPO for the preparation of such diplomatic conference.

(3)(a) Each Contracting Party that is a State shall have one vote and shall vote only in its own name.

(b) Any Contracting Party that is an intergovernmental organization may participate in the vote, in place of its Member States, with a number of votes equal to the number of its Member States which are party to this Treaty. No such intergovernmental organization shall participate in the vote if any one of its Member States exercises its right to vote and *vice versa.*

(4) The Assembly shall meet in ordinary session once every two years upon convocation by the Director General of WIPO.

(5) The Assembly shall establish its own rules of procedure, including the convocation of extraordinary sessions, the requirements of a quorum and, subject to the provisions of this Treaty, the required majority for various kinds of decisions.

Article 16

International Bureau

The International Bureau of WIPO shall perform the administrative tasks concerning the Treaty.

Article 17

Eligibility for Becoming Party to the Treaty

(1) Any Member State of WIPO may become party to this Treaty.

(2) The Assembly may decide to admit any intergovernmental organization to become party to this Treaty which declares that it is competent in respect of, and has its own legislation binding on all its Member States on, matters covered by this Treaty and that it has been duly authorized, in accordance with its internal procedures, to become party to this Treaty.

(3) The European Community, having made the declaration referred to in the preceding paragraph in the Diplomatic Conference that has adopted this Treaty, may become party to this Treaty.

Article 18

Rights and Obligations under the Treaty

Subject to any specific provisions to the contrary in this Treaty, each Contracting Party shall enjoy all of the rights and assume all of the obligations under this Treaty.

Article 19

Signature of the Treaty

This Treaty shall be open for signature until December 31, 1997, by any Member State of WIPO and by the European Community.

Article 20

Entry into Force of the Treaty

This Treaty shall enter into force three months after 30 instruments of ratification or accession by States have been deposited with the Director General of WIPO.

Article 21

Effective Date of Becoming Party to the Treaty

This Treaty shall bind
  (i) the 30 States referred to in Article 20, from the date on which this Treaty has entered into force;
 (ii) each other State from the expiration of three months from the date on which the State has deposited its instrument with the Director General of WIPO;
(iii) the European Community, from the expiration of three months after the deposit of its instrument of ratification or accession if such instrument has been deposited after the entry into force of this Treaty according to Article 20, or, three months after the entry into force of this Treaty if such instrument has been deposited before the entry into force of this Treaty;
(iv) any other intergovernmental organization that is admitted to become party to this Treaty, from the expiration of three months after the deposit of its instrument of accession.

Article 22

No Reservations to the Treaty

No reservation to this Treaty shall be admitted.

Article 23

Denunciation of the Treaty

This Treaty may be denounced by any Contracting Party by notification addressed to the Director General of WIPO. Any denunciation shall take effect one year from the date on which the Director General of WIPO received the notification.

Article 24

Languages of the Treaty

(1) This Treaty is signed in a single original in English, Arabic, Chinese, French, Russian and Spanish languages, the versions in all these languages being equally authentic.

(2) An official text in any language other than those referred to in paragraph (1) shall be established by the Director General of WIPO on the request of an interested party, after consultation with all the interested parties. For the purposes of this paragraph, "interested party" means any Member State of WIPO whose official language, or one of whose official languages, is involved and the European Community, and any other intergovernmental organization that may become party to this Treaty, if one of its official languages is involved.

Article 25

Depositary

The Director General of WIPO is the depositary of this Treaty.

Agreed Statements Concerning the WIPO Copyright Treaty

Geneva, December 2 to 20, 1996

Concerning Article 1(4)

The reproduction right, as set out in Article 9 of the Berne Convention, and the exceptions permitted thereunder, fully apply in the digital environment, in particular to the use of works in digital form. It is understood that the storage of protected work in digital form in an electronic medium constitutes a reproduction within the meaning of Article 9 of the Berne Convention.

Concerning Article 3

It is understood that in applying Article 3 of this Treaty, the expression "country of the Union" in Articles 2 to 6 of the Berne Convention will be read as if it were a reference to a Contracting Party to this Treaty, in the application of those Berne Articles in respect of protection provided for in this Treaty. It is also understood that the expression "country outside the Union" in those Articles in the Berne Convention will, in the same circumstances, be read as if it were a reference to a country that is not a Contracting Party to this Treaty, and that "this Convention" in Articles 2(8), 2*bis*(2), 3, 4 and 5 of the Berne Convention will be read as if it were a reference to the Berne Convention and this Treaty. Finally, it is understood that a reference in Articles 3 to 6 of the Berne Convention to a "national of one of the countries of the Union" will, when these Articles are applied to this Treaty, mean, in regard to an intergovernmental organization that is a Contracting Party to this Treaty, a national of one of the countries that is member of that organization.

Concerning Article 4

The scope of protection for computer programs under Article 4 of this Treaty, read with Article 2, is consistent with Article 2 of the Berne Convention and on a par with the relevant provisions of the TRIPS Agreement.

Concerning Article 5

The scope of protection for compilations of data (databases) under Article 5 of this Treaty, read with Article 2, is consistent with Article 2 of the Berne Convention and on a par with the relevant provisions of the TRIPS Agreement.

Concerning Articles 6 and 7

As used in these Articles, the expressions "copies" and "original and copies," being subject to the right of distribution and the right of rental under the said Articles, refer exclusively to fixed copies that can be put into circulation as tangible objects.

Concerning Article 7

It is understood that the obligation under Article 7(1) does not require a Contracting Party to provide an exclusive right of commercial rental to authors who, under that Contracting Party's law, are not granted rights in respect of phonograms. It is understood that this obligation is consistent with Article 14(4) of the TRIPS Agreement.

Concerning Article 8

It is understood that the mere provision of physical facilities for enabling or making a communication does not in itself amount to communication within the meaning of this Treaty or the Berne Convention. It is further understood that nothing in Article 8 precludes a Contracting Party from applying Article 11*bis*(2).

Concerning Article 10

It is understood that the provisions of Article 10 permit Contracting Parties to carry forward and appropriately extend into the digital environment limitations and exceptions in their national laws which have been considered acceptable under the Berne Convention.

Similarly, these provisions should be understood to permit Contracting Parties to devise new exceptions and limitations that are appropriate in the digital network environment.

It is also understood that Article 10(2) neither reduces nor extends the scope of applicability of the limitations and exceptions permitted by the Berne Convention.

Concerning Article 12

It is understood that the reference to "infringement of any right covered by this Treaty or the Berne Convention" includes both exclusive rights and rights of remuneration.

It is further understood that Contracting Parties will not rely on this Article to devise or implement rights management systems that would have the effect of imposing formalities which are not permitted under the Berne Convention or this Treaty, prohibiting the free movement of goods or impeding the enjoyment of rights under this Treaty.

F14. WIPO Performances and Phonograms Treaty

Geneva, December 2 to 20, 1996

Contents

Preamble

Chapter I
General Provisions

Chapter II
Rights of Performers

Chapter III
Rights of Producers of Phonograms

Chapter IV
Common Provisions

Chapter V
Administrative and Final Clauses

Article 33:　Depositary

PREAMBLE

THE CONTRACTING PARTIES,

Desiring to develop and maintain the protection of the rights of performers and producers of phonograms in a manner as effective and uniform as possible,

Recognizing the need to introduce new international rules in order to provide adequate solutions to the questions raised by economic, social, cultural and technological developments,

Recognizing the profound impact of the development and convergence of information and communication technologies on the production and use of performances and phonograms,

Recognizing the need to maintain a balance between the rights of performers and producers of phonograms and the larger public interest, particularly education, research and access to information,

Have agreed as follows:

CHPATER I

GENERAL PROVISIONS

Article 1

Relation to Other Conventions

(1) Nothing in this Treaty shall derogate from existing obligations that Contracting Parties have to each other under the International Convention for the Protection of Performers, Producers of Phonograms and Broadcasting Organizations done in Rome, October 26, 1961 (hereinafter the "Rome Convention").

(2) Protection granted under this Treaty shall leave intact and shall in no way affect the protection of copyright in literary and artistic works. Consequently, no provision of this Treaty may be interpreted as prejudicing such protection.

(3) This Treaty shall not have any connection with, or shall it prejudice any rights and obligations under, any other treaties.

Article 2

Definitions

For the purposes of this Treaty:

(a) "performers" are actors, singers, musicians, dancers, and other persons who act, sing, deliver, declaim, play in, interpret, or otherwise perform literary or artistic works (or expressions of folk-lore);

(b) "phonogram" means the fixation of the sounds of a performance or of other sounds, or of a representation of sounds, other than in the form of a fixation incorporated in a cinematographic or other audiovisual work;

(c) "fixation" means the embodiment of sounds, or of the representations thereof, from which they can be perceived, reproduced or communicated through a device;

(d) "producer of a phonogram" means the person, or the legal entity, who or which takes the initiative and has the responsibility for the first fixation of the sounds of a performance or other sounds, or the representations of sounds;

(e) "publication" of a fixed performance or a phonogram means the offering of copies of the fixed performance or the phonogram to the public, with the consent of the rightholder, and provided that copies are offered to the public in reasonable quantity;

(f) "broadcasting" means the transmission by wireless means for public reception of sounds or of images and sounds or of the representations thereof; such transmission by satellite is also "broadcasting"; transmission of encrypted signals is "broadcasting" where the means for decrypting are provided to the public by the broadcasting organization or with its consent;

(g) "communication to the public" of a performance or a phonogram means the transmission to the public by any medium, otherwise than by broadcasting, of sounds of a performance or the sounds or the representations of sounds fixed in a phonogram. For the purposes of Article 15, "communication to the public" includes making the sounds or representations of sounds fixed in a phonogram audible to the public.

Article 3

Beneficiaries of Protection under this Treaty

(1) Contracting Parties shall accord the protection provided under this Treaty to the performers and producers of phonograms who are nationals of other Contracting Parties.

(2) The nationals of other Contracting Parties shall be understood to be those performers or producers of phonograms who would meet the criteria for eligibility for protection provided under the Rome Convention, were all the Contracting Parties to this Treaty Contracting States of that Convention. In respect of these criteria of eligibility, Contracting Parties shall apply the relevant definitions in Article 2 of this Treaty.

(3) Any Contracting Party availing itself of the possibilities provided in Article 5(3) of the Rome Convention or, for the purposes of Article 5 of the same Convention, Article 17 thereof shall make a notification as foreseen in those provisions to the Director General of the World Intellectual Property Organization (WIPO).

Article 4

National Treatment

(1) Each Contracting Party shall accord to nationals of other Contracting Parties, as defined in Article 3(2), the treatment it accords to its own nationals with regard to the exclusive rights specifically granted in this Treaty, and to the right to equitable remuneration provided for in Article 15 of this Treaty.

(2) The obligation provided for in paragraph (1) does not apply to the extent that another Contracting Party makes use of the reservations permitted by Article 15(3) of this Treaty.

CHAPTER II

RIGHTS OF PERFORMERS

Article 5

Moral Rights of Performers

(1) Independently of a performer's economic rights, and even after the transfer of those rights, the performer shall, as regards his live aural performances or performances fixed in phonograms, have the right to claim to be identified as the performer of his performances, except where omission is dictated by the manner of the use of the performance, and to object to any distortion, mutilation or other modification of his performances that would be prejudicial to his reputation.

(2) The rights granted to a performer in accordance with paragraph (1) shall, after his death, be maintained, at least until the expiry of the economic rights, and

shall be exercisable by the persons or institutions authorized by the legislation of the Contracting Party where protection is claimed. However, those Contracting Parties whose legislation, at the moment of their ratification of or accession to this Treaty, does not provide for protection after the death of the performer of all rights set out in the preceding paragraph may provide that some of these rights will, after his death, cease to be maintained.

(3) The means of redress for safeguarding the rights granted under this Article shall be governed by the legislation of the Contracting Party where protection is claimed.

Article 6

Economic Rights of Performers in their Unfixed Performances

Performers shall enjoy the exclusive right of authorizing, as regards their performances:

   (i) the broadcasting and communication to the public of their unfixed performances except where the performance is already a broadcast performance; and

  (ii) the fixation of their unfixed performances.

Article 7

Right of Reproduction

Performers shall enjoy the exclusive right of authorizing the direct or indirect reproduction of their performances fixed in phonograms, in any manner or form.

Article 8

Right of Distribution

(1) Performers shall enjoy the exclusive right of authorizing the making available to the public of the original and copies of their performances fixed in phonograms through sale or other transfer of ownership.

(2) Nothing in this Treaty shall affect the freedom of Contracting Parties to determine the conditions, if any, under which the exhaustion of the right in paragraph (1) applies after the first sale or other transfer of ownership of the original or a copy of the fixed performance with the authorization of the performer.

Article 9

Right of Rental

(1) Performers shall enjoy the exclusive right of authorizing the commercial rental to the public of the original and copies of their performances fixed in phonograms as determined in the national law of Contracting Parties, even after distribution of them by, or pursuant to, authorization by the performer.

(2) Notwithstanding the provisions of paragraph (1), a Contracting Party that, on April 15, 1994, had and continues to have in force a system of equitable remuneration of performers for the rental of copies of their performances fixed in phonograms, may maintain that system provided that the commercial rental of phonograms is not giving rise to the material impairment of the exclusive right of reproduction of performers.

Article 10

Right of Making Available of Fixed Performances

Performers shall enjoy the exclusive right of authorizing the making available to the public of their performances fixed in phonograms, by wire or wireless means, in such a way that members of the public may access them from a place and at a time individually chosen by them.

CHAPTER III

RIGHTS OF PRODUCERS OF PHONOGRAMS

Article 11

Right of Reproduction

Producers of phonograms shall enjoy the exclusive right of authorizing the direct or indirect reproduction of their phonograms, in any manner or form.

Article 12

Right of Distribution

(1) Producers of phonograms shall enjoy the exclusive right of authorizing the making available to the public of the original and copies of their phonograms through sale or other transfer of ownership.

(2) Nothing in this Treaty shall affect the freedom of Contracting Parties to determine the conditions, if any, under which the exhaustion of the right in paragraph (1) applies after the first sale or other transfer of ownership of the original or a copy of the phonogram with the authorization of the producer of the phonogram.

Article 13

Right of Rental

(1) Producers of phonograms shall enjoy the exclusive right of authorizing the commercial rental to the public of the original and copies of their phonograms, even after distribution of them by or pursuant to authorization by the producer.

(2) Notwithstanding the provisions of paragraph (1), a Contracting Party that, on April 15, 1994, had and continues to have in force a system of equitable remuneration of producers of phonograms for the rental of copies of their phonograms, may maintain that system provided that the commercial rental of phonograms is not giving rise to the material impairment of the exclusive rights of reproduction of producers of phonograms.

Article 14

Right of Making Available of Phonograms

Producers of phonograms shall enjoy the exclusive right of authorizing the making available to the public of their phonograms, by wire or wireless means, in such a way that members of the public may access them from a place and at a time individually chosen by them.

CHAPTER IV

COMMON PROVISIONS

Article 15

Right to Remuneration for Broadcasting and Communication to the Public

(1) Performers and producers of phonograms shall enjoy the right to a single

equitable remuneration for the direct or indirect use of phonograms published for commercial purposes for broadcasting or for any communication to the public.

(2) Contracting Parties may establish in their national legislation that the single equitable remuneration shall be claimed from the user by the performer or by the producer of a phonogram or by both. Contracting Parties may enact national legislation that, in the absence of an agreement between the performer and the producer of a phonogram, sets the terms according to which performers and producers of phonograms shall share the single equitable remuneration.

(3) Any Contracting Party may in a notification deposited with the Director General of WIPO, declare that it will apply the provisions of paragraph (1) only in respect of certain uses, or that it will limit their application in some other way, or that it will not apply these provisions at all.

(4) For the purposes of this Article, phonograms made available to the public by wire or wireless means in such a way that members of the public may access them from a place and at a time individually chosen by them shall be considered as if they had been published for commercial purposes.

Article 16

Limitations and Exceptions

(1) Contracting Parties may, in their national legislation, provide for the same kinds of limitations or exceptions with regard to the protection of performers and producers of phonograms as they provide for, in their national legislation, in connection with the protection of copyright in literary and artistic works.

(2) Contracting Parties shall confine any limitations of or exceptions to rights provided for in this Treaty to certain special cases which do not conflict with a normal exploitation of the performance or phonogram and do not unreasonably prejudice the legitimate interests of the performer or of the producer of the phonogram.

Article 17

Term of Protection

(1) The term of protection to be granted to performers under this Treaty shall last, at least, until the end of a period of 50 years computed from the end of the year in which the performance was fixed in a phonogram.

(2) The term of protection to be granted to producers of phonograms under this Treaty shall last, at least, until the end of a period of 50 years computed from the end of the year in which the phonogram was published, or failing such publication within 50 years from fixation of the phonogram, 50 years from the end of the year in which the fixation was made.

Article 18

Obligations concerning Technological Measures

Contracting Parties shall provide adequate legal protection and effective legal remedies against the circumvention of effective technological measures that are used by performers or producers of phonograms in connection with the exercise of their rights under this Treaty and that restrict acts, in respect of their performances or phonograms, which are not authorized by the performers or the producers of phonograms concerned or permitted by law.

Article 19

Obligations concerning Rights Management Information

(1) Contracting Parties shall provide adequate and effective legal remedies

against any person knowingly performing any of the following acts knowing, or with respect to civil remedies having reasonable grounds to know, that it will induce, enable, facilitate or conceal an infringement of any right covered by this Treaty:

(i) to remove or alter any electronic rights management information without authority;

(ii) to distribute, import for distribution, broadcast, communicate or make available to the public, without authority, performances, copies of fixed performances or phonograms knowing that electronic rights management information has been removed or altered without authority.

(2) As used in this Article, "rights management information" means information which identifies the performer, the performance of the performer, the producer of the phonogram, the phonogram, the owner of any right in the performance or phonogram, or information about the terms and conditions of use of the performance or phonogram, and any numbers or codes that represent such information, when any of these items of information is attached to a copy of a fixed performance or a phonogram or appears in connection with the communication or making available of a fixed performance or a phonogram to the public.

Article 20
Formalities

The enjoyment and exercise of the rights provided for in this Treaty shall not be subject to any formality.

Article 21
Reservations

Subject to the provisions of Article 15(3), no reservations to this Treaty shall be permitted.

Article 22
Application in Time

(1) Contracting Parties shall apply the provisions of Article 18 of the Berne Convention, *mutatis mutandis*, to the rights of performers and producers of phonograms provided for in this Treaty.

(2) Notwithstanding paragraph (1), a Contracting Party may limit the application of Article 5 of this Treaty to performances which occurred after the entry into force of this Treaty for that Party.

Article 23
Provisions on Enforcement of Rights

(1) Contracting Parties undertake to adopt, in accordance with their legal systems, the measures necessary to ensure the application of this Treaty.

(2) Contracting Parties shall ensure that enforcement procedures are available under their law so as to permit effective action against any act of infringement of rights covered by this Treaty, including expeditious remedies to prevent infringements and remedies which constitute a deterrent to further infringements.

CHAPTER V

ADMINISTRATIVE AND FINAL CLAUSES

Article 24
Assembly

(1)(a)The Contracting Parties shall have an Assembly.

(b) Each Contracting Party shall be represented by one delegate who may be assisted by alternate delegates, advisors and experts.

(c) The expenses of each delegation shall be borne by the Contracting Party that has appointed the delegation. The Assembly may ask WIPO to grant financial assistance to facilitate the participation of delegations of Contracting Parties that are regarded as developing countries in conformity with the established practice of the General Assembly of the United Nations or that are countries in transition to a market economy.

(2)(a)The Assembly shall deal with matters concerning the maintenance and development of this Treaty and the application and operation of this Treaty.

(b) The Assembly shall perform the function allocated to it under Article 26(2) in respect of the admission of certain intergovernmental organizations to become party to this Treaty.

(c) The Assembly shall decide the convocation of any diplomatic conference for the revision of this Treaty and give the necessary instructions to the Director General of WIPO for the preparation of such diplomatic conference.

(3)(a)Each Contracting Party that is a State shall have one vote and shall vote only in its own name.

(b) Any Contracting Party that is an intergovernmental organization may participate in the vote, in place of its Member States, with a number of votes equal to the number of its Member States which are party to this Treaty. No such intergovernmental organization shall participate in the vote if any one of its Member States exercises its right to vote and vice versa.

(4) The Assembly shall meet in ordinary session once every two years upon convocation by the Director General of WIPO.

(5) The Assembly shall establish its own rules of procedure, including the convocation of extraordinary sessions, the requirements of a quorum and, subject to the provisions of this Treaty, the required majority for various kinds of decisions.

Article 25

International Bureau

The International Bureau of WIPO shall perform the administrative tasks concerning the Treaty.

Article 26

Eligibility for Becoming Party to the Treaty

(1) Any Member State of WIPO may become party to this Treaty.

(2) The Assembly may decide to admit any intergovernmental organization to become party to this Treaty which declares that it is competent in respect of, and has its own legislation binding on all its Member States on, matters covered by this Treaty and that it has been duly authorized, in accordance with its internal procedures, to become party to this Treaty.

(3) The European Community, having made the declaration referred to in the preceding paragraph in the Diplomatic Conference that has adopted this Treaty, may become party to this Treaty.

Article 27

Rights and Obligations under the Treaty

Subject to any specific provisions to the contrary in this Treaty, each Contracting Party shall enjoy all of the rights and assume all of the obligations under this Treaty.

Article 28

Signature of the Treaty

This Treaty shall be open for signature until December 31, 1997, by any Member State of WIPO and by the European Community.

Article 29

Entry into Force of the Treaty

This Treaty shall enter into force three months after 30 instruments of ratification or accession by States have been deposited with the Director General of WIPO.

Article 30

Effective Date of Becoming Party to the Treaty

This Treaty shall bind
  (i) the 30 States referred to in Article 29, from the date on which this Treaty has entered into force;
 (ii) each other State from the expiration of three months from the date on which the State has deposited its instrument with the Director General of WIPO;
(iii) the European Community, from the expiration of three months after the deposit of its instrument of ratification or accession if such instrument has been deposited after the entry into force of this Treaty according to Article 29, or, three months after the entry into force of this Treaty if such instrument has been deposited before the entry into force of this Treaty;
(iv) any other intergovernmental organization that is admitted to become party to this Treaty, from the expiration of three months after the deposit of its instrument of accession.

Article 31

Denunciation of the Treaty

This Treaty may be denounced by any Contracting Party by notification addressed to the Director General of WIPO. Any denunciation shall take effect one year from the date on which the Director General of WIPO received the notification.

Article 32

Languages of the Treaty

(1) This Treaty is signed in a single original in English, Arabic, Chinese, French, Russian and Spanish languages, the versions in all these languages being equally authentic.

(2) An official text in any language other than those referred to in paragraph (1) shall be established by the Director General of WIPO on the request of an interested party, after consultation with all the interested parties. For the purposes of this paragraph, "interested party" means any Member State of WIPO whose official language, or one of whose official languages, is involved and the European Community, and any other intergovernmental organization that may become party to this Treaty, if one of its official languages is involved.

Article 33
Depositary

The Director General of WIPO is the depositary of this Treaty.

Agreed Statements Concerning The WIPO Performances and Phonograms Treaty

Geneva, December 2 to 20, 1996

Concerning Article 1

It is understood that Article 1(2) clarifies the relationship between rights in phonograms under this Treaty and copyright in works embodied in the phonograms. In cases where authorization is needed from both the author of a work embodied in the phonogram and a performer or producer owning rights in the phonogram, the need for the authorization of the author does not cease to exist because the authorization of the performer or producer is also required, and vice versa.

It is further understood that nothing in Article 1(2) precludes a Contracting Party from providing exclusive rights to a performer or producer of phonograms beyond those required to be provided under this Treaty.

Concerning Article 2(b)

It is understood that the definition of phonogram provided in Article 2(b) does not suggest that rights in the phonogram are in any way affected through their incorporation into a cinematographic or other audiovisual work.

Concerning Articles 2(e), 8, 9, 12, and 13

As used in these Articles, the expressions "copies" and "original and copies," being subject to the right of distribution and the right of rental under the said Articles, refer exclusively to fixed copies that can be put into circulation as tangible objects.

Concerning Article 3

It is understood that the reference in Articles 5(a) and 16(a)(iv) of the Rome Convention to "national of another Contracting State" will, when applied to this Treaty, mean, in regard to an intergovernmental organization that is a Contracting Party to this Treaty, a national of one of the countries that is a member of that organization.

Concerning Article 3(2)

For the application of Article 3(2), it is understood that fixation means the finalization of the master tape ("bande-mère").

Concerning Articles 7, 11 and 16

The reproduction right, as set out in Articles 7 and 11, and the exceptions permitted thereunder through Article 16, fully apply in the digital environment, in particular to the use of performances and phonograms in digital form. It is understood that the storage of a protected performance or phonogram in digital form in an electronic medium constitutes a reproduction within the meaning of these Articles.

Concerning Article 15

It is understood that Article 15 does not represent a complete resolution of the level of rights of broadcasting and communication to the public that should be enjoyed by performers and phonogram producers in the digital age. Delegations were unable to achieve consensus on differing proposals for aspects of exclusivity to be provided in certain circumstances or for rights to be provided without the possibility of reservations, and have therefore left the issue to future resolution.

Concerning Article 15

It is understood that Article 15 does not prevent the granting of the right conferred by this Article to performers of folklore and producers of phonograms recording folklore where such phonograms have not been published for commercial gain.

Concerning Article 16

The agreed statement concerning Article 10 (on Limitations and Exceptions) of the WIPO Copyright Treaty is applicable *mutatis mutandis* also to Article 16 (on Limitations and Exceptions) of the WIPO Performances and Phonograms Treaty.

Concerning Article 19

The agreed statement concerning Article 12 (on Obligations concerning Rights Management Information) of the WIPO Copyright Treaty is applicable *mutatis mutandis* also to Article 19 (on Obligations concerning Rights Management Information) of the WIPO Performances and Phonograms Treaty.

F15. CONVENTION ON CYBERCRIME

Budapest, November 23, 2001

CONTENTS

Preamble

PREAMBLE

The member States of the Council of Europe and the other States signatory hereto,

Considering that the aim of the Council of Europe is to achieve a greater unity between its members;

Recognising the value of fostering co-operation with the other States parties to this Convention;

Convinced of the need to pursue, as a matter of priority, a common criminal policy aimed at the protection of society against cybercrime, inter alia, by adopting appropriate legislation and fostering international co-operation;

Conscious of the profound changes brought about by the digitalisation, convergence and continuing globalisation of computer networks;

Concerned by the risk that computer networks and electronic information may also be used for committing criminal offences and that evidence relating to such offences may be stored and transferred by these networks;

Recognising the need for co-operation between States and private industry in combating cybercrime and the need to protect legitimate interests in the use and development of information technologies;

Believing that an effective fight against cybercrime requires increased, rapid and well-functioning international co-operation in criminal matters;

Convinced that the present Convention is necessary to deter action directed against the confidentiality, integrity and availability of computer systems, networks and computer data as well as the misuse of such systems, networks and data by providing for the criminalisation of such conduct, as described in this Convention, and the adoption of powers sufficient for effectively combating such criminal offences, by facilitating their detection, investigation and prosecution at both the domestic and international levels and by providing arrangements for fast and reliable international co-operation;

Mindful of the need to ensure a proper balance between the interests of law enforcement and respect for fundamental human rights as enshrined in the 1950 Council of Europe Convention for the Protection of Human Rights and Fundamental Freedoms, the 1966 United Nations International Covenant on Civil and Political Rights and other applicable international human rights treaties, which reaffirm the right of everyone to hold opinions without interference, as well as the right to freedom of expression, including the freedom to seek, receive, and impart information and ideas of all kinds, regardless of frontiers, and the rights concerning the respect for privacy;

Mindful also of the right to the protection of personal data, as conferred, for example, by the 1981 Council of Europe Convention for the Protection of Individuals with regard to Automatic Processing of Personal Data;

Considering the 1989 United Nations Convention on the Rights of the Child and the 1999 International Labour Organization Worst Forms of Child Labour Convention;

Taking into account the existing Council of Europe conventions on co-operation in the penal field, as well as similar treaties which exist between Council of Europe member States and other States, and stressing that the present Convention is intended to supplement those conventions in order to make criminal investigations and proceedings concerning criminal offences related to computer systems and data more effective and to enable the collection of evidence in electronic form of a criminal offence;

Welcoming recent developments which further advance international understanding and co-operation in combating cybercrime, including action taken by the United Nations, the OECD, the European Union and the G8;

Recalling Committee of Ministers Recommendations No. R (85) 10 concerning the practical application of the European Convention on Mutual Assistance in Criminal Matters in respect of letters rogatory for the interception of telecommunications, No. R (88) 2 on piracy in the field of copyright and neighbouring rights, No. R (87) 15 regulating the use of personal data in the police sector, No. R (95) 4 on the protection of personal data in the area of telecommunication services, with particular reference to telephone services, as well as No. R (89) 9 on computer-related crime providing guidelines for national legislatures concerning the definition of certain computer crimes and No. R (95) 13 concerning problems of criminal procedural law connected with information technology;

Having regard to Resolution No. 1 adopted by the European Ministers of Justice at their 21st Conference (Prague, 10 and 11 June 1997), which recommended that the Committee of Ministers support the work on cybercrime carried out by the European Committee on Crime Problems (CDPC) in order to bring domestic criminal law provisions closer to each other and enable the use of effective means of investigation into such offences, as well as to Resolution No. 3 adopted at the 23rd Conference of the European Ministers of Justice (London, 8 and 9 June 2000), which encouraged the negotiating parties to pursue their efforts with a view to finding appropriate solutions to enable the largest possible number of States to become parties to the Convention and acknowledged the need for a swift and efficient system of international co-operation, which duly takes into account the specific requirements of the fight against cybercrime;

Having also regard to the Action Plan adopted by the Heads of State and Government of the Council of Europe on the occasion of their Second Summit (Strasbourg, 10 and 11 October 1997), to seek common responses to the development of the new information technologies based on the standards and values of the Council of Europe;

HAVE AGREED AS FOLLOWS:

CHAPTER I

USE OF TERMS

Article 1

Definitions

For the purposes of this Convention:

a "computer system" means any device or a group of interconnected or related devices, one or more of which, pursuant to a program, performs automatic processing of data;

b "computer data" means any representation of facts, information or concepts in a form suitable for processing in a computer system, including a program suitable to cause a computer system to perform a function;

c "service provider" means:

i any public or private entity that provides to users of its service the ability to communicate by means of a computer system, and

ii any other entity that processes or stores computer data on behalf of such communication service or users of such service;

d "traffic data" means any computer data relating to a communication by means of a computer system, generated by a computer system that formed a part in the chain of communication, indicating the communication's origin, destination, route, time, date, size, duration, or type of underlying service.

CHAPTER II

MEASURES TO BE TAKEN AT THE NATIONAL LEVEL

Section 1 —Substantive criminal law

TITLE 1—Offences against the confidentiality, integrity and availability of computer data and systems

Article 2

Illegal access

Each Party shall adopt such legislative and other measures as may be necessary to establish as criminal offences under its domestic law, when committed intentionally, the access to the whole or any part of a computer system without right. A Party may require that the offence be committed by infringing security measures, with the intent of obtaining computer data or other dishonest intent, or in relation to a computer system that is connected to another computer system.

Article 3

Illegal interception

Each Party shall adopt such legislative and other measures as may be necessary to establish as criminal offences under its domestic law, when committed intentionally, the interception without right, made by technical means, of non-public transmissions of computer data to, from or within a computer system, including electromagnetic emissions from a computer system carrying such computer data. A Party may require that the offence be committed with dishonest intent, or in relation to a computer system that is connected to another computer system.

Article 4

Data interference

1 Each Party shall adopt such legislative and other measures as may be necessary to establish as criminal offences under its domestic law, when committed intentionally, the damaging, deletion, deterioration, alteration or suppression of computer data without right.

2 A Party may reserve the right to require that the conduct described in paragraph 1 result in serious harm.

Article 5
System interference

Each Party shall adopt such legislative and other measures as may be necessary to establish as criminal offences under its domestic law, when committed intentionally, the serious hindering without right of the functioning of a computer system by inputting, transmitting, damaging, deleting, deteriorating, altering or suppressing computer data.

Article 6
Misuse of devices

1 Each Party shall adopt such legislative and other measures as may be necessary to establish as criminal offences under its domestic law, when committed intentionally and without right:

a the production, sale, procurement for use, import, distribution or otherwise making available of:

i a device, including a computer program, designed or adapted primarily for the purpose of committing any of the offences established in accordance with the above Articles 2 through 5;

ii a computer password, access code, or similar data by which the whole or any part of a computer system is capable of being accessed,

with intent that it be used for the purpose of committing any of the offences established in Articles 2 through 5; and

b the possession of an item referred to in paragraphs a.i or ii above, with intent that it be used for the purpose of committing any of the offences established in Articles 2 through 5. A Party may require by law that a number of such items be possessed before criminal liability attaches.

2 This article shall not be interpreted as imposing criminal liability where the production, sale, procurement for use, import, distribution or otherwise making available or possession referred to in paragraph 1 of this article is not for the purpose of committing an offence established in accordance with Articles 2 through 5 of this Convention, such as for the authorised testing or protection of a computer system.

3 Each Party may reserve the right not to apply paragraph 1 of this article, provided that the reservation does not concern the sale, distribution or otherwise making available of the items referred to in paragraph 1 a.ii of this article.

TITLE 2C—Computer-related offences

Article 7
Computer-related forgery

Each Party shall adopt such legislative and other measures as may be necessary to establish as criminal offences under its domestic law, when committed intentionally and without right, the input, alteration, deletion, or suppression of computer data, resulting in inauthentic data with the intent that it be considered or acted upon for legal purposes as if it were authentic, regardless whether or not the data is directly readable and intelligible. A Party may require an intent to defraud, or similar dishonest intent, before criminal liability attaches.

Article 8
Computer-related fraud

Each Party shall adopt such legislative and other measures as may be necessary to establish as criminal offences under its domestic law, when committed intentionally and without right, the causing of a loss of property to another person by:

a any input, alteration, deletion or suppression of computer data;

b any interference with the functioning of a computer system,

with fraudulent or dishonest intent of procuring, without right, an economic benefit for oneself or for another person.

TITLE 3—Content-related offences

Article 9

Offences related to child pornography

1 Each Party shall adopt such legislative and other measures as may be necessary to establish as criminal offences under its domestic law, when committed intentionally and without right, the following conduct:

a producing child pornography for the purpose of its distribution through a computer system;

b offering or making available child pornography through a computer system;

c distributing or transmitting child pornography through a computer system;

d procuring child pornography through a computer system for oneself or for another person;

e possessing child pornography in a computer system or on a computer-data storage medium.

2 For the purpose of paragraph 1 above, the term "child pornography" shall include pornographic material that visually depicts:

a a minor engaged in sexually explicit conduct;

b a person appearing to be a minor engaged in sexually explicit conduct;

c realistic images representing a minor engaged in sexually explicit conduct.

3 For the purpose of paragraph 2 above, the term "minor" shall include all persons under 18 years of age. A Party may, however, require a lower age-limit, which shall be not less than 16 years.

4 Each Party may reserve the right not to apply, in whole or in part, paragraphs 1, sub-paragraphs d. and e, and 2, sub-paragraphs b. and c.

TITLE 4—Offences related to infringements of copyright and related rights

Article 10

Offences related to infringements of copyright and related rights

1 Each Party shall adopt such legislative and other measures as may be necessary to establish as criminal offences under its domestic law the infringement of copyright, as defined under the law of that Party, pursuant to the obligations it has undertaken under the Paris Act of 24 July 1971 revising the Berne Convention for the Protection of Literary and Artistic Works, the Agreement on Trade-Related Aspects of Intellectual Property Rights and the WIPO Copyright Treaty, with the exception of any moral rights conferred by such conventions, where such acts are committed wilfully, on a commercial scale and by means of a computer system.

2 Each Party shall adopt such legislative and other measures as may be necessary to establish as criminal offences under its domestic law the infringement of related rights, as defined under the law of that Party, pursuant to the obligations it

has undertaken under the International Convention for the Protection of Performers, Producers of Phonograms and Broadcasting Organisations (Rome Convention), the Agreement on Trade-Related Aspects of Intellectual Property Rights and the WIPO Performances and Phonograms Treaty, with the exception of any moral rights conferred by such conventions, where such acts are committed wilfully, on a commercial scale and by means of a computer system.

3 A Party may reserve the right not to impose criminal liability under paragraphs 1 and 2 of this article in limited circumstances, provided that other effective remedies are available and that such reservation does not derogate from the Party's international obligations set forth in the international instruments referred to in paragraphs 1 and 2 of this article.

TITLE 5—Ancillary liability and sanctions

Article 11
Attempt and aiding or abetting

1 Each Party shall adopt such legislative and other measures as may be necessary to establish as criminal offences under its domestic law, when committed intentionally, aiding or abetting the commission of any of the offences established in accordance with Articles 2 through 10 of the present Convention with intent that such offence be committed.

2 Each Party shall adopt such legislative and other measures as may be necessary to establish as criminal offences under its domestic law, when committed intentionally, an attempt to commit any of the offences established in accordance with Articles 3 through 5, 7, 8, and 9.1.a and c. of this Convention.

3 Each Party may reserve the right not to apply, in whole or in part, paragraph 2 of this article.

Article 12
Corporate liability

1 Each Party shall adopt such legislative and other measures as may be necessary to ensure that legal persons can be held liable for a criminal offence established in accordance with this Convention, committed for their benefit by any natural person, acting either individually or as part of an organ of the legal person, who has a leading position within it, based on:

    a a power of representation of the legal person;

    b an authority to take decisions on behalf of the legal person;

    c an authority to exercise control within the legal person.

2 In addition to the cases already provided for in paragraph 1 of this article, each Party shall take the measures necessary to ensure that a legal person can be held liable where the lack of supervision or control by a natural person referred to in paragraph 1 has made possible the commission of a criminal offence established in accordance with this Convention for the benefit of that legal person by a natural person acting under its authority.

3 Subject to the legal principles of the Party, the liability of a legal person may be criminal, civil or administrative.

4 Such liability shall be without prejudice to the criminal liability of the natural persons who have committed the offence.

Article 13
Sanctions and measures

1 Each Party shall adopt such legislative and other measures as may be neces-

sary to ensure that the criminal offences established in accordance with Articles 2 through 11 are punishable by effective, proportionate and dissuasive sanctions, which include deprivation of liberty.

2 Each Party shall ensure that legal persons held liable in accordance with Article 12 shall be subject to effective, proportionate and dissuasive criminal or non-criminal sanctions or measures, including monetary sanctions.

Section 2 —Procedural law

TITLE 1—Common provisions

Article 14

Scope of procedural provisions

1 Each Party shall adopt such legislative and other measures as may be necessary to establish the powers and procedures provided for in this section for the purpose of specific criminal investigations or proceedings.

2 Except as specifically provided otherwise in Article 21, each Party shall apply the powers and procedures referred to in paragraph 1 of this article to:

    a the criminal offences established in accordance with Articles 2 through 11 of this Convention;

    b other criminal offences committed by means of a computer system; and

    c the collection of evidence in electronic form of a criminal offence.

    a Each Party may reserve the right to apply the measures referred to in Article 20 only to offences or categories of offences specified in the reservation, provided that the range of such offences or categories of offences is not more restricted than the range of offences to which it applies the measures referred to in Article 21. Each Party shall consider restricting such a reservation to enable the broadest application of the measure referred to in Article 20.

    b Where a Party, due to limitations in its legislation in force at the time of the adoption of the present Convention, is not able to apply the measures referred to in Articles 20 and 21 to communications being transmitted within a computer system of a service provider, which system:

        i is being operated for the benefit of a closed group of users, and

        ii does not employ public communications networks and is not connected with another computer system, whether public or private,

    that Party may reserve the right not to apply these measures to such communications. Each Party shall consider restricting such a reservation to enable the broadest application of the measures referred to in Articles 20 and 21.

Article 15

Conditions and safeguards

1 Each Party shall ensure that the establishment, implementation and application of the powers and procedures provided for in this Section are subject to conditions and safeguards provided for under its domestic law, which shall provide for the adequate protection of human rights and liberties, including rights arising pursuant to obligations it has undertaken under the 1950 Council of Europe Convention for the Protection of Human Rights and Fundamental Freedoms, the 1966 United Nations International Covenant on Civil and Political Rights, and other applicable international human rights instruments, and which shall incorporate the principle of proportionality.

2 Such conditions and safeguards shall, as appropriate in view of the nature of the procedure or power concerned, inter alia, include judicial or other independent supervision, grounds justifying application, and limitation of the scope and the duration of such power or procedure.

3 To the extent that it is consistent with the public interest, in particular the sound administration of justice, each Party shall consider the impact of the powers and procedures in this section upon the rights, responsibilities and legitimate interests of third parties.

TITLE 2—Expedited preservation of stored computer data

Article 16

Expedited preservation of stored computer data

1 Each Party shall adopt such legislative and other measures as may be necessary to enable its competent authorities to order or similarly obtain the expeditious preservation of specified computer data, including traffic data, that has been stored by means of a computer system, in particular where there are grounds to believe that the computer data is particularly vulnerable to loss or modification.

2 Where a Party gives effect to paragraph 1 above by means of an order to a person to preserve specified stored computer data in the person's possession or control, the Party shall adopt such legislative and other measures as may be necessary to oblige that person to preserve and maintain the integrity of that computer data for a period of time as long as necessary, up to a maximum of ninety days, to enable the competent authorities to seek its disclosure. A Party may provide for such an order to be subsequently renewed.

3 Each Party shall adopt such legislative and other measures as may be necessary to oblige the custodian or other person who is to preserve the computer data to keep confidential the undertaking of such procedures for the period of time provided for by its domestic law.

4 The powers and procedures referred to in this article shall be subject to Articles 14 and 15.

Article 17

Expedited preservation and partial disclosure of traffic data

1 Each Party shall adopt, in respect of traffic data that is to be preserved under Article 16, such legislative and other measures as may be necessary to:

    a ensure that such expeditious preservation of traffic data is available regardless of whether one or more service providers were involved in the transmission of that communication; and

    b ensure the expeditious disclosure to the Party's competent authority, or a person designated by that authority, of a sufficient amount of traffic data to enable the Party to identify the service providers and the path through which the communication was transmitted.

2 The powers and procedures referred to in this article shall be subject to Articles 14 and 15.

TITLE 3—Production order

Article 18

Production order

1 Each Party shall adopt such legislative and other measures as may be necessary to empower its competent authorities to order:

a a person in its territory to submit specified computer data in that person's possession or control, which is stored in a computer system or a computer-data storage medium; and

b a service provider offering its services in the territory of the Party to submit subscriber information relating to such services in that service provider's possession or control.

2 The powers and procedures referred to in this article shall be subject to Articles 14 and 15.

3 For the purpose of this article, the term "subscriber information" means any information contained in the form of computer data or any other form that is held by a service provider, relating to subscribers of its services other than traffic or content data and by which can be established:

a the type of communication service used, the technical provisions taken thereto and the period of service;

b the subscriber's identity, postal or geographic address, telephone and other access number, billing and payment information, available on the basis of the service agreement or arrangement;

c any other information on the site of the installation of communication equipment, available on the basis of the service agreement or arrangement.

TITLE 4—Search and seizure of stored computer data

Article 19
Search and seizure of stored computer data

1 Each Party shall adopt such legislative and other measures as may be necessary to empower its competent authorities to search or similarly access:

a a computer system or part of it and computer data stored therein; and

b a computer-data storage medium in which computer data may be stored in its territory.

2 Each Party shall adopt such legislative and other measures as may be necessary to ensure that where its authorities search or similarly access a specific computer system or part of it, pursuant to paragraph 1.a, and have grounds to believe that the data sought is stored in another computer system or part of it in its territory, and such data is lawfully accessible from or available to the initial system, the authorities shall be able to expeditiously extend the search or similar accessing to the other system.

3 Each Party shall adopt such legislative and other measures as may be necessary to empower its competent authorities to seize or similarly secure computer data accessed according to paragraphs 1 or 2. These measures shall include the power to:

a seize or similarly secure a computer system or part of it or a computer-data storage medium;

b make and retain a copy of those computer data;

c maintain the integrity of the relevant stored computer data;

d render inaccessible or remove those computer data in the accessed computer system.

4 Each Party shall adopt such legislative and other measures as may be necessary to empower its competent authorities to order any person who has knowledge about the functioning of the computer system or measures applied to protect the computer data therein to provide, as is reasonable, the necessary information, to enable the undertaking of the measures referred to in paragraphs 1 and 2.

5 The powers and procedures referred to in this article shall be subject to Articles 14 and 15.

TITLE 5—Real-time collection of computer data

Article 20

Real-time collection of traffic data

1 Each Party shall adopt such legislative and other measures as may be necessary to empower its competent authorities to:

    a collect or record through the application of technical means on the territory of that Party, and

    b compel a service provider, within its existing technical capability:

        i to collect or record through the application of technical means on the territory of that Party; or

        ii to co-operate and assist the competent authorities in the collection or recording of,

    traffic data, in real-time, associated with specified communications in its territory transmitted by means of a computer system.

2 Where a Party, due to the established principles of its domestic legal system, cannot adopt the measures referred to in paragraph 1.a, it may instead adopt legislative and other measures as may be necessary to ensure the real-time collection or recording of traffic data associated with specified communications transmitted in its territory, through the application of technical means on that territory.

3 Each Party shall adopt such legislative and other measures as may be necessary to oblige a service provider to keep confidential the fact of the execution of any power provided for in this article and any information relating to it.

4 The powers and procedures referred to in this article shall be subject to Articles 14 and 15.

Article 21

Interception of content data

1 Each Party shall adopt such legislative and other measures as may be necessary, in relation to a range of serious offences to be determined by domestic law, to empower its competent authorities to:

    a collect or record through the application of technical means on the territory of that Party, and

    b compel a service provider, within its existing technical capability:

        i to collect or record through the application of technical means on the territory of that Party, or

        ii to co-operate and assist the competent authorities in the collection or recording of,

content data, in real-time, of specified communications in its territory transmitted by means of a computer system.

2 Where a Party, due to the established principles of its domestic legal system, cannot adopt the measures referred to in paragraph 1.a, it may instead adopt legislative and other measures as may be necessary to ensure the real-time collection or recording of content data on specified communications in its territory through the application of technical means on that territory.

3 Each Party shall adopt such legislative and other measures as may be necessary to oblige a service provider to keep confidential the fact of the execution of any power provided for in this article and any information relating to it.

4 The powers and procedures referred to in this article shall be subject to Articles 14 and 15.

Section 3 —Jurisdiction

Article 22

Jurisdiction

1 Each Party shall adopt such legislative and other measures as may be necessary to establish jurisdiction over any offence established in accordance with Articles 2 through 11 of this Convention, when the offence is committed:

  a in its territory; or

  b on board a ship flying the flag of that Party; or

  c on board an aircraft registered under the laws of that Party; or

  d by one of its nationals, if the offence is punishable under criminal law where it was committed or if the offence is committed outside the territorial jurisdiction of any State.

2 Each Party may reserve the right not to apply or to apply only in specific cases or conditions the jurisdiction rules laid down in paragraphs 1.b through 1.d of this article or any part thereof.

3 Each Party shall adopt such measures as may be necessary to establish jurisdiction over the offences referred to in Article 24, paragraph 1, of this Convention, in cases where an alleged offender is present in its territory and it does not extradite him or her to another Party, solely on the basis of his or her nationality, after a request for extradition.

4 This Convention does not exclude any criminal jurisdiction exercised by a Party in accordance with its domestic law.

5 When more than one Party claims jurisdiction over an alleged offence established in accordance with this Convention, the Parties involved shall, where appropriate, consult with a view to determining the most appropriate jurisdiction for prosecution.

CHAPTER III

INTERNATIONAL CO-OPERATION

Section 1 —General principles

TITLE 1—General principles relating to international co-operation

Article 23

General principles relating to international co-operation

The Parties shall co-operate with each other, in accordance with the provisions of this chapter, and through the application of relevant international instruments on international co-operation in criminal matters, arrangements agreed on the basis of uniform or reciprocal legislation, and domestic laws, to the widest extent possible for the purposes of investigations or proceedings concerning criminal offences related to computer systems and data, or for the collection of evidence in electronic form of a criminal offence.

TITLE 2   Principles relating to extradition

Article 24

Extradition

  a This article applies to extradition between Parties for the criminal offences established in accordance with Articles 2 through 11 of this Convention, provided that they are punishable under the laws of both Parties concerned by deprivation of liberty for a maximum period of at least one year, or by a more severe penalty.

b Where a different minimum penalty is to be applied under an arrangement agreed on the basis of uniform or reciprocal legislation or an extradition treaty, including the European Convention on Extradition (ETS No. 24), applicablle between two or more parties, the minimum penalty provided for under such arrangement or treaty shall apply.

2 The criminal offences described in paragraph 1 of this article shall be deemed to be included as extraditable offences in any extradition treaty existing between or among the Parties. The Parties undertake to include such offences as extraditable offences in any extradition treaty to be concluded between or among them.

3 If a Party that makes extradition conditional on the existence of a treaty receives a request for extradition from another Party with which it does not have an extradition treaty, it may consider this Convention as the legal basis for extradition with respect to any criminal offence referred to in paragraph 1 of this article.

4 Parties that do not make extradition conditional on the existence of a treaty shall recognise the criminal offences referred to in paragraph 1 of this article as extraditable offences between themselves.

5 Extradition shall be subject to the conditions provided for by the law of the requested Party or by applicable extradition treaties, including the grounds on which the requested Party may refuse extradition.

6 If extradition for a criminal offence referred to in paragraph 1 of this article is refused solely on the basis of the nationality of the person sought, or because the requested Party deems that it has jurisdiction over the offence, the requested Party shall submit the case at the request of the requesting Party to its competent authorities for the purpose of prosecution and shall report the final outcome to the requesting Party in due course. Those authorities shall take their decision and conduct their investigations and proceedings in the same manner as for any other offence of a comparable nature under the law of that Party.

a Each Party shall, at the time of signature or when depositing its instrument of ratification, acceptance, approval or accession, communicate to the Secretary General of the Council of Europe the name and address of each authority responsible for making or receiving requests for extradition or provisional arrest in the absence of a treaty.

b The Secretary General of the Council of Europe shall set up and keep updated a register of authorities so designated by the Parties. Each Party shall ensure that the details held on the register are correct at all times.

TITLE 3—General principles relating to mutual assistance

Article 25

General principles relating to mutual assistance

1 The Parties shall afford one another mutual assistance to the widest extent possible for the purpose of investigations or proceedings concerning criminal offences related to computer systems and data, or for the collection of evidence in electronic form of a criminal offence.

2 Each Party shall also adopt such legislative and other measures as may be necessary to carry out the obligations set forth in Articles 27 through 35.

3 Each Party may, in urgent circumstances, make requests for mutual assistance or communications related thereto by expedited means of communication,

including fax or e-mail, to the extent that such means provide appropriate levels of security and authentication (including the use of encryption, where necessary), with formal confirmation to follow, where required by the requested Party. The requested Party shall accept and respond to the request by any such expedited means of communication.

4 Except as otherwise specifically provided in articles in this chapter, mutual assistance shall be subject to the conditions provided for by the law of the requested Party or by applicable mutual assistance treaties, including the grounds on which the requested Party may refuse co-operation. The requested Party shall not exercise the right to refuse mutual assistance in relation to the offences referred to in Articles 2 through 11 solely on the ground that the request concerns an offence which it considers a fiscal offence.

5 Where, in accordance with the provisions of this chapter, the requested Party is permitted to make mutual assistance conditional upon the existence of dual criminality, that condition shall be deemed fulfilled, irrespective of whether its laws place the offence within the same category of offence or denominate the offence by the same terminology as the requesting Party, if the conduct underlying the offence for which assistance is sought is a criminal offence under its laws.

Article 26

Spontaneous information

1 A Party may, within the limits of its domestic law and without prior request, forward to another Party information obtained within the framework of its own investigations when it considers that the disclosure of such information might assist the receiving Party in initiating or carrying out investigations or proceedings concerning criminal offences established in accordance with this Convention or might lead to a request for co-operation by that Party under this chapter.

2 Prior to providing such information, the providing Party may request that it be kept confidential or only used subject to conditions. If the receiving Party cannot comply with such request, it shall notify the providing Party, which shall then determine whether the information should nevertheless be provided. If the receiving Party accepts the information subject to the conditions, it shall be bound by them.

TITLE 4—Procedures pertaining to mutual assistance requests in the absence of applicable international agreements

Article 27

Procedures pertaining to mutual assistance requests in the absence of applicable international agreements

1 Where there is no mutual assistance treaty or arrangement on the basis of uniform or reciprocal legislation in force between the requesting and requested Parties, the provisions of paragraphs 2 through 9 of this article shall apply. The provisions of this article shall not apply where such treaty, arrangement or legislation exists, unless the Parties concerned agree to apply any or all of the remainder of this article in lieu thereof.

a Each Party shall designate a central authority or authorities responsible for sending and answering requests for mutual assistance, the execution of such requests or their transmission to the authorities competent for their execution.

b The central authorities shall communicate directly with each other;

c Each Party shall, at the time of signature or when depositing its instrument of ratification, acceptance, approval or accession, communicate to the Secretary General of the Council of Europe the names and addresses of the authorities designated in pursuance of this paragraph;

d The Secretary General of the Council of Europe shall set up and keep updated a register of central authorities designated by the Parties. Each Party shall ensure that the details held on the register are correct at all times.

3 Mutual assistance requests under this article shall be executed in accordance with the procedures specified by the requesting Party, except where incompatible with the law of the requested Party.

4 The requested Party may, in addition to the grounds for refusal established in Article 25, paragraph 4, refuse assistance if:

a the request concerns an offence which the requested Party considers a political offence or an offence connected with a political offence, or

b it considers that execution of the request is likely to prejudice its sovereignty, security, ordre public or other essential interests.

5 The requested Party may postpone action on a request if such action would prejudice criminal investigations or proceedings conducted by its authorities.

6 Before refusing or postponing assistance, the requested Party shall, where appropriate after having consulted with the requesting Party, consider whether the request may be granted partially or subject to such conditions as it deems necessary.

7 The requested Party shall promptly inform the requesting Party of the outcome of the execution of a request for assistance. Reasons shall be given for any refusal or postponement of the request. The requested Party shall also inform the requesting Party of any reasons that render impossible the execution of the request or are likely to delay it significantly.

8 The requesting Party may request that the requested Party keep confidential the fact of any request made under this chapter as well as its subject, except to the extent necessary for its execution. If the requested Party cannot comply with the request for confidentiality, it shall promptly inform the requesting Party, which shall then determine whether the request should nevertheless be executed.

a In the event of urgency, requests for mutual assistance or communications related thereto may be sent directly by judicial authorities of the requesting Party to such authorities of the requested Party. In any such cases, a copy shall be sent at the same time to the central authority of the requested Party through the central authority of the requesting Party.

b Any request or communication under this paragraph may be made through the International Criminal Police Organisation (Interpol).

c Where a request is made pursuant to sub-paragraph a. of this article and the authority is not competent to deal with the request, it shall refer the request to the competent national authority and inform directly the requesting Party that it has done so.

d Requests or communications made under this paragraph that do not involve coercive action may be directly transmitted by the competent authorities of the requesting Party to the competent authorities of the requested Party.

e Each Party may, at the time of signature or when depositing its instrument of ratification, acceptance, approval or accession, inform the Secretary General of the Council of Europe that, for reasons of efficiency, requests made under this paragraph are to be addressed to its central authority.

Article 28

Confidentiality and limitation on use

1 When there is no mutual assistance treaty or arrangement on the basis of uniform or reciprocal legislation in force between the requesting and the requested Parties, the provisions of this article shall apply. The provisions of this article shall not apply where such treaty, arrangement or legislation exists, unless the Parties concerned agree to apply any or all of the remainder of this article in lieu thereof.

2 The requested Party may make the supply of information or material in response to a request dependent on the condition that it is:

a kept confidential where the request for mutual legal assistance could not be complied with in the absence of such condition, or

b not used for investigations or proceedings other than those stated in the request.

3 If the requesting Party cannot comply with a condition referred to in paragraph 2, it shall promptly inform the other Party, which shall then determine whether the information should nevertheless be provided. When the requesting Party accepts the condition, it shall be bound by it.

4 Any Party that supplies information or material subject to a condition referred to in paragraph 2 may require the other Party to explain, in relation to that condition, the use made of such information or material.

Section 2 —Specific provisions

TITLE 1—Mutual assistance regarding provisional measures

Article 29

Expedited preservation of stored computer data

1 A Party may request another Party to order or otherwise obtain the expeditious preservation of data stored by means of a computer system, located within the territory of that other Party and in respect of which the requesting Party intends to submit a request for mutual assistance for the search or similar access, seizure or similar securing, or disclosure of the data.

2 A request for preservation made under paragraph 1 shall specify:

a the authority seeking the preservation;

b the offence that is the subject of a criminal investigation or proceedings and a brief summary of the related facts;

c the stored computer data to be preserved and its relationship to the offence;

d any available information identifying the custodian of the stored computer data or the location of the computer system;

e the necessity of the preservation; and

f that the Party intends to submit a request for mutual assistance for the search or similar access, seizure or similar securing, or disclosure of the stored computer data.

3 Upon receiving the request from another Party, the requested Party shall take all appropriate measures to preserve expeditiously the specified data in accordance with its domestic law. For the purposes of responding to a request, dual criminality shall not be required as a condition to providing such preservation.

4 A Party that requires dual criminality as a condition for responding to a request for mutual assistance for the search or similar access, seizure or similar

securing, or disclosure of stored data may, in respect of offences other than those established in accordance with Articles 2 through 11 of this Convention, reserve the right to refuse the request for preservation under this article in cases where it has reasons to believe that at the time of disclosure the condition of dual criminality cannot be fulfilled.

5　In addition, a request for preservation may only be refused if:

　　a　the request concerns an offence which the requested Party considers a political offence or an offence connected with a political offence, or

　　b　the requested Party considers that execution of the request is likely to prejudice its sovereignty, security, ordre public or other essential interests.

6　Where the requested Party believes that preservation will not ensure the future availability of the data or will threaten the confidentiality of or otherwise prejudice the requesting Party's investigation, it shall promptly so inform the requesting Party, which shall then determine whether the request should nevertheless be executed.

7　Any preservation effected in response to the request referred to in paragraph 1 shall be for a period not less than sixty days, in order to enable the requesting Party to submit a request for the search or similar access, seizure or similar securing, or disclosure of the data. Following the receipt of such a request, the data shall continue to be preserved pending a decision on that request.

Article 30

Expedited disclosure of preserved traffic data

1　Where, in the course of the execution of a request made pursuant to Article 29 to preserve traffic data concerning a specific communication, the requested Party discovers that a service provider in another State was involved in the transmission of the communication, the requested Party shall expeditiously disclose to the requesting Party a sufficient amount of traffic data to identify that service provider and the path through which the communication was transmitted.

2　Disclosure of traffic data under paragraph 1 may only be withheld if:

　　a　the request concerns an offence which the requested Party considers a political offence or an offence connected with a political offence; or

　　b　the requested Party considers that execution of the request is likely to prejudice its sovereignty, security, ordre public or other essential interests.

TITLE 2—Mutual assistance regarding investigative powers

Article 31

Mutual assistance regarding accessing of stored computer data

1　A Party may request another Party to search or similarly access, seize or similarly secure, and disclose data stored by means of a computer system located within the territory of the requested Party, including data that has been preserved pursuant to Article 29.

2　The requested Party shall respond to the request through the application of international instruments, arrangements and laws referred to in Article 23, and in accordance with other relevant provisions of this chapter.

3　The request shall be responded to on an expedited basis where:

　　a　there are grounds to believe that relevant data is particularly vulnerable to loss or modification; or

　　b　the instruments, arrangements and laws referred to in paragraph 2 otherwise provide for expedited co-operation.

Article 32

Trans-border access to stored computer data with consent or where publicly available

A Party may, without the authorisation of another Party:

a access publicly available (open source) stored computer data, regardless of where the data is located geographically; or

b access or receive, through a computer system in its territory, stored computer data located in another Party, if the Party obtains the lawful and voluntary consent of the person who has the lawful authority to disclose the data to the Party through that computer system.

Article 33

Mutual assistance in the real-time collection of traffic data

1 The Parties shall provide mutual assistance to each other in the real-time collection of traffic data associated with specified communications in their territory transmitted by means of a computer system. Subject to the provisions of paragraph 2, this assistance shall be governed by the conditions and procedures provided for under domestic law.

2 Each Party shall provide such assistance at least with respect to criminal offences for which real-time collection of traffic data would be available in a similar domestic case.

Article 34

Mutual assistance regarding the interception of content data

The Parties shall provide mutual assistance to each other in the real-time collection or recording of content data of specified communications transmitted by means of a computer system to the extent permitted under their applicable treaties and domestic laws.

TITLE 3—24/7 Network

Article 35

24/7 Network

1 Each Party shall designate a point of contact available on a twenty-four hour, seven-day-a-week basis, in order to ensure the provision of immediate assistance for the purpose of investigations or proceedings concerning criminal offences related to computer systems and data, or for the collection of evidence in electronic form of a criminal offence. Such assistance shall include facilitating, or, if permitted by its domestic law and practice, directly carrying out the following measures:

a the provision of technical advice;

b the preservation of data pursuant to Articles 29 and 30;

c the collection of evidence, the provision of legal information, and locating of suspects.

a A Party's point of contact shall have the capacity to carry out communications with the point of contact of another Party on an expedited basis.

b If the point of contact designated by a Party is not part of that Party's authority or authorities responsible for international mutual assistance or extradition, the point of contact shall ensure that it is able to co-ordinate with such authority or authorities on an expedited basis.

3 Each Party shall ensure that trained and equipped personnel are available, in order to facilitate the operation of the network.

Chapter IV

Final provisions

Article 36

Signature and entry into force

1 This Convention shall be open for signature by the member States of the Council of Europe and by non-member States which have participated in its elaboration.

2 This Convention is subject to ratification, acceptance or approval. Instruments of ratification, acceptance or approval shall be deposited with the Secretary General of the Council of Europe.

3 This Convention shall enter into force on the first day of the month following the expiration of a period of three months after the date on which five States, including at least three member States of the Council of Europe, have expressed their consent to be bound by the Convention in accordance with the provisions of paragraphs 1 and 2.

4 In respect of any signatory State which subsequently expresses its consent to be bound by it, the Convention shall enter into force on the first day of the month following the expiration of a period of three months after the date of the expression of its consent to be bound by the Convention in accordance with the provisions of paragraphs 1 and 2.

Article 37

Accession to the Convention

1 After the entry into force of this Convention, the Committee of Ministers of the Council of Europe, after consulting with and obtaining the unanimous consent of the Contracting States to the Convention, may invite any State which is not a member of the Council and which has not participated in its elaboration to accede to this Convention. The decision shall be taken by the majority provided for in Article 20.d. of the Statute of the Council of Europe and by the unanimous vote of the representatives of the Contracting States entitled to sit on the Committee of Ministers.

2 In respect of any State acceding to the Convention under paragraph 1 above, the Convention shall enter into force on the first day of the month following the expiration of a period of three months after the date of deposit of the instrument of accession with the Secretary General of the Council of Europe.

Article 38

Territorial application

1 Any State may, at the time of signature or when depositing its instrument of ratification, acceptance, approval or accession, specify the territory or territories to which this Convention shall apply.

2 Any State may, at any later date, by a declaration addressed to the Secretary General of the Council of Europe, extend the application of this Convention to any other territory specified in the declaration. In respect of such territory the Convention shall enter into force on the first day of the month following the expiration of a period of three months after the date of receipt of the declaration by the Secretary General.

3 Any declaration made under the two preceding paragraphs may, in respect of any territory specified in such declaration, be withdrawn by a notification addressed to the Secretary General of the Council of Europe. The withdrawal shall become effective on the first day of the month following the expiration of a period of three months after the date of receipt of such notification by the Secretary General.

Article 39

Effects of the Convention

1 The purpose of the present Convention is to supplement applicable multilateral or bilateral treaties or arrangements as between the Parties, including the provisions of:
- the European Convention on Extradition, opened for signature in Paris, on 13 December 1957 (ETS No. 24);
- the European Convention on Mutual Assistance in Criminal Matters, opened for signature in Strasbourg, on 20 April 1959 (ETS No. 30);
- the Additional Protocol to the European Convention on Mutual Assistance in Criminal Matters, opened for signature in Strasbourg, on 17 March 1978 (ETS No. 99).

2 If two or more Parties have already concluded an agreement or treaty on the matters dealt with in this Convention or have otherwise established their relations on such matters, or should they in future do so, they shall also be entitled to apply that agreement or treaty or to regulate those relations accordingly. However, where Parties establish their relations in respect of the matters dealt with in the present Convention other than as regulated therein, they shall do so in a manner that is not inconsistent with the Convention's objectives and principles.

3 Nothing in this Convention shall affect other rights, restrictions, obligations and responsibilities of a Party.

Article 40

Declarations

By a written notification addressed to the Secretary General of the Council of Europe, any State may, at the time of signature or when depositing its instrument of ratification, acceptance, approval or accession, declare that it avails itself of the possibility of requiring additional elements as provided for under Articles 2, 3, 6 paragraph 1.b, 7, 9 paragraph 3, and 27, paragraph 9.e.

Article 41

Federal clause

1 A federal State may reserve the right to assume obligations under Chapter II of this Convention consistent with its fundamental principles governing the relationship between its central government and constituent States or other similar territorial entities provided that it is still able to co-operate under Chapter III.

2 When making a reservation under paragraph 1, a federal State may not apply the terms of such reservation to exclude or substantially diminish its obligations to provide for measures set forth in Chapter II. Overall, it shall provide for a broad and effective law enforcement capability with respect to those measures.

3 With regard to the provisions of this Convention, the application of which comes under the jurisdiction of constituent States or other similar territorial entities, that are not obliged by the constitutional system of the federation to take legislative measures, the federal government shall inform the competent authori-

ties of such States of the said provisions with its favourable opinion, encouraging them to take appropriate action to give them effect.

Article 42
Reservations

By a written notification addressed to the Secretary General of the Council of Europe, any State may, at the time of signature or when depositing its instrument of ratification, acceptance, approval or accession, declare that it avails itself of the reservation(s) provided for in Article 4, paragraph 2, Article 6, paragraph 3, Article 9, paragraph 4, Article 10, paragraph 3, Article 11, paragraph 3, Article 14, paragraph 3, Article 22, paragraph 2, Article 29, paragraph 4, and Article 41, paragraph 1. No other reservation may be made.

Article 43
Status and withdrawal of reservations

1 A Party that has made a reservation in accordance with Article 42 may wholly or partially withdraw it by means of a notification addressed to the Secretary General of the Council of Europe. Such withdrawal shall take effect on the date of receipt of such notification by the Secretary General. If the notification states that the withdrawal of a reservation is to take effect on a date specified therein, and such date is later than the date on which the notification is received by the Secretary General, the withdrawal shall take effect on such a later date.

2 A Party that has made a reservation as referred to in Article 42 shall withdraw such reservation, in whole or in part, as soon as circumstances so permit.

3 The Secretary General of the Council of Europe may periodically enquire with Parties that have made one or more reservations as referred to in Article 42 as to the prospects for withdrawing such reservation(s).

Article 44
Amendments

1 Amendments to this Convention may be proposed by any Party, and shall be communicated by the Secretary General of the Council of Europe to the member States of the Council of Europe, to the non-member States which have participated in the elaboration of this Convention as well as to any State which has acceded to, or has been invited to accede to, this Convention in accordance with the provisions of Article 37.

2 Any amendment proposed by a Party shall be communicated to the European Committee on Crime Problems (CDPC), which shall submit to the Committee of Ministers its opinion on that proposed amendment.

3 The Committee of Ministers shall consider the proposed amendment and the opinion submitted by the CDPC and, following consultation with the non-member States Parties to this Convention, may adopt the amendment.

4 The text of any amendment adopted by the Committee of Ministers in accordance with paragraph 3 of this article shall be forwarded to the Parties for acceptance.

5 Any amendment adopted in accordance with paragraph 3 of this article shall come into force on the thirtieth day after all Parties have informed the Secretary General of their acceptance thereof.

Article 45
Settlement of disputes

1 The European Committee on Crime Problems (CDPC) shall be kept informed regarding the interpretation and application of this Convention.

2 In case of a dispute between Parties as to the interpretation or application of this Convention, they shall seek a settlement of the dispute through negotiation or any other peaceful means of their choice, including submission of the dispute to the CDPC, to an arbitral tribunal whose decisions shall be binding upon the Parties, or to the International Court of Justice, as agreed upon by the Parties concerned.

Article 46

Consultations of the Parties

1 The Parties shall, as appropriate, consult periodically with a view to facilitating:

a the effective use and implementation of this Convention, including the identification of any problems thereof, as well as the effects of any declaration or reservation made under this Convention;

b the exchange of information on significant legal, policy or technological developments pertaining to cybercrime and the collection of evidence in electronic form;

c consideration of possible supplementation or amendment of the Convention.

2 The European Committee on Crime Problems (CDPC) shall be kept periodically informed regarding the result of consultations referred to in paragraph 1.

3 The CDPC shall, as appropriate, facilitate the consultations referred to in paragraph 1 and take the measures necessary to assist the Parties in their efforts to supplement or amend the Convention. At the latest three years after the present Convention enters into force, the European Committee on Crime Problems (CDPC) shall, in co-operation with the Parties, conduct a review of all of the Convention's provisions and, if necessary, recommend any appropriate amendments.

4 Except where assumed by the Council of Europe, expenses incurred in carrying out the provisions of paragraph 1 shall be borne by the Parties in the manner to be determined by them.

5 The Parties shall be assisted by the Secretariat of the Council of Europe in carrying out their functions pursuant to this article.

Article 47

Denunciation

1 Any Party may, at any time, denounce this Convention by means of a notification addressed to the Secretary General of the Council of Europe.

2 Such denunciation shall become effective on the first day of the month following the expiration of a period of three months after the date of receipt of the notification by the Secretary General.

Article 48

Notification

The Secretary General of the Council of Europe shall notify the member States of the Council of Europe, the non-member States which have participated in the elaboration of this Convention as well as any State which has acceded to, or has been invited to accede to, this Convention of:

a any signature;

b the deposit of any instrument of ratification, acceptance, approval or accession;

c any date of entry into force of this Convention in accordance with Articles 36 and 37;

d any declaration made under Article 40 or reservation made in accordance with Article 42;

e any other act, notification or communication relating to this Convention.

In witness whereof the undersigned, being duly authorised thereto, have signed this Convention.

Done at Budapest, this 23rd day of November 2001, in English and in French, both texts being equally authentic, in a single copy which shall be deposited in the archives of the Council of Europe. The Secretary General of the Council of Europe shall transmit certified copies to each member State of the Council of Europe, to the non-member States which have participated in the elaboration of this Convention, and to any State invited to accede to it.

F16. ADDITIONAL PROTOCOL TO THE CONVENTION ON CYBERCRIME, CONCERNING THE CRIMINALISATION OF ACTS OF A RACIST AND XENOPHOBIC NATURE COMMITTED THROUGH COMPUTER SYSTEMS

Strasbourg, January 28, 2003

Contents

CHAPTER I
COMMON PROVISIONS

CHAPTER II
MEASURES TO BE TAKEN AT NATIONAL LEVEL

CHAPTER III
RELATIONS BETWEEN THE CONVENTION AND THIS PROTOCOL

CHAPTER IV
FINAL PROVISIONS

The member States of the Council of Europe and the other States Parties to the Convention on Cybercrime, opened for signature in Budapest on 23 November 2001, signatory hereto;

Considering that the aim of the Council of Europe is to achieve a greater unity between its members;

Recalling that all human beings are born free and equal in dignity and rights;

Stressing the need to secure a full and effective implementation of all human rights without any discrimination or distinction, as enshrined in European and other international instruments;

Convinced that acts of a racist and xenophobic nature constitute a violation of human rights and a threat to the rule of law and democratic stability;

Considering that national and international law need to provide adequate legal responses to propaganda of a racist and xenophobic nature committed through computer systems;

Aware of the fact that propaganda to such acts is often subject to criminalisation in national legislation;

Having regard to the Convention on Cybercrime, which provides for modern and flexible means of international co-operation and convinced of the need to harmonise substantive law provisions concerning the fight against racist and xenophobic propaganda;

Aware that computer systems offer an unprecedented means of facilitating freedom of expression and communication around the globe;

Recognising that freedom of expression constitutes one of the essential foundations of a democratic society, and is one of the basic conditions for its progress and for the development of every human being;

Concerned, however, by the risk of misuse or abuse of such computer systems to disseminate racist and xenophobic propaganda;

Mindful of the need to ensure a proper balance between freedom of expression and an effective fight against acts of a racist and xenophobic nature;

Recognising that this Protocol is not intended to affect established principles relating to freedom of expression in national legal systems;

Taking into account the relevant international legal instruments in this field, and in particular the Convention for the Protection of Human Rights and Fundamental Freedoms and its Protocol No. 12 concerning the general prohibition of discrimination, the existing Council of Europe conventions on co-operation in the penal field, in particular the Convention on Cybercrime, the United Nations International Convention on the Elimination of All Forms of Racial Discrimination of 21 December 1965, the European Union Joint Action of 15 July 1996 adopted by the Council on the basis of Article K.3 of the Treaty on European Union, concerning action to combat racism and xenophobia;

Welcoming the recent developments which further advance international understanding and co-operation in combating cybercrime and racism and xenophobia;

Having regard to the Action Plan adopted by the Heads of State and Government of the Council of Europe on the occasion of their Second Summit (Strasbourg, 10-11 October 1997) to seek common responses to the developments of the new technologies based on the standards and values of the Council of Europe;

HAVE AGREED AS FOLLOWS:

CHAPTER I

COMMON PROVISIONS

Article 1

Purpose

The purpose of this Protocol is to supplement, as between the Parties to the Protocol, the provisions of the Convention on Cybercrime, opened for signature in Budapest on 23 November 2001 (hereinafter referred to as "the Convention"), as regards the criminalisation of acts of a racist and xenophobic nature committed through computer systems.

Article 2

Definition

1 For the purposes of this Protocol:

"racist and xenophobic material" means any written material, any image or any other representation of ideas or theories, which advocates, promotes or incites hatred, discrimination or violence, against any individual or group of individuals, based on race, colour, descent or national or ethnic origin, as well as religion if used as a pretext for any of these factors.

2 The terms and expressions used in this Protocol shall be interpreted in the same manner as they are interpreted under the Convention.

CHAPTER II

MEASURES TO BE TAKEN AT NATIONAL LEVEL

Article 3

Dissemination of racist and xenophobic material through computer systems

1 Each Party shall adopt such legislative and other measures as may be necessary to establish as criminal offences under its domestic law, when committed intentionally and without right, the following conduct:

distributing, or otherwise making available, racist and xenophobic material to the public through a computer system.

2 A Party may reserve the right not to attach criminal liability to conduct as defined by paragraph 1 of this article, where the material, as defined in Article 2, paragraph 1, advocates, promotes or incites discrimination that is not associated with hatred or violence, provided that other effective remedies are available.

3 Notwithstanding paragraph 2 of this article, a Party may reserve the right not to apply paragraph 1 to those cases of discrimination for which, due to established principles in its national legal system concerning freedom of expression, it cannot provide for effective remedies as referred to in the said paragraph 2.

Article 4

Racist and xenophobic motivated threat

Each Party shall adopt such legislative and other measures as may be necessary to establish as criminal offences under its domestic law, when committed intentionally and without right, the following conduct:

threatening, through a computer system, with the commission of a serious criminal offence as defined under its domestic law, (i) persons for the reason that they belong to a group, distinguished by race, colour, descent or national or ethnic origin, as well as religion, if used as a pretext for any of these factors, or (ii) a group of persons which is distinguished by any of these characteristics.

Article 5

Racist and xenophobic motivated insult

1 Each Party shall adopt such legislative and other measures as may be necessary to establish as criminal offences under its domestic law, when committed intentionally and without right, the following conduct:

insulting publicly, through a computer system, (i) persons for the reason that they belong to a group distinguished by race, colour, descent or national or ethnic origin, as well as religion, if used as a pretext for any of these factors; or (ii) a group of persons which is distinguished by any of these characteristics.

2 A Party may either:

    a require that the offence referred to in paragraph 1 of this article has the effect that the person or group of persons referred to in paragraph 1 is exposed to hatred, contempt or ridicule; or

    b reserve the right not to apply, in whole or in part, paragraph 1 of this article.

Article 6

Denial, gross minimisation, approval or justification of genocide or crimes against humanity

1 Each Party shall adopt such legislative measures as may be necessary to establish the following conduct as criminal offences under its domestic law, when committed intentionally and without right:

distributing or otherwise making available, through a computer system to the public, material which denies, grossly minimises, approves or justifies acts constituting genocide or crimes against humanity, as defined by international law and recognised as such by final and binding decisions of the International Military Tribunal, established by the London Agreement of 8 August 1945, or of any other international court established by relevant international instruments and whose jurisdiction is recognised by that Party.

2 A Party may either

  a require that the denial or the gross minimisation referred to in paragraph 1 of this article is committed with the intent to incite hatred, discrimination or violence against any individual or group of individuals, based on race, colour, descent or national or ethnic origin, as well as religion if used as a pretext for any of these factors, or otherwise

  b reserve the right not to apply, in whole or in part, paragraph 1 of this article.

Article 7

Aiding and abetting

Each Party shall adopt such legislative and other measures as may be necessary to establish as criminal offences under its domestic law, when committed intentionally and without right, aiding or abetting the commission of any of the offences established in accordance with this Protocol, with intent that such offence be committed.

CHAPTER III

RELATIONS BETWEEN THE CONVENTION AND THIS PROTOCOL

Article 8

Relations between the Convention and this Protocol

1 Articles 1, 12, 13, 22, 41, 44, 45 and 46 of the Convention shall apply, *mutatis mutandis*, to this Protocol.

2 The Parties shall extend the scope of application of the measures defined in Articles 14 to 21 and Articles 23 to 35 of the Convention, to Articles 2 to 7 of this Protocol.

CHAPTER IV

FINAL PROVISIONS

Article 9

Expression of consent to be bound

1 This Protocol shall be open for signature by the States which have signed the Convention, which may express their consent to be bound by either:

a signature without reservation as to ratification, acceptance or approval; or

b signature subject to ratification, acceptance or approval, followed by ratification, acceptance or approval.

2 A State may not sign this Protocol without reservation as to ratification, acceptance or approval, or deposit an instrument of ratification, acceptance or approval, unless it has already deposited or simultaneously deposits an instrument of ratification, acceptance or approval of the Convention.

3 The instruments of ratification, acceptance or approval shall be deposited with the Secretary General of the Council of Europe.

Article 10
Entry into force

1 This Protocol shall enter into force on the first day of the month following the expiration of a period of three months after the date on which five States have expressed their consent to be bound by the Protocol, in accordance with the provisions of Article 9.

2 In respect of any State which subsequently expresses its consent to be bound by it, the Protocol shall enter into force on the first day of the month following the expiration of a period of three months after the date of its signature without reservation as to ratification, acceptance or approval or deposit of its instrument of ratification, acceptance or approval.

Article 11
Accession

1 After the entry into force of this Protocol, any State which has acceded to the Convention may also accede to the Protocol.

2 Accession shall be effected by the deposit with the Secretary General of the Council of Europe of an instrument of accession which shall take effect on the first day of the month following the expiration of a period of three months after the date of its deposit.

Article 12
Reservations and declarations

1 Reservations and declarations made by a Party to a provision of the Convention shall be applicable also to this Protocol, unless that Party declares otherwise at the time of signature or when depositing its instrument of ratification, acceptance, approval or accession.

2 By a written notification addressed to the Secretary General of the Council of Europe, any Party may, at the time of signature or when depositing its instrument of ratification, acceptance, approval or accession, declare that it avails itself of the reservation(s) provided for in Articles 3, 5 and 6 of this Protocol. At the same time, a Party may avail itself, with respect to the provisions of this Protocol, of the reservation(s) provided for in Article 22, paragraph 2, and Article 41, paragraph 1, of the Convention, irrespective of the implementation made by that Party under the Convention. No other reservations may be made.

3 By a written notification addressed to the Secretary General of the Council of Europe, any State may, at the time of signature or when depositing its instrument of ratification, acceptance, approval or accession, declare that it avails itself of the possibility of requiring additional elements as provided for in Article 5, paragraph 2.a, and Article 6, paragraph 2.a, of this Protocol.

Article 13
Status and withdrawal of reservations

1 A Party that has made a reservation in accordance with Article 12 above

shall withdraw such reservation, in whole or in part, as soon as circumstances so permit. Such withdrawal shall take effect on the date of receipt of a notification addressed to the Secretary General of the Council of Europe. If the notification states that the withdrawal of a reservation is to take effect on a date specified therein, and such date is later than the date on which the notification is received by the Secretary General, the withdrawal shall take effect on such a later date.

2 The Secretary General of the Council of Europe may periodically enquire with Parties that have made one or more reservations in accordance with Article 12 as to the prospects for withdrawing such reservation(s).

Article 14

Territorial application

1 Any Party may at the time of signature or when depositing its instrument of ratification, acceptance, approval or accession, specify the territory or territories to which this Protocol shall apply.

2 Any Party may, at any later date, by a declaration addressed to the Secretary General of the Council of Europe, extend the application of this Protocol to any other territory specified in the declaration. In respect of such territory, the Protocol shall enter into force on the first day of the month following the expiration of a period of three months after the date of receipt of the declaration by the Secretary General.

3 Any declaration made under the two preceding paragraphs may, in respect of any territory specified in such declaration, be withdrawn by a notification addressed to the Secretary General of the Council of Europe. The withdrawal shall become effective on the first day of the month following the expiration of a period of three months after the date of receipt of such notification by the Secretary General.

Article 15

Denunciation

1 Any Party may, at any time, denounce this Protocol by means of a notification addressed to the Secretary General of the Council of Europe.

2 Such denunciation shall become effective on the first day of the month following the expiration of a period of three months after the date of receipt of the notification by the Secretary General.

Article 16

Notification

The Secretary General of the Council of Europe shall notify the member States of the Council of Europe, the non-member States which have participated in the elaboration of this Protocol as well as any State which has acceded to, or has been invited to accede to, this Protocol of:

    a   any signature;

    b   the deposit of any instrument of ratification, acceptance, approval or accession;

    c   any date of entry into force of this Protocol in accordance with its Articles 9, 10 and 11;

    d   any other act, notification or communication relating to this Protocol.

In witness whereof the undersigned, being duly authorised thereto, have signed this Protocol.

Done at Strasbourg, this 28 January 2003, in English and in French, both texts being equally authentic, in a single copy which shall be deposited in the archives of the Council of Europe. The Secretary General of the Council of Europe shall transmit certified copies to each member State of the Council of Europe, to the non-member States which have participated in the elaboration of this Protocol, and to any State invited to accede to it.

F17. ANTI-COUNTERFEITING TRADE AGREEMENT

[Opened for signature on May 1, 2011.]

The Parties to this Agreement,

Noting that effective enforcement of intellectual property rights is critical to sustaining economic growth across all industries and globally;

Noting further that the proliferation of counterfeit and pirated goods, as well as of services that distribute infringing material, undermines legitimate trade and sustainable development of the world economy, causes significant financial losses for right holders and for legitimate businesses, and, in some cases, provides a source of revenue for organized crime and otherwise poses risks to the public;

Desiring to combat such proliferation through enhanced international cooperation and more effective international enforcement;

Intending to provide effective and appropriate means, complementing the TRIPS Agreement, for the enforcement of intellectual property rights, taking into account differences in their respective legal systems and practices;

Desiring to ensure that measures and procedures to enforce intellectual property rights do not themselves become barriers to legitimate trade;

Desiring to address the problem of infringement of intellectual property rights, including infringement taking place in the digital environment, in particular with respect to copyright or related rights, in a manner that balances the rights and interests of the relevant right holders, service providers, and users;

Desiring to promote cooperation between service providers and right holders to address relevant infringements in the digital environment;

Desiring that this Agreement operates in a manner mutually supportive of international enforcement work and cooperation conducted within relevant international organizations;

Recognizing the principles set forth in the Doha Declaration on the TRIPS Agreement and Public Health, adopted on 14 November 2001, at the Fourth WTO Ministerial Conference;

Hereby agree as follows:

CHAPTER I INITIAL PROVISIONS AND DEFINITIONS

Section 1: —Initial Provisions

Article 1: Relation to Other Agreements

Nothing in this Agreement shall derogate from any obligation of a Party with respect to any other Party under existing agreements, including the TRIPS Agreement.

Article 2: Nature and Scope of Obligations

1. Each Party shall give effect to the provisions of this Agreement. A Party may implement in its law more extensive enforcement of intellectual property rights than is required by this Agreement, provided that such enforcement does not contravene the provisions of this Agreement. Each Party shall be free to determine the appropriate method of implementing the provisions of this Agreement within its own legal system and practice.

2. Nothing in this Agreement creates any obligation with respect to the distribution of resources as between enforcement of intellectual property rights and enforcement of law in general.

3. The objectives and principles set forth in Part I of the TRIPS Agreement, in particular in Articles 7 and 8, shall apply, mutatis mutandis, to this Agreement.

Article 3: Relation to Standards concerning the Availability and Scope of Intellectual Property Rights

1. This Agreement shall be without prejudice to provisions in a Party's law governing the availability, acquisition, scope, and maintenance of intellectual property rights.
2. This Agreement does not create any obligation on a Party to apply measures where a right in intellectual property is not protected under its laws and regulations.

Article 4: Privacy and Disclosure of Information

1. Nothing in this Agreement shall require a Party to disclose:
   (a) information, the disclosure of which would be contrary to its law, including laws protecting privacy rights, or international agreements to which it is party;
   (b) confidential information, the disclosure of which would impede law enforcement or otherwise be contrary to the public interest; or
   (c) confidential information, the disclosure of which would prejudice the legitimate commercial interests of particular enterprises, public or private.
2. When a Party provides written information pursuant to the provisions of this Agreement, the Party receiving the information shall, subject to its law and practice, refrain from disclosing or using the information for a purpose other than that for which the information was provided, except with the prior consent of the Party providing the information.

Section 2: —General Definitions

Article 5: General Definitions

For the purposes of this Agreement, unless otherwise specified:
(a) **ACTA** means the *Anti-Counterfeiting Trade Agreement*;
(b) **Committee** means the ACTA Committee established under Chapter V (Institutional Arrangements);
(c) **competent authorities** includes the appropriate judicial, administrative, or law enforcement authorities under a Party's law;
(d) **counterfeit trademark goods** means any goods, including packaging, bearing without authorization a trademark which is identical to the trademark validly registered in respect of such goods, or which cannot be distinguished in its essential aspects from such a trademark, and which thereby infringes the rights of the owner of the trademark in question under the law of the country in which the procedures set forth in Chapter II (Legal Framework for Enforcement of Intellectual Property Rights) are invoked;
(e) **country** is to be understood to have the same meaning as that set forth in the Explanatory Notes to the WTO Agreement;
(f) **customs transit** means the customs procedure under which goods are transported under customs control from one customs office to another;
(g) **days** means calendar days;
(h) **intellectual property** refers to all categories of intellectual property that are the subject of Sections 1 through 7 of Part II of the TRIPS Agreement;
(i) **in-transit goods** means goods under customs transit or transhipment;
(j) **person** means either a natural person or a legal person;

(k) **pirated copyright goods** means any goods which are copies made without the consent of the right holder or person duly authorized by the right holder in the country of production and which are made directly or indirectly from an article where the making of that copy would have constituted an infringement of a copyright or a related right under the law of the country in which the procedures set forth in Chapter II (Legal Framework for Enforcement of Intellectual Property Rights) are invoked;

(l) **right holder** includes a federation or an association having the legal standing to assert rights in intellectual property;

(m) **territory**, for the purposes of Section 3 (Border Measures) of Chapter II (Legal Framework for Enforcement of Intellectual Property Rights), means the customs territory and all free zones[1] of a Party;

(n) **transhipment** means the customs procedure under which goods are transferred under customs control from the importing means of transport to the exporting means of transport within the area of one customs office which is the office of both importation and exportation;

(o) **TRIPS Agreement** means the Agreement on Trade-Related Aspects of Intellectual Property Rights, contained in Annex 1C to the WTO Agreement;

(p) **WTO** means the World Trade Organization; and

(q) **WTO Agreement** means the Marrakesh Agreement Establishing the World Trade Organization, done on April 15, 1994;

Chapter II Legal Framework for Enforcement of Intellectual Property Rights

Section 1: —General Obligations

Article 6: General Obligations with Respect to Enforcement

1. Each Party shall ensure that enforcement procedures are available under its law so as to permit effective action against any act of infringement of intellectual property rights covered by this Agreement, including expeditious remedies to prevent infringements and remedies which constitute a deterrent to further infringements. These procedures shall be applied in such a manner as to avoid the creation of barriers to legitimate trade and to provide for safeguards against their abuse.

2. Procedures adopted, maintained, or applied to implement the provisions of this Chapter shall be fair and equitable, and shall provide for the rights of all participants subject to such procedures to be appropriately protected. These procedures shall not be unnecessarily complicated or costly, or entail unreasonable time-limits or unwarranted delays.

3. In implementing the provisions of this Chapter, each Party shall take into account the need for proportionality between the seriousness of the infringement, the interests of third parties, and the applicable measures, remedies and penalties.

4. No provision of this Chapter shall be construed to require a Party to make its officials subject to liability for acts undertaken in the performance of their official duties.

---

[1] For greater certainty, the Parties acknowledge that free zone means a part of the territory of a Party where any goods introduced are generally regarded, insofar as import duties and taxes are concerned, as being outside the customs territory.

Section 2: —Civil Enforcement[2]

Article 7: Availability of Civil Procedures

1. Each Party shall make available to right holders civil judicial procedures concerning the enforcement of any intellectual property right as specified in this Section.

2. To the extent that any civil remedy can be ordered as a result of administrative procedures on the merits of a case, each Party shall provide that such procedures shall conform to principles equivalent in substance to those set forth in this Section.

Article 8: Injunctions

1. Each Party shall provide that, in civil judicial proceedings concerning the enforcement of intellectual property rights, its judicial authorities have the authority to issue an order against a party to desist from an infringement, and inter alia, an order to that party or, where appropriate, to a third party over whom the relevant judicial authority exercises jurisdiction, to prevent goods that involve the infringement of an intellectual property right from entering into the channels of commerce.

2. Notwithstanding the other provisions of this Section, a Party may limit the remedies available against use by governments, or by third parties authorized by a government, without the authorization of the right holder, to the payment of remuneration, provided that the Party complies with the provisions of Part II of the TRIPS Agreement specifically addressing such use. In other cases, the remedies under this Section shall apply or, where these remedies are inconsistent with a Party's law, declaratory judgments and adequate compensation shall be available.

Article 9: Damages

1. Each Party shall provide that, in civil judicial proceedings concerning the enforcement of intellectual property rights, its judicial authorities have the authority to order the infringer who, knowingly or with reasonable grounds to know, engaged in infringing activity to pay the right holder damages adequate to compensate for the injury the right holder has suffered as a result of the infringement. In determining the amount of damages for infringement of intellectual property rights, a Party's judicial authorities shall have the authority to consider, inter alia, any legitimate measure of value the right holder submits, which may include lost profits, the value of the infringed goods or services measured by the market price, or the suggested retail price.

2. At least in cases of copyright or related rights infringement and trademark counterfeiting, each Party shall provide that, in civil judicial proceedings, its judicial authorities have the authority to order the infringer to pay the right holder the infringer's profits that are attributable to the infringement. A Party may presume those profits to be the amount of damages referred to in paragraph 1.

3. At least with respect to infringement of copyright or related rights protecting works, phonograms, and performances, and in cases of trademark counterfeiting, each Party shall also establish or maintain a system that provides for one or more of the following:

   (a) pre-established damages, or

---

[2] A Party may exclude patents and protection of undisclosed information from the scope of this Section.

    (b) presumptions[3] for determining the amount of damages sufficient to compensate the right holder for the harm caused by the infringement; or

    (c) at least for copyright, additional damages.

4. Where a Party provides the remedy referred to in subparagraph 3(a) or the presumptions referred to in subparagraph 3(b), it shall ensure that either its judicial authorities or the right holder has the right to choose such a remedy or presumptions as an alternative to the remedies referred to in paragraphs 1 and 2.

5. Each Party shall provide that its judicial authorities, where appropriate, have the authority to order, at the conclusion of civil judicial proceedings concerning infringement of at least copyright or related rights, or trademarks, that the prevailing party be awarded payment by the losing party of court costs or fees and appropriate attorney's fees, or any other expenses as provided for under that Party's law.

Article 10: Other Remedies

1. At least with respect to pirated copyright goods and counterfeit trademark goods, each Party shall provide that, in civil judicial proceedings, at the right holder's request, its judicial authorities have the authority to order that such infringing goods be destroyed, except in exceptional circumstances, without compensation of any sort.

2. Each Party shall further provide that its judicial authorities have the authority to order that materials and implements, the predominant use of which has been in the manufacture or creation of such infringing goods, be, without undue delay and without compensation of any sort, destroyed or disposed of outside the channels of commerce in such a manner as to minimize the risks of further infringements.

3. A Party may provide for the remedies described in this Article to be carried out at the infringer's expense.

Article 11: Information Related to Infringement

Without prejudice to its law governing privilege, the protection of confidentiality of information sources, or the processing of personal data, each Party shall provide that, in civil judicial proceedings concerning the enforcement of intellectual property rights, its judicial authorities have the authority, upon a justified request of the right holder, to order the infringer or, in the alternative, the alleged infringer, to provide to the right holder or to the judicial authorities, at least for the purpose of collecting evidence, relevant information as provided for in its applicable laws and regulations that the infringer or alleged infringer possesses or controls. Such information may include information regarding any person involved in any aspect of the infringement or alleged infringement and regarding the means of production or the channels of distribution of the infringing or allegedly infringing goods or services, including the identification of third persons alleged to be involved in the production and distribution of such goods or services and of their channels of distribution.

---

[3] The presumptions referred to in subparagraph 3(b) may include a presumption that the amount of damages is: (i) the quantity of the goods infringing the right holder's intellectual property right in question and actually assigned to third persons, multiplied by the amount of profit per unit of goods which would have been sold by the right holder if there had not been the act of infringement; or (ii) a reasonable royalty; or (iii) a lump sum on the basis of elements such as at least the amount of royalties or fees which would have been due if the infringer had requested authorization to use the intellectual property right in question.

Article 12: Provisional Measures

1. Each Party shall provide that its judicial authorities have the authority to order prompt and effective provisional measures:

   (a) against a party or, where appropriate, a third party over whom the relevant judicial authority exercises jurisdiction, to prevent an infringement of any intellectual property right from occurring, and in particular, to prevent goods that involve the infringement of an intellectual property right from entering into the channels of commerce;

   (b) to preserve relevant evidence in regard to the alleged infringement.

2. Each Party shall provide that its judicial authorities have the authority to adopt provisional measures *inaudita altera parte* where appropriate, in particular where any delay is likely to cause irreparable harm to the right holder, or where there is a demonstrable risk of evidence being destroyed. In proceedings conducted *inaudita altera parte*, each Party shall provide its judicial authorities with the authority to act expeditiously on requests for provisional measures and to make a decision without undue delay.

3. At least in cases of copyright or related rights infringement and trademark counterfeiting, each Party shall provide that, in civil judicial proceedings, its judicial authorities have the authority to order the seizure or other taking into custody of suspect goods, and of materials and implements relevant to the act of infringement, and, at least for trademark counterfeiting, documentary evidence, either originals or copies thereof, relevant to the infringement.

4. Each Party shall provide that its authorities have the authority to require the applicant, with respect to provisional measures, to provide any reasonably available evidence in order to satisfy themselves with a sufficient degree of certainty that the applicant's right is being infringed or that such infringement is imminent, and to order the applicant to provide a security or equivalent assurance sufficient to protect the defendant and to prevent abuse. Such security or equivalent assurance shall not unreasonably deter recourse to procedures for such provisional measures.

5. Where the provisional measures are revoked or where they lapse due to any act or omission by the applicant, or where it is subsequently found that there has been no infringement of an intellectual property right, the judicial authorities shall have the authority to order the applicant, upon request of the defendant, to provide the defendant appropriate compensation for any injury caused by these measures.

Section 3: —Border Measures[4, 5]

Article 13: Scope of the Border Measures[6]

In providing, as appropriate, and consistent with its domestic system of intellectual property rights protection and without prejudice to the requirements of the TRIPS Agreement, for effective border enforcement of intellectual property rights, a Party should do so in a manner that does not discriminate unjustifiably between intellectual property rights and that avoids the creation of barriers to legitimate trade.

---

[4] Where a Party has dismantled substantially all controls over movement of goods across its border with another Party with which it forms part of a customs union, it shall not be required to apply the provisions of this Section at that border.

[5] It is understood that there shall be no obligation to apply the procedures set forth in this Section to goods put on the market in another country by or with the consent of the right holder.

[6] The Parties agree that patents and protection of undisclosed information do not fall within the scope of this Section.

Article 14: Small Consignments and Personal Luggage

1. Each Party shall include in the application of this Section goods of a commercial nature sent in small consignments.

2. A Party may exclude from the application of this Section small quantities of goods of a non-commercial nature contained in travellers' personal luggage.

Article 15: Provision of Information from the Right Holder

Each Party shall permit its competent authorities to request a right holder to supply relevant information to assist the competent authorities in taking the border measures referred to in this Section. A Party may also allow a right holder to supply relevant information to its competent authorities.

Article 16: Border Measures

1. Each Party shall adopt or maintain procedures with respect to import and export shipments under which:

   (a) its customs authorities may act upon their own initiative to suspend the release of suspect goods; and

   (b) where appropriate, a right holder may request its competent authorities to suspend the release of suspect goods.

2. A Party may adopt or maintain procedures with respect to suspect intransit goods or in other situations where the goods are under customs control under which:

   (a) its customs authorities may act upon their own initiative to suspend the release of, or to detain, suspect goods; and

   (b) where appropriate, a right holder may request its competent authorities to suspend the release of, or to detain, suspect goods.

Article 17: Application by the Right Holder

1. Each Party shall provide that its competent authorities require a right holder that requests the procedures described in subparagraphs 1(b) and 2(b) of Article 16 (Border Measures) to provide adequate evidence to satisfy the competent authorities that, under the law of the Party providing the procedures, there is prima facie an infringement of the right holder's intellectual property right, and to supply sufficient information that may reasonably be expected to be within the right holder's knowledge to make the suspect goods reasonably recognizable by the competent authorities. The requirement to provide sufficient information shall not unreasonably deter recourse to the procedures described in subparagraphs 1(b) and 2(b) of Article 16 (Border Measures).

2. Each Party shall provide for applications to suspend the release of, or to detain, any suspect goods[7] under customs control in its territory. A Party may provide for such applications to apply to multiple shipments. A Party may provide that, at the request of the right holder, the application to suspend the release of, or to detain, suspect goods may apply to selected points of entry and exit under customs control.

3. Each Party shall ensure that its competent authorities inform the applicant within a reasonable period whether they have accepted the application. Where its competent authorities have accepted the application, they shall also inform the applicant of the period of validity of the application.

---

[7] The requirement to provide for such applications is subject to the obligations to provide procedures referred to in subparagraphs 1(b) and 2(b) of Article 16 (Border Measures).

4. A Party may provide that, where the applicant has abused the procedures described in subparagraphs 1(b) and 2(b) of Article 16 (Border Measures), or where there is due cause, its competent authorities have the authority to deny, suspend, or void an application.

Article 18: Security or Equivalent Assurance

Each Party shall provide that its competent authorities have the authority to require a right holder that requests the procedures described in subparagraphs 1(b) and 2(b) of Article 16 (Border Measures) to provide a reasonable security or equivalent assurance sufficient to protect the defendant and the competent authorities and to prevent abuse. Each Party shall provide that such security or equivalent assurance shall not unreasonably deter recourse to these procedures. A Party may provide that such security may be in the form of a bond conditioned to hold the defendant harmless from any loss or damage resulting from any suspension of the release of, or detention of, the goods in the event the competent authorities determine that the goods are not infringing. A Party may, only in exceptional circumstances or pursuant to a judicial order, permit the defendant to obtain possession of suspect goods by posting a bond or other security.

Article 19: Determination as to Infringement

Each Party shall adopt or maintain procedures by which its competent authorities may determine, within a reasonable period after the initiation of the procedures described in Article 16 (Border Measures), whether the suspect goods infringe an intellectual property right.

Article 20: Remedies

1. Each Party shall provide that its competent authorities have the authority to order the destruction of goods following a determination referred to in Article 19 (Determination as to Infringement) that the goods are infringing. In cases where such goods are not destroyed, each Party shall ensure that, except in exceptional circumstances, such goods are disposed of outside the channels of commerce in such a manner as to avoid any harm to the right holder.

2. In regard to counterfeit trademark goods, the simple removal of the trademark unlawfully affixed shall not be sufficient, other than in exceptional cases, to permit release of the goods into the channels of commerce.

3. A Party may provide that its competent authorities have the authority to impose administrative penalties following a determination referred to in Article 19 (Determination as to Infringement) that the goods are infringing.

Article 21: Fees

Each Party shall provide that any application fee, storage fee, or destruction fee to be assessed by its competent authorities in connection with the procedures described in this Section shall not be used to unreasonably deter recourse to these procedures.

Article 22: Disclosure of Information

Without prejudice to a Party's laws pertaining to the privacy or confidentiality of information:

(a) a Party may authorize its competent authorities to provide a right holder with information about specific shipments of goods, including the description and quantity of the goods, to assist in the detection of infringing goods;

(b) a Party may authorize its competent authorities to provide a right holder with information about goods, including, but not limited to, the description and quantity of the goods, the name and address of the consignor, importer, exporter, or consignee, and, if known, the country of origin of the goods, and the name and address of the manufacturer of the goods, to assist in the determination referred to in Article 19 (Determination as to Infringement);

(c) unless a Party has provided its competent authorities with the authority described in subparagraph (b), at least in cases of imported goods, where its competent authorities have seized suspect goods or, in the alternative, made a determination referred to in Article 19 (Determination as to Infringement) that the goods are infringing, the Party shall authorize its competent authorities to provide a right holder, within thirty days[8] of the seizure or determination, with information about such goods, including, but not limited to, the description and quantity of the goods, the name and address of the consignor, importer, exporter, or consignee, and, if known, the country of origin of the goods, and the name and address of the manufacturer of the goods.

Section 4: —Criminal Enforcement
Article 23: Criminal Offences

1. Each Party shall provide for criminal procedures and penalties to be applied at least in cases of wilful trademark counterfeiting or copyright or related rights piracy on a commercial scale.[9] For the purposes of this Section, acts carried out on a commercial scale include at least those carried out as commercial activities for direct or indirect economic or commercial advantage.

2. Each Party shall provide for criminal procedures and penalties to be applied in cases of wilful importation[10] and domestic use, in the course of trade and on a commercial scale, of labels or packaging[11];

   (a) to which a mark has been applied without authorization which is identical to, or cannot be distinguished from, a trademark registered in its territory; and

   (b) which are intended to be used in the course of trade on goods or in relation to services which are identical to goods or services for which such trademark is registered.

3. A Party may provide criminal procedures and penalties in appropriate cases for the unauthorized copying of cinematographic works from a performance in a motion picture exhibition facility generally open to the public.

4. With respect to the offences specified in this Article for which a Party provides criminal procedures and penalties, that Party shall ensure that criminal liability for aiding and abetting is available under its law.

5. Each Party shall adopt such measures as may be necessary, consistent

---

[8] For the purposes of this Article, days means business days.

[9] Each Party shall treat wilful importation or exportation of counterfeit trademark goods or pirated copyright goods on a commercial scale as unlawful activities subject to criminal penalties under this Article. A Party may comply with its obligation relating to importation and exportation of counterfeit trademark goods or pirated copyright goods by providing for distribution, sale or offer for sale of such goods on a commercial scale as unlawful activities subject to criminal penalties.

[10] A Party may comply with its obligation relating to importation of labels or packaging through its measures concerning distribution.

[11] A Party may comply with its obligations under this paragraph by providing for criminal procedures and penalties to be applied to attempts to commit a trademark offence.

with its legal principles, to establish the liability, which may be criminal, of legal persons for the offences specified in this Article for which the Party provides criminal procedures and penalties. Such liability shall be without prejudice to the criminal liability of the natural persons who have committed the criminal offences.

Article 24: Penalties

For offences specified in paragraphs 1, 2, and 4 of Article 23 (Criminal Offences), each Party shall provide penalties that include imprisonment as well as monetary fines[12] sufficiently high to provide a deterrent to future acts of infringement, consistently with the level of penalties applied for crimes of a corresponding gravity.

Article 25: Seizure, Forfeiture and Destruction

1. With respect to the offences specified in paragraphs 1, 2, 3, and 4 of Article 23 (Criminal Offences) for which a Party provides criminal procedures and penalties, that Party shall provide that its competent authorities have the authority to order the seizure of suspected counterfeit trademark goods or pirated copyright goods, any related materials and implements used in the commission of the alleged offence, documentary evidence relevant to the alleged offence, and the assets derived from, or obtained directly or indirectly through, the alleged infringing activity.

2. Where a Party requires the identification of items subject to seizure as a prerequisite for issuing an order referred to in paragraph 1, that Party shall not require the items to be described in greater detail than necessary to identify them for the purpose of seizure.

3. With respect to the offences specified in paragraphs 1, 2, 3, and 4 of Article 23 (Criminal Offences) for which a Party provides criminal procedures and penalties, that Party shall provide that its competent authorities have the authority to order the forfeiture or destruction of all counterfeit trademark goods or pirated copyright goods. In cases where counterfeit trademark goods and pirated copyright goods are not destroyed, the competent authorities shall ensure that, except in exceptional circumstances, such goods shall be disposed of outside the channels of commerce in such a manner as to avoid causing any harm to the right holder. Each Party shall ensure that the forfeiture or destruction of such goods shall occur without compensation of any sort to the infringer.

4. With respect to the offences specified in paragraphs 1, 2, 3, and 4 of Article 23 (Criminal Offences) for which a Party provides criminal procedures and penalties, that Party shall provide that its competent authorities have the authority to order the forfeiture or destruction of materials and implements predominantly used in the creation of counterfeit trademark goods or pirated copyright goods and, at least for serious offences, of the assets derived from, or obtained directly or indirectly through, the infringing activity. Each Party shall ensure that the forfeiture or destruction of such materials, implements, or assets shall occur without compensation of any sort to the infringer.

5. With respect to the offences specified in paragraphs 1, 2, 3, and 4 of Article 23 (Criminal Offences) for which a Party provides criminal procedures and penalties, that Party may provide that its judicial authorities have the authority to order:

---

[12] It is understood that there is no obligation for a Party to provide for the possibility of imprisonment and monetary fines to be imposed in parallel.

(a) the seizure of assets the value of which corresponds to that of the assets derived from, or obtained directly or indirectly through, the allegedly infringing activity; and

(b) the forfeiture of assets the value of which corresponds to that of the assets derived from, or obtained directly or indirectly through, the infringing activity.

Article 26: Ex Officio Criminal Enforcement

Each Party shall provide that, in appropriate cases, its competent authorities may act upon their own initiative to initiate investigation or legal action with respect to the criminal offences specified in paragraphs 1, 2, 3, and 4 of Article 23 (Criminal Offences) for which that Party provides criminal procedures and penalties.

Section 5: —Enforcement of Intellectual Property Rights in the Digital Environment

Article 27: Enforcement in the Digital Environment

1. Each Party shall ensure that enforcement procedures, to the extent set forth in Sections 2 (Civil Enforcement) and 4 (Criminal Enforcement), are available under its law so as to permit effective action against an act of infringement of intellectual property rights which takes place in the digital environment, including expeditious remedies to prevent infringement and remedies which constitute a deterrent to further infringements.

2. Further to paragraph 1, each Party's enforcement procedures shall apply to infringement of copyright or related rights over digital networks, which may include the unlawful use of means of widespread distribution for infringing purposes. These procedures shall be implemented in a manner that avoids the creation of barriers to legitimate activity, including electronic commerce, and, consistent with that Party's law, preserves fundamental principles such as freedom of expression, fair process, and privacy.[13]

3. Each Party shall endeavour to promote cooperative efforts within the business community to effectively address trademark and copyright or related rights infringement while preserving legitimate competition and, consistent with that Party's law, preserving fundamental principles such as freedom of expression, fair process, and privacy.

4. A Party may provide, in accordance with its laws and regulations, its competent authorities with the authority to order an online service provider to disclose expeditiously to a right holder information sufficient to identify a subscriber whose account was allegedly used for infringement, where that right holder has filed a legally sufficient claim of trademark or copyright or related rights infringement, and where such information is being sought for the purpose of protecting or enforcing those rights. These procedures shall be implemented in a manner that avoids the creation of barriers to legitimate activity, including electronic commerce, and, consistent with that Party's law, preserves fundamental principles such as freedom of expression, fair process, and privacy.

5. Each Party shall provide adequate legal protection and effective legal

---

[13] For instance, without prejudice to a Party's law, adopting or maintaining a regime providing for limitations on the liability of, or on the remedies available against, online service providers while preserving the legitimate interests of right holder.

remedies against the circumvention of effective technological measures[14] that are used by authors, performers or producers of phonograms in connection with the exercise of their rights in, and that restrict acts in respect of, their works, performances, and phonograms, which are not authorized by the authors, the performers or the producers of phonograms concerned or permitted by law.

6. In order to provide the adequate legal protection and effective legal remedies referred to in paragraph 5, each Party shall provide protection at least against:

(a) to the extent provided by its law:

   (i) the unauthorized circumvention of an effective technological measure carried out knowingly or with reasonable grounds to know; and

   (ii) the offering to the public by marketing of a device or product, including computer programs, or a service, as a means of circumventing an effective technological measure; and

(b) the manufacture, importation, or distribution of a device or product, including computer programs, or provision of a service that:

   (i) is primarily designed or produced for the purpose of circumventing an effective technological measure; or

   (ii) has only a limited commercially significant purpose other than circumventing an effective technological measure.[15]

7. To protect electronic rights management information,[16] each Party shall provide adequate legal protection and effective legal remedies against any person knowingly performing without authority any of the following acts knowing, or with respect to civil remedies, having reasonable grounds to know, that it will induce, enable, facilitate, or conceal an infringement of any copyright or related rights:

(a) to remove or alter any electronic right management information

(b) to distribute, import for distribution, broadcast, communicate, or make available to the public copies of works, performances, or phonograms, knowing that electronic rights management information has been removed or altered without authority.

8. In providing adequate legal protection and effective legal remedies pursuant to the provisions of paragraphs 5 and 7, a Party may adopt or maintain appropriate limitations or exceptions to measures implementing the provi-

---

[14] For the purposes of this Article, **technological measures** means any technology, device, or component that, in the normal course of its operation, is designed to prevent or restrict acts, in respect of works, performances, or phonograms, which are not authorized by authors, performers or producers of phonograms, as provided for by a Party's law. Without prejudice to the scope of copyright or related rights contained in a Party's law, technological measures shall be deemed effective where the use of protected works, performances, or phonograms is controlled by authors, performers or producers of phonograms through the application of a relevant access control or protection process, such as encryption or scrambling, or a copy control mechanism, which achieves the objective of protection.

[15] In implementing paragraphs 5 and 6, no Party shall be obligated to require that the design of, or the design and selection of parts and components for, a consumer electronics, telecommunications, or computing product provide for a response to any particular technological measure, so long as the product does not otherwise contravene its measures implementing these paragraphs.

[16] For the purposes of this Article, **rights management information** means: (a) information that identifies the work, the performance, or the phonogram; the author of the work, the performer of the performance, or the producer of the phonogram; or the owner of any right in the work, performance, or phonogram; (b) information about the terms and conditions of use of the work, performance, or phonogram; or (c) any numbers or codes that represent the information described in (a) and (b) above; when any of these items of information is attached to a copy of a work, performance, or phonogram, or appears in connection with the communication or making available of a work, performance, or phonogram to the public.

sions of paragraphs 5, 6, and 7. The obligations set forth in paragraphs 5, 6, and 7 are without prejudice to the rights, limitations, exceptions, or defences to copyright or related rights infringement under a Party's law.

CHAPTER III ENFORCEMENT PRACTICES

Article 28: Enforcement Expertise, Information and Domestic Coordination

1. Each Party shall encourage the development of specialized expertise within its competent authorities responsible for the enforcement of intellectual property rights.

2. Each Party shall promote the collection and analysis of statistical data and other relevant information concerning intellectual property rights infringements as well as the collection of information on best practices to prevent and combat infringements.

3. Each Party shall, as appropriate, promote internal coordination among, and facilitate joint actions by, its competent authorities responsible for the enforcement of intellectual property rights.

4. Each Party shall endeavour to promote, where appropriate, the establishment and maintenance of formal or informal mechanisms, such as advisory groups, whereby its competent authorities may receive the views of right holders and other relevant stakeholders.

Article 29: Management of Risk at Border

1. In order to enhance the effectiveness of border enforcement of intellectual property rights, the competent authorities of a Party may:

   (a) consult with the relevant stakeholders, and the competent authorities of other Parties responsible for the enforcement of intellectual property rights to identify and address significant risks, and promote actions to mitigate those risks; and

   (b) share information with the competent authorities of other Parties on border enforcement of intellectual property rights, including relevant information to better identify and target for inspection shipments suspected of containing infringing goods.

2. Where a Party seizes imported goods infringing an intellectual property right, its competent authorities may provide the Party of export with information necessary for identification of the parties and goods involved in the exportation of the seized goods. The competent authorities of the Party of export may take action against those parties and future shipments in accordance with that Party's law.

Article 30: Transparency

To promote transparency in the administration of its intellectual property rights enforcement system, each Party shall take appropriate measures, pursuant to its law and policies, to publish or otherwise make available to the public information on:

(a) procedures available under its law for enforcing intellectual property rights, its competent authorities responsible for such enforcement, and contact points available for assistance;

(b) relevant laws, regulations, final judicial decisions, and administrative rulings of general application pertaining to the enforcement of intellectual property rights; and

(c) its efforts to ensure an effective system of enforcement and protection of intellectual property rights.

Article 31: Public Awareness

Each Party shall, as appropriate, promote the adoption of measures to enhance public awareness of the importance of respecting intellectual property rights and the detrimental effects of intellectual property rights infringement.

Article 32: Environmental Considerations in Destruction of Infringing Goods

The destruction of goods infringing intellectual property rights shall be done consistently with the laws and regulations on environmental matters of the Party in which the destruction takes place.

CHAPTER IV INTERNATIONAL COOPERATION

Article 33: International Cooperation

1. Each Party recognizes that international cooperation is vital to realizing effective protection of intellectual property rights and that it should be encouraged regardless of the origin of the goods infringing intellectual property rights, or the location or nationality of the right holder.

2. In order to combat intellectual property rights infringement, in particular trademark counterfeiting and copyright or related rights piracy, the Parties shall promote cooperation, where appropriate, among their competent authorities responsible for the enforcement of intellectual property rights. Such cooperation may include law enforcement cooperation with respect to criminal enforcement and border measures covered by this Agreement.

3. Cooperation under this Chapter shall be conducted consistent with relevant international agreements, and subject to the laws, policies, resource allocation, and law enforcement priorities of each Party.

Article 34: Information Sharing

Without prejudice to the provisions of Article 29 (Management of Risk at Border), each Party shall endeavour to exchange with other Parties:

(a) information the Party collects under the provisions of Chapter III (Enforcement Practices), including statistical data and information on best practices;

(b) information on its legislative and regulatory measures related to the protection and enforcement of intellectual property rights; and

(c) other information as appropriate and mutually agreed.

Article 35: Capacity Building and Technical Assistance

1. Each Party shall endeavour to provide, upon request and on mutually agreed terms and conditions, assistance in capacity building and technical assistance in improving the enforcement of intellectual property rights to other Parties to this Agreement and, where appropriate, to prospective Parties. The capacity building and technical assistance may cover such areas as:

(a) enhancement of public awareness on intellectual property rights;

(b) development and implementation of national legislation related to the enforcement of intellectual property rights;

(c) training of officials on the enforcement of intellectual property rights; and

(d) coordinated operations conducted at the regional and multilateral levels.

2. Each Party shall endeavour to work closely with other Parties and, where

appropriate, non-Parties to this Agreement for the purpose of implementing the provisions of paragraph 1.

3. A Party may undertake the activities described in this Article in conjunction with relevant private sector or international organizations. Each Party shall strive to avoid unnecessary duplication between the activities described in this Article and other international cooperation activities.

CHAPTER V INSTITUTIONAL ARRANGEMENTS
Article 36: The ACTA Committee

1. The Parties hereby establish the ACTA Committee. Each Party shall be represented on the Committee.

2. The Committee shall:

    (a) review the implementation and operation of this Agreement;

    (b) consider matters concerning the development of this Agreement;

    (c) consider any proposed amendments to this Agreement in accordance with Article 42 (Amendments);

    (d) decide, in accordance with paragraph 2 of Article 43 (Accession), upon the terms of accession to this Agreement of any Member of the WTO; and

    (e) consider any other matter that may affect the implementation and operation of this Agreement.

3. The Committee may decide to:

    (a) establish *ad hoc* committees or working groups to assist the Committee in carrying out its responsibilities under paragraph 2, or to assist a prospective Party upon its request in acceding to this Agreement in accordance with Article 43 (Accession);

    (b) seek the advice of non-governmental persons or groups;

    (c) make recommendations regarding the implementation and operation of this Agreement, including by endorsing best practice guidelines related thereto;

    (d) share information and best practices with third parties on reducing intellectual property rights infringements, including techniques for identifying and monitoring piracy and counterfeiting; and

    (e) take other actions in the exercise of its functions.

4. All decisions of the Committee shall be taken by consensus, except as the Committee may otherwise decide by consensus. The Committee shall be deemed to have acted by consensus on a matter submitted for its consideration, if no Party present at the meeting when the decision is taken formally objects to the proposed decision. English shall be the working language of the Committee and the documents supporting its work shall be in the English language.

5. The Committee shall adopt its rules and procedures within a reasonable period after the entry into force of this Agreement, and shall invite those Signatories not Parties to this Agreement to participate in the Committee's deliberations on those rules and procedures. The rules and procedures:

    (a) shall address such matters as chairing and hosting meetings, and the performance of organizational duties relevant to this Agreement and its operation; and

    (b) may also address such matters as granting observer status, and any other matter the Committee decides necessary for its proper operation.

6. The Committee may amend the rules and procedures.

7. Notwithstanding the provisions of paragraph 4, during the first five years following the entry into force of this Agreement, the Committee's decisions to adopt or amend the rules and procedures shall be taken by consensus of the Parties and those Signatories not Parties to this Agreement.

8. After the period specified in paragraph 7, the Committee may adopt or amend the rules and procedures upon the consensus of the Parties to this Agreement.

9. Notwithstanding the provisions of paragraph 8, the Committee may decide that the adoption or amendment of a particular rule or procedure requires the consensus of the Parties and those Signatories not Parties to this Agreement.

10. The Committee shall convene at least once every year unless the Committee decides otherwise. The first meeting of the Committee shall be held within a reasonable period after the entry into force of this Agreement.

11. For greater certainty, the Committee shall not oversee or supervise domestic or international enforcement or criminal investigations of specific intellectual property cases.

12. The Committee shall strive to avoid unnecessary duplication between its activities and other international efforts regarding the enforcement of intellectual property rights.

Article 37: Contact Points

1. Each Party shall designate a contact point to facilitate communications between the Parties on any matter covered by this Agreement.

2. On the request of another Party, a Party's contact point shall identify an appropriate office or official to whom the requesting Party's inquiry may be addressed, and assist, as necessary, in facilitating communications between the office or official concerned and the requesting Party.

Article 38: Consultations

1. A Party may request in writing consultations with another Party with respect to any matter affecting the implementation of this Agreement. The requested Party shall accord sympathetic consideration to such a request, provide a response, and afford adequate opportunity to consult.

2. The consultations, including particular positions taken by consulting Parties, shall be kept confidential and be without prejudice to the rights or positions of either Party in any other proceeding, including a proceeding under the auspices of the Understanding on Rules and Procedures Governing the Settlement of Disputes contained in Annex 2 to the WTO Agreement.

3. The consulting Parties may, by mutual consent, notify the Committee of the result of their consultations under this Article.

Chapter VI Final Provisions

Article 39: Signature

This Agreement shall remain open for signature by participants in its negotiation,[17] and by any other WTO Members the participants may agree to by consensus, from 1 May 2011 until 1 May 2013.

---

[17] Australia, the Republic of Austria, the Kingdom of Belgium, the Republic of Bulgaria, Canada,

Article 40: Entry Into Force

1. This Agreement shall enter into force thirty days after the date of deposit of the sixth instrument of ratification, acceptance, or approval as between those Signatories that have deposited their respective instruments of ratification, acceptance, or approval.

2. This Agreement shall enter into force for each Signatory that deposits its instrument of ratification, acceptance, or approval after the deposit of the sixth instrument of ratification, acceptance, or approval, thirty days after the date of deposit by such Signatory of its instrument of ratification, acceptance, or approval.

Article 41: Withdrawal

A Party may withdraw from this Agreement by means of a written notification to the Depositary. The withdrawal shall take effect 180 days after the Depositary receives the notification.

Article 42: Amendments

1. A Party may propose amendments to this Agreement to the Committee. The Committee shall decide whether to present a proposed amendment to the Parties for ratification, acceptance, or approval.

2. Any amendment shall enter into force ninety days after the date that all the Parties have deposited their respective instruments of ratification, acceptance, or approval with the Depositary.

Article 43: Accession

1. After the expiration of the period provided in Article 39 (Signature), any Member of the WTO may apply to accede to this Agreement.

2. The Committee shall decide upon the terms of accession for each applicant.

3. This Agreement shall enter into force for the applicant thirty days after the date of deposit of its instrument of accession based upon the terms of accession referred to in paragraph 2.

Article 44: Texts of the Agreement

This Agreement shall be signed in a single original in the English, French, and Spanish languages, each version being equally authentic.

Article 45: Depositary

The Government of Japan shall be the Depositary of this Agreement.

---

the Republic of Cyprus, the Czech Republic, the Kingdom of Denmark, the Republic of Estonia, the European Union, the Republic of Finland, the French Republic, the Federal Republic of Germany, the Hellenic Republic, the Republic of Hungary, Ireland, the Italian Republic, Japan, the Republic of Korea, the Republic of Latvia, the Republic of Lithuania, the Grand Duchy of Luxembourg, the Republic of Malta, the United Mexican States, the Kingdom of Morocco, the Kingdom of the Netherlands, New Zealand, the Republic of Poland, the Portuguese Republic, Romania, the Republic of Singapore, the Slovak Republic, the Republic of Slovenia, the Kingdom of Spain, the Kingdom of Sweden, the Swiss Confederation, the United Kingdom of Great Britain and Northern Ireland, and the United States of America.

F18. BEIJING TREATY ON AUDIOVISUAL PERFORMANCES

adopted by the Diplomatic Conference on June 24, 2012

CONTENTS

Preamble

PREAMBLE

The Contracting Parties,

Desiring to develop and maintain the protection of the rights of performers in their audiovisual performances in a manner as effective and uniform as possible,

Recalling the importance of the Development Agenda recommendations, adopted in 2007 by the General Assembly of the Convention Establishing the World Intellectual Property Organization (WIPO), which aim to ensure that development considerations form an integral part of the Organization's work,

Recognizing the need to introduce new international rules in order to provide adequate solutions to the questions raised by economic, social, cultural and technological developments,

Recognizing the profound impact of the development and convergence of information and communication technologies on the production and use of audiovisual performances,

Recognizing the need to maintain a balance between the rights of performers in their audiovisual performances and the larger public interest, particularly education, research and access to information,

Recognizing that the WIPO Performances and Phonograms Treaty (WPPT) done in Geneva on December 20, 1996, does not extend protection to performers in respect of their performances fixed in audiovisual fixations,

Referring to the Resolution concerning Audiovisual Performances adopted by the Diplomatic Conference on Certain Copyright and Neighboring Rights Questions on December 20, 1996,

Have agreed as follows:

Article 1

Relation to Other Conventions and Treaties

(1) Nothing in this Treaty shall derogate from existing obligations that Contracting Parties have to each other under the WPPT or the International Convention for the Protection of Performers, Producers of Phonograms and Broadcasting Organizations done in Rome on October 26, 1961.

(2) Protection granted under this Treaty shall leave intact and shall in no way affect the protection of copyright in literary and artistic works. Consequently, no provision of this Treaty may be interpreted as prejudicing such protection.

(3) This Treaty shall not have any connection with treaties other than the WPPT, nor shall it prejudice any rights and obligations under any other treaties.[1,2]

Article 2

Definitions

For the purposes of this Treaty:

(a) "performers" are actors, singers, musicians, dancers, and other persons who act, sing, deliver, declaim, play in, interpret, or otherwise perform literary or artistic works or expressions of folklore[3];

(b) "audiovisual fixation" means the embodiment of moving images, whether or not accompanied by sounds or by the representations thereof, from which they can be perceived, reproduced or communicated through a device[4];

(c) "broadcasting" means the transmission by wireless means for public

---

[1] Agreed statement concerning Article 1: It is understood that nothing in this Treaty affects any rights or obligations under the WIPO Performances and Phonograms Treaty (WPPT) or their interpretation and it is further understood that paragraph 3 does not create any obligations for a Contracting Party to this Treaty to ratify or accede to the WPPT or to comply with any of its provisions.

[2] Agreed statement concerning Article 1(3): It is understood that Contracting Parties who are members of the World Trade Organization (WTO) acknowledge all the principles and objectives of the Agreement on Trade-Related Aspects of Intellectual Property Rights (TRIPS Agreement) and understand that nothing in this Treaty affects the provisions of the TRIPS Agreement, including, but not limited to, the provisions relating to anti-competitive practices.

[3] Agreed statement concerning Article 2(a): It is understood that the definition of "performers" includes those who perform a literary or artistic work that is created or first fixed in the course of a performance.

[4] Agreed statement concerning Article 2(b): It is hereby confirmed that the definition of "audiovisual fixation" contained in Article 2(b) is without prejudice to Article 2(c) of the WPPT.

reception of sounds or of images or of images and sounds or of the representations thereof; such transmission by satellite is also "broadcasting"; transmission of encrypted signals is "broadcasting" where the means for decrypting are provided to the public by the broadcasting organization or with its consent;

(d) "communication to the public" of a performance means the transmission to the public by any medium, otherwise than by broadcasting, of an unfixed performance, or of a performance fixed in an audiovisual fixation. For the purposes of Article 11, "communication to the public" includes making a performance fixed in an audiovisual fixation audible or visible or audible and visible to the public.

Article 3
Beneficiaries of Protection

(1) Contracting Parties shall accord the protection granted under this Treaty to performers who are nationals of other Contracting Parties.

(2) Performers who are not nationals of one of the Contracting Parties but who have their habitual residence in one of them shall, for the purposes of this Treaty, be assimilated to nationals of that Contracting Party.

Article 4
National Treatment

(1) Each Contracting Party shall accord to nationals of other Contracting Parties the treatment it accords to its own nationals with regard to the exclusive rights specifically granted in this Treaty and the right to equitable remuneration provided for in Article 11 of this Treaty.

(2) A Contracting Party shall be entitled to limit the extent and term of the protection accorded to nationals of another Contracting Party under paragraph (1), with respect to the rights granted in Article 11(1) and 11(2) of this Treaty, to those rights that its own nationals enjoy in that other Contracting Party.

(3) The obligation provided for in paragraph (1) does not apply to a Contracting Party to the extent that another Contracting Party makes use of the reservations permitted by Article 11(3) of this Treaty, nor does it apply to a Contracting Party, to the extent that it has made such reservation.

Article 5
Moral Rights

(1) Independently of a performer's economic rights, and even after the transfer of those rights, the performer shall, as regards his live performances or performances fixed in audiovisual fixations, have the right:

(i) to claim to be identified as the performer of his performances, except where omission is dictated by the manner of the use of the performance; and

(ii) to object to any distortion, mutilation or other modification of his performances that would be prejudicial to his reputation, taking due account of the nature of audiovisual fixations.

(2) The rights granted to a performer in accordance with paragraph (1) shall, after his death, be maintained, at least until the expiry of the economic rights, and shall be exercisable by the persons or institutions authorized by the legislation of the Contracting Party where protection is claimed.

However, those Contracting Parties whose legislation, at the moment of their ratification of or accession to this Treaty, does not provide for protection after the death of the performer of all rights set out in the preceding paragraph may provide that some of these rights will, after his death, cease to be maintained.

(3) The means of redress for safeguarding the rights granted under this Article shall be governed by the legislation of the Contracting Party where protection is claimed.[5]

Article 6
Economic Rights of Performers in their Unfixed Performances

Performers shall enjoy the exclusive right of authorizing, as regards their performances:

(i) the broadcasting and communication to the public of their unfixed performances except where the performance is already a broadcast performance; and

(ii) the fixation of their unfixed performances.

Article 7
Right of Reproduction

Performers shall enjoy the exclusive right of authorizing the direct or indirect reproduction of their performances fixed in audiovisual fixations, in any manner or form.[6]

Article 8
Right of Distribution

(1) Performers shall enjoy the exclusive right of authorizing the making available to the public of the original and copies of their performances fixed in audiovisual fixations through sale or other transfer of ownership.

(2) Nothing in this Treaty shall affect the freedom of Contracting Parties to determine the conditions, if any, under which the exhaustion of the right in paragraph (1) applies after the first sale or other transfer of ownership of the original or a copy of the fixed performance with the authorization of the performer.[7]

Article 9
Right of Rental

(1) Performers shall enjoy the exclusive right of authorizing the commercial

---

[5] Agreed statement concerning Article 5: For the purposes of this Treaty and without prejudice to any other treaty, it is understood that, considering the nature of audiovisual fixations and their production and distribution, modifications of a performance that are made in the normal course of exploitation of the performance, such as editing, compression, dubbing, or formatting, in existing or new media or formats, and that are made in the course of a use authorized by the performer, would not in themselves amount to modifications within the meaning of Article 5(1)(ii). Rights under Article 5(1)(ii) are concerned only with changes that are objectively prejudicial to the performer's reputation in a substantial way. It is also understood that the mere use of new or changed technology or media, as such, does not amount to modification within the meaning of Article 5(1)(ii).

[6] Agreed statement concerning Article 7: The reproduction right, as set out in Article 7, and the exceptions permitted thereunder through Article 13, fully apply in the digital environment, in particular to the use of performances in digital form. It is understood that the storage of a protected performance in digital form in an electronic medium constitutes a reproduction within the meaning of this Article.

[7] Agreed statement concerning Articles 8 and 9: As used in these Articles, the expression "original and copies," being subject to the right of distribution and the right of rental under the said Articles, refers exclusively to fixed copies that can be put into circulation as tangible objects.

rental to the public of the original and copies of their performances fixed in audiovisual fixations as determined in the national law of Contracting Parties, even after distribution of them by, or pursuant to, authorization by the performer.

(2) Contracting Parties are exempt from the obligation of paragraph (1) unless the commercial rental has led to widespread copying of such fixations materially impairing the exclusive right of reproduction of performers.[8]

Article 10

Right of Making Available of Fixed Performances

Performers shall enjoy the exclusive right of authorizing the making available to the public of their performances fixed in audiovisual fixations, by wire or wireless means, in such a way that members of the public may access them from a place and at a time individually chosen by them.

Article 11

Right of Broadcasting and Communication to the Public

(1) Performers shall enjoy the exclusive right of authorizing the broadcasting and communication to the public of their performances fixed in audiovisual fixations.

(2) Contracting Parties may in a notification deposited with the Director General of WIPO declare that, instead of the right of authorization provided for in paragraph (1), they will establish a right to equitable remuneration for the direct or indirect use of performances fixed in audiovisual fixations for broadcasting or for communication to the public. Contracting Parties may also declare that they will set conditions in their legislation for the exercise of the right to equitable remuneration.

(3) Any Contracting Party may declare that it will apply the provisions of paragraphs (1) or (2) only in respect of certain uses, or that it will limit their application in some other way, or that it will not apply the provisions of paragraphs (1) and (2) at all.

Article 12

Transfer of Rights

(1) A Contracting Party may provide in its national law that once a performer has consented to fixation of his or her performance in an audiovisual fixation, the exclusive rights of authorization provided for in Articles 7 to 11 of this Treaty shall be owned or exercised by or transferred to the producer of such audiovisual fixation subject to any contract to the contrary between the performer and the producer of the audiovisual fixation as determined by the national law.

(2) A Contracting Party may require with respect to audiovisual fixations produced under its national law that such consent or contract be in writing and signed by both parties to the contract or by their duly authorized representatives.

(3) Independent of the transfer of exclusive rights described above, national laws or individual, collective or other agreements may provide the

---

[8] Agreed statement concerning Articles 8 and 9: As used in these Articles, the expression "original and copies," being subject to the right of distribution and the right of rental under the said Articles, refers exclusively to fixed copies that can be put into circulation as tangible objects.

performer with the right to receive royalties or equitable remuneration for any use of the performance, as provided for under this Treaty including as regards Articles 10 and 11.

Article 13

Limitations and Exceptions

(1) Contracting Parties may, in their national legislation, provide for the same kinds of limitations or exceptions with regard to the protection of performers as they provide for, in their national legislation, in connection with the protection of copyright in literary and artistic works.

(2) Contracting Parties shall confine any limitations of or exceptions to rights provided for in this Treaty to certain special cases which do not conflict with a normal exploitation of the performance and do not unreasonably prejudice the legitimate interests of the performer[9].

Article 14

Term of Protection

The term of protection to be granted to performers under this Treaty shall last, at least, until the end of a period of 50 years computed from the end of the year in which the performance was fixed.

Article 15

Obligations concerning Technological Measures

Contracting Parties shall provide adequate legal protection and effective legal remedies against the circumvention of effective technological measures that are used by performers in connection with the exercise of their rights under this Treaty and that restrict acts, in respect of their performances, which are not authorized by the performers concerned or permitted by law.[10,11]

Article 16

Obligations concerning Rights Management Information

(1) Contracting Parties shall provide adequate and effective legal remedies against any person knowingly performing any of the following acts knowing, or with respect to civil remedies having reasonable grounds to know, that it will induce, enable, facilitate, or conceal an infringement of any right covered by this Treaty:

---

[9] Agreed statement concerning Article 13: The Agreed statement concerning Article 10 (on Limitations and Exceptions) of the WIPO Copyright Treaty (WCT) is applicable mutatis mutandis also to Article 13 (on Limitations and Exceptions) of the Treaty.

[10] Agreed statement concerning Article 15 as it relates to Article 13: It is understood that nothing in this Article prevents a Contracting Party from adopting effective and necessary measures to ensure that a beneficiary may enjoy limitations and exceptions provided in that Contracting Party's national law, in accordance with Article 13, where technological measures have been applied to an audiovisual performance and the beneficiary has legal access to that performance, in circumstances such as where appropriate and effective measures have not been taken by rights holders in relation to that performance to enable the beneficiary to enjoy the limitations and exceptions under that Contracting Party's national law. Without prejudice to the legal protection of an audiovisual work in which a performance is fixed, it is further understood that the obligations under Article 15 are not applicable to performances unprotected or no longer protected under the national law giving effect to this Treaty.

[11] Agreed statement concerning Article 15: The expression "technological measures used by performers" should, as this is the case regarding the WPPT, be construed broadly, referring also to those acting on behalf of performers, including their representatives, licensees or assignees, including producers, service providers, and persons engaged in communication or broadcasting using performances on the basis of due authorization.

    (i) to remove or alter any electronic rights management information without authority;

    (ii) to distribute, import for distribution, broadcast, communicate or make available to the public, without authority, performances or copies of performances fixed in audiovisual fixations knowing that electronic rights management information has been removed or altered without authority.

(2) As used in this Article, "rights management information" means information which identifies the performer, the performance of the performer, or the owner of any right in the performance, or information about the terms and conditions of use of the performance, and any numbers or codes that represent such information, when any of these items of information is attached to a performance fixed in an audiovisual fixation.[12]

Article 17

Formalities

The enjoyment and exercise of the rights provided for in this Treaty shall not be subject to any formality.

Article 18

Reservations and Notifications

(1) Subject to provisions of Article 11(3), no reservations to this Treaty shall be permitted.

(2) Any notification under Article 11(2) or 19(2) may be made in instruments of ratification or accession, and the effective date of the notification shall be the same as the date of entry into force of this Treaty with respect to the Contracting Party having made the notification. Any such notification may also be made later, in which case the notification shall have effect three months after its receipt by the Director General of WIPO or at any later date indicated in the notification.

Article 19

Application in Time

(1) Contracting Parties shall accord the protection granted under this Treaty to fixed performances that exist at the moment of the entry into force of this Treaty and to all performances that occur after the entry into force of this Treaty for each Contracting Party.

(2) Notwithstanding the provisions of paragraph (1), a Contracting Party may declare in a notification deposited with the Director General of WIPO that it will not apply the provisions of Articles 7 to 11 of this Treaty, or any one or more of those, to fixed performances that existed at the moment of the entry into force of this Treaty for each Contracting Party. In respect of such Contracting Party, other Contracting Parties may limit the application of the said Articles to performances that occurred after the entry into force of this Treaty for that Contracting Party.

(3) The protection provided for in this Treaty shall be without prejudice to any acts committed, agreements concluded or rights acquired before the entry into force of this Treaty for each Contracting Party.

---

[12] Agreed statement concerning Article 16: The Agreed statement concerning Article 12 (on Obligations concerning Rights Management Information) of the WCT is applicable mutatis mutandis also to Article 16 (on Obligations concerning Rights Management Information) of the Treaty.

(4) Contracting Parties may in their legislation establish transitional provisions under which any person who, prior to the entry into force of this Treaty, engaged in lawful acts with respect to a performance, may undertake with respect to the same performance acts within the scope of the rights provided for in Articles 5 and 7 to 11 after the entry into force of this Treaty for the respective Contracting Parties.

Article 20
Provisions on Enforcement of Rights

(1) Contracting Parties undertake to adopt, in accordance with their legal systems, the measures necessary to ensure the application of this Treaty.

(2) Contracting Parties shall ensure that enforcement procedures are available under their law so as to permit effective action against any act of infringement of rights covered by this Treaty, including expeditious remedies to prevent infringements and remedies which constitute a deterrent to further infringements.

Artticle 21
Assembly

(a) The Contracting Parties shall have an Assembly.

(b) Each Contracting Party shall be represented in the Assembly by one delegate who may be assisted by alternate delegates, advisors and experts.

(c) The expenses of each delegation shall be borne by the Contracting Party that has appointed the delegation. The Assembly may ask WIPO to grant financial assistance to facilitate the participation of delegations of Contracting Parties that are regarded as developing countries in conformity with the established practice of the General Assembly of the United Nations or that are countries in transition to a market economy.

(a) The Assembly shall deal with matters concerning the maintenance and development of this Treaty and the application and operation of this Treaty.

(b) The Assembly shall perform the function allocated to it under Article 23(2) in respect of the admission of certain intergovernmental organizations to become party to this Treaty.

(c) The Assembly shall decide the convocation of any diplomatic conference for the revision of this Treaty and give the necessary instructions to the Director General of WIPO for the preparation of such diplomatic conference.

(a) Each Contracting Party that is a State shall have one vote and shall vote only in its own name.

(b) Any Contracting Party that is an intergovernmental organization may participate in the vote, in place of its Member States, with a number of votes equal to the number of its Member States which are party to this Treaty. No such intergovernmental organization shall participate in the vote if any one of its Member States exercises its right to vote and vice versa.

(4) The Assembly shall meet upon convocation by the Director General and, in the absence of exceptional circumstances, during the same period and at the same place as the General Assembly of WIPO.

(5) The Assembly shall endeavor to take its decisions by consensus and shall establish its own rules of procedure, including the convocation of extraordinary sessions, the requirements of a quorum and, subject to the provisions of this Treaty, the required majority for various kinds of decisions.

Article 22
International Bureau

The International Bureau of WIPO shall perform the administrative tasks concerning the Treaty.

Article 23
Eligibility for Becoming Party to the Treaty

(1) Any Member State of WIPO may become party to this Treaty.

(2) The Assembly may decide to admit any intergovernmental organization to become party to this Treaty which declares that it is competent in respect of, and has its own legislation binding on all its Member States on, matters covered by this Treaty and that it has been duly authorized, in accordance with its internal procedures, to become party to this Treaty.

(3) The European Union, having made the declaration referred to in the preceding paragraph in the Diplomatic Conference that has adopted this Treaty, may become party to this Treaty.

Article 24
Rights and Obligations under the Treaty

Subject to any specific provisions to the contrary in this Treaty, each Contracting Party shall enjoy all of the rights and assume all of the obligations under this Treaty.

Article 25
Signature of the Treaty

This Treaty shall be open for signature at the headquarters of WIPO by any eligible party for one year after its adoption.

Article 26
Entry into Force of the Treaty

This Treaty shall enter into force three months after 30 eligible parties referred to in Article 23 have deposited their instruments of ratification or accession.

Article 27
Effective Date of Becoming Party to the Treaty

This Treaty shall bind:

(i) the 30 eligible parties referred to in Article 26, from the date on which this Treaty has entered into force;

(ii) each other eligible party referred to in Article 23, from the expiration of three months from the date on which it has deposited its instrument of ratification or accession with the Director General of WIPO.

Article 28
Denunciation of the Treaty

This Treaty may be denounced by any Contracting Party by notification addressed to the Director General of WIPO. Any denunciation shall take effect one year from the date on which the Director General of WIPO received the notification.

Article 29
Languages of the Treaty

(1) This Treaty is signed in a single original in English, Arabic, Chinese, French, Russian and Spanish languages, the versions in all these languages being equally authentic.

(2) An official text in any language other than those referred to in paragraph (1) shall be established by the Director General of WIPO on the request of an interested party, after consultation with all the interested parties. For the purposes of this paragraph, "interested party" means any Member State of WIPO whose official language, or one of whose official languages, is involved and the European Union, and any other intergovernmental organization that may become party to this Treaty, if one of its official languages is involved.

Article 30
Depositary

The Director General of WIPO is the depositary of this Treaty.

Agreed Statements concerning the Beijing Treaty on Audiovisual Performances

(adopted by the Diplomatic Conference on the Protection of Audiovisual Performances in Beijing, on June 24, 2012)

Concerning Article 1

It is understood that nothing in this Treaty affects any rights or obligations under the WIPO Performances and Phonograms Treaty (WPPT) or their interpretation and it is further understood that paragraph 3 does not create any obligations for a Contracting Party to this Treaty to ratify or accede to the WPPT or to comply with any of its provisions.

Concerning Article 1(3)

It is understood that Contracting Parties who are members of the World Trade Organization (WTO) acknowledge all the principles and objectives of the Agreement on Trade- Related Aspects of Intellectual Property Rights (TRIPS Agreement) and understand that nothing in this Treaty affects the provisions of the TRIPS Agreement, including, but not limited to, the provisions relating to anti-competitive practices.

Concerning Article 2(a)

It is understood that the definition of "performers" includes those who perform a literary or artistic work that is created or first fixed in the course of a performance.

Concerning Article 2(b)

It is hereby confirmed that the definition of "audiovisual fixation" contained in Article 2(b) is without prejudice to Article 2(c) of the WPPT.

Concerning Article 5

For the purposes of this Treaty and without prejudice to any other treaty, it is understood that, considering the nature of audiovisual fixations and their production and distribution, modifications of a performance that are made in the normal course of exploitation of the performance, such as editing, compression, dubbing, or formatting, in existing or new media or formats, and that are made in the course of a use authorized by the performer, would not in themselves amount to modifications within the meaning of Article 5(1)(ii). Rights under Article 5(1)(ii) are concerned only with changes that are objectively prejudicial to the performer's reputation in a substantial way. It is also understood that the mere use of new or changed technology or media, as such, does not amount to modification within the meaning of Article 5(1)(ii).

Concerning Article 7

The reproduction right, as set out in Article 7, and the exceptions permitted thereunder through

Article 13, fully apply in the digital environment, in particular to the use of performances in digital form. It is understood that the storage of a protected performance in digital form in an electronic medium constitutes a reproduction within the meaning of this Article.

Concerning Articles 8 and 9

As used in these Articles, the expression "original and copies," being subject to the right of distribution and the right of rental under the said Articles, refers exclusively to fixed copies that can be put into circulation as tangible objects.

Concerning Article 13

The Agreed statement concerning Article 10 (on Limitations and Exceptions) of the WIPO Copyright Treaty (WCT) is applicable mutatis mutandis also to Article 13 (on Limitations and Exceptions) of the Treaty.

Concerning Article 15 as it relates to Article 13

It is understood that nothing in this Article prevents a Contracting Party from adopting effective and necessary measures to ensure that a beneficiary may enjoy limitations and exceptions provided in that Contracting Party's national law, in accordance with Article 13, where technological measures have been applied to an audiovisual performance and the beneficiary has legal access to that performance, in circumstances such as where appropriate and effective measures have not been taken by rights holders in relation to that performance to enable the beneficiary to enjoy the limitations and exceptions under that Contracting Party's national law. Without prejudice to the legal protection of an audiovisual work in which a performance is fixed, it is further understood that the obligations under Article 15 are not applicable to performances unprotected or no longer protected under the national law giving effect to this Treaty.

Concerning Article 15

The expression "technological measures used by performers" should, as this is the case regarding the WPPT, be construed broadly, referring also to those acting on behalf of performers, including their representatives, licensees or assignees, including producers, service providers, and persons engaged in communication or broadcasting using performances on the basis of due authorization.

Concerning Article 16

The Agreed statement concerning Article 12 (on Obligations concerning Rights Management Information) of the WCT is applicable mutatis mutandis also to Article 16 (on Obligations concerning Rights Management Information) of the Treaty.

F19. MARRAKESH TREATY TO FACILTATE ACCESS TO PUBLISHED WORKS FOR PERSONS WHO ARE BLIND, VISUALLY IMPAIRED, OR OTHERWISE PRINT DISABLED

adopted by the Diplomatic Conference on June 28, 2013

PREAMBLE

Recalling the principles of non-discrimination, equal opportunity, accessibility and full and effective participation and inclusion in society, proclaimed in the Universal Declaration of Human Rights and the United Nations Convention on the Rights of Persons with Disabilities,

Mindful of the challenges that are prejudicial to the complete development of persons with visual impairments or with other print disabilities, which limit their freedom of expression, including the freedom to seek, receive and impart information and ideas of all kinds on an equal basis with others, including through all forms of communication of their choice, their enjoyment of the right to education, and the opportunity to conduct research,

Emphasizing the importance of copyright protection as an incentive and reward for literary and artistic creations and of enhancing opportunities for everyone, including persons with visual impairments or with other print disabilities, to participate in the cultural life of the community, to enjoy the arts and to share scientific progress and its benefits,

Aware of the barriers of persons with visual impairments or with other print disabilities to access published works in achieving equal opportunities in society, and the need to both expand the number of works in accessible formats and to improve the circulation of such works,

Taking into account that the majority of persons with visual impairments or with other print disabilities live in developing and least-developed countries, Recognizing that, despite the differences in national copyright laws, the positive impact of new information and communication technologies on the lives of persons with visual impairments or with other print disabilities may be reinforced by an enhanced legal framework at the international level,

Recognizing that many Member States have established limitations and exceptions in their national copyright laws for persons with visual impairments or with other print disabilities, yet there is a continuing shortage of available works in accessible format copies for such persons, and that considerable resources are required for their effort of making works accessible to these persons, and that the lack of possibilities of cross-border exchange of accessible format copies has necessitated duplication of these efforts,

Recognizing both the importance of rightholders' role in making their works accessible to persons with visual impairments or with other print disabilities and the importance of appropriate limitations and exceptions to make works accessible to these persons, particularly when the market is unable to provide such access,

Recognizing the need to maintain a balance between the effective protection of the rights of authors and the larger public interest, particularly education, research and access to information, and that such a balance must facilitate effective and timely access to works for the benefit of persons with visual impairments or with other print disabilities,

Reaffirming the obligations of Contracting Parties under the existing international treaties on the protection of copyright and the importance and flexibility of the three-step test for limitations and exceptions established in Article 9(2) of the Berne Convention for the Protection of Literary and Artistic Works and other international instruments,

Recalling the importance of the Development Agenda recommendations, adopted in 2007 by the General Assembly of the World Intellectual Property Organization (WIPO), which aim to ensure that development considerations form an integral part of the Organization's work,

Recognizing the importance of the international copyright system and desiring to harmonize limitations and exceptions with a view to facilitating access to and use of works by persons with visual impairments or with other print disabilities,

Have agreed as follows:

Article 1

Relation to Other Conventions and Treaties

Nothing in this Treaty shall derogate from any obligations that Contracting Parties have to each other under any other treaties, nor shall it prejudice any rights that a Contracting Party has under any other treaties.

Article 2

Definitions

For the purposes of this Treaty:

(a) "works" means literary and artistic works within the meaning of Article 2(1) of the Berne Convention for the Protection of Literary and Artistic Works, in the form of text, notation and/or related illustrations, whether published or otherwise made publicly available in any media.[1]

(b) "accessible format copy" means a copy of a work in an alternative manner or form which gives a beneficiary person access to the work, including to permit the person to have access as feasibly and comfortably as a person without visual impairment or other print disability. The accessible format copy is used exclusively by beneficiary persons and it must respect the integrity of the original work, taking due consideration of the changes needed to make the work accessible in the alternative format and of the accessibility needs of the beneficiary persons;

(c) "authorized entity" means an entity that is authorized or recognized by the government to provide education, instructional training, adaptive reading or information access to beneficiary persons on a non-profit basis. It also includes a government institution or non-profit organization that provides the same services to beneficiary persons as one of its primary activities or institutional obligations.[2]

An authorized entity establishes and follows its own practices:

(i) to establish that the persons it serves are beneficiary persons;

(ii) to limit to beneficiary persons and/or authorized entities its distribution and making available of accessible format copies;

(iii) to discourage the reproduction, distribution and making available of unauthorized copies; and

(iv) to maintain due care in, and records of, its handling of copies of works, while respecting the privacy of beneficiary persons in accordance with Article 8.

---

[1] Agreed statement concerning Article 2(a): For the purposes of this Treaty, it is understood that this definition includes such works in audio form, such as audiobooks.

[2] Agreed statement concerning Article 2(c): For the purposes of this Treaty, it is understood that "entities recognized by the government" may include entities receiving financial support from the government to provide education, instructional training, adaptive reading or information access to beneficiary persons on a non-profit basis.

Article 3

Beneficiary Persons

A beneficiary person is a person who:

(a) is blind;

(b) has a visual impairment or a perceptual or reading disability which cannot be improved to give visual function substantially equivalent to that of a person who has no such impairment or disability and so is unable to read printed works to substantially the same degree as a person without an impairment or disability; or[3]

(c) is otherwise unable, through physical disability, to hold or manipulate a book or to focus or move the eyes to the extent that would be normally acceptable for reading;

regardless of any other disabilities.

Article 4

National Law Limitations and Exceptions Regarding Accessible Format Copies

(a) Contracting Parties shall provide in their national copyright laws for a limitation or exception to the right of reproduction, the right of distribution, and the right of making available to the public as provided by the WIPO Copyright Treaty (WCT), to facilitate the availability of works in accessible format copies for beneficiary persons. The limitation or exception provided in national law should permit changes needed to make the work accessible in the alternative format.

(b) Contracting Parties may also provide a limitation or exception to the right of public performance to facilitate access to works for beneficiary persons.

2. A Contracting Party may fulfill Article 4(1) for all rights identified therein by providing a limitation or exception in its national copyright law such that:

(a) Authorized entities shall be permitted, without the authorization of the copyright rightholder, to make an accessible format copy of a work, obtain from another authorized entity an accessible format copy, and supply those copies to beneficiary persons by any means, including by non-commercial lending or by electronic communication by wire or wireless means, and undertake any intermediate steps to achieve those objectives, when all of the following conditions are met:

   (i) the authorized entity wishing to undertake said activity has lawful access to that work or a copy of that work;

   (ii) the work is converted to an accessible format copy, which may include any means needed to navigate information in the accessible format, but does not introduce changes other than those needed to make the work accessible to the beneficiary person;

   (iii) such accessible format copies are supplied exclusively to be used by beneficiary persons; and

   (iv) the activity is undertaken on a non-profit basis; and

---

[3] Agreed statement concerning Article 3(b): Nothing in this language implies that "cannot be improved" requires the use of all possible medical diagnostic procedures and treatments.

(b) A beneficiary person, or someone acting on his or her behalf including a primary caretaker or caregiver, may make an accessible format copy of a work for the personal use of the beneficiary person or otherwise may assist the beneficiary person to make and use accessible format copies where the beneficiary person has lawful access to that work or a copy of that work.

3. A Contracting Party may fulfill Article 4(1) by providing other limitations or exceptions in its national copyright law pursuant to Articles 10 and 11.[4]

4. A Contracting Party may confine limitations or exceptions under this Article to works which, in the particular accessible format, cannot be obtained commercially under reasonable terms for beneficiary persons in that market. Any Contracting Party availing itself of this possibility shall so declare in a notification deposited with the Director General of WIPO at the time of ratifi- cation of, acceptance of or accession to this Treaty or at any time thereafter.[5]

5. It shall be a matter for national law to determine whether limitations or exceptions under this Article are subject to remuneration.

Article 5

Cross-Border Exchange of Accessible Format Copies

1. Contracting Parties shall provide that if an accessible format copy is made under a limitation or exception or pursuant to operation of law, that accessible format copy may be distributed or made available by an authorized entity to a beneficiary person or an authorized entity in another Contracting Party.[6]

2. A Contracting Party may fulfill Article 5(1) by providing a limitation or exception in its national copyright law such that:

(a) authorized entities shall be permitted, without the authorization of the rightholder, to distribute or make available for the exclusive use of beneficiary persons accessible format copies to an authorized entity in another Contracting Party; and

(b) authorized entities shall be permitted, without the authorization of the rightholder and pursuant to Article 2(c), to distribute or make available accessible format copies to a beneficiary person in another Contracting Party;

provided that prior to the distribution or making available the originating authorized entity did not know or have reasonable grounds to know that the accessible format copy would be used for other than beneficiary persons.[7]

3. A Contracting Party may fulfill Article 5(1) by providing other limitations

---

[4] Agreed statement concerning Article 4(3): It is understood that this paragraph neither reduces nor extends the scope of applicability of limitations and exceptions permitted under the Berne Convention, as regards the right of translation, with respect to persons with visual impairments or with other print disabilities.

[5] Agreed statement concerning Article 4(4): It is understood that a commercial availability requirement does not prejudge whether or not a limitation or exception under this Article is consistent with the three-step test.

[6] Agreed statement concerning Article 5(1): It is further understood that nothing in this Treaty reduces or extends the scope of exclusive rights under any other treaty.

[7] Agreed statement concerning Article 5(2): It is understood that, to distribute or make available accessible format copies directly to a beneficiary person in another Contracting Party, it may be appropriate for an authorized entity to apply further measures to confirm that the person it is serving is a beneficiary person and to follow its own practices as described in Article 2(c).

or exceptions in its national copyright law pursuant to Articles 5(4), 10 and 11.

(a) When an authorized entity in a Contracting Party receives accessible format copies pursuant to Article 5(1) and that Contracting Party does not have obligations under Article 9 of the Berne Convention, it will ensure, consistent with its own legal system and practices, that the accessible format copies are only reproduced, distributed or made available for the benefit of beneficiary persons in that Contracting Party's jurisdiction.

(b) The distribution and making available of accessible format copies by an authorized entity pursuant to Article 5(1) shall be limited to that jurisdiction unless the Contracting Party is a Party to the WIPO Copyright Treaty or otherwise limits limitations and exceptions implementing this Treaty to the right of distribution and the right of making available to the public to certain special cases which do not conflict with a normal exploitation of the work and do not unreasonably prejudice the legitimate interests of the rightholder.[8,9].

(c) Nothing in this Article affects the determination of what constitutes an act of distribution or an act of making available to the public.

5. Nothing in this Treaty shall be used to address the issue of exhaustion of rights.

Article 6
Importation of Accessible Format Copies

To the extent that the national law of a Contracting Party would permit a beneficiary person, someone acting on his or her behalf, or an authorized entity, to make an accessible format copy of a work, the national law of that Contracting Party shall also permit them to import an accessible format copy for the benefit of beneficiary persons, without the authorization of the rightholder.[10]

Article 7
Obligations Concerning Technological Measures

Contracting Parties shall take appropriate measures, as necessary, to ensure that when they provide adequate legal protection and effective legal remedies against the circumvention of effective technological measures, this legal protection does not prevent beneficiary persons from enjoying the limitations and exceptions provided for in this Treaty.[11]

Article 8
Respect for Privacy

In the implementation of the limitations and exceptions provided for in this

---

[8] Agreed statement concerning Article 5(4)(b): It is understood that nothing in this Treaty requires or implies that a Contracting Party adopt or apply the three-step test beyond its obligations under this instrument or under other international treaties.

[9] Agreed statement concerning Article 5(4)(b): It is understood that nothing in this Treaty creates any obligations for a Contracting Party to ratify or accede to the WCT or to comply with any of its provisions and nothing in this Treaty prejudices any rights, limitations and exceptions contained in the WCT.

[10] Agreed statement concerning Article 6: It is understood that the Contracting Parties have the same flexibilities set out in Article 4 when implementing their obligations under Article 6.

[11] Agreed statement concerning Article 7: It is understood that authorized entities, in various circumstances, choose to apply technological measures in the making, distribution and making available of accessible format copies and nothing herein disturbs such practices when in accordance with national law.

Treaty, Contracting Parties shall endeavor to protect the privacy of beneficiary persons on an equal basis with others.

Article 9

Cooperation to Facilitate Cross-Border Exchange

1. Contracting Parties shall endeavor to foster the cross-border exchange of accessible format copies by encouraging the voluntary sharing of information to assist authorized entities in identifying one another. The International Bureau of WIPO shall establish an information access point for this purpose.

2. Contracting Parties undertake to assist their authorized entities engaged in activities under Article 5 to make information available regarding their practices pursuant to Article 2(c), both through the sharing of information among authorized entities, and through making available information on their policies and practices, including related to cross-border exchange of accessible format copies, to interested parties and members of the public as appropriate.

3. The International Bureau of WIPO is invited to share information, where available, about the functioning of this Treaty.

4. Contracting Parties recognize the importance of international cooperation and its promotion, in support of national efforts for realization of the purpose and objectives of this Treaty.[12]

Article 10

General Principles on Implementation

1. Contracting Parties undertake to adopt the measures necessary to ensure the application of this Treaty.

2. Nothing shall prevent Contracting Parties from determining the appropriate method of implementing the provisions of this Treaty within their own legal system and practice.[13]

3. Contracting Parties may fulfill their rights and obligations under this Treaty through limitations or exceptions specifically for the benefit of beneficiary persons, other limitations or exceptions, or a combination thereof, within their national legal system and practice. These may include judicial, administrative or regulatory determinations for the benefit of beneficiary persons as to fair practices, dealings or uses to meet their needs consistent with the Contracting Parties' rights and obligations under the Berne Convention, other international treaties, and Article 11.

Article 11

General Obligations on Limitations and Exceptions

In adopting measures necessary to ensure the application of this Treaty, a Contracting Party may exercise the rights and shall comply with the obligations

---

[12] Agreed statement concerning Article 9: It is understood that Article 9 does not imply mandatory registration for authorized entities nor does it constitute a precondition for authorized entities to engage in activities recognized under this Treaty; but it provides for a possibility for sharing information to facilitate the cross-border exchange of accessible format copies.

[13] Agreed statement concerning Article 10(2): It is understood that when a work qualifies as a work under Article 2(a), including such works in audio form, the limitations and exceptions provided for by this Treaty apply mutatis mutandis to related rights as necessary to make the accessible format copy, to distribute it and to make it available to beneficiary persons.

that that Contracting Party has under the Berne Convention, the Agreement on Trade-Related Aspects of Intellectual Property Rights and the WIPO Copyright Treaty, including their interpretative agreements so that:

(a) in accordance with Article 9(2) of the Berne Convention, a Contracting Party may permit the reproduction of works in certain special cases provided that such reproduction does not conflict with a normal exploitation of the work and does not unreasonably prejudice the legitimate interests of the author;

(b) in accordance with Article 13 of the Agreement on Trade-Related Aspects of Intellectual Property Rights, a Contracting Party shall confine limitations or exceptions to exclusive rights to certain special cases which do not conflict with a normal exploitation of the work and do not unreasonably prejudice the legitimate interests of the rightholder;

(c) in accordance with Article 10(1) of the WIPO Copyright Treaty, a Contracting Party may provide for limitations of or exceptions to the rights granted to authors under the WCT in certain special cases, that do not conflict with a normal exploitation of the work and do not unreasonably prejudice the legitimate interests of the author;

(d) in accordance with Article 10(2) of the WIPO Copyright Treaty, a Contracting Party shall confine, when applying the Berne Convention, any limitations of or exceptions to rights to certain special cases that do not conflict with a normal exploitation of the work and do not unreasonably prejudice the legitimate interests of the author.

Article 12

Other Limitations and Exceptions

1. Contracting Parties recognize that a Contracting Party may implement in its national law other copyright limitations and exceptions for the benefit of beneficiary persons than are provided by this Treaty having regard to that Contracting Party's economic situation, and its social and cultural needs, in conformity with that Contracting Party's international rights and obligations, and in the case of a least-developed country taking into account its special needs and its particular international rights and obligations and flexibilities thereof.

2. This Treaty is without prejudice to other limitations and exceptions for persons with disabilities provided by national law.

Article 13

Assembly

(a) The Contracting Parties shall have an Assembly.

(b) Each Contracting Party shall be represented in the Assembly by one delegate who may be assisted by alternate delegates, advisors and experts.

(c) The expenses of each delegation shall be borne by the Contracting Party that has appointed the delegation. The Assembly may ask WIPO to grant financial assistance to facilitate the participation of delegations of Contracting Parties that are regarded as developing countries in conformity with the established practice of the General Assembly of the United Nations or that are countries in transition to a market economy.

(a) The Assembly shall deal with matters concerning the maintenance and development of this Treaty and the application and operation of this Treaty.

(b) The Assembly shall perform the function allocated to it under Article 15 in respect of the admission of certain intergovernmental organizations to become party to this Treaty.

(c) The Assembly shall decide the convocation of any diplomatic conference for the revision of this Treaty and give the necessary instructions to the Director General of WIPO for the preparation of such diplomatic conference.

(a) Each Contracting Party that is a State shall have one vote and shall vote only in its own name.

(b) Any Contracting Party that is an intergovernmental organization may participate in the vote, in place of its Member States, with a number of votes equal to the number of its Member States which are party to this Treaty. No such intergovernmental organization shall participate in the vote if any one of its Member States exercises its right to vote and vice versa.

4. The Assembly shall meet upon convocation by the Director General and, in the absence of exceptional circumstances, during the same period and at the same place as the General Assembly of WIPO.

5. The Assembly shall endeavor to take its decisions by consensus and shall establish its own rules of procedure, including the convocation of extraordinary sessions, the requirements of a quorum and, subject to the provisions of this Treaty, the required majority for various kinds of decisions.

Article 14

International Bureau

The International Bureau of WIPO shall perform the administrative tasks concerning this Treaty.

Article 15

Eligibility for Becoming Party to the Treaty

1. Any Member State of WIPO may become party to this Treaty.

2. The Assembly may decide to admit any intergovernmental organization to become party to this Treaty which declares that it is competent in respect of, and has its own legislation binding on all its Member States on, matters covered by this Treaty and that it has been duly authorized, in accordance with its internal procedures, to become party to this Treaty.

3. The European Union, having made the declaration referred to in the preceding paragraph at the Diplomatic Conference that has adopted this Treaty, may become party to this Treaty.

Article 16

Rights and Obligations Under the Treaty

Subject to any specific provisions to the contrary in this Treaty, each Contracting Party shall enjoy all of the rights and assume all of the obligations under this Treaty.

Article 17

Signature of the Treaty

This Treaty shall be open for signature at the Diplomatic Conference in Marrakesh, and thereafter at the headquarters of WIPO by any eligible party for one year after its adoption.

Article 18

Entry into Force of the Treaty

This Treaty shall enter into force three months after 20 eligible parties referred to in Article 15 have deposited their instruments of ratification or accession.

Article 19

Effective Date of Becoming Party to the Treaty

This Treaty shall bind:

(a) the 20 eligible parties referred to in Article 18, from the date on which this Treaty has entered into force;

(b) each other eligible party referred to in Article 15, from the expiration of three months from the date on which it has deposited its instrument of ratification or accession with the Director General of WIPO.

Article 20

Denunciation of the Treaty

This Treaty may be denounced by any Contracting Party by notification addressed to the Director General of WIPO. Any denunciation shall take effect one year from the date on which the Director General of WIPO received the notification.

Article 21

Languages of the Treaty

1. This Treaty is signed in a single original in English, Arabic, Chinese, French, Russian and Spanish languages, the versions in all these languages being equally authentic.

2. An official text in any language other than those referred to in Article 21(1) shall be established by the Director General of WIPO on the request of an interested party, after consultation with all the interested parties. For the purposes of this paragraph, "interested party" means any Member State of WIPO whose official language, or one of whose official languages, is involved and the European Union, and any other intergovernmental organization that may become party to this Treaty, if one of its official languages is involved.

Article 22

Depositary

The Director General of WIPO is the depositary of this Treaty.

Done in Marrakesh on the 27th day of June, 2013.

PART G

TREATY ON THE FUNCTIONING OF THE EUROPEAN UNION (TFEU)

PART G

TREATY ON THE FUNCTIONING OF THE EUROPEAN UNION (TFEU)

G1. Extracts From the Consolidated Version of the Treaty on the Functioning of the European Union[i]

(Formerly Known as the European Community Treaty of Rome)

(March 25, 1957)

PART ONE—PRINCIPLES

Article 1 (new)

1. This Treaty organises the functioning of the Union and determines the areas of, delimitation of, and arrangements for exercising its competencies.

2. This Treaty and the Treaty on European Union constitute the Treaties on which the Union is founded. These two Treaties, which have the same legal value, shall be referred to as 'the Treaties'.

TITLE I—Categories and Areas of Union Competence

Article 2 (new)

1. When the Treaties confer on the Union exclusive competence in a specific area, only the Union may legislate and adopt legally binding acts, the Member States being able to do so themselves only if so empowered by the Union or for the implementation of Union acts.

2. When the Treaties confer on the Union a competence shared with the Member States in a specific area, the Union and the Member States may legislate and adopt legally binding acts in that area. The Member States shall exercise their competence to the extent that the Union has not exercised its competence. The Member States shall again exercise their competence to the extent that the Union has decided to cease exercising its competence.

3. The Member States shall coordinate their economic and employment policies within arrangements as determined by this Treaty, which the Union shall have competence to provide.

4. The Union shall have competence, in accordance with the provisions of the Treaty on European Union, to define and implement a common foreign and security policy, including the progressive framing of a common defence policy.

5. In certain areas and under the conditions laid down in the Treaties, the Union shall have competence to carry out actions to support, coordinate or supplement the actions of the Member States, without thereby superseding their competence in these areas. Legally binding acts of the Union adopted on the basis of the provisions of the Treaties relating to these areas shall not entail harmonisation of Member States' laws or regulations.

6. The scope of and arrangements for exercising the Union's competences shall be determined by the provisions of the Treaties relating to each area.

Article 3 (new)

1. The Union shall have exclusive competence in the following areas:
(a) customs union;

---

[i] *Editorial Note*: As Amended by the Single European Act of February 17, 1986, the Maastricht Treaty of February 7, 1992, the Treaty of Amsterdam of October 2, 1997, the Treaty of Nice of March 10, 2001 and the Treaty of Lisbon of December 13, 2007.

(b) the establishing of the competition rules necessary for the functioning of the internal market;

(c) monetary policy for the member states whose currency is the euro;

(d) the conservation of marine biological resources under the common fisheries policy;

(e) common commercial policy.

2. The Union shall also have exclusive competence for the conclusion of an international agreement when its conclusion is provided for in a legislative act of the Union or is necessary to enable the Union to exercise its internal competence, or in so far as its conclusion may affect common rules or alter their scope.

Article 4 (new)

1. The Union shall share competence with the Member States where the Treaties confer on it a competence which does not relate to the areas referred to in Articles 3 and 6.

2. Shared competence between the Union and the Member States applies in the following principal areas:

(a) internal market;

(b) social policy, for the aspects defined in this Treaty;

(c) economic, social and territorial cohesion;

(d) agriculture and fisheries, excluding the conservation of marine biological resources;

(e) environment;

(f) consumer protection;

(g) transport;

(h) trans-European networks;

(i) energy;

(j) area of freedom, security and justice;

(k) common safety concerns in public health matters, for the aspects defined in this Treaty.

3. In the areas of research, technological development and space, the Union shall have competence to carry out activities, in particular to define and implement programmes; however, the exercise of that competence shall not result in Member States being prevented from exercising theirs.

4. In the areas of development cooperation and humanitarian aid, the Union shall have competence to carry out activities and conduct a common policy; however, the exercise of that competence shall not result in Member States being prevented from exercising theirs.

Article 5 (new)

1. The Member States shall coordinate their economic policies within the Union. To this end, the Council shall adopt measures, in particular broad guidelines for these policies. Specific provisions shall apply to those Member States whose currency is the euro.

2. The Union shall take measures to ensure coordination of the employment policies of the Member States, in particular by defining guidelines for these policies.

3. The Union may take initiatives to ensure coordination of Member States' social policies.

Article 6 (new)

The Union shall have competence to carry out actions to support, coordinate or supplement the actions of the Member States. The areas of such action shall, at European level, be:

(a) protection and improvement of human health;
(b) industry;
(c) culture;
(d) tourism;
(e) education, vocational training, youth and sport;
(f) civil protection;
(g) administrative cooperation.

TITLE II—Provisions Having General Application

Article 8 (ex Article 3, paragraph 2; previously Article 3, paragraph 2)

In all its activities the Union shall aim to eliminate inequalities, and to promote equality, between men and women.

PART TWO—NON-DISCRIMINATION AND CITIZENSHIP OF THE UNION

Article 18 (ex Article 12; previously Article 6)

Within the scope of application of the Treaties, and without prejudice to any special provisions contained therein, any discrimination on grounds of nationality shall be prohibited.

The European Parliament and the Council, acting in accordance with the ordinary legislative procedure, may adopt rules designed to prohibit such discrimination.

PART THREE—UNION POLICIES AND INTERNAL ACTIONS

TITLE I—The Internal Market

Article 26 (ex Article 14; previously Article 7a)

1. The Union shall adopt measures with the aim of establishing or ensuring the functioning of the internal market in accordance with the relevant provisions of the Treaties.

2. The internal market shall comprise an area without internal frontiers in which the free movement of goods, persons, services and capital is ensured in accordance with the provisions of the Treaties.

3. The Council, on a proposal from the Commission, shall determine the guidelines and conditions necessary to ensure balanced progress in all the sectors concerned.

TITLE II—Free Movement of Goods

CHAPTER 3 Prohibition of Quantitative Restrictions between Member States

Article 34 (ex Article 28; previously Article 30)

Quantitative restrictions on imports and all measures having equivalent effect shall be prohibited between Member States.

Article 35 (ex Article 29; previously Article 34)

Quantitative restrictions on exports, and all measures having equivalent effect, shall be prohibited between Member States.

Article 36 (ex Article 30; previously Article 36)

The provisions of Articles 34 and 35 shall not preclude prohibitions or restrictions on imports, exports or goods in transit justified on grounds of public morality, public policy or public security; the protection of health and life of humans, animals or plants; the protection of national treasures possessing artistic, historic or archaeological value; or the protection of industrial and commercial property. Such prohibitions or restrictions shall not, however, constitute a means of arbitrary discrimination or a disguised restriction on trade between Member States.

TITLE IV—Free Movement of Persons, Services and Capital

CHAPTER 3 SERVICES

Article 56 (ex Article 49; previously Article 59)

Within the framework of the provisions set out below, restrictions on freedom to provide services within the Union shall be prohibited in respect of nationals of Member States who are established in a Member State other than that of the person for whom the services are intended.

The European Parliament and the Council, acting in accordance with the ordinary legislative procedure, may extend the provisions of the Chapter to nationals of a third country who provide services and who are established within the Union.

Article 57 (ex Article 50; previously Article 60)

Services shall be considered to be "services" within the meaning of the Treaties where they are normally provided for remuneration, insofar as they are not governed by the provisions relating to freedom of movement for goods, capital and persons.

"Services" shall in particular include:

(a) activities of an industrial character;

(b) activities of a commercial character;

(c) activities of craftsmen;

(d) activities of the professions.

Without prejudice to the provisions of the Chapter relating to the right of establishment, the person providing a service may, in order to do so, temporarily pursue his activity in the Member State where the service is provided, under the same conditions as are imposed by that State on its own nationals.

TITLE VII—Common Rules on Competition, Taxation and Approximation of Laws

CHAPTER 1 RULES ON COMPETITION

Section 1 —RULES APPLYING TO UNDERTAKINGS

Article 101 (ex Article 81; previously Article 85)

1. The following shall be prohibited as incompatible with the internal market: all agreements between undertakings, decisions by associations of undertakings and concerted practices which may affect trade between Member States and which have as their object or effect the prevention, restriction or distortion of competition within the internal market, and in particular those which:

(a) directly or indirectly fix purchase or selling prices or any other trading conditions;

(b) limit or control production, markets, technical development, or investment;

(c) share markets or sources of supply;

(d) apply dissimilar conditions to equivalent transactions with other trading parties, thereby placing them at a competitive disadvantage;

(e) make the conclusion of contracts subject to acceptance by the other parties of supplementary obligations which, by their nature or according to commercial usage, have no connection with the subject of such contracts.

2. Any agreements or decisions prohibited pursuant to this Article shall be automatically void.

3. The provisions of paragraph 1 may, however, be declared inapplicable in the case of:

— any agreement or category of agreements between undertakings;

— any decision or category of decisions by associations of undertakings;

— any concerted practice or category of concerted practices, which contributes to improving the production or distribution of goods or to promoting technical or economic progress, while allowing consumers a fair share of the resulting benefit, and which does not:

    (a) impose on the undertakings concerned restrictions which are not indispensable to the attainment of these objectives;

    (b) afford such undertakings the possibility of eliminating competition in respect of a substantial part of the products in question.

Article 102 (ex Article 82; previously Article 86)

Any abuse by one or more undertakings of a dominant position within the internal market or in a substantial part of it shall be prohibited as incompatible with the internal market insofar as it may affect trade between Member States.

Such abuse may, in particular, consist in:

(a) directly or indirectly imposing unfair purchase or selling prices or other unfair trading conditions;

(b) limiting production, markets or technical development to the prejudice of consumers;

(c) applying dissimilar conditions to equivalent transactions with other trading parties, thereby placing them at a competitive disadvantage;

(d) making the conclusion of contracts subject to acceptance by the other parties of supplementary obligations which, by their nature or according to commercial usage, have no connection with the subject of such contracts.

CHAPTER 3 APPROXIMATION OF LAWS

Article 114 (ex Article 95; previously 100a)

1. Save where otherwise provided in the Treaties, the following provisions shall apply for the achievement of the objectives set out in Article 26. The European Parliament and the Council shall, acting in accordance with the ordinary legislative procedure and after consulting the Economic and Social Committee, adopt the measures for the approximation of the provisions laid down by law, regulation or administrative action in Member States which have as their object the establishment and functioning of the internal market.

2. Paragraph 1 shall not apply to fiscal provisions, to those relating to the free movement of persons nor to those relating to the rights and interests of employed persons.

3. . The Commission, in its proposals envisaged in paragraph 1 concerning health, safety, environmental protection and consumer protection, will take as a base a high level of protection, taking account in particular of any new development based on scientific facts. Within their respective powers, the European Parliament and the Council will also seek to achieve this objective.

4. If, after the adoption of a harmonisation measure by the European Parliament and the Council, by the Council or by the Commission, a Member State deems it necessary to maintain national provisions on grounds of major needs referred to in Article 36, or relating to the protection of the environment or the working environment, it shall notify the Commission of these provisions as well as the grounds for maintaining them.

5. Moreover, without prejudice to paragraph 4, if, after the adoption of a harmonisation measure, by the European Parliament and the Council, by the Council or by the Commission, a Member State deems it necessary to introduce national provisions based on new scientific evidence relating to the protection of the environment or the working environment on grounds of a problem specific to that Member State arising after the adoption of the harmonisation measure, it shall notify the Commission of the envisaged provisions as well as the grounds for introducing them.

6. The Commission shall, within six months of the notifications as referred to in paragraphs 4 and 5, approve or reject the national provisions involved after having verified whether or not they are a means of arbitrary discrimination or a disguised restriction on trade between Member Sates and whether or not they shall constitute an obstacle to the functioning of the internal market.

In the absence of a decision by the Commission within this period the national provisions referred to in paragraphs 4 and 5 shall be deemed to have been approved.

When justified by the complexity of the matter and in the absence of danger for human health, the Commission may notify the Member State concerned that the period referred to in this paragraph may be extended for a further period of up to six months.

7. When, pursuant to paragraph 6, a Member State is authorised to maintain or introduce national provisions derogating from a harmonisation measure, the Commission shall immediately examine whether to propose an adaptation to that measure.

8. When a Member State raises a specific problem on public health in a field which has been the subject of prior harmonisation measures, it shall bring it to the attention of the Commission which shall immediately examine whether to propose appropriate measures to the Council.

9. By way of derogation from the procedure laid down in Articles 258 and 259, the Commission and any Member State may bring the matter directly before the Court of Justice of the European Union if it considers that another Member State is making improper use of the powers provided for in this Article.

10. The harmonisation measures referred to above shall, in appropriate cases, include a safeguard clause authorising the Member States to take, for one or more of the non-economic reasons referred to in Article 36, provisional measures subject to a Union control procedure.

Article 115 (ex Article 94; previously Article 100)

Without prejudice to Article 114, the Council shall, acting unanimously in accordance wit h a special legislative procedure and after consulting the European Parliament and the Economic and Social Committee, issue directives for the approximation of such laws, regulations or administrative provisions of the Member States as directly affect the establishment or functioning of the internal market.

Article 118 (New)

In the context of the establishment and functioning of the internal market, the European Parliament and the Council, acting in accordance with the ordinary legislative procedure, shall establish measures for the creation of European intellectual property rights to provide uniform protection of intellectual property rights throughout the Union and for the setting up of centralised Union-wide authorisation, coordination and supervision arrangements.

The Council, acting in accordance with a special legislative procedure, shall by means of regulations establish language arrangements for the European intellectual property rights. The Council shall act unanimously after consulting the European Parliament.

TITLE VIII—Economic and Monetary Policy

Article 119 (ex Article 4; previously Article 3a)

1. For the purposes set out in Article 3 of the Treaty on European Union, the activities of the Member States and the Union shall include, as provided in the Treaties, the adoption of an economic policy which is based on the close coordination of Member States' economic policies, on the internal market and on the definition of common objectives, and conducted in accordance with the principle of an open market economy with free competition.

2. Concurrently with the foregoing, and as provided in the Treaties and in accordance with the procedures set out therein, these activities shall include a single currency, the euro, and the definition and conduct of a single monetary policy and exchange-rate policy the primary objective of both of which shall be to maintain price stability and, without prejudice to this objective, to support the general economic policies in the Union, in accordance with the principle of an open market economy with free competition.

3. These activities of the Member States and the Union shall entail compliance with the following guiding principles: stable prices, sound public finances and monetary conditions and a sustainable balance of payments.

TITLE XIII—Culture

Article 167 (ex Article 151; previously Article 128)

1. The Union shall contribute to the flowering of the cultures of the Member States, while respecting their national and regional diversity and at the same time bringing the common cultural heritage to the fore.

2. Action by the Union shall be aimed at encouraging cooperation between Member States and, if necessary, supporting and supplementing their action in the following areas:

— improvement of the knowledge and dissemination of the culture and history of the European peoples,

— conservation and safeguarding of cultural heritage of European significance,

— non-commercial cultural exchanges,

— artistic and literary creation, including in the audiovisual sector.

3. The Union and the Member States shall foster cooperation with third countries and the competent international organisations in the sphere of culture, in particular the Council of Europe.

4. The Union shall take cultural aspects into account in its action under other provisions of the Treaties, in particular in order to respect and to promote the diversity of its cultures.

5. In order to contribute to the achievement of the objectives referred to in this Article:
— the European Parliament and the Council acting in accordance with the ordinary legislative procedure and after consulting the Committee of the Regions, shall adopt incentive measures, excluding any harmonisation of the laws and regulations of the Member States,
— the Council, on a proposal from the Commission, shall adopt recommendations.

TITLE XIX—Research and Technological Development and Space

Article 179 (ex Article 163; previously Article 130f)

1. The Union shall have the objective of strengthening its scientific and technological bases by achieving a European research area in which researchers, scientific knowledge and technology circulate freely, and encouraging it to become more competitive, including in its industry, while promoting all the research activities deemed necessary by virtue of other Chapters of the Treaties.

2. For this purpose the Union shall, throughout the Union, encourage undertakings, including small and medium-sized undertakings, research centres and universities in their research and technological development activities of high quality; it shall support their efforts to cooperate with one another, aiming, notably, at permitting researchers to cooperate freely across borders and at enabling undertakings to exploit the internal market potential to the full, in particular through the opening-up of national public contracts, the definition of common standards and the removal of legal and fiscal obstacles to that cooperation.

3. All Union activities under the Treaties in the area of research and technological development, including demonstration projects, shall be decided on and implemented in accordance with the provisions of this Title.

Article 180 (ex Article 164; previously Article 130g)

In pursuing these objectives, the Union shall carry out the following activities, complementing the activities carried out in the Member States:
(a) implementation of research, technological development and demonstration programmes, by promoting cooperation with and between undertakings, research centres and universities;
(b) promotion of cooperation in the field of Union research, technological development and demonstration with third countries and international organisations;
(c) dissemination and optimisation of the results of activities in Union research, technological development and demonstration;
(d) stimulation of the training and mobility of researchers in the Union.

PART SIX—INSTITUTIONAL AND FINANCIAL PROVISIONS

TITLE I—Institutional Provisions

Section 5 —THE COURT OF JUSTICE OF THE EUROPEAN UNION

Article 267 (Article 234; previously Article 177)

The Court of Justice of the European Union shall have jurisdiction to give preliminary rulings concerning:
(a) the interpretation of the Treaties;
(b) the validity and interpretation of acts of the institutions, bodies, offices or agencies of the Union.

Where such a question is raised before any court or tribunal of a Member State, that court or tribunal may, if it considers that a decision on the question is necessary to enable it to give judgment, request the Court to give a ruling thereon.

Where any such question is raised in a case pending before a court or tribunal of a Member State against whose decisions there is no judicial remedy under national law, that court or tribunal shall bring the matter before the Court.

If such a question is raised in a case pending before a court or tribunal of a Member State with regard to a person in custody, the Court of Justice of the European Union shall act with the minimum of delay.

CHAPTER 2 LEGAL ACTS OF THE UNION, ADOPTION PROCEDURES AND OTHER PROVISIONS

Section 1 —The Legal Acts of the Union

Article 288 (ex Article 249; previously Article 189)

To exercise the Union's competences, the institutions shall adopt regulations, directives, decisions, recommendations and opinions.

A regulation shall have general application. It shall be binding in its entirety and directly applicable in all Member States.

A directive shall be binding, as to the result to be achieved, upon each Member State to which it is addressed, but shall leave to the national authorities the choice of form and methods.

A decision shall be binding in its entirety.

A decision which specifies those to whom it is addressed shall be binding only on them.

Recommendations and opinions shall have no binding force.

PART SEVEN—GENERAL AND FINAL PROVISIONS

Article 345 (Article 295; previously Article 222)

The Treaties shall in no way prejudice the rules in Member States governing the system of property ownership.

G2. EXTRACT FROM THE TREATY OF LISBON AMENDING THE TREATY ON EUROPEAN UNION AND THE TREATY ESTABLISHING THE EUROPEAN COMMUNITY

Signed at Lisbon, 13 December 2007 and entered into force on 1 December 2009

AMENDMENTS TO THE TREATY ON EUROPEAN UNION AND TO THE TREATY ESTABLISHING THE EUROPEAN COMMUNITY

Section I—The Legal Acts of the Union

Article 5

1. The articles, sections, chapters, titles and parts of the Treaty on European Union and of the Treaty establishing the European Community, as amended by this Treaty, shall be renumbered in accordance with the tables of equivalences set out in the Annex to this Treaty, and which form an integral part of this Treaty.

2. The cross-references to the articles, sections, chapters, titles and parts of the Treaty on European Union and of the Treaty on the Functioning of the European Union, as well as between them, shall be adapted pursuant to paragraph 1 and the references to paragraphs of the said articles as renumbered or re-ordered by the provisions of this Treaty shall be adapted in accordance with those provisions. References to the articles, sections, chapters, titles and parts of the Treaty on European Union and of the Treaty establishing the European Community contained inthe other treaties and acts of primary legislation on which the Union is founded shall be adapted pursuant to paragraph 1 of this Article. References to recitals of the Treaty on European Union or to paragraphs or articles of the Treaty on European Union or of the Treaty establishing the European Community as re-numbered or re-arranged by the provisions of this Treaty shall be adapted pursuant to this latter. Such adaptations shall, where necessary, also apply in the event that the provision in question has been repealed.

3. The references to the recitals, articles, sections, chapters, titles and parts of the Treaty on European Union and of the Treaty establishing the European Community, as amended by this Treaty, contained in other instruments or acts shall be understood as referring to the recitals, articles, sections, chapters, titles and parts of those Treaties as renumbered pursuant to paragraph 1 and, respectively, to the paragraphs of the said articles, as renumbered or re-arranged by certain provisions of this Treaty.

PART H

EU DIRECTIVES

PART H

EU DIRECTIVES

Council Directive 87/54/EEC of December 16, 1986 on the legal protection of topographies of semiconductor products

([1987] O.J. L24/36)

The Council of the European Communities,

Having regard to the Treaty establishing the European Economic Community and in particular Article 100 thereof,

Having regard to the proposal from the Commission,

Having regard to the opinion of the European Parliament,

Having regard to the opinion of the Economic and Social Committee,

(1) Whereas semiconductor products are playing an increasingly important role in a broad range of industries and semiconductor technology can accordingly be considered as being of fundamental importance for the Community's industrial development;

(2) Whereas the functions of semiconductor products depend in large part on the topographies of such products and whereas the development of such topographies requires the investment of considerable resources, human, technical and financial, while topographies of such products can be copied at a fraction of the cost needed to develop them independently;

(3) Whereas topographies of semiconductor products are at present not clearly protected in all Member States by existing legislation and such protection, where it exists, has different attributes;

(4) Whereas certain existing differences in the legal protection of semiconductor products offered by the laws of the Member States have direct and negative effects on the functioning of the common market as regards semiconductor products and such differences could well become greater as Member States introduce new legislation on this subject;

(5) Whereas existing differences having such effects need to be removed and new ones having a negative effect on the common market prevented from arising;

(6) Whereas, in relation to extension of protection to persons outside the Community, Member States should be free to act on their behalf in so far as Community decisions have not been taken within a limited period of time;

(7) Whereas the Community's legal framework on the protection of topographies of semiconductor products can, in the first instance, be limited to certain basic principles by provisions specifying whom and what should be protected, the exclusive rights on which protected persons should be able to rely to authorize or prohibit certain acts, exceptions to these rights and for how long the protection should last;

(8) Whereas other matters can for the time being be decided in accordance with national law, in particular, whether registration or deposit is required as a condition for protection and, subject to an exclusion of licences granted for the sole reason that a certain period of time has elapsed, whether and on what conditions non-voluntary licences may be granted in respect of protected topographies;

(9) Whereas protection of topographies of semiconductor products in accordance with this Directive should be without prejudice to the application of some other forms of protection;

(10) Whereas further measures concerning the legal protection of topographies of semiconductor products in the Community can be considered at a later stage, if necessary, while the application of common basic principles by all Member States in accordance with the provisions of this Directive is an urgent necessity,

Has Adopted this Directive:

Chapter 1

Definitions

Article 1

1. For the purposes of this Directive:
 (a) a "semiconductor product" shall mean the final or an intermediate form of any product:
   (i) consisting of a body of material which includes a layer of semiconducting material; and
   (ii) having one or more other layers composed of conducting, insulating or semiconducting material, the layers being arranged in accordance with a predetermined three-dimensional pattern; and
   (iii) intended to perform, exclusively or together with other functions, an electronic function;
 (b) the "topography" of a semiconductor product shall mean a series of related images, however fixed or encoded;
   (i) representing the three-dimensional pattern of the layers of which a semiconductor product is composed; and
   (ii) in which series, each image has the pattern or part of the pattern of a surface of the semiconductor product at any stage of its manufacture;
 (c) "commercial exploitation" means the sale, rental, leasing or any other method of commercial distribution, or an offer for these purposes. However, for the purposes of Articles 3(4), 4(1), 7(1), (3) and (4) "commercial exploitation" shall not include exploitation under conditions of confidentiality to the extent that no further distribution to third parties occurs, except where exploitation of a topography takes place under conditions of confidentiality required by a measure taken in conformity with Article 223(1)(b) of the Treaty.

2. The Council acting by qualified majority on a proposal from the Commission, may amend paragraph 1(a)(i) and (ii) in order to adapt these provisions in the light of technical progress.

Chapter 2

Protection of Topographies of Semiconductor Products

Article 2

1. Member States shall protect the topographies of semiconductor products by adopting legislative provisions conferring exclusive rights in accordance with the provisions of the Directive.

2. The topography of a semiconductor product shall be protected in so far as it satisfies the conditions that it is the result of its creator's own intellectual effort and is not commonplace in the semiconductor industry. Where the topography of a semiconductor product consists of elements that are commonplace in the semiconductor industry, it shall be protected only to the extent that the combination of such elements, taken as a whole, fulfils the abovementioned conditions.

Article 3

1. Subject to paragraphs 2 to 5, the right to protection shall apply in favour of persons who are the creators of the topographies of semiconductor products.

2. Member States may provide that,

(a) where a topography is created in the course of the creator's employment, the right to protection shall apply in favour of the creator's employer unless the terms of employment provide to the contrary;

(b) where a topography is created under a contract other than a contract of employment, the right to protection shall apply in favour of a party to the contract by whom the topography has been commissioned, unless the contract provides to the contrary.

3.

(a) As regards the persons referred to in paragraph 1, the right to protection shall apply in favour of natural persons who are nationals of a Member State or who have their habitual residence on the territory of a Member State.

(b) Where Member States make provision in accordance with paragraph 2, the right to protection shall apply in favour of:

   (i) natural persons who are nationals of a Member State or who have their habitual residence on the territory of a Member State;

   (ii) companies or other legal persons which have a real and effective industrial or commercial establishment on the territory of a Member State.

4. Where no right to protection exists in accordance with other provisions of this Article, the right to protection shall also apply in favour of the persons referred to in paragraphs 3(b)(i) and (ii) who:

(a) first commercially exploit within a Member State a topography which has not yet been exploited commercially anywhere in the world; and

(b) have been exclusively authorised to exploit commercially the topography throughout the Community by the person entitled to dispose of it.

5. The right to protection shall also apply in favour of the successors in title of the persons mentioned in paragraphs 1 to 4.

6. Subject to paragraph 7, Member States may negotiate and conclude agreements or understandings with third States and multilateral Conventions concerning the legal protection of topographies of semiconductor products whilst respecting Community law and in particular the rules laid down in this Directive.

7. Member States may enter into negotiations with[i] third States with a view to extending the right to protection to persons who do not benefit from the right to protection according to the provisions of this Directive. Member States who enter into such negotiations shall inform the Commission thereof.

When a Member State wishes to extend protection to persons who otherwise do not benefit from the right to protection according to the provisions of this Directive or to conclude an agreement or understanding on the extension of protection with a non-Member State it shall notify the Commission. The Commission shall inform the other Member States thereof.

The Member State shall hold the extension of protection or the conclusion of the agreement or understanding in abeyance for one month from the date on which it notifies the Commission. However, if within that period the Commission notifies the Member State concerned of its intention to submit a proposal to the Council for all Member States to extend protection in respect of the persons or non-Member State concerned, the Member State shall hold the extension of protection or the conclusion of the agreement or understanding in abeyance for a period of two months from the date of the notification by the Member State.

---

[i] *Editorial Note:* O.J. text has "which".

Where, before the end of this two-month period, the Commission submits such a proposal to the Council, the Member State shall hold the extension of protection or the conclusion of the agreement or understanding in abeyance for a further period of four months from the date on which the proposal was submitted.

In the absence of a Commission notification or proposal or a Council decision within the time limits prescribed above, the Member State may extend protection or conclude the agreement or understanding.

A proposal by the Commission to extend protection, whether or not it is made following a notification by a Member State in accordance with the preceding paragraphs shall be adopted by the Council acting by qualified majority.

A Decision of the Council on the basis of a Commission proposal shall not prevent a Member State from extending protection to persons, in addition to those to benefit from protection in all Member States, who were included in the envisaged extension, agreement or understanding as notified, unless the Council acting by qualified majority has decided otherwise.

8. Commission proposals and Council decisions pursuant to paragraph 7 shall be published for information in the *Official Journal of the European Communities*.

Article 4

1. Member States may provide that the exclusive rights conferred in conformity with Article 2 shall not come into existence or shall no longer apply to the topography of a semiconductor product unless an application for registration in due form has been filed with a public authority within two years of its first commercial exploitation. Member States may require in addition to such registration that material identifying or exemplifying the topography or any combination thereof has been deposited with a public authority, as well as a statement as to the date of first commercial exploitation of the topography where it precedes the date of the application for registration.

2. Member States shall ensure that material deposited in conformity with paragraph 1 is not made available to the public where it is a trade secret. This provision shall be without prejudice to the disclosure of such material pursuant to an order of a court or other competent authority to persons involved in litigation concerning the validity or infringement of the exclusive rights referred to in Article 2.

3. Member States may require that transfers of rights in protected topographies be registered.

4. Member States may subject registration and deposit in accordance with paragraphs 1 and 3 to the payment of fees not exceeding their administrative costs.

5. Conditions prescribing the fulfilment of additional formalities for obtaining or maintaining protection shall not be admitted.

6. Member States which require registration shall provide for legal remedies in favour of a person having the right to protection in accordance with the provisions of this Directive who can prove that another person has applied for or obtained the registration of a topography without his authorisation.

Article 5

1. The exclusive rights referred to in Article 2 shall include the rights to authorise or prohibit any of the following acts:

(a) reproduction of a topography in so far as it is protected under Article 2(2);

(b) commercial exploitation or the importation for that purpose of a topography or of a semiconductor product manufactured by using the topography.

2. Notwithstanding paragraph 1, a Member State may permit the reproduction of a topography privately for non commercial aims.

3. The exclusive rights referred to in paragraph 1(a) shall not apply to reproduction for the purpose of analysing, evaluating or teaching the concepts, processes, systems or techniques embodied in the topography or the topography itself.

4. The exclusive rights referred to in paragraph 1 shall not extend to any such act in relation to a topography meeting the requirements of Article 2(2) and created on the basis of an analysis and evaluation of another topography carried out in conformity with paragraph 3.

5. The exclusive rights to authorise or prohibit the acts specified in paragraph 1(b) shall not apply to any such act committed after the topography or the semiconductor product has been put on the market in a Member State by the person entitled to authorise its marketing or with his consent.

6. A person who, when he acquires a semiconductor product, does not know, or has no reasonable grounds to believe, that the product is protected by an exclusive right conferred by a Member State in conformity with this Directive shall not be prevented from commercially exploiting that product.

However, for acts committed after that person knows, or has reasonable grounds to believe, that the semiconductor product is so protected, Member States shall ensure that on the demand of the rightholder a tribunal may require, in accordance with the provisions of the national law applicable, the payment of adequate remuneration.

7. The provisions of paragraph 6 shall apply to the successors in title of the person referred to in the first sentence of that paragraph.

Article 6

Member States shall not subject the exclusive rights referred to in Article 2 to licences granted, for the sole reason that a certain period of time has elapsed, automatically, and by operation of law.

Article 7

1. Member States shall provide that the exclusive rights referred to in Article 2 shall come into existence:
(a) where registration is the condition for the coming into existence of the exclusive rights in accordance with Article 4, on the earlier of the following dates:
    (i) the date when the topography is first commercially exploited anywhere in the world;
    (ii) the date when an application or registration has been filed in due form; or
(b) when the topography is first commercially exploited anywhere in the world; or
(c) when the topography is first fixed or encoded.

2. Where the exclusive rights come into existence in accordance with paragraph 1(a) or (b), the Member States shall provide, for the period prior to those rights coming into existence, legal remedies in favour of a person having the right to protection in accordance with the provisions of this Directive who can prove that another person has fraudulently reproduced or commercially exploited or imported for that purpose a topography. This paragraph shall be without prejudice to legal remedies made available to enforce the exclusive rights conferred in conformity with Article 2.

3. The exclusive rights shall come to an end 10 years from the end of the calendar year in which the topography is first commercially exploited anywhere

in the world or, where registration is a condition for the coming into existence or continuing application of the exclusive rights, 10 years from the earlier of the following dates:

(a) the end of the calendar year in which the topography is first commercially exploited anywhere in the world;

(b the end of the calendar year in which the application for registration has been filed in due form.

4. Where a topography has not been commercially exploited anywhere in the world within a period of 15 years from its first fixation or encoding, any exclusive rights in existence pursuant to paragraph 1 shall come to an end and no new exclusive rights shall come into existence unless an application for registration in due form has been filed within that period in those Member States where registration is a condition for the coming into existence or continuing application of the exclusive rights.

Article 8

The protection granted to the topographies of semiconductor products in accordance with Article 2 shall not extend to any concept, process, system, technique or encoded information embodied in the topography other than the topography itself.

Article 9

Where the legislation of Member States provides that semiconductor products manufactured using protected topographies may carry an indication, the indication to be used shall be a capital T as follows: T, "T", [T], "T" or [T].

CHAPTER 3

CONTINUED APPLICATION OF OTHER LEGAL PROVISIONS

Article 10

1. The provisions of this Directive shall be without prejudice to legal provisions concerning patent and utility model rights.

2. The provisions of this Directive shall be without prejudice:

(a) to rights conferred by the Member States in fulfillment of their obligations under international agreements, including provisions extending such rights to nationals of, or residents in, the territory of the Member State concerned;

(b) to the law of copyright in Member States, restricting the reproduction of drawing or other artistic representations of topographies by copying them in two dimensions.

3. Protection granted by national law to topographies of semiconductor products fixed or encoded before the entry into force of the national provisions enacting the Directive, but no later than the date set out in Article 11(1), shall not be affected by the provisions of this Directive.

CHAPTER 4

FINAL PROVISIONS

Article 11

1. Member States shall bring into force the laws, regulations or administrative provisions necessary to comply with this Directive by November 7 1987.

2. Member States shall ensure that they communicate to the Commission the texts of the main provisions of national law which they adopt in the field covered by this Directive.

Article 12

This Directive is addressed to the Member States.

Done at Brussels, 16 December 1986.

H2. COUNCIL DIRECTIVE 93/83/EEC

Council Directive 93/83/EEC of September 27, 1993 on the coordination of certain rules concerning copyright and rights related to copyright applicable to satellite broadcasting and cable retransmission

([1993] O.J. L248)

THE COUNCIL OF THE EUROPEAN COMMUNITIES,

Having regard to the Treaty establishing the European Economic Community, and in particular Articles 57(2) and 66 thereof,

Having regard to the proposal from the Commission,

In cooperation with the European Parliament,

Having regard to the opinion of the Economic and Social Committee,

(1) Whereas the objectives of the Community as laid down in the Treaty include establishing an ever closer union among the peoples of Europe, fostering closer relations between the States belonging to the Community and ensuring the economic and social progress of the Community countries by common action to eliminate the barriers which divide Europe;

(2) Whereas, to that end, the Treaty provides for the establishment of a common market and an area without internal frontiers; whereas measures to achieve this include the abolition of obstacles to the free movement of services and the institution of a system ensuring that competition in the common market is not distorted; whereas, to that end, the Council may adopt directives for the coordination of the provisions laid down by law, regulation or administrative action in Member States concerning the taking up and pursuit of activities as self-employed persons;

(3) Whereas broadcasts transmitted across frontiers within the Community, in particular by satellite and cable, are one of the most important ways of pursuing these Community objectives, which are at the same time political, economic, social, cultural and legal;

(4) Whereas the Council has already adopted Directive 89/552/EEC of 3 October 1989 on the coordination of certain provisions laid down by law, regulation or administrative action in Member States concerning the pursuit of television broadcasting activities, which makes provision for the promotion of the distribution and production of European television programmes and for advertising and sponsorship, the protection of minors and the right of reply;

(5) Whereas, however, the achievement of these objectives in respect of cross-border satellite broadcasting and the cable retransmission of programmes from other Member States is currently still obstructed by a series of differences between national rules of copyright and some degree of legal uncertainty; whereas this means that holders of rights are exposed to the threat of seeing their works exploited without payment of remuneration or that the individual holders of exclusive rights in various Member States block the exploitation of their rights; whereas the legal uncertainty in particular constitutes a direct obstacle in the free circulation of programmes within the Community;

(6) Whereas a distinction is currently drawn for copyright purposes between communication to the public by direct satellite and communication to the public by communications satellite; whereas, since individual reception is possible and affordable nowadays with both types of satellite, there is no longer any justification for this differing legal treatment;

(7) Whereas the free broadcasting of programmes is further impeded by the current legal uncertainty over whether broadcasting by a satellite whose signals can be received directly affects the rights in the country of transmission only or in all countries of reception together; whereas, since communications satellites and direct satellites are treated alike for copyright purposes, this legal uncertainty now affects almost all programmes broadcast in the Community by satellite;

(8) Whereas, furthermore, legal certainty, which is a prerequisite for the free movement of broadcasts within the Community, is missing where programmes transmitted across frontiers are fed into and retransmitted through cable networks;

(9) Whereas the development of the acquisition of rights on a contractual basis by authorization is already making a vigorous contribution to the creation of the desired European audiovisual area; whereas the continuation of such contractual agreements should be ensured and their smooth application in practice should be promoted wherever possible;

(10) Whereas at present cable operators in particular cannot be sure that they have actually acquired all the programme rights covered by such an agreement;

(11) Whereas, lastly, parties in different Member States are not all similarly bound by obligations which prevent them from refusing without valid reason to negotiate on the acquisition of the rights necessary for cable distribution or allowing such negotiations to fail;

(12) Whereas the legal framework for the creation of a single audio-visual area laid down in Directive 89/552/EEC must, therefore, be supplemented with reference to copyright;

(13) Whereas, therefore, an end should be put to the differences of treatment of the transmission of programmes by communications satellite which exist in the Member States, so that the vital distinction throughout the Community becomes whether works and other protected subject matter are communicated to the public; whereas this will also ensure equal treatment of the supplies of cross-border broadcasts, regardless of whether they use a direct broadcasting or a communications satellite;

(14) Whereas the legal uncertainty regarding the rights to be acquired which impedes cross-border satellite broadcasting should be overcome by defining the notion of communication to the public by satellite at a Community level; whereas this definition should at the same time specify where the act of communication takes place; whereas such a definition is necessary to avoid the cumulative application of several national laws to one single act of broadcasting; whereas communication to the public by satellite occurs only when, and in the Member State where, the programme-carrying signals are introduced under the control and responsibility of the broadcasting organization into an uninterrupted chain of communication leading to the satellite and down towards the earth; whereas normal technical procedures relating to the programme-carrying signals should not be considered as interruptions to the chain of broadcasting;

(15) Whereas the acquisition on a contractual basis of exclusive broadcasting rights should comply with any legislation on copyright and rights related to copyright in the Member State in which communication to the public by satellite occurs;

(16) Whereas the principle of contractual freedom on which this Directive is based will make it possible to continue limiting the exploitation of these rights, especially as far as certain technical means of transmission or certain language versions are concerned;

(17) Whereas, in arriving at the amount of the payment to be made for the rights acquired, the parties should take account of all aspects of the broadcast, such as the actual audience, the potential audience and the language version;

(18) Whereas the application of the country-of-origin principle contained in this Directive could pose a problem with regard to existing contracts; whereas this Directive should provide for a period of five years for existing contracts to be adapted, where necessary, in the light of the Directive; whereas the said country-of-origin principle should not, therefore, apply to existing contracts which expire before 1 January 2000; whereas if by that date parties still have an interest in the contract, the same parties should be entitled to renegotiate the conditions of the contract;

(19) Whereas existing international co-production agreements must be interpreted in the light of the economic purpose and scope envisaged by the parties upon signature; whereas in the past international co-production agreements have often not expressly and specifically addressed communication to the public by satellite within the meaning of this Directive a particular form of exploitation; whereas the underlying philosophy of many Cexisting international co-production agreements is that the rights in the co-production are exercised separately and independently by each co-producer, by dividing the exploitation rights between them along territorial lines; whereas, as a general rule, in the situation where a communication to the public by satellite authorized by one co-producer, the interpretation of such an existing agreement would normally suggest that the latter co-producer would have to give his consent to the authorization, by the former co-producer, of the communication to the public by satellite; whereas the language exclusivity of the latter co-producer will be prejudiced where the language version or versions of the communication to the public, including where the version is dubbed or subtitled, coincide(s) with the language or the languages widely understood in the territory allotted by the agreement to the latter co-producer; whereas the notion of exclusivity should be understood in a wider sense where the communication to the public by satellite concerns a work which consists merely of images and contains no dialogue or subtitles; whereas a clear rule is necessary in cases where the international co-production agreement does not expressly regulate the division of rights in the specific case of communication to the public by satellite within the meaning of this Directive;

(20) Whereas communications to the public by satellite from non-member countries will under certain conditions be deemed to occur within a Member State of the Community;

(21) Whereas it is necessary to ensure that protection for authors, performers, producers of phonograms and broadcasting organizations is accorded in all Member States and that this protection is not subject to a statutory licence system; whereas only in this way is it possible to ensure that any difference in the level of protection within the common market will not create distortions of competition;

(22) Whereas the advent of new technologies is likely to have an impact on both the quality and the quantity of the exploitation of works and other subject matter;

(23) Whereas in the light of these developments the level of protection granted pursuant to this Directive to all rightholders in the areas covered by this Directive should remain under consideration;

(24) Whereas the harmonization of legislation envisaged in this Directive entails the harmonization of the provisions ensuring a high level of protection of authors, performers, phonogram producers and broadcasting organizations; whereas this harmonization should not allow a broadcasting organization to take advantage of differences in levels of protection by relocating activities, to the detriment of audiovisual productions;

(25) Whereas the protection provided for rights related to copyright should be aligned on that contained in Council Directive 92/100/EEC of 19 November 1992 on rental right and lending right and on certain rights related to copyright in the field of intellectual property for the purposes of communication to the public by satellite; whereas, in particular, this will ensure that performers and phonogram producers are guaranteed an appropriate remuneration for the communication to the public by satellite of their performances or phonograms;

(26) Whereas the provisions of Article 4 do not prevent Member States from extending the presumption set out in Article 2(5) of Directive 92/100/EEC to the exclusive rights referred to in Article 4; whereas, furthermore, the provisions of Article 4 do not prevent Member States from providing for a rebuttable presumption of the authorization of exploitation in respect of the exclusive rights of performers referred to in that Article, in so far as such presumption is compatible with the International Convention for the Protection of Performers, Producers of Phonograms and Broadcasting Organizations;

(27) Whereas the cable retransmission of programmes from other Member States is an act subject to copyright and, as the case may be, rights related to copyright; whereas the cable operator must, therefore, obtain the authorization from every holder of rights in each part of the programme retransmitted; whereas, pursuant to this Directive, the authorizations should be granted contractually unless a temporary exception is provided for in the case of existing legal licence schemes;

(28) Whereas, in order to ensure that the smooth operation of contractual arrangements is not called into question by the intervention of outsiders holding rights in individual parts of the programme, provision should be made, through the obligation to have recourse to a collecting society, for the exclusive collective exercise of the authorization right to the extent that this is required by the special features of cable retransmission; whereas the authorization right as such remains intact and only the exercise of this right is regulated to some extent, so that the right to authorize a cable retransmission can still be assigned; whereas this Directive does not affect the exercise of moral rights;

(29) Whereas the exemption provided for in Article 10 should not limit the choice of holders of rights to transfer their rights to a collecting society and thereby have a direct share in the remuneration paid by the cable distributor for cable retransmission;

(30) Whereas contractual arrangements regarding the authorization of cable retransmission should be promoted by additional measures; whereas a party seeking the conclusion of a general contract should, for its part, be obliged to submit collective proposals for an agreement; whereas furthermore, any party shall be entitled, at any moment, to call upon the assistance of impartial mediators whose task is to assist negotiations and who may submit proposals; whereas any such proposals and any opposition thereto should be served on the parties concerned in accordance with the applicable rules concerning the service of legal documents, in particular as set out in existing international conventions; whereas, finally, it is necessary to ensure that the negotiations are not blocked without valid justification or that individual holders are not prevented without valid justification from taking part in the negotiations; whereas none of these measures for the promotion of the acquisition of rights calls into question the contractual nature of the acquisition of cable retransmission rights;

(31) Whereas for a transitional period Member States should be allowed to retain existing bodies with jurisdiction in their territory over cases where the right to retransmit a programme by cable to the public has been unreasonably refused or offered on unreasonable terms by a broadcasting organization; whereas it is understood that the right of parties concerned to be heard by the body should

be guaranteed and that the existence of the body should not prevent the parties concerned from having normal access to the courts;

(32) Whereas, however, Community rules are not needed to deal with all of those matters, the effects of which perhaps with some commercially insignificant exceptions, are felt only inside the borders of a single Member State;

(33) Whereas minimum rules should be laid down in order to establish and guarantee free and uninterrupted cross-border broadcasting by satellite and simultaneous, unaltered cable retransmission of programmes broadcast from other Member States, on an essentially contractual basis;

(34) Whereas this Directive should not prejudice further harmonization in the field of copyright and rights related to copyright and the collective administration of such rights; whereas the possibility for Member States to regulate the activities of collecting societies should not prejudice the freedom of contractual negotiation of the rights provided for in this Directive, on the understanding that such negotiation takes place within the framework of general or specific national rules with regard to competition law or the prevention of abuse of monopolies;

(35) Whereas it should, therefore, be for the Member States to supplement the general provisions needed to achieve the objectives of this Directive by taking legislative and administrative measures in their domestic law, provided that these do not run counter to the objectives of this Directive and are compatible with Community law;

(36) Whereas this Directive does not affect the applicability of the competition rules in Articles 85 and 86 of the Treaty,

HAS ADOPTED THIS DIRECTIVE:

CHAPTER I

DEFINITIONS

Article 1

Definitions

1. For the purpose of this Directive, "satellite" means any satellite operating on frequency bands which, under telecommunications law, are reserved for the broadcast of signals for reception by the public or which are reserved for closed, point-to-point communication. In the latter case, however, the circumstances in which individual reception of the signals takes place must be comparable to those which apply in the first case.

2.

(a) For the purpose of this Directive, "communication to the public by satellite" means the act of introducing, under the control and responsibility of the broadcasting organization, the programme-carrying signals intended for reception by the public into an uninterrupted chain of communication leading to the satellite and down towards the earth.

(b) The act of communication to the public by satellite occurs solely in the Member State where, under the control and responsibility of the broadcasting organization, the programme-carrying signals are introduced into an uninterrupted chain of communication leading to the satellite and down towards the earth.

(c) If the programme-carrying signals are encrypted, then there is communication to the public by satellite on condition that the means for decrypting the broadcast are provided to the public by the broadcasting organization or with its consent.

(d) Where an act of communication to the public by satellite occurs in a non-Community State which does not provide the level of protection provided for under Chapter II,

    (i) if the programme-carrying signals are transmitted to the satellite from an uplink station[ii] situated in a Member State, that act of communication to the public by satellite shall be deemed to have occurred in that Member State and the rights provided for under Chapter II shall be exercisable against the person operating the uplink station; or

    (ii) if there is no use of an uplink station situated in a Member State but a broadcasting organization established in a Member State has commissioned the act of communication to the public by satellite, that act shall be deemed to have occurred in the Member State in which the broadcasting organization has its principal establishment in the Community and the rights provided for under Chapter II shall be exercisable against the broadcasting organization.

3. For the purposes of this Directive, "cable retransmission" means the simultaneous unaltered and unabridged retransmission by a cable or microwave system for reception by the public of an initial transmission from another Member State, by wire or over the air, including that by satellite, of television or radio programmes intended for reception by the public.

4. For the purposes of this Directive "collecting society" means any organization which manages or administers copyright or rights related to copyright as its sole purpose or as one of its main purposes.

5. For the purposes of this Directive, the principal director of a cinematographic or audiovisual work shall be considered as its author or one of its authors. Member States may provide for others to be considered as its co-authors.

CHAPTER II

BROADCASTING OF PROGRAMMES BY SATELLITE

Article 2

Broadcasting right

Member States shall provide an exclusive right for the author to authorize the communication to the public by satellite of copyright works, subject to the provisions set out in this chapter.

Article 3

Acquisition of broadcasting rights

1. Member States shall ensure that the authorization referred to in Article 2 may be acquired only by agreement.

2. A Member State may provide that a collective agreement between a collecting society and a broadcasting organization concerning a given category of works may be extended to rightholders of the same category who are not represented by the collecting society, provided that:

— the communication to the public by satellite simulcasts a terrestrial broadcast by the same broadcaster, and

— the unrepresented rightholder shall, at any time, have the possibility of excluding the extension of the collective agreement to his works and of exercising his rights either individually or collectively.

[ii] *Editorial Note*: O.J. text has "situation".

3. Paragraph 2 shall not apply to cinematographic works, including works created by a process analogous to cinematography.

4. Where the law of a Member State provides for the extension of a collective agreement in accordance with the provisions of paragraph 2, that Member State[iii] shall inform the Commission which broadcasting organizations are entitled to avail themselves of that law. The Commission shall publish this information in the *Official Journal of the European Communities* (C series).

Article 4

Rights of performers, phonogram producers and broadcasting organizations

1. For the purposes of communication to the public by satellite, the rights of performers, phonogram producers and broadcasting organizations shall be protected in accordance with the provisions of Articles 6, 7, 8 and 10 of Directive 92/100/EEC.

2. For the purposes of paragraph 1, "broadcasting by wireless means" in Directive 92/100/EEC shall be understood as including communication to the public by satellite.

3. With regard to the exercise of the rights referred to in paragraph 1, Articles 2(7) and 12 of Directive 92/100/EEC shall apply.

Article 5

Relation between copyright and related rights

Protection of copyright-related rights under this Directive shall leave intact and shall in no way affect the protection of copyright.

Article 6

Minimum protection

1. Member States may provide for more far-reaching protection for holders of rights related to copyright than that required by Article 8 of Directive 92/100/EEC.

2. In applying paragraph 1 Member States shall observe the definitions contained in Article 1(1) and (2).

Article 7

Transitional provisions

1. With regard to the application in time of the rights referred to in Article 4(1) of this Directive, Article 13(1), (2), (6) and (7) of Directive 92/100/EEC shall apply. Article 13(4) and (5) of Directive 92/100/EEC shall apply *mutatis mutandis*.

2. Agreements concerning the exploitation of works and other protected subject matter which are in force on the date mentioned in Article 14(1) shall be subject to the provisions of Articles 1(2), 2 and 3 as from 1 January 2000 if they expire after that date.

3. When an international co-production agreement concluded before the date mentioned in Article 14(1) between a co-producer from a Member State and one or more co-producers from other Member States or third countries expressly provides for a system of division of exploitation rights between the co-producers

---

iii *Editorial Note*: O.J. text has "States".

by geographical areas for all means of communication to the public, without distinguishing the arrangements applicable to communication to the public by satellite from the provisions applicable to the other means of communication, and where communication to the public by satellite of the co-production would prejudice the exclusivity, in particular the language exclusivity, of one of the co-producers or his assignees in a given territory, the authorization by one of the co-producers or his assignees for a communication to the public by satellite shall require the prior consent of the holder of that exclusivity, whether co-producer or assignee.

Chapter III

Cable Retransmission

Article 8

Cable retransmission right

1. Member States shall ensure that when programmes from other Member States are retransmitted by cable in their territory the applicable copyright and related rights are observed and that such retransmission takes place on the basis of individual or collective contractual agreements between copyright owners, holders of related rights and cable operators.

2. Notwithstanding paragraph 1, Member States may retain until 31 December 1997 such statutory licence systems which are in operation or expressly provided for by national law on 31 July 1991.

Article 9

Exercise of the cable retransmission right

1. Member States shall ensure that the right of copyright owners and holders of related rights to grant or refuse authorization to a cable operator for a cable retransmission may be exercised only through a collecting society.

2. Where a rightholder has not transferred the management of his rights to a collecting society, the collecting society which manages rights of the same category shall be deemed to be mandated to manage his rights. Where more than one collecting society manages rights of that category, the rightholder shall be free to choose which of those collecting societies is deemed to be mandated to manage his rights. A rightholder referred to in this paragraph shall have the same rights and obligations resulting from the agreement between the cable operator and the collecting society which is deemed to be mandated to manage his rights as the rightholders who have mandated that collecting society and he shall be able to claim those rights within a period, to be fixed by the Member State concerned, which shall not be shorter than three years from the date of the cable retransmission which includes his work or other protected subject matter.

3. A Member State may provide that, when a rightholder authorizes the initial transmission within its territory of a work or other protected subject matter, he shall be deemed to have agreed not to exercise his cable retransmission rights on an individual basis but to exercise them in accordance with the provisions of this Directive.

Article 10

Exercise of the cable retransmission right by broadcasting organizations

Member States shall ensure that Article 9 does not apply to the rights exercised by a broadcasting organization in respect of its own transmission, irrespective of whether the rights concerned are its own or have been transferred to it by other copyright owners and/or holders of related rights.

Article 11

Mediators

1. Where no agreement is concluded regarding authorization of the cable retransmission of a broadcast, Member States shall ensure that either party may call upon the assistance of one or more mediators.

2. The task of the mediators shall be to provide assistance with negotiation. They may also submit proposals to the parties.

3. It shall be assumed that all the parties accept a proposal as referred to in paragraph 2 if none of them expresses its opposition within a period of three months. Notice of the proposal and of any opposition thereto shall be served on the parties concerned in accordance with the applicable rules concerning the service of legal documents.

4. The mediators shall be so selected that their independence and impartiality are beyond reasonable doubt.

Article 12

Prevention of the abuse of negotiating positions

1. Member States shall ensure by means of civil or administrative law, as appropriate, that the parties enter and conduct negotiations regarding authorization for cable retransmission in good faith and do not prevent or hinder negotiation without valid justification.

2. A Member State which, on the date mentioned in Article 14(1), has a body with jurisdiction in its territory over cases where the right to retransmit a programme by cable to the public in that Member State has been unreasonably refused or offered on unreasonable terms by a broadcasting organization may retain that body.

3. Paragraph 2 shall apply for a transitional period of eight years from the date mentioned in Article 14(1).

CHAPTER IV

GENERAL PROVISIONS

Article 13

Collective administration of rights

This Directive shall be without prejudice to the regulation of the activities of collecting societies by the Member States.

Article 14

Final provisions

1. Member States shall bring into force the laws, regulations and administrative provisions necessary to comply with this Directive before 1 January 1995. They shall immediately inform the Commission thereof.

When Member States adopt these measures, the latter shall contain a reference to this Directive or shall be accompanied by such reference at the time of their official publication. The methods of making such a reference shall be laid down by the Member States.

2. Member States shall communicate to the Commission the provisions of national law which they adopt in the field covered by this Directive.

3. Not later than 1 January 2000, the Commission shall submit to the European Parliament, the Council and the Economic and Social Committee a report on the application of this Directive and, if necessary, make further proposals to adapt it to developments in the audio and audio-visual sector.

Article 15

This Directive is addressed to the Member States.
Done at Brussels, 27 September 1993.

H3. DIRECTIVE 96/9/EC

Directive 96/9/EC of the European Parliament and of the Council of 11 March 1996 on the legal protection of databases[i]

([1996] O.J. L77/20)

THE EUROPEAN PARLIAMENT AND THE COUNCIL OF THE EUROPEAN UNION

Having regard to the Treaty establishing the European Community, and in particular Article 57(2), 66 and 100a thereof,

Having regard to the proposal from the Commission[1],

Having regard to the opinion of the Economic and Social Committee[2],

Acting in accordance with the procedure laid down in Article 189b of the Treaty[3],

(1) Whereas databases are at present not sufficiently protected in all Member States by existing legislation; whereas such protection, where it exists, has different attributes;

(2) Whereas such differences in the legal protection of databases offered by the legislation of the Member States have direct negative effects on the functioning of the internal market as regards databases and in particular on the freedom of natural and legal persons to provide on-line database goods and services on the basis of harmonized legal arrangements throughout the Community; whereas such differences could well become more pronounced as Member States introduce new legislation in this field, which is now taking on an increasingly international dimension;

(3) Whereas existing differences distorting the functioning of the internal market need to be removed and new ones prevented from arising, while differences not adversely affecting the functioning of the internal market or the development of an information market within the Community need not be removed or prevented from arising;

(4) Whereas copyright protection for databases exists in varying forms in the Member States according to legislation or case-law, and whereas, if differences in legislation in the scope and conditions of protection remain between the Member States, such unharmonized intellectual property rights can have the effect of preventing the free movement of goods or services within the Community;

(5)Whereas copyright remains an appropriate form of exclusive right for authors who have created databases;

---

[i] *Editorial note*: The footnote numbering in the original Directive is reproduced below.
[1] OJ No. C 156, 23, 6, 1992, p. 4 and OJ No. C 308, 15, 11, 1993, p. 1.
[2] OJ No. C 19, 25, 1, 1993, p. 3.
[3] Opinion of the European Parliament of 23 June 1993 (OJ No. C 194, 19, 7, 1993, p. 144), Common Position of the Council of 10 July 1995 (OJ No. C 288, 30, 10, 1995, p. 1), Decision of the European Parliament of 14 December 1995 (OJ No. C 17, 22, 1, 1996) and Council Decision of 26 February 1996.

(6) Whereas, nevertheless, in the absence of a harmonized system of unfair-competition legislation or of case-law, other measures are required in addition to prevent the unauthorized extraction and/or re-utilization of the contents of a database;

(7) Whereas the making of databases requires the investment of considerable human, technical and financial resources while such databases can be copied or accessed at a fraction of the cost needed to design them independently;

(8) Whereas the unauthorized extraction and/or re-utilization of the contents of a database constitute acts which can have serious economic and technical consequences;

(9) Whereas databases are a vital tool in the development of an information market within the Community; whereas this tool will also be of use in many other fields;

(10) Whereas the exponential growth, in the Community and worldwide, in the amount of information generated and processed annually in all sectors of commerce and industry calls for investment in all the Member States in advanced information processing systems;

(11) Whereas there is at present a very great imbalance in the level of investment in the database sector both as between the Member States and between the Community and the world's largest database producing third countries;

(12) Whereas such an investment in modern information storage and processing systems will not take place within the Community unless a stable and uniform legal protection regime is introduced for the protection of the rights of makers of databases;

(13) Whereas this Directive protects collections, sometimes called 'compilations', of works, data or other materials which are arranged, stored and accessed by means which include electronic, electromagnetic or electro-optical processes or analogous processes;

(14) Whereas protection under this Directive should be extended to cover non-electronic databases;

(15) Whereas the criteria used to determine whether a database should be protected by copyright should be defined to the fact that the selection or the arrangement of the contents of the database is the author's own intellectual creation; whereas such protection should cover the structure of the database;

(16) Whereas no criterion other than originality in the sense of the author's intellectual creation should be applied to determine the eligibility of the database for copyright protection, and in particular no aesthetic or qualitative criteria should be applied;

(17) Whereas the term 'database' should be understood to include literary, artistic, musical or other collections of works or collections of other material such as texts, sound images, numbers, facts, and data; whereas it should cover collections of independent works, data or other materials which are systematically or methodically arranged and can be individually accessed; whereas this means that a recording or an audio-visual, cinematographic, literary or musical work as such does not fall within the scope of this Directive;

(18) Whereas this Directive is without prejudice to the freedom of authors to decide whether, or in what manner, they will allow their works to be included in a database, in particular whether or not the authorization given is exclusive; whereas the protection of databases by the *sui generis* right is without prejudice to existing rights over their contents, and whereas in particular where an author or the holder of a related right permits some of his works or subject matter to be included in a database pursuant to a non-exclusive agreement, a third party may make use of those works or subject matter subject to the required consent of the

author or of the holder of the related right without the *sui generis* right of the maker of the database being invoked to prevent him doing so, on condition that those works or subject matter are neither extracted from the database nor re-utilized on the basis thereof;

(19) Whereas, as a rule, the compilation of several recordings of musical performances on a CD does not come within the scope of this Directive, both because, as a compilation, it does not meet the conditions for copyright protection and because it does not represent a substantial enough investment to be eligible under the *sui generis* right;

(20) Whereas protection under this Directive may also apply to the materials necessary for the operation or consultation of certain databases such as thesaurus and indexation systems;

(21) Whereas the protection provided for in this Directive relates to databases in which works, data or other materials have been arranged systematically or methodically; whereas it is not necessary for those materials to have been physically stored in an organized manner;

(22) Whereas electronic databases within the meaning of this Directive may also include devices such as CD-ROM and CD-i;

(23) Whereas the term 'database' should not be taken to extend to computer programs used in the making or operation of a database which are protected by Council Directive 91/250/EEC of 14 May 1991 on the legal protection of computer programs[4];

(24) Whereas the rental and lending of databases in the field of copyright and related rights are governed exclusively by Council Directive 92/100/EEC of 19 November 1992 on rental right and lending right and on certain rights related to copyright in the field of intellectual property[5];

(25) Whereas the term of copyright is already governed by Council Directive 93/98/EEC of 29 October 1993 harmonizing the term of protection of copyright and certain related rights[6];

(26) Whereas works protected by copyright and subject matter protected by related rights, which are incorporated into a database, remain nevertheless protected by the respective exclusive rights and may not be incorporated into, or extracted from, the database without the permission of the rightholder or his successors in title;

(27) Whereas copyright in such works and related rights in subject matter thus incorporated into a database are in no way affected by the existence of a separate right in the selection or arrangement of these works and subject matter in a database;

(28) Whereas the moral rights of the natural person who created the database belong to the author and should be exercised according to the legislation of the Member States and the provisions of the Berne Convention for the Protection of Literary and Artistic Works; whereas such moral rights remain outside the scope of this Directive;

(29) Whereas the arrangements applicable to databases created by employees are left to the discretion of the Member States; whereas, therefore nothing in this Directive prevents Member States from stipulating in their legislation that where a database is created by an employee in the execution of his duties or following the instructions given by his employer, the employer exclusively shall be entitled

---

[4] OJ No. L 122, 17. 5. 1991, p. 42. Directive as last amended by Directive 93/98/EEC (OJ No. L 290, 24. 11. 1993, p. 9).

[5] OJ No. L 346, 27. 1. 1992, p. 61.

[6] OJ No. L 290, 24. 11. 1993, p. 9.

to exercise all economic rights in the database so created, unless otherwise provided by contract;

(30) Whereas the author's exclusive rights should include the right to determine the way in which his work is exploited and by whom, and in particular to control the distribution of his work to unauthorized persons;

(31) Whereas the copyright protection of databases includes making databases available by means other than the distribution of copies;

(32) Whereas Member States are required to ensure that their national provisions are at least materially equivalent in the case of such acts subject to restrictions as are provided for by this Directive;

(33) Whereas the question of exhaustion of the right of distribution does not arise in the case of on-line databases, which come within the field of provision of services; whereas this also applies with regard to a material copy of such a database made by the user of such a service with the consent of the rightholder, whereas, unlike CD-ROM or CD-i, where the intellectual property is incorporated in a material medium, namely an item of goods, every on-line service is in fact an act which will have to be subject to authorization where the copyright so provides;

(34) Whereas, nevertheless, once the rightholder has chosen to make available a copy of the database to a user, whether by an on-line service or by other means of distribution, that lawful user must be able to access and use the database for the purposes and in the way set out in the agreement with the rightholder, even if such access and use necessitate performance of otherwise restricted acts;

(35) Whereas a list should be drawn up of exceptions to restricted acts, taking into account the fact that copyright as covered by this Directive applies only to the selection or arrangements of the contents of a database; whereas Member States should be given the option of providing for such exceptions in certain cases; whereas, however, this option should be exercised in accordance with the Berne Convention and to the extent that the exceptions relate to the structure of the database; whereas a distinction should be drawn between exceptions for private use and exceptions for reproduction for private purposes, which concerns provisions under national legislation of some Member States on levies on blank media or recording equipment;

(36) Whereas the term 'scientific research' within the meaning of this Directive covers both the natural sciences and the human sciences;

(37) Whereas Article 10(1) of the Berne Convention is not affected by this Directive;

(38) Whereas the increasing use of digital recording technology exposes the database maker to the risk that the contents of his database may be copied and rearranged electronically, without his authorization, to produce a database of identical content which, however, does not infringe any copyright in the arrangement of his database;

(39) Whereas, in addition to aiming to protect the copyright in the original selection or arrangement of the contents of a database, this Directive seeks to safeguard the position of makers of databases against misappropriation of the results of the financial and professional investment made in obtaining and collection the contents by protecting the whole or substantial parts of a database against certain acts by a user or competitor;

(40) Whereas the object of this *sui generis* right is to ensure protection of any investment in obtaining, verifying or presenting the contents of a database for the limited duration of the right; whereas such investment may consist in the deployment of financial resources and/or the expending of time, effort and energy;

(41) Whereas the objective of the *sui generis* right is to give the maker of a database the option of preventing the unauthorized extraction and/or re-utilization

of all or a substantial part of the contents of that database; whereas the maker of a database is the person who takes the initiative and the risk of investing; whereas this excludes subcontractors in particular from the definition of maker;

(42) Whereas the special right to prevent unauthorized extraction and/or re-utilization relates to acts by the user which go beyond his legitimate rights and thereby harm the investment; whereas the right to prohibit extraction and/or re-utilization of all or a substantial part of the contents relates not only to the manufacture of a parasitical competing product but also to any user who, through his acts, causes significant detriment, evaluated qualitatively or quantitatively, to the investment;

(43) Whereas, in the case of on-line transmission, the right to prohibit re-utilization is not exhausted either as regards the database or as regards a material copy of the database or of part thereof made by the addressee of the transmission with the consent of the rightholder;

(44) Whereas, when on-screen display of the contents of a database necessitates the permanent or temporary transfer of all or a substantial part of such contents to another medium, that act should be subject to authorization by the rightholder;

(45) Whereas the right to prevent unauthorized extraction and/or re-utilization does not in any way constitute an extension of copyright protection to mere facts or data;

(46) Whereas the existence of a right to prevent the unauthorized extraction and/or re-utilization of the whole or a substantial part of works, data or materials from a database should not give rise to the creation of a new right in the works, data or materials themselves;

(47) Whereas, in the interests of competition between suppliers of information products and services, protection by the *sui generis* right must not be afforded in such a way as to facilitate abuses of a dominant position, in particular as regards the creation and distribution of new products and services which have an intellectual, documentary, technical, economic or commercial added value; whereas, therefore, the provisions of this Directive are without prejudice to the application of Community or national competition rules;

(48) Whereas the objective of this Directive, which is to afford an appropriate and uniform level of protection of databases as a means to secure the remuneration of the maker of the database, is different from the aim of Directive 95/46/EC of the European Parliament and of the Council of 24 October 1995 on the protection of individuals with regard to the processing of personal data and on the free movement of such data[7], which is to guarantee free circulation of personal data on the basis of harmonized rules designed to protect fundamental rights, notably the right to privacy which is recognized in Article 8 of the European Convention for the Protection of Human Rights and Fundamental Freedoms; whereas the provisions of this Directive are without prejudice to data processing legislation;

(49) Whereas, notwithstanding the right to prevent extraction and/or re-utilization of all or a substantial part of a database, it should be laid down that the maker of a database or rightholder may not prevent a lawful user of the database from extracting and re-utilizing insubstantial parts; whereas, however, that user may not unreasonably prejudice either the legitimate interests of the holder of the *sui generis* right or the holder of copyright or a related right in respect of the works or subject matter contained in the database;

(50) Whereas the Member States should be given the option of providing for exceptions to the right to prevent the unauthorized extraction and/or re-utilization

---

[7] OJ No. L 281, 23. 11. 1995, p. 31.

of a substantial part of the contents of a database in the case of extraction for private purposes, for the purpose of illustration for teaching or scientific research, or where extraction and/or re-utilization are/is carried out in the interests of public security or for the purposes of an administrative or judicial procedure; whereas such operations must not prejudice the exclusive rights of the maker to exploit the database and their purpose must not be commercial;

(51) Whereas the Member States, where they avail themselves of the option to permit a lawful user of a database to extract a substantial part of the contents for the purposes of illustration for teaching or scientific research, may limit that permission to certain categories of teaching or scientific research institution;

(52) Whereas those Member States which have specific rules providing for a right comparable to the *sui generis* right provided for in this Directive should be permitted to retain, as far as the new right is concerned, the expectations traditionally specified by such rules;

(53) Whereas the burden of proof regarding the date of completion of the making of a database lies with the maker of the database;

(54) Whereas the burden of proof that the criteria exist for concluding that a substantial modification of the contents of a database is to be regarded as a substantial new investment lies with the maker of the database resulting from such investment;

(55) Whereas a substantial new investment involving a new term of protection may include a substantial verification of the contents of the database;

(56) Whereas the right to prevent unauthorized extraction and/or re-utilization in respect of a database should apply to databases whose makers are nationals or habitual residents of third countries or to those produced by legal persons not established in a Member State, within the meaning of the Treaty, only if such third countries offer compatible protection to databases produced by nationals of a Member State or persons who have their habitual residence in the territory of the Community;

(57) Whereas, in addition to remedies provided under the legislation of the Member States for infringements of copyright or other rights, Member States should provide for appropriate extraction and/or re-utilization of the contents of a database;

(58) Whereas, in addition to the protection given under this Directive to the structure of the database by copyright, and to its contents against unauthorized extraction and/or re-utilization under the *sui generis* right, other legal provisions in the Member States relevant to the supply of database goods and services continue to apply;

(59) Whereas this Directive is without prejudice to the application to databases composed of audiovisual works of any rules recognized by a Member State's legislation concerning the broadcasting of audio-visual programmes;

(60) Whereas some Member States currently protect under copyright arrangements databases which do not meet the criteria for eligibility for copyright protection laid down in this Directive; whereas, even if the databases concerned are eligible for protection under the right laid down in this Directive to prevent unauthorized extraction and/or re-utilization of their contents, the term of protection under that right is considerably shorter than that which they enjoy under the national arrangements currently in force; whereas harmonization of the criteria for determining whether a database is to be protected by copyright may not have the effect of reducing the term of protection currently enjoyed by the right-holders concerned; whereas a derogation should be laid down to that effect; whereas the effects of such derogation must be confined to the territories of the Member States concerned,

HAVE ADOPTED THIS DIRECTIVE:

Chapter I

Scope

Article 1

Scope

1. This Directive concerns the legal protection of databases in any form.

2. For the purposes of this Directive, 'database' shall mean a collection of independent works, data or other materials arranged in a systematic or methodical way and individually accessible by electronic or other means.

3. Protection under this Directive shall not apply to computer programs used in the making or operation of databases accessible by electronic means.

Article 2

Limitations on the scope

This Directive shall apply without prejudice to Community provisions relating to:

   (a) the legal protection of computer programs;
   (b) rental right, lending right and certain rights related to copyright in the field of intellectual property;
   (c) the term of protection of copyright and certain related rights.

Chapter II

Copyright

Article 3

Object of protection

1. In accordance with this Directive, databases which, by reason of the selection or arrangement of their contents, constitute the author's own intellectual creation shall be protected as such by copyright. No other criteria shall be applied to determine their eligibility for that protection.

2. The copyright protection of databases provided for by this Directive shall not extend to their contents and shall be without prejudice to any rights subsisting in those contents themselves.

Article 4

Database authorship

1. The author of a database shall be the natural person or group of natural persons who created the base or, where the legislation of the Member States so permits, the legal person designated as the rightholder by that legislation.

2. Where collective works are recognized by the legislation of a Member State, the economic rights shall be owned by the person holding the copyright.

3. In respect of a database created by a group of natural persons jointly, the exclusive rights shall be owned jointly.

Article 5

Restricted acts

In respect of the expression of the database which is protectable by copyright, the author of a database shall have the exclusive right to carry out or to authorize:

(a) temporary or permanent reproduction by any means and in any form, in whole or in part;

(b) translation, adaptation, arrangement and any other alteration;

(c) any form of distribution to the public of the database or of copies thereof. The first sale in the Community of a copy of the database by the rightholder or with his consent shall exhaust the right to control resale of that copy within the Community;

(d) any communication, display or performance to the public;

(e) any reproduction, distribution, communication, display or performance to the public of the results of the acts referred to in (b).

Article 6

Exceptions to restricted acts

1. The performance by the lawful user of a database or of a copy thereof of any of the acts listed in Article 5 which is necessary for the purposes of access to the contents of the databases and normal use of the contents by the lawful user shall not require the authorization of the author of the database. Where the lawful user is authorised to use only part of the database, this provision shall apply only to that part.

2. Member States shall have the option of providing for limitations on the rights set out in Article 5 in the following cases:

(a) in the case of reproduction for private purposes of a non-electronic database;

(b) where there is use for the sole purpose of illustration for teaching or scientific research, as long as the source is indicated and to the extent justified by the non-commercial purpose to be achieved;

(c) where there is use for the purposes of public security of for the purposes of an administrative or judicial procedure;

(d) where other exceptions to copyright which are traditionally authorized under national law are involved, without prejudice to points (a), (b) and (c).

3. In accordance with the Berne Convention for the protection of Literary and Artistic Works, this Article may not be interpreted in such a way as to allow its application to be used in a manner which unreasonably prejudices the rightholder's legitimate interests or conflicts with normal exploitation of the database.

CHAPTER III

SUI GENERIS RIGHT

Article 7

Object of protection

1. Member States shall provide for a right for the maker of a database which shows that there has been qualitatively and/or quantitatively a substantial investment in either the obtaining, verification or presentation of the contents to prevent extraction and/or re-utilization of the whole or of a substantial part, evaluated qualitatively and/or quantitatively, of the contents of that database.

2. For the purposes of this Chapter:

(a) 'extraction' shall mean the permanent or temporary transfer of all or a substantial part of the contents of a database to another medium by any means or in any form;

(b) 're-utilization' shall mean any form of making available to the public all or a substantial part of the contents of a database by the distribution of copies, by renting, by on-line or other forms of transmission. The first sale of a copy of a database within the Community by the rightholder or with his consent shall exhaust the right to control resale of that copy within the Community;

Public lending is not an act of extraction or re-utilization.

3. The right referred to in paragraph 1 may be transferred, assigned or granted under contractual licence.

4. The right provided for in paragraph 1 shall apply irrespective of the eligibility of that database for protection by copyright or by other rights. Moreover, it shall apply irrespective of eligibility of the contents of that database for protection by copyright or by other rights. Protection of databases under the right provided for in paragraph 1 shall be without prejudice to rights existing in respect of their contents.

5. The repeated and systematic extraction and/or re-utilization of insubstantial parts of the contents of the database implying acts which conflict with a normal exploitation of that database or which unreasonably prejudice the legitimate interests of the maker of the database shall not be permitted.

Article 8

Rights and obligations of lawful users

1. The maker of a database which is made available to the public in whatever manner may not prevent a lawful user of the database from extracting and/or re-utilizing insubstantial parts of its contents, evaluated qualitatively and/or quantitatively, for any purpose whatsoever. Where the lawful user is authorized to extract and/or re-utilize only part of the database, this paragraph shall apply only to that part.

2. A lawful user of a database which is made available to the public in whatever manner may not perform acts which conflict with normal exploitation of the database or unreasonably prejudice the legitimate interests of the maker of the database.

3. A lawful user of a database which is made available to the public in any manner may not cause prejudice to the holder of a copyright or related right in respect of the works or subject matter contained in the database.

Article 9

Exceptions to the sui generis right

Member States may stipulate that lawful users of a database which is made available to the public in whatever manner may, without the authorization of its maker, extract or re-utilize a substantial part of its contents:

(a) in the case of extraction for private purposes of the contents of a non-electronic database;

(b) in the case of extraction for the purposes of illustration for teaching or scientific research, as long as the source is indicated and to the extent justified by the non-commercial purpose to be achieved;

(c) in the case of extraction and/or re-utilization for the purposes of public security or an administrative or judicial procedure.

Article 10

Term of protection

1. The right provided for in Article 7 shall run from the date of completion of the making of the database. It shall expire fifteen years from the first of January of the year following the date of completion.

2. In the case of a database which is made available to the public in whatever manner before expiry of the period provided for in paragraph 1, the term of protection by the right shall expire fifteen years from the first of January of the year following the date when the database was first made available to the public.

3. Any substantial change, evaluated qualitatively or quantitatively, to the contents of a database, including any substantial change resulting from the accumulation of successive additions, deletions or alterations, which would result in the database being considered to be a substantial new investment, evaluated qualitatively or quantitatively, shall qualify the database resulting from that investment for its own term of protection.

Article 11

Beneficiaries of protection under the sui generis right

1. The right provided for in Article 7 shall apply to database whose makers or rightholders are nationals of a Member State or who have their habitual residence in the territory of the Community.

2. Paragraph 1 shall also apply to companies and firms formed in accordance with the law of a Member State and having their registered office, central administration or principal place of business within the Community; however, where such a company or firm has only its registered office in the territory of the Community, its operations must be genuinely linked on an ongoing basis with the economy of a Member State.

3. Agreements extending the right provided for in Article 7 to databases made in third countries and falling outside the provisions of paragraphs 1 and 2 shall be concluded by the Council acting on a proposal from the Commission. The term of any protection extended to databases by virtue of that procedure shall not exceed that available pursuant to Article 10.

CHAPTER IV

COMMON PROVISIONS

Article 12

Remedies

Member States shall provide appropriate remedies in respect of infringements of the rights provided for in this Directive.

Article 13

Continued application of other legal provisions

This Directive shall be without prejudice to provisions concerning in particular copyright, rights related to copyright or any other rights or obligations subsisting in the data, works or other materials incorporated into a database, patent rights, trade marks, design rights, the protection of national treasures, laws on restrictive practices and unfair competition, trade secrets, security, confidentiality, data protection and privacy, access to public documents, and the law of contract.

Article 14

Application over time

1. Protection pursuant to this Directive as regards copyright shall also be available in respect of databases created prior to the date referred to in Article 16(1) which on that date fulfil the requirements laid down in this Directive as regards copyright protection of databases.

2. Notwithstanding paragraph 1, where a database protected under copyright arrangements in a Member State on the date of publication of this Directive does not fulfil the eligibility criteria for copyright protection laid down in Article 3(1), this Directive shall not result in any curtailing in that Member State of the remaining term of protection afforded under those arrangements.

3. Protection pursuant to the provisions of this Directive as regards the right provided for in Article 7 shall also be available in respect of databases the making of which was completed not more than fifteen years prior to the date referred to in Article 16(1) and which on that date fulfil the requirements laid down in Article 7.

4. The protection provided for in paragraphs 1 and 3 shall be without prejudice to any acts concluded and rights acquired before the date referred to in those paragraphs.

5. In the case of a database the making of which was completed not more than fifteen years prior to the date referred to in Article 16(1), the term of protection by the right provided for in Article 7 shall expire fifteen years from the first of January following that date.

Article 15

Binding nature of certain provisions

Any contractual provision contrary to Articles 6(1) and 8 shall be null and void.

Article 16

Final provisions

1. Member States shall bring into force the laws, regulations and administrative provisions necessary to comply with this Directive before 1 January 1998.

When Member States adopt these provisions, they shall contain a reference to this Directive or shall be accompanied by such reference on the occasion of their official publication. The methods of making such reference shall be laid down by Member States.

2. Member States shall communicate to the Commission the text of the provisions of domestic law which they adopt in the field governed by this Directive.

3. Not later than at the end of the third year after the date referred to in paragraph 1, and every three years thereafter, the Commission shall submit to the European Parliament, the Council and the Economic and Social Committee a report on the application of this Directive, in which, *inter alia*, on the basis of specific information supplied by the Member States, it shall examine in particular the application of the *sui generis* right, including Articles 8 and 9, and shall verify especially whether the application of this right has led to abuse of a dominant position or other interference with free competition which would justify appropriate measures being taken, including the establishment of non-voluntary licensing arrangements. Where necessary, it shall submit proposals for adjustments of this Directive in line with developments in the area of databases.

Article 17

This Directive is addressed to the Member States.

Done at Strasbourg, 11 March 1996.

H4. COUNCIL DIRECTIVE 98/34/EC

Directive 98/34/EC of the European Parliament and of the Council of 22 June 1998 laying down a procedure for the provision of information in the field of technical standards (as amended by Directive 98/48/EC) (Extract)[i]

([1998] O.J. L204/37)

Article 1

For the purposes of this Directive, the following meanings shall apply:

2. "service", any Information Society Directive service, that is to say, any service normally provided for remuneration, at a distance, by electronic means and at the individual request of a receipt of services.

For the purposes of this definition:

— "at a distance" means that the service is provided without the parties being simultaneously present,

— "by electronic means" means that the service is sent initially and received at its destination by means of electronic equipment for the processing (including digital compression) and storage of data, and entirely transmitted, conveyed and received by wire, by radio, by optical means or by other electromagnetic means,

— "at the individual request of a receipt of services" means that the service is provided through the transmission of data on individual request.

An indicative list of services not covered by this definition is set out in Annex V.

This Directive shall not apply to:

— radio broadcasting services,

— television broadcasting services covered by point (a) of Article 1 of Directive 89/552/EEC.[1]

Annex V

Indicative list of services not covered by the second subparagraph of point 2 of Article 1

1. Services not provided "at a distance".

Services provides in the physical presence of the provider and the recipient, even if they involve the use of electronic devices.

(a) medical examinations or treatment at a doctor's surgery using electronic equipment where the patient is physically present;

(b) consultations of an electronic catalogue in a shop with the customer on site;

(c) plane ticket reservation at a travel agency in the physical presence of the customer by means of a network of computers;

(d) electronic games made available in a video-arcade where the customer is physically present.

2. Services not provided "by electronic means"

— Services having material content even though provided via electronic devices:

(a) automatic cash or ticket dispensing machines (banknotes, rail tickets);

(b) access to road networks, car parks, etc., charging for use, even if there

---

[i] *Editorial note*: The footnote numbering in the original Directive is reproduced below.
[1] [1989] O.J. L298/23. Directive as last amended by Directive 97/36/EC ([1997] O.J. L202/1).

are electronic devices at the entrance/exit controlling access and/or ensuring correct payment is made;
— Off-line services: distribution of CD roms or software on diskettes,
— Services which are not provided via electronic processing/inventory systems:

(a) voice telephony services;

(b) telefax/telex services;

(c) services provided via voice telephony or fax;

(d) telephone/telex consultation of a doctor;

(e) telephone/telefax consultation of a lawyer;

(f) telephone/telefax direct marketing.

3. Services not supplied "at the individual request of a recipient of services". Services provided by transmitting data without individual demand without demand for simultaneous reception by an unlimited number of individual receivers (point to mulitpoint transmission):

(a) television broadcasting services (including near-video on-demand services), covered by point (a) of Article 1 of Directive 89/552/EEC;

(b) radio broadcasting services;

(c) (televised) teletext.

H5. DIRECTIVE 98/71/EC

Directive 98/71/EC of the European Parliament and of the Council of 13 October 1998 on the legal protection of designs[i]

([1998] O.J. L289/28)

THE EUROPEAN PARLIAMENT AND THE COUNCIL OF THE EUROPEAN UNION

Having regard to the Treaty establishing the European Community and in particular Article 100a thereof,

Having regard to the proposal by the Commission[1],

Having regard to the opinion of the Economic and Social Committee[2],

Acting in accordance with the procedure laid down in Article 189b of the Treaty[3], in the light of the joint text approved by the Conciliation Committee on 29 July 1998,

(1) Whereas the objectives of the Community, as laid down in the Treaty, include laying the foundations of an ever closer union among the peoples of Europe, fostering closer relations between Member States of the Community, and ensuring the economic and social progress of the Community countries by common action to eliminate the barriers which divide Europe; whereas to that end the Treaty provides for the establishment of an internal market characterised by the abolition of obstacles to the free movement of goods and also for the institution of a system ensuring that competition in the internal market is not distorted; whereas an approximation of the laws of the Member States on the legal protection of designs would further those objectives;

(2) Whereas the differences in the legal protection of designs offered by the

---

[i] *Editorial note*: The footnote numbering in the original Directive is reproduced below.

[1] OJ C 345, 23. 12. 1993, p. 14 and OJ C 142, 14. 5. 1996, p. 7.

[2] OJ C 388, 31. 12. 1994, p. 9 and OJ C 110, 2. 5. 1995, p. 12.

[3] Opinion of the European Parliament of 12 October 1995 (OJ C 287, 30. 10. 1995, p. 157), common position of the Council of 17 June 1997 (OJ C 237, 4. 8. 1997, p. 1), Decision of the European Parliament of 22 October 1997 (OJ C 339, 10. 11. 1997, p. 52). Decision of the European Parliament of 15 September 1998. Decision of the Council of 24 September 1998.

legislation of the Member States directly affect the establishment and functioning of the internal market as regards goods embodying designs; whereas such differences can distort competition within the internal market;

(3) Whereas it is therefore necessary for the smooth functioning of the internal market to approximate the design protection laws of the Member States;

(4) Whereas, in doing so, it is important to take into consideration the solutions and the advantages with which the Community design system will provide undertakings wishing to acquire design rights;

(5) Whereas it is unnecessary to undertake a full-scale approximation of the design laws of the Member States, and it will be sufficient if approximation is limited to those national provisions of law which most directly affect the functioning of the internal market; whereas provisions on sanctions, remedies and enforcement should be left to national law; whereas the objectives of this limited approximation cannot be sufficiently achieved by the Member States acting alone;

(6) Whereas Member States should accordingly remain free to fix the procedural provisions concerning registration, renewal and invalidation of design rights and provisions concerning the effects of such invalidity;

(7) Whereas this Directive does not exclude the application to designs of national or Community legislation providing for protection other than that conferred by registration or publication as design, such as legislation relating to unregistered design rights, trade marks, patents and utility models, unfair competition or civil liability;

(8) Whereas, in the absence of harmonisation of copyright law, it is important to establish the principle of cumulation of protection under specific registered design protection law and under copyright law, whilst leaving Member States free to establish the extent of copyright protection and the conditions under which such protection is conferred;

(9) Whereas the attainment of the objectives of the internal market requires that the conditions for obtaining a registered design right be identical in all the Member States; whereas to that end it is necessary to give a unitary definition of the notion of design and of the requirements as to novelty and individual character with which registered design rights must comply;

(10) Whereas it is essential, in order to facilitate the free movement of goods, to ensure in principle that registered design rights confer upon the right holder equivalent protection in all Member States;

(11) Whereas protection is conferred by way of registration upon the right holder for those design features of a product, in whole or in part, which are shown visibly in an application and made available to the public by way of publication or consultation of the relevant file;

(12) Whereas protection should not be extended to those component parts which are not visible during normal use of a product, or to those features of such part which are not visible when the part is mounted, or which would not, in themselves, fulfil the requirements as to novelty and individual character; whereas features of design which are excluded from protection for these reasons should not be taken into consideration for the purpose of assessing whether other features of the design fulfil the requirements for protection;

(13) Whereas the assessment as to whether a design has individual character should be based on whether the overall impression produced on an informed user viewing the design clearly differs from that produced on him by the existing design corpus, taking into consideration the nature of the product to which the design is applied or in which it is incorporated, and in particular the industrial sector to which it belongs and the degree of freedom of the designer in developing the design;

(14) Whereas technological innovation should not be hampered by granting

design protection to features dictated solely by a technical function; whereas it is understood that this does not entail that a design must have an aesthetic quality; whereas, likewise, the interoperability of products of different makes should not be hindered by extending protection to the design of mechanical fittings; whereas features of a design which are excluded from protection for these reasons should not be taken into consideration for the purpose of assessing whether other features of the design fulfil the requirements for protection;

(15) Whereas the mechanical fittings of modular products may nevertheless constitute an important element of the innovative characteristics of modular products and present a major marketing asset and therefore should be eligible for protection;

(16) Whereas a design right shall not subsist in a design which is contrary to public policy or to accepted principles of morality; whereas this Directive does not constitute a harmonisation of national concepts of public policy or accepted principles of morality;

(17) Whereas it is fundamental for the smooth functioning of the internal market to unify the term of protection afforded by registered design rights;

(18) Whereas the provisions of this Directive are without prejudice to the application of the competition rules under Articles 85 and 86 of the Treaty;

(19) Whereas the rapid adoption of this Directive has become a matter of urgency for a number of industrial sectors; whereas full-scale approximation of the laws of the Member States on the use of protected designs for the purpose of permitting the repair of a complex product so as to restore its original appearance, where the product incorporating the design or to which the design is applied constitutes a component part of a complex product upon whose appearance the protected design is dependent, cannot be introduced at the present stage; whereas the lack of full-scale approximation of the laws of the Member States on the use of protected designs for such repair of a complex product should not constitute an obstacle to the approximation of those other national provisions of design law which most directly affect the functioning of the internal market; whereas for this reason Member States should in the meantime maintain in force any provisions in conformity with the Treaty relating to the use of the design of a component part used for the purpose of the repair of a complex product so as to restore its original appearance, or, if they introduce any new provisions relating to such use, the purpose of these provisions should be only to liberalise the market in such parts; whereas those Member States which, on the date of entry into force of this Directive, do not provide for protection for designs of component parts are not required to introduce registration of designs for such parts; whereas three years after the implementation date the Commission should submit an analysis of the consequences of the provisions of this Directive for Community industry, for consumers, for competition and for the functioning of the internal market; whereas, in respect of component parts of complex products, the analysis should, in particular, consider harmonisation on the basis of possible options, including a remuneration system and a limited term of exclusivity; whereas, at the latest one year after the submission of its analysis, the Commission should, after consultation with the parties most affected, propose to the European Parliament and the Council any changes to this Directive needed to complete the internal market in respect of component parts of complex products, and any other changes which it considers necessary;

(20) Whereas the transitional provision in Article 14 concerning the design of a component part used for the purpose of the repair of a complex product so as to restore its original appearance is in no case to be construed as constituting an obstacle to the free movement of a product which constitutes such a component part;

(21) Whereas the substantive grounds for refusal of registration in those Member States which provide for substantive examination of applications prior to registration, and the substantive grounds for the invalidation of registered design rights in all the Member States, must be exhaustively enumerated,

HAVE ADOPTED THIS DIRECTIVE:

Article 1

Definitions

For the purpose of this Directive:

(a) 'design' means the appearance of the whole or a part of a product resulting from the features of, in particular, the lines, contours, colours, shape, texture and/or materials of the product itself and/or its ornamentation;

(b) 'product' means any industrial or handicraft item, including *inter alia* parts intended to be assembled into a complex product, packaging, get-up, graphic symbols and typographic typefaces, but excluding computer programs;

(c) 'complex product' means a product which is composed of multiple components which can be replaced permitting disassembly and reassembly of the product.

Article 2

Scope of application

1. This Directive shall apply to:

(a) design rights registered with the central industrial property offices of the Member States;

(b) design rights registered at the Benelux Design Office;

(c) design rights registered under international arrangements which have effect in a Member State;

(d) applications for design rights referred to under (a), (b) and (c).

2. For the purpose of this Directive, design registration shall also comprise the publication following filing of the design with the industrial property office of a Member State in which such publication has the effect of bringing a design right into existence.

Article 3

Protection requirements

1. Member States shall protect designs by registration, and shall confer exclusive rights upon their holders in accordance with the provisions of this Directive.

2. A design shall be protected by a design right to the extent that it is new and has individual character.

3. A design applied to or incorporated in a product which constitutes a component part of a complex product shall only be considered to be new and to have individual character:

(a) if the component part, once it has been incorporated into the complex product, remains visible during normal use of the latter, and

(b) to the extent that those visible features of the component part fulfil in themselves the requirements as to novelty and individual character.

4. 'Normal use' within the meaning of paragraph (3)(a) shall mean use by the end user, excluding maintenance, servicing or repair work.

Article 4

Novelty

A design shall be considered new if no identical design has been made available to the public before the date of filing of the application for registration or, if priority is claimed, the date of priority. Designs shall be deemed to be identical if their features differ only in immaterial details.

Article 5

Individual character

1. A design shall be considered to have individual character if the overall impression it produces on the informed user differs from the overall impression produced on such a user by any design which has been made available to the public before the date of filing of the application for registration or, if priority is claimed, the date of priority.

2. In assessing individual character, the degree of freedom of the designer in developing the design shall be taken into consideration.

Article 6

Disclosure

1. For the purpose of applying Articles 4 and 5, a design shall be deemed to have been made available to the public if it has been published following registration or otherwise, or exhibited, used in trade or otherwise disclosed, except where these events could not reasonably have become known in the normal course of business to the circles specialised in the sector concerned, operating within the Community, before the date of filing of the application for registration or, if priority is claimed, the date of priority. The design shall not, however, be deemed to have been made available to the public for the sole reason that it has been disclosed to a third person under explicit or implicit conditions of confidentiality.

2. A disclosure shall not be taken into consideration for the purpose of applying Articles 4 and 5 if a design for which protection is claimed under a registered design right of a Member State has been made available to the public:

(a) by the designer, his successor in title, or a third person as a result of information provided or action taken by the designer, or his successor in title; and

(b) during the 12-month period preceding the date of filing of the application or, if priority is claimed, the date of priority.

3. Paragraph 2 shall also apply if the design has been made available to the public as a consequence of an abuse in relation to the designer or his successor in title.

Article 7

Designs dictated by their technical function and designs of interconnections

1. A design right shall not subsist in features of appearance of a product which are solely dictated by its technical function.

2. A design right shall not subsist in features of appearance of a product which must necessarily be reproduced in their exact form and dimensions in order to permit the product in which the design is incorporated or to which it is applied to be mechanically connected to or placed in, around or against another product so that either product may perform its function.

3. Notwithstanding paragraph 2, a design right shall, under the conditions set

out in Articles 4 and 5, subsist in a design serving the purpose of allowing multiple assembly or connection of mutually interchangeable products within a modular system.

Article 8

Designs contrary to public policy or morality

A design right shall not subsist in a design which is contrary to public policy or to accepted principles of morality.

Article 9

Scope of protection

1. The scope of the protection conferred by a design right shall include any design which does not produce on the informed user a different overall impression.

2. In assessing the scope of protection, the degree of freedom of the designer in developing his design shall be taken into consideration.

Article 10

Term of protection

Upon registration, a design which meets the requirements of Article 3(2) shall be protected by a design right for one or more periods of five years from the date of filing of the application. The right holder may have the term of protection renewed for one or more periods of five years each, up to a total term of 25 years from the date of filing.

Article 11

Invalidity or refusal of registration

1. A design shall be refused registration, or, if the design has been registered, the design right shall be declared invalid:

(a) if the design is not a design within the meaning of Article 1(a); or

(b) if it does not fulfil the requirements of Articles 3 to 8; or

(c) if the applicant for or the holder of the design right is not entitled to it under the law of the Member State concerned; or

(d) if the design is in conflict with a prior design which has been made available to the public after the date of filing of the application or, if priority is claimed, the date of priority, and which is protected from a date prior to the said date by a registered Community design or an application for a registered Community design or by a design right of the Member State concerned, or by an application for such a right.

2. Any Member State may provide that a design shall be refused registration, or, if the design has been registered, that the design right shall be declared invalid:

(a) if a distinctive sign is used in a subsequent design, and Community law or the law of the Member State concerned governing that sign confers on the right holder of the sign the right to prohibit such use; or

(b) if the design constitutes an unauthorised use of a work protected under the copyright law of the Member State concerned; or

(c) if the design constitutes an improper use of any of the items listed in Article 6b of the Paris Convention for the Protection of Industrial Property, or of badges, emblems and escutcheons other than those covered by Article 6b of the said Convention which are of particular public interest in the Member State concerned.

3. The ground provided for in paragraph 1(c) may be invoked solely by the person who is entitled to the design right under the law of the Member State concerned.

4. The grounds provided for in paragraph 1(d) and in paragraph 2(a) and (b) may be invoked solely by the applicant for or the holder of the conflicting right.

5. The ground provided for in paragraph 2(c) may be invoked solely by the person or entity concerned by the use.

6. Paragraphs 4 and 5 shall be without prejudice to the freedom of Member States to provide that the grounds provided for in paragraphs 1(d) and 2(c) may also be invoked by the appropriate authority of the Member State in question on its own initiative.

7. When a design has been refused registration or a design right has been declared invalid pursuant to paragraph 1(b) or to paragraph 2, the design may be registered or the design right maintained in an amended form, if in that form it complies with the requirements for protection and the identity of the design is retained. Registration or maintenance in an amended form may include registration accompanied by a partial disclaimer by the holder of the design right or entry in the design Register of a court decision declaring the partial invalidity of the design right.

8. Any Member State may provide that, by way of derogation from paragraphs 1 to 7, the grounds for refusal of registration or for invalidation in force in that State prior to the date on which the provisions necessary to comply with this Directive enter into force shall apply to design applications which have been made prior to that date and to resulting registrations.

9. A design right may be declared invalid even after it has lapsed or has been surrendered.

Article 12
Rights conferred by the design right

1. The registration of a design shall confer on its holder the exclusive right to use it and to prevent any third party not having his consent from using it. The aforementioned use shall cover, in particular, the making, offering, putting on the market, importing, exporting or using of a product in which the design is incorporated or to which it is applied, or stocking such a product for those purposes.

2. Where, under the law of a Member State, acts referred to in paragraph 1 could not be prevented before the date on which the provisions necessary to comply with this Directive entered into force, the rights conferred by the design right may not be invoked to prevent continuation of such acts by any person who had begun such acts prior to that date.

Article 13
Limitation of the rights conferred by the design right

1. The rights conferred by a design right upon registration shall not be exercised in respect of:
   (a) acts done privately and for non-commercial purposes;
   (b) acts done for experimental purposes;
   (c) acts of reproduction for the purposes of making citations or of teaching, provided that such acts are compatible with fair trade practice and do not unduly prejudice the normal exploitation of the design, and that mention is made of the source.

2. In addition, the rights conferred by a design right upon registration shall not be exercised in respect of:

(a) the equipment on ships and aircraft registered in another country when these temporarily enter the territory of the Member State concerned;

(b) the importation in the Member State concerned of spare parts and accessories for the purpose of repairing such craft;

(c) the execution of repairs on such craft.

Article 14

Transitional provision

Until such time as amendments to this Directive are adopted on a proposal from the Commission in accordance with the provisions of Article 18, Member States shall maintain in force their existing legal provisions relating to the use of the design of a component part used for the purpose of the repair of a complex product so as to restore its original appearance and shall introduce changes to those provisions only if the purpose is to liberalise the market for such parts.

Article 15

Exhaustion of rights

The rights conferred by a design right upon registration shall not extend to acts relating to a product in which a design included within the scope of protection of the design right is incorporated or to which it is applied, when the product has been put on the market in the Community by the holder of the design right or with his consent.

Article 16

Relationship to other forms of protection

The provisions of this Directive shall be without prejudice to any provisions of Community law or of the law of the Member State concerned relating to unregistered design rights, trade marks or other distinctive signs, patents and utility models, typefaces, civil liability or unfair competition.

Article 17

Relationship to copyright

A design protected by a design right registered in or in respect of a Member State in accordance with this Directive shall also be eligible for protection under the law of copyright of that State as from the date on which the design was created or fixed in any form. The extent to which, and the conditions under which, such a protection is conferred, including the level of originality required, shall be determined by each Member State.

Article 18

Revision

Three years after the implementation date specified in Article 19, the Commission shall submit an analysis of the consequences of the provisions of this Directive for Community industry, in particular the industrial sectors which are most affected, particularly manufacturers of complex products and component parts, for consumers, for competition and for the functioning of the internal market. At the latest one year later the Commission shall propose to the European Parliament and the Council any changes to this Directive needed to complete the internal market in respect of component parts of complex products and any other changes which it considers necessary in light of its consultations with the parties most affected.

Article 19

Implementation

1. Member States shall bring into force the laws, regulations or administrative provisions necessary to comply with this Directive not later than 28 October 2001.

When Member States adopt these provisions, they shall contain a reference to this Directive or shall be accompanied by such reference on the occasion of their official publication. The methods of making such reference shall be laid down by Member States.

2. Member States shall communicate to the Commission the provisions of national law which they adopt in the field governed by this Directive.

Article 20

Entry into force

This Directive shall enter into force on the 20th day following its publication in the *Official Journal of the European Communities*.

Article 21

Addressees

This Directive is addressed to the Member States.

Done at Luxembourg, 13 October 1998.

For the European Parliament	*For the Council*
The President	*The President*
J. M. GIL-ROBLES	C. EINEM

H6. DIRECTIVE 98/84/EC

Directive 98/84/EC of the European Parliament and of the Council of 20 November 1998 on the legal protection of services based on, or consisting of, conditional access[i]

([1998] O.J. L320/54)

THE EUROPEAN PARLIAMENT AND THE COUNCIL OF THE EUROPEAN UNION

Having regard to the Treaty establishing the European Community, and in particular Articles 57(2), 66 and 100a thereof,

Having regard to the proposal from the Commission[1],

Having regard to the opinion of the Economic and Social Committee[2],

Acting in accordance with the procedure laid down in Article 189b of the Treaty[3],

(1) Whereas the objectives of the Community as laid down in the Treaty include creating an ever closer union among the peoples of Europe and ensuring economic and social progress, by eliminating the barriers which divide them;

(2) Whereas the cross-border provision of broadcasting and information soci-

---

[i] *Editorial note*: The footnote numbering in the original Directive is reproduced below.

[1] OJ C 314, 16. 10. 1997, p. 7 and OJ C 203, 30. 6. 1998, p. 12.

[2] OJ C 129, 27. 4. 1998, p. 16.

[3] Opinion of the European Parliament of 30 April 1998 (OJ C 152, 18. 5. 1998, p. 59), Council Common Position of 29 June 1998 (OJ C 262, 19. 8. 1998, p. 34) and Decision of the European Parliament of 8 October 1998 (OJ C 328, 26. 10. 1998). Council Decision of 9 November 1998.

ety services may contribute, from the individual point of view, to the full effectiveness of freedom of expression as a fundamental right and, from the collective point of view, to the achievement of the objectives laid down in the Treaty;

(3) Whereas the Treaty provides for the free movement of all services which are normally provided for remuneration;

whereas this right, as applied to broadcasting and information society services, is also a specific manifestation in Community law of a more general principle, namely freedom of expression as enshrined in Article 10 of the European Convention for the Protection of Human Rights and Fundamental Freedoms;

whereas that Article explicitly recognizes the right of citizens to receive and impart information regardless of frontiers and whereas any restriction of that right must be based on due consideration of other legitimate interests deserving of legal protection;

(4) Whereas the Commission undertook a wide-ranging consultation based on the Green Paper 'Legal Protection of Encrypted Services in the Internal Market';

whereas the results of that consultation confirmed the need for a Community legal instrument ensuring the legal protection of all those services whose remuneration relies on conditional access;

(5) Whereas the European Parliament, in its Resolution of 13 May 1997 on the Green Paper[4], called on the Commission to present a proposal for a Directive covering all encoded services in respect of which encoding is used to ensure payment of a fee, and agreed that this should include information society services provided at a distance by electronic means and at the individual request of a service receiver, as well as broadcasting services;

(6) Whereas the opportunities offered by digital technologies provide the potential for increasing consumer choice and contributing to cultural pluralism, by developing an even wider range of services within the meaning of Articles 59 and 60 of the Treaty;

whereas the viability of those services will often depend on the use of conditional access in order to obtain the remuneration of the service provider;

whereas, accordingly, the legal protection of service providers against illicit devices which allow access to these services free of charge seems necessary in order to ensure the economic viability of the services;

(7) Whereas the importance of this issue was recognized by the Commission Communication on 'A European Initiative in Electronic Commerce';

(8) Whereas, in accordance with Article 7a of the Treaty, the internal market is to comprise an area without internal frontiers in which the free movement of services and goods is ensured;

whereas Article 128(4) of the Treaty requires the Community to take cultural aspects into account in its action under other provisions of the Treaty;

whereas by virtue of Article 130(3) of the Treaty, the Community must, through the policies and activities it pursues, contribute to creating the conditions necessary for the competitiveness of its industry;

(9) Whereas this Directive is without prejudice to possible future Community or national provisions meant to ensure that a number of broadcasting services, recognized as being of public interest, are not based on conditional access;

(10) Whereas this Directive is without prejudice to the cultural aspects of any further Community action concerning new services;

(11) Whereas the disparity between national rules concerning the legal protection of services based on, or consisting of, conditional access is liable to create obstacles to the free movement of services and goods;

4 OJ C 167, 2. 6. 1997, p. 31.

(12) Whereas the application of the Treaty is not sufficient to remove these internal market obstacles; whereas those obstacles should therefore be removed by providing for an equivalent level of protection between Member States; whereas this implies an approximation of the national rules relating to the commercial activities which concern illicit devices;

(13) Whereas it seems necessary to ensure that Member States provide appropriate legal protection against the placing on the market, for direct or indirect financial gain, of an illicit device which enables or facilitates without authority the circumvention of any technological measures designed to protect the remuneration of a legally provided service;

(14) Whereas those commercial activities which concern illicit devices include commercial communications covering all forms of advertising, direct marketing, sponsorship, sales promotion and public relations promoting such products and services;

(15) Whereas those commercial activities are detrimental to consumers who are misled about the origin of illicit devices; whereas a high level of consumer protection is needed in order to fight against this kind of consumer fraud; whereas Article 129a(1) of the Treaty provides that the Community should contribute to the achievement of a high level of consumer protection by the measures it adopts pursuant to Article 100a thereof;

(16) Whereas, therefore, the legal framework for the creation of a single audio-visual area laid down in Council Directive 89/552/EEC of 3 October 1989 on the coordination of certain provisions laid down by law, regulation or administrative action in Member States concerning the pursuit of television broadcasting activities[5] should be supplemented with reference to conditional access techniques as laid down in this Directive, in order, not least, to ensure equal treatment of the suppliers of cross-border broadcasts, regardless of their place of establishment;

(17) Whereas, in accordance with the Council Resolution of 29 June 1995 on the effective uniform application of Community law and on the penalties applicable for breaches of Community law in the internal market[6], Member States are required to take action to ensure that Community law is duly applied with the same effectiveness and thoroughness as national law;

(18) Whereas, in accordance with Article 5 of the Treaty, Member States are required to take all appropriate measures to guarantee the application and effectiveness of Community law, in particular by ensuring that the sanctions chosen are effective, dissuasive and proportionate and the remedies appropriate;

(19) Whereas the approximation of the laws, regulations and administrative provisions of the Member States should be limited to what is needed in order to achieve the objectives of the internal market, in accordance with the principle of proportionality as set out in the third paragraph of Article 3b of the Treaty;

(20) Whereas the distribution of illicit devices includes transfer by any means and putting such devices on the market for circulation inside or outside the Community;

(21) Whereas this Directive is without prejudice to the application of any national provisions which may prohibit the private possession of illicit devices, to the application of Community competition rules and to the application of Community rules concerning intellectual property rights;

(22) Whereas national law concerning sanctions and remedies for infringing commercial activities may provide that the activities have to be carried out in the

---

[5] OJ L 298, 17. 10. 1989, p. 23. Directive as amended by Directive 97/36/EC of the European Parliament and of the Council (OJ L 202, 30. 7. 1997, p. 60).
[6] OJ C 188, 22. 7. 1995, p. 1.

knowledge or with reasonable grounds for knowing that the devices in question were illicit;

(23) Whereas the sanctions and remedies provided for under this Directive are without prejudice to any other sanction or remedy for which provision may be made under national law, such as preventive measures in general or seizure of illicit devices; whereas Member States are not obliged to provide criminal sanctions for infringing activities covered by this Directive;

whereas Member States' provisions for actions for damages are to be be in conformity with their national legislative and judicial systems;

(24) Whereas this Directive is without prejudice to the application of national rules which do not fall within the field herein coordinated, such as those adopted for the protection of minors, including those in compliance with Directive 89/552/EEC, or national provisions concerned with public policy or public security,

HAVE ADOPTED THIS DIRECTIVE:

Article 1

Scope

The objective of this Directive is to approximate provisions in the Member States concerning measures against illicit devices which give unauthorised access to protected services.

Article 2

Definitions

For the purposes of this Directive:

(a) protected service shall mean any of the following services, where provided against remuneration and on the basis of conditional access:
   — television broadcasting, as defined in Article 1(a) of Directive 89/552/EEC,
   — radio broadcasting, meaning any transmission by wire or over the air, including by satellite, of radio programmes intended for reception by the public,
   — information society services within the meaning of Article 1(2) of Directive 98/34/EC of the European Parliament and of the Council of 22 June 1998 laying down a procedure for the provision of information in the field of technical standards and regulations and of rules on information society services[7],
   or the provision of conditional access to the above services considered as a service in its own right;

(b) conditional access shall mean any technical measure and/or arrangement whereby access to the protected service in an intelligible form is made conditional upon prior individual authorisation;

(c) conditional access device shall mean any equipment or software designed or adapted to give access to a protected service in an intelligible form;

(d) associated service shall mean the installation, maintenance or replacement of conditional access devices, as well as the provision of commercial communication services in relation to them or to protected services;

(e) illicit device shall mean any equipment or software designed or adapted to give access to a protected service in an intelligible form without the authorisation of the service provider;

---

[7] OJ L 204, 21. 7. 1998, p. 37. Directive as amended by Directive 98/48/EC (OJ L 217, 5. 8. 1998, p. 18).

(f) field coordinated by this Directive shall mean any provision relating to the infringing activities specified in Article 4.

Article 3

Internal market principles

1. Each Member State shall take the measures necessary to prohibit on its territory the activities listed in Article 4, and to provide for the sanctions and remedies laid down in Article 5.

2. Without prejudice to paragraph 1, Member States may not:

(a) restrict the provision of protected services, or associated services, which originate in another Member State; or

(b) restrict the free movement of conditional access devices; for reasons falling within the field coordinated by this Directive.

Article 4

Infringing activities

Member States shall prohibit on their territory all of the following activities:

(a) the manufacture, import, distribution, sale, rental or possession for commercial purposes of illicit devices;

(b) the installation, maintenance or replacement for commercial purposes of an illicit device;

(c) the use of commercial communications to promote illicit devices.

Article 5

Sanctions and remedies

1. The sanctions shall be effective, dissuasive and proportionate to the potential impact of the infringing activity.

2. Member States shall take the necessary measures to ensure that providers of protected services whose interests are affected by an infringing activity as specified in Article 4, carried out on their territory, have access to appropriate remedies, including bringing an action for damages and obtaining an injunction or other preventive measure, and where appropriate, applying for disposal outside commercial channels of illicit devices.

Article 6

Implementation

1. Member States shall bring into force the laws, regulations and administrative provisions necessary to comply with this Directive by 28 May 2000. They shall notify them to the Commission forthwith.

When Member States adopt such measures, they shall contain a reference to this Directive or shall be accompanied by such reference at the time of their official publication. The methods of making such reference shall be laid down by Member States.

2. Member States shall communicate to the Commission the text of the provisions of national law which they adopt in the field coordinated by this Directive.

Article 7

Reports

Not later than three years after the entry into force of this Directive, and every two years thereafter, the Commission shall present a report to the European Parliament, the Council and the Economic and Social Committee concerning the implementation of this Directive accompanied, where appropriate, by proposals, in particular as regards the definitions under Article 2, for adapting it in light of technical and economic developments and of the consultations carried out by the Commission.

Article 8

Entry into force

This Directive shall enter into force on the day of its publication in the Official Journal of the European Communities.

Article 9

Addressees

This Directive is addressed to the Member States.
Done at Brussels, 20 November 1998.
For the European Parliament
The President
J. M. GIL-ROBLES
For the Council
The President
E. HOSTASCH

H7. DIRECTIVE 2000/31/EC

Directive 2000/31/EC of the European Parliament and of the Council of 8 June 2000 on certain legal aspects of information society services, in particular electronic commerce, in the Internal Market (Directive on electronic commerce)[i]

([2000] O.J. L178/1)

THE EUROPEAN PARLIAMENT AND THE COUNCIL OF THE EUROPEAN UNION,

Having regard to the Treaty establishing the European Community, and in particular Articles 47(2), 55 and 95 thereof,

Having regard to the proposal from the Commission[1],

Having regard to the opinion of the Economic and Social Committee[2],

Acting in accordance with the procedure laid down in Article 251 of the Treaty[3],

Whereas:

(1) The European Union is seeking to forge ever closer links between the States and peoples of Europe, to ensure economic and social progress; in accordance with Article 14(2) of the Treaty, the internal market comprises an area without internal frontiers in which the free movements of goods, services and the freedom of establishment are ensured; the development of information society services within the area without internal frontiers is vital to eliminating the barriers which divide the European peoples.

---

[i] *Editorial note*: The footnote numbering in the original Directive is reproduced below.
[1] OJ C 30, 5.2.1999, p. 4.
[2] OJ C 169, 16.6.1999, p. 36.
[3] Opinion of the European Parliament of 6 May 1999 (OJ C 279, 1.10.1999, p. 389), Council common position of 28 February 2000 (OJ C 128, 8.5.2000, p. 32) and Decision of the European Parliament of 4 May 2000 (not yet published in the Official Journal).

(2) The development of electronic commerce within the information society offers significant employment opportunities in the Community, particularly in small and medium-sized enterprises, and will stimulate economic growth and investment in innovation by European companies, and can also enhance the competitiveness of European industry, provided that everyone has access to the Internet.

(3) Community law and the characteristics of the Community legal order are a vital asset to enable European citizens and operators to take full advantage, without consideration of borders, of the opportunities afforded by electronic commerce; this Directive therefore has the purpose of ensuring a high level of Community legal integration in order to establish a real area without internal borders for information society services.

(4) It is important to ensure that electronic commerce could fully benefit from the internal market and therefore that, as with Council Directive 89/552/EEC of 3 October 1989 on the coordination of certain provisions laid down by law, regulation or administrative action in Member States concerning the pursuit of television broadcasting activities[4], a high level of Community integration is achieved.

(5) The development of information society services within the Community is hampered by a number of legal obstacles to the proper functioning of the internal market which make less attractive the exercise of the freedom of establishment and the freedom to provide services; these obstacles arise from divergences in legislation and from the legal uncertainty as to which national rules apply to such services; in the absence of coordination and adjustment of legislation in the relevant areas, obstacles might be justified in the light of the case-law of the Court of Justice of the European Communities; legal uncertainty exists with regard to the extent to which Member States may control services originating from another Member State.

(6) In the light of Community objectives, of Articles 43 and 49 of the Treaty and of secondary Community law, these obstacles should be eliminated by coordinating certain national laws and by clarifying certain legal concepts at Community level to the extent necessary for the proper functioning of the internal market; by dealing only with certain specific matters which give rise to problems for the internal market, this Directive is fully consistent with the need to respect the principle of subsidiarity as set out in Article 5 of the Treaty.

(7) In order to ensure legal certainty and consumer confidence, this Directive must lay down a clear and general framework to cover certain legal aspects of electronic commerce in the internal market.

(8) The objective of this Directive is to create a legal framework to ensure the free movement of information society services between Member States and not to harmonise the field of criminal law as such.

(9) The free movement of information society services can in many cases be a specific reflection in Community law of a more general principle, namely freedom of expression as enshrined in Article 10(1) of the Convention for the Protection of Human Rights and Fundamental Freedoms, which has been ratified by all the Member States; for this reason, directives covering the supply of information society services must ensure that this activity may be engaged in freely in the light of that Article, subject only to the restrictions laid down in paragraph 2 of that Article and in Article 46(1) of the Treaty; this Directive is not intended to affect national fundamental rules and principles relating to freedom of expression.

(10) In accordance with the principle of proportionality, the measures provided

---

[4] OJ L 298, 17.10.1989, p. 23. Directive as amended by Directive 97/36/EC of the European Parliament and of the Council (OJ L 202, 30.7.1997, p. 60).

for in this Directive are strictly limited to the minimum needed to achieve the objective of the proper functioning of the internal market; where action at Community level is necessary, and in order to guarantee an area which is truly without internal frontiers as far as electronic commerce is concerned, the Directive must ensure a high level of protection of objectives of general interest, in particular the protection of minors and human dignity, consumer protection and the protection of public health; according to Article 152 of the Treaty, the protection of public health is an essential component of other Community policies.

[...]

(12) It is necessary to exclude certain activities from the scope of this Directive, on the grounds that the freedom to provide services in these fields cannot, at this stage, be guaranteed under the Treaty or existing secondary legislation; excluding these activities does not preclude any instruments which might prove necessary for the proper functioning of the internal market; taxation, particularly value added tax imposed on a large number of the services covered by this Directive, must be excluded form the scope of this Directive.

(13) This Directive does not aim to establish rules on fiscal obligations nor does it pre-empt the drawing up of Community instruments concerning fiscal aspects of electronic commerce.

(14) The protection of individuals with regard to the processing of personal data is solely governed by Directive 95/46/EC of the European Parliament and of the Council of 24 October 1995 on the protection of individuals with regard to the processing of personal data and on the free movement of such data[5] and Directive 97/66/EC of the European Parliament and of the Council of 15 December 1997 concerning the processing of personal data and the protection of privacy in the telecommunications sector[6] which are fully applicable to information society services; these Directives already establish a Community legal framework in the field of personal data and therefore it is not necessary to cover this issue in this Directive in order to ensure the smooth functioning of the internal market, in particular the free movement of personal data between Member States; the implementation and application of this Directive should be made in full compliance with the principles relating to the protection of personal data, in particular as regards unsolicited commercial communication and the liability of intermediaries; this Directive cannot prevent the anonymous use of open networks such as the Internet.

(15) The confidentiality of communications is guaranteed by Article 5 Directive 97/66/EC; in accordance with that Directive, Member States must prohibit any kind of interception or surveillance of such communications by others than the senders and receivers, except when legally authorised.

(16) The exclusion of gambling activities from the scope of application of this Directive covers only games of chance, lotteries and betting transactions, which involve wagering a stake with monetary value; this does not cover promotional competitions or games where the purpose is to encourage the sale of goods or services and where payments, if they arise, serve only to acquire the promoted goods or services.

(17) The definition of information society services already exists in Community law in Directive 98/34/EC of the European Parliament and of the Council of 22 June 1998 laying down a procedure for the provision of information in the field of technical standards and regulations and of rules on information society

---

[5] OJ L 281, 23.11.1995, p. 31.
[6] OJ L 24, 30.1.1998, p. 1.

services[7] and in Directive 98/84/EC of the European Parliament and of the Council of 20 November 1998 on the legal protection of services based on, or consisting of, conditional access[8]; this definition covers any service normally provided for remuneration, at a distance, by means of electronic equipment for the processing (including digital compression) and storage of data, and at the individual request of a recipient of a service; those services referred to in the indicative list in Annex V to Directive 98/34/EC which do not imply data processing and storage are not covered by this definition.

(18) Information society services span a wide range of economic activities which take place on-line; these activities can, in particular, consist of selling goods on-line; activities such as the delivery of goods as such or the provision of services off-line are not covered; information society services are not solely restricted to services giving rise to on-line contracting but also, in so far as they represent an economic activity, extend to services which are not remunerated by those who receive them, such as those offering on-line information or commercial communications, or those providing tools allowing for search, access and retrieval of data; information society services also include services consisting of the transmission of information via a communication network, in providing access to a communication network or in hosting information provided by a recipient of the service; television broadcasting within the meaning of Directive EEC/89/552 and radio broadcasting are not information society services because they are not provided at individual request; by contrast, services which are transmitted point to point, such as video-on-demand or the provision of commercial communications by electronic mail are information society services; the use of electronic mail or equivalent individual communications for instance by natural persons acting outside their trade, business or profession including their use for the conclusion of contracts between such persons is not an information society service; the contractual relationship between an employee and his employer is not an information society service; activities which by their very nature cannot be carried out at a distance and by electronic means, such as the statutory auditing of company accounts or medical advice requiring the physical examination of a patient are not information society services.

[...]

(40) Both existing and emerging disparities in Member States' legislation and case-law concerning liability of service providers acting as intermediaries prevent the smooth functioning of the internal market, in particular by impairing the development of cross-border services and producing distortions of competition; service providers have a duty to act, under certain circumstances, with a view to preventing or stopping illegal activities; this Directive should constitute the appropriate basis for the development of rapid and reliable procedures for removing and disabling access to illegal information; such mechanisms could be developed on the basis of voluntary agreements between all parties concerned and should be encouraged by Member States; it is in the interest of all parties involved in the provision of information society services to adopt and implement such procedures; the provisions of this Directive relating to liability should not preclude the development and effective operation, by the different interested parties, of technical systems of protection and identification and of technical surveillance instruments made possible by digital technology within the limits laid down by Directives 95/46/EC and 97/66/EC.

(41) This Directive strikes a balance between the different interests at stake

---

[7] OJ L 204, 21.7.1998, p. 37. Directive as amended by Directive 98/48/EC (OJ L 217, 5.8.1998, p. 18).

[8] OJ L 320, 28.11.1998, p. 54.

and establishes principles upon which industry agreements and standards can be based.

(42) The exemptions from liability established in this Directive cover only cases where the activity of the information society service provider is limited to the technical process of operating and giving access to a communication network over which information made available by third parties is transmitted or temporarily stored, for the sole purpose of making the transmission more efficient; this activity is of a mere technical, automatic and passive nature, which implies that the information society service provider has neither knowledge of nor control over the information which is transmitted or stored.

(43) A service provider can benefit from the exemptions for 'mere conduit' and for 'caching' when he is in no way involved with the information transmitted; this requires among other things that he does not modify the information that he transmitted; this requirement does not cover manipulations of a technical nature which take place in the course of the transmission as they do not alter the integrity of the information contained in the transmission.

(44) A service provider who deliberately collaborates with one of the recipients of his service in order to undertake illegal acts goes beyond the activities of 'mere conduit' or 'caching' and as a result cannot benefit from the liability exemptions established for these activities.

(45) The limitations of the liability of intermediary service providers established in this Directive do not affect the possibility of injunctions of different kinds; such injunctions can in particular consist of orders by courts or administrative authorities requiring the termination or prevention of any infringement, including the removal of illegal information or the disabling of access to it.

(46) In order to benefit from a limitation of liability, the provider of an information society service, consisting of the storage of information, upon obtaining actual knowledge or awareness of illegal activities has to act expeditiously to remove or to disable access to the information concerned; the removal or disabling of access has to be undertaken in the observance of the principle of freedom of expression and of procedures established for this purpose at national level; this Directive does not affect Member States' possibility of establishing specific requirements which must be fulfilled expeditiously prior to the removal or disabling of information.

(47) Member States are prevented from imposing a monitoring obligation on service providers only with respect to obligations of a general nature; this does not concern monitoring obligations in a specific case and, in particular, does not affect orders by national authorities in accordance with national legislation.

(48) This Directive does not affect the possibility for Member States of requiring service providers, who host information provided by recipients of their service, to apply duties of care, which can reasonably be expected from them and which are specified by national law, in order to detect and prevent certain types of illegal activities.

(49) Member States and the Commission are to encourage the drawing-up of codes of conduct; this is not to impair the voluntary nature of such codes and the possibility for interested parties of deciding freely whether to adhere to such codes.

(50) It is important that the proposed directive on the harmonisation of certain aspects of copyright and related rights in the information society and this Directive come into force within a similar time scale with a view to establishing a clear framework of rules relevant to the issue of liability of intermediaries for copyright and relating rights infringements at Community level.

(51) Each Member State should be required, where necessary, to amend any legislation which is liable to hamper the use of schemes for the out-of-court

settlement of disputes through electronic channels; the result of this amendment must be to make the functioning of such schemes genuinely and effectively possible in law and in practice, even across borders.

(52) The effective exercise of the freedoms of the internal market makes it necessary to guarantee victims effective access to means of settling disputes; damage which may arise in connection with information society services is characterised both by its rapidity and by its geographical extent; in view of this specific character and the need to ensure that national authorities do not endanger the mutual confidence which they should have in one another, this Directive requests Member States to ensure that appropriate court actions are available; Member States should examine the need to provide access to judicial procedures by appropriate electronic means.

(53) Directive 98/27/EC, which is applicable to information society services, provides a mechanism relating to actions for an injunction aimed at the protection of the collective interests of consumers; this mechanism will contribute to the free movement of information society services by ensuring a high level of consumer protection.

(54) The sanctions provided for under this Directive are without prejudice to any other sanction or remedy provided under national law; Member States are not obliged to provide criminal sanctions for infringement of national provisions adopted pursuant to this Directive.

[...]

HAVE ADOPTED THIS DIRECTIVE:

CHAPTER I

GENERAL PROVISIONS

Article 1

Objective and scope

1. This Directive seeks to contribute to the proper functioning of the internal market by ensuring the free movement of information society services between the Member States.

2. This Directive approximates, to the extent necessary for the achievement of the objective set out in paragraph 1, certain national provisions on information society services relating to the internal market, the establishment of service providers, commercial communications, electronic contracts, the liability of intermediaries, codes of conduct, out-of-court dispute settlements, court actions and cooperation between Member States.

3. This Directive complements Community law applicable to information society services without prejudice to the level of protection for, in particular, public health and consumer interests, as established by Community acts and national legislation implementing them in so far as this does not restrict the freedom to provide information society services.

4. This Directive does not establish additional rules on private international law nor does it deal with the jurisdiction of Courts.

5. This Directive shall not apply to:

(a) the field of taxation;

(b) questions relating to information society services covered by Directives 95/46/EC and 97/66/EC;

(c) questions relating to agreements or practices governed by cartel law;

(d) the following activities of information society services:

— the activities of notaries or equivalent professions to the extent that they involve a direct and specific connection with the exercise of public authority,

— the representation of a client and defence of his interests before the courts,

— gambling activities which involve wagering a stake with monetary value in games of chance, including lotteries and betting transactions.

6. This Directive does not affect measures taken at Community or national level, in the respect of Community law, in order to promote cultural and linguistic diversity and to ensure the defence of pluralism.

Article 2

Definitions

For the purpose of this Directive, the following terms shall bear the following meanings:

(a) 'information society services': services within the meaning of Article 1(2) of Directive 98/34/EC as amended by Directive 98/48/EC;

(b) 'service provider': any natural or legal person providing an information society service;

(c) 'established service provider': a service provider who effectively pursues an economic activity using a fixed establishment for an indefinite period. The presence and use of the technical means and technologies required to provide the service do not, in themselves, constitute an establishment of the provider;

(d) 'recipient of the service': any natural or legal person who, for professional ends or otherwise, uses an information society service, in particular for the purposes of seeking information or making it accessible;

(e) 'consumer': any natural person who is acting for purposes which are outside his or her trade, business or profession;

(f) 'commercial communication': any form of communication designed to promote, directly or indirectly, the goods, services or image of a company, organisation or person pursuing a commercial, industrial or craft activity or exercising a regulated profession. The following do not in themselves constitute commercial communications:

— information allowing direct access to the activity of the company, organisation or person, in particular a domain name or an electronic-mail address,

— communications relating to the goods, services or image of the company, organisation or person compiled in an independent manner, particularly when this is without financial consideration;

(g) 'regulated profession': any profession within the meaning of either Article 1(d) of Council directive 89/48/EEC of 21 December 1988 on a general system for the recognition of higher-education diplomas awarded on completion of professional education and training of at least three-years' duration[9] or of Article 1(f) of Council Directive 92/51/EEC of 18 June 1992 on a second general system for the recognition of professional education and training to supplement Directive 89/48/EEC[10];

(h) 'coordinated field': requirements laid down in Member States' legal

---

[9] OJ L 19, 24.1.1989, p.16.
[10] OJ L 209, 24.7.1992, p. 25. Directive as last amended by Commission Directive 97/38/EC (OJ L 184, 12.7.1997, p. 31).

systems applicable to information society service providers or information society services, regardless of whether they are of a general nature or specifically designed for them.

(i) The coordinated field concerns requirements with which the service provider has to comply in respect of:

— the taking up of the activity of an information society service, such as requirements concerning qualifications, authorisation or notification,

— the pursuit of the activity of an information society service, such as requirements concerning the behaviour of the service provider, requirements regarding the quality or content of the service including those applicable to advertising and contracts, or requirements concerning the liability of the service provider;

(ii) The coordinated field does not cover requirements such as:

— requirements applicable to goods as such,

— requirements applicable to the delivery of goods,

— requirements applicable to services not provided by electronic means.

CHAPTER II

PRINCIPLES

SECTION 4:

LIABILITY OF INTERMEDIARY SERVICE PROVIDERS

Article 12

'Mere conduit'

1. Where an information society service is provided that consists of the transmission in a communication network of information provided by a recipient of the service, or the provision of access to a communication network, Member States shall ensure that the service provider is not liable for the information transmitted, on condition that the provider:

(a) does not initiate the transmission;

(b) does not select the receiver of the transmission; and

(c) does not select or modify the information contained in the transmission.

2. The acts of transmission and of provision of access referred to in paragraph 1 include the automatic, intermediate and transient storage of the information transmitted in so far as this takes place for the sole purpose of carrying out the transmission in the communication network, and provided that the information is not stored for any period longer than is reasonably necessary for the transmission.

3. This Article shall not affect the possibility for a court or administrative authority, in accordance with Member States' legal systems, of requiring the service provider to terminate or prevent an infringement.

Article 13

'Caching'

1. Where an information society service is provided that consists of the transmission in a communication network of information provided by a recipient of the service, Member States shall ensure that the service provider is not liable for the automatic, intermediate and temporary storage of that information, performed for the sole purpose of making more efficient the information's onward transmission to other recipients of the service upon their request, on condition that:

(a) the provider does not modify the information;

(b) the provider complies with conditions on access to the information;

(c) the provider complies with rules regarding the updating of the information, specified in a manner widely recognised and used by industry;

(d) the provider does not interfere with the lawful use of technology, widely recognised and used by industry, to obtain data on the use of the information; and

(e) the provider acts expeditiously to remove or to disable access to the information it has stored upon obtaining actual knowledge of the fact that the information at the initial source of the transmission has been removed from the network, or access to it has been disabled, or that a court or an administrative authority has ordered such removal or disablement.

2. This Article shall not affect the possibility for a court or administrative authority, in accordance with Member States' legal systems, of requiring the service provider to terminate or prevent an infringement.

Article 14

Hosting

1. Where an information society service is provided that consists of the storage of information provided by a recipient of the service, Member States shall ensure that the service provider is not liable for the information stored at the request of a recipient of the service, on condition that:

(a) the provider does not have actual knowledge of illegal activity or information and, as regards claims for damages, is not aware of facts or circumstances from which the illegal activity or information is apparent; or

(b) the provider, upon obtaining such knowledge or awareness, acts expeditiously to remove or to disable access to the information.

2. Paragraph 1 shall not apply when the recipient of the service is acting under the authority or the control of the provider.

3. This Article shall not affect the possibility for a court or administrative authority, in accordance with Member States' legal systems, of requiring the service provider to terminate or prevent an infringement, nor does it affect the possibility for Member States of establishing procedures governing the removal or disabling of access to information.

Article 15

No general obligation to monitor

1. Member States shall not impose a general obligation on providers, when providing the services covered by Articles 12, 13 and 14, to monitor the information which they transmit or store, nor a general obligation actively to seek facts or circumstances indicating illegal activity.

2. Member States may establish obligations for information society service providers promptly to inform the competent public authorities of alleged illegal activities undertaken or information provided by recipients of their service or obligations to communicate to the competent authorities, at their request, information enabling the identification of recipients of their service with whom they have storage agreements.

CHAPTER III

IMPLEMENTATION

Article 16

Codes of conduct

1. Member States and the Commission shall encourage:

(a) the drawing up of codes of conduct at Community level, by trade, professional and consumer associations or organisations, designed to contribute to the proper implementation of Article 5 to 15;

(b) the voluntary transmission of draft codes of conduct at national or Community level to the Commission;

(c) the accessibility of these codes of conduct in the Community languages by electronic means;

(d) the communication to the Member States and the Commission, by trade, professional and consumer associations or organisations, of their assessment of the application of their codes of conduct and their impact upon practices, habits or customs relating to electronic commerce;

(e) the drawing up of codes of conduct regarding the protection of minors and human dignity.

2. Member States and the Commission shall encourage the involvement of associations or organisations representing consumers in the drafting and implementation of codes of conduct affecting their interests and drawn up in accordance with paragraph 1(a). Where appropriate, to take account of their specific needs, associations representing the visually impaired and disabled should be consulted.

Article 17

Out-of-court dispute settlement

1. Member States shall ensure that, in the event of disagreement between an information society service provider and the recipient of the service, their legislation does not hamper the use of out-of-court schemes, available under national law, for dispute settlement, including appropriate electronic means.

2. Member States shall encourage bodies responsible for the out-of-court settlement of, in particular, consumer disputes to operate in a way which provides adequate procedural guarantees for the parties concerned.

3. Member States shall encourage bodies responsible for out-of-court dispute settlement to inform the Commission of the significant decisions they take regarding information society services and to transmit any other information on the practices, usages or customs relating to electronic commerce.

Article 18

Court actions

1. Member States shall ensure that court actions available under national law concerning information society services' activities allow for the rapid adoption of measures, including interim measures, designed to terminate any alleged infringement and to prevent any further impairment of the interests involved.

2. The Annex to Directive 98/27/EC shall be supplemented as follows:

'11. Directive 2000/31/EC of the European Parliament and of the Council of 8 June 2000 on certain legal aspects on information society services, in particular electronic commerce, in the internal market (Directive on electronic commerce) (OJ L 178, 17.7.2000, p. 1).'

Article 19

Cooperation

1. Member States shall have adequate means of supervision and investigation necessary to implement this Directive effectively and shall ensure that service providers supply them with the requisite information.

2. Member States shall cooperate with other Member States; they shall, to that end, appoint one or several contact points, whose details they shall communicate to the other Member States and to the Commission.

3. Member States shall, as quickly as possible, and in conformity with national law, provide the assistance and information requested by other Member States or by the Commission, including by appropriate electronic means.

4. Member States shall establish contact points which shall be accessible at least by electronic means and from which recipients and service providers may:

(a) obtain general information on contractual rights and obligations as well as on the complaint and redress mechanisms available in the event of disputes, including practical aspects involved in the use of such mechanisms;

(b) obtain the details of authorities, associations or organisations from which they may obtain further information or practical assistance.

5. Member States shall encourage the communication to the Commission of any significant administrative or judicial decisions taken in their territory regarding disputes relating to information society services and practices, usages and customs relating to electronic commerce. The Commission shall communicate these decisions to the other Member States.

Article 20

Sanctions

Member States shall determine the sanctions applicable to infringements of national provisions adopted pursuant to this Directive and shall take all measures necessary to ensure that they are enforced. The sanctions they provide for shall be effective, proportionate and dissuasive.

H8. DIRECTIVE 2001/29/EC

Directive 2001/29/EC of the European Parliament and of the Council of 22 May 2001 on the harmonisation of certain aspects of copyright and related rights in the information society[i]

([2001] O.J. L167/10)

THE EUROPEAN PARLIAMENT AND THE COUNCIL OF THE EUROPEAN UNION,

Having regard to the Treaty establishing the European Community, and in particular Articles 47(2), 55 and 95 thereof,

Having regard to the proposal from the Commission[1],

Having regard to the opinion of the Economic and Social Committee[2],

Acting in accordance with the procedure laid down in Article 251 of the Treaty[3],

Whereas:

---

[i] *Editorial note.* The footnote numbering in the original Directive is reproduced below.

[1] OJ C 108, 7.4.1998, p. 6 and OJ C 180, 25.6.1999, p. 6.

[2] OJ C 407, 28.12.1998, p. 30.

[3] Opinion of the European Parliament of 10 February 1999 (OJ C 150, 28.5.1999, p. 171), Council

(1) The Treaty provides for the establishment of an internal market and the institution of a system ensuring that competition in the internal market is not distorted. Harmonisation of the laws of the Member States on copyright and related rights contributes to the achievement of these objectives.

(2) The European Council, meeting at Corfu on 24 and 25 June 1994, stressed the need to create a general and flexible legal framework at Community level in order to foster the development of the information society in Europe. This requires, *inter alia*, the existence of an internal market for new products and services. Important Community legislation to ensure such a regulatory framework is already in place or its adoption is well under way. Copyright and related rights play an important role in this context as they protect and stimulate the development and marketing of new products and services and the creation and exploitation of their creative content.

(3) The proposed harmonisation will help to implement the four freedoms of the internal market and relates to compliance with the fundamental principles of law and especially of property, including intellectual property, and freedom of expression and the public interest.

(4) A harmonised legal framework on copyright and related rights, through increased legal certainty and while providing for a high level of protection of intellectual property, will foster substantial investment in creativity and innovation, including network infrastructure, and lead in turn to growth and increased competitiveness of European industry, both in the area of content provision and information technology and more generally across a wide range of industrial and cultural sectors. This will safeguard employment and encourage new job creation.

(5) Technological development has multiplied and diversified the vectors for creation, production and exploitation. While no new concepts for the protection of intellectual property are needed, the current law on copyright and related rights should be adapted and supplemented to respond adequately to economic realities such as new forms of exploitation.

(6) Without harmonisation at Community level, legislative activities at national level which have already been initiated in a number of Member States in order to respond to the technological challenges might result in significant differences in protection and thereby in restrictions on the free movement of services and products incorporating, or based on, intellectual property, leading to a refragmentation of the internal market and legislative inconsistency. The impact of such legislative differences and uncertainties will become more significant with the further development of the information society, which has already greatly increased transborder exploitation of intellectual property. This development will and should further increase. Significant legal differences and uncertainties in protection may hinder economies of scale for new products and services containing copyright and related rights.

(7) The Community legal framework for the protection of copyright and related rights must, therefore, also be adapted and supplemented as far as is necessary for the smooth functioning of the internal market. To that end, those national provisions on copyright and related rights which vary considerably from one Member State to another or which cause legal uncertainties hindering the smooth functioning of the internal market and the proper development of the information society in Europe should be adjusted, and inconsistent national responses to the technological developments should be avoided, whilst differences not adversely affecting the functioning of the internal market need not be removed or prevented.

Common Position of 28 September 2000 (OJ C 344, 1.12.2000, p. 1) and Decision of the European Parliament of 14 February 2001 (not yet published in the Official Journal). Council Decision of 9 April 2001.

(8) The various social, societal and cultural implications of the information society require that account be taken of the specific features of the content of products and services.

(9) Any harmonisation of copyright and related rights must take as a basis a high level of protection, since such rights are crucial to intellectual creation. Their protection helps to ensure the maintenance and development of creativity in the interests of authors, performers, producers, consumers, culture, industry and the public at large. Intellectual property has therefore been recognised as an integral part of property.

(10) If authors or performers are to continue their creative and artistic work, they have to receive an appropriate reward for the use of their work, as must producers in order to be able to finance this work. The investment required to produce products such as phonograms, films or multimedia products, and services such as 'ondemand' services, is considerable. Adequate legal protection of intellectual property rights is necessary in order to guarantee the availability of such a reward and provide the opportunity for satisfactory returns on this investment.

(11) A rigorous, effective system for the protection of copyright and related rights is one of the main ways of ensuring that European cultural creativity and production receive the necessary resources and of safeguarding the independence and dignity of artistic creators and performers.

(12) Adequate protection of copyright works and subject-matter of related rights is also of great importance from a cultural standpoint. Article 151 of the Treaty requires the Community to take cultural aspects into account in its action.

(13) A common search for, and consistent application at European level of, technical measures to protect works and other subject-matter and to provide the necessary information on rights are essential insofar as the ultimate aim of these measures is to give effect to the principles and guarantees laid down in law.

(14) This Directive should seek to promote learning and culture by protecting works and other subject-matter while permitting exceptions or limitations in the public interest for the purpose of education and teaching.

(15) The Diplomatic Conference held under the auspices of the World Intellectual Property Organisation (WIPO) in December 1996 led to the adoption of two new Treaties, the 'WIPO Copyright Treaty' and the 'WIPO Performances and Phonograms Treaty', dealing respectively with the protection of authors and the protection of performers and phonogram producers. Those Treaties update the international protection for copyright and related rights significantly, not least with regard to the so-called 'digital agenda', and improve the means to fight piracy world-wide. The Community and a majority of Member States have already signed the Treaties and the process of making arrangements for the ratification of the Treaties by the Community and the Member States is under way. This Directive also serves to implement a number of the new international obligations.

(16) Liability for activities in the network environment concerns not only copyright and related rights but also other areas, such as defamation, misleading advertising, or infringement of trademarks, and is addressed horizontally in Directive 2000/31/EC of the European Parliament and of the Council of 8 June 2000 on certain legal aspects of information society services, in particular electronic commerce, in the internal market ('Directive on electronic commerce')[4], which clarifies and harmonises various legal issues relating to information society services including electronic commerce. This Directive should be implemented within a timescale similar to that for the implementation of the

---

[4] OJ L 178, 17.7.2000, p. 1.

Directive on electronic commerce, since that Directive provides a harmonised framework of principles and provisions relevant *inter alia* to important parts of this Directive. This Directive is without prejudice to provisions relating to liability in that Directive.

(17) It is necessary, especially in the light of the requirements arising out of the digital environment, to ensure that collecting societies achieve a higher level of rationalisation and transparency with regard to compliance with competition rules.

(18) This Directive is without prejudice to the arrangements in the Member States concerning the management of rights such as extended collective licences.

(19) The moral rights of rightholders should be exercised according to the legislation of the Member States and the provisions of the Berne Convention for the Protection of Literary and Artistic Works, of the WIPO Copyright Treaty and of the WIPO Performances and Phonograms Treaty. Such moral rights remain outside the scope of this Directive.

(20) This Directive is based on principles and rules already laid down in the Directives currently in force in this area, in particular Directives 91/250/EEC[5], 92/100/EEC[6], 93/83/EEC[7], 93/98/EEC[8] and 96/9/EC[9], and it develops those principles and rules and places them in the context of the information society. The provisions of this Directive should be without prejudice to the provisions of those Directives, unless otherwise provided in this Directive.

(21) This Directive should define the scope of the acts covered by the reproduction right with regard to the different beneficiaries. This should be done in conformity with the acquis communautaire. A broad definition of these acts is needed to ensure legal certainty within the internal market.

(22) The objective of proper support for the dissemination of culture must not be achieved by sacrificing strict protection of rights or by tolerating illegal forms of distribution of counterfeited or pirated works.

(23) This Directive should harmonise further the author's right of communication to the public. This right should be understood in a broad sense covering all communication to the public not present at the place where the communication originates. This right should cover any such transmission or retransmission of a work to the public by wire or wireless means, including broadcasting. This right should not cover any other acts.

(24) The right to make available to the public subject-matter referred to in Article 3(2) should be understood as covering all acts of making available such subject-matter to members of the public not present at the place where the act of making available originates, and as not covering any other acts.

(25) The legal uncertainty regarding the nature and the level of protection of acts of on-demand transmission of copyright works and subject-matter protected by related rights over networks should be overcome by providing for harmonised protection at Community level. It should be made clear that all rightholders recognised by this Directive should have an exclusive right to make available to the

---

[5] Council Directive 91/250/EEC of 14 May 1991 on the legal protection of computer programs (OJ L 122, 17.5.1991, p. 42). Directive as amended by Directive 93/98/EEC.

[6] Council Directive 92/100/EEC of 19 November 1992 on rental right and lending right and on certain rights related to copyright in the field of intellectual property (OJ L 346, 27.11.1992, p. 61). Directive as amended by Directive 93/98/EEC.

[7] Council Directive 93/83/EEC of 27 September 1993 on the coordination of certain rules concerning copyright and rights related to copyright applicable to satellite broadcasting and cable retransmission (OJ L 248, 6.10.1993, p. 15).

[8] Council Directive 93/98/EEC of 29 October 1993 harmonising the term of protection of copyright and certain related rights (OJ L 290, 24.11.1993, p. 9).

[9] Directive 96/9/EC of the European Parliament and of the Council of 11 March 1996 on the legal protection of databases (OJ L 77, 27.3.1996, p. 20).

public copyright works or any other subjectmatter by way of interactive on-demand transmissions. Such interactive on-demand transmissions are characterised by the fact that members of the public may access them from a place and at a time individually chosen by them.

(26) With regard to the making available in on-demand services by broadcasters of their radio or television productions incorporating music from commercial phonograms as an integral part thereof, collective licensing arrangements are to be encouraged in order to facilitate the clearance of the rights concerned.

(27) The mere provision of physical facilities for enabling or making a communication does not in itself amount to communication within the meaning of this Directive.

(28) Copyright protection under this Directive includes the exclusive right to control distribution of the work incorporated in a tangible article. The first sale in the Community of the original of a work or copies thereof by the rightholder or with his consent exhausts the right to control resale of that object in the Community. This right should not be exhausted in respect of the original or of copies thereof sold by the rightholder or with his consent outside the Community. Rental and lending rights for authors have been established in Directive 92/100/EEC. The distribution right provided for in this Directive is without prejudice to the provisions relating to the rental and lending rights contained in Chapter I of that Directive.

(29) The question of exhaustion does not arise in the case of services and on-line services in particular. This also applies with regard to a material copy of a work or other subject-matter made by a user of such a service with the consent of the rightholder. Therefore, the same applies to rental and lending of the original and copies of works or other subject-matter which are services by nature. Unlike CD-ROM or CD-I, where the intellectual property is incorporated in a material medium, namely an item of goods, every on-line service is in fact an act which should be subject to authorisation where the copyright or related right so provides.

(30) The rights referred to in this Directive may be transferred, assigned or subject to the granting of contractual licences, without prejudice to the relevant national legislation on copyright and related rights.

(31) A fair balance of rights and interests between the different categories of rightholders, as well as between the different categories of rightholders and users of protected subject-matter must be safeguarded. The existing exceptions and limitations to the rights as set out by the Member States have to be reassessed in the light of the new electronic environment. Existing differences in the exceptions and limitations to certain restricted acts have direct negative effects on the functioning of the internal market of copyright and related rights. Such differences could well become more pronounced in view of the further development of transborder exploitation of works and cross-border activities. In order to ensure the proper functioning of the internal market, such exceptions and limitations should be defined more harmoniously. The degree of their harmonisation should be based on their impact on the smooth functioning of the internal market.

(32) This Directive provides for an exhaustive enumeration of exceptions and limitations to the reproduction right and the right of communication to the public. Some exceptions or limitations only apply to the reproduction right, where appropriate. This list takes due account of the different legal traditions in Member States, while, at the same time, aiming to ensure a functioning internal market. Member States should arrive at a coherent application of these exceptions and limitations, which will be assessed when reviewing implementing legislation in the future.

(33) The exclusive right of reproduction should be subject to an exception to allow certain acts of temporary reproduction, which are transient or incidental

reproductions, forming an integral and essential part of a technological process and carried out for the sole purpose of enabling either efficient transmission in a network between third parties by an intermediary, or a lawful use of a work or other subject-matter to be made. The acts of reproduction concerned should have no separate economic value on their own. To the extent that they meet these conditions, this exception should include acts which enable browsing as well as acts of caching to take place, including those which enable transmission systems to function efficiently, provided that the intermediary does not modify the information and does not interfere with the lawful use of technology, widely recognised and used by industry, to obtain data on the use of the information. A use should be considered lawful where it is authorised by the rightholder or not restricted by law.

(34) Member States should be given the option of providing for certain exceptions or limitations for cases such as educational and scientific purposes, for the benefit of public institutions such as libraries and archives, for purposes of news reporting, for quotations, for use by people with disabilities, for public security uses and for uses in administrative and judicial proceedings.

(35) In certain cases of exceptions or limitations, rightholders should receive fair compensation to compensate them adequately for the use made of their protected works or other subject-matter. When determining the form, detailed arrangements and possible level of such fair compensation, account should be taken of the particular circumstances of each case. When evaluating these circumstances, a valuable criterion would be the possible harm to the rightholders resulting from the act in question. In cases where rightholders have already received payment in some other form, for instance as part of a licence fee, no specific or separate payment may be due. The level of fair compensation should take full account of the degree of use of technological protection measures referred to in this Directive. In certain situations where the prejudice to the rightholder would be minimal, no obligation for payment may arise.

(36) The Member States may provide for fair compensation for rightholders also when applying the optional provisions on exceptions or limitations which do not require such compensation.

(37) Existing national schemes on reprography, where they exist, do not create major barriers to the internal market. Member States should be allowed to provide for an exception or limitation in respect of reprography.

(38) Member States should be allowed to provide for an exception or limitation to the reproduction right for certain types of reproduction of audio, visual and audiovisual material for private use, accompanied by fair compensation. This may include the introduction or continuation of remuneration schemes to compensate for the prejudice to rightholders. Although differences between those remuneration schemes affect the functioning of the internal market, those differences, with respect to analogue private reproduction, should not have a significant impact on the development of the information society. Digital private copying is likely to be more widespread and have a greater economic impact. Due account should therefore be taken of the differences between digital and analogue private copying and a distinction should be made in certain respects between them.

(39) When applying the exception or limitation on private copying, Member States should take due account of technological and economic developments, in particular with respect to digital private copying and remuneration schemes, when effective technological protection measures are available. Such exceptions or limitations should not inhibit the use of technological measures or their enforcement against circumvention.

(40) Member States may provide for an exception or limitation for the benefit

of certain non-profit making establishments, such as publicly accessible libraries and equivalent institutions, as well as archives. However, this should be limited to certain special cases covered by the reproduction right. Such an exception or limitation should not cover uses made in the context of on-line delivery of protected works or other subject-matter. This Directive should be without prejudice to the Member States' option to derogate from the exclusive public lending right in accordance with Article 5 of Directive 92/100/EEC. Therefore, specific contracts or licences should be promoted which, without creating imbalances, favour such establishments and the disseminative purposes they serve.

(41) When applying the exception or limitation in respect of ephemeral recordings made by broadcasting organisations it is understood that a broadcaster's own facilities include those of a person acting on behalf of and under the responsibility of the broadcasting organisation.

(42) When applying the exception or limitation for noncommercial educational and scientific research purposes, including distance learning, the non-commercial nature of the activity in question should be determined by that activity as such. The organisational structure and the means of funding of the establishment concerned are not the decisive factors in this respect.

(43) It is in any case important for the Member States to adopt all necessary measures to facilitate access to works by persons suffering from a disability which constitutes an obstacle to the use of the works themselves, and to pay particular attention to accessible formats.

(44) When applying the exceptions and limitations provided for in this Directive, they should be exercised in accordance with international obligations. Such exceptions and limitations may not be applied in a way which prejudices the legitimate interests of the rightholder or which conflicts with the normal exploitation of his work or other subject-matter. The provision of such exceptions or limitations by Member States should, in particular, duly reflect the increased economic impact that such exceptions or limitations may have in the context of the new electronic environment. Therefore, the scope of certain exceptions or limitations may have to be even more limited when it comes to certain new uses of copyright works and other subject-matter.

(45) The exceptions and limitations referred to in Article 5(2), (3) and (4) should not, however, prevent the definition of contractual relations designed to ensure fair compensation for the rightholders insofar as permitted by national law.

(46) Recourse to mediation could help users and rightholders to settle disputes. The Commission, in cooperation with the Member States within the Contact Committee, should undertake a study to consider new legal ways of settling disputes concerning copyright and related rights.

(47) Technological development will allow rightholders to make use of technological measures designed to prevent or restrict acts not authorised by the rightholders of any copyright, rights related to copyright or the *sui generis* right in databases. The danger, however, exists that illegal activities might be carried out in order to enable or facilitate the circumvention of the technical protection provided by these measures. In order to avoid fragmented legal approaches that could potentially hinder the functioning of the internal market, there is a need to provide for harmonised legal protection against circumvention of effective technological measures and against provision of devices and products or services to this effect.

(48) Such legal protection should be provided in respect of technological measures that effectively restrict acts not authorised by the rightholders of any copyright, rights related to copyright or the *sui generis* right in databases without, however, preventing the normal operation of electronic equipment and its

technological development. Such legal protection implies no obligation to design devices, products, components or services to correspond to technological measures, so long as such device, product, component or service does not otherwise fall under the prohibition of Article 6. Such legal protection should respect proportionality and should not prohibit those devices or activities which have a commercially significant purpose or use other than to circumvent the technical protection. In particular, this protection should not hinder research into cryptography.

(49) The legal protection of technological measures is without prejudice to the application of any national provisions which may prohibit the private possession of devices, products or components for the circumvention of technological measures.

(50) Such a harmonised legal protection does not affect the specific provisions on protection provided for by Directive 91/250/EEC. In particular, it should not apply to the protection of technological measures used in connection with computer programs, which is exclusively addressed in that Directive. It should neither inhibit nor prevent the development or use of any means of circumventing a technological measure that is necessary to enable acts to be undertaken in accordance with the terms of Article 5(3) or Article 6 of Directive 91/250/EEC. Articles 5 and 6 of that Directive exclusively determine exceptions to the exclusive rights applicable to computer programs.

(51) The legal protection of technological measures applies without prejudice to public policy, as reflected in Article 5, or public security. Member States should promote voluntary measures taken by rightholders, including the conclusion and implementation of agreements between rightholders and other parties concerned, to accommodate achieving the objectives of certain exceptions or limitations provided for in national law in accordance with this Directive. In the absence of such voluntary measures or agreements within a reasonable period of time, Member States should take appropriate measures to ensure that rightholders provide beneficiaries of such exceptions or limitations with appropriate means of benefiting from them, by modifying an implemented technological measure or by other means. However, in order to prevent abuse of such measures taken by rightholders, including within the framework of agreements, or taken by a Member State, any technological measures applied in implementation of such measures should enjoy legal protection.

(52) When implementing an exception or limitation for private copying in accordance with Article 5(2)(b), Member States should likewise promote the use of voluntary measures to accommodate achieving the objectives of such exception or limitation. If, within a reasonable period of time, no such voluntary measures to make reproduction for private use possible have been taken, Member States may take measures to enable beneficiaries of the exception or limitation concerned to benefit from it. Voluntary measures taken by rightholders, including agreements between rightholders and other parties concerned, as well as measures taken by Member States, do not prevent rightholders from using technological measures which are consistent with the exceptions or limitations on private copying in national law in accordance with Article 5(2)(b), taking account of the condition of fair compensation under that provision and the possible differentiation between various conditions of use in accordance with Article 5(5), such as controlling the number of reproductions. In order to prevent abuse of such measures, any technological measures applied in their implementation should enjoy legal protection.

(53) The protection of technological measures should ensure a secure environment for the provision of interactive on-demand services, in such a way that members of the public may access works or other subject-matter from a place

and at a time individually chosen by them. Where such services are governed by contractual arrangements, the first and second subparagraphs of Article 6(4) should not apply. Non-interactive forms of online use should remain subject to those provisions.

(54) Important progress has been made in the international standardisation of technical systems of identification of works and protected subject-matter in digital format. In an increasingly networked environment, differences between technological measures could lead to an incompatibility of systems within the Community. Compatibility and interoperability of the different systems should be encouraged. It would be highly desirable to encourage the development of global systems.

(55) Technological development will facilitate the distribution of works, notably on networks, and this will entail the need for rightholders to identify better the work or other subject-matter, the author or any other rightholder, and to provide information about the terms and conditions of use of the work or other subject-matter in order to render easier the management of rights attached to them. Rightholders should be encouraged to use markings indicating, in addition to the information referred to above, *inter alia* their authorisation when putting works or other subject-matter on networks.

(56) There is, however, the danger that illegal activities might be carried out in order to remove or alter the electronic copyright-management information attached to it, or otherwise to distribute, import for distribution, broadcast, communicate to the public or make available to the public works or other protected subject-matter from which such information has been removed without authority. In order to avoid fragmented legal approaches that could potentially hinder the functioning of the internal market, there is a need to provide for harmonised legal protection against any of these activities.

(57) Any such rights-management information systems referred to above may, depending on their design, at the same time process personal data about the consumption patterns of protected subject-matter by individuals and allow for tracing of on-line behaviour. These technical means, in their technical functions, should incorporate privacy safeguards in accordance with Directive 95/ 46/EC of the European Parliament and of the Council of 24 October 1995 on the protection of individuals with regard to the processing of personal data and the free movement of such data[10].

(58) Member States should provide for effective sanctions and remedies for infringements of rights and obligations as set out in this Directive. They should take all the measures necessary to ensure that those sanctions and remedies are applied. The sanctions thus provided for should be effective, proportionate and dissuasive and should include the possibility of seeking damages and/or injunctive relief and, where appropriate, of applying for seizure of infringing material.

(59) In the digital environment, in particular, the services of intermediaries may increasingly be used by third parties for infringing activities. In many cases such intermediaries are best placed to bring such infringing activities to an end. Therefore, without prejudice to any other sanctions and remedies available, rightholders should have the possibility of applying for an injunction against an intermediary who carries a third party's infringement of a protected work or other subject-matter in a network. This possibility should be available even where the acts carried out by the intermediary are exempted under Article 5. The conditions and modalities relating to such injunctions should be left to the national law of the Member States.

---

[10] OJ L 281, 23.11.1995, p. 31.

(60) The protection provided under this Directive should be without prejudice to national or Community legal provisions in other areas, such as industrial property, data protection, conditional access, access to public documents, and the rule of media exploitation chronology, which may affect the protection of copyright or related rights.

(61) In order to comply with the WIPO Performances and Phonograms Treaty, Directives 92/100/EEC and 93/ 98/EEC should be amended,

HAVE ADOPTED THIS DIRECTIVE:

CHAPTER I

OBJECTIVE AND SCOPE

Article 1
Scope

1. This Directive concerns the legal protection of copyright and related rights in the framework of the internal market, with particular emphasis on the information society.

2. Except in the cases referred to in Article 11, this Directive shall leave intact and shall in no way affect existing Community provisions relating to:

(a) the legal protection of computer programs;
(b) rental right, lending right and certain rights related to copyright in the field of intellectual property;
(c) copyright and related rights applicable to broadcasting of programmes by satellite and cable retransmission;
(d) the term of protection of copyright and certain related rights;
(e) the legal protection of databases.

CHAPTER II

RIGHTS AND EXCEPTIONS

Article 2
Reproduction right

Member States shall provide for the exclusive right to authorise or prohibit direct or indirect, temporary or permanent reproduction by any means and in any form, in whole or in part:

(a) for authors, of their works;
(b) for performers, of fixations of their performances;
(c) for phonogram producers, of their phonograms;
(d) for the producers of the first fixations of films, in respect of the original and copies of their films;
(e) for broadcasting organisations, of fixations of their broadcasts, whether those broadcasts are transmitted by wire or over the air, including by cable or satellite.

Article 3
Right of communication to the public of works and right of making available to the public other subject-matter

1. Member States shall provide authors with the exclusive right to authorise or

prohibit any communication to the public of their works, by wire or wireless means, including the making available to the public of their works in such a way that members of the public may access them from a place and at a time individually chosen by them.

2. Member States shall provide for the exclusive right to authorise or prohibit the making available to the public, by wire or wireless means, in such a way that members of the public may access them from a place and at a time individually chosen by them:

(a) for performers, of fixations of their performances;

(b) for phonogram producers, of their phonograms;

(c) for the producers of the first fixations of films, of the original and copies of their films;

(d) for broadcasting organisations, of fixations of their broadcasts, whether these broadcasts are transmitted by wire or over the air, including by cable or satellite.

3. The rights referred to in paragraphs 1 and 2 shall not be exhausted by any act of communication to the public or making available to the public as set out in this Article.

Article 4

Distribution right

1. Member States shall provide for authors, in respect of the original of their works or of copies thereof, the exclusive right to authorise or prohibit any form of distribution to the public by sale or otherwise.

2. The distribution right shall not be exhausted within the Community in respect of the original or copies of the work, except where the first sale or other transfer of ownership in the Community of that object is made by the rightholder or with his consent.

Article 5

Exceptions and limitations

1. Temporary acts of reproduction referred to in Article 2, which are transient or incidental [and] an integral and essential part of a technological process and whose sole purpose is to enable:

(a) a transmission in a network between third parties by an intermediary, or

(b) a lawful use

of a work or other subject-matter to be made, and which have no independent economic significance, shall be exempted from the reproduction right provided for in Article 2.

2. Member States may provide for exceptions or limitations to the reproduction right provided for in Article 2 in the following cases:

(a) in respect of reproductions on paper or any similar medium, effected by the use of any kind of photographic technique or by some other process having similar effects, with the exception of sheet music, provided that the rightholders receive fair compensation;

(b) in respect of reproductions on any medium made by a natural person for private use and for ends that are neither directly nor indirectly commercial, on condition that the rightholders receive fair compensation which takes account of the application or non-application of technological measures referred to in Article 6 to the work or subjectmatter concerned;

(c) in respect of specific acts of reproduction made by publicly accessible libraries, educational establishments or museums, or by archives, which are not for direct or indirect economic or commercial advantage;

(d) in respect of ephemeral recordings of works made by broadcasting organisations by means of their own facilities and for their own broadcasts; the preservation of these recordings in official archives may, on the grounds of their exceptional documentary character, be permitted;

(e) in respect of reproductions of broadcasts made by social institutions pursuing non-commercial purposes, such as hospitals or prisons, on condition that the rightholders receive fair compensation.

3. Member States may provide for exceptions or limitations to the rights provided for in Articles 2 and 3 in the following cases:

(a) use for the sole purpose of illustration for teaching or scientific research, as long as the source, including the author's name, is indicated, unless this turns out to be impossible and to the extent justified by the non-commercial purpose to be achieved;

(b) uses, for the benefit of people with a disability, which are directly related to the disability and of a non-commercial nature, to the extent required by the specific disability;

(c) reproduction by the press, communication to the public or making available of published articles on current economic, political or religious topics or of broadcast works or other subject-matter of the same character, in cases where such use is not expressly reserved, and as long as the source, including the author's name, is indicated, or use of works or other subject-matter in connection with the reporting of current events, to the extent justified by the informatory purpose and as long as the source, including the author's name, is indicated, unless this turns out to be impossible;

(d) quotations for purposes such as criticism or review, provided that they relate to a work or other subject-matter which has already been lawfully made available to the public, that, unless this turns out to be impossible, the source, including the author's name, is indicated, and that their use is in accordance with fair practice, and to the extent required by the specific purpose;

(e) use for the purposes of public security or to ensure the proper performance or reporting of administrative, parliamentary or judicial proceedings;

(f) use of political speeches as well as extracts of public lectures or similar works or subject-matter to the extent justified by the informatory purpose and provided that the source, including the author's name, is indicated, except where this turns out to be impossible;

(g) use during religious celebrations or official celebrations organised by a public authority;

(h) use of works, such as works of architecture or sculpture, made to be located permanently in public places;

(i) incidental inclusion of a work or other subject-matter in other material;

(j) use for the purpose of advertising the public exhibition or sale of artistic works, to the extent necessary to promote the event, excluding any other commercial use;

(k) use for the purpose of caricature, parody or pastiche;

(l) use in connection with the demonstration or repair of equipment;

(m) use of an artistic work in the form of a building or a drawing or plan of a building for the purposes of reconstructing the building;

(n) use by communication or making available, for the purpose of research or private study, to individual members of the public by dedicated terminals on the premises of establishments referred to in paragraph 2(c) of works and other subject-matter not subject to purchase or licensing terms which are contained in their collections;

(o) use in certain other cases of minor importance where exceptions or limitations already exist under national law, provided that they only concern analogue uses and do not affect the free circulation of goods and services within the Community, without prejudice to the other exceptions and limitations contained in this Article.

4. Where the Member States may provide for an exception or limitation to the right of reproduction pursuant to paragraphs 2 and 3, they may provide similarly for an exception or limitation to the right of distribution as referred to in Article 4 to the extent justified by the purpose of the authorised act of reproduction.

5. The exceptions and limitations provided for in paragraphs 1, 2, 3 and 4 shall only be applied in certain special cases which do not conflict with a normal exploitation of the work or other subject-matter and do not unreasonably prejudice the legitimate interests of the rightholder.

CHAPTER III

PROTECTION OF TECHNOLOGICAL MEASURES AND RIGHTS-MANAGEMENT INFORMATION

Article 6

Obligations as to technological measures

1. Member States shall provide adequate legal protection against the circumvention of any effective technological measures, which the person concerned carries out in the knowledge, or with reasonable grounds to know, that he or she is pursuing that objective.

2. Member States shall provide adequate legal protection against the manufacture, import, distribution, sale, rental, advertisement for sale or rental, or possession for commercial purposes of devices, products or components or the provision of services which:

(a) are promoted, advertised or marketed for the purpose of circumvention of, or

(b) have only a limited commercially significant purpose or use other than to circumvent, or

(c) are primarily designed, produced, adapted or performed for the purpose of enabling or facilitating the circumvention of,

any effective technological measures.

3. For the purposes of this Directive, the expression 'technological measures' means any technology, device or component that, in the normal course of its operation, is designed to prevent or restrict acts, in respect of works or other subjec-tmatter, which are not authorised by the rightholder of any copyright or any right related to copyright as provided for by law or the *sui generis* right provided for in Chapter III of Directive 96/9/EC. Technological measures shall be deemed 'effective' where the use of a protected work or other subject-matter is controlled by the rightholders through application of an access control or protection process, such as encryption, scrambling or other transformation of the work or other subject-matter or a copy control mechanism, which achieves the protection objective.

4. Notwithstanding the legal protection provided for in paragraph 1, in the absence of voluntary measures taken by rightholders, including agreements be-

tween rightholders and other parties concerned, Member States shall take appropriate measures to ensure that rightholders make available to the beneficiary of an exception or limitation provided for in national law in accordance with Article 5(2)(a), (2)(c), (2)(d), (2)(e), (3)(a), (3)(b) or (3)(e) the means of benefiting from that exception or limitation, to the extent necessary to benefit from that exception or limitation and where that beneficiary has legal access to the protected work or subject-matter concerned.

A Member State may also take such measures in respect of a beneficiary of an exception or limitation provided for in accordance with Article 5(2)(b), unless reproduction for private use has already been made possible by rightholders to the extent necessary to benefit from the exception or limitation concerned and in accordance with the provisions of Article 5(2)(b) and (5), without preventing rightholders from adopting adequate measures regarding the number of reproductions in accordance with these provisions.

The technological measures applied voluntarily by rightholders, including those applied in implementation of voluntary agreements, and technological measures applied in implementation of the measures taken by Member States, shall enjoy the legal protection provided for in paragraph 1.

The provisions of the first and second subparagraphs shall not apply to works or other subject-matter made available to the public on agreed contractual terms in such a way that members of the public may access them from a place and at a time individually chosen by them.

When this Article is applied in the context of Directives 92/100/EEC and 96/9/EC, this paragraph shall apply *mutatis mutandis*.

Article 7

Obligations concerning rights-management information

1. Member States shall provide for adequate legal protection against any person knowingly performing without authority any of the following acts:

(a) the removal or alteration of any electronic rights-management information;

(b) the distribution, importation for distribution, broadcasting, communication or making available to the public of works or other subject-matter protected under this Directive or under Chapter III of Directive 96/9/EC from which electronic rights-management information has been removed or altered without authority,

if such person knows, or has reasonable grounds to know, that by so doing he is inducing, enabling, facilitating or concealing an infringement of any copyright or any rights related to copyright as provided by law, or of the *sui generis* right provided for in Chapter III of Directive 96/9/EC.

2. For the purposes of this Directive, the expression 'rights-management information' means any information provided by rightholders which identifies the work or other subject-matter referred to in this Directive or covered by the *sui generis* right provided for in Chapter III of Directive 96/9/EC, the author or any other rightholder, or information about the terms and conditions of use of the work or other subject-matter, and any numbers or codes that represent such information.

The first subparagraph shall apply when any of these items of information is associated with a copy of, or appears in connection with the communication to the public of, a work or other subject-matter referred to in this Directive or covered by the *sui generis* right provided for in Chapter III of Directive 96/9/EC.

CHAPTER IV

COMMON PROVISIONS

Article 8

Sanctions and remedies

1. Member States shall provide appropriate sanctions and remedies in respect of infringements of the rights and obligations set out in this Directive and shall take all the measures necessary to ensure that those sanctions and remedies are applied. The sanctions thus provided for shall be effective, proportionate and dissuasive.

2. Each Member State shall take the measures necessary to ensure that right-holders whose interests are affected by an infringing activity carried out on its territory can bring an action for damages and/or apply for an injunction and, where appropriate, for the seizure of infringing material as well as of devices, products or components referred to in Article 6(2).

3. Member States shall ensure that rightholders are in a position to apply for an injunction against intermediaries whose services are used by a third party to infringe a copyright or related right.

Article 9

Continued application of other legal provisions

This Directive shall be without prejudice to provisions concerning in particular patent rights, trade marks, design rights, utility models, topographies of semi-conductor products, type faces, conditional access, access to cable of broadcasting services, protection of national treasures, legal deposit requirements, laws on restrictive practices and unfair competition, trade secrets, security, confidentiality, data protection and privacy, access to public documents, the law of contract.

Article 10

Application over time

1. The provisions of this Directive shall apply in respect of all works and other subject-matter referred to in this Directive which are, on 22 December 2002, protected by the Member States' legislation in the field of copyright and related rights, or which meet the criteria for protection under the provisions of this Directive or the provisions referred to in Article 1(2).

2. This Directive shall apply without prejudice to any acts concluded and rights acquired before 22 December 2002.

Article 11

1. [...]
2. [...]

Notes:

(1) Article 11(1) was repealed by Directive 2006/115/EC of the European Parliament and of the council of 12 December 2006 on rental right and lending right and on certain rights related to copyright in the field of intellectual property [2006] O.J. L376/28, Annex 1, with effect from January 8, 2007. Article 11(1) formerly read:

"1. *Directive 92/100/EEC is hereby amended as follows:*

(a) *Article 7 shall be deleted;*

(b) *Article 10(3) shall be replaced by the following:*

'3. *The limitations shall only be applied in certain special cases which do not conflict with a normal exploitation of the subject-matter and do not unreasonably prejudice the legitimate interests of the rightholder.'"*

H EU DIRECTIVES

(2) Article 11(2) was repealed by Directive 2006/116/EEC of the European Parliament and of the council of 12 December 2006 on the term of protection of copyright and certain related rights [2006] O.J. L372/12, Annex I, with effect from January 8, 2007. Article 11(2) formerly read:

"2. *Article 3(2) of Directive 93/98/EEC shall be replaced by the following:*

'2. *The rights of producers of phonograms shall expire 50 years after the fixation is made. However, if the phonogram has been lawfully published within this period, the said rights shall expire 50 years from the date of the first lawful publication. If no lawful publication has taken place within the period mentioned in the first sentence, and if the phonogram has been lawfully communicated to the public within this period, the said rights shall expire 50 years from the date of the first lawful communication to the public.*

However, where through the expiry of the term of protection granted pursuant to this paragraph in its version before amendment by Directive 2001/29/EC of the European Parliament and of the Council of 22 May 2001 on the harmonisation of certain aspects of copyright and related rights in the information society[11] the rights of producers of phonograms are no longer protected on 22 December 2002, this paragraph shall not have the effect of protecting those rights anew. '"

Article 12

Final provisions

1. Not later than 22 December 2004 and every three years thereafter, the Commission shall submit to the European Parliament, the Council and the Economic and Social Committee a report on the application of this Directive, in which, *inter alia*, on the basis of specific information supplied by the Member States, it shall examine in particular the application of Articles 5, 6 and 8 in the light of the development of the digital market. In the case of Article 6, it shall examine in particular whether that Article confers a sufficient level of protection and whether acts which are permitted by law are being adversely affected by the use of effective technological measures. Where necessary, in particular to ensure the functioning of the internal market pursuant to Article 14 of the Treaty, it shall submit proposals for amendments to this Directive.

2. Protection of rights related to copyright under this Directive shall leave intact and shall in no way affect the protection of copyright.

3. A contact committee is hereby established. It shall be composed of representatives of the competent authorities of the Member States. It shall be chaired by a representative of the Commission and shall meet either on the initiative of the chairman or at the request of the delegation of a Member State.

4. The tasks of the committee shall be as follows:

(a) to examine the impact of this Directive on the functioning of the internal market, and to highlight any difficulties;

(b) to organise consultations on all questions deriving from the application of this Directive;

(c) to facilitate the exchange of information on relevant developments in legislation and case-law, as well as relevant economic, social, cultural and technological developments;

(d) to act as a forum for the assessment of the digital market in works and other items, including private copying and the use of technological measures.

Article 13

Implementation

1. Member States shall bring into force the laws, regulations and administra-

---

[11] OJ L 167, 22.6.2001, p. 10.

tive provisions necessary to comply with this Directive before 22 December 2002. They shall forthwith inform the Commission thereof.

When Member States adopt these measures, they shall contain a reference to this Directive or shall be accompanied by such reference on the occasion of their official publication. The methods of making such reference shall be laid down by Member States.

2. Member States shall communicate to the Commission the text of the provisions of domestic law which they adopt in the field governed by this Directive.

Article 14

Entry into force

This Directive shall enter into force on the day of its publication in the *Official Journal of the European Communities*.

Article 15

Addressees

This Directive is addressed to the Member States.
Done at Brussels, 22 May 2001.

For the European Parliament	*For the Council*
The President	*The President*
N. FONTAINE	M. WINBERG

H9. DIRECTIVE 2001/84/EC

Directive 2001/84/EC of the European Parliament and of the Council of 27 September 2001 on the resale right for the benefit of the author of an original work of art[i]

([2001] O.J. L272/32)

THE EUROPEAN PARLIAMENT AND THE COUNCIL OF THE EUROPEAN UNION,

Having regard to the Treaty establishing the European Community, and in particular Article 95 thereof,

Having regard to the proposal from the Commission[1],

Having regard to the opinion of the Economic and Social Committee[2],

Acting in accordance with the procedure laid down in Article 251 of the Treaty[3], and in the light of the joint text approved by the Conciliation Committee on 6 June 2001,

Whereas:

(1) In the field of copyright, the resale right is an unassignable and inalienable right, enjoyed by the author of an original work of graphic or plastic art, to an economic interest in successive sales of the work concerned.

(2) The resale right is a right of a productive character which enables the author/artist to receive consideration for successive transfers of the work. The

---

[i] *Editorial note*: The footnote numbering in the original Directive is reproduced below.

[1] OJ C 178, 21.6.1996, p. 16 and OJ C 125, 23.4.1998, p. 8.

[2] OJ C 75, 10.3.1997, p. 17.

[3] Opinion of the European Parliament of 9 April 1997 (OJ C 132, 28.4.1997, p. 88), confirmed on 27 October 1999, Council Common Position of 19 June 2000 (OJ C 300, 20.10.2000, p. 1) and Decision of the European Parliament of 13 December 2000 (OJ C 232, 17.8.2001, p. 173). Decision of the European Parliament of 3 July 2001 and Decision of the Council of 19 July 2001.

subject-matter of the resale right is the physical work, namely the medium in which the protected work is incorporated.

(3) The resale right is intended to ensure that authors of graphic and plastic works of art share in the economic success of their original works of art. It helps to redress the balance between the economic situation of authors of graphic and plastic works of art and that of other creators who benefit from successive exploitations of their works.

(4) The resale right forms an integral part of copyright and is an essential prerogative for authors. The imposition of such a right in all Member States meets the need for providing creators with an adequate and standard level of protection.

(5) Under Article 151(4) of the Treaty the Community is to take cultural aspects into account in its action under other provisions of the Treaty.

(6) The Berne Convention for the Protection of Literary and Artistic Works provides that the resale right is available only if legislation in the country to which the author belongs so permits. The right is therefore optional and subject to the rule of reciprocity. It follows from the case-law of the Court of Justice of the European Communities on the application of the principle of nondiscrimination laid down in Article 12 of the Treaty, as shown in the judgment of 20 October 1993 in Joined Cases C-92/92 and C-326/92 *Phil Collins and Others*[4], that domestic provisions containing reciprocity clauses cannot be relied upon in order to deny nationals of other Member States rights conferred on national authors. The application of such clauses in the Community context runs counter to the principle of equal treatment resulting from the prohibition of any discrimination on grounds of nationality.

(7) The process of internationalisation of the Community market in modern and contemporary art, which is now being speeded up by the effects of the new economy, in a regulatory context in which few States outside the EU recognise the resale right, makes it essential for the European Community, in the external sphere, to open negotiations with a view to making Article 14b of the Berne Convention compulsory.

(8) The fact that this international market exists, combined with the lack of a resale right in several Member States and the current disparity as regards national systems which recognise that right, make it essential to lay down transitional provisions as regards both entry into force and the substantive regulation of the right, which will preserve the competitiveness of the European market.

(9) The resale right is currently provided for by the domestic legislation of a majority of Member States. Such laws, where they exist, display certain differences, notably as regards the works covered, those entitled to receive royalties, the rate applied, the transactions subject to payment of a royalty, and the basis on which these are calculated. The application or non-application of such a right has a significant impact on the competitive environment within the internal market, since the existence or absence of an obligation to pay on the basis of the resale right is an element which must be taken into account by each individual wishing to sell a work of art. This right is therefore a factor which contributes to the creation of distortions of competition as well as displacement of sales within the Community.

(10) Such disparities with regard to the existence of the resale right and its application by the Member States have a direct negative impact on the proper functioning of the internal market in works of art as provided for by Article 14 of the Treaty. In such a situation Article 95 of the Treaty constitutes the appropriate legal basis.

---

[4] [1993] ECR I-5145.

(11) The objectives of the Community as set out in the Treaty include laying the foundations of an ever closer union among the peoples of Europe, promoting closer relations between the Member States belonging to the Community, and ensuring their economic and social progress by common action to eliminate the barriers which divide Europe. To that end the Treaty provides for the establishment of an internal market which presupposes the abolition of obstacles to the free movement of goods, freedom to provide services and freedom of establishment, and for the introduction of a system ensuring that competition in the common market is not distorted. Harmonisation of Member States' laws on the resale right contributes to the attainment of these objectives.

(12) The Sixth Council Directive (77/388/EEC) of 17 May 1977 on the harmonisation of the laws of the Member States relating to turnover taxes—common system of value added tax: uniform basis of assessment[5], progressively introduces a Community system of taxation applicable *inter alia* to works of art. Measures confined to the tax field are not sufficient to guarantee the harmonious functioning of the art market. This objective cannot be attained without harmonisation in the field of the resale right.

(13) Existing differences between laws should be eliminated where they have a distorting effect on the functioning of the internal market, and the emergence of any new differences of that kind should be prevented. There is no need to eliminate, or prevent the emergence of, differences which cannot be expected to affect the functioning of the internal market.

(14) A precondition of the proper functioning of the internal market is the existence of conditions of competition which are not distorted. The existence of differences between national provisions on the resale right creates distortions of competition and displacement of sales within the Community and leads to unequal treatment between artists depending on where their works are sold. The issue under consideration has therefore transnational aspects which cannot be satisfactorily regulated by action by Member States. A lack of Community action would conflict with the requirement of the Treaty to correct distortions of competition and unequal treatment.

(15) In view of the scale of divergences between national provisions it is therefore necessary to adopt harmonising measures to deal with disparities between the laws of the Member States in areas where such disparities are liable to create or maintain distorted conditions of competition. It is not however necessary to harmonise every provision of the Member States' laws on the resale right and, in order to leave as much scope for national decision as possible, it is sufficient to limit the harmonisation exercise to those domestic provisions that have the most direct impact on the functioning of the internal market.

(16) This Directive complies therefore, in its entirety, with the principles of subsidiarity and proportionality as laid down in Article 5 of the Treaty.

(17) Pursuant to Council Directive 93/98/EEC of 29 October 1993 harmonising the term of protection of copyright and certain related rights[6], the term of copyright runs for 70 years after the author's death. The same period should be laid down for the resale right. Consequently, only the originals of works of modern and contemporary art may fall within the scope of the resale right. However, in order to allow the legal systems of Member States which do not, at the time of the adoption of this Directive, apply a resale right for the benefit of artists to incorporate this right into their respective legal systems and, moreover, to enable the economic operators in those Member States to adapt gradually to the

---

[5] OJ L 145, 13.6.1977, p. 1. Directive as last amended by Directive 1999/85/EC (OJ L 277, 28.10.1999, p. 34).
[6] OJ L 290, 24.11.1993, p. 9.

aforementioned right whilst maintaining their economic viability, the Member States concerned should be allowed a limited transitional period during which they may choose not to apply the resale right for the benefit of those entitled under the artist after his death.

(18) The scope of the resale right should be extended to all acts of resale, with the exception of those effected directly between persons acting in their private capacity without the participation of an art market professional. This right should not extend to acts of resale by persons acting in their private capacity to museums which are not for profit and which are open to the public. With regard to the particular situation of art galleries which acquire works directly from the author, Member States should be allowed the option of exempting from the resale right acts of resale of those works which take place within three years of that acquisition. The interests of the artist should also be taken into account by limiting this exemption to such acts of resale where the resale price does not exceed EUR10 000.

(19) It should be made clear that the harmonisation brought about by this Directive does not apply to original manuscripts of writers and composers.

(20) Effective rules should be laid down based on experience already gained at national level with the resale right. It is appropriate to calculate the royalty as a percentage of the sale price and not of the increase in value of works whose original value has increased.

(21) The categories of works of art subject to the resale right should be harmonised.

(22) The non-application of royalties below the minimum threshold may help to avoid disproportionately high collection and administration costs compared with the profit for the artist. However, in accordance with the principle of subsidiarity, the Member States should be allowed to establish national thresholds lower than the Community threshold, so as to promote the interests of new artists. Given the small amounts involved, this derogation is not likely to have a significant effect on the proper functioning of the internal market.

(23) The rates set by the different Member States for the application of the resale right vary considerably at present. The effective functioning of the internal market in works of modern and contemporary art requires the fixing of uniform rates to the widest possible extent.

(24) It is desirable to establish, with the intention of reconciling the various interests involved in the market for original works of art, a system consisting of a tapering scale of rates for several price bands. It is important to reduce the risk of sales relocating and of the circumvention of the Community rules on the resale right.

(25) The person by whom the royalty is payable should, in principle, be the seller. Member States should be given the option to provide for derogations from this principle in respect of liability for payment. The seller is the person or undertaking on whose behalf the sale is concluded.

(26) Provision should be made for the possibility of periodic adjustment of the threshold and rates. To this end, it is appropriate to entrust to the Commission the task of drawing up periodic reports on the actual application of the resale right in the Member States and on the impact on the art market in the Community and, where appropriate, of making proposals relating to the amendment of this Directive.

(27) The persons entitled to receive royalties must be specified, due regard being had to the principle of subsidiarity. It is not appropriate to take action through this Directive in relation to Member States' laws of succession. However, those entitled under the author must be able to benefit fully from the resale right after his death, at least following the expiry of the transitional period referred to above.

(28) The Member States are responsible for regulating the exercise of the resale right, particularly with regard to the way this is managed. In this respect management by a collecting society is one possibility. Member States should ensure that collecting societies operate in a transparent and efficient manner. Member States must also ensure that amounts intended for authors who are nationals of other Member States are in fact collected and distributed. This Directive is without prejudice to arrangements in Member States for collection and distribution.

(29) Enjoyment of the resale right should be restricted to Community nationals as well as to foreign authors whose countries afford such protection to authors who are nationals of Member States. A Member State should have the option of extending enjoyment of this right to foreign authors who have their habitual residence in that Member State.

(30) Appropriate procedures for monitoring transactions should be introduced so as to ensure by practical means that the resale right is effectively applied by Member States. This implies also a right on the part of the author or his authorised representative to obtain any necessary information from the natural or legal person liable for payment of royalties. Member States which provide for collective management of the resale right may also provide that the bodies responsible for that collective management should alone be entitled to obtain information,

HAVE ADOPTED THIS DIRECTIVE:

CHAPTER I

SCOPE

Article 1

Subject matter of the resale right

1. Member States shall provide, for the benefit of the author of an original work of art, a resale right, to be defined as an inalienable right, which cannot be waived, even in advance, to receive a royalty based on the sale price obtained for any resale of the work, subsequent to the first transfer of the work by the author.

2. The right referred to in paragraph 1 shall apply to all acts of resale involving as sellers, buyers or intermediaries art market professionals, such as salesrooms, art galleries and, in general, any dealers in works of art.

3. Member States may provide that the right referred to in paragraph 1 shall not apply to acts of resale where the seller has acquired the work directly from the author less than three years before that resale and where the resale price does not exceed EUR10 000.

4. The royalty shall be payable by the seller. Member States may provide that one of the natural or legal persons referred to in paragraph 2 other than the seller shall alone be liable or shall share liability with the seller for payment of the royalty.

Article 2

Works of art to which the resale right relates

1. For the purposes of this Directive, 'original work of art' means works of graphic or plastic art such as pictures, collages, paintings, drawings, engravings, prints, lithographs, sculptures, tapestries, ceramics, glassware and photographs, provided they are made by the artist himself or are copies considered to be original works of art.

2. Copies of works of art covered by this Directive, which have been made in limited numbers by the artist himself or under his authority, shall be considered

to be original works of art for the purposes of this Directive. Such copies will normally have been numbered, signed or otherwise duly authorised by the artist.

Chapter II

Particular Provisions

Article 3

Threshold

1. It shall be for the Member States to set a minimum sale price from which the sales referred to in Article 1 shall be subject to resale right.

2. This minimum sale price may not under any circumstances exceed EUR3 000.

Article 4

Rates

1. The royalty provided for in Article 1 shall be set at the following rates:

(a) 4% for the portion of the sale price up to EUR50 000;

(b) 3% for the portion of the sale price from EUR50 000,01 to EUR200 000;

(c) 1% for the portion of the sale price from EUR200 000,01 to EUR350 000;

(d) 0,5% for the portion of the sale price from EUR350 000,01 to EUR500 000;

(e) 0,25% for the portion of the sale price exceeding EUR500 000.

However, the total amount of the royalty may not exceed EUR12 500.

2. By way of derogation from paragraph 1, Member States may apply a rate of 5% for the portion of the sale price referred to in paragraph 1(a).

3. If the minimum sale price set should be lower than EUR3 000, the Member State shall also determine the rate applicable to the portion of the sale price up to EUR3 000; this rate may not be lower than 4%.

Article 5

Calculation basis

The sale prices referred to in Articles 3 and 4 are net of tax.

Article 6

Persons entitled to receive royalties

1. The royalty provided for under Article 1 shall be payable to the author of the work and, subject to Article 8(2), after his death to those entitled under him/her.

2. Member States may provide for compulsory or optional collective management of the royalty provided for under Article 1.

Article 7

Third-country nationals entitled to receive royalties

1. Member States shall provide that authors who are nationals of third countries and, subject to Article 8(2), their successors in title shall enjoy the resale right in accordance with this Directive and the legislation of the Member State concerned only if legislation in the country of which the author or his/her successor in title is a national permits resale right protection in that country for authors from the Member States and their successors in title.

2. On the basis of information provided by the Member States, the Commission shall publish as soon as possible an indicative list of those third countries which fulfil the condition set out in paragraph 1. This list shall be kept up to date.

3. Any Member State may treat authors who are not nationals of a Member State but who have their habitual residence in that Member State in the same way as its own nationals for the purpose of resale right protection.

Article 8
Term of protection of the resale right

1. The term of protection of the resale right shall correspond to that laid down in Article 1 of Directive 93/98/EEC.

2. By way of derogation from paragraph 1, those Member States which do not apply the resale right on (the entry into force date referred to in Article 13), shall not be required, for a period expiring not later than 1 January 2010, to apply the resale right for the benefit of those entitled under the artist after his/her death.

3. A Member State to which paragraph 2 applies may have up to two more years, if necessary to enable the economic operators in that Member State to adapt gradually to the resale right system while maintaining their economic viability, before it is required to apply the resale right for the benefit of those entitled under the artist after his/her death. At least 12 months before the end of the period referred to in paragraph 2, the Member State concerned shall inform the Commission giving its reasons, so that the Commission can give an opinion, after appropriate consultations, within three months following the receipt of such information. If the Member State does not follow the opinion of the Commission, it shall within one month inform the Commission and justify its decision. The notification and justification of the Member State and the opinion of the Commission shall be published in the *Official Journal of the European Communities* and forwarded to the European Parliament.

4. In the event of the successful conclusion, within the periods referred to in Article 8(2) and (3), of international negotiations aimed at extending the resale right at international level, the Commission shall submit appropriate proposals.

Article 9
Right to obtain information

The Member States shall provide that for a period of three years after the resale, the persons entitled under Article 6 may require from any art market professional mentioned in Article 1(2) to furnish any information that may be necessary in order to secure payment of royalties in respect of the resale.

CHAPTER III

FINAL PROVISIONS

Article 10
Application in time

This Directive shall apply in respect of all original works of art as defined in Article 2 which, on 1 January 2006, are still protected by the legislation of the Member States in the field of copyright or meet the criteria for protection under the provisions of this Directive at that date.

Article 11
Revision clause

1. The Commission shall submit to the European Parliament, the Council and

the Economic and Social Committee not later than 1 January 2009 and every four years thereafter a report on the implementation and the effect of this Directive, paying particular attention to the competitiveness of the market in modern and contemporary art in the Community, especially as regards the position of the Community in relation to relevant markets that do not apply the resale right and the fostering of artistic creativity and the management procedures in the Member States. It shall examine in particular its impact on the internal market and the effect of the introduction of the resale right in those Member States that did not apply the right in national law prior to the entry into force of this Directive. Where appropriate, the Commission shall submit proposals for adapting the minimum threshold and the rates of royalty to take account of changes in the sector, proposals relating to the maximum amount laid down in Article 4(1) and any other proposal it may deem necessary in order to enhance the effectiveness of this Directive.

2. A Contact Committee is hereby established. It shall be composed of representatives of the competent authorities of the Member States. It shall be chaired by a representative of the Commission and shall meet either on the initiative of the Chairman or at the request of the delegation of a Member State.

3. The task of the Committee shall be as follows:

— to organise consultations on all questions deriving from application of this Directive,

— to facilitate the exchange of information between the Commission and the Member States on relevant developments in the art market in the Community.

Article 12

Implementation

1. Member States shall bring into force the laws, regulations and administrative provisions necessary to comply with this Directive before 1 January 2006. They shall forthwith inform the Commission thereof.

When Member States adopt these measures, they shall contain a reference to this Directive or shall be accompanied by such reference on the occasion of their official publication. The methods of making such a reference shall be laid down by the Member States.

2. Member States shall communicate to the Commission the provisions of national law which they adopt in the field covered by this Directive.

Article 13

Entry into force

This Directive shall enter into force on the day of its publication in the *Official Journal of the European Communities*.

Article 14

Addressees

This Directive is addressed to the Member States.

Done at Brussels, 27 September 2001.

For the European Parliament	*For the Council*
The President	*The President*
N. FONTAINE	C. PICQUÉ

H10. DIRECTIVE 2003/98/EC

Directive 2003/98/EC of the European Parliament and of the Council of 17 November 2003 on the re-use of public sector information[i]

([2003] O.J. L345/90)

THE EUROPEAN PARLIAMENT AND THE COUNCIL OF THE EUROPEAN UNION,

Having regard to the Treaty establishing the European Community, and in particular Article 95 thereof,

Having regard to the proposal from the Commission,[1]

Having regard to the opinion of the European Economic and Social Committee,[2]

Having regard to the opinion of the Committee of the Regions,[3]

Acting in accordance with the procedure set out in Article 251 of the Treaty,[4]

Whereas:

(1) The Treaty provides for the establishment of an internal market and of a system ensuring that competition in the internal market is not distorted. Harmonisation of the rules and practices in the Member States relating to the exploitation of public sector information contributes to the achievement of these objectives.

(2) The evolution towards an information and knowledge society influences the life of every citizen in the Community, *inter alia*, by enabling them to gain new ways of accessing and acquiring knowledge.

(3) Digital content plays an important role in this evolution. Content production has given rise to rapid job creation in recent years and continues to do so. Most of these jobs are created in small emerging companies.

(4) The public sector collects, produces, reproduces and disseminates a wide range of information in many areas of activity, such as social, economic, geographical, weather, tourist, business, patent and educational information.

(5) One of the principal aims of the establishment of an internal market is the creation of conditions conducive to the development of Community-wide services. Public sector information is an important primary material for digital content products and services and will become an even more important content resource with the development of wireless content services. Broad cross-border geographical coverage will also be essential in this context. Wider possibilities of re-using public sector information should *inter alia* allow European companies to exploit its potential and contribute to economic growth and job creation.

(6) There are considerable differences in the rules and practices in the Member States relating to the exploitation of public sector information resources, which constitute barriers to bringing out the full economic potential of this key docu-

---

[i] *Editorial note*: The footnote numbering in the original Directive is reproduced below. This Directive was amended by Directive 2013/37/EU with effect from July 17, 2013, being the twentieth day after the date of publication in the Official Journal of the European Union (June 27, 2013, see OJ L.175, 27.6.2013, p.1; see also Directive 2013/37/EU, Article 3).The text below is the consolidated version including the amendments in Directive 2013/37/EU: see http://eur-lex.europa.eu/legal-content/EN/TXT/?qid=1438262403357&uri=CELEX:02003L0098-20130717 [Accessed July 28, 2015]. It was published in OJ L 345, 31.12.2003, p.90 with the following disclaimer "This document is meant purely as a documentation tool and the institutions do not assume any liability for its contents".

[1] OJ C 227 E, 24.9.2002, p. 382.

[2] OJ C 85, 8.4.2003, p. 25.

[3] OJ C 73, 26.3.2003, p. 38.

[4] Opinion of the European Parliament of 12 February 2003 (not yet published in the Official Journal), Council Common Position of 26 May 2003 (OJ C 159 E, 8.7.2003, p. 1) and Position of the European Parliament of 25 September 2003 (not yet published in the Official Journal). Council Decision of 27 October 2003.

ment resource. Traditional practice in public sector bodies in exploiting public sector information has developed in very disparate ways. That should be taken into account. Minimum harmonisation of national rules and practices on the re-use of public sector documents should therefore be undertaken, in cases where the differences in national regulations and practices or the absence of clarity hinder the smooth functioning of the internal market and the proper development of the information society in the Community.

(7) Moreover, without minimum harmonisation at Community level, legislative activities at national level, which have already been initiated in a number of Member States in order to respond to the technological challenges, might result in even more significant differences. The impact of such legislative differences and uncertainties will become more significant with the further development of the information society, which has already greatly increased cross-border exploitation of information.

(8) A general framework for the conditions governing reuse of public sector documents is needed in order to ensure fair, proportionate and non-discriminatory conditions for the re-use of such information. Public sector bodies collect, produce, reproduce and disseminate documents to fulfil their public tasks. Use of such documents for other reasons constitutes a re-use. Member States' policies can go beyond the minimum standards established in this Directive, thus allowing for more extensive re-use.

(9) This Directive does not contain an obligation to allow re-use of documents. The decision whether or not to authorise re-use will remain with the Member States or the public sector body concerned. This Directive should apply to documents that are made accessible for re-use when public sector bodies license, sell, disseminate, exchange or give out information. To avoid cross-subsidies, re-use should include further use of documents within the organisation itself for activities falling outside the scope of its public tasks. Activities falling outside the public task will typically include supply of documents that are produced and charged for exclusively on a commercial basis and in competition with others in the market. The definition of 'document' is not intended to cover computer programmes. The Directive builds on the existing access regimes in the Member States and does not change the national rules for access to documents. It does not apply in cases in which citizens or companies can, under the relevant access regime, only obtain a document if they can prove a particular interest. At Community level, Articles 41 (right to good administration) and 42 of the Charter of Fundamental Rights of the European Union recognise the right of any citizen of the Union and any natural or legal person residing or having its registered office in a Member State to have access to European Parliament, Council and Commission documents. Public sector bodies should be encouraged to make available for re-use any documents held by them. Public sector bodies should promote and encourage re-use of documents, including official texts of a legislative and administrative nature in those cases where the public sector body has the right to authorise their re-use.

(10) The definitions of 'public sector body' and 'body governed by public law' are taken from the public procurement Directives (92/50/EEC,[5] 93/36/EEC[6] and 93/37/EEC[7] and 98/4/EC[8]). Public undertakings are not covered by these definitions.

---

[5] OJ L 209, 24.7.1992, p. 1. Directive as last amended by Commission Directive 2001/78/EC (OJ L 285, 29.10.2001, p. 1).

[6] OJ L 199, 9.8.1993, p. 1. Directive as last amended by Commission Directive 2001/78/EC.

[7] OJ L 199, 9.8.1993, p.54. Directive as last amended by Commission Directive 2001/78/EC.

[8] OJ L 101, 1.4.1998, p. 1.

(11) This Directive lays down a generic definition of the term 'document', in line with developments in the information society. It covers any representation of acts, facts or information—and any compilation of such acts, facts or information—whatever its medium (written on paper, or stored in electronic form or as a sound, visual or audiovisual recording), held by public sector bodies. A document held by a public sector body is a document where the public sector body has the right to authorise re-use.

(12) The time limit for replying to requests for re-use should be reasonable and in line with the equivalent time for requests to access the document under the relevant access regimes. Reasonable time limits throughout the Union will stimulate the creation of new aggregated information products and services at pan-European level. Once a request for re-use has been granted, public sector bodies should make the documents available in a timeframe that allows their full economic potential to be exploited. This is particularly important for dynamic content (e.g. traffic data), the economic value of which depends on the immediate availability of the information and of regular updates. Should a licence be used, the timely availability of documents may be a part of the terms of the licence.

(13) The possibilities for re-use can be improved by limiting the need to digitise paper-based documents or to process digital files to make them mutually compatible. Therefore, public sector bodies should make documents available in any pre-existing format or language, through electronic means where possible and appropriate. Public sector bodies should view requests for extracts from existing documents favourably when to grant such a request would involve only a simple operation. Public sector bodies should not, however, be obliged to provide an extract from a document where this involves disproportionate effort. To facilitate re-use, public sector bodies should make their own documents available in a format which, as far as possible and appropriate, is not dependent on the use of specific software. Where possible and appropriate, public sector bodies should take into account the possibilities for the re-use of documents by and for people with disabilities.

(14) Where charges are made, the total income should not exceed the total costs of collecting, producing, reproducing and disseminating documents, together with a reasonable return on investment, having due regard to the self-financing requirements of the public sector body concerned, where applicable. Production includes creation and collation, and dissemination may also include user support. Recovery of costs, together with a reasonable return on investment, consistent with applicable accounting principles and the relevant cost calculation method of the public sector body concerned, constitutes an upper limit to the charges, as any excessive prices should be precluded. The upper limit for charges set in this Directive is without prejudice to the right of Member States or public sector bodies to apply lower charges or no charges at all, and Member States should encourage public sector bodies to make documents available at charges that do not exceed the marginal costs for reproducing and disseminating the documents.

(15) Ensuring that the conditions for re-use of public sector documents are clear and publicly available is a precondition for the development of a Community-wide information market. Therefore all applicable conditions for the re-use of the documents should be made clear to the potential re-users. Member States should encourage the creation of indices accessible on line, where appropriate, of available documents so as to promote and facilitate requests for re-use. Applicants for re-use of documents should be informed of available means of redress relating to decisions or practices affecting them. This will be particularly important for SMEs which may not be familiar with interactions with public sector bodies from other Member States and corresponding means of redress.

H EU DIRECTIVES

(16) Making public all generally available documents held by the public sector—concerning not only the political process but also the legal and administrative process—is a fundamental instrument for extending the right to knowledge, which is a basic principle of democracy. This objective is applicable to institutions at every level, be it local, national or international.

(17) In some cases the re-use of documents will take place without a licence being agreed. In other cases a licence will be issued imposing conditions on the re-use by the licensee dealing with issues such as liability, the proper use of documents, guaranteeing non-alteration and the acknowledgement of source. If public sector bodies license documents for re-use, the licence conditions should be fair and transparent. Standard licences that are available online may also play an important role in this respect. Therefore Member States should provide for the availability of standard licences.

(18) If the competent authority decides to no longer make available certain documents for re-use, or to cease updating these documents, it should make these decisions publicly known, at the earliest opportunity, via electronic means whenever possible.

(19) Conditions for re-use should be non-discriminatory for comparable categories of re-use. This should, for example, not prevent the exchange of information between public sector bodies free of charge for the exercise of public tasks, whilst other parties are charged for the re-use of the same documents. Neither should it prevent the adoption of a differentiated charging policy for commercial and non-commercial re-use.

(20) Public sector bodies should respect competition rules when establishing the principles for re-use of documents avoiding as far as possible exclusive agreements between themselves and private partners. However, in order to provide a service of general economic interest, an exclusive right to re-use specific public sector documents may sometimes be necessary. This may be the case if no commercial publisher would publish the information without such an exclusive right.

(21) This Directive should be implemented and applied in full compliance with the principles relating to the protection of personal data in accordance with Directive 95/46/EC of the European Parliament and of the Council of 24 October 1995 on the protection of individuals with regard to the processing of personal data and of the free movement of such data.[9]

(22) The intellectual property rights of third parties are not affected by this Directive. For the avoidance of doubt, the term 'intellectual property rights' refers to copyright and related rights only (including *sui generis* forms of protection). This Directive does not apply to documents covered by industrial property rights, such as patents, registered designs and trademarks. The Directive does not affect the existence or ownership of intellectual property rights of public sector bodies, nor does it limit the exercise of these rights in any way beyond the boundaries set by this Directive. The obligations imposed by this Directive should apply only insofar as they are compatible with the provisions of international agreements on the protection of intellectual property rights, in particular the Berne Convention for the Protection of Literary and Artistic Works (the Berne Convention) and the Agreement on Trade-Related Aspects of Intellectual Property Rights (the TRIPS Agreement). Public sector bodies should, however, exercise their copyright in a way that facilitates re-use.

(23) Tools that help potential re-users to find documents available for re-use and the conditions for re-use can facilitate considerably the cross-border use of public sector documents. Member States should therefore ensure that practical

---

[9] OJ L 281, 23.11.1995, p. 31.

arrangements are in place that help re-users in their search for documents available for reuse. Assets lists, accessible preferably online, of main documents (documents that are extensively re-used or that have the potential to be extensively re-used), and portal sites that are linked to decentralised assets lists are examples of such practical arrangements.

(24) This Directive is without prejudice to Directive 2001/29/ EC of the European Parliament and of the Council of 22 May 2001 on the harmonisation of certain aspects of copyright and related rights in the information society[10] and Directive 96/9/EC of the European Parliament and of the Council of 11 March 1996 on the legal protection of databases.[11] It spells out the conditions within which public sector bodies can exercise their intellectual property rights in the internal information market when allowing re-use of documents.

(25) Since the objectives of the proposed action, namely to facilitate the creation of Community-wide information products and services based on public sector documents, to enhance an effective cross-border use of public sector documents by private companies for added-value information products and services and to limit distortions of competition on the Community market, cannot be sufficiently achieved by the Member States and can therefore, in view of the intrinsic Community scope and impact of the said action, be better achieved at Community level, the Community may adopt measures, in accordance with the principle of subsidiarity as set out in Article 5 of the Treaty. In accordance with the principle of proportionality, as set out in that Article, this Directive does not go beyond what is necessary in order to achieve those objectives. This Directive should achieve minimum harmonisation, thereby avoiding further disparities between the Member States in dealing with the re-use of public sector documents,

HAVE ADOPTED THIS DIRECTIVE:

CHAPTER I

GENERAL PROVISIONS

Article 1

Subject matter and scope

1. This Directive establishes a minimum set of rules governing the re-use and the practical means of facilitating re-use of existing documents held by public sector bodies of the Member States.

2. This Directive shall not apply to:

(a) documents the supply of which is an activity falling outside the scope of the public task of the public sector bodies concerned as defined by law or by other binding rules in the Member State, or in the absence of such rules, as defined in line with common administrative practice in the Member State in question, provided that the scope of the public tasks is transparent and subject to review;

(b) documents for which third parties hold intellectual property rights;

(c) documents which are excluded from access by virtue of the access regimes in the Member States, including on the grounds of:

— the protection of national security (i.e. State security), defence, or public security,

— statistical confidentiality,

— commercial confidentiality (e.g. business, professional or company secrets);

(ca) documents access to which is restricted by virtue of the access regimes in the Member States, including cases whereby citizens or companies have to prove a particular interest to obtain access to documents;

(cb) parts of documents containing only logos, crests and insignia;

(cc) documents access to which is excluded or restricted by virtue of the access regimes on the grounds of protection of personal data, and parts of documents accessible by virtue of those regimes which contain personal data the re-use of which has been defined by law as being incompatible with the law concerning the protection of individuals with regard to the processing of personal data;

(d) documents held by public service broadcasters and their subsidiaries, and by other bodies or their subsidiaries for the fulfilment of a public service broadcasting remit;

(e) documents held by educational and research establishments, including organisations established for the transfer of research results, schools and universities, except university libraries and

(f) documents held by cultural establishments other than libraries, museums and archives.

3. This Directive builds on and is without prejudice to access regimes in the Member States.

4. This Directive leaves intact and in no way affects the level of protection of individuals with regard to the processing of personal data under the provisions of Union and national law, and in particular does not alter the obligations and rights set out in Directive 95/46/EC.

5. The obligations imposed by this Directive shall apply only insofar as they are compatible with the provisions of international agreements on the protection of intellectual property rights, in particular the Berne Convention and the TRIPS Agreement.

Article 2

Definitions

For the purpose of this Directive the following definitions shall apply:

1. 'public sector body' means the State, regional or local authorities, bodies governed by public law and associations formed by one or several such authorities or one or several such bodies governed by public law;

2. 'body governed by public law' means any body:

(a) established for the specific purpose of meeting needs in the general interest, not having an industrial or commercial character; and

(b) having legal personality; and

(c) financed, for the most part by the State, or regional or local authorities, or other bodies governed by public law; or subject to management supervision by those bodies; or having an administrative, managerial or supervisory board, more than half of whose members are appointed by the State, regional or local authorities or by other bodies governed by public law;

3. 'document' means:

(a) any content whatever its medium (written on paper or stored in electronic form or as a sound, visual or audiovisual recording);

(b) any part of such content;

4. 're-use' means the use by persons or legal entities of documents held by

public sector bodies, for commercial or non-commercial purposes other than the initial purpose within the public task for which the documents were produced. Exchange of documents between public sector bodies purely in pursuit of their public tasks does not constitute re-use;

5. 'personal data' means data as defined in Article 2(a) of Directive 95/46/EC.

6. 'machine-readable format' means a file format structured so that software applications can easily identify, recognize and extract specific data, including individual statements of fact, and their internal structure;

7. 'open format' means a file format that is platform-independent and made available to the public without any restriction that impedes the re-use of documents;

8. 'formal open standard' means a standard which has been laid down in written form, detailing specifications for the requirements on how to ensure software interoperability;

9. 'university' means any public sector body that provides post-secondary-school higher education leading to academic degrees.

Article 3

General principle

1. Subject to paragraph 2 Member States shall ensure that documents to which this Directive applies in accordance with Article 1 shall be re-usable for commercial or non-commercial purposes in accordance with the conditions set out in Chapters III and IV.

2. For documents in which libraries, including university libraries, museums and archives hold intellectual property rights, Member States shall ensure that, where the re-use of such documents is allowed, these documents shall be re-usable for commercial or non-commercial purposes in accordance with the conditions set out in Chapters III and IV.

CHAPTER II

REQUESTS FOR RE-USE

Article 4

Requirements applicable to the processing of requests for re-use

1. Public sector bodies shall, through electronic means where possible and appropriate, process requests for re-use and shall make the document available for re-use to the applicant or, if a licence is needed, finalise the licence offer to the applicant within a reasonable time that is consistent with the time-frames laid down for the processing of requests for access to documents.

2. Where no time limits or other rules regulating the timely provision of documents have been established, public sector bodies shall process the request and shall deliver the documents for re-use to the applicant or, if a licence is needed, finalise the licence offer to the applicant within a timeframe of not more than 20 working days after its receipt. This timeframe may be extended by another 20 working days for extensive or complex requests. In such cases the applicant shall be notified within three weeks after the initial request that more time is needed to process it.

3. In the event of a negative decision, the public sector bodies shall communicate the grounds for refusal to the applicant on the basis of the relevant provisions of the access regime in that Member State or of the national provisions adopted pursuant to this Directive, in particular points (a) to (cc) of Article 1(2)

or Article 3. Where a negative decision is based on Article 1(2)(b), the public sector body shall include a reference to the natural or legal person who is the rightholder, where known, or alternatively to the licensor from which the public sector body has obtained the relevant material. Libraries, including university libraries, museums and archives shall not be required to include such a reference.

4. Any decision on re-use shall contain a reference to the means of redress in case the applicant wishes to appeal the decision. The means of redress shall include the possibility of review by an impartial review body with the appropriate expertise, such as the national competition authority, the national access to documents authority or a national judicial authority, whose decisions are binding upon the public sector body concerned.

5. Public sector bodies covered under Article 1(2)(d), (e) and (f) shall not be required to comply with the requirements of this Article.

CHAPTER III

CONDITIONS FOR RE-USE

Article 5

Available formats

1. Public sector bodies shall make their documents available in any pre-existing format or language, and, where possible and appropriate, in open and machine-readable format together with their metadata. Both the format and the metadata should, in so far as possible, comply with formal open standards.

2. Paragraph 1 shall not imply an obligation for public sector bodies to create or adapt documents or provide extracts in order to comply with that paragraph where this would involve disproportionate effort, going beyond a simple operation.

3. On the basis of this Directive, public sector bodies cannot be required to continue the production and storage of a certain type of documents with a view to the re-use of such documents by a private or public sector organisation.

Article 6

Principles governing charging

1. Where charges are made for the re-use of documents, those charges shall be limited to the marginal costs incurred for their reproduction, provision and dissemination.

2. Paragraph 1 shall not apply to the following:

(a) public sector bodies that are required to generate revenue to cover a substantial part of their costs relating to the performance of their public tasks;

(b) by way of exception, documents for which the public sector body concerned is required to generate sufficient revenue to cover a substantial part of the costs relating to their collection, production, reproduction and dissemination. Those requirements shall be defined by law or by other binding rules in the Member State. In the absence of such rules, the requirements shall be defined in accordance with common administrative practice in the Member State;

(c) libraries, including university libraries, museums and archives.

3. In the cases referred to in points (a) and (b) of paragraph 2, the public sector bodies concerned shall calculate the total charges according to objective, trans-

parent and verifiable criteria to be laid down by the Member States. The total income of those bodies from supplying and allowing re-use of documents over the appropriate accounting period shall not exceed the cost of collection, production, reproduction and dissemination, together with a reasonable return on investment. Charges shall be calculated in line with the accounting principles applicable to the public sector bodies involved.

4. Where charges are made by the public sector bodies referred to in point (c) of paragraph 2, the total income from supplying and allowing re-use of documents over the appropriate accounting period shall not exceed the cost of collection, production, reproduction, dissemination, preservation and rights clearance, together with a reasonable return on investment. Charges shall be calculated in line with the accounting principles applicable to the public sector bodies involved.

Article 7

Transparency

1. In the case of standard charges for the re-use of documents held by public sector bodies, any applicable conditions and the actual amount of those charges, including the calculation basis for such charges, shall be pre-established and published, through electronic means where possible and appropriate.

2. In the case of charges for the re-use other than those referred to in paragraph 1, the public sector body in question shall indicate at the outset which factors are taken into account in the calculation of those charges. Upon request, the public sector body in question shall also indicate the way in which such charges have been calculated in relation to the specific re-use request.

3. The requirements referred to in point (b) of Article 6(2) shall be pre-established. They shall be published by electronic means, where possible and appropriate.

4. Public sector bodies shall ensure that applicants for re-use of documents are informed of available means of redress relating to decisions or practices affecting them.

Article 8

Licences

1. Public sector bodies may allow re-use without conditions or may impose conditions, where appropriate through a licence. These conditions shall not unnecessarily restrict possibilities for re-use and shall not be used to restrict competition.

2. In Member States where licences are used, Member States shall ensure that standard licences for the re-use of public sector documents, which can be adapted to meet particular licence applications, are available in digital format and can be processed electronically. Member States shall encourage all public sector bodies to use the standard licences.

Article 9

Practical arrangements

Member States shall make practical arrangements facilitating the search for documents available for re-use, such as asset lists of main documents with relevant metadata, accessible where possible and appropriate online and in machine-readable format, and portal sites that are linked to the asset lists. Where possible Member States shall facilitate the cross-linguistic search for documents.

CHAPTER IV

NON-DISCRIMINATION AND FAIR TRADING

Article 10

Non-discrimination

1. Any applicable conditions for the re-use of documents shall be non-discriminatory for comparable categories of re-use.

2. If documents are re-used by a public sector body as input for its commercial activities which fall outside the scope of its public tasks, the same charges and other conditions shall apply to the supply of the documents for those activities as apply to other users.

Article 11

Prohibition of exclusive arrangements

1. The re-use of documents shall be open to all potential actors in the market, even if one or more market players already exploit added-value products based on these documents. Contracts or other arrangements between the public sector bodies holding the documents and third parties shall not grant exclusive rights.

2. However, where an exclusive right is necessary for the provision of a service in the public interest, the validity of the reason for granting such an exclusive right shall be subject to regular review, and shall, in any event, be reviewed every three years. The exclusive arrangements established after the entry into force of this Directive shall be transparent and made public.

This paragraph shall not apply to digitisation of cultural resources.

2a. Notwithstanding paragraph 1, where an exclusive right relates to digitisation of cultural resources, the period of exclusivity shall in general not exceed 10 years. In case where that period exceeds 10 years, its duration shall be subject to review during the 11th year and, if applicable, every seven years thereafter.

The arrangements granting exclusive rights referred to in the first subparagraph shall be transparent and made public.

In the case of an exclusive right referred to in the first subparagraph, the public sector body concerned shall be provided free of charge with a copy of the digitised cultural resources as part of those arrangements. That copy shall be available for re-use at the end of the period of exclusivity.

3. Exclusive arrangements existing on 1 July 2005 that do not qualify for the exceptions under paragraph 2 shall be terminated at the end of the contract or in any event not later than 31 December 2008.

4. Without prejudice to paragraph 3, exclusive arrangements existing on 17 July 2013 that do not qualify for the exceptions under paragraphs 2 and 2a shall be terminated at the end of the contract or in any event not later than 18 July 2043.

CHAPTER V

FINAL PROVISIONS

Article 12

Implementation

Member States shall bring into force the laws, regulations and administrative provisions necessary to comply with this Directive by 1 July 2005. They shall forthwith inform the Commission thereof. When Member States adopt those measures, they shall contain a reference to this Directive or be accompanied by such a reference on the occasion of their official publication. Member States shall determine how such reference is to be made.

Article 13

Review

1. The Commission shall carry out a review of the application of this Directive before 18 July 2018 and shall communicate the results of that review, together with any proposals for amendments to this Directive, to the European Parliament and the Council.

2. Member States shall submit a report every 3 years to the Commission on the availability of public sector information for re-use and the conditions under which it is made available and the redress practices. On the basis of that report, which shall be made public, Member States shall carry out a review of the implementation of Article 6, in particular as regards charging above marginal cost.

3. The review referred to in paragraph 1 shall in particular address the scope and impact of this Directive, including the extent of the increase in re-use of public sector documents, the effects of the principles applied to charging and the re-use of official texts of a legislative and administrative nature, the interaction between data protection rules and re-use possibilities, as well as further possibilities of improving the proper functioning of the internal market and the development of the European content industry.

Article 14

Entry into force

This Directive shall enter into force on the day of its publication in the Official Journal of the European Union.

Article 15

Addressees

This Directive is addressed to the Member States.
Done at Brussels, 17 November 2003.

For the Parliament   *For the Council*
P. COX   G. ALEMANNO
The President   *The President*

H11. DIRECTIVE 2004/48/EC

Directive 2004/48/EC of the European Parliament and of the Council of 29 April 2004 on the enforcement of intellectual property rights[i]

([2004] O.J. L195/16)

THE EUROPEAN PARLIAMENT AND THE COUNCIL OF THE EUROPEAN UNION,

Having regard to the Treaty establishing the European Community, and in particular Article 95 thereof,

Having regard to the proposal from the Commission,

---

[i] *Editorial note*: The footnote numbering in the original Directive is reproduced below.

Having regard to the opinion of the European Economic and Social Committee[1],

After consulting the Committee of the Regions,

Acting in accordance with the procedure laid down in Article 251 of the Treaty[2],

Whereas:

(1) The achievement of the internal market entails eliminating restrictions on freedom of movement and distortions of competition, while creating an environment conducive to innovation and investment. In this context, the protection of intellectual property is an essential element for the success of the internal market. The protection of intellectual property is important not only for promoting innovation and creativity, but also for developing employment and improving competitiveness.

(2) The protection of intellectual property should allow the inventor or creator to derive a legitimate profit from his/ her invention or creation. It should also allow the widest possible dissemination of works, ideas and new knowhow. At the same time, it should not hamper freedom of expression, the free movement of information, or the protection of personal data, including on the Internet.

(3) However, without effective means of enforcing intellectual property rights, innovation and creativity are discouraged and investment diminished. It is therefore necessary to ensure that the substantive law on intellectual property, which is nowadays largely part of the *acquis communautaire*, is applied effectively in the Community. In this respect, the means of enforcing intellectual property rights are of paramount importance for the success of the internal market.

(4) At international level, all Member States, as well as the Community itself as regards matters within its competence, are bound by the Agreement on trade-related aspects of intellectual property (the TRIPS Agreement), approved, as part of the multilateral negotiations of the Uruguay Round, by Council Decision 94/ 800/EC[3] and concluded in the framework of the World Trade Organisation.

(5) The TRIPS Agreement contains, in particular, provisions on the means of enforcing intellectual property rights, which are common standards applicable at international level and implemented in all Member States. This Directive should not affect Member States' international obligations, including those under the TRIPS Agreement.

(6) There are also international conventions to which all Member States are parties and which also contain provisions on the means of enforcing intellectual property rights. These include, in particular, the Paris Convention for the Protection of Industrial Property, the Berne Convention for the Protection of Literary and Artistic Works, and the Rome Convention for the Protection of Performers, Producers of Phonograms and Broadcasting Organisations.

(7) It emerges from the consultations held by the Commission on this question that, in the Member States, and despite the TRIPS Agreement, there are still major disparities as regards the means of enforcing intellectual property rights. For instance, the arrangements for applying provisional measures, which are used in particular to preserve evidence, the calculation of damages, or the arrangements for applying injunctions, vary widely from one Member State to another. In some Member States, there are no measures, procedures and remedies such as the right

---

[1] OJ C 32, 5.2.2004, p. 15.
[2] Opinion of the European Parliament of 9 March 2004 (not yet published in the Official Journal) and Council Decision of 26 April 2004.
[3] OJ L 336, 23.12.1994, p. 1.

of information and the recall, at the infringer's expense, of the infringing goods placed on the market.

(8) The disparities between the systems of the Member States as regards the means of enforcing intellectual property rights are prejudicial to the proper functioning of the Internal Market and make it impossible to ensure that intellectual property rights enjoy an equivalent level of protection throughout the Community. This situation does not promote free movement within the internal market or create an environment conducive to healthy competition.

(9) The current disparities also lead to a weakening of the substantive law on intellectual property and to a fragmentation of the internal market in this field. This causes a loss of confidence in the internal market in business circles, with a consequent reduction in investment in innovation and creation. Infringements of intellectual property rights appear to be increasingly linked to organised crime. Increasing use of the Internet enables pirated products to be distributed instantly around the globe. Effective enforcement of the substantive law on intellectual property should be ensured by specific action at Community level. Approximation of the legislation of the Member States in this field is therefore an essential prerequisite for the proper functioning of the internal market.

(10) The objective of this Directive is to approximate legislative systems so as to ensure a high, equivalent and homogeneous level of protection in the internal market.

(11) This Directive does not aim to establish harmonised rules for judicial cooperation, jurisdiction, the recognition and enforcement of decisions in civil and commercial matters, or deal with applicable law. There are Community instruments which govern such matters in general terms and are, in principle, equally applicable to intellectual property.

(12) This Directive should not affect the application of the rules of competition, and in particular Articles 81 and 82 of the Treaty. The measures provided for in this Directive should not be used to restrict competition unduly in a manner contrary to the Treaty.

(13) It is necessary to define the scope of this Directive as widely as possible in order to encompass all the intellectual property rights covered by Community provisions in this field and/or by the national law of the Member State concerned. Nevertheless, that requirement does not affect the possibility, on the part of those Member States which so wish, to extend, for internal purposes, the provisions of this Directive to include acts involving unfair competition, including parasitic copies, or similar activities.

(14) The measures provided for in Articles 6(2), 8(1) and 9(2) need to be applied only in respect of acts carried out on a commercial scale. This is without prejudice to the possibility for Member States to apply those measures also in respect of other acts. Acts carried out on a commercial scale are those carried out for direct or indirect economic or commercial advantage; this would normally exclude acts carried out by end consumers acting in good faith.

(15) This Directive should not affect substantive law on intellectual property, Directive 95/46/EC of 24 October 1995 of the European Parliament and of the Council on the protection of individuals with regard to the processing of personal data and on the free movement of such data[4], Directive 1999/93/EC of the European Parliament and of the Council of 13 December 1999 on a Community

---

[4] OJ L 281, 23.11.1995, p. 31. Directive as amended by Regulation (EC) No 1882/2003 (OJ L 284, 31.10.2003, p. 1).

framework for electronic signatures[5] and Directive 2000/31/EC of the European Parliament and of the Council of 8 June 2000 on certain legal aspects of information society services, in particular electronic commerce, in the internal market[6]...

(16) The provisions of this Directive should be without prejudice to the particular provisions for the enforcement of rights and on exceptions in the domain of copyright and related rights set out in Community instruments and notably those found in Council Directive 91/250/EEC of 14 May 1991 on the legal protection of computer programs[7] or in Directive 2001/29/EC of the European Parliament and of the Council of 22 May 2001 on the harmonisation of certain aspects of copyright and related rights in the information society[8].

(17) The measures, procedures and remedies provided for in this Directive should be determined in each case in such a manner as to take due account of the specific characteristics of that case, including the specific features of each intellectual property right and, where appropriate, the intentional or unintentional character of the infringement.

(18) The persons entitled to request application of those measures, procedures and remedies should be not only the rightholders but also persons who have a direct interest and legal standing in so far as permitted by and in accordance with the applicable law, which may include professional organisations in charge of the management of those rights or for the defence of the collective and individual interests for which they are responsible.

(19) Since copyright exists from the creation of a work and does not require formal registration, it is appropriate to adopt the rule laid down in Article 15 of the Berne Convention, which establishes the presumption whereby the author of a literary or artistic work is regarded as such if his/her name appears on the work. A similar presumption should be applied to the owners of related rights since it is often the holder of a related right, such as a phonogram producer, who will seek to defend rights and engage in fighting acts of piracy.

(20) Given that evidence is an element of paramount importance for establishing the infringement of intellectual property rights, it is appropriate to ensure that effective means of presenting, obtaining and preserving evidence are available. The procedures should have regard to the rights of the defence and provide the necessary guarantees, including the protection of confidential information. For infringements committed on a commercial scale it is also important that the courts may order access, where appropriate, to banking, financial or commercial documents under the control of the alleged infringer.

(21) Other measures designed to ensure a high level of protection exist in certain Member States and should be made available in all the Member States. This is the case with the right of information, which allows precise information to be obtained on the origin of the infringing goods or services, the distribution channels and the identity of any third parties involved in the infringement.

(22) It is also essential to provide for provisional measures for the immediate termination of infringements, without awaiting a decision on the substance of the case, while observing the rights of the defence, ensuring the proportionality of the provisional measures as appropriate to the characteristics of the case in question and providing the guarantees needed to cover the costs and the injury caused to the defendant by an unjustified request. Such measures are particularly justified where any delay would cause irreparable harm to the holder of an intellectual property right.

---

[5] OJ L 13, 19.1.2000, p. 12.

[6] OJ L 178, 17.7.2000, p. 1

[7] OJ L 122, 17.5.1991, p. 42. Directive as amended by Directive 93/98/EEC (OJ L 290, 24.11.1993, p. 9).

[8] OJ L 167, 22.6.2001, p. 10.

(23) Without prejudice to any other measures, procedures and remedies available, rightholders should have the possibility of applying for an injunction against an intermediary whose services are being used by a third party to infringe the rightholder's industrial property right. The conditions and procedures relating to such injunctions should be left to the national law of the Member States. As far as infringements of copyright and related rights are concerned, a comprehensive level of harmonisation is already provided for in Directive 2001/29/EC. Article 8(3) of Directive 2001/29/EC should therefore not be affected by this Directive.

(24) Depending on the particular case, and if justified by the circumstances, the measures, procedures and remedies to be provided for should include prohibitory measures aimed at preventing further infringements of intellectual property rights. Moreover there should be corrective measures, where appropriate at the expense of the infringer, such as the recall and definitive removal from the channels of commerce, or destruction, of the infringing goods and, in appropriate cases, of the materials and implements principally used in the creation or manufacture of these goods. These corrective measures should take account of the interests of third parties including, in particular, consumers and private parties acting in good faith.

(25) Where an infringement is committed unintentionally and without negligence and where the corrective measures or injunctions provided for by this Directive would be disproportionate, Member States should have the option of providing for the possibility, in appropriate cases, of pecuniary compensation being awarded to the injured party as an alternative measure. However, where the commercial use of counterfeit goods or the supply of services would constitute an infringement of law other than intellectual property law or would be likely to harm consumers, such use or supply should remain prohibited.

(26) With a view to compensating for the prejudice suffered as a result of an infringement committed by an infringer who engaged in an activity in the knowledge, or with reasonable grounds for knowing, that it would give rise to such an infringement, the amount of damages awarded to the rightholder should take account of all appropriate aspects, such as loss of earnings incurred by the rightholder, or unfair profits made by the infringer and, where appropriate, any moral prejudice caused to the rightholder. As an alternative, for example where it would be difficult to determine the amount of the actual prejudice suffered, the amount of the damages might be derived from elements such as the royalties or fees which would have been due if the infringer had requested authorisation to use the intellectual property right in question. The aim is not to introduce an obligation to provide for punitive damages but to allow for compensation based on an objective criterion while taking account of the expenses incurred by the rightholder, such as the costs of identification and research.

(27) To act as a supplementary deterrent to future infringers and to contribute to the awareness of the public at large, it is useful to publicise decisions in intellectual property infringement cases.

(28) In addition to the civil and administrative measures, procedures and remedies provided for under this Directive, criminal sanctions also constitute, in appropriate cases, a means of ensuring the enforcement of intellectual property rights.

(29) Industry should take an active part in the fight against piracy and counterfeiting. The development of codes of conduct in the circles directly affected is a supplementary means of bolstering the regulatory framework. The Member States, in collaboration with the Commission, should encourage the development of codes of conduct in general. Monitoring of the manufacture of optical discs, particularly by means of an identification code embedded in discs produced in the Community, helps to limit infringements of intellectual property

rights in this sector, which suffers from piracy on a large scale. However, these technical protection measures should not be misused to protect markets and prevent parallel imports.

(30) In order to facilitate the uniform application of this Directive, it is appropriate to provide for systems of cooperation and the exchange of information between Member States, on the one hand, and between the Member States and the Commission on the other, in particular by creating a network of correspondents designated by the Member States and by providing regular reports assessing the application of this Directive and the effectiveness of the measures taken by the various national bodies.

(31) Since, for the reasons already described, the objective of this Directive can best be achieved at Community level, the Community may adopt measures, in accordance with the principle of subsidiarity as set out in Article 5 of the Treaty. In accordance with the principle of proportionality as set out in that Article, this Directive does not go beyond what is necessary in order to achieve that objective.

(32) This Directive respects the fundamental rights and observes the principles recognised in particular by the Charter of Fundamental Rights of the European Union. In particular, this Directive seeks to ensure full respect for intellectual property, in accordance with Article 17(2) of that Charter,

HAVE ADOPTED THIS DIRECTIVE:

CHAPTER I

OBJECTIVE AND SCOPE

Article 1

Subject matter

This Directive concerns the measures, procedures and remedies necessary to ensure the enforcement of intellectual property rights. For the purposes of this Directive, the term 'intellectual property rights' includes industrial property rights.

Article 2

Scope

1. Without prejudice to the means which are or may be provided for in Community or national legislation, in so far as those means may be more favourable for rightholders, the measures, procedures and remedies provided for by this Directive shall apply, in accordance with Article 3, to any infringement of intellectual property rights as provided for by Community law and/or by the national law of the Member State concerned.

2. This Directive shall be without prejudice to the specific provisions on the enforcement of rights and on exceptions contained in Community legislation concerning copyright and rights related to copyright, notably those found in Directive 91/250/EEC and, in particular, Article 7 thereof or in Directive 2001/29/EC and, in particular, Articles 2 to 6 and Article 8 thereof.

3. This Directive shall not affect:

(a) the Community provisions governing the substantive law on intellectual property, Directive 95/46/EC, Directive 1999/93/EC or Directive 2000/31/EC, in general, and Articles 12 to 15 of Directive 2000/31/EC in particular;

(b) Member States' international obligations and notably the TRIPS Agreement, including those relating to criminal procedures and penalties;

(c) any national provisions in Member States relating to criminal procedures or penalties in respect of infringement of intellectual property rights.

CHAPTER II

MEASURES, PROCEDURES AND REMEDIES

SECTION 1

GENERAL PROVISIONS

Article 3

General obligation

1. Member States shall provide for the measures, procedures and remedies necessary to ensure the enforcement of the intellectual property rights covered by this Directive. Those measures, procedures and remedies shall be fair and equitable and shall not be unnecessarily complicated or costly, or entail unreasonable time-limits or unwarranted delays.

2. Those measures, procedures and remedies shall also be effective, proportionate and dissuasive and shall be applied in such a manner as to avoid the creation of barriers to legitimate trade and to provide for safeguards against their abuse.

Article 4

Persons entitled to apply for the application of the measures, procedures and remedies

Member States shall recognise as persons entitled to seek application of the measures, procedures and remedies referred to in this chapter:

(a) the holders of intellectual property rights, in accordance with the provisions of the applicable law;

(b) all other persons authorised to use those rights, in particular licensees, in so far as permitted by and in accordance with the provisions of the applicable law;

(c) intellectual property collective rights-management bodies which are regularly recognised as having a right to represent holders of intellectual property rights, in so far as permitted by and in accordance with the provisions of the applicable law;

(d) professional defence bodies which are regularly recognised as having a right to represent holders of intellectual property rights, in so far as permitted by and in accordance with the provisions of the applicable law.

Article 5

Presumption of authorship or ownership

For the purposes of applying the measures, procedures and remedies provided for in this Directive,

(a) for the author of a literary or artistic work, in the absence of proof to the contrary, to be regarded as such, and consequently to be entitled to institute infringement proceedings, it shall be sufficient for his/her name to appear on the work in the usual manner;

(b) the provision under (a) shall apply *mutatis mutandis* to the holders of rights related to copyright with regard to their protected subject matter.

SECTION 2

EVIDENCE

Article 6

Evidence

1. Member States shall ensure that, on application by a party which has presented reasonably available evidence sufficient to support its claims, and has, in substantiating those claims, specified evidence which lies in the control of the opposing party, the competent judicial authorities may order that such evidence be presented by the opposing party, subject to the protection of confidential information. For the purposes of this paragraph, Member States may provide that a reasonable sample of a substantial number of copies of a work or any other protected object be considered by the competent judicial authorities to constitute reasonable evidence.

2. Under the same conditions, in the case of an infringement committed on a commercial scale Member States shall take such measures as are necessary to enable the competent judicial authorities to order, where appropriate, on application by a party, the communication of banking, financial or commercial documents under the control of the opposing party, subject to the protection of confidential information.

Article 7

Measures for preserving evidence

1. Member States shall ensure that, even before the commencement of proceedings on the merits of the case, the competent judicial authorities may, on application by a party who has presented reasonably available evidence to support his/her claims that his/her intellectual property right has been infringed or is about to be infringed, order prompt and effective provisional measures to preserve relevant evidence in respect of the alleged infringement, subject to the protection of confidential information. Such measures may include the detailed description, with or without the taking of samples, or the physical seizure of the infringing goods, and, in appropriate cases, the materials and implements used in the production and/or distribution of these goods and the documents relating thereto. Those measures shall be taken, if necessary without the other party having been heard, in particular where any delay is likely to cause irreparable harm to the rightholder or where there is a demonstrable risk of evidence being destroyed.

Where measures to preserve evidence are adopted without the other party having been heard, the parties affected shall be given notice, without delay after the execution of the measures at the latest. A review, including a right to be heard, shall take place upon request of the parties affected with a view to deciding, within a reasonable period after the notification of the measures, whether the measures shall be modified, revoked or confirmed.

2. Member States shall ensure that the measures to preserve evidence may be subject to the lodging by the applicant of adequate security or an equivalent assurance intended to ensure compensation for any prejudice suffered by the defendant as provided for in paragraph 4.

3. Member States shall ensure that the measures to preserve evidence are revoked or otherwise cease to have effect, upon request of the defendant, without prejudice to the damages which may be claimed, if the applicant does not institute, within a reasonable period, proceedings leading to a decision on the merits of the case before the competent judicial authority, the period to be determined by the judicial authority ordering the measures where the law of a

Member State so permits or, in the absence of such determination, within a period not exceeding 20 working days or 31 calendar days, whichever is the longer.

4. Where the measures to preserve evidence are revoked, or where they lapse due to any act or omission by the applicant, or where it is subsequently found that there has been no infringement or threat of infringement of an intellectual property right, the judicial authorities shall have the authority to order the applicant, upon request of the defendant, to provide the defendant appropriate compensation for any injury caused by those measures.

5. Member States may take measures to protect witnesses' identity.

SECTION 3

RIGHT OF INFORMATION

Article 8

Right of information

1. Member States shall ensure that, in the context of proceedings concerning an infringement of an intellectual property right and in response to a justified and proportionate request of the claimant, the competent judicial authorities may order that information on the origin and distribution networks of the goods or services which infringe an intellectual property right be provided by the infringer and/or any other person who:

(a) was found in possession of the infringing goods on a commercial scale;

(b) was found to be using the infringing services on a commercial scale;

(c) was found to be providing on a commercial scale services used in infringing activities;
    or

(d) was indicated by the person referred to in point (a), (b) or (c) as being involved in the production, manufacture or distribution of the goods or the provision of the services.

2. The information referred to in paragraph 1 shall, as appropriate, comprise:

(a) the names and addresses of the producers, manufacturers, distributors, suppliers and other previous holders of the goods or services, as well as the intended wholesalers and retailers;

(b) information on the quantities produced, manufactured, delivered, received or ordered, as well as the price obtained for the goods or services in question.

3. Paragraphs 1 and 2 shall apply without prejudice to other statutory provisions which:

(a) grant the rightholder rights to receive fuller information;

(b) govern the use in civil or criminal proceedings of the information communicated pursuant to this Article;

(c) govern responsibility for misuse of the right of information;
    or

(d) afford an opportunity for refusing to provide information which would force the person referred to in paragraph 1 to admit to his/her own participation or that of his/her close relatives in an infringement of an intellectual property right;
    or

(e) govern the protection of confidentiality of information sources or the processing of personal data.

SECTION 4

PROVISIONAL AND PRECAUTIONARY MEASURES

Article 9

Provisional and precautionary measures

1. Member States shall ensure that the judicial authorities may, at the request of the applicant:

(a) issue against the alleged infringer an interlocutory injunction intended to prevent any imminent infringement of an intellectual property right, or to forbid, on a provisional basis and subject, where appropriate, to a recurring penalty payment where provided for by national law, the continuation of the alleged infringements of that right, or to make such continuation subject to the lodging of guarantees intended to ensure the compensation of the rightholder; an interlocutory injunction may also be issued, under the same conditions, against an intermediary whose services are being used by a third party to infringe an intellectual property right; injunctions against intermediaries whose services are used by a third party to infringe a copyright or a related right are covered by Directive 2001/29/EC;

(b) order the seizure or delivery up of the goods suspected of infringing an intellectual property right so as to prevent their entry into or movement within the channels of commerce.

2. In the case of an infringement committed on a commercial scale, the Member States shall ensure that, if the injured party demonstrates circumstances likely to endanger the recovery of damages, the judicial authorities may order the precautionary seizure of the movable and immovable property of the alleged infringer, including the blocking of his/her bank accounts and other assets. To that end, the competent authorities may order the communication of bank, financial or commercial documents, or appropriate access to the relevant information.

3. The judicial authorities shall, in respect of the measures referred to in paragraphs 1 and 2, have the authority to require the applicant to provide any reasonably available evidence in order to satisfy themselves with a sufficient degree of certainty that the applicant is the rightholder and that the applicant's right is being infringed, or that such infringement is imminent.

4. Member States shall ensure that the provisional measures referred to in paragraphs 1 and 2 may, in appropriate cases, be taken without the defendant having been heard, in particular where any delay would cause irreparable harm to the rightholder. In that event, the parties shall be so informed without delay after the execution of the measures at the latest.

A review, including a right to be heard, shall take place upon request of the defendant with a view to deciding, within a reasonable time after notification of the measures, whether those measures shall be modified, revoked or confirmed.

5. Member States shall ensure that the provisional measures referred to in paragraphs 1 and 2 are revoked or otherwise cease to have effect, upon request of the defendant, if the applicant does not institute, within a reasonable period, proceedings leading to a decision on the merits of the case before the competent judicial authority, the period to be determined by the judicial authority ordering the measures where the law of a Member State so permits or, in the absence of such determination, within a period not exceeding 20 working days or 31 calendar days, whichever is the longer.

6. The competent judicial authorities may make the provisional measures referred to in paragraphs 1 and 2 subject to the lodging by the applicant of ade-

quate security or an equivalent assurance intended to ensure compensation for any prejudice suffered by the defendant as provided for in paragraph 7.

7. Where the provisional measures are revoked or where they lapse due to any act or omission by the applicant, or where it is subsequently found that there has been no infringement or threat of infringement of an intellectual property right, the judicial authorities shall have the authority to order the applicant, upon request of the defendant, to provide the defendant appropriate compensation for any injury caused by those measures.

SECTION 5

MEASURES RESULTING FROM A DECISION ON THE MERITS OF THE CASE

Article 10

Corrective measures

1. Without prejudice to any damages due to the rightholder by reason of the infringement, and without compensation of any sort, Member States shall ensure that the competent judicial authorities may order, at the request of the applicant, that appropriate measures be taken with regard to goods that they have found to be infringing an intellectual property right and, in appropriate cases, with regard to materials and implements principally used in the creation or manufacture of those goods. Such measures shall include:

(a) recall from the channels of commerce;

(b) definitive removal from the channels of commerce;

  or

(c) destruction.

2. The judicial authorities shall order that those measures be carried out at the expense of the infringer, unless particular reasons are invoked for not doing so.

3. In considering a request for corrective measures, the need for proportionality between the seriousness of the infringement and the remedies ordered as well as the interests of third parties shall be taken into account.

Article 11

Injunctions

Member States shall ensure that, where a judicial decision is taken finding an infringement of an intellectual property right, the judicial authorities may issue against the infringer an injunction aimed at prohibiting the continuation of the infringement. Where provided for by national law, non-compliance with an injunction shall, where appropriate, be subject to a recurring penalty payment, with a view to ensuring compliance. Member States shall also ensure that rightholders are in a position to apply for an injunction against intermediaries whose services are used by a third party to infringe an intellectual property right, without prejudice to Article 8(3) of Directive 2001/29/EC.

Article 12

Alternative measures

Member States may provide that, in appropriate cases and at the request of the person liable to be subject to the measures provided for in this section, the competent judicial authorities may order pecuniary compensation to be paid to the injured party instead of applying the measures provided for in this section if that person acted unintentionally and without negligence, if execution of the measures in question would cause him/her disproportionate harm and if pecuniary compensation to the injured party appears reasonably satisfactory.

Article 13

Damages

1. Member States shall ensure that the competent judicial authorities, on application of the injured party, order the infringer who knowingly, or with reasonable grounds to know, engaged in an infringing activity, to pay the rightholder damages appropriate to the actual prejudice suffered by him/her as a result of the infringement.

When the judicial authorities set the damages:

(a) they shall take into account all appropriate aspects, such as the negative economic consequences, including lost profits, which the injured party has suffered, any unfair profits made by the infringer and, in appropriate cases, elements other than economic factors, such as the moral prejudice caused to the rightholder by the infringement;

   or

(b) as an alternative to (a), they may, in appropriate cases, set the damages as a lump sum on the basis of elements such as at least the amount of royalties or fees which would have been due if the infringer had requested authorisation to use the intellectual property right in question.

2. Where the infringer did not knowingly, or with reasonable grounds know, engage in infringing activity, Member States may lay down that the judicial authorities may order the recovery of profits or the payment of damages, which may be pre-established.

Article 14

Legal costs

Member States shall ensure that reasonable and proportionate legal costs and other expenses incurred by the successful party shall, as a general rule, be borne by the unsuccessful party, unless equity does not allow this.

SECTION 7

PUBLICITY MEASURES

Article 15

Publication of judicial decisions

Member States shall ensure that, in legal proceedings instituted for infringement of an intellectual property right, the judicial authorities may order, at the request of the applicant and at the expense of the infringer, appropriate measures for the dissemination of the information concerning the decision, including displaying the decision and publishing it in full or in part. Member States may provide for other additional publicity measures which are appropriate to the particular circumstances, including prominent advertising.

CHAPTER III

SANCTIONS BY MEMBER STATES

Article 16

Sanctions by Member States

Without prejudice to the civil and administrative measures, procedures and remedies laid down by this Directive, Member States may apply other appropriate sanctions in cases where intellectual property rights have been infringed.

Chapter IV

Codes of Conduct and Administrative Cooperation

Article 17
Codes of conduct

Member States shall encourage:
(a) the development by trade or professional associations or organisations of codes of conduct at Community level aimed at contributing towards the enforcement of the intellectual property rights, particularly by recommending the use on optical discs of a code enabling the identification of the origin of their manufacture;
(b) the submission to the Commission of draft codes of conduct at national and Community level and of any evaluations of the application of these codes of conduct.

Article 18
Assessment

1. Three years after the date laid down in Article 20(1), each Member State shall submit to the Commission a report on the implementation of this Directive. On the basis of those reports, the Commission shall draw up a report on the application of this Directive, including an assessment of the effectiveness of the measures taken, as well as an evaluation of its impact on innovation and the development of the information society. That report shall then be transmitted to the European Parliament, the Council and the European Economic and Social Committee. It shall be accompanied, if necessary and in the light of developments in the Community legal order, by proposals for amendments to this Directive.

2. Member States shall provide the Commission with all the aid and assistance it may need when drawing up the report referred to in the second subparagraph of paragraph 1.

Article 19
Exchange of information and correspondents

For the purpose of promoting cooperation, including the exchange of information, among Member States and between Member States and the Commission, each Member State shall designate one or more national correspondents for any question relating to the implementation of the measures provided for by this Directive. It shall communicate the details of the national correspondent(s) to the other Member States and to the Commission.

Chapter V

Final Provisions

Article 20
Implementation

1. Member States shall bring into force the laws, regulations and administrative provisions necessary to comply with this Directive by 29 April 2006. They

shall forthwith inform the Commission thereof. When Member States adopt these measures, they shall contain a reference to this Directive or shall be accompanied by such reference on the occasion of their official publication. The methods of making such reference shall be laid down by Member States.

2. Member States shall communicate to the Commission the texts of the provisions of national law which they adopt in the field governed by this Directive.

Article 21

Entry into force

This Directive shall enter into force on the 20th day following that of its publication in the *Official Journal of the European Union*.

Article 22

Addressees

This Directive is addressed to the Member States.

Done at Strasbourg, 29 April 2004.

For the European Parliament   *For the Council*
The President   *The President*
P. COX   M. McDOWELL

H12. DIRECTIVE 2006/115/EC

Directive 2006/115/EC of the European Parliament and of the Council of 12 December 2006 on rental right and lending right and on certain rights related to copyright in the field of intellectual property[i]

([2006] O.J. L376/28)

THE EUROPEAN PARLIAMENT AND THE COUNCIL OF THE EUROPEAN UNION,

Having regard to the Treaty establishing the European Community, and in particular Articles 47(2), 55 and 95 thereof,

Having regard to the proposal from the Commission,

Having regard to the opinion of the European Economic and Social Committee,

Acting in accordance with the procedure laid down in Article 251 of the Treaty[1],

(1) Council Directive 92/100/EEC of 19 November 1992 on rental right and lending right and on certain rights related to copyright in the field of intellectual property[2] has been substantially amended several times.[3] In the interests of clarity and rationality the said Directive should be codified.

(2) Rental and lending of copyright works and the subject matter of related rights protection is playing an increasingly important role in particular for authors, performers and producers of phonograms and films. Piracy is becoming an increasing threat.

(3) The adequate protection of copyright works and subject matter of related

---

[i] *Editorial note*: The footnote numbering in the original Directive is reproduced below.

[1] Opinion of the European Parliament delivered on 12 October 2006 (not yet published in the Official Journal).

[2] OJ L 346, 27.11.1992, p. 61. Directive as last amended by Directive 2001/29/EC of the European Parliament and of the Council (OJ L 167, 22.6.2001, p. 10).

[3] See Annex I, Part A.

rights protection by rental and lending rights as well as the protection of the subject matter of related rights protection by the fixation right, distribution right, right to broadcast and communication to the public can accordingly be considered as being of fundamental importance for the economic and cultural development of the Community.

(4) Copyright and related rights protection must adapt to new economic developments such as new forms of exploitation.

(5) The creative and artistic work of authors and performers necessitates an adequate income as a basis for further creative and artistic work, and the investments required particularly for the production of phonograms and films are especially high and risky. The possibility of securing that income and recouping that investment can be effectively guaranteed only through adequate legal protection of the rightholders concerned.

(6) These creative, artistic and entrepreneurial activities are, to a large extent, activities of self-employed persons. The pursuit of such activities should be made easier by providing a harmonised legal protection within the Community. To the extent that these activities principally constitute services, their provision should equally be facilitated by a harmonised legal framework in the Community.

(7) The legislation of the Member States should be approximated in such a way as not to conflict with the international conventions on which the copyright and related rights laws of many Member States are based.

(8) The legal framework of the Community on the rental right and lending right and on certain rights related to copyright can be limited to establishing that Member States provide rights with respect to rental and lending for certain groups of rightholders and further to establishing the rights of fixation, distribution, broadcasting and communication to the public for certain groups of rightholders in the field of related rights protection.

(9) It is necessary to define the concepts of rental and lending for the purposes of this Directive.

(10) It is desirable, with a view to clarity, to exclude from rental and lending within the meaning of this Directive certain forms of making available, as for instance making available phonograms or films for the purpose of public performance or broadcasting, making available for the purpose of exhibition, or making available for on-the-spot reference use. Lending within the meaning of this Directive should not include making available between establishments which are accessible to the public.

(11) Where lending by an establishment accessible to the public gives rise to a payment the amount of which does not go beyond what is necessary to cover the operating costs of the establishment, there is no direct or indirect economic or commercial advantage within the meaning of this Directive.

(12) It is necessary to introduce arrangements ensuring that an unwaivable equitable remuneration is obtained by authors and performers who must remain able to entrust the administration of this right to collecting societies representing them.

(13) The equitable remuneration may be paid on the basis of one or several payments at any time on or after the conclusion of the contract. It should take account of the importance of the contribution of the authors and performers concerned to the phonogram or film.

(14) It is also necessary to protect the rights at least of authors as regards public lending by providing for specific arrangements. However, any measures taken by way of derogation from the exclusive public lending right should comply in particular with Article 12 of the Treaty.

(15) The provisions laid down in this Directive as to rights related to copyright

should not prevent Member States from extending to those exclusive rights the presumption provided for in this Directive with regard to contracts concerning film production concluded individually or collectively by performers with a film producer. Furthermore, those provisions should not prevent Member States from providing for a rebuttable presumption of the authorisation of exploitation in respect of the exclusive rights of performers provided for in the relevant provisions of this Directive, in so far as such presumption is compatible with the International Convention for the Protection of Performers, Producers of Phonograms and Broadcasting Organisations (hereinafter referred to as the Rome Convention).

(16) Member States should be able to provide for more farreaching protection for owners of rights related to copyright than that required by the provisions laid down in this Directive in respect of broadcasting and communication to the public.

(17) The harmonised rental and lending rights and the harmonised protection in the field of rights related to copyright should not be exercised in a way which constitutes a disguised restriction on trade between Member States or in a way which is contrary to the rule of media exploitation chronology, as recognised in the judgment handed down in Société Cinéthèque v. FNCF.[4]

(18) This Directive should be without prejudice to the obligations of the Member States relating to the time-limits for transposition into national law of the Directives as set out in Part B of Annex I,

HAVE ADOPTED THIS DIRECTIVE:

CHAPTER I

RENTAL AND LENDING RIGHT

Article 1

Object of harmonisation

1. In accordance with the provisions of this Chapter, Member States shall provide, subject to Article 6, a right to authorise or prohibit the rental and lending of originals and copies of copyright works, and other subject matter as set out in Article 3(1).

2. The rights referred to in paragraph 1 shall not be exhausted by any sale or other act of distribution of originals and copies of copyright works and other subject matter as set out in Article 3(1).

Article 2

Definitions

1. For the purposes of this Directive the following definitions shall apply:
   (a) 'rental' means making available for use, for a limited period of time and for direct or indirect economic or commercial advantage;
   (b) 'lending' means making available for use, for a limited period of time and not for direct or indirect economic or commercial advantage, when it is made through establishments which are accessible to the public;
   (c) 'film' means a cinematographic or audiovisual work or moving images, whether or not accompanied by sound.

2. The principal director of a cinematographic or audiovisual work shall be considered as its author or one of its authors. Member States may provide for others to be considered as its co-authors.

---

[4] Joined Cases 60/84 and 61/84 [1985] ECR 2 605.

Article 3

Rightholders and subject matter of rental and lending right

1. The exclusive right to authorise or prohibit rental and lending shall belong to the following:

(a) the author in respect of the original and copies of his work;

(b) the performer in respect of fixations of his performance;

(c) the phonogram producer in respect of his phonograms;

(d) the producer of the first fixation of a film in respect of the original and copies of his film.

2. This Directive shall not cover rental and lending rights in relation to buildings and to works of applied art.

3. The rights referred to in paragraph 1 may be transferred, assigned or subject to the granting of contractual licences.

4. Without prejudice to paragraph 6, when a contract concerning film production is concluded, individually or collectively, by performers with a film producer, the performer covered by this contract shall be presumed, subject to contractual clauses to the contrary, to have transferred his rental right, subject to Article 5.

5. Member States may provide for a similar presumption as set out in paragraph 4 with respect to authors.

6. Member States may provide that the signing of a contract concluded between a performer and a film producer concerning the production of a film has the effect of authorising rental, provided that such contract provides for an equitable remuneration within the meaning of Article 5. Member States may also provide that this paragraph shall apply mutatis mutandis to the rights included in Chapter II.

Article 4

Rental of computer programs

This Directive shall be without prejudice to Article 4(c) of Council Directive 91/250/EEC of 14 May 1991 on the legal protection of computer programs.[5]

Article 5

Unwaivable right to equitable remuneration

1. Where an author or performer has transferred or assigned his rental right concerning a phonogram or an original or copy of a film to a phonogram or film producer, that author or performer shall retain the right to obtain an equitable remuneration for the rental.

2. The right to obtain an equitable remuneration for rental cannot be waived by authors or performers.

3. The administration of this right to obtain an equitable remuneration may be entrusted to collecting societies representing authors or performers.

4. Member States may regulate whether and to what extent administration by collecting societies of the right to obtain an equitable remuneration may be imposed, as well as the question from whom this remuneration may be claimed or collected.

---

[5] OJ L 122, 17.5.1991, p. 42. Directive as amended by Directive 93/98/EEC (OJ L 290, 24.11.1993, p. 9).

Article 6
Derogation from the exclusive public lending right

1. Member States may derogate from the exclusive right provided for in Article 1 in respect of public lending, provided that at least authors obtain a remuneration for such lending. Member States shall be free to determine this remuneration taking account of their cultural promotion objectives.

2. Where Member States do not apply the exclusive lending right provided for in Article 1 as regards phonograms, films and computer programs, they shall introduce, at least for authors, a remuneration.

3. Member States may exempt certain categories of establishments from the payment of the remuneration referred to in paragraphs 1 and 2.

CHAPTER II

RIGHTS RELATED TO COPYRIGHT

Article 7
Fixation right

1. Member States shall provide for performers the exclusive right to authorise or prohibit the fixation of their performances.

2. Member States shall provide for broadcasting organisations the exclusive right to authorise or prohibit the fixation of their broadcasts, whether these broadcasts are transmitted by wire or over the air, including by cable or satellite.

3. A cable distributor shall not have the right provided for in paragraph 2 where it merely retransmits by cable the broadcasts of broadcasting organisations.

Article 8
Broadcasting and communication to the public

1. Member States shall provide for performers the exclusive right to authorise or prohibit the broadcasting by wireless means and the communication to the public of their performances, except where the performance is itself already a broadcast performance or is made from a fixation.

2. Member States shall provide a right in order to ensure that a single equitable remuneration is paid by the user, if a phonogram published for commercial purposes, or a reproduction of such phonogram, is used for broadcasting by wireless means or for any communication to the public, and to ensure that this remuneration is shared between the relevant performers and phonogram producers. Member States may, in the absence of agreement between the performers and phonogram producers, lay down the conditions as to the sharing of this remuneration between them.

3. Member States shall provide for broadcasting organisations the exclusive right to authorise or prohibit the rebroadcasting of their broadcasts by wireless means, as well as the communication to the public of their broadcasts if such communication is made in places accessible to the public against payment of an entrance fee.

Article 9
Distribution right

1. Member States shall provide the exclusive right to make available to the public, by sale or otherwise, the objects indicated in points (a) to (d), including copies thereof, hereinafter 'the distribution right':

(a) for performers, in respect of fixations of their performances;

(b) for phonogram producers, in respect of their phonograms;

(c) for producers of the first fixations of films, in respect of the original and copies of their films;

(d) for broadcasting organisations, in respect of fixations of their broadcasts as set out in Article 7(2).

2. The distribution right shall not be exhausted within the Community in respect of an object as referred to in paragraph 1, except where the first sale in the Community of that object is made by the rightholder or with his consent.

3. The distribution right shall be without prejudice to the specific provisions of Chapter I, in particular Article 1(2).

4. The distribution right may be transferred, assigned or subject to the granting of contractual licences.

Article 10

Limitations to rights

1. Member States may provide for limitations to the rights referred to in this Chapter in respect of:

(a) private use;

(b) use of short excerpts in connection with the reporting of current events;

(c) ephemeral fixation by a broadcasting organisation by means of its own facilities and for its own broadcasts;

(d) use solely for the purposes of teaching or scientific research.

2. Irrespective of paragraph 1, any Member State may provide for the same kinds of limitations with regard to the protection of performers, producers of phonograms, broadcasting organisations and of producers of the first fixations of films, as it provides for in connection with the protection of copyright in literary and artistic works.

However, compulsory licences may be provided for only to the extent to which they are compatible with the Rome Convention.

3. The limitations referred to in paragraphs 1 and 2 shall be applied only in certain special cases which do not conflict with a normal exploitation of the subject matter and do not unreasonably prejudice the legitimate interests of the rightholder.

CHAPTER III

COMMON PROVISIONS

Article 11

Application in time

1. This Directive shall apply in respect of all copyright works, performances, phonograms, broadcasts and first fixations of films referred to in this Directive which were, on 1 July 1994, still protected by the legislation of the Member States in the field of copyright and related rights or which met the criteria for protection under this Directive on that date.

2. This Directive shall apply without prejudice to any acts of exploitation performed before 1 July 1994.

3. Member States may provide that the rightholders are deemed to have given their authorisation to the rental or lending of an object referred to in points (a) to (d) of Article 3(1) which is proven to have been made available to third parties for this purpose or to have been acquired before 1 July 1994.

However, in particular where such an object is a digital recording, Member States may provide that rightholders shall have a right to obtain an adequate remuneration for the rental or lending of that object.

4. Member States need not apply the provisions of Article 2(2) to cinematographic or audiovisual works created before 1 July 1994.

5. This Directive shall, without prejudice to paragraph 3 and subject to paragraph 7, not affect any contracts concluded before 19 November 1992.

6. Member States may provide, subject to the provisions of paragraph 7, that when rightholders who acquire new rights under the national provisions adopted in implementation of this Directive have, before 1 July 1994, given their consent for exploitation, they shall be presumed to have transferred the new exclusive rights.

7. For contracts concluded before 1 July 1994, the unwaivable right to an equitable remuneration provided for in Article 5 shall apply only where authors or performers or those representing them have submitted a request to that effect before 1 January 1997. In the absence of agreement between rightholders concerning the level of remuneration, Member States may fix the level of equitable remuneration.

Article 12

Relation between copyright and related rights

Protection of copyright-related rights under this Directive shall leave intact and shall in no way affect the protection of copyright.

Article 13

Communication

Member States shall communicate to the Commission the main provisions of national law adopted in the field covered by this Directive.

Article 14

Repeal

Directive 92/100/EEC is hereby repealed, without prejudice to the obligations of the Member States relating to the time-limits for transposition into national law of the Directives as set out in Part B of Annex I.

References made to the repealed Directive shall be construed as being made to this Directive and should be read in accordance with the correlation table in Annex II.

Article 15

Entry into force

This Directive shall enter into force on the twentieth day following that of its publication in the Official Journal of the European Union.

Article 16

Addressees

This Directive is addressed to the Member States.

Done at Strasbourg, 12 December 2006.

<table>
<tr><td>For the European Parliament</td><td>For the Council</td></tr>
<tr><td>The President</td><td>The President</td></tr>
</table>

J. BORRELL FONTELLES   M. PEKKARINEN

ANNEX I

PART A

REPEALED DIRECTIVE WITH ITS SUCCESSIVE AMENDMENTS

Council Directive 92/100/EEC
(OJ L 346, 27.11.1992, p. 61)
Council Directive 93/98/EEC   Article 11(2) only
(OJ L 290, 24.11.1993, p.9)
Directive 2001/29/EC of the European Parliament   Article 11(1) only
and of the Council
(O) L 167, 22.6.2001, p.10)

PART B

LIST OF TIME-LIMITS FOR TRANSPOSITION INTO NATIONAL LAW

(referred to in Article 14)

Directive	Time-limit for transposition
92/100/EEC	1 July 1994
93/98/EEC	30 June 1995
2001/29/EC	21 December 2002

ANNEX II

CORRELATION TABLE

Directive 92/100/EEC	This Directive
Article 1(1)	Article 1(1)
Article 1(2)	Article 2(1), introductory words and point (a)
Article 1(3)	Article 2(1), point (b)
Article 1(4)	Article 1(2)
Article 2(1), introductory words	Article 3(1), introductory words
Article 2(1), first indent	Article 3(1)(a)
Article 2(1), second indent	Article 3(1)(b)
Article 2(1), third indent	Article 3(1)(c)
Article 2(1), fourth indent, first sentence	Article 3(1)(d)
Article 2(1), fourth indent, second sentence	Article 2(1), point (c)
Article 2(2)	Article 2(2)
Article 2(3)	Article 3(2)
Article 2(4)	Article 3(3)
Article 2(5)	Article 3(4)
Article 2(6)	Article 3(5)
Article 2(7)	Article 3(6)
Article 3	Article 4

H EU DIRECTIVES

Directive 92/100/EEC	This Directive
Article 4	Article 5
Article 5(1) to (3)	Article 6(1) to (3)
Article 5(4)	—
Article 6	Article 7
Article 8	Article 8
Article 9(1), introductory words and final words	Article 9(1), introductory words
Article 9(1), first indent	Article 9(1)(a)
Article 9(1), first indent	Article 9(1)(a)
Article 9(1), second indent	Article 9(1)(b)
Article 9(1), third indent	Article 9(1)(c)
Article 9(1), fourth indent	Article 9(1)(d)
Article 9(2), (3) and (4)	Article 9(2), (3) and (4)
Article 10(1)	Article 10(1)
Article 10(2), first sentence	Article 10(2), first subparagraph
Article 10(2), second sentence	Article 10(2), second subparagraph
Article 10(3)	Article 10(3)
Article 13(1), and (2)	Article 11(1), and (2)
Article 13(3), first sentence	Article 11(3), first subparagraph
Article 13(3), second sentence	Article 11(3), second subparagraph
Article 13(4)	Article 11(4)
Article 13(5)	—
Article 13(6)	Article 11(5)
Article 13(7)	Article 11(6)
Article 13(8)	—
Article 13(9)	Article 11(7)
Article 14	Article 12
Article 15(1)	—
Article 15(2)	Article 13
—	Article 14
—	Article 15
Article 16	Article 16
—	Annex I
—	Annex II

H13. DIRECTIVE 2006/116/EC

Directive 2006/116/EC of the European Parliament and of the Council of 12 December 2006 on the term of protection of copyright and certain related rights[i]

([2006] O.J. L372/12)[ii]

---

[i] *Editorial Note*: The footnote numbering in the original Directive is reproduced below. This Directive was amended by Directive 2011/77/EU with effect from October 31, 2011 (see OJ L.265, 11.10.2011, p.1 and Directive 2011/77/EU, Article 4).This Directive was amended by The text below is the consolidated version including the amendments in Directive 2011/77/EU: :see

THE EUROPEAN PARLIAMENT AND THE COUNCIL OF THE EUROPEAN UNION,

Having regard to the Treaty establishing the European Community, and in particular Articles 47(2), 55 and 95 thereof,

Having regard to the proposal from the Commission,

Having regard to the opinion of the European Economic and Social Committee[1],

Acting in accordance with the procedure laid down in Article 251 of the Treaty[2],

Whereas:

(1) Council Directive 93/98/EEC of 29 October 1993 harmonising the term of protection of copyright and certain related rights[3] has been substantially amended.[4] In the interests of clarity and rationality the said Directive should be codified.

(2) The Berne Convention for the protection of literary and artistic works and the International Convention for the protection of performers, producers of phonograms and broadcasting organisations (Rome Convention) lay down only minimum terms of protection of the rights they refer to, leaving the Contracting States free to grant longer terms. Certain Member States have exercised this entitlement. In addition, some Member States have not yet become party to the Rome Convention.

(3) There are consequently differences between the national laws governing the terms of protection of copyright and related rights, which are liable to impede the free movement of goods and freedom to provide services and to distort competition in the common market. Therefore, with a view to the smooth operation of the internal market, the laws of the Member States should be harmonised so as to make terms of protection identical throughout the Community.

(4) It is important to lay down not only the terms of protection as such, but also certain implementing arrangements, such as the date from which each term of protection is calculated.

(5) The provisions of this Directive should not affect the application by the Member States of the provisions of Article 14 bis (2)(b), (c) and (d) and (3) of the Berne Convention.

(6) The minimum term of protection laid down by the Berne Convention, namely the life of the author and 50 years after his death, was intended to provide protection for the author and the first two generations of his descendants. The average lifespan in the Community has grown longer, to the point where this term is no longer sufficient to cover two generations.

(7) Certain Member States have granted a term longer than 50 years after the death of the author in order to offset the effects of the world wars on the exploitation of authors' works.

(8) For the protection of related rights certain Member States have introduced a term of 50 years after lawful publication or lawful communication to the public.

(9) The Diplomatic Conference held in December 1996, under the auspices of

http://eur-lex.europa.eu/legal-content/EN/TXT/
?qid=1438272591949&uri=CELEX:02006L0116-20111031.

[ii] *Editorial Note*: [Accessed July 28, 2015]. It was published in OJ L 372, 27.12.2006, p.12 with the following disclaimer "This document is meant purely as a documentation tool and the institutions do not assume any liability for its contents"

[1] Opinion of 26 October 2006 (not yet published in the Official Journal).

[2] Opinion of the European Parliament of 12 October 2006 (not yet published in the Official Journal) and Council Decision of 30 November 2006.

[3] OJ L 290, 24.11.1993, p. 9. Directive as amended by Directive 2001/ 29/EC of the European Parliament and of the Council (OJ L 167, 22.6.2001, p. 10).

[4] See Annex I, Part A.

the World Intellectual Property Organization (WIPO), led to the adoption of the WIPO Performances and Phonograms Treaty, which deals with the protection of performers and producers of phonograms. This Treaty took the form of a substantial up-date of the international protection of related rights.

(10) Due regard for established rights is one of the general principles of law protected by the Community legal order. Therefore, the terms of protection of copyright and related rights established by Community law cannot have the effect of reducing the protection enjoyed by rightholders in the Community before the entry into force of Directive 93/98/ EEC. In order to keep the effects of transitional measures to a minimum and to allow the internal market to function smoothly, those terms of protection should be applied for long periods.

(11) The level of protection of copyright and related rights should be high, since those rights are fundamental to intellectual creation. Their protection ensures the maintenance and development of creativity in the interest of authors, cultural industries, consumers and society as a whole.

(12) In order to establish a high level of protection which at the same time meets the requirements of the internal market and the need to establish a legal environment conducive to the harmonious development of literary and artistic creation in the Community, the term of protection for copyright should be harmonised at 70 years after the death of the author or 70 years after the work is lawfully made available to the public, and for related rights at 50 years after the event which sets the term running.

(13) Collections are protected according to Article 2(5) of the Berne Convention when, by reason of the selection and arrangement of their content, they constitute intellectual creations. Those works are protected as such, without prejudice to the copyright in each of the works forming part of such collections. Consequently, specific terms of protection may apply to works included in collections.

(14) In all cases where one or more physical persons are identified as authors, the term of protection should be calculated after their death. The question of authorship of the whole or a part of a work is a question of fact which the national courts may have to decide.

(15) Terms of protection should be calculated from the first day of January of the year following the relevant event, as they are in the Berne and Rome Conventions.

(16) The protection of photographs in the Member States is the subject of varying regimes. A photographic work within the meaning of the Berne Convention is to be considered original if it is the author's own intellectual creation reflecting his personality, no other criteria such as merit or purpose being taken into account. The protection of other photographs should be left to national law.

(17) In order to avoid differences in the term of protection as regards related rights it is necessary to provide the same starting point for the calculation of the term throughout the Community. The performance, fixation, transmission, lawful publication, and lawful communication to the public, that is to say the means of making a subject of a related right perceptible in all appropriate ways to persons in general, should be taken into account for the calculation of the term of protection regardless of the country where this performance, fixation, transmission, lawful publication, or lawful communication to the public takes place.

(18) The rights of broadcasting organisations in their broadcasts, whether these broadcasts are transmitted by wire or over the air, including by cable or satellite, should not be perpetual. It is therefore necessary to have the term of protection running from the first transmission of a particular broadcast only. This provision is understood to avoid a new term running in cases where a broadcast is identical to a previous one.

(19) The Member States should remain free to maintain or introduce other rights related to copyright in particular in relation to the protection of critical and scientific publications. In order to ensure transparency at Community level, it is however necessary for Member States which introduce new related rights to notify the Commission.

(20) It should be made clear that this Directive does not apply to moral rights.

(21) For works whose country of origin within the meaning of the Berne Convention is a third country and whose author is not a Community national, comparison of terms of protection should be applied, provided that the term accorded in the Community does not exceed the term laid down in this Directive.

(22) Where a rightholder who is not a Community national qualifies for protection under an international agreement, the term of protection of related rights should be the same as that laid down in this Directive. However, this term should not exceed that fixed in the third country of which the rightholder is a national.

(23) Comparison of terms should not result in Member States being brought into conflict with their international obligations.

(24) Member States should remain free to adopt provisions on the interpretation, adaptation and further execution of contracts on the exploitation of protected works and other subject matter which were concluded before the extension of the term of protection resulting from this Directive.

(25) Respect of acquired rights and legitimate expectations is part of the Community legal order. Member States may provide in particular that in certain circumstances the copyright and related rights which are revived pursuant to this Directive may not give rise to payments by persons who undertook in good faith the exploitation of the works at the time when such works lay within the public domain.

(26) This Directive should be without prejudice to the obligations of the Member States relating to the time-limits for transposition into national law and application of the Directives, as set out in Part B of Annex I,

HAVE ADOPTED THIS DIRECTIVE:

Article 1

Duration of authors' rights

1. The rights of an author of a literary or artistic work within the meaning of Article 2 of the Berne Convention shall run for the life of the author and for 70 years after his death, irrespective of the date when the work is lawfully made available to the public.

2. In the case of a work of joint authorship, the term referred to in paragraph 1 shall be calculated from the death of the last surviving author.

3. In the case of anonymous or pseudonymous works, the term of protection shall run for 70 years after the work is lawfully made available to the public. However, when the pseudonym adopted by the author leaves no doubt as to his identity, or if the author discloses his identity during the period referred to in the first sentence, the term of protection applicable shall be that laid down in paragraph 1.

4. Where a Member State provides for particular provisions on copyright in respect of collective works or for a legal person to be designated as the rightholder, the term of protection shall be calculated according to the provisions of paragraph 3, except if the natural persons who have created the work are identified as such in the versions of the work which are made available to the public. This paragraph is without prejudice to the rights of identified authors whose identifiable contributions are included in such works, to which contributions paragraph 1 or 2 shall apply.

5. Where a work is published in volumes, parts, instalments, issues or episodes and the term of protection runs from the time when the work was lawfully made available to the public, the term of protection shall run for each such item separately.

6. In the case of works for which the term of protection is not calculated from the death of the author or authors and which have not been lawfully made available to the public within 70 years from their creation, the protection shall terminate.

7. The term of protection of a musical composition with words shall expire 70 years after the death of the last of the following persons to survive, whether or not those persons are designated as co-authors: the author of the lyrics and the composer of the musical composition, provided that both contributions were specifically created for the respective musical composition with words.

Article 2

Cinematographic or audiovisual works

1. The principal director of a cinematographic or audiovisual work shall be considered as its author or one of its authors. Member States shall be free to designate other co-authors.

2. The term of protection of cinematographic or audiovisual works shall expire 70 years after the death of the last of the following persons to survive, whether or not these persons are designated as co-authors: the principal director, the author of the screenplay, the author of the dialogue and the composer of music specifically created for use in the cinematographic or audiovisual work.

Article 3

Duration of related rights

1. The rights of performers shall expire 50 years after the date of the performance. However, if a fixation of the performance is lawfully published or lawfully communicated to the public within this period, the rights shall expire 50 years from the date of the first such publication or the first such communication to the public, whichever is the earlier.

However,

— if a fixation of the performance otherwise than in a phonogram is lawfully published or lawfully communicated to the public within this period, the rights shall expire 50 years from the date of the first such publication or the first such communication to the public, whichever is the earlier,

— if a fixation of the performance in a phonogram is lawfully published or lawfully communicated to the public within this period, the rights shall expire 70 years from the date of the first such publication or the first such communication to the public, whichever is the earlier.

2. The rights of producers of phonograms shall expire 50 years after the fixation is made. However, if the phonogram has been lawfully published within this period, the said rights shall expire 70 years from the date of the first lawful publication. If no lawful publication has taken place within the period mentioned in the first sentence, and if the phonogram has been lawfully communicated to the public within this period, the said rights shall expire 70 years from the date of the first lawful communication to the public.

However, this paragraph shall not have the effect of protecting anew the rights of producers of phonograms where, through the expiry of the term of protection granted them pursuant to Article 3(2) of Directive 93/98/EEC in its version before amendment by Directive 2001/29/EEC, they were no longer protected on 22 December 2002.

2a. If, 50 years after the phonogram was lawfully published or, failing such publication, 50 years after it was lawfully communicated to the public, the phonogram producer does not offer copies of the phonogram for sale in sufficient quantity or does not make it available to the public, by wire or wireless means, in such a way that members of the public may access it from a place and at a time individually chosen by them, the performer may terminate the contract by which the performer has transferred or assigned his rights in the fixation of his performance to a phonogram producer (hereinafter a 'contract on transfer or assignment'). The right to terminate the contract on transfer or assignment may be exercised if the producer, within a year from the notification by the performer of his intention to terminate the contract on transfer or assignment pursuant to the previous sentence, fails to carry out both of the acts of exploitation referred to in that sentence. This right to terminate may not be waived by the performer. Where a phonogram contains the fixation of the performances of a plurality of performers, they may terminate their contracts on transfer or assignment in accordance with applicable national law. If the contract on transfer or assignment is terminated pursuant to this paragraph, the rights of the phonogram producer in the phonogram shall expire.

2b. Where a contract on transfer or assignment gives the performer a right to claim a non-recurring remuneration, the performer shall have the right to obtain an annual supplementary remuneration from the phonogram producer for each full year immediately following the 50th year after the phonogram was lawfully published or, failing such publication, the 50th year after it was lawfully communicated to the public. The right to obtain such annual supplementary remuneration may not be waived by the performer.

2c. The overall amount to be set aside by a phonogram producer for payment of the annual supplementary remuneration referred to in paragraph 2b shall correspond to 20% of the revenue which the phonogram producer has derived, during the year preceding that for which the said remuneration is paid, from the reproduction, distribution and making available of the phonogram in question, following the 50th year after it was lawfully published or, failing such publication, the 50th year after it was lawfully communicated to the public.

Member States shall ensure that phonogram producers are required on request to provide to performers who are entitled to the annual supplementary remuneration referred to in paragraph 2b any information which may be necessary in order to secure payment of that remuneration.

2d. Member States shall ensure that the right to obtain an annual supplementary remuneration as referred to in paragraph 2b is administered by collecting societies.

2e. Where a performer is entitled to recurring payments, neither advance payments nor any contractually defined deductions shall be deducted from the payments made to the performer following the 50th year after the phonogram was lawfully published or, failing such publication, the 50th year after it was lawfully communicated to the public.

3. The rights of producers of the first fixation of a film shall expire 50 years after the fixation is made. However, if the film is lawfully published or lawfully communicated to the public during this period, the rights shall expire 50 years from the date of the first such publication or the first such communication to the public, whichever is the earlier. The term 'film' shall designate a cinematographic or audiovisual work or moving images, whether or not accompanied by sound.

4. The rights of broadcasting organisations shall expire 50 years after the first transmission of a broadcast, whether this broadcast is transmitted by wire or over the air, including by cable or satellite.

H EU DIRECTIVES

Article 4

Protection of previously unpublished works

Any person who, after the expiry of copyright protection, for the first time lawfully publishes or lawfully communicates to the public a previously unpublished work, shall benefit from a protection equivalent to the economic rights of the author. The term of protection of such rights shall be 25 years from the time when the work was first lawfully published or lawfully communicated to the public.

Article 5

Critical and scientific publications

Member States may protect critical and scientific publications of works which have come into the public domain. The maximum term of protection of such rights shall be 30 years from the time when the publication was first lawfully published.

Article 6

Protection of photographs

Photographs which are original in the sense that they are the author's own intellectual creation shall be protected in accordance with Article 1. No other criteria shall be applied to determine their eligibility for protection. Member States may provide for the protection of other photographs.

Article 7

Protection vis-à-vis third countries

1. Where the country of origin of a work, within the meaning of the Berne Convention, is a third country, and the author of the work is not a Community national, the term of protection granted by the Member States shall expire on the date of expiry of the protection granted in the country of origin of the work, but may not exceed the term laid down in Article 1.

2. The terms of protection laid down in Article 3 shall also apply in the case of rightholders who are not Community nationals, provided Member States grant them protection. However, without prejudice to the international obligations of the Member States, the term of protection granted by Member States shall expire no later than the date of expiry of the protection granted in the country of which the rightholder is a national and may not exceed the term laid down in Article 3.

3. Member States which, on 29 October 1993, in particular pursuant to their international obligations, granted a longer term of protection than that which would result from the provisions of paragraphs 1 and 2 may maintain this protection until the conclusion of international agreements on the term of protection of copyright or related rights.

Article 8

Calculation of terms

The terms laid down in this Directive shall be calculated from the first day of January of the year following the event which gives rise to them.

Article 9

Distribution right

Moral rights This Directive shall be without prejudice to the provisions of the Member States regulating moral rights.

Article 10

Application in time

1. Where a term of protection which is longer than the corresponding term provided for by this Directive was already running in a Member State on 1 July 1995, this Directive shall not have the effect of shortening that term of protection in that Member State.

2. The terms of protection provided for in this Directive shall apply to all works and subject matter which were protected in at least one Member State on the date referred to in paragraph 1, pursuant to national provisions on copyright or related rights, or which meet the criteria for protection under [Council Directive 92/100/EEC of 19 November 1992 on rental right and lending right and on certain rights related to copyright in the field of intellectual property][5].

3. This Directive shall be without prejudice to any acts of exploitation performed before the date referred to in paragraph 1. Member States shall adopt the necessary provisions to protect in particular acquired rights of third parties.

4. Member States need not apply the provisions of Article 2(1) to cinematographic or audiovisual works created before 1 July 1994.

5. Article 3(1) to (2e) in the version thereof in force on 31 October 2011 shall apply to fixations of performances and phonograms in regard to which the performer and the phonogram producer are still protected, by virtue of those provisions in the version thereof in force on 30 October 2011, as at 1 November 2013 and to fixations of performances and phonograms which come into being after that date.

6. Article 1(7) shall apply to musical compositions with words of which at least the musical composition or the lyrics are protected in at least one Member State on 1 November 2013, and to musical compositions with words which come into being after that date. The first subparagraph of this paragraph shall be without prejudice to any acts of exploitation performed before 1 November 2013. Member States shall adopt the necessary provisions to protect, in particular, acquired rights of third parties.

Article 10a

Transitional measures

1. In the absence of clear contractual indications to the contrary, a contract on transfer or assignment concluded before 1 November 2013 shall be deemed to continue to produce its effects beyond the moment at which, by virtue of Article 3(1) in the version thereof in force on 30 October 2011, the performer would no longer be protected.

2. Member States may provide that contracts on transfer or assignment which entitle a performer to recurring payments and which are concluded before 1 November 2013 can be modified following the 50th year after the phonogram was lawfully published or, failing such publication, the 50th year after it was lawfully communicated to the public.

Article 11

Notification and communication

1. Member States shall immediately notify the Commission of any governmental plan to grant new related rights, including the basic reasons for their introduction and the term of protection envisaged.

---

[5] OJ L 346, 27.11.1992, p. 61. Directive as last amended by Directive 2001/29/EC.

2. Member States shall communicate to the Commission the texts of the provisions of internal law which they adopt in the field governed by this Directive.

Article 12

Repeal

Directive 93/98/EEC is hereby repealed, without prejudice to the obligations of the Member States relating to the time-limits for transposition into national law, as set out in Part B of Annex I, of the Directives, and their application.

References made to the repealed Directive shall be construed as being made to this Directive and should be read in accordance with the correlation table in Annex II.

Article 13

Entry into force

This Directive shall enter into force on the twentieth day following that of its publication in the *Official Journal of the European Union*.

Article 14

Addressees

This Directive is addressed to the Member States.
Done at Strasbourg, 12 December 2006.

For the European Parliament	*For the Council*
The President	*The President*
J. BORRELL FONTELLES	M. PEKKARINEN

ANNEX I

PART A

REPEALED DIRECTIVE WITH ITS AMENDMENT

Council Directive 93/98/EEC
(OJ L 290, 24.11.1993, p. 9)

Article 11(2) only

Directive 2001/29/EC of the European Parliament
and of the Council (OJ L 167, 22.6.2001, p. 10)

PART B

LIST OF TIME-LIMITS FOR TRANSPOSITION INTO NATIONAL LAW AND APPLICATION

(referred to in Article 12)

Directive	Time-limit for transposition	Date of application
93/98/EEC	1 July 1995 (Articles 1 to 11)	19 November 1993 (Article 12) 1 July 1997 at the latest as regards Article 2(1) (Article 10(5))
2001/29/EC	22 December 2002	

ANNEX II

CORRELATION TABLE

Directive 92/100/EEC	This Directive
Articles 1 to 9	Articles 1 to 9
Article 10(1) to (4)	Article 10(1) to (4)
Article 10(5)	—
Article 11	—
Article 12	Article 11(1)
Article 13(1), first subparagraph	—
Article 13(1), second subparagraph	—
Article 13(1), third subparagraph	Article 11(2)
Article 13(2)	—
—	Article 12
—	Article 13
Article 14	Article 14
—	Annex I
—	Annex II

H14. DIRECTIVE 2009/24/EC

Directive 2009/24/EC of the European Parliament and of the Council of 23 April 2009 on the legal protection of computer programs[i]

([2009] OJ L111/16)

THE EUROPEAN PARLIAMENT AND THE COUNCIL OF THE EUROPEAN UNION,

Having regard to the Treaty establishing the European Community and in particular Article 95 thereof,

Having regard to the proposal from the Commission,

Having regard to the opinion of the European Economic and Social Committee[1],

Acting in accordance with the procedure laid down in Article 251 of the Treaty[2],

Whereas:

(1) The content of Council Directive 91/250/EEC of 14 May 1991 on the legal protection of computer programs[3] has been amended[4]. In the interests of clarity and rationality the said Directive should be codified.

(2) The development of computer programs requires the investment of

---

[i] *Editorial note*: The footnote numbering in the original Directive is reproduced below.
[1] OJ C 204, 9.8.2008, p. 24.
[2] Opinion of the European Parliament of 17 June 2008 (not yet published in the Official Journal) and Council Decision of 23 March 2009.
[3] OJ L 122, 17.5.1991, p. 42.
[4] See Annex I, Part A.

considerable human, technical and financial resources while computer programs can be copied at a fraction of the cost needed to develop them independently.

(3) Computer programs are playing an increasingly important role in a broad range of industries and computer program technology can accordingly be considered as being of fundamental importance for the Community's industrial development.

Certain differences in the legal protection of computer programs offered by the laws of the Member States have direct and negative effects on the functioning of the internal market as regards computer programs.

(5) Existing differences having such effects need to be removed and new ones prevented from arising, while differences not adversely affecting the functioning of the internal market to a substantial degree need not be removed or prevented from arising.

(6) The Community's legal framework on the protection of computer programs can accordingly in the first instance be limited to establishing that Member States should accord protection to computer programs under copyright law as literary works and, further, to establishing who and what should be protected, the exclusive rights on which protected persons should be able to rely in order to authorise or prohibit certain acts and for how long the protection should apply.

(7) For the purpose of this Directive, the term 'computer program' shall include programs in any form, including those which are incorporated into hardware. This term also includes preparatory design work leading to the development of a computer program provided that the nature of the preparatory work is such that a computer program can result from it at a later stage.

(8) In respect of the criteria to be applied in determining whether or not a computer program is an original work, no tests as to the qualitative or aesthetic merits of the program should be applied.

(9) The Community is fully committed to the promotion of international standardisation.

(10) The function of a computer program is to communicate and work together with other components of a computer system and with users and, for this purpose, a logical and, where appropriate, physical interconnection and interaction is required to permit all elements of software and hardware to work with other software and hardware and with users in all the ways in which they are intended to function. The parts of the program which provide for such interconnection and interaction between elements of software and hardware are generally known as 'interfaces'. This functional interconnection and interaction is generally known as 'interoperability'; such interoperability can be defined as the ability to exchange information and mutually to use the information which has been exchanged.

(11) For the avoidance of doubt, it has to be made clear that only the expression of a computer program is protected and that ideas and principles which underlie any element of a program, including those which underlie its interfaces, are not protected by copyright under this Directive. In accordance with this principle of copyright, to the extent that logic, algorithms and programming languages comprise ideas and principles, those ideas and principles are not protected under this Directive. In accordance with the legislation and case-law of the Member States and the international copyright conventions, the expression of those ideas and principles is to be protected by copyright.

(12) For the purposes of this Directive, the term 'rental' means the making available for use, for a limited period of time and for profit-making purposes, of a computer program or a copy thereof. This term does not include public lending, which, accordingly, remains outside the scope of this Directive.

(13) The exclusive rights of the author to prevent the unauthorised reproduc-

tion of his work should be subject to a limited exception in the case of a computer program to allow the reproduction technically necessary for the use of that program by the lawful acquirer. This means that the acts of loading and running necessary for the use of a copy of a program which has been lawfully acquired, and the act of correction of its errors, may not be prohibited by contract. In the absence of specific contractual provisions, including when a copy of the program has been sold, any other act necessary for the use of the copy of a program may be performed in accordance with its intended purpose by a lawful acquirer of that copy.

(14) A person having a right to use a computer program should not be prevented from performing acts necessary to observe, study or test the functioning of the program, provided that those acts do not infringe the copyright in the program.

(15) The unauthorised reproduction, translation, adaptation or transformation of the form of the code in which a copy of a computer program has been made available constitutes an infringement of the exclusive rights of the author. Nevertheless, circumstances may exist when such a reproduction of the code and translation of its form are indispensable to obtain the necessary information to achieve the interoperability of an independently created program with other programs. It has therefore to be considered that, in these limited circumstances only, performance of the acts of reproduction and translation by or on behalf of a person having a right to use a copy of the program is legitimate and compatible with fair practice and must therefore be deemed not to require the authorisation of the rightholder. An objective of this exception is to make it possible to connect all components of a computer system, including those of different manufacturers, so that they can work together. Such an exception to the author's exclusive rights may not be used in a way which prejudices the legitimate interests of the rightholder or which conflicts with a normal exploitation of the program.

(16) Protection of computer programs under copyright laws should be without prejudice to the application, in appropriate cases, of other forms of protection. However, any contractual provisions contrary to the provisions of this Directive laid down in respect of decompilation or to the exceptions provided for by this Directive with regard to the making of a back-up copy or to observation, study or testing of the functioning of a program should be null and void.

(17) The provisions of this Directive are without prejudice to the application of the competition rules under Articles 81 and 82 of the Treaty if a dominant supplier refuses to make information available which is necessary for interoperability as defined in this Directive.

(18) The provisions of this Directive should be without prejudice to specific requirements of Community law already enacted in respect of the publication of interfaces in the telecommunications sector or Council Decisions relating to standardisation in the field of information technology and telecommunication.

(19) This Directive does not affect derogations provided for under national legislation in accordance with the Berne Convention on points not covered by this Directive.

(20) This Directive should be without prejudice to the obligations of the Member States relating to the time-limits for transposition into national law of the Directives set out in Annex I, Part B,

HAVE ADOPTED THIS DIRECTIVE:

Article 1

Object of protection

(1) In accordance with the provisions of this Directive, Member States shall

protect computer programs, by copyright, as literary works within the meaning of the Berne Convention for the Protection of Literary and Artistic Works. For the purposes of this Directive, the term 'computer programs' shall include their preparatory design material.

(2) Protection in accordance with this Directive shall apply to the expression in any form of a computer program. Ideas and principles which underlie any element of a computer program, including those which underlie its interfaces, are not protected by copyright under this Directive.

(3) A computer program shall be protected if it is original in the sense that it is the author's own intellectual creation. No other criteria shall be applied to determine its eligibility for protection.

(4) The provisions of this Directive shall apply also to programs created before 1 January 1993, without prejudice to any acts concluded and rights acquired before that date.

Article 2

Authorship of computer programs

(1) The author of a computer program shall be the natural person or group of natural persons who has created the program or, where the legislation of the Member State permits, the legal person designated as the rightholder by that legislation.

Where collective works are recognised by the legislation of a Member State, the person considered by the legislation of the Member State to have created the work shall be deemed to be its author.

(2) In respect of a computer program created by a group of natural persons jointly, the exclusive rights shall be owned jointly.

(3) Where a computer program is created by an employee in the execution of his duties or following the instructions given by his employer, the employer exclusively shall be entitled to exercise all economic rights in the program so created, unless otherwise provided by contract.

Article 3

Beneficiaries of protection

Protection shall be granted to all natural or legal persons eligible under national copyright legislation as applied to literary works.

Article 4

Restricted acts

(1) Subject to the provisions of Articles 5 and 6, the exclusive rights of the rightholder within the meaning of Article 2 shall include the right to do or to authorise:

(a) the permanent or temporary reproduction of a computer program by any means and in any form, in part or in whole; in so far as loading, displaying, running, transmission or storage of the computer program necessitate such reproduction, such acts shall be subject to authorisation by the rightholder;

(b) the translation, adaptation, arrangement and any other alteration of a computer program and the reproduction of the results thereof, without prejudice to the rights of the person who alters the program;

(c) any form of distribution to the public, including the rental, of the original computer program or of copies thereof.

(2) The first sale in the Community of a copy of a program by the rightholder

or with his consent shall exhaust the distribution right within the Community of that copy, with the exception of the right to control further rental of the program or a copy thereof.

Article 5
Exceptions to the restricted acts

(1) In the absence of specific contractual provisions, the acts referred to in points (a) and (b) of Article 4(1) shall not require authorisation by the rightholder where they are necessary for the use of the computer program by the lawful acquirer in accordance with its intended purpose, including for error correction.

(2) The making of a back-up copy by a person having a right to use the computer program may not be prevented by contract in so far as it is necessary for that use.

(3) The person having a right to use a copy of a computer program shall be entitled, without the authorisation of the rightholder, to observe, study or test the functioning of the program in order to determine the ideas and principles which underlie any element of the program if he does so while performing any of the acts of loading, displaying, running, transmitting or storing the program which he is entitled to do.

Article 6
Decompilation

(1) The authorisation of the rightholder shall not be required where reproduction of the code and translation of its form within the meaning of points (a) and (b) of Article 4(1) are indispensable to obtain the information necessary to achieve the interoperability of an independently created computer program with other programs, provided that the following conditions are met:

(a) those acts are performed by the licensee or by another person having a right to use a copy of a program, or on their behalf by a person authorised to do so;

(b) the information necessary to achieve interoperability has not previously been readily available to the persons referred to in point (a); and

(c) those acts are confined to the parts of the original program which are necessary in order to achieve interoperability.

(2) The provisions of paragraph 1 shall not permit the information obtained through its application:

(a) to be used for goals other than to achieve the interoperability of the independently created computer program;

(b) to be given to others, except when necessary for the interoperability of the independently created computer program; or

(c) to be used for the development, production or marketing of a computer program substantially similar in its expression, or for any other act which infringes copyright.

(3) In accordance with the provisions of the Berne Convention for the protection of Literary and Artistic Works, the provisions of this Article may not be interpreted in such a way as to allow its application to be used in a manner which unreasonably prejudices the rightholder's legitimate interests or conflicts with a normal exploitation of the computer program.

Article 7
Special measures of protection

(1) Without prejudice to the provisions of Articles 4, 5 and 6, Member States

shall provide, in accordance with their national legislation, appropriate remedies against a person committing any of the following acts:

(a) any act of putting into circulation a copy of a computer program knowing, or having reason to believe, that it is an infringing copy;

(b) the possession, for commercial purposes, of a copy of a computer program knowing, or having reason to believe, that it is an infringing copy;

(c) any act of putting into circulation, or the possession for commercial purposes of, any means the sole intended purpose of which is to facilitate the unauthorised removal or circumvention of any technical device which may have been applied to protect a computer program.

(2) Any infringing copy of a computer program shall be liable to seizure in accordance with the legislation of the Member State concerned.

(3) Member States may provide for the seizure of any means referred to in point (c) of paragraph 1.

Article 8

Continued application of other legal provisions

The provisions of this Directive shall be without prejudice to any other legal provisions such as those concerning patent rights, trade-marks, unfair competition, trade secrets, protection of semi-conductor products or the law of contract.

Any contractual provisions contrary to Article 6 or to the exceptions provided for in Article 5(2) and (3) shall be null and void.

Article 9

Communication

Member States shall communicate to the Commission the provisions of national law adopted in the field governed by this Directive.

Article 10

Repeal

Directive 91/250/EEC, as amended by the Directive indicated in Annex I, Part A, is repealed, without prejudice to the obligations of the Member States relating to the time-limits for transposition into national law of the Directives set out in Annex I, Part B.

References to the repealed Directive shall be construed as references to this Directive and shall be read in accordance with the correlation table in Annex II.

Article 11

Entry into force

This Directive shall enter into force on the 20th day following its publication in the *Official Journal of the European Union*.

Article 12

Addressees

This Directive is addressed to the Member States.

ANNEX I

PART A

REPEALED DIRECTIVE WITH ITS AMENDMENT (REFERRED TO IN ARTICLE 10)

Council Directive 91/250/EEC (OJ L 122, 17.5.1991, p. 42)
Council Directive 93/98/EEC (OJ L 290, 24.11.1993, p. 9)   Article 11(1) only

PART B

LIST OF TIME-LIMITS FOR TRANSPOSITION INTO NATIONAL LAW (REFERRED TO IN ARTICLE 10)

Directive	Time-limit for transposition
91/250/EEC	31 December 1992
93/98/EEC	30 June 1995

ANNEX II

Correlation table

Directive 91/250/EEC	This Directive
Article 1(1), (2) and (3)	Article 1(1), (2) and (3)
Article 2(1), first sentence	Article 2(1), first subparagraph
Article 2(1), second sentence	Article 2(1), second subparagraph
Article 2(2) and (3)	Article 2(2) and (3)
Article 3	Article 3
Article 4, introductory words	Article 4(1), introductory words
Article 4(a)	Article 4(1), point (a)
Article 4(b)	Article 4(1), point (b)
Article 4(c), first sentence	Article 4(1), point (c)
Article 4(c), second sentence	Article 4(2)
Articles 5, 6 and 7	Articles 5, 6 and 7
Article 9(1), first sentence	Article 8, first paragraph
Article 9(1), second sentence	Article 8, second paragraph
Article 9(2)	Article 1(4)
Article 10(1)	—
Article 10(2)	Article 9
—	Article 10
—	Article 11
Article 11	Article 12
—	Annex I
—	Annex II

H15. DIRECTIVE 2011/77

Directive 2011/77/EU of the European Parliament and of the Council of 27 September 2011 amending Directive 2006/116/EC on the term of protection of copyright and certain related rights

THE EUROPEAN PARLIAMENT AND THE COUNCIL OF THE EUROPEAN UNION,

Having regard to the Treaty on the Functioning of the European Union, and in particular Articles 53(1), 62 and 114 thereof,

Having regard to the proposal from the European Commission,

Having regard to the opinion of the European Economic and Social Committee[1],

Acting in accordance with the ordinary legislative procedure[2],

Whereas:

(1) Under Directive 2006/116/EC of the European Parliament and of the Council[3], the term of protection for performers and producers of phonograms is 50 years.

(2) In the case of performers this period starts with the performance or, when the fixation of the performance is lawfully published or lawfully communicated to the public within 50 years after the performance is made, with the first such publication or the first such communication to the public, whichever is the earliest.

(3) For phonogram producers the period starts with the fixation of the phonogram or its lawful publication within 50 years after fixation, or, if it is not so published, its lawful communication to the public within 50 years after fixation.

(4) The socially recognised importance of the creative contribution of performers should be reflected in a level of protection that acknowledges their creative and artistic contribution.

(5) Performers generally start their careers young and the current term of protection of 50 years applicable to fixations of performances often does not protect their performances for their entire lifetime. Therefore, some performers face an income gap at the end of their lifetime. In addition, performers are often unable to rely on their rights to prevent or restrict an objectionable use of their performances that may occur during their lifetime.

(6) The revenue derived from the exclusive rights of reproduction and making available, as provided for in Directive 2001/29/EC of the European Parliament and of the Council of 22 May 2001 on the harmonisation of certain aspects of copyright and related rights in the information society[4], as well as fair compensation for reproductions for private use within the meaning of that Directive, and from the exclusive rights of distribution and rental within the meaning of Directive 2006/115/EC of the European Parliament and of the Council of 12 December 2006 on rental right and lending right and on certain rights related to copyright in the field of intellectual property[5], should be available to performers for at least their lifetime.

(7) The term of protection for fixations of performances and for phonograms should therefore be extended to 70 years after the relevant event.

(8) The rights in the fixation of the performance should revert to the performer if a phonogram producer refrains from offering for sale in sufficient quantity, within the meaning of the International Convention on the Protection of Performers, Producers of Phonograms and Broadcasting Organisations, copies of a phonogram which, but for the term extension, would be in the public domain, or refrains from making such a phonogram available to the public. That option should be available on expiry of a reasonable period of time for the phonogram producer to carry out both of these acts of exploitation. The rights of the phonogram producer in the phonogram should therefore expire, in order to avoid a situation in which these rights would coexist with those of the performer in the fixa-

---

[1] OJ C 182, 4.8.2009, p. 36.
[2] Position of the European Parliament of 23 April 2009 (OJ C 184 E, 8.7.2010, p. 331) and Decision of the Council of 12 September 2011.
[3] OJ L 372, 27.12.2006, p. 12.
[4] OJ L 167, 22.6.2001, p. 10.
[5] OJ L 376, 27.12.2006, p. 28.

tion of the performance while the latter rights are no longer transferred or assigned to the phonogram producer.

(9) Upon entering into a contractual relationship with a phonogram producer, performers normally have to transfer or assign to the phonogram producer their exclusive rights of reproduction, distribution, rental and making available of fixations of their performances. In exchange, some performers are paid an advance on royalties and enjoy payments only once the phonogram producer has recouped the initial advance and made any contractually defined deductions. Other performers transfer or assign their exclusive rights in return for a one-off payment (non-recurring remuneration). This is particularly the case for performers who play in the background and do not appear in the credits (non-featured performers) but sometimes also for performers who appear in the credits (featured performers).

(10) In order to ensure that performers who have transferred or assigned their exclusive rights to phonogram producers actually benefit from the term extension, a series of accompanying measures should be introduced.

(11) A first accompanying measure should be the imposition on phonogram producers of an obligation to set aside, at least once a year, a sum corresponding to 20% of the revenue from the exclusive rights of distribution, reproduction and making available of phonograms. 'Revenue' means the revenue derived by the phonogram producer before deducting costs.

(12) Payment of those sums should be reserved solely for the benefit of performers whose performances are fixed in a phonogram and who have transferred or assigned their rights to the phonogram producer in return for a one-off payment. The sums set aside in this manner should be distributed to non-featured performers at least once a year on an individual basis. Such distribution should be entrusted to collecting societies and national rules on non-distributable revenue may be applied. In order to avoid the imposition of a disproportionate burden in the collection and administration of that revenue, Member States should be able to regulate the extent to which micro-enterprises are subject to the obligation to contribute where such payments would appear unreasonable in relation to the costs of collecting and administering such revenue.

(13) However, Article 5 of Directive 2006/115/EC already grants performers an unwaivable right to equitable remuneration for the rental of, inter alia, phonograms. Likewise, in contractual practice performers do not usually transfer or assign to phonogram producers their rights to claim a single equitable remuneration for broadcasting and communication to the public under Article 8(2) of Directive 2006/115/EC and to fair compensation for reproductions for private use under point (b) of Article 5(2) of Directive 2001/29/EC. Therefore, in the calculation of the overall amount to be dedicated by a phonogram producer to payments of the supplementary remuneration, no account should be taken of revenue which the phonogram producer has derived from the rental of phonograms, of the single equitable remuneration received for broadcasting and communication to the public or of the fair compensation received for private copying.

(14) A second accompanying measure designed to rebalance contracts whereby performers transfer their exclusive rights on a royalty basis to a phonogram producer, should be a 'clean slate' for those performers who have assigned their above-mentioned exclusive rights to phonogram producers in return for royalties or remuneration. In order for performers to benefit fully from the extended term of protection, Member States should ensure that, under agreements between phonogram producers and performers, a royalty or remuneration rate unencumbered by advance payments or contractually defined deductions is paid to performers during the extended period.

(15) For the sake of legal certainty it should be provided that, in the absence of

clear indications to the contrary in the contract, a contractual transfer or assignment of rights in the fixation of the performance concluded before the date by which Member States are to adopt measures implementing this Directive shall continue to produce its effects for the extended term.

(16) Member States should be able to provide that certain terms in those contracts which provide for recurring payments can be renegotiated for the benefit of performers. Member States should have procedures in place to cover the eventuality that the renegotiation fails.

(17) This Directive should not affect national rules and agreements which are compatible with its provisions, such as collective agreements concluded in Member States between organisations representing performers and organisations representing producers.

(18) In some Member States, musical compositions with words are given a single term of protection, calculated from the death of the last surviving author, while in other Member States separate terms of protection apply for music and lyrics. Musical compositions with words are overwhelmingly co-written. For example, an opera is often the work of a librettist and a composer. Moreover, in musical genres such as jazz, rock and pop music, the creative process is often collaborative in nature.

(19) Consequently, the harmonisation of the term of protection in respect of musical compositions with words the lyrics and music of which were created in order to be used together is incomplete, giving rise to obstacles to the free movement of goods and services, such as cross-border collective management services. In order to ensure the removal of such obstacles, all such works in protection at the date by which the Member States are required to transpose this Directive should have the same harmonised term of protection in all Member States.

(20) Directive 2006/116/EC should therefore be amended accordingly.

(21) Since the objectives of the accompanying measures cannot be sufficiently achieved by the Member States, inasmuch as national measures in that field would either lead to distortion of competition or affect the scope of exclusive rights of the phonogram producer which are defined by Union legislation, and can therefore be better achieved at Union level, the Union may adopt measures, in accordance with the principle of subsidiarity as set out in Article 5 of the Treaty on European Union. In accordance with the principle of proportionality, as set out in that Article, this Directive does not go beyond what is necessary in order to achieve those objectives.

(22) In accordance with point 34 of the interinstitutional agreement on better law-making[6], Member States are encouraged to draw up, for themselves and in the interests of the Union, their own tables which will, as far as possible, illustrate the correlation between this Directive and their transposition measures, and to make them public,

HAVE ADOPTED THIS DIRECTIVE:

[*Art.1 amends Directive 2006/116 and is not reproduced here. Directive 2006/ 116 is printed as amended at H13 above.*]

Article 2

Transposition

1. Member States shall bring into force the laws, regulations and administrative provisions necessary to comply with this Directive by 1 November 2013. They shall forthwith inform the Commission thereof.

---

[6] OJ C 321, 31.12.2003, p. 1.

When Member States adopt those measures, they shall contain a reference to this Directive or shall be accompanied by such a reference on the occasion of their official publication. The methods of making such reference shall be laid down by Member States.

2. Member States shall communicate to the Commission the text of the main provisions of national law which they adopt in the field covered by this Directive.

Article 3

Reporting

1. By 1 November 2016, the Commission shall submit to the European Parliament, the Council and the European Economic and Social Committee a report on the application of this Directive in the light of the development of the digital market, accompanied, where appropriate, by a proposal for the further amendment of Directive 2006/116/EC.

2. By 1 January 2012, the Commission shall submit a report to the European Parliament, the Council and the European Economic and Social Committee, assessing the possible need for an extension of the term of protection of rights to performers and producers in the audiovisual sector. If appropriate, the Commission shall submit a proposal for the further amendment of Directive 2006/116/EC.

Article 4

Entry into force

This Directive shall enter into force on the 20th day following its publication in the *Official Journal of the European Union*.

Article 5

Addressees

This Directive is addressed to the Member States.

Done at Strasbourg, 27 September 2011.

For the European Parliament	*For the Council*
The President	*The President*
J. BUZEK	M. DOWGIELEWICZ

H16. DIRECTIVE 2012/28/EU

Directive 2012/28/EU of the European Parliament and of the Council of 25 October 2012 on certain permitted uses of orphan works[i]

([2012] OJ L299/5)

(Text with EEA relevance)

THE EUROPEAN PARLIAMENT AND THE COUNCIL OF THE EUROPEAN UNION,

Having regard to the Treaty on the Functioning of the European Union, and in particular Articles 53(1), 62 and 114 thereof,

Having regard to the proposal from the European Commission,

After transmission of the draft legislative act to the national parliaments,

---

[i] *Editorial note*: The footnote numbering in the original Directive is reproduced below.

Having regard to the opinion of the European Economic and Social Committee[1],

Acting in accordance with the ordinary legislative procedure[2],

Whereas:

(1) Publicly accessible libraries, educational establishments and museums, as well as archives, film or audio heritage institutions and public-service broadcasting organisations, established in the Member States, are engaged in large-scale digitisation of their collections or archives in order to create European Digital Libraries. They contribute to the preservation and dissemination of European cultural heritage, which is also important for the creation of European Digital Libraries, such as Europeana. Technologies for mass digitisation of print materials and for search and indexing enhance the research value of the libraries' collections. Creating large online libraries facilitates electronic search and discovery tools which open up new sources of discovery for researchers and academics who would otherwise have to content themselves with more traditional and analogue search methods.

(2) The need to promote free movement of knowledge and innovation in the internal market is an important component of the Europe 2020 Strategy, as set out in the Communication from the Commission entitled "Europe 2020: A strategy for smart, sustainable and inclusive growth", which includes as one of its flagship initiatives the development of a Digital Agenda for Europe.

(3) Creating a legal framework to facilitate the digitisation and dissemination of works and other subject-matter which are protected by copyright or related rights and for which no rightholder is identified or for which the rightholder, even if identified, is not located—so-called orphan works—is a key action of the Digital Agenda for Europe, as set out in the Communication from the Commission entitled "A Digital Agenda for Europe". This Directive targets the specific problem of the legal determination of orphan work status and its consequences in terms of the permitted users and permitted uses of works or phonograms considered to be orphan works.

(4) This Directive is without prejudice to specific solutions being developed in the Member States to address larger mass digitisation issues, such as in the case of so-called "out-of-commerce" works. Such solutions take into account the specificities of different types of content and different users and build upon the consensus of the relevant stakeholders. This approach has also been followed in the Memorandum of Understanding on key principles on the digitisation and making available of out-of-commerce works, signed on 20 September 2011 by representatives of European libraries, authors, publishers and collecting societies and witnessed by the Commission. This Directive is without prejudice to that Memorandum of Understanding, which calls on Member States and the Commission to ensure that voluntary agreements concluded between users, rightholders and collective rights management organisations to licence the use of out-of-commerce works on the basis of the principles contained therein benefit from the requisite legal certainty in a national and cross-border context.

(5) Copyright is the economic foundation for the creative industry, since it stimulates innovation, creation, investment and production. Mass digitisation and dissemination of works is therefore a means of protecting Europe's cultural heritage. Copyright is an important tool for ensuring that the creative sector is rewarded for its work.

(6) The rightholders' exclusive rights of reproduction of their works and other

---

[1] OJ C376, 22.12.2011, p.66.

[2] Position of the European Parliament of 13 September 2012 (not yet published in the Official Journal) and decision of the Council of 4 October 2012.

protected subject-matter and of making them available to the public, as harmonised under Directive 2001/29/EC of the European Parliament and of the Council of 22 May 2001 on the harmonisation of certain aspects of copyright and related rights in the information society[3], necessitate the prior consent of right-holders to the digitisation and the making available to the public of a work or other protected subject-matter.

(7) In the case of orphan works, it is not possible to obtain such prior consent to the carrying-out of acts of reproduction or of making available to the public.

(8) Different approaches in the Member States to the recognition of orphan work status can present obstacles to the functioning of the internal market and the use of, and cross-border access to, orphan works. Such different approaches can also result in restrictions on the free movement of goods and services which incorporate cultural content. Therefore, ensuring the mutual recognition of such status is appropriate, since it will allow access to orphan works in all Member States.

(9) In particular, a common approach to determining the orphan work status and the permitted uses of orphan works is necessary in order to ensure legal certainty in the internal market with respect to the use of orphan works by publicly accessible libraries, educational establishments and museums, as well as by archives, film or audio heritage institutions and public-service broadcasting organisations.

(10) Cinematographic or audiovisual works and phonograms in the archives of public-service broadcasting organisations and produced by them include orphan works. Taking into account the special position of broadcasters as producers of phonograms and audiovisual material and the need to adopt measures to limit the phenomenon of orphan works in the future, it is appropriate to set a cut-off date for the application of this Directive to works and phonograms in the archives of broadcasting organisations.

(11) Cinematographic and audiovisual works and phonograms contained in the archives of public-service broadcasting organisations and produced by them, should for the purposes of this Directive be regarded as including cinematographic and audiovisual works and phonograms which are commissioned by such organisations for the exclusive exploitation by them or other co-producing public-service broadcasting organisations. Cinematographic and audiovisual works and phonograms contained in the archives of public-service broadcasting organisations which have not been produced or commissioned by such organisations, but which those organisations have been authorised to use under a licensing agreement, should not fall within the scope of this Directive.

(12) For reasons of international comity, this Directive should apply only to works and phonograms that are first published in the territory of a Member State or, in the absence of publication, first broadcast in the territory of a Member State or, in the absence of publication or broadcast, made publicly accessible by the beneficiaries of this Directive with the consent of the rightholders. In the latter case, this Directive should only apply provided that it is reasonable to assume that the rightholders would not oppose the use allowed by this Directive.

(13) Before a work or phonogram can be considered an orphan work, a diligent search for the rightholders in the work or phonogram, including rightholders in works and other protected subject-matter that are embedded or incorporated in the work or phonogram, should be carried out in good faith. Member States should be permitted to provide that such diligent search may be carried out by the organisations referred to in this Directive or by other organisations. Such other organisations may charge for the service of carrying out a diligent search.

---

[3] OJ L167, 22.6.2001, p.10.

(14) It is appropriate to provide for a harmonised approach concerning such diligent search in order to ensure a high level of protection of copyright and related rights in the Union. A diligent search should involve the consultation of sources that supply information on the works and other protected subject-matter as determined, in accordance with this Directive, by the Member State where the diligent search has to be carried out. In so doing, Member States could refer to the diligent search guidelines agreed in the context of the High Level Working Group on Digital Libraries established as part of the i2010 digital library initiative.

(15) In order to avoid duplication of search efforts, a diligent search should be carried out in the Member State where the work or phonogram was first published or, in cases where no publication has taken place, where it was first broadcast. The diligent search in respect of cinematographic or audiovisual works the producer of which has his headquarters or habitual residence in a Member State should be carried out in that Member State. In the case of cinematographic or audiovisual works which are co-produced by producers established in different Member States, the diligent search should be carried out in each of those Member States. With regard to works and phonograms which have neither been published nor broadcast but which have been made publicly accessible by the beneficiaries of this Directive with the consent of the rightholders, the diligent search should be carried out in the Member State where the organisation that made the work or phonogram publicly accessible with the consent of the rightholder is established. Diligent searches for the rightholders in works and other protected subject-matter that are embedded or incorporated in a work or phonogram should be carried out in the Member State where the diligent search for the work or phonogram containing the embedded or incorporated work or other protected subject-matter is carried out. Sources of information available in other countries should also be consulted if there is evidence to suggest that relevant information on rightholders is to be found in those other countries. The carrying-out of diligent searches may generate various kinds of information, such as a search record and the result of the search. The search record should be kept on file in order for the relevant organisation to be able to substantiate that the search was diligent.

(16) Member States should ensure that the organisations concerned keep records of their diligent searches and that the results of such searches, consisting in particular of any finding that a work or phonogram is to be considered an orphan work within the meaning of this Directive, as well as information on the change of status and on the use which those organisations make of orphan works, are collected and made available to the public at large, in particular through the recording of the relevant information in an online database. Considering in particular the pan-European dimension, and in order to avoid duplication of efforts, it is appropriate to make provision for the creation of a single online database for the Union containing such information and for making it available to the public at large in a transparent manner. This can enable both the organisations which are carrying out diligent searches and the rightholders easily to access such information. The database could also play an important role in preventing and bringing to an end possible copyright infringements, particularly in the case of changes to the orphan work status of the works and phonograms. Under Regulation (EU) No 386/2012[4], the Office for Harmonization in the Internal Market ("the Office") is entrusted with certain tasks and activities, financed by making

---

[4] Regulation (EU) No 386/2012 of the European Parliament and of the Council of 19 April 2012 on entrusting the Office for Harmonization in the Internal Market (Trade Marks and Designs) with tasks related to the enforcement of intellectual property rights, including the assembling of public and private-sector representatives as a European Observatory on Infringements of Intellectual Property Rights (OJ L129, 16.5.2012, p.1).

use of its own budgetary means, aimed at facilitating and supporting the activities of national authorities, the private sector and the Union institutions in the fight against, including the prevention of, infringement of intellectual property rights.

In particular, pursuant to point (g) of Article 2(1) of that Regulation, those tasks include providing mechanisms which help to improve the online exchange of relevant information between the Member States' authorities concerned and fostering cooperation between those authorities. It is therefore appropriate to rely on the Office to establish and manage the European database containing information related to orphan works referred to in this Directive.

(17) There can be several rightholders in respect of a particular work or phonogram, and works and phonograms can themselves include other works or protected subject-matter. This Directive should not affect the rights of identified and located rightholders. If at least one rightholder has been identified and located, a work or phonogram should not be considered an orphan work. The beneficiaries of this Directive should only be permitted to use a work or phonogram one or more of the rightholders in which are not identified or not located, if they are authorised to carry out the acts of reproduction and of making available to the public covered by Articles 2 and 3 respectively of Directive 2001/29/EC by those rightholders that have been identified and located, including the rightholders of works and other protected subject-matter which are embedded or incorporated in the works or phonograms. Rightholders that have been identified and located can give this authorisation only in relation to the rights that they themselves hold, either because the rights are their own rights or because the rights were transferred to them, and should not be able to authorise under this Directive any use on behalf of rightholders that have not been identified and located. Correspondingly, when previously non-identified or non-located rightholders come forward in order to claim their rights in the work or phonogram, the lawful use of the work or phonogram by the beneficiaries can continue only if those rightholders give their authorisation to do so under Directive 2001/29/EC in relation to the rights that they hold.

(18) Rightholders should be entitled to put an end to the orphan work status in the event that they come forward to claim their rights in the work or other protected subject-matter. Rightholders that put an end to the orphan work status of a work or other protected subject-matter should receive fair compensation for the use that has been made of their works or other protected subject-matter under this Directive, to be determined by the Member State where the organisation that uses an orphan work is established. Member States should be free to determine the circumstances under which the payment of such compensation may be organised, including the point in time at which the payment is due. For the purposes of determining the possible level of fair compensation, due account should be taken, inter alia, of Member States' cultural promotion objectives, of the non-commercial nature of the use made by the organisations in question in order to achieve aims related to their public-interest missions, such as promoting learning and disseminating culture, and of the possible harm to rightholders.

(19) If a work or phonogram has been wrongly found to be an orphan work, following a search which was not diligent, the remedies for copyright infringement in Member States' legislation, provided for in accordance with the relevant national provisions and Union law, remain available.

(20) In order to promote learning and the dissemination of culture, Member States should provide for an exception or limitation in addition to those provided for in Article 5 of Directive 2001/29/EC. That exception or limitation should permit certain organisations, as referred to in point (c) of Article 5(2) of Directive 2001/29/EC and film or audio heritage institutions which operate on a non-profit making basis, as well as public-service broadcasting organisations, to reproduce

and make available to the public, within the meaning of that Directive, orphan works, provided that such use fulfils their public interest missions, in particular the preservation of, the restoration of, and the provision of cultural and educational access to, their collections, including their digital collections. Film or audio heritage institutions should, for the purposes of this Directive, cover organisations designated by Member States to collect, catalogue, preserve and restore films and other audiovisual works or phonograms forming part of their cultural heritage. Public-service broadcasters should, for the purposes of this Directive, cover broadcasters with a public-service remit as conferred, defined and organised by each Member State. The exception or limitation established by this Directive to permit the use of orphan works is without prejudice to the exceptions and limitations provided for in Article 5 of Directive 2001/29/EC. It can be applied only in certain special cases which do not conflict with the normal exploitation of the work or other protected subject-matter and do not unreasonably prejudice the legitimate interests of the rightholder.

(21) In order to incentivise digitisation, the beneficiaries of this Directive should be allowed to generate revenues in relation to their use of orphan works under this Directive in order to achieve aims related to their public-interest missions, including in the context of public-private partnership agreements.

(22) Contractual arrangements may play a role in fostering the digitisation of European cultural heritage, it being understood that publicly accessible libraries, educational establishments and museums, as well as archives, film or audio heritage institutions and public-service broadcasting organisations, should be allowed, with a view to undertaking the uses permitted under this Directive, to conclude agreements with commercial partners for the digitisation and making available to the public of orphan works. Those agreements may include financial contributions by such partners. Such agreements should not impose any restrictions on the beneficiaries of this Directive as to their use of orphan works and should not grant the commercial partner any rights to use, or control the use of, the orphan works.

(23) In order to foster access by the Union's citizens to Europe's cultural heritage, it is also necessary to ensure that orphan works which have been digitised and made available to the public in one Member State may also be made available to the public in other Member States. Publicly accessible libraries, educational establishments and museums, as well as archives, film or audio heritage institutions and public-service broadcasting organisations that use an orphan work in order to achieve their public-interest missions should be able to make the orphan work available to the public in other Member States.

(24) This Directive is without prejudice to the arrangements in the Member States concerning the management of rights such as extended collective licences, legal presumptions of representation or transfer, collective management or similar arrangements or a combination of them, including for mass digitisation.

(25) Since the objective of this Directive, namely ensuring legal certainty with respect to the use of orphan works, cannot be sufficiently achieved by the Member States and can therefore, by reason of the need for uniformity of the rules governing the use of orphan works, be better achieved at Union level, the Union may adopt measures, in accordance with the principle of subsidiarity as set out in Article 5 of the Treaty on European Union. In accordance with the principle of proportionality, as set out in that Article, this Directive does not go beyond what is necessary in order to achieve that objective,

HAVE ADOPTED THIS DIRECTIVE:

Article 1

Subject-matter and scope

1. This Directive concerns certain uses made of orphan works by publicly ac-

cessible libraries, educational establishments and museums, as well as by archives, film or audio heritage institutions and public-service broadcasting organisations, established in the Member States, in order to achieve aims related to their public-interest missions.

2. This Directive applies to:

(a) works published in the form of books, journals, newspapers, magazines or other writings contained in the collections of publicly accessible libraries, educational establishments or museums as well as in the collections of archives or of film or audio heritage institutions;

(b) cinematographic or audiovisual works and phonograms contained in the collections of publicly accessible libraries, educational establishments or museums as well as in the collections of archives or of film or audio heritage institutions; and

(c) cinematographic or audiovisual works and phonograms produced by public-service broadcasting organisations up to and including 31 December 2002 and contained in their archives;

which are protected by copyright or related rights and which are first published in a Member State or, in the absence of publication, first broadcast in a Member State.

3. This Directive also applies to works and phonograms referred to in paragraph 2 which have never been published or broadcast but which have been made publicly accessible by the organisations referred to in paragraph 1 with the consent of the rightholders, provided that it is reasonable to assume that the rightholders would not oppose the uses referred to in Article 6. Member States may limit the application of this paragraph to works and phonograms which have been deposited with those organisations before 29 October 2014.

4. This Directive shall also apply to works and other protected subject-matter that are embedded or incorporated in, or constitute an integral part of, the works or phonograms referred to in paragraphs 2 and 3.

5. This Directive does not interfere with any arrangements concerning the management of rights at national level.

Article 2

Orphan works

1. A work or a phonogram shall be considered an orphan work if none of the rightholders in that work or phonogram is identified or, even if one or more of them is identified, none is located despite a diligent search for the rightholders having been carried out and recorded in accordance with Article 3.

2. Where there is more than one rightholder in a work or phonogram, and not all of them have been identified or, even if identified, located after a diligent search has been carried out and recorded in accordance with Article 3, the work or phonogram may be used in accordance with this Directive provided that the rightholders that have been identified and located have, in relation to the rights they hold, authorised the organisations referred to in Article 1(1) to carry out the acts of reproduction and making available to the public covered respectively by Articles 2 and 3 of Directive 2001/29/EC.

3. Paragraph 2 shall be without prejudice to the rights in the work or phonogram of rightholders that have been identified and located.

4. Article 5 shall apply mutatis mutandis to the rightholders that have not been identified and located in the works referred to in paragraph 2.

5. This Directive shall be without prejudice to national provisions on anonymous or pseudonymous works.

Article 3
Diligent search

1. For the purposes of establishing whether a work or phonogram is an orphan work, the organisations referred to in Article 1(1) shall ensure that a diligent search is carried out in good faith in respect of each work or other protected subject-matter, by consulting the appropriate sources for the category of works and other protected subject-matter in question. The diligent search shall be carried out prior to the use of the work or phonogram.

2. The sources that are appropriate for each category of works or phonogram in question shall be determined by each Member State, in consultation with rightholders and users, and shall include at least the relevant sources listed in the Annex.

3. A diligent search shall be carried out in the Member State of first publication or, in the absence of publication, first broadcast, except in the case of cinematographic or audiovisual works the producer of which has his headquarters or habitual residence in a Member State, in which case the diligent search shall be carried out in the Member State of his headquarters or habitual residence. In the case referred to in Article 1(3), the diligent search shall be carried out in the Member State where the organisation that made the work or phonogram publicly accessible with the consent of the rightholder is established.

4. If there is evidence to suggest that relevant information on rightholders is to be found in other countries, sources of information available in those other countries shall also be consulted.

5. Member States shall ensure that the organisations referred to in Article 1(1) maintain records of their diligent searches and that those organisations provide the following information to the competent national authorities:

(a) the results of the diligent searches that the organisations have carried out and which have led to the conclusion that a work or a phonogram is considered an orphan work;

(b) the use that the organisations make of orphan works in accordance with this Directive;

(c) any change, pursuant to Article 5, of the orphan work status of works and phonograms that the organisations use;

(d) the relevant contact information of the organisation concerned.

6. Member States shall take the necessary measures to ensure that the information referred to in paragraph 5 is recorded in a single publicly accessible online database established and managed by the Office for Harmonization in the Internal Market ("the Office") in accordance with Regulation (EU) No 386/2012. To that end, they shall forward that information to the Office without delay upon receiving it from the organisations referred to in Article 1(1).

Article 4
Mutual recognition of orphan work status

A work or phonogram which is considered an orphan work according to Article 2 in a Member State shall be considered an orphan work in all Member States. That work or phonogram may be used and accessed in accordance with this Directive in all Member States. This also applies to works and phonograms referred to in Article 2(2) in so far as the rights of the non-identified or non-located rightholders are concerned.

Article 5
End of orphan work status

Member States shall ensure that a rightholder in a work or phonogram considered to be an orphan work has, at any time, the possibility of putting an end to the orphan work status in so far as his rights are concerned.

Article 6

Permitted uses of orphan works

1. Member States shall provide for an exception or limitation to the right of reproduction and the right of making available to the public provided for respectively in Articles 2 and 3 of Directive 2001/29/EC to ensure that the organisations referred to in Article 1(1) are permitted to use orphan works contained in their collections in the following ways:

    (a) by making the orphan work available to the public, within the meaning of Article 3 of Directive 2001/29/EC;

    (b) by acts of reproduction, within the meaning of Article 2 of Directive 2001/29/EC, for the purposes of digitisation, making available, indexing, cataloguing, preservation or restoration.

2. The organisations referred to in Article 1(1) shall use an orphan work in accordance with paragraph 1 of this Article only in order to achieve aims related to their public-interest missions, in particular the preservation of, the restoration of, and the provision of cultural and educational access to, works and phonograms contained in their collection. The organisations may generate revenues in the course of such uses, for the exclusive purpose of covering their costs of digitising orphan works and making them available to the public.

3. Member States shall ensure that the organisations referred to in Article 1(1) indicate the name of identified authors and other rightholders in any use of an orphan work.

4. This Directive is without prejudice to the freedom of contract of such organisations in the pursuit of their public-interest missions, particularly in respect of public-private partnership agreements.

5. Member States shall provide that a fair compensation is due to rightholders that put an end to the orphan work status of their works or other protected subject-matter for the use that has been made by the organisations referred to in Article 1(1) of such works and other protected subject-matter in accordance with paragraph 1 of this Article. Member States shall be free to determine the circumstances under which the payment of such compensation may be organised. The level of the compensation shall be determined, within the limits imposed by Union law, by the law of the Member State in which the organisation which uses the orphan work in question is established.

Article 7

Continued application of other legal provisions

This Directive shall be without prejudice to provisions concerning, in particular, patent rights, trade marks, design rights, utility models, the topographies of semi-conductor products, type faces, conditional access, access to cable of broadcasting services, the protection of national treasures, legal deposit requirements, laws on restrictive practices and unfair competition, trade secrets, security, confidentiality, data protection and privacy, access to public documents, the law of contract, and rules on the freedom of the press and freedom of expression in the media.

Article 8

Application in time

1. This Directive shall apply in respect of all works and phonograms referred

to in Article 1 which are protected by the Member States' legislation in the field of copyright on or after 29 October 2014.

2. This Directive shall apply without prejudice to any acts concluded and rights acquired before 29 October 2014.

Article 9

Transposition

1. Member States shall bring into force the laws, regulations and administrative provisions necessary to comply with this Directive by 29 October 2014. They shall forthwith communicate to the Commission the text of those provisions. When Member States adopt those provisions, they shall contain a reference to this Directive or shall be accompanied by such a reference on the occasion of their official publication. The methods of making such reference shall be laid down by Member States.

2. Member States shall communicate to the Commission the text of the main provisions of national law which they adopt in the field covered by this Directive.

Article 10

Review clause

The Commission shall keep under constant review the development of rights information sources and shall by 29 October 2015, and at annual intervals thereafter, submit a report concerning the possible inclusion in the scope of application of this Directive of publishers and of works or other protected subject-matter not currently included in its scope, and in particular stand-alone photographs and other images.

By 29 October 2015, the Commission shall submit to the European Parliament, the Council and the European Economic and Social Committee a report on the application of this Directive, in the light of the development of digital libraries.

When necessary, in particular to ensure the functioning of the internal market, the Commission shall submit proposals for amendment of this Directive.

A Member State that has valid reasons to consider that the implementation of this Directive hinders one of the national arrangements concerning the management of rights referred to in Article 1(5) may bring the matter to the attention of the Commission together with all relevant evidence. The Commission shall take such evidence into account when drawing up the report referred to in the second paragraph of this Article and when assessing whether it is necessary to submit proposals for amendment of this Directive.

Article 11

Entry into force

This Directive shall enter into force on the day following that of its publication in the Official Journal of the European Union.

Article 12

Addressees

This Directive is addressed to the Member States.

ANNEX

The sources referred to in Article 3(2) include the following:

(1) for published books:
(a) legal deposit, library catalogues and authority files maintained by libraries and other institutions;
(b) the publishers' and authors' associations in the respective country;
(c) existing databases and registries, WATCH (Writers, Artists and their Copyright Holders), the ISBN (International Standard Book Number) and databases listing books in print;
(d) the databases of the relevant collecting societies, in particular reproduction rights organisations;
(e) sources that integrate multiple databases and registries, including VIAF (Virtual International Authority Files) and ARROW (Accessible Registries of Rights Information and Orphan Works);
(2) for newspapers, magazines, journals and periodicals:
(a) the ISSN (International Standard Serial Number) for periodical publications;
(b) indexes and catalogues from library holdings and collections;
(c) legal deposit;
(d) the publishers' associations and the authors' and journalists' associations in the respective country;
(e) the databases of relevant collecting societies including reproduction rights organisations;
(3) for visual works, including fine art, photography, illustration, design, architecture, sketches of the latter works and other such works that are contained in books, journals, newspapers and magazines or other works:
(a) the sources referred to in points (1) and (2);
(b) the databases of the relevant collecting societies, in particular for visual arts, and including reproduction rights organisations;
(c) the databases of picture agencies, where applicable;
(4) for audiovisual works and phonograms:
(a) legal deposit;
(b) the producers' associations in the respective country;
(c) databases of film or audio heritage institutions and national libraries;
(d) databases with relevant standards and identifiers such as ISAN (International Standard Audiovisual Number) for audiovisual material, ISWC (International Standard Music Work Code) for musical works and ISRC (International Standard Recording Code) for phonograms;
(e) the databases of the relevant collecting societies, in particular for authors, performers, phonogram producers and audiovisual producers;
(f) credits and other information appearing on the work's packaging;
(g) databases of other relevant associations representing a specific category of rightholders.

H17. DIRECTIVE 2014/26/EU

Directive 2014/26/EU of the European Parliament and of the Council of 26 February 2014 on collective management of copyright and related rights and multi-territorial licensing of rights in musical works for online use in the internal market[i]

([2014] OJ L84/72)
(Text with EEA relevance)

THE EUROPEAN PARLIAMENT AND THE COUNCIL OF THE EUROPEAN UNION,
    Having regard to the Treaty on the Functioning of the European Union, and in particular Articles 50(1) and 53(1) and Article 62 thereof,

---

[i] *Editorial note*: The footnote numbering in the original Directive is reproduced below.

Having regard to the proposal from the European Commission,

After transmission of the draft legislative act to the national parliaments,

Having regard to the opinion of the European Economic and Social Committee[1],

Acting in accordance with the ordinary legislative procedure[2],

Whereas:

(1) The Union Directives which have been adopted in the area of copyright and related rights already provide a high level of protection for rightholders and thereby a framework wherein the exploitation of content protected by those rights can take place. Those Directives contribute to the development and maintenance of creativity. In an internal market where competition is not distorted, protecting innovation and intellectual creation also encourages investment in innovative services and products.

(2) The dissemination of content which is protected by copyright and related rights, including books, audiovisual productions and recorded music, and services linked thereto, requires the licensing of rights by different holders of copyright and related rights, such as authors, performers, producers and publishers. It is normally for the rightholder to choose between the individual or collective management of his rights, unless Member States provide otherwise, in compliance with Union law and the international obligations of the Union and its Member States. Management of copyright and related rights includes granting of licences to users, auditing of users, monitoring of the use of rights, enforcement of copyright and related rights, collection of rights revenue derived from the exploitation of rights and the distribution of the amounts due to rightholders. Collective management organisations enable rightholders to be remunerated for uses which they would not be in a position to control or enforce themselves, including in non-domestic markets.

(3) Article 167 of the Treaty on the Functioning of the European Union (TFEU) requires the Union to take cultural diversity into account in its action and to contribute to the flowering of the cultures of the Member States, while respecting their national and regional diversity and at the same time bringing the common cultural heritage to the fore. Collective management organisations play, and should continue to play, an important role as promoters of the diversity of cultural expression, both by enabling the smallest and less popular repertoires to access the market and by providing social, cultural and educational services for the benefit of their rightholders and the public.

(4) When established in the Union, collective management organisations should be able to enjoy the freedoms provided by the Treaties when representing rightholders who are resident or established in other Member States or granting licences to users who are resident or established in other Member States.

(5) There are significant differences in the national rules governing the functioning of collective management organisations, in particular as regards their transparency and accountability to their members and rightholders. This has led in a number of instances to difficulties, in particular for non-domestic rightholders when they seek to exercise their rights, and to poor financial management of the revenues collected. Problems with the functioning of collective management organisations lead to inefficiencies in the exploitation of copyright and related rights across the internal market, to the detriment of the members of collective management organisations, rightholders and users.

---

[1] OJ C44, 15.2.2013, p.104.

[2] Position of the European Parliament of 4 February 2014 (not yet published in the Official Journal) and decision of the Council of 20 February 2014.

(6) The need to improve the functioning of collective management organisations has already been identified in Commission Recommendation 2005/737/EC[3]. That Recommendation set out a number of principles, such as the freedom of rightholders to choose their collective management organisations, equal treatment of categories of rightholders and equitable distribution of royalties. It called on collective management organisations to provide users with sufficient information on tariffs and repertoire in advance of negotiations between them. It also contained recommendations on accountability, rightholder representation in the decision-making bodies of collective management organisations and dispute resolution. However, the Recommendation has been unevenly followed.

(7) The protection of the interests of the members of collective management organisations, rightholders and third parties requires that the laws of the Member States relating to copyright management and multi-territorial licensing of online rights in musical works should be coordinated with a view to having equivalent safeguards throughout the Union. Therefore, this Directive should have as a legal base Article 50(1) TFEU.

(8) The aim of this Directive is to provide for coordination of national rules concerning access to the activity of managing copyright and related rights by collective management organisations, the modalities for their governance, and their supervisory framework, and it should therefore also have as a legal base Article 53(1) TFEU. In addition, since it is concerned with a sector offering services across the Union, this Directive should have as a legal base Article 62 TFEU.

(9) The aim of this Directive is to lay down requirements applicable to collective management organisations, in order to ensure a high standard of governance, financial management, transparency and reporting. This should not, however, prevent Member States from maintaining or imposing, in relation to collective management organisations established in their territories, more stringent standards than those laid down in Title II of this Directive, provided that such more stringent standards are compatible with Union law.

(10) Nothing in this Directive should preclude a Member State from applying the same or similar provisions to collective management organisations which are established outside the Union but which operate in that Member State.

(11) Nothing in this Directive should preclude collective management organisations from concluding representation agreements with other collective management organisations—in compliance with the competition rules laid down by Articles 101 and 102 TFEU—in the area of rights management in order to facilitate, improve and simplify the procedures for granting licences to users, including for the purposes of single invoicing, under equal, non-discriminatory and transparent conditions, and to offer multi-territorial licences also in areas other than those referred to in Title III of this Directive.

(12) This Directive, while applying to all collective management organisations, with the exception of Title III, which applies only to collective management organisations managing authors' rights in musical works for online use on a multi-territorial basis, does not interfere with arrangements concerning the management of rights in the Member States such as individual management, the extended effect of an agreement between a representative collective management organisation and a user, i.e. extended collective licensing, mandatory collective management, legal presumptions of representation and transfer of rights to collective management organisations.

(13) This Directive does not affect the possibility for Member States to

---

[3] Commission Recommendation 2005/737/EC of 18 May 2005 on collective cross-border management of copyright and related rights for legitimate online music services (OJ L276, 21.10.2005, p.54).

determine by law, by regulation or by any other specific mechanism to that effect, rightholders' fair compensation for exceptions or limitations to the reproduction right provided for in Directive 2001/29/EC of the European Parliament and of the Council[4] and rightholders' remuneration for derogations from the exclusive right in respect of public lending provided for in Directive 2006/115/EC of the European Parliament and of the Council[5] applicable in their territory as well as the conditions applicable for their collection.

(14) This Directive does not require collective management organisations to adopt a specific legal form. In practice, those organisations operate in various legal forms such as associations, cooperatives or limited liability companies, which are controlled or owned by holders of copyright and related rights or by entities representing such rightholders. In some exceptional cases, however, due to the legal form of a collective management organisation, the element of ownership or control is not present. This is, for example, the case for foundations, which do not have members. None the less, the provisions of this Directive should also apply to those organisations. Similarly, Member States should take appropriate measures to prevent the circumvention of the obligations under this Directive through the choice of legal form. It should be noted that entities which represent rightholders, and which are members of collective management organisations, may be other collective management organisations, associations of rightholders, unions or other organisations.

(15) Rightholders should be free to entrust the management of their rights to independent management entities. Such independent management entities are commercial entities which differ from collective management organisations, inter alia, because they are not owned or controlled by rightholders. However, to the extent that such independent management entities carry out the same activities as collective management organisations, they should be obliged to provide certain information to the rightholders they represent, collective management organisations, users and the public.

(16) Audiovisual producers, record producers and broadcasters license their own rights, in certain cases alongside rights that have been transferred to them by, for instance, performers, on the basis of individually negotiated agreements, and act in their own interest. Book, music or newspaper publishers license rights that have been transferred to them on the basis of individually negotiated agreements and act in their own interest. Therefore audiovisual producers, record producers, broadcasters and publishers should not be regarded as 'independent management entities'. Furthermore, authors' and performers' managers and agents acting as intermediaries and representing rightholders in their relations with collective management organisations should not be regarded as 'independent management entities' since they do not manage rights in the sense of setting tariffs, granting licences or collecting money from users.

(17) Collective management organisations should be free to choose to have certain of their activities, such as the invoicing of users or the distribution of amounts due to rightholders, carried out by subsidiaries or by other entities that they control. In such cases, those provisions of this Directive that would be applicable if the relevant activity were carried out directly by a collective management organisation should be applicable to the activities of the subsidiaries or other entities.

---

[4] Directive 2001/29/EC of the European Parliament and of the Council of 22 May 2001 on the harmonisation of certain aspects of copyright and related rights in the information society (OJ L167, 22.6.2001, p.10).

[5] Directive 2006/115/EC of the European Parliament and of the Council of 12 December 2006 on rental right and lending right and on certain rights related to copyright in the field of intellectual property (OJ L376, 27.12.2006, p.28).

(18) In order to ensure that holders of copyright and related rights can benefit fully from the internal market when their rights are being managed collectively and that their freedom to exercise their rights is not unduly affected, it is necessary to provide for the inclusion of appropriate safeguards in the statute of collective management organisations. Moreover, a collective management organisation should not, when providing its management services, discriminate directly or indirectly between rightholders on the basis of their nationality, place of residence or place of establishment.

(19) Having regard to the freedoms established in the TFEU, collective management of copyright and related rights should entail a rightholder being able freely to choose a collective management organisation for the management of his rights, whether those rights be rights of communication to the public or reproduction rights, or categories of rights related to forms of exploitation such as broadcasting, theatrical exhibition or reproduction for online distribution, provided that the collective management organisation that the rightholder wishes to choose already manages such rights or categories of rights.

The rights, categories of rights or types of works and other subject-matter managed by the collective management organisation should be determined by the general assembly of members of that organisation if they are not already determined in its statute or prescribed by law. It is important that the rights and categories of rights be determined in a manner that maintains a balance between the freedom of rightholders to dispose of their works and other subject-matter and the ability of the organisation to manage the rights effectively, taking into account in particular the category of rights managed by the organisation and the creative sector in which it operates. Taking due account of that balance, rightholders should be able easily to withdraw such rights or categories of rights from a collective management organisation and to manage those rights individually or to entrust or transfer the management of all or part of them to another collective management organisation or another entity, irrespective of the Member State of nationality, residence or establishment of the collective management organisation, the other entity or the rightholder. Where a Member State, in compliance with Union law and the international obligations of the Union and its Member States, provides for mandatory collective management of rights, rightholders' choice would be limited to other collective management organisations.

Collective management organisations managing different types of works and other subject-matter, such as literary, musical or photographic works, should also allow this flexibility to rightholders as regards the management of different types of works and other subject-matter. As far as non-commercial uses are concerned, Member States should provide that collective management organisations take the necessary steps to ensure that their rightholders can exercise the right to grant licences for such uses. Such steps should include, inter alia, a decision by the collective management organisation on the conditions attached to the exercise of that right as well as the provision to their members of information on those conditions. Collective management organisations should inform rightholders of their choices and allow them to exercise the rights related to those choices as easily as possible. Rightholders who have already authorised the collective management organisation may be informed via the website of the organisation. A requirement for the consent of rightholders in the authorisation to the management of each right, category of rights or type of works and other subject-matter should not prevent the rightholders from accepting proposed subsequent amendments to that authorisation by tacit agreement in accordance with the conditions set out in national law. Neither contractual arrangements according to which a termination or withdrawal by rightholders has an immediate effect on licences granted prior to such termination or withdrawal, nor contractual arrangements according to

H EU DIRECTIVES

which such licences remain unaffected for a certain period of time after such termination or withdrawal, are, as such, precluded by this Directive. Such arrangements should not, however, create an obstacle to the full application of this Directive. This Directive should not prejudice the possibility for rightholders to manage their rights individually, including for non-commercial uses.

(20) Membership of collective management organisations should be based on objective, transparent and non-discriminatory criteria, including as regards publishers who by virtue of an agreement on the exploitation of rights are entitled to a share of the income from the rights managed by collective management organisations and to collect such income from the collective management organisations. Those criteria should not oblige collective management organisations to accept members the management of whose rights, categories of rights or types of works or other subject-matter falls outside their scope of activity. The records kept by a collective management organisation should allow for the identification and location of its members and rightholders whose rights the organisation represents on the basis of authorisations given by those rightholders.

(21) In order to protect those rightholders whose rights are directly represented by the collective management organisation but who do not fulfil its membership requirements, it is appropriate to require that certain provisions of this Directive relating to members be also applied to such rightholders. Member States should be able also to provide such rightholders with rights to participate in the decision-making process of the collective management organisation.

(22) Collective management organisations should act in the best collective interests of the rightholders they represent. It is therefore important to provide for systems which enable the members of a collective management organisation to exercise their membership rights by participating in the organisation's decision-making process. Some collective management organisations have different categories of members, which may represent different types of rightholders, such as producers and performers. The representation in the decision-making process of those different categories of members should be fair and balanced. The effectiveness of the rules on the general assembly of members of collective management organisations would be undermined if there were no provisions on how the general assembly should be run. Thus, it is necessary to ensure that the general assembly is convened regularly, and at least annually, and that the most important decisions in the collective management organisation are taken by the general assembly.

(23) All members of collective management organisations should be allowed to participate and vote in the general assembly of members. The exercise of those rights should be subject only to fair and proportionate restrictions. In some exceptional cases, collective management organisations are established in the legal form of a foundation, and thus have no members. In such cases, the powers of the general assembly of members should be exercised by the body entrusted with the supervisory function. Where collective management organisations have entities representing rightholders as their members, as may be the case where a collective management organisation is a limited liability company and its members are associations of rightholders, Member States should be able to provide that some or all powers of the general assembly of members are to be exercised by an assembly of those rightholders. The general assembly of members should, at least, have the power to set the framework of the activities of the management, in particular with respect to the use of rights revenue by the collective management organisation. This should, however, be without prejudice to the possibility for Member States to provide for more stringent rules on, for example, investments, mergers or taking out loans, including a prohibition on any such transactions. Collective management organisations should encourage the active

participation of their members in the general assembly. The exercise of voting rights should be facilitated for members who attend the general assembly and also for those who do not. In addition to being able to exercise their rights by electronic means, members should be allowed to participate and vote in the general assembly of members through a proxy. Proxy voting should be restricted in cases of conflicts of interest. At the same time, Member States should provide for restrictions as regards proxies only if this does not prejudice the appropriate and effective participation of members in the decision-making process. In particular, the appointment of proxy-holders contributes to the appropriate and effective participation of members in the decision-making process and allows rightholders to have a true opportunity to opt for a collective management organisation of their choice, irrespective of the Member State of establishment of the organisation.

(24) Members should be allowed to participate in the continuous monitoring of the management of collective management organisations. To that end, those organisations should have a supervisory function appropriate to their organisational structure and should allow members to be represented in the body that exercises that function. Depending on the organisational structure of the collective management organisation, the supervisory function may be exercised by a separate body, such as a supervisory board, or by some or all of the directors in the administrative board who do not manage the business of the collective management organisation. The requirement of fair and balanced representation of members should not prevent the collective management organisation from appointing third parties to exercise the supervisory function, including persons with relevant professional expertise and rightholders who do not fulfil the membership requirements or who are represented by the organisation not directly but via an entity which is a member of the collective management organisation.

(25) For reasons of sound management, the management of a collective management organisation must be independent. Managers, whether elected as directors or hired or employed by the organisation on the basis of a contract, should be required to declare, prior to taking up their position and thereafter on a yearly basis, whether there are conflicts between their interests and those of the rightholders that are represented by the collective management organisation. Such annual statements should be also made by persons exercising the supervisory function. Member States should be free to require collective management organisations to make such statements public or to submit them to public authorities.

(26) Collective management organisations collect, manage and distribute revenue from the exploitation of the rights entrusted to them by rightholders. That revenue is ultimately due to rightholders, who may have a direct legal relationship with the organisation, or may be represented via an entity which is a member of the collective management organisation or via a representation agreement. It is therefore important that a collective management organisation exercise the utmost diligence in collecting, managing and distributing that revenue. Accurate distribution is only possible where the collective management organisation maintains proper records of membership, licences and use of works and other subject-matter. Relevant data that are required for the efficient collective management of rights should also be provided by rightholders and users and verified by the collective management organisation.

(27) Amounts collected and due to rightholders should be kept separately in the accounts from any own assets the organisation may have. Without prejudice to the possibility for Member States to provide for more stringent rules on investment, including a prohibition of investment of the rights revenue, where such amounts are invested, this should be carried out in accordance with the general investment and risk management policy of the collective management

organisation. In order to maintain a high level of protection of the rights of right-holders and to ensure that any income that may arise from the exploitation of such rights accrues to their benefit, the investments made and held by the collective management organisation should be managed in accordance with criteria which would oblige the organisation to act prudently, while allowing it to decide on the most secure and efficient investment policy. This should allow the collective management organisation to opt for an asset allocation that suits the precise nature and duration of any exposure to risk of any rights revenue invested and does not unduly prejudice any rights revenue owed to rightholders.

(28) Since rightholders are entitled to be remunerated for the exploitation of their rights, it is important that management fees do not exceed justified costs of the management of the rights and that any deduction other than in respect of management fees, for example a deduction for social, cultural or educational purposes, should be decided by the members of the collective management organisation. The collective management organisations should be transparent towards rightholders regarding the rules governing such deductions. The same requirements should apply to any decision to use the rights revenue for collective distribution, such as scholarships. Rightholders should have access, on a non-discriminatory basis, to any social, cultural or educational service funded through such deductions. This Directive should not affect deductions under national law, such as deductions for the provision of social services by collective management organisations to rightholders, as regards any aspects that are not regulated by this Directive, provided that such deductions are in compliance with Union law.

(29) The distribution and payment of amounts due to individual rightholders or, as the case may be, to categories of rightholders, should be carried out in a timely manner and in accordance with the general policy on distribution of the collective management organisation concerned, including when they are performed via another entity representing the rightholders. Only objective reasons beyond the control of a collective management organisation can justify delay in the distribution and payment of amounts due to rightholders. Therefore, circumstances such as the rights revenue having been invested subject to a maturity date should not qualify as valid reasons for such a delay. It is appropriate to leave it to Member States to decide on rules ensuring timely distribution and the effective search for, and identification of, rightholders in cases where such objective reasons occur. In order to ensure that the amounts due to rightholders are appropriately and effectively distributed, without prejudice to the possibility for Member States to provide for more stringent rules, it is necessary to require collective management organisations to take reasonable and diligent measures, on the basis of good faith, to identify and locate the relevant rightholders. It is also appropriate that members of a collective management organisation, to the extent allowed for under national law, should decide on the use of any amounts that cannot be distributed in situations where rightholders entitled to those amounts cannot be identified or located.

(30) Collective management organisations should be able to manage rights and collect revenue from their exploitation under representation agreements with other organisations. To protect the rights of the members of the other collective management organisation, a collective management organisation should not distinguish between the rights it manages under representation agreements and those it manages directly for its rightholders. Nor should the collective management organisation be allowed to apply deductions to the rights revenue collected on behalf of another collective management organisation, other than deductions in respect of management fees, without the express consent of the other organisation. It is also appropriate to require collective management organisations to distribute and make payments to other organisations on the basis of such

representation agreements no later than when they distribute and make payments to their own members and to non-member rightholders whom they represent. Furthermore, the recipient organisation should in turn be required to distribute the amounts due to the rightholders it represents without delay.

(31) Fair and non-discriminatory commercial terms in licensing are particularly important to ensure that users can obtain licences for works and other subject-matter in respect of which a collective management organisation represents rights, and to ensure the appropriate remuneration of rightholders. Collective management organisations and users should therefore conduct licensing negotiations in good faith and apply tariffs which should be determined on the basis of objective and non-discriminatory criteria. It is appropriate to require that the licence fee or remuneration determined by collective management organisations be reasonable in relation to, inter alia, the economic value of the use of the rights in a particular context. Finally, collective management organisations should respond without undue delay to users' requests for licences.

(32) In the digital environment, collective management organisations are regularly required to license their repertoire for totally new forms of exploitation and business models. In such cases, and in order to foster an environment conducive to the development of such licences, without prejudice to the application of competition law rules, collective management organisations should have the flexibility required to provide, as swiftly as possible, individualised licences for innovative online services, without the risk that the terms of those licences could be used as a precedent for determining the terms for other licences.

(33) In order to ensure that collective management organisations can comply with the obligations set out in this Directive, users should provide those organisations with relevant information on the use of the rights represented by the collective management organisations. This obligation should not apply to natural persons acting for purposes outside their trade, business, craft or profession, who therefore fall outside the definition of user as laid down in this Directive. Moreover, the information required by collective management organisations should be limited to what is reasonable, necessary and at the users' disposal in order to enable such organisations to perform their functions, taking into account the specific situation of small and medium-sized enterprises. That obligation could be included in an agreement between a collective management organisation and a user; this does not preclude national statutory rights to information. The deadlines applicable to the provision of information by users should be such as to allow collective management organisations to meet the deadlines set for the distribution of amounts due to rightholders. This Directive should be without prejudice to the possibility for Member States to require collective management organisations established in their territory to issue joint invoices.

(34) In order to enhance the trust of rightholders, users and other collective management organisations in the management of rights by collective management organisations, each collective management organisation should comply with specific transparency requirements. Each collective management organisation or its member being an entity responsible for attribution or payment of amounts due to rightholders should therefore be required to provide certain information to individual rightholders at least once a year, such as the amounts attributed or paid to them and the deductions made. Collective management organisations should also be required to provide sufficient information, including financial information, to the other collective management organisations whose rights they manage under representation agreements.

(35) In order to ensure that rightholders, other collective management organisations and users have access to information on the scope of activity of the organisation and the works or other subject-matter that it represents, a collective

management organisation should provide information on those issues in response to a duly justified request. The question whether, and to what extent, reasonable fees can be charged for providing this service should be left to national law. Each collective management organisation should also make public information on its structure and on the way in which it carries out its activities, including in particular its statutes and general policies on management fees, deductions and tariffs.

(36) In order to ensure that rightholders are in a position to monitor and compare the respective performances of collective management organisations, such organisations should make public an annual transparency report comprising comparable audited financial information specific to their activities. Collective management organisations should also make public an annual special report, forming part of the annual transparency report, on the use of amounts dedicated to social, cultural and educational services. This Directive should not prevent a collective management organisation from publishing the information required by the annual transparency report in a single document, for example as part of its annual financial statements, or in separate reports.

(37) Providers of online services which make use of musical works, such as music services that allow consumers to download music or to listen to it in streaming mode, as well as other services providing access to films or games where music is an important element, must first obtain the right to use such works. Directive 2001/29/EC requires that a licence be obtained for each of the rights in the online exploitation of musical works. In respect of authors, those rights are the exclusive right of reproduction and the exclusive right of communication to the public of musical works, which includes the right of making available. Those rights may be managed by the individual rightholders themselves, such as authors or music publishers, or by collective management organisations that provide collective management services to rightholders. Different collective management organisations may manage authors' rights of reproduction and communication to the public. Furthermore, there are cases where several rightholders have rights in the same work and may have authorised different organisations to license their respective shares of rights in the work. Any user wishing to provide an online service offering a wide choice of musical works to consumers needs to aggregate rights in works from different rightholders and collective management organisations.

(38) While the internet knows no borders, the online market for music services in the Union is still fragmented, and a digital single market has not yet been fully achieved. The complexity and difficulty associated with the collective management of rights in Europe has, in a number of cases, exacerbated the fragmentation of the European digital market for online music services. This situation is in stark contrast to the rapidly growing demand on the part of consumers for access to digital content and associated innovative services, including across national borders.

(39) Commission Recommendation 2005/737/EC promoted a new regulatory environment better suited to the management, at Union level, of copyright and related rights for the provision of legitimate online music services. It recognised that, in an era of online exploitation of musical works, commercial users need a licensing policy that corresponds to the ubiquity of the online environment and is multi-territorial. However, the Recommendation has not been sufficient to encourage the widespread multi-territorial licensing of online rights in musical works or to address the specific demands of multi-territorial licensing.

(40) In the online music sector, where collective management of authors' rights on a territorial basis remains the norm, it is essential to create conditions conducive to the most effective licensing practices by collective management organisations in an increasingly cross-border context. It is therefore appropriate to

provide a set of rules prescribing basic conditions for the provision by collective management organisations of multi-territorial collective licensing of authors' rights in musical works for online use, including lyrics. The same rules should apply to such licensing for all musical works, including musical works incorporated in audiovisual works. However, online services solely providing access to musical works in sheet music form should not be covered. The provisions of this Directive should ensure the necessary minimum quality of cross-border services provided by collective management organisations, notably in terms of transparency of repertoire represented and accuracy of financial flows related to the use of the rights. They should also set out a framework for facilitating the voluntary aggregation of music repertoire and rights, thus reducing the number of licences a user needs to operate a multi-territory, multi-repertoire service. Those provisions should enable a collective management organisation to request another organisation to represent its repertoire on a multi-territorial basis where it cannot or does not wish to fulfil the requirements itself. There should be an obligation on the requested organisation, provided that it already aggregates repertoire and offers or grants multi-territorial licences, to accept the mandate of the requesting organisation. The development of legal online music services across the Union should also contribute to the fight against online infringements of copyright.

(41) The availability of accurate and comprehensive information on musical works, rightholders and the rights that each collective management organisation is authorised to represent in a given territory is of particular importance for an effective and transparent licensing process, for the subsequent processing of the users' reports and the related invoicing of service providers, and for the distribution of amounts due. For that reason, collective management organisations granting multi-territorial licences for musical works should be able to process such detailed data quickly and accurately. This requires the use of databases on ownership of rights that are licensed on a multi-territorial basis, containing data that allow for the identification of works, rights and rightholders that a collective management organisation is authorised to represent and of the territories covered by the authorisation. Any changes to that information should be taken into account without undue delay and the databases should be continually updated. Those databases should also help to match information on works with information on phonograms or any other fixation in which the work has been incorporated. It is also important to ensure that prospective users and rightholders, as well as collective management organisations, have access to the information they need in order to identify the repertoire that those organisations are representing. Collective management organisations should be able to take measures to protect the accuracy and integrity of the data, to control their reuse or to protect commercially sensitive information.

(42) In order to ensure that the data on the music repertoire they process are as accurate as possible, collective management organisations granting multi-territorial licences in musical works should be required to update their databases continuously and without delay as necessary. They should establish easily accessible procedures to enable online service providers, as well as rightholders and other collective management organisations, to inform them of any inaccuracy that the organisations' databases may contain in respect of works they own or control, including rights — in whole or in part—and territories for which they have mandated the relevant collective management organisation to act, without however jeopardising the veracity and integrity of the data held by the collective management organisation. Since Directive 95/46/EC of the European Parliament

and of the Council[6] grants to every data subject the right to obtain rectification, erasure or blocking of inaccurate or incomplete data, this Directive should also ensure that inaccurate information regarding rightholders or other collective management organisations in the case of multi-territorial licences is to be corrected without undue delay. Collective management organisations should also have the capacity to process electronically the registration of works and authorisations to manage rights. Given the importance of information automation for the fast and effective processing of data, collective management organisations should provide for the use of electronic means for the structured communication of that information by rightholders. Collective management organisations should, as far as possible, ensure that such electronic means take into account the relevant voluntary industry standards or practices developed at international or Union level.

(43) Industry standards for music use, sales reporting and invoicing are instrumental in improving efficiency in the exchange of data between collective management organisations and users. Monitoring the use of licences should respect fundamental rights, including the right to respect for private and family life and the right to protection of personal data. In order to ensure that these efficiency gains result in faster financial processing and ultimately in earlier payments to rightholders, collective management organisations should be required to invoice service providers and to distribute amounts due to rightholders without delay. For this requirement to be effective, it is necessary that users provide collective management organisations with accurate and timely reports on the use of works. Collective management organisations should not be required to accept users' reports in proprietary formats when widely used industry standards are available. Collective management organisations should not be prevented from outsourcing services relating to the granting of multi-territorial licences for online rights in musical works. Sharing or consolidation of back-office capabilities should help the organisations to improve management services and rationalise investments in data management tools.

(44) Aggregating different music repertoires for multi-territorial licensing facilitates the licensing process and, by making all repertoires accessible to the market for multi-territorial licensing, enhances cultural diversity and contributes to reducing the number of transactions an online service provider needs in order to offer services. This aggregation of repertoires should facilitate the development of new online services, and should also result in a reduction of transaction costs being passed on to consumers. Therefore, collective management organisations that are not willing or not able to grant multi-territorial licences directly in their own music repertoire should be encouraged on a voluntary basis to mandate other collective management organisations to manage their repertoire on a non-discriminatory basis. Exclusivity in agreements on multi-territorial licences would restrict the choices available to users seeking multi-territorial licences and also restrict the choices available to collective management organisations seeking administration services for their repertoire on a multi-territorial basis. Therefore, all representation agreements between collective management organisations providing for multi-territorial licensing should be concluded on a non-exclusive basis.

(45) The transparency of the conditions under which collective management organisations manage online rights is of particular importance to members of collective management organisations. Collective management organisations should therefore provide sufficient information to their members on the main terms of

---

[6] Directive 95/46/EC of the European Parliament and of the Council of 24 October 1995 on the protection of individuals with regard to the processing of personal data and on the free movement of such data (OJ L281, 23.11.1995, p.31).

any agreement mandating any other collective management organisation to represent those members' online music rights for the purposes of multi-territorial licensing.

(46) It is also important to require any collective management organisations that offer or grant multi-territorial licences to agree to represent the repertoire of any collective management organisations that decide not to do so directly. To ensure that this requirement is not disproportionate and does not go beyond what is necessary, the requested collective management organisation should only be required to accept the representation if the request is limited to the online right or categories of online rights that it represents itself. Moreover, this requirement should only apply to collective management organisations which aggregate repertoire and should not extend to collective management organisations which provide multi-territorial licences for their own repertoire only. Nor should it apply to collective management organisations which merely aggregate rights in the same works for the purpose of being able to license jointly both the right of reproduction and the right of communication to the public in respect of such works. To protect the interests of the rightholders of the mandating collective management organisation and to ensure that small and less well-known repertoires in Member States can access the internal market on equal terms, it is important that the repertoire of the mandating collective management organisation be managed on the same conditions as the repertoire of the mandated collective management organisation and that it is included in offers addressed by the mandated collective management organisation to online service providers. The management fee charged by the mandated collective management organisation should allow that organisation to recoup the necessary and reasonable investments incurred. Any agreement whereby a collective management organisation mandates another organisation or organisations to grant multi-territorial licences in its own music repertoire for online use should not prevent the first-mentioned collective management organisation from continuing to grant licences limited to the territory of the Member State where that organisation is established, in its own repertoire and in any other repertoire it may be authorised to represent in that territory.

(47) The objectives and effectiveness of the rules on multi-territorial licensing by collective management organisations would be significantly jeopardised if rightholders were not able to exercise such rights in respect of multi-territorial licences when the collective management organisation to which they have granted their rights did not grant or offer multi-territorial licences and furthermore did not want to mandate another collective management organisation to do so. For this reason, it would be important in such circumstances to enable rightholders to exercise the right to grant the multi-territorial licences required by online service providers themselves or through another party or parties, by withdrawing from their original collective management organisation their rights to the extent necessary for multi-territorial licensing for online uses, and to leave the same rights with their original organisation for the purposes of mono-territorial licensing.

(48) Broadcasting organisations generally rely on a licence from a local collective management organisation for their own broadcasts of television and radio programmes which include musical works. That licence is often limited to broadcasting activities. A licence for online rights in musical works would be required in order to allow such television or radio broadcasts to be also available online. To facilitate the licensing of online rights in musical works for the purposes of simultaneous and delayed transmission online of television and radio broadcasts, it is necessary to provide for a derogation from the rules that would otherwise apply to the multi-territorial licensing of online rights in musical works. Such a derogation should be limited to what is necessary in order to allow access

to television or radio programmes online and to material having a clear and subordinate relationship to the original broadcast produced for purposes such as supplementing, previewing or reviewing the television or radio programme concerned. That derogation should not operate so as to distort competition with other services which give consumers access to individual musical or audiovisual works online, nor lead to restrictive practices, such as market or customer sharing, which would be in breach of Article 101 or 102 TFEU.

(49) It is necessary to ensure the effective enforcement of the provisions of national law adopted pursuant to this Directive. Collective management organisations should offer their members specific procedures for handling complaints. Those procedures should also be made available to other rightholders directly represented by the organisation and to other collective management organisations on whose behalf it manages rights under a representation agreement. Furthermore, Member States should be able to provide that disputes between collective management organisations, their members, rightholders or users as to the application of this Directive can be submitted to a rapid, independent and impartial alternative dispute resolution procedure. In particular, the effectiveness of the rules on multi-territorial licensing of online rights in musical works could be undermined if disputes between collective management organisations and other parties were not resolved quickly and efficiently. As a result, it is appropriate to provide, without prejudice to the right of access to a tribunal, for the possibility of easily accessible, efficient and impartial out-of-court procedures, such as mediation or arbitration, for resolving conflicts between, on the one hand, collective management organisations granting multi-territorial licences and, on the other, online service providers, rightholders or other collective management organisations. This Directive neither prescribes a specific manner in which such alternative dispute resolution should be organised, nor determines which body should carry it out, provided that its independence, impartiality and efficiency are guaranteed. Finally, it is also appropriate to require that Member States have independent, impartial and effective dispute resolution procedures, via bodies possessing expertise in intellectual property law or via courts, suitable for settling commercial disputes between collective management organisations and users on existing or proposed licensing conditions or on a breach of contract.

(50) Member States should establish appropriate procedures by means of which it will be possible to monitor compliance by collective management organisations with this Directive. While it is not appropriate for this Directive to restrict the choice of Member States as to competent authorities, nor as regards the ex-ante or ex-post nature of the control over collective management organisations, it should be ensured that such authorities are capable of addressing in an effective and timely manner any concern that may arise in the application of this Directive. Member States should not be obliged to set up new competent authorities. Moreover, it should also be possible for members of a collective management organisation, rightholders, users, collective management organisations and other interested parties to notify a competent authority in respect of activities or circumstances which, in their opinion, constitute a breach of law by collective management organisations and, where relevant, users. Member States should ensure that competent authorities have the power to impose sanctions or measures where provisions of national law implementing this Directive are not complied with. This Directive does not provide for specific types of sanctions or measures, provided that they are effective, proportionate and dissuasive. Such sanctions or measures may include orders to dismiss directors who have acted negligently, inspections at the premises of a collective management organisation or, in cases where an authorisation is issued for an organisation to operate, the withdrawal of such authorisation. This Directive should remain neutral as regards the prior

authorisation and supervision regimes in the Member States, including a requirement for the representativeness of the collective management organisation, in so far as those regimes are compatible with Union law and do not create an obstacle to the full application of this Directive.

(51) In order to ensure that the requirements for multi-territorial licensing are complied with, specific provisions on the monitoring of their implementation should be laid down. The competent authorities of the Member States and the Commission should cooperate with each other to that end. Member States should provide each other with mutual assistance by way of exchange of information between their competent authorities in order to facilitate the monitoring of collective management organisations.

(52) It is important for collective management organisations to respect the rights to private life and personal data protection of any rightholder, member, user and other individual whose personal data they process. Directive 95/46/EC governs the processing of personal data carried out in the Member States in the context of that Directive and under the supervision of the Member States' competent authorities, in particular the public independent authorities designated by the Member States. Rightholders should be given appropriate information about the processing of their data, the recipients of those data, time limits for the retention of such data in any database, and the way in which rightholders can exercise their rights to access, correct or delete their personal data concerning them in accordance with Directive 95/46/EC. In particular, unique identifiers which allow for the indirect identification of a person should be treated as personal data within the meaning of that Directive.

(53) Provisions on enforcement measures should be without prejudice to the competencies of national independent public authorities established by the Member States pursuant to Directive 95/46/EC to monitor compliance with national provisions adopted in implementation of that Directive.

(54) This Directive respects the fundamental rights and observes the principles enshrined in the Charter of Fundamental Rights of the European Union ('the Charter'). Provisions in this Directive relating to dispute resolution should not prevent parties from exercising their right of access to a tribunal as guaranteed in the Charter.

(55) Since the objectives of this Directive, namely to improve the ability of their members to exercise control over the activities of collective management organisations, to guarantee sufficient transparency by collective management organisations and to improve the multi-territorial licensing of authors' rights in musical works for online use, cannot be sufficiently achieved by Member States but can rather, by reason of their scale and effects, be better achieved at Union level, the Union may adopt measures in accordance with the principle of subsidiarity as set out in Article 5 of the Treaty on European Union. In accordance with the principle of proportionality, as set out in that Article, this Directive does not go beyond what is necessary in order to achieve those objectives.

(56) The provisions of this Directive are without prejudice to the application of rules on competition, and any other relevant law in other areas including confidentiality, trade secrets, privacy, access to documents, the law of contract and private international law relating to the conflict of laws and the jurisdiction of courts, and workers' and employers' freedom of association and their right to organise.

(57) In accordance with the Joint Political Declaration of 28 September 2011

of Member States and the Commission on explanatory documents,[7] Member States have undertaken to accompany, in justified cases, the notification of their transposition measures with one or more documents explaining the relationship between the components of a directive and the corresponding parts of national transposition instruments. With regard to this Directive, the legislator considers the transmission of such documents to be justified.

(58) The European Data Protection Supervisor was consulted in accordance with Article 28(2) of Regulation (EC) No 45/2001 of the European Parliament and of the Council[8] and delivered an opinion on 9 October 2012,

HAVE ADOPTED THIS DIRECTIVE:

TITLE I

GENERAL PROVISIONS

Article 1

Subject-matter

This Directive lays down requirements necessary to ensure the proper functioning of the management of copyright and related rights by collective management organisations. It also lays down requirements for multi-territorial licensing by collective management organisations of authors' rights in musical works for online use.

Article 2

Scope

1. Titles I, II, IV and V with the exception of Article 34(2) and Article 38 apply to all collective management organisations established in the Union.

2. Title III and Article 34(2) and Article 38 apply to collective management organisations established in the Union managing authors' rights in musical works for online use on a multi-territorial basis.

3. The relevant provisions of this Directive apply to entities directly or indirectly owned or controlled, wholly or in part, by a collective management organisation, provided that such entities carry out an activity which, if carried out by the collective management organisation, would be subject to the provisions of this Directive.

4. Article 16(1), Articles 18 and 20, points (a), (b), (c), (e), (f) and (g) of Article 21(1) and Articles 36 and 42 apply to all independent management entities established in the Union.

Article 3

Definitions

For the purposes of this Directive, the following definitions shall apply:

(a) 'collective management organisation' means any organisation which is authorised by law or by way of assignment, licence or any other contractual arrangement to manage copyright or rights related to copyright on behalf of more than one rightholder, for the collective benefit of those rightholders,

---

[7] OJ C369, 17.12.2011, p.14.

[8] Regulation (EC) No 45/2001 of the European Parliament and of the Council of 18 December 2000 on the protection of individuals with regard to the processing of personal data by the Community institutions and bodies and on the free movement of such data (OJ L8, 12.1.2001, p.1).

as its sole or main purpose, and which fulfils one or both of the following criteria:

(i) it is owned or controlled by its members;

(ii) it is organised on a not-for-profit basis;

(b) 'independent management entity' means any organisation which is authorised by law or by way of assignment, licence or any other contractual arrangement to manage copyright or rights related to copyright on behalf of more than one rightholder, for the collective benefit of those rightholders, as its sole or main purpose, and which is:

(i) neither owned nor controlled, directly or indirectly, wholly or in part, by rightholders; and

(ii) organised on a for-profit basis;

(c) 'rightholder' means any person or entity, other than a collective management organisation, that holds a copyright or related right or, under an agreement for the exploitation of rights or by law, is entitled to a share of the rights revenue;

(d) 'member ' means a rightholder or an entity representing rightholders, including other collective management organisations and associations of rightholders, fulfilling the membership requirements of the collective management organisation and admitted by it;

(e) 'statute' means the memorandum and articles of association, the statute, the rules or documents of constitution of a collective management organisation;

(f) 'general assembly of members' means the body in the collective management organisation wherein members participate and exercise their voting rights, regardless of the legal form of the organisation;

(g) 'director' means:

(i) where national law or the statute of the collective management organisation provides for a unitary board, any member of the administrative board;

(ii) where national law or the statute of the collective management organisation provides for a dual board, any member of the management board or the supervisory board;

(h) 'rights revenue' means income collected by a collective management organisation on behalf of rightholders, whether deriving from an exclusive right, a right to remuneration or a right to compensation;

(i) 'management fees' means the amounts charged, deducted or offset by a collective management organisation from rights revenue or from any income arising from the investment of rights revenue in order to cover the costs of its management of copyright or related rights;

(j) 'representation agreement' means any agreement between collective management organisations whereby one collective management organisation mandates another collective management organisation to manage the rights it represents, including an agreement concluded under Articles 29 and 30;

(k) 'user' means any person or entity that is carrying out acts subject to the authorisation of rightholders, remuneration of rightholders or payment of compensation to rightholders and is not acting in the capacity of a consumer;

(l) 'repertoire' means the works in respect of which a collective management organisation manages rights;

(m) 'multi-territorial licence' means a licence which covers the territory of more than one Member State;

(n) 'online rights in musical works' means any of the rights of an author in a musical work provided for under Articles 2 and 3 of Directive 2001/29/EC which are required for the provision of an online service.

Title II

Collective Management Organisations

Chapter 1

Representation of rightholders and membership and organisation of collective management organisations

Article 4

General principles

Member States shall ensure that collective management organisations act in the best interests of the rightholders whose rights they represent and that they do not impose on them any obligations which are not objectively necessary for the protection of their rights and interests or for the effective management of their rights.

Article 5

Rights of rightholders

1. Member States shall ensure that rightholders have the rights laid down in paragraphs 2 to 8 and that those rights are set out in the statute or membership terms of the collective management organisation.

2. Rightholders shall have the right to authorise a collective management organisation of their choice to manage the rights, categories of rights or types of works and other subject-matter of their choice, for the territories of their choice, irrespective of the Member State of nationality, residence or establishment of either the collective management organisation or the rightholder. Unless the collective management organisation has objectively justified reasons to refuse management, it shall be obliged to manage such rights, categories of rights or types of works and other subject-matter, provided that their management falls within the scope of its activity.

3. Rightholders shall have the right to grant licences for non-commercial uses of any rights, categories of rights or types of works and other subject-matter that they may choose.

4. Rightholders shall have the right to terminate the authorisation to manage rights, categories of rights or types of works and other subject-matter granted by them to a collective management organisation or to withdraw from a collective management organisation any of the rights, categories of rights or types of works and other subject-matter of their choice, as determined pursuant to paragraph 2, for the territories of their choice, upon serving reasonable notice not exceeding six months. The collective management organisation may decide that such termination or withdrawal is to take effect only at the end of the financial year.

5. If there are amounts due to a rightholder for acts of exploitation which occurred before the termination of the authorisation or the withdrawal of rights took effect, or under a licence granted before such termination or withdrawal took effect, the rightholder shall retain his rights under Articles 12, 13, 18, 20, 28 and 33.

6. A collective management organisation shall not restrict the exercise of rights provided for under paragraphs 4 and 5 by requiring, as a condition for the exercise of those rights, that the management of rights or categories of rights or types of works and other subject-matter which are subject to the termination or the withdrawal be entrusted to another collective management organisation.

7. In cases where a rightholder authorises a collective management organisation to manage his rights, he shall give consent specifically for each right or category of rights or type of works and other subject-matter which he authorises the collective management organisation to manage. Any such consent shall be evidenced in documentary form.

8. A collective management organisation shall inform rightholders of their rights under paragraphs 1 to 7, as well as of any conditions attached to the right set out in paragraph 3, before obtaining their consent to its managing any right or category of rights or type of works and other subject-matter.

A collective management organisation shall inform those rightholders who have already authorised it of their rights under paragraphs 1 to 7, as well as of any conditions attached to the right set out in paragraph 3, by 10 October 2016.

Article 6

Membership rules of collective management organisations

1. Member States shall ensure that collective management organisations comply with the rules laid down in paragraphs 2 to 5.

2. A collective management organisation shall accept rightholders and entities representing rightholders, including other collective management organisations and associations of rightholders, as members if they fulfil the membership requirements, which shall be based on objective, transparent and non-discriminatory criteria. Those membership requirements shall be included in the statute or membership terms of the collective management organisation and shall be made publicly available. In cases where a collective management organisation refuses to accept a request for membership, it shall provide the rightholder with a clear explanation of the reasons for its decision.

3. The statute of a collective management organisation shall provide for appropriate and effective mechanisms for the participation of its members in the organisation's decision-making process. The representation of the different categories of members in the decision-making process shall be fair and balanced.

4. A collective management organisation shall allow its members to communicate with it by electronic means, including for the purposes of exercising members' rights.

5. A collective management organisation shall keep records of its members and shall regularly update those records.

Article 7

Rights of rightholders who are not members of the collective management organisation

1. Member States shall ensure that collective management organisations comply with the rules laid down in Article 6(4), Article 20, Article 29(2) and Article 33 in respect of rightholders who have a direct legal relationship by law or by way of assignment, licence or any other contractual arrangement with them but are not their members.

2. Member States may apply other provisions of this Directive to the rightholders referred to in paragraph 1.

Article 8

General assembly of members of the collective management organisation

1. Member States shall ensure that the general assembly of members is organised in accordance with the rules laid down in paragraphs 2 to 10.

2. A general assembly of members shall be convened at least once a year.

3. The general assembly of members shall decide on any amendments to the statute and to the membership terms of the collective management organisation, where those terms are not regulated by the statute.

4. The general assembly of members shall decide on the appointment or dismissal of the directors, review their general performance and approve their remuneration and other benefits such as monetary and non-monetary benefits, pension awards and entitlements, rights to other awards and rights to severance pay.

In a collective management organisation with a dual board system, the general assembly of members shall not decide on the appointment or dismissal of members of the management board or approve their remuneration and other benefits where the power to take such decisions is delegated to the supervisory board.

5. In accordance with the provisions laid down in Chapter 2 of Title II, the general assembly of members shall decide at least on the following issues:

(a) the general policy on the distribution of amounts due to rightholders;

(b) the general policy on the use of non-distributable amounts;

(c) the general investment policy with regard to rights revenue and to any income arising from the investment of rights revenue;

(d) the general policy on deductions from rights revenue and from any income arising from the investment of rights revenue;

(e) the use of non-distributable amounts;

(f) the risk management policy;

(g) the approval of any acquisition, sale or hypothecation of immovable property;

(h) the approval of mergers and alliances, the setting-up of subsidiaries, and the acquisition of other entities or shares or rights in other entities;

(i) the approval of taking out loans, granting loans or providing security for loans.

6. The general assembly of members may delegate the powers listed in points (f), (g), (h) and (i) of paragraph 5, by a resolution or by a provision in the statute, to the body exercising the supervisory function.

7. For the purposes of points (a) to (d) of paragraph 5, Member States may require the general assembly of members to determine more detailed conditions for the use of the rights revenue and the income arising from the investment of rights revenue.

8. The general assembly of members shall control the activities of the collective management organisation by, at least, deciding on the appointment and removal of the auditor and approving the annual transparency report referred to in Article 22.

Member States may allow alternative systems or modalities for the appointment and removal of the auditor, provided that those systems or modalities are designed to ensure the independence of the auditor from the persons who manage the business of the collective management organisation.

9. All members of the collective management organisation shall have the right to participate in, and the right to vote at, the general assembly of members. However, Member States may allow for restrictions on the right of the members

of the collective management organisation to participate in, and to exercise voting rights at, the general assembly of members, on the basis of one or both of the following criteria:

(a) duration of membership;

(b) amounts received or due to a member,

provided that such criteria are determined and applied in a manner that is fair and proportionate. The criteria laid down in points (a) and (b) of the first subparagraph shall be included in the statute or the membership terms of the collective management organisation and shall be made publicly available in accordance with Articles 19 and 21.

10. Every member of a collective management organisation shall have the right to appoint any other person or entity as a proxy holder to participate in, and vote at, the general assembly of members on his behalf, provided that such appointment does not result in a conflict of interest which might occur, for example, where the appointing member and the proxy holder belong to different categories of rightholders within the collective management organisation.

However, Member States may provide for restrictions concerning the appointment of proxy holders and the exercise of the voting rights of the members they represent if such restrictions do not prejudice the appropriate and effective participation of members in the decision-making process of a collective management organisation.

Each proxy shall be valid for a single general assembly of members. The proxy holder shall enjoy the same rights in the general assembly of members as those to which the appointing member would be entitled. The proxy holder shall cast votes in accordance with the instructions issued by the appointing member.

11. Member States may decide that the powers of the general assembly of members may be exercised by an assembly of delegates elected at least every four years by the members of the collective management organisation, provided that:

(a) appropriate and effective participation of members in the collective management organisation's decision-making process is ensured; and

(b) the representation of the different categories of members in the assembly of delegates is fair and balanced.

The rules laid down in paragraphs 2 to 10 shall apply to the assembly of delegates mutatis mutandis.

(12. Member States may decide that where a collective management organisation, by reason of its legal form, does not have a general assembly of members, the powers of that assembly are to be exercised by the body exercising the supervisory function. The rules laid down in paragraphs 2 to 5, 7 and 8 shall apply mutatis mutandis to such body exercising the supervisory function.

13. Member States may decide that where a collective management organisation has members who are entities representing rightholders, all or some of the powers of the general assembly of members are to be exercised by an assembly of those rightholders. The rules laid down in paragraphs 2 to 10 shall apply mutatis mutandis to the assembly of rightholders.

Article 9

Supervisory function

1. Member States shall ensure that each collective management organisation has in place a supervisory function for continuously monitoring the activities and the performance of the duties of the persons who manage the business of the organisation.

2. There shall be fair and balanced representation of the different categories of members of the collective management organisation in the body exercising the supervisory function.

3. Each person exercising the supervisory function shall make an annual individual statement on conflicts of interest, containing the information referred to in the second subparagraph of Article 10(2), to the general assembly of members.

4. The body exercising the supervisory function shall meet regularly and shall have at least the following powers:

(a) to exercise the powers delegated to it by the general assembly of members, including under Article 8(4) and (6);

(b) to monitor the activities and the performance of the duties of the persons referred to in Article 10, including the implementation of the decisions of the general assembly of members and, in particular, of the general policies listed in points (a) to (d) of Article 8(5).

5. The body exercising the supervisory function shall report on the exercise of its powers to the general assembly of members at least once a year.

Article 10

Obligations of the persons who manage the business of the collective management organisation

1. Member States shall ensure that each collective management organisation takes all necessary measures so that the persons who manage its business do so in a sound, prudent and appropriate manner, using sound administrative and accounting procedures and internal control mechanisms.

2. Member States shall ensure that collective management organisations put in place and apply procedures to avoid conflicts of interest, and where such conflicts cannot be avoided, to identify, manage, monitor and disclose actual or potential conflicts of interest in such a way as to prevent them from adversely affecting the collective interests of the rightholders whom the organisation represents.

The procedures referred to in the first subparagraph shall include an annual individual statement by each of the persons referred to in paragraph 1 to the general assembly of members, containing the following information:

(a) any interests in the collective management organisation;

(b) any remuneration received in the preceding financial year from the collective management organisation, including in the form of pension schemes, benefits in kind and other types of benefits;

(c) any amounts received in the preceding financial year as a rightholder from the collective management organisation;

(d) a declaration concerning any actual or potential conflict between any personal interests and those of the collective management organisation or between any obligations owed to the collective management organisation and any duty owed to any other natural or legal person.

CHAPTER 2

MANAGEMENT OF RIGHTS REVENUE

Article 11

Collection and use of rights revenue

1. Member States shall ensure that collective management organisations comply with the rules laid down in paragraphs 2 to 5.

2. A collective management organisation shall be diligent in the collection and management of rights revenue.

3. A collective management organisation shall keep separate in its accounts:

(a) rights revenue and any income arising from the investment of rights revenue; and

(b) any own assets it may have and income arising from such assets, from management fees or from other activities.

4. A collective management organisation shall not be permitted to use rights revenue or any income arising from the investment of rights revenue for purposes other than distribution to rightholders, except where it is allowed to deduct or offset its management fees in compliance with a decision taken in accordance with point (d) of Article 8(5) or to use the rights revenue or any income arising from the investment of rights revenue in compliance with a decision taken in accordance with Article 8(5).

5. Where a collective management organisation invests rights revenue or any income arising from the investment of rights revenue, it shall do so in the best interests of the rightholders whose rights it represents, in accordance with the general investment and risk management policy referred to in points (c) and (f) of Article 8(5) and having regard to the following rules:

(a) where there is any potential conflict of interest, the collective management organisation shall ensure that the investment is made in the sole interest of those rightholders;

(b) the assets shall be invested in order to ensure the security, quality, liquidity and profitability of the portfolio as a whole;

(c) the assets shall be properly diversified in order to avoid excessive reliance on any particular asset and accumulations of risks in the portfolio as a whole.

Article 12

Deductions

1. Member States shall ensure that where a rightholder authorises a collective management organisation to manage his rights, the collective management organisation is required to provide the rightholder with information on management fees and other deductions from the rights revenue and from any income arising from the investment of rights revenue, before obtaining his consent to its managing his rights.

2. Deductions shall be reasonable in relation to the services provided by the collective management organisation to rightholders, including, where appropriate, the services referred to in paragraph 4, and shall be established on the basis of objective criteria.

3. Management fees shall not exceed the justified and documented costs incurred by the collective management organisation in managing copyright and related rights.

Member States shall ensure that the requirements applicable to the use and the transparency of the use of amounts deducted or offset in respect of management fees apply to any other deductions made in order to cover the costs of managing copyright and related rights.

4. Where a collective management organisation provides social, cultural or educational services funded through deductions from rights revenue or from any income arising from the investment of rights revenue, such services shall be provided on the basis of fair criteria, in particular as regards access to, and the extent of, those services.

Article 13
Distribution of amounts due to rightholders

1. Without prejudice to Article 15(3) and Article 28, Member States shall ensure that each collective management organisation regularly, diligently and accurately distributes and pays amounts due to rightholders in accordance with the general policy on distribution referred to in point (a) of Article 8(5).

Member States shall also ensure that collective management organisations or their members who are entities representing rightholders distribute and pay those amounts to rightholders as soon as possible but no later than nine months from the end of the financial year in which the rights revenue was collected, unless objective reasons relating in particular to reporting by users, identification of rights, rightholders or matching of information on works and other subject-matter with rightholders prevent the collective management organisation or, where applicable, its members from meeting that deadline.

2. Where the amounts due to rightholders cannot be distributed within the deadline set in paragraph 1 because the relevant rightholders cannot be identified or located and the exception to that deadline does not apply, those amounts shall be kept separate in the accounts of the collective management organisation.

3. The collective management organisation shall take all necessary measures, consistent with paragraph 1, to identify and locate the rightholders. In particular, at the latest three months after the expiry of the deadline set in paragraph 1, the collective management organisation shall make available information on works and other subject-matter for which one or more rightholders have not been identified or located to:

(a) the rightholders that it represents or the entities representing rightholders, where such entities are members of the collective management organisation; and

(b) all collective management organisations with which it has concluded representation agreements.

The information referred to in the first subparagraph shall include, where available, the following:

(a) the title of the work or other subject-matter;

(b) the name of the rightholder;

(c) the name of the relevant publisher or producer; and

(d) any other relevant information available which could assist in identifying the rightholder.

The collective management organisation shall also verify the records referred to in Article 6(5) and other readily available records. If the abovementioned measures fail to produce results, the collective management organisation shall make that information available to the public at the latest one year after the expiry of the three-month period.

4. Where the amounts due to rightholders cannot be distributed after three years from the end of the financial year in which the collection of the rights revenue occurred, and provided that the collective management organisation has taken all necessary measures to identify and locate the rightholders referred to in paragraph 3, those amounts shall be deemed non-distributable.

5. The general assembly of members of a collective management organisation shall decide on the use of the non-distributable amounts in accordance with point (b) of Article 8(5), without prejudice to the right of rightholders to claim such amounts from the collective management organisation in accordance with the laws of the Member States on the statute of limitations of claims.

6. Member States may limit or determine the permitted uses of non-

distributable amounts, inter alia, by ensuring that such amounts are used in a separate and independent way in order to fund social, cultural and educational activities for the benefit of rightholders.

CHAPTER 3

MANAGEMENT OF RIGHTS ON BEHALF OF OTHER COLLECTIVE MANAGEMENT ORGANISATIONS

Article 14

Rights managed under representation agreements

Member States shall ensure that a collective management organisation does not discriminate against any rightholder whose rights it manages under a representation agreement, in particular with respect to applicable tariffs, management fees, and the conditions for the collection of the rights revenue and distribution of amounts due to rightholders.

Article 15

Deductions and payments in representation agreements

1. Member States shall ensure that a collective management organisation does not make deductions, other than in respect of management fees, from the rights revenue derived from the rights it manages on the basis of a representation agreement, or from any income arising from the investment of that rights revenue, unless the other collective management organisation that is party to the representation agreement expressly consents to such deductions.

2. The collective management organisation shall regularly, diligently and accurately distribute and pay amounts due to other collective management organisations.

3. The collective management organisation shall carry out such distribution and payments to the other collective management organisation as soon as possible but no later than nine months from the end of the financial year in which the rights revenue was collected, unless objective reasons relating in particular to reporting by users, identification of rights, rightholders or matching of information on works and other subject-matter with rightholders prevent the collective management organisation from meeting that deadline.

The other collective management organisation, or, where it has as members entities representing rightholders, those members, shall distribute and pay the amounts due to rightholders as soon as possible but no later than six months from receipt of those amounts, unless objective reasons relating in particular to reporting by users, identification of rights, rightholders or matching of information on works and other subject-matter with rightholders prevent the collective management organisation or, where applicable, its members from meeting that deadline.

CHAPTER 4

RELATIONS WITH USERS

Article 16

Licensing

1. Member States shall ensure that collective management organisations and users conduct negotiations for the licensing of rights in good faith. Collective management organisations and users shall provide each other with all necessary information.

2. Licensing terms shall be based on objective and non-discriminatory criteria. When licensing rights, collective management organisations shall not be required to use, as a precedent for other online services, licensing terms agreed with a user where the user is providing a new type of online service which has been available to the public in the Union for less than three years.

Rightholders shall receive appropriate remuneration for the use of their rights. Tariffs for exclusive rights and rights to remuneration shall be reasonable in relation to, inter alia, the economic value of the use of the rights in trade, taking into account the nature and scope of the use of the work and other subject-matter, as well as in relation to the economic value of the service provided by the collective management organisation. Collective management organisations shall inform the user concerned of the criteria used for the setting of those tariffs.

3. Collective management organisations shall reply without undue delay to requests from users, indicating, inter alia, the information needed in order for the collective management organisation to offer a licence.

Upon receipt of all relevant information, the collective management organisation shall, without undue delay, either offer a licence or provide the user with a reasoned statement explaining why it does not intend to license a particular service.

4. A collective management organisation shall allow users to communicate with it by electronic means, including, where appropriate, for the purpose of reporting on the use of the licence.

Article 17

Users' obligations

Member States shall adopt provisions to ensure that users provide a collective management organisation, within an agreed or pre-established time and in an agreed or pre-established format, with such relevant information at their disposal on the use of the rights represented by the collective management organisation as is necessary for the collection of rights revenue and for the distribution and payment of amounts due to rightholders. When deciding on the format for the provision of such information, collective management organisations and users shall take into account, as far as possible, voluntary industry standards.

CHAPTER 5

TRANSPARENCY AND REPORTING

Article 18

Information provided to rightholders on the management of their rights

1. Without prejudice to paragraph 2 of this Article and Article 19 and Article 28(2), Member States shall ensure that a collective management organisation makes available, not less than once a year, to each rightholder to whom it has attributed rights revenue or made payments in the period to which the information relates, at least the following information:

(a) any contact details which the rightholder has authorised the collective management organisation to use in order to identify and locate the rightholder;

(b) the rights revenue attributed to the rightholder;

(c) the amounts paid by the collective management organisation to the rightholder per category of rights managed and per type of use;

(d) the period during which the use took place for which amounts were attributed and paid to the rightholder, unless objective reasons relating to reporting by users prevent the collective management organisation from providing this information;

(e) deductions made in respect of management fees;

(f) deductions made for any purpose other than in respect of management fees, including those that may be required by national law for the provision of any social, cultural or educational services;

(g) any rights revenue attributed to the rightholder which is outstanding for any period.

2. Where a collective management organisation attributes rights revenue and has as members entities which are responsible for the distribution of rights revenue to rightholders, the collective management organisation shall provide the information listed in paragraph 1 to those entities, provided that they do not have that information in their possession. Member States shall ensure that the entities make at least the information listed in paragraph 1 available, not less than once a year, to each rightholder to whom they have attributed rights revenue or made payments in the period to which the information relates.

Article 19

Information provided to other collective management organisations on the management of rights under representation agreements

Member States shall ensure that a collective management organisation makes at least the following information available, not less than once a year and by electronic means, to collective management organisations on whose behalf it manages rights under a representation agreement, for the period to which the information relates:

(a) the rights revenue attributed, the amounts paid by the collective management organisation per category of rights managed, and per type of use, for the rights it manages under the representation agreement, and any rights revenue attributed which is outstanding for any period;

(b) deductions made in respect of management fees;

(c) deductions made for any purpose other than in respect of management fees as referred to in Article 15;

(d) information on any licences granted or refused with regard to works and other subject-matter covered by the representation agreement;

(e) resolutions adopted by the general assembly of members in so far as those resolutions are relevant to the management of the rights under the representation agreement.

Article 20

Information provided to rightholders, other collective management organisations and users on request

Without prejudice to Article 25, Member States shall ensure that, in response to a duly justified request, a collective management organisation makes at least the following information available by electronic means and without undue delay to any collective management organisation on whose behalf it manages rights under a representation agreement or to any rightholder or to any user:

(a) the works or other subject-matter it represents, the rights it manages, directly or under representation agreements, and the territories covered; or

(b) where, due to the scope of activity of the collective management organisation, such works or other subject-matter cannot be determined, the types of works or of other subject-matter it represents, the rights it manages and the territories covered.

Article 21

Disclosure of information to the public

1. Member States shall ensure that a collective management organisation makes public at least the following information:

(a) its statute;

(b) its membership terms and the terms of termination of authorisation to manage rights, if these are not included in the statute;

(c) standard licensing contracts and standard applicable tariffs, including discounts;

(d) the list of the persons referred to in Article 10;

(e) its general policy on distribution of amounts due to rightholders;

(f) its general policy on management fees;

(g) its general policy on deductions, other than in respect of management fees, from rights revenue and from any income arising from the investment of rights revenue, including deductions for the purposes of social, cultural and educational services;

(h) a list of the representation agreements it has entered into, and the names of the collective management organisations with which those representation agreements have been concluded;

(i) the general policy on the use of non-distributable amounts;

(j) the complaint handling and dispute resolution procedures available in accordance with Articles 33, 34 and 35.

2. The collective management organisation shall publish, and keep up to date, on its public website the information referred to in paragraph 1.

Article 22

Annual transparency report

1. Member States shall ensure that a collective management organisation, irrespective of its legal form under national law, draws up and makes public an annual transparency report, including the special report referred to in paragraph 3, for each financial year no later than eight months following the end of that financial year.

The collective management organisation shall publish on its website the annual transparency report, which shall remain available to the public on that website for at least five years.

2. The annual transparency report shall contain at least the information set out in the Annex.

3. A special report shall address the use of the amounts deducted for the purposes of social, cultural and educational services and shall contain at least the information set out in point 3 of the Annex.

4. The accounting information included in the annual transparency report shall be audited by one or more persons empowered by law to audit accounts in accordance with Directive 2006/43/EC of the European Parliament and of the Council.[9] The audit report, including any qualifications thereto, shall be reproduced in full in the annual transparency report.

---

[9] Directive 2006/43/EC of the European Parliament and of the Council of 17 May 2006 on statutory audits of annual accounts and consolidated account, amending Council Directives 78/660/EEC and 83/349/EEC and repealing Council Directive 84/253/EEC (OJ L157, 9.6.2006, p.87).

For the purposes of this paragraph, accounting information shall comprise the financial statements referred to in point 1(a) of the Annex and any financial information referred to in points (g) and (h) of point 1 and in point 2 of the Annex.

TITLE III

MULTI-TERRITORIAL LICENSING OF ONLINE RIGHTS IN MUSICAL WORKS BY COLLECTIVE MANAGEMENT ORGANISATIONS

Article 23

Multi-territorial licensing in the internal market

Member States shall ensure that collective management organisations established in their territory comply with the requirements of this Title when granting multi-territorial licences for online rights in musical works.

Article 24

Capacity to process multi-territorial licences

1. Member States shall ensure that a collective management organisation which grants multi-territorial licences for online rights in musical works has sufficient capacity to process electronically, in an efficient and transparent manner, data needed for the administration of such licences, including for the purposes of identifying the repertoire and monitoring its use, invoicing users, collecting rights revenue and distributing amounts due to rightholders.

2. For the purposes of paragraph 1, a collective management organisation shall comply, at least, with the following conditions:

(a) to have the ability to identify accurately the musical works, wholly or in part, which the collective management organisation is authorised to represent;

(b) to have the ability to identify accurately, wholly or in part, with respect to each relevant territory, the rights and their corresponding rightholders for each musical work or share therein which the collective management organisation is authorised to represent;

(c) to make use of unique identifiers in order to identify rightholders and musical works, taking into account, as far as possible, voluntary industry standards and practices developed at international or Union level;

(d) to make use of adequate means in order to identify and resolve in a timely and effective manner inconsistencies in data held by other collective management organisations granting multi-territorial licences for online rights in musical works.

Article 25

Transparency of multi-territorial repertoire information

1. Member States shall ensure that a collective management organisation which grants multi-territorial licences for online rights in musical works provides to online service providers, to rightholders whose rights it represents and to other collective management organisations, by electronic means, in response to a duly justified request, up-to-date information allowing the identification of the online music repertoire it represents. This shall include:

(a) the musical works represented;

(b) the rights represented wholly or in part; and

(c) the territories covered.

2. The collective management organisation may take reasonable measures, where necessary, to protect the accuracy and integrity of the data, to control their reuse and to protect commercially sensitive information.

Article 26

Accuracy of multi-territorial repertoire information

1. Member States shall ensure that a collective management organisation which grants multi-territorial licences for online rights in musical works has in place arrangements to enable rightholders, other collective management organisations and online service providers to request a correction of the data referred to in the list of conditions under Article 24(2) or the information provided under Article 25, where such rightholders, collective management organisations and online service providers, on the basis of reasonable evidence, believe that the data or the information are inaccurate in respect of their online rights in musical works. Where the claims are sufficiently substantiated, the collective management organisation shall ensure that the data or the information are corrected without undue delay.

2. The collective management organisation shall provide rightholders whose musical works are included in its own music repertoire and rightholders who have entrusted the management of their online rights in musical works to it in accordance with Article 31 with the means of submitting to it in electronic form information concerning their musical works, their rights in those works and the territories in respect of which the rightholders authorise the organisation. When doing so, the collective management organisation and the rightholders shall take into account, as far as possible, voluntary industry standards or practices regarding the exchange of data developed at international or Union level, allowing rightholders to specify the musical work, wholly or in part, the online rights, wholly or in part, and the territories in respect of which they authorise the organisation.

3. Where a collective management organisation mandates another collective management organisation to grant multi-territorial licences for the online rights in musical works under Articles 29 and 30, the mandated collective management organisation shall also apply paragraph 2 of this Article with respect to the rightholders whose musical works are included in the repertoire of the mandating collective management organisation, unless the collective management organisations agree otherwise.

Article 27

Accurate and timely reporting and invoicing

1. Member States shall ensure that a collective management organisation monitors the use of online rights in musical works which it represents, wholly or in part, by online service providers to which it has granted a multi-territorial licence for those rights.

2. The collective management organisation shall offer online service providers the possibility of reporting by electronic means the actual use of online rights in musical works and online service providers shall accurately report the actual use of those works. The collective management organisation shall offer the use of a least one method of reporting which takes into account voluntary industry standards or practices developed at international or Union level for the electronic exchange of such data. The collective management organisation may refuse to accept reporting by the online service provider in a proprietary format if the organisation allows for reporting using an industry standard for the electronic exchange of data.

3. The collective management organisation shall invoice the online service provider by electronic means. The collective management organisation shall offer the use of a least one format which takes into account voluntary industry standards or practices developed at international or Union level. The invoice shall identify the works and rights which are licensed, wholly or in part, on the basis of the data referred to in the list of conditions under Article 24(2), and the corresponding actual uses, to the extent that this is possible on the basis of the information provided by the online service provider and the format used to provide that information. The online service provider may not refuse to accept the invoice because of its format if the collective management organisation is using an industry standard.

4. The collective management organisation shall invoice the online service provider accurately and without delay after the actual use of the online rights in that musical work is reported, except where this is not possible for reasons attributable to the online service provider.

5. The collective management organisation shall have in place adequate arrangements enabling the online service provider to challenge the accuracy of the invoice, including when the online service provider receives invoices from one or more collective management organisations for the same online rights in the same musical work.

Article 28

Accurate and timely payment to rightholders

1. Without prejudice to paragraph 3, Member States shall ensure that a collective management organisation which grants multi-territorial licences for online rights in musical works distributes amounts due to rightholders accruing from such licences accurately and without delay after the actual use of the work is reported, except where this is not possible for reasons attributable to the online service provider.

2. Without prejudice to paragraph 3, the collective management organisation shall provide at least the following information to rightholders together with each payment it makes under paragraph 1:

(a) the period during which the uses took place for which amounts are due to rightholders and the territories in which the uses took place;

(b) the amounts collected, deductions made and amounts distributed by the collective management organisation for each online right in any musical work which rightholders have authorised the collective management organisation, wholly or in part, to represent;

(c) the amounts collected for rightholders, deductions made, and amounts distributed by the collective management organisation in respect of each online service provider.

3. Where a collective management organisation mandates another collective management organisation to grant multi-territorial licences for the online rights in musical works under Articles 29 and 30, the mandated collective management organisation shall distribute the amounts referred to in paragraph 1 accurately and without delay, and shall provide the information referred to in paragraph 2 to the mandating collective management organisation. The mandating collective management organisation shall be responsible for the subsequent distribution of such amounts and the provision of such information to rightholders, unless the collective management organisations agree otherwise.

Article 29

Agreements between collective management organisations for multi-territorial licensing

1. Member States shall ensure that any representation agreement between collective management organisations whereby a collective management organisation mandates another collective management organisation to grant multi-territorial licences for the online rights in musical works in its own music repertoire is of a non-exclusive nature. The mandated collective management organisation shall manage those online rights on a non-discriminatory basis.

2. The mandating collective management organisation shall inform its members of the main terms of the agreement, including its duration and the costs of the services provided by the mandated collective management organisation.

3. The mandated collective management organisation shall inform the mandating collective management organisation of the main terms according to which the latter's online rights are to be licensed, including the nature of the exploitation, all provisions which relate to or affect the licence fee, the duration of the licence, the accounting periods and the territories covered.

Article 30

Obligation to represent another collective management organisation for multi-territorial licensing

1. Member States shall ensure that where a collective management organisation which does not grant or offer to grant multi-territorial licences for the online rights in musical works in its own repertoire requests another collective management organisation to enter into a representation agreement to represent those rights, the requested collective management organisation is required to agree to such a request if it is already granting or offering to grant multi-territorial licences for the same category of online rights in musical works in the repertoire of one or more other collective management organisations.

2. The requested collective management organisation shall respond to the requesting collective management organisation in writing and without undue delay.

3. Without prejudice to paragraphs 5 and 6, the requested collective management organisation shall manage the represented repertoire of the requesting collective management organisation on the same conditions as those which it applies to the management of its own repertoire.

4. The requested collective management organisation shall include the represented repertoire of the requesting collective management organisation in all offers it addresses to online service providers.

5. The management fee for the service provided by the requested collective management organisation to the requesting organisation shall not exceed the costs reasonably incurred by the requested collective management organisation.

6. The requesting collective management organisation shall make available to the requested collective management organisation information relating to its own music repertoire required for the provision of multi-territorial licences for online rights in musical works. Where information is insufficient or provided in a form that does not allow the requested collective management organisation to meet the requirements of this Title, the requested collective management organisation shall be entitled to charge for the costs reasonably incurred in meeting such requirements or to exclude those works for which information is insufficient or cannot be used.

Article 31

Access to multi-territorial licensing

Member States shall ensure that where a collective management organisation does not grant or offer to grant multi-territorial licences for online rights in musical works or does not allow another collective management organisation to represent those rights for such purpose by 10 April 2017, rightholders who have authorised that collective management organisation to represent their online rights in musical works can withdraw from that collective management organisation the online rights in musical works for the purposes of multi-territorial licensing in respect of all territories without having to withdraw the online rights in musical works for the purposes of mono-territorial licensing, so as to grant multi-territorial licences for their online rights in musical works themselves or through any other party they authorise or through any collective management organisation complying with the provisions of this Title.

Article 32

Derogation for online music rights required for radio and television programmes

The requirements under this Title shall not apply to collective management organisations when they grant, on the basis of the voluntary aggregation of the required rights, in compliance with the competition rules under Articles 101 and 102 TFEU, a multi-territorial licence for the online rights in musical works required by a broadcaster to communicate or make available to the public its radio or television programmes simultaneously with or after their initial broadcast as well as any online material, including previews, produced by or for the broadcaster which is ancillary to the initial broadcast of its radio or television programme.

TITLE IV

ENFORCEMENT MEASURES

Article 33

Complaints procedures

1. Member States shall ensure that collective management organisations make available to their members, and to collective management organisations on whose behalf they manage rights under a representation agreement, effective and timely procedures for dealing with complaints, particularly in relation to authorisation to manage rights and termination or withdrawal of rights, membership terms, the collection of amounts due to rightholders, deductions and distributions.

2. Collective management organisations shall respond in writing to complaints by members or by collective management organisations on whose behalf they manage rights under a representation agreement. Where the collective management organisation rejects a complaint, it shall give reasons.

Article 34

Alternative dispute resolution procedures

1. Member States may provide that disputes between collective management organisations, members of collective management organisations, rightholders or users regarding the provisions of national law adopted pursuant to the requirements of this Directive can be submitted to a rapid, independent and impartial alternative dispute resolution procedure.

2. Member States shall ensure, for the purposes of Title III, that the following disputes relating to a collective management organisation established in their territory which grants or offers to grant multi-territorial licences for online rights in musical works can be submitted to an independent and impartial alternative dispute resolution procedure:

(a) disputes with an actual or potential online service provider regarding the application of Articles 16, 25, 26 and 27;

(b) disputes with one or more rightholders regarding the application of Articles 25, 26, 27, 28, 29, 30 and 31;

(c) disputes with another collective management organisation regarding the application of Articles 25, 26, 27, 28, 29 and 30.

Article 35

Dispute resolution

1. Member States shall ensure that disputes between collective management organisations and users concerning, in particular, existing and proposed licensing conditions or a breach of contract can be submitted to a court, or if appropriate, to another independent and impartial dispute resolution body where that body has expertise in intellectual property law.

2. Articles 33 and 34 and paragraph 1 of this Article shall be without prejudice to the right of parties to assert and defend their rights by bringing an action before a court.

Article 36

Compliance

1. Member States shall ensure that compliance by collective management organisations established in their territory with the provisions of national law adopted pursuant to the requirements laid down in this Directive is monitored by competent authorities designated for that purpose.

2. Member States shall ensure that procedures exist enabling members of a collective management organisation, rightholders, users, collective management organisations and other interested parties to notify the competent authorities designated for that purpose of activities or circumstances which, in their opinion, constitute a breach of the provisions of national law adopted pursuant to the requirements laid down in this Directive.

3. Member States shall ensure that the competent authorities designated for that purpose have the power to impose appropriate sanctions or to take appropriate measures where the provisions of national law adopted in implementation of this Directive have not been complied with. Those sanctions and measures shall be effective, proportionate and dissuasive. Member States shall notify the Commission of the competent authorities referred to in this Article and in Articles 37 and 38 by 10 April 2016. The Commission shall publish the information received in that regard.

Article 37

Exchange of information between competent authorities

1. In order to facilitate the monitoring of the application of this Directive, each Member State shall ensure that a request for information received from a competent authority of another Member State, designated for that purpose, concerning matters relevant to the application of this Directive, in particular with regard to the activities of collective management organisations established in the

territory of the requested Member State, is responded to without undue delay by the competent authority designated for that purpose, provided that the request is duly justified.

2. Where a competent authority considers that a collective management organisation established in another Member State but acting within its territory may not be complying with the provisions of the national law of the Member State in which that collective management organisation is established which have been adopted pursuant to the requirements laid down in this Directive, it may transmit all relevant information to the competent authority of the Member State in which the collective management organisation is established, accompanied where appropriate by a request to that authority that it take appropriate action within its competence. The requested competent authority shall provide a reasoned reply within three months.

3. Matters as referred to in paragraph 2 may also be referred by the competent authority making such a request to the expert group established in accordance with Article 41.

Article 38

Cooperation for the development of multi-territorial licensing

1. The Commission shall foster a regular exchange of information between the competent authorities designated for that purpose in Member States, and between those authorities and the Commission, on the situation and development of multi-territorial licensing.

2. The Commission shall conduct regular consultations with representatives of rightholders, collective management organisations, users, consumers and other interested parties on their experience with the application of the provisions of Title III of this Directive. The Commission shall provide competent authorities with all relevant information that emerges from those consultations, within the framework of the exchange of information provided for in paragraph 1.

3. Member States shall ensure that by 10 October 2017, their competent authorities provide the Commission with a report on the situation and development of multi-territorial licensing in their territory. The report shall include information on, in particular, the availability of multi-territorial licences in the Member State concerned and compliance by collective management organisations with the provisions of national law adopted in implementation of Title III of this Directive, together with an assessment of the development of multi-territorial licensing of online rights in musical works by users, consumers, rightholders and other interested parties.

4. On the basis of the reports received pursuant to paragraph 3 and the information gathered pursuant to paragraphs 1 and 2, the Commission shall assess the application of Title III of this Directive. If necessary, and where appropriate on the basis of a specific report, it shall consider further steps to address any identified problems. That assessment shall cover, in particular, the following:

(a) the number of collective management organisations meeting the requirements of Title III;

(b) the application of Articles 29 and 30, including the number of representation agreements concluded by collective management organisations pursuant to those Articles;

(c) the proportion of repertoire in the Member States which is available for licensing on a multi-territorial basis.

TITLE V

REPORTING AND FINAL PROVISIONS

Article 39

Notification of collective management organisations

By 10 April 2016, Member States shall provide the Commission, on the basis of the information at their disposal, with a list of the collective management organisations established in their territories. Member States shall notify any changes to that list to the Commission without undue delay. The Commission shall publish that information and keep it up to date.

Article 40

Report

By 10 April 2021, the Commission shall assess the application of this Directive and submit to the European Parliament and to the Council a report on the application of this Directive. That report shall include an assessment of the impact of this Directive on the development of cross-border services, on cultural diversity, on the relations between collective management organisations and users and on the operation in the Union of collective management organisations established outside the Union, and, if necessary, on the need for a review. The Commission's report shall be accompanied, if appropriate, by a legislative proposal.

Article 41

Expert group

An expert group is hereby established. It shall be composed of representatives of the competent authorities of the Member States. The expert group shall be chaired by a representative of the Commission and shall meet either on the initiative of the chairman or at the request of the delegation of a Member State. The tasks of the group shall be as follows:

(a) to examine the impact of the transposition of this Directive on the functioning of collective management organisations and independent management entities in the internal market, and to highlight any difficulties;

(b) to organise consultations on all questions arising from the application of this Directive;

(c) to facilitate the exchange of information on relevant developments in legislation and case-law, as well as relevant economic, social, cultural and technological developments, especially in relation to the digital market in works and other subject-matter.

Article 42

Protection of personal data

The processing of personal data carried out within the framework of this Directive shall be subject to Directive 95/46/EC.

Article 43

Transposition

1. Member States shall bring into force the laws, regulations and administrative provisions necessary to comply with this Directive by 10 April 2016. They shall immediately inform the Commission thereof.

When Member States adopt those measures, they shall contain a reference to this Directive or shall be accompanied by such reference on the occasion of their official publication. The methods of making such reference shall be laid down by Member States.

2. Member States shall communicate to the Commission the text of the main measures of national law which they adopt in the field covered by this Directive.

Article 44

Entry into force

This Directive shall enter into force on the twentieth day following that of its publication in the Official Journal of the European Union.

Article 45

Addressees

This Directive is addressed to the Member States.

ANNEX

1. Information to be provided in the annual transparency report referred to in Article 22(2):

(a) financial statements comprising a balance-sheet or a statement of assets and liabilities, an income and expenditure account for the financial year and a cash-flow statement;

(b) a report on the activities in the financial year;

(c) information on refusals to grant a licence pursuant to Article 16(3);

(d) a description of the legal and governance structure of the collective management organisation;

(e) information on any entities directly or indirectly owned or controlled, wholly or in part, by the collective management organisation;

(f) information on the total amount of remuneration paid to the persons referred in Article 9(3) and Article 10 in the previous year, and on other benefits granted to them;

(g) the financial information referred to in point 2 of this Annex;

(h) a special report on the use of any amounts deducted for the purposes of social, cultural and educational services, containing the information referred to in point 3 of this Annex.

2. Financial information to be provided in the annual transparency report:

(a) financial information on rights revenue, per category of rights managed and per type of use (e.g. broadcasting, online, public performance), including information on the income arising from the investment of rights revenue and the use of such income (whether it is distributed to rightholders or other collective management organisations, or otherwise used);

(b) financial information on the cost of rights management and other services provided by the collective management organisation to rightholders, with a comprehensive description of at least the following items:

(i) all operating and financial costs, with a breakdown per category of rights managed and, where costs are indirect and cannot be attributed to one or more categories of rights, an explanation of the method used to allocate such indirect costs;

(ii) operating and financial costs, with a breakdown per category of rights managed and, where costs are indirect and cannot be attributed to one or more categories of rights, an explanation of the method used to allocate such indirect costs, only with regard to the management of rights, including management fees deducted from or offset against rights revenue or any income arising from the investment of rights revenue in accordance with Article 11(4) and Article 12(1), (2) and (3);

   (iii) operating and financial costs with regard to services other than the management of rights, but including social, cultural and educational services;

   (iv) resources used to cover costs;

   (v) deductions made from rights revenues, with a breakdown per category of rights managed and per type of use and the purpose of the deduction, such as costs relating to the management of rights or to social, cultural or educational services;

   (vi) the percentages that the cost of the rights management and other services provided by the collective management organisation to rightholders represents compared to the rights revenue in the relevant financial year, per category of rights managed, and, where costs are indirect and cannot be attributed to one or more categories of rights, an explanation of the method used to allocate such indirect costs;

(c) financial information on amounts due to rightholders, with a comprehensive description of at least the following items:

   (i) the total amount attributed to rightholders, with a breakdown per category of rights managed and type of use;

   (ii) the total amount paid to rightholders, with a breakdown per category of rights managed and type of use;

   (iii) the frequency of payments, with a breakdown per category of rights managed and per type of use;

   (iv) the total amount collected but not yet attributed to rightholders, with a breakdown per category of rights managed and type of use, and indicating the financial year in which those amounts were collected;

   (v) the total amount attributed to but not yet distributed to rightholders, with a breakdown per category of rights managed and type of use, and indicating the financial year in which those amounts were collected;

   (vi) where a collective management organisation has not carried out the distribution and payments within the deadline set in Article 13(1), the reasons for the delay;

   (vii) the total non-distributable amounts, along with an explanation of the use to which those amounts have been put;

(d) information on relationships with other collective management organisations, with a description of at least the following items:

   (i) amounts received from other collective management organisations and amounts paid to other collective management organisations, with a breakdown per category of rights, per type of use and per organisation;

   (ii) management fees and other deductions from the rights revenue due to other collective management organisations, with a breakdown per category of rights, per type of use and per organisation;

   (iii) management fees and other deductions from the amounts paid by other collective management organisations, with a breakdown per category of rights and per organisation;

   (iv) amounts distributed directly to rightholders originating from other collective management organisations, with a breakdown per category of rights and per organisation.

3. Information to be provided in the special report referred to in Article 22(3):

(a) the amounts deducted for the purposes of social, cultural and educational services in the financial year, with a breakdown per type of purpose and, for each type of purpose, with a breakdown per category of rights managed and per type of use;

(b) an explanation of the use of those amounts, with a breakdown per type of purpose including the costs of managing amounts deducted to fund social, cultural and educational services and of the separate amounts used for social, cultural and educational services.

PART I

RELATED EU INSTRUMENTS

PART I

RELATED EU INSTRUMENTS

Council Decision[i] of March 16, 2000 on the approval, on behalf of the European Community, of the WIPO Copyright Treaty and the WIPO Performances and Phonograms Treaty[1]

([2001] O.J. L89/6)

THE COUNCIL OF THE EUROPEAN UNION

Having regard to the Treaty establishing the European Community, and in particular Articles 47(2), 55 and 95 thereof, in conjunction with the first sentence of Article 300(2) and the second subparagraph of Article 300(3),

Having regard to the proposal from the Commission,[2]

Having regard to the assent of the European Parliament,[3]

Whereas:

(1) The WIPO Copyright Treaty (WCT) and the WIPO Performances and Phonograms Treaty (WPPT) adopted in Geneva on 20 December 1996 under the auspices of the World Intellectual Property Organisation will help to ensure a balanced level of protection for works and other subject matter, while allowing the public access to material available via networks.

(2) The competence of the Community to conclude or accede to international agreements or treaties does not derive only from explicit conferral by the Treaty but may also derive from other provisions of the Treaty and from acts adopted pursuant to those provisions by Community institutions.

(3) The subject-matter of the WCT and the WPPT falls to a large extent within the scope of existing Community directives in this field.

(4) It follows that the approval of the WCT and the WPPT is a matter for both the Community and its Member States.

(5) The WCT and the WPPT should therefore be approved on behalf of the Community with regard to matters within its competence.

(6) The Community has already signed the WCT and the WPPT, subject to final conclusion.

(7) The deposit of the instruments of conclusion of the Community should take place as far as possible simultaneously with the deposit of the instruments of ratification of the Member States,

HAS DECIDED AS FOLLOWS;

Article 1

1. The WIPO Copyright Treaty (WCT) is hereby approved on behalf of the Community with regard to matters within its competence.

2. The WIPO Performances and Phonograms Treaty (WPPT) is hereby approved on behalf of the Community with regard to matters within its competence.

3. The texts of the Treaties are attached to this Decision.

Article 2

The President of the Council is hereby authorised to deposit the instru-

---

[i] *Editorial Note*: The footnotenumbering in the original Decision is reproduced below.

[1] Two statements relating to this Decision are set out in [2000] O.J. C103/1.

[2] [1998] O.J. C165/8.

[3] Assent of February 16, 2000 (Bull. 1/2-2000; point 1.3.58).

ments of conclusion with the Director-General of the World Intellectual Property Organisation as from the date by which the Member States will have to bring into force the measures adopted by the European Parliament and the Council necessary to adapt the existing Community legislation to the obligations deriving from the WCT and the WPPT.

Article 3

1. The Commission is hereby authorised to represent the Community at the meetings of the Assemblies referred to in the WCT and WPPT.

2. On all matters within the sphere of competence of the Community, the Commission shall negotiate in the Assemblies of the WCT and the WPPT on behalf of the Community in accordance with the applicable rules of the EC Treaty, in particular Article 300 thereof.

3. The position which the Community may adopt within the Assemblies shall be prepared by the relevant council working party.

Done at Brussels, 16 March 2000.

I2. COMMISSION RECOMMENDATION 2005/737/EC

Commission Recommendation of May 18, 2005 on collective cross-border management of copyright and related rights for legitimate online music services[i]

([2005] O.J. L276/54)

THE COMMISSION OF THE EUROPEAN COMMUNITIES,

Having regard to the Treaty establishing the European Community, and in particular Article 211 thereof,

Whereas:

(1) In April 2004 the Commission adopted a Communication on the Management of Copyright and Related Rights in the Internal Market.

(2) The European Parliament, in its report of 15 January 2004,[1] stated that right-holders should be able to enjoy copyright and related rights protection wherever such rights are established, independent of national borders or modes of use during the whole term of their validity.

(3) The European Parliament further emphasised that any action by the Community in respect of the collective cross-border management of copyright and related rights should strengthen the confidence of artists, including writers and musicians, that the pan-European use of their creative works will be financially rewarded.[2]

(4) New technologies have led to the emergence of a new generation of commercial users that make use of musical works and other subject matter online. The provision of legitimate online music services requires management of a series of copyright and related rights.

(5) One category of those rights is the exclusive right of reproduction which covers all reproductions made in the process of online distribution of a musical work. Other categories of rights are the right of communication to the public of musical works, the right to equitable remuneration for the communication to the public of other subject matter and the exclusive right of making available a musical work or other subject matter.

(6) Pursuant to Directive 2001/29/EC of the European Parliament and of the Council of 22 May 2001 on the harmonisation of certain aspects of copyright and related rights in the information society[3] and Council Directive 92/100/EEC of 19 November 1992 on rental right and lending right and on certain rights related to copyright in the field of intellectual property,[4] a licence is required for each of the rights in the online exploitation of musical works. These rights may be managed by collective rights managers that provide certain management services to right-holders as agents or by individual right-holders themselves.

(7) Licensing of online rights is often restricted by territory, and commercial users negotiate in each Member State with each of the respective collective rights managers for each right that is included in the online exploitation.

(8) In the era of online exploitation of musical works, however, commercial users need a licensing policy that corresponds to the ubiquity of the online environment and which is multi-territorial. It is therefore appropriate to

---

[i] *Editorial note:* The footnote numbering in the original Recommendation is reproduced below.
[1] A5-0478/2003.
[2] See recital 29.
[3] [2001] O.J. L167/10.
[4] [1992] O.J. L346/61. Directive as amended by Directive 2001/29/EC.

provide for multi-territorial licensing in order to enhance greater legal certainty to commercial users in relation to their activity and to foster the development of legitimate online services, increasing, in turn, the revenue stream for right-holders.

(9) Freedom to provide collective management services across national borders entails that right-holders are able to freely choose the collective rights manager for the management of the rights necessary to operate legitimate online music services across the Community. That right implies the possibility to entrust or transfer all or a part of the online rights to another collective rights manager irrespective of the Member State of residence or the nationality of either the collective rights manager or the rights-holder.

(10) Fostering effective structures for cross-border management of rights should also ensure that collective rights managers achieve a higher level of rationalisation and transparency, with regard to compliance with competition rules, especially in the light of the requirements arising out of the digital environment.

(11) The relationship between right-holders and collective rights managers, whether based on contract or statutory membership rules, should include a minimum protection for right-holders with respect to all categories of rights that are necessary for the provision of legitimate online music services. There should be no difference in treatment of right-holders by rights managers on the basis of the Member State of residence or nationality.

(12) Royalties collected on behalf of right-holders should be distributed equitably and without discrimination on the grounds of residence, nationality, or category of rightholder. In particular, royalties collected on behalf of right-holders in Member States other than those in which the right-holders are resident or of which they are nationals should be distributed as effectively and efficiently as possible.

(13) Additional recommendations on accountability, rightholder representation in the decision-making bodies of collective rights managers and dispute resolution should ensure that collective rights managers achieve a higher level of rationalisation and transparency and that rightholders and commercial users can make informed choices. There should be no difference in treatment on the basis of category of membership in the collective rights management society: all right-holders, be they authors, composers, publishers, record producers, performers or others, should be treated equally.

(14) It is appropriate to continuously assess the development of the online music market,

HEREBY RECOMMENDS;

Definitions

1. For the purposes of this Recommendation the following definitions are applied:

(a) 'management of copyright and related rights for the provision of legitimate online music services at Community level' means the provision of the following services: the grant of licences to commercial users, the auditing and monitoring of rights, the enforcement of copyright and related rights, the collection of royalties and the distribution of royalties to rightholders;

(b) 'musical works' means any musical work or other protected subject matter;

(c) 'repertoire' means the catalogue of musical works which is administered by a collective rights manager;

(d) 'multi-territorial licence' means a licence which covers the territory of more than one Member state;

(e) 'collective rights manager' means any person providing the services set out in point (a) to several right-holders;

(f) 'online rights' means any of the following rights:

    (i) the exclusive right of reproduction that covers all reproductions provided for under Directive 2001/29/EC in the form of intangible copies, made in the process of online distribution of musical works;

    (ii) the right of communication to the public of a musical work, either in the form of a right to authorise or prohibit pursuant to Directive 2001/29/EC or a right to equitable remuneration in accordance with Directive 92/100/EEC, which includes webcasting, internet radio and simulcasting or near-on-demand services received either on a personal computer or on a mobile telephone;

    (iii) the exclusive right of making available a musical work pursuant to Directive 2001/29/EC, which includes on-demand or other interactive services;

(g) 'right-holder' means any natural or legal person that holds online rights;

(h) 'commercial user' means any person involved in the provision of online music services who needs a licence from right-holders in order to provide legitimate online music services;

(i) 'reciprocal representation agreement' means any bilateral agreement between collective rights managers whereby one collective rights manager grants to the other the right to represent its repertoire in the territory of the other.

General

2. Member States are invited to take the steps necessary to facilitate the growth of legitimate online services in the Community by promoting a regulatory environment which is best suited to the management, at Community level, of copyright and related rights for the provision of legitimate online music services.

The relationship between right-holders, collective rights managers and commercial users

3. Right-holders should have the right to entrust the management of any of the online rights necessary to operate legitimate online music services, on a territorial scope of their choice, to a collective rights manager of their choice, irrespective of the Member State of residence or the nationality of either the collective rights manager or the right-holder.

4. Collective rights managers should apply the utmost diligence in representing the interests of right-holders.

5. With respect to the licensing of online rights the relationship between right-holders and collective rights managers, whether based on contract or statutory membership rules, should, at least be governed by the following:

(a) right-holders should be able to determine the online rights to be entrusted for collective management;

(b) right-holders should be able to determine the territorial scope of the mandate of the collective rights managers;

(c) right-holders should, upon reasonable notice of their intention to do so, have the right to withdraw any of the online rights and transfer the multi territorial management of those rights to another collective rights manager, irrespective of the Member State of residence or the nationality of either the collective rights manager or the right-holder;

(d) where a right-holder has transferred the management of an online right to another collective rights manager, without prejudice to other forms of cooperation among rights managers, all collective rights managers concerned should ensure that those online rights are withdrawn from any existing reciprocal representation agreement concluded amongst them.

6. Collective rights managers should inform right-holders and commercial users of the repertoire they represent, any existing reciprocal representation agreements, the territorial scope of their mandates for that repertoire and the applicable tariffs.

7. Collective rights managers should give reasonable notice to each other and commercial users of changes in the repertoire they represent.

8. Commercial users should inform collective right managers of the different features of the services for which they want to acquire online rights.

9. Collective rights managers should grant commercial users licences on the basis of objective criteria and without any discrimination among users.

Equitable distribution and deductions

10. Collective rights managers should distribute royalties to all right-holders or category of right-holders they represent in an equitable manner.

11. Contracts and statutory membership rules governing the relationship between collective rights managers and rightholders for the management, at Community level, of musical works for online use should specify whether and to what extent, there will be deductions from the royalties to be distributed for purposes other than for the management services provided.

12. Upon payment of the royalties collective rights managers should specify vis-a-vis all the right-holders they represent, the deductions made for purposes other than for the management services provided.

Non-discrimination and representation

13. The relationship between collective rights managers and right-holders, whether based on contract or statutory membership rules should be based on the following principles:

(a) any category of right-holder is treated equally in relation to all elements of the management service provided;

(b) the representation of right-holders in the internal decision making process is fair and balanced.

Accountability

14. Collective rights managers should report regularly to all right-holders they represent, whether directly or under reciprocal representation agreements, on any licences granted, applicable tariffs and royalties collected and distributed.

Dispute settlement

15. Member States are invited to provide for effective dispute resolution mechanisms, in particular in relation to tariffs, licensing conditions, entrustment of online rights for management and withdrawal of online rights.

Follow-up

16. Member States and collective rights managers are invited to report, on

a yearly basis, to the Commission on the measures they have taken in relation to this Recommendation and on the management, at Community level, of copyright and related rights for the provision of legitimate online music services.

17. The Commission intends to assess, on a continuous basis, the development of the online music sector and in the light of this Recommendation.

18. The Commission will to consider, on the basis of the assessment referred to in point 17, the need for further action at Community level.

Addressees

19. This Recommendation is addressed to the Member States and to all economic operators which are involved in the management of copyright and related rights within the Community.

Done at Brussels, 18 May 2005.

PART J

PRECEDENTS AND COURT FORMS

PART J

PRECEDENTS AND COURT FORMS

J1. PRECEDENTS[1]

J1.i Assignment of Copyright[2]

ASSIGNMENT

DATE:

PARTIES:

(1) [*Assignor*] of [*or* whose registered office] [*or* whose principal place of business is at] [*address*] ("the Assignor"); and

(2) [*Assignee*] of [*or* whose registered office] [*or* whose principal place of business is at] [*address*] ("the Assignee").

IT IS AGREED AS FOLLOWS:

1. Definitions

In this assignment the following words or phrases shall have the following meanings:

Rights	the copyright[3] and all rights in the nature of copyright throughout the Territory in the Work for all the residue of the term of copyright[4] and such rights in the Work and all extensions and renewals thereof[5] together with all accrued causes of action in respect thereof[6]
Territory	the world[7]
Work	[*description of work*[8]]

2. Background

   (1) The Assignor is [the author of the Work and] the owner of the Rights.
   (2) The Assignor has agreed to assign the Rights to the Assignee.

[*Set out any other background facts it is wished to recite.*]

---

[1] Precedents provided are only the very basic forms of assignments and other instruments. It is beyond the scope of this work to provide more detailed precedents.

[2] See CDPA 1988 s.90 and paras 5–83 et seq., above. An assignment must be in writing, signed by or on behalf of the assignor, but need not be by deed. It should be borne in mind that rights may also be granted by way of licence, and care should be taken to make it clear what is intended. Thus a grant of a licence should use some such words as "by way of licence only." As with an assignment, a licence should make clear the extent of the rights granted, the term and territory.

[3] A simple assignment of "the copyright" will assign all the things which the copyright owner has the exclusive right to do. See para. 5–88, above. Alternatively, the assignment may be limited, so as to transfer some only of the copyright owner's exclusive rights. See CDPA 1988 s.90(2)(a) and paras 5–97 et seq. above.

[4] The assignment may be limited to part only of the period for which the copyright subsists, e.g. "for the period of ten years from the date hereof".

[5] This provision is directed to certain foreign systems of law, such as those of the United States of America, which provide for copyright to be periodically renewed or extended.

[6] This provision will ensure that the assignee can recover damages in respect of any infringement which may have taken place before the date of the assignment. Notice of the assignment should be given to the proposed defendant. See Law of Property Act 1925 s.136, and para. 5–95, above.

[7] The assignment may of course be limited in its geographical extent, e.g. to the United Kingdom.

[8] Care should be taken to identify the work or works precisely, perhaps by reference to a Schedule, bearing in mind that a number of different copyright works may make up the "work" which is to be the subject-matter of the assignment.

J PRECEDENTS AND COURT FORMS

3. Assignment

[In consideration of the sum of £[   ] now paid by the Assignee to the Assignor (the receipt of which the Assignor hereby acknowledges),] the Assignor hereby assigns with [full] [limited] title guarantee[9] to the Assignee for use in the Territory the Rights.

[4. [Assertion] [Waiver] of Moral Rights

Assertion of right to be identified as author (see Precedent J1.v) alternatively waiver of moral rights (see Precedent J1.vi).]

5. Further Assurances

The Assignor shall at any time and from time to time hereafter at the request and expense of the Assignee execute all such documents and do all such further acts as the Assignee may require in order to vest the Rights in the Assignee.[10]

EXECUTION

The parties have shown their acceptance of the terms of this assignment by signing at the end of it.[11]

SIGNED BY	)
[duly authorised	)
for and on behalf of]	)
[*assignor*]	)
in the presence of	)
SIGNED BY	)
[duly authorised	)
for and on behalf of]	)
[*assignee*]	)
in the presence of	)

J1.ii Assignment of Future Copyright[12]

DATE:

---

[9] If an assignment is made with title guarantees (either limited or full), then certain covenants as to title will be implied: see Pt I of the Law of Property (Miscellaneous Provisions) Act 1994 (c.36). The covenants are implied whether or not a disposition is for valuable consideration, but the absence of consideration may well affect the availability of equitable remedies such as specific performance in respect of the covenants. For discussion of the nature and effect of the covenants see, for example, *Emmet on Title*, Ch.16.

[10] cf. the covenant implied (by Law of Property (Miscellaneous Provisions) Act 1994 (c.36) s.2(1)(b), where a full or limited title guarantee is given: "that the person making the disposition will at his own cost do all that he reasonably can to give the person to whom he disposes of the property the title he purports to give." This statutorily implied covenant may be excluded or limited by the terms of the assignment (as may all covenants implied by the 1994 Act: see s.8(1)).

[11] In the case of a body corporate, the requirement that the assignment be signed will be satisfied by affixing the company's seal. See CDPA 1988 s.176(1). However, a registered company need not have a common seal, and whether or not it does, a document signed by two "authorised signatories" or by a director in the presence of a witness who attests his signature and expressed to be executed by the company has the same effect as if executed under the common seal: Companies Act 2006 s.46(4). For these purposes every director and the secretary or a joint secretary are "authorised signatories".

[12] By s.91(1) of the CDPA 1988, an agreement made in relation to future copyright, and signed by or on behalf of the prospective owner of the copyright, whereby the owner purports to assign the future copyright, shall as provided by the section (see para. 5–109, above) cause the copyright, when it comes into existence, to vest in the assignee or his successor in title. It should be noted that an agreement in this form will not necessarily have the same effect outside the United Kingdom, which is why a covenant for further assurances is desirable. The agreement should

PARTIES:

(1) [*Assignor*] of [*or* whose registered office is at] [*or* whose principal place of business is at] [*address*] ("the Assignor"); and

(2) [*Assignee*] of [*or* whose registered office is at] [*or* whose principal place of business is at] [*address*] ("the Assignee").

IT IS AGREED AS FOLLOWS:

1. Definitions

In this assignment the following words or phrases shall have the following meanings:

Rights	the copyright and all rights in the nature of copyright throughout the Territory in the Work about to be created by the Assignor for the full term of copyright and such rights in the Work and all extensions and renewals thereof
Territory	the world
Work	[*description of work*]

2. Background

(1) The Assignor is about to create the Work;

(2) The Assignor has agreed to assign the Rights to the Assignee.

[*Set out any other background facts it is wished to recite.*]

3. Assignment

[In consideration of the sum of £[   ] now paid by the Assignee to the Assignor (the receipt of which the Assignor hereby acknowledges),] the Assignor hereby assigns with [full] [limited] title guarantee to the Assignee for use in the Territory the Rights, with the intention that the Rights should forthwith upon completion of the Work vest in the Assignee.

4. [Assertion] [Waiver] of Moral Rights

[*Assertion of right to be identified as author (see Precedent J1.v), alternatively waiver of moral rights (see Precedent J1.vi).*]

5. Further Assurances

[*Covenant for further assurances—see Precedent J1.i, clause 5.*]

EXECUTION

The parties have shown their acceptance of the terms of this assignment by signing at the end of it.

SIGNED BY	)
[duly authorised	)
for and on behalf of]	)

---

always be supported by valuable consideration even when made by deed (see para. 5–109, above), not least to make the covenant for further assurances specifically enforceable. See also the notes to Precedent J1.i in relation to the present form generally.

[*assignor*]   )
in the presence of   )
SIGNED BY   )
[duly authorised   )
for and on behalf of]   )
[*assignee*]   )
in the presence of   )

J1.iii Assignment of Unregistered United Kingdom Design Right[13]

DATE:

PARTIES:

(1) [*Assignor*] of [*or* whose registered office is at] [*or* whose principal place of business is at] [*address*] ("the Assignor"); and

(2) [*Assignee*] of [*or* whose registered office is at] *or* whose principal place of business is at] [*address*] ("the Assignee").

IT IS AGREED AS FOLLOWS:

1. Definitions

In this assignment the following words or phrases shall have the following meanings:

Design Right	the design right as conferred by Part III of the Copyright, Designs and Patents Act 1988 or any statutory modification or re-enactment thereof in the Design for all the residue of the term of design right therein together with all accrued causes of action in respect thereof[14]
Design	[*description of design*]

2. Background

[*Set out any background facts it is wished to recite, such as the assignor's ownership of and agreement to assign the Design Right.*]

3. Assignment

[In consideration of the sum of £[   ] now paid by the Assignee to the Assignor (the receipt of which the Assignor hereby acknowledges),] the Assignor hereby assigns with [full] [limited] title guarantee[15] to the Assignee the Design Right.

4. Further Assurances

---

[13] See CDPA 1988 s.222. The assignment must be in writing, signed by or on behalf of the assignor, but need not be by deed. As with copyright, the design right may also be licensed. See CDPA 1988 s.222(4).

[14] This provision will ensure that the assignee can recover damages in respect of any infringement which may have taken place before the date of the assignment. Notice of the assignment should be given to the proposed defendant. See Law of Property Act 1925 s.136, and para. 5–95, above.

[15] If an assignment is made with title guarantees (either limited or full), then certain covenants as to title will be implied: see Pt I of the Law of Property (Miscellaneous Provisions) Act 1994 (c.36). The covenants are implied whether or not a disposition is for valuable consideration, but the absence of consideration may well affect the availability of equitable remedies such as specific

[Covenant for further assurances—see Precedent J1.i, clause 5 but delete "Rights" and substitute "Design Right".]

EXECUTION

The parties have shown their acceptance of the terms of this assignment by signing at the end of it.[16]

SIGNED BY	)
[duly authorised	)
for and on behalf of]	)
[*assignor*]	)
in the presence of	)
SIGNED BY	)
[duly authorised	)
for and on behalf of]	)
[*assignee*]	)
in the presence of	)

J1.iv Assignment of Future Unregistered United Kingdom Design Right[17]

DATE:

PARTIES:

(1) [*Assignor*] of [*or* whose registered office is at] [*or* whose principal place of business is at] [*address*] ("the Assignor"); and

(2) [*Assignee*] of [*or* whose registered office is at] [*or* whose principal place of business is at] [*address*] ("the Assignee").

IT IS AGREED AS FOLLOWS:

1. Definitions

In this assignment the following words or phrases shall have the following meanings:

Design Right	the design right as conferred by Part III of the Copyright, Designs and Patents Act 1988 or any statutory modification or re-enactment thereof in the Design about to be created by the Assignor for the full term of design right therein
Design	[*description of design*]

2. Background

[Set out any background facts it is wished to recite, such as the fact that the

---

performance in respect of the covenants. For discussion of the nature and effect of the covenants see, for example, *Emmet on Title*, Ch.16.

[16] In the case of a body corporate, the requirement that the assignment be signed will be satisfied by affixing the company's seal. See CDPA 1988 s.176(1). However, a registered company need not have a common seal, and whether or not it does, a document signed by two "authorised signatories" or by a director in the presence of a witness who attests his signature and expressed to be executed by the company has the same effect as if executed under the common seal: Companies Act 2006 s.46(4). For these purposes every director and the secretary or a joint secretary are "authorised signatories".

[17] See CDPA 1988 s.223. The provisions dealing with assignments of future copyright and future design right are in identical terms.

Design is about to be created by the assignor, and his/her agreement to assign the Design Right.]

3. Assignment

[In consideration of the sum of £[   ] now paid by the Assignee to the Assignor (the receipt of which the Assignor hereby acknowledges),] the Assignor hereby assigns with [full] [limited] title guarantee to the Assignee the Design Right, with the intention that the Design Right should forthwith upon completion of the Design vest in the Assignee.

4. Further Assurances

[*Covenant for further assurances—see Precedent J1.i, clause 5 but delete "Rights" and substitute "Design Right".*]

EXECUTION

The parties have shown their acceptance of the terms of this assignment by signing at the end of it

SIGNED BY   )
[duly authorised   )
for and on behalf of]   )
[*assignor*]   )
in the presence of   )
SIGNED BY   )
[duly authorised   )
for and on behalf of]   )
[*assignee*]   )
in the presence of   )

J1.v Assertion of Right to be Identified as Author[18]

THIS INSTRUMENT is made on [date] by A.B. of [*address*].

1. A.B. is the author of [*insert description of work*].

2. Notice is hereby given that A.B. hereby asserts his right generally[19] to be identified as the author of the said work.

Signed....................

J1.vi Waiver of Moral Rights[20]

THIS WAIVER is made on [date] by A.B. of [*address*].

---

[18] See CDPA 1988 s.78 and paras 11–22 et seq., above. The form included here is intended to be a simple instrument in writing signed by the author, so as to satisfy s.78(2)(b) of the 1988 Act. It may be adapted to be included in an assignment of copyright (see Precedent J1.i) so as to satisfy s78(2)(a), or to be applicable to a director of a film.

[19] The right may be asserted generally or in relation to any specified act or description of acts. See CDPA 1988 s.78(2).

[20] The CDPA 1988 s.87 provides that any of the moral rights may be waived by an instrument in writing signed by or on behalf of the person giving up the right. See paras 11–91, et seq., above. The present form contains a waiver in respect of the right to be identified as the author of a literary, dramatic, musical or artistic work, or the director of a film, and the right not to have such works subjected to derogatory treatment.

1. 1, A.B., hereby unconditionally and irrevocably[21] waive my rights [to be identified as the author[22] of [*insert description of work*[23]]] [to be identified as the director of [*insert description of film*]] and not to have the said [work]/[film] subjected to derogatory treatment.[24]

2. This waiver is made expressly in favour of C.D.[25] and for the avoidance of doubt shall extend to licensees and successors in title to the copyright in the said [work]/[film].[26]

Signed....................

---

[21] The waiver may be conditional or unconditional, and may be expressed to be subject to revocation. See CDPA 1988 s.87(3)(b).

[22] CDPA 1988 s.77; paras 11–08 et seq., above.

[23] The waiver may relate to a specific work, to works of a specified description or to works generally, and may relate to existing or future works. See CDPA 1988 s.87(3)(a).

[24] See CDPA 1988 s.80 and paras 11–34 et seq., above.

[25] i.e. the owner or the prospective owner of the copyright in the work.

[26] If the waiver is made in favour of the owner or the prospective owner of the copyright in the work, it shall be presumed, unless the contrary intention is expressed, to extend to his licensees and successors in title. See CDPA 1988 s.87(2).

J2. COURT FORMS

J2.i Infringement of Copyright: Entries for Claim Form[27]

Brief details of claim

The claimant's claim is for:

1. An order that the defendant ([whether acting by himself his employees or agents or otherwise howsoever] [whether acting by its directors, officers, employees or agents or otherwise howsoever[28]]) must not do the following acts or any of them, that is to say, without the claimant's licence.

(1) reproduce [*description of the copyright work*] ("the claimant's work") or any substantial part thereof[29] ;

(2) issue to the public copies of the claimant's work or any substantial part thereof[30] ;

(3) possess in the course of a business, sell, offer for sale, expose for sale or in the course of a business exhibit in public, or distribute infringing copies of the claimant's work[31] ;

(4) authorise any of the above acts[32] ;

(5) in any other manner infringe the claimant's copyright in the claimant's work.

2. An inquiry as to damages for infringement of copyright (including damages under reg.3 of the Intellectual Property (Enforcement, etc.) Regulations, and additional damages under section 97(2) of the Copyright, Designs and Patents Act 1988[33]) alternatively and at the claimant's option an account of profits, together with an order for the payment to the claimant of all sums found due upon the making of the said inquiry or the taking of the said account.

3. Interest pursuant to section 35A of the Supreme Court Act 1981, alternatively the court's equitable jurisdiction.

4. Delivery up of:

(a) all infringing copies of the claimant's work in the defendant's possession custody or control[34] ; and

(b) any article in the defendant's possession custody or control specifically designed or adapted for making copies of the claimant's work.[35]

5. An order that all infringing copies or articles delivered up pursuant to the

---

[27] Form N1. Except in the case of claims started in the IPEC, the words "Intellectual Property" must appear below the title of the court in which the claim is issued: PD63, para.17.1. The form given here is suitable for a case of infringement of copyright in a literary, dramatic, musical or artistic work. See generally, Chs 7 and 8. In suitable cases there may be added a claim relating to the claimant's moral rights (see Court Forms J2.iv and J2.v, below).

[28] In the case of a corporate defendant

[29] As to this act of primary infringement, see CDPA 1988 s.17 and Ch.7.

[30] As to this act of primary infringement, see CDPA 1988 s.18 and Ch.7.

[31] As to these acts of secondary infringement, see CDPA 1988 s.23 and Ch.8.

[32] Authorising acts of primary infringement is itself an act of primary infringement: see CDPA 1988 s.16(2). Although the 1988 Act does not expressly provide that authorising secondary infringement is itself an act of infringement, a person who does so authorise is normally liable as a joint tortfeasor with the infringer: see paras 21–45 et seq., above

[33] As to these damages, see paras 21–282 et seq. and paras 21–298 et seq., respectively.

[34] See CDPA 1988 s.99(1)(a), and para. 21–329, above.

[35] See CDPA 1988 s.99(1)(b), and para. 21–329, above.

previous paragraph 4 be forfeited to the claimant alternatively be destroyed or otherwise dealt with as the court shall think fit.[36]

6. An order that measures be taken at the defendant's expense for the dissemination and publication of any judgment herein.

7. Further or other relief.

8. Costs.

Value

The claimant expects to recover more than £100,000.[37]

J2.ii Infringement of Copyright: Particulars of Claim[38]

Claim No.

IN THE HIGH COURT OF JUSTICE

CHANCERY DIVISION

INTELLECTUAL PROPERTY

BETWEEN:

A.B.

Claimant

and

B. C.

Defendant

PARTICULARS OF CLAIM

1. The claimant is the owner of the copyright in [*description of copyright work*] ("the claimant's work").

PARTICULARS OF SUBSISTENCE[39]

[*Insert details of how it is said that copyright subsists in the claimant's work,* e.g.:

    (1) The claimant's work is an original[40] literary work and was made on *date*]/ [between [*date*] and [*date when work was completed*]].

    (2) The claimant's work was made by E.F., who, when the claimant's work

---

[36] See CDPA 1988 s.114(1) and paras 21–331 et seq., above. Until a decision is made as to whether to make an order under this section, the claimant must retain any item ordered to be delivered up. See CDPA 1988 s.99(3).

[37] See paras 21–358 et seq., above, for the difficulties that arise where the claimant does not expect to recover more than £100,000 .

[38] The precedent given here follows on from the previous precedent, and is suitable to the case of infringement of copyright in a literary work.

[39] As to the qualification requirements for copyright subsistence, see CDPA 1988 ss.153–156 and paras 3–279 et seq., above.

[40] As to originality, see paras 3–198 et seq., above. If the author of the work is dead, or his/her identity cannot be ascertained by reasonable inquiry, then there is a statutory presumption of originality, in the absence of evidence to the contrary: CDPA 1988 s.104(5).

was made, was [a British citizen]/[a British subject]/[domiciled/resident in the United Kingdom].

(3) The claimant's work was first published on [*date*] in [the United Kingdom]. At that time E.F. remained [a British citizen]/[a British subject]/[domiciled/resident in the United Kingdom].]

PARTICULARS OF OWNERSHIP[41]

[Insert details of how it is said that the claimant owns the copyright, e.g.:

(1) The claimant's work was created by E.F.[42]

(2) By an assignment in writing dated [*date*], E.F. assigned the copyright in the claimant's work to the claimant [together with all accrued causes of action in respect thereof].[A copy of the assignment is annexed to these Particulars of Claim marked "A"]

2. Before the issue of the claim form herein, the defendant has infringed the claimant's copyright in the claimant's work by, without the licence of the claimant:

(1) reproducing a substantial part of the claimant's work in a material form[43];

(2) putting into circulation copies of a substantial part of the claimant's work not previously put into circulation[44]; and/or

(3) authorising the said acts[45];
and

(4) possessing in the course of its business;

(5) selling, offering and exposing for sale;

(6) exhibiting in public and distributing in the course of its business articles which were, and which the defendant knew or had reason to believe were, infringing copies of the claimant's work[46]; and/or

(7) authorising the said acts.[47]

PARTICULARS OF INFRINGEMENT

[Give details of infringement, e.g.:

The claimant will seek to recover in respect of all acts of infringement but before disclosure and/or further information herein will rely upon the following facts and matters:

(1) the printing by or for the defendant of copies of a work entitled [*title*] ("the defendant's work"), which reproduces a substantial part of the claimant's work. A Schedule of the passages of the claimant's work which are reproduced in the defendant's work is served separately.]

(2) the sale by the defendant of the defendant's work.

(3) [*Set out any other known instances of infringement.*]

PARTICULARS OF KNOWLEDGE

Before disclosure and/or further information herein the claimant relies upon:

---

[41] As to the considerations affecting authorship and ownership, see CDPA 1988 ss.9–11 and 90–93, and Chs 4 and 5, above.

[42] As to the statutory presumptions as to authorship in the case of literary, dramatic and musical works, see CDPA 1988 s.104 and paras 21–381 et seq., above.

[43] See CDPA 1988 s.17 and Ch.7, above.

[44] See CDPA 1988 s.18 and Ch.7, above.

[45] See CDPA 1988 s.16(2).

[46] See CDPA 1988 s.23 and Ch.8, above.

[47] Authorising a secondary infringement will normally give rise to liability as a joint tortfeasor: see paras 21–45 et seq., above.

(1) [*Set out relevant facts, e.g.* that the claimant's work is very well known, and that there is an obvious and very high degree of similarity between the claimant's work and the defendant's work.]

(2) the claimant's solicitors' letter to the defendant dated [*date*].

3. All copies of the defendant's work are infringing copies of the claimant's work, and the claimant is entitled to delivery up of the same.

4. By reason of the matters aforesaid, the claimant has suffered loss and damage.

5. By its acts of infringement aforesaid, well knowing that it was thereby infringing the copyright in the claimant's work, the defendant has acted in flagrant disregard of the claimant's rights. In the premises the claimant is entitled to and claims from the defendant additional damages pursuant to section 97(2) of the Copyright, Designs and Patents Act 1988.

PARTICULARS[48]

Before disclosure and/or further information herein, the claimant will rely upon:

(1) the defendant's knowledge that the defendant's work was an infringing copy of the claimant's work, and in particular the Particulars of Knowledge stated above;

(2) [*Set out any benefit received by the defendant on which the claimant relies.*]

6. Unless restrained by the court, the defendant threatens and intends further to infringe the copyright in the claimant's work, whereby the claimant will suffer further loss and damage.

7. The claimant claims interest pursuant to section 35A of the Supreme Court Act 1981, alternatively the court's equitable jurisdiction, for such period and at such rate as the court thinks fit.

AND THE CLAIMANT CLAIMS:

[*Insert prayer for relief*—see Court Form J2.i]

[*Statement of truth*][49]

[*Claimant's address for service*][50]

J2.iii Infringement of Unregistered United Kingdom Design Right: Particulars of Claim[51]

[*Heading—See Court Form J2.ii*]

PARTICULARS OF CLAIM

1. The claimant is the owner of the design right ("the claimant's design right")

---

[48] Where a claim is made for additional damages under s.97(2), the particulars of claim must include a statement to that effect and the grounds for claiming them: PD63 para.22.1.

[49] See CPR 22.1(1)(a).

[50] The particulars of claim must include the claimant's address for service if they are served separately from the claim form: PD16 para.3.8(4).

[51] As to design right, see Ch.13, and, in particular, as to jurisdiction, see paras 13–213 et seq., above.

in the design ("the claimant's design") of the external and internal shape and configuration of [*insert description of the article*].

PARTICULARS OF QUALIFICATIONS FOR PROTECTION[52]

[*Insert details of how it is said that the design right qualifies for protection, e.g.*:
(1) The claimant's design was recorded in a design document consisting of [*insert description of design document*] on [*date*] and an article was first made to the claimant's design on [*date*].
(2) When it was created, the claimant's design was original.
(3) The designer of the claimant's design was E.F., who did not create the design in pursuance of a commission or in the course of employment and who, when the claimant's design was made, was [a British citizen]/[a British subject]/[habitually resident in the United Kingdom.]]

PARTICULARS OF OWNERSHIP[53]

[*Insert details of how it is said that the claimant owns the claimant's design right, e.g.*:
(1) E.F. was, in the premises, the first owner of the claimant's design right.
(2) By an assignment in writing dated [*date*], E.F. assigned the claimant's design right to the claimant together with all accrued causes of action in respect thereof.]]

2. Before the issue of the claim form herein, the defendant has infringed the claimant's design right by, without the claimant's licence:
(1) reproducing the claimant's design for commercial purposes by:
   (i) making articles to the claimant's design;
   (ii) making design documents recording the claimant's design for the purpose of enabling such articles to be made[54] ; and/or
(2) authorising the said acts[55]
   and/or
(3) possessing for commercial purposes;
(4) selling, offering and exposing for sale in the course of its business articles which were, and which the defendant knew or had reason to believe were, articles whose making was an infringement of the claimant's design right.[56]

PARTICULARS OF INFRINGEMENT

The claimant will seek to recover in respect of all acts of infringement but before disclosure and/or further information herein relies on the manufacture by or for the defendant, and the sale by the defendant of [*insert description of articles*] ("the defendant's articles"), which are copies of the claimant's design such as to be exactly or substantially to the claimant's design.

---

[52] As to the qualification requirements for design right protection, see CDPA 1988 ss.217–221 and paras 13–99 et seq., above.

[53] As to the considerations affecting ownership, see CDPA 1988 ss.215, 222–224, and paras 13–122 et seq., above.

[54] As to the acts of primary infringement of the design right, see CDPA 1988 s.226 and paras 13–162 et seq., above.

[55] Authorising primary infringement of design right is itself a primary infringement: see CDPA 1988 s.226(3).

[56] As to the acts of secondary infringement of the design right, see CDPA 1988 s.227 and paras 13–178 et seq., above.

PARTICULARS OF KNOWLEDGE

Before disclosure and/or further information herein the claimant relies upon:

(1) [*Set out relevant facts*]

(2) the claimant's solicitors' letter to the defendant dated [*date*].

3. All copies of the defendant's articles are infringing articles and the claimant is entitled to delivery up of the same.

4. By reason of the matters aforesaid, the claimant has suffered loss and damage.

5. By its acts of infringement aforesaid, well knowing that it was thereby infringing the copyright in the claimant's works, the defendant has acted in flagrant disregard of the claimant's rights. In the premises the claimant is entitled to and claims from the defendant additional damages pursuant to section 229(3) of the Copyright, Designs and Patents Act 1988.

PARTICULARS[57]

Before disclosure and/or further information herein, the claimant will rely upon:

(1) the defendant's knowledge that the defendant's work was an infringing copy of the claimant's works, and in particular the facts pleaded in sub-paragraph (1) of the Particulars of Knowledge;

(2) [*Set out any benefit received by the defendant on which the claimant relies.*]

[*Continue as in Court Form J2.ii, paragraphs 6–7 mutatis mutandis*]

AND THE CLAIMANT CLAIMS:

1. An order that the defendant ([whether acting by himself, his employees or agents or otherwise howsoever] [whether acting by its directors, officers, employees or agents or otherwise howsoever[58]]) must not do the following acts or any of them that is to say, without the licence of the claimant:

(1) reproduce the internal and external shape and configuration of [*insert description of article*] ("the claimant's design") by

    (i) making articles to the claimant's design;

    (ii) making any design document recording the claimant's design for the purpose of enabling such articles to be made; and/or

(2) possess for commercial purposes any article which was without the claimant's licence made to the claimant's design ("infringing article");

(3) sell, offer or expose for sale in the course of a business any infringing article;

(4) authorise any such act[59]; or

(5) otherwise infringe the claimant's design right.

2. An inquiry as to damages for infringement of the claimant's design right (including damages under reg.3 of the Intellectual Property (Enforcement, etc.) Regulations 2006, and under section 229(3) of the Copyright, Designs and Patents

---

[57] Where a claim is made for additional damages under s.229(3), the particulars of claim must include a statement to that effect and the grounds for claiming them: PD63 para.22.1.

[58] In the case of a corporate defendant.

[59] Although the 1988 Act does not expressly provide that authorising secondary infringement of design right is itself an act of infringement, a person who does so authorise is normally liable as a joint tortfeasor with the infringer: see paras 21–45 et seq. above.

Act 1988), alternatively and at the claimant's option an account of profits together with an order for the payment to the claimant of all sums found due upon the making of the said inquiry or the taking of the said account.

3. Interest pursuant to s.35A of the Supreme Court Act 1981, alternatively the court's equitable jurisdiction.

4. Delivery up[60] of:
   (a) all articles in the defendant's possession custody or control the making of which infringed the claimant's design right; and
   (b) anything in the defendant's possession custody or control specifically designed or adapted for making articles to the claimant's design.

5. An order that all articles and things delivered up pursuant to the previous paragraph be forfeited to the claimant alternatively be destroyed or otherwise dealt with as the court shall think fit.[61]

6. An order that measures be taken at the defendant's expense for the dissemination and publication of any judgment herein.

7. Further or other relief.

8. Costs.

[*Statement of truth*][62]

[*Claimant's address for service*][63] .

J2.iv Infringement of Right to be Identified as Author: Particulars of Claim[64]

[*Heading—See Court Form J2.i*]

PARTICULARS OF CLAIM

1. The claimant is the author of the copyright literary work [*insert description of work*] ("the claimant's work").

2. By an assignment in writing dated [*date*], the claimant assigned the copyright in the claimant's work to E.F. Included in the assignment was a statement that the claimant asserted his right to be identified as the author of the claimant's work ("the claimant's right").[65]

3. Before the issue of the claim form herein, the defendant has published the claimant's work commercially[66] in the form of [*insert form of publication*].

4. The defendant claims to be entitled to publish the claimant's work as afore-

---

[60] See CDPA 1988 s.230.

[61] See CDPA 1988 s.231(1). Until a decision is made on whether to make an order under this section, the claimant must retain any item ordered to be delivered up. See CDPA 1988 s.230(6).

[62] See CPR 22.1(1)(a).

[63] The particulars of claim must include the claimant's address for service if they are served separately from the claim form: PD16 para.3.8(4).

[64] As to infringement of the right to be identified as the author of a literary, dramatic, musical or artistic work, see CDPA 1988 ss.77–79 and paras 11–14 et seq., and 11–86 et seq., above.

[65] The right is not infringed unless (a) it has been asserted and (b) the defendant is bound by that assertion. One of the ways in which the right may be asserted is on an assignment of the copyright, when the assignee and anyone claiming through him will be bound. See CDPA 1988 ss.77(1) and 78, and paras 11–22 et seq., above.

[66] As to the acts of infringement, see CDPA 1988 s.77 and paras 11–14 et seq., above.

said by virtue of a licence from E.F. In the premises, the defendant is bound by the claimant's said assertion of the claimant's right.[67]

5. When the claimant's work was published as aforesaid the claimant was not identified as the author of the claimant's work. Further, the claimant did not consent to such publication. In the premises, the claimant's right was thereby infringed.

6. By reason of the matters aforesaid, the claimant has suffered loss and damage.

7. Unless restrained by the court, the defendant threatens and intends further to infringe the claimant's right, whereby the claimant will suffer further loss and damage.

8. The claimant claims interest pursuant to section 35A of the Supreme Court Act 1981, alternatively the equitable jurisdiction of the court for such period and at such rate as the court thinks fit.

AND THE CLAIMANT CLAIMS[68] :

1. An order that the defendant (whether acting by himself his employees or agents or otherwise howsoever] [whether acting by its directors, officers, employees or agents or otherwise howsoever[69]]) must not do the following acts or any of them, that is to say, without the claimant's consent:
    (1) commercially publish the claimant's work without identifying the claimant as the author thereof;
    (2) otherwise infringe the claimant's right to be identified as the author of the claimant's work ("the claimant's right").

2. An inquiry as to damages ,including damages under reg.3 of the Intellectual Property (Enforcement, etc.) Regulations 2006, for infringement of the claimant's right, alternatively and at the claimant's option, an account of profits together with an order for the payment to the claimant of all sums found due upon the making of the said inquiry or the taking of the said account.

3. Interest pursuant to section 35A of the Supreme Court Act 1981, alternatively the court's equitable jurisdiction.

4. An order that measures be taken at the defendant's expense for the dissemination and publication of any judgment herein.

5. Further or other relief.

6. Costs.

[*Conclude as Court Form J2.i*]

J2.v Infringement of Right not to have Work Subjected to Derogatory Treatment: Particulars of Claim[70]

[*Heading—See Court Form J2.ii*]

---

[67] See paras 11–23 et seq., above.
[68] An infringement of the right is actionable as a breach of statutory duty. See CDPA 1988 s.103(1) and para. 11–86, above.
[69] In the case of a corporate defendant.
[70] As to such right, see CDPA 1988 ss.80–83 and paras 11–34 et seq., above.

PARTICULARS OF CLAIM

1. The claimant is the author of the copyright literary work [*description of work*] ("the claimant's work"). [The defendant is the owner of the copyright in the claimant's work.][71]

2. Before the issue of the claim form herein, the defendant has published commercially a derogatory treatment of the claimant's work.

PARTICULARS

[*State form of derogatory publication, e.g.*:

The claimant will rely on the version of the claimant's work entitled [*insert title*] ("the defendant's version") published by the defendant, in which passages were variously added to and deleted from the claimant's work as set out in the Schedule served herewith, with the result that the claimant's work was distorted and/or mutilated and/or treated in a manner prejudicial to the honour and/or reputation of the claimant.][72]

3. The claimant did not consent to such publication. [Further, the claimant was identified in the defendant's version as the author thereof yet such publication took place without any clear or reasonably prominent indication being given at the time of publication that the claimant's work had been subjected to treatment to which the claimant had not consented.[73]] In the premises, the claimant's right not to have the claimant's work subjected to derogatory treatment ("the claimant's right") was thereby infringed by the defendant.

4. The defendant has further infringed the claimant's right by without the claimant's consent possessing in the course of his business, selling, offering and exposing for sale and distributing in the course of his business copies of the defendant's version knowing or having reason to believe that by the defendant's version the claimant's work had been distorted and/or mutilated and/or treated in a manner prejudicial to the honour and/or reputation of the claimant.[74]

PARTICULARS OF KNOWLEDGE

Before disclosure and/or further information herein the claimant relies upon:
    (1) [*Set out relevant facts*]
    (2) the claimant's solicitors' letter to the defendant dated [*date*].

[*Continue as in Court Form J2.ii, paragraphs 6–7 mutatis mutandis*]

AND THE CLAIMANT CLAIMS[75] :

1. An order that the defendant (whether acting by himself his employees or agents or otherwise howsoever] [whether acting by its directors, officers, employ-

---

[71] In the precedent given here it is assumed that the defendant is the owner of the copyright in the work. In certain cases where this is so (works produced in the course of employment and other cases where the author is not the first owner of the copyright—see CDPA 1988 s.82(1) and paras 5–01 et seq., above), the right will not be infringed unless matters of the kind pleaded in the second sentence of para.3 of this precedent can be established. See CDPA 1988 s.82(2).

[72] As to the acts of infringement, see CDPA 1988 s.80 and paras 11–43 et seq., above.

[73] See CDPA 1988 s.82(2).

[74] As to such acts of infringement, see CDPA 1988 s.83 and paras 11–48 et seq., above.

[75] An infringement of the right is actionable as a breach of statutory duty. See CDPA 1988 s.103(1) and para. 11–84, above.

ees or agents or otherwise howsoever[76]]) must not do the following acts or any of them, that is to say, without the claimant's consent:

(1) publish commercially the claimant's work in the form of the version referred to in paragraph 2 above ("the defendant's version");

(2) sell, offer or expose for sale or distribute in the course of a business copies of the defendant's version [unless in every such case a disclaimer is made on such terms and in such manner as may be approved by the court dissociating the claimant from the defendant's version[77]];

(3) otherwise infringe the claimant's right not to have the claimant's work subjected to derogatory treatment ("the claimant's right").

2. An inquiry as to damages for infringement of the claimant's right, including damages under reg.3 of the Intellectual Property (Enforcement, etc.) Regulations 2006, alternatively and at the claimant's option, an account of profits together with an order for the payment to the claimant of all sums found due upon the making of the said inquiry or the taking of the said account.

3. Delivery up for destruction of all copies of the defendant's version which are in the defendant's possession custody or control.[78]

4. Interest pursuant to section 35A of the Supreme Court Act 1981, alternatively the court's equitable jurisdiction.

5. An order that measures be taken at the defendant's expense for the dissemination and publication of any judgment herein.

6. Further or other relief.

7. Costs.

[*Conclude as Court Form J2.ii*]

J2.vi Box 3 of Application Notice for Interim Injunction[79]

1. An order that the defendant until after judgment or further order in the meantime (whether acting by himself his employees or agents or otherwise howsoever) must not do the following acts or any of them that is to say [*insert appropriate relief, e.g.*

Manufacture, or authorise the manufacture of, sell, offer, advertise or expose for sale, distribute, destroy or otherwise dispose of any product an example of which forms exhibit "AB1" to the first witness statement of A.B. made in this action on [*date*].[80]

2. Such further or other relief as the court shall think fit.

3. An order providing for the costs of this application.

J2.vii Infringement of Copyright: Final Judgment

[*Heading—See Court Form J2.ii*]

---

[76] In the case of a corporate defendant.
[77] See CDPA 1988 s.103(2) and para 11–88, above.
[78] i.e. under the Court's inherent jurisdiction. See *Hole v Bradbury* (1879) 12 Ch.D. 886 and para. 21–330, above.
[79] Form N244. As to interim injunctions, see paras 21–181 et seq., above.
[80] Interim relief should generally not be framed in such terms as, for example, to restrain the defendant "from infringing the claimant's copyright". On a committal application, this may raise the very issues which must be resolved at trial.

UPON THE TRIAL of this action

AND UPON HEARING oral evidence

AND UPON HEARING counsel for the claimant and for the defendant

AND UPON READING the documents filed

IT IS ORDERED THAT

(1) The defendant must not ([whether acting by himself his employees or agents or otherwise howsoever] [whether acting by its directors, officers, employees or agents or otherwise howsoever[81]]) do the following acts or any of them that is to say, without the claimant's licence:

(i) reproduce [*insert description of work*] ("the claimant's work"), or any substantial part thereof; or

(ii) issue to the public copies of the claimant's work or any substantial part thereof; or

(iii) sell, offer or expose for sale or exhibit in public or distribute copies of the claimant's work made without the claimant's licence; or

(iv) authorise any of the acts aforesaid; or

(v) otherwise infringe the claimant's copyright in the claimant's work.

(2) The defendant must within 21 days hereof [by its proper officer][82] make a witness statement setting forth sufficient information to enable the claimant to make an informed election between an inquiry as to damages or an account of profits,[83] that is to say:

(i) the number of [*identify infringing product*] made and sold;

(ii) the sums received and receivable from sales of the [*infringing product*]; and

(iii) an approximate estimate of the costs incurred (that approximate estimate to include a statement of how the estimate was made);

and must serve a copy of the said affidavit and all copiable exhibits on the solicitors for the claimant.

(3) The claimant must within 21 days of service upon it elect, by notice in writing served on the defendant's solicitors, whether an account of profits should be taken, or whether an inquiry should be made as to what damages the claimant has suffered by reason of the infringement of the claimant's copyright in the claimant's work committed by the defendant; any failure to elect an account of profits within the aforesaid period to be final unless the Court shall hereafter be of the opinion that the aforesaid statement was inadequate for the purpose of enabling a properly informed election to be made.

---

[81] In the case of a corporate defendant.
[82] The words in brackets are to be inserted in the case of a corporate defendant.
[83] See *Island Records Ltd v Tring International Plc* [1996] 1 W.L.R. 1256; *Brugger v Medicaid* [1996] F.S.R. 362.

[(4) The inquiry as to damages, or as the case may be, the account of profits and the costs thereof shall be reserved to the trial judge.][84]

(5) The following inquiries be made[85]:

(i) An inquiry as to what damages the claimant has suffered by reason of the infringement of the claimant's copyright in the claimant's work committed by the defendant by

(a) (without the licence of the claimant) reproducing or issuing to the public copies of the claimant's work or any substantial part thereof or authorising any of the acts aforesaid or

(b) (without the licence of the claimant) selling offering or exposing for sale or exhibiting in public or distributing after [*insert date when sale, etc., with knowledge first took place*] copies of the claimant's work made without the claimant's licence

(ii) An inquiry as to what damages (if any) the claimant is entitled to under reg.3 of the Intellectual Property (Enforcement, etc.) Regulations and under section 97(2) of the Copyright Designs and Patents Act 1988 [In considering whether the justice of the case requires an award of additional damages under section 97(2) of the 1988 Act, the court taking the inquiry shall have particular regard to the findings as to the flagrancy of the infringement made in the judgment][86]

(iii) An inquiry as to what interest (if any) the claimant is entitled to on the said damages pursuant to section 35A of the Supreme Court Act 1981.

(6) The defendant shall pay the claimant the sums (if any) found due to the claimant upon the making of the said inquiries.

(7) The defendant must within 14 days after service of this order upon him deliver or cause to be delivered up to the claimant at the defendant's own expense:

(i) all copies of the claimant's work made without the claimant's licence in the defendant's possession custody or control;

(ii) all articles specifically designed or adapted for making copies of the claimant's work in the defendant's possession custody or control;

and must within 7 days thereafter make and serve upon the claimant's solicitors a witness statement verifying that he no longer has in his possession custody or control any such copies or articles.

(5) All such copies or articles as are delivered up by the defendant as aforesaid shall be forfeited to the claimant.[87]

(6) The defendant shall display on the homepage of its website for a period of one year or until further order of the court a short statement in the form set out in

---

[84] Normally, the inquiry or account is heard by a Chancery Master. If, however, there is a substantial overlap between the evidence at trial and that which would be before the Master, it may be desirable for the Judge also to deal with quantum.

[85] This assumes the claimant has opted for damages at the conclusion of the trial, and does not therefore need the *Tring* information ordered in paragraph (2) of this order.

[86] The words in square brackets are applicable where the trial Judge has made a finding that the infringement was flagrant: see *MCA Records Inc v Charly Records Ltd* [2001] EWCA Civ 1441 [2002] E.C.D.R. 37 [2002] E.M.L.R. 1 at para.66.

[87] See CDPA 1988 s.114(1) and paras 21–331 et seq., above.

the Schedule to this Order together with a hyperlink to the judgment on the BAILLI website.[88]

(7) The defendant shall pay the claimant his costs of this action down to and including this judgment such costs to be assessed on the standard basis if not agreed

AND the costs of the said inquiries are reserved.

---

[88] See *Vestergaard Fransden A/S v Bestnet Europe Ltd* [2009] EWHC 1456 Ch at para.114.